Reading
for
Understanding

READING for UNDERSTANDING

THIRD EDITION

MAURICE B. McNAMEE
Saint Louis University

Holt, Rinehart and Winston, Inc.
New York Chicago San Francisco Atlanta Dallas

Library of Congress Catalog Card Number: 68-16791

2685154

Printed in the United States of America

2 3 4 5 6 7 8 9

Preface

The title, *Reading for Understanding,* indicates very well the purpose of this book. The primary aim of freshman courses in English is to foster an understanding of the rhetorical structure of expository prose. Students just entering college are frequently not aware of structure either in what they read or in what they write. One of the indispensable means of developing their awareness is a reading program in which students are guided through a considerable amount of good expository writing.

The selections in this reader have been chosen with two objects in mind. My first concern was to provide readings of substantial length that exemplify some of the methods of rhetorical development. Secondly, I was concerned to find essays of current interest and on related topics so that they might invite the kind of comparison and contrast that illustrates the process of a liberal education. This process is a matter of discovering relationships between things we already know and those we continue to learn, and it is aided by collections of readings which themselves complement one another.

Reading for Understanding is divided into two parts. Part I is composed of expository essays that are arranged by topic, and during the first semester it might serve as the nucleus of a course in which the rhetoric of exposition is the point of focus. Part II contains a section of expository essays on the nature and function of art, literature, and music; a section that illustrates the chronological development of the essay as a literary form; sections on description and on the oration; and a section devoted to short stories. Part II might be used as an introduction to literature, where that is the emphasis in the second semester, or as a preparation for the sophomore course in literature.

The topical sections in Part I are closely related to the interests and problems of college freshmen. Section 1 introduces them to the whole problem of the relationship between their reading and their writing—which should be their major concern all through their freshman composition course. Section 2 expands the students' thinking about logic and rhetoric, and the ways in which propaganda and advertising impinge upon their everyday experience through the public media of communication. Section 3 should increase their awareness of the roots, history, and present sources of change in the English language and give them a respect for its richness and versatility.

I have found that students have a perennial interest in discussions of the purpose of college education, especially as this purpose has become increasingly complex in modern technological society. Section 4 provides a variety of recent essays on problems of a liberal education in an age of technology, and it also contains an essay from the mid-nineteenth century by John Henry Newman, which serves as a preview of the current conflict and dialogue between the humanists and the technologists. Perhaps even more interesting to the college freshman than the academic world into which he is moving is the larger world of thought in which he is increasingly involved. In that world he will be confronted with the ideas of modern science and philosophy and with shifting concepts of social organization and the role of the United States in the world, as well as with the whole problem and potential of modern technology. These topics are all discussed in Section 5 by some of the leading thinkers of the day in essays that are models of rhetorical exposition.

Section 6 is a collection of expository essays on the concept of the hero, on some of the chief epic heroes, and the place of the hero in the modern world. This section has been included to provide an introduction to an outside reading program in the epics and tragedies of Western literature. This reading program is designed to serve two purposes. First, it introduces student to the whole mythological background of their own literary tradition and to two of the major literary genres in that tradition. Secondly, and more importantly for a course in freshman composition, it provides endless subject matter for themes and gives students what they frequently lack—something to write about and a wealth of illustrative material upon which to draw as they learn to develop an idea by such methods as multiple example and comparison and contrast.

Most of the selections used in *Reading for Understanding* are followed by a study guide. The study guides are closely focused on the theme of the essay, the structure of the author's thought, and the patterns of rhetorical development, because these are the areas in which students are weakest and in which they need most continued exercise both in their reading and writing. In the later sections of this book, attention is given to such stylistic matters as sentence structure, diction, imagery, and tone. For reference, there is an appendix on the chief principles of rhetorical development and effectiveness.

At this point I wish to make the following important acknowledgments to Dr. Joseph Rogers for allowing me to use his analysis of "The Gentleman from San Francisco"; and to the members of the English faculty at Saint Louis University and other colleges and universities whose suggestions have assisted me in preparing what is essentially a new book, not merely a revision of an old one. I also wish to express my gratitude to the following instructors who read the prospectus of this new edition of *Reading for Understanding* and who gave me the benefit of their constructive criticism: Robert D. Crozier, S.J., Fordham Community College; John Gerrietts, Loyola University, Chicago; Sister M. Romaine, S.S.J., Villa Marie College; and J. M. Stiker, Lewis College. My thanks also go to Mrs. Judith Rau and Mrs. Wylla Munsell for their help in preparing the manuscript.

M. B. McN.

Saint Louis, Missouri
January 1968

Contents

Rhetorical Contents of the Expository Essays

DEFINITION

CLASSIFICATION

ANALYSIS

COMPARISON AND CONTRAST

ANALOGY

CAUSE AND EFFECT

INDUCTION

NARRATION

CONCRETE EXAMPLES

MULTIPLE EXAMPLES

Expository Essays: A Rhetorical Guide

PART I

Understanding the Rhetoric of Exposition

SECTION 1

Reading and Writing for Understanding

WHAT EVERY FRESHMAN SHOULD KNOW

Roger W. Holmes

1 I never face a class without wondering what would happen if students were not so docile. Why do you meet your professors and the academic taradiddle of college with such fear and respect? You are everywhere in chains because you accept a tradition about college work which at cost to you misrepresents its values and overestimates its importance. You remind me of the elephant chained to his stake at the circus. If the poor devil knew his own strength! And if you and your classmates but knew *yours!* The good things that might happen to our colleges if you would take matters into your own hands and pull up a few of the rotted stakes of academic tradition are worth dreaming about. Consider some confidential advice from one who would like to see you gain your freedom, who knows the weaknesses of academic life from the inside, and can give a few pointers on how to pull at those stakes.

2 One of the first things you are told is that you must study hard. But that is only half of the story. The other half is that beyond a certain point which is easily reached, the more you work the poorer the results. In my particular college you would be supposed to devote not more than fifteen

"What Every Freshman Should Know," by Roger W. Holmes, *The American Mercury* (November 1940), pp. 273–280. Reprinted by permission of *The American Mercury*, P.O. Box 1306, Torrance, Calif.

hours a week to classes and another thirty to outside assignments. That means that you should be able to escape academic duties for one whole day each week and to take either the afternoon or the evening off almost every day. Work hard when you work. Mornings are the best times. But never work through both afternoon and evening. And take off part of Saturday and most of Sunday. Use three afternoons for exercise in the open air and three evenings for movies or concerts or plays or for that novel you want to read. Your college work will benefit.

3 You will be told that classes are the most important thing at college. Don't believe it. President Eliot of Harvard said that if he wished to found a college the first thing he would build would be a dormitory. If there were money left over, he would erect a library and fill it with books. And if he had money to burn he would hire a faculty and build a classroom building. Those of us who are willing to remember find it easy to recollect that the most valuable things that happened to us in college usually happened in our dormitories, and most of them after midnight. We also recall with considerable pleasure the few occasions when we had the time and audacity to enter the college library and just browse among books utterly unconnected with our courses. Somehow we remember those books. We read them not because we had to, but because we wanted to. The difference is tremendous.

4 You will be told that marks are important. But they are a meager indication of a student's worth. Someday we shall have the courage to scuttle the whole marking system, and with it, I hope, will go that awful and meaningless sheepskin. Marks provide the outward and visible sign of the whole academic tradition. I wish every college student might come behind the scenes and watch his instructors doling out grades on papers and bluebooks. We have such curious foibles. The odds are definitely in favor of a paper read after rather than before dinner. A typewritten paper stands a better chance than one in longhand. And that factor of length! I know one student who got himself an A by sandwiching a dozen pages of economics notes into a long term-paper on Beethoven. It is a matter of record that given the same set of papers twice we will grade them differently. Given the same paper, moreover, various teachers will assign it grades ranging from D to A, even in mathematics. Some departments give as many as 40 per cent of their students A's, while others in the same institution allow only 5 per cent of the same students to get the highest marks.

5 You have probably been told that your academic record as an undergraduate will make or break your life. That simply is not so. Are you going into teaching? There is not a college president worth his salt who does not know that a Phi Beta Kappa key is small indication of your promise as a teacher. Are you going to professional school? Countless men and women with average grades as undergraduates have done brilliantly in professional

school. And in getting jobs, it is what they have been able to do in professional school that counts. Are you going to seek work as soon as you finish college? Letters of recommendation these days cover numerous items which have nothing to do with your academic achievement but are just as important. It would not be true to say that marks mean nothing, but if you will remember these facts every time you enter a classroom you will be on the right track.

6 Your professors form part of the academic taradiddle too. We stand on little raised platforms, the academic equivalents of the pedestal; we call ourselves "doctors" and smile with patient condescension when mistaken for medical men; we put high-sounding letters after our names; and we march in academic processions, clothed in magnificent medieval costumes. All in all we manage by such devices to convey the impression that we know what we are talking about. To be sure, we are not as pompous as some of our European colleagues in crime. Some of us even have the courage to sit on the same level and at the same seminar table with our students and listen to what they have to say. But it is not difficult to get the impression that your professors are founts of wisdom.

7 You will be told to take careful notes on their lectures and to commit those notes to memory. This whole business of note-taking is outmoded. Students started taking notes in the Middle Ages, before the printing press was invented. The student wrote his own books. Today, with large college libraries and with textbooks crowding and jostling one another for attention, the taking of notes is anachronistic. What you will do, if you are like the rest of the sheep, will be to produce pages and pages of notes, study them religiously for the examinations, then store them away. If you ever look at them again it will be simply to realize that the information they convey is far better presented in at least a dozen books immediately available, or that it is so thoroughly out of date that the notes are useless.

8 One of the major instruments of torture in collegiate education is the course examination. By this device the professor is enabled to discover how much of what he has said in class you have committed to memory. The night before the examination you cram the notes into your head. Next morning you enter a room heavy with the atmosphere of suspicion. You leave all notes and books in the hall, and you write on questions the answers to which you will have forgotten within a week, answers which in ordinary life no one in his right mind would ask you to remember because the information is available in the reference books where it belongs. Either you are working under the honor system, an unwitting accessory to the hocus-pocus, or you are annoyed and upset by a proctor who marches around among the desks looking for trouble. The more you understand why you are in college, the less seriously you will take examinations. Some day you may even educate us to the point where we will compose tests

which will measure your ability to use your knowledge with originality, rather than your ability to ape teacher. When that day arrives we shall let you bring notes, texts and even the *Encyclopaedia Britannica* to examinations. And then you may take examinations seriously.

9 Now that you are in college and going to classes, pause long enough to ask yourself why *we* are teaching and *you* are learning. In spite of what you may have heard from us or your high school teachers or your parents, the answer is not that we know the final answers to the problems we are discussing. We are teaching because we have studied carefully subjects in which you are a beginner, and because we have had more worldly experience than you. But neither of these facts makes us omniscient. If the truth be known, there are those of you in our classes who are more intelligent than we are—who will outstrip us in our chosen fields. Question us. Doubt us. Raise objections. Make us think! Avoid us when we measure your achievement in terms of the proximity of your thinking to our own. Welcome us when we admit that we do not know the answers to your questions, when we help you to find your own answers, when we encourage you to consider views with which we do not agree.

10 Why are you going to college? Not to enhance your parents' social position; not to get high marks; not to get the ultimate answers, which not even *we* can furnish. To use our own professional jargon, you come to college to get a liberal education. We must admit that we do not altogether know what a liberal education is, but we have some fairly good ideas on the subject. We do not entirely follow these ideas. None of us, for example, believes that there is a magic in piling up a certain number of hour-credits. Yet, sixty credits and you get your diploma. And that diploma is supposed to admit you to the company of educated men and women. Why not fifty-five, or sixty-five? We do not know. Indeed if you pressed us we should have to admit that some students are liberally educated with thirty credits while others will not belong to the educated company if they take sixty times sixty hours of credit. Do not measure your education by simple arithmetic.

11 Elect your courses with care. If you go to a college which requires that you juggle five courses at once, you will do well to find one easy berth and sleep in it; otherwise you cannot do justice to the other four. This is a secret practice acceptable and accepted by all. But in general easy courses should be avoided simply because they are easy and do not give you your father's money's worth.

12 Do not select your courses with an eye to a specific job or type of occupation. More of you will make this mistake than not, and it is one of the most serious you can make. In the first place, we know at least that a liberal education involves a balance and harmony of interests. Secondly, your interests and talents are by no means fully appreciated or explored when

you come to us. You do not want to wake up in your senior year and wish that you had not missed many important and interesting things. Thousands of seniors do.

13 When you come to college you are intellectually very young and have not yet learned to proceed safely or efficiently under your own intellectual power. You are what your environment and your elders have made you. Your ideas are not your own. The first thing you must learn is to stand on your own ideas. This is why one should not take us and our ideas too seriously. Broaden your horizon so that as you become more and more able to take care of yourself you will move intelligently. Do considerable mental visiting in your first years in college. Try to encounter the major points of view represented on the faculty and among the students. Entertain them the more seriously the more they differ from your own. You may return to your own, but if you do it will be with greater tolerance and broader understanding.

14 You come to college to gain a liberal perspective. In gaining this perspective you must come to know the nature which surrounds and compels you, the society with which you must live and cooperate, the creative spirit which is your heritage, and the tools of language and of thought. To express it in this specific manner is helpful. It suggests certain intellectual virtues which you must possess before you can be considered an educated man or woman. This does not mean that there are particular courses which can alone provide you with these virtues. Do not take a course solely for its specific content.

15 For example, we have said that you must come to know the natural world. This does not mean that you must study physics *and* chemistry *and* astronomy *and* geology. It means that you must acquire the scientific attitude, understand the atmosphere and significance of the exact sciences, know their fundamental assumptions, their key concepts, their major contributions. And the same is true of the biological sciences. A course in botany *or* zoology *or* physiology *or* psychology is enough to give you an understanding of the important aspects of biology. You have not time for them all. But one is essential. Far too many are ignorant of the biological forces affecting human conduct. You should get into the laboratory while you are in college, and you should work in both the exact and the biological sciences.

16 You want also to know the society with which you must live and cooperate. And one of the ways in which you want to know it is the historical. You must be historically minded. You must recognize the importance of the past for the present. Man learns by experience, and history is social experience. Greek, Roman, European, American history—you cannot study them all, *but* you can become historically minded. And you can become socially minded in your view of the present world. Economic, social and

political forces have your world in their grips. You must study these forces, measure them, evaluate them.

17 Our heritage in the field of the arts has always been recognized as liberalizing. Not so much need to urge you here. Most of the greatest interpretation of human living is to be found in painting, sculpture, music and literature. What are some of the things which the great creative geniuses have told us about ourselves? What are modern artists trying to do? You must find out these things, not just that you may go to museums and concerts, but that you may *want* to go to museums and concerts. Elect some art or music, for pleasure, but also to increase your knowledge. Also, get a full and enthusiastic knowledge of the literature of your mother tongue. You will have discovered a source of wisdom, good taste and pleasure. Such studies need no recommendation.

18 Finally, you must come to understand the tools of language and of thought. And here urging is necessary. You ought to know another language, ancient or modern, inflected or non-inflected, so well that you dream in it. Such knowledge gives a far better understanding of your own tongue, both as a tool and as an art, than you could otherwise obtain. And you will have open to you another literature. Furthermore, you should be conversant with the structures and powers of thought as an intellectual tool, and you should be willing to examine fundamental assumptions. Mathematics, logic and philosophy are helpful here. You may think them difficult, but do not avoid them altogether.

19 If you will examine this program for the enlarging of your intellectual horison you will see that it involves some eight subjects spread throughout the departments of your college. It is a program which you can complete in your freshman and sophomore years and one which you should carry through in order that you may be equipped intellectually to proceed to the second part of your college education. It will give you necessary breadth.

20 But you must also specialize, when the foundation has been laid. You must do this not because specialization will prepare you for a specific job, but because a certain degree of specialization is the second essential of true intellectual endeavor. Without specialization your college work is in danger of becoming that thin veneer of "culture" which we all recognize as superficial. And now you will find the faculty more cooperative. We are specialists and we like to encourage specialization. But still be on your guard, for we shall mislead you by overemphasizing the importance of our particular little corners of learning. The important matter is not *what* you specialize in, but that you specialize. Specialization for its own sake, that is my point. If you are going on to graduate work you will find the overwhelming advice of graduate school faculties to be that you specialize in *anything but* your subject of graduate study. If you are going into medicine, you might major in history. If you will be a lawyer, major in art or music.

21 Even your specialization should be carefully planned. In the first place, it will probably be advisable for you to do advanced work in each of the four major fields of study: natural science; social science; art and literature; and language, mathematics or philosophy. If you studied chemistry as a freshman, you might go on to more advanced chemistry and take elementary astronomy or geology as allied work. In short, in each major field in which you took two elementary courses as an underclassman, you should follow one elementary course into advanced work and at the same time gain some knowledge in an allied field.

22 But this will take only half of your time as an upperclassman. You should devote the other half of your last two years to intensive specialization in one subject in which you have the greatest interest and for which you have shown marked talent. Perhaps you have found history the most absorbing of subjects. Good! Go on in it. Devote half of your junior and senior years to history. Show that you can work intensively on the details of your chosen major, manipulate these details correctly, and fit them into a comprehensive picture of the whole. But remember—though your teachers will work against you here—remember that you are studying primarily for the sake of the intensive specialization and not of the history. Your roommate is getting the same thing from majoring in mathematics or English literature.

23 When you have avoided the Scylla of heterogeneous meanderings among elementary facts and concepts and the Charybdis of a study so narrow that you are ignorant of what is going on outside your own little corner of interest, you will have intellectual balance and perspective. Do not take us as your models. We represent a special world and we are an academic people. You are going into a broader world and non-academic environment. Make us realize that our interests and understandings should spread into every field. Make us see that our students are at least as important as the subjects we teach. Make us understand that marks and examinations are mere administrative conveniences to be taken far less seriously than we take them. In short, insist that we get together as a unified organization and provide you with a liberal education. Strength to you! If you will do these things you will be performing a service to us and to yourselves.

STUDY GUIDE

Structure

1. Every serious writer has some *central idea* that he is trying to develop in his essay or chapter in a book. To understand a writer's meaning, it is important that readers determine as quickly as possible what his central idea is. To do so, you should first read through the whole essay or chapter and try to decide what the writer is really talking about—in other words, his *subject matter*—and then what he has to say about it—his *thesis* or *theme*. Some-

times a writer will state his thesis or thematic idea succinctly in the essay itself, but sometimes he does not, in which case readers have to arrive at it themselves by examining the whole essay. Holmes states his main idea in paragraph 14, where he says that to gain a liberal perspective in college, one must come to know the nature that surrounds one, the society with which one must live and cooperate, the creative spirit of one's heritage, and the tools of language and thought. What curricular subjects discussed in the rest of the essay does this liberal perspective demand of the student? Why?

2. In a well-developed essay there are clearly discernible parts, each of which contributes something to the development of the main idea. These parts frequently include more than one paragraph. This essay falls logically into four main divisions: paragraphs 1–5, 6–9, 10–19, and 20–23. In analyzing the thought structure of an essay or section of a book, students should develop the habit of summarizing what is said in each major part in a complete declarative sentence. This summary will evolve into a *sentence outline*. Holmes's essay is outlined as an example. Fill in the blanks with the proper predicates suggested by the information in the essay.

THESIS SENTENCE: To gain a liberal perspective in college, one must come to know the *nature* that surrounds one, the *society* with which one must live and cooperate, the *creative spirit* of one's heritage, and the *tools of language and thought.*

I. College freshmen themselves are apt to overestimate things of secondary importance in their college education (paragraphs 1–5).
   A. The first of these is _______.
   B. The second of these is _______.
   C. And the third is _______.

II. A. Professors may also help to encourage these mistaken ideas about what is important in college education (paragraphs 6–9).
      1. One of these mistaken ideas is _______.
      2. Another mistaken idea is _______.
   B. But it is important for the student to know why professors are teaching and students are learning in college.

III. The real purpose of college is to develop a liberal perspective, which involves coming to know nature, society, the creative spirit of one's heritage, and the tools of language and thought (paragraphs 10–19).
   A. To know nature, one must study _______.
   B. To know society, one must study _______.
   C. To know one's artistic heritage, one must study _______.
   D. Finally, to understand the tools of language and thought, one must study _______.

IV. All the above elements lay the foundation of a general education in the first years of college but a superstructure must be built on this foundation by both intensification and specialization in the later years (paragraphs 20–23).
   A. The intensification is achieved by _______.
   B. The specialization is achieved by _______.

3. By employing proper connectives (conjunctions, reflexive pronouns, and so on), a good writer tries to help readers follow his thought from part to

part of his composition. Study the first sentences of paragraphs 6, 10, and 20, and see how the author has used connective words or sentence structure to point back to what has preceded or ahead to what is to come.

4. How would you describe the tone of the first and second parts of the essay? What are some of the ways in which the author has achieved that tone? Look up what is said about the connotation of the imperative sentence in the Appendix. Do the multiple imperatives in this essay help establish its tone?

5. Discuss the effectiveness of the sustained simile of the chained elephant in paragraph 1. How successfully does it express the author's attitude toward his student readers in the early part of the essay?

6. Discuss the last paragraph as a summary of the entire essay.

"WHY THE DEVIL DON'T YOU TEACH FRESHMEN TO WRITE?"

Edwin R. Clapp

1 Despite all the outcry and accusation in recent years, despite the growing mass and competence of professional assaults upon the problem, it seems that Johnny still "can't write." One reason is, I think, a misunderstanding, both lay and learned, of what writing means. When the man next to me in the Chicago plane discovers that I teach English, he mumbles something about watching his grammar. When Dr. Stackblower, associate professor of anthropology, bears down on me roaring, "Why the devil don't you teach the freshmen to write?" I know that he has just read some paper rich in orthographical mayhem. If Johnny makes a gross blunder in usage or spelling, both businessman and academic are shocked by his "English." But if Johnny scrambles the logic of his argument, or drifts into irrelevance, or dishes out bland generalizations innocent of support, or winds up in Timbuktu when he set out for Oshkosh—the man in the plane (or the street) is unlikely to be aware of error. And if Dr. Stackblower is, he will charge it to incompetence in anthropology. That "English" is implicated never crosses either of their minds.

2 I think we need to be clearer about what writing involves, what we want of Johnny, and what in practice we are willing to do to get it. Though "Johnny" may stand for any of his avatars from the elementary to the graduate school, let our Johnny be a college undergraduate, while "we" are all those charged with his education. In this context, let us look at him and at writing and at ourselves.

"Why the Devil Don't You Teach Freshmen to Write?" by Edwin R. Clapp, reprinted from *Saturday Review* (February 20, 1965) by permission of the author and publisher.

3 Writing has two dimensions: literacy and competence. Literacy involves what is often called "correctness" or "mechanics"—the ability to spell, to punctuate, to follow accepted conventions of grammar and usage, to employ everyday words in their common meanings. Such ability is certainly necessary. Writing in which it is lacking is at best irritating and distracting, at worst incomprehensible. As a description of writing, however, literacy is incomplete, external, and negative; it represents the capacity not to make mistakes. But it is an easy definition. The capacity it represents is clearly visible within the framework of the sentence. It lends itself to measure. Misspellings and grammatical errors can be counted. Tests based upon them can be devised and used as indices of verbal skill. Spelling above all—both to Professor Stackblower and the man in the plane for Chicago—is the great sign and symbol of the command of language. Be thou as chaste as ice, as pure as snow—and misspell "cat"—thou shalt not escape calumny. By and large the great world, lay and learned, equates "good English" with literacy, and particularly with spelling.

4 In contrast with literacy, competence means the ability to control language as the vehicle of thought and feeling, to recognize a subject and its boundaries, to order and support ideas, to conduct an argument or define a quality, to distinguish what is relevant from what is not, to express with precision differences of mood and force and meaning. Usually it is consistent with and inclusive of literacy as a substructure above and beyond which it grows, but this is not always true. Otherwise competent writers may, for instance, spell badly. Competence is manifested in the substance, organization, and texture of discourse in its larger units as well as in the sentence. Subtler and more complex than literacy, it is not hard to recognize but does not lend itself to counting. And when recognized, competence may by its very nature be thought of less as mastery of expression than as an aspect of the thing expressed. Thus it may go undervalued or even unnoted when Johnny's writing is assessed. And yet, competence—far more than literacy—is the true goal, both for Johnny and for all of us.

5 If we fret over Johnny's English, we must be clear what we are asking of him. We have confused literacy and competence, as definitions of ability and as desired ends. We have demanded literacy, when we *ought* to demand competence—not as a flat alternative, which it is not, but as an ability of greater value that in the fullness of its attainment will bring literacy with it, if only as a kind of by-product. Spelling we must make a special case. It is as much a matter of social decorum as an essential of communication; and when a genuine problem, it must be attacked as a distinctive one, often in terms of both psychology and language. (I hope not to be misunderstood; I want Johnny to spell. But spelling has come to occupy a place in the public mind out of all proportion to its significance, and thus to obscure more important issues.) We can have more of competence and

literacy (*and* better spelling) than we now have; we can have it tomorrow in the college and the day after in the schools, but only at the price of looking harder at ourselves as well as at Johnny. We shall need more dollars in some places, and—as competence in writing is inextricably involved with competence in reading, and this with thought—perhaps more sweat and tears. But to begin with, more light.

6 *Why* is the ability to write well seemingly attained so seldom, so incompletely, and with such difficulty? A full answer would require a book. It would involve the nature of language and our understanding of language, the character of American society and education, and the whole fabric of the modern world—all interwoven and all changing. I can attempt here only a sketch of some chapters.

7 First, Johnny's failures are sometimes more apparent than real; or, more accurately, they are of differing orders of magnitude. Demanding literacy as we do, we may overlook genuine if partial competence. I have struggled with more than one Johnny whose knowledge and insight were matched by his command of expression in everything save spelling, but whose feats in this department so occupied the foreground of attention as to obscure his real merits. Professor Stackblower naturally writes him down as another example of the inadequacies of the English Department. But to make due allowance for such anomalies is no more than to nibble off an edge of the problem.

8 Second, the teaching of "English," particularly but not only in the elementary and secondary school, has often meant a formally conceived literacy of labels and categories abstracted from the communicative and expressive functions of language, a literacy operating with equally external tools and devices—rote memory, workbooks, rigid and sometimes quite wrong grammatical dicta divorced from the plain facts of usage, the taxonomy of discourse. There is no doubt an element of necessity in all this. Much remains to be learned about the teaching of the language skills. But much is a product of confused aims, ignorance, and acceptance of the easy way, and for this the institution that educates the teacher bears a substantial responsibility.

9 Third, in the schools the basic relationships (differences as well as similarities) between spoken and written language, reading and writing, bread-and-butter prose and imaginative literature, and their implications for teaching have remained relatively undeveloped. In particular, the coupled reading and writing of expository prose, the prose of thought, seems to have been neglected; and this coupling is crucial for competence. There are all sorts of reasons: the overloaded teacher struggling with too many and too large classes (one place where more dollars are needed), the resultant impossibility of an adequate amount of critical attention to an adequate amount of student writing, the nice questions of the kinds of

reading appropriate to the several stages of Johnny's development and of how best to explore with him the processes of the mind expressed in an ordered world of prose—plus the brute fact that thought is hard.

10 Fourth, the universality of English as the language of all the disciplines has had mixed consequences for the teaching and learning of reading and writing. Successful expression everywhere involves the same elements: precision, clarity, order, relevance. But this very commonalty, this fact that he takes the vehicle of language for granted, gives the teacher of biology or history or economics an option between meaningful exploitation of reading and writing in *his* area and buck passing, between opportunity and escape. He may consider English, construed as literacy, strictly the business of the English teacher, and ignore the shared world of competence. With honorable exceptions, lip service, if that, has for the most part been given the idea that every teacher has a responsibility for how his students write; and the idea that he has a vested interest, let alone a responsibility, in how they read has not even been suggested—even though to distinguish reading and writing from thinking and knowing is almost an exercise in tautology. Nor does this situation represent merely inertia or indifference, or one more expression of that academic tribalism to which the departmentalization of learning gives rise—though all these may contribute.

11 A fifth consideration, closely related to the last but more basic, is the nature of language itself. If "all art constantly aspires to the condition of music," because in music content and form are one, in language the separation of the thing said from the way of saying, the what from the how, is in some partial and superficial sense possible. Thus "English" comes to be considered the garment of thought, discrete from the substance, which alone is biology or history or economics. One can detach the conventions, the mechanics, the "rules" of punctuation, grammar, usage (and of course spelling!) from fact and idea, keep the latter for oneself, and relegate the former to the exclusive custody of the English teacher, who thus becomes essentially a glorified proofreader. This is no fancy. I have been approached more than once by a professor of, let us say, engineering, who wanted me to find him a colleague to attend to the English of a report writing course while *his* staff took care of the engineering. Now, it is certainly true that the instructor in English is not *per se* qualified in engineering. It is just as true that the engineer really qualified as engineer ought also to be qualified in the world of discourse that engineering shares. We have returned to, perhaps in part accounted for, the dichotomy between literacy and competence. If the teacher of whatever subject thinks of English as only literacy, incidental or alien to the subject itself, the student is to be forgiven if *he* comes to regard English as a garb to be put on primarily or exclusively for the eccentrics who teach it. And his indignation is to be understood, if not

pardoned, when he is confronted by the instructor in biology or history or economics or engineering who insists that thought and expression are facets of the same thing and that the student is accountable to him for both. Fortunately, this instructor is as little a figure of fiction as Professor Stackblower; unfortunately, there are not so many of him.

12 A last reason for Johnny's parlous condition is that in school and out "good English," whether construed as literacy or competence, is in our time and society an artefact and a minority attainment. Very likely *good* English or French or Greek has always been a mark of education. For language itself is speech and usage, but popular and educated speech and usage are not identical, and *written* language (that which is read and composed to be read) is not identical with either, although closer to and largely governed by the standards of the latter. We expect educated speech to be in appropriate ways literate; we expect educated writing to be competent as well. We Americans are a democratic and heterogeneous society, divided by region and sometimes by origin; mobile, often in a significant sense homeless; quite variously schooled; instructed to a degree by sound and picture (as in popular conversation, radio, television); often lacking in bookish background and tradition; in tastes and ideals much drawn to the immediate and physical, the practical and technological. Should we be surprised that in such a context literacy in terms of upper-middle-class usage (not to mention competence in a form of discourse reaching toward art) is imperfectly attained by our young through the limited process of formal education? If this sketch gives something like a true picture of the reasons why "English" is the way it is, what is to be done about Johnny?

13 Education, like politics, is an art of the possible. The beginning of wisdom is, in the cant phrase, to "take the student where he is." Where is Johnny? He is, you will recall, a college undergraduate, let's say a freshman. He has typically been exposed to a number of years of drill founded on a traditional and dubious grammar; he has done some writing of quite variable amount and character; he has read a few standard works of literature and probably a slender but startling miscellany of contemporary fare; he doesn't know how to pursue an idea through a piece of prose that has one; he concocts what *he* considers English for his English teacher and is shocked if anybody else expects this odd behavior of him; and, as there is no guarantee that he spells correctly, Professor Stackblower is quite likely to be displeased with him. He has grown up believing that English means literacy because this is what he has been taught, and if it hasn't taken very well he is rather apologetic about it. Probably nobody has had time, strength, or inclination to help him very far toward competence. But, perhaps just because he is now eighteen or thereabouts, he can be helped toward competence and, if necessary, literacy into the bargain.

14 The initial help must come from the English Department. "Fresh-

man composition" has, of course, been taught in a fantastic variety of ways, and I have no pet formula to peddle, certainly no panacea. The essentials are, negatively, not to rehash the conventions of grammar again *seriatim et ad nauseam;* positively, to read a certain amount of serious well-fabricated exposition in order to discover the subject, its parts, their ordonnance and function—in short what it says and how and why; and to do some writing of the same kind and in the same spirit. Johnny is to discover, if he hasn't, that reading, writing, and thinking are a kind of three-wheeler which will take him down a number of roads. *En route,* he is firmly reminded that literacy is expected of him (spelling, too). He may find the going tough, but all the roads will take him toward competence, whatever incidental signs they bear. They are long roads, and he may not get all the way.

15 He will not—any more often than he does now—unless what happens to him in his English class is reinforced by what happens to him elsewhere. Johnny must come to believe that how he writes matters, not just to his English instructor, but to everybody else. He *won't* believe this unless in the first place he writes—instead of filling in boxes in multiple-choice tests. He won't, unless in the second place his instructor in history or biology or economics also believes it, and shows Johnny that he does. Even Professor Stackblower, if he would trouble only to circle Johnny's misspellings in a paper or two and give Johnny to understand that his grades have taken a shocking turn for the worse because of them, might be surprised by Johnny's improvement. I have seen it happen. Strangely enough, this simple step does not always occur to Stackblower.

16 To some it will seem platitudinous, and to others (especially battle-hardened academicians) utopian, to propose that college faculties take reasonable responsibility for whatever standards of literacy and/or competence they profess. The grounds for misgiving were succinctly put by the dean of a school of business administration who had requested the English Department to provide additional discipline in writing for his students. When I asked why his faculty shouldn't undertake this task themselves, he lowered his voice and said, "Frankly, I don't think they know enough—and besides, it's too hard work!" It may well be that Professor Kitzhaber is right in doubting (in his useful little book *Themes, Theories, and Therapy*) that any general and sustained faculty acceptance of "reasonable responsibility" is forthcoming. If so, in my opinion Johnny will stay where he is.

17 But mine is a genuinely modest proposal. By "reasonable responsibility" I mean that when in any course in any department student writing is demanded, the judgment of this writing should be consistent with accepted institutional standards applicable to the occasion, and that this judgment should be reflected in grades. I don't ask that all members of a faculty set themselves up as grammarians or rhetoricians, or that as readers

they devote the time and energy to style and structure one expects of the instructor in English. I ask that the faculty member who professes to be scandalized by misspelling and other gross errors at the level of literacy make known his displeasure in terms Johnny will understand. Neither great *expertise* nor effort would be required merely to check these off, particularly if some institution-wide code were adopted. As to competence, it is this that the faculty member who is baffled and offended by vagueness, confusion, and general impenetrability is seeking, although he may not consciously set out to demand clarity, order, or even evidence. One recalls the astonished delight with which M. Jourdain discovered that he was talking prose. I wish my colleagues to become aware that prose on the level of competence, the prose of written discourse, is what they really want of students. I think that they can get it, or get more of it than they have. Johnny is capable of writing better than he does—on demand. Such a demand would be far more potent than any addition to the standard formal requirements in English.

18 We have been talking about Johnny—and Joanne—simply as undergraduates. They may be destined for business, or the professions, or government service, or housewifery. If they come, however painfully, to understand that "English" means something more and other than literacy, this is a gain not only today for them as individuals and for the microcosm of the college, but also tomorrow for their children and the macrocosm of society and the schools. Faculty responsibility means much more than merely pacifying Professor Stackblower.

19 But to say "tomorrow" brings us back to my colleagues in English. If Johnny and Joanne are headed for careers as *English* teachers, they ought to be better equipped than their predecessors. I have been saying that undergraduate Johnny, whether in spite of or because of his experience in the schools, can be got to write. His teachers can be educated to do more for him, to help him further and earlier up the ladder of literacy and competency. I can attempt no blueprint here, but let my colleagues read and take to themselves Dr. Conant's description of typical faculty attitudes in *The Education of American Teachers*. We in college English need to accept responsibility for educating the public-school teacher, as we do the graduate student. We need to make a larger place in our curricula for language and writing alongside literature (which is what everybody, including me, yearns to teach). If we can—and I think we can—get Johnny to put whatever brains he has into learning *really* to read and *really* to write, we shall have done our whole duty as teachers of English, including our duty to literature. Perhaps it is the first duty of all teachers.

STUDY GUIDE

Structure

1. This essay, like the previous one, is well organized and illustrates several of the most usual methods of developing an idea in expository prose. It does two things: First, it discusses some of the reasons why most freshmen cannot write either correctly or competently, and then it makes some positive suggestions about how they may be brought to some competence in writing. Do you agree that the *thesis idea* of the whole essay is stated in the following sentence from paragraph 14? "The essentials [for developing competence] are, negatively, not to rehash the conventions of grammar again *seriatim et ad nauseam;* positively, to read a certain amount of serious well-fabricated exposition in order to discover the subject, its parts, their ordonnance and function —in short what it says and how and why; and to do some writing of the same kind and in the same spirit."

2. The following *thought divisions* may be easily discerned in this essay: paragraphs 1 and 2 (an introduction), paragraphs 3–5 (a definition of and distinction between literacy and competence), paragraphs 6–12 (a discussion of some of the reasons for the freshman's inability to write), paragraphs 13–17 (some positive suggestions for teaching him competence), and paragraphs 18 and 19 (a conclusion). Using the sentence outline in the study guide to the first essay as a model, construct a similar outline for this essay. Be sure to take account of the thought divisions indicated here.

3. In almost any piece of expository prose it is necessary to define one's terms. Where has the author employed *definition* to clarify the state of the question in this essay?

4. Another frequent method of developing an idea is to supply the reasons for or causes of a given effect or factual situation. Study closely how the author has employed this method of development in paragraphs 6–12. What has the author done verbally to help readers understand that he is providing an enumeration of reasons here?

THE LITERATURE OF KNOWLEDGE AND THE LITERATURE OF POWER

Thomas De Quincey

1 What is it that we mean by *literature?* Popularly, and amongst the thoughtless, it is held to include everything that is printed in a book. Little logic is required to disturb *that* definition; the most thoughtless person is

Reprinted from Thomas De Quincey, "The Literature of Knowledge and the Literature of Power," *North British Review* (1848).

easily made aware that in the idea of *literature* one essential element is,—some relation to a general and common interest of man, so that what applies only to a local, or professional, or merely personal interest, even though presenting itself in the shape of a book, will not belong to literature. So far the definition is easily narrowed; and it is as easily expanded. For not only is much that takes a station in books not literature; but, inversely, much that really *is* literature never reaches a station in books. The weekly sermons of Christendom, that vast pulpit literature which acts so extensively upon the popular mind—to warn, to uphold, to renew, to comfort, to alarm—does not attain the sanctuary of libraries in the ten thousandth part of its extent. The drama again, as, for instance, the finest of Shakespeare's plays in England, and all leading Athenian plays in the noontide of the Attic stage, operated as a literature on the public mind, and were (according to the strictest letter of that term) *published* through the audiences that witnessed their representation some time before they were published as things to be read; and they were published in this scenical mode of publication with much more effect than they could have had as books, during ages of costly copying or of costly printing.

2 Books, therefore, do not suggest an idea coextensive and interchangeable with the idea of literature; since much literature, scenic, forensic, or didactic (as from lecturers and public orators), may never come into books; and much that *does* come into books may connect itself with no literary interest. But a far more important correction, applicable to the common vague idea of literature, is to be sought—not so much in a better definition of literature, as in a sharper distinction of the two functions which it fulfils. In that great social organ, which collectively we call literature, there may be distinguished two separate offices that may blend and often *do* so, but capable severally of a severe insulation, and naturally fitted for reciprocal repulsion. There is, first, the literature of *knowledge*, and secondly, the literature of *power*. The function of the first is, to *teach*; the function of the second is, to *move:* the first is a rudder, the second an oar or a sail. The first speaks to the *mere* discursive understanding; the second speaks ultimately, it may happen, to the higher understanding or reason, but always *through* affections of pleasure and sympathy. Remotely, it may travel towards an object seated in what Lord Bacon calls *dry* light; but proximately it does and must operate, else it ceases to be a literature of *power*, on and through that *humid* light which clothes itself in the mists and glittering *iris* of human passions, desires, and genial emotions. Men have so little reflected on the higher functions of literature, as to find it a paradox if one should describe it as a mean or subordinate purpose of books to give information. But this is a paradox only in the sense which makes it honorable to be paradoxical. Whenever we talk in ordinary language of seeking information or gaining knowledge, we understand the words as connected with

something of absolute novelty. But it is the grandeur of all truth which *can* occupy a very high place in human interests, that it is never absolutely novel to the meanest of minds: it exists eternally by way of germ or latent principle in the lowest as in the highest, needing to be developed but never to be planted. To be capable of transplantation is the immediate criterion of a truth that ranges on a lower scale. Besides which, there is a rarer thing than truth, namely, *power* or deep sympathy with truth. What is the effect, for instance, upon society, of children? By the pity, by the tenderness, and by the peculiar modes of admiration, which connect themselves with the helplessness, with the innocence, and with the simplicity of children, not only are the primal affections strengthened and continually renewed, but the qualities which are dearest in the sight of Heaven—the frailty, for instance, which appeals to forbearance, the innocence which symbolizes the heavenly, and the simplicity which is most alien from the worldly, are kept up in perpetual remembrance, and their ideals are continually refreshed. A purpose of the same nature is answered by the higher literature, namely, the literature of power. What do you learn from *Paradise Lost?* Nothing at all. What do you learn from a cookery-book? Something new, something that you did not know before, in every paragraph. But would you therefore put the wretched cookery-book on a higher level of estimation than the divine poem? What you owe to Milton is not any knowledge, of which a million separate items are still but a million of advancing steps on the same earthly level; what you owe, is *power*, that is, exercise and expansion to your own latent capacity of sympathy with the infinite, where every pulse and each separate influx is a step upwards—a step ascending as upon a Jacob's ladder from earth to mysterious altitudes above the earth. *All* the steps of knowledge, from first to last, carry you further on the same plane, but could never raise you one foot above your ancient level of earth; whereas, the very *first* step in power is a flight—is an ascending into another element where earth is forgotten.

3 Were it not that human sensibilities are ventilated and continually called out into exercise by the great phenomena of infancy, or of real life as it moves through chance and change, or of literature as it recombines these elements in the mimicries of poetry, romance, &c., it is certain that, like any animal power or muscular energy falling into disuse, all such sensibilities would gradually droop and dwindle. It is in relation to these great *moral* capacities of man that the literature of power, as contradistinguished from that of knowledge, lives and has its field of action. It is concerned with what is highest in man; for the Scriptures themselves never condescended to deal by suggestion or coöperation, with the mere discursive understanding. When speaking of man in his intellectual capacity, the Scriptures speak not of the understanding, but of "*the understanding heart*," —making the heart, that is, the great *intuitive* (or non-discursive) organ, to

be the interchangeable formula for man in his highest state of capacity for the infinite. Tragedy, romance, fairy tale, or epopee, all alike restore to man's mind the ideals of justice, of hope, of truth, of mercy, of retribution, which else (left to the support of daily life in its realities) would languish for want of sufficient illustration. What is meant, for instance, by *poetic justice?*—It does not mean a justice that differs by its object from the ordinary justice of human jurisprudence; for then it must be confessedly a very bad kind of justice; but it means a justice that differs from common forensic justice, by the degree in which it *attains* its object, a justice that is more omnipotent over its own ends, as dealing—not with the refractory elements of earthly life—but with elements of its own creation, and with materials flexible to its own purest preconceptions. It is certain that, were it not for the literature of power, these ideals would often remain amongst us as mere arid national forms; whereas, by the creative forces of man put forth in literature, they gain a vernal life of restoration, and germinate into vital activities. The commonest novel, by moving in alliance with human fears and hopes, with human instincts of wrong and right, sustains and quickens those affections. Calling them into action, it rescues them from torpor. And hence the preeminency over all authors that merely *teach*, of the meanest that *moves*; or that teaches, if at all, indirectly *by* moving. The very highest work that has ever existed in the literature of knowledge is but a *provisional* work: a book upon trial and sufferance, and *quamdiu bene se gesserit.*[1] Let its teaching be even partially revised, let it be but expanded, nay, even let its teaching be but placed in a better order, and instantly it is superseded. Whereas the feeblest works in the literature of power, surviving at all, survive as finished and unalterable amongst men. For instance, the *Principia* of Sir Isaac Newton was a book *militant* on earth from the first. In all stages of its progress it would have to fight for its existence; first, as regards absolute truth; secondly, when that combat is over, as regards its form or mode of presenting the truth. And as soon as a La Place, or anybody else, builds higher upon the foundations laid by this book, effectually he throws it out of the sunshine into decay and darkness; by weapons won from this book he superannuates and destroys this book, so that soon the name of Newton remains, as a mere *nominis umbra,* but his book, as a living power, has transmigrated into other forms. Now, on the contrary, the *Iliad,* the *Prometheus* of Æschylus, the *Othello* or *King Lear,* the *Hamlet* or *Macbeth,* and the *Paradise Lost,* are not militant but triumphant forever as long as the languages exist in which they speak or can be taught to speak. They never *can* transmigrate into new incarnations. To reproduce *these* in new forms, or variations, even if in some things they should be improved, would be to plagiarize. A good steam-engine is prop-

[1] This Latin phrase means, "As long as it bore itself well."—Ed.

erly superseded by a better. But one lovely pastoral valley is not superseded by another, nor a statue of Praxiteles by a statue of Michael Angelo. These things are not separated by imparity, but by disparity. They are not thought of as unequal under the same standard, but as different in *kind*, and as equal under a different standard. Human works of immortal beauty and works of nature in one respect stand on the same footing: they never absolutely repeat each other; never approach so near as not to differ; and they differ not as better and worse, or simply by more and less; they differ by undecipherable and incommunicable differences, that cannot be caught by mimicries, nor be reflected in the mirror of copies, nor become ponderable in the scales of vulgar comparison.

STUDY GUIDE

Structure

1. In this essay the three paragraphs actually mark the three main thought divisions of the essay. (More frequently, as was the case in the two previous essays, several paragraphs may be employed to develop each of the chief thought divisions of an essay.) What is the main idea developed in each of the three paragraphs? State each main idea in a complete sentence.

2. Indicate the various ways in which the author has established a coherent transition in words and in thought between the three paragraphs. Underline the connecting words or phrases at the beginning of the second and third paragraphs.

Methods of Development

1. An almost indispensable method of developing an idea in a piece of expository prose is definition. A writer can define an object negatively by telling readers what it is not or positively by indicating the general traits that all objects included under the definition possess and the specific traits that differentiate these objects from all other objects. (Look up the detailed discussion of *definition* in the Appendix.) Show how De Quincey employs the negative method of definition in paragraph 1 to develop the idea of literature in general. Does he anywhere approach a positive definition of literature in general in paragraph 1?

2. *Concrete examples* are often more helpful for explaining something than the definition itself. Indicate how De Quincey has employed concrete examples in paragraph 1 to help clarify his notion of what literature is or is not.

3. Could you provide concrete examples of books that are not literature because they are concerned too narrowly with a "local, or professional, or merely personal interest"?

4. Since De Quincey's main purpose in this selection is not to give a definition of literature in general but to distinguish between literature of knowledge and literature of power, his chief methods of development in the second paragraph are *classification* and *contrast*. Show how the sustained contrast between the two kinds of literature builds up the whole structure of this

paragraph. Draw up a list of the ways in which the two kinds of literature are distinguished by De Quincey.

5. Show how the author has clarified his distinction between the purposes of the two types of literature by the use of metaphors.

6. How does the comparison of the effect of children on society help to clarify the purpose and function of the literature of power?

7. What precisely does De Quincey mean by the "*moral* capacities" of man in the last paragraph? Can you draw up a definition of them from what he says about them in this paragraph?

8. In paragraph 3, De Quincey provides a further distinction between the literature of knowledge and the literature of power. What is it? What concrete examples has he used to help clarify it?

DEEP READERS OF THE WORLD, BEWARE!

Saul Bellow

1 Interviewed as he was getting on the train for Boston, E. M. Forster was asked how he felt on the eve of his first visit to Harvard. He replied that he had heard that there were some particularly deep readers of his books to be found in Cambridge. He expected to be questioned closely by them, and this worried him. The reason is perfectly understandable.

2 In this age of ours serious people are more serious than they ever were, and lightness of heart like Mr. Forster's is hard to find. To the serious a novel is a work of art; art has a role to play in the drama of civilized life; civilized life is set upon a grim and dangerous course—and so we may assume if we are truly serious that no good novelist is going to invite us to a picnic merely to eat egg salad and chase butterflies over the English meadows or through the Tuscan woods. Butterflies are gay, all right, but in them lies the secret of metamorphosis. As for eggs, life's mystery hides in the egg. We all know that. So much for butterflies and egg salad.

3 It would be unjust to say that the responsibility for this sort of thing belongs entirely to the reader. Often the writer himself is at fault. He doesn't mind if he *is* a little deeper than average. Why not?

4 Nevertheless deep reading has gone very far. It has become dangerous to literature.

5 "Why, sir," the student asks, "does Achilles drag the body of Hector

around the walls of Troy?" "That sounds like a stimulating question. Most interesting. I'll bite," says the professor. "Well, you see, sir, the *Iliad* is full of circles—shields, chariot wheels and other round figures. And you know what Plato said about circles. The Greeks were all mad for geometry." "Bless your crew-cut head," says the professor, "for such a beautiful thought. You have exquisite sensibility. Your approach is both deep and serious. Still I always believed that Achilles did it because he was so angry."

6 It would take an unusual professor to realize that Achilles *was* angry. To many teachers he would represent much, but he would not *be* anything in particular. To be is too obvious. Our professor however is a "square," and the bright student is annoyed with him. Anger! What good is anger? Great literature is subtle, dignified, profound. Homer is as good as Plato anytime; and if Plato thought, Homer must surely have done so, too, thought just as beautifully circle for circle.

7 Things are not what they seem. And anyway, unless they represent something large and worthy, writers will not bother with them. Any deep reader can tell you that picking up a bus transfer is the *reise-motif* (journey motif) when it happens in a novel. A travel folder signifies Death. Coal holes represent the Underworld. Soda crackers are the Host. Three bottles of beer are—it's obvious. The busy mind can hardly miss at this game, and every player is a winner.

8 Are you a Marxist? Then Herman Melville's Pequod in *Moby Dick* can be a factory, Ahab the manager, the crew the working class. Is your point of view religious? The Pequod sailed on Christmas morning, a floating cathedral headed south. Do you follow Freud or Jung? Then your interpretations may be rich and multitudinous. I recently had a new explanation of *Moby Dick* from the young man in charge of an electronic brain. "Once and for all," he said, "that whale is everybody's mother wallowing in her watery bed. Ahab has the Oedipus complex and wants to slay the hell out of her."

9 This is deep reading. But it is only fair to remember that the best novelists and poets of the century have done much to promote it. When Mairy (in James Joyce's *Ulysses*) loses the pin of her drawers, she doesn't know what to do to keep them up; the mind of Bloom goes from grammar to painting, from painting to religion. It is all accomplished in a few words. Joyce's genius holds all the elements in balance.

10 The deep reader, however, is apt to lose his head. He falls wildly on any particle of philosophy or religion and blows it up bigger than the Graf Zeppelin. Does Bloom dust Stephen's clothes and brush off the wood shavings? They are no ordinary shavings but the shavings from Stephen's cross.

11 What else: All the little monkish peculiarities at which Robert Browning poked fun in the "Soliloquy in a Spanish Cloister," crossing

knife and fork on the platter at the end of a meal and the rest of it, have become the pillars of the new system.

12 Are we to attach meaning to whatever is grazed by the writer? Is modern literature Scripture? Is criticism Talmud, theology? Deep readers of the world, beware! You had better be sure that your seriousness is indeed high seriousness and not, God forbid, low seriousness.

13 A true symbol is substantial, not accidental. You cannot avoid it, you cannot remove it. You can't take the handkerchief from *Othello*, or the sea from *The Nigger of the Narcissus*, or the disfigured feet from *Oedipus Rex*. You can, however, read *Ulysses* without suspecting that wood shavings have to do with the Crucifixion or that the name Simon refers to the sin of Simony or that the hunger of the Dubliners at noon parallels that of the Lestrigonians. These are purely peripheral matters; fringe benefits, if you like. The beauty of the book cannot escape you if you are any sort of reader, and it is better to approach it from the side of naivete than from that of culture-idolatry, sophistication and snobbery. Of course it's hard in our time to be as naive as one would like. Information does filter through. It leaks, as we have taken to saying. Still the knowledge of even the sophisticated is rather thin, and even the most wised-up devils, stuffed to the ears with arcana, turned out to be fairly simple.

14 Perhaps the deepest readers are those who are least sure of themselves. An even more disturbing suspicion is that they prefer meaning to feeling. What again about the feelings? Yes, it's too bad. I'm sorry to have to ring in this tiresome subject, but there's no help for it. The reason why the schoolboy takes refuge in circles is that the wrath of Achilles and the death of Hector are too much for him. He is doing no more than most civilized people do when confronted with passion and death. They contrive somehow to avoid them.

15 The practice of avoidance is so widespread that it is probably not fair to single out any group for blame. But if nothing is to be said or done, we might as well make ready to abandon literature altogether. Novels are being published today which consist entirely of abstractions, meanings, and while our need for meanings is certainly great our need for concreteness, for particulars, is even greater. We need to see how human beings act after they have appropriated or assimilated the meanings. Meanings themselves are a dime a dozen. In literature humankind becomes abstract when we begin to dislike it. And . . .

16 Interruption by a deep reader: Yes, yes, we know all that. But just look at the novels of the concrete and the particular, people opening doors and lighting cigarettes. Aren't they boring? Besides, do you want us to adopt a program to curtail the fear of feeling and to pretend to *like* the creature of flesh and bone?

17 Certainly not. No programs.

18 A pretty pass we have come to!

19 We must leave it to inspiration to redeem the concrete and the particular and to recover the value of flesh and bone. Meanwhile, let Plato have his circles and let the soda crackers be soda crackers and the wood shavings wood shavings. They are mysterious enough as it is.

STUDY GUIDE

Structure

This essay is a lightly satirical treatment of one of the exaggerations of modern criticism—what the author calls "deep reading." He nowhere explicitly defines deep reading but rather allows concrete examples to define it for him. The essay might be divided into an introduction (paragraphs 1–3), the body of the essay (paragraphs 4–18), and a conclusion (paragraph 19).

1. What rhetorical devices has Bellow used in the introduction to capture the interest of the reader and introduce his subject? (See the discussion of the rhetoric of the *exordium*, or introduction, in the Appendix.)

2. How is his handling of the egg and the butterfly in paragraph 2 already an exemplification of deep reading?

3. One method of developing an idea is to provide multiple concrete examples that illustrate rather than define it. List the concrete examples of deep reading that the author offers us in paragraphs 5–11. How do they show what he means by deep reading?

4. Is Bellow against all symbolism in literature? Where does he illustrate concretely the difference between what he considers legitimate and exaggerated symbolism in the analysis of literature?

5. Indicate how paragraph 19 alludes concretely to both deep reading and its opposite?

6. Do you see any connection between what Bellow is pleading for in paragraph 15 and what De Quincey discusses in connection with the literature of power?

ON FAMILIAR STYLE

William Hazlitt

1 It is not easy to write a familiar style. Many people mistake a familiar for a vulgar style, and suppose that to write without affectation is to write at random. On the contrary, there is nothing that requires more precision,

Reprinted from William Hazlitt, *Table-Talk* (1821).

and, if I may so say, purity of expression, than the style I am speaking of. It utterly rejects not only all unmeaning pomp, but all low, cant phrases, and loose, unconnected, *slipshod* allusions. It is not to take the first word that offers, but the best word in common use; it is not to throw words together in any combinations we please, but to follow and avail ourselves of the true idiom of the language. To write a genuine familiar or truly English style, is to write as any one would speak in common conversation, who had a thorough command and choice of words, or who could discourse with ease, force, and perspicuity, setting aside all pedantic and oratorical flourishes. Or to give another illustration, to write naturally is the same thing in regard to common conversation, as to read naturally is in regard to common speech. It does not follow that it is an easy thing to give the true accent and inflection to the words you utter, because you do not attempt to rise above the level of ordinary life and colloquial speaking. You do not assume indeed the solemnity of the pulpit, or the tone of stage-declamation: neither are you at liberty to gabble on at a venture, without emphasis or discretion, or to resort to vulgar dialect or clownish pronunciation. You must steer a middle course. You are tied down to a given and appropriate articulation, which is determined by the habitual associations between sense and sound, and which you can only hit by entering into the author's meaning, as you must find the proper words and style to express yourself by fixing your thoughts on the subject you have to write about. Any one may mouth out a passage with a theatrical cadence, or get upon stilts to tell his thoughts: but to write or speak with propriety and simplicity is a more difficult task. Thus it is easy to affect a pompous style, to use a word twice as big as the thing you want to express: it is not so easy to pitch upon the very word that exactly fits it. Out of eight or ten words equally common, equally intelligible, with nearly equal pretensions, it is a matter of some nicety and discrimination to pick out the very one, the preferableness of which is scarcely perceptible, but decisive. . . .

2 The proper force of words lies not in the words themselves, but in their application. A word may be a fine-sounding word, of an unusual length, and very imposing from its learning and novelty, and yet in the connection in which it is introduced, may be quite pointless and irrelevant. It is not pomp or pretension, but the adaptation of the expression to the idea that clenches a writer's meaning:—as it is not the size or glossiness of the materials, but their being fitted each to its place, that gives strength to the arch; or as the pegs and nails are as necessary to the support of the building as the larger timbers, and more so than the mere shewy, unsubstantial ornaments. I hate any thing that occupies more space than it is worth. I hate to see a load of band-boxes go along the street, and I hate to see a parcel of big words without any thing in them. A person who does not de-

liberately dispose of all his thoughts alike in cumbrous draperies and flimsy disguises, may strike out twenty varieties of familiar everyday language, each coming somewhat nearer to the feeling he wants to convey, and at last not hit upon that particular and only one, which may be said to be identical with the exact impression in his mind. This would seem to shew that Mr. Cobbett is hardly right in saying that the first word that occurs is always the best. It may be a very good one; and yet a better may present itself on reflection or from time to time. It should be suggested naturally, however, and spontaneously, from a fresh and lively conception of the subject. We seldom succeed by trying at improvement, or by merely substituting one word for another that we are not satisfied with, as we cannot recollect the name of a place or person by merely plaguing ourselves about it. We wander farther from the point by persisting in a wrong scent; but it starts up accidentally in the memory when we least expected it, by touching some link in the chain of previous association.

STUDY GUIDE

Structure

1. A definition in a piece of literary exposition is not built with the same precision as a logical definition by genus and specific difference in a philosophical treatise. It may proceed by eliminating false ideas of the thing being discussed, by listing qualities that pertain to it alone, by comparing or contrasting it with something else, and eventually stating more precisely in what the thing being defined actually consists. There are, of course, dozens of different ways of building such a rhetorical definition. The procedures listed here, however, are roughly those which Hazlitt uses to define the familiar style in paragraph 1. Trace through his use of these methods in his paragraph sentence by sentence.

2. Indicate in a similar manner what methods of development Hazlitt uses to define "the proper force of words" or good diction in paragraph 2 of this essay.

3. Take any word you like that needs clarification and try to write a paragraph in which you define, expand, and illustrate its meaning in somewhat the same way that Hazlitt enlarges upon the idea of the familiar style and forceful diction in these paragraphs. You might, for instance, try to define the difference between *familiarity* and *vulgarity* that Hazlitt says is frequently not understood. You will have to begin with your own discovery of the exact dictionary definitions of these terms. From there you can work into an enlargement of the two ideas by elimination of false ideas about them, by comparisons and contrasts, concrete examples, a listing of specific qualities of *familiarity* and *vulgarity*, and so on.

WHAT IS STYLE?

F. L. Lucas

1 When it was suggested to Walt Whitman that one of his works should be bound in vellum, he was outraged—"Pshaw!" he snorted, "—hangings, curtains, finger bowls, chinaware, Matthew Arnold!" And he might have been equally irritated by talk of style; for he boasted of "my barbaric yawp"—he would *not* be literary; his readers should touch not a book but a man. Yet Whitman took the pains to rewrite *Leaves of Grass* four times, and his style is unmistakable. Samuel Butler maintained that writers who bothered about their style became unreadable but he bothered about his own. "Style" has got a bad name by growing associated with precious and superior persons who, like Oscar Wilde, spend a morning putting in a comma, and the afternoon (so he said) taking it out again. But such abuse of "style" is misuse of English. For the word means merely "a way of expressing oneself, in language, manner, or appearance"; or, secondly, "a *good* way of so expressing oneself"—as when one says, "Her behavior never lacked style."

2 Now there is no crime in expressing oneself (though to try to *impress* oneself on others easily grows revolting or ridiculous). Indeed one cannot help expressing oneself, unless one passes one's life in a cupboard. Even the most rigid Communist, or Organization-man, is compelled by Nature to have a unique voice, unique fingerprints, unique handwriting. Even the signatures of the letters on your breakfast table may reveal more than their writers guess. There are blustering signatures that swish across the page like cornstalks bowed before a tempest. There are cryptic signatures, like a scrabble of lightning across a cloud, suggesting that behind is a lofty divinity whom all must know, or an aloof divinity whom none is worthy to know (though, as this might be highly inconvenient, a docile typist sometimes interprets the mystery in a bracket underneath). There are impetuous squiggles implying that the author is a sort of strenuous Sputnik streaking round the globe every eighty minutes. There are florid signatures, all curlicues and danglements and flamboyance, like the youthful Disraeli (though these seem rather out of fashion). There are humble, humdrum signatures. And there are also, sometimes, signatures that are courteously clear, yet mindful of a certain simple grace and artistic economy—in short, of style.

3 Since, then, not one of us can put pen to paper, or even open his mouth, without giving something of himself away to shrewd observers, it seems mere common sense to give the matter a little thought. Yet it does not seem very common. Ladies may take infinite pains about having style in their clothes, but many of us remain curiously indifferent about having it in our words. How many women would dream of polishing not only their nails but also their tongues? They may play freely on that perilous little organ, but they cannot often be bothered to tune it. And how many men think of improving their talk as well as their golf handicap?

4 No doubt strong silent men, speaking only in gruff monosyllables, may despise "mere words." No doubt the world does suffer from an endemic plague of verbal dysentery. But that, precisely, is bad style. And consider the amazing power of mere words. Adolf Hitler was a bad artist, bad statesman, bad general, and bad man. But largely because he could tune his rant, with psychological nicety, to the exact wave length of his audiences and make millions quarrelsome-drunk all at the same time by his command of windy nonsense, skilled statesmen, soldiers, scientists were blown away like chaff, and he came near to rule the world. If Sir Winston Churchill had been a mere speechifier, we might well have lost the war; yet his speeches did quite a lot to win it.

5 No man was less of a literary aesthete than Benjamin Franklin; yet this tallow-chandler's son, who changed world history, regarded as "a principal means of my advancement" that pungent style which he acquired partly by working in youth over old *Spectators;* but mainly by being Benjamin Franklin. The squinting demagogue, John Wilkes, as ugly as his many sins, had yet a tongue so winning that he asked only half an hour's start (to counteract his face) against any rival for a woman's favor. "Vote for you!" growled a surly elector in his constituency. "I'd sooner vote for the devil!" "But in case your friend should not stand . . . ?" Cleopatra, that ensnarer of world conquerors, owed less to the shape of her nose than to the charm of her tongue. Shakespeare himself has often poor plots and thin ideas; even his mastery of character has been questioned; what does remain unchallenged is his verbal magic. Men are often taken, like rabbits, by the ears. And though the tongue has no bones, it can sometimes break millions of them.

6 "But," the reader may grumble, "I am neither Hitler, Cleopatra, nor Shakespeare. What is all this to me?" Yet we all talk—often too much; we all have to write letters—often too many. We live not by bread alone but also by words. And not always with remarkable efficiency. Strikes, lawsuits, divorces, all sorts of public nuisance and private misery, often come just from the gaggling incompetence with which we express ourselves. Americans and British get at cross-purposes because they use the same words

with different meanings. Men have been hanged on a comma in a statute. And in the valley of Balaclava a mere verbal ambiguity, about *which* guns were to be captured, sent the whole Light Brigade to futile annihilation.

7 Words can be more powerful, and more treacherous, than we sometimes suspect; communication more difficult than we may think. We are all serving life sentences of solitary confinement within our own bodies; like prisoners, we have, as it were, to tap in awkward code to our fellow men in their neighboring cells. Further, when A and B converse, there take part in their dialogue not two characters, as they suppose, but six. For there is A's real self—call it A_1, there is also A's picture of himself—A_2; there is also B's picture of A—A_3. And there are three corresponding personalities of B. With six characters involved even in a simple tête-à-tête, no wonder we fall into muddles and misunderstandings.

8 Perhaps, then, there are five main reasons for trying to gain some mastery of language:

9 We have no other way of understanding, informing, misinforming, or persuading one another.

10 Even alone, we think mainly in words; if our language is muddy, so will our thinking be.

11 By our handling of words we are often revealed and judged. "Has he written anything?" said Napoleon of a candidate for an appointment. "Let me see his *style*."

12 Without a feeling for language one remains half-blind and deaf to literature.

13 Our mother tongue is bettered or worsened by the way each generation uses it. Languages evolve like species. They can degenerate; just as oysters and barnacles have lost their heads. Compare ancient Greek with modern. A heavy responsibility, though often forgotten.

14 Why and how did I become interested in style? The main answer, I suppose, is that I was born that way. Then I was, till ten, an only child running loose in a house packed with books, and in a world (thank goodness) still undistracted by radio and television. So at three I groaned to my mother, "Oh, I *wish* I could read," and at four I read. Now travel among books is the best travel of all, and the easiest, and the cheapest. (Not that I belittle ordinary travel—which I regard as one of the three main pleasures in life.) One learns to write by reading good books, as one learns to talk by hearing good talkers. And if I have learned anything of writing, it is largely from writers like Montaigne, Dorothy Osborne, Horace Walpole, Johnson, Goldsmith, Montesquieu, Voltaire, Flaubert and Anatole France. Again, I was reared on Greek and Latin, and one can learn much from translating Homer or the Greek Anthology, Horace or Tacitus, if one is thrilled by

the originals and tries, however vainly, to recapture some of that thrill in English. . . .

15 For forty years at Cambridge I have tried to teach young men to write well, and have come to think it impossible. To write really well is a gift inborn; those who have it teach themselves; one can only try to help and hasten the process. After all, the uneducated sometimes express themselves far better than their "betters." In language, as in life, it is possible to be perfectly correct—and yet perfectly tedious, or odious. The illiterate last letter of the doomed Vanzetti was more moving than most professional orators; eighteenth-century ladies, who should have been spanked for their spelling, could yet write far better letters than most professors of English; and the talk of Synge's Irish peasants seems to me vastly more vivid than the later style of Henry James. Yet Synge averred that his characters owed far less of their eloquence to what he invented for them than to what he had overheard in the cottages of Wicklow and Kerry:

16 "*Christy*. 'It's little you'll think if my love's a poacher's, or an earl's itself, when you'll feel my two hands stretched around you, and I squeezing kisses on your puckered lips, till I'd feel a kind of pity for the Lord God is all ages sitting lonesome in His golden chair.'

17 "*Pegeen*. 'That'll be right fun, Christy Mahon, and any girl would walk her heart out before she'd meet a young man was your like for eloquence, or talk at all.' "

18 Well she might! It's not like that they talk in universities—more's the pity.

19 But though one cannot teach people to write well, one can sometimes teach them to write rather better. One can give a certain number of hints, which often seem boringly obvious—only experience shows they are not.

20 One can say: Beware of pronouns—they are devils. Look at even Addison, describing the type of pedant who chatters of style without having any: "Upon enquiry I found my learned friend had dined that day with Mr. Swan, the famous punster; and desiring *him* to give me some account of Mr. Swan's conversation, *he* told me that *he* generally talked in the Paronomasia, that *he* sometimes gave in to the Plocé, but that in *his* humble opinion *he* shone most in the Antanaclasis." What a sluttish muddle of *he* and *him* and *his*! It all needs rewording. Far better repeat a noun, or a name, than puzzle the reader, even for a moment, with ambiguous pronouns. Thou shalt not puzzle thy reader.

21 Or one can say: Avoid jingles. The B.B.C. news bulletins seem compiled by earless persons, capable of crying round the globe: "The enemy is re*port*ed to have seized this im*port*ant *port*, and reinforcements are hurrying up in sup*port*." Any fool, once told, can hear such things to be insupportable.

22 Or one can say: Be sparing with relative clauses. Don't string them together like sausages, or jam them inside one another like Chinese boxes or the receptacles of Buddha's tooth. Or one can say: Don't flaunt jargon, like Addison's Mr. Swan, or the type of modern critic who gurgles more technical terms in a page than Johnson used in all his *Lives* or Sainte-Beuve in thirty volumes. But dozens of such snippety precepts, though they may sometimes save people from writing badly, will help them little toward writing well. Are there no general rules of a more positive kind, and of more positive use?

23 Perhaps. There *are* certain basic principles which seem to me observed by many authors I admire, which I think have served me and which may serve others. I am not talking of geniuses, who are a law to themselves (and do not always write a very good style, either); nor of poetry, which has different laws from prose; nor of poetic prose, like Sir Thomas Browne's or De Quincey's, which is often more akin to poetry; but of the plain prose of ordinary books and documents, letters and talk.

24 The writer should respect truth and himself; therefore honesty. He should respect his readers; therefore courtesy. These are two of the cornerstones of style. Confucius saw it, twenty-five centuries ago: "The Master said, The gentleman is courteous, but not pliable: common men are pliable, but not courteous."

25 First, honesty. In literature, as in life, one of the fundamentals is to find, and be, one's true self. One's true self may indeed be unpleasant (though one can try to better it); but a false self, sooner or later, becomes disgusting—just as a nice plain woman, painted to the eyebrows, can become horrid. In writing, in the long run, pretense does not work. As the police put it, anything you say may be used as evidence against you. If handwriting reveals character, writing reveals it still more. You cannot fool *all* your judges *all* the time.

26 Most style is not honest enough. Easy to say, but hard to practice. A writer may take to long words, as young men to beards—to impress. But long words, like long beards, are often the badge of charlatans. Or a writer may cultivate the obscure, to seem profound. But even carefully muddied puddles are soon fathomed. Or he may cultivate eccentricity, to seem original. But really original people do not have to think about being original—they can no more help it than they can help breathing. They do not need to dye their hair green. The fame of Meredith, Wilde or Bernard Shaw might now shine brighter, had they struggled less to be brilliant; whereas Johnson remains great, not merely because his gifts were formidable but also because, with all his prejudice and passion, he fought no less passionately to "clear his mind of cant."

27 Secondly, courtesy—respect for the reader. From this follow several other basic principles of style. Clarity is one. For it is boorish to make your

reader rack his brains to understand. One should aim at being impossible to misunderstand—though men's capacity for misunderstanding approaches infinity. Hence Molière and Po Chu-i tried their work on their cooks; and Swift his on his menservants—"which, if they did not comprehend, he would alter and amend, until they understood it perfectly." Our bureaucrats and pundits, unfortunately, are less considerate.

28 Brevity is another basic principle. For it is boorish, also, to waste your reader's time. People who would not dream of stealing a penny of one's money turn not a hair at stealing hours of one's life. But that does not make them less exasperating. Therefore there is no excuse for the sort of writer who takes as long as a marching army corps to pass a given point. Besides, brevity is often more effective; the half can say more than the whole, and to imply things may strike far deeper than to state them at length. And because one is particularly apt to waste words on preambles before coming to the substance, there was sense in the Scots professor who always asked his pupils—"Did ye remember to tear up that fir-r-st page?"

29 Here are some instances that would only lose by lengthening:

> *It is useless to go to bed to save the light, if the result is twins.* (Chinese proverb.)
>
> *My barn is burnt down—*
> *Nothing hides the moon.* (Complete Japanese poem.)
>
> *Je me regrette.* (Dying words of the gay vicomtesse d'Houdetot.)
>
> *I have seen their backs before.* (Wellington, when French marshals turned their backs on him at a reception.)
>
> *Continue until the tanks stop, then get out and walk.* (Patton to the Twelfth Corps, halted for fuel supplies at St. Dizier, 8/30/44.)

30 Or there is the most laconic diplomatic note on record: when Philip of Macedon wrote to the Spartans that, if he came within their borders, he would leave not one stone of their city, they wrote back the one word—"If."

31 Clarity comes before even brevity. But it is a fallacy that wordiness is necessarily clearer. Metternich when he thought something he had written was obscure would simply go through it crossing out everything irrelevant. What remained, he found, often became clear. Wellington, asked to recommend three names for the post of Commander-in-Chief, India, took a piece of paper and wrote three times—"Napier." Pages could not have been clearer—or as forcible. On the other hand the lectures, and the sentences, of Coleridge became at times bewildering because his mind was often "wiggle-waggle"; just as he could not even walk straight on a path.

32 But clarity and brevity, though a good beginning, are only a beginning. By themselves, they may remain bare and bleak. When Calvin Coolidge, asked by his wife what the preacher had preached on, replied "Sin," and, asked what the preacher had said, replied, "He was against it," he was brief enough. But one hardly envies Mrs. Coolidge.

33 An attractive style requires, of course, all kinds of further gifts—such as variety, good humor, good sense, vitality, imagination. Variety means avoiding monotony of rhythm, of language, of mood. One needs to vary one's sentence length (this present article has too many short sentences; but so vast a subject grows here as cramped as a djin in a bottle); to amplify one's vocabulary; to diversify one's tone. There are books that petrify one throughout, with the rigidly pompous solemnity of an owl perched on a leafless tree. But ceaseless facetiousness can be as bad; or perpetual irony. Even the smile of Voltaire can seem at times a fixed grin, a disagreeable wrinkle. Constant peevishness is far worse, as often in Swift; even on the stage too much irritable dialogue may irritate an audience, without its knowing why.

34 Still more are vitality, energy, imagination gifts that must be inborn before they can be cultivated. But under the head of imagination two common devices may be mentioned that have been the making of many a style —metaphor and simile. Why such magic power should reside in simply saying, or implying, that A is like B remains a little mysterious. But even our unconscious seems to love symbols; again, language often tends to lose itself in clouds of vaporous abstraction, and simile or metaphor can bring it back to concrete solidity; and, again, such imagery can gild the gray flats of prose with sudden sun-glints of poetry.

35 If a foreigner may for a moment be impertinent, I admire the native gift of Americans for imagery as much as I wince at their fondness for slang. (Slang seems to me a kind of linguistic fungus; as poisonous, and as short-lived, as toadstools.) When Matthew Arnold lectured in the United States, he was likened by one newspaper to "an elderly macaw pecking at a trellis of grapes"; he observed, very justly, "How lively journalistic fancy is among the Americans!" General Grant, again, unable to hear him, remarked: "Well, wife, we've paid to see the British lion, but as we can't hear him roar, we'd better go home." By simile and metaphor, these two quotations bring before us the slightly pompous, fastidious, inaudible Arnold as no direct description could have done.

36 Or consider how language comes alive in the Chinese saying that lending to the feckless is "like pelting a stray dog with dumplings," or in the Arab proverb: "They came to shoe the pasha's horse, and the beetle stretched forth his leg"; in the Greek phrase for a perilous cape—"stepmother of ships"; or the Hebrew adage that "as the climbing up a sandy

way is to the feet of the aged, so is a wife full of words to a quiet man"; in Shakespeare's phrase for a little England lost in the world's vastness—"in a great Poole, a Swan's-nest"; or Fuller's libel on tall men—"Ofttimes such who are built four stories high are observed to have little in their cockloft"; in Chateaubriand's "I go yawning my life"; or in Jules Renard's portrait of a cat, "well buttoned in her fur." Or, to take a modern instance, there is Churchill on dealings with Russia: "Trying to maintain good relations with a Communist is like wooing a crocodile. You do not know whether to tickle it under the chin or beat it over the head. When it opens its mouth, you cannot tell whether it is trying to smile or preparing to eat you up." What a miracle human speech can be, and how dull is most that one hears! Would one hold one's hearers, it is far less help, I suspect, to read manuals on style than to cultivate one's own imagination and imagery.

37 I will end with two remarks by two wise old women of the civilized eighteenth century.

38 The first is from the blind Mme. du Deffand (the friend of Horace Walpole) to that Mlle. de Lespinasse with whom, alas, she was to quarrel so unwisely: "You must make up your mind, my queen, to live with me in the greatest truth and sincerity. You will be charming so long as you let yourself be natural, and remain without pretension and without artifice." The second is from Mme. de Charrière, the Zélide whom Boswell had once loved at Utrecht in vain, to a Swiss girl friend: "Lucinde, my clever Lucinde, while you wait for the Romeos to arrive, you have nothing better to do than become perfect. Have ideas that are clear, and expressions that are simple." ("*Ayez des idées nettes et des expressions simples.*") More than half the bad writing in the world, I believe, comes from neglecting those two very simple pieces of advice.

39 In many ways, no doubt, our world grows more and more complex; sputniks cannot be simple; yet how many of our complexities remain futile, how many of our artificialities false. Simplicity too can be subtle—as the straight lines of a Greek temple, like the Parthenon at Athens, are delicately curved, in order to look straighter still.

STUDY GUIDE

Structure

1. F. L. Lucas is here concerned with something that concerns everyone—style. He defines style as *good self-expression.* People express themselves every moment of the day whether they intend to or not, and especially by the language they use. This is his reason for discussing the nature and effects of good style and some of the means of achieving it. His discussion is a beautifully organized piece of writing, and hence it is worth studying his organization in detail. The essay is made up of the following thought divisions: an introduction

(paragraphs 1–3), the body of the essay (paragraphs 4–36), and a conclusion (paragraphs 37–39). The body of the essay itself is divided into the following topics: the power of words (paragraphs 4–6); the difficulty of communication (paragraph 7); some reasons for gaining a mastery of language (paragraphs 8–13); some reasons for the author's interest in style (paragraph 14); the fact that writing really well cannot be taught (paragraphs 15–18); the possibility of teaching students to write better by observing a few *don'ts* (paragraphs 19–22), and a few positive principles for writing better (paragraphs 23–36). Draw up a careful sentence outline of the essay in which you take account of all these general thought divisions and in which you show by proper subordination and parallelism the various divisions and thought development within each part.

2. One of Lucas' favorite methods of developing an idea is by multiple concrete examples. Point out several paragraphs that are effectively developed through this method.

3. One means of adding vitality and variety to one's writing is by the judicious use of the *concrete anecdote.* Point out several instances of the effective use of this device in this essay.

4. Lucas himself says that well-chosen *similes* or *metaphors* are a writer's chief means of adding sprightliness to his expression. He says they can "gild the gray flats of prose with sudden sun-glints of poetry." He has used two metaphors himself in this statement. Discuss their effectiveness here. Find four or five other examples in the essay in which the author has both clarified his ideas and added zest to his expression by the imaginative appeal of a simile or metaphor. If you need some clarification of the difference between the simile and metaphor, look up the discussion of the two figures in the Appendix.

FENIMORE COOPER'S FURTHER LITERARY OFFENSES

Mark Twain

1 *Young Gentlemen*: In studying Cooper you will find it profitable to study him in detail—word by word, sentence by sentence. For every sentence of his is interesting. Interesting because of its make-up; its peculiar make-up, its original make-up. Let us examine a sentence or two, and see. Here is a passage from Chapter XI of *The Last of the Mohicans,* one of the most famous and most admired of Cooper's books:

> Notwithstanding the swiftness of their flight, one of the Indians had found an opportunity to strike a straggling fawn with an arrow, and had

borne the more preferable fragments of the victim, patiently on his shoulders, to the stopping-place. Without any aid from the science of cookery, he was immediately employed, in common with his fellows, in gorging himself with this digestible sustenance. Magua alone sat apart, without participating in the revolting meal, and apparently buried in the deepest thought.

2 This little paragraph is full of matter for reflection and inquiry. The remark about the swiftness of the flight was unnecessary, as it was merely put in to forestall the possible objection of some over-particular reader that the Indian couldn't have found the needed "opportunity" while fleeing swiftly. The reader would not have made that objection. He would care nothing about having that small matter explained and justified. But that is Cooper's way; frequently he will explain and justify little things that do not need it and then make up for this by as frequently failing to explain important ones that do need it. For instance he allowed that astute and cautious person, Deerslayer-Hawkeye, to throw his rifle heedlessly down and leave it lying on the ground where some hostile Indians would presently be sure to find it—a rifle prized by that person above all things else in the earth—and the reader gets no word of explanation of that strange act. There was a reason, but it wouldn't bear exposure. Cooper meant to get a fine dramatic effect out of the finding of the rifle by the Indians, and he accomplished this at the happy time; but all the same, Hawkeye could have hidden the rifle in a quarter of a minute where the Indians could not have found it. Cooper couldn't think of any way to explain why Hawkeye didn't do that, so he just shirked the difficulty and did not explain at all. In another place Cooper allowed Heyward to shoot at an Indian with a pistol that wasn't loaded—and grants us not a word of explanation as to how the man did it.

3 No, the remark about the swiftness of their flight was not necessary; neither was the one which said that the Indian found an opportunity; neither was the one which said he *struck* the fawn; neither was the one which explained that it was a "straggling" fawn; neither was the one which said the striking was done with an arrow; neither was the one which said the Indian bore the "fragments;" nor the remark that they were preferable fragments; nor the remark that they were *more* preferable fragments; nor the explanation that they were fragments of the "victim;" nor the over-particular explanation that specifies the Indian's "shoulders" as the part of him that supported the fragments; nor the statement that the Indian bore the fragments patiently. None of those details has any value. We don't care what the Indian struck the fawn with; we don't care whether it was a straggling fawn or an unstraggling one; we don't care which fragments the Indian saved; we don't care why he saved the "more" preferable ones when

the merely preferable ones would have amounted to just the same thing and couldn't have been told from the more preferable ones by anybody, dead or alive; we don't care whether the Indian carried them on his shoulders or in his handkerchief; and finally, we don't care whether he carried them patiently or struck for higher pay and shorter hours. We are indifferent to that Indian and all his affairs.

4 There was only one fact in that long sentence that was worth stating, and it could have been squeezed into these few words—and with advantage to the narrative, too:

5 "During the flight one of the Indians had killed a fawn, and he brought it into camp." You will notice that "During the flight one of the Indians had killed a fawn and he brought it into camp," is more straightforward and businesslike, and less mincing and smirky, than it is to say "Notwithstanding the swiftness of their flight, one of the Indians had found an opportunity to strike a straggling fawn with an arrow, and had borne the more preferable fragments of the victim, patiently on his shoulders, to the stopping-place." You will notice that the form "During the flight one of the Indians had killed a fawn and he brought it into camp" holds up its chin and moves to the front with the steady strike of a grenadier, whereas the form "Notwithstanding the swiftness of their flight, one of the Indians had found an opportunity to strike a straggling fawn with an arrow, and had borne the more preferable fragments of the victim, patiently on his shoulders, to the stopping-place," simpers along with an airy, complacent, monkey-with-a-parasol gait which is not suited to the transportation of raw meat.

6 I beg to remind you that an author's way of setting forth a matter is called his Style, and that an author's style is a main part of his equipment for business. The style of some authors has variety in it, but Cooper's style is remarkable for the absence of this feature. Cooper's style is always grand and stately and noble. Style may be likened to an army, the author to its general, the book to the campaign. Some authors proportion an attacking force to the strength or weakness, the importance or unimportance, of the object to be attacked; but Cooper doesn't. It doesn't make any difference to Cooper whether the object of attack is a hundred thousand men or a cow; he hurls his entire force against it. He comes thundering down with all his battalions at his back, cavalry in the van, artillery on the flanks, infantry massed in the middle, forty bands braying, a thousand banners streaming in the wind; and whether the object be an army or a cow you will see him come marching sublimely in, at the end of the engagement, bearing the more preferable fragments of the victim patiently on his shoulders, to the stopping-place. Cooper's style is grand, awful, beautiful; but it is sacred to Cooper, it is his very own, and no student of the Veterinary College of Arizona will be allowed to filch it from him.

7 In one of his chapters Cooper throws an ungentle slur at one Gamut because he is not exact enough in his choice of words. But Cooper has that failing himself, as was remarked in our first Lecture. If the Indian had "struck" the fawn with a brick, or with a club, or with his fist, no one could find fault with the word used. And one cannot find much fault when he strikes it with an arrow; still it sounds affected, and it might have been a little better to lean to simplicity and say he shot it with an arrow.

8 "Fragments" is well enough, perhaps, when one is speaking of the parts of a dismembered deer, yet it hasn't just exactly the right sound—and sound is something; in fact sound is a good deal. It makes the difference between good music and poor music, and it can sometimes make the difference between good literature and indifferent literature. "Fragments" sounds all right when we are talking about the wreckage of a breakable thing that has been smashed; it also sounds all right when applied to cat's-meat; but when we use it to describe large hunks and chunks like the fore- and hind-quarters of a fawn, it grates upon the fastidious ear.

9 "Without any aid from the science of cookery, he was immediately employed, in common with his fellows, in gorging himself with this digestible sustenance."

10 This was a mere statistic; just a mere cold, colorless statistic; yet you see Cooper has made a chromo out of it. To use another figure, he has clothed a humble statistic in flowing, voluminous and costly raiment, whereas both good taste and economy suggest that he ought to have saved these splendors for a king, and dressed the humble statistic in a simple breech-clout. Cooper spent twenty-four words here on a thing not really worth more than eight. We will reduce the statistic to its proper proportions and state it in this way:

11 "He and the others ate the meat raw."

12 "Digestible sustenance" is a handsome phrase, but it was out of place there, because we do not know these Indians or care for them; and so it cannot interest us to know whether the meat was going to agree with them or not. Details which do not assist a story are better left out.

13 "Magua alone sat apart, without participating in the revolting meal," is a statement which we understand, but that is our merit, not Cooper's. Cooper is not clear. He does not say who it is that is revolted by the meal. It is really Cooper himself, but there is nothing in the statement to indicate that it isn't Magua. Magua is an Indian and likes raw meat.

14 The word "alone" could have been left out and space saved. It has no value where it is.

15 I must come back with some frequency, in the course of these Lectures, to the matter of Cooper's inaccuracy as an Observer. In this way I shall hope to persuade you that it is well to look at a thing carefully before you try to describe it; but I shall rest you between times with other mat-

ters and thus try to avoid over-fatiguing you with that detail of our theme. In *The Last of the Mohicans* Cooper gets up a stirring "situation" on an island flanked by great cataracts—a lofty island with steep sides—a sort of tongue which projects downstream from the midst of the divided waterfall. There are caverns in this mass of rock, and a party of Cooper people hide themselves in one of these to get away from some hostile Indians. There is a small exit at each end of this cavern. These exits are closed with blankets and the light excluded. The exploring hostiles back themselves up against the blankets and rave and rage in a blood-curdling way, but they are Cooper Indians and of course fail to discover the blankets; so they presently go away baffled and disappointed. Alice, in her gratitude for this deliverance, flings herself on her knees to return thanks. The darkness in there must have been pretty solid; yet if we may believe Cooper, it was a darkness which could not have been told from daylight; for here are some nice details which were visible in it:

16 "Both Heyward and the more tempered Cora witnessed the act of involuntary emotion with powerful sympathy, the former secretly believing that piety had never worn a form so lovely as it had now assumed in the youthful person of Alice. Her eyes were radiant with the glow of grateful feelings; the flush of her beauty was again seated on her cheeks, and her whole soul seemed ready and anxious to pour out its thanksgivings, through the medium of her eloquent features. But when her lips moved, the words they should have uttered appeared frozen by some new and sudden chill. Her bloom gave place to the paleness of death; her soft and melting eyes grew hard, and seemed contracting with horror; while those hands which she had raised, clasped in each other, towards heaven, dropped in horizontal lines before her, the fingers pointed forward in convulsed motion."

17 It is a case of strikingly inexact observation. Heyward and the more tempered Cora could not have seen the half of it in the dark that way.

18 I must call your attention to certain details of this work of art which invite particular examination. "Involuntary" is surplusage, and violates Rule 14.[1] All emotion is involuntary when genuine, and then the qualifying term is not needed; a qualifying term is needed only when the emotion is pumped-up and ungenuine. "Secretly" is surplusage, too; because Heyward was not believing out loud, but all to himself; and a person cannot believe a thing all to himself without doing it privately. I do not approve of the word "seated," to describe the process of locating a flush. No one can seat a flush. A flush is not a deposit on an exterior surface, it is a something which squashes out from within.

19 I cannot approve of the word "new." If Alice had had an old chill,

[1] Rule 14: "Eschew surplusage." In the published essay, Twain wrote: "There are nineteen rules governing literary art in the domain of romantic fiction—some say twenty-two. In *Deerslayer* Cooper violated eighteen of them."

formerly, it would be all right to distinguish this one from that one by calling this one the new chill; but she had not had any old chill, this one was the only chill she had had, up till now, and so the tacit reference to an old anterior chill is unwarranted and misleading. And I do not altogether like the phrase "while those hands which she had raised." It seems to imply that she had some other hands—some other ones which she had put on the shelf a minute so as to give her a better chance to raise those ones; but it is not true; she had only the one pair. The phrase is in the last degree misleading. But I like to see her extend these ones in front of her and work the fingers. I think that that is a very good effect. And it would have almost doubled the effect if the more tempered Cora had done it some, too.

20 A Cooper Indian who has been washed is a poor thing, and commonplace; it is the Cooper Indian in his paint that thrills. Cooper's extra words are Cooper's paint—his paint, his feathers, his tomahawk, his war-whoop.

21 In the two-thirds of a page elsewhere referred to, wherein Cooper scored 114 literary transgressions out of a possible 115, he appears before us with all his things on. As follows, the italics are mine—they indicate violations of Rule 14:

> In a minute he was once more fastened to the tree, *a helpless object of any insult or wrong that might be offered. So eagerly did every one now act, that nothing was said.* The fire was immediately lighted *in the pile, and the end of all was anxiously expected.*
>
> It was not the intention of the Hurons *absolutely* to destroy *the life of* their victim by *means of* fire. They designed merely to put his *physical fortitude* to the severest proofs it could endure, short of that extremity. In the end, they fully intended to carry his scalp into their village, but it was their wish first to break down his resolution, and to reduce him to *the level of* a complaining sufferer. With this view, the pile of brush *and branches* had been placed at a *proper* distance, *or one* at which it was thought the heat would soon become intolerable, though *it might* not *be* immediately dangerous. *As often happened, however, on these occasions,* this distance had been miscalculated, and the flames *began to wave their forked tongues in a proximity to the face of the victim that* would have proved fatal in another instant had not Hetty rushed through the crowd, armed with a stick, and scattered the blazing pile in a *dozen directions.* More than one hand was raised to strike the *presumptuous* intruder to the earth; but the chiefs prevented the blows by reminding their *irritated* followers of the state of her mind. Hetty, herself, was insensible to the risk she ran; but, *as soon as she had performed this bold act, she* stood looking about her in frowning resentment, as if to rebuke the *crowd of attentive* savages *for their cruelty.*
>
> "God bless you, dearest *sister,* for that brave and ready act," murmured Judith, *herself unnerved so much as to be incapable of exertion,* "Heaven itself has sent you on its holy errand."

22 Number of words, 320; necessary ones, 220; words wasted by the generous spendthrift, 100.

23 In our day those 100 unnecessary words would have to come out. We will take them out presently and make the episode approximate the modern requirement in the matter of compression.

24 If we may consider each unnecessary word in Cooper's report of that barbecue a separate and individual violation of Rule 14, then that rule is violated 100 times in that report. Other rules are violated in it. Rule 12, two instances; [2] Rule 13, three instances; [3] Rule 15, one instance; [4] Rule 16, two instances; [5] Rule 17, one or two little instances; [6] the Report in its entirety is an offense against Rule 18 [7]—also against Rule 16. Total score, about 114 violations of the laws of literary art out of a possible 115.

25 Let us now bring forward the Report again, with the most of the unnecessary words knocked out. By departing from Cooper's style and manner, all the facts could be put into 150 words, and the effects heightened at the same time—this is manifest, of course—but that would not be desirable. We must stick to Cooper's language as closely as we can:

> In a minute he was once more fastened to the tree. The fire was immediately lighted. It was not the intention of the Hurons to destroy Deerslayer's life by fire; they designed merely to put his fortitude to the severest proofs it could endure short of that extremity. In the end, they fully intended to take his life, but it was their wish first to break down his resolution and reduce him to a complaining sufferer. With this view the pile of brush had been placed at a distance at which it was thought the heat would soon become intolerable, without being immediately dangerous. But this distance had been miscalculated; the fire was so close to the victim that he would have been fatally burned in another instant if Hetty had not rushed through the crowd and scattered the brands with a stick. More than one Indian raised his hand to strike her down but the chiefs saved her by reminding them of the state of her mind. Hetty herself was insensible to the risk she ran; she stood looking about her in frowning resentment, as if to rebuke the savages for their cruelty.
> "God bless you, dear!" cried Judith, "for that brave and ready act. Heaven itself has sent you on its holy errand, and you shall have a chromo."

26 Number of words, 220—and the facts are all in.

[2] Rule 12: "*Say* what he is proposing to say, not merely come near it."
[3] Rule 13: "Use the right word, not its second cousin."
[4] Rule 15: "Not omit necessary details."
[5] Rule 16: "Avoid slovenliness of form."
[6] Rule 17: "Use good grammar."
[7] Rule 18: "Employ a simple and straightforward style."

STUDY GUIDE

Structure

1. Mark Twain is here concerned with the same qualities of clarity, brevity, and variety that F. L. Lucas mentioned in the previous essay. With which of these qualities is Twain chiefly concerned in his criticism of Fenimore Cooper?

2. In the opening paragraph the author makes several statements that set the ironic tone of the whole piece; in other words, he says the opposite of what he means. What are these statements?

3. This essay has a deliberately loose structure to fit its casual, semi-humorous, and satiric tone. But Twain helps us to notice when he is indulging in an aside or digression. Show how he does this in paragraphs 15–17.

4. Twain is also a master of the simile and metaphor used frequently for ironic and humorous effects. Discuss his use of simile or metaphor in paragraphs 5, 6, and 10.

5. Lucas says that a writer reveals a great deal about himself through his style or manner of self-expression. What kind of person seems to be revealed by the style of Fenimore Cooper in the passage analyzed here? What kind of a person is revealed by the style of Mark Twain in this essay?

POLITICS AND THE ENGLISH LANGUAGE

George Orwell

1 Most people who bother with the matter at all would admit that the English language is in a bad way, but it is generally assumed that we cannot by conscious action do anything about it. Our civilization is decadent and our language—so the argument runs—must inevitably share in the general collapse. It follows that any struggle against the abuse of language is a sentimental archaism, like preferring candles to electric light or hansom cabs to aeroplanes. Underneath this lies the half-conscious belief that language is a natural growth and not an instrument which we shape for our own purposes.

2 Now, it is clear that the decline of a language must ultimately have

political and economic causes: it is not due simply to the bad influence of this or that individual writer. But an effect can become a cause, reinforcing the original cause and producing the same effect in an intensified form, and so on indefinitely. A man may take to drink because he feels himself to be a failure, and then fail all the more completely because he drinks. It is rather the same thing that is happening to the English language. It becomes ugly and inaccurate because our thoughts are foolish, but the slovenliness of our language makes it easier for us to have foolish thoughts. The point is that the process is reversible. Modern English, especially written English, is full of bad habits which spread by imitation and which can be avoided if one is willing to take the necessary trouble. If one gets rid of these habits one can think more clearly, and to think clearly is a necessary first step towards political regeneration: so that the fight against bad English is not frivolous and is not the exclusive concern of professional writers. I will come back to this presently, and I hope that by that time the meaning of what I have said here will have become clearer. Meanwhile, here are five specimens of the English language as it is now habitually written.

3 These five passages have not been picked out because they are especially bad—I could have quoted far worse if I had chosen—but because they illustrate various of the mental vices from which we now suffer. They are a little below the average, but are fairly representative samples. I number them so that I can refer back to them when necessary:

> (1) I am not, indeed, sure whether it is not true to say that the Milton who once seemed not unlike a seventeenth-century Shelley had not become, out of an experience ever more bitter in each year, more alien [sic] to the founder of that Jesuit sect which nothing could induce him to tolerate.
>
> Professor Harold Laski
> (Essay in *Freedom of Expression*).

> (2) Above all, we cannot play ducks and drakes with a native battery of idioms which prescribes such egregious collocations of vocables as the Basic *put up with* for *tolerate* or *put at a loss* for *bewilder*.
>
> Professor Lancelot Hogben (*Interglossa*).

> (3) On the one side we have the free personality: by definition it is not neurotic, for it has neither conflict nor dream. Its desires, such as they are, are transparent, for they are just what institutional approval keeps in the forefront of consciousness; another institutional pattern would alter their number and intensity; there is little in them that is natural, irreducible, or culturally dangerous. But *on the other side*, the social bond itself is nothing but the mutual reflection of these self-secure integrities. Recall the definition of love. Is not this the very picture of a small

academic? Where is there a place in this hall of mirrors for either personality or fraternity?

Essay on psychology in *Politics* (New York).

(4) All the "best people" from the gentlemen's clubs, and all the frantic fascist captains, united in common hatred of Socialism and bestial horror of the rising tide of the mass revolutionary movement, have turned to acts of provocation, to foul incendiarism, to medieval legends of poisoned wells, to legalize their own destruction of proletarian organizations, and rouse the agitated petty-bourgeoisie to chauvinistic fervor on behalf of the fight against the revolutionary way out of the crisis.

Communist pamphlet.

(5) If a new spirit is to be infused into this old country, there is one thorny and contentious reform which must be tackled, and that is the humanization and galvanization of the B.B.C. Timidity here will bespeak canker and atrophy of the soul. The heart of Britain may be sound and of strong beat, for instance, but the British lion's roar at present is like that of Bottom in Shakespeare's *Midsummer Night's Dream*—as gentle as any sucking dove. A virile new Britain cannot continue indefinitely to be traduced in the eyes, or rather ears, of the world by the effete languors of Langham Place, brazenly masquerading as "standard English." When the Voice of Britain is heard at nine o'clock, better far and infinitely less ludicrous to hear aitches honestly dropped than the present priggish, inflated, inhibited, school-ma'amish arch braying of blameless bashful mewing maidens!

Letter in *Tribune*

4 Each of these passages has faults of its own, but, quite apart from avoidable ugliness, two qualities are common to all of them. The first is staleness of imagery; the other is lack of precision. The writer either has a meaning and cannot express it, or he inadvertently says something else, or he is almost indifferent as to whether his words mean anything or not. This mixture of vagueness and sheer incompetence is the most marked characteristic of modern English prose, and especially of any kind of political writing. As soon as certain topics are raised, the concrete melts into the abstract and no one seems able to think of turns of speech that are not hackneyed: prose consists less and less of *words* chosen for the sake of their meaning, and more and more of *phrases* tacked together like the sections of a prefabricated hen-house. I list below, with notes and examples, various of the tricks by means of which the work of prose-construction is habitually dodged:

5 DYING METAPHORS A newly invented metaphor assists thought by evoking a visual image, while on the other hand a metaphor which is technically "dead" (e.g. *iron resolution*) has in effect reverted to being an ordinary word and can generally be used without loss of vividness. But in

between these two classes there is a huge dump of worn-out metaphors which have lost all evocative power and are merely used because they save people the trouble of inventing phrases for themselves. Examples are: *Ring the changes on, take up the cudgels for, toe the line, ride roughshod over, stand shoulder to shoulder with, play into the hands of, no axe to grind, grist to the mill, fishing in troubled waters, on the order of the day, Achilles' heel, swan song, hotbed.* Many of these are used without knowledge of their meaning (what is a "rift," for instance?), and incompatible metaphors are frequently mixed, a sure sign that the writer is not interested in what he is saying. Some metaphors now current have been twisted out of their original meaning without those who use them even being aware of the fact. For example, *toe the line* is sometimes written *tow the line.* Another example is *the hammer and the anvil,* now always used with the implication that the anvil gets the worst of it. In real life it is always the anvil that breaks the hammer, never the other way about: a writer who stopped to think what he was saying would be aware of this, and would avoid perverting the original phrase.

6 OPERATORS OR VERBAL FALSE LIMBS These save the trouble of picking out appropriate verbs and nouns, and at the same time pad each sentence with extra syllables which give it an appearance of symmetry. Characteristic phrases are *render inoperative, militate against, make contact with, be subjected to, give rise to, give grounds for, have the effect of, play a leading part* (*role*) *in, make itself felt, take effect, exhibit a tendency to, serve the purpose of, etc., etc.* The keynote is the elimination of simple verbs. Instead of being a single word, such as *break, stop, spoil, mend, kill,* a verb becomes a *phrase,* made up of a noun or adjective tacked on to some general-purposes verb such as *prove, serve, form, play, render.* In addition, the passive voice is wherever possible used in preference to the active, and noun constructions are used instead of gerunds (*by examination of* instead of *by examining*). The range of verbs is further cut down by means of the *-ize* and *de-* formations, and the banal statements are given an appearance of profundity by means of the *not un-* formation. Simple conjunctions and prepositions are replaced by such phrases as *with respect to, having regard to, the fact that, by dint of, in view of, in the interests of, on the hypothesis that;* and the ends of sentences are saved by anticlimax by such resounding common-places as *greatly to be desired, cannot be left out of account, a development to be expected in the near future, deserving of serious consideration, brought to a satisfactory conclusion,* and so on and so forth.

7 PRETENTIOUS DICTION Words like *phenomenon, element, individual* (as noun), *objective, categorical, effective, virtual, basic, primary, promote, constitute, exhibit, exploit, utilize, eliminate, liquidate* are used to dress up simple statement and give an air of scientific impartiality to bi-

ased judgments. Adjectives like *epoch-making, epic, historic, unforgettable, triumphant, age-old, inevitable, inexorable, veritable* are used to dignify the sordid processes of international politics, while writing that aims at glorifying war usually takes on an archaic color, its characteristic words being: *realm, throne, chariot, mailed fist, trident, sword, shield, buckler, banner, jackboot, clarion.* Foreign words and expressions such as *cul de sac, ancien régime, deux ex machina, mutatis mutandis, status quo, gleichschaltung, weltanschauung,* are used to give an air of culture and elegance. Except for the useful abbreviations *i.e., e.g.,* and *etc.,* there is no real need for any of the hundreds of foreign phrases now current in English. Bad writers, and especially scientific, political and sociological writers, are nearly always haunted by the notion that Latin or Greek words are grander than Saxon ones, and unnecessary words like *expedite, ameliorate, predict, extraneous, deracinated, clandestine, subaqueous* and hundreds of others constantly gain ground from their Anglo-Saxon opposite numbers.[1] The jargon peculiar to Marxist writing (*hyena, hangman, cannibal, petty bourgeois, these gentry, lacquey, flunkey, mad dog, White Guard,* etc.) consists largely of words and phrases translated from Russian, German or French; but the normal way of coining a new word is to use a Latin or Greek root with the appropriate affix and, where necessary, the size formation. It is often easier to make up words of this kind (*deregionalize, impermissible, extramarital, nonfragmentary* and so forth) than to think up the English words that will cover one's meaning. The result, in general, is an increase in slovenliness and vagueness.

8 MEANINGLESS WORDS In certain kinds of writing, particularly in art criticism and literary criticism, it is normal to come across long passages which are almost completely lacking in meaning.[2] Words like *romantic, plastic, values, human, dead, sentimental, natural, vitality* as used in art criticism, are strictly meaningless, in the sense that they not only do not point to any discoverable object, but are hardly ever expected to do so by the reader. When one critic writes, "The outstanding feature of Mr. X's work is its living quality," while another writes, "The immediately striking thing about Mr. X's work is its peculiar deadness," the reader accepts this as a simple difference of opinion. If words like *black* and *white* were in-

[1] An interesting illustration of this is the way in which the English flower names which were in use till very recently are being ousted by Greek ones, *Snapdragon* becoming *antirrhinum, forget-me-not* becoming myosotis, etc. It is hard to see any practical reason for this change of fashion: it is probably due to an instinctive turning-away from the more homely word and a vague feeling that the Greek word is scientific.

[2] Example: "Comfort's catholicity of perception and image, strangely Whitmanesque in range, almost the exact opposite in aesthetic compulsion, continues to evoke that trembling atmospheric accumulative hinting at a cruel, an inexorably serene timelessness. . . . Wrey Gardiner scores by aiming at simple bull's-eyes with precision. Only they are not so simple, and through this contented sadness runs more than the surface bitter-sweet of resignation." (*Poetry Quarterly.*)

volved, instead of the jargon words *dead* and *living*, he would see at once that language was being used in an improper way. Many political words are similarly abused. The word *Fascism* has now no meaning except in so far as it signifies "something not desirable." The words *democracy, socialism, freedom, patriotic, realistic, justice,* have each of them several different meanings which cannot be reconciled with one another. In the case of a word like *democracy,* not only is there no agreed definition, but the attempt to make one is resisted from all sides. It is almost universally felt that when we call a country democratic we are praising it: consequently the defenders of every kind of régime claim that it is a democracy, and fear that they might have to stop using the word if it were tied down to any one meaning. Words of this kind are often used in a consciously dishonest way. That is, the person who uses them has his own private definition, but allows his hearer to think he means something quite different. Statements like *Marshal Pétain was a true patriot, The Soviet Press is the freest in the world, The Catholic Church is opposed to persecution,* are almost always made with intent to deceive. Other words used in variable meanings, in most cases more or less dishonestly, are: *class, totalitarian, science, progressive, reactionary, bourgeois, equality.*

9 Now that I have made this catalogue of swindles and perversions, let me give another example of the kind of writing that they lead to. This time it must of its nature be an imaginary one. I am going to translate a passage of good English into modern English of the worst sort. Here is a well-known verse from *Ecclesiastes:*

10 "I returned and saw under the sun, that the race is not to the swift, nor the battle to the strong, neither yet bread to the wise, nor yet riches to men of understanding, nor yet favour to men of skill; but time and chance happeneth to them all."

11 Here it is in modern English:

12 "Objective consideration of contemporary phenomena compels the conclusion that success or failure in competitive activities exhibits no tendency to be commensurate with innate capacity, but that a considerable element of the unpredictable must invariably be taken into account."

13 This is a parody, but not a very gross one. Exhibit (3), above, for instance, contains several patches of the same kind of English. It will be seen that I have not made a full translation. The beginning and ending of the sentence follow the original meaning fairly closely, but in the middle the concrete illustrations—race, battle, bread—dissolve into the vague phrase "success or failure in competitive activities." This had to be so, because no modern writer of the kind I am discussing—no one capable of using phrases like "objective consideration of contemporary phenomena"—would ever tabulate his thoughts in that precise and detailed way. The whole tendency of modern prose is away from concreteness. Now analyse these two

sentences a little more closely. The first contains forty-nine words but only sixty syllables, and all its words are those of everyday life. The second contains thirty-eight words of ninety syllables; eighteen of its words are from Latin roots, and one from Greek. The first sentence contains six vivid images, and only one phrase ("time and chance") that could be called vague. The second contains not a single fresh, arresting phrase, and in spite of its ninety syllables it gives only a shortened version of the meaning contained in the first. Yet without a doubt it is the second kind of sentence that is gaining ground in modern English. I do not want to exaggerate. This kind of writing is not yet universal, and outcrops of simplicity will occur here and there in the worst-written page. Still, if you or I were told to write a few lines on the uncertainty of human fortunes, we should probably come much nearer to my imaginary sentence than to the one from *Ecclesiastes*.

14 As I have tried to show, modern writing at its worst does not consist in picking out words for the sake of their meaning and inventing images in order to make the meaning clearer. It consists in gumming together long strips of words which have already been set in order by someone else, and making the results presentable by sheer humbug. The attraction of this way of writing is that it is easy. It is easier—even quicker, once you have the habit—to say *In my opinion it is not an unjustifiable assumption that* than to say *I think*. If you use ready-made phrases, you not only don't have to hunt about for words; you also don't have to bother with the rhythms of your sentences, since these phrases are generally so arranged as to be more or less euphonious. When you are composing in a hurry—when you are dictating to a stenographer, for instance, or making a public speech—it is natural to fall into a pretentious, Latinized style. Tags like *a consideration which we should do well to bear in mind* or *a conclusion to which all of us would readily assent* will save many a sentence from coming down with a bump. By using stale metaphors, similes and idioms, you save much mental effort, at the cost of leaving your meaning vague, not only for your reader but for yourself. This is the significance of mixed metaphors. The sole aim of a metaphor is to call up a visual image. When these images clash—as in *The Fascist octopus has sung its swan song, the jackboot is thrown into the melting pot*—it can be taken as certain that the writer is not seeing a mental image of the objects he is naming; in other words he is not really thinking. Look again at the examples I gave at the beginning of this essay. Professor Laski (1) uses five negatives in fifty-three words. One of these is superfluous, making nonsense of the whole passage, and in addition there is the slip *alien* for akin, making further nonsense, and several avoidable pieces of clumsiness which increase the general vagueness. Professor Hogben (2) plays ducks and drakes with a battery which is able

to write prescriptions, and, while disapproving of the everyday phrase *put up with,* is unwilling to look *egregious* up in the dictionary and see what it means; (3), if one takes an uncharitable attitude towards it, is simply meaningless: probably one could work out its intended meaning by reading the whole of the article in which it occurs. In (4), the writer knows more or less what he wants to say, but an accumulation of stale phrases chokes him like tea leaves blocking a sink. In (5), words and meaning have almost parted company. People who write in this manner usually have a general emotional meaning—they dislike one thing and want to express solidarity with another—but they are not interested in the detail of what they are saying. A scrupulous writer, in every sentence that he writes, will ask himself at least four questions, thus: What am I trying to say? What words will express it? What image or idiom will make it clearer? Is this image fresh enough to have an effect? And he will probably ask himself two more: Could I put it more shortly? Have I said anything that is avoidably ugly? But you are not obliged to go to all this trouble. You can shirk it by simply throwing your mind open and letting the ready-made phrases come crowding in. They will construct your sentences for you—even think your thoughts for you, to a certain extent—and at need they will perform the important service of partially concealing your meaning even from yourself. It is at this point that the special connection between politics and the debasement of language becomes clear.

15 In our time it is broadly true that political writing is bad writing. Where it is not true, it will generally be found that the writer is some kind of rebel, expressing his private opinions and not a "party line." Orthodoxy, of whatever color, seems to demand a lifeless, imitative style. The political dialects to be found in pamphlets, leading articles, manifestos, White Papers and the speeches of under-secretaries do, of course, vary from party to party, but they are all alike in that one almost never finds in them a fresh, vivid, home-made turn of speech. When one watches some tired hack on the platform mechanically repeating the familiar phrases—*bestial atrocities, iron heel, bloodstained tyranny, free peoples of the world, stand shoulder to shoulder*—one often has a curious feeling that one is not watching a live human being but some kind of dummy: a feeling which suddenly becomes stronger at moments when the light catches the speaker's spectacles and turns them into blank discs which seem to have no eyes behind them. And this is not altogether fanciful. A speaker who uses that kind of phraseology has gone some distance towards turning himself into a machine. The appropriate noises are coming out of his larynx, but his brain is not involved as it would be if he were choosing his words for himself. If the speech he is making is one that he is accustomed to make over and over again, he may be almost unconscious of what he is saying, as one is

when one utters the responses in church. And this reduced state of consciousness, if not indispensable, is at any rate favorable to political conformity.

16 In our time, political speech and writing are largely the defence of the indefensible. Things like the continuance of British rule in India, the Russian purges and deportations, the dropping of the atom bombs on Japan, can indeed be defended, but only by arguments which are too brutal for most people to face, and which do not square with the professed aims of political parties. Thus political language has to consist largely of euphemism, question-begging and sheer cloudy vagueness. Defenceless villages are bombarded from the air, the inhabitants driven out into the countryside, the cattle machine-gunned, the huts set on fire with incendiary bullets: this is called *pacification*. Millions of peasants are robbed of their farms and sent trudging along the roads with no more than they can carry: this is called *transfer of population* or *rectification of frontiers*. People are imprisoned for years without trial, or shot in the back of the neck or sent to die of scurvy in Arctic lumber camps: this is called *elimination of unreliable elements*. Such phraseology is needed if one wants to name things without calling up mental pictures of them. Consider for instance some comfortable English professor defending Russian totalitarianism. He cannot say outright, "I believe in killing off your opponents when you can get good results by doing so." Probably, therefore, he will say something like this:

17 "While freely conceding that the Soviet régime exhibits certain features which the humanitarian may be inclined to deplore, we must, I think, agree that a certain curtailment of the right to political opposition is an unavoidable concomitant of transitional periods, and that the rigors which the Russian people have been called upon to undergo have been amply justified in the sphere of concrete achievement."

18 The inflated style is itself a kind of euphemism. A mass of Latin words falls upon the facts like soft snow, blurring the outlines and covering up all the details. The great enemy of clear language is insincerity. When there is a gap between one's real and one's declared aims, one turns as it were instinctively to long words and exhausted idioms, like a cuttlefish squirting out ink. In our age there is no such thing as "keeping out of politics." All issues are political issues, and politics itself is a mass of lies, evasions, folly, hatred and schizophrenia. When the general atmosphere is bad, language must suffer. I should expect to find—this is a guess which I have not sufficient knowledge to verify—that the German, Russian, and Italian languages have all deteriorated in the last ten or fifteen years, as a result of dictatorship.

19 But if thought corrupts language, language can also corrupt thought. A bad usage can spread by tradition and imitation, even among people who

should and do know better. The debased language that I have been discussing is in some ways very convenient. Phrases like *a not unjustifiable assumption, leaves much to be desired, would serve no good purpose, a consideration which we should do well to bear in mind,* are a continuous temptation, a packet of aspirins always at one's elbow. Look back through this essay, and for certain you will find that I have again and again committed the very faults I am protesting against. By this morning's post I have received a pamphlet dealing with conditions in Germany. The author tells me that he "felt impelled" to write it. I open it at random, and here is almost the first sentence that I see: "[The Allies] have an opportunity not only of achieving a radical transformation of Germany's social and political structure in such a way as to avoid a nationalistic reaction in Germany itself, but at the same time of laying the foundations of a co-operative and unified Europe." You see, he "feels impelled" to write—feels, presumably, that he has something new to say—and yet his words, like cavalry horses answering the bugle, group themselves automatically into the familiar dreary pattern. This invasion of one's mind by ready-made phrases (*lay the foundations, achieve a radical transformation*) can only be prevented if one is constantly on guard against them, and every such phrase anaesthetizes a portion of one's brain.

20 I said earlier that the decadence of our language is probably curable. Those who deny this would argue, if they produced an argument at all, that language merely reflects existing social conditions, and that we cannot influence its development by any direct tinkering with words and constructions. So far as the general tone or spirit of a language goes, this may be true, but it is not true in detail. Silly words and expressions have often disappeared, not through any evolutionary process but owing to the conscious action of a minority. Two recent examples were *explore every avenue* and *leave no stone unturned,* which were killed by the jeers of a few journalists. There is a long list of flyblown metaphors which could similarly be got rid of if enough people would interest themselves in the job; and it should also be possible to laugh the *not un-* formation out of existence,[3] to reduce the amount of Latin and Greek in the average sentence, to drive out foreign phrases and strayed scientific words, and, in general, to make pretentiousness unfashionable. But all these are minor points. The defence of the English language implies more than this, and perhaps it is best to start by saying what it does *not* imply.

21 To begin with it has nothing to do with archaism, with the salvaging of obsolete words and turns of speech, or with the setting up of a "standard English" which must never be departed from. On the contrary, it is

[3] One can cure oneself of the *not un-*formation by memorizing this sentence: A not unblack dog was chasing a not unsmall rabbit across a not ungreen field.

especially concerned with the scrapping of every word or idiom which has outworn its usefulness. It has nothing to do with correct grammar and syntax, which are of no importance so long as one makes one's meaning clear, or with the avoidance of Americanisms, or with having what is called a "good prose style." On the other hand it is not concerned with fake simplicity and the attempt to make written English colloquial. Nor does it even imply in every case preferring the Saxon word to the Latin one, though it does imply using the fewest and shortest words that will cover one's meaning. What is above all needed is to let the meaning choose the word, and not the other way about. In prose, the worst thing one can do with words is to surrender to them. When you think of a concrete object, you think wordlessly, and then, if you want to describe the thing you have been visualizing, you probably hunt about till you find the exact words that seem to fit it. When you think of something abstract you are more inclined to use words from the start, and unless you make a conscious effort to prevent it, the existing dialect will come rushing in and do the job for you, at the expense of blurring or even changing your meaning. Probably it is better to put off using words as long as possible and get one's meaning as clear as one can through pictures or sensations. Afterwards one can choose—not simply *accept*—the phrases that will best cover the meaning, and then switch round and decide what impression one's words are likely to make on another person. This last effort of the mind cuts out all stale or mixed images, all prefabricated phrases, needless repetitions, and humbug and vagueness generally. But one can often be in doubt about the effect of a word or a phrase, and one needs rules that one can rely on when instinct fails. I think the following rules will cover most cases:

(i) Never use a metaphor, simile or other figure of speech which you are used to seeing in print.
(ii) Never use a long word where a short one will do.
(iii) If it is possible to cut a word out, always cut it out.
(iv) Never use the passive where you can use the active.
(v) Never use a foreign phrase, a scientific word or a jargon word if you can think of an everyday English equivalent.
(vi) Break any of these rules sooner than say anything outright barbarous.

These rules sound elementary, and so they are, but they demand a deep change of attitude in anyone who has grown used to writing in the style now fashionable. One could keep all of them and still write bad English, but one could not write the kind of stuff I quoted in those five specimens at the beginning of this article.

22 I have not here been considering the literary use of language, but merely language as an instrument for expressing and not for concealing or

preventing thought. Stuart Chase and others have come near to claiming that all abstract words are meaningless, and have used this as a pretext for advocating a kind of political quietism. Since you don't know what Fascism is, how can you struggle against Fascism? One need not swallow such absurdities as this, but one ought to recognize that the present political chaos is connected with the decay of language, and that one can probably bring about some improvement by starting at the verbal end. If you simplify your English, you are freed from the worst follies of orthodoxy. You cannot speak any of the necessary dialects, and when you make a stupid remark its stupidity will be obvious, even to yourself. Political language—and with variations this is true of all political parties, from Conservatives to Anarchists—is designed to make lies sound truthful and murder respectable, and to give an appearance of solidity to pure wind. One cannot change this all in a moment, but one can at least change one's own habits, and from time to time one can even, if one jeers loudly enough, send some worn-out and useless phrase—some *jackboot, Achilles' heel, hotbed, melting pot, acid test, veritable inferno* or other lump of verbal refuse—into the dustbin where it belongs.

STUDY GUIDE

Structure and Content

1. George Orwell says he is not considering the literary use of language in this essay but merely language as an instrument for expressing thought. And yet the qualities of expression that he praises correspond rather closely to those enumerated by Lucas and Mark Twain. What are they?

2. Orwell says in another essay that he hardly ever wrote anything that did not have serious political implications. What connections does he see here between politics and language?

3. Is his attitude toward the present condition of the language predominantly pessimistic or optimistic? Give evidence for your answer from the essay itself.

4. Indicate the structural parts of this essay and the paragraphs that are devoted to each part, and then state in a sentence what the author is doing in each of these parts.

5. Orwell in general writes in a serious but rather straightforward manner throughout the essay, but in some places he becomes animated and employs strongly connotative diction and imagery to express his more intensely critical attitude. Study the diction and imagery in paragraph 15, for example, as an indication of his sharply critical attitude toward political speakers who abuse language.

6. By culling current newspapers and news magazines, see whether you can find some examples of the kind of political abuse of language that Orwell cites in paragraphs 16 and 17.

7. Show how Orwell has clarified his idea of the cause-and-effect relation-

ship between politics and economics and the decay of language by his use of an *analogy* in paragraph 2.

8. The essay is largely developed through an analysis and classification of the bad qualities of much modern writing. What are these qualities?

HOW TO WRITE AN "F" PAPER:
Fresh Advice for Students of Freshman English

Joseph C. Pattison

Writing an "F" paper is admittedly not an easy task, but one can learn to do it by grasp of the principles to use. The thirteen below, if practiced at all diligently, should lead any student to that fortune in his writing.

OBSCURE THE IDEAS:

1. Select a topic that is big enough to let you wander around the main idea without ever being forced to state it precisely. If an assigned topic has been limited for you, take a detour that will allow you to amble away from it for a while.
2. Pad! Pad! Pad! Do not develop your ideas. Simply restate them in safe, spongy generalizations to avoid the need to find evidence to support what you say. Always point out repetition with the phrase, "As previously noted. . . ." Better yet, repeat word-for-word at least one or two of your statements.
3. Disorganize your discussion. For example, if you are using the time order to present your material, keep the reader alert by making a jump from the past to the present only to spring back into the past preparatory to a leap into the future preceding a return hop into the present just before the finish of the point about the past. Devise comparable strategems to use with such other principles for organizing a discussion as space, contrast, cause-effect, and climax.
4. Begin a new paragraph every sentence or two.
   By generous use of white space, make the reader aware that he is looking at a page blank of sustained thought.
   Like this.

"How to Write an 'F' Paper," by Joseph C. Pattison, in *College English* (October 1963). Reprinted with the permission of the National Council of Teachers of English and Joseph C. Pattison.

Mangle the Sentences:

5. Fill all the areas of your sentences with deadwood. Incidentally, "the area of" will deaden almost any sentence, and it is particularly flat when displayed prominently at the beginning of a sentence.
6. Using fragments and run-on or comma-spliced sentences. Do not use a main subject and a main verb, for the reader will get the complete thought too easily. Just toss him part of the idea at a time, as in "Using fragments. . . ." To gain sentence variety, throw in an occasional run-on sentence thus the reader will have to read slowly and carefully to get the idea.
7. Your sentence order invert for statement of the least important matters. That will force the reader to be attentive to understand even the simplest points you make.
8. You, in the introduction, body, and conclusion of your paper, to show that you can contrive ornate, graceful sentences, should use involution. Frequent separation of subjects from verbs by insertion of involved phrases and clauses will prove that you know what can be done to a sentence.

Slovenize the Diction:

9. Add the popular "-wise" and "-ize" endings to words. Say, "Timewise, it is fastest to go by U.S. 40," rather than simply, "It is fastest to go by U.S. 40." Choose "circularize" in preference to "circulate." Practice will smartenize your style.
10. Use vague words in place of precise ones. From the start, establish vagueness of tone by saying, "The thing is . . ." instead of, "The issue is. . . ." Make the reader be imaginative throughout his reading of your paper.
11. Employ lengthy Latinate locutions wherever possible. Shun the simplicity of style that comes from apt use of short, old, familiar words, especially those of Anglo-Saxon origin. Show that you can get the *maximum* (L.), not merely the *most (AS.)*, from every word choice you make.
12. Inject humor into your writing by using the wrong word occasionally. Write "then" when you mean "than" or "to" when you mean "too." Every reader likes a laugh.
13. Find a "tried and true" phrase to use to clinch a point. It will have a comfortingly folksy sound for the reader. Best of all, since you want to end in a conversational and friendly way, sprinkle your conclusion with clichés. "Put a little frosting on the cake," as the saying goes.

Well, to ensconce this whole business in a nutshell, you, above all, an erudite discourse on nothing in the field of your topic should pen. Thereby gaining the reader's credence in what you say.

Suggestion-wise, one last thing: file-ize this list for handy reference the next time you a paper write.

STUDY GUIDE

This facetious little essay serves as a kind of summary *in reverse* of all the qualities of good self-expression or style that have been discussed in the previous essays of this unit. List the positive stylistic virtue that is opposed to the stylistic vice stated or implied in each numbered section of this essay.

SECTION 2

Understanding the Patterns of Logic, Propaganda, and Advertising

INDUCTIVE AND DEDUCTIVE REASONING

Thomas Henry Huxley

1 The method of scientific investigation is nothing but the expression of the necessary mode of working of the human mind. It is simply the mode at which all phenomena are reasoned about, rendered precise and exact. There is no more difference, but there is just the same kind of difference, between the mental operations of a man of science and those of an ordinary person, as there is between the operations and methods of a baker or of a butcher weighing out his goods in common scales, and the operation of a chemist in performing a difficult and complex analysis by means of his balance and finely graduated weights. It is not that the action of the scales in the one case, and the balance in the other, differ in the principles of their construction or manner of working; but the beam of one is set on an infinitely finer axis than the other, and of course turns by the addition of a much smaller weight.

2 You will understand this better, perhaps, if I give you some familiar example. You have all heard it repeated, I dare say, that men of science work by means of induction and deduction, and that by the help of these

Reprinted from Thomas Henry Huxley, "The Method of Scientific Investigation," in *Collected Essays* (1894).

operations, they, in a sort of sense, wring from Nature certain other things, which are called natural laws, and causes, and that out of these, by some cunning skill of their own, they build up hypotheses and theories. And it is imagined by many, that the operations of the common mind can be by no means compared with these processes, and that they have to be acquired by a sort of special apprenticeship to the craft. To hear all these large words, you would think that the mind of a man of science must be constituted differently from that of his fellow men; but if you will not be frightened by terms, you will discover that you are quite wrong, and that all these terrible apparatus are being used by yourselves every day and every hour of your lives.

3 There is a well-known incident in one of Molière's plays, where the author makes the hero express unbounded delight on being told that he has been talking prose during the whole of his life. In the same way, I trust that you will take comfort, and be delighted with yourselves, on the discovery that you have been acting on the principles of inductive and deductive philosophy during the same period. Probably there is not one here who has not in the course of the day had occasion to set in motion a complex train of reasoning, of the very same kind, though differing of course in degree, as that which a scientific man goes through in tracing the causes of natural phenomena.

4 A very trivial circumstance will serve to exemplify this. Suppose you go into a fruiterer's shop, wanting an apple—you take one up, and, on biting, you find it is sour; you look at it, and see that it is hard, and green. You take up another one and that too is hard, green, and sour. The shopman offers you a third; but, before biting it, you examine it, and find that it is hard and green, and you immediately say that you will not have it, as it must be sour, like those that you have already tried.

5 Nothing can be more simple than that, you think; but if you will take the trouble to analyze and trace out into its logical elements what has been done by the mind, you will be greatly surprised. In the first place, you have performed the operation of induction. You found, that, in two experiences, hardness and greenness in apples went together with sourness. It was so in the first case, and it was confirmed by the second. True, it is a very small basis, but still it is enough to make an induction from; you generalize the facts, and you expect to find sourness in apples where you get hardness and greenness. You found upon that a general law, that all hard and green apples are sour; and that, so far as it goes, is a perfect induction. Well, having got your natural law in this way, when you are offered another apple which you find is hard and green, you say, "All hard and green apples are sour; this apple is hard and green, therefore this apple is sour." That train of reasoning is what logicians call a syllogism, and has all its various parts and

terms—its major premise, its minor premise, and its conclusion. And, by the help of further reasoning, which, if drawn out, would have to be exhibited in two or three other syllogisms, you arrive at your final determination. "I will not have that apple." So that, you see, you have, in the first place, established a law by induction, and upon that you have founded a deduction, and reasoned out the special conclusion of the particular case. Well now, suppose, having got your law, that at some time afterwards, you are discussing the qualities of apples with a friend: you will say to him, "It is a very curious thing—but I find that all hard and green apples are sour!" Your friend says to you, "But how do you know that?" You at once reply, "Oh, because I have tried them over and over again, and have always found them to be so." Well, if we were talking science instead of common sense, we should call that an experimental verification. And, if still opposed, you go further, and say, "I have heard from the people in Somersetshire and Devonshire, where a large number of apples are grown, that they have observed the same thing. It is also found to be the case in Normandy, and in North America. In short, I find it to be the universal experience of mankind wherever attention has been directed to the subject." Whereupon your friend, unless he is a very unreasonable man, agrees with you, and is convinced that you are quite right in the conclusion you have drawn. He believes, although perhaps he does not know he believes it, that the more extensive verifications are—the more frequently experiments have been made, and results of the same kind arrived at—that the more varied the conditions under which the same results are attained, the more certain is the ultimate conclusion, and he disputes the question no further. He sees that the experiment has been tried under all sorts of conditions, as to time, place, and people, with the same results; and he says with you, therefore, that the law you have laid down must be a good one, and he must believe it.

6 In science we do the same thing; the philosopher exercises precisely the same faculties, though in a much more delicate manner. In scientific inquiry it becomes a matter of duty to expose a supposed law to every possible kind of verification, and to take care, moreover, that this is done intentionally, and not left to a mere accident, as in the case of the apples. And in science, as in common life, our confidence in a law is in exact proportion to the absence of variation in the result of our experimental verifications. For instance, if you let go your grasp of an article you may have in your hand, it will immediately fall to the ground. That is a very common verification of one of the best established laws of nature—that of gravitation. The method by which men of science establish the existence of that law is exactly the same as that by which we have established the trivial proposition about the sourness of hard and green apples. But we believe it

in such an extensive, thorough, and unhesitating manner because the universal experience of mankind verifies it, and we can verify it ourselves at any time; and that is the strongest possible foundation on which any natural law can rest.

STUDY GUIDE

Word Study

Give the exact etymology of the words *induction* and *deduction.* How do the prefixes used in these words help to indicate the points of departure and arrival in inductive and deductive argumentation?

Theme and Thought Structure

1. Huxley is discussing inductive and deductive reasoning in this essay. What precise point concerning them is he trying to bring home to his readers? Where in the essay does he come closest to stating that point?

2. A. How does the allusion to the incident in Molière's play (paragraph 3) bring out the main point of the essay?

B. How does the analogy drawn in paragraph 1 help to clarify this point?

3. Show how the main example used in paragraphs 4 and 5 illustrate the point concerning induction and deduction which Huxley is discussing.

Content and Suggestions for Writing

1. In rhetoric the equivalent of an induction is a theme or paragraph developed by *multiple examples.* To be effective such a theme must have a sufficient number of examples to warrant the general conclusion, and each example must clearly be a particular case of the general truth stated in the conclusion. Write a theme on a topic of your own choosing in which each paragraph develops an example of the general truth stated either in the first or last paragraph.

2. In rhetoric the equivalent of a deduction is an *enthymeme* or a form of argumentation in which one or both of the major premises are presupposed but not expressed. For example: He is opposed to a liberal education, since he will admit nothing but practical and technical subjects into the curriculum. The major premise from which the conclusion "He is opposed to a liberal education" is deduced is not expressed but presumed. In full syllogistic form, the idea would be expressed as follows:

> Anyone who tolerates only practical and technical subjects in a college curriculum is opposed to a liberal education.
> But he tolerates only practical and technical subjects in a college curriculum.
> Therefore he is opposed to a liberal education.

Conclusions expressed in such arguments are as valid as the assumed premises from which they are derived. To test the logical validity of such incomplete statements in your own and others' writing, expand them into their full syllogistic form, and then you can more easily investigate the validity of the premises or primary assumptions upon which the conclusions are based. For practice, supply the general assumptions or premises implied in the following statements in syllogistic form, and then state whether the premises are valid or not.

A. Since he is a literary genius, he can be expected to hide his deepest meaning.
B. As a scientist, he is intolerant of poetry and all the arts.
C. Since education trains a man for successful living, it is evident that practical and professional courses are the most important in the curriculum.

A Note on the Inductive and Deductive Methods of Reasoning

1. Induction is the process by which the mind passes from sufficiently enumerated instances to a universal truth. For example, the many deaths of particular men down through history justifies the *general conclusion* that all men are mortal. The validity of this generalization rests on the certainty about the many, identical, particular instances. The observation of a great many identical instances for long periods of time result in the most valid and universal laws. It is this inductive method of reasoning that the scientist uses to form his general laws.

2. Deduction is the form of argumentation in which the mind passes from a more universal truth to a less universal truth distinct from the first but implied in it. A deduction always works from a general law of some kind which has been arrived at through an induction. It applies this general law to a particular instance. For example, to say that some individual man will die is to make a deduction from the general law that all men will die concerning this particular man. The formal expression of the deductive process is the syllogism. For example:

All men are mortal (a conclusion from an induction).
James is a man.
Therefore James is mortal.

The universal statement is the *major premise*. The grammatical subject of the major premise always names the objects (here "all men") of which the predicate states the common characteristics (here "mortal"). The objects named may be very unlike in a hundred and one ways, but they are identical in the one point named in the predicate. The *minor premise* merely states that a definite individual is included in the class named in the major premise. The conclusion of a syllogism is always made up of the grammatical subject of the minor premise and the grammatical predicate of the major premise. If this procedure is followed closely the conclusion will always be valid, provided, of course, that both the major and minor premises are demonstrably true.

You need not always express all the steps of the process of deductive reasoning; but to test the validity of the reasoning, it is always helpful to supply the missing steps. When this is done, the logic or illogicality of the argument is more easily discerned. For practice, expand the following statements into the implied syllogisms that lie behind them, and then evaluate the validity of the conclusions.

A. I attend college in order to get into the higher income bracket.
B. Since he favors socialized medicine, he is obviously a Communist.

C. Most child prodigies do not succeed very well in adult life, so Jimmie will be a disappointment when he grows up.
D. He is obviously against progress, since he defends a liberal education.
E. As a poet, he could be expected to be impractical.

It is fairly easy to detect the fallacy of the assumptions upon which these segregated generalizations are based, but it is not always easy to detect such unjustified statements when they are embedded in full-length essays. The wary reader must be on the lookout for them, and not accept conclusions and particularly applications before he has determined the validity of the assumed premises from which they are derived.

HAIR-TRIGGER PLAINTIFFS

Westbrook Pegler

1 In deploring the ethics of the legal profession it is customary to forget that a large proportion of the citizens have become shyster-minded themselves and go through life hoping to be flicked on the flask by a rich man's limousine, disappointed in love, thrown out of a solvent hotel, insulted, libeled, frightened, humiliated or barked at by a dog whose owner lives in a big house.

2 Quite aside from the small criminal element of professional plaintiffs who are constantly having painful accidents on the common carriers and in department stores and suing for $100,000, there is a tendency among people to think in terms of damage, evidence, and lawsuits in every conceivable mishap or close call that befalls them. This is no special failing of the poor, being common also among people who are middling well to do, and is the cause of much of the clutter, delay, and perjury in the Courts.

3 Not to deny that a person who has suffered actual injury through the negligence or evil intent of another should receive compensation, it must be admitted that many injuries, physical and otherwise, are brought to court which would be laughed off or accepted as the rub of the green if people had an honest mind about them.

4 A man crosses a street against a traffic light, leaps to avoid a car, barks his shin against a curb, yells murder with great presence of mind, demands an ambulance and puts in a week's time malingering in a hospital over an injury whose proper treatment would be a dab of iodine and a jolt of scotch. In due time his attorneys notify the attorneys for the insurance

From *'T Aint Right* (New York: Doubleday & Company, Inc., 1936), pp. 188–191. Reprinted by permission of the author.

company that he has suffered great pain and will have to go on crutches for the rest of his life, in addition to which his little woman has suffered a loss of his services, the whole bill amounting to $100,000.

5 A grocery boy who plays football on the high school team slips on an icy stoop delivering a dozen eggs and falls eighteen inches. This does him great bodily harm, and his lawyer sues the owner of the house for an endowment to see the young man the rest of his way through life, not failing to point out that he is the principal support of his parents and numerous brothers and sisters on his $3.00 a week from the grocer.

6 A suburban lady comes staggering out of the cocktail bar of a hotel which is making money, begins to yodel and perform the split in the lobby and is firmly but gently shoved outside by the house detective in the honest performance of his duty. Two weeks later it develops through the affidavits of friends who were lushing with her at the bar, that the plaintiff drank nothing but mild, nutritious stingers, prescribed by her physician as a remedy for anemia, and that she was not plastered but just suddenly faint, not yodeling but crying for help, not doing the split but swooning. Therefore she has been publicly humiliated to an extent which cannot be compensated for a nickel less than $50,000.

7 When Jack Dempsey was heavyweight champion of the world he was sued for $100,000 by the father of a little girl who was said to have been snapped at by a dog which wandered onto premises which Dempsey had rented for his training. When Gene Tunney was heavyweight champion, he was warned not to possess or drive any automobile because an ordinary hub scrape with a fifty-dollar flivver in a traffic jam would develop into a shambles with dead and wounded strewn over a wide area by the time the plaintiffs got to Court. Nobody ever sued a poor man for breach of promise or alienation. The brutality of the hit-and-run driver might be palliated in certain cases by the fear in the heart of every driver that no matter how carefully and well he drives his car an accident which is imposed on him by the victim's own recklessness must inevitably involve him in litigation and might cost him everything he owns if he has the decency to stop and give assistance. I recall a case in which a child sliding on a sled on a public highway broke his nose against a car which was parked compliant to the law and then brought suit against the owner's employer, though the mishap occurred on the owner's day off.

8 The vast profusion of lawyers with nothing much to do for eating dollars doubtless accounts for much of this abuse, but the thieves' psychology of the people themselves is most to blame. The instinct now is not to avoid accident or other distress but to meet it at least halfway with a mind already at work on the scene in Court and a row of big numbers typed out in the plaintiff's petition. The shyster spirit of the citizens is fouling the Courts with many claims for injuries which in people of reasonably decent

conscience could be repaired with a nickel's worth of sticking plaster, a rock thrown at the barking dog, or a stein on the table and a good song ringing clear.

STUDY GUIDE

Theme and Thought Structure

1. Pegler is trying to convince us that it is not only lawyers but also the public who are shyster-minded. What does he mean by *shyster-mindedness*? What is the dictionary definition of the term?

2. This essay is a good instance of a whole theme developed inductively by multiple examples.

A. Show how the topic in paragraph 1 is developed by multiple examples within that paragraph.

B. The multiple examples introduced by Pegler to prove his generalization about the public are developed in paragraphs 4–7. Show how these examples are well chosen to give a fairly good cross section of the public mind—a fairly broad induction? Do they all show the common characteristic of shyster-mindedness—the desire to get all you can from a person who can pay?

3. Pegler is satirizing the tendency to shyster-mindedness in the public. In satire the writer tries to make the thing he is satirizing look ridiculous. Point out words or phrases in the following sentences which put the shyster mind in a ridiculous light: the opening sentence, the first sentences of paragraphs 4, 5, and 6, and the concluding sentences of paragraph 8.

4. Write a theme in which you try to show the prevalence of some abuse among students or among the public at large which you think ought to be corrected. Try to develop your theme by multiple concrete examples organized somewhat after the pattern employed by Pegler in this essay. Try to make the abuse you are discussing look ridiculous as Pegler makes the shyster-mindedness of the public look ridiculous here. Do not say it is ridiculous; make it look ridiculous.

RATS AND HISTORY

Hans Zinsser

1 A rat census is obviously impossible. It is quite certain, however, that they breed more rapidly than they are destroyed in many places in the world. We can appraise the rat population only by the numbers that are

From *Rats, Lice, and History* (Boston: Little, Brown & Company for *Atlantic Monthly Press*, 1935), pp. 204–211.

killed in organized rat campaigns and by the amount of destruction they cause. In about 1860, Shipley tells us, there was a slaughterhouse for horses on Montfaucon, which it was planned to remove farther away from Paris. The carcasses of horses amounted to sometimes thirty-five a day, and were regularly cleaned up completely by rats in the following night. Dusaussois had the idea of trying to find out how many rats were engaged in this gruesome traffic. He set horse-meat bait in enclosures from which the exit of rats could be prevented, and in the course of the first night killed 2650. By the end of a month, he had killed over 16,000. Shipley estimates that there are about forty million rats in England at one time. In 1881 there was a rat plague in certain districts of India. The crops of the preceding two years were below average and a large part of them had been destroyed by rats. Rewards offered for rat destruction led to a killing of over 12,000,000 rats. Shipley estimates that a single rat does about 7s.6d. worth of damage in a year, which makes a charge of £15,000,000 upon Great Britain and Ireland. It costs about sixty cents to two dollars a year to feed a rat on grain. Every rat on a farm costs about fifty cents a year. Lantz adds to this that hotel managers estimate five dollars a year as a low estimate of the loss inflicted by a rat. He thinks that in the thickly populated parts of the country an estimate of one rat per acre is not excessive, and that in most of our cities there are as many rats as people. He investigated, in 1909, the approximate total damage by rats in the cities of Washington and Baltimore. From the data he obtained, he calculated the annual damage in the two cities as amounting to $400,000 and $700,000 respectively—which, considering the populations, amounted to an average loss of $1.27 a year per person. On the same basis, the urban population of the United States, at that time 28,000,000 people, sustained an annual direct injury of $35,000,000 a year. In Denmark, the estimated rat cost is about $1.20 a person; in Germany, eighty-five cents a person; in France, a little over a dollar. Add to this the inestimable depreciation of property and the costs of protection.

2 All this has nothing to do with our main subject, but we were started on rats, and it is just as well to give thought to the problem of what rat extermination for sanitary purposes is likely to mean in other respects.

3 The tremendous speed with which rats swarmed over the continents of the world can be readily understood if one reads the observations of actual rat migrations made in modern times. The seasonal migration of rats from buildings to the open fields takes place with the coming of the warm weather and the growth of vegetation; and a return to shelter follows with the cold weather. Doctor Lantz tells us that in 1903 hordes of rats migrated over several counties in western Illinois, suddenly appearing when for several years no abnormal numbers had been seen. An eyewitness stated to Lantz that, as he was returning to his home on a moonlight night, he heard a rustling in a near-by field, and saw a great army of rats cross the road

in front of him. The army of rats stretched away as far as he could see in the moonlight. This to be sure, was before the Eighteenth Amendment, but there must have been some fact behind it, since heavy damage was caused by rats in the entire surrounding country of farms and villages in the ensuing winter and summer. On one farm, in the month of April, about 3500 rats were caught in traps. Lantz himself saw a similar migration in the valley of the Kansas River, in 1904; and Lantz, being at that time an officer and gentleman of the United States Agricultural Service, cannot be under any suspicion that is aroused by accounts of armies of rats seen by moonshine. In England, a general movement of rats inland from the coast occurs every October, and this migration is connected with the closing of the herring season. During the herring catch, rats swarm all over the coast, attracted by the food supply of herring cleaning; when it is over, they go back to their regular haunts. In South America, Lantz advises us, rat plagues are periodic in Parana, in Brazil, and occur at intervals of about thirty years. In Chile, the same thing has been observed, at intervals of fifteen to twenty-five years. Studies of these migrations have shown that the rat plagues are associated with the ripening and decay of a dominant species of bamboo in each country. For a year or two, the ripening seed in the forests supplies a favorite food for the rats. They multiply enormously, and eventually, this food supply failing, they go back to the cultivated areas. A famine was caused in 1878 in the state of Parana by the wholesale destruction of the corn, rice, and mandioca crops by rats. The invasion of Bermuda by rats in 1615, and their sudden disappearance, are as dramatic as the rise and fall of some of the short-lived Indian empires of Central and South America. Black rats appeared in that year, and within the two following ones increased with alarming rapidity. They devoured fruits, plants, and trees to such an extent that a famine resulted, and a law required every man in the islands to keep twelve traps set. Nothing, however, was of any use, until finally the rats disappeared with a suddenness that makes it almost necessary to assume that they died of a pestilence.

4 As we have indicated in a preceding paragraph, the natural history of the rat is tragically similar to that of man. Offspring of widely divergent evolutionary directions, men and rats reached present stages of physical development within a few hundred thousand years of each other—since remnants of both are found in the fossils of the glacial period.

5 Some of the more obvious qualities in which rats resemble men—ferocity, omnivorousness, and adaptability to all climates—have been mentioned above. We have also alluded to the irresponsible fecundity with which both species breed at all seasons of the year with a heedlessness of consequences which subjects them to wholesale disaster on the inevitable, occasional failure of the food supply. In this regard, it is only fair to state—in justice to man—that, as far as we can tell, the rat does this of its own

free and stupid gluttony, while man has tradition, piety, and the duty of furnishing cannon fodder to contend with, in addition to his lower instincts. But these are, after all, phenomena of human biology, and man cannot be absolved of responsibility for his stupidities because they are the results of wrong-headedness rather than the consequences of pure instinct —certainly not if they result in identical disasters.

6 Neither rat nor man has achieved social, commercial, or economic stability. This has been either perfectly or to some extent, achieved by ants and by bees, by some birds, and by some of the fishes in the sea. Man and the rat are merely, so far, the most successful animals of prey. They are utterly destructive of other forms of life. Neither of them is of the slightest earthly use to any other species of living things. Bacteria nourish plants; plants nourish man and beast. Insects, in their well-organized societies, are destructive of one form of living creature, but helpful to another. Most other animals are content to lead peaceful and adjusted lives, rejoicing in vigor, grateful for this gift of living, and doing the minimum of injury to obtain the things they require. Man and the rat are utterly destructive. All that nature offers is taken for their own purposes, plant or beast.

7 Gradually these two have spread across the earth, keeping pace with each other and unable to destroy each other, though continually hostile. They have wandered from East to West, driven by their physical needs, and—unlike any other species of living things—have made war upon their own kind. The gradual, relentless, progressive extermination of the black rat by the brown has no parallel in nature so close as that of the similar extermination of one race of man by another. Did the Danes conquer England; or the Normans the Saxon-Danes; or the Normans the Sicilian-Mohammedans; or the Moors the Latin-Iberians; or the Franks the Moors; or the Spanish the Aztecs and the Incas; or the Europeans in general the simple aborigines of the world by qualities other than those by which *Mus decumanus* has driven out *Mus rattus*? In both species, the battle has been pitilessly to the strong. And the strong have been pitiless. The physically weak have been driven before the strong—annihilated, or constrained to the slavery of doing without the bounties which were provided for all equally. Isolated colonies of black rats survive, as weaker nations survive until the stronger ones desire the little they still possess.

8 The rat has an excuse. As far as we know, it does not appear to have developed a soul, or that intangible quality of justice, mercy, and reason that psychic evolution has bestowed upon man. We must not expect too much. It takes a hundred thousand years to alter the protuberances on a bone, the direction of a muscle; much longer than this to develop a lung from a gill, or to atrophy a tail. It is only about twenty-five hundred years since Plato, Buddha, and Confucius; only two thousand years since Christ.

In the meantime, we have had Homer and Saint Francis, Copernicus and Galileo; Shakespeare, Pascal, Newton, Goethe, Bach, and Beethoven, and a great number of lesser men and women of genius who have demonstrated the evolutionary possibilities of the human spirit. If such minds have been rare, and spread thinly over three thousand years, after all they still represent the sports that indicate the high possibilities of fortunate genetic combinations. And these must inevitably increase if the environment remains at all favorable. If no upward progress in spirit or intelligence seems apparent, let us say, between the best modern minds and that of Aristotle, we must remember that, in terms of evolutionary change, three thousand years are negligible. If, as in the last war and its subsequent imbecilities, mankind returns completely to the rat stage of civilization, this surely shows how very rudimentary an emergence from the Neanderthal our present civilization represents—how easily the thin, spiritual veneer is cracked under any strain that awakens the neolithic beast within. Nevertheless, for perhaps three or five thousand years, the beast has begun to ponder and grope. Isolated achievements have demonstrated of what the mind and spirit are capable when a happy combination of genes occurs under circumstances that permit the favored individual to mature. And the most incomprehensible but hopeful aspect of the matter is the fact that successive generations have always bred an adequate number of individuals sufficiently superior to the brutal mass to keep alive a reverence for these supreme achievements and make them a cumulative heritage. It is more than likely—biologically considered—that by reason of this progressive accumulation of the best that superior specimens of our species have produced, the evolution toward higher things may gain velocity with time, and that in another hundred thousand years the comparison of the race of men with that of rats may be less humiliatingly obvious.

STUDY GUIDE

1. In paragraph 2 the author says that all his talk about rats has nothing to do with his main subject. What is his main subject? Does he state his main point succinctly anywhere or only imply it? Make a statement of your own which expresses the main point Zinsser is trying to make in the selection.

2. What are the topics developed in paragraphs 1 and 3? Show how the method of induction is employed to develop these topics. Are the instances proffered sufficient in number and extent to warrant the general statements made in these paragraphs?

3. From paragraph 4 to the end of the selection Zinsser is no longer proceeding inductively. He is rather arguing from a general assumption about man's origins which he makes no attempt to prove. What is that general assumption? Select at least three sentences which indicate clearly that Zinsser is making this general assumption.

4. The proper use of the inductive method in paragraphs 1 and 3 give the reader the impression that he is dealing with a carefully scientific mind. There is no equivalent inductive evidence to give for the generalizations made or implied about man's origin in paragraphs 4–9. The author, however, tries to give the appearance of an inductive proof for some of his statements. Point out instances where he does this in paragraphs 6, 7, and 8.

CLASSICAL EDUCATION

Bertrand Russell

1 One defect does seem inherent in a purely classical education—namely, a too exclusive emphasis on the past. By the study of what is absolutely ended and can never be renewed, a habit of criticism towards the present and the future is engendered. The qualities in which the present excels are qualities to which the study of the past does not direct attention, and to which, therefore, the student of Greek civilization may easily become blind. In what is new and growing there is apt to be something crude, insolent, even a little vulgar, which is shocking to the man of sensitive taste; quivering from the rough contact, he retires to the trim gardens of a polished past, forgetting that they were reclaimed from the wilderness by men as rough and earth-soiled as those from whom he shrinks in his own day. The habit of being unable to recognize merit until it is dead is too apt to be the result of a purely bookish life, and a culture based wholly on the past will seldom be able to pierce through everyday surroundings to the essential splendour of contemporary things or to the hope of still greater splendour in the future.

. . . .

2 Our whole life is built about a certain number—not a very small number—of primary instincts and impulses. Only what is in some way connected with these instincts and impulses appears to us desirable or important; there is no faculty, whether "reason" or "virtue" or whatever it may be called, that can take our active life and our hopes and fears outside the region controlled by these first movers of all desire. Each of them is like a queen-bee, aided by a hive of workers gathering honey; but when the queen is gone the workers languish and die, and the cells remain empty of their expected sweetness. So with each primary impulse in civilised man: it is surrounded and protected by a busy swarm of attendant derivative de-

From Bertrand Russell, "The Place of Science in a Liberal Education," *Mysticism and Logic* (New York: David McKay Company, Inc., 1925), pp. 35–38.

sires, which store up in its service whatever honey the surrounding world affords. But if the queen-impulse dies, the death-dealing influence, though retarded a little by habit, spreads slowly through all the subsidiary impulses, and a whole tract of life becomes inexplicably colourless. What was formerly full of zest, and so obviously worth doing that it raised no questions, has now grown dreary and purposeless: with a sense of disillusion we inquire the meaning of life, and decide, perhaps, that all is vanity. The search for an outside meaning that can *compel* an inner response must always be disappointed: all "meaning" must be at bottom related to our primary desires, and when they are extinct no miracle can restore to the world that value which they reflected upon it.

EFFECTS OF SCIENCE

J. B. S. Haldane

But civilization as we know it is a poor thing. And if it is to be improved there is no hope save in science. A hundred and forty years ago men, women, and children were being hanged in England for stealing any property valued at over a shilling; miners were hereditary slaves in Scotland; criminals were publicly and legally tortured to death in France. Europe was definitely rather worse off, whether in health, wealth, or morals, than the Roman Empire under Antonius Pius in A.D. 150. Since then we have improved very greatly in all these respects. We are far from perfect, but we live about twice as long, and we do not hang starving children for stealing food, raid the coast of Africa for slaves, or imprison debtors for life. These advances are the direct and indirect consequences of science. Physics and chemistry have made us rich, biology healthy, and the application of scientific thought to ethics by such men as Bentham has done more than any dozen saints to make us good. The process can only continue if science continues.

MODERN ARTS

Thomas Craven

1 Art has lost its historical connection with dominant idealisms—lost its most important function. There is no need to disguise this fact. Its claims, for the most part, are preposterous; its accomplishments negligible. Modern art, the art succeeding Impressionism, which seemed to promise so much, now promises nothing. Its exhibits are stale and nonsensical—of no value whatever save as adjuncts to the vanity of wealthy collectors who find in it the parallel of their own spiritual emptiness. Its obscurities and aberrations still inspire the drivel of the esoteric scribes; but it has no meaning save that which is read into it by the dictates of idiosyncrasy.

2 Democracy, you see, has provided no mythology adaptable to the symbolical apparatus of painting; its ideals have been continually shifting, have accommodated themselves to the rapid changes in the mechanics of production and distribution. Democratic society has created no background of vital belief, no general conviction that behind the shifting dance of expedients there exists a spiritual reality, absolute and unchangeable. Democracy has drained the substance from the old illusions to which art was faithfully united: the illusion that eternal life actually lay beyond the horizon of fact; that the King was divine and his antics inspired. Today the King is not even a figurehead—he is an obsolete dunce; and the Church, like the old aristocracy with its ideals of power, grandeur and gentility, survives as a clearing house for social indulgences.

STUDY GUIDE

There are certain statements made in each of the three preceding selections which are based on false assumptions. Expand each of these statements into full syllogistic form, and then, in each case, point out the false assumption upon which the conclusion is based.

From Thomas Craven, "Art and Propaganda," *Modern Art* (New York: Simon and Schuster, Inc., 1934), p. 351. Reprinted from *Modern Art* by permission of Simon and Schuster, publishers.

HOW TO DETECT PROPAGANDA

The Institute of Propaganda Analysis

1 If American citizens are to have a clear understanding of present-day conditions and what to do about them, they must be able to recognize propaganda, to analyze it, and to appraise it.

2 But what is propaganda? As generally understood, propaganda is expression of opinion or action by individuals or groups deliberately designed to influence opinions or actions of other individuals or groups with reference to predetermined ends. Thus propaganda differs from scientific analysis. The propagandist is trying to "put something across," good or bad; whereas the scientist is trying to discover truth and fact. Often the propagandist does not want careful scrutiny and criticism; he wants to bring about a specific action. Because the action may be socially beneficial or socially harmful to millions of people, it is necessary to focus upon the propagandist and his activities the searchlight of scientific scrutiny. Socially desirable propaganda will not suffer from such examination, but the opposite type will be detected and revealed for what it is.

3 We are fooled by propaganda chiefly because we do not recognize it when we see it. We can more easily recognize it if we are familiar with the seven devices commonly employed by the propagandist. These devices are: (1) name calling, (2) glittering generalities, (3) the transfer, (4) the testimonial, (5) the plain folks device, (6) card stacking, and (7) the band wagon.

4 We are fooled by these devices because they appeal to our emotions rather than to our reason. They make us believe and do something we would not believe or do if we thought about it calmly, dispassionately. In examining these devices, note that they work most effectively at those times when we are too lazy to think for ourselves, and that they also tie into emotions which sway us to be "for" or "against" nations, races, religions, ideals, economic and political policies and practices, and so on through automobiles, cigarettes, radios, toothpastes, presidents, and wars. With our emotions stirred, it may be fun to be fooled by these propaganda devices, but it is more fun and infinitely more to our interest to

know how they work. Lincoln must have had in mind citizens who could balance their emotions with intelligence when he made his remark: ". . . but you can't fool all the people all of the time."

5 "Name Calling" is a device to make us form a judgment without examining the evidence on which it should be based. Here the propagandist appeals to our hate and fear. He does this by giving "bad names" to those individuals, groups, nations, races, policies, practices, beliefs, and ideals which he would have us condemn and reject. For centuries the name "heretic" was bad. Anybody who dissented from popular or group belief or practice was in danger of being called a heretic and of receiving the punishment of heretics. Today's bad names include: Fascist, demagogue, dictator, Red, financial oligarchy, Communist, muckraker, alien, outside agitator, Utopian, rabble-rouser, Constitution wrecker.

6 Use of "bad names" without presentation of their essential meaning, without all their pertinent implications, comprises perhaps the most common of all propaganda devices. Those who want to *maintain* the status quo apply bad names to those who would change it. For example, the Hearst press applies bad names to Communists and Socialists. Those who want to *change* the status quo apply bad names to those who would maintain it. For example, the *Daily Worker* and the *American Guardian* apply bad names to conservative Republicans and Democrats.

7 "Glittering Generalities" is a device by which the propagandist identifies his program with virtue by use of "virtue words." Here he appeals to our emotions of love, generosity, and Brotherhood. He uses words like truth, freedom, honor, liberty, social justice, public service, the right to work, loyalty, progress, democracy, the American way, Constitution defender. These words suggest shining ideals which all persons of good will believe. Hence the propagandist by identifying his individual group, nation, race, policy, practice, or belief with such ideals, seeks to win us to his cause. As Name Calling is a device to make us form judgments to *reject and condemn,* without examining the evidence, Glittering Generalities is a device to make us *accept and approve,* without examining the evidence. For example, use of the phrases, "the right to work" and "social justice," may be a device to make us accept programs for meeting the labor-capital problem which, if we examined them critically, we would not accept at all.

8 In the Name Calling and Glittering Generalities devices, words are used to stir up our emotions and to befog our thinking. In one device "bad names" are used to make us mad; in the other "good words" are used to make us glad. The propagandist is most effective in use of these devices when his words make us create devils to fight or gods to adore. By his use of "bad words" we personify as a "devil" some nation, race, group, individual policy, practice, or ideal; we are made fighting mad to destroy

it. By use of "good words" we personify as a godlike idol some nation, race, group, etc. From considerations of names, "bad" and "good," we pass to institutions and symbols, also "bad" and "good." These we see in the next device.

9 "Transfer" is a device by which the propagandist carries over the authority, sanction, and prestige of something we respect and revere to something he would have us accept. For example, most of us respect and revere our church and our nation. If the propagandist succeeds in getting church or nation to approve a campaign in behalf of some program, he thereby transfers its authority, sanction, and prestige to that program. Thus we may accept something which otherwise we might reject.

10 In the Transfer device, symbols are constantly used. The cross represents the Christian Church; the flag represents the nation; cartoons like Uncle Sam represent a consensus of public opinion. Those symbols stir emotions. At their very sight, with the speed of light, is aroused the whole complex of feelings we have with respect to church or nation. A cartoonist by having Uncle Sam disapprove a budget for unemployment relief would have us feel that the whole United States disapproves relief costs. By drawing an Uncle Sam who approves the same budget, the cartoonist would have us feel that the American people approve it. Thus, the Transfer device is used both for and against causes and ideas.

11 The "Testimonial" is a device to make us accept anything from a patent medicine or a cigarette to a program or national policy. In this device the propagandist makes use of testimonials. "When I feel tired, I smoke a Camel and get the grandest 'lift.' " "We believe the John L. Lewis plan of labor organization is splendid; C.I.O. should be supported." This device works in reverse also; counter-testimonials may be employed. Seldom are these used against commercial products like patent medicines and cigarettes; but they are constantly employed in social, economic, and political issues. For example, "We believe that the John L. Lewis plan of labor organization is bad; C.I.O. should not be supported."

12 "Plain Folks" is a device used by politicians, labor leaders, business men, and even by ministers and educators to win our confidence by appearing to be people like ourselves—"just plain folks among the neighbors." In election years especially do candidates show their devotion to little children and the common, homey things of life. They have front porch campaigns. For the newspaper men they raid the icebox finding there some of the good wife's apple pie. They go to country picnics; they attend service at the old frame church; they pitch hay and go fishing; they show their belief in home and mother. In short, they would win our votes by showing that they're just as common as the rest of us—"just plain folks"—and, therefore, wise and good. Business men are often "plain folks" with the factory hands. Even distillers use the device. "It's our family's whiskey, neighbor; and neighbor, it's your price."

13 "Card Stacking" is a device in which the propagandist employs all the arts of deception to win our support for himself, his group, nation, race, policy, practice, belief, or ideal. He stacks the cards against the truth. He uses under-emphasis and over-emphasis to dodge issues and evade facts. He offers false testimony. He creates a smoke-screen of clamor by raising a new issue when he wants an embarrassing matter forgotten. He draws a red herring across the trail to confuse and divert those in quest of facts he does not want revealed. He makes the unreal appear real and the real appear unreal. He lets half-truth masquerade as truth. By the Card Stacking device a mediocre candidate, through the "build-up" is made to appear an intellectual titan; an ordinary prize-fighter a probable world champion; a worthless patent medicine a beneficent cure. By means of this device propagandists would convince us that ruthless war of aggression is a crusade for righteousness. Card Stacking employs sham, hypocrisy, effrontery.

14 The "Band Wagon" is a device to make us follow the crowd, to accept the propagandist's program en masse. Here his theme is "Everybody's doing it." His techniques range from those of medicine show to dramatic spectacle. He hires a hall, fills a great stadium, marches a million men in parade. He employs symbols, colors, music, movement, all the dramatic arts. He appeals to the desire, common to most of us, to "follow the crowd." Because he wants us to "follow the crowd," in masses, he directs his appeal to groups held together by common ties of nationality, religion, race, environment, sex, vocation. Thus propagandists campaigning for or against a program will appeal to us as Catholics, Protestants, or Jews; as members of the Nordic race or as Negroes; as farmers or as school teachers; as housewives or as miners. All the artifices of flattery are used to harness the fears and hatreds, prejudices, and biases, convictions and ideals common to the group; thus emotion is made to push and pull the group onto the Band Wagon. In newspaper articles and in the spoken word this device is also found. "Don't throw your vote away; vote for our candidate; he's sure to win." Nearly every candidate wins in every election—before the votes are in.

15 Observe that in all these devices our emotion is the stuff with which propagandists work. Without it they are helpless; with it, harnessing it to their purposes, they can make us glow with pride or burn with hatred, they can make us zealots in behalf of the program they espouse. As we said in the beginning, propaganda as generally understood is expression of opinion or action by individuals or groups with reference to predetermined ends. Without the appeal of our emotions—to our fears and our courage, to our selfishness and unselfishness, to our loves and to our hates—propagandists would influence few opinions and few actions.

16 To say this is not to condemn emotion, an essential part of life, or to assert that all predetermined ends of propagandists are "bad." What we mean is that the intelligent citizen does not want propagandists to utilize

his emotions, even to the attainment of "good ends" without his knowing what is going on. He does not want to be "used" in the attainment of ends he may later consider "bad." He does not want to be gullible; he does not want to be fooled; he does not want to be duped, even in a "good" cause. He wants to know the facts and among these is included the fact of the utilization of his emotions.

17 Keeping in mind the seven common propaganda devices, turn to today's newspapers and almost immediately you can spot examples of them all. At election time or during any campaign, Plain Folks and Band Wagons are common. Card Stacking is hardest to detect because it is adroitly executed or because we lack the information necessary to nail the lie. A little practice with the daily newspapers in detecting these propaganda devices soon enables us to detect them elsewhere—in radio, news-reel, books, magazines, and in expressions of labor unions, business groups, churches, schools, and political parties.

STUDY GUIDE

Word Study

1. Look up the etymology of the word *propaganda*. What was its original meaning in English? Why has its reputation changed from good to bad?

2. Distinguish clearly among *proving, persuading*, and *propagandizing*.

Thought Structure

This essay contains a very handy listing of the chief devices employed by the propagandist to influence people through the substitution of the emotional for the logical appeal. It is developed by definition, classification, and concrete examples.

It has been pointed out by experts, however, that these seven devices are really not equally parallel. Name calling, glittering generalities, and transfer are really all specific kinds of card stacking, of deliberately prejudicing someone in favor of or against someone or something.

Content and Application

1. In any current edition of a magazine which carries advertisements, find and analyze advertisements which employ some of the devices discussed in this essay. Especially frequent are the transfer and the testimonial. Advertisers must be cautious in using name calling, but they do employ the device covertly.

2. In some instances the advertiser wishes to give the appearance of logical proof when he really has no proof. In the testimonial device, for instance, he will give the impression of an inductive argument by citing many testimonials

from a wide variety of people. Find examples of this among current advertisements.

In the second part of Zinsser's essay "Rats and History" we saw him parading multiple examples to give the impression of inductive proof. Find other examples of such pseudoinductions.

3. Sometimes the advertiser even simulates the deductive process by using incomplete syllogisms either verbally or pictorially. For example: Clear Heads Choose Calvert. The advertiser knows that we will finish the syllogism for him:

> Clear heads choose Calvert.
> But I have a clear head.
> Therefore I choose Calvert.

or:

> Men of distinction choose Calvert.
> But ______ is a man of distinction.
> Therefore ______ chooses Calvert.

The advertiser knows that, if I think I am a man of distinction, I will flatter myself into the minor of another syllogism, which will read:

> Men of distinction choose Calvert.
> But I am a man of distinction.
> Therefore I choose Calvert.

Or if I am not that presumptuous, he hopes that my admiration for the distinguished sportsman, novelist, or musician whom he pictures enjoying a Calvert highball, will be transferred from the person to the highball, and that I will be satisfied with nothing less than a Calvert highball.

Find several other examples of implied syllogisms in current advertisements. Notice particularly how the minor premise, in which the product being advertised is mentioned, is glamorized in color and picture.

4. Look up some recent political campaign speeches or literature and point out instances of these propaganda devices in them.

5. Get copies of periodicals such as *The Daily Worker*, and find examples of antireligious, anticapitalist, or antigovernment propaganda in which some of these devices are employed.

6. Find examples of the use of some of these devices in newspaper cartoons.

7. The technique of the propagandist is not new. Whenever a man has wanted to influence others not by convincing them logically but by playing upon their emotions, he has used these devices of propaganda.

Mark Antony, in Shakespeare's *Julius Caesar*, uses several of them masterfully to win an unsympathetic audience to his own cause and to incite it against Brutus and Cassius. Study his speech in Act III, sc. 2, ll. 78–266, and indicate which of these seven devices he employs. Notice the effect of these devices on the unthinking mob Mark Antony is addressing.

THE ART OF MORALS

Havelock Ellis

1 There is a certain indefiniteness about the conception of morality as an artistic impulse, to be judged by an aesthetic criterion, which is profoundly repugnant to at least two classes of minds fully entitled to make their antipathy felt. In the first place, it makes no appeal to the abstract reasoner, indifferent to the manifoldly concrete problems of living. For the man whose brain is hypertrophied and his practical life shrivelled to an insignificant routine—the man of whom Kant is the supreme type—it is always a temptation to rationalize morality. Such a pure intellectualist, overlooking the fact that human beings are not mathematical figures, may even desire to transform ethics into a species of geometry. That we may see in Spinoza, a nobler and more inspiring figure, no doubt, but of much the same temperament as Kant. The impulses and desires of ordinary men and women are manifold, inconstant, often conflicting, and sometimes overwhelming. "Morality is a fact of sensibility," remarks Jules de Gaultier; "it has no need to have recourse to reason for its affirmations." But to men of the intellectualist type this consideration is almost negligible; all the passions and affections of humanity seem to them meek as sheep which they may shepherd, and pen within the flimsiest hurdles. William Blake, who could cut down to that central core of the world where all things are fused together, knew better when he said that the only golden rule of life is "the great and golden rule of art." James Hinton was forever expatiating on the close resemblance between the methods of art, as shown especially in painting, and the methods of moral action. Thoreau, who also belonged to this tribe, declared, in the same spirit as Blake, that there is no golden rule in morals, for rules are only current silver; "it is golden not to have any rule at all."

2 There is another quite different type of person who shares this antipathy to the indefiniteness of aesthetic morality: the ambitious moral reformer. The man of this class is usually by no means devoid of strong passions; but for the most part he possesses no great intellectual calibre and so is unable to estimate the force and complexity of human impulses. The moral reformer, eager to introduce the millennium here and now by the aid of the newest mechanical devices, is righteously indignant with anything so vague as an aesthetic morality. He must have definite rules and

From *The Dance of Life* (Boston: Houghton Mifflin Company, 1923), pp. 280–283.

regulations, clear-cut laws and bylaws, with an arbitrary list of penalties attached, to be duly inflicted in this world or the next. The popular conception of Moses, descending from the "sacred" mount with a "brand new" table of commandments, which he declares have been delivered to him by God, though he is ready to smash them to pieces on the slightest provocation, furnishes a delightful image of the typical moral reformer of every age. It is, however, only in savage and barbarous stages of society, or among the uncultivated classes of civilization, that the men of this type can find their faithful followers.

3 Yet there is more to be said. That very indefiniteness of the criterion of moral action, falsely supposed to be a disadvantage, is really the prime condition for effective moral action. The academic philosophers of ethics, had they possessed virility enough to enter the field of real life, would have realized—as we cannot expect the moral reformers blinded by the smoke of their own fanaticism to realize—that the slavery to rigid formulas which they preached was the death of all high moral responsibility. Life must always be a great adventure, with risks on every hand; a clear-sighted eye, a many-sided sympathy, a fine daring, an endless patience, are forever necessary to all good living. With such qualities alone may the artist in life reach success; without them even the most devoted slave to formulas can only meet disaster. No reasonable being may draw breath in the world without an open-eyed freedom of choice, and if the moral world is to be governed by laws, better to people it with automatic machines than with living men and women.

STUDY GUIDE

1. The task of the propagandist is to get his audience to dislike the person, thing, or idea against which he is working, and to like the person, thing, or idea for which he is working. His chief instrument in achieving his end is the *connotation* of words. "Connotation," someone has said, "creates values —either good or bad." Hence the propagandist piles up words that have an unfavorable connotation in connection with the thing he is opposing and words with a favorable connotation in connection with the thing he is advocating. The former practice is really name calling—associating vice words with the thing you wish damned; the latter is an example of glittering generalities—associating virtue words with the thing you wish accepted or idolized.

In this selection Ellis is trying to put those who oppose the concept of morals as art in an unfavorable light and those who accept it in a favorable light.

List all the unfavorably connotative words or phrases in the passage associated with Ellis' opponents and all the favorably connotative ones associated with those who agree with him.

2. Find other examples of propaganda writing and be ready to show how positive or negative values have been created through the use of connotation.

THEY MADE THE CIGAR RESPECTABLE

Keith Monroe

1 Suppose you were a manufacturer whose product was steadily falling into disfavor. Previously bought by millions, like the button shoe or the high collar, it was now scorned except by oldsters too stubborn to change, and by bums too ignorant to care. Your sales were sinking toward the bankruptcy point. What would you do?

2 The problem is an old one. Few businessmen who have faced it have ever solved it, except by flight into some other line of work. It wiped out the fletchers and the blacksmiths. It defeated the makers of corsets and gas lights and stereoscopes. But it has not defeated one present-day group of manufacturers.

3 They have met this problem in our generation and have conquered it, after a fight for survival which only recently has seemed securely won. In ten years of studied undercover work they have rolled back the tide of public distaste, thereby almost literally rescuing their product from the gutter and themselves from limbo.

4 The men by whom—or for whom—this miracle was performed are the cigar makers. There are around forty fairly big ones today, and around 4,000 small ones. They are the smart survivors of the 27,000 who flourished before World War I, and they survived because they gambled part of their fast-shrinking bankrolls on a public-relations campaign.

5 What saved them was pervasive low-pressure propaganda, which was brought to bear long before the cigarette was publicly associated with lung cancer; the pressure was so invisible and imperceptible that most people never noticed it even though it reversed their attitude toward cigars. Among public-relations wizards, the "cigar campaign" is recognized as one of the great classics of their art.

6 Perhaps the reader does not smoke cigars and therefore thinks that this campaign did not sway him. But if he is under fifty, let him ask himself if he feels any prejudice against cigars today—and then let him think back twenty years. Around 1935 how did cigar-smokers look to him? Didn't they seem rather lowbrow and crude? Or else pitiably old-fashioned?

Wouldn't he have been taken aback to see a young man of good family puffing a stogie?

7 If the reader is a lady, let her recall how she reacted to cigar smoke in the thirties. Does her nose wrinkle today as it did then? Let her remember the many parlors in which cigar fumes, if anyone had dared to generate them, would have seemed shamefully offensive. Is she shocked today if a gentlemen lights a cigar in her home?

8 The answers seem beyond dispute, at least satistically. Public-opinion pollsters recently found that 90 per cent of American women no longer object to cigar smoking by men. Of all American men, 40 per cent now smoke cigars at least occasionally, and they start young, at the average age of twenty-three. Cigar sales, which were down to $225 million a year when the manufacturers kittied up for their campaign, have soared to $550 million.

9 This is still a cut below the majestic old days of $650 million annual sales in the first decades of the century. But the sales curve, which dropped steeply from 1920 to 1936, has climbed ever since, and in recent years has gone up at the rate of 2 per cent a year. In the last three years an estimated 1,500,000 new men have become cigar-smokers.

10 Perhaps the curve would eventually have gone up anyway, without pushing by propagandists. Public taste runs in mysterious waves. There is no sure way of telling when, or why, people will change their minds en masse. (One of many examples is the strange lettuce market of 1930. For unknown reasons, housewives simply weren't in the mood to buy lettuce that year. The price plummeted, but lettuce didn't sell at any price. Lettuce growers and speculators went broke, lettuce fields were abandoned and left to rot. Then, over one weekend, an army of women from Maine to Mexico began asking their grocers for lettuce. Prices climbed to ten-year highs and shattered fortunes were rebuilt in a few weeks, as women kept on buying lettuce.)

11 The cigar has survived several such violent ups and downs. Columbus brought it back from the New World and showed Spanish nobility how the Indians smoked it. It became so much the rage that professors of smoking set up salons to teach both sexes how to light up, how to blow smoke rings, and a few other tricks still used by cigar-smokers today.

12 Cigars grew so popular that Pope Urban VIII had to issue a bull against priests who smoked while saying mass. The interior of St. Peter's itself was sometimes so gray with cigar haze that Innocent X finally threatened smokers with excommunication. This almost killed the cigar in Europe.

13 But the Vatican's attitude changed later, and cigar-manufacturing became a papal prerogative. In 1851 the Secretary to the Papal States warned that anyone who disseminated anti-cigar propaganda would be jailed.

Cigars were hotly controversial by then. Not only were prohibitionists preaching against them, but in 1848 cigar-smokers were pursued by mobs and lynched in the streets of Milan. It wasn't that the Milanese found cigar odor as obnoxious as all that; they hated it for ideological reasons. The cigar was a symbol of their Austrian rulers. All cigars in Milan were imported by the Austrian government, but boycotted by nationalists, so a cheroot in the mouth was emblematic of an 1848-style collaborationist.

14 There were cigar stores in America before the Revolution. One in Lancaster, Pennsylvania, was opened in 1770 and is still owned by the same family. The earliest cigar-makers in this country were Colonial dames, who rolled them by hand and sold them to itinerant peddlers for pin money. These good wives sampled their own wares as a matter of course. In colonial days cigar-smoking was no less ladylike than cigarette-smoking is today.

15 The first world war came closer to killing the cigar than any other event had. During that war, men switched to cigarettes. Until then the cigarette had seemed vaguely degenerate. Almost nobody smoked it except mysterious Orientals, absinthe drinkers, Tenderloin girls, and other slinky characters. But the doughboys, burdened with bulkier equipment than any warriors since the Crusades, discovered the advantages of the handy little pack in an outside pocket. They learned to enjoy a quick puff at odd moments in the trenches. Suddenly a cigarette was a he-man's pleasure.

16 This trend started by default, because cigars weren't in the field. Service men had yearned for cigars in the early months of the war, so Washington had ordered millions for distribution to the armed forces. Unfortunately its policy was to buy from the lowest bidders.

17 "Many bidders for cigar contracts," the Cigar Institute of America records bitterly, "were neither experienced nor reputable. It was their practice to produce something that had the appearance of a cigar, deliver it to government depots, then disappear with their profit. Much of this product was in no condition for anything but the incinerator. It was moldy or dried or wormy, or the most sordid combination of assorted vegetables and wrapping paper."

18 So the AEF tried cigarettes. Soon all the armies of the Allied and the Central Powers were smoking them too. Cigarette manufacturers shrewdly reinvested their profits in massive advertising and distribution drives which led to complete saturation of their markets.

19 By 1920 they were strong enough to suggest that women might smoke too. They began cautiously, with advertisements which showed winsome and fashionable girls imploring men to "Blow Some My Way." Finally they risked a picture of a girl actually smoking. Another barrier between the sexes fell, and millions of women bought cigarettes.

20 Meanwhile, trainloads of war-surplus cigars were being dumped on

civilians. Retailers put baskets of cigars in their stores with signs like "Take a handful for 5 cents" and "Free cigars with every purchase." Only the most hardened roughnecks could smoke them at any price. A cigar in the mouth became the mark of a tough mug.

21 The infant movie industry noticed this. Thrifty casting directors realized they didn't need a good actor to play a house detective, gangster, or ward heeler. All they needed was a $5-a-day extra with plug hat and cigar.

22 Movie audiences learned to identify the cigar-smoker as the villain. The impact of Hollywood on our folkways has been felt many times. This time it knocked cigars out the mouths of almost everyone except Grandpa. Without malice aforethought, the movie-makers nearly finished off the cigar-makers.

23 Dealers buried cigars on bottom counters, and stopped bothering to humidify them. Four of every five cigar factories closed. In 1933 most of the remaining manufacturers sat down in one room to form the Cigar Manufacturers Association.

24 They were a jealous and suspicious crowd: Cubans, Puerto Ricans, New Yorkers and Southerners and New Englanders. Each considered his product a work of art, and was as egoistic as a chef or a novelist. No one would agree to anything smacking of standardization. No system of classifying cigar shapes or sizes would suit them—nor has, to this day. "Perfecto" or "Panatela" can mean almost anything in length and thickness, depending on which company is doing the labeling.

25 However, the manufacturers did agree to hire a market-research man. But when he recommended spending $150,000 on publicity to make cigar-smoking fashionable, the CMA shuddered and voted him down.

26 Another two years passed. Cigars were becoming as old-fashioned as chin whiskers. Then the sales curve took a feeble turn upward. Why? Some tobacco men said cigar sales had followed the prosperity graph downward, and now would follow it up again. Others noted that Cremo, Dutch Masters, and Bayuk Phillies had lashed out on their own with vigorous advertising; perhaps they were pulling the whole industry upward.

27 Not until 1940, when the "national defense" boom had failed to bring prosperity to them, did the cigar-makers pull out their checkbooks and agree on joint, bold action. They would finance a subtle but widespread promotion to stop Americans' drift away from cigars.

28 The manufacturers rented offices in Rockefeller Center, established the Cigar Institute of America, and hired a manager: Berthold Nussbaum, an adman who had wrestled for years with cigar-company accounts.

29 Mr. Nussbaum remembered the blunder of the movie men, who wasted vast sums bellowing "Movies Are Your Best Entertainment." (Their billboards, banners, radio commercials, and newspaper pages were

hastily canceled when someone pointed out that the initials of the slogan spelled MAYBE. But even when reborn as "Motion Pictures Are Your Best Entertainment" the campaign flopped.) He knew that a blatant smoke-more-cigars theme would merely remind people that few cigars were being smoked.

30 When the meat packers had wanted to sell more bacon, he remembered, they had sought the advice of the legendary Ivy Lee, a public relations counsel who believed in persuasion by indirection. Mr. Lee had sprinkled the newspapers with statements from doctors urging people to eat bigger breakfasts. The doctors never mentioned bacon. But millions of people bought bacon, because a big breakfast usually includes bacon and eggs.

31 Mr. Nussbaum devised an even more oblique approach. His campaign did not urge anybody to do anything. Instead he sent emissaries to newspaper offices, empty-handed. They bore no mimeographed press releases, no invitations to press conferences. They had nothing in writing—but they discreetly passed the word to news photographers that there would be cash prizes each month for the best published photos of people smoking cigars.

32 Cameramen, who had previously suggested to a cigar-smoking subject that he hide his cigar before posing, now decided that he looked better with cigar. They sometimes went so far as to offer him one if he didn't have it. News pictures began to show cigars in the mouths of the Duke of Windsor, Lauritz Melchior, Darryl Zanuck, Benny Goodman. When American wire-service men photographed Winston Churchill, they waited patiently for chances to catch him with cigar in teeth.

33 By text as well as by photo, cigars eased into newspapers and magazines. Cigar Institute agents had begun feeding copy to editors. The nation heard cigars mentioned casually amid the thunder of big names. There were reminders of Churchill's fifteen cigars a day; of the five-dollar Havanas Coolidge had cherished, and the humidor Roosevelt kept for distinguished visitors; of Babe Ruth's passion for expensive Perfectos, and Douglas MacArthur's habit of sitting down with a cigar to mull a military problem.

34 Cigar sales showed a walloping increase of one billion in 1941. Mr. Nussbaum died of a heart attack the week before Pearl Harbor, but the manufacturers kept their campaign rolling. As their new manager they picked Harry W. McHose, fresh from Lexington, Kentucky, where he had been a publicity man for American Tobacco Company during the government's monopoly suit against cigarette manufacturers.

35 Mr. McHose saw that the new war threatened final ruin of the cigar business if the government repeated its 1917 policy. He persuaded Washington to buy only from established cigar-makers. Cigars for the armed forces

were as good as those for civilians, and service men asked for more and more. The first Allied soldier to land in France was reported to be a young American paratrooper who arrived bolt upright with a lighted cigar in his mouth. The Cigar Institute, naturally, prevented this incident from being overlooked.

36 By 1944 there was a world-wide cigar shortage. Manufacturers could not keep up with demand. They had only 36,000 factory workers, with no hope of hiring more while the war lasted. But they knew that even if they made enough cigars for everyone who wanted them, sales would be far below the eight-billion peak of 1910. Mr. McHose kept hatching ideas.

37 He had plenty of problems. Younger men by no means overwhelmed cigar counters. Women still complained about the "vile smell." Hollywood still used cigars incessantly as a prop for heavies.

38 Mr. McHose begged Hollywood to stop putting stogies in the mouths of Edward G. Robinson and his ilk. Hollywood paid no attention. Finally he loaded a briefcase and stormed the studios in person.

39 He showed movie magnates a tabulation which revealed that 27,500,000 people a week passed cigar counters near theaters. "Whenever you make a movie with a good cigar scene," he offered, "I'll put posters advertising it on 25,000 cigar counters across the nation. Free of charge."

40 Free advertising is meat and drink to showmen. Hollywood heavies stopped smoking, and heroes started. Tyrone Power puffed cigar smoke all over the screen in "Blood and Sand." So did Gary Cooper as Sergeant York. When the Cigar Institute heard that Hollywood was filming George Gershwin's life story, it hastened to concoct twenty-five pages of alleged historical data about Gershwin's cigar-smoking. The subsequent movie showed Gershwin wreathed in smoke at each high point of triumph or delight. In "Saratoga Trunk," Gary Cooper flourished Havanas intermittently, and Ingrid Bergman cooed, "A house isn't really a house unless it has about it the scent of a good cigar after breakfast."

41 If they thought about it at all, men may have been puzzled that cigar counters were all flaunting movie posters. But movie patronage picked up. By the end of 1947 the Cigar Institute was able to boast that forty major movies of that year contained "good cigar scenes" and that "Seldom, if ever, is a cigar misused today in action or dialogue."

42 Mr. McHose combed literature for endorsements of cigars. Robert Louis Stevenson, he found, had advised women never to marry a non-smoker. Bert Leston Taylor had suggested that when things go wrong it is a good idea to "meditate on interstellar spaces,/And smoke a mild seegar." Bulwer-Lytton called the cigar "as great a comfort to a man as a good cry to a woman." Thackeray called it "a kind companion, a gentle stimulant,

an amiable anodyne, a cementer of friendship." Kipling wrote "A woman is only a woman, but a good cigar is a smoke!"

43 People softened up toward cigars. Without analyzing why, men began smoking them and women did not protest. Cigar missionaries kept the vogue growing. Boxes of cigars became prizes on radio shows. Store-window displays urged cigars for Father's Day and Christmas. Service clubs and American Legion posts presented cigars to boys entering the armed forces. Elks gave them away to new fathers.

44 A painting of a young father surrounded by stacks of cigar boxes turned up on the cover of *Coronet*. Cigars got into male fashion pictures. The Cigar Institute persuaded the Veterans of Foreign Wars to send a humidor of costly cigars to Lord Mountbatten as a gift for the royal wedding, and wangled newsreel coverage. It organized the Cigar Bowl football game in Tampa, and lined up a radio network to broadcast it, though fifteen other "bowl" games were already booked for the same day.

45 These feats led to Mr. McHose's election as president of the American Public Relations Association. In 1947 he departed to conquer new fields, but the Cigar Institute still campaigns more or less invisibly. It has recently persuaded some airlines to relax their long-standing taboo against cigar-smoking on planes; several luxury flights now offer cigars to passengers. Amy Vanderbilt has issued a guide to "The Good Manners of Cigar Smoking." Newsreels show today's jet aces chewing cigars, not gum.

46 The Cigar Institute now uses paid advertising as well as the other kind. It began spending the major portion of its budget on advertisements in 1949, and bought $350,000 worth last year. Its present director, Eugene L. Raymond, says "The CIA is subtly wooing younger men in its ads, by soliciting testimonials from baseball and other sports figures whom the younger element lionizes." Individual manufacturers have even begun to slant advertising to women: General Cigar used the headline, "America's first cigar ad for women only," and Bayuk gave this advice to women, "Be glad your husband smokes cigars."

47 There are still a few cigar counters which let cigars get so dry that only a subhuman could enjoy them, but such counters are far rarer than they were a few years ago. The public-relations counsel of the Cigar Institute, Lynn Farnol, says, "Humidification and the care of cigars are now the beginning of the industry bible. Mr. Raymond has spoken at the Cigar Clinics in every major city in America on this subject."

48 Cigar men decline to harp on the fact that cigar-smokers apparently are not nearly as susceptible to lung cancer as cigarette-smokers. There is no pseudo-medical lore in their campaigns. Nor are there any veiled cracks at competition. Cigar men are doing all right as it is. Maybe their propaganda hasn't changed your mind about cigars, but it has certainly changed a lot of other minds.

STUDY GUIDE

1. According to this article, which of the propaganda devices proved most effective in making the cigar respectable?
2. Check on the devices employed currently in magazine advertisements and television commercials that are keeping the cigar respectable, and write a report on them.
3. Analyze the propaganda or rhetorical devices currently employed in the communication media—magazines, billboards, radio, and television—in popularizing a new product, and write an essay on them.

THE AD AND THE ID

Vance Packard

1 The early nineteen fifties witnessed the beginnings of a revolution in American advertising: Madison Avenue became conscious of the *unconscious*. Evidence had piled up that the responses of consumers to the questions of market researchers were frequently unreliable—in other words, that people often don't want what they say they want. Some years ago, for instance, a great automobile company committed one of the costliest blunders in automobile history through reliance on the old-style "nose counting" methods. Direct consumer surveys indicated that people wanted a sensible car in tune with the times—without frills, maneuverable and easy to park. A glance at today's cars—elongated, fish-finned and in riotous technicolor—shows how misleading were the results of the survey. Errors of this sort convinced manufacturers and advertisers that they must take into account the irrationality of consumer behavior—that they must carry their surveys into the submerged areas of the human mind. The result is a strange and rather exotic phenomenon entirely new to the market place —the use of a kind of mass psychoanalysis to guide campaigns of persuasion. The ad is being tailored to meet the needs of the id.

2 The so-called "depth approach" to selling problems is known as motivational research, or simply M. R. Social scientists by the hundreds have been recruited for this massive exploration of the consumer's psyche, and hundreds of millions of dollars are being spent on it. Two-thirds of the na-

From *Harper's Bazaar* (August 1957).

tion's leading advertising agencies have been using the depth approach (along with the more conventional methods), and one major agency resorts to it for every single product it handles, to detect possible hidden appeals and resistances.

3 A number of factors have contributed to the rapid growth of motivational research. By the mid-nineteen fifties, American producers were achieving a fabulous output. This meant that we must be persuaded to buy more and more to keep the wheels of the economy turning. As the president of National Sales Executives exclaimed: "Capitalism is dead—consumerism is king!" Another formidable obstacle that faced the merchandisers in our advanced technology was the increasing similarity of competing products. While it might still be possible for people of discrimination to distinguish between brands of cigarettes, whiskey, detergent, and so on, it became increasingly difficult to teach them to do so on any rational basis. Still, loyalty to a particular brand had to be created, and it was done in many instances by "building a personality"—playful, conservative or showy—into the brand. In this way, Procter and Gamble's image makers have projected a living personification for each of their brands of soap (Ivory is mother and daughter on a sort of pedestal of purity; Camay a glamorous woman), and a Chicago chain of food stores decided that the image which would give it the edge over its competitors should have "the traits we like in our friends"—generosity, cleanliness, etc.

4 What the depth researchers are looking for, of course, are the hidden *whys* of our behavior—why many people are intimidated by banks, why men are drawn into showrooms by convertibles but emerge with sedans, why women go into a trancelike state at the supermarket and why junior likes noisy cereal. The principal tools of M. R. are the techniques of psychiatry—interviews "in depth" (but without the couch, which might make the consumer guinea pig wary); Rorschach (ink blot) tests; stress tests, in which the rate at which you blink your eyes is recorded by hidden cameras; lie detectors; word association tests; and finally the group interview, which, surprisingly, has the effect of breaking down inhibitions. (One candid statement prompts another and presently a roomful of people are freely discussing laxatives, deodorants, weight reducers and athlete's foot.)

5 The efforts of the persuaders to probe our everyday habits for hidden meanings are often fascinating purely for the revelations—some amusing, some rather appalling—which they offer us about ourselves. The average American likes to think of himself as a rugged individualist and, above all, a thoughtful, hardheaded consumer of the products of American enterprise. But in the findings of the motivational researchers, we are apt to emerge as comic actors in a genial if twitchy Thurberian world—bundles of daydreams, secret yearnings and curious emotional quirks.

6 In learning to sell to our subconscious, the persuaders soon dis-

covered unsuspected areas of tension and guilt. Self-indulgent and easy-does-it products are a significant sector of the total American market, yet Americans, it seems, have in them a larger streak of Puritanism than is generally recognized. For instance, the hidden attitude of women toward labor-saving devices is decidedly surprising. Working wives can accept them, but the full-time housewife is liable to feel that they threaten her importance and creativity. The research director of an ad agency sadly explained the situation as follows: "If you tell the housewife that by using your washing machine, drier or dishwasher she can be free to play bridge, you're dead!—the housewife today already feels guilty about the fact that she is not working as hard as her mother. Instead, you should emphasize that appliances free her to have more time with her children." Makers of ready-mixes and foods with "built-in maid service" ran into the same sort of problem. In the early days, the packages promised to take over all the work, but wives were not grateful for this boon. A leading motivational analyst, James Vicary, has stated the reason. Cake-making, he finds, is steeped in creative symbolism for women—it is, in fact, "a traditional acting out of the birth of a child." This feeling shows up in our folklore in such jokes as the one which says that brides whose cakes fall obviously can't produce a baby yet. (A Chicago analyst has noted that gardening, too, is a symbolic "pregnancy activity" and thus is particularly popular with women past the child-bearing age who need creative outlets.)

7 Subconscious tensions about food also rose to plague the makers of Jello a few years ago. Jello had become known to millions of households as a quick dessert, simple and shirt-sleeved in character. Then the ad-men, trying to make it more captivating, started showing it in beautiful, layered, lavishly decorated concoctions. The ads were not a success, and the Institute for Motivational Research was able to tell why. Many women, looking at these feats of fussy preparation, wondered if they could duplicate them, and often concluded that if they had to go to all that work, they would much rather make their own dessert without someone standing over their shoulder telling them how to do it. The Jello people, alerted, went back to showing simple mounds of the stuff, and added to their attraction largely by such simple devices as fairy-tale drawings.

8 The whole area of food, in fact, would seem to be booby-trapped with hidden problems for women. Mr. Vicary noticed, for instance, that young wives in particular tended to avoid the smaller, clerk-manned grocery stores in favor of the supermarket. He was able to isolate the explanation: newly married women are more ignorant about food than older women and are afraid the clerk will find them out. A Midwestern grocery chain found that this state of fearfulness centered around butcher clerks in particular. Faced with a discussion of cuts of meat, where their lack of knowledge is often profound, many women feel anxiety. After "depth-probing" the situ-

ation, the chain began training its butchers to exhibit extraordinary patience and garrulity with younger women, and the strategy has paid off by turning the chain into a haven for innocents.

9 Supermarkets, on the other hand, are so tension-free as to make many women fall into a state bordering on hypnotic trance. Anxious to trace the reasons for the enormous rise in so-called impulse buying in American supermarkets (today seven out of ten purchases in supermarkets are made on impulse—the shopping list of old is becoming obsolete), Mr. James Vicary made a remarkable test. He had assumed that some special psychology must be at work to put women in an impulsive state when they got into supermarkets, possibly the tension of confronting so many products and having to make rapid decisions. Since our blink rate is one rough index of our inner tension, Mr. Vicary installed hidden cameras to record the blink rate of women shoppers. Normally, we blink about thirty-two times a minute, and he expected to see the rate go up as the ladies faced their decisions. Nothing of the sort occurred. The rate went down, down, down to a subnormal fourteen blinks a minute for the average woman—a condition of hypnoidal trance. Many of the women collided with boxes or passed the whirring cameras without noticing them. But when they approached the checkout counters with their loaded carts, their blink rate would start rising back toward normal; and when they heard the bell of the cash register, the rate shot up to the abnormal figure of forty-five a minute, a symptom of acute anxiety. Mr. Vicary's explanation of the trance: the woman feels herself a queen in a fairyland filled with lovely, accessible objects, unimaginable in former years and all whispering "buy me, buy me."

10 The calorie consciousness which swept the country, beginning a few years ago, created other psychological troubles for food-makers. A number of brewing companies, who had thought to capitalize on the phenomenon, tried to outdo one another in plugging low-caloried beer, and for a time sales did go up. Mr. M. R. hoisted warning flags. Dr. Ernest Dichter, head of the Institute for Motivational Research, warned that calorie consciousness is a sort of psychological penance. People go on diets because they are trying to punish themselves for past indulgence. Hence, low-calorie diets are not supposed to be pleasant. What the brewers were conveying, in effect, was that real beer must be fattening and that low-calorie beer was somehow denatured. "Thus," said the Institute, "when a beer advertises itself as low in calories, the consumer reacts by feeling the beer has a poor taste." Perhaps this cautionary note was responsible for one brewer's recent clarion call: "Made by people who like beer for people who drink beer, and plenty of it!"

11 Another product which found its market temporarily constricted because of too much harping on calories was Ry-Krisp, which ran advertisements containing calorie tables and showing very slim people nibbling the

wafers. Motivational analysts found that Ry-Krisp had developed for itself a self-punishment image as a food that was "good" for people—an image which drove away people not in a self-punishing mood. Corrective action was taken: in advertisements, Ry-Krisp began appearing with tempting foods and was described as delicious and festive. This more permissive approach nearly doubled sales in test areas.

12 Even in travel we have hidden anxieties which marketers find it profitable to take into account. A number of years ago, an airline became disturbed by the fact that so many passengers flew only when pressed for time, and it hired a conventional research firm to find out why. The simple answer came back that they didn't fly because they were afraid of being killed, but an intensive advertising campaign emphasizing safety yielded disappointing results. At last Dr. Dichter was called in. His answer, based on picture tests which encouraged potential travelers to imagine themselves involved in airline crashes, was different and astonishing. What the traveler feared was not death but a sort of posthumous embarrassment. The husband pictured his wife receiving the news and saying, "The damned fool, he should have gone by train." The obvious answer was to convince wives of the common sense of flying, which would bring their husbands home faster from business trips, and to get them in the air (to get their feet wet, as it were) with tempting family flying plans.

13 Still other subconscious fears, and not always the obvious ones, relate to money. Motivational studies have proved, for example, that it is not guilt about owing money which makes people hesitate to approach the bank for a loan. The fear is of the bank itself, which is seen as an angry father-figure who will disapprove of our untidy financial affairs. Many people would rather go to a loan company, in spite of the higher interest rate, simply because the moral tone associated with it is lower; in fact, there is a complete shift in moral dominance in which the borrower becomes a righteous fellow, temporarily forced into low company, and the higher cost of the loan is a small price to pay for such a changed view of ourselves. It is worth noting that a good many banks today are trying to mellow the stern image of themselves by removing the bars on teller windows, making wider use of glass fronts and staging folksy little exhibits which depict them—at worst—as rather crusty but charming old gentlemen in Scotch hats.

14 It will surprise nobody to learn that sex plays an enormously important part in selling. But how it works *is* frequently surprising. Sex images have, of course, long been cherished by ad-makers, but in the depth approach sex takes on some extraordinary ramifications and subtleties. A classic example is the study of automobiles made by Dr. Dichter which became known as "Mistress Versus Wife"—a study responsible for the invention of the most successful new car style introduced to the American market for several years. Dealers had long been aware that a convertible in the

window drew the male customer into the showroom. They also knew that he usually ended by choosing a four-door sedan. The convertible, said Dr. Dichter, had associations of youth and adventure—it was symbolic of the mistress. But the sedan was the girl one married because she would make a good wife and mother. How could an automobile symbolically combine the appeals of mistress and wife? The answer was the celebrated hardtop, which Dr. Dichter's organization takes full credit for inspiring.

15 A company advertising a home permanent wave ran into another sexual problem, which was solved by M. R. They had thought it would be a brilliant idea to picture a mother and daughter with identical hairdos captioned: "A Double Header Hit with Dad." Wives, interviewed at the conscious level, said they didn't object at all to the implied idea of competition for the husband-father's admiration, but the company was still apprehensive—rightly, as it turned out. Depth interviews revealed that women would indeed deeply resent the "hit with dad" theme, and it was hastily dropped.

16 As for the American male, he stands in equal need of sexual reassurance, particularly as women continue to invade his traditional strongholds. The fact that cigar makers have been enjoying their greatest prosperity in twenty years has been credited by many to the man-at-bay, and at least one ad agency disagrees with the efforts of the Cigar Institute of America's efforts to draw women into the picture. This agency, puzzled by the failure of a campaign which had pictured a smiling woman offering cigars to a group of men, ordered a depth survey to uncover the reason. The conclusion was that men enjoy cigars precisely because they are objectionable to women; nor is the man sincere who politely asks if the ladies mind his lighting up. As the head of the agency put it: "He knows . . . he is going to stink up the room."

17 Motivational analysis has even discovered certain products to be sexually "maladjusted," and it is responsible for several spectacular cases of planned transvestitism. When the cancer scare drove millions of men to try filter tips, the makers of Marlboro cigarettes decided to cash in by changing the sex of a cigarette originally designed for women. The ads began to show a series of rugged males, engaged in virile occupations and all of them, by an extraordinary coincidence, tattooed. The tattoo motif puzzled a good many people, since the tattoo is a common phenomenon among delinquents in reformatories. Marlboro, however, decided it was exactly what was needed to give its men a virile and "interesting past" look—the same look arrived at, by other means, in the one-eyed man in the Hathaway shirt.

18 When Lloyd Warner published his book, *Social Class in America*, in 1948, it created a respectful stir in academic circles; but in later years it was to create an even greater one among merchandisers. Like David Ries-

man in his classic, *The Lonely Crowd,* or Russell Lynes, whose famous dissection of high-, middle- and low-brows charted the social significance of such items as tossed salad and rye whiskey, Warner defined social classes less in terms of wealth and power than criteria of status, and merchandisers have begun to give considerable thought to his conclusions. Burleigh Gardener, for example, founder of the M. R. Firm of Social Research, Inc., has taken Warner's concepts as his guiding thesis. Social Research has put a class label on many sorts of house-furnishing: the solid color carpet, it appears, is upper class; the "knickknack" shelf lower class: Venetian blinds are upper middle class.

19 Chicago's Color Research Institute (a psychoanalytically minded group) ran into some of the intricacies of class structure when it was asked to design two candy boxes, one intended to sell to lower class buyers at $1.95, the other to an upper class clientele at $3.50. The Institute's researches led it to a curious recommendation: the box for the cheaper candy would be in vermilion metal tied with a bright blue ribbon, and it would have to cost fifty cents; the box for the expensive candy could be made of pale pink pasteboard at a cost of no more than nine cents. The reason? Candy-giving is an important rite in the lower class, and the girl is likely to treasure the box, whereas the upper-class girl will ignore the box (the candy is what counts) and will probably throw it away.

20 Many advertising men have filled the air above their Madison Avenue rookeries with arguments over the validity and potency of M. R. And the researchers themselves have added to the confusion by disagreeing with each other's methods and results. Of more concern, however, to the average citizen are the possibilities for mass manipulation opened up by motivational research. Disturbing examples of such manipulation have, unfortunately, appeared in politics, industrial relations (a California engineering school boasts that its graduates are "custom-built men") and even in the church, where ministers are being advised how they can more effectively control their congregations. The manipulative approach to politics is not, of course, new—Machiavelli was perfectly familiar with it. But the manipulation of the people by a tyrant is an infinitely simpler problem than that of dealing with the citizens of a free society, who can spurn your solicitations if they want to. Now, however, mass persuasion in this kind of situation has been greatly reinforced by the techniques of the symbol manipulators, who have drawn on Pavlov and his conditioned reflexes, Freud and his father images, Riesman and his concept of modern American voters as spectator-consumers of politics. In the last election, both parties tried to "merchandise" their candidates by commerical marketing methods, using on billboards slogans of scientifically tested appeal, hammering out key messages until the public was saturation-bombed, and grooming their candidates to look "sincere" in front of the TV camera. As one advertising

man put it: "I think of a man in a voting booth who hesitates between the two levers as if he were pausing between competing tubes of tooth paste in a drugstore. The brand that has made the highest penetration in his brain will win his choice."

21 What are the implications of all this persuasion in terms of morality? The social scientists and psychiatrists have a workable rationale for explaining their co-operation with, say, the merchandisers. They are broadening the world's knowledge of human behavior; and knowledge, as Alfred Whitehead has said, keeps no better than fish. But there remains the disturbing fact that by scientifically catering to the irrational, the persuaders are working toward a progressively less rational society. We may wonder if, in a few decades when it becomes technically feasible, we will be ripe for biocontrol, a brand new science for controlling mental processes, emotional reactions and sense perceptions by bioelectrical signals. Already, rats with full bellies have been made to feel ravenously hungry, and to feel fear when they had nothing to be afraid of. As one electronic engineer has said: "The ultimate achievement of biocontrol may be the control of man himself. . . . The controlled subjects would never be permitted to think as individuals. A few months after birth, a surgeon would equip each child with a socket mounted under the scalp and electrodes reaching selected areas of brain tissue. . . . The child's sensory perceptions and muscular activity could either be modified or completely controlled by bioelectric signals radiating from state-controlled transmitters." He added that the electrodes would cause no discomfort.

22 I'm sure the persuaders of 1957 would be appalled by such a prospect. Most of them are likeable, earnest men who just want to control us a little bit, to maneuver us into buying something that we may actually need. But when you start manipulating people, where exactly do you stop?

STUDY GUIDE

Theme and Structure

1. This essay sets out to define and illustrate motivational research as it touches on advertising. What is Packard's definition of it?

2. The essay might be divided into the following chief sections: paragraphs 1–5, 6–19, and 20–22. What is the topic discussed in each of these major sections?

3. In the second section, Packard gives illustrations of how motivational research has been used to guide advertising in several areas of human experience. What are these areas?

4. Find examples from current advertising that illustrate the appeal to some of the hidden motives discussed in this essay.

5. Write an essay of your own in which you discuss some of the possible abuses that you foresee in the use of motivational research.

SECTION 3

Understanding Our Language

WHAT IS A LANGUAGE?

L. M. Myers

1 It is quite possible to spend years studying or even teaching various languages without ever having a very firm or useful notion of what a language is. But to proceed in this way naturally involves a good deal of waste motion and makes the learning of a language much more difficult than it need be. This is probably the principal reason why so many Americans say: "Of course I don't really know any French—I just had it in college." This casual pessimism is bad enough when applied to a foreign language. When extended, as it often is, to the native tongue, it can cause very serious worry and outright suffering. Our confusion about the nature of languages is such that many people who speak excellent English never have the satisfaction of knowing that they do, but go through life with recurrent feelings of guilt about their supposed inadequacy.

2 It would be pleasant to avoid such dangers by agreeing on a nice, efficient definition, but unfortunately no such convenient solution will work. A language is much too complicated an affair to be effectively summarized in any sacred set of words. If we adopted one we should continually find that we were either stretching the definition to cover some aspect we had not previously considered or narrowing our ideas of language to fit the definition. Such stretching and narrowing are quite legitimate when they are done explicitly and for specified purposes by qualified scholars; but they are dangerously misleading when offered to the general public. What most people need is not a definition of language, but some informa-

tion about how a few languages have developed and how they work; some discussion of what we actually know about languages and what we can only guess at; and (perhaps most of all) a demonstration that some of our most widely cherished beliefs about language are inaccurate to the point of supersitition.

3 To begin with the obvious, language is what human beings talk with. Anybody who wants to may of course define the word *language* so as to include the noises made by crows or the wing-signals made by bees, but I am simply not using the word that way. Without language the human race would hardly be human in any very important sense. We couldn't even think as we now use the term, because most of our thinking is done in language and couldn't be done without it; and it seems most unlikely that we could have developed even the simplest kind of stone-age culture.

4 I have just mentioned the wing-signals of bees, and we all know that some of the social life of dogs seems to be carried on by sniffing. The fact that our main system of signals is composed of sounds is therefore a matter of choice rather than of necessity, but there is little doubt that our ancestors made a wise choice. If we consider each of the five senses we can see at once that a really extensive set of symbols based on smell or taste would be rather hard to organize and transmit. We might use touch, but not at a distance, and sight has various disadvantages as a *basic* system. It won't work in the dark or in thick brush or under many other conditions; there is no generally satisfactory way of attracting the attention of the one you want to communicate with; and it interferes too much with other activities. On the whole hearing seems to be the most promising sense to receive with, and that is the one our ancestors somehow selected. Maybe they tried all five and that one simply worked out best.

5 Of course there are many ways of making sound. Crickets rub their legs together and ruffed grouse drum on hollow logs, but neither method seems to permit of much variety. By using their mouths and some nearby organs our ancestors developed a much more flexible system. Nobody knows how the first steps were made. One very old theory is that some sounds just naturally represent some things, and man somehow made the connection. This has been expressed metaphorically by saying that when early man for the first time saw a cow, somehow "a bell rang" in his brain, and he said *cow*. People who do not care for the explanation have called this the "*ding-dong theory*." Another guess is that language began by imitation of natural sounds. According to this the first words were the ancient equivalents of *bow-wow, meow, gurgle, swish*, etc. There certainly are words of this sort, which may be called "echoic" or "onomatopoetic"; but there is no proof that they are among the earliest words, and there are not enough of them to make a very satisfactory basis for all language. Unbelievers have accordingly called this the "*bow-wow theory*."

6 A third theory is that vocal sounds were at first merely an accidental accompaniment of gestures. A man who was disgusted, for instance, might make a face to indicate his disgust, perhaps rounding and pushing out his lips. If he did this forcefully enough some breath might escape and he would make a noise. At first it was the face that had the meaning; then the sound which accompanied the face began to have a share of the meaning; and finally, since the sound was more convenient, it took over the job of conveying the meaning all by itself. If you try to make such a face and noise you may guess that people who don't accept it call this the "*pooh-pooh theory*."

7 There is also the *yo-he-ho* theory which argues that men engaged in heavy shared labor automatically made grunts, which gradually became symbols of the activities that called them forth; and there are various others. But no one of them really explains very much, and certainly no one is now generally accepted as satisfactory. We just don't know how language began, and there is no sound reason to suppose that we ever shall.

8 However they began, the early speakers of a language had to make the following steps, though presumably not in such a clearcut and logical order as here indicated:

1. Select, from innumberable possibilities, a few dozen sounds to serve as the building blocks of their speech. No two of them could possibly pronounce the sounds exactly alike, but the variations had to lie within recognizable limits. These sounds, or rather sound-classes, are called *phonemes*. They are not pronunciations of letters; letters are indications, often very ambiguous, of phonemes.

2. Arrange these phonemes into some thousands of meaningful units, which may be either complete words or significant parts of words, called *morphemes*. For instance, *fire* contains only one morpheme; *fire-man* contains two, each of which could occur alone; and *fireman's* contains three, one of which occurs only in combinations. Though the morpheme indicated by *'s* is not a word, it is an important unit in the structure of the language.

3. Develop a *syntax*, consisting of some habitual patterns for arranging the morphemes into longer utterances, such as sentences. The three most obvious elements in the patterns are:

a. word-order

b. "inflectional" morphemes, such as those found in *walk, walks, walked, walking*, or *big, bigger, biggest*.

c. "function words," such as prepositions and auxiliary verbs, which are often more important as structural elements in sentences than for any exact meanings of their own.

Just as real, though not so clearly indicated in writing, are the elements of pitch, stress, and transition between sounds, which can often give different ways of saying the "same" sentence entirely different meanings.

9 This is obviously the barest outline of the sort of thing that happened. The actual process must have been incredibly complicated, and it is not surprising that no group ever managed to make these steps with complete uniformity. There is no reason to believe that even two people can either speak exactly alike or understand each other perfectly and consistently, or that one person can speak at seventy exactly as he did at twenty. When the communicating group consists of hundreds of millions of people spread over millions of square miles and developing through fifteen centuries of an ever-changing world, a complete and tidy analysis of their language is an obvious impossibility. It is, however, entirely feasible to discuss some of the forces at work in language, and some of the events which directed the particular course that these forces should take as Modern English evolved from its earliest discoverable sources.

10 Language developed for a good many thousand years, and apparently became as complicated as it ever got to be, before any way of writing it down was invented. The old and apparently logical idea that uncivilized and illiterate people must speak a very simple kind of language has been completely destroyed by modern investigation. Linguists have found that African Bushmen and Amazonian Indians speak languages of a grammatical complexity that would make most of us shudder. The spoken form of language is therefore primary, and the written form, however important it may be, is secondary. Most of us realize this—in a way, and part of the time. It seems perfectly obvious when we think of history. But when it comes to our everyday use of language we often think of the written form as the true one, and of speech as an often very imperfect reflection. For instance, our usual pronunciations are often considered careless or sloppy when they do not contain all the sounds that seem to be indicated by the established spelling. It seldom occurs to most people that when writing and speech differ, the simplest explanation is that writing is falling down on its job of reflecting speech.

11 Of course the simplest explanation may be a little too simple to be entirely accurate. Writing began simply as a secondary representation of speech, but for many purposes it has obvious advantages, especially in its comparative permanence; and among literate people it always develops some independent characteristics of its own, and exerts some influence on the original spoken form. Even the English spoken by a man who personally is illiterate is very different from what it would have been if our society had no tradition of literacy. It is therefore natural—as most things that happen consistently are—that the comparative importance of the written form should often be exaggerated in schools. When the teacher writes a sentence

on the blackboard or calls attention to one in a textbook, it is there for all to consider uniformly and at leisure. It seems both more real and more important than a spoken sentence which disappears as soon as it is uttered; and it is certainly more convenient to consider and discuss. So the teacher uses it as a model for rather than a record of speech, and says things like, "Danny, don't say *ol' knight*, say *old knight*. Can't you see the *d*? You must learn to pronounce words the way they are written." The fact that even the teacher does not pronounce the *k*, the *g*, or the *h* in knight is seldom considered at this point.

12 The importance given to the written form of language, in schools and in many other situations, is an undeniable fact, and not necessarily a shameful one; but we will find it very useful to remember that the spoken form is not only the earlier, but for most purposes still the primary one.

13 This last point is easy enough to accept in theory, but quite hard to grasp firmly as a working principle; and the better educated we are, and the more our education has concentrated on English, the more likely we are to feel that the language really lives in books and is only imperfectly reflected in speech. Perhaps the best way to illustrate this tendency is to examine a passage that was printed before our conventions of writing had become comparatively uniform:

> And certaynly our langage now vsed varyeth ferre from that whiche was vsed and spoken whan I was borne; for we Englysshe men ben borne vnder the domynacyon of the mone, whiche is neuer steadfaste, but euer wauerynge, wexynge one season, and waneth and dyscreaseth another season. And that comyn Englysshe that is spoken in one shyre varyeth from a-nother in so moche, that in my dayes happened that certayn marchauntes were in a shippe in Tamyse, for to haue sayled ouer the see into Zelande; and for lacke of wynde thei taryed atte forlond, and wente to lande for to refreshe them. And one of theym, named Sheffelde, a mercer, cam in-to an hows, and axed for mete; and specyally he axed after eggys. And the goode wyf answerde, that she coude speke no Frenshe. And the marchaunt was angry, for he also coude speke no Frenshe, but wolde haue hadde egges, and she vnderstode hym not. And thenne at laste a-nother sayd that he wolde haue eyren. Then the good wyf sayd that she vnderstod hym wel! Loo, what sholde a man in thyse dayes now wryte, egges or eyren? Certaynly it is harde to playse euery man by cause of dyuersite and chaunge of langage.[1]
>
> [From Caxton's Preface to his *Eneydos*, 1490]

14 It is really quite amazing how differently people of approximately equal intelligence will react to such a passage as this. One man will read it almost at sight, possibly pausing for a second or so at *vsed* and *wauervnge*,

[1] Rolf Kaiser, *Medieval English* (Berlin-Wilmersdorf, 1961), p. 567, lines 195–211.

but adapting himself almost immediately, and quickly recognizing every word except perhaps *forlond* and *mercer*. Another will find it almost unintelligible at first glance, and almost intolerable even after a good deal of study. For anybody who finds it difficult the following steps are suggested:

1. Make up your mind that there is not a misspelled word in the passage. Never mind whether this statement is true—it is useful. The man who wrote the passage was simply using the letters he knew to indicate the sounds of the words he used, and he is fairly, though far from perfectly, consistent. If he happened to spell a word two different ways—for instance *eggys* and *egges*—there was no way he could find out which was right, because there was no dictionary of the language in existence, and he could find plenty of practice on both sides.

2. Notice that he tends to use some conventions quite different from ours. If we reversed his *u*'s and *v*'s the passage would look far more normal, and if we reversed his *i*'s and *y*'s we should gain about as much as we lost.

3. Use your ears to help your eyes. A number of words which seem strange to the sight are immediately clear to the ear, especially if they are pronounced in context and with no excess of precision. For instance, *comyn* alone might suggest nothing, but if you read aloud and rather casually "that comyn Englysshe" it could hardly be anything but "that common English."

15 What we have, in other words, is a spoken language represented somewhat inadequately, but not hopelessly, in print; and the way to understand this language is to look through the groups of letters for the sounds that lie behind them. (Semi-literate people sometimes seem to understand this better than the thoroughly educated.) In studying Modern English it is possible, if not reasonable, to think of a word as a group of letters which should be pronounced in a certain way; but in studying the earlier stages it is absolutely necessary to remember that a word is a group of sounds, which the spelling suggests but does not control.

16 This particular passage of Caxton's is also interesting for another reason. Nearly five hundred years ago the man who introduced printing into English was considerably worried by the "dyuersite & chaunge of langage." He would have had just as much reason for worry if he had lived five hundred or a thousand years earlier; and he has successors who are just as much worried now. Uniformity and stability in language would certainly have their advantages, but before we yearn for them too passionately perhaps we should consider whether they are even theoretically possible.

17 To begin with, nobody talks simply language—we have to talk English or Spanish or German. Several hundred millions of us talk English,

in one way or another. The Americans don't talk just like the British, and the Americans in South Carolina don't talk just like the Americans in Cleveland. In fact, nobody talks simply English—we have to talk one dialect or another. Of course there are snobbish people who think that what they talk is pure English, and anything different is a dialect; and there are humble people who realize that they talk a dialect, but credit other more fortunate people with talking the language pure. However, all qualified students of the subject now seem to agree that the language is composed exclusively of dialects. They also agree that we are on pretty slippery ground if we argue that some dialects are *intrinsically* better than others, though of course it is obvious that some have more prestige, and may therefore be worth learning.

18 If we go one step further we will realize that no two speakers of a given dialect talk exactly alike. Each has his own *idiolect*, or individual language, which differs at least a little from all others. And if we consider our own idiolects we realize that no one of us talks exactly the same way all the time. So language is really languages, which are really collections of dialects, which are really collections of idiolects—and even these aren't quite uniform and dependable.

19 We are now faced with a very difficult question. Are the dialects and idiolects merely group and individual departures from the true language? Or is a language simply the sum total of what the idiolects that compose its dialects happen to add up to? Unfortunately, each answer looks quite reasonable from one point of view, but entirely impossible from another. We are then reminded of the ancient puzzle of which came first, the chicken or the egg; the situation seems to be completely paradoxical. No solution so far proposed squares with all the evidence, or satisfies all competent linguists. Probably the best way to approach the question is to remove the word *merely* from the second sentence of this paragraph, and the word *simply* from the third. Anybody who wants to keep either word in and answer *yes* to the question in which it occurs is interested in defending a dogma rather than forming an opinion. And anybody who really wants to learn anything about the subject will find it profitable to devote most of his effort to understanding the point of view he finds least attractive. There really is important evidence on both sides.

20 About sixty years ago the great Swiss linguist, Saussure,[2] attempted

[2] Ferdinand de Saussure, *Cours de Linguistique Générale* (Paris, 1916). Unfortunately, this book was not actually written by Saussure, but was compiled by two of his students from notes on his three series of lectures, delivered between 1906 and 1911. It is impossible to determine whether certain contradictions which mar an exceedingly valuable book are due to changes in his thinking or to inaccurate reporting and editing. The book has been translated into English by Wade Baskin as *Course in General Linguistics* (New York, 1959). The quotations and references in this chapter are all from pages 14 to 20 of the English version.

to clarify the problem by dividing human speech into two components—*langue*, an impersonal set of conventions to which all members of a speech community must (subconsciously) subscribe in order to understand and make themselves understood; and *parole*, a collective term for individual acts of speaking. *Parole* would be utterly meaningless if it were not based on *langue*; but it never reflects *langue* quite perfectly, and it inevitably involves certain physical phenomena which are no more a part of *langue* than the chalk mark with which a circle may be represented on a blackboard is part of the circle which it represents. Saussure says that *langue* is "the social side of speech, outside the individual who can never create or modify it by himself; it exists only by virtue of a sort of contract signed by the members of a community." A little later he adds that it "exists in the form of a sum of impressions deposited in the brain of each member of a community, almost like a dictionary of which identical copies have been distributed to each individual." [3]

21 Saussure says that one might, if really necessary, apply the term "linguistics" to each of the two branches, and speak of a linguistics of *parole*; but that such a science must not be confused with linguistics proper, whose sole object is *langue*. Since his time most European linguists have followed his lead, while American linguists have emphasized *parole*, denying with considerable vigor his statement that it was no part of "linguistics proper." During the past decade many American linguists have adopted the Saussurean attitude. . . .

22 To a non-linguist the Saussurean emphasis on *langue* is likely to seem merely a more precise statement of a theory that all sensible people have always (if rather vaguely) taken for granted. According to this theory a language is a set of conventions, an agreement that certain combinations of sounds (or letters) stand for certain things and activities and ideas; and that these combinations must be arranged in a limited number of grammatical patterns. Whether we believe that these conventions are ultimately based on logic or are purely arbitrary makes, for the moment, little difference. At any rate our ancestors have somehow decided, for instance, that Rags is to be called a *dog*, and not a *chien* or a *cane* or a *perro* (as other sets of ancestors have decided elsewhere). They have likewise decided that

[3] *Langue* is often translated as *language*, and some of Saussure's more zealous followers seem to think that this settles the question of what language really is. It seems unlikely that he would have agreed with them, since he says:

> Note that I have defined things rather than words; these definitions are not endangered by certain ambiguous words that do not have identical meanings in various languages. . . . No word corresponds exactly to any of the notions specified above; that is why all definitions of words are made in vain; starting from words in defining things is a bad procedure.

Since *language* is used here (and in many other books) to include both components, I use the French terms to avoid confusion.

we should say *a black dog,* and not *a dog black,* which would be the normal word-order in some other languages. This is not merely a matter of style, but an important signalling device. We recognize at once the difference between *business college* and *college business;* but Frenchman, whose language has the opposite conventions, would be likely to get the two reversed. Countless other decisions of the same general nature were made before we were born, and as children we could neither understand nor talk to our elders until we somehow began to be aware of their conventions, and to imitate them—at first pretty crudely. After a few years of steady effort, imitation, practice, and correction much of the crudeness disappeared, and we eventually learned to reflect the conventions in our own speaking with some degree of accuracy. Whenever we failed we simply made a mistake; the language was already in existence, and we had neither the right nor the power to modify it. The mistake might be a purely personal one, or it might be one picked up from our parents and other elders who had already departed from the true path, and thus spoke a dialect rather than the pure language.

23 Obviously, the more closely we adhere to the established conventions, the more dependable our communication will be. Every conceivable effort should therefore be made to encourage uniformity, and to discourage any departures in pronunciation, word-forms, patterns of arrangement, meanings assigned to each word, or any other variations from the established system. And whenever any group of people, whether from geographical isolation, social submergence, foreign influence, or any other reason, develops a system noticeably different from the pure and original one, their kind of language should be considered an inferior dialect, and they should be penalized (not nastily, of course, but firmly) for speaking it.

24 The trouble with this theory is that there is no such thing in nature as that intrinsically pure, good, or correct English that we would like so much to teach; and there never has been. Neither can we find a uniquely pure form of French, German, or Latin, though it is easy enough to talk as if we could. There is nothing to prevent Harris from talking about "pure, Parisian French" if he wants to; but there is likewise nothing to prevent Clarke from replying, "What do you mean, pure Parisian? They speak with a horrible twang in Paris. If you want to hear really good French you should go to Tours." Meanwhile Reade is thinking how silly they both are, since he has known for years that the only *really* good French is spoken in Geneva, the entire French nation having lost the true way some generations back. And of course if we actually went to Paris (or Tours or Geneva) we should find that its inhabitants spoke with much variety and argued about certain points, that the older ones accused the younger ones of corrupting the language, and so forth.

25 A linguist—even one who concentrates on *langue*—knows all this,

and has no theories at all about how people ought to use a language. His approach is purely descriptive; and what he wants to describe is not the infinitely varied acts of *parole*, but the underlying system of conventions which these acts imperfectly reflect. His basic theory is that all members of a speech community must have the same "set of impressions deposited in the brain" in order to communicate. Their performance may vary enormously, but their "competence"—their mastery of the system—is identical.

26 This is a very useful hypothesis, since it frees him from having to take account of all the physical irregularities of *parole*, and it has resulted in some important advances in our knowledge. Its chief defect is that there is no precise way of determining the exact membership of a speech community sharing an identical set of conventions. Probably no two adults anywhere in the world know exactly the same list of words, and certainly no two people know exactly the same things about them, or pronounce, arrange, and react to them identically. Some of the differences can be dismissed as matters of *parole*, but others seem to be based on a difference in the *langue* itself. This certainly varies from one dialect to another; and there is satisfactory evidence that it varies in a small degree within each dialect. Language, like everything else, is always and necessarily changing. No speaker ever reflects his underlying conventions (whatever they are) quite perfectly, and of course speakers are influenced to some extent by each other. With each act of speech there is at least the possibility of a tiny modification in the conventions of a group, and a good many of these possibilities eventually take obvious effect, so that in time the whole set of conventions changes beyond easy recognition.

27 Until very recently most American linguists paid little attention to the theories of Saussure, but followed what is called the structural approach of Leonard Bloomfield.[4] They started with the basic assumption that language is simply people talking, and that if we want to study it scientifically we should not (at least in the beginning) try to look *behind* the talking for some system assumed to underlie it. We should look directly *at* the talking, and try to describe it as accurately and completely as possible. Like other scientists we should begin by observing the phenomena, and we should do this with absolute impartiality. When we have made enough observations we may try to arrange them into a system; but our procedure must be purely inductive, and we can neither make value judgments nor discard inconvenient evidence in order to do this. We cannot, for instance, say that *ellum* is a mispronunciation of *elm*, but only that two different pronunciations of this word occur. Similarly, we must record the fact that some people say "He don't like them apples" where others would say "He

[4] *Language* (New York, 1933).

doesn't like those apples" without permitting ourselves to make any prejudiced comment about "bad grammar."

28 This inductive, objective approach was developed in studying previously unwritten languages, such as those of American Indians, and proved extremely fruitful for this purpose. It reduced the temptation for an investigator to distort his description to make it fit any preconceived theory about how the language ought to be constructed. Anything a native speaker said had to be accepted as part of the data. A particular pronunciation, for instance, might be comparatively unusual, but it simply could not be wrong, any more than a pebble can be of a wrong shape.

29 Attempts to apply this approach to English immediately run into two difficulties. In my ignorance, I am perfectly willing to postulate that any three Papago Indians who consent to act as informants can give me a satisfactory sample of their language. After all, there are not very many of them, and they are a fairly homogeneous group. But English is spoken by hundreds of millions of people, and spoken with such variety that it is hard to find a sample small enough to study intensively, and at the same time widely acceptable as typical of the whole. Moreover, I have no reason to suppose that any Papago is dissatisfied with his own use of his language, or contemptuous of his neighbor's use. His *langue*, to the best of my knowledge, is completely subconscious. He knows what words and grammatical patterns mean, and use them accordingly. But an American usually has two kinds of *langue*, one as subconscious as the Papago's, the other quite explicit, though perhaps not completely mastered. For instance, he knows perfectly well what *ain't* means, whether or not he himself uses it. But even if he does use it, he is conscious that it is often regarded as wrong. Whether he tries to conform or decides to go on living comfortably in a state of grammatical sin, he seldom quarrels with the idea that the explicit conventions are somehow right.

30 A few structural linguists want to treat English exactly like Papago, and take the stand that anything a native speaker says (except a slip that he would himself correct) must be right because he says it—a language is simply what its speakers talk, and all attempts to legislate about it are illegitimate. Most structuralists, however, are willing to admit that "standard English" has so much social importance that we are justified in teaching it in our schools. They insist only that such instruction should be based only on careful observation of how certain speakers do actually talk, and not on any theories about how they should. Such an attitude immediately arouses the fury of a good many people. To anybody who feels outraged I can only say that I am not advocating it as *the* true approach; but that I do most urgently suggest that the more it annoys him, the harder he should try to understand its possible value for some purposes, because it simply cannot be tossed aside as worthless. The pronunciation of English has

changed a good deal since Anglo-Saxon times, and quite noticeably even since the time of Dr. Johnson, and the structure has changed along with it. It would probably be impossible to find a single correct sentence today that would not have been wrong once. Take such an innocent-looking one as "Those little girls are very nice." If the repeated mistakes of our ancestors had not somehow come to be sanctified as "good grammar," *those* should be *tho*—the *s* got in by mistaken analogy with other plurals; *little* should have a special ending to agree with the noun it modifies; *are* should be something else, though it is hard to say what, since this Scandinavian form drove out several perfectly good English ones; and *very*, having started life as an adjective, should not be permitted to modify another adjective without adding-*ly*. Perhaps we should add that *nice* meant "ignorant" before it meant "foolish," "foolishly precise" and "precise" on its way to its current meaning of something like "mildly admirable"; and that *girls* formerly meant something like "teenagers"—young people of either sex.

31 In short, all the evidence we have tells us that any language is always changing, and never quite uniform at any one time. It seems a little naive to assume that all the changes that took place up to about Aunt Emma's day were improvements, while all those that have been taking place since are calamities.

32 Since neither the "chicken first" nor the "egg first" theory is entirely satisfactory, some sort of compromise seems necessary. It would be ridiculous for me to pretend that I can offer a final solution to a question that divides the linguists of the world, but I feel bound to make a clear statement of where I stand so that readers who prefer a different approach can make appropriate allowances. We have already seen that no two people can possibly *use* a language in exactly the same way. The critical question is, do they differ merely in *performance*—the degree of accuracy with which their *parole* reflects the *langue* which has been built into their nervous systems and is identical for them all? Or is the *langue* itself a little different for each speaker? Saussure chose the first answer, which has an obvious advantage, since it allows us to investigate the underlying system without being distracted by insignificant physical differences. But it is of course an assumption, not a demonstrable fact; and its adherents are likely (in my experience) to shy away from the question of exactly how widely a particular *langue* is spread. They admit differences in dialects, but (like everybody else) have found it impossible to give the precise boundaries of a homogeneous dialect group.

33 It seems to me more reasonable to assume that all speakers differ somewhat in their *langue* as well as their *parole*. We can say then that each speaker of a language must somehow have in his mind a chart of that language which his acts of speech must approximately reflect, or they would

have no meaning at all, even to him. And each of the neighbors with whom he talks must also have a chart, somewhat similar to his, or they could not interchange ideas; but not quite the same, because all men are different. In any group of speakers the various charts must overlap considerably to make some communication possible; but they are never quite identical, and the possibilities of variation in the degree of overlap are practically infinite. In other words, our idiolects do not differ from each other simply as imperfect reflections of one perfect chart. Rather, each is based on its own chart—imperfectly constructed in imitation of other charts already imperfect. When we speak of the chart for a whole language we are using a fiction, useful for some purposes, very troublesome for others. In this book, for instance, I shall sometimes use the term "standard English" because it will save an intolerable amount of qualification: but a reader should be careful not to take it for more than it is worth. I use it simply to mean the kinds of English that cultivated (and don't ask me how cultivated) speakers generally use or accept as satisfactory. Such speakers agree almost unanimously on some points, such as a preference for *I saw* rather than *I seen.* They differ rather casually on many others, and quite bitterly on a few. Some of the usages they condemn can be shown to be sounder, either historically or logically, than the ones they prefer; but these usages will remain non-standard unless and until enough standard speakers take them up.

STUDY GUIDE

Theme and Structure

1. After reading through the essay carefully, can you formulate an answer to the question "What is language?" Where does the author come closest to answering that question succinctly himself? What are some of the difficulties involved in giving a simple answer to that question?

2. There are ten thought divisions that are easily discernible in this essay: paragraphs 1–4, 5–7, 8 and 9, 10–12, 13–15, 16–18, 19–21, 22–26, 27–31, and 32 and 33. State the subject matter that the author is concerned with in each of these divisions.

3. Study the opening sentences of these thought divisions and indicate what method the author has used to connect each of them with what has preceded. Is it by a conjunction, demonstrative pronoun, word repetition, or some other device? Underline the connecting words.

4. What is the exact meaning of *dialect, ideolect, langue,* and *parole,* as the author uses them? How do the ideas they express help to clarify the nature of language? How has the author used the last two to express his idea of language in paragraph 33?

5. What method of development has the author used in paragraph 4?

ENGLISH: HIS SISTERS AND HIS COUSINS AND HIS AUNTS

Charlton Laird

1 "Who sees things grow from their origin," Aristotle says, "will have the most advantageous view of them." No arch-Methuselah has seen language grow from its origin, but we have now glimpsed the origin and growth of English and its sister languages from Indo-European. Without this fundamental understanding—that English is one of a family of languages and partakes of the qualities of that family—no one can ask significant questions about the background of our speech. But now we can propound some of the most searching questions. Let us try to do so.

2 *What is the nature of the English language, and how did it acquire this nature?*

3 This question is too large to answer all at once, but we can start on it by breaking it down a bit. Pretty clearly English, like most languages, is made up of symbols for meaning (words), and some method of putting these words together so that they convey enlarged meaning (grammar). Of these two, the words are the more obvious; everybody is aware of words, whereas much grammar is unconscious. Accordingly let us start with words, and ask ourselves where our words came from—later we can ask how they came to be what they are today.

4 In view of the previous chapter, part of the answer must be obvious. If English came from Anglo-Saxon, and Anglo-Saxon came from Indo-European, at least part of our vocabulary must descend to us from Indo-European through Anglo-Saxon. How much of it, and which parts of it? To start an answer, one might start counting the words in ordinary prose, dividing them into those which came from Anglo-Saxon and those which did not. On the assumption that the stuff you are now reading is ordinary prose, the next paragraph will be printed with *as* for *Anglo-Saxon* over the words which come from that language, and *o* for *other* over the remaining words.

as as as as as o o as as o o as

5 There is, of course, a preliminary question. Did the Anglo-Saxons get

as o as as o o as as o as as o o as
all their words from Indo-European, or did they have some secret cache of

as as as o as o o o as as
words from which they could surreptitiously augment their word stock?

o as o as as as as o as as as o
Presenting the evidence for an answer would require our going into Anglo-

o asas o as as as as o as as o as as o
Saxon as a language, and that, at the moment, we are scarcely in a position

as as as o as as as as as o as o as as
to do. But fortunately the answer is not in dispute. The Angles and the

o as as o o o o as as as
Saxons came from relatively isolated Germanic peoples. Having been in

o as o o o as as&o? as as as o as as
contact with Roman traders, they had picked up a few Latin words. All

o as as as o as o o as as o
their neighbors spoke some derivative of Indo-European, and from them

as o o as as as as as as as as as
the Anglo-Saxons borrowed a few more words. Thus even the borrowed

as as o o as as o o as as o o
words in Anglo-Saxon came from Indo-European, but the important fact

as as as as as as o o as&o? as as
is that although speakers of West Germanic acquired scattered words here

as as as as o as o as as as as o o as
and there, the great bulk of their word stock came to them directly from

o o as as as o o as as o o
Proto-Germanic, and most of Proto-Germanic came from Indo-European.

6 We are now ready to look at the paragraph above. The first result is obvious; the *as*'s predominate. That is, in this passage more words come from Anglo-Saxon than from all other sources combined. The subject

matter influences these results a little; had the subject been *pterodactyls* instead of *words*, the *pterodactyls* would have been marked *o*. On the other hand, had the subject been *farm grains and animals*, there would have been still more words marked *as*. The linguistic habits of the writer make some difference, also. The writer could have changed *would require our going* to *would necessitate going*, and thus drop out one *as* word. Or he could have written *we should have to go*, and thus drop out one word. But he could not have changed the result much if he had tried, because of the nature of the words themselves.

7 A little study of this passage will reveal the reason. The bulk of the words marked *o* fall into a few categories. They are learned words, like *Proto-Germanic* and *language*; they are qualifying words, like *fortunately*, *relatively*, *surreptitiously*; they are the sort of words used in sophisticated discussion, like *preliminary*, *question*, *derivative*, and *dispute*. The words marked *as* include the bulk of the common names for things, like *word* and *neighbor*; the words for customary actions, like *go* and *speak*; the words which have little meaning in themselves, but which are essential to any coherent use of the language, like *a*, *the*, *of*, *from*, *get*, *do*, *had*, *there*. In short, most of the common words of the language come from Anglo-Saxon; most of the words not from Anglo-Saxon are comparatively uncommon. There are exceptions, of course. *They*, *their*, and *them* are the most striking exceptions; there are special circumstances accounting for them, to which we shall return. Some borrowed words, like *question*, have become relatively common. But the exceptions are obviously exceptions; the core of functioning English vocabulary is Anglo-Saxon vocabulary.

8 Just to keep the record straight, we might remind ourselves that counting words in a piece of prose is not the only plausible check of vocabulary. We might, for instance, count a page in a dictionary. Were we to do so, we should get another answer, but we might postpone that test until we have followed further the Anglo-Saxons and the linguistic habits they brought with them.

9 We have already observed that the somewhat barbaric farmers who came to the island of Britain in the fifth and sixth centuries were a mixture of West Germanic-speaking lowlanders, mostly Angles and Saxons. Strictly speaking their language was not Anglo-Saxon and no such language existed; there were only Anglian dialects, Saxon dialects, and other Germanic dialects, which have descended with variations until this day. But Anglo-Saxon is a convenient term; not everybody knows what it means, but nobody confuses it with anything else, as they do its synonym, *Old English*. "Oh, I just love those Old English novels," an acquaintance of mine gushed, in speaking of Thomas Hardy. At least, nobody thinks Thomas Hardy wrote Anglo-Saxon. Roughly, then, the Hengist and Horsa of the

Venerable Bede and all their rude pirate friends spoke what we may call Anglo-Saxon.

10 They continued to speak it for some hundreds of years, disturbed by nothing more than a few obstreperous Celts and one another's battle-axes. It took them a century or so to drive out or to pacify the Celts. Some of the Celts died in battle; others took sanctuary on convenient islands, Ireland and the Isle of Man, for instance. Some fled to the continent and founded a colony in what is now Brittany—named, presumably, from the British immigrants. But probably most of them stayed on the island of Britain. Those who could not live with the Germans fled to the mountains of Scotland and Wales where the invaders were not disposed to follow. The invaders were farmers, and wooded mountains are not good farming country; besides, it is often unhealthy to go among mountains if somebody on top of the mountain does not like you.

11 Many Celts stayed where they were, reduced to subsidiary or servile positions under the invaders. Apparently the Germans were not shockingly hard on them, provided they would surrender anything the Germans wanted, especially the best farming land. The Celtic graveyards of the period are in villages up on the hilltops, connected by the ancient Celtic trackways. Down in the rich valleys are the Germanic graveyards. In defense of the invaders one should add, perhaps, that the Celts had not bothered with that land; it was covered with oak trees, which were hard to get rid of, and the Celts had not taken much to farming anyhow. But whether they were treated badly or not, the Celts did not love their Germanic fellow Indo-Europeans. In fact, they seem to have hated them so much that although the Celts had become Roman Christians they took no chances of seeing any Germans in the Christian heaven. They declined to convert them to Christianity, thereby dooming them expeditiously to hell.

12 So the invading Germans fought a slow war of conquest with the native Celts, and continued fighting small dynastic wars among themselves after they had subdued the natives. They settled down and became natives themselves, and soon an ancestor of the English language was the native speech. In all this, they absorbed almost no Celtic language, as they absorbed no Celtic religion. Many Celtic names for places survive, mostly old Celtic roots with Latin endings, now changed beyond all ready recognition; for instance, *Eboracum* became *York*, and *Caer Luguvalium* became *Carlisle*. But you can search for hours through a dictionary without finding any other sort of word which the Anglo-Saxons in the valleys got from the Celts on the hilltops or the Celtic servants in the kitchen. A few Celtic words we have. A few words for place names have become common nouns, *down* for *hill*, for instance. Later we acquired Celtic words with

Celtic goods. We borrowed Celtic *whisky*, and corrupted the Celtic word for it, *usquebaugh* (water of life), but all that happened long after. The early Celts had no whisky to lend. The explanation for the meager Celtic influence upon English supposedly is that the invaders conquered slowly, keeping their own ranks intact, taking new land only when they needed it; hence there were never a few conquering Gemans surrounded by large numbers of native Celts. The Celts who stayed had to learn Anglo-Saxon; Germans never bothered to learn Celtic. The experience of the white people in what became the United States is somewhat analogous; since on the whole the whites drove the Indians before them, and kept the Indians in a servile position and few in number when the two peoples mixed, relatively few Indian words except place names have found their way into standard English. Many of our Indian words date from the day when a small number of white trappers or traders lived in a predominantly Indian culture. That seemingly did not happen in Britain; any German who found himself in a predominantly Celtic culture did not live long.

13 Thus the Angles and the Saxons, their friends and their dialects, became established in England. Christianity eventually found its way to them in spite of the native Celts, partly from Ireland and partly from the Continent. Several relatively large political areas, or kingdoms, took something like shape on the island. To the north and east were Northumbria and Mercia, mainly Anglian areas; to the south and west were various divisions of Saxons; at the extreme southeast tip were the descendants of the Jutes—whoever they were. They were apparently the first comers among the Germanic people. The Venerable Bede, with a handy etymological guess, said they came from Jutland, but we now know they did not. The best guess seems to be that they were professional soldiers—that is, professional international robbers; anyhow, their descendants lived mostly in what is now Kent. This was the situation when some strong-minded relative of the Germanic invaders came to visit. They announced their arrival by sacking the Abbey of Lindisfarne late in the eighth century, and not until about the year 900 did the Anglo-Saxons have reason to hope they had stopped coming.

14 These guests were some of the same Vikings who figured in the previous chapter. They came mainly from Norway and Denmark, and they brought with them techniques which the intrepid northern sailors had worked out. They possessed long, open boats, pushed by crude sails or manned with long oars. If the oarsmen were hardy enough, these boats could be taken across the Atlantic Ocean. And they were, for the oarsmen were hardy. The combination of boats and boatmen constituted the best navy in Europe. It constituted, also, a threat to the very existence of the civilization of western Europe, for once again offense had advanced faster

than defense, and civilization appeared helpless before the onslaughts of the Nordic seafarers.

15 They had a tactic. A few boats with a few hundred armed men would sail into a harbor or row up a river—the shallow draft of the boats permitted entry, especially at high tide, into many rivers. The men would land to murder, rape, burn, or do what they pleased; mainly, of course, they wanted to rob, but other inconveniences usually attended the robbing. Before the residents could muster a fighting force, the marauders had filled their boats with plunder and were gone, ready to sail into another harbor or up another river and repeat the process.

16 Against this attack Europe had little defense. The Vikings overran Ireland, they pillaged all over France, they sacked in Spain and the Mediterranean areas. For a time they held most of England. They swept in from the north and east, butchering and plundering. Men hid in the woods, eating what they could find, and there were no virgins in the land. How all this was stopped is not to be told here. Partly, of course, it stopped because the North ran out of excess Vikings, for in spite of their prowess, Vikings tended to die suddenly. In England the Norsemen were stopped partly because King Alfred built a better navy than they had. On the Continent the feudal system, based upon the fortress, deterred the Vikings, or Creek Men, by providing a refuge near the creek. It was a long, complicated, bloody business. But we are concerned with linguistics, not with bloodletting.

17 By the end of the ninth century, King Alfred and his West Saxons had stopped the Vikings in England. By beating them in battle, by outsmarting them in geopolitics, by converting them to Christianity and threatening them with the terrors of hell, he got them to agree, sporadically, to stop looting and settle down. They had come in such great numbers that they could not be driven out. They were mostly Danes and, like the Anglo-Saxons, they were mostly farmers who wanted land. The habitable parts of the island of Britain—the outlying areas harbored only wolves, Welshmen, and Scotsmen, who did not count—were divided along a line running roughly from modern London to modern Liverpool, which just happened to be about the line between the Anglian-speaking and the Saxon-speaking groups. The area to the northeast of this line became Danelaw, the country in which the law of the Danes was the law of the land, the country in which the Vikings could do as they pleased; the area to the southwest remained Saxon.

18 This line is the line of cleavage of British dialects until this day. To the south and west are forms descending from the Saxon dialects. To the north and the east the forms descend from Anglian, as these have been altered, corrupted, and augmented with influence from Old Norse. Most medieval

works composed in the north can be recognized at once, not only by grammatical differences, but also by the Norse words in the vocabulary. Many of these words have been lost in Modern English or are preserved only in certain dialects not now considered standard English, which has descended mainly from the dialect of London (*bushy* in southern England can be bosky in the north), but to see how Viking influence upon vocabulary has persisted, one has only to look at a map of Britain. In Anglo-Saxon a common word for an inhabited place was *tun*, which in Modern English can appear as *town, ton, don, dun,* and the like. A corresponding word in Old Norse is *ham*. A glance at the map will show that southern and western areas are seeded with *Wimbledon, Brighton, Taunton, Swindon*. In the occasional occurrences of *ham* in the south, as in *Hampton, Southampton, ham* is presumably the Anglo-Saxon word for *home*, or a similar word meaning "meadow" or "river land," which did not come from Old Norse. To the north are *Nottingham, Birmingham, Durham,* and *Bullingham,* and in a truly Danish area, *North Ham, South Ham,* and *West Ham* surround *Ham*.

19 In this manner the Vikings left a lasting imprint upon the language of Britain, partly because so many of them stayed, and stayed clustered in their own little groups, partly because they were so important—after all, King Canute was King of Denmark before he was King of England—and partly because the languages of the invaders and the invaded were so similar that subsequent inhabitants of Britain did not always know whether they were talking North Germanic Old Norse or West Germanic Anglo-Saxon. Nor do we always know. For instance, most dictionaries say that the origin of our word *gutter* was Old French *goutiere*, from a word meaning "a drop" (Modern French *goutte*), which has certainly given us English *gout*. But it could also have come from an Old Norse word. When Robert Mannyng of Brunne wrote:

"He toke the gate and went thru the gate"

he means to say that a man walked along the path (Old Norse *gata*) and went through the gate (Anglo-Saxon *gæt*).[1] We should note, furthermore, that the nominative masculine form of the word *gata* in Old Norse ended in *r*, that is, *gatr*, and that if Robert Mannyng had been trying to write this sound he would probably have written *gater* or *gutter*, just as we do. Did the Old Norse word for path, *gatr*, become the path along the side of the street, where, when there was water, the water ran? Or did the Old French *goutiere*, a trough to catch the drops from the eaves, become a place for water to run along a road as well as a way for water to run along a house?

[1] The ligature æ is an Anglo-Saxon spelling roughly equivalent to the modern sound of *a* in *hat*.

The answer is not easy. Often we do not know whether we are speaking Old Norse or not.

20 The most spectacular borrowing from Old Norse is probably that to be found in the Modern English plural third person pronoun. The Anglo-Saxon pronouns *hie, hiera, heom, hie* became so corrupted that they were readily confused with singulars (the nominative plural became *he,* identical with the masculine singular; the possessive became *her,* identical with the feminine singular; the dative and accusative merged and became *hem,* identical with a variant spelling of *him*). When this happened, speakers of Middle English gradually adopted the Old Norse plural pronoun, which has given us our *they, their, them.*

21 No sooner had the Angles and Saxons learned to live more or less at ease with their obstreperous relatives from the North, than more relatives arrived, beginning in the summer of 1066. These, too, were Vikings, but they had been living in France and had become sophisticated. Or somewhat sophisticated. They had not been tractable folk when they arrived. They had harried widely and laid siege to Paris. They finally agreed to being bought off, accepting a large chunk of France on the promise of keeping other Vikings out of that country. The story is that when their leader was asked to kiss the French king's foot in sign of fealty he picked it up so high the king went over backward. After they settled in France these reformed Vikings learned to talk French of a sort, greedily acquired the advantages of western European culture, and proceeded to set up a Norman empire which was eventually to stretch from Scotland to Sicily. They took advantage of some dynastic changes on the neighboring island of Britain—their home was just across the channel from England in what is still called Normandy—moved in rapidly, defeated a hastily gathered army near Hastings, and established themselves, under William the Conqueror, as rulers of the country.

22 The victors acted like the winners in a political election. There was little raping or pillaging. Anybody who accepted the results of the hustings at Hastings was allowed to go about his business. Many an Englishman probably did not notice the change much more than many a Democrat does when the Republicans come in. Of course the winners appropriated all of the best jobs, including the important posts in the church and in education, which was part of the church, as well as in government. Norman Frenchmen became the governors, the administrators, the preachers, the teachers, the big landowners, and the like. These people used French, and forced those who dealt with them to use French—or rather, the Scandinavianized French which we call Anglo-Norman. Meanwhile, intellectual matters were in the hands of the Universal Church, which wrote and even spoke Latin. English, as a written language, almost disappeared.

23 Anyone examining the preserved writings of this time, and making

up his mind solely on bulk and importance of written work, would inevitably conclude that the English people must thereafter have spoken French or Latin or some kind of mixture of them. Letters were written in French, cases at Law were conducted in French, sermons were delivered in French, handbooks of agriculture and conduct were written in French, stories were told in French. Meanwhile, learned disquisitions were conducted in Latin, the schools were based upon Latin, and great international works like Geoffrey of Monmouth's *History of the Kings of Britain,* which was known and venerated all over Europe, were written in Latin. Only stray pieces of script have been preserved from that time of anything that stems from Anglo-Saxon, and these, like Lawman's *Brut,* were even then little known.

24 But what happened? English survived to become again the official language of England, and all the works written in French or Latin, if they any longer had any importance, had to be translated into Middle English. Obviously most Englishmen must have gone right on talking Anglo-Saxon while they wrote French. Or at least their wives went on talking Anglo-Saxon, and little Athelwold learned Anglo-Saxon as he learned to toddle. Little Athelwold's daddy, if he had to sue his neighbor, may have sued him in French, and he prayed to the Virgin Mary in Latin; but when he spanked little Athelwold he spanked him in Anglo-Saxon, and the evidence that he did is all over the language. The words *bottom, buttocks, butt,* and *rump* are all from Germanic roots, along with some other terms now considered vulgar.

25 Furthermore, the impact of the Norman French upon the English language was much slighter than is commonly supposed. A very large percentage of the words in any dictionary came into English from Latin or Greek, and many of them by way of French. The natural assumption has been that William the Conqueror and his Normans brought these words along with him. The argument—or the presumption, for supposed truth was long taken for granted—ran somewhat as follows: English vocabulary is heavily French; the Normans conquered England; the Normans spoke French; *ergo* the conquering Normans forced their French vocabulary upon the English people. This assumption is written into many conventional reference works and assumed in most of the others. The most interesting fact about it is that it is not true.

26 Doubtless the Normans would have been glad to fasten their language on the country. Within limits they tried to. But they were too few, and they were too remote from English life. After a while everybody forgot who had been Normans and who had been Anglo-Saxons, and most people did not care. But meanwhile, little Athelwold had been whopped in Anglo-Saxon, and he learned the language with a sense of intimacy which he never acquired for French. Anyhow, only relatively few Englishmen ever

learned French, even Anglo-Norman. Educated people did, of course, but not many people were educated.

27 This sounds like theorizing. How can we know that French vocabulary in English does not come mainly and directly from the Norman Conquest? In several ways, but here are two.

28 Comparatively few French words were borrowed into English during Anglo-Norman times, and the great bulk of them were borrowed after French ceased to be spoken as a native language in England. For instance, the following is a tabulation of about a thousand words selected objectively, and arranged by the half century of their first appearance in English, so far as the word is recorded in the *New English Dictionary*. The *New English Dictionary* (1928), in its revised re-issue (1933), called the *Oxford English Dictionary*, is the monumental thirteen-volume work which is the standard authority for the history of English words.

*Date of first appearance in English**	*Number of words*	*Date of first appearance in English*	*Number of words*
1050	2	1451–1500	90
1051–1100	0	1501–1550	62
1101–1150	2	1551–1600	95
1151–1200	7	1601–1650	61
1201–1250	35	1651–1700	37
1251–1300	99	1701–1750	33
1301–1350	108	1751–1800	26
1351–1400	198	1801–1850	46
1401–1450	74	1851–1900	25

* Table, page 214 in *A History of the English Language*, Second Edition, by Albert C. Baugh. Copyright © 1957 by Appleton-Century-Crofts, Inc. Reprinted by permission of Appleton-Century Crofts, Division of Meredith Corporation.

29 The study was begun many years ago by the distinguished Danish grammarian, Otto Jespersen, and concluded by Professor Albert C. Baugh of the University of Pennsylvania. These men would be the first to point out that the figures cannot be taken at their face value. But these figures, less than one percent (9 out of 1000 words) were borrowed from French into English during the first 134 years of Norman occupancy. This is obviously not correct. Part of the paucity of Anglo-Norman words results, surely, from the scarcity of written Middle English from that period. Furthermore, the results of the *New English Dictionary*, though they reveal a mine of information, are far from complete. The *Middle English Dictionary* now being published will certainly increase this percentage somewhat. But even after all possible qualifications, exceptions, probable errors, and the like have been allowed for, the basic fact remains obvious. The bulk of

French words appeared in the English language long after Anglo-Norman was no longer spoken as a native tongue.

30 Now for the second piece of evidence, which perhaps need not be labored, the more because the evidence requires going into grammatical forms. The words which were borrowed appear mostly in the dialect of the French of Paris, not in the dialect of Normandy, the home of the conquerors. Evidence for a statement like this must inevitably be detailed, but the following may provide an index which is roughly reliable. Anyone who knows Modern French recognizes most of the French words at once. These French words are recognizable because they come mostly from the French of Paris, and standard Modern French also stems from the French of Paris. Words which came into English from Anglo-Norman are often not readily recognizable as French. For instance, our word *carrefour*, a square or crossroads, comes to us from something like standard Old French. But the main intersection in the old town of Oxford, England, is called Carfax, somewhat to the wonder of some local people who associate the word by folk etymology with car tracks, although there are no car tracks there. The explanation is that this place name preserves the Anglo-Norman form, sometimes spelled *carfoukes*, from Medieval Latin *quadrifurcus*, having four forks. And so it goes. The bulk of the French words which we use today did not come into English in Anglo-Norman times, and when they did come, they came in a form the Normans in England would never have used—the whole of France laughed at the way those Hrolf-come-lately Norsemen tried to talk French. Only the exceptions, like *Carfax*, are Anglo-Norman.

31 The Norman Conquest ended the direct invasions of the English language by military means. The effects of both the Viking and Norman invasions, as invasions, were meager in language, much more meager than most people suppose. The Viking invasion eventually affected the language, not because the Danes invaded, but because so many of them settled down. The Norman Conquest had great indirect effect, because Normans cemented English connections with the Continent; the invasion was followed by a flow of Continental goods and fashions, and these eventually brought their words along with them. But the evidence in England as elsewhere is that conquest alone seldom influences language very much. Language is too fundamental, too much rooted in childhood, in the family, in eating and sleeping and making a living, ever to be directly influenced much by war. Language grows from life, not from death.

32 Most of the relatives of English have remained peacefully at home, minding their own meanings. If they have come to English speech, they have done so through change. To understand their impact upon our language we must become acquainted with the concept of *cognates*. The word means "born together," and it refers specifically to words which have

descended in various languages from a common parent. Naturally, any word in English which has descended through Anglo-Saxon from Indo-European is likely to have sisters, cousins, and aunts scattered over a fair share of the civilized world. Any of tens of thousands of examples would suffice, but let us take the word *mother*.

33 This word certainly occurred in Indo-European, supposedly in a form something like **mater*.[2] If so, Latin has preserved it intact. The Greek *meter* is not much different, nor is the Celtic *maither*—Celtic is etymologically close to Latin. Sanskrit has *matar;* Slavic, *mati* and *mote.* The Proto-Germanic form must have been something like **modor,* judging from the occurrence of the word in Old High German, Plattdeutsch, and Old Norse; German *Mutter* and English *mother* develop from Old High German *mouter* and Anglo-Saxon *mordor* respectively. Thus, modern equivalents of *mother* like French *mère,* German *Mutter,* and Spanish *madre* are cognates, distant cousins which have all descended from old great-grandmother Indo-European, each through its own line of descent by the various aunts and uncles.

34 Sometimes the cousins go visiting, in entirely peaceful ways. *Maternal* obviously comes from *mater,* and thus an English-speaking mother can have either of two cognate forms applied to her; she may be *maternal* from the Latin or *motherly* from the English. The synonyms *matriarchy* and *Mutterrecht* are cognates from Greek and German respectively. *Maiden* and *matron,* though to a degree antonyms, can probably be traced to the same root. Our dictionaries and our language are scattered with the cousins, the second cousins, the third, eighth and tenth cousins of English, many of them readily recognizable, but many of them obscure to all but the experts. They are numerous, so numerous that most of the English vocabulary which has not come directly from Indo-European by way of Anglo-Saxon has come indirectly from Indo-European by way of some more or less distant relative. English is deeply indebted to its far-flung linguistic family.

STUDY GUIDE

Structure and Content

1. The principle of organization in this essay is chronology. Laird is detailing the successive influences on the development of the English language. Draw up an outline in which you indicate these successive influences and the

[2] The asterisk before **mater* is intended to indicate that the form does not occur in any extant manuscript, but has been inferred from what it has done, very much as atoms are inferred from what they do. In this book all inferred forms will be preceded by an asterisk.

contributions each made to the language. Indicate in each case the paragraphs devoted to the various influences.

2. Show how an *analogy* is used to good effect in paragraph 11 to clarify the relationship between the invading Anglo-Saxons and the Celts.

3. What proof does the author give for the slight direct influence of Anglo-Norman on the English language?

4. Why did Anglo-Saxon rather than the older Celtic language become the foundation of English?

CHANGING MEANINGS AND VALUES OF WORDS

Stuart Robertson and Frederic G. Cassidy

1 The study of meaning in language is called Semasiology or Semantics. The latter term, however, has recently been used widely to refer to what is properly called General Semantics, a study allied more closely to the field of philosophy than to that of linguistics, and which therefore will not be dealt with in this book. The term *Semantics* nevertheless has application within the field of linguistics; there it is limited at present to the description of the meanings which words or other units of language convey, and, when these are seen historically, also to the various types of meaning-change that occur.

2 But the word "meaning" itself poses difficult problems. What is the meaning of "meaning"? We all recognize that language is a give-and-take of speech-signals, a series of stimuli by speakers and responses by hearers; also that some non-linguistic stimuli produce linguistic responses, and *vice versa*. (Thus a kiss may produce the response "Darling!"—and *vice versa*.) When the hearer of a linguistic stimulus responds to it in some predictable way, we say, in common parlance, that he has "understood" the speaker. But we are by no means certain—here we must throw ourselves upon the psychologists—what goes on inside the hearer's nervous system between his hearing of the words and his response to them. The student of language therefore limits himself to an investigation of the parts of the process which are clearly accessible, and with which he can deal with some degree of objectivity. Less and less do linguists raise the question of "ideas" or "concepts" in the mind; today they generally define meaning

as simply the situation out of which language comes and the response that it elicits.

3 If this is meaning, how does it change? It is clear that, for speakers of the same language, there must be a large measure of consistency in the response to linguistic signals—otherwise, communication would be impossible. Nevertheless, since no two situations can ever be exactly alike, there is always some area of variation, and over a period of time the increment of slight variations will alter the reference of the linguistic signal. Let us take an example. Since meaning involves both the situation out of which a word comes (which makes the speaker say it) and the hearer's response, every speech situation is complex, with many components. But the relative prominence of these components will not always be the same. When the word *green* is first said it ordinarily brings a response in terms of color; but if the context concerns a fruit, this primary element of color may become associated with a secondary element—unripeness. Repetition may then establish this association until the element of unripeness becomes more prominent than that of color—so much so that it becomes possible to say, without fear of misunderstanding, "Blackberries are red when they are green."

4 Every new focus of prominence, once established, may beget others: when fruit and young people are associated, the element of unripeness may be paralleled with inexperience, and the latter may then assume primary prominence in such a statement as, "Those freshmen are pretty green." Thus a series of shifts in focus, from one element in a situation to others, will produce shifts in meaning—or "new meanings"—for words. In this example, *green* has acquired two new meanings and lost none; but many a word, after shifting, has lost its first meaning entirely. Indeed, over the centuries meanings grow and decay in a surprising variety of ways, the chief of which we are to examine in this chapter.

5 Yet before proceeding we must give attention to one more point. Even though it is generally recognized that meanings change, many people still cling, curiously enough, to the quite contradictory notion that words all have "true" meanings, that changes somehow take us away from the "true" meaning, and that the way to find out what a word "really means" is to find out what it once meant. This is particularly true in respect to borrowed words in English, the belief evidently being that the meaning of the word in contemporary English and the meaning of the Latin or Greek word from which the English word is derived must be one and the same. A little reflection should show that an appeal to etymology in order to establish the present meaning of the word is as untrustworthy as an appeal to spelling in order to establish its present pronunciation. And for a reason that is almost exactly parallel: change of *meaning* is likely to have altered the etymological sense, which is thereby rendered archaic or obsolete, just

as change of *sound* is likely to be unrecorded in the "antiquarian" spelling that so frequently characterizes Modern English. The study of etymology has great value and interest—a point to which we shall later return—but its usefulness in settling the question of what a word means is subject to considerable qualification.

6 Let us see what results when one ignores the idea that a word may change its meaning, and appeals to its etymology in order to determine its present meaning. A handbook of only twenty-odd years ago on "correct English" sets forth the following dictum: "*Dilapidated* . . . Said of a building or other structure. But the word is from the Latin *lapis,* a stone, and cannot properly be used of any but a stone structure." One might just as reasonably argue that because *candidate* is related to the Latin *candidus* (white), it cannot properly be used of an aspirant for political office unless he is clothed in a suit of white material. More clearly even, one might protest that *holiday* properly describes Christmas or Easter, but should never be used of Independence Day or Labor Day; or that *bonfire* should not be applied except where the combustible material is bone. These arguments are not much more grotesque than some that have been seriously maintained in defense of an etymological crotchet, while ignoring the fact of change of meaning. Indeed, one who argues on this basis is a victim of the "etymological fallacy."

7 The fact is that what a word once meant is not necessarily what it now means; the etymological meaning has often died out, and a quite new development is the living descendant. This is particularly true of words in common or popular use. Words, after all, are for the most part purely conventional symbols. They mean only what those who are using them agree to make them mean. Exactly the same principles apply to "learned" words, but because their traditional users have generally known the language from which they were borrowed, or of whose elements they were composed, they have tended to preserve the etymological meaning—indeed, it is conventional to use such words with an eye to their source; thus they are less prone to alterations of meaning than are popular words. It is in this way, incidentally, that a cultural tradition holds in check, to some extent, the constant tendency of language to change.

8 Change of meaning, however, though usually unpredictable, is not utterly arbitrary; as we shall see in a moment, it often proceeds along familiar paths. Furthermore, though it takes place in all languages, it does not proceed at the same rate even in related ones. If we look at cognate words in English and German, for example, which might have been expected to have the same meaning, we often find them widely different, and the difference is most commonly the result of some radical change of sense in the English word. Opposite instances can be found, admittedly, in which the English word has stood still and the German one changed; yet it

is usually the latter which is conservative. Examples of this characteristic English shift in meaning are the following: *Schlagen* and *slay* are originally the same word, but the German word retains the general meaning of "smite" or "strike" while the English word has become narrowed to mean "strike with fatal consequences" or "kill." *Knabe* is the cognate in German of Old English *cnapa* or *cnafa*, and has the same meaning, "boy"; but Modern English *knave* has a radically different one; the German *Tier* means any kind of animal, as did the cognate Old English *deor*, but in Modern English *deer* means one particular kind of animal.

9 GENERALIZATION AND SPECIALIZATION One very common type of change is that in which the "area" of the meaning is changed. When a word that has referred broadly or inclusively begins instead to refer narrowly or exclusively, this is an example of "specialization" of meaning; the contrary is called "generalization." Interestingly enough, the same word may undergo both processes at different stages of the development of its meaning. *Go*, for example, is a verb of motion that seems as general as possible in meaning, and presumably this is also the basic meaning; early in its history in English, however, it must have specialized, for Old English *gān* sometimes means "walk," and in Middle English *ryde or gon* (ride or walk) is a familiar formula. Although the present meaning is the generalized one, the specialization "walk" was still possible in the late seventeenth century, as we see in these phrases from Bunyan: "I am resolved to run when I can, to go when I cannot run, and to creep when I cannot go."

10 Borrowed words are quite as likely as native ones to undergo such transformations in meaning. *Virtue* is connected with Latin *vir* (man). Thus, *virtue* first meant "manliness" in general; but its meaning later specialized to stand for the manly quality most in demand in the military state, namely "fortitude" or "warlike prowess"—the meaning familiar in Cæsar's *Commentaries*. But a still later Latin meaning is more comprehensive, and it was this very general meaning that was attached to *virtue* when it was borrowed in English through French. One possible specialization was "power," as in "Virtue had gone out of him," or even "magical power," as in "the virtue of the spell" or Milton's "virtuous ring and glass." More commonly, however, the word in English retained a general sense of "noble quality"—though more and more with reference to moral rather than to mental or physical characteristics. But another specialization limits its application to women; for example, "All the sons were brave, and all the daughters virtuous," where *virtuous* is equivalent to "chaste." "A woman's virtue" will today be interpreted in only the last sense. A curious evolution, indeed, when one recalls that the etymological meaning is "manliness." . . .

11 But generalization of meaning does not always stay within bounds; under some conditions the meaning becomes so broad that, in extreme cases, there is hardly any meaning left. We have a whole set of words, used conversationally when we either do not know, or cannot remember, or perhaps will not take the trouble to search for a more precise term: the *what-you-may-call it* kind of word—*thingumabob, doohickie, jigger,* and so on. Not so long ago *gadget* was imported into the U.S. from England, and has found a very hearty welcome into this company.

12 Another type, in which generalization goes even farther, has aroused strong opposition from guardians of literary style, who realize that emptiness and "jargon" result from the indiscriminate use of "words that mean little or nothing, but may stand for almost anything": such words are *thing, business, concern, condition, matter, article, circumstance.* As we all recognize at once, these are words that have a fairly exact sense, but which also have acquired the ability to fit into a wide variety of everyday contexts, in which their meaning becomes extremely vague—in fact, almost wholly dependent on the context. The word *deal* is the current American favorite in this group, its gamut of meaning running all the way from perfectly favorable ("Your job sounds like a pretty fine deal") to thoroughly unfavorable ("I won't take part in any of his deals"). This word serves the purpose, and is going through the same general sort of development, that *proposition* did a generation ago.

13 Even more frequent than generalization, and even more readily illustrated in numberless familiar instances, is the opposite process of specialization. *Steorfan* is an Old English word, cognate with the German *sterben,* which meant "die"; but the standard Modern English meaning ("Starve") is a specialized one, namely "die from hunger." Another specialization, "die from cold," is found in certain Modern English dialects: "[he] . . . bid her come . . . sit close by the fire: he was sure she was starved" is from the Yorkshire dialect of *Wuthering Heights* (Chapter XXX). The older meaning of *meat* was "food" in general, as one might suspect from the archaic phrase *meat and drink* and from the compound *sweetmeat.* For the meaning "meat," the older term was *flesh* or *flesh meat.* It is interesting to observe, incidentally, that the German cognate for *flesh, Fleisch,* suggests first of all the specialized sense of "meat"; this is the present meaning, too, of French *viande,* while the English *viands* retains the general sense of "food." *Coast* is a borrowing, through French, from a Latin word for "side" or "rib" (compare Modern English *intercostal*), and once meant "border" or "frontier"—the "coast of Bohemia" was not always an absurdity. But *coast* in present use not only has the usual specialization "seashore"; as employed in the eastern United States, it means specifically "Pacific coast." *Shore,* on the other hand, means, in parts of the east at any rate, "Atlantic shore." In some of the same localities, however, "eastern shore"

means what elsewhere would have to be expanded into "eastern shore of the Chesapeake in Maryland," just as in part of New England "the cape" means definitely "Cape Cod." *Token* formerly had the broad meaning "sign," but was long ago specialized to mean a physical thing that is a sign (of something)—as in *love token*, or the metal tokens used on streetcars or buses.

14 An *undertaker* once could undertake to do anything; nowadays he only undertakes to manage funerals. So, to people in general, *doctor* stands only for *doctor of medicine*. *Liquor*, which once was synonymous with *liquid*, is now definitely specialized. *Reek*, like German *rauchen*, once had the broad meaning "smoke," as it still has in the Scotch dialect; but the standard Modern English use limits it quite definitely to unpleasant exhalations. *Disease* meant "discomfort"—"lack of ease" in general. *Girl* meant "young person (of either sex)." The limitation of *corpse* to "dead body" made it necessary to re-borrow the word in its Modern French form *corps* for another possible meaning of "body," and to make occasional use of the original Latin, *corpus*, for still another sense, "complete collection of writings." *Corn*, in general American use, will be immediately understood as "Indian corn" or "maize." But the word itself once meant simply "grain," and so, in other parts of the English-speaking world, it is differently specialized—in Scotland, to mean "oats," and in England "wheat." Keats's allusion to "Ruth amid the alien corn" probably calls up, to many American readers, a very different picture from what the poet had in mind.

15 What are the factors that account for specialization of meaning? One is, of course, that localities and groups of people have their own specialized associations for words that otherwise may convey a broader meaning. It has been well remarked that "every man is his own specializer." *Pipe*, for example, calls up different ideas in the mind of the smoker, the plumber, and the organist. *Ring* may be thought of in connection with jewelry, opera, politics, or pugilism—even though, in the last connection, the "squared circle" has long since superseded the original truly circular shape. Quite apart from particular or local specializations, however, there are a great many words whose meaning has become specialized for nearly everybody. A second factor that helps to account for both generalization and specialization is the fading of the etymological significance of the word. Thus, to illustrate the one point, *arrive* [<Lat. *ad* (to) + *ripa* (shore)] originally applied to the end of a voyage only, and was used without the preposition, since this was included in the word. Milton's "ere he arrive the happy isle" illustrates a use that is in strict accord with the *etymology* of the word. When, however, consciousness of the Latin parts that made up the word was weakened, it was no longer used transitively, but in the phrase "arrive at," and with the more generalized application to the end of any journey.

16 Yet another factor is the competition among synonymous words. The borrowing of the Latin *animal* and the French *beast* meant that, with the native *deer*, English would have possessed three exactly synonymous terms for one idea; it is obviously in the interests of economy that *deer* should have specialized to mean one particular species of animal rather than "animal" in general, and that *beast* should have acquired connotations that limit its sphere. *Bird* and *fowl, dog* and *hound, boy* and *knave, chair* and *stool* are further instances of words that were once synonyms but that have been differentiated in meaning here by the specialization of the second term of each pair.

17 A further remark about generalization and specialization is suggested by some of the words just alluded to. The degree of specialization which a language exhibits seems to depend on cultural need. In a culture in which the coconut is essential—as in Polynesia—an extremely complex vocabulary is said to have grown up, with different terms for many stages or ripeness of the fruit. So also, the Eskimos have different terms for falling snow, snow on the ground, snow packed hard like ice, slushy snow, wind-driven flying snow, and other kinds. Many similar examples could be cited, for the languages of undeveloped culture appear to be particularly rich in specialized terms. At one time in the course of the English language it must have seemed desirable to speakers to make verbal distinctions in connection with groups of animals—mostly those of interest to farmers and hunters. An elaborate set of what are called "company terms" was accordingly developed, some (but by no means all) of which survive today. The better known ones include a *herd* or a *drove* of cattle, but a *flock* of sheep or birds, a *school* of fish, a *pack* of wolves (or hounds), a *covey* of partridges, and a *swarm* of bees. But there are others far more esoteric, such as *nye* of pheasants, *cete* of badgers, *sord* of mallards, *wisp* of snipe, *doylt* of tame swine, *gaggle* of geese, *harras* of horses, and *kennel* of raches. There is a similar profusion of names for the same animal (*cow, heifer, bull, calf, steer*, and *ox*), the young of various animals (*puppy, kitten, kid, calf, colt, lamb*, and so forth), and the male and female of the same species *gander* and *goose, drake* and *duck, horse* and *mare, cock* and *hen, dog* and *bitch*). The need for a generic term is of course particularly felt here, and it is supplied, not quite satisfactorily, by the convention of making either the name of the male (*horse* and *dog*) or of the female (*cow, duck*, and *goose*), or even that of the young of the species (*chicken* and *pig*), perform a larger duty.

18 ELEVATION AND DEGRADATION If generalization and specialization may be said to involve a change in the "area" of meaning, elevation and degradation involve the rising or falling of meaning in a scale of values. Thus a word which once denominated something bad (or at least

neutral) but comes to refer to something good, has undergone *elevation* of meaning; the reverse of this process, obviously, represents a *degradation* of meaning.

19 And here a word of warning: we must not confuse the linguistic signal with the thing it stands for, though that error is too often made. It is not the word as such which is bad or good, or which becomes elevated or degraded, but only the meaning which society chooses to put upon it. As we shall see, society often reverses itself in the course of time, and words which were once disapproved may become "respectable," while others that had social favor may lose it. This would not be possible if the value were inherent in the word. With this in mind, then, let us illustrate degradation of meaning.

20 Many terms that are now descriptive of moral depravity were once quite without this suggestion. *Lust*, for example, meant simply "pleasure," as in German; *wanton* was "untaught"; *lewd* was merely "ignorant," "lerned and lewed" being a phrase commonly standing for "clergy and laity"; *immoral* was "not customary"; *vice*, "flaw"; *hussy*, "housewife"; *wench*, "young girl"; and *harlot*, "fellow" (of either sex). In a similar way, words that impute rascality have often been thoroughly innocent labels: *villain*, for example, was "farm laborer"; *counterfeiter*, "imitator" or "copyist"; *pirate* (at least in its earlier Greek sense), "one who adventures or tries"; *buccaneer*, "one who smokes meat"; *ringleader*, simply "leader" (in a good or a neutral sense), *varlet*, *knave*, and *imp* meant merely "boy"; and *sly*, *crafty*, and *cunning* all implied the compliment "skilful." A perennial form of humor—the city man's ridicule of the countryman—is witnessed in the degradation of such nouns as *peasant*, *boor* (compare German *Bauer* and Dutch *Boer*), and *churl*, and in the frequent implication of such adjectives as *bucolic*, *rural*, *rustic*, and *provincial*.

21 When a word may be applied in two possible ways, one favorable or complimentary and the other the reverse, it is extremely likely that it will specialize in the less desirable sense. Thus, *suggestive* is likely to mean only "evilly suggestive," though it *may* still mean "informative" or "illuminating," and though the noun *suggestion* has escaped any such specialization—just as the verb *to harbor* is limited to unworthy or illegal concealment (as in "harboring a criminal" or "harboring thoughts of revenge"), while the noun *harbor* retains the old broad and literal meaning of "haven." *Asylum*, through association with the idea of "refuge for the insane," has followed a course like that of the verb *harbor*. A *libel*, in Middle English and early Modern English, was simply a "brief bit of writing" (from Lat. *libellum*, little book); now it is definitely limited to something malicious or defamatory. *Doom* once meant "judgment"; now it means only "condemnation." *Reek*, as we have seen, can now stand only for unpleasant distillations; *stink* and *stench* have specialized in the same way from a

formerly neutral meaning, and *smell* and even *odor* seem likely to follow their lead. A *smirk* was once merely a smile, without the suggestion of affectation. One could formerly *resent* benefits as well as injuries, and *retaliate* for favors as well as slights; compare with the present meanings of these words the ordinary implications of the phrase "get even with" or "get square with."

22 On the other hand, instances of words that have traveled an opposite path, from the humble to the exalted, or from the base to the refined, are not far to seek. The institution of chivalry brought about the elevation of *knight* (youth) and *squire* (shield-bearer); and *chivalry* itself was invested by the Romantic Revival with a glamor that the word (as we see from its source, Fr. *cheval*, horse) did not originally possess. "Romantic" ideas in the late eighteenth and early nineteenth centuries were similarly responsible for the gain in dignity of such words as *bard*, once a term of contempt like *vagabond; minstrel*, once applicable to juggler and buffoon as well as musician; and *enthusiasm*, in the earlier eighteenth century akin to *fanaticism*. Like *knight*, other terms for rank or position have had the good fortune to take on added prestige when the offices for which they stood changed their character, and when their own etymological meanings were forgotten. Such is the history of *marshal* (originally, "horse-servant"), *chamberlain* (room-attendant), *minister* (servant), *constable* (stable-attendant), *governor* (pilot), and *steward* (sty-guardian). It is true that in a number of these words the extent of the elevation fluctuates: *marshal* is a less dignified title when it is applied to the lone policeman of an American village than when it is applied to the highest ranking officers of the English or the French army; there is a similar variation between the American and the British connotations for *constable*, just as *steward* may suggest a club attendant as well as the Lord High Steward of England, or even the royal dynasty of the *Stewarts* (or *Stuarts*); likewise, *governor* may mean the warden of an English prison or the chief administrative officer of one of our American states. On the whole, however, the fact that any present implication of these words represents a gain in dignity over the etymological one is patent enough. So too it is with a number of political and religious labels: *Tory, Whig, Puritan, Quaker*, and *Methodist* are well-known examples of names that were originally applied in contempt but that have taken on dignified associations (though, to some, *Puritan* and perhaps *Tory* still convey a derisive significance). Archibishop Trench long ago pointed out that the influence of Christianity elevated *angel* from merely "messenger," *martyr* from "witness," and *paradise* from "park," through the Biblical application to the abode of our first parents (as in *Paradise Lost* and "*earthly* paradise") to the "blisful waiting-place of faithful departed spirits." Miscellaneous further illustrations of elevation are *pretty* from the early meaning "sly," through "clever," to something approaching

"beautiful"; *nice* from an etymological meaning "ignorant," through its earliest English sense "foolish," and later ones like "particular," to its present broad and vague colloquial meaning of "pleasant" or "acceptable"; and *fond* from "foolish" to "affectionate."

23 The usual view of degradation and elevation has been that the downward path is far the more common. Despite McKnight's protest to the effect that elevation has been less noticed simply because it is less dramatic, there seems to be every reason to agree with the general verdict. Examples of elevation, after all, are far less easy to find than examples of degradation, which indeed meet us at every turn. Besides, most of the words that have been cited as undergoing elevation fall into a few obvious categories, while the types of degradation are extremely various. The truth of the matter would appear to be that degradation has been more noticed not because it is more spectacular but simply because it is omnipresent, as elevation is not. Why should this be so, and why should the use of words be made difficult by a lurking leer, a hint of unpleasant connotation that makes a word that appears to be absolutely right in denotation impossible for a given occasion? It is hard to escape the conclusion that there is a disagreeable commentary on human nature here. How difficult it is for superlatives to retain their superlative force—because the general tendency is to apply them on light occasion and hence to weaken their meaning! So *fair* comes to mean "passable," and indeed is often equivalent to "not good"; and *quite* has passed, in its usual American application at least, from "entirely" or "completely" to "moderately." The tendency to procrastinate finds illustration in a whole series of words or phrases—*by and by, presently, anon, immediately, directly,* and *soon* itself—that have "slowed up," changing their meaning from "now" or "at once" to "soon" or "after a time." It is scarcely a far-fetched interpretation to see in the narrowing of *demure* to apply to *mock* modesty, of *genteel* to *spurious* gentility, of *sophistication* to *worldly* wisdom, of *egregious* to notoriety rather than fame, of *sanctimonious* to *pretended* holiness, and of *grandiose* to *tinsel* (itself an example of degradation) grandeur—to see in all these, and dozens of others that might be mentioned, the workings of human motives like suspicion, contempt, and general pessimism.

STUDY GUIDE

Structure

1. This is only a small part of a much longer essay on the changing meaning and values of words. The entire essay is developed as this section is—by definition and multiple examples. Show how the examples clarify the ideas

of generalization and specialization and of elevation and degradation that are defined in this section of the essay.

2. The later part of this same essay is an excellent discussion of *slang*. It might be interesting for one of the students to look it up, outline it, and give an oral report on the way slang originates and affects the language.

Content

1. Does what is said about the nature of language in paragraph 3 agree with Myers' and Laird's fundamental ideas about it?

2. Why does the study of *etymology* seldom help us to learn the present meaning of a word? In what kind of words, popular or learned, is the etymology apt to be closer to the modern meaning? Why?

3. Is the modern meaning of *politician* or *statesman* closer to the etymological meaning?

THE ENGLISH LANGUAGE

Lincoln Barnett

1 To Americans, who use it all their lives, the English language is a commonplace thing, to be treated casually and taken entirely for granted. But few Americans realize how commonplace their language really is. Today 250 million of the world's people—nearly one in 10—use English as their primary language. And 600 million people—nearly one in four—understand it in some degree. In our own lifetime English has become the most widely spoken language on earth.

2 Few events in man's turbulent history compare in scope or significance with this global linguistic conquest. At the time of the Norman Conquest in 1066, English had no more than 1.5 million speakers. In the ensuing five centuries it evolved slowly into the rich, flexible medium of the Elizabethan poets who, while cherishing their language, never dreamed it might become a universal tongue. In 1582 Richard Mulcaster, the most famous English educator of his day, remarked, "The English tongue is of small reach, stretching no further than this island of ours, nay not there over all." As recently as the 18th Century, English was still outranked by French, Latin (for scholarship), German, Spanish, Russian and Italian, and European academicians deplored the fact that English writers wrote only in English.

3 Today English is written, spoken, broadcast and understood on every

From *Life* (March 2, 1962). Reprinted by permission of the author and publisher.

continent. There are few civilized areas where it has any competition as the international language of commerce, diplomacy, science and scholarship. Its speakers cover one quarter of the globe, ranging from the fair-skinned people of the British Isles through every gradation of color and race the world around. It is spoken by Christians, Jews, Moslems, Buddhists, Hindus and adherents of every major religious faith on earth. It is still spreading around the planet at a constantly accelerating tempo.

4 Among the leading disseminators of English are the Russians and Chinese, who are attempting to woo friends and influence nations with it in uncommitted regions of the earth. The Russians use English for propaganda broadcasts to the Far East. Radio listeners in Kenya, Nyasaland and Zanzibar, whose entertainment formerly came from Cairo in Arabic and Swahili, now receive loud, clear broadcasts from Peiping Radio in Red China—all in English. Freight shipments of heavy machinery and other commodities from Russia to the Near East are stamped "Made in U.S.S.R."—in English. In many cities Russian cultural offices compete with British and American centers in advertising English courses. And of the 30 million books which the Russians annually distribute to former British dominions in Africa and Asia, a large proportion are in English—among them technical books, novels and children's books, including "*Goldilocks and the Three Bears* by Leo Tolstoy" (actual author: Robert Southey).

5 English is also the language of international aviation, spoken by pilots and airport control tower operators on all the airways of the world. The West German Luftwaffe and even the fliers of East Germany use it. The French, though ever jealous of their proud and beautiful language, find English far more efficient for air-ground communication. It takes less time, for example, to say *jet* than *avion à réaction,* or to talk of *flaps* rather than *volets de flexions.* There are other areas of mankind's diverse activities within which English now reigns virtually supreme. It is the international language of sport in every country where people play *futbol* or *beisbol.* It is the international language of jazz, whose followers in all lands know the difference between *le bebop* and *buki-buki* (boogie-woogie). It is the language of international youth—of teen-agers everywhere who wear *blue djins* and *pulova* sweaters, chew *gomma americana* (specifically, bubble gum), smoke *Looky Strooky* cigarets (as in Russia), and enjoy hot dogs and Coke (or, as in Japan, *Koka-Kora* and its rival *Pepusi-Kora*).

6 It is in the realm of statesmanship, however, that English has attained the status of a universal tongue to a degree never approached by Latin in the heyday of the Roman Empire or by French in the 18th and 19th centuries. At the Bandung Conference of 1955, attended by representatives from 29 Asian and African countries, the proceedings were conducted entirely in English—not for any love of England or America, but because it was the only means by which the multilingual delegates could

communicate with one another. More recently, when Egypt and Indonesia drew up a cultural treaty, it was specified that the definitive version of the agreement between these two Moslem countries, neither one an ardent admirer of the Western world, would be the English-language copy. When a trade delegation from Ceylon journeyed to the U.S.S.R. for a conference, their Russian hosts, who met them in Kabul, greeted them in English. And when the Dalai Lama fled down from his Tibetan highlands to seek sanctuary in India, he was welcomed by Prime Minister Nehru on the northern frontier.

7 "How are you?" Nehru asked in English.

8 "Very nice," the Dalai Lama said.

9 The most spectacular advances made by English are in the so-called underdeveloped areas of the world. The polyglot populations of Asia and Africa often find it much easier to learn English than to try to comprehend the speech of their nearest neighbors. Contrary to popular supposition, languages evolve in the direction of simplicity. English, being a highly evolved, cosmopolitan, sophisticated language, has been refined and revised, planed down and polished through centuries of use so that today it is far less complex in grammar and syntax than any primitive tongue. Some of the most difficult languages in the world are spoken by some of the world's most backward people—*e.g.*, the Australian aborigines, the Eskimos, the Hottentots and the Yaghan Indians of Tierra del Fuego. In West Africa alone some 60 million tribesmen speak more than 400 different languages; hence wherever European influence has left its mark, Africans often talk to one another in English (or to a lesser extent in French) when they leave their own local language district—which in some cities may mean across the street. Ghana has proclaimed English its official language and requires English instruction from primary school on. In East Africa, whose tribes have communicated for centuries in Swahili, even rabid nationalists today favor English as the common tongue.

10 The swift and astonishing spread of English around the globe has not occurred without some opposition. The French in particular have endeavored to hold the linguistic lines in their former colonies in Asia and Africa. In France itself the Office du Vocabulaire Français continually exhorts newspapers and magazines to avoid the *snobisme* of using English words where French equivalents exist. The Spanish are also reluctant to let their ancient romantic language suffer the incursions of a foreign idiom. Of all European countries Spain has been least receptive to English, partly because of its geographical isolation, partly because Spaniards historically profess little love for the homeland of Sir Francis Drake. Even in Latin America, where English is now virtually mandatory for business and professional men, purists recurrently plead for the preservation of Spanish as "the most beautiful, majestic and sonorous language in the world."

11 Perhaps the most notable victory of the English language over nationalistic resistance was recently won in India. In an effort to expunge relics of the British Raj, the Central Government had proclaimed in 1950 that the official language of India would henceforth be Hindi and that the transition away from English must be complete by 1965. While this pleased the Hindu populatons in the north, the reaction was quite different in the rest of the vast subcontinent, which encompasses 845 distinct languages and dialects. The Bengali-speakers in the east did not like the decree, and in the south the millions of speakers of Tamil and related Dravidian languages protested that 15 years was too brief an interval in which to adopt a tongue as alien to them as any in the Occidental world. For more than a century English has been the common tongue, and although not more than 3% of India's population of 438 million employ it with any degree of fluency, they represent the ruling 3%—administrators, judges, legislators and other educated groups. If English were expunged, they pointed out, there would be no way for all the peoples of the huge land to communicate with each other. Months of argument ensued, marred recurrently by bloody riots. At the University of Lucknow, which switched at once from English to Hindi, levels of learning went into an alarming decline. Faculty members evolved a kind of Anglo-Hindi jargon, inventing hybrid words for technical terms in an attempt to comply with the government edict. The result was Babel.

12 Finally the so-called "Save Hindi" campaign was called off. The announcement, significantly, was published in English. Prime Minister Nehru declared that for an indefinite period English would continue as an "associate official language." While Hindus listened in silence and non-Hindi-speaking legislators cheered, Nehru termed English "the major window for us to the outside world."

13 "We dare not close that window," he said. "And if we do, it will spell peril to our future."

14 In Nehru's words lies one explanation for the virtually unopposed diffusion of English around the globe. For not only in Asia and Africa, but in Europe, crisscrossed by linguistic frontiers and dissected by deep-rooted cultural loyalties, people of all classes now look to English as a window, a magic casement opening on every horizon of loquacious man.

15 West German schools require six to nine years of English. The obligation meets with no emotional resistance, for the Germans, unlike the French, feel no sense of linguistic betrayal in studying English: they are eager to learn and experience little difficulty in the process. Even in East German (where Russian used to be, but is no longer, a compulsory subject) English holds first place among the optional language courses in secondary schools, with 12 applicants for every available departmental vacancy. English classes are equally in demand in Poland and Yugoslavia. Within the

U.S.S.R. itself schools offer English from the fourth or fifth grades on, and in some of the largest cities it is the one compulsory language in the curriculum. One of the best-sellers in the bookshops of Moscow is an English grammar.

16 The teaching of languages in schools, however, represents only one of many channels through which the torrent of English is inundating all lands. Other tributary freshets include radio and television, motion pictures, recordings of popular songs, English language publications, adult education courses, language centers, mobile libraries and exchange fellowships sponsored by government agencies and private foundations, and, perhaps most important of all, the incomputable numbers of informal encounters that occur every day among businessmen, professional men, politicians, scientists, technicians, students and just plain tourists.

17 Although the flood of English dates only from the end of World War II, its incipient stage actually began more than three centuries ago when British adventurers first carried their speech to the far places of the earth, erecting the initial bastions of empire. In the wake of the conquerors came traders, and after them missionaries—who still exercise a potent force in Africa and Asia. But the major catalyst in the English language explosion was war—especially the two great conflicts of this century.

18 "War is perhaps the most rapidly effectual excitant of language," a British etymologist has observed. The occupation troops that moved into defeated countries after World War I and on an incomparably greater scale after World War II did more to spread English (particularly American English) than any other agency of dissemination. From the hundreds of thousands of soldiers and their dependents deployed throughout both hemispheres, English words and phrases filtered down to every level of the diverse populations in every one of the nations and zones. No longer was English speech the limited possession of the educated, the wealthy and the peripatetic social elite. It became the economically valuable property of all, from shopkeepers and salesgirls, bellboys and bartenders, down to barefoot urchins in the streets of Tokyo and Teheran, Berlin and Baghdad who swiftly learned to chirp, "Hey, Joe, gimme gum."

19 The popular desire to learn English has increased each year as America's international interests and commercial commitments continue to radiate in widening circles across the seas. The desire has been met by a vast complex of organizations, both national and international, British and American, public and private. The U.S. Information Service maintains 389 cultural centers in 80 countries, ranging from small circulating libraries offering English books and magazines to elaborate establishments like Amerika House in Berlin which provides programs of lectures, concerts, dances and language instruction to as many as 1,800 visitors a day. During the last year 28 million persons used the facilities of USIS centers scat-

tered around the world. Of these more than a million attended English language seminars, among them 5,000 local teachers whose combined classes represented more than two million pupils.

20 How can this worldwide and apparently insatiable demand for English be explained? None of the external factors—commercial motivations, the extended military and economic influence of the English-speaking people, circumglobal pathways of communications and travel—can adequately account for the phenomenon. The essential catalyst lies in the internal anatomy of the language itself.

21 To the advanced practitioner—the poet, novelist, essayist—English poses great difficulties by virtue of its lush vocabulary of more than half a million words and the flexibility with which they can be employed. But literature is one thing and plain talk is another. It is in the realm of plain talk that English excels. It excels by reason of its basically simple rudiments—a hard core of perhaps 1,000 energetic words which fill all the needs of ordinary communication, a few tolerant rules governing their use, and a logical underlying structure which can be taught and learned more quickly than is possible in any other language spoken today. During World War II when foreign fliers were brought to the U.S for training, it was found that a good working knowledge of English could be imparted in about 60 hours of concentrated instruction.

22 These assets, which make English so useful as an international language, derive from its history and cosmopolitan antecedents. For in the course of centuries of development it has been periodically enriched and invigorated by elements of many other tongues. Whatever its original foundations may have been, as laid down by Germanic tribes, they were altered and revised by repeated waves of invaders that crossed the Channel in historic times—the Romans, Jutes, Saxons, Angles, Viking and finally the Normans. Today English is classified as a member of the Teutonic linguistic family that also includes German, Dutch and the Scandinavian group. However more than half its vocabulary is of Latin origin, implanted either directly during the four centuries of the Roman occupation and the permanent Norman conquest or indirectly by borrowings from modern French, Spanish, Italian and Portuguese.

23 The diversified, cosmopolitan ancestry of the words in the English lexicon has been a major asset in the diffusion of the language. Of equal value is the simplicity of the grammatical conventions that govern their use. Foremost among these is the logical, down-to-earth and wholesome attitude of the English language toward sex. In the Romance languages all nouns are arbitrarily either masculine or feminine. In French, for example, *la ville* (city) and *la lune* (moon) are feminine while *le village* (village) and *le soleil* (sun) are masculine. And in German, where there are three genders to cope with, *Sonne*, (sun) is feminine, *Mond* (moon) is mascu-

line while *Weib* (woman) is neuter. To British or American students of foreign languages such distinctions seem to impose an additional task of memorizing gender as well as meaning and make no sense in a world populated by men and women, fathers and mothers, boys and girls.

24 Consider, for example, a simple French sentence: *La plume noire du vieux monsieur est perdue* (The black pen of the old gentleman is lost). The arbitrary femininity of the pen is relentlessly reiterated in the article *la,* the adjective *noire* and the participle *perdue.* There is no question, no possible shadow of doubt, that pens are female objects. But had the old gentleman lost his pencil instead of his pen, the sentence would read: *Le crayon noir du vieux monsieur est perdu,* thus establishing the maleness of pencils through every auxiliary word. And if the loss of either implement had been suffered by an old lady instead of an old gentleman, the possessive phrase would become *de la vieille dame,* involving a strikingly different form of the adjective meaning "old" and a metamorphosis of the masculine particle *du* ("of the") into the feminine *de la.*

25 Gender is only one of the many brier patches eliminated by common English usage through centuries of hacking and pruning in the thickets of grammar. The inflections (changes that reflect gender, tense, number, person, etc.) that complicate most other languages have almost entirely disappeared from English. Nouns change only to denote the possessive or plural forms and these variations are extremely simple ones. The possessive case is formed by the addition of *'s* (or by the apostrophe alone for some words already ending in *s*). The plural is formed by the easy addition of *s* (with a very few exceptions such as *foot, feet; child, children; mouse, mice; deer, deer; knife, knives*).

26 Pronouns retain some inflections, especially in the first person: *I, me, mine, we, us, ours.* But even here erosion has been at work. The second person *you* is both singular and plural, both subject and object. *Ye* has disappeared entirely, and *thou* and *thee* hold their own only among the Quakers. The relative pronoun *whom* is still mandatory in writing and in the conversation of all who cherish traditional usage, but it has given way to *who* in colloquial speech and in time will doubtless follow other inflected forms into linguistic oblivion.

27 English adjectives and adverbs completely ignore the words they modify. They change only to denote comparison, and there are only three degrees: *bright, brighter, brightest; brightly, more brightly, most brightly.*

28 Finally verbs—source of the severest headaches among language students—have lost most of their tortuous variations. In classical Greek, for example, a verb may progress through as many as 500 inflections to indicate complex interactions of tense, mood, voice, person and number. Most modern languages have reduced these complexities, but English has gone further than any other Western language in the process of evolutionary

simplification. A conjugation of the English verb *to love* clearly reveals this development, when compared with conjugations of its French and Latin equivalents, *aimer* and *amare:*

I love	J'aime	Amo
You love	Tu aimes	Amas
He loves	Il aime	Amat
She loves	Elle aime	Amat
We love	Nous aimons	Amamus
You love	Vous aimez	Amatis
They love	Ils aiment	Amant
They love	Elles aiment	Amant

29 Thus, where Latin requires six personal endings and French five, English asks only two—the attachment of an *s* to the third person singular. And in the past tense—*I loved, you loved, he loved, she loved, we loved, you loved, they loved*—there are no inflections at all.

30 The absence, or decay, of inflections in English is not an unmitigated blessing to the foreign-born student. Although it vastly reduces the amount of time which he would expend in memorizing verbal mutations in another language, it may also leave him with a sense of being adrift in an uncharted sea of new words without any formal rules of navigation. It is often difficult in English to distinguish a verb from a noun. For example, one may *slice* cheese or eat a *slice* of cheese; one may *swim* or go for a *swim;* one may *call* a friend on the telephone or receive a telephone *call,* or *call* for help, or leave a *call* for 7 A.M. Such free interchange of function among the parts of speech, while one of the delights of the English language, also creates a condition which the late Edward Sapir, Sterling Professor of Anthropology and Linguistics at Yale, described as "masked complexity." "Anyone who takes the trouble to examine these [difficulties] carefully," Sapir observed, "will soon see that behind the superficial appearance of simplicity there is concealed a perfect hornet's nest of bizarre and arbitrary usages."

31 The heart of the hornet's nest lies in the realm of little words. In the vast lexicon of English, thousands of precise, highly specialized and often elegant words flower side by side with small, easy-to-learn, highly flexible parts of speech. It is one of the marvelous endowments of English that these two species of words—the specialized and the general—complement, augment, define and analyze each other. Thus one may *extinguish a fire* or *put out a fire; dismount* or *get off; ascend* or *go up.*

32 The special formula of little-verb-plus-preposition is the key to a quick grasp of English speech, if not necessarily to a gracious literary style. In 1920 two Cambridge scholars, Dr. I. A. Richards, now of Harvard, and the late C. K. Ogden, discovered while collaborating on a book about Eng-

lish semantics (entitled *The Meaning of Meaning*) that a few hundred key words could do all the real work in their analyses of other words and idioms. After 10 years of lexicological labor Ogden evolved what is known as Basic English—an elixir, distilled from the ancient wine of our language, of 850 volatile, versatile words that can say just about anything that needs to be said in ordinary talk.

33 The critical discovery made by Richards and Ogden was that their stripped-down lexicon required only 18 verbs—as against 4,000 to 10,000 that may be available in the vocabulary of a college-educated man. The 18 vital verbs are: *be, come, do, get, give, go, have, keep, let, make, may, put, say, see, seem, send, take* and *will*. The ability of these verbs to do the work of all the others stems from their gift of entering into an astonishing number of mergers with prepositions. Thus a combination like *give up* can cover the pivotal meanings of *abandon, abdicate, abjure, cease, cede, desert, desist, discontinue, forego, forsake, relinquish, renounce, resign, sacrifice, stop, succumb, surrender, vacate, withdraw* and *yield*.

34 It is evident that the little words of English constitute a kind of inner voice—a language within a language—capable of understudying most of the flashier ornaments of the Oxford English Dictionary and Webster's Unabridged. Because they cover so much ground they can be of enormous value to the English novitiate. Each one pinch-hits for hundreds of more complex if subtler words, and they are relatively simple to spell and pronounce.

35 But their simplicity is deceptive. They can be used in so many ways that their very versatility can create confusion in the mind of the learner. Contemplate, for example, the little word *up*. Most of the time it behaves like a preposition, indicating direction (*He lives up the street*). But it can also masquerade as an adverb (*It's time to get up*), a noun (*Every life has its ups and downs*), a verb (*I'll up you five dollars*) or an adjective (*The sun is up*). In addition to its multiple function in the combination *give up*, it plays a ubiquitous and sometimes superfluous role in a variety of other expressions, such as *add up, clean up, do up, drink up, hurry up, join up, line up, lock up, mix up, offer up, pay up, play up, ring up, set up, stop up, tie up, tidy up, wake up, wash up, work up, wrap up, up to now* and *up to you*. To the foreign student it seems paradoxical that the same meaning is conveyed by *his house burned up* and *his house burned down; my wife isn't up yet* and *my wife isn't down yet; the train slowed up* and *the train slowed down*. Even more bewildering are those situations where utterly unrelated concepts are evoked by one and the same phrase—*e.g., make up*, whose transient meaning depends on whether the context is cosmetics (*She takes an hour to make up her face*), indecision (*I just can't make up my mind*), domesticity (*Let's make up the bed*), forgiveness (*Kiss and make up*), fiction (*I'll make up some kind of a story*) or atonement (*Some day I'll make up for this mistake*).

36 The puzzles presented by prepositions confuse not only the foreign student but also those born to the English tongue and most particularly those teachers and writers whose obligation it is to employ them correctly. The little words are sticky, fussy, elusive words even for those who have lived and worked with them all their lives. However, the pragmatic glory of English is that it is able to convey meaning even when grammar goes out the window. It matters little if a Frenchman, instead of saying, "I have been here for two hours," says "I am here since two hours." Either is intelligible to anyone who understands English. And it is because of the infinite elasticity of the English language that the many varieties of broken English have evolved, giving rise to such immortal phrases as "*Him big chief paleface*" and "*No tickee, no shirtee,*" and making possible communication without grammar the world around.

37 This language form recently has achieved an ultimate in richness and conciseness among its new creators in Nigeria. There according to Professor Frederick W. Harbison, a Princeton economist who has often visited Nigeria, a boy who finishes grade school is known as a *megotbuk* (pronounced me-got-book). A boy who graduates from college is a *bigbigbuk*. And the exceptional young man who has studied at Oxford and returns home trailing clouds of culture is a *bintojaguarfridgful*—a handy contraction for "He has been to England and come home with a Jaguar and enough money to keep a refrigerator full of frozen foods."

38 The most excruciating difficulties encountered by the serious foreign student who wishes to learn to write English, as well as speak it, involve neither grammar nor syntax but rather the chaotic lack of correlation between its spelling and pronunciation. The inconsistencies are so multifarious and grotesque that foreigners are not alone in deploring them. Most Americans cannot spell correctly, and for even the most cultivated of professional men on both shores of the Atlantic the incoherent character of English orthography is a timeless problem. It is when the novice endeavors to discern some trace of conformity between the sound and spelling of English words that he gets in trouble.

39 The favorite scapegoat of critics of English orthography is the vestigial *ough* monstrosity, which can be pronounced in nine different ways, none of them related phonetically to the letters involved—viz., *tough, though, thought, thorough, through, bough, cough, drought, hiccough*. In another ambush the foreign student encounters homonyms—words that sound alike but are spelled differently and have different meanings—such as *pair, pear* and *pare; beat* and *beet, meat* and *meet; grate* and *great; peace* and *piece; sew* and *so; there, their* and *they're*. But in another part of the forest he is waylaid by pairs of words, twins of identical spelling, which are pronounced quite differently and serve different grammatical functions e.g., the verb *read* (present tense) and *read* (past tense); the nouns *tear*

(in the eye) and *tear* (in the sheet); the verb *lead* and the noun *lead;* the noun *con'tract* and verb *contract'*.

40 Periodically professional and amateur apostles of consistency and simplicity have tried to get rid of these difficulties. The most notable recent crusader was the late George Bernard Shaw, who provided in his will for a bequest of £500 to be awarded to the inventor of a new alphabet that would most nearly effect a phonetic wedding of sound and symbol. As an example of the lunacy of English spelling, Shaw constructed the word *ghoti*. He pointed out the *gh* combination is pronounced like *f* in *cough;* the vowel *o* is pronounced like a short i in the word *women;* and the *ti* combination is pronounced like *sh* in the word *nation*. Hence *ghoti* is pronounced *fish*.

41 Although Shaw's bequest was disposed of two years ago—divided equally among four contestants—the Oxford English Dictionary remains intact today. For despite all the idiosyncrasies of English spelling and the continual complaints against it, those who use the language cherish it. Defenders of the traditional spelling point out, quite correctly, that the written form of any English word reveals its etymology; it may afford no clue as to pronunciation, but its ancestry is clearly disclosed. In the diversified letter combinations of English words one may read the long, tumultuous history of the British Isles. So far as American spelling is concerned, about all that has been effected since the days of Noah Webster are a few minuscule changes: the u has been dropped from *honour* and *colour*, for example, and occasionally one encounters words like *tonite, thruway* and *altho*. It would seem that the English-speaking people of the U.S., like those of the U.K., are reluctant to surrender their antiquated, irrational, exasperating, obsolete, indefensible, crazy, mixed-up system of spelling. The American attitude was perhaps epitomized by Mark Twain when he remarked, "Simplified spelling is all right; but, like chastity, you can carry it too far."

42 For all its flaws, however, English is being adopted everywhere in the most insidious way of all, by infiltrating the other languages. Many English and American words are now completely international, not merely understood but spoken and published around the world. Among the most familiar of these, universally employed on every continent, are: *baby sitter, bar, bridge, boyfriend, best-seller, bus, beefsteak, cocktail, cover girl, cowboy, gangster, goddam, hamburger, holdup, hot dog, ice cream, jazz, juice, jeep, knockout, nightclub, party, pipeline, pin-up, racket, sandwich, shorts, sex appeal, striptease, whisky* and *weekend*. It goes without saying that for years *okay* has been a universal expression of assent. It underwent a significant variation when Premier Khrushchev added a modifier, during his tour of the U.S., by exclaiming on several occasions, "Very okay."

43 This diffusion would have pleased one of the great architects of the language, Dr. Samuel Johnson, who cherished his mother tongue. "Wondrous the English language," he once exclaimed, "language of live men!"

STUDY GUIDE

Structure

1. This essay, like the previous one, is an excellent example of the development of ideas through the use of multiple concrete examples. Study particularly paragraphs 4, 5, and 6, 15 and 16, 18, 20, 40, and 43 from this viewpoint.

2. In paragraphs 23–30, Barnett develops the idea that the English language is easily spread because of assets which it derives from its history. What are these assets?

3. Show how the last two paragraphs of the essay serve as an interesting conclusion and bring the reader around to the point with which the essay began.

Imagery

1. There are several striking *metaphors* that add interest and life to the expression. Study, for instance, the effect of the sequence of metaphors in paragraphs 17 and 18: "one of many *channels*," "*torrent* of English is inundating all lands," "other tributary *freshets*," "the *flood* of English," "the incipient *stage*."

2. Barnett writes that "Gender is only one of the many *brier patches* eliminated by common English usage through centuries of *hacking* and *pruning* in the *thickets* of grammar." Discuss the added expressiveness that metaphor has given to this sentence in contrast to the revision which follows: "Gender is only one of the difficulties eliminated by common English usage through centuries of simplifying some of the complexities of gender agreement in other languages."

3. Discuss the relative expressiveness of the following two sentences: "Although it [the absence of inflections] vastly reduces the amount of time which he would expend in memorizing verbal mutations in another language, it may also leave him with a sense of *being adrift in an uncharted sea* of new words *without any formal rules of navigation*" and ". . . it may also leave him *with a sense of confusion* and *without any rules to guide him*."

AMERICAN PROSE TODAY

Geoffrey Moore

It is a natural, simple, and unaffected speech
that I love, so written as it is spoken, and
such upon the paper as it is in the mouth,

Reprinted from pp. 47–70, *New World Writing* (New York: New American Library of World Literature, Inc., 1955), by permission of the author.

a pithy, sinewy, full, strong, conpendious
and material speech, not so delicate and
affected as vehement and piercing. . . .
—FLORIO'S MONTAIGNE

1 "We have really everything in common with America—except, of course, the language." Oscar Wilde's witticism still has some truth, although, like mother-of-pearl, it changes colour according to the angle of view. It is true that some British readers have, or pretend to have, difficulty with some American writing. Different terms for the same thing can sometimes be puzzling; unfamiliar idioms, reference to objects or institutions unknown in England, and a slicker, wilder sense of humour even more so. Fashionables, particularly literary fashionables, affect remarks like "I couldn't quite follow all the jokes—that peculiar dialect, is it *Bronx?*" (see G. S. Fraser, "The Aesthete and the Sensationalist," *Partisan Review*, April, 1955). And there are even a dogged few of the Old Guard who cry "Beaver!" whenever they recognise an Americanism, and send a fiery letter to their favourite fourpenny. However, the majority of the English are by now hopelessly lost. It's not merely that "O.K." is widely used among the working-class and lower-middle-class and that errand boys and young clerks say "I don't get you" and "I haven't seen him in years." But—oh, more horrible still—even our distinguished worthies use American words and phrases, and in their written style, moreover. H. W. Horwill once made a list, including "proposition," "up against" (it), "disgruntled," and "out to" (increase efficiency) which had been used by such unimpeachably British personages as Sir Winston Churchill, the Archbishop of York, Sir Michael Sadler, and Sir William Holdsworth. In fact, the process has gone so far that even those purists who would rather die than be discovered committing an Americanism unconsciously use words of American origin in normal usage. Leafing through a dictionary of American English, one finds, on almost every page, words which are now commonly accepted in England as English—"in the neighbourhood of" (say, a million pounds), "landslide" (for the English "landslip"), "to take a cut" (in wages). Even "boarding-house," "business man," "graveyard," "law-abiding," "overcoat" and "telegram" are American importations; and there are a great many more, some of them now abandoned in their country of origin.

2 The influence of American usages, most of them new, but some from an English older than that now current in Britain, may be put to detailed proof by reference to the dictionary of Sir William Craigie and Professor Hulbert and that of Professor M. M. Mathews, and, among numerous other books, to H. L. Mencken's cocksure but massively documented *The American Language* and its *Supplements*. But most readers would, I think, be willing to accept, without proof, the statement that, in certain respects, American English has a dynamic which British English no longer possesses.

It can be found in that popular and picturesque style common to detective stories and Hollywood movies (so popular in fact that English writers like Peter Cheyney and James Hadley Chase have worked hard to supply a pastiche of it). It can be found in the vivid American phrases of each new generation, from "what makes him tick" and "to blow one's top" to "out of this world" and "strictly from hunger" (when I was at school it was "Sez you!")—embarrassing clichés already, of course, but nonethelss vivid. It can be found more pervasively, however, in less sensational words which, for over a hundred and fifty years, have been forcing their way into general Anglo-American usage—words like "belittle," "demoralizing," and "lengthy."

3 But, say we accept these facts, what do they tell us? Merely that a great new nation, in an expanding and optimistic frame of mind, has been striking out in all directions, coining new words and phrases, and using accepted ones in new contexts. It is, after all, only what we might have expected. What is more interesting is to inquire whether this great new nation has by now developed a distinctive prose, expressive of its spirit. We do not quarrel these days about whether there is not an American literature. There plainly is, and we can point to its various aspects and analyse, within reason, its characteristics. But is there such a thing as an American prose? I refer here to nonfiction, the prose of exposition, the ordinary literary means of communication.

4 The sophist might answer: Yes, American prose is prose written by Americans. But, we persist: Is it different from English prose, and, if so, how? Or, alternatively: Is there "an American style"? The answer might be that there are a number of American styles and that they owe their nature to the circumstances of American development. Not merely racial, or religious, or social differences, but, as Mr. Wallace Stevens once said, physical ones too, have made the attitude of the people different, and the attitude of a people is reflected in its prose. Add to this the spirit which founded the United States, the early struggles, the theocratic art-banishing society of New England, the early establishment of a unique kind of democracy, the distrust of aristocratic virtues (elegance, propriety, mannered grace, intellect) and the acceptance of brotherhood-become-chumminess, and you have a taste of the brew which might be expected to make American prose different from British. From the first, the American moved about a lot and so, despite the difference in accent between, say, South Carolina and New Hampshire, usage was sufficiently standard that he could be understood in any part of the country. In England, however, as Mr. Harold Whitehall has pointed out, the inhabitants of, for example, Howden in Yorkshire used to find it very difficult to understand the inhabitants of Dewsbury, forty miles away. And so, largely on the basis of aristocratic speech, Britain developed a *lingua franca*, Received Standard English, the

rules of which could be laid down and accepted as gospel. H. W. Fowler could write a *Modern English Usage,* but no American ever either dared to write, or felt the necessity of writing, a *Modern American Usage.* Mr. Horwill, an Englishman, did, of course, produce one, but that was for the aid of the British. However, there seems, by this time, to have developed a generally accepted and, as it were, legitimate body of American usage which can be called Standard without fear of offending Americans' own susceptibilities. At least I take it to be so and, with this in mind, I should like to examine various examples of modern "expositional" American prose in an effort to discover whether they have the "independence and vigour" which, in 1954, *The Times Literary Supplement* found so marked in American creative writing. Although this will involve commenting on usage, I do not propose to single out American usages which are now perfectly acceptable in Britain.

Political Prose

> *My purpose was to sketch the genesis and set in some crude historical perspective the present troubled world scene, and then to attempt to defrost a tiny segment of the opaque window through which we see others and others see us—and to do it briefly, having listened to many lectures myself!*

5 This is from the foreword to Adlai Stevenson's *Call to Greatness.* Two things are immediately noticeable: first, the modest tone, and, second, the use of an original figure of speech which has been drawn naturally and unaffectedly from American experience. Almost all Americans, except those who live in the extreme Southern states, find it necessary at some time during the winter to "defrost," either manually or by aid of a device built into their cars, a driving window which has been made opaque by frost or frozen snow. The style might be described as "literary" (e.g., "genesis," "present troubled world scene"), yet it gives an impression of ease. It has the ring of sincerity and makes us feel that we can trust a man who is at once so unpretentious and yet so quietly convinced that he can clarify our vision of world affairs.

6 Having come to the above conclusion about this passage, I was surprised, on re-reading it, to find that it is actually ungrammatical. I say "surprised" since, as a teacher, my eye is, if anything over-alert to such things. The fault is in the first line, in which, to make grammatical sense, there should be an "of" after "genesis." It gives a very awkward ring to the sentence, however, and the writer, being American, was led to reject it. An Englishman would probably either have put it in or re-worded the sentence. It is, I think, a good example of how even the most educated and highly

literate of Americans have, when they feel like it, a cavalier attitude toward the niceties of grammar. I have noticed that in the *non solum, sed etiam* construction, for example, Americans rarely put in the "also."

Scientific Prose

> (a) *It was not until the nineteenth century and Faraday that the full richness of space began to be understood: how it could be the seat not only of gravitational forces produced by the mass of material particles but of electric and magnetic forces produced by their charges. Even in Newton's day it was clear that there were very strong forces at work in lending to material objects their solidity.*

> (b) *In regard to sexual response there is very little precise information concerning the role of those portions of the cord which lie above (anterior) to the sacro-lumbar area. As long as genital and pelvic responses were considered the major portion or even the whole of sexual response, and as long as the demonstrated function of the sacro-lumbar area seemed to account for all genital and pelvic responses, there was a tacit assumption that the thoracic and cervical areas of the cord had little or no direct connection with sexual behavior.*

7 The first extract is from J. Robert Oppenheimer's BBC Reith Lectures for 1953; the second is from Dr. Alfred C. Kinsey's (and others') *Sexual Behavior in the Human Female.* In both, fairly long sentences are handled with skill. But there is a great difference in tone between the two pieces. Although both deal with factual scientific material, the writer of the first piece seems alive to the larger, even metaphysical implications, of his subject matter. His prose has an imagination and breadth of understanding which light up the scientific detail. This is shown by the choice of such words as "richness" (to describe space) and "seat" (a less imaginative writer might have written "source"). The skilful use of the colon and the writing of the last sentence, particularly, reveal a writer who has an ear for English prose. A more ham-fisted writer might have reversed the last few words, ending with a dull and factual thud on "lending solidity to material objects." But, as it is, the writing is instinct with personality, yet with a personality which is in no sense exploited.

8 The second passage, although authoritative, has an institutional ring, as might perhaps be expected of the work of a group of zoologists and statisticians. The dullness of the tone is set, first of all, by the consistent, even persistent, use of the third person, elsewhere combined with the passive voice (the first person plural would have been unexceptionable, and lighter on the ear). "In regard to" is an ungraceful worn-out phrase, the insensitive writer's self-starter. A happier phrasing might have run "We have very little precise information about the role in sexual response of those

portions. . . ." etc. The "there was a tacit assumption" of the last sentence is orotund, a cliché, in fact, much used by people who wish to give an impression of sonorousness and authority. It shows the same lack of care for language which allowed the writers to forget that, in the third line, the preposition "to" belongs *inside* the bracket.

Historical Prose

(a) *As the sectional tension increased, the sense of irrepressible differences, long buried in the national consciousness, began to burst into the clear. The growing pressure on the North had finally persuaded many Northerners that the slavery system embodied a fundamental threat to free society.*

(b) *August gave way to September, September to October, and the clamor grew increasingly furious. Jackson men paraded the streets in the glare of torches, singing campaign songs, carrying hickory poles, gathering around huge bonfires blazing high into the night.*

9 These two extracts are both from Arthur M. Schlesinger, Jr.'s *The Age of Jackson*. Together they make a point better than one alone, and that point is that the methods and the vocabulary of the journalist have invaded the writing of history. (cf., *Time,* April 22, 1955, "Warm in the April sunshine, London's upper-crust horseplayers crowded the club enclosure at Kempton Park Race Track. Peeresses in Dior tweeds appraised each other. . . ." etc.) The tone is different. *Time's* is not merely colourful; it is impertinent. Mr. Schlesinger is not writing sensationally, he is merely trying to "bring the scene to life." Although he is in no sense perverting the facts, he is nonetheless "popularising" history. And since he is not merely a famous historian, but also an academic one, approved of academically, the method is worth remarking on. It is not entirely new. Strachey was, of course, a populariser and, so to pick an example from a number of others, was Philip Guedalla; but the texture of these English writers was finer grained, more glittering. Mr. Schlesinger's style, although it is not bad, is without flair, bouncy yet workaday ("as sectional tension increased," "embodied a fundamental threat"), with an occasional, rather disconcerting vernacular phrase (e.g., "into the clear"). It is the style of a man who has not thought much about language. The four parts of Mr. Schlesinger's first sentence create four different effects. The first gives us the sense of *pulling,* the second of energy contained under *pressure,* like steam in a kettle, the third *buries* this steam kettle, the fourth allows it to "burst into the clear" which seems superficially to fit with the idea of "irrepressible differences," but is vaguely disconcerting until we realize that the stress is on "into the clear," which is a hunting term. There is, in other words, a confusion of

different kinds of language. This is for me a most interesting discovery, since I did not pick Mr. Schlesinger invidiously, but in a spirit of enquiry, knowing him to be one of the most outstanding of the younger American historians.

Critical Prose

(a) *Such an art when it pretends to measure life is essentially vicarious; it is a substitute for something that never was—like a tin soldier, or Peter Pan. It has all the flourish of life and every sentimental sincerity. Taken for what it is, it is charming and even instructive. Taken solemnly, as it is meant to be, the distortion by which it exists is too much for it, and it seems a kind of baby-talk.*

(b) . . . *aesthetic value has been defined as conformity to or expression of a culture. This is the side of formism most prevalent today. A work of art has aesthetic value in proportion as it gives expression to its age. This definition tends to run over into a cultural relativism very congenial to contemporary art historians, and in marked contrast to the universality of aesthetic values emphasized in the first formulation of aesthetic value for formism above as representation of the universal.*

(c) *There is nothing to do different from what we already do: if poets write poems and readers read them, each as best they can—if they try to live not as soldiers or voters or intellectuals or economic men, but as human beings—they are doing all that can be done. But to expect them (by, say, reciting one-syllable poems over the radio) to bring back that Yesterday in which people stood on chairs to look at Lord Tennyson, is to believe that General Motors can bring back "the tradition of craftsmanship" by giving, as it does, prizes to Boy Scouts for their scale-models of Napoleonic coaches; to believe that the manners of the past can be restored by encouraging country-people to say* Grüss Gott *or* Howdy, stranger *to the tourists they meet along summer lanes.*

10 The first extract is from R. P. Blackmur's essay on the verse of E. E. Cummings in *The Double Agent*; the second is from Stephen C. Pepper's *The Basis of Criticism in the Arts*; and the third from Randall Jarrell's *Poetry and the Age*. The field of criticism in the United States is so rich that I should have preferred to take at least two or three more examples—from Edmund Wilson, say, or Van Wyck Brooks, or the late F. O. Matthiessen. However, these three samples do at least reveal three important aspects of American criticism. The second passage is of the kind which is so often the target for British writers—jargon criticism. I could have quoted more extreme examples (from Kenneth Burke, for instance) for there is a great deal of this kind of thing, particularly in academic or semi-academic writing, of which there is so much more in the United

States than anywhere else. I think of it sometimes as a Germanic derivation. "The side of formism," "cultural relativism," and the garbled mumble of the end of the final sentence—this is the antithesis of clarity. Perhaps it is the result of Coleridge's example; he learnt from Germany too. Perhaps it is the overseriousness and earnestness of the American commentator. Perhaps it is a little of the unconscious desire to blind the vulgar with science. Perhaps it is an attempt to order a frighteningly vast world of thought and feeling. Perhaps it is—as Marius Bewley suggested of Kenneth Burke—that these "methodological" critics have developed their jargon and their unreadable style in order to isolate them "against the shock of the work of art itself." But, whatever the reason, the effect is both exasperating and perturbing.

11 The Blackmur passage, on the other hand, is a good illustration of what we mean when we say that someone's writing "has style." The language is both elegant and precise, the manner judicious but not portentous, flavored by just the right amount of everyday reference ("tin soldier, or Peter Pan" and "baby-talk"). It is the writing of an acute sensibility. We cannot help feeling the force of the conviction behind the sentiments, not only because of what they say but because of the manner of their expression. The language is faintly Jamesian, ("all the flourish of life and every sentimental sincerity"). The final effect is of a man who respects literature too much to make it merely a stamping-ground for pseudo-scientific theories.

12 Mr. Jarrell, in his conversational ease, his common sense and his liveliness, is representative of the younger generation of American critics. He will not allow his individual perception and spirit to be subdued by the acceptances of academic style and theory. His is a style of wit and irony, which can sometimes approach the self-consciously brilliant but is anchored to earth (and this is why it is so effective for most readers) by the essential rightness of the sentiments. The style is more noticeably idiosyncratic than Mr. Blackmur's. It is perceptive, impressionistic, and opinionated. But in the last resort it obtains its effects by laying the cards on the table and saying, as it were, "Now, after all. . . ." Only a man with a wide cultural background and a sureness of judgment based on good taste can afford to do this. Finally, the style achieves a vividness and concreteness by reference to manners and institutions well known in American life.

Humorous Prose

(a) *I have a lot of other notes jotted down about why I hate women, but I seem to have lost them all, except one. That one is to the effect that I hate women because, while they never lose old snapshots or anything of that sort they invariably lose one glove. I believe that I have never gone anywhere with any woman in my whole life who did not lose one glove. I have searched for single gloves under tables in crowded restaurants and under feet of people in darkened movie theatres. I have spent some part of every day or night hunting for a woman's glove. If there were no other reason in the world for hating women, that one would be enough. In fact, you can leave all the others out.*

(b) *I first heard pure Slurvian fluently spoken by a co-worker of mine who told me that his closest friend was a man named Hard (Howard). Hard was once in an automobile accident, his car, unfortunately, cliding with another, causing Hard's wife, Dorthy, who was with him, to claps. Dorthy didn't have much stamina but was a sweet woman—sweet as surp.*

13 The first passage is from James Thurber's *Let Your Mind Alone!*, the second is from John Davenport's "Slurvian Self-Taught." They seem to me to show two sides of American humour, both deriving perhaps from the frontier tradition. Despite its urbanity, the Thurber piece is in the tradition of Mark Twain, the father of the American natural style and one of the first to use the device of exaggeration (the "tall tale") successfully as a literary mode. As Mark Twain in his descriptive passages and essays used the simple, common "conversational" style and idiom of his day, so Mr. Thurber uses the natural "conversational" style of our day. I perhaps ought to explain what I mean by "conversational." By this I understand the vernacular of the ordinary educated person translated into literature (notice the direct "I," and "in my whole life"). While, therefore, it is "a conversational style," it is not exactly as it would be in spontaneous speech. "Invariably," for example, and "I have" would sound a little mannered if actually spoken by one friend to another. Actual speech usage would be too clumsy for a writer whose effects are as subtly obtained as Mr. Thurber's. The humour, which I find irresistible, arises from exaggerating a fairly common situation. The writer is half-serious, half-joking, and the hit-on the funny-bone effect is helped by the direct and simple language, and by the masterly sense of timing. The last sentence is both a parting shot and an ending which gathers up the whole of the essay.

14 The second extract is deadpan, and achieves its effect by being written as if it were a sort of anecdotal reminiscence by a professional investigator of linguistics. This level is allowed to merge into the level of overt humour, as in the last sentence of the passage quoted. It could not, I feel, have been written by anyone but an American, because no one but an American could have the knowledge of and feeling for the vernacular (slurred or otherwise) which this writer displays. The sense of timing which both writers exploit so magnificently seems to be a part of the American temperament (to ask why arouses some interesting anthro-

pological and sociological speculations). It is displayed outside literature by such comedians as Jack Benny and Fred Allen. The former, particularly, builds easily on the natural cadences of American speech, in which there runs a faint but constant undercurrent of humour.

Letters: Official and Otherwise

(a) *Keeping company with these people in their notion is the man who gets a hard-to-understand Government letter. To be sure, he is peeved upon being muddled by a phrase such as "noncompensable evaluation heretofore assigned," but he is seldom really mad.*

15 This is not from a letter but from an American government manual telling officials how to write letters more economically and less pretentiously (*Plain Letters*, published by the U. S. National Archives and Records Service in Washington, March 1955). The writer, Miss Mona Sheppard, "staff specialist in correspondence management," has fallen, in her desire to avoid officialese and use what she calls, after Franklin K. Lane, "straightaway English," into another kind of jargon, the jargon of chumminess. Perhaps I am morbidly sensitive, but to read this passage chills my spine and raises my hackles. It is full of the kind of matey journalese which is found not only in the newspapers and on the radio but in bank circulars, advertising letters, exhortations from alumni associations, or invitations to Old Home Week with the Elks. My complaint is not with colloquial American, as such, which is extremely effective when used with skill and discrimination, by, say, Thurber, or Robert Benchley, or E. B. White, or the general run of *New Yorker* writers (or funny in a sad sort of way, when used creatively, by, say, Ring Lardner). My complaint is rather with the barbarous tone of this specimen, the absence of feeling for the values of words, the sheer lack of grace. "Keeping company with these people in their notion" is roundabout and ugly. "Hard-to-understand" is an example of the prostitution of English which is increasingly found in British as well as American daily journalism. But if I spend any longer on this passage I shall get mad too.

16 The language of the model letters which the Manual holds up for approval is not quite so ungraceful as the language of the instructions, but it is frequently inept, equally lacking in any sort of ear for the English language. And since, at this point, I anticipate cries of rage, and, possibly, of misunderstanding, from the direction of Washington, let me say that Style, as I understand it, is at the farthest possible remove from ornament, flourish, or affectation. It is, in Sir Arthur Quiller-Couch's words, "the power to touch with ease, grace, precision, any note in the gamut of human thought or emotion." "But essentially," Sir Arthur goes on, "it resembles

good manners. It comes of endeavouring to understand others, of thinking for them rather than for yourself. . . ." (This is a point that the jargon critics would well bear in mind.)

> (b) *You make me feel very much at home in Pittsburgh. I like the people I meet there; and I am enthusiastic about the job you are doing. But I would be showing rank favoritism if I were to move to go out there to start off your Institute. I have to catch up with my obligations in other parts of the country. I am, of course, flattered that you asked me to come.*

17 This extract, from a letter held up as a good example for Government letter writers, breathes insincerity through its very heartiness. The punctuation and grammar (the placing of the semicolon and the use of "would" instead of "should") are the work of an imperfectly educated man, and the cliché, "showing rank favoritism," clashes horribly with the self-consciously colloquial "to move to go out there to start off. . . ." This is the literary equivalent of the glad hand, and just as distasteful.

18 The fact that the best letter in *Plain Letters* is by Abraham Lincoln is ominous. President Lincoln's letter is exact, entirely unaffected, and through its very simplicity, a noble piece of writing, worthy to be quoted in full. It runs:

> WASHINGTON, July 13, 1863
>
> MAJOR GENERAL GRANT. *My Dear General: I do not remember that you and I ever met personally. I write this now as a grateful acknowledgment for the almost inestimable service you have done the country. I wish to say a word further. When you first reached the vicinity of Vicksburg, I thought you should do what you finally did—march the troops across the neck, run the batteries with the transports, and thus go below; and I never had any faith, except a general hope that you knew better than I, that the Yazoo Pass expedition and the like could succeed. When you got below and took Port Gibson, Grand Gulf, and vicinity, I thought you should go down the river and join General Banks, and when you turned northward, east of the Big Black, I feared it was a mistake. I now wish to make the personal acknowledgment that you were right and I was wrong.*
>
> *Yours very truly,*
> *A. Lincoln*

19 There is one last, interesting point about this American government manual. It concerns itself only with letters written by officials to the general public. The British Government publication, *The Complete Plain Words* (1954), written by Sir Ernest Gowers, (who is not a "staff specialist in correspondence management" but merely an educated man) is by comparison "pure," being concerned with the encouragement of good, clear prose in whatever kind of communication. The idea that clear prose

ought to be encouraged *because* it establishes better communication, and relations, between the Government and the public, would, I am sure, be abhorrent to Sir Ernest, as it would to any man of principle.

Journalistic Prose

20 In a democratic country, in which almost everyone can read and in which everyone is supposed to have equal opportunities for education, or for anything else, one might expect to find a "typical" or "representative" American style, in the kind of publication which is read by the majority. According to figures taken from the polls of the Princeton Institute of Public Opinion and Mr. J. K. Wood's *Magazines of the United States*, although only approximately 20 per cent of Americans read books at all, 83 per cent regularly read newspapers and magazines.

NEWSPAPERS

(a) *Secretary of Agriculture Ezra Taft Benson has called on western Kansas farmers to begin a day of "prayer and supplication to ask God in heaven to send rain." Well, that's one way of stopping the good Kansas dirt from blowing over to Russia. It's certainly not the best way. The secretary has made a tour; he's impressed. But first and foremost the secretary is a politician, not a conservationist. It will take a little more than politics to keep that western Kansas dirt on the ground.*

21 This passage from a student newspaper editorial seems clear and direct—"conversational," "natural," in fact, yet not altogether or ingenuously so. The tone is cocky. "Secretary of Agriculture Ezra Taft Benson" is borrowed from *Time's* style, which was presumably invented to give the impression that everybody's time, including *Time's*, was limited. Yet the saving of one three-letter word and two commas is not worth the ungracefulness of the usage. One feels that the writer is breathing down one's neck. A cliché slips in ("first and foremost"). "Impressed" gives one a feeling of inadequately describing Mr. Benson's possible reactions. Noticeable American usages are "called on," which has a Town Meeting ring, and "politician," which in England means someone in politics but in the United States is a bad word.

(b) *Reed's number one problem is working capital. So in order to get money for equipment and to meet his payroll until he gets to rolling, he is incorporating the business and plans to sell stock. The telephone switchboard will be installed soon and within the next few weeks he plans to have a grand opening.*

22 This is from an article in the *St. Louis Post-Dispatch*, and is subcolloquial. It reads like a cross between the vernacular and the language of

radio copy-writers—more the latter. Few in conversation talk about their "number one" problem, but writers of "commercials" do. "Meet his payroll" and "get to rolling" are examples of those vivid coinages which arise out of a forceful expanding society in which the tone of general prose is set by the majority, who have no ear for subtlety of language. They are designed to give an impressionistic picture to people whose range of communication, understanding, and imagination is narrow. This kind of prose does not work through the intelligence but through the emotions. The repetition of "get" and "plan" emphasises the narrowness of the vocabulary. Within its limits it is a most effective kind of communication, and sufficiently hard-punching to penetrate the dullest mind capable of reading words on a page. It is an example of American pragmatism. It is probably inevitable in a democratic society in which the mass media have superseded the printed page as the chief means of communication. It reflects the speech and the habits of mind of the majority of people and it would be sentimental, ineffectual, and entirely unrealistic (not to say reactionary) for one to regret that this particular form of speech ever invaded prose. But one does.

> (c) *The Pakistan grain storage contract presents a flagrant case of official negligence and mismanagement. Any monkey business with government contracts can and should be a matter of public concern. So we have this relatively small item of grain elevators grown into a national story.*

> (d) *For the present, and with all due consideration of both Soviet aims and motivations, it appears as if the Soviets are prepared to give ground at least in part and at least at one point—Austria. After stalling and sabotaging the Austrian treaty in more than 260 treaty meetings stretching over nearly a decade, they have now reached agreement with Austria on the terms of liberation which, barring new Soviet demands, the West is likely to accept.*

23 These two passages are from editorials, the first in the *Kansas City Star* for May 4, 1955, the second from *The New York Times* for May 2, 1955. The most noticeable thing about the first is the way in which it combines an elevated and judicious style with colloquialisms. "Presents a flagrant case" in the first passage consorts oddly with "monkey business." The grave "can and should be a matter of public concern" is immediately followed by the colloquial "So we have this . . . ," as one might say, to a friend, "So we have this fellow (or car, or problem) on our hands." This lack of taste, of consistency of tone, of feeling for what is appropriate in the context may arise from the comparative lack of literary training in American, particularly Middle Western schools. *The New York Times* passage is a much better piece of writing and much more of a piece. It is

much less "literary" than a leader in the London *Times* would be, but more pompous. To some extent, "stalling," which is vivid and vernacular, conflicts with the high editorial style ("all due consideration").

MAGAZINES

(a) *The only comment on the American economy that can be made with perfect assurance is that nobody really understands it. On the whole, this is a good thing. An economy capable of being thoroughly understood would probably prove treacherous. Of course, there are always a few professionals who like to believe that they understand the American economy, and these people turn up at Congressional hearings to explain why the market acts the way it does, but it is quite obvious that they are just groping their way along, the same as everybody else.*

24 This is from the editorial page of *The New Yorker* entitled "Talk of the Town," the nearest thing to the essay one can find in the United States today. It is highly intelligent and professionally polished, yet intimate and engaging in its manner. The man who wrote this passage did have an ear, and he did have taste. The short second sentence picks up an echo both of the New York Yiddish colloquialism "This is a good thing?" and the British (*1066 and All That*) "a Good Thing," and yet is simply effective without these probably unintended connotations. The third sentence is disarming. It is as sensitively balanced as a line of verse. "Treacherous" strikes one as being just the right word; no other will do. It is meaningful, connotative, and funny, yet not fancy. "Of course," "these people," and "the same as everybody else" keep the level down, an important thing in a milieu in which ceremony or over-refinement are quickly smelled out. This kind of prose mirrors the most attractive kind of American personality, that of a man, who is polite but not deferential, droll, easy in manner, and responsive.

(b) *Barsov went. At his own request, the U.S. authorities flew him to Linz. "Are you sure you want to go back?" they asked him at the end. He was.*

The Soviets had a propaganda bonanza in Barsov; they pointed to him as an example of what happens to those who desert the Soviets and trust the West.

25 This quotation from an article in the *Reader's Digest* is an example of "bright" snappy journalism. The clipped style ("Barsov went," "He was.") probably owes something to the Walter Winchell manner of radio reporting. The American slang word "bonanza" (a rich strike) is a good choice since it adds, like a raccoon's tail to a streamlined car, a human touch to prose which is in danger of becoming cold through its professional terseness. This prose is tailored for "modern people," who, after a

day in the office or the factory, believe that the best way to relax is by not mentally taxing themselves. It has, therefore, a "cat on the mat" simplicity and clarity, otherwise a number of readers (who knows how many?) would consider themselves too tired even to try to grasp its import. This kind of prose must also have a reasonable quota of direct speech and be sharply paragraphed, for unrelieved indirect speech and normal paragraphing would be too dull and difficult to lure the fickle attention of the new kind of reader. Such devices are, of course, used in other publications, too, both inside and outside the United States. In Britain, for example, the *Daily Express*, which is much influenced by the fashions of the United States, is an extreme example of bright journalism.

26 Mention of the *Reader's Digest* brings up the matter of condensing and rewriting which is practiced in a much more open, thoroughgoing, and ruthless way in the United States than anywhere else, mainly in the interests of efficient marketing. Morally, the practice is highly questionable, but I will confine myself to its effect on prose in magazines. It is said that the *Reader's Digest* not only condenses articles and novels already published, but that to a considerable extent it commissions articles, has them rewritten to exactly the right style and length, and then, by agreement, places them in selected magazines, so that it will seem in any given month that there is a choice from the nation's periodicals. In the case of *The New Yorker*, a magazine of a different breed, I have also often heard the complaint that articles and even stories pass through the editorial mill to such an extent that some are completely rewritten. How much this is true I have no way of telling since the workings of *The New Yorker* are clothed in comparative mystery. I judge that it is probably exaggerated, owing to the nature of the contributors, for one thing. Where an ordinary working journalist might have few misgivings about having his prose tampered with, the respected critics and writers whose work appears in *The New Yorker* might be expected to have more to say. At any rate, there is a noticeable difference, as might be expected, between the style of a book-piece by Anthony West, or Edmund Wilson, and an article on television by Philip Hamburger, or between a short story by Eudora Welty and one by John Cheever. Whatever editing there is is probably not only less extreme but different in kind from that of the *Reader's Digest*. *Reader's Digest* prose is excellent up to a point—clear, uninvolved, and pithy; but it is no vehicle for conveying ideas of any subtlety. Nuances of language it will not bear; that is not its purpose. Subtle, imaginative language and original figures of speech—if they are ever present in the contributions—must be smoothed into prose which can be easily grasped by the meanest intelligence. The magazine must be an efficient machine, and it is. But a steady diet of its prose has the same effect on the mind, as a steady diet of pap on the teeth. *The New*

Yorker, on the other hand, communicates at a level of intelligence and imagination which is probably higher than that of any other general magazine written in English. Both the *Reader's Digest* and *The New Yorker* probably have an ideal reader in mind, but they are very different kinds of people. The *Reader's Digest* aims at the Everyman of the Twentieth Century, the lowest common denominator of reader. Given that purpose the *Reader's Digest* editors do an extremely efficient job. Considering the editorial policy of maximum human interest and maximum optimism, the success with which the editors manipulate their material this side of sentimentality is extraordinary. What is important in this comparison, however, is, I believe, the difference in intention. The editors of the *Reader's Digest* seem, like the writers for *Time*, to be working in a region below their own natural range. The editors of *The New Yorker*, on the other hand, seem to be aiming at men and women like themselves. It is this, I imagine, which is responsible for the difference in tone, depth, and degree of idiosyncrasy between the prose of the two magazines.

> (c) *The speaker rustled his notes, clinked a pocketful of keys and stared at the ceiling while he fumbled for words. Then his wife's voice cut through the jangle: "Put your keys down, honey." Meekly, irascible Columnist Westbrook Pegler obeyed. For once the foaming temper was in check. Mellow with memory, onetime Sportswriter Pegler had turned out for the Tucson, Ariz. Press Club dinner, greeting the new baseball season.*
>
> *Peg. . . .*

27 This passage is, of course from *Time* (April 11, 1955). The formula is familiar and highly successful: first, the dramatic opening, the deliberate holding back of the name. Who can this Milquetoast be? To our surprise, it is none other than irascible Columnist Westbrook Pegler, who, having been introduced in a cloud of unknowing, soon becomes, in the democratic fashion, our friend, "Peg." This richly staged introduction, as designing as an advertiser's banquet, achieves its purpose admirably, again within the imaginative scope and vocabulary of the lowest common denominator of readers, although the level is, one suspects, rather higher than that of the *Reader's Digest*. It is the most lavish example so far of the presentation of factual material in an emotional way. It was prophesied by Tocqueville as a concomitant of the Age of Democracy. Everyone can read, but few can or want to read properly. Even to say "properly" is suspect in this time of the triumph of the mindless. Must democracy inevitably lead to the relaxing of standards and pandering to increasingly jaded palates? It is a nice question. The "average reader" cannot be expected to use his brain because he wants "relaxation" after his day's work, or because he has no time to spare, or because he wasn't taught properly in High School. So the writers of *Time* labour (and they prob-

ably have some fun doing it, too) to present him with ever more brightly written and attractively presented material. If they did not, their public would go off and read *Newsweek*, no doubt.

ADVERTISING PROSE

> (a) *Yes, only Viceroy has this filter composed of 20,000 tiny filter traps. You cannot obtain the same filtering action in* any other cigarette. . . . *That's why more college men and women smoke Viceroys than any other filter cigarette. . . .*

28 This passage, taken from an advertisement by the makers of Viceroy cigarettes in a student newspaper, is typical of nationwide current advertising technique for cigarettes, and of the kind of prose used in such advertisements.

29 The copywriters have apparently now reached their nadir, for they are using the same formula in print as on the radio. Perhaps this is significant in terms of the relationship of speech to literature in the United States, but I doubt it. The method is one of insidious hammering, as if with a little rubber hammer which the torturer wields tirelessly, so that, in the end, one's whole body is in tune with the nagging rhythmic blows. Four (at least four) things are constant: first, the meaningless and tiresome "yes," worn like a charm to scare away the advertising man's bogey (lack of smoothness, lack of a "friendly" yet authoritative, selling ring); second, the appeal to "science"; third, the "You cannot . . . in *any other cigarette*" (which varies in some cases to "No other cigarette made . . . etc.); and, fourth, the repetition on the same, though slightly modulated note ("That's why . . . than any other filter smoke"). Writers on the traditional ballad tell us that their anonymous authors used the device of "incremental repetition" in order that a rhythmic, memorable pattern might be retained in the minds of an audience which lived in an oral tradition. Here is incremental repetition today, serving other ends in another society.

> WHY SWELTER? JUST A TWIST OF THE WRIST CHANGES
> HOT MISERY . . . TO COOL COMFORT!
> LIVE AND WORK IN G-E "COMFORT-CONDITIONED AIR"!
> *Simply dial out swelter with this great new General Electric Room Air Conditioner! You can sleep dry and cool* tonight *in G-E. Comfort-Conditioned Air"—air that's always cool, dry and filtered to reduce dust, dirt and pollen.*
>
> WHY NOT CALL ON YOUR GENERAL ELECTRIC DEALER NOW?

30 The most noticeable thing about this passage, which is taken from an advertisement in *Life*, is its colourful and highly sensory use of language.

This, coupled with the exclamatory style, creates an effect of pseudo-momentousness. Nothing more, possibly, in the way of emotive effect, could have been crammed into the headline. The advertising copywriters are, as I believe Mr. Hayakawa once pointed out, the folk-poets of modern commercial civilisation. They know all the tricks of language that a poet or a short story writer knows, but they put them to the service, not of art, but of commercial persuasion. As Tocqueville said, "Democracy not only infuses a taste for letters among the trading classes, but introduces a trading spirit into literature." The writer of this copy ("Just a Twist of the Wrist") had an ear for the fundamental rhythms of the English language, a language which naturally and easily falls into patterns of rhyme, alliteration and onomatopoeia. These are patterns which can be found as easily in literature as in ordinary speech, from "A faire felde ful of folke/Fonde I there bytwene," of William Langland to "The breezes blew, the white foam flew,/The furrow follow'd free" of Coleridge, from Cockney rhyming slang to the "What's cookin', good-lookin' " of the American high school boy.

31 "Dial it out" is another example of verbal ingenuity devoted to the end of persuading. The effect is concentrated and dramatic. One can see oneself just dialling away "swelter," (i.e. the state of sweltering) by that "twist of the wrist." The use of "swelter" here, incidentally, is an interesting illustration of the extreme grammatical flexibility of the English language in communicating sensations, and also of the streamlining tendency of American English.

32 Another interesting invention is "Comfort-Conditioned Air." Perhaps the copywriter, like Fleming with his moulds, made the discovery by sheer accident. At any rate, it seems to be a reversal of the familiar "Air-Conditioned Comfort." And the wonder of it is that it means something. The poet, fiddling with words, struck rich ore (a bonanza). The effect of it was so heady that when he came to compose the whole line he made the very air, now "cool, dry and filtered," the property of General Electric. What kind of air have you there, Mr. Jones? I have G.E. Comfort-Conditioned Air in here, Mr. Smith.

33 One last point calls for mention and that is the use of "great," which, second to "beautiful," seems to be the most overworked word in the English language. If this air-conditioner is "great," what then was the invention of the aeroplane or the propounding of the Theory of Relativity?

34 I trust that my own tone, in commenting on these examples, has not at times seemed like that of the Reverend John Witherspoon. The Reverend John was mild in comparison with later British commentators who were apt to report on the misuse of language in the United States with shouts of glee, thus arousing the animosity and eventually the triumphant counter-cries of H. L. Mencken. A pre-Revolutionary (immigrant) Ameri-

can, the Reverend John hoped for a specifically American style, to be watched over by some "center of learning and politeness." In the meantime he thought it his duty to point out the various misuses of the English language in America, which he listed under the headings of: (1) Americanisms, (2) vulgarisms in England and America, (3) vulgarisms in America alone, (4) local phrases or terms, (5) common blunders arising from ignorance, (6) cant phrases, (7) personal blunders, and (8) technical terms introduced into the language.

35 On subjects like America and Prose one's mind cannot be made a blank. One has impressions, and my impression, before examining the samples I have chosen, was that in spite of some obvious examples of excessive rhetoric, of ineptness in handling words, of crudeness, of a peculiarly American kind of inflation, American prose as a whole had more naturalness than the English and at its best a transparent sincerity and simplicity worthy of American ideals. I did not, however, choose my quotations to prove this point. I threw my net as wide as I could, examined the pieces as objectively as possible, and relied on my findings to provide me with some conclusions which might or might not prove what I had previously accepted.

36 I find, on the whole, that my preconceptions are borne out only in so far as the best topical commentary, the best political writing, the best criticism and, above all, the best humorous writing is concerned. Elsewhere, there are great variations. Of course, the reader might object that he could have chosen a whole set of other samples which would alter the emphasis, or alternatively, that the quotations were far too short for judgment. This might be true, but short of conducting a statistical survey I do not see what else could be done. Perhaps, before our time runs out, one of the great Foundations will have provided funds for such an enterprise. But since language cannot be gauged like physical reactions, and the value of the comments depends on the taste of the investigator, it would be a difficult task. In the meantime, and in the light of my own crude sampling, I offer, diffidently, some general conclusions.

37 In the first place, it seems to me that American "expositional prose" is much weaker than American creative prose. Only in the case of people of acute sensibility, at the highest level, do we find a kind of prose which, by its tasteful natural diction, its use of figures drawn from American life, and its ease of manner can be held up as an example of the use of English which is both good and distinctively American. The American temperament seems better fitted to explore the creative possibilities of language, and one can find all kinds of examples to support this from the ebullience but relative crudeness of Thomas Wolfe to the fine-grained yet almost overwhelmingly rhetorical "immediacy" of William Faulkner. In the hands of the modern American short story writer, particularly, American prose is

both beautiful and exciting to read. Life leaps from the page: sights, colours, smells, all the multifarious aspects of common and uncommon human existence make an impact which British creative prose rarely achieves. But the cultural climate of the United States in the 20th century has apparently not been conducive to the development of a widespread and distinctively American instrument for conveying facts, ideas, and comment at the general level. Feelings and emotions get in the way, for one thing. There is too commonly an inability to express a logical sequence of thought with "ease, grace, precision," what I have called "having no ear" for the English language. One reason for this lies, I am sure, in the deep-seated American feeling that "style" is something ornamental, part of a way of life that is variously called "British" or "aristocratic." It does not matter that the reaction, which is an emotional one, is understandable. What matters is that it is bad for American prose. To quote Sir Arthur Quiller-Couch again:

> The editor of a mining paper in Denver, U.S.A., boldly the other day laid down this law, that niceties of language were mere "frills": all a man needed was "to get there," that is, to say what he wished in his own way. But just here . . . lies the mischief. You will not get there by hammering away on your own untutored impulse. You must first be your own reader, chiselling out the thought definitely for yourself: and, after that, must carve out the intaglio more sharply and neatly, if you would impress its image accurately upon the wax of other men's minds.

38 But there is another reason, I believe, for the comparative lack of literary ability in all but the exceptional in the United States and this lies in the tendency to "educate for life" and to relegate literature to an inferior place. A questionnaire sent out in 1949 for *Harper's Magazine* by Norman Lewis revealed what Mr. Lewis called a "linguistic liberalism" among those people in the United States who "use the English language as a direct means of earning a livelihood." This meant accepting such expressions as "His work is different *than* mine," "I encountered *less* difficulties than I had expected" (attributed to Mr. Arthur Schlesinger, Jr.), and "The reason I'm worried is *because* I think she's ill." If we substitute "sloppy English" for "linguistic liberalism" we are, I think, nearer the mark. Yet, as against ninety-three American College Professors of English who rejected the first expression, there were sixty-two who accepted it as worthy of currency in educated speech. Forty-nine out of the one hundred and fifty-five even accepted the barbarous second example, and the astounding total of eighty-nine out of one hundred and fifty-five the third. This perhaps partly explains why college students' essays are such examples of bad prose. But what is far more perturbing than uneducated usage in educated exposition is the sheer muddle of the language, the lack of an ability, in the college group, to express ideas lucidly and coherently. Yet even those who seem on

the page to be semi-literate morons can make good sense when they speak, be ready in comment, even advance ideas. One's conclusion cannot but be that American conditions, educational and otherwise, have militated against clear and graceful literary expression. Yet Abraham Lincoln, that self-educated man, could express himself simply, cogently, and with style. Could he have learnt it had he grown up in America today? Where would he find models? Well, he could find them for one thing in Mr. Stevenson's prose, or in Mr. Oppenheimer's, or Mr. Randall Jarrell's, or Mr. Thurber's. He could read *The New Yorker*, or the *Atlantic*, or *Harper's*. The compilers of college textbooks of exposition certainly seem to strive to put good examples of prose before their readers. One wonders what the 40 per cent of college professors of English who say "His work is different *than* mine" do with them. Point out their queer usage perhaps?

39 It seems, then, that "independence and vigour," which the United States has in abundance, may produce good novels and stories but does not make a good climate for expositional prose which, unlike creative writing, touches everybody. In fact, the outstanding exceptions which I have noted would be classified by some as outside the mainstream of American culture. It almost seems as if there were, as Disraeli said of 19th century English society, "two nations" in America, but instead of these two nations being the rich and the poor, they are the educated and the uneducated, the literate and the semi-literate. One remembers some of Tocqueville's prophecies:

> The most common expedient employed by democratic nations to make an innovation in language consists in giving some unwonted meaning to an expression already in use. This method is very simple, prompt, and convenient; no learning is required to use it aright, and ignorance itself rather facilitates the practice; but that practice is most dangerous to the language.

40 There will always, I feel, be Americans to whom these practices will be abhorrent. They will uphold the standards of American prose to the end. But to whom will they make their communication, except to each other?

41 All this raises, no doubt, most interesting questions, some as basic as one could wish for, such as: Does literacy matter? It is true that one can be intelligent without being literate. But Western Civilisation is built upon such principles and traditions as demand literacy. To deny it is to deny Western Civilisation as an idea and to prepare the way for barbarism. Yet some years ago a Californian professor seriously suggested, not merely that the oral might eventually entirely supersede the written communication, but that it was a good thing that it should do so. Perhaps in the end it will be so. Perhaps the triumph of the mass media and the encouragement of "speech" rather than literature in schools has started a tide which cannot

be turned. And what, when it is upon them, will the publishers and manufacturers of typewriters do then, poor things? If they are, like the rest of us, still here, that is.

STUDY GUIDE

Structure

1. Moore tries in this essay to determine whether there is in America "a distinctive prose, expressive of its spirit" (paragraph 3). He later admits to such a prose in the area of fiction and narrows his inquiry to expositional prose (paragraph 4). He attempts to arrive at a conclusion through an *induction* (see Huxley's essay on "Inductive and Deductive Reasoning" in Section 2 and the notes on induction in the Study Guide following that selection). The induction proceeds through the examination and evaluation of a wide variety of passages of American expository prose (paragraphs 5–33). What are the considered conclusions to this induction? Where does Moore express them? Considering the qualifications he himself puts upon his conclusions, do you think they are valid?

2. What are some of the reasons Moore suggests for the general low level of American expository prose?

Suggestions for Writing

1. Find what you consider typical examples of expository prose in the *Reader's Digest*, *The New Yorker*, and *Time*, and show by a close analysis of sentence structure, diction, imagery, and allusion what kind of reader each selection envisions.

2. Find other examples of advertising copy that show the "insidious hammering" technique that Moore speaks of in paragraph 29. Indicate how this effect is achieved through elements of diction and sentence structure.

3. Make a study of reports on the same news item from *The London Times*, *The New York Times*, your own local newspaper, and the magazine *Time*, and see whether you can detect some of the characteristics that Moore attributes to these various news outlets in his article.

ENGLISH IN 2061: A FORECAST

Mario Pei

1 If a modern-day Rip Van Winkle went to sleep and didn't wake up for 100 years, how well would he be able to understand an American of 2061?

From *Saturday Review* (January 14, 1961). Reprinted by permission of the author and publisher.

2 It does not take a linguist to know that the language changes. Educated laymen know that the language they speak was once Elizabethan English (a little difficult to follow today, especially in the pronunciation of Shakespearian actors), and before that the half-incomprehensible language of Chaucer, and before that the Anglo-Saxon that no one today can read, let alone speak, unless he has had a graduate course in it.

3 Yet many people fail to realize that language is also going to change in the future. The English of 1,000 years from now (granted that English is still a living tongue by the year 2961 A.D.) will probably be as different from the language of *Saturday Review* as the latter is from the spoken tongue of the Venerable Bede.

4 The big difference between the past and the future is that we know, or can reconstruct with some degree of accuracy, what has happened in the past while we have no way of knowing—or so it sometimes seems—what course the future will take.

5 But is the last proposition altogether true? We know that governments, business organizations, even private individuals make projections into the future, based on present tendencies and trends. These forecasts do not, of course, have the same value as recorded history, since they may be thrown completely out of kilter by the unexpected or accidental. Nevertheless, barring the unexpected, it is quite possible for our government experts to say: "We anticipate that the population of the United States, growing at an average yearly rate of about 2,000,000 will reach the 200 million mark, more or less, by 1970." In like manner, a business firm may say: "Our profits have grown about $1,000,000 a year over the past ten years. Barring a major depression, we estimate that by 1965 they will be about $5,000,000 higher than they are today." When you estimate your income tax for a year that is just beginning, as the Treasury Department somewhat unreasonably asks you to do, you go through this process of reasoning: "My income over the past five years has been about $10,000. As of this moment, I cannot anticipate any sizable change. Therefore, I am putting down the same figures for 1961 that appear in my 1960 declaration."

6 It is quite possible to do the same thing with language, always with the understanding that some outside factor may come along to knock the calculation into a cocked hat. One such factor in the development of the English language, for instance, was the Danish invasions of England that antedated the Norman Conquest. One effect of them is that today we say, "Take the knife and cut the steak" instead of "Nim the metter and sned the oxflesh," which is the logical development of the Anglo-Saxon of King Alfred without Scandinavian interference. Another factor was 1066 itself, by reason of which we say, "The army pays out large sums of money" instead of "The here tells out great tales of gild."

7 A projection of the English language into the future on the basis of present-day indications is something like the predictions of an IBM ma-

chine on election night when only the first 2,000,000 votes are in. It can be fascinating, though many things may come along to upset our predictions. Nevertheless, despite the hazards, the questions can legitimately be asked: What can we prophesy at this moment about the English of 100 years hence? How will our descendants of 2061 A.D. speak and write?

8 By looking at the changes that have taken place in the past, and at the way the language is changing now, I think we can make some reasonable predictions.

9 Let us first of all recall that language consists of sounds (or phonemes, which are sounds that are distinctively significant to the speakers); of grammatical forms (like *love, loves, loved*, or *see, sees, saw, seen*, or *child, children*); of word arrangements like the characteristic "John loves Mary," which indicates that John, coming before the verb, is the doer of the action, and Mary, coming after the verb, the recipient; and of individual words, laden with their distinctive meanings. Language change may and does occur in any of these four divisions: phonology, morphology, syntax, and vocabulary.

10 But the changes do not occur at the same rate or to the same extent in all four. In times of trouble and stress, when communities become isolated, or when an alien tongue comes in direct contact with the native language of an area, changes in sound and grammatical structure seem favored; when conditions are stable, sounds and grammar change moderately, but vocabulary grows quickly.

11 For this reason, the big sound-and-grammar changes in the English tongue took place primarily in the days of the Anglo-Saxons, the Danes, and the Normans, then again through the troublous times that preceded the stabilization of English society down to the days of Queen Elizabeth I. There were numerous vocabulary changes in those days, too, but the most dramatic vocabulary accretions have come since the dawn of the scientific era.

12 Our projection for the next hundred years, assuming there will be no major cataclysm (such as an atomic war that plunges us back into medieval conditions), therefore involves a very limited amount of sound changes, a very moderate amount of grammatical transformation, and extensive vocabulary changes, mainly along the lines of accretion.

13 In the sounds of our language, the omens point to a process of stabilization and standardization, with local dialectal variants tending to be replaced by a uniform style of pronunciation. Indeed, it is likely that even the cleavage between British and American English will tend to be effaced. There are many reasons for this. Large, centralized government units, easy communication between speakers of different areas, widespread trade and travel, and widespread education all favor unification and standardization. This was proved in the days of the Roman Empire, when a strong central

government, good roads, unrestricted trade among the provinces and a fairly good educational system (at least for that period) led to the use of a standardized Latin throughout the western part of the Empire and a standardized Greek in the eastern regions. Today we have not only the American Union and the British Commonwealth, with their highly centralized features; we also have highways, railroads, swift ships, and jet planes, bringing the speakers of the various English-speaking areas into fast and easy contact with one another; we have public schooling for all social classes, with illiteracy practically eliminated; above all, we have the ubiquitous printing presses, radio, TV, and spoken films, bringing a standard King's English and a standard General American to all readers, viewers, and listeners. The local dialects will probably never quite disappear; but they will be driven more and more undergound, particularly with the new generations of speakers. Only those mispronunciations that have spread throughout the country, like *marjerine* for *margarine* and *Febuary* for *February*, will come out on top. As for the cleavage between British and American English, the tendency has been toward reunification since the First World War. Spoken British films were almost incomprehensible to American audiences when they first appeared, while American plays presented in England often were accompanied by printed glossaries in the programs (or should we spell it programmes?). Today, a British accent barely causes us to strain our ears, while the British have grown quite accustomed to the Midwestern voice. Actually, we are slowly and insensibly modifying some of our forms of pronunciation to conform with the British, and they are doing the same with regard to ours.

14 The pronunciation of the year 2061 will probably not differ very widely from the General American of our best radio and TV announcers today. There will be an elimination of marked vulgarisms and localisms, which will be looked upon as old-fashioned (Cicero, writing in the first century B.C., used such expressions as *rustici dicebant*, "the rustics used to say," and *rustico sermone significabat*, "in rustic speech used to mean"; his use of the imperfect past in this connection is a dead giveaway that these local forms of speech had gone out of fashion by his day).

15 In the matter of grammatical forms and arrangements, our language today is far too standardized to permit of much change. It is possible that a few stray levelings may take place (*oxes* and *deers* for *oxen* and *deer*, for instance; or *I heared him* in the place of *I heard him*). But despite the widespread rantings of the apostles of "usage" (however that much-belabored word may be defined), it is not likely that substandard forms will make much headway. The primary reason for this is that such substandard forms are normally in the nature of localisms. Such rank atrocities as "Them dogs are us'ns," "I seen the both'n of 'em," and "I'll call you up, without I can't" are too localized to survive the impact of schools and TV.

The only grammatical changes that have a real chance of becoming part of the standard language are those that have nation-wide currency, such as "It's me," "Who did you see?" and "ain't." Judgment may be suspended for some ignorant uses in sentences like "I should of done it" and "I seen him."

16 One historical factor that may blast our calculations to smithereens, however, is the possible growth of a pidginized form of English for international use, and its influence upon the native speakers. If this happens, it is possible that we may get such analogical standardizations as *childs, mouses, gooses, foots* (so that all nouns may form their plurals the same way without exception), and *I did see, I did go* for *I saw, I went* (so that the basically simple English verb may be further simplified by having a universally regular past).

17 The really big changes will come in vocabulary. It will be the multiplicity of new words that will really make the English of 2061 a startlingly different language from that of today.

18 Here there are several factors at work. As man's activities become increasingly complex and multiform, new words have to be coined, combined, borrowed, or otherwise created to take care of such activities. All we have to do is to go over the list of vocabulary accretions since 1900 to realize what is in store for the language in the next hundred years. Think of *futurama, micromatic, jitterbug, genocide, corny, snafu, gremlin, smog, zoot suit*—all words that would have been meaningless to Dickens or Edgar Allan Poe. Add to these the words of specialized fields of activity (*megavolt* and *psychosomatic, electronic* and *morphophonemic, isotope* and *positron, kodak* and *latex*), and consider also the words that pre-existed the turn of the century, but which are now used in a variety of new acceptances (*atomic fission, integration, featherbed, release,* etc.). It is easy to see that the language of the future will be only partly comprehensible to the speaker of present-day English, even if the basic sounds, forms, sentence structures, and connecting words remain largely unchanged.

19 The future tongue will sound, from the point of view of present-day speakers, somewhat like double-talk or, better yet, those nonsense sentences that linguists often construct when they want to get away from meaning and concentrate on form—sentences in which the sounds, the grammatical forms, the word order, and the connecting words are all standard English, but in which the vocabulary is imaginary: something like "Foring mests larry no granning sunners in the rones." Yet this vocabulary will of course be easily understood by speakers who have grown up with it.

20 How many of our present, current, everyday words will be altogether obsolete, or even archaic, by 2061? A good many, no doubt. All we have to do is to look closely at the vocabulary of 100 years ago and notice how many words were in current use that we can still recognize, but would not

think of using ourselves, words like *drawing-room* and *trencher, conscript* and *sparking light, eximious* and *mansuetude,* or, to go a little further, *vocular* and *viduous, gossipaceous* and *dandiacal.* If we care to go a few centuries further back, we can find *deruncinate* and *suppeditate, whirlicote* and *begeck, yuke* and *pringle, toom* and *mizzle, jarkmen* and *priggers, assation* and *clancular, dignotion* and *exolution.*

21 Since the language of radio and TV, in the English-speaking countries, is largely a matter of commercial promotion, a special word may be in order for the future ramifications of the Madison Avenue tongue.

22 In the field of sounds, the promotional language tends to avoid, save for occasional picturesque effect, localism and special accents. It is a powerful, perhaps the most powerful, factor in the standardization we anticipate. It is only occasionally that we get a deliberate distortion of pronunciation, like *halo* for hello. This laudable conservatism does not, by the way, extend to spelling. Forms like *nite, kool, Duz,* and *chaise lounge* are there to plague us, and to confuse the foreigner and even the native learner of English.

23 In grammar and syntax, the language of promotion tends toward those vulgarisms that are nation-wide ("like a cigarette should" is a good example), but not toward local or extreme forms.

24 In the advertising vocabulary, two distinct and contradictory trends are noticeable. One is the tendency to stress the short, pithy, monosyllabic elements of vocabulary, as when an earlier "If headaches persist or recur frequently" was replaced by "if headaches hang on too long or keep coming back." But side by side with this, we have droves of commercialized scientific and pseudoscientific long words, like *hydramatic* and *irradiated, homogenized* and *naugahyde, chlorophyll* and *duridium,* even *oldsmobility* and *beaverette.*

25 One grammatical peculiarity of the language of commercialism is the avoidance of the personal pronouns *it* and *they,* replaced with endless and annoying repetitions of the name of the sponsor or product. This may eventually lead an as yet unborn chronicler of the English language to say in the year 2061: "Personal pronouns, still quite alive in British English, are obsolescent in American. This is particularly true of the third person neuter pronoun *it,* which only the older generation of American English speakers occasionally use today. Instead, Americans prefer to repeat the noun over and over again, often with ludicrous effects."

26 But all in all, despite the multiplying of human activity, the advances of science and its nomenclature, the ravages of commercialism, it seems to this writer that we are not justified in expecting too radical a change in the language, particularly in its sound-and-grammar structure, provided the present trends continue.

27 Remember, though, that this picture may be violently changed by

the unexpected and unforeseeable. A historical upset, a political upheaval, a military disaster may place the English language in swift motion once more, so that a century or two could bring on the same differences that appear between the Anglo-Saxon of Aelfric and the Middle English of Chaucer.

STUDY GUIDE

Structure

1. This essay by Mario Pei is very neatly structured. Study carefully paragraph 1 and paragraphs 25 and 26 as effective introductory and concluding paragraphs.

2. The whole essay can be divided into the following major thought divisions: paragraphs 1–8, 9–12, 13–20, 21–25, and 26 and 27. Work out carefully in a sentence outline how each of these parts is related to the author's purpose of forecasting what English will be like in 2061.

3. Show how he has used analogy to develop the first part.

4. Show how the author repeats the organization of the second and third parts to develop what he has to say about the possible future effects of radio and television on the development of the English language in four part.

Content and a Suggestion for Writing

1. What connection has the forecast of greatest change in the vocabulary of English with the technology and the knowledge explosion which is the concern of the selection that follows?

2. Write an eassy in which you represent how incomprehensible a casual discussion by contemporary students on almost any topic—their studies, their homes, their recreation, their travel and vacations, modern politics or science—might be to even a well-informed nineteenth-century person because of the vocabulary changes that have taken place in the language since his time.

A SCHOOLMAN'S GUIDE TO MARSHALL McLUHAN

John M. Culkin

1 Education, a seven-year-old assures me, is "how kids learn stuff." Few definitions are as satisfying. It includes all that is essential—a who, a what, and a process. It excludes all the people, places, and things which are only

From *Saturday Review* (March 18, 1967). Reprinted by permission of the author and publisher.

sometimes involved in learning. The economy and accuracy of the definition, however, are more useful in locating the problem than in solving it. We know little enough about *kids*, less about *learning*, and considerably more than we would like to know about *stuff*.

2 In addition, the whole process of formal schooling is now wrapped inside an environment of speeded-up technological change which is constantly influencing kids and learning and stuff. The jet-speed of this technological revolution, especially in the area of communications, has left us with more reactions to it than reflections about it. Meanwhile back at the school, the student, whose psyche is being programed for tempo, information, and relevance by his electronic environment, is still being processed in classrooms operating on the postulates of another day. The cold war existing between these two worlds is upsetting for both the student and the schools. One thing is certain: It is hardly a time for educators to plan with nostalgia, timidity, or old formulas. Enter Marshall McLuhan.

3 He enters from the North, from the University of Toronto where he teaches English and is director of the Center for Culture and Technology. He enters with the reputation as "the oracle of the electric age" and as "the most provocative and controversial writer of this generation." More importantly for the schools, he enters as a man with fresh eyes, with new ways of looking at old problems. He is a man who gets his ideas first and judges them later. Most of these ideas are summed up in his book, *Understanding Media*. His critics tried him for not delivering these insights in their most lucid and practical form. It isn't always cricket, however, to ask the same man to crush the grapes and serve the wine. Not all of McLu is nu or tru, but then again neither is *all* of anybody else. This article is an attempt to select and order those elements of McLuhanism which are most relevant to the schools and to provide the schoolman with some new ways of thinking about the schools.

4 McLuhan's promise is modest enough: "All I have to offer is an enterprise of investigation into a world that's quite unusual and quite unlike any previous world and for which no models of perception will serve." This unexplored world happens to be the present. McLuhan feels that very few men look at the present with a present eye, that they tend to miss the present by translating it into the past, seeing it through a rear-view mirror. The unnoticed fact of our present is the electronic environment created by the new communications media. It is as pervasive as the air we breathe (and some would add that it is just as polluted), yet its full import eludes the judgments of commonsense or content-oriented perception. The environments set up by different media are not just containers for people; they are processes which shape people. Such influence is deterministic only

if ignored. There is no inevitability as long as there is a willingness to contemplate what is happening.

5 Theorists can keep reality at arm's length for long periods of time. Teachers and administrators can't. They are closeted with reality all day long. In many instances they are co-prisoners with electronic-age students in the old pencil box cell. And it is the best teachers and the best students who are in the most trouble because they are challenging the system constantly. It is the system which has to come under scrutiny. Teachers and students can say, in the words of the Late Late Show, "Baby, this thing is bigger than both of us." It won't be ameliorated by a few dashes of good will or a little more hard work. It is a question of understanding these new kids and these new media and of getting the schools to deal with the new electronic environment. It's not easy. And the defenders of the old may prove to be the ones least able to defend and preserve the values of the old.

6 For some people, analysis of these newer technologies automatically implies approbation of them. Their world is so full of *shoulds* that it is hard to squeeze in an *is*. McLuhan suggests a more positive line of exploration:

> At the moment, it is important that we understand cause and process. The aim is to develop an awareness about print and the newer technologies of communication so that we can orchestrate them, minimize their mutual frustrations and clashes, and get the best out of each in the educational process. The present conflict leads to elimination of the motive to learn and to diminution of interest in all previous achievement: It leads to loss of the sense of relevance. Without an understanding of media grammars, we cannot hope to achieve a contemporary awareness of the world in which we live.

7 We have been told that it is the property of true genius to disturb all settled ideas. McLuhan is disturbing in both his medium and his message. His ideas challenge the normal way in which people perceive reality. They can create a very deep and personal threat since they touch on everything in a person's experience. They are just as threatening to the establishment whose way of life is predicated on the postulates he is questioning. The establishment has no history of organizing parades to greet its disturbers.

8 His medium is perhaps more disturbing than his message. From his earliest work he has described his enterprise as "explorations in communication." The word he uses most frequently today is "probe." His books demand a high degree of involvement from the reader. They are poetic and intuitive rather than logical and analytic. Structurally, his unit is the sentence. Most of them are topic sentences—which are left undeveloped.

The style is oral and breathless and frequently obscure. It's a different kind of medium.

9 "The medium is the message," announced McLuhan a dozen years ago in a cryptic and uncompromising aphorism whose meaning is still being explored. The title of his latest book, an illustrated popular paperback treatment of his theories, playfully proclaims that *The Medium is the Massage* —a title calculated to drive typesetters and critics to hashish and beyond. The original dictum can be looked at in four ways, the third of which includes a massage of importance.

10 The first meaning would be better communicated orally—"The *medium* is the message." The *medium* is the thing to study. The *medium* is the thing you're missing. Everybody's hooked on content; pay attention to form, structure, framework, *medium*. The play's the thing. The medium's the thing. McLuhan makes the truth stand on its head to attract attention. Why the medium is worthy of attention derives from its other three meanings.

11 Meaning number two stresses the relation of the medium to the content. The form of communication not only alters the content, but each form also has preferences for certain kinds of messages. Content always exists in some form and is, therefore, to some degree governed by the dynamics of that form. If you don't know the medium, you don't know the message. The insight is neatly summed up by Dr. Edmund Carpenter: "English is a mass medium. All languages are mass media. The new mass media—film, radio, TV—are new languages, their grammars as yet unknown. Each codifies reality differently; each conceals a unique metaphysics. Linguists tell us it's possible to say anything in any language if you use enough words or images, but there's rarely time; the natural course is for a culture to exploit its media biases. . . ."

12 It is always content-in-form which is mediated. In this sense, the medium is co-message. The third meaning for the M-M formula emphasizes the relation of the medium to the individual psyche. The medium alters the perceptual habits of its users. Independent of the content, the medium itself gets through. Pre-literate, literate, and post-literate cultures see the world through different-colored glasses. In the process of delivering content the medium also works over the sensorium of the consumer. To get this subtle insight across, McLuhan punned on m*e*ssage and came up with m*a*ssage. The switch is intended to draw attention to the fact that a medium is not something neutral—it does something to people. It takes hold of them, it jostles them, it bumps them around, it massages them. It opens and closes windows in their sensorium. Proof? Look out the window at the TV generation. They are rediscovering texture, movement, color, and sound as they retribalize the race. TV is a real grabber; it really massages those lazy, unused senses.

13 The fourth meaning underscores the relation of the medium to society. Whitehead said, "The major advances in civilization are processes that all but wreck the societies in which they occur." The media massage the society as well as the individual. The results pass unnoticed for long periods of time because people tend to view the new as just a little bit more of the old. Whitehead again: "The greatest invention of the nineteenth century was the invention of the method of invention. A new method entered into life. In order to understand our epoch, we can neglect all details of change, such as railways, telegraphs, radios, spinning machines, synthetic dyes. We must concentrate on the method in itself: That is the real novelty which has broken up the foundations of the old civilization." Understanding the medium or process involved is the key to control.

14 The media shape both content and consumer and do so practically undetected. We recall the story of the Russian worker whose wheelbarrow was searched every day as he left the factory grounds. He was, of course, stealing wheelbarrows. When your medium is your message and they're only investigating content, you can get away with a lot of things—like wheelbarrows, for instance. It's not the picture but the frame. Not the contents but the box. The blank page is not neutral; nor is the classroom.

15 McLuhan's writings abound with aphorisms, insights, for-instances, and irrelevancies which float loosely around recurring themes. They provide the raw materials of a do-it-yourself kit for tidier types who prefer to do their exploring with clearer charts. What follows is one man's McLuhan served up in barbarously brief form. Five postulates, spanning nearly 4,000 years, will serve as the fingers in this endeavor to grasp McLuhan:

16 1) 1967 B.C.—*All the senses get into the act.* A conveniently symmetrical year for a thesis which is partially cyclic. It gets us back to man before the Phoenician alphabet. We know from our contemporary ancestors in the jungles of New Guinea and the wastes of the Arctic that preliterate man lives in an all-at-once sense world. The reality which bombards him from all directions is picked up with the omni-directional antennae of sight, hearing, touch, smell, and taste. Films such as *The Hunters* and *Nanook of the North* depict primitive men tracking game with an across-the-board sensitivity which mystifies Western, literate man. We mystify them too. And it is this cross-mystification which makes inter-cultural abrasions so worthwhile.

17 Most people presume that their way of perceiving the world is *the* way of perceiving the world. If they hang around with people like themselves, their mode of perception may never be challenged. It is at the poles (literally and figuratively) that the violent contrasts illumine our own unarticulated perceptual prejudices. Toward the North Pole, for example, live Eskimos. A typical Eskimo family consists of a father, a mother, two

children, and an anthropologist. When the anthropologist goes into the igloo to study Eskimos, he learns a lot about himself. Eskimos see pictures and maps equally well from all angles. They can draw equally well on top of a table or underneath it. They have phenomenal memories. They travel without visual bearings in their white-on-white world and can sketch cartographically accurate maps of shifting shorelines. They have forty or fifty words for what we call "snow." They live in a world without linearity, a world of acoustic space. They are Eskimos. Their natural way of perceiving the world is different from our natural way of perceiving the world.

18 Each culture develops its own balance of the senses in response to the demands of its environment. The most generalized formulation of the theory would maintain that the individual's modes of cognition and perception are influenced by the culture he is in, the language he speaks, and the media to which he is exposed. Each culture, as it were, provides its constituents with a custom-made set of goggles. The differences in perception are a question of degree. Some cultures are close enough to each other in perceptual patterns so that the differences pass unnoticed. Other cultural groups, such as the Eskimo and the American teen-ager, are far enough away from us to provide esthetic distance.

19 2) *Art imitates life.* In *The Silent Language* Edward T. Hall offers the thesis that all art and technology is an extension of some physical or psychic element of man. Today man has developed extension for practically everything he used to do with his body: stone axe for hand, wheel for foot, glasses for eyes, radio for voice and ears. Money is a way of storing energy. This externalizing of individual, specialized functions is now, by definition, at its most advanced stage. Through the electronic media of telegraph, telephone, radio, and television, man has now equipped his world with a nervous system similar to the one within his own body. President Kennedy is shot and the world instantaneously reels from the impact of the bullets. Space and time dissolve under electronic conditions. Current concern for the United Nations, the Common Market, ecumenism, reflects this organic thrust toward the new convergence and unity which is "blowing in the wind." Now in the electric age, our extended faculties and senses constitute a single instantaneous and coexistent field of experience. It's all-at-once. It's shared-by-all. McLuhan calls the world "a global village."

20 3) *Life imitates art.* We shape our tools and thereafter they shape us. These extensions of our senses begin to interact with our senses. These media become a massage. The new change in the environment creates a new balance among the senses. No sense operates in isolation. The full sensorium seeks fulfillment in almost every sense experience. And since

there is a limited quantum of energy available for any sensory experience, the sense-ratio will differ for different media.

21 The nature of the sensory effect will be determined by the medium used. McLuhan divides the media according to the quality or definition of their physical signal. The content is not relevant in this kind of analysis. The same picture from the same camera can appear as a glossy photograph or as a newspaper wirephoto. The photograph is well-defined, of excellent pictorial quality, hi-fi within its own medium. McLuhan calls this kind of medium "hot." The newspaper photo is grainy, made up of little dots, low definition. McLuhan calls this kind of medium "cool." Film is hot; television is cool. Radio is hot; telephone is cool. The cool medium or person invites participation and involvement. It leaves room for the response of the consumer. A lecture is hot; all the work is done. A seminar is cool; it gets everyone into the game. Whether all the connections are causal may be debated, but it's interesting that the kids of the cool TV generation want to be so involved and so much a part of what's happening.

22 4) *We shaped the alphabet and it shaped us.* In keeping with the McLuhan postulate that "the medium is the message," a literate culture should be more than mildly eager to know what books do to people. Everyone is familiar enough with all the enrichment to living mediated through fine books to allow us to pass on to the subtler effects which might be attributed to the print medium, independent of the content involved. Whether one uses the medium to say that *God is dead* or that *God is love* (--- -- ----), the structure of the medium itself remains unchanged. Nine little black marks with no intrinsic meaning of their own are strung along a line with spaces left after the third and fifth marks. It is this stripping away of meaning which allows us to X-ray the form itself.

23 As an example, while lecturing to a large audience in a modern hotel in Chicago, a distinguished professor is bitten in the leg by a cobra. The whole experience takes three seconds. He is affected through the touch of the reptile, the gasp of the crowd, the swimming sights before his eyes. His memory, imagination, and emotions come into emergency action. A lot of things happen in three seconds. Two weeks later he is fully recovered and wants to write up the experience in a letter to a colleague. To communicate this experience through print means that it must first be broken down into parts and then mediated, eyedropper fashion, one thing at a time, in an abstract, linear, fragmented, sequential way. That is the essential structure of print. And once a culture uses such a medium for a few centuries, it begins to perceive the world in a one-thing-at-a-time, abstract, linear, fragmented, sequential way. And it shapes its organizations and schools according to the same premises. The form of print has become the form of thought. The medium has become the message.

24 For centuries now, according to McLuhan, the straight line has been the hidden metaphor of literate man. It was unconsciously but inexorably used as the measure of things. It went unnoticed, unquestioned. It was presumed as natural and universal. It is neither. Like everything else it is good for the things it is good for. To say that it is not everything is not to say that it is nothing. The electronic media have broken the monopoly of print; they have altered our sensory profiles by heightening our awareness of aural, tactile, and kinetic values.

25 5) 1967 A.D.—*All the senses want to get into the act.* Print repressed most sense-life in favor of the visual. The end of print's monopoly also marks the end of a visual monopoly. As the early warning system of art and popular culture indicates, all the senses want to get into the act. Some of the excesses in the current excursions into aural, oral, tactile, and kinetic experience may in fact be directly responsive to the sensory deprivation of the print culture. Nature abhors a vacuum. No one glories in the sight of kids totally out of control in reaction to the Beatles. Some say, "What are the Beatles doing to these kids?" Others say, "What have we done to these kids?" All the data isn't in on what it means to be a balanced human being.

26 Kids are what the game is all about. Given an honest game with enough equipment to go around, it is the mental, emotional, and volitional capacity of the student which most determines the outcome. The whole complicated system of formal education is in business to get through to kids, to motivate kids, to help kids learn stuff. Schools are not in business to label kids, to grade them for the job market or to babysit. They are there to communicate with them.

27 Communication is a funny business. There isn't as much of it going on as most people think. Many feel that it consists in saying things in the presence of others. Not so. It consists not in saying things but in having things heard. Beautiful English speeches delivered to monolingual Arabs are not beautiful speeches. You have to speak the language of the audience —of the *whom* in the "who-says-what-to-whom" communications diagram. Sometimes the language is lexical (Chinese, Japanese, Portuguese), sometimes it is regional or personal (125th Street-ese, Holden Caulfield-ese, anybody-ese). It has little to do with words and much to do with understanding the audience. The word for good communication is "Whom-ese" —the language of the audience, of the "whom."

28 All good communicators use Whom-ese. The best writers, film-makers, advertising men, lovers, preachers, and teachers all have the knack for thinking about the hopes, fears, and capacity of the other person and of being able to translate their communication into terms which are *relevant* for that person. Whitehead called "inert ideas" the bane of education.

Relevance, however, is one of those subjective words. It doesn't pertain to the object in itself but to the object as perceived by someone. The school may decide that history is *important for* the student, but the role of the teacher is to make history *relevant to* the student.

29 If *what* has to be tailored to the *whom*, the teacher has to be constantly engaged in audience research. It's not a question of keeping up with the latest slang or of selling out to the current mores of the kids. Neither of these tactics helps either learning or kids. But it is a question of knowing what values are strong in their world, of understanding the obstacles to communication, of sensing their style of life. Communication doesn't have to end there, but it can start nowhere else. If they are tuned in to FM and you are broadcasting on AM, there's no communication. Communication forces you to pay a lot of attention to other people.

30 McLuhan has been paying a great deal of attention to modern kids. Of necessity they live in the present since they have no theories to diffract or reflect what is happening. They are also the first generation to be born into a world in which there was always television. McLuhan finds them a great deal different from their counterparts at the turn of the century when the electric age was just getting up steam.

31 A lot of things have happened since 1900 and most of them plug into walls. Today's six-year-old has already learned a lot of stuff by the time he shows up for the first day of school. Soon after his umbilical cord was cut he was planted in front of a TV set "to keep him quiet." He liked it enough there to stay for some 3,000 to 4,000 hours before he started the first grade. By the time he graduates from high school he has clocked 15,000 hours of TV time and 10,800 hours of school time. He lives in a world which bombards him from all sides with information from radios, films, telephones, magazines, recordings, and people. He learns more things from the windows of cars, trains, and even planes. Through travel and communications he has experienced the war in Vietnam, the wide world of sports, the civil rights movement, the death of a President, thousands of commercials, a walk in space, a thousand innocuous shows, and, one may hope, plenty of Captain Kangaroo.

32 This is all merely descriptive, an effort to lay out what *is*, not what should be. Today's student can hardly be described by any of the old educational analogies comparing him to an empty bucket or a blank page. He comes to the information machine called school and he is already brimming over with information. As he grows his standards for relevance are determined more by what he receives outside the school than what he receives inside. A recent Canadian film tells the story of a bright, articulate middle class teen-ager who leaves school because there's "no reason to stay." He daydreams about Vietnam while his teacher drones on about the four reasons for the spread of Christianity and the five points such informa-

tion is worth on the exam. Only the need for a diploma was holding him in school; learning wasn't, and he left. He decided the union ticket wasn't worth the gaff. He left. Some call him a dropout. Some call him a pushout.

33 The kids have one foot on the dock and one foot on the ferryboat. Living in two centuries makes for that kind of tension. The gap between the classroom and the outside world and the gap between the generations is wider than it has ever been. Those tedious people who quote Socrates on the conduct of the young are trying vainly to reassure themselves that this is just the perennial problem of communication between generations. 'Tain't so. "Today's child is growing up absurd, because he lives in two worlds, and neither of them inclines him to grow up." Says McLuhan in *The Medium is the Massage*. "Growing up—that is our new work, and it is *total*. Mere instruction will not suffice."

34 Learning is something that people do for themselves. People, places, and things can facilitate or impede learning; they can't make it happen without some cooperation from the learner. The learner these days comes to school with a vast reservoir of vicarious experiences and loosely related facts; he wants to use all his senses in his learning as an active agent in the process of discovery; he knows that all the answers aren't in. The new learner is the result of the new media, says McLuhan. And a new learner calls for a new kind of learning.

35 Leo Irrera said, "If God had anticipated the eventual structure of the school system, surely he would have shaped man differently." Kids are being tailored to fit the Procrustean forms of schedules, classrooms, memorizing, testing, etc., which are frequently relics from an obsolete approach to learning. It is the total environment which contains the philosophy of education, not the title page in the school catalogue. And it is the total environment which is invincible because it is invisible to most people. They tend to move things around within the old boxes or to build new and cleaner boxes. They should be asking whether or not there should be a box in the first place.

36 The new learner, who is the product of the all-at-once electronic environment, often feels out of it in a linear, one-thing-at-a-time school environment. The total environment is now the great teacher; the student has competence models against which to measure the effectiveness of his teachers. Nuclear students in linear schools make for some tense times in education. Students with well developed interests in science, the arts and humanities, or current events need assistance to suit their pace, not that of the state syllabus. The straight line theory of development and the uniformity of performance which it so frequently encourages just don't fit many needs of the new learner. Interestingly, the one thing which most of the current educational innovations share is their break with linear or print-oriented patterns: team teaching, nongraded schools, audio-lingual language

training, multimedia learning situations, seminars, student research at all levels of education, individualized learning, and the whole shift of responsibility for learning from the teacher to the student. Needless to say, these are not as widespread as they should be, nor were they brought about through any conscious attention to the premises put forward by McLuhan. Like the print-oriented and linear mentality they now modify, these premises were plagiarized from the atmosphere. McLuhan's value is in the power he gives us to predict and control these changes.

37 There is too much stuff to learn today. McLuhan calls it an age of "information overload." And the information levels outside the classroom are now higher than those in the classroom. Schools used to have a virtual monopoly on information; now they are part-time competitors in the electronic informational surround. And all human knowledge is expanding at computer speed.

38 Every choice involves a rejection. If we can't do everything, what priorities will govern our educational policies? "The medium is the message" may not be bad for openers. We can no longer teach kids all about a subject; we can teach them what a subject is all about. We have to introduce them to the form, structure, gestalt, grammar, and process of the knowledge involved. What does a math man do when a math man does do math? This approach to the formal element of a discipline can provide a channel of communication between specialists. Its focus is not on content or detail but on the postulates, ground rules, frames of reference, and premises of each discipline. It stresses the modes of cognition and perception proper to each field. Most failures in communication are based on disagreement about items which are only corollaries of a larger thesis. It happens between disciplines, individuals, media, and cultures.

39 The arts play a new role in education because they are explorations in perception. Formerly conceived as a curricular luxury item, they now become a dynamic way of tuning up the sensorium and of providing fresh ways of looking at familiar things. When exploration and discovery become the themes, the old lines between art and science begin to fade. We have to guide students to becoming their own data processors to operate through pattern recognition. The media themselves serve as both aids to learning and as proper objects of study in this search for an all-media literacy. Current interest in film criticism will expand to include all art and communication forms.

40 And since the knowledge explosion has blown out the walls between subjects, there will be a continued move toward interdisciplinary swapping and understanding. Many of the categorical walls between things are artifacts left over from the packaging days of print. The specialist's life will be even lonelier as we move further from the Gutenberg era. The trends are all toward wholeness and convergence.

41 These things aren't true just because Marshall McLuhan says they are. They work. They explain problems in education that nobody else is laying a glove on. When presented clearly and with all the necessary examples and footnotes added, they have proven to be a liberating force for hundreds of teachers who were living through the tension of this cultural fission without realizing that the causes for the tension lay outside themselves. McLuhan's relevance for education demands the work of teams of simultaneous translators and researchers who can both shape and substantiate the insights which are scattered through his work. McLuhan didn't invent electricity or put kids in front of TV sets; he is merely trying to describe what's happening out there so that it can be dealt with intelligently. When someone warns you of an oncoming truck, it's frightfully impolite to accuse him of driving the thing. McLuhan can help kids to learn stuff better.

STUDY GUIDE

Structure

1. Work up a sentence outline of this essay taking account of the following probable thought divisions: paragraphs 1–3, 4–9, 10–14, 15–25, and 26–41.

2. The heart of Father Culkin's essay is a summary of Marshall McLuhan's thought and hence it turns out to be largely a listing, or enumeration, of McLuhan's chief ideas. In what parts of the essay is this method most obvious?

Questions of Content and Style

1. What do you consider the insight by McLuhan that most radically effects the situation of both teacher and student in the modern college?

2. What would be some practical applications in curriculum planning of the blown-out walls between subjects discussed by Culkin in paragraph 40?

3. Culkin says that in McLuhan's style the structural unit is the sentence. "Most of them are topic sentences—which are left undeveloped. The style is oral and breathless and frequently obscure." This is another way of saying that McLuhan's style is aphoristic, or Senecan—in which ideas are expressed in curt, disparate aphorisms that the reader is invited to consider and to develop for himself. It was the manner of writing popular among the ancient stoic philosophers when they were making moral observations or jotting down observations in physical science. It is the style of Bacon's first edition of his *Essays*. Compare, for instance, the following brief passage from McLuhan's *The Medium is the Massage* with the first version of Bacon's essay "Of Studies in Section 8." There is no logical progression in either selection but only a succession of aphoristic statements.

> Television completes the cycle of the human sensorium. With the omnipresent ear and the moving eye, we have abolished writing, the

specialized acoustic-visual metaphor that established the dynamics of Western civilization.

In television there occurs an extension of the sense of active, exploratory touch which involves all the senses simultaneously, rather than that of sight alone. You have to be "with" it. But in all electric phenomena, the visual is only one component in a complex interplay. Since, in the age of information, most transactions are managed electrically, the electric technology has meant for Western man a considerable drop in the visual component, in his experience, and a corresponding increase in the activity of his other senses.

Television demands participation and involvement in depth of the whole being. It will not work as a background. It engages you. Perhaps this is why so many people feel that their identity has been threatened. This charge of the light brigade has heightened our general awareness of the shape and meaning of lives and events to a level of extreme sensitivity.

It was the funeral of President Kennedy that most strongly proved the power of television to invest an occasion with the character of corporate participation. It involves an entire population in a ritual process. (By comparison, press, movies, and radio are mere packaging devices for consumers.) In television, images are projected at you. You are the screen. The images wrap around you. You are the vanishing point. This creates a sort of inwardness, a sort of reverse perspective which has much in common with Oriental art.[1]

4. Using Geoffrey Moore's analyses of American expository style as a guide, where would you place the literary style of Father Culkin? Give concrete evidence from the essay itself that definitely places it in a special category of American expository prose. Does its being there perhaps illustrate some of the ideas about the necessary conditions of communication inculcated by the author at the end of his essay?

5. Discuss the effectiveness of McLuhan's metaphors of the rearview mirror (paragraph 4) and of the medium as the massage (paragraph 9) referred to by Father Culkin.

6. Father Culkin has some interesting metaphors of his own. Discuss the effectiveness of the FM and AM metaphor in paragraph 29 and the dock and ferryboat metaphor in paragraph 33.

[1] Marshall McLuhan, *The Medium is the Massage* (New York: Random House, Inc., 1967), p. 125.

SECTION 4

Understanding the Nature and Purpose of a Liberal Education in a Technological Society

ENGLISH AND AMERICAN EDUCATION

Sir Geoffrey Crowther

1 For the past three years I have been engaged, with my colleagues of the Central Advisory Council on Education in England, in a comprehensive study of the English educational system. I had some of my own education in the United States, and I have been a frequent visitor to America ever since. This double experience has bred in me a growing sense of astonishment that two countries which share the same language, so many of the same cultural traditions and ways of life, whose political, religious, and social aspirations are so largely identical, should have educational systems so utterly different as to provide almost no basis for a comparison between them.

2 That is a strong statement, and my present purpose is to try to justify it. Let me first say, however, that I have no intention whatever of trying to show that one national system is, on balance, better than the other; only that they are much more different than is usually realized.

3 The American and the English educational systems are different in purpose, structure, and method. Let us start with purpose. The two systems

grew up in response to very different pressures and needs. In America, you have always been very conscious of the need to build up a new society. You have wanted to construct something bigger, richer, better than you have. This is said to arise from something in the American national character, but that seems to me to turn the logic upside down; it is the American national character that has arisen from the circumstances in which the American people have found themselves. From the start it was necessary to create a supply of ministers of religion, of lawyers, and of skilled artisans —I place them in the order of importance in which they were regarded at the time. Later on there came the obvious necessity of incorporating the great waves of immigrants into your society. Still later came the great task, in which you are still engaged, of knitting your varied economic, social, and racial groups into the harmonious and balanced society in which the principles of democratic government can work properly.

4 Consciously or unconsciously, American education has at all times been designed to serve these social purposes. It has been regarded as an instrument by which society can build its own future. From its nature, it has inescapably been concerned with the rank and file of the people. Its chief concern for many generations has been to do something to the masses—and I think the word is *to*, not *for*—in the interests of the American dream.

5 All this, of course, is platitude in America. What may not be quite so familiar is the contrast in the historical situation in England. We have never been very conscious of the necessity to build a new society. At all relevant times we have had a fully developed society already in being. And at all relevant times we have also, I am sorry to say, been on the whole pretty satisfied with the society we have. For most of the last two hundred years, American education has been designed to do a job of construction; English education has been designed primarily for maintenance, with improvement coming second. In the very latest period, perhaps, those attitudes have started to change. As with so many aspects of education, there seem to be the first signs of a tendency to change sides. Your education is becoming socially more conservative just when ours is becoming more consciously radical.

6 But that is a speculation for the future, on which I will not enlarge. I am talking of the influences of the past, which have shaped the structures of today. American education has always had to concern itself with the common man in his multitudes. The concern of English education has until very recently been with the maintenance of society, in the words of the old prayer which you will often hear in school and college chapels, "that there may never be wanting a succession of persons duly qualified to serve God in church and state." This is a conception which does not necessarily embrace the education of the great mass. There is a fine, rich, broad

educational tradition in England. But it is not a tradition of education, above the minimum level, for the multitude. Post-primary education has always been thought of as a privilege in England; it was not until 1944 that the principle of secondary education for all was established, and it is hardly yet fully effective.

7 Let me pursue this contrast a little further. Let me give you two of the consequences, of which I would guess that one will shock you, while the other may perhaps surprise you more favorably.

8 I will start with the shocker. The consequence of our different attitude is that the sheer size, the volume or quantity, of English education is very much smaller than American. The age at which the legal compulsion to attend school expires is still only fifteen. Moreover, that is an effective leaving age, and more than four children out of five in fact leave school before they are sixteen. Of the sixteen-year-old age group—those between their sixteenth and seventeenth birthdays—only 22 per cent are still in full-time education. In the seventeen-year-olds, the figure falls to 13 per cent of the boys and 11 per cent of the girls. Among eighteen-year-olds, it is 8 per cent of the boys and 5.5 per cent of the girls.

9 What strikes Americans, I find, as even odder than these figures is the fact that we are not, as a nation, greatly disturbed by them, although many of us think they ought to be larger. But we cannot assume that public opinion is on our side. I am very doubtful whether there would be any support in public opinion for a policy of keeping the majority of children in school after sixteen, and I am certain that you would find hardly anyone in England who believes, as you do, in keeping all children at school until eighteen. Our college students represent about 3 per cent of each age group, and there is an expansion program in hand that will raise it to about 5 per cent. Anybody who suggested that we needed any more than that would meet with the strongest resistance, and not least from the universities themselves.

10 This attitude does not arise from any lack of love for our children. It is not because we think we can't afford it. The proportion of our national income that we spend on general welfare services—social security, health, and the like—is about the highest in the world. It is not from lack of generosity or lack of means that we confine education after the middle teens to a minority. It is because we sincerely believe that it is the right thing to do, in the interests of the children themselves. After all, there can be no absolute rules about education. Nobody believes that any child should be allowed to leave school at twelve. I do not suppose a time will ever come when, even in America, it will become legal or compulsory for everyone to stay in full-time education until twenty-five. Where you fix the age between those limits is surely a matter of judgment. And why should it be the same age for all children? Our belief in England is that, balancing what can be

got out of school against what can be got out of life, the average boy or girl has probably had the optimum dose after eleven years of schooling—and do not forget that we begin, by legal compulsion, at the age of five. Eleven years, after all, is one year out of every six or seven of the average lifetime.

11 Now let me give you the other side of the medal. Because education after fifteen or sixteen is confined to a minority, that minority gets every assistance that the state can provide. It is nowadays, to an overwhelming extent, a minority chosen for intelligence and attainment. There are, of course, still the independent schools, where very substantial fees have to be paid. But the pressure of numbers upon them is such that a stupid boy or girl will have great difficulty getting in. And in the state schools, selection is by merit only. But once selected, a boy finds himself with his foot not so much on a ladder as an escalator. He will have the best resources of the best schools concentrated on him. If he can secure a place in a university, and that also is a matter of selection by merit, the state will pay his tuition fees and his living expenses, not only during the session but during the vacation as well. There is no such thing as working your way through college in England. We do not need a National Merit Scholarship scheme because we have one already. Nor is this a recent thing. It has been expanded in recent years, but it has always existed.

12 Let me move on to structure. The outstanding difference here lies in the fact that we have a very much smaller degree of local control than you do. There are about 50,000 school boards in the United States, each of them, I suppose, more or less free to run the schools as it thinks best. That gives a total population in the average school board area of about 3500 persons. In England there are about 130 local education authorities, which gives an average population per area of about 300,000. Moreover, there are two other differences, apart from this sharp difference in size. Your school boards consist, I believe, in most states, of persons specially elected for the purpose, with no other duties. In England the schools are run by the county council, or the borough council, which is the general-purpose government of the area.

13 Second, your school boards raise their own money by direct taxes, or at least the greater part of it. In England about 70 per cent of the expenditure of the local education authorities is met out of grants from the central government in London. There are advantages and disadvantages in this. It means that we do not have the enormous range in standards between rich areas and poor areas that you do. It means a much greater degree of standardization of conditions of employment among the teachers, and therefore of interchangeability between school and school and between area and area. But it also inevitably means a greater degree of uniformity imposed from the center. We think our system is decentralized, because it allows

much more local freedom and variety than exist in the school systems of most Continental European countries. But there is no doubt that it is much more highly centralized than the American system.

14 The other great difference under the heading of structure is the principle of selection upon which our system is based. All children, except the minority in fee-paying schools, go to undifferentiated schools from the age of five to the age of eleven. At eleven or thereabouts, a proportion of them, varying from area to area but averaging between 20 and 25 per cent, is selected for what we call grammar schools, which include children to the age of eighteen, though not all the pupils stay that long. The remainder go to what are called secondary modern schools, which include children to age fifteen and increasingly to sixteen, but no older.

15 You will see from this description that the crucial time for an English child is at the age of eleven or a little more. The selection test then applied—the famous or infamous eleven-plus examination—is supposed to be a classification purely by ability and aptitude, without any suspicion of being derogatory to those who are not selected. But, of course, everybody wants to be selected, and with the growing pressure of numbers as a result of the post-war bulge of population, the selection has been getting steadily more competitive. As the result of agitation, the Labor Party has adopted the policy of abolishing the eleven-plus examination by sending all children at that age to the same schools, the so-called comprehensive secondary schools. The Labor Party has moved toward this system in several of the areas where it controls the local council, and even in Conservative areas there is a distinct movement to experiment with systems that do not involve sending children to different schools at the age of eleven.

16 I have several times seen this movement quoted in America as evidence that English education is turning away from selection. I think this is a grave misunderstanding. The public objection to selection at eleven is social and political, not educational. It is an objection on the part of parents to having their children sent to different schools, not to their having different educations. And the remedies that are being applied are wholly in terms of institutions, not in terms of the education they provide. I know, for example, one large new comprehensive school built by a Labor council. Every child entering that school is tested and placed in one of fifteen "streams," differentiated by the children's intelligence and aptitude. This selection is done by the teachers; the parents have nothing to do with it; and the children are not even supposed to know which stream is which in intelligence grading. A child placed in one of the top streams will have an almost wholly different education from a child placed even in one of the middle streams. If this is not selection, I do not know the meaning of the term. But this is what we mean by a comprehensive school. Many people in England will tell you that the comprehensive school has been

copied from the American comprehensive high school, some meaning it as a compliment, some as the reverse. I have often told them that they could hardly be more mistaken.

17 Nonselection—if that is the opposite of selection—as it is practiced in America is totally unknown in England. By nonselection I mean the principle of treating all children alike, allowing them to sort themselves out by their choice of courses, by what they find easy and difficult, or by their varying ambitions—with counseling assistance, no doubt, but without any compulsory segregations. I am sure that your system seems as odd to us as ours does to you. There is no retreat from selection in England; the only change is that a growing number of people—but still a minority—think that the selection should be within a common school, not between schools.

18 The differences between the two countries in educational method make an enormous subject, and I must restrict myself to four points out of many that it would be possible to make.

19 The first of these differences in method lies in the position of the teacher, in the relative positions of the teacher and the textbook. One of the things about American education that most strikes the English visitor is the importance you attach to textbooks. We have no parallel to that. To begin with, I do not think there are more than two or three, at most, of the local education authorities in England that tell their schools what textbooks to use. That is left to the teacher, occasionally the principal, or the head of department in a large school. And in the higher grades, more often than not, there is not a textbook at all. A teacher will often recommend a book as covering the subject pretty well and as being useful for reference but will not make any attempt to go through it chapter by chapter.

20 This system places a much greater responsibility on the individual teacher, and I have often been asked in America whether we do not have a lot of trouble with it. So far as the political and social responsibility of the teacher is concerned, I cannot recall having heard of a single case arising through a teacher's being accused of using a book which seems offensive or objectionable to somebody in authority. That is partly, perhaps mainly, because our system of large authorities and rather remote and indirect public control puts the individual teacher largely out of the reach of vigilance committees, whether of parents or of the local chamber of commerce. There is also a strong tradition against anything that smacks of political interference with the schools.

21 Educational responsibility, however, is another matter. Quite clearly, a system like ours, which places so much responsibility on the individual teacher, cannot work well unless the average standard of intelligence, knowledge, and teaching competence is high. Up to the present, we have been able to maintain that standard. It is partly, of course, a matter of

numbers. In the whole of England last year there were only some 260,000 schoolteachers. We were a little short, but 300,000 would have given us all we need. And this is in a country about one quarter the size of the United States. I do not know how many schoolteachers there are in the United States, but I am very sure it is many more than four times 300,000. I do not see how you could possibly have coped with the enormous increase in the American school population in the past forty years without being willing to take thousands of young men and women who needed close support from a textbook before they could teach. Indeed, under the pressure of rising numbers in the schools, I fear we shall find before long that we shall have to give the teacher more assistance, and that implies more external control on his teaching. This particular contrast is not, however, entirely a matter of numbers. It is partly also the result of a different tradition of teacher training, which, in England, has always laid a much greater emphasis on the content of what is to be taught than in America and much less on questions of pedagogic method.

22 The second difference in method is the absence in England of the course system which is so universal in your schools and colleges. Indeed, the word "course" has a wholly different meaning in the two countries. If you asked an English school child what courses he was taking, he wouldn't know what you meant. If you asked him what subjects he was taking, he would answer English, Latin, mathematics, history, and so forth. But that would not mean, as it would in America, that those were the subjects he had chosen to take. They would be the subjects that his form, or class, was taking, and therefore that he was taking with the rest of the class. Until the boy is about fifteen or sixteen, it is unlikely that he or his parents have had any say in the choice of form in which he is placed. And at no age does he have any say in deciding the curriculum of that form. At the higher ages, there is a choice between three or four different curriculums, but each curriculum has to be taken, within narrow limits, as it stands.

23 Here, indeed, is a contrast with the American system. Perhaps it is not quite so sharp a contrast in practice as it is in principle, as I observe that, more and more, those American boys and girls who have ambition to gain admittance to a good college find their choice of courses in high school made for them by the college entrance requirements. But there is one important consequence for teaching that is worth bringing out. In an English school, in any year but one (and that one is what we call the fifth form year, about the age of fourteen or fifteen), you can assume that the pupils who are taking a subject in one year will be taking the same subject next year. The study of a subject can therefore be planned as a continuous process over a period of years. That is what we mean when we use the word "course." We mean a whole balanced curriculum of six or seven or eight subjects, planned to continue over three or four or five years. Once a

boy or girl enters on such a course, he or she will normally pursue it to the end. And all the boys and girls in a course will take substantially the same subjects, with perhaps slight options, as between a second classical or a second modern language. You will therefore understand how bewildered we are when we contemplate one of your neat, packaged, self-contained, nine-month courses, such as high school physics. It is no good asking an English schoolboy when he enters college how many years of French he has had at school. Two boys might both truthfully answer nine years. But they might mean totally different things, and neither one would mean what you thought he meant.

24 How, then, do we measure what a student has accomplished, if we cannot count up the number of courses he has satisfactorily taken? The answer is that we rely, to an extent wholly unknown to you, on general examinations. Every year—sometimes every term—the pupil has to take a written examination in all the subjects of the curriculum, and his further progress depends, sometimes entirely, on his performance in that examination. Most of these examinations are set and assessed within the school itself, by his own teachers. But at three crucial points in his career the examination is set and assessed by an external body. The first of these is the eleven-plus examination, which determines to which sort of secondary school the child should go. The second comes at fifteen or sixteen and is called the Ordinary Level of the General Certificate of Education, set and assessed by one of nine examining boards closely associated with the universities. This examination can be taken in any number of subjects from one upwards, but the most usual practice is to take it in from five to nine subjects. Third, there is the Advanced Level of the General Certificate of Education, which is taken at eighteen or thereabouts and which plays a large part in university entrance.

25 I have been describing the practice of the grammar schools; that is, the schools for the brightest 20 to 25 per cent of the children. Examinations, especially written examinations, play a much smaller part in the life of the less intelligent children. Even in this case, however, they play a much larger part than they do in America; and there is a rising demand for public examinations, at lower standards of intelligence than those of the General Certificate of Education, for these less gifted children. I cannot honestly say that the children themselves clamor for examinations, but employers do, and therefore so do the parents. All the questions that Americans ask and answer in terms of the number and variety of courses a student has taken we ask and answer in terms of the examinations he has passed.

26 I have left to the last what is the sharpest difference of all between our two systems. This is our system of specialization, in which England is, I think, unique in the world. A student will take the examination for the

Ordinary Level of the General Certificate of Education at the age of fifteen or sixteen in a wide range of subjects drawn both from the humanities and from the natural sciences. But once he has passed that examination, he will specialize. That is to say, he will devote two thirds, or perhaps even more, of his time in school to a narrow range of subjects. In one boy's case, it may be physics, chemistry, and mathematics; in another's it may be chemistry and biology, or it may be history or modern languages and literature, or classical languages and philosophy. But, whatever the choice, the greater part of the pupil's attention, in the classroom and in his private study time, is given to his specialty, and he will take the advanced level examination at eighteen in his special subjects only. When he gets to the university, the specialization is even more intense. The range of subjects does not usually get any narrower, but the student gives 100 per cent of his time to it.

27 I have found that to Americans, and indeed to educationalists from every country in the world except England, this seems a very strange system indeed. Perhaps you will have difficulty in believing that I really mean what I say. So let me cite my own case, though it is now more than thirty years old. I was a modern languages specialist. For my last three years at school, from the ages of fifteen to eighteen, I studied mostly French and German language and literature, perhaps three or four hours a week of history, and one hour of Scripture on Sundays. For another two years at Cambridge, even the history and the Scripture were cut out, and I studied French and German exclusively. Five years of my life were given to those languages. My experience was perhaps a little extreme; I think the admixture of general and contrasting subjects would nowadays, in a good school, be a little bigger. But the difference would not be great. The English boy or girl is a specialist from the age of fifteen or sixteen.

28 The advisory council of which I am chairman was specifically requested by the Minister of Education to review this system of specialization. We examined it most carefully and discussed it at great length, both with witnesses and among ourselves. In the end we came to the conclusion that we wanted to see it continued. We found that it was being pushed too far, and we have made a number of suggestions for removing what we think are abuses. But we have reported in favor of this system of specialization. And that is a unanimous conclusion reached by a council made up of educators of all kinds. Perhaps you will find that fact as extraordinary as the system itself, and I must try to give you some of our reasons for thinking that, in this matter, we in England are in step and the whole of the rest of the world is out of step.

29 Let me begin by telling you of one argument that we reject. This is the argument that every intelligent citizen, or every educated man, ought to know something about each subject in a range so wide that it compels a

balanced curriculum; that no one can afford to be ignorant of history, government, science, languages, and so forth. To this, we would give our answer in two parts. First, it is true that there are certain elementary skills and knowledges that everyone must have—reading, writing, arithmetic, and several more. But these essential elements can be, and should be, provided by the age of sixteen. If you go on with them after that age, you will be wasting your time, because the knowledge you instill will be forgotten unless it can be attached to the main intellectual interest of a boy's or girl's life, which begins to emerge at about that age.

30 The second part of the answer is that it is only when you have got these essential elementary skills and knowledges out of the way that you can confront the real task of education. The acquisition of factual knowledge is by itself a poor test of any education and a lamentably poor test of the education of boys and girls of seventeen and eighteen. It has been said that the process of education is not to be compared to that of filling up an empty pot, but rather to that of lighting a fire. The proper test of an education is whether it teaches the pupil to think and whether it awakens his interest in applying his brain to the various problems and opportunities that life presents. If these have once been done, then factual knowledge can easily be assimilated. If these have not been done, then no amount of nodding acquaintance with widely varying fields of human knowledge will equip a boy or girl with an educated mind. We in England argue the case for specialization not primarily on the score of the information it provides but because it awakens interest, teaches clear thinking, and induces self-discipline in study.

31 We believe that, if you can find which of the recognized intellectual disciplines most arouses a boy's interest—and we confine his choice to five or six recognized disciplines, chosen for their intellectual content, not for their vocational value—if you can let him spend his time on what interests him, but insist that he must work hard at it, go deep into it, follow it up in the library or the laboratory, get around behind the stage scenery that defines the formal academic subject, you will really be teaching him how to use the mind that God has given him. This sort of intensive study takes a great deal of time, and that is why it can only be applied, for any one student, to a restricted range of subjects. No doubt you will say that the boy must be very narrow as a result. That may be. Are you sure that being narrow is worse than being shallow?

32 I find that English education has a high reputation among Americans. I am often asked, for example, whether it is not true that the eighteen-year-old boy in England is a year or two ahead of his American contemporary. I always answer that question, or assertion, by asking some others. What boy? If an English boy is still at school at eighteen, he is necessarily in the upper quartile in intelligence. Are you comparing him

with the average American high school graduate, who is of average intelligence? And ahead in what? In the subjects to which he has been giving nearly all his time and attention for two years? It would be strange if he were not a long way ahead in those. Or over the whole range of a broad curriculum? He has been taught different things, by different methods, with a different purpose in view, in a different sort of school. There is no fair basis for a comparative judgment.

STUDY GUIDE

Structure

1. This is in every way an admirably organized essay. In a tightly knit piece of expository prose the introduction frequently states the precise purpose of the writer and the conclusion in some way implies or refers to what the writer has announced in his introduction and actually done in the body of his essay. Show how the introduction (paragraphs 1 and 2) and the conclusion (paragraph 32) fulfill these functions.

2. The essay is an excellent example of the development of an idea by comparison and contrast. American and English education are compared on the basis of their purposes, their structure, and their method. Work out a sentence outline in which you show how the two systems of education are contrasted in each of these areas.

3. The writer here achieves a fine coherence by the well-placed connecting elements between the various parts of his essay. Underline these connecting elements in the following paragraphs and show how they help the reader to follow the author's sequence of thought: paragraphs 3, 8, 11, 12, 18, 26, and 32.

ON THE FUTURE OF HUMANISTIC EDUCATION

John Courtney Murray

1 The issue of the future of humanistic education arises, I suppose, because the future of man himself has become an issue in our day. Is the present moment the portent of a new epoch of history, a new age of humanity, a new sort of humanism, a new type of man? Must there consequently be a new kind of education, for which the tradition offers no model? . . .

2 For my part, I see nothing in the prognosis of a new age of humanity that would require us to abandon or radically to alter the fourfold structure of aims in terms of which the tradition of humanistic education has stated its ideal. The ideal has been to put the student in the way of developing a power of diction, a view of reality, a set of values, and a sense of style.

3 By diction I mean, for the moment, all that traditional humanism, in dependence on Quintilian (A.D. 35–c. 100), has meant by a finished power of utterance (*perfecta eloquentia*). In his *Institutio oratoria* (*The Training of an Orator*), Quintilian defined the majestic verb "eloqui" simply as the power "to utter, and to convey to the listener, what you have in mind." Diction in this sense means command of words, the ability to find in language the exact equivalent of the thought in mind, and the further quality of fluency. Diction, however, also includes the capacity to order discourse with a sense of logic and thus endow it with force, and to compose discourse with the care that issues in elegance, which is a thing of restraint, propriety, polish, grace. This art of utterance stands highest in the order of the skills which education seeks to develop. The mark of the humanist is the manner in which he uses his tongue, in the several senses of that word. Today we might speak of a power of communication, except that Quintilian would wince at the shallowness of meaning that the word has taken on. His orator was trained to fulfill Cato's definition, "a good man skilled in speaking," a man who had the public in mind, and who also had in mind something that needed utterance, because it was true, and therefore would serve the public good.

4 What the humanist is supposed to have in mind, needing utterance, is, in the end, a view of reality in Newman's sense of the word "view." In *The Idea of a University*, he contrasts the "genuine philosophical habit of mind," which is at once the possession and the quest for a view, with "that spurious philosophism which shows itself in what, for want of a word, I may call 'viewiness.' " The contrast is between a grasp of things in their ordered intelligibility and what is pejoratively called "knowledgeability," which is a thing of bits and pieces, the property of the famous gentleman who "knew everything—and nothing else." This aspect of the ideal of humanistic education serves more often as the measure of its failure than of its success. In 1953–54 a survey of twenty-one colleges and universities, made for the Fund for the Advancement of Education, discovered that the "pervasive problem" was the problem of "coherence." The discovery was not new. Long before, Woodrow Wilson had spoken of "the feudal system of learning," in which "there is no common mastery, but everywhere separate baronies of knowledge, where a few strong men rule and many ignorant men are held vassals." My concern, however, is not with the factual state of education but with its ideal. The survey itself acknowl-

edged the ideal in multiple references to the need for synthesis, integration, coherence, a unifying purpose and idea, a design, a synoptic view.

5 To achieve a view requires a certain comprehensiveness and versatility of intellect, a command over the mind's full range of powers, the faculty of entering with comparative ease into any subject of thought, the active power of insight that prompts one to ask the right questions, a flexibility of intelligence that enables one to assume a variety of viewpoints, the capacity to grasp the relations between things and to throw them into system. The effort to build a view begins with the profound sense that intelligence is, as Aristotle said it was, *capax fieri omnia,* a universally responsive capacity for spiritual identification with, and therefore knowledge of, all that is real. To put it more simply, the quest for a view begins with the awakening of the spirit of wonder that is the root of the desire for understanding.

6 The spirit of wonder is man's native endowment. What is not an endowment but a most painful acquisition is an understanding of what Wilson called the "constitution of learning." Little success will attend any effort to order one's knowledge, unless one understands what the order of knowledge is and why it is an order. Therefore one must come to understand what understanding is, and what the ways of understanding are, and why there are several, not just one. From another point of view, one must come to understand the virtualities of man's intellectual consciousness—how they are multiple, not single. In a metaphor, one must understand that truth is not a ranch-style structure, all on one level, with a single door of entry, but a many-storied edifice through which one ascends by those different modes of access which are the variant methodologies of inquiry. To say all this is, of course, to raise a whole spectrum of philosophical issues. They are precisely the issues that must be raised in the course of a humanistic education, because its aim is to put the student in the way of building a view of reality. The essential humanist refusal is to diminish the range of man's intelligence and thus contract the dimensions of reality.

7 I am implying, of course, that the subject matter of a humanistic education is the whole of reality, or, if you will, all truth, in its unity and in all the inner differentiations within its unity. Out of this implication a multitude of educational problems arise which cannot be touched here. I must, however, note that within the tradition of humanistic education the canon for the inclusion or exclusion of this or that subject matter or field of study was never considered to be relevance. The canon is too vague to serve as a heuristic principle. Relevance to whom? Why? When? Under what circumstances? How? And what precisely does relevance mean? The issue of relevance is best left to be solved *ambulando*. One must wait to discover by experience the uses of what one knows and the consequences of ignorance. The humanist is not greatly disposed to argue the issue of

relevance. Not being a pedant, he is prepared to agree with Whitehead that all education is and ought to be useful, in the sense that all understanding is useful.

8 The tradition of humanistic education has never regarded the student as a naked intelligence inhabiting a world of concepts and propositions, in which the only issues are truth and error, certitude and probability, adequacy or inadequacy of formulation, logic or fallacy in argument. The student's attention was directed to the real world as it is, a world of good and evil, beauty and ugliness, order and disorder, in which man is called upon not only to think but also to act—to do things and make things. The aim, therefore, was to cultivate a power of moral judgment and the esthetic sense that is called taste. Newman has the phrase for this aim: "the instinctive just estimate of things as they pass before us." The estimate, whether moral or esthetic, is instinctive, but only because the sense of right and wrong, of the beautiful and the ugly, has been subjected to rigorous discipline and refined by the further necessary tutelage of experience. The estimate is just, because it is not merely visceral; valid reasons can be adduced for it, if need be. The right word here might be "appreciation," the capacity to set a just value on what presents itself, not only in the intellectual order of thought but in the practical orders of doing and making. The power of evaluation supposes the possession of a set of values, anchored in the order of reality and order in proper hierarchy. Humanistic education, therefore, has looked to the development of a set of values, moral and esthetic.

9 Finally, the tradition has considered that humanistic education should somehow instill what Whitehead called "the most austere of all mental qualities," the sense for style. In the well-known passage in his Presidential Address to the Mathematical Association of England in 1916, he spoke of the sense for style as "the ultimate morality of mind" and also the final utility of education. "It is," he said, "an aesthetic sense, based on admiration for the direct attainment of a foreseen end, simply and without waste." In all the affairs of men, certainly in all the affairs of intelligence, blindness or lack of focus with regard to the end in view, roundaboutness and muddle and wastage of effort in pursuit of the end assume somewhat the character of *hamartia*, sin. Where they are found, something essential is "missing" (the root meaning of *hamartia*), and the privation is a manner of evil. "Style," Whitehead concludes, "is the last acquirement of the educated mind; it is also the most useful. It pervades the whole being." Style is not, indeed, wisdom, which remains the highest of the intellectual virtues. Style is, however, a quality of wisdom as of the four other intellectual virtues—knowledge and understanding, art and prudence.

10 The foregoing may do as a highly condensed and generalized sum-

mary of the four traditional aims of humanistic education—diction, a view, values, and style. I maintain that this ideal, in its fourfold structure, will be as valid in the future as it has been in the past. The only objection to the ideal is that it may be impossible of attainment in the course of "what goes on in schools and colleges." The objection is irrelevant. The ideal always lay beyond reach; but one became an educated man in the process of reaching for it.

11 The whole issue, however, is not thus easily disposed of. There is some substance to the talk about the new epoch of history and the new man. Moreover, I happen to be a conservative who believes in innovation, as true conservatives must, lest in the end they find themselves with nothing worth conserving. Therefore, I further maintain that the educational tradition, in order to be true to itself, must undergo that organic process of change which is known as "growth." It only remains to know what the dynamism of growth is, what directions the progress in the tradition should take, and what new forms the development should show forth.

12 In the realm of doctrine or theory the dynamism of development is readily identified. It is the change of perspective that is brought about by the asking of either a new question, or of an old question in a new mode of statement or with a new note of urgency. The classic theological instance is Nicaea. The new question asked by Arius altered the perspective in which the writings of the New Testament had viewed the Logos-Son. The New Testament question was asked in intersubjective categories, I and Thou, and formally raised the issue of presence and function: Art thou the Christ—the Lord-with-us, the Savior-of-us? The Arian question was asked in ontological categories and formally raised the issue of being and nature: Is the Son God or creature? The Nicene answer, given in the famous *homoousion,* affirmed the scriptural doctrine but in the new perspective. Thus it was a development, a growth in understanding. Another theological instance confronts us today, as the polemical question (Who has the one true faith—Catholic, Protestant, Orthodox?) gives place to the ecumenical question (How shall Catholic, Protestant, and Orthodox move together toward unity in the true faith?). A change of perspective has occurred which affects almost every single theological issue and will surely result in an enrichment of the Christian tradition.

13 The same dynamism of development has operated in the field of political theory. There has been in the West a political tradition, a tradition of growth in the understanding and practice of politics. Its growth has been occasioned by changes of perspective; these in turn occurred as new questions arose, or, more exactly, as one or other essential political question took precedence over others; and this in turn happened in consequence of the changing experiences of particular cultures in different periods of history. For classical antiquity the political question was justice;

for medieval times it was the political relationship, its origin and limits—that is, the question of authority; for modern times it was the freedom of the individual citizen. In our own times, as Hans Morgenthau tirelessly points out, the political question is power and the struggle for power. The experience of totalitarianism has raised the question—that is, given primacy to it. And its primacy creates a new perspective within which the Western political tradition is given an opportunity for new growth in the understanding of itself.

14 The same complex of factors—new experience, new question, new perspective on an old problem—could furnish the dynamism for organic developments in the tradition of humanistic education. The new experience is easily identified; it prompts all the talk about the new age and the new man. It is the scientific experience, using the term in its broadest meaning. The new educational question, however, has not yet been formulated with clarity. A confused argument is, indeed, going on, but it seems to be hardly more than a reverberating echo of the seventeenth-century quarrel between the "ancients" and the "moderns," which was satirized by Jonathan Swift in "The Battle of the Books." In Swift's version, which has the truth of caricature, the quarrel concerned occupancy of the higher and larger of the two tops of the Parnassus. Traditionally, it had belonged to the ancients; the Moderns coveted it. Hence they sent the demand, "either that the ancients would remove themselves and their effects down to the lower summit, which the moderns would graciously surrender to them, and advance in their place; or else the said ancients will give leave to the moderns to come with shovels and mattocks, and level the said hill as low as they shall think it convenient."

15 The same issue seems to appear in today's battle of the books, when the state of the question is conceived to be science *versus* the humanities. This conception of the issue releases only a sectarian quarrel, not a useful argument. The state of the question is altered when the positivist philosophers of science join the fray, as they enthusiastically do. (For the most part, scientists themselves are above the battle, or possibly beneath it; generally they want to get on with their work in the laboratory or at the desk, and not be bothered about education.) The positivist or pragmatist takes up the position that there are not two tops to Parnassus—the hill of true and certain knowledge—but only one, and now it is securely occupied by science. The humanities can make no valid cognitive claims for themselves; all such claims must be submitted to the test of scientific verification. In its extreme form, the position seems to assert that there is no Parnassus at all, but only a way of climbing it—that is, there is no definitive and universal truth, but only a method for its endless pursuit.

16 There are, moreover, those who attempt to reconcile the contending parties by saying that science deals with "facts," whereas the humani-

ties deal with "values," and therefore there should be no quarrel. This position, of course, stultifies the humanist and makes the scientist quite rightly mad. His rejoinder is that science today is not value-free, that it is itself a value, and that it creates values for society as for the individual. The contention is true enough, but, so far from advancing the argument, it disguises or further confuses the real issue. And the confusion is worse confounded when the humanities are reduced to literature and the fine arts, under exclusion of philosophy, on the ground, as Douglas Bush has pointed out, that "modern philosophy seems to be suspended somewhere between linguistics and mathematics," both of which, incidentally, are now considered to be scientific disciplines. Thus the old battle of the books, which was at least serious and even sprightly in its day, runs drearily down to the level of the trivial and nugatory, the partisan and the passionate. . . .

17 I do not think that this battle, which is only an engagement in a larger war, can be fought to a conclusion in the course of "what goes on in schools and colleges." (I really should not use the military image. The issue is a schism in the soul of civilization. And in a case of spiritual schism an image from the world of medicine, "healing," or from the higher world of religion, "conversion," would be more apt.) What, then, can education undertake to do, in response to today's dominant experience? What might be the directions and the forms of progress? Some few suggestions can be offered with regard to ways in which the four traditional aims of education may be enlarged and also brought to new focus.

18 A new issue of diction has arisen. If the Faustian man has arrived on the scene, it is important that the humanist should be able to talk to him. This means that his language must be learned. I do not mean his jargon, but his nonverbal language, which is mathematics, and his logic, which is the special logic of the scientific method of inquiry. As Ernest Nagel said, "To accept the conclusions of science without a thorough familiarity with its method of warranting them is to remain ignorant of the critical spirit that is the life of science." No educated man today can afford this ignorance. There is moreover, the need to obviate the danger to which Margaret Mead has called attention, the danger of developing, as other civilizations before us have developed, "special esoteric groups," whose members can communicate only with one another. This development she says, is "schismogenic," self-perpetuating and self-aggravating. Again, if it be true that these esoteric groups, in combination, are fashioning a new age of man, the humanist cannot afford to be left out of their conversation. Its subject matter is his own—man and the world of man. Moreover, the scientific conversation is political in some Greek sense, as the scientific enterprise is a public enterprise. Scientists frequently vaunt the latter fact (though some of them make the disastrous mistake of supposing that

humanism, like religion, is a purely private matter). The conversation ought, therefore, to be somehow open to the public. Furthermore, since the scientists are talking, not just about themselves and about what they are doing, but about the future of man, their conversation is of universal import. We the People should know what they are saying and what they are up to. There is, therefore, the problem of translation downward, so to speak, from the world of expertise to the world in which the rest of us live. The humanist, the man of diction, who is in command of all the forms of literary art, from the learned essay to the light theater-piece, and who is also the "good man speaking skilfully," should somehow let us know what is in store for us—in some more responsible ways than by scary stories of unsafe fail-safe systems.

19 Finally, there is the problem of diction as it touches the scientist himself. Privately, he may, indeed, be dealing with the ineffable, with what can be communicated only in nonverbal symbols. The ineffable is, however, useless to political man, who lives in a world whose motive power is chiefly the power of speech. If, therefore, science is relevant to political man, as science says it is, the scientist must somehow learn intelligibly to use his tongue. Above all, he is not permitted to ascend to the arrogance of saying, as he sometimes does, "You would not understand." The rest of us would be tempted to the quick retort: "The trouble is that you do not understand what understanding is." We know today the scientific fact, verified in experiment, that a child of ten can be brought to understand almost anything if the teacher understands not only his subject but also the nature and processes of understanding in any subject. Incidentally, the arrogant statement and the just retort embody an implicit statement of an aspect of our current cultural schism. Part of the trouble does seem to be that Science understands science, but it does not understand understanding.

20 In what concerns the second aim of education—the quest of a view of reality—the new perspective derivative from the scientific experiences makes possible a development. The central reality of which traditional humanism sought to fashion a view was man, taking "man" to mean "I-with-the-others-in-the-world," that is, the person, society, and the human environment in both its cosmic and in its humanly created aspects. In an older humanism man was simply the subject who undertook the inquiry. He was Ulysses, setting out "to gain experience of the world and of the vices and worth of men," pressing onward even into the "unpeopled world to be discovered by following the sun," and still further daring to pursue his quest into the transcendent world where God dwells in inaccessible light. Moreover, he had at his disposal, as his tool of research, only his own intelligence, tutored in the logic of philosophical inquiry, stored with knowledge of what men had thought and said, made and done. Finally,

what aroused his wonder was simply the world of common human experience; this was the world of which he had to render an account, in all the aspects of it that progressively aroused his curiosity. In our day, however, man is no longer simply the inquiring subject; he is also the object of inquiry. The inquiry is objective, skeptical, professionally neutral. And man has at his disposal, as tools of research, whole batteries of scientific instruments, new kinds of mathematics, new techniques of statistical estimate and so on. Finally, these new artificial hands, so to speak, have made accessible to man a whole new world of experience, the special experience, unknown to the old humanist, which is called "scientific."

21 The instant question is: What has science found out about man? The detailed and unfolding answer to this question needs to be made the common property of all educated men and women today. Therefore, as part of its aim to put the student in the way of acquiring a view of reality, humanistic education needs to develop what Robert J. Henle, S.J., calls a "program of cultural assimilation of science." It is not simply that the student must be exposed to the scientific experience by serious study of the scientific disciplines, to some depth at least in one or other of them. It is a matter of conveying to the student—to adapt Henle's terms—the scientific "story" of the cosmos and the scientific "picture" of man in the cosmos, in so far as the story and the picture can presently be constructed out of the certified findings of all the sciences, from genetics to geopolitics. We know today how important the body-image is to the individual, how panic ensues when it is lost—in the course, for instance, of controlled experiments in the limited environment, so called. This body-image is largely an affair of the unconscious. For his own spiritual security man also needs a conscious image of himself and his world—the kind of image that every age has needed to construct for itself, if only by recourse to myth and fantasy. Science can now construct this image with a relative measure of factual accuracy. And the rest of us ought to know what it is; it belongs, as it were, to us, as a man's body-image is a part of himself.

22 If the scientific view of man and his world were to become the common intellectual possession of scientist and humanist, expert and non-expert, some small step would have been taken toward the integration of science and humanism in our culture. There is, however, a more compelling reason why this effort at the cultural assimilation of science is imperative in education. Unless the student comes to know the scientific story of the world and the scientific picture of man (together, as I said, with a firm grasp of the method whereby the story was put together and the picture drawn, and thus of the level of explanation on which the picture and the story have their validity), he cannot intelligently get on toward his higher aim, which is the building of a view of *all* reality. That is to say, he cannot grapple with the question of whether the scientific perspective

is the only perspective within which the truth about man comes into view; whether the scientific view is therefore the total view; or whether it is open to completion by inclusion within a wider framework of systematic understanding whose architecture is designed by philosophy and theology.

23 This question pertains to the pervasive issue with which humanistic education must continually concern itself—the spiritual and intellectual schism in our culture. I state the issue in the first instance as that of openness, in a reciprocal sense. Is the scientific story and picture of man open to, or closed against, the story and the picture which, in different ways, philosophy and theology have to tell or draw, and does this openness also reveal itself from the standpoint of philosophy and theology? Christian theology begins in biblical "recital-theology," so called, a telling of the story of the world and man—the story of creation and redemption—and a foretelling of the way in which the story will come out. Christian theology goes on to systematize the content and meaning of the story in the form of doctrine, which, in synthesis with such propositions about man and the world as philosophy may certify, presents a picture of man-in-his-world. There are, therefore, two stories and two pictures. How are they related? Does one cancel the other or complete the other? Is man to acquiesce in an irreducibly dualistic view of himself? Or is he to reduce the dualism to some sort of monism? Or can he account for the difference of views, render intelligible the diversity of perspectives, and compose the views into one, under respect for the respective character of the explanatory value of each? Here, I suggest, is a stimulating new focus for the second traditional aim of education. (I am supposing, of course, that theology will gradually find place in the higher education of the future.)

24 The third aim is the cultivation of the capacity to make valid judgments both of worth and of utility. Here the new focus would concern such judgments as they bear on science and technology, in themselves, and in their relation to other areas of intellectual achievement and moral aspiration. The sciences today present themselves for judgment in a variety of ways. They are systems of true statements, in the scientific sense of truth, which are conclusions of controlled investigation; these systems are part of the public knowledge. The sciences are disciplines that employ a distinctive logic of inquiry, by whose canons and criteria they evaluate claims to knowledge. They are disciplines whose pursuit forms the mind and imparts to it a special quality and a characteristic bent. They are sets of techniques whose import is pragmatic, in that they make it possible to manipulate, regulate, impart chosen directions to the energies of the cosmos and of man himself, and also to manage the course of events. They are collectively a massive enterprise within the liberal society, which profoundly affects its ethos and the whole moral as well as material condition of man. In their ensemble they constitute a revelation of the spirit

of man, a manifestation of his power over his own history and nature. In all these aspects science presents itself for value-judgment with regard to both its worth and its utility. Therefore, it becomes an aim of humanistic education to see that the student is equipped to pass this multiple judgment with discriminating nicety, in the light of both fact and rational standards.

25 The educated man is not permitted to be contemptuous of science, as if it were all an affair of "atoms and the void." Conversely, he will not permit himself to be seduced by science, as if it were the contemporary golden bull, symbol of divinity. In particular, he will stand against the temptation inherent in the contemporary climate, which is to be intimidated by science, as if it were Doctor Faustus.

26 Nothing need be added, I think, about the sense for style. Whitehead may or may not have been wholly right when he said, "Civilization advances by extending the number of important operations which we can perform without thinking about them." In any case, style is what you don't think about when in action, on penalty of awkwardness. Similarly, style is what you don't talk about when discoursing on education, on penalty of superfluity. In a true sense, style is not really an aim of education but a result. Aims need to be defined; but one must simply wait for results.

STUDY GUIDE

Structure

1. Father Murray says in paragraph 13 that he is a "conservative who believes in innovation." He expresses what he thinks should be conserved from the past in part one (paragraphs 1–10) and the innovations that he considers necessary in part two (paragraphs 11–26). State briefly the main ideas of each part.

2. The first part (paragraphs 1–10) is developed almost as a separate essay with an introductory and concluding paragraph. Make a sentence outline of this part of the essay in which you show the thought relationship between its sections.

3. Show how the author has made the reader conscious of the transition to a new part of the essay in paragraph 13.

4. What exactly does the author mean by dynamism in paragraph 13 and following? What connection does the discussion of the theological question and the political question in paragraphs 12 and 13 have with the dynamism or sense of growth that the author is talking about here?

5. How are paragraphs 17–26 related to the thought structure that you have outlined?

Diction and Content

1. In this essay the author has his own meaning for the term *style*. Has he

by it? How does his meaning differ from what a writer like Lucas in Section 3 means by it?

2. The author's definition of diction (paragraph 3) is also considerably more inclusive than the ordinary definition of that word. How is it ordinarily defined? Look it up in your dictionary. Does Murray's definition approach the usual meaning of literary style?

3. Look up the background of Quintilian, Newman, Wilson, and Whitehead. Why did each of them have some authority to speak about the nature and aims of education?

4. Look up the etymology of *appreciation* (paragraph 8) and show how even etymologically the word means "the capacity to set a *just value* on what presents itself."

5. What, according to the author, is the main problem between the humanists and the scientists in modern society? What does he suggest that the humanists and scientists can do to help solve the problem?

6. There are several unfamiliar words in this eassy. Look up the exact meaning of the following words and discuss their meaning in the context of this essay: *prognosis, synoptic, heuristic,* and *polemical. Ecumenical* is not an unfamiliar word today, but what is its exact meaning?

THE AGE OF OVERWRITE AND UNDERTHINK

Stephen Spender

1 In the famous controversy about the two cultures, one important point seems to have been overlooked: that if there truly is a gulf between the literary and the scientific culture, it cannot be bridged by science, but only by language. Language is the only means of communication between specialities as far apart as every individual's unique experience of his own life. Scientific specialization itself is human experience, and if it is to become part of the general culture it can only be so by communication through language. When there is a question of discussing and explaining our experiences of the other arts, music, or painting, we use words. If architecture aspires to the condition of music, all human experience aspires to words.

2 This very simple point, that we communicate by means of language, seems to be largely overlooked by our educators. Our own language is thought of as just one thing taught like all the others, not as an inter-

mediary between all things taught. Before the end of the last century, English, I believe, was not a subject at English universities. There was no English school at Oxford and Cambridge. Everyone was supposed to know English literature, and apart from the grammar taught in one's childhood, how to write English was a benefit conferred by, or inferred from, a classical education. I suppose that some of those who hotly contested the introduction of the study of English literature must have argued, with reason, that if English becomes a subject, then reading and writing English literature becomes a specialization among other specializations. The main road of communication becomes a cellar occupied by people who make a profession of reading and writing. In our own time an attempt is being made to turn the tables on those who have made English one subject among other subjects by giving it the status of principal subject. Dr. Leavis and his followers argue that English should be the main study at the new universities. They argue that in the era of the breakdown of values, and in the absence of religion, our only connection with the past of the "organic community" is through the English books of the Great Tradition, as chosen by the Leavisite priesthood.

3 This seems an attempt to replace compulsory religious teaching with compulsory study of English literature. It seems an extreme position only serving to dramatize that it is a desperate one in the age of nuclear fission when the people who are studying either to reinvent us or to completely destroy us have no time for any other work than their frenetic pursuit of bigger and better means of doing one or the other.

4 What one may insist on, though, is that life attains significance through the consciousness of the individual who lives it, and who is able to understand that significance through comparing his own experiences with those of other people. Language is the only means of communicating experiences, realizing consciousness. One cannot, I think, reasonably argue that everyone ought to be a New Critic, or a doctrinaire of the Great Tradition, but one can point out that it is urgent for people to be able to communicate, and that they can only do this through being able to read the works that illuminate their experiences. This means developing a capacity to speak, think, and write clearly.

5 It seems to be universally recognized that everyone should learn to read and write. Not to be able to do so is to be illiterate. Little importance, however, is attached to *what* you read and how you write. The idea that writing is not just a physical attainment, like using a knife and fork, but is communication, and that everyone should be concerned with it to the degree that he has experiences and ideas to express, seems to be regarded as eccentric. Yet it is doubtful whether you can carry on an intelligent conversation without being able to write down the ideas conversed about. Anyone can demonstrate this to himself by simply turning on the

radio or TV and listening to the dismal attempts of experts in politics and government to communicate their expertise. What one witnesses again and again is the breakdown of language.

6 We groan over specialization, but we accept it as inevitable, reflecting that specialists are so specialized in matters of which we are so ignorant that even if they could tell us about the things they know, we would not understand. Yet there exist, especially in France and England, a few masters of exposition who show that the most specialized subject is often far more communicable than we would anticipate its being. Moreover, it is doubtful whether what we need or want to know from the specialist is really that which is highly technical and particular to his research. What we need to know from scientists is how their scientific picture of the world should affect and qualify our life. A good deal of this can be explained. And if—as Robert Oppenheimer seems to think—there is a highly important kind of scientific experience that cannot be communicated to the nonspecialist then the significance of noncommunicability is something that also needs to be explained, because it may be a factor, or, rather a blank, in the picture of life we need to allow for. In the past it was considered important to understand that there were incommunicable mysteries. But these were communicated as *experience of the incommunicable*, in that people realized there were mysteries of knowledge and priesthood. If there is a kind of scientific experience that is central to modern life and cannot be explained, then this is something different from mere "specialization," and it can and should be understood.

7 Whether what scientists have to explain to us is communicable, or whether they have to explain that it is incommunicable, the fact is that the present breakdown in communication is due at least partly to the neglect of English. It is slovenly to accept without question the cliché that we cannot communicate because we live in "an age of specialization." One only has to look at the essays of most sociologists to realize that language, the medium of communication, is often the last thing that people who have very important things to tell about the state of our society have taken trouble about. We enter the era of mass communication when the study of the traditional, and the ultimate, means of communication, the English language, is looked at as a matter concerning only literary specialists.

8 I do not see why an attempt should not be made at school through the widened study of writing and speaking English to break down some barriers of incommunicability. The basic condition for making such an attempt possible would be that everyone, in whatever discipline, wrote an essay on some general subject once a week or fortnight. Some of these essays might take the form of communications from members of one discipline to another. For example, students on the science side of the school might be

asked to write essays directed to those studying history, explaining, in words that the science student hoped the historian would understand, what some aspect of his science was about, and vice versa. The historians, or the scientists, would then read the best essays from the science students, and perhaps both classes would meet to discuss the essays.

9 Another exercise that I have thought about (without being able to fire anyone else with my own enthusiasm) is that a day of a term or a year should be set aside for general academic exercise in which speakers from different specialized disciplines would explain before an audience what they thought was the meaning and importance of their work. A good classroom exercise might be to make students listen to TV interviews with Senators, ex-Presidents, etc., taking with them notebooks in which they would write down sentences in the interview that strike them as particularly good, or particularly bad, considered not for their content but as language—to be followed by a general discussion of these by the class. This might prove linguistically therapeutic.

10 I think, then, that we should regard English literature—fiction, non-fiction, poetry, etc.—primarily as teaching people to communicate with one another and in that way helping them to live their lives. We are not, even in the university creative writing course, teaching them to be writers. We are concerned only with teaching them to read, to express themselves, to appreciate language, to discuss and talk better because they are trying to read and write. Instead of giving them a specialist view of writing, we should try to break this down, to emphasize the importance of writing everything as well as possible: a letter to a friend or to a member of the family, a private journal. We should make them think of reading and writing as two sides of the same medal. One reads better because one writes better, one writes better because one reads better.

11 That students often distinguish sharply between reading and writing is painfully evident. Some years ago, after reading an essay by one of my students I suggested to her that she should read Samuel Butler's essays. "Oh, I don't read, Mr. Spender," she protested, "I write."

12 As I suggested above, every student at school ought to write a weekly essay. Students ought to be given a wide choice of subjects, with a view, perhaps, to their sometimes being very close to themselves and sometimes demanding that they should get away from their self-absorption, their subjectivity, into their opposite, the objective. But it is a mistake to produce the impression that this kind of belles-lettres is literature, or, at any rate, more literary, than the subject I suggested previously, of a scientist writing for a historian about his scientific studies. Everything that is well written can be literature, if literature is what we are concerned with. One of the masterpieces of English literature is a handbook on angling.

STUDY GUIDE

Suggested Exercise

Father Murray says, in paragraph 19 of his essay, that "If . . . science is relevant to political man, as science says it is, the scientist must somehow learn intelligibly to use his tongue." Spender in the opening paragraph of this essay refers to the "two cultures." The term is that of the novelist and scientist C. P. Snow, who has written extensively about the seemingly unbridgeable gulf which stretches between the world of scientists and that of literary intellectuals. Spender, like Father Murray, takes a more hopeful view than Snow. He says that "if there truly is a gulf between the literary and the scientific culture, it cannot be bridged by science, but only by language." He further suggests that some of that incommunicability might be broken down even in the freshman composition class by exercises in writing. In these exercises, students in the sciences would write an explanation of a scientific fact or principle for the nonscientific members of the class.

Spender's suggestion is an experiment worth trying. The following essay, "The Truth about the Bomb" by William L. Laurence, may provide a helpful model of the kind of language necessary for the communication of scientific knowledge to a nonscientific audience.

THE TRUTH ABOUT THE BOMB

William L. Laurence

1 Five years after the first announcement of the explosion of the A-bomb over Hiroshima, even the most intelligent Americans still have only the vaguest idea about the facts. Yet these facts are within the understanding of the average man. If we keep the analogy of the match in mind, it becomes simple to understand the principles underlying both the A-bomb, now more correctly identified as the "fission bomb," and the hydrogen bomb, more properly described as the "fusion bomb."

2 Our principal fuel is coal, which, as everyone knows, is "bottled sunshine," stored up in plants that grew about two hundred million years ago. When we apply the small amount of heat energy from a match, the bottled energy is released in the form of light and heat, which we can use in a great variety of ways. The point here is that it requires only the application of a very small amount of energy from a match to release a very

From *The Hell Bomb* by William L. Laurence, published by Alfred A. Knopf, New York, 1951.

large amount of energy that has been stored for millions of years in the ancient plants we know as coal.

3 Now, during the past half century we discovered that the nuclei, or centers, of the smallest units of which the ninety-odd elements of the material universe are made up—units we know as atoms—had stored up within them since the beginning of creation amounts of energy millions of times greater than is stored up by the sun in coal. But we had no match with which to start an atomic fire burning.

4 Then, in January 1939, came the world-shaking discovery of the phenomenon known as uranium fission. In simple language, we had found a proper "match" for lighting a fire with a twin of uranium, the ninety-second, and last, natural element. This twin is a rare form of uranium known as uranium 235—the figure signifying that it is 235 times heavier than common hydrogen. Doubly phenomenal, the discovery of uranium fission meant that to light the atomic fire, with the release of stored-up energy three million times greater than that of coal and twenty million times that of TNT (on an equal-weight basis), would require no match at all. When proper conditions are met, the atomic fire would be lighted automatically by spontaneous combustion.

5 What are these proper conditions? In the presence of certain chemical agencies, spontaneous combustion will take place when an easily burning substance, such as sawdust, for example, accumulates heat until it reaches the kindling temperature at which it ignites. The chemical agencies here are the equivalent of a match.

6 The requirement to start the spontaneous combustion of uranium 235, and also of two man-made elements named plutonium and uranium 233 (all three known as fissionable materials or nuclear fuels), is just as simple. In this operation you do not need a critical temperature, but what is known as a critical mass. This simply means that spontaneous combustion of any one of the three atomic fuels takes place as soon as you assemble a lump of a certain weight. The actual critical mass is a top secret. But the noted British physicist, Dr. M. L. E. Oliphant, of radar fame, published in 1946 his own estimate, which places its weight between ten and thirty kilograms. If so, this would mean that a lump of uranium 235 (U-235), plutonium, or U-233, weighing ten or thirty kilograms, as the case may be, would explode automatically by spontaneous combustion and release an explosive force of 20,000 tons of TNT for each kilogram undergoing complete combustion. In the conventional A-bomb a critical mass is assembled in the last split second by a timing mechanism that brings together, let us say, one tenth and nine tenths of a critical mass. The spontaneous combustion that followed such a consummation on August 6 and 9, 1945, destroyed Hiroshima and Nagasaki.

7 Thus, if we substitute the familiar phrase "spontaneous combustion"

for the less familiar word "fission," we get a clear understanding of what is known in scientific jargon as the "fission process," a "self-multiplying chain reaction with neutrons," and similar technical mumbo-jumbo. These terms simply mean the lighting of an atomic fire and the release of great amounts of the energy stored in the nuclei of U-235 since the beginning of the universe. The two so-called man-made elements are not really created. They are merely transformed out of two natural heavy elements in such a way that their stored energy is liberated by the process of spontaneous combustion.

8 Why, one may ask, does not spontaneous combustion of U-235 take place in nature? Why, indeed, has not all the U-235 in nature caught fire automatically long ago? To this also there is a simple answer. Just as in the spontaneous combustion of sawdust the material must be dry enough to burn, so must the U-235. Only in place of the word "dry" we must use the word "concentrated." The U-235 found in nature is very much diluted with another element that makes it "wet." It therefore must be separated first, by a very laborious and costly process, from the nonfissionable, or "wetting," element. Even then it won't catch fire, and could not be made to burn by any means, until the amount separated ("dried") reaches the critical mass. When these two conditions—conditions that do not exist in nature—are met, the U-235 catches fire just as sawdust does when it reaches the critical temperature.

9 The fact that as soon as a critical mass is assembled the three elemental atomic fuels burst into flame automatically thus puts a definite limit to the amount of material that can be used in the conventional A-bomb. The best you can do is to incorporate into a bomb two fragments, let us say, of nine tenths of a critical mass each. To enclose more than two such fragments would present difficulties that appear impossible to overcome. It is this limitation of size, an insurmountable roadblock put there by mother nature, that makes the basic difference between the A-bomb and the H-bomb.

10 For, as we have already seen, to light an atomic fire with deuterium it is necessary to strike a match generating a flame with a temperature of about 50,000,000 degrees centigrade. As long as no such match is applied, no fire can start. It thus becomes obvious that deuterium is not limited by nature to a critical mass. A quantity of deuterium a thousand times the amount of the U-235, and hence a thousand times more powerful, can therefore be incorporated in an ordinary A-bomb, where it would remain quiescent until the A-bomb match is struck. Weight for weight, deuterium has only a little more energy content than U-235, so that a bomb incorporating 1,000 kilograms (one ton) of deuterium would thus have an energy of 20,000,000 tons of TNT.

11 Here must be mentioned another form of hydrogen, named trit-

ium. It has long ago disappeared from nature but it is now being re-created in ponderable amounts in our atomic furnaces. Tritium, the nucleus of which is known as a triton, weighs three times as much as the lightest form of hydrogen. It has an energy content nearly twice that of deuterium. But it is very difficult to make and is extremely expensive. Its cost per kilogram at present AEC prices is close to a billion dollars, as compared with no more than $4,500 for a kilogram of deuterium. A combination of deuterons and tritons would release the greatest energy of all, 3.5 times the energy of deuterons alone. It would reduce the amount of tritons required to half the volume and three fifths of the weight required in a pure triton bomb, thus making the cost considerably lower.

12 But why bother with such fantastically costly tritons when we can get all the deuterium we want at no more than $4,500 a kilogram, while we can make up the difference in energy by merely incorporating two to three and a half times as much deuterium? Here we are dealing with what is probably the most ticklish question in the design of the H-bomb.

13 To light a fire successfully, it is not enough merely to have a match. The match must burn for a time long enough for its flame to act. If you try to light a cigarette in a strong wind, the wind may blow out your match so fast that your cigarette will not light. The same question presents itself here, but on a much greater scale. The match for lighting deuterium—namely, the A-bomb—burns only for about a hundred billionths of a second. Is this time long enough to light the "cigarette" with this one and only "match"?

14 It is known that the time is much too slow for lighting deuterium in its gaseous form. But it is also known that the inflammability is much faster when the gas is compressed to its liquid form, at which its density is 790 times greater. At this density it would take only seven liters (about 7.4 quarts) per one kilogram (2.2 pounds), as compared with 5,555 liters for gaseous deuterium. And it catches fire in a much shorter time.

15 Is this time long enough? On the answer to this question will depend whether the hydrogen bomb will consist of deuterium alone or of deuterium and tritium, for it is known that the deuteron-triton combination catches fire much faster than deutrons or tritons alone.

16 We were already working with tritium in Los Alamos as far back as 1945. I remember the time when Dr. Oppenheimer, wartime scientific director of Los Alamos, went to a large safe and brought out a small vial of a clear liquid that looked like water. It was the first highly diluted minute sample of a superheavy water, composed of tritium and oxygen, ever to exist in the world, or anywhere in the universe, for that matter. We both looked at it in silent, rapt admiration. Though we did not speak, each of us knew what the other was thinking. Here was something, our thoughts ran, that existed on earth in gaseous form some two billion years ago, long

before there were any waters or any forms of life. Here was something with the power to return the earth to its lifeless state of two billion years ago.

17 The question of what type of hydrogen is to be used in the H-bomb therefore hangs on the question of which one of the possible combinations will catch fire by the light of a match that is blown out after an interval of about a hundred billionths of a second. On the answer to this question will also depend the time it will take us to complete the H-bomb and its cost. To make a bomb of a thousand times the power of the A-bomb would require 1,000 kilograms of deuterium at a cost of $4,500,000 or 171 kilograms of tritium and 114 kilograms of deuterium at a total cost of more than $166,000,000,000 at current prices, not counting the cost of the A-bomb trigger. Large-scale production of tritium, however, will most certainly reduce its cost enormously, possibly by a factor of ten thousand or more, while . . . the amount of tritium, if required, may turn out to be much smaller.

18 We can thus see that if deuterium alone is found to be all that is required to set off an H-bomb it will be cheap and relatively easy to make in a short time—both for us and for Russia. Furthermore, such a deuterium bomb would be practically limitless in size. One of a million times the power of the Hiroshima bomb is possible, since deuterium can be extracted in limitless amounts from plain water. On the other hand, if sizable amounts of tritium are found necessary, the cost will be much higher and it will take a considerably longer time, since the production of tritium is very slow and costly. This, in turn, will place a definite limit on the power of the H-bomb, since, unlike deuterium, the amounts of tritium will necessarily always be limited. . . . We are at present in a much more advantageous position to produce tritium than is Russia, so that if tritium is found necessary, we have a head start on her in H-bomb development.

19 The radius of destructiveness by the blast of a bomb with a thousand times the energy of the A-bomb will be only ten times greater, since the increase goes by the cube root of the energy. The radius of total destruction by blast in Hiroshima was one mile. Therefore the radius of a super-bomb a thousand times more powerful will be ten miles, or a total area of 314 square miles. A bomb a million times the power of the Hiroshima bomb would require 1,000 tons of deuterium. Such a super-superduper could be exploded at a distance from an abandoned, innocent-looking tramp ship. It would have a radius of destruction by blast of 100 miles and a destructive area of more than 30,000 square miles. The time may come when we shall have to search every vessel several hundred miles off shore. And the time may be nearer than we think.

20 The radius over which the tremendous heat generated by a bomb of a thousandfold the energy would produce fatal burns would be as far as twenty miles from the center of the explosion. This radius increases as the

square root, instead of the cube root, of the power. The Hiroshima bomb caused fatal burns at a radius of two thirds of a mile.

21 The effects of the radiations from a hydrogen bomb are so terrifying that by describing them I run the risk of being branded a fearmonger. Yet facts are facts, and they have been known to scientists for a long time. It would be a disservice to the people if the facts were further denied to them. We have already paid too high a price for a secrecy that now turns out never to have been secret at all. . . .

STUDY GUIDE

Analogy

1. The chief means by which Laurence enables the nonspecialist reader to follow his explanation of the nature of atomic fission is *analogy*. Study his use of an everyday object, the match, and familiar processes, spontaneous combustion and lighting a cigarette in the wind, to help his readers understand the process of nuclear fission.

2. Some of the science students might take a scientific process with which they are familiar and try, by similar concrete analogies, to explain it to nonscientific members of the class.

IS TECHNOLOGY TAKING OVER?

Charles E. Silberman

1 "I think of art, at its most significant, as a DEW line, a Distant Early Warning system that can always be relied on to tell the old culture what is beginning to happen to it." The author of the analogy is Marshall McLuhan, director of the University of Toronto's Center for Culture and Technology. McLuhan's ideas about art, culture, and technology are very much in the wind these days. He believes that art is a guide to what is happening because the big changes, initiated through new technologies, alter "sense ratios or patterns of perception"; and because the artist is peculiarly sensitive to such changes. What is happening to our culture under the assaults of radio, television, computers, jet travel, satellite communication, etc., McLuhan argues, is a new merging of time and space, a return

Reprinted from the February 1966 issue of *Fortune* Magazine by special permission;

to the interdependence of the tribal village, a growing demand for "involvement" and for sensory experience.

2 Some of these themes are evoked in the "kinetic" (moving) sculpture of Nicolas Schöffer, recently on display in the Jewish Museum in New York. . . . Schöffer calls his sculptures "programed environments" and has written that "the role of the artist no longer is to create a work of art, but to create creation." He designed the sculpture . . . so as to involve the spectator himself in the process of creation—i.e., as he looks into the mirrors and moves about he is incorporated into, and endlessly redesigns, the work of art. Schöffer's art is at once a product of new technologies and evidence that these technologies are leading artists to try new styles and forms, indeed to construct new visions of the world.

3 "Man rushes first to be saved *by* technology," the novelist Gerald Sykes wrote two months ago, "and then to be saved *from* it." Of late, the latter rushing has been more noticeable; indeed, Man as Victim of his Technology is emerging as one of the most insistent and characteristic themes of our time. Fear of technology lay at the root of the gloomy talk about automation and unemployment that filled the mass media in the early 1960's. It was manifest in last year's student revolts at Berkeley and elsewhere: "I am a human being; do not fold, bend, or mutilate," the students had written on the signs they carried. The fear erupted in the wake of the massive power failure that blacked out New York City and most of the Northeast last November. "The British author E. M. Forster once drew a frightening picture of a civilization that surrendered to automation, then collapsed from the weight of its own complexity," the New York *Times* science editor, Walter Sullivan, recalled, adding, "The consequences of Tuesday's electric blackout have given new meaning to this vision."

4 The theme is hardly new; men have always felt an irresistible urge to try to master nature, and have always harbored a deep-seated fear that the attempt would anger the gods and bring about their own downfall. This ambivalence is one of the most persistent themes of mythology and legend. The price of eating of the Tree of Knowledge—of daring "to be as God"—was expulsion from Eden. For daring to give man the gift of fire, Prometheus was condemned to savage torture. And every age has had its own variation on the theme of the sorcerer's apprentice: the young apprentice, too lazy to fill his master's water barrel by his own labor, invokes some fragments of an incantation he has overheard and puts the broom to work fetching water. The broom does so with dispatch; but soon the barrel begins to overflow, and the lad is powerless to intervene, being ignorant of the incantation needed to stop the broom.

5 In the traditional version, the sorcerer returns in time to stop the broom and save the boy from drowning. In the contemporary myth, however, disaster seems to be irreversible; it is inherent in the technologies man

creates. "During the past two centuries," writes the English social scientist, Sir Geoffrey Vickers, "men gained knowledge and power," which they used "to make a world increasingly unpredictable and uncontrollable." The belief that increased power to alter the environment permits increased control over it "is a manifest delusion," Sir Geoffrey argues, adding, "The rate of change increases at an accelerating speed, without a corresponding acceleration in the rate at which further responses can be made; and this brings ever nearer the threshold beyond which control is lost."

6 In the opinion of some, control has already been lost. The French sociologist Jacques Ellul has announced that "a technical take-over" has occurred, and that it is irreversible. Ellul's American translator and advocate, John Wilkinson of the Center for the Study of Democratic Institutions, writes of an "autonomous technology" that is said to be "taking over the traditional values of every society without exception, subverting and suppressing these values to produce at last a monolithic world culture in which all nontechnological difference and variety is mere appearance." According to Ellul and Wilkinson, men can no longer turn technology to their own ends; rather, it "has become an end-in-itself, to which men must adapt themselves"—even though the process subverts so many human values. Technology has placed itself "beyond good and evil"; indeed, it has such "power and autonomy . . . that it, in its turn, has become the judge of what is moral, the creator of a new morality." The result is bound to be the dehumanization of man himself. When "the edifice of the technical society" is completed, Ellul grimly concludes, "the stains of human passion will be lost amid the chromium gleam."

7 This degree of pessimism is extreme, of course. But the unquestioning optimism that marked so much nineteenth-century talk about technology has virtually disappeared. An optimist nowadays is someone who thinks we have a pretty good chance to solve the problems posed by technology; he is nevertheless apt to betray a certain brooding uneasiness about the future. "Can We Survive Technology?" the late John von Neumann asked in the title of an essay he wrote, eleven years ago, as part of *Fortune's* twenty-fifth anniversary celebration. His answer was yes, but there was no doubt that he regarded the question as a real one.

8 The prospect of "dehumanization" is not the only concern about technology being expressed these days. Another arises out of the possibility of nuclear destruction. A third concern has to do with the future of democracy, the argument being that ordinary citizens and government officials are losing the capacity to understand national policy decisions. The English scientist-turned-novelist, C. P. Snow, is perhaps the best known of those who hold that critical governmental decisions now involve such complex technical questions that only scientists are capable of making them. Finally, there is the specter of mass idleness—i.e., the fear that automation of pro-

duction and distribution will eliminate the need for human labor. Some writers see this primarily as an economic problem. Others view it as primarily social or psychological, and have argued that, without work to occupy the bulk of their waking hours, Americans might find life meaningless. "What we fear to face," writes Professor David Riesman of Harvard, one of the first to raise this issue, "is more than total destruction: it is total meaninglessness."

9 The fear of dehumanization has been the most pervasive of all, however. One reason for its pervasiveness may be that those who try to dispel the fear have not always done a satisfactory job. The traditional argument is that the impact of technology depends on us—on the purpose to which we put our knowledge, the tasks to which we apply our technology. "We are too prone to make technological instruments the scapegoats for the sins of those who wield them," R.C.A. Chairman David Sarnoff has said. "The products of modern science are not in themselves good or bad; it is the way they are used that determines their value."

10 In arguing thus, General Sarnoff was following a long and honorable philosophic tradition. "If mankind can rise to the occasion," Alfred North Whitehead wrote some forty years ago, in *Science and the Modern World*, "there lies in front a golden age of beneficent creativeness. But material power in itself is ethically neutral. It can equally well work in the wrong direction." Von Neumann argued in almost identical terms in his 1955 *Fortune* article: "Technology—like science—is neutral all through, providing only means of control applicable to any purpose, indifferent to all."

11 This view is a half-truth that obscures more than it illuminates. Its opponents are on strong enough ground when they deny that technology *determines* our destinies. The trouble arises when they fail to recognize that technology directly *affects* both the individual and society. For purpose does not exist in a vacuum; men do not choose from an infinite array of alternatives. On the contrary, the alternatives from which they choose are in large part given by their technology; any major advance in science or change in technology throws up new alternatives and erases old ones.

12 A new technology, moreover, frequently produces unexpected and unintended effects quite independent of its ostensible purpose. Thus the automobile has changed American life—and is now changing life around the globe—in ways that have little to do with the speed at which people drive or their destinations. Both the pattern and the pace of suburbanization, for example, changed drastically in the 1920's, when cars became an item of mass consumption; and dissertations could be—indeed, have been—written on the way the automobile changed sexual behavior. The assembly line, whether it turns out corn flakes or Cadillacs, has had effects far beyond the developers' original purpose, which was simply to reduce production costs; among other things, the assembly line has drastically changed

the nature of work, altered the function of management and reordered the relations among workers and between workers and management.

13 Some writers, including Daniel Bell, Raymond Aron, and Georges Friedmann, have described the way in which industrialization is imposing a set of "imperatives"—insistent pressures for urbanization, the professionalization of management, the rapid growth of professional and technical employment—that lead to a number of striking similarities in all industrial nations. These pressures operate under both capitalism and socialism, as Bell, for one, has recently argued in a paper on the decline of the Marxist-Leninist ideology in the Soviet Union.

14 Science and technology alter human purpose in another and more fundamental, if less apparent, way: by affecting our basic and frequently unconscious concepts of the good, the true, and the beautiful. According to Marshall McLuhan, the most stimulating—and controversial—student of technology to have emerged in some years, technology literally changes the way in which we perceive the world. "Like it or not," Richard Schickel wrote recently in *Harper's*, McLuhan "is on his way to becoming one of those annoying 'seminal' thinkers whose arguments you must adapt, incorporate, or dispose of before pressing ahead in his field."

15 McLuhan sees each new technology or "medium" as an extension of some part of the human body or capability. For example, the wheel is an extension of the foot, the lever an extension of the arm, tools an extension of the hand. The alphabet and print are extensions of the eye; they translate sounds into sight—i.e., into letters that can be seen on the printed page. "All media are active metaphors in their power to translate experience into new forms."

16 The extension of any one sense, McLuhan believes, alters the relation among all the senses; it creates a new "sense ratio," a new interplay among the senses. This interplay not only alters concepts of style and content, as the printing press did with literature, but changes the way in which we perceive the world. For perception, as Jerome Bruner and others have demonstrated, is not simply a passive or objective relationship between a viewer and the object being viewed. On the contrary, it is a highly subjective and active process, in which events totally outside the stimulus affect (in some cases determine) what we perceive, and how. As E. H. Gombrich has shown, "the innocent eye sees nothing." We see what we are disposed to see. And what disposes us—what determines the anticipation or expectation that is crucial to perception—is only in small degree biological. It is primarily cultural; we see what our culture (which includes our technology) disposes us to see.

17 What happens, then, when our culture and technology change? What happens is that we see things we don't now see, and we see familiar things in a very different way, if indeed we see them at all. If the changes are

large, a culture's whole perceptual style is likely to change. These changes are most evident in the arts, since the nature of the artist—his function, so to speak—is to be most sensitive to them. "Why is it," Gombrich asks in the opening paragraph of his classic *Art and Illusion*, "that different ages and different nations have represented the visible world in such different ways?" The answer is not, as earlier art historians assumed, that techniques improved. "If styles have differed," Gombrich suggests, "it must be because intentions have changed"—because artists in different periods and different nations have perceived "the visible world" in very different ways, reflecting the different technologies and different modes of thought around them.

18 To say this is not to suggest as McLuhan frequently seems to that technology has taken hold and effaced human will, any more than to acknowledge the role and power of the unconscious in individual behavior is to deny the reality of individual choice. It is, rather, to argue that we can enlarge the sphere of choice and use technology to serve human purpose only if we recognize that it affects our purpose, both individually and collectively, and so make the effort to understand how. We need to understand what is fixed and what is changeable; in an era of radical change, we particularly need to be able to distinguish the new from the old—the elements of continuity from those of discontinuity. The need, in short, is not for some new "adjustment" to the imperatives of technology; it is for recognition of what those imperatives are, in order that choices may be made and control may be exercised.

19 Before looking more closely at McLuhan's controversial notions of how technology is changing thought, behavior, and society, it will pay to return to the thesis of Jacques Ellul, whose book, *The Technological Society*, has been enjoying something of a vogue since an English translation was published in this country two years ago. "Just as postwar France established what we call the theatre of the absurd," Arnold Beichman wrote in reviewing the book in the *Christian Science Monitor*, "Professor Ellul may now claim to have produced the sociology of the absurd with his continuing emphasis on man's bewilderment, his helplessness, his utter futility in the world of Technique." What gives Ellul his significance, other reviewers pointed out, is not any special originality of theme—his thesis has roots in Spengler, Veblen, Huxley, Orwell, Mumford—but rather the systematic, rigorous way in which he presents it and the relentlessness with which he carries it to a logical conclusion—and beyond. *The Technological Society* is the sharpest and least ambiguous of the recent arguments that technology is bringing about a loss of freedom and a subversion of human values. Because of this strong theme—and perhaps also because it had supported American publication of the book—the Center for the Study of Democratic Institutions last December assembled in Santa Barbara a group of

thirty-two scholars, philosophers, and scientists from around the world to discuss Ellul's analysis.

20 The enemy, according to Ellul, is not the machine; it is not any single technology or group of technologies. It is, rather, what Ellul calls "technique," a concept embracing the machine but going far beyond it. By technique, Ellul principally means the drive to rationalize every human activity, the search for "the one best means in every field"; sometimes, however, he defines technique as "the ensemble of means," i.e., the whole complex of standardized means that have developed. Unfortunately, Ellul is sometimes maddeningly vague about his central concept. His introductory "Note to the Reader" talks of technique as "the totality of methods rationally arrived at and having absolute efficiency (for a given stage of development) in every field of human activity."

21 What seems to be crucial about technique, however, is its tendency to take over all of man's activities, to "transform everything it touches into a machine." The search for "the one best means" so dominates every activity that this search itself becomes the end; efficiency becomes the purpose of all activity. The end result, Ellul argues, is that "when technique enters into every area of life, including the human, it ceases to be external to man and becomes his very substance." Hence his conclusion that "technique has become autonomous"—that instead of technique serving man, man now serves technique.

22 Without doubt, Ellul is describing certain clear and disturbing tendencies in contemporary society—tendencies that, if carried to their logical conclusion, would subvert quite a few cherished human values. But is our society's commitment to "the one best way" really so inexorable? Will it —must it—carry that commitment to the extreme foreseen by Ellul?

23 The answer is no. Certainly Ellul offers no convincing evidence to support his thesis; and many of his arguments are just foolish. Throughout the book, for example, the technique-ridden present is compared with a beautiful, pastoral—and wholly imaginary—past, when man lived in accordance with "the traditional rhythms of life and nature." "Think of our dehumanized factories, our unsatisfied senses, our working women, our estrangement from nature," Ellul demands. But with what shall we contrast this dehumanized world? The beautiful, harmonious life being lived by, say, the Chinese or Vietnamese peasant woman, who works in the fields, close to nature, for twelve hours a day—roughly the conditions under which the great bulk of women (and men) have worked, at least in the temperate zones, through all of human history? For that is the condition that Ellul idealizes. In the Middle Ages, he assures us, "Man sought open spaces, large rooms, the possibility of moving about, of seeing beyond his nose, of not constantly colliding with other people." This would have

been startling news to the medieval peasant, who lived with his wife and children, other relatives, and probably animals as well in a one-room thatched cottage. And even for the nobility, was there really more "possibility of moving about" in the Middle Ages, when travel was by foot or hoof, than today, when steelworkers spend their sabbaticals in Europe?

24 Ellul's pages are filled with this sort of doubtful history. "Consider . . . our hospitals," he pleads, "in which [man] is only a number"—but in which, one has to add, the chances of his becoming well are quite a lot better than they were in any hospital in the harmonious past. Shall we contrast the dehumanizing medical care of our time with, say, that of the idyllic fourteenth century, when man lived in harmony with the rhythms of nature—and perhaps half the population of England died in just two years as a result of the Black Death?

25 When he writes of technique's tendency to take over, to subordinate ends to means, Ellul is often equally silly:

26 The politician, he tells us, "no longer has any real choice; decision follows automatically from the preparatory technical labors." The evidence? In the U.S., we are informed, on the authority of a German writer, "unchallengeable decisions have already been made by 'electronic brains' in the service of the National Bureau of Standards; for example, by the EAC, surnamed the 'Washington Oracle.' The EAC is said to have been the machine which made the decision to recall General MacArthur after it had solved equations containing all the strategic and economic variables of his plan." The fact, of course, is that Harry S. Truman made the decision. The Bureau of Standards did then have a computer (its correct name was SEAC), which did make some decisions for the Pentagon—for example, how many Army raincoats to order, and in what sizes.

27 Technique, Ellul asserts, "possesses monopoly of action. No human activity is possible except as it is mediated and censored by the technical medium . . . Not even the simplest initiative can have an original, independent existence."

28 The evidence? "Suppose one were to write a revolutionary book," Ellul explains. "If it is to be published, it must enter into the framework of the technical organization of book publishing. In a predominantly capitalistic technical culture, the book can be published only if it can return a profit. Thus, it must appeal to some public and hence must refrain from attacking the real taboos of the public for which it is destined"—a statement that will come as news to such angry social critics as Paul Goodman and Norman Mailer. "Any author who seeks to have his manuscript published must make it conform to certain lines laid down by the potential publishers," Ellul goes on to explain. Thus, "the bourgeois publishing house will not publish Lenin; the 'revolutionary' publishing house will not publish Paul Bourget; and no one will publish a book attacking the real re-

ligion of our times, by which I mean the dominant social forces of the technological society." As the English philosopher J. P. Corbett of the University of Sussex sardonically asked in a critique of Ellul, "What more need be said about Professor Ellul's methods of handling evidence, except to wonder whether he had much difficulty in getting *his* book published?"

29 Ellul's conspiratorial view of events rushing headlong toward the Apocalypse may be taken as a prime example of what the historian Richard Hofstadter calls "the paranoid style"—a kind of literature to which Americans seem addicted. (Other recent examples include Rachel Carson's *Silent Spring,* Vance Packard's *The Hidden Persuaders,* and Paul Goodman's *Growing Up Absurd.*) This approach to the contemporary scene, Professor Corbett says, involves "taking hold of some social phenomenon or other, describing it with an impressive array of pejorative terms, illustrating it by a series of spine-chilling examples, making the reader feel, like the reader of a good ghost story, that all his ordinary assumptions are in jeopardy, but then leaving him with the impression that nothing whatever can be done, whether in theory or in practice, to put things right." The appeal is understandably great. "You thus get all the thrills of virtue with all the comforts of inaction; you are taken to the brink of destiny only to find yourself tucked up snugly in the electric blanket of existing institutions; your guilty conscience is given a salubrious airing, and yet everything is allowed to go on precisely as before."

30 What distinguishes Marshall McLuhan from most other grand theorists of the technological society is his avoidance of the paranoid style. For McLuhan joyously welcomes the technological and cultural changes that other writers fear or criticize, and has succeeded in changing the terms of the debate over what is happening to man in this era of radical change. "Other observers," the art critic Harold Rosenberg wrote in reviewing McLuhan's *Understanding Media* for *The New Yorker,* "have been content to repeat criticisms of industrial society that were formulated a century ago, as if civilization had been steadily emptied out since the advent of the power loom. As against the image of our time as a faded photograph of a richly pigmented past, McLuhan, for all his abstractness, has found positive, humanistic meaning and the color of life in supermarkets, stratospheric flight, the lights blinking on broadcasting towers." Looking at the same phenomena that Ellul and others see as dehumanizing man, McLuhan "has dared to seek the cure in the disease, and his vision of going forward into primitive wholeness is a good enough reply to those who would go back to it." Indeed, McLuhan's work is a "concrete testimonial" to the conviction "that man is certain to find his footing in the new world he is in the process of creating."

31 McLuhan's ideas about what is happening now can be understood best in relation to his ideas about technology's past impact on human so-

ciety, particularly in the past several hundred years. The theory is summed up in McLuhan's epigram, "The medium is the message," by which he means that *societies are shaped more by the nature of the media through which men communicate than by the content of their communications.* In its most general form, as originally developed, for example, by the historian Harold Innis, on whom McLuhan relies very heavily, this idea is less paradoxical or controversial than it sounds. It is now widely believed, for example, that the invention of hand tools and spoken language are what differentiated man from the beasts, enabling him to create social systems of an elaborateness and duration unknown among any other species. Just when or how this happened is shrouded in mystery. But most students of evolution now believe that it was the development of language and of tools that led to the development of the human brain and its differentiation from the brain of any other species—rather than the other way around.

32 The next great "technological" development, in McLuhan's view, was the invention of writing—a clear example of the "medium" being more important than the "message." For once men start to write, they become conscious of time in a way never possible before; writing enormously enlarges society's collective memory, and so social organization begins to extend backward into the past and forward into the future in a way impossible in a completely preliterate society. More important, perhaps, writing also leads to the breakup of tribal society and the emergence of individualism in the Western sense—the phenomenon nineteenth-century English historians referred to as the shift from "status" to "contract."

33 The point is that individualism is virtually a byproduct of literacy. Preliterate societies are oral societies; they live in a world of sound. Whereas for us "seeing is believing," for the preliterate hearing is believing; reality resides in what is heard and said. Because oral communication requires proximity, oral societies tend to be collective. As David Riesman has put it, "When a whole society depends on what individuals can remember, it can hardly help depending on every device of the demagogue and the poet: rhyme, rhythm, melody, structure, repetition." Since people "tend to remember best the things they have felt most deeply," the memorable words in an oral culture will tend to be "those most charged with group feeling;" communication will "keep alive in an individual the childhood sense of dependence, childhood's terrors and elations, and something of its awe for the old." Indeed, "one can hardly speak of *individuals* in the modern sense in such cultures."

34 Once books enter the environment, it can never be the same again; in Riesman's phrase, books are "the gunpowder of the mind." They "bring with them detachment and a critical attitude that is not possible in oral tradition . . . If oral communication keeps people together, print is the isolating medium par excellence." For the invention of writing, as Profes-

sor Kenneth Boulding writes, "made it possible for the present to speak to the future, and to hear from the past. It also made it possible for one man to communicate with people far beyond the range of his voice." In McLuhan's phrase, the book substitutes the eye for the ear; this substitution causes "the most radical explosion that can occur in any culture."

35 In the West the explosion occurred in two stages, widely separated over time. The first was the development of the phonetic alphabet, which transformed Greek life in the sixth and fifth centuries B.C. and laid the groundwork for what we consider Western civilization. Socrates was the last great product—and champion—of the oral tradition. Plato used the new medium of prose (poetry had been the medium before, since it is easier to remember than prose) to record Socrates' conversation—an attempt to preserve the power of the spoken word on the written page. With Aristotle, the world passed from exclusive reliance on oral instruction to the new habit of reading. Even so, the oral tradition remained very strong until the invention of the printing press in the fifteenth century.

36 It was this invention and its aftereffects—what McLuhan calls "The Gutenberg Galaxy"—that completed the "detribalization of Western man." For printing enormously amplified the effects of the written word. The effects were not just quantitative, however; the printing press did not simply mean more of the same. For print, unlike manuscript, is uniform and endlessly repeatable. The printed book "was the first teaching machine," McLuhan writes. "By putting the same text in front of any given number of students or readers, print ended the scholastic regime of oral disputation very quickly." The Elluls of that period were convinced, of course, that the printing press would bring about the dehumanization of the individual.

37 The result was precisely the opposite—the flowering of the individual. For the portability of the book allowed "typographic man" to learn by himself, thus encouraging individualism, as well as the peculiarly modern distinction (first celebrated in *Hamlet*) between knowing and doing. And the repetitiveness of print, by permitting the almost endless multiplication of messages, carried men away from the intimate, complex—and confining—relationships of what was still a predominantly tribal society. Together with the emphasis on linear sequence and continuity, this made possible the development of large-scale organization and of abstract human relationships. Hence print, as Kenneth Boulding writes in summarizing McLuhan's thesis, led Western man "from tribalism into nationhood, from feudalism into capitalism, from craftsmanship into mass production, from lore into science."

38 Now, McLuhan argues, all this is being reversed; the history of the past four hundred years—in a sense, of the past 2,500 years—is being played backward. Print produced an "explosion" that shattered tribal unity and

broke society up into separate elements. Electric and electronic technology—television, radio, the telephone, the computer—is causing what he insists on calling an "implosion," forcing people back together in tribal unity, albeit on a global scale, returning us to the world of the oral and the simultaneous, the world of emotion and sensory expression.

39 For one thing, the ear is becoming much more important. People are again getting information by hearing it—over the telephone, the radio, and increasingly via television, which McLuhan considers an aural rather than a visual medium (see below). Here again, his ideas in their more generalized forms have considerable scholarly support. It is widely agreed that, even apart from new media, more and more of today's communication is verbal in the traditional face-to-face sense. "Everything is moving so fast," says geneticist Ruth Sager of Columbia University, "that most important scientific communication is verbal. Things do get published in journals, of course, but that's for documentation." The new communication media, moreover, extend man's ear around the globe the way the book extended his vision.

40 Oral communication, we have seen, immerses the individual in the group, involves him (to use a favorite McLuhan term) in the feelings and affairs of others. The speed of electric and electronic circuitry substitute the simultaneous for the sequential, ending both time and space as we have known them for the past several centuries. Thus contemporary man, peering into his television screen, is in much the same position as preliterate or tribal man; he is forming his view of the world through direct, firsthand observation, the only difference being that his village is the whole world. As with his tribal ancestor, "action and reaction occur almost at the same time."

41 Television heightens the need of, and the search for, involvement in several other ways. The most important arises out of the fact that it provides what engineers call a "low-definition image." Compared to a photograph, for example, television provides relatively little information per square inch. A sixteen-inch-square photograph can show several dozen people clearly and sharply; if you try to show that many people on a TV screen, it comes out as one big blur. The result is that television, to use the language of psychology, provides an "incomplete loop"; the viewer feels the need to complete the loop himself.

42 Ours is the first society in history, McLuhan believes, to have the opportunity to escape technological determinism; this belief is the major source of his optimism. "Hitherto most people have accepted their cultures as a fate, like climate or vernacular," McLuhan argued in *The Gutenberg Galaxy* (a much better and more convincing book than his more recent *Understanding Media*). We can free ourselves from fate, however,

for "we can transcend the limitations of our own assumptions by a critique of them. We can now live, not just amphibiously in divided and distinguished worlds, but pluralistically in many worlds and cultures simultaneously. We are no more committed to one culture—to a single ratio among the human senses—than to one book or to one language or to one technology." But freedom of choice, McLuhan warns, depends on making the effort to understand the process by which technology affects our culture. "Our need today is, culturally, the same as the scientist's who seeks to become aware of the bias of the instruments of research in order to correct that bias."

43 What makes McLuhan one of the major intellectual influences of our time is the fact that he is one of the few people making the effort to understand how technology really is affecting us. His attempt to fit miscellaneous phenomena, from the Beatles to false eyelashes to pop art, into his grand scheme of things can be exasperating; but this same attempt to discover the meaning of the commonplace provides occasional blinding flashes of illumination.

44 Against this achievement, the question of whether McLuhan is right or wrong in his specific interpretation of the meaning of current technological change is relatively unimportant, if not irrelevant. As Kenneth Boulding puts it, "It is perhaps typical of very creative minds that they hit very large nails not quite on the head." For all its faults, McLuhan's work offers one possible answer to those looking for encouragement about man's ability to survive.

45 Certainly there is another possible answer, however. The answer may begin by observing that the question has been asked before, and answered in the affirmative. "From the dawn of history," Whitehead wrote in *Science and the Modern World*, in many ways still the best treatment of the impact of science, "mankind has always been losing its religious faith, has always suffered from the malignant use of material power, has always suffered from the infertility of its best intellectual types, has always witnessed the periodical decadence of art." And yet, Whitehead argues, "mankind has progressed. Even if you take a tiny oasis of peculiar excellence, the type of modern man who would have most chance of happiness in ancient Greece at its best period is probably (as now) an average professional heavyweight boxer, and not an average Greek scholar from Oxford or Germany. Indeed, the main use of the Oxford scholar would have been his capability of writing an ode in glorification of the boxer. Nothing does more harm in unnerving men for their duties in the present," he concludes, "than the attention devoted to the points of excellence in the past as compared with the average failure of the present day."

46 And yet complacency about the impact of science and technology is

hardly in order. There have been periods of decadence and destruction in the past. And our age *is* different, in ways we do not, as yet, fully understand; we are living in an era of radical change. One critical difference about our age, according to Emmanuel G. Mesthene, executive director of the Harvard University Program on Technology and Society, is that modern technology puts the traditional problems of choice in a totally different context. Until the present, Professor Mesthene argues, the arena of human action was limited by the state of the physical world. Politics, for example, was carried on within the context of weapons of a certain power and mobility, of oceans and mountains of a given width and height, of weather that could be neither controlled nor predicted, of communication and transportation networks of given speeds and capacities. "Of course, weapons, and speeds, and technologies all changed over time. Even mountains did." But the changes occurred so slowly that they were seen, if indeed they were seen at all, as effects, after they had occurred. For practical purposes, the physical and technological constraints were fixed and certain. "The decision-maker couldn't change them, just as the baseball manager can't move the short left-field fence when the star right-hander of the opposing team comes to bat." Hence the role of thought was to distinguish what was possible from what was not. And the question of choice—"can we do this?"—meant, in practice, "do the rules allow it?"

47 The critical characteristic of today's technology, Mesthene argues, is the way it has collapsed the old time span. By shortening the process of change, technology is shifting the way in which the question of choice is formulated. "Can we do this?" no longer means "can we do this within the rules?" but rather, "can we change the rules?" Frequently—more frequently than McLuhan or Mesthene suppose—the answer is no. But certainly there are times when it is yes—when the old physical and technological constraints are no longer given. Both radar and the atom bomb, which affected the course of World War II, were developed during that war. Similarly, new devices to detect underground nuclear explosions were developed while the arms-control talks were going on, and they affected the outcome of those talks. As Mesthene puts it, "It is now possible, for the first time ever, to move the left-field fence *during* the game."

48 The result is to enlarge rather than to restrict the sphere of human action and choice—to make it possible, if you will, for steelworkers to vacation in Europe or Hawaii, or even Miami Beach. It is also to create new dangers—which is something *not* new. "It is the business of the future to be dangerous," Whitehead wrote, adding, "In the immediate future there will be less security than in the immediate past, less stability. It must be admitted that there is a degree of instability which is inconsistent with civilization. But, on the whole, the great ages have been unstable ages."

STUDY GUIDE

Theme and Structure

1. This essay concerning the effects of technology on modern society is interesting because it expresses a rather balanced view between extreme pessimism and unqualified optimism. Make a statement of your own, based on the content of this essay, that expresses Silberman's views. Where does he come closest to expressing his own views in the essay?

2. Paragraphs 1 and 2 serve as an introduction and paragraphs 45–48 as a conclusion. The rest of the essay might be divided roughly into two sections: paragraphs 3–22 and paragraphs 23–44. What is the author's chief concern in each part?

3. Paragraphs 3, 4, and 5 are developed by multiple examples. List the examples that give force to the generalizations made in these paragraphs.

4. Show how the ideas developed in the two main parts of the essay are made more effective by associating them with specific writers.

THE REAL FUNCTION OF A UNIVERSITY

John Henry Newman

1 I suppose the *primâ-facie* view which the public at large would take of a University, considering it as a place of Education, is nothing more or less than a place for acquiring a great deal of knowledge on a great many subjects. Memory is one of the first developed of the mental faculties; a boy's business when he goes to school is to learn, that is, to store up things in his memory. For some years his intellect is little more than an instrument for taking in facts, or a receptacle for storing them; he welcomes them as fast as they come to him; he lives on what is without; he has his eyes ever about him; he has a lively susceptibility of impressions; he imbibes information of every kind; and little does he make his own in a true sense of the word, living rather upon his neighbours all around him. He has opinions, religious, political, and literary, and, for a boy, is very positive in them and sure about them; but he gets them from his schoolfellows, or his masters, or his parents, as the case may be. Such as he is in his other rela-

Reprinted from John Henry Newman, *The Idea of a University* (1873).

tions, such also is he in his school exercises; his mind is observant, sharp, ready, retentive; he is almost passive in the acquisition of knowledge. I say this in no disparagement of the idea of a clever boy. Geography, chronology, history, language, natural history, he heaps up the matter of these studies as treasures for a future day. It is the seven years of plenty with him: he gathers in by handfuls, like the Egyptians, without counting; and though, as time goes on, there is exercise for his argumentative powers in the Elements of Mathematics, and for his taste in the Poets and Orators, still, while at school, or at least, till quite the last years of his time, he acquires, and little more; and when he is leaving for the University, he is mainly the creature of foreign influences and circumstances, and made up of accidents, homogeneous or not, as the case may be. Moreover, the moral habits, which are a boy's praise, encourage and assist this result; that is, diligence, assiduity, regularity, despatch, perservering application; for these are the direct conditions of acquisition, and naturally lead to it. Acquirements, again, are emphatically producible, and at a moment; they are a something to show, both for master and scholar; an audience, even though ignorant themselves of the subjects of an examination, can comprehend when questions are answered and when they are not. Here again is a reason why mental culture is in the minds of men identified with the acquisition of knowledge.

2 The same notion possesses the public mind, when it passes on from the thought of a school to that of a University: and with the best of reasons so far as this, that there is no true culture without requirements, and that philosophy presupposes knowledge. It requires a great deal of reading, or a wide range of information, to warrant us in putting forth our opinions on any serious subject; and without such learning the most original mind may be able indeed to dazzle, to amuse, to refute, to perplex, but not to come to any useful result or any trustworthy conclusion. . . .

3 The communication of knowledge certainly is either a condition or the means of that sense of enlargement or enlightenment, of which at this day we hear so much in certain quarters: this cannot be denied; but next, it is equally plain, that such communication is not the whole of the process. The enlargement consists, not merely in the passive reception into the mind of a number of ideas hitherto unknown to it, but in the mind's energetic and simultaneous action upon and towards and among those new ideas, which are rushing in upon it. It is the action of a formative power, reducing to order and meaning the matter of our acquirements; it is a making the objects of our knowledge subjectively our own, or, to use a familiar word, it is a digestion of what we receive, into the substance of our previous state of thought; and without this no enlargement is said to follow. There is no enlargement, unless there be a comparison of ideas one

with another, as they come before the mind, and a systematizing of them. We feel our minds to be growing and expanding *then,* when we not only learn, but refer what we learn to what we know already. It is not the mere addition to our knowledge that is the illumination; but the locomotion, the movement onwards, of that mental centre, to which both what we know, and what we are learning, the accumulating mass of our acquirements, gravitates. And therefore a truly great intellect, and recognized to be such by the common opinion of mankind, such as the intellect of Aristotle, or of St. Thomas, or of Newton, or of Goethe, . . . is one which takes a connected view of old and new, past and present, far and near, and which has an insight into the influence of all these one on another; without which there is no whole, and no centre. It possesses the knowledge, not only of things, but also of their mutual and true relations; knowledge, not merely considered as acquirement, but as philosophy.

4 Accordingly, when this analytical, distributive, harmonizing process is away, the mind experiences no enlargement, and is not reckoned as enlightened or comprehensive, whatever it may add to its knowledge. For instance, a great memory, as I have already said, does not make a philosopher, any more than a dictionary can be called a grammar. There are men who embrace in their minds a vast multitude of ideas, but with little sensibility about their real relations towards each other. These may be antiquarians, annalists, naturalists; they may be learned in the law; they may be versed in statistics; they are most useful in their own place; I should shrink from speaking disrespectfully of them; still, there is nothing in such attainments to guarantee the absence of narrowness of mind. If they are nothing more than well-read men, or men of information, they have not what specially deserves the name of culture of mind, or fulfils the type of Liberal Education.

5 In like manner, we sometimes fall in with persons who have seen much of the world, and of the men who, in their day, have played a conspicuous part in it, but who generalize nothing, and have no observation, in the true sense of the word. They abound in information in detail, curious and entertaining, about men and things; and, having lived under the influence of no very clear or settled principles, religious or political, they speak of every one and every thing, only as so many phenomena, which are complete in themselves, and lead to nothing, not discussing them, or teaching any truth, or instructing the hearer, but simply talking. No one would say that these persons, well informed as they are, had attained to any great culture of intellect or to philosophy.

6 The case is the same still more strikingly where the persons in question are beyond dispute men of inferior powers and deficient education. Perhaps they have been much in foreign countries, and they receive,

in a passive, otiose, unfruitful way, the various facts which are forced upon them there. Seafaring men, for example, range from one end of the earth to the other; but the multiplicity of external objects, which they have encountered, forms no symmetrical and consistent picture upon their imagination; they see the tapestry of human life, as it were on the wrong side, and it tells no story. They sleep, and they rise up, and they find themselves, now in Europe, now in Asia; they see visions of great cities and wild regions; they are in the marts of commerce, or amid the islands of the South; they gaze on Pompey's Pillar, or on the Andes; and nothing which meets them carries them forward or backward, to any idea beyond itself. Nothing has a drift or relation; nothing has a history or a promise. Every thing stands by itself, and comes and goes in its turn, like the shifting scenes of a show, which leave the spectator where he was. Perhaps you are near such a man on a particular occasion, and expect him to be shocked or perplexed at something which occurs; but one thing is much the same to him as another, or, if he is perplexed, it is as not knowing what to say, whether it is right to admire, or to ridicule, or to disapprove, while conscious that some expression of opinion is expected from him; for in fact he has no standard of judgment at all, and no landmarks to guide him to a conclusion. Such is mere acquisition, and, I repeat, no one would dream of calling it philosophy.

7 Instances, such as these, confirm, by the contrast, the conclusion I have already drawn from those which preceded them. That only is true enlargement of mind which is the power of viewing many things at once as one whole, of referring them severally to their true place in the universal system, of understanding their respective values, and determining their mutual dependence. Thus is that form of Universal Knowledge, of which I have on a former occasion spoken, set up in the individual intellect, and constitutes its perfection. Possessed of this real illumination, the mind never views any part of the extended subject-matter of Knowledge without recollecting that it is but a part, or without the associations which spring from this recollection. It makes every thing in some sort lead to every thing else; it would communicate the image of the whole to every separate portion, till that whole becomes in imagination like a spirit, every where pervading and penetrating its component parts, and giving them one definite meaning. Just as our bodily organs, when mentioned, recall their function in the body, as the word "creation" suggests the Creator, and "subjects" a sovereign, so, in the mind of the Philosopher, as we are abstractedly conceiving of him, the elements of the physical and moral world, sciences, arts, pursuits, ranks, offices, events, opinions, individualities, are all viewed as one, with correlative functions, and as gradually by successive combinations converging, one and all, to the true centre.

8 To have even a portion of this illuminative reason and true philosophy is the highest state to which nature can aspire, in the way of intellect; it puts the mind above the influences of chance and necessity, above anxiety, suspense, unsettlement, and superstition, which is the lot of the many. Men, whose minds are possessed with some one object, take exaggerated views of its importance, are feverish in the pursuit of it, make it the measure of things which are utterly foreign to it, and are startled and despond if it happens to fail them. They are ever in alarm or in transport. Those on the other hand who have no object or principle whatever to hold by, lose their way, every step they take. They are thrown out, and do not know what to think or say, at every fresh juncture; they have no view of persons, or occurrences, or facts, which come suddenly upon them, and they hang upon the opinion of others, for want of internal resources. But the intellect, which has been disciplined to the perfection of its powers, which knows, and thinks while it knows, which has learned to leaven the dense mass of facts and events with the elastic force of reason, such an intellect cannot be partial, cannot be exclusive, cannot be impetuous, cannot be at a loss, cannot but be patient, collected, and majestically calm, because it discerns the end in every beginning, the origin in every end, the law in every interruption, the limit in each delay; because it ever knows where it stands, and how its path lies from one point to another. . . .

9 There are men who, when in difficulties, originate at the moment vast ideas or dazzling projects; who, under the influence of excitement, are able to cast a light, almost as if from inspiration, on a subject or course of action which comes before them; who have a sudden presence of mind equal to any emergency, rising with the occasion, and an undaunted magnanimous bearing, and an energy and keenness which is but made intense by opposition. This is genius, this is heroism; it is the exhibition of a natural gift, which no culture can teach, at which no Institution can aim; here, on the contrary, we are concerned, not with mere nature, but with training and teaching. That perfection of the Intellect, which is the result of Education, and its *beau ideal,* to be imparted to individuals in their respective measures, is the clear, calm, accurate vision and comprehension of all things, as far as the finite mind can embrace them, each in its place, and with its own characteristics upon it. It is almost prophetic from its knowledge of history; it is almost heart-searching from its knowledge of human nature; it has almost supernatural charity from its freedom from littleness and prejudice; it has almost the repose of faith, because nothing can startle it; it has almost the beauty and harmony of heavenly contemplation, so intimate is it with the eternal order of things and the music of the spheres.

STUDY GUIDE

Theme and Structure

1. In this selection from *The Idea of a University*, Newman is trying to answer the statement, made by Thomas Babington Macaulay, that a liberal education is useless. Newman is trying to dispel the idea that a university education should merely consist in the dissemination of useful information. Select the sentence in the essay that best expresses Newman's idea of what the heart of a liberal education really is.

Even in the nineteenth century there was a controversy between the advocates of the new science and the defenders of a traditional humanism comparable to that between C. P. Snow's two cultures or between the scientists and humanists of which Father Murray speaks. The historian Macaulay expressed the utilitarian view of many of his contemporaries that an education not resulting in immediate physical benefit to mankind was useless. Macaulay pointed, correctly or not, to Francis Bacon in the sixteenth century as the man who first advanced that view. In his essay "On Bacon," Macaulay makes this invidious comparison between the Platonic and the Baconian philosophies:

> To sum up the whole, we should say that the aim of the Platonic philosophy was to exalt man into a god. The aim of the Baconian philosophy was to provide man with what he requires while he continues to be man. The aim of the Platonic philosophy was to raise us far above vulgar wants. The aim of the Baconian philosophy was to supply our vulgar wants. The former aim was noble; but the latter was attainable. Plato drew a good bow; but, like Acestes in Virgil, he aimed at the stars; and therefore, though there was no want of strength or skill, the shot was thrown away. His arrow was indeed followed by a track of dazzling radiance, but it struck nothing. . . .
>
> Bacon fixed his eye on a mark which was placed on the earth, and within bow-shot, and hit it in the white. The philosophy of Plato began in words and ended in words, noble words indeed, words such as were to be expected from the finest of human intellects exercising boundless dominion over the finest of human languages. The philosophy of Bacon began in observations and ended in arts.
>
> The boast of the ancient philosophers was that their doctrine formed the minds of men to a high degree of wisdom and virtue. This was indeed the only practical good which the most celebrated of those teachers even pretended to effect; and undoubtedly, if they had effected this, they would have deserved far higher praise than if they had discovered the most salutary medicines or constructed the most powerful machines. But the truth is that, in those very matters in which alone they professed to do any good to mankind, in those very matters for the sake of which they neglected all the vulgar interests of mankind, they did nothing, or worse than nothing. They promised what was impracticable; they despised what was practicable; they filled the world with long words and long beards; and they left it as wicked and as ignorant as they found it.
>
> An acre in Middlesex is better than a principality in Utopia. The smallest actual good is better than the most magnificent promises of impossibilities. The wise man of the Stoics would, no doubt, be a grander object than a

steam-engine. But there are steam engines. And the wise man of the Stoics is yet to be born. A philosophy which should enable a man to feel perfectly happy while in agonies of pain would be better than a philosophy which assuages pain. But we know there are remedies which will assuage pain; and we know that the ancient sages liked the toothache just as little as their neighbours. A philosophy which should extinguish cupidity would be better than a philosophy which should devise laws for the security of property. But it is possible to make laws which shall, to a very great extent, secure property. And we do not understand how any motives which the ancient philosophy furnished could extinguish cupidity. We know indeed that the philosophers were no better than other men. From the testimony of friends as well as of foes, from the confessions of Epictetus and Seneca, as well as from the sneers of Lucian and the fierce invectives of Juvenal, it is plain that these teachers of virtue had all the vices of their neighbours, with the additional vice of hypocrisy. Some people may think the object of the Baconian philosophy a low object, but they cannot deny that, high or low, it has been attained. They cannot deny that every year makes an addition to what Bacon called "fruit." They cannot deny that mankind have made, and are making, great and constant progress in the road which he pointed out to them. Was there any such progressive movement among the ancient philosophers?

One of the students might read all of this essay "On Bacon" and make a report on it to the class.

2. Select the *topic sentence* of each paragraph and state which of the following methods Newman has employed in developing the idea expressed in each of the topic sentences: the method of tracing an effect back to its cause, multiple examples, definition, classification, or a combination of these.

3. It is one thing to state an idea and quite another thing to explain and develop it. Show where and how Newman makes his readers understand what a trained intellect really is.

4. Beginning with paragraph 2, encircle the *connective* at the opening of each paragraph which expresses the relationship of the thought content of that paragraph to what has preceded.

5. How does Newman's idea of the purpose of a university education compare with that of Father Murray?

Specific and Concrete Diction

1. Show how Newman has used *specific terms* as a means of obtaining emphasis in the next-to-last sentence of paragraph 3 and in the third sentence of paragraph 4.

Discover as many concrete terms as you can in paragraph 7. Do they make the paragraph more emphatic? Why?

Figurative Language

The test of proper figurative language in expository prose is this: Does the figure really help to clarify the idea being discussed?

1. Point out the figure in each of the following sentences: sentence 3 in paragraph 1, sentence 3 in paragraph 3, sentence 3 in paragraph 6, and sentence 6 in paragraph 6. How do they help to clarify what Newman is talking about?

2. What is the *literary allusion* in sentences 7 and 8 of paragraph 1? Does this allusion help to clarify the idea being expressed there? How?

Sentence Structure

1. Why is the sentence structure of sentences 3–7 in paragraph 1 appropriate?
2. What type of sentence structure predominates in the first part of paragraph 3? Is it appropriate to the thoughts Newman is expressing there?
3. In good expository prose there is apt to be a fair amount of parallel structure because it is often necessary for an author to compare and contrast ideas or to make cumulative statements of parallel ideas. It sometimes helps to write out sentences exhibiting parallelism in sense lines to emphasize their structure. Sentence 2 in paragraph 8, for instance, would appear in sense lines as follows:

Men,
    whose minds are possessed with some object,
take exaggerated views of its importance,
are feverish in the pursuit of it,
make it the measure of things
                        which are utterly foreign to it,
and *are startled*
and *despond*
        if it happens to fail them.

And sentence 6 in the same paragraph:

But *the intellect,*
    which has been disciplined to the perfection of its powers,
    which knows,
      and *thinks*
            while it knows,
    which has learned to leaven the dense mass of facts and events
                with the elastic force of reason,

such *an intellect*
    cannot be partial,
    cannot be exclusive,
    cannot be impetuous,
    cannot be at a loss,
    cannot but *be patient,*
                collected,
                and majestically *calm,*
    because *it discerns the end in every beginning,*
                the origin in every end,
                the law in every interruption,
                the limit in each delay;
    because *it* ever *knows where* it stands.
                and *how* its path leads from one point to another.

Write out other sentences from the passage in sense lines to display their parallel structure.

4. Which type of sentence does Newman employ most? Does it fit the thought, purpose, and audience implied in this passage?
5. For what kind of an audience was Newman writing? How is this clear from his diction, his figurative language, and his sentence structure?

SECTION 5

Understanding Our World

A CHAIN OF JUNGLE LIFE

William Beebe

1 I offer a living chain of ten links—the first, a tiny delicate being, one hundred to the inch, deep in the jungle, with the strangest home in the world—my last, you, the present reader of these lines. Between, there befell certain things, of which I attempt falteringly to write. To know and think them is very worth while, to have discovered them is sheer joy, but to write of them is impertinence, so exciting and unreal are they in reality, and so tame and humdrum are any combinations of our twenty-six letters.

2 Somewhere today a worm has given up existence, a mouse has been slain, a spider snatched from the web, a jungle bird torn sleeping from its perch; else we should have no song of robin, nor flash of reynard's red, no humming flight of wasp, nor grace of crouching ocelot. In tropical jungles, in Northern home orchards, anywhere you will, unnumbered activities of bird and beast and insect require daily toll of life.

3 Now and then we actually witness one of these tragedies or successes —whichever point of view we take—appearing to us as an exciting but isolated event. When once we grasp the idea of chains of life, each of these occurrences assumes a new meaning. Like everything else in the world it is not isolated, but closely linked with other similar happenings. I have sometimes traced even closed chains, one of the shortest of which consisted of predacious flycatchers which fed upon young lizards of a species which, when it grew up, climbed trees and devoured the nestling flycatchers!

4 One of the most wonderful zoological "Houses that Jack built" was this of Opalina's, a long, swinging, exciting chain, including in its links a Protozoan, two stages of Amphibians, a Fish, a Reptile, two Birds, and (unless some intervening act of legislature bars the fact as immoral, and illegal) three Mammals—myself, the Editor, and You. . . .

5 I left my Kartabo laboratory one morning with my gun, headed for the old Dutch stelling. Happening to glance up I saw a mote, lit with the oblique rays of the morning sun. The mote drifted about in circles, which became spirals; the mote became a dot, then a spot, then an oblong; and down the heavens from unknown heights, with the whole of British Guiana spread out beneath him from which to choose, swept a vulture into my path. We had a quintet, a small flock of our own vultures who came sifting down the sky, day after day, to the feasts of monkey bodies and wild peccaries which we spread for them. I knew all these by sight, from one peculiarity or another, for I was accustomed to watch them hour after hour, striving to learn something of that wonderful soaring, of which all my many hours of flying had taught me nothing.

6 This bird was a stranger, perhaps from the coast or the inland savannas, for to these birds great spaces are only matters of brief moments. I wanted a yellow-headed vulture, both for the painting of its marvellous head colors, and for the strange, intensely interesting, one-sided, down-at-the-heel syrinx, which, with the voice, had dissolved long ages ago, leaving only a whistling breath, and an irregular complex of bones straggling over the windpipe. Some day I shall dilate upon vultures as pets—being surpassed in cleanliness, affectionateness, and tameness only by baby bears, sloths, and certain monkeys.

7 But today I wanted the newcomer as a specimen. I was surprised to see that he did not head for the regular vulture table, but slid along the slant of the east wind, banked around its side, spreading and curling upward his wing finger-tips and finally resting against its front edge. Down this he sank slowly, balancing with the grace of perfect mastery, and again swung round and settled suddenly down shore, beyond a web of mangrove roots. This took me by surprise, and I changed my route and pushed through the undergrowth of young palms. Before I came within sight, the bird heard me, rose with a whipping of great pinions, and swept around three-fourths of a circle before I could catch enough of a glimpse to drop him. The impetus carried him on and completed the circle; and, when I came out on the Cuyuni shore, I saw him spread out on what must have been the exact spot from which he had risen.

8 I walked along a greenheart log with little crabs scuttling off on each side, and as I looked ahead at the vulture I saw to my great surprise that it had more colors than any yellow-headed vulture should have, and that its plumage was somehow very different. This excited me so that I promptly

slipped off the log and joined the crabs in the mud. Paying more attention to my steps, I did not again look up until I had reached the tuft of low reeds on which the bird lay. Now at last I understood why my bird had metamorphosed in death, and also why it had chosen to descend to this spot. Instead of one bird, there were two, and a reptile. Another tragedy had taken place a few hours earlier, before dawn, a double death; and the sight of these three creatures brought to mind at once the chain for which I am always on the lookout. I picked up my chain by the middle and began searching both ways for the missing links.

9 The vulture lay with magnificent wings outspread, partly covering a big, spectacled owl, whose plumage was in turn wrapped about by several coils of a moderate-sized anaconda. Here was an excellent beginning for my chain, and at once I visualized myself and the snake, although alternate links, yet coupled in contradistinction to my editor and the vulture, the first two having entered the chain by means of death, whereas the vulture had simply joined in the pacifistic manner of its kind; and, as my editor has dealt gently with me heretofore, I allowed myself to believe that his entrance might also be through no more rough handling than a blue slip.

10 The head of the vulture was already losing some of its brilliant chrome and saffron; so I took it up, noted the conditions of the surrounding sandy mud, and gathered together my spoils. I would have passed within a few feet of the owl and the snake and never discovered them, so close were they in color to the dark reddish beach; yet the vulture with its small eyes and minute nerves had detected this tragedy when still perhaps a mile high in the air, or half a mile up-river. There could have been no odor; nor had this bird any adequate nostrils to detect it, had there been one. It was sheer keenness of vision. I looked at the bird's claws, and their weakness showed the necessity of the eternal search for carrion or recently killed creatures. Here in a half minute, it had devoured an eye of the owl and both of those of the serpent. It is a curious thing, this predilection for eyes; give a monkey a fish, and the eyes are the first titbits taken.

11 Through the vulture I came to the owl link, a splendid bird clad in the colors of its time of hunting; a great, soft, dark, shadow of a bird, with tiny body and long fluffy plumage of twilight buff and ebony night, lit by twin, orange moons of eyes. The name "spectacled owl" is really more applicable to the downy nestling which is like a white powder puff with two dark feathery spectacles around the eyes. Its name is one of those I am fond of repeating rapidly—*Pulsatrix perspicillata perspicillata.* Etymologies do not grow in the jungle and my memory is noted only for its consistent vagueness; but, if the owl's title does not mean *The Eye-browed One Who Strikes*, it ought to, especially as the subspecific trinomial grants it two eyebrows.

12 I would give much to know just what the beginning of the combat

was like. The middle I could reconstruct without question, and the end was only too apparent. By a most singular coincidence, a few years before, and less than three miles away, I had found the desiccated remains of another spectacled owl mingled with the bones of a snake; only, in that instance, the fangs indicated a small fer-de-lance, the owl having succumbed to its venom. This time the owl had rashly attacked a serpent far too heavy for it to lift, or even, as it turned out, successfully to battle with. The mud had been churned up for a foot in all directions, and the bird's plumage showed that it must have rolled over and over. The anaconda, having just fed, had come out of the water and was probably stretched out on the sand and mud, as I have seen them, both by full sun and in the moonlight. These owls are birds rather of the creeks and river banks than of the deep jungle; and in their food I have found shrimps, crabs, fish, and young birds. Once a few snake vertebrae showed that these reptiles are occasionally killed and devoured.

13 Whatever possessed the bird to strike its talons deep into the neck and back of this anaconda, none but the owl could say; but from then on the story was written by the combatants and their environment. The snake, like a flash, threw two coils around bird, wings and all, and clamped these tight with a cross-vise of muscle. The tighter the coils compressed the deeper the talons of the bird were driven in, but the damage was done with the first strike, and if the owl and the snake had parted at this moment, neither could have survived. It was a swift, terrible, and short fight. The snake could not use its teeth and the bird had no time to bring its beak into play, and there in the night, with the lapping waves of the falling tide only two or three feet away, the two creatures of prey met and fought and died, in darkness and silence, locked fast together.

14 A few nights before I had heard, on the opposite side of the bungalow, the deep, sonorous cry of the spectacled owl; within a week I had passed the line-and-crescents track of anacondas, one about the size of this snake and another much larger. And now fate had linked their lives, or rather deaths, with my life, using as her divining rod, the focusing of a sky-soaring vulture.

15 The owl had not fed that evening, although the bird was so well nourished that it could never have been driven to its fool-hardy feat by stress of hunger. Hopeful of lengthening the chain, I rejoiced to see a suspicious swelling about the middle of the snake, which dissection resolved into a good-sized fish—itself carnivorous, locally called a basha. This was the first time I had known one of these fish to fall a victim to a land creature, except in the case of a big kingfisher who had caught two small ones. Like the owl and anaconda, bashas are nocturnal in their activities, and, according to their size, feed on small shrimps, big shrimps, and so on up to six

or eight inch catfish. They are built on swift, torpedo-like lines, and clad in iridescent silver mail.

16 From what I have seen of the habits of anacondas, I should say that this one had left its hole high up among the upper beach roots late in the night, and softly wound its way down into the rising tide. Here after drinking, the snake sometimes pursues and catches small fish and frogs, but the usual method is to coil up beside a half-buried stick or log and await the tide and the manna it brings. In the van of the waters comes a host of small fry, followed by their pursuers or by larger vegetable feeders, and the serpent has but to choose. In this mangrove lagoon, then, there must have been a swirl and a splash, a passive holding fast by the snake for a while until the right opportunity offered, and then a swift throw of coils. There must then be no mistake as to orientation of the fish. It would be a fatal error to attempt the tail first, with scales on end and serried spines to pierce the thickest tissues. It is beyond my knowledge how one of these fish can be swallowed even head first without serious laceration. But here was optical proof of its possibility, a newly swallowed basha, so recently caught that he appeared as in life, with even the delicate turquoise pigment beneath his scales, acting on his silvery armor as quicksilver under glass. The tooth marks of the snake were still clearly visible on the scales—another link, going steadily down the classes of vertebrates, mammal, bird, reptile and fish, and still my magic boxes were unexhausted.

17 Excitedly I cut open the fish. An organism more unlike that of the snake would be hard to imagine. There I had followed an elongated stomach and had left unexplored many feet of alimentary canal. Here, the fish had his heart literally in his mouth, while his liver and lights were only a short distance behind, followed by a great expanse of tail to wag him at its will, and drive him through the water with the speed of twin propellers. His eyes are wonderful for night hunting, large, wide, and bent in the middle so he can see both above and on each side. But all this wide-angled vision availed nothing against the lidless, motionless watch of the ambushed anaconda. Searching the crevices of the rocks and logs for timorous small fry, the basha had sculled too close, and the jaws which closed upon him were backed by too much muscle, and too perfect a throttling machine to allow of the least chance of escape. It was a big basha compared with the moderate-size snake, but the fierce eyes had judged well, as the evidence before me proved.

18 Still my chain held true, and in the stomach of the basha I found what I wanted—another link, and more than I could have hoped for—a representative of the fifth and last class of vertebrate animals living on the earth, an Amphibian, an enormous frog. This too had been a swift-forged link, so recent that digestion had only affected the head of the creature. I

drew it out, set it upon its great squat legs, and there was a grandmother frog almost as in life, a Pok-poke as the Indians call it, or, as a herpetologist would prefer, *Leptodactylus caliginosus*—the Smoky Jungle Frog.

19 She lived in the jungle just behind, where she and a sister of hers had their curious nests of foam, which they guarded from danger, while the tadpoles grew and squirmed within its sudsy mesh as if there were no water in the world. I had watched one of the two, perhaps this one, for hours; and I saw her dart angrily after little fish which came too near. Then, this night, the high full-moon tides had swept over the barrier back of the mangrove roots and set the tadpoles free, and the mother frogs were at liberty to go where they pleased.

20 From my cot in the bungalow to the south, I had heard in the early part of the night, the death scream of a frog; it must have been at that moment that somehow the basha had caught the great amphibian. This frog is one of the fiercest of its class, and captures mice, reptiles, and small fish without trouble. It is even cannibalistic on very slight provocation, and two of equal size will sometimes endeavor to swallow one another in the most appallingly matter-of-fact manner.

21 They represent the opposite extreme in temperament from the pleasantly philosophical giant toads. In outward appearance in the dim light of dusk, the two groups are not unlike; but the moment they are taken in the hand all doubt ceases. After one dive for freedom, the toad resigns himself to fate, only venting his spleen in much puffing out of his sides; while the frog either fights until exhausted, or pretends death until opportunity offers for a last mad dash.

22 In this case the frog must have leaped into the deep water beyond the usual barrier and while swimming been attacked by the equally voracious fish. In addition to the regular croak of this species, it has a most unexpected and unamphibian yell or scream, given only when it thinks itself at the last extremity. It is most unnerving when the frog, held firmly by the hind legs, suddenly puts its whole soul into an ear splitting *peent! peent! peent! peent! peent! peent!*

23 Many a time they are probably saved from death by this cry which startles like a sudden blow, but tonight no utterance in the world could have saved it; its assailant was dumb and all but deaf to aerial sounds. Its cries were smothered in the water as the fish dived and nuzzled it about the roots, as bashas do with their food—and it became another link in the chain.

24 Like a miser with one unfilled coffer, or a gambler with an unfilled royal flush, I went eagerly at the frog with forceps and scalpal. But beyond the meagre residuum of eggs, there was nothing but shrunken organs in its body. The rashness of its venture into river water was perhaps prompted by

hunger after its long maternal fast while it watched over its egg-filled nest of foam.

25 Hopeful to the last, I scrape some mucus from its food-canal, place it in a drop of water under my microscope, and—discover Opalina, my last link which in the course of its most astonishing life history gives me still another.

26 To the naked eye there is nothing visible—the water seems clear, but when I enlarge the diameter of magnification I lift the veil on another world, and there swim into view a dozen minute lives, oval little beings covered with curving lines, giving the appearance of wandering fingerprints. In some lights these are iridescent and they then well deserve the name of Opalina. As for their personality, they are oval and rather flat; it would take one hundred of them to stretch an inch; they have no mouth; and they are covered with a fur of flagella with which they whip themselves through the water. Indeed the whole of their little selves consists of a multitude of nuclei, sometimes as many as two hundred, exactly alike—facial expression, profile, torso, limbs, pose, all are summed up in rounded nuclei, partly obscured by a mist of vibrating flagella.

27 As for their gait, they move along with colorful waves, steadily and gently, not keeping an absolutely straight course and making rather much leeway, as any rounded, keelless craft, surrounded with its own paddle-wheels, must expect to do.

28 I have placed Opalina under very strange and unpleasant conditions in thus subjecting it to the inhospitable qualities of a drop of clear water. Even as I watch, it begins to slow down; and the flagella move less rapidly and evenly. It prefers an environment far different, where I discovered it living happily and contentedly in the stomach and intestines of a frog, where its iridescence was lost, or rather, had never existed in the absolute darkness; where its delicate hairs must often be unmercifully crushed and bent in the ever-moving tube; and where air and sky, trees and sun, sound and color were forever unknown; in their place only bits of half-digested ants and beetles, thousand-legs and worms, rolled and tumbled along in the dense gastric stream of acid pepsin; a strange choice of home for one of our fellow living beings on the earth.

29 After an Opalina has flagellated itself about, and fed for a time in its strange, almost crystalline way on the juices of its host's food, its body begins to contract, and narrow across the center until it looks something like a map of the New World. Finally its isthmus thread breaks and two Opalinas swim placidly off, both identical, except that they have half the number of nuclei as before. We cannot wonder that there is no backward glance or wave of cilia, or even memory of their body, for they are themselves, or rather it is they, or it is each; our whole vocabulary, our entire

stock of pronouns breaks down, our very conception of individuality is shattered by the life of Opalina.

30 Each daughter cell or self-twin, or whatever we choose to conceive it, divides in turn. Finally there comes a day (or rather some Einstein period of space-time, for there are no days in a frog's stomach!) when Opalina's fraction has reached a stage with only two nuclei. When this has creased and stretched and finally broken like two bits of drawn-out molasses candy, we have the last divisional possibility. The time for the great adventure had arrived, with decks cleared for action, or, as a protozoologist would put it, with the flagellate's protoplasm uninucleate, approximating encystment.

31 The encysting process is but slightly understood, but the tiny one-two-hundredth-of-its-former-self Opalina curls up, its paddlewheels run down; it forms a shell, and rolls into the current which it has withstood for a Protozoan's lifetime. Out into the world drifts the minute ball of latent life, a plaything of the cosmos, permitted neither to see, hear, eat, nor to move of its own volition. It hopes (only it cannot even desire) to find itself in water; it must fall or be washed into a pool with tadpoles, one of which must come along at the right moment and swallow it with the debris upon which it rests. The possibility of this elaborate concatenation of events has everything against it, and yet it must occur or death will result. No wonder that the population of Opalinas does not overstock its limited and retired environment!

32 Supposing that all happens as it should, and that the only chance in a hundred thousand comes to pass; the encysted being knows or is affected in some mysterious way by entrance into the body of the tadpole. The cyst is dissolved and the infant Opalina begins to feed and to develop new nuclei. Like the queen ant after she has been walled forever into her chamber, the life of the little One-cell would seem to be extremely sedentary and humdrum, in fact, monotonous, until its turn comes to fractionize itself, and again severally to go into the outside world, multiplied and by installments. But as the queen ant had her one superlative day of sunlight, heavenly flight, and a mate; so Opalina, while she is still wholly herself, has a little adventure all her own.

33 Let us strive to visualize her environment as it would appear to her if she could find time and ability, with her single cell, to do more than feed and bisect herself. Once free from her horny cyst, she stretches her drop of a body, sets all her paddle-hairs in motion and swims slowly off. If we suppose that she has been swallowed by a tadpole an inch long, her living quarters are astonishingly spacious or rather elongated. Passing from end to end she would find a living tube two feet in length, a dizzy path to traverse, as it curled in a tight, many-whorled spiral—the stairway, the domicile, the universe at present for Opalina. She is compelled to be a vegetarian, for nothing but masses of decayed leaf tissue and black mud and algae come

down the stairway. For many days there is only the sound of water gurgling past the tadpole's gills, or glimpses of sticks and leaves and the occasional flash of a small fish through the thin skin periscope of its body.

34 Then the tadpole's mumbling even of half-rotted leaves comes to an end, and both it and its guests begin to fast. Down the whorls comes less and less vegetable detritus, and Opalina must feel like the crew of a submarine when the food supply runs short. At the same time something very strange happens, the experience of which eludes our utmost imagination. Poe wrote a memorable tale of a prison cell which day by day grew smaller, and Opalina goes through much the same adventure. If she frequently traverses her tube, she finds it growing shorter and shorter. As it contracts, the spiral untwists and straightens out, while all the time the rations are cut off. A dark curtain of pigment is drawn across the epidermal periscope; and, as books of dire adventure say, the "horror of darkness is added to the terrible uncertainty." The whole movement of the organism changes; there is no longer the rush and swish of water; and the even, undulatory motion alters to a series of spasmodic jerks—quite the opposite of ordinary transition from water to land. Instead of water rushing through the gills of her host, Opalina might now hear strange musical sounds, loud and low, the singing of insects, the soughing of swamp palms.

35 Opalina, about this time, should be feeling very low in her mind from lack of food, and from the uncertainty of explanation of why the larger her host grew, the smaller, more confined became her quarters. The tension is relieved at last by a new influx of provender, but no more inert mold or distintegrated leaves. Down the short, straight tube appears a live millipede, kicking as only a millipede can, with its thousand heels. Deserting for a moment Opalina's point of view, my scientific conscience insists on asserting itself to the effect that no millipede with which I am acquainted has even half a thousand legs. But not to quibble over details, even a few hundred kicking legs must make quite a commotion in Opalina's home, before the pepsin puts a quietus on the unwilling invader.

36 From now on there is no lack of food, for at each sudden jerk of the whole amphibian there comes down some animal or other. The vegetarian tadpole, with its enormously lengthened digestive apparatus, has crawled out on land, fasting, while the miracle is being wrought with its plumbing; and, when the readjustment is made to more easily assimilating animal food, and it has become a frog, it forgets all about leaves and algae, and leaps after, and captures almost any living creature which crosses its path and which is small enough to be engulfed.

37 With the refurnishing of her apartment and the sudden and complete change of diet, the exigencies of life are past for Opalina. She has now but to move blindly about, bathed in a stream of nutriment, and from time to time, nonchalantly to cut herself in twain. Only one other possibility

awaits, that which occurred in the case of our Opalina. There comes a time when the sudden leap is not followed by an inrush of food, but by another leap and still another, and finally a headlong dive, a plash and a rush of water, which, were protozoans given to reincarnated memory, might recall times long past. Suddenly came a violent spasm, then a terrible struggle, ending in a strange quiet; Opalina has become a link.

38 All motion is at an end; and instead of food comes compression; closer and closer shut the walls; and soon they break down and a new fluid pours in. Opalina's cyst had dissolved readily in the tadpole's stomach, but her own body was able to withstand what all the food of tadpole and frog could not. If I had not wanted the painting of a vulture's head, little Opalina, together with the body of her life-long host, would have corroded and melted; and in the dark depths of the tropical waters, her multitude of paddle-hairs, her more or fewer nuclei, all would have dissolved and been reabsorbed, to furnish their iota of energy to the swift silvery fish.

39 This flimsy, little sky scraper castle of Jack's, built of isolated bricks of facts, gives a hint of the wonderland of correlation. Facts are necessary, but even a pack-rat can assemble a gallon of beans in a single night. To link facts together, to see them forming into a concrete whole; to make A fit in ARCH and ARCH into ARCHITECTURE, that is one great joy of life which, of all the links in my chain, only the Editor, You and I—the Mammals—can know.

STUDY GUIDE

Word Study

1. Give the dictionary definition which best fits Beebe's use of the following words: *impertinence* (paragraph 1), *predacious* (paragraph 3), *stelling* (paragraph 5), *savannas* (paragraph 6), *metamorphosed* (paragraph 8), *carrion* and *predilection* (paragraph 10), *desiccated* (paragraph 12), *serried* (paragraph 16), *encystment* (paragraph 30), *concatenation* (paragraph 31), *detritus* and *epidermal* (paragraph 34), and *provender* (paragraph 35).

2. Give an exact definition of the following words: *ocelot, sloth, anaconda, algae,* and *peccaries.*

3. What are the biological distinctions among the following: algae, fish, reptile, bird, and mammal?

4. A. By using their etymologies explain the meaning of the following words: *impertinence* (paragraph 1), *protozoan* and *amphibian* (paragraph 4), *trinomial* (paragraph 11), *herpetologist* (paragraph 18), and *undulatory* (paragraph 34).

B. Give the etymology of *flagella* (paragraph 26), and show how the etymological meaning is implied in Beebe's use of the term.

C. Give the etymology of *exigence* (paragraph 37) and of *indigence.*

Thought Structure

1. State the subject matter and theme of the whole essay, and give the sentence or sentences in which the author comes closest to stating his theme.

2. Make a careful sentence outline of the entire essay. Indicate the paragraphs devoted to each major thought division.

Effective Sentence Structure

One of the chief effects to be attained in descriptive narrative, especially when a series of actions is being described, is swift movement from detail to detail. Compression and economy of expression are essential here. The chief means of obtaining this effect are the deft use of (1) appositives, (2) participial modifiers, (3) compound predicates, (4) short simple sentences, and (5) compound sentences with short concise clauses.

This selection from Beebe is especially good in its use of these devices.

1. List at least ten sentences in which Beebe has made good use of *appositives* for his descriptive or narrative purposes.

2. List five sentences in which he has attained compression of expression through a good use of *participial modifiers.*

3. List ten sentences in which an impression of quick action has been achieved through the use of compound predicates.

4. Point out five places in the essay in which Beebe uses a series of short simple sentences or of compound sentences with short clauses to create an effect of swift action.

Effective Diction

1. Verbs are the action words in any language. Hence to express action exactly you must be careful in your choice of verbs and verbals. Show how Beebe has made a good choice of verbs or verbals to denote or connote a very precise action or motion in the following sentences: paragraph 5, sentences 3 and 4; paragraph 7, sentences 3 and 5; paragraph 8, sentence 1; paragraph 12, sentence 5; paragraph 13, sentence 2; paragraph 16, sentence 1; paragraph 17, sentence 6; paragraph 19, sentences 1 and 2; paragraph 26, sentence 3; paragraph 28, sentence 3; paragraph 31, sentences 1 and 2; and paragraph 33, sentence 2.

2. The use of *concrete language* is another way of enabling us to experience what you are trying to describe. Show how the use of concrete nouns has made Beebe's expression particularly effective in the opening sentences of paragraphs 2 and 11.

3. *Figurative language* (especially simile and metaphor) enhances any kind of description or narrative, but it is absolutely essential when you are describing a scene or action unfamiliar to the reader. Discuss the propriety of the similes or metaphors employed by Beebe in the following sentences: paragraph 5, sentence 2; paragraph 7, sentences 2 and 3; paragraph 11, sentence 2; paragraph 13, sentence 2; paragraph 15, sentence 5; paragraph 16, sentences 2 and 7; paragraph 24, sentence 1; paragraph 26, sentences 1 and 4; paragraph 27, sentence 1; paragraph 29, sentences 1 and 2; paragraph 30, sentence 3; paragraph 33, sentence 5; paragraph 34, sentences 2 and 7; and paragraph 36, sentence 2.

4. Show how the author has used a sustained *personification* in the section about Opalina to help us sense the life of this microscopic creature.

5. An *allusion* is a reference to some well-known fact, event, or literary quotation to clarify the thing you are describing or discussing. Show how Beebe has made literary allusions in paragraphs 4 and 34 to express his ideas. What precise elements of the stories to which he alludes does he wish us to transfer to the things he is describing?

Suggestion for Writing

Have you ever observed even a short chain of life in the physical world about you? If you have, try to describe it as vividly as Beebe has described this long one.

MAN AND ANIMAL: THE CITY AND THE HIVE

Susanne K. Langer

1 Within the past five or six decades, the human scene has probably changed more radically than ever before in history. The outward changes in our own setting are already an old story: the disappearance of horse-drawn vehicles, riders, children walking to school, and the advent of the long, low, powerful Thing in their stead; the transformation of the mile-wide farm into a tic-tac-toe of lots, each sprouting a split-level dream home. These are the obvious changes, more apparent in the country than in the city. The great cities have grown greater, brighter, more mechanized, but their basic patterns seem less shaken by the new power and speed in which the long industrial revolution culminates.

2 The deepest change, however, is really a change in our picture of mankind; and that is most spectacular where mankind is teeming and concentrated—in the city. Our old picture of human life was a picture of local groups, each speaking its mother-tongue, observing some established religion, following its own customs. It might be a civilized community or a savage tribe, but it had its distinct traditions. And in it were subdivisions, usually families, with their more special local ties and human relations.

3 Today, natural tribes and isolated communities have all but disappeared. The ease and speed of travel, the swift economic changes that send people in search of new kinds of work, the two wars that swept over all boundaries, have wiped out most of our traditions. The old family structure is tottering. Society tends to break up into new and smaller units

—in fact, into its ultimate units, the human individuals that compose it.

4 This atomization of society is most obvious in a great cosmopolitan city. The city seems to be composed of millions of unrelated individuals, each scrambling for himself, yet each caught in the stream of all the others.

5 Discerning eyes saw this a hundred years ago, especially in industrial cities, where individuals from far or near came to do what other individuals from far or near had also come to do—each a cog in the new machine. Most of the cogs had no other relation to each other. And ever since this shakeup in society began, a new picture of society has been in the making—the picture of *human masses*, brought together by some outside force, some imposed function, into a super-personal unit; masses of people, each representing an atom of "manpower" in a new sort of organism, the industrial State.

6 The idea of the State as a higher organism—the State as a superindividual—is old. But our conception of such a State is new, because our industrial civilization, which begets our atomized society, is new. The old picture was not one of masses driven by some imposed economic power, or any other outside power. The superindividual was a rational being, directed by a mind within it. The guardians of the State, the rulers, were its mind. Plato described the State as "the man writ large." Hobbes, two thousand years later, called it "Leviathan," the great Creature. A city-state like ancient Athens or Sparta might be "a man writ large," but England was too big for that. It was the big fish in the big pond. The mind of Hobbes's fish was perhaps subhuman, but it was still single and sovereign in the organism.

7 Another couple of centuries later, Rudyard Kipling, faced with a democratic, industrialized civilization, called his allegory of England "The Mother Hive." Here, a common will, dictated by complicated instincts, replaced even Leviathan's mind; each individual was kept in line by the blind forces of the collective life.

8 The image of the hive has had a great success as an ideal of collaborative social action. Every modern Utopia (except the completely wishful Shangri-La) reflects the beehive ideal. Even a statesman of highest caliber, Jan Smuts, has praised it as a pattern for industrial society. Plato's personified State and Hobbes's sea monster impress us as fantasies, but the hive looks like more than a poetic figure; it seems really to buzz around us.

9 I think the concept of the State as a collective organism, composed of multitudes of little workers, guided by social forces that none of the little workers can fathom, and accomplishing some greater destiny, is supported by another factor than our mechanized industry; that other factor is a momentous event in our intellectual history: the spread of the theory of evolution.

10 First biologists, then psychologists, and finally sociologists and mor-

alists have become newly aware that man belongs to the animal kingdom. The impact of the concept of evolution on scientific discovery has been immense, and it has not stopped at laboratory science; it has also produced some less sober and sound inspirations. The concept of continuous animal evolution has made most psychologists belittle the differences between man and his non-human relatives, and led some of them, indeed, to think of *homo sapiens* as just one kind of primate among others, like the others in all essential respects—differing from apes and monkeys not much more than they differ from species to species among themselves. Gradually the notion of the human animal became common currency, questioned only by some religious minds. This in turn has made it natural for social theorists with scientific leanings to model their concepts of human society on animal societies, the ant hill and the beehive.

11 Perhaps it were well, at this point, to say that I myself stand entirely in the scientific camp. I do not argue against any religious or even vitalistic doctrines; such things are not arguable. I speak not *for*, but *from*, a naturalist's point of view, and anyone who does not share it can make his own reservations in judging what I say.

12 Despite Man's zoölogical status, which I wholeheartedly accept, there is a deep gulf between the highest animal and the most primitive normal human being: a difference in mentality that is fundamental. It stems from the development of one new process in the human brain—a process that seems to be entirely peculiar to that brain: the use of *symbols for ideas*. By "symbols" I mean all kinds of signs that can be used and understood whether the things they refer to are there or not. The word "symbol" has, unfortunately, many different meanings for different people. Some people reserve it for mystic signs, like Rosicrucian symbols; some mean by it *significant images*, such as Keats' "Huge cloudy symbols of a high romance"; some use it quite the opposite way and speak of "mere symbols," meaning empty gestures, signs that have lost their meanings; and some, notably logicians, use the term for mathematical signs, marks that constitute a code, a brief, concise language. In their sense, ordinary words are symbols, too. Ordinary language is a symbolism.

13 When I say that the distinctive function of the human brain is the use of symbols, I mean any and all of these kinds. They are all different from signs that animals use. Animals interpret signs, too, but only as pointers to actual things and events: cues to action or expectation, threats and promises, landmarks and earmarks in the world. Human beings use such signs, too; but above all they use symbols—especially words—to think and talk about things that are neither present nor expected. The words convey *ideas*, that may or may not have counterparts in actuality. This power of thinking *about* things expresses itself in language, imagina-

tion, and speculation—the chief products of human mentality that animals do not share.

14 Language, the most versatile and indispensable of all symbolisms, has put its stamp on all our mental functions, so that I think they always differ from even their closet analogues in animal life. Language has invaded our feeling and dreaming and action, as well as our reasoning, which is really a product of it. The greatest change wrought by language is the increased scope of awareness in speech-gifted beings. An animal's awareness is always of things in its own place and life. In human awareness, the present, actual situation is often the least part. We have not only memories and expectations; we have *a past* in which we locate our memories, and *a future* that vastly over-reaches our own anticipations. Our past is a story, our future a piece of imagination. Likewise our ambient is a place in a wider, symbolically conceived place, the universe. We live in *a world.*

15 This difference of mentality between man and animal seems to me to make a cleft between them almost as great as the division between animals and plants. There is continuity between the orders, but the division is real nevertheless. Human life differs radically from animal life. By virtue of our incomparably wider awareness, our power of envisagement of things and events beyond any actual perception, we have acquired needs and aims that animals do not have; and even the most savage human society, having to meet those needs and implement those aims, is not really comparable to any animal society. The two may have some analogous functions, but the essential structure must be different, because man and beast live differently in every way.

16 Probably the profoundest difference between human and animal needs is made by one piece of human awareness, one fact that is not present to animals, because it is never learned in any direct experience: that is our foreknowledge of Death. The fact that we ourselves must die is not a simple and isolated fact. It is built on a wide survey of facts, that discloses the structure of history as a succession of overlapping brief lives, the patterns of youth and age, growth and decline; and above all that, it is built on the logical insight that *one's own life is a case in point.* Only a creature that can think symbolically *about* life can conceive of its own death. Our knowledge of death is part of our knowledge of life.

17 What, then, do we—all of us—know about life?

18 Every life that we know is generated from other life. Each living thing springs from some other living thing or things. Its birth is a process of new individuation, in a life-stream whose beginning we do not know.

19 *Individuation* is a word we do not often meet. We hear about individuality, sometimes spoken in praise, sometimes as an excuse for being slightly crazy. We hear and read about "the Individual," a being that is

forever adjusting, like a problem child, to something called "Society." But how does individuality arise? What makes an individual? A fundamental, biological process of *individuation*, that marks the life of every stock, plant or animal. Life is a series of individuations, and these can be of various sorts, and reach various degrees.

20 Most people would agree, off-hand, that every creature lives its life and then dies. This might, indeed, be called a truism. But, like some other truisms, it is not true. The lowest forms of life, such as the amoeba, normally (that is, barring accidents) do not die. When they grow very large and might be expected to lay eggs, or in some other way raise a family, they do no such thing: they divide, and make two small ones ready to grow. Well now, where is the old one? It did not die. But it is gone. Its individuation was only an episode in the life of the stock, a phase, a transient form that changed again. Amoebae are individuated in space—they move and feed as independent, whole organisms—but in time they are not self-identical individuals. They do not generate young ones while they themselves grow old; they grow old and *become* young ones.

21 All the higher animals, however, are final individuations that end in death. They spring from a common stock, but they do not merge back into it. Each one is an end. Somewhere on its way toward death it usually produces a new life to succeed it, but its own story is finished by death.

22 That is our pattern, too. Each human individual is a culmination of an inestimably long line—its ancestry—and each is destined to die. The living stock is like a palm tree, a trunk composed of its own past leaves. Each leaf springs from the trunk, unfolds, grows, and dies off; its past is incorporated in the trunk, where new life has usually arisen from it. So there constantly are ends, but the stock lives on, and each leaf has that whole life behind it.

23 The momentous difference between us and our animal cousins is that they do not know they are going to die. Animals spend their lives avoiding death, until it gets them. They do not know it is going to. Neither do they know that they are part of a greater life, but pass on the torch without knowing. Their aim, then, is simply to keep going, to function, to escape trouble, to live from moment to moment in an endless Now.

24 Our power of symbolic conception has given us each a glimpse of himself as one final individuation from the great human stock. We do not know when or what the end will be, but we know that there will be one. We also envisage a past and future, a stretch of time so vastly longer than any creature's memory, and a world so much richer than any world of sense, that it makes our time in that world seem infinitesimal. This is the price of the great gift of symbolism.

25 In the face of such uncomfortable prospects (probably conceived long before the dawn of any religious ideas), human beings have evolved

aims different from any other creatures. Since we cannot have our fill of existence by going on and on, we want to have *as much life as possible* in our short span. If our individuation must be brief, we want to make it complete; so we are inspired to think, act, dream our desires, create things, express our ideas, and in all sorts of ways make up by concentration what we cannot have by length of days. We seek the greatest possible individuation, or development of personality. In doing this, we have set up a new demand, not for mere continuity of existence, but for *self-realization*. That is a uniquely human aim.

26 But obviously, the social structure could not arise on this principle alone. Vast numbers of individualists realizing themselves with a vengeance would not make up an ideal society. A small number might try it; there is a place, far away from here, called the Self-Realization Golden World Colony. But most of us have no golden world to colonize. You can only do that south of Los Angeles.

27 Seriously, however, an ideal is not disposed of by pointing out that it cannot be implemented under existing conditions. It may still be a true ideal; and if it is very important we may have to change the conditions, as we will have to for the ideal of world peace. If complete individuation were really the whole aim of human life, our society would be geared to it much more than it is. It is not the golden world that is wanting, but something else; the complete individualist is notoriously not the happy man, even if good fortune permits his antics.

28 The fact is that *the greatest possible individuation* is usually taken to mean, "as much as is possible without curtailing the rights of others." But that is not the real measure of how much is possible. The measure is provided in the individual himself, and is as fundamental as his knowledge of death. It is the other part of his insight into nature—his knowledge of life, of the great unbroken stream, the life of the stock from which his individuation stems.

29 One individual life, however rich, still looks infinitesimal: no matter how much self-realization is concentrated in it, it is a tiny atom—and we don't like to be tiny atoms, not even hydrogen atoms. We need more than fullness of personal life to counter our terrible knowledge of all it implies. And we have more; we have our history, our commitments made for us before we were born, our relatedness to the rest of mankind. The counterpart of individuation from the great life of the stock is our rootedness in that life, our involvement with the whole human race, past and present.

30 Each person is not only a free, single end, like the green palm leaf that unfolds, grows in a curve of beauty, and dies in its season; he is like the whole palm leaf, the part inside the trunk, too. He is the culmination of his entire ancestry, and *represents* that whole human past. In his brief individuation he is an *expression* of all humanity. That is what makes each

person's life sacred and all-important. A single ruined life is the bankruptcy of a long line. This is what I mean by the individual's involvement with all mankind.

31 All animals are unconsciously involved with their kind. Heredity governs not only their growth, color and form, but their actions, too. They carry their past about with them in everything they do. But they do not know it. They don't need to, because they never could lose it. Their involvement with the greater life of the race is implicit in their limited selfhood.

32 Our knowledge that life is finite and, in fact, precarious and brief, drives us on to greater individuation than animals attain. Our mental talents have largely freed us from that built-in behavior called instinct. The scope of our imagination gives each of us a separate world, and a separate consciousness, and threatens to break the instinctual ties of brotherhood that make all the herrings swim into one net, and all the geese turn their heads at the same moment. Yet we cannot afford to lose the feeling of involvement with our kind; for if we do, personal life shrinks up to nothingness.

33 The sense of involvement is our social sense. We have it by nature, originally just as animals do, and just as unconsciously. It is the direct feeling of needing our own kind, caring what happens. Social sense is an instinctive sense of being somehow one with all other people—a feeling that reflects the rootedness of our existence in a human past. Human society rests on this feeling. It is often said to rest on the need of collaboration, or on domination of the weak by the strong, or some other circumstance, but I think such theories deal with its modes, and ignore its deeper structure; at the bottom of it is the feeling of involvement, or social sense. If we lose that, no coercion will hold us to our duties, because they do not feel like commitments; and no achievements will matter, because they are doomed to be snuffed out with the individual, without being laid to account in the continuity of life.

34 Great individual development, such as human beings are driven by their intellectual insights to seek, does of course always threaten to break the bonds of direct social involvement, that give animal life its happy unconscious continuity. When the strain gets hard, we have social turmoil, anarchy, irresponsibility, and in private lives the sense of loneliness and infinite smallness that lands some people in nihilism and cynicism, and leads others to existentialism or less intellectual cults.

35 It is then that social philosophers look upon animal societies as models for human society. There is no revolt, no strike, no competition, no anti-anything party, in a beehive. As Kipling, fifty years or more ago, represented his British Utopia that he called the Mother Hive, that ideal State had a completely cooperative economy, an army that went into action

without a murmur, each man with the same impulse, the moment an enemy threatened to intrude, and a populace of such tribal solidarity that it would promptly run out any stranger that tried to become established in the State and disrupt its traditions. Any native individual that could not fit into the whole had to be liquidated; the loss was regrettable, but couldn't be helped, and would be made up.

36 Yet the beehive really has no possible bearing on human affairs; for it owes its harmonious existence to the fact that its members are *incompletely individuated,* even as animals go. None of them perform all of a creature's essential functions: feeding, food-getting, nest-building, mating, and procreating. The queen has to be fed and tended; she has only procreative functions. She doesn't even bring up her own children; they have nurses. The drones are born and reared only as her suitors, and when the romance is finished they are killed, like proper romantic heroes. The building, nursing, food-getting, and fighting are done by sterile females who cannot procreate; amazons who do all their own housework. So there is not only division of labor, but division of organs, functional and physical incompleteness. This direct involvement of each bee with the whole lets the hive function with an organic rhythm that makes its members appear wonderfully socialized. But they are really not socialized at all, any more than the cells in our tissues are socialized; they are associated, by being un-individuated.

37 That is as far away from a human ideal as one can get. We need, above all, a world in which we can realize our capacities, develop and act as personalities. That means giving up our instinctive patterns of habit and prejudice, our herd-instincts. Yet we need the emotional security of the greater, continuous life—the awareness of our involvement with all mankind. How can we eat that cake, and have it, too?

38 The same mental talent that makes us need so much individuation, comes to the rescue of our social involvement: I mean the peculiarly human talent of holding ideas in the mind by means of symbols. Human life, even in the simplest forms we know, is shot through and through with *social symbols.* All fantastic beliefs in a Great Ancestor are symbolic of the original and permanent life of the stock from which every individual life stems. The Totem, the Hero, the Sacred Cow, these are the most elementary social symbols. With a maturer view of the world, and the development of religious ideas, the symbolic image of Man is usually taken up into the greater view of a divine world-order and a moral law. We are sons of Adam and daughters of Eve. If Adam and Eve were simply some human couple supposed to have lived in the Near East before it was so difficult, this would be an odd way of speaking; we don't ordinarily refer to our neighbor's children as Mr. Brown's boys and Mrs. Brown's girls. But Adam is Man, and Eve is Woman (the names even mean that): and among us

transient little mites, every man is Man, every woman is Woman. That is the source of human dignity, the sense of which has to be upheld at all levels of social life.

39 Most people have some religious ritual that supports their knowledge of a greater life; but even in purely secular affairs we constantly express our faith in the continuity of human existence. Animals provide lairs or nests for their immediate offspring. Man builds for the future—often for nothing else; his earliest great buildings were not mansions, but monuments. And not only physical edifices, but above all laws and institutions are intended for the future, and often justified by showing that they have a precedent, or are in accord with the past. They are conveniences of their day, but symbols of more than their day. They are symbols of Society, and of each individual's inalienable membership in Society.

40 What, then, is the measure of our possible individuation, without loss of social sense? It is the power of social symbolism. We can give up our actual, instinctual involvements with our kind just to the extent that we can replace them by symbolic ones. This is the prime function of social symbols, from a handshake, to the assembly of robed judges in a Supreme Court. In protocol and ritual, in the investment of authority, in sanctions and honors, lies our security against loss of involvement with mankind; in such bonds lies our freedom to be individuals.

41 It has been said that an animal society, like a beehive, is really an organism, and the separate bees its organic parts. I think this statement requires many reservations, but it contains some truth. The hive is an organic structure, a super-individual, something like an organism. A human city, however, is an *organization*. It is above all a symbolic structure, a mental reality. Its citizens are the whole and only individuals. They are not a "living mass," like a swarm of semi-individuated bees. The model of the hive has brought with it the concept of human masses, to be cared for in times of peace, deployed in times of war, educated for use or sacrificed for the higher good of their state. In the specious analogy of animal and human society, the hive and the city, lies, I think, the basic philosophical fallacy of all totalitarian theory, even the most sincere and idealistic—even the thoroughly noble political thought of Plato.

42 We are like leaves of the palm tree, each deeply embedded in the tree, a part of the trunk, each opening to the light in a final, separate life. Our world is a human world, organized to implement our highest individuation. There may be ten thousand of us working in one factory. There are several millions of us living in a city like New York. But we are not the Masses: we are the Public.

STUDY GUIDE

Theme and Structure

1. Although the author recognizes many similarities between animal and human life and admits that human life probably evolved from animal life, she also sees very fundamental differences between animal and human life as they now function. What are these chief differences? Where does she discuss them?

2. What are the two fundamental needs that must be realized to establish a human society? Which parts of the essay are devoted to a discussion of each?

3. Work out a sentence outline of the essay, indicating how each of the thought divisions helps develop the thematic idea of the whole essay. Begin with a thesis sentence that expresses the main idea developed in the whole essay. The thought divisions are paragraphs 1–4, 5–8, 9–11, 12–16, 17–25, 26–34, 35–40, and 41 and 42.

Figurative Language

1. The author discusses three separate images that have been employed to symbolize the state: Individual Man Writ Large, the Leviathan, the Beehive. Who is responsible for each of these images? What are the connotations of each that make them unacceptable to the author as images of the state as it actually functions? What are some of the particular features of life in the beehive that make it an unsuitable analogy to life in a human city?

2. The author introduces an image of her own that she thinks better suggests the elements of strong personal individuation and the social sense, an image that involves a memory of the past and a look to the future. What is her image? How does it help to express the main ideas developed in the essay?

3. Why are human buildings and laws symbols of social consciousness (see paragraph 39) in a way in which animal lairs and nests are not?

Suggestion for Writing

The author makes the following statement in paragraph 27: "The complete individualist is notoriously not the happy man, even if fortune permits his antics." Using this as a thematic idea, write an essay in which you develop it by using multiple examples and by tracing the effect back to its cause.

EVOLUTION AND CYCLICISM IN OUR TIME

Walter J. Ong

1 There can be no doubt that the discovery of the process of evolution, cosmic and organic, has been one of the greatest achievements of the human mind. In a sense, this is the central discovery in the Western world

since Renaissance times, and in a still further sense it is the central corporate discovery of all mankind.

2 The discovery of cosmic and organic evolution is part of man's discovery of himself in history. Early man had no effective way of putting together really extended history. Preliterate man could not control enough data to enable him to reconstruct a lengthy sequence of events in time. There had been, of course, data gathered and reported by eyewitnesses, but when this information had been passed on through even a few generations without the help of writing, fact—provided one had it in the first place—became inextricable from fictional accretion. Instead of a historical account of their past, preliterate peoples even today have only myth, related perhaps to fact at certain points but related so erratically as to make historical reconstruction very difficult.

3 With the invention and spread of writing, extended records began to create a new and important dimension in human thinking. As records accumulated, it was only a matter of time until persons would begin to notice that the state of affairs in the past had been quite different from what it was in the present. In their hieroglyphic writing the ancient Egyptians accumulated great masses of records. The Hebrews, coeval with the later Egyptians, and, if in some ways less civilized, still advanced beyond the Egyptians in possessing the alphabet, had a far-developed historical sense, as the Old Testament shows. Their way of conceiving history is not so developed as ours, yet they have an unmistakable historical instinct and outlook. In Aristotle's day, when alphabetic writing was probably only about fifteen hundred years old, the historical dimension had begun to intrude even in scientific thinking. Near the beginning of his *Metaphysics* Aristotle inserts a quite sketchy and primitive, and yet portentous history of philosophy.

4 From the ancient Mediterranean civilizations, modern man's sense of history develops in a rather direct line through medieval and Renaissance European civilization into the age of the Enlightenment and thence into the present one world, where it is now in one way or another shared by all men. In this line of development, the sense of a past accessible through circumstantial records grew in the human consciousness as it had never grown at other earlier times or in other civilizations. In the Chinese civilization, perhaps because of the different kind of commitment to time involved in character writing as against alphabetic writing, perhaps because of specialization in other awarenesses made possible by this same remarkble character writing, perhaps because of relative lack of contact with the Hebrew and Christian religious sense of time, or because of all these factors and some others as well, so strong a historical sense did not develop. The Chinese would have to acquire this sense later from the West, most forcefully in its Marxist manifestation. Other civilizations, too, performed

more like the Chinese than like the Western segment of mankind. The Hindu, the Central American, the African did not themselves develop the modern sense of a temporal dimension in the cosmos. These and other civilizations have learned this, with modern science, from the West. The margin by which the West outdistanced other civilizations in achieving this sense of history, however, has been in reality slight. If man has been here for some five hundred thousand years, the segment of mankind which first developed this historical sense did not begin to do so until nearly all this five hundred thousand years had elapsed—that is, until roughly some three thousand years ago.

5 What we mean by this historical sense should be noted carefully. By the eighteenth century in the West, when this sense had pretty well matured, what had happened was not simply that man had become speculatively interested in time. Speculative interest in time he had had for centuries. Nor was it that man had developed a sense of reality as embedded in a flow of time such as Heraclitus had registered six centuries before Christ in his logion, *Panta rhei*, or "All things are in flux." A sense of flux is an old awareness, too. What had happened by the age of the Enlightenment was that man had achieved a sense that the present he knew was growing out of a past with which he was in some kind of verifiable contact and which was different from the present, and that this same present was pointed into a future destined itself to be vastly different from both the present and the past. Today we are taught from elementary school on that earlier ages of the universe differed vastly from later ones, and this notion has become so commonplace that we find it hard to imagine human beings unaware of it. Yet it is safe to say that until quite recent generations most human beings were generally unaware of this fact. Man could become aware of it only when he had methods of probing into the past far enough and accurately enough to be struck by the changes between one period and another, in human culture, learning, and finally in physical and cosmic environment.

6 By the time of Diderot's *Pensées sur l'interprétation de la nature* in 1754, the sense of a present involved in a past and future vastly different from itself and from one another is manifestly part of the informed Western outlook:

> Could not the philosopher . . . suspect that life had its individual elements scattered and mixed in the mass of matter; that it happened that these elements united because it was possible for this to happen; that the embryo formed of these elements has passed through an infinitude of organization and development; that it has acquired in succession movement, sensation, ideas, thought, reflection, conscience [*conscience* in the original French, which means either consciousness or conscience but seems to signify the latter here], feelings, emotions, signs, gestures,

> sounds, articulation, language, laws, sciences, and arts; that millions of years have elapsed between each of these developments; that there are perhaps other developments to be undergone and other paths of growth to be followed which are as yet unknown to us.[1]

7 This passage from Diderot and other passages quoted in H. F. Osborn, *From the Greeks to Darwin*, can serve to remind us that perhaps the ultimate triumph to date of the evolutionary outlook is the knowledge that the evolutionary outlook itself was arrived at by an evolutionary process. Diderot is writing over a century before Charles Darwin's great work *On the Origin of Species*, and yet it is no discredit to Darwin's genius to state that, given the awareness evident in the Diderot passage, the discovery of the principle of natural selection, not only in its primordial Darwinian form but also in its later modifications and refinements was only a matter of time. The insight which Darwin was to crystallize in his work, so brilliantly and scrupulously written and so often painstakingly revised, and to make current with the aid of his remarkable gift for catch phrases—"origin of species," "natural selection," "survival of the fittest," "struggle for life," to name only a few—was not entirely his own. This insight was itself evolving in the minds of men as they passed on from generation to generation their accumulated records of past experience and their growing reflections on what they knew of the past.

8 Indeed, by some strange sort of fatality, the very origin of the *Origin of Species* provides evidence of the most explicit and spectacular sort concerning the corporate and gradual origin of human discoveries. For a great many of Darwin's most original insights were on his own humble admission arrived at by at least one other individual at the same time in the same intellectual milieu. The correspondence in 1858 between Darwin and the somewhat younger Alfred Russel Wallace is a commonplace item in the history of ideas. In it we can see the convergence of the two men's individual lights in the theory of natural selection, made explicit in their famous joint communication to the Linnean Society. The case alerts us to a state of affairs which other cases confirm: discoveries are not so much stumbled upon as developed. Knowledge itself is a communal affair and evolves communally. The most an individual can hope to contribute to the process is what we have recently learned to style a "breakthrough" in a front of activity which must be on the whole cooperative rather than purely personal. Because it develops communally, the structure of human knowledge must be explained not only in terms of its various logics. It must also be explained sociologically. The accounts of Henry Ford or Thomas Alva Edison of Max Planck or Albert Einstein working out utterly

[1] Reprinted from H. F. Osborn, *From the Greeks to Darwin* (1904).

new inventions all by themselves—normally in cold and ill-lighted attics—belong with Horatio Alger literature or the old Tom Swift books. Reality is something different.

9 When we look back of the Darwin-Wallace correspondence to the discoveries and reflections of men who preceded them, we find even more unmistakably how thoroughly their great discovery or "breakthrough" was dependent on the painstaking work, brilliant intellectual risks, and brilliant insights of others and how much it was dependent also upon obscure and individually uncontrollable, but immensely influential, psychological and sociological forces of which Darwin's own age could hardly be explicitly aware since we are only now learning to identify them.

10 Evolutionary thinking can be discerned taking dim but real shape in the philosophy and science of the rather remote pre-Darwinian age and in a general build-up of the historical dimension of all thinking. In his *Scienza nuova* Giambattista Vico (1668–1744) focuses attention on development, and this focus is intensified in philosophical thought through Hegel (1770–1831) and Schelling (1775–1854). Auguste Comte (1798–1857) proposed a philosophy built on considerable knowledge of social development as well as on massive theories about the nature of this development. Karl Marx's 1848 *Communist Manifesto* involves still more theories about the nature and inevitability of change, social and other.

11 Evolutionary thinking was found taking shape at an early date not only in philosophy itself but also in the natural sciences, which even as late as the nineteenth century were regarded, as they were through the Middle Ages and the Renaissance, as part of philosophy, as "natural philosophy." The German philosopher Kant (1724–1804) like the French astronomer Laplace (1749–1827) faced into the problems of the cosmos as it was known to the new astronomy and proposed nebular hypotheses to account for the present state of the universe by a theory of stellar evolution. Descartes and Leibnitz had already bruited abroad the idea that the earth could have gone through a molten stage. Such unfamiliar stages had tended to be explained as aberrations or catastrophes. But in the eighteenth and the nineteenth centuries the English geologists James Hutton (1726–97) and Charles Lyell (1797–1875) discarded the older catastrophic theories in favor of uniformitarian explanations. Catastrophism had viewed the present state of the universe as due to earlier, mysteriously violent deviations from some more pacific "natural" order. These deviations or catastrophes were supposed to be inexplicable in terms of still operating physical processes. Uniformitarianism took for granted that past states of the universe which account for present conditions are themselves explainable in terms of processes subject to the same physical laws as are now operating and verifiable.

12 Hutton and Lyell did not of course destroy catastrophism. Such a the-

ory still persists in our own day in the minds of many who feel that the only cosmology possible to the devout is one which proceeds by a series of abrupt changes initiated by special interventions of God. To this mind, although the universe was evolving for billions of years toward the point where life, at least on our planet, became possible, nothing short of an abrupt divine intervention breaking sharply with earlier processes can account for the appearance of the first living organisms. In this catastrophic view, although the first human remains in the five or ten billion year history of our universe appear after the patient elaboration over billions of years first of larger and larger molecules out of which organic substances can be synthesized and then of more and more highly developed organisms which finally approximate man in external form, and although these first human remains appear in the very epoch when the organisms approximating man were in full developmental career, one must conceive of the human body as having nothing to do with this stupendous cosmic process. Rather, one must imagine it as being formed quite suddenly from those materials alone —various aluminum salts or other clay-like matter—which had reached their more or less stable forms relatively early in the process of cosmic development and had not passed through any of the later organic transmutations.

13 The survival of catastrophism in one or another form and the tendency to link catastrophism with a religious view of the universe confused the issues in many religious circles, but it could not stop the development of evolutionary theory in the natural sciences. By the late eighteenth century Erasmus Darwin (1731–1802), Charles Darwin's grandfather, was working with the idea that species are not separated by chasms from one another but rather connected through intermediate forms in lines of descent, and Lamarck (1744–1829) had produced his theory of use inheritance which Charles Darwin's theory of natural selection superseded. At this time, the term "biology" itself, proposed independently in 1802 by Lamarck and S. T. Treviranus, came into use, so that the very science of biology, insofar as it can be considered a distinct knowledge, is itself a product of the evolutionary milieu.

14 In both philosophy and the natural sciences the interest in evolution was a product of the visions of history which were forming in men's minds. These visions were not very clear, and yet they were both fascinating and productive. Although they had to do with change, these new visions were not quite the same as those of the older philosophies which had been more interested in becoming in general, with coming into being as contrasted with the act of existence. The newer visions concerned themselves with series of individual events which were each unique and yet in some sense, real but difficult to fix, a part of a pattern.

15 One can, of course, make a distinction between evolution and history.

Evolution can refer to developments in the cosmos independent of human culture, and history can refer to developments within human culture itself. Of these two concepts, history, while in a way more constricted, is nevertheless the dominant notion in the sense that the discovery of evolution is a historical event, since it takes place in human culture and not outside. Moreover, since history is closer to him, man has approached evolution by reflection on history first, so that evolution will always remain for him something associated with history and understandable in terms of this association. Here we shall speak of history in the common intertwined sense in which it refers primarily to human history but also involves as occasion offers, the development of the universe itself before men and since.

16 Determining what the pattern of history is had long disturbed men and still disturbs us. For, although there are true histories and false histories, all history is selective, so that one can have as many histories—and true ones, too—as he wishes, depending on what items one selects in one's reporting. The number of histories is potentially infinite. The difficulty in finding a pattern which is *the* pattern lodges in the fact that history, whatever else it does, never really repeats itself. Every event is unique. This is what brought Aristotle to state in his *Art of Poetry* that history is less philosophical than poetry itself, which is certainly unphilosophical enough if by philosophical one means, as Aristotle did, capable of treatment in universal terms.

17 The one way to cast history in these terms is to transmute its singular happenings into universals, and the readiest way to effect this transmutation is to imagine that time is cyclic and as a consequence the history of the universe is, too. That is to say, everything that is now happening has happened before an infinite number of times and will happen an infinite number of times again, so that there is really nothing singular ever possible at all. One can bolster this view by selecting details in history which, put together, form a pattern of rise and fall, waxing and waning, ascent and decline, and so on—spring, summer, autumn, winter. These cyclic patterns are of course really there, provided only that one takes note of the proper details (those which relate to such patterns) and passes by the others (those which do not).

18 From the time of the most ancient philosophies men have been adept at noting the proper details to discern the cyclic patterns. Cyclic views of history have apparently been the dominant views. They appear in Hindu thought, in the pre-Socratic philosophers and through the ancient Greeks generally, on down through Joachim de Flora (1145–1202) and others to Spengler and Toynbee in our own day. Cyclicism is so pervasive that it obtrudes itself unnoticed in historians, artists, and others who seemingly have never adverted to the fact that their frames of thought have an unmistakably cyclic cast. Thus we have cultural developments explained in terms

of a New England spring, summer, Indian summer, and so on—although no winter has been acknowledged as yet. A recent literary historian, Robert E. Spiller, organizes not merely North Atlantic literature but all American literature circularly in his title *The Cycle of American Literature: An Essay in Historical Criticism* (1955), just as E. I. Watkin in his *Catholic Art and Culture* had organized the history of Western art into a classical autumn, Christian spring, medieval summer, Renaissance Indian summer, baroque autumn, and modern winter, thereby making it rather evident that either art is going to have to go completely out of existence because its possibilities are all exhausted or we are headed directly into a glorious spring. There are many early and detailed precedents for this sort of thing. Between 1720 and 1750 Iohannes Nicolaus Funccius had published in Marburg and Lemgo his five books in Latin entitled respectively (in translation) *The Childhood, Adolescence, Imminent Old Age, Vigorous Old Age,* and *Helpless Broken-Down Old Age of the Latin Language.* This kind of construct is revealing. It works so long as one views Latin and Roman culture as not particularly derivative from anything else and as not destined to feed into anything else. The moment one regards Italian, Provençal, Catalan, French, Spanish, Portuguese, Rhaeto-Romanic and Roumanian as variants of Latin—which they are—the entire picture shifts and the rise-and-fall construct no longer accounts for the facts, since in modern French Latin is still on the rise, unless one detects a cycle in French literature, too.

19 These cyclic patterns occur not only among historians operating in the field of belles-lettres but in the visions of painters, too. The well-known series of paintings by the English-born American Thomas Cole (1801–1848) entitled "The Course of Empire" is a case in point. It is discussed in the next study here.

20 In his brilliant book *The Myth of the Eternal Return* Mircea Eliade has exposed the psychological roots of the drive to detect among the details of history a cyclic pattern which will make plausible a totally cyclic view of time itself. Cyclic theories of time accomplish for the learned what the mythological rituals of the seasons accomplish for the intellectually unsophisticated. Both mitigate the terror of history, in which events, and most of all man's personal decisions, are set forever in an irreversible pattern. Cyclic theories tend to cushion or distract from time's impact, dissociating time from unique acts, for in the extreme or pure cyclic view of the universe nothing is unique at all, since even our most personal decisions have been and will be made over and over again. Mythological rituals, more or less seasonal in their celebration and to this extent associated with a cyclic pattern, draw attention from real events to mythological archetypes which are not referable to any real time. To ask a Greek, for example, when, in what year of the universe, Dionysus was torn to pieces by the Maenads is to miss the whole point of the myth. These things took place somewhere

outside time. Their extra-temporal status gave the myths their psychological value. By referring actual temporal occurrences in one way or another to them, these temporal occurrences could be disinfected of the curse of time. Pagan religious views generally register a human aversion to time, providing at least a subconscious refuge from time's evils.

21 By contrast the Hebrew and even more the Christian revelation presents time as a good. This point has become a commonplace one in contemporary theology, Protestant as well as Catholic. For the Hebrew, revelation, initially given to an ancestor, Abraham, who was seen quite definitely as inside history, was kept alive through a historical people, Abraham's descendants. For Christians, the Hebrew view was retained and supplemented by a more momentous historical incident, the Incarnation of the Son of God, Himself God, together with His subsequent death and resurrection—all events datable, even today, with greater surety than all but a few events of secular history. The Christian view sees Christ as anchored in time in at least three ways. First, like other men, He is born and dies at one certain time and no other. But secondly, unlike other men, He appears at the maturing of a special long-term development which calls for His appearance. He is expected as other men are not. He culminates the history of the Chosen People by putting an end to an intent wait of centuries. And thirdly, the centuries-long history of this Chosen People was itself, according to the common Christian teaching, not only a wait or watchful preparation but also a prefiguration or foreshadowing of His own life and work.

22 Thus faced squarely into time and at home in it, the Christian as such has no need for either mythological archetypes or cyclic theories of the sort studied by Eliade. Yet we do find both these pagan phenomena widespread among certain Christian populations. Notably, in medieval European culture biography is written according to these patterns. The medieval saint's life is too frequently fitted to a pre-existent archetypal pattern in which even the points at which the miracles are supposed to occur are predetermined, and the familiar secular biography such as is found in the *Mirror for Magistrates* or Lydgate's *Fall of Princes* is often based on a spectacularly cyclic design, the wheel of Fortune. When such pagan patterns occur among Christians, they can be regarded as pagan survivals. Only after the Renaissance did Christians learn to write biography in a more genuinely Christian way by centering attention on the shaping action of the human will and its decisions.

23 Modern theology has come to speak of the Christian (and Hebrew) sense of time as "linear" rather than cyclic. Oscar Cullimann and many others have made much of this view. The concept of linearity has its disadvantages here, for the Christian and Hebrew sense of time is by no means so spatialized as the term "linear" suggests. It is more interior and

psychological, or "human," and, besides, it does involve certain considerations which, when they are handled geometrically, are best handled by analogy not with straight lines but with circles, as Père Gaston Fessard has shown in his brilliant study, *La dialectique des Exercices spirituels de Saint Ignace de Loyola*. Nevertheless, there is a sense in which the Christian and Hebrew sense of time can be said to be linear by contrast with cyclic views. For the Christian the soul's journey through time is a development: the soul starts out in one state and ends in quite a different one in which its career or spiritual evolution has fixed it. In a parallel fashion, the Hebrew and Christian world vision sees the universe in linear time: contrary to the conviction of Aristotle and a host of others, matter is not eternal, but the universe is created in one state and at the end of time will somehow be transfigured, different from what it has been. Christ is incarnate at a certain point in time, and this point is never reached again.

24 It is true that earlier Christians were ignorant of the full dimensions of cosmic time. As late as St. Robert Bellarmine and even later, we find theologians and others as well quite convinced that from the creation of the world to the expected end of time was a matter of some six thousand years, and the first Christians had done their thinking, it seems, in an even more telescoped temporal world view. It is likewise true that earlier Christians had no idea of the fact that the universe was actually evolving from day to day during their own lives, if on a scale so disproportionate to a single human life that no one person alone could be directly aware of the changes going on. What is important, however, in the Chrisitan tradition is not the statistical errors or observational deficiencies of earlier Christians, but the total frame of mind which Christian teaching fosters. The Church herself has never been specific about the age or life expectancy of the present universe or about its day-to-day stability. Chiliasm in various forms has been recurrent, it is true, but always as an aberration. Hence, despite the defects of the world view in which Christians conceived revelation to be operating, the way for an evolutionary view was as a matter of fact kept open by Christian teaching. For in any view, however otherwise scientifically erroneous, a Christian who followed the teachings of the Catholic Church had to allow for a beginning of the universe and an ending which was different from the beginning. This sense of difference between beginning and end is congenial to evolutionary views. Cyclic views of time and the universe are not.

25 When one reviews in the larger perspective suggested here the developments in thought and in world outlook which precede and accompany the work of Charles Darwin, one is struck by certain relationships between the evolutionary outlook and Christianity. The two seem curiously congenial to each other. The evolutionary outlook has grown up in an intellectual setting prepared by Christianity under the influence of the time sense

which Christianity very really if not always with full consciousness encourages. For, like the Christian view, the evolutionary view involves a certain "linear" rather than cyclic sense of time.

26 The discovery of evolution has opened a vision of the universe which at the beginning is in a condition from which it departs never to return. The progressive changes in the cosmos, moreover, do not consist simply in a running down, as was thought when the second law of thermodynamics, the Carnot-Clausius law, was taken as the ultimate determinant of cosmic activity. According to this law, the universe is tending toward a state of complete equilibrium. The mountains will all eventually wash into the sea, hot things will lose heat to cooler things until all are of a uniform temperature and so on. We know now that the story is more complicated than this. There is also a winding-up process in the universe, the process according to which life evolves upward in more and more complex, more and more intense forms. For, although there is some regressive organic evolution, the pattern of life on the whole is certainly one of progress.

27 Life is a struggle upward, a struggle against odds, but on the whole a victorious process. This conviction lies back of Darwinian and other evolutionary views in which the whole of organic evolution is a kind of ascesis, a struggle from worse to better, curiously like the career of the Christian soul. Indeed, it is not difficult to show that Christian asceticism, subtly transmuted, has formed much of the framework for Darwin's thinking. This is all the more interesting when one recalls that this same framework could not be provided by many other religions which regard life as a process in which one relaxes his hold on himself to lose himself finally in some dissolution.

28 But does what we know of cosmic evolution really accord with Christianity by rigidly excluding the possibility of cyclic time? Is not a throbbing universe possible, and does not such a universe involve cyclic time? That is to say, speaking in a somewhat oversimplified fashion, could it not be that the present expanding universe arose from the explosion of some sort of super-atom and that this universe will ultimately contract into the super-atom only to explode again, and so on indefinitely, so as to give us an infinite series of successive universes? And does not all this suggest cyclic time, with the same events recurring infinitely?

29 It would seem not. The discovery of evolution has undermined cyclic views even more than would at first blush appear. In the universe as we now know it, there exists no real model or analogue for cyclicism—that is, for identical and inevitable repetition of an event at two (much less at an infinite number of) points in time.

30 The grossest model for cyclicism is and has been the path of the earth around the sun. The old cyclic myths and cyclic cosmologies had assumed the permanence of the earth-sun relationship, which they commonly con-

ceived in terms of a path of the sun around the earth. But today we know this relationship is not permanent. The path of the earth around the sun is by no means stable. It has come into being by a series of changes, and continues to undergo evolution at a rate which is measurable, although quite disproportionate to the span of human life. No season is, as a matter of fact, quite like any other, and in their succession, although there are so-called cycles of approximate repetitions, the over-all pattern is that of a one-directional change.

31 Even if the universe is expanding as the result of a primordial explosion of some sort of super-atom (as George Gamow and others conjecture), and one assumes that it will eventually contract back into the super-atom only to explode and begin evolving again, all the indications we have from the world-in-time-around-us would suggest that, if we face into real particulars and details, the second of these two evolutions would be not the same as the first, but different from it somewhat as year differs from year, or one chain of evolution (European fauna and flora) from another (American fauna and flora). One assumes that two successive cosmic evolutions would be identical on the suspicion that they are like two successive years or eras; but we know now that two successive years or eras are not quite identical. One can set up a mathematical model for cyclic succession, of course, but there remains the problem of finding something in reality which at least hints reality accords with the mathematical model. Nothing appears to be available. It appears that cyclic theories of cosmic evolution and of history depend upon setting up such a model or construct, for which one can find no exact counterpart anywhere in the universe, and upon using this model, despite everything, as though it applied to reality.

32 Perhaps it should be added that the highly poetic continuous creation theory put forth by Professor Fred Hoyle seems to leave even less room for exact repetition of events than any of the theories it proposes to replace. It is designed to counteract the Carnot-Clausius law rather than to contradict the view that individual things are different in the end from in the beginning. In this theory, although the universe as a whole does not begin all at once, every assignable item in it most certainly does begin and move through irreversible developmental states. The "background material" continuously created for the formation of clouds of interstellar gas and galaxies is certainly different at the time of its creation from what it is afterward.

33 Cyclicism is even further disqualified when one considers something further about the evolution of the cosmos which is all too often left out of consideration. That is that the cosmos gives birth to the human person in utter particularity and uniqueness. In *The Phenomenon of Man* and elsewhere, Pierre Teilhard de Chardin, S.J., has made the point that cosmologies which view the physical universe without regard to the fact that it

has given birth to the human person are not only incomplete but impossibly distorted and misleading. Too often a cosmology accounts to some degree of satisfaction for everything except human beings, who appear as some sort of monstrous intrusion on the scene. This is true even when a cosmology does account in some way for the evolution of the human body, explaining its relationship to, and probable line of development from prehuman forms. For, frequently enough, such a cosmology lets the matter go at that, failing even to ask the question as to what the human person, this mysterious self, this interiority, inviolable, known only to me and to God, has to do with the process of cosmic evolution. For it certainly has something to do with this evolution. The universe prepared itself for some five or ten billion years for the advent of just this mysterious self, this interiority, this uniqueness which I am—and which every human being is. How is the process of cosmic evolution related to me?

34 Both the Christian and the pagan must face this question. And up to the present seldom has either done so. Indeed, it seems that neither knows how to do so as yet. Yet the fact is that the development of the universe to date has had direction and that the direction leads not up to or around or parallel to but into the human consciousness itself. Cosmic evolution has certainly been a process of greater and greater complexification or interiorization of existent things. Without opting for any one of the various theories regarding the initial stages of our universe, we know that there was a time when the matter of which our globe is composed was simply too hot to make it possible for anything more complicated than simple inorganic molecules to exist—probably for a time too hot for even molecules to exist at all, so that everything was retained in a simple atomic structure. Cooling made possible the formation of crystals, organized according to a pattern which is interior in that it is determined by the internal molecular structure of the crystal but which is not very intensely interior in the sense that a crystalline structure is open: it tends to hook on to its borders further molecules without any particular limit. As the earth cools still more and the present continents and seas take shape, the gigantic protein molecules form. Despite their relatively massive sizes, these molecules are more organized in terms of an interior than are the molecules making up inorganic crystals. They do not grow by simple accretion, but have their own peculiar structural equilibrium to maintain without accretion. Their interior exists in a state of tension with the exterior around them. It seems that some of the protein molecules or some of the things very close to them such as viruses, are able to reproduce themselves, not out of their own substance but by generating next to themselves, in certain media with which they may be surrounded, others like themselves. Higher forms of organization, which are generally regarded as properly living, have a still higher interiorizing component. Out of their interior organization, they

generate other beings with there own interior organizations. The build-up of interiority reaches its maximum in man, who has the reproducing capacity of lower forms of life plus an interior and transcendent awareness of self which is so peculiarly his own that it cannot be communicated to others. But inside this awareness communication with others can take place. Indeed communication in human society, although it uses external media of all sorts, is basically a transaction between two or more unique and inviolable interiors.

35 This is a most inadequate sketch of incredibly complex and beautiful stages in cosmic development. But it may help to convey a sense of the way in which the human person is not adventitious but in a very profound sense native to the material universe. Each human soul, it is true, is created by a direct act of God. When I reflect on the interior self which I am, examine this sense of "I" which I alone have, it yields no evidence that it is descended from anything at all. I alone know what it feels like to be myself. Even my father and mother have not known what it feels like to be me. They have no direct consciousness of me such as my own consciousness of myself, nor do I have any direct consciousness of them. To say that my soul, as evidenced to me in my consciousness, is "descended" or derived from these or any other souls has no meaning. This "I" is unique and inaccessible. This isolation of each person, his being on his own, underived from other consciousnesses, is the glory and the terror of human existence. I cannot be duplicated even in the intelligence of another man, as I should have to be were he to know me as immediately as I know myself. Moreover, I know my uniqueness and induplicability in simply knowing myself as I do. With some three billion people in the world, no person in complete possession of his faculties is in the least worried that one of the other three billion will turn out to be a duplication of himself. The present population figure could be doubled or squared without occasioning the slightest alarm on this score. No man is an island, and yet each possesses himself alone. Each of these individual selves is the product of a direct act of God which is truly "special" in the sense that it brings into existence a special soul and consciousness, which will always remain unlike every other, a true person.

36 And yet these persons are born of the universe in which they live. They do not arise outside it. Matter is prepared for the human soul not merely by the body of a mother and a father; long before any human generation becomes even thinkable, it has to be organized by the evolution of the entire universe over a period of billions of years. For the material things around us, the inorganic matter and even more the organic matter from which we derive our nourishment, are not constitutive of the material universe in its primitive state. Primitive atomic matter must be elaborated by mighty cosmic forces which simultaneously distribute it into

the galaxies and solar systems of today and give it the progressively higher and higher interior organization which produces the complex chemical forms with which we are surrounded and inside which we must live. The material in our bodies is billions of years old, and during these billions of years it has not been lying about in a relatively stable condition as had been supposed by Western man up until some few hundred years ago, when the material things around us had been regularly explained in terms of varying combinations of the stable elements earth, water, air, and fire. Built up of these, things were differentiated, it had been thought, without reference to time, by specific natures. Today we know that the very organization of matter is a coefficient of its age. Four billion years ago a protein molecule was not a possibility anywhere in our surroundings. Matter had not sufficiently developed to produce this elaborate structure.

37 It took much longer for matter to be capable of the incredibly tight organization found in the human body. Nevertheless, over a period beginning with the emergence of life some one billion or more years ago, living beings did develop progressively more and more elaborate organization, more and more "complexification" or intensity of life. At a point where living organisms approximating the present human body finally were appearing, the first human soul is created by God, infused within a body in the material universe. This is, of course, a special act of God, for the creation of the human soul is always a special act of His, since the soul in its spirituality transcends the merely material. Moreover, God's freedom to create or not to create the universe at the start was of course absolute. But given the created and developing universe, it seems to compromise the divine wisdom to suggest that the creation of the first human soul was not called for at this point in a way analogous to that in which the creation of one's soul was called for when the germ cells from the bodies of his parents united. Is it possible to think that after five or ten billion years of elaboration, God might have simply let the ripeness of time go by? might have out of some whim simply failed to bring into being the first soul? To think this would seem to compromise God's fidelity to Himself. For we know enough of the story of an evolving cosmos to know that cosmic development had been pointing for billions upon billions of years to a certain fullness of time when material being had finally reached a point in which its spiritualization through a rational animal was possible. Because of this gigantic cosmic preparation, of which the preparation of the human ovum and sperm is only a kind of tiny echo, it seems quite proper and necessary to say that the whole cosmos gave birth to man. As a mother, it prepared the material for his body and, while not creating his human soul, presented him to the light of day.

38 The birth of man in the cosmos is striking evidence against cyclicism if further evidence is really needed. For here we have the cosmic processes

terminating not in repetition but in its antithesis, the utterly unrepeatable and unique human person.

39 But the story of the universe is not complete with the appearance of man, or even with the evolution of human society up to the present. As the story of the universe moves on today, man is finding out more and more about his origins in the physical world in which he lives. We are living in an age in which man is identifying himself more and more with the material universe by pinponting the network of connections between himself and the rest of God's material creation. Darwin's discoveries mark a stage in this movement whereby man finds himself more and more truly by finding the cosmos in which he lives. This movement is the contrary of that of Platonism and other ancient philosophies which drift away from a consideration of this world to a world of separated and supposedly "pure" ideas. The Platonic ideas are visually conceived in the sense that they are conceived by considering intellectual activity as analogous to vision and what we know intellectually by analogy with the objects of sight. *Idea* itself is the Greek cognate of the Latin *video* and of our English "vision." This reliance on vision yields a world of "objects" which are "clear and distinct," and quite directly produces the old Platonic and Aristotelian notion of "species," each cut off from one another, or, to use the more standard word signifying the same thing, "defined" one against the other. Darwin's discoveries represent a direct assault on this visualism, for in his account of the origin of species all distinctness is lost in a blur of variants, potentially infinite in quantity and always at least incipient in the mere differentiation of individual from individual, although how far incipient depends somewhat on how far macroevolution dominates microevolution (if the two are effectively distinct at all).

40 The complaint has been made that the Darwinian view as against the Platonic focuses on this world and not on the world of spirit. Darwin is preoccupied with the story of the human body rather than of the human soul. Plato is interested in the soul and his "eternal verities." And what is the story of the body compared to my immortal soul? Yet there is something profoundly Christian in the Darwinian conception which is missing in the Platonic. For, although the Christian knows by his faith that the human soul is immortal, insistence upon the survival of the soul after death is not a distinguishing feature of divine revelation. It is not met with in most of the Old Testament, and in the New Testament, while it is supposed, it is enveloped in the more important Christian doctrine of the resurrection of the body. Fascination with the survival of the soul is a mark of certain pagan philosophies. The resurrection of the body—born of this universe—is an article of faith distinctively Christian. Christian writers such as Father Robert W. Gleason in *The World to Come* have made this point, and the point needs making more frequently. The pagan may look forward to getting rid

of his body and of this universe. The Christian does not look forward to this at all.

41 The world view which is opening out before us in our post-Darwinian world is thus one eminently congenial to a follower of Christ. For the universe in which we are finding man to be so profoundly at home—if at the same time so profoundly ill at ease, for we cannot deny this side of his experience although for want of time we must scant it here—is after all God's universe. It is said that to date Christians are so ill-equipped intellectually to appreciate this universe, much less to elucidate it in a Christian light to others. If one were to ask what is most needed in Catholic intellectual and educational circles today, I should reply without hesitation a real cosmology, and a philosophy and theology which see man in the full time perspectives of the universe we know and which talk about him habitually in these perspectives.

42 But in the evolutionary picture is not man shrunk to a mere nothing? A conservative low figure for the age of the universe is five billion years. If we imagine that a moving-picture film had been made of the universe from a beginning five billion years ago up to today and that the film is shown in fast motion, speeded up so that the five-billion-year-long run is crowded into two hours, the period from the time when the first acquatic vertebrates evolved to the present day would be just over nine and a half minutes. The period of roughly five hundred thousand years from the time of the earliest known chipped stone tools to the present would be a little more than one-half second—a one-half second which would be the most important era of all. If this one-half second of film were itself slowed down to run two hours, the period from the first domestication of animals and plants to the present would occupy only about the last two minutes, and the period between the life of Christ and the present would take the last twenty-nine seconds.

43 This seems to make man impossibly small and insignificant. And so it does if we view him as though he were a tiny speck fetched from some realm of separated Platonic ideas and inserted into the vast reaches of time and space which the universe fills, or as a being coming into existence in an Aristotelian-type universe, an eternal datum cyclically organized. And yet if we view man as something which this universe has built up to out of these vast reaches of time and space, he is not insignificant at all. Before him, the prehuman universe is insignificant. For the supposition we have just made about viewing the universe in its early stages is an impossible one. The universe, for most of its early life, was one in which vision, and a fortiori photography, was an impossibility. For vision becomes possible only with living things, and the universe at first is a universe which will not tolerate any life at all. One cannot validly imagine oneself as picking up by sight a universe which would destroy any seeing organ or indeed any living thing,

even though at a later time when it has evolved to another state this same universe will produce sight. This would be like trying to imagine what a mass of molten steel in a blast furnace looks like to one sitting inside the molten steel. One can imagine various combinations of bright yellows and reds and blues and whites. But none really represent the actuality, which is simply and totally invisible—try sitting inside a mass of molten steel and see what you see—because it is simply intolerant of the conditions necessary for sight, or indeed for any of the other senses. Hence it is that any attempt to understand the early universe starting from a sensory image can never be fully successful. Any sensory image we can form of it must give us only an analogue of the reality which of its very nature precluded all possibility of its being sensed. However impressive it may be when we reconstruct it now in our imaginations and minds, and however agitated its hyperactivated molecules and masses, this was a dull and helpless universe at its start, intolerant of anything which might register even the fact that it was there. With the advent of man, this fact is registered. And thus the reconstruction of the brute facts of four or five billion—perhaps ten billion—years ago in man's mind today is more wonderful and impressive than the original facts themselves. Against the backdrop of the infrahuman universe which has given him birth, man remains more impressive than the rest of this universe. For he, as nothing before him, really includes it all. It comes to life and fruition in him.

44 Even if this were not so, it is against this cosmic backdrop that man must be viewed and, indeed, that God's Providence and revelation to man must be conceived. Against this backdrop the Incarnation took place. Any educated man, and much more any Catholic educator, must view himself and all mankind and God's action in this cosmic scene, and must do so not occasionally but habitually. A Christ projected by our imginations, consciously or subconsciously, into any universe other than this real one is to that extent unreal. Only with as full as possible an understanding of the universe as it actually has been and is can we hope to realize effectively, with His grace, what is the meaning of His Incarnation in this evolving creation and in this always more and more closely knit human society which through Him was brought into being and through Him and with Him and in Him is being brought to its mysterious fruition.

STUDY GUIDE

Theme and Structure

1. Father Ong says in paragraph 1 that "the discovery of the process of evolution, cosmic and organic, has been one of the greatest achievements of the human mind." After you have read through his essay, write a paragraph in which you enumerate some of the reasons for the truth of his statement.

2. Write a sentence outline in which you state the ideas developed in each of the following parts of the essay paragraphs: 1–4, 5–6, 7–8, 9–13, 14–20, 21–24, 25–32, 33–38, 39–41, and 42.

3. Do you see any connection between what Father Ong says about the development of the "historical sense" in paragraphs 5 and 6 and what Susanne K. Langer said about the central human awareness in her essay?

4. What is the chief difference between the cyclic and linear views of history? What are some of the reasons for the congeniality of the linear view to Christianity?

5. Why does the very presence of man in the universe at least partly disqualify an exaggerated cyclic view of history?

6. Some critics would say that Father Ong may be extreme in the opposition he sees between the cyclic and linear views of history. Thus, for instance, John McLaughlin says in *America* (April 29, 1967):

> Must cyclicism and evolution be antithetical orientations? Only, it seems to me, if you accept Fr. Ong's semantics, namely, that cyclicism is "the identical and inevitable repetition of an event." The operative word is "identical." But what cyclicist holds that? One may think of man's passage through time as neither linear (Ong) nor cyclic (Toynbee *et al.*) but spiral and upward. Such a view would preserve the plain truth that history does frequently and substantially repeat itself. . . . The spiral model would simultaneously stress man's forward progression.

Father Ong's insight about the essential linearity of history as seen from a Christian perspective is an extremely valuable one. The notion of McLaughlin that it is not exactly a straightforward linear movement, but a spiral one, but still forward and upward, may add a helpful and necessary qualification to the idea. Can you see, for instance, any way in which the history of art and literature might illustrate both a linear and spiral movement—a forward evolution in which patterns and tastes do partly reoccur?

7. Why does the evolutionary concept of the cosmos and history add to rather than detract from the dignity of man?

8. Why is the complete uniqueness of every "I," or person, both the glory and the terror of human existence?

Diction and Imagery

1. What is the exact meaning of *chiliasm* and *ascesis*? What is the point of the analogy made in paragraph 27 between the *ascetical* life and the evolutionary process?

2. Discuss the analogy (paragraph 37) between the ovum and the sperm in the formation of the human body and the evolutionary process and the creative action of God in bringing into existence the individual human person.

3. Why does the device of the fast-motion film in paragraph 42 help make the point of man's seeming insignificance?

4. How does the use of the analogy of trying to *see* molten steel from within the mass of molten steel itself help to emphasize the evolutionary process as a preparation for man's *sensing* anything?

5. Why is the Christian concept of the resurrection of the body peculiarly congenial to the evolutionary view of the cosmos and man? In this

connection it might be interesting to read the poem "That Nature Is a Heraclitean Fire and the Comfort of the Resurrection" by Gerard Manley Hopkins, and write a paper in which you show how the poem relates to ideas discussed in this essay.

WHAT IS EXISTENTIALISM?

Roger Troisfontaines

1 Existentialism at the present moment is not quite so fashionable as it was a few years ago, but perhaps this very fact provides us with an opportunity for examining this philosophical movement with great detachment.

2 The word "existentialism" covers a great variety of attitudes and opinions and to attempt to treat them all in a single article presents something of a challenge. However, in order to meet the challenge as well as possible I should like to exclude from the very beginning two concepts of existentialism which are incorrect or too restricted. The one considers existentialism merely as a sort of postwar dilettantism, and is represented particularly by the young men and young women who frequent the cellars of the left bank in Paris; the other, which errs by being too restricted, identifies existentialism with the philosophy of Jean-Paul Sartre. Then, from a more positive point of view, we shall be able to define the existentialist movement in general as a philosophy of subjectivity, or selfhood, whose fundamental doctrine proclaims man's freedom in the accomplishment of his destiny, and whose principal method is consequently that of description, or phenomenology.

3 With this common basis as a background we shall be in a better position to distinguish and to understand the divergent tendencies resulting from the different interpretations of human destiny and of man's freedom which the existentialist philosophers propose, and whose characteristic operations they describe.

4 We shall illustrate these different tendencies by an extremely simplified exposition of the two principal French representatives of existentialism, Jean-Paul Sartre and Gabriel Marcel. From this I believe it will be evident that contemporary existentialism, although it is an important movement in philosophy, is certainly not *the* Philosophy.

"What Is Existentialism?" by Roger Troisfontaines, *Thought*, Vol. 32 (Winter 1957), pp. 516–532.

5 The most popular postwar conception of existentialism is that it is the eccentric attitude of young men and women with uncombed hair, who dance the latest gyrations and who, when they remember to do so, declare that the world is absurd; a fact which permits them to take all the liberty they like with even the most elementary moral obligations.

6 This ridiculous new way of being "cool" or "zazou," sprung from the Parisian night clubs in the neighborhood of the "Café de Flore" where Jean-Paul Sartre wrote his books, has nothing to do with existential philosophy. If it did in fact borrow the name, such a transposition is unwarranted. Is there an explanation of how this transposition came about? Perhaps, but before an answer is suggested a few brief observations concerning one French word are in order. They will be useful for an understanding of the explanation to follow.

7 The French language, as is well known, makes frequent use of the impersonal pronoun *on*. The nearest literal equivalent in English is the use of the word "one," as in the expression, "one never knows, does one?" Such a use of "one" is usually regarded as stiff and formal, and, in modern American usage, is practically nonexistent. This, however, is not the case in French, in which *on* is used incessantly. In translation, it can be the equivalent of almost any of the English pronouns. Thus *on dit* means "they say"; *on m'a dit* means "someone told me"; *on se reverra,* "we shall meet again"; *on ne sait jamais,* "you never know." But what is characteristic of the French *on* is that it is not personal, that is to say, it is impersonal. It designates anyone, everyone, people in general. It is completely devoid of individuality and personality.

8 Now, to return to the question of how the term "existentialist" came to be applied to the eccentric young people of Saint-Germain-des-Prés. All the existentialists insist on the fact that man is free and responsible, and that he should take into his own hands the direction of his personal life. The impersonal pronoun *on* (one) is opposed to the personal subject "I." The man who acts and thinks like everyone else or anyone at all remains under the domination of the impersonal *on*. As a result, he becomes a mere statistical unit, one specimen among an infinity of others, a grain of dust, an atom caught up in a whirlwind, a sheep in a herd.

9 The ideas such a man calls his own are merely those which come to him from his milieu, through the medium of the daily press, the radio, and television. He thinks what "everyone" *(on)* thinks. All his actions are motivated by a spirit of conformity or by human respect; he does what "one" does. On the contrary, only that man has the right to say "I" who judges for himself, who takes a position, who is willing to go against the accepted opinion and even run grave personal risks, if necessary; in a word, he is the man who commits himself and who, by that very fact, modifies the existing situations and forms his own personality.

10 Of this doctrine concerning the necessity of commitment (*engagement* in French) and of personal creation, certain superficial individuals have retained only the negative aspect: namely, that they must not act as "everybody else" acts. Alas! They do this to shock others, without realizing that snobbishly following a new vogue merely tightens the circle of the impersonal *on*. Far from delivering them from it, this attitude subjects them to it even more completely, and in a very grotesque way.

11 It is in the name of Sartre that these thoughtless individuals consider themselves authorized to proclaim their nausea in the face of the universe and to assert that for them "anything goes." But Jean-Paul Sartre himself admits that he is not the whole of existentialism. In the manifesto which he delivered just about everywhere, and later published under the title *Existentialism is a humanism*, he himself points out that there are at least "*two* types of existentialists: a first group, who are Christians and among whom," says Sartre, "I number Karl Jaspers and Gabriel Marcel; and on the other hand the atheistic existentialists, among whom should be numbered Heidegger and myself." We should note in passing that Heidegger protests against this imputation of atheism. It is well to remark also that the three authors mentioned by Sartre are, on the average, twenty years older than he (he was born in 1905), and that as Mounier says, "Existentialism already represented the richest and fullest current of contemporary philosophy, at a time when the great talents of Jean-Paul Sartre were interested in marmalade under aspects much more immediate than those of existential psychoanalysis." The reference to "marmalade" is an allusion to a long analysis of viscosity in *Being and Nothingness*. Viscous people, explains Sartre, are like a drop of marmalade or, better, like a honey drop falling into a jar of honey. For a while, the drop seems to retain its individuality. After a few seconds, however, it vanishes into the mass. This is a good picture of *la mort sucrée du pour-soi*, "the sugary death of consciousness." The vanishing "I" becomes an anonymous *on*.

12 Thus Sartre is neither the whole nor the first of existentialism. In France, in particular, Gabriel Marcel, who was born in 1889, had developed the broad outlines of an existential philosophy long before Sartre had published anything at all. Although Marcel accepted, at the Congress of Rome in 1946, the title of "Christian Existentialist," and although he allowed a similar title to be given to one of the volumes of the collections "Présences"; still, since 1948 he simply has not permitted anyone to call him an existentialist. In his opinion, the word itself is ugly, and besides, Sartre has hopelessly soiled it in his literary work, which Mauriac has described as "excrementalism." However, Marcel does not for that reason consider himself any less *existentiel*; just as Heidegger calls himself "existential" in opposition to Jaspers. I shall not discuss these distinctions here,

important though they be, and, since all of these authors have a special interest in concrete existence, which, however, each one understands in his own way, I shall consider them all as existential philosophers.

13 All of them, as a matter of fact, acknowledge that they have certain traits in common, although that does not always mean that one actually exercises an influence upon another. Thus, when Marcel published in 1923 his article "Existence and Objectivity," which is really the charter of French existentialism, he knew nothing of the works of his German contemporaries, Jaspers and Heidegger, nor even of the writings of the Dane, Sören Kierkegaard (who died in 1855), and whom all recognize as the first of the philosophers of existence.

14 But what then are the characteristics common to these philosophers and to many others, who profess to be of the same cloth, such as Berdyaev, Chestov, Le Senne, Merleau-Ponty and others? The point on which they all agree is that of the extreme importance of subjectivity. As has happened so often in the history of philosophy, with the "know thyself" of Socrates, the *cogito* of Descartes and the Transcendental Ego of Kant, the present movement brings back our attention from the consideration of things and ideas to man, but this time to man under the aspect which is strictly personal to him, the subject, the incommunicable "I." The subject of Descartes's *cogito* or of Kant's Pure Reason could be you as well as I. It is"anyone," it is still the impersonal *on*. But it is evident that the spiritual experiences which mean the most to me exclude precisely this appropriation to "just anyone." What is truly "subjective" is incommunicable and nontransferable.

15 To take a very simple example, I can give, lend or sell this pen, because, it is, in the etymological sense of the word, an object (from the Latin *ob-jicere*), something that I can throw before me, separate from myself, look at from the outside, and give away to another. Any pen of the same type could render me the same services as this one. But I am attached to this particular one. Why? Because it belonged to my father, or because I received it from a friend, or because it is my sole daily reminder of a certain period in my life; my university studies, for instance, or my captivity in Germany, and so on. This relationship of habit or affection, the real reason for my attachment to this particular pen, is not at all objective. I cannot separate it from myself, nor sell it, nor transfer it. It is subjective.

16 Subjectivity, as this example clearly shows, is not to be confused with subjectivism. A subjectivist interpretation in the pejorative sense is a false interpretation. I claim to see as white what is in fact gray, because I would prefer to have it that way. I declare some good action evil, because it is performed by someone whom I dislike, or I declare innocent a man who is guilty, because he belongs to my party. Subjectivism falsifies the object; it is one of the many forms of error or of lying. Subjectivity, on the

contrary, goes beyond the merely objective, but without changing it. Objectively the house in which I spent my childhood is the same for me and for any prospective buyer. Subjectively, it is completely different for me, because of my dear ones who lived there and perhaps even died there, and because of the innumerable memories which fill every corner of the house and constitute a sort of presence, even without my being able to recall them consciously. This house is not just before me as an object, it is within me. Into the knowledge which I have of this house, I have put what is most individual and personal in me. The subjective then, this time in the nonpejorative sense, is that which I alone can understand or do; it is such that no one else can take my place in regard to it.

17 On the street, two young men pass a young lady. It is possible that objectively one of them knows her better than the other; he knows just about everything that "one" (*on*) can say about her; the date and place of her birth, her family history and education, her marks at school, her financial status, the color of her eyes, the talents and defects which people recognize in her, and so on. But the other young man has a knowledge of her which is unique, because he loves her and is loved by her, because they have already promised themselves to each other. No one sees a young lady as her fiancé does, and, if subjectivism can be the basis of illusion in this matter, there is nevertheless a subjectivity which comes into play and which is perfectly legitimate; he knows her differently and better than anyone else, because she penetrates his consciousness and he hers, infinitely beyond anything which can be called "objective."

18 Subjectivity, then, is the realm of those realities which belong most profoundly to my personal being, those which constitute it in its innermost reality, and which, for that very reason, I cannot separate from myself. It is the mystery in which I am immersed, and in which I constantly live, but which I cannot express in terms of "problems" without altering its very nature. The word "problem" (which comes from the Greek *pro-ballo*, to throw before) has exactly the same etymology as the word "object." A problem is before me. I can walk around it, examine it from all possible angles; but, when it trespasses on the domain of my own experience, that is, when it is likewise within me, and when I cannot legitimately abstract myself from it, then it becomes a mystery. For the medical student or for the physician, sickness is a problem; the facts are there and he must find a solution. But when I am ill, my situation is something completely different. Insofar as I try to treat myself, I can adopt the objective point of view of the doctor, but, as a subject, I have to react personally to my sickness; for, from a human viewpoint, here—as in all the other circumstances of my life—I can grow spiritually or I can fail miserably. Sickness is a mystery inasmuch as it is a trial, in which I am forced to get to know myself and to take certain attitudes with regard to good or evil, that is,

either open myself up to the love of God and of my neighbor, or shut myself up in pouting pride and demanding selfishness. No one can make this decision for me, not even the well-intentioned visitor, who may come to explain to me that sickness is a trial. Except in the case in which his words are the expression of a sympathy which is such that it is evident that my trial is equally his own, he would do better to say nothing.

19 There is no way of rendering exterior what is really subjective. If I want to speak of my love or of my religious faith in the language of objective science, or if I simply want to talk about them, the core of intimacy and warmth, which gives my love and my faith their value, disappears at once, and I am exposed to the ridicule of others or to theories of analysis. I have no difficulty in speaking *to* God in prayer or in silent communion, for God is within me just as much as He is outside of me, and therefore He shares in the mystery of my own being, but when I try to speak *about* God, the formulae which I employ designate a quasi-exterior being, the God of philosophers and scientists, so different from my God, with whom I am in contact when I pray!

20 Subjectivity is never more evident than when I commit myself personally, that is, in my free acts. Here, in opposition to every form of totalitarianism and in opposition to all determinist doctrines, the existentialist philosophers all agree in affirming man's freedom. They have no trouble in showing that this sector of our life, in which man freely implicates himself, is the one which each of us considers as the most important, and the one in which each of us finds his reasons for both living and dying. In order for men to dedicate and sacrifice themselves, it is not sufficient that there be *before* them some purely objective datum; they need a reality which is also *within* them and a reality which is such that their action will contribute in one way or another to its growth or manifestation, whether that reality be their work, their family, their country or their religion.

21 Leaving to technical science the objective world, existential philosophy, which some of its followers identify, though wrongly, with philosophy as such, reserves for itself the sphere of the subjective. To dominate matter and to know the laws which determine it does not interest the existentialists. A scientific judgment is true for anyone at all, and a good technique is at the disposal of anyone who takes the trouble to learn it. Science and technology perfect the realm of the impersonal *on*, but they do not free man from it. Existential philosophy is interested in the human subject, who is always unique, and who has to complete his own creation by his free actions.

22 Our situation at the point of departure on our adventure of life is in fact imposed upon us. None of us chose to come into this world, nor to be born at a certain time, in a certain country, a certain family, a certain

social milieu, with a body more or less healthy, more or less attractive; with a character more or less agreeable or easy to get along with, and so on. This is what Marcel calls "existence" (from the Latin *ex-istere*, to be outside of), I am conditioned by what is outside of me, and I am not conscious of myself except in a certain relationship with the external world. Sartre calls the same thing "facticity" (because it is a "fact"). But the important thing is what I am going to make out of all the various elements of this initial situation. As a matter of fact, it is in view of my "project," that is, of the way in which I "commit myself" in the universe, that all these elements take on a meaning. To use another example: the same objective sky is for the artist a harmony of volumes and colors, for the farmer either a sprinkler or a heater, for the hiker a threat or a promise, for the scientist an unstable equilibrium and an occasion for study and calculation, for the contemplative a divine gift and an invitation to eternal love. All of these affirmations are true, but each in a different way.

23 In the last analysis, it depends on me whether I succeed or fail in this life—the only life that is given to me. The success may not be external, for that depends on too many circumstances not under my control, but there can be an internal subjective success. What sort of a man am I going to make out of myself? This is the only important question, and every man must answer it. For, even though I receive the help of my neighbor or of God, in the end it is I and I alone who must decide. For what is essential, no one can take my place. I am responsible for myself, and when I realize that, I cannot help feeling an anguish in the face of the task which is mine. As Scripture says, man is put in the hands of his own counsel. It is I who condemn myself or who accept salvation, and we are well authorized in using this religious language, for the themes of existentialism are originally, and explicitly in Kierkegaard its founder, Christian themes. The great choice for him was and is, as we shall see, that of faith, to say Yes or No to God. Although these themes have been secularized and perverted by certain of our contemporaries, they cannot be well understood except in this perspective.

24 Since freedom is something which, by its very nature, is unpredictable and since it cannot be forced, the only way to speak about it and to urge others toward it, is to describe its operations, in order to give others food for thought, for reflection and for personal decision. The philosopher is a man who tries to make a success of his life, and who expresses, as well as he can, his own way of looking at things and his own way of acting, so that others may profit by his experience. Far from being a system of constructions or deductions, an existential philosophy is an appeal, an exhortation, a sermon. With the intention of giving philosophy a solid and universal experimental basis, Husserl developed a method of description of essences, which he called phenomenology. His disciple Heidegger applied this

method to the description of existence. All the contemporary existentialists are phenomenologists; that is to say, they try to render explicit, by means of description, what is implicit in the realities which we live in our daily lives, but which we live without being sufficiently aware of them. Thus, for instance, we all hope for any number of things: that our train will be on time, that some loved one will not stay away long, that our son will pass his examinations, that our partner in marriage will remain faithful, that God will receive us into everlasting happiness, and so on. Starting from the most ordinary, everyday experiences, Marcel analyzes this human attitude for some fifty pages. It would be absurd to sum them up, for their interest consists precisely in the progressive discovery. Let us say only that Marcel proposes the formulation of this virtue as follows: "I hope in you for us," that is to say, "I have trust in you whom I love, because you also love me and I can count on you to maintain the community of life which we live together." He shows also that all our hopes are ultimately based upon an unshakeable trust in an absolute "You," or "Thou" whose Love cannot fail. But Sartre in his turn describes, in an extremely vivid way, the manner in which bad faith operates. He discovers in every one of our actions a way of being-what-we-are-not and of not-being-what-we-are.

25 This existential method explains the introduction into philosophy of certain literary forms, which previously were not considered suitable; for example, confessions (and here St. Augustine is invoked as the ancestor of the movement), reflections or aphorisms (which have Pascal as a precursor), diaries, novels, plays; in short, any form which enables a person to say "I." Let us not be too quick to condemn the hateful "I." The existentialists would reply that to express the "I" is still the best means of attaining the truly universal, because in every spiritual experience a concrete "I," analogous to mine, is involved. I am less unfaithful to reality in describing my own experience in its singularity than in trying to universalize an experience which is supposedly "common to all men," and it is the reflection on my experience which is most likely to suggest elements which other subjects, as subjects, will be able to assimilate.

26 There is a good example of the existentialist approach in the recently translated book *The Fall* by Albert Camus. This monologue, according to Robert Gorham David in the *New York Times Book Review* (February, 17, 1957, p. 33), "is an irresistibly brilliant examination of the modern conscience. Only a very obdurate reader could finish it without finding himself much more honest about the character of his motives and the contradictions in his values. Despite his external ambiguity and apparent negations, the book has a positive effect of a uniquely personal kind."

27 The theater is a particularly useful vehicle for existentialist expression, since it puts on the stage several characters, all of whom express themselves in the first person. The situation here is more simplified than in real

life, the reactions more clearly defined, and the spectator is concerned in the play without at the same time being "put on the spot." He can examine himself and judge more clearly.

28 As far as the philosophers themselves are concerned, they write plays for two very different reasons.

29 Some see in it a means of propaganda, or of popularizing their ideas. Such is the case of Sartre; his play, *The Devil and God,* for example, is supposed to prove to us that God does not exist. Here is how Sartre goes about it: A German cavalry officer of the sixteenth century, named Goetz, enjoys doing evil, because, as he says, "What is good has already been done . . . by God the Father. As for me I invent!" He rejoices over the fact that he has killed his brother, because by so doing he has "made God's heart bleed." "God, who is the only adversary worthy of me." "I shall crucify God tonight," he boasts, as he decides upon the massacre of the twenty thousand inhabitants of the city of Worms, because, as he says, "God's suffering is infinite, and that makes the one who makes Him suffer likewise infinite." When someone points out to him that to do good is even more difficult than to do evil, he agrees, on a bet, to do good, because, he says, "It is still the best way to be *alone.*" For a year and a day, he will play the role of a saint, and Sartre would like to convince us of the spiritual value of such a questionable conversion. We are more inclined to share the reserve and suspicion of the peasants to whom Goetz distributes his fortune. The adventure becomes a catastrophe. We are in the midst of the Wars of Religion, and the City of Love, which Goetz was trying to establish, is destroyed by fire and sword. Does not God have any care for those who are faithful to Him?

30 After this failure in the apostolic life Goetz dedicates himself to what Sartre imagines is a life of asceticism and mysticism. Goetz decides to destroy the man within him, because, as he discovers, "God created man to be destroyed." He fasts and vows perfect chastity. Such a vow, however, does not prevent this remarkable hermit from living with a woman, and from falling into sins of the flesh regularly. But again, Sartre thinks that such a murderer needed this occasion to practice penance, and he does so by having himself whipped by the woman in the most classical masochistic manner.

31 Finally, after a year and a day, comes the great enlightenment. "I prayed, I begged for a sign. I sent messages to heaven," says Goetz. "No answer. Now I know the answer: it is: nothing. . . . You see the void above our heads? That is God. . . . Silence . . . that is God. Absence . . . that is God. God is the solitude of man. There was only me: I alone determined what was evil and I alone invented the good. *I,* man. If God exists, then man is nothing: but if man exists. . . . Heinrich, I'm going to let you in on a big joke: God does not exist. . . . He does not exist . . .

Joy, tears of joy, Alleluia. . . . I have liberated us. No more heaven; no more hell; just the earth. Farewell to the monsters, farewell to the saints. Only men exist." Despite the talent of Sartre and that of Pierre Brasseur who made the play a success, it is hard to imagine anyone being convinced by such naive propaganda, inferior in many ways to the very worst type of didactic plays for children.

32 But the theater can be used for other purposes and for Marcel in particular it is truly a metaphysical experiment. No preconceived doctrine dictates the words and actions; the persons come first, and the author, who places them in a situation which he has imagined or, more frequently, actually encountered, observes them and listens to them react as living persons. He does not know ahead of time where that will lead him; and, as a matter of fact, there are a great number of unfinished plays in Marcel's files: he has not yet been able to resolve the situation. On the other hand, sometimes he takes up and continues a play which he began years before, because now he finally sees the way in which the characters should develop. None of his heroes is the spokesman of the author. He generally prefers to dramatize the contradictory of his own philosophical positions, in order to make of it a sort of proof *a contrario*. Thus, to cite but one example, fidelity to the dead is a favorite theme of Marcel's philosophy. In *La Chapelle Ardente*, he represents a mother, completely absorbed in the memory of her son killed during the war. Psychologically warped by what she thinks is fidelity, she unconsciously goes about ruining her own life and torturing all those around her. First of all, she succeeds in turning the ex-fiancée of her son away from a happy marriage, and then she pushes her into the arms of a weakling, who will be less capable of taking her mind off her dead fiancé. Finally, the woman's husband, who cannot endure this funeral-parlor atmosphere any longer, divorces her in order to escape her nagging. The play is "gloomy," as is often the case with Marcel, but it is left up to the spectator himself to judge where the mistake lies and to react in consequence.

33 With this common basis of a philosophy of subjectivity, which takes the form of a description intended to stimulate our freedom, it is easy to see that there can exist completely divergent points of view among the existential philosophers, depending on the use which each one makes of his freedom. Man can either shut himself up within himself in a selfish and proud isolation, or, on the contrary, he can open up his heart to God and to his neighbor in a humble spirit of friendliness, receptiveness, and generosity.

34 Let us illustrate again, by means of an example—that of testimony. Unfortunately we cannot develop this example as fully as the phenomenological method would demand. Let us suppose that, quite by chance, I am present at an accident or a crime. Just as in the case of my existence, which

I have not chosen, I find that, whether I like it or not, I am engaged (passively) in a situation; for I have seen what took place. The important thing, however, is the attitude which I am going to take actively in regard to this event. We can distinguish four attitudes:

35 1. When I am questioned, on the spot, at the police station or in courtroom I can transform my observation into testimony; that is to say, I can personally assume the responsibility for what I say, I can commit myself in the trial and bind myself under oath. The one who gives testimony is always a definite individual: anyone (*on*) can observe, but I testify. I am able to testify because I am a conscious and free person. What is more, I feel that I am obliged to testify. Why? Because I possess a certain amount of light upon what took place, and because, as a result of my testimony, justice will be done. This of course implies that I believe fundamentally in a certain human order, which is to be established or re-established, and that I recognize the role which is mine, if I consent, in the organization of the world.

36 2. But it is equally possible that I fear to compromise myself. If I give testimony, I shall necessarily be for one party and against the other; I run the risk of provoking trouble for myself. It is always dangerous to commit oneself. Thus, whatever the case may have been, I declare, from the first questioning on, that "I didn't see very clearly," that "I don't remember," or "I couldn't say if . . ." and so on. I declare myself incompetent to give testimony. I take refuge in the anonymous, I prefer the impersonal *on*. I refuse to be a responsible subject. The honey drop vanishes into the mass.

37 3. It is possible that I adopt this attitude out of simple cowardice, but certain authors try to justify it by a theory such as the following: "What good does it do to testify? What difference does it make whether the trial turns out well or badly? The world is absurd, isn't it? It has no meaning. Justice here below . . . or the preparation of eternal life, what a joke!" "Whatever exists," says Sartre, "is born without a reason, prolongs its existence by weakness and dies by accident."

38 4. Finally, certain other authors, who profess this same fundamental absurdity of the universe and of life, still find a reason for giving testimony, but only now and then, to amuse themselves. Their testimony might just as well be false as true; that has no importance for them; the main thing is to create something arbitrarily, to make a pretense at committing oneself, without believing in it, "just for fun."

39 An absurd and criminal attitude? Certainly, but it is an attitude which, in the great trial of life, is proclaimed by a certain number of contemporary writers. This seems to be the doctrine of Malraux in *The Royal Road, The Human Condition,* and *Hope*; to commit yourself completely,

in the Communist revolution in China, for example, or in the civil war in Spain, without believing in either, without any concern for the values involved, and with the intention of passing over to the other camp, if ever the one which you are serving triumphs. This is also the theory of the gratuitous act developed by André Gide and his disciples, as well as the *Myth of Sisyphus* of Camus: to find one's happiness in rolling a stone, *because* it is useless.

40 There is no commitment in the second and in the third attitudes: they belong to the impersonal *on*. The first and the fourth attitudes, on the contrary, are really existentialist. But they are completely divergent; the first is a personal commitment according to the truth and the reality; the fourth is an individualistic pretension of being the only important creature —or even the only creator.

41 We can say that such is the attitude which Sartre claims to justify in philosophy. According to his own feeling the fundamental metaphysical experience is nausea, the discovery of primordial absurdity. Far from looking upon consciousness as a progress over matter, he denounces it as a "sickness of being," the introduction of the nothingness in the fullness of the material thing. Similarly, he considers freedom as a "curse." "We are condemned to be free." But he chooses to exercise the liberty for its own sake, in any manner whatsoever: "thus, there is no difference between getting drunk by myself or leading a nation," and he loudly claims as his own the possibility which is, in fact, his, that of sinning and of damning himself. The exaltation of self-sufficiency is insane, or more exactly and explicitly, diabolical. The rejection of others and of God is the pivot of Sartre's ethics. The ideal would be to be completely alone, the sole center of the universe. "Original sin is the arrival of others," says Sartre, who is very fond of theological vocabulary, but who always perverts it. Every other subject is considered as a "drain," through which my universe leaks away. Others steal my world! And, as the characters in *Huis Clos (No Exit)* they discover, "Hell is other people." "The first duty of the creature," we are taught, "is to deny its creator." In *The Flies*, Orestes, who has just killed his mother, and thus implicated himself in a crime which will overturn the whole moral, political, familial and religious order, defies God: "You will have no power over me except the power which I myself acknowledge. You created me, but you did not have to create me free. You are God and I am free. We are both equally alone." In Sartre's opinion, humanism must be based on atheism, or more exactly, on antitheism. To be sure, all men dream of being God, and the seven hundred pages of *Being and Nothingness* claim to describe, from this viewpoint, all human attitudes and projects. But all such attempts are doomed to failure, says Sartre, and here are the last words of his ontology: "The passion of man is the exact opposite

of that of Christ, for man loses himself as man, in order that God may be born. But the idea of God is contradictory, and we lose ourselves in vain; man is a useless passion" (*L'Être et le Néant*, p. 708).

42 It is hardly necessary to emphasize the harmfulness of such a doctrine, nor should we be surprised at the condemnations which it has provoked. But the general public, victim of a very cleverly directed propaganda, too often identifies Sartre with existentialism, and the rejection which the former deserves is extended also to the latter.

43 However, other types of existentialism are possible and have, in fact, developed; for there are other directions in which man can orientate his freedom. Thus Gabriel Marcel has devoted himself for forty years to an analysis of the spiritual life and of love for others. Brought up in a non-religious atmosphere, he has tried to understand what new intelligibility, what new vision of the world, faith gives to the man who lives by it. After twenty years of study, he was finally touched by grace and was converted and baptized in 1929, at the age of thirty-nine.

44 Where Sartre sees in the initial situation which makes us men, nothing but an absurd and incomprehensible accident, Marcel sees the gracious gift of a Transcendent Lover, who invites us to collaborate with Him in the perfecting of our own being. The great and unique task of man here below is to pass from existence to being; that is, from the initial participation in which he is immersed independently of his own will, to a new participation, this time conscious and freely willed, with the world, himself, other men, and God. Every man should recognize his vocation, dedicate himself to it and remain faithful to it, whatever may be the trials of his life. All the concepts of classical philosophy are renewed by phenomenology, and many of its searching analyses treat of our relationships of love for the universe, for our close friends, for our neighbor and for God. This itself is a proof that a religious existentialism is possible and that it contributes some extremely interesting elements for Christian thought.

45 Does this mean that this form of philosophy should replace those which have preceded it? Certainly not. Interesting as it may be, a description of subjectivity, by itself remains fundamentally insufficient. The disagreement among the existentialists themselves shows this. Each one analyzes his experience, but the experiences themselves are radically opposed to one another. When we turn our backs upon one another, at the seaside, for example, our visions of the world no longer coincide, and they can even contradict one another.

46 In regard to phenomenology itself, several points of view are possible. While it constitutes an excellent method of explanation and illustration, it does not provide the basis for a universal metaphysic. Each one claims to be right from his own viewpoint. Who will decide? Who will determine

the hierarchy of these perspectives? Who will show where truth and goodness lie, or where, on the contrary, there is a perversion? Under pain of falling into subjectivism, subjectivity has to base itself on an objective foundation, and it must do so according to criteria and norms which, far from crushing freedom, will be the sole means of enabling it not to degrade itself. Subjectivity and objectivity have complementary roles to play, and it would be equally harmful to abandon the one as to reject the other.

47 The fact of emphasizing human freedom is the chief benefit of existentialism. But the great lesson which contemporary philosophy has already taught us is that freedom is not the final end. Like the tongues of Aesop, it is capable of both the best and the worst. Everything depends on the use that I make of it. It is impossible to love without being free, but, for a creature, freedom includes the possibility of sinning.

48 The experience of Sartre, oscillating between a nauseous universe and a selfish isolation, is a lesson for us. So is that of Marcel, who teaches us how to pass from the existential situation, to a participation of "being" here below, to blossom, after the final trial of death, in the universal communion of charity. But it is up to each one of us to choose in which direction he will orientate his liberty, toward selfishness or toward love.

STUDY GUIDE

Theme and Structure

1. The author sets out to answer the question in the title "What Is Existentialism?" Hence the essay is a good example of an *extended definition.* In such a definition the false notions of the thing being defined are frequently excluded and then the positive definition is stated and expanded. Where, in this essay, are these two functions of a definition performed?

2. What are the two chief elements that the author discovers in all types of existentialists?

3. What are the two main groups of existentialists?

4. Concrete examples are often the best means of specifying and clarifying an idea to be defined. Who are the two individuals who serve as concrete examples of the two groups of existentialists being discussed here? What do they have in common? How do they differ from one another?

5. Susanne K. Langer in paragraph 34 of her essay says that exaggerated individualism "lands some people in nihilism and cynicism, and leads others to existentialism. . . ." Using Troisfontaines' discussion of existentialism, indicate in what sense Miss Langer is using the term in the above statement.

6. Do you see any connection between Miss Langer's discussion of *individuation* and *social involvement* as marks of the human situation and Troisfontaines' discussion of *subjectivity* and free *social commitment* as marks of the existentialist point of view?

7. Considering the emphasis on subjectivity and personal freedom in existentialism, do you think it is almost necessary for existentialists to express themselves in literary forms—plays, novels, short stories, and so on?

Diction and Imagery

1. The author emphasizes the difference between *objectivity, subjectivity,* and *subjectivism.* What is the exact meaning of each? How do concrete examples help to clarify the difference between these ideas in paragraphs 16, 17, and 18?

2. How do comparisons help define the Sartrean and Marcelian type of existentialist in paragraph 33?

3. What is the exact definition of *phenomenology?* Why is it a natural accompaniment to an existentialist emphasis in philosophy?

A WORLD THEY NEVER MADE

D. W. Brogan

1 "A world they never made." I am fully aware of the dangers inherent in applying to a people of one hundred seventy millions a poet's insight into personal psychology. And in beginning my discussion of the world in which the American people to their great discomfort find themselves, I am not professing to expound an exact or even an approximately verifiable science. I am attempting something both more humble and more bold, the calling of the attention of Americans to what I, a sympathetic foreigner but nevertheless a foreigner, think is the first cause of their discomfort, the first cause of the degree of suspicion, apprehension, bewilderment with which many, many Americans regard the world of 1959 and the world that they see lying beyond 1959.

2 To begin with, it is a world they never made. In making that judgment on the contemporary world the average American is not indulging in more than the usual human allowance of permissible shorthand. In one sense the United States is most decidedly one of the makers of the modern world; in some respects the United States is the chief maker of the modern world. But in the sense in which I am using the metaphor, the poet's insight, the world that the American today is forced to regard and fear is one that he feels little responsibility for making and little consequent capacity for understanding. Not only is it a world defying his sense

From *America in the Modern World,* by D. W. Brogan. Copyright 1960. Reprinted by permission of Rutgers University Press.

of both what is reasonable and what is right. It is a world that somehow or other has replaced the other, better, happier, more harmless world that lay alongside the United States, in few relations with it but those relations friendly, hopeful, innocent.

3 The American does not like the world in which he finds himself (who does?), but he dislikes it the more because it has replaced a world that may indeed never have existed. It certainly did not exist in the simple innocent form in which the American tradition remembers it, but it was not totally mythical and had some if not all of the attractiveness that the tradition lends it. The American today, it seems to me, has slowly accepted the fact that this is a case of Paradise Lost, not just Paradise Mislaid, and naturally he laments his exile from Eden. Naturally he fears the flaming sword that sweeps between him and the innocent garden of his youth.

4 It is time, I am sure, to leave metaphor, to leave poetry, and to try to present in more prosaic terms the nature of the present dilemma that perplexes the American, the nature of some of the varying characteristics of the world in which the American has to live. What is the first that has to be stressed, the first American disillusionment?

5 It is, I think, the discovery that progress is an ambiguous term. All of us, or most of us, know that progress—the view that the world more or less inevitably and easily got better and better—is a novel idea in the history of the human mind. It seemed more natural until quite recently in our human story to look to the past, to a golden age in which mankind lived happily under the benevolent protection of the "laws of nature and of nature's God" for the epoch of human felicity. I do not know that at any time in past history mankind thought it was living in the golden age or even in the silver age. At best it was the age of iron that each generation saw itself embedded in. But in the past things were better till we paid for "the crude apple that corrupted Eve."

6 It was against this traditional pessimism of the human race, reflected in legend all over the earth, that the idea of progress—the idea that the present was better than the past, the future better than the present—was a protest and one that since, say, the late fifteenth century began to captivate the Western mind. To find the line of progress, to move along that line, to cooperate with the winning forces of destiny, to welcome with open hand the gifts of nature, given the more lavishly when those hands were capable of using and developing the gifts—these were the first duties of modern man. And if man did his duty he would be rewarded from a horn of plenty of an unprecedented size and generosity.

> The world's great age begins anew,
> The golden years return.

They return; but far more golden than in the past, for Shelley saw the future of the free man in the free society as much more attractive than the golden age of the Greeks. We stand on the shoulders of the ancients, said Bacon, and naturally we see farther and reach higher. I could multiply the citations but I need hardly do so. The theme is the commonplace of our Western tradition, finding some of its most eloquent expression in America in the Declaration of Independence, some of its most adroit and plausible exemplification in the writings and achievements of Franklin. "He snatched the lightning from heaven, and the sceptre from tyrants." So wrote Turgot of the American who, as political and technological innovator, best justified American hopes at the birth of the American Republic. Franklin, Jefferson, the names say a lot.

7 But more important than the great names of great men is a fact about American life that I want to emphasize now and shall have occasion to emphasize again. It was not only the great Americans who believed in progress, it was all Americans. This country was born in the age of progress, baptized in the religion of progress, created and peopled by men and women who believed in progress, in some amelioration for themselves, in more for their children; it was in hope as well as in resentment and rebellion that they had crossed the Atlantic to a new world that, often unconsciously, they knew they had to make and resolve, again often unconsciously, to make better. Many attempts have been made, some of them profound and just, to characterize the American people. Surely one of their marks, until very recent times, has been that they have been a people of hope, of believers in amelioration. They have been a people for whom the bonds of tradition have not been allowed to justify inertia, the acceptance of visibly inferior conditions simply because that was the way of the fathers.

8 This hopefulness of the American view of life can be illustrated in many ways. Professor Perry Miller has shown us how the early American Calvinists, grim, fatalistic, pessimistic as they may seem, as they must seem to preachers of "togetherness," were in fact by the standards of seventeenth-century Europe optimistic, ill-disciplined, cheerfully inconsistent. With them, as with Dr. Johnson's would-be philosopher friend, "cheerfulness would keep breaking in." The new world offered new possibilities and "no man who had been born in Boston needed to be born again."

9 It would be possible to cast shadows on this picture. The greatest of Americans, that is, the man I consider the greatest of Americans, had a strong streak of pessimism in his nature. As much as Dr. Reinhold Niebuhr, Lincoln had a sense of man's essentially tragic situation. So it is expressed in that great but not 100 per cent American document, the Second Inaugural; so it is revealed in Lincoln's quotation from *Macbeth* at the moment of his triumphant return from captured Richmond:

Duncan is in his grave;
After life's fitful fever he sleeps well.

But the greatest men of a nation are too great to be fully or merely representative and the representative American has, until recently, seen the story of the human race as on the whole a success story and one part of it as undoubtedly a success story, the history of the United States, the creation here, on this continent, of the last, best hope of earth. And if melodramatic pessimism is a luxury Americans could allow themselves because they did not really doubt that theirs was a success story, the pessimism that I seem to note today is not merely melodramatic; it is real, alarmed, and shows for the first time a realization that the human story may go wrong, that the old pessimistic cyclical theory of human destiny may be the true one—and that the American people are inextricably involved in the common, dangerous, and only intermittently hopeful destiny of the human race. For the American is beginning to realize that he can neither remake the world according to the American plan (for many Americans, necessarily God's plan) nor contract out. If the human race would obey or imitate, all would be well soon, if not now. But the hope of obedience or imitation is weak if not dead.

10 This, it seems to me, is the first ground for American discontent and alarm. The world is not visibly going the American way and is still less visibly content to let the Americans go their way, "the world forgetting, by the world forgot."

11 What were the American hopes that have been shattered? The first is that the United States having made herself by her exertions would save the world by her example. How deep that faith was, how justified, a cursory glance at history abundantly illustrates. In an international as well as in a national sense, America had erected a standard to which all good men could and, it was confidently believed, *would* repair. It was not for nothing that the founders of the Republic adopted a proud Latin motto: "Novus ordo seclorum," a new order of the ages. (You will find this device on one of the three sacred documents of the Republic: not on the Declaration, not on the Constitution, but on the dollar bill.)

12 In a world still sunk in tyranny, empty tradition, political and religious servility, the new Republic shone, free from the sins of the past, bright with the greatest hopes known in the upward history of man-upward, for no one, in America at least, doubted that, as an American poet was to put it with great effect if bad Latin, the banner with the strange device bore the inspiring motto "excelsior." It is easy to make fun of the poem, of the poet, of the sentiment, but to do so is to sin against the spirit of America—and to fail to understand both the greatness of the hopes and the present chill of the fears.

13 It was not a matter of mere national pride or conceit. The virtuous republic of Washington was a model, not a mere pattern laid up in heaven but taking form in the remote American forest. The very hostility of conservative thinkers like de Maistre was proof of the fascination of the new state and the new society. Hopes dashed by the course of the French Revolution came to life again as the mild rule of Washington and then of Jefferson was contrasted with the Reign of Terror and the baleful, cometlike career of Napoleon. The great news was out; a free and orderly society could be created and mankind had far more hope of happiness open to him than had, until this happy day, been dreamed of. Again I could multiply the instances, from the repentance of his early hostility by William Cobbett to Goethe's famous praise of the new society:

> Amerika, du hast es besser.

But chronology supplies the most adequate example. It is a hundred years since the most profound and permanently valuable foreign commentator on the American scene and the American system died. And one of the lessons that Alexis de Tocqueville wanted to teach Europe—and especially France—was that the possibilities of human happiness, if not of exceptional human achievement, were greater than Europeans, especially conservative Europeans regretting the old order that America condemned by her success, had ever admitted to be possible. That way the Western world was going and that way, drab or dull as it might be, the greatest happiness of the greatest number lay.

14 On that shining picture a most ominous shadow lay—slavery. So the Civil War was both the punishment of American sin and the justification of faith in America. The victory of the North was a triumph for the cause of human freedom and dignity and John Bright, addressing a great meeting in favor of extending the franchise, interrupted his oration to give out the simple but meaningful message, "Richmond has fallen." So Walt Whitman was hailed by Swinburne; so all liberal Europe (including that semirepresentative figure, Karl Marx) welcomed the triumph of the Union. And the victors felt—and rightly felt—that this triumph not only was theirs but was the most manifest proof that faith in human progress and in a kindly destiny for mankind was justified.

15 That faith was naïve, so naïve that quite a different triumph, that of Bismarck's Prussia, was welcomed as a victory for the same good cause and the unification of Italy was welcomed both because national unity was a good thing and because it meant a decline, perhaps a fatal decline, in the power of Giant Pope. And the homage of imitation and admiration was not confined to statesmen and poets. It was made more manifest in the floods of immigrants who poured in, the greatest folk movement of which

we have any adequate record. The Statue of Liberty was no more eloquent of America's role in the upward spiral of mankind than was Castle Garden and then Ellis Island. Every immigrant was a vote for America and the American way of life. It is my belief that the memory of this golden day still colors the American attitude toward the outside world and that some of the average American's discontent with that outside world springs from a deep regret that those days of automatic leadership for all the advancing peoples of the world seem to be over. They have of course been over for a long time. It was pointless to stress the sentiments of the poem of Emma Lazarus when the United States no longer welcomed the poor and the oppressed in the old, generous and, if you like, reckless way. Moreover, as Socialist criticism of the capitalist order grew in strength in Europe, the determinedly un-Socialist economy and political system of the United States became a stumbling block, a stone of offense to the makers and shakers of Europe. The United States became less the country that had freed the slaves than the country that had hanged the Chicago anarchists, less the country of Lincoln than of the Standard Oil Company. And it was not only on the Left that the American image lost some of its dazzling brilliance.

16 The success story of Bismarck's Germany to some degree offset the success story of the United States. If it was Commodore Perry who forced the Japanese to go to school, they went to school at least as much to Prussia as to the United States or to Britain. Nor was this the only disillusionment. The formal imitation of American constitutional methods in Latin America gave only ambiguously gratifying results. The innocence with which Louis Kossuth had been hailed after the failure of the Hungarian rising of 1849 was hard to recapture when the finally triumphant Magyars turned out to be oppressors themselves.

17 The innocent, egalitarian farmer's republic had become the greatest industrial power in the world with all the problems of social order and justice that this dangerous promotion involved. America was virtuous; America was right; America was promises; but America was not quite so innocent, not quite so conscious of deserved and spontaneous admiration.

18 The year 1914 was, it is now easy to see, the watershed. Then began our dangerous, disorderly, unpredictable world. Then the faith in automatic progress received its first, perhaps its greatest, blow. Yet to the innocent American, on the farm, in the corner store, in the White House, the lesson of 1914 seemed plain. America had it better; the murderous quarrels of Europe had not been and should not be exported. America should stay above the battle and with malice toward none should only step in to bind up the nations' wounds. Such was the high ambition of the most famous New Jersey statesman, and who can think that Woodrow Wilson was wrong in his first ambition, which was to be a mediator and not a victor? It

is not my place to discuss or decide why that ambition failed and Wilson had to combine the two so different roles of being the head of a victorious coalition and the creator of a just and lasting peace. My purpose is to remind you that the Wilson of the last months of 1918, the first months of 1919, was the last American to revive in Europe (and outside Europe) the old faith in the good faith, the healing power, the moral superiority of the United States. With him there crashed a faith that has never been fully restored.

19 And that crash was all the more important because a new and baleful star had arisen, for surely the most important result of the First World War was not the Russian Revolution, that might have come anyway, but the Bolshevik Revolution, which I believe was made possible only by the war—and by the Allied victory, for that saved the Bolsheviks from destruction by the Germans.

20 The Russian Revolution is so much one of the turning points in world history that I need do no more than remind you of the fact, but the point I want to stress is that it had, among other results, one highly relevant for our purpose, the setting up of a rival and deeply hostile center of attraction to that still exercised by the United States.

21 In 1919 the American people made a desperate and totally hopeless effort to return to the peace that they had known yesterday. How quickly the crusading fervor wore off! How soon it was implausibly asserted that all American policy need do was to reverse the sins and errors of 1914–1919! Let America mind her own business; let her remember in a phrase of President Coolidge's (that may have been misunderstood) that "the business of the United States is business." Much could be said about this policy, if that it can be called. But it had one fatal fault. It ignored the fact that the world of 1919 was a world that owed its shape very largely to the power and policy of the United States. That policy may have been an error, that power may have been wrongly asserted, but the fact was there. The new and disillusioning world that the American people turned their back on was a world in whose making the American people had had a great share. For the sin of 1914 the innocent Republic had had no share of guilt. For the world of 1919–1939 the Republic, still in its own estimation innocent, had if not guilt at least a share in its creation.

22 Nothing could be further from my intentions than to indict American policy or the American people. It is easy to see how tempting it was to withdraw from the sinful outer world and to give only such leadership as was compatible with formal irresponsibility. But America had a share in the responsibility for the destruction of the hopes of 1919. Just before the outbreak of the second war an intelligent Frenchman, said that *all* the great powers involved—Britain, France, Germany, Russia, America—had committed enough sins, positively and negatively, to account for the

disastrous state of the world. Perhaps the sins of the United States were mainly negative, but sins there were. But the American people did not see it in that light. They saw a series of undeserved slurs, a mass of undeserved hate, a degree of unprecedented ingratitude descend on the innocent Republic. They saw, with bitterness, what had happened to democracy in the world that they had hoped to make safe for it. They forgot, as Chesterton said at the time, that the world could not simply be made safe for democracy, for it is a dangerous trade.

23 Yet the contrast between impoverished Europe and booming America, if it fed hatred, envy and malice, also bred reluctant admiration. Europe, even the Soviet Union, was ready to go to school to the masters of them that knew. André Siegfried declared that the world would have to choose between Gandhi and Henry Ford, and in a more material, less ideologically impressive fashion the United States was for a brief moment, again, the last best hope of earth. Then came the catastrophe from which, in my opinion, American prestige has not fully recovered and whose reverberations still weaken her world position.

24 It is again far from my intention to assess responsibility for the smash of 1929 or for the long and slow haul of the American economy out of the slough of despond into which the American people were plunged and in which they, in a sense, remained until the coming of the Second World War. What I am concerned with is the impact on the outer world and the rebounding of that impact on the American view of the outer world.

25 It seems to me to matter little whether Europe made the smash or whether the United States pursued its own destruction. Seen from the outside, what mattered was that the great exemplar of a liberal economy had failed, that the policy of abundance had failed, that the secret of high wages (as it had been optimistically described) had been lost.

26 The decline in European faith in the American political way of life that had occurred so precipitately in 1919–1920 was followed by an equally precipitate decline in faith in the American economic way of life. All the radical, Socialist fear and suspicion of American capitalism was revived; it was reinforced, made more formidable by the rise of communism, now the doctrine, the political weapon of a great state. Everywhere democratic values plummeted down like so many overpriced stocks. In the crash the feeble new democratic institutions and habits of Germany and Japan were smashed as the feeble democratic institutions of Italy had been smashed in the previous decade. Whether on the Left or on the Right, the day seemed to be to the authoritarian way of life. The answer lay not in free cooperation but in some form or other of dictatorship. True, in the first years of the New Deal the spectacle of a democratic leader taking the initiative was a refreshing novelty. But the successes of the New Deal were

limited and not easily imitable in countries with less abundant resources. Franklin D. Roosevelt remained a symbolic leader in a world of dictators or of drab and timid parliamentary chiefs like Chamberlain and Daladier, but the American people were too committed to isolation for him to do more than exemplify principles and moral passions. He could advise; he could not lead, even if he had been determined to lead—which it is not quite certain that he was.

27 The world that drifted to war or was rapidly pushed to war (I think the latter is the truer view) was a world for which the United States, by her immediate past and by her power, had a great responsibility but in which her role was played ineffectually and evasively. As far as the second war was "the unnecessary war," as Sir Winston Churchill was later to call it, the main fault for not avoiding it must fall on the rulers—and peoples—of Britain and France. But there is some American share to be noted and I am convinced that much of the faith that the American people later put into the United Nations came from a sense of inadequacy and guilt in the recent past.

28 In the Second Word War the role of the United States was curiously reversed. In the first war the American material contribution, although decisive, was limited in time and extent. In the second it was immense in time, in extent, in impact. It can be justly said that only for the United States was the Second World War truly a world war, that the United States alone threw her massive power into all theaters of war and that power was an indispensable condition of victory in all parts of the globe. It is true that the United States did not suffer as much as Russia or Britain—not to speak of Germany. But the world had an unforgettable lesson in the realities of American power. That lesson has not been forgotten.

29 On the ideological side the picture is not quite so impressive. True, President Roosevelt had difficulties to face that did not face President Wilson. He had an ally in the Soviet Union as embarrassing, at times, as the czardom would have been to Wilson had it survived. The very violence of the defiance of the democratic dogma by Nazi Germany was a kind of handicap. Imperial Germany and Republican America had more in common than had the Third Reich and the United States, and whether the policy of "unconditional surrender" was a mistake or not it was a natural mistake. But for these and other reasons, some personal and some political, the United States in the Second World War was not the admitted and solitary center of an ideological crusade. It was not in F.D.R.'s power, adroit orator as he was, to stir the masses of the world as Wilson had done and perhaps Wilson's successor was too conscious of Wilson's mistakes and Wilson's fate to wish to imitate him. Then death came before Roose-

velt's policy was tested, before he could use the fund of good will and trust that he had accumulated.

30 Whatever the reasons, the United States in 1945 stood rather on a pinnacle of material power than on a peak of political leadership. Nothing in a sense was further from the minds of the American people than a desire to mount the peak of leadership. Innocently, the American people knew that they had won and deserved victory and believed that they had won, as they had deserved, peace. The new United Nations, the amicable continuance of wartime relations with the Allies (of whom the cunning British were as much to be feared as the rude Russians), would deal with the urgent questions. Meantime the American people could busily beat swords into plowshares or their equivalent and resume the slow upward climb to the old prosperity that had been temporarily lost. That climb proved easier and quicker than had been feared. What proved harder was the seeking of peace and the ensuring of it.

31 There was no question in 1945 of the United States not being a maker of the world of 1945. If the American public underestimated the difficulty and the duration of the task that fell on it, it did not for a moment deny that it had a share and a responsibility for the state of the world and for its salvation. Indeed, one of the most remarkable and comforting and creditable signs of the maturity of the American people has been found in the fact that no challenge put to them since 1945 has found them wanting in either generosity or courage. Even wisdom has been in more abundant supply than veterans of 1919 might have feared.

32 But it was soon found that virtue and good will were not enough. For one thing, they were supposed to call out equivalent virtues in other people and they did not conspicuously do so. The liberated and saved countries of Western Europe were barely capable of mere survival. The great power of Eastern Europe, in its most desperate need, yet preferred power to plenty and showed neither will to true accommodation of interests nor capacity to understand the real roots of American policy.

33 There were faults on both sides, faults committed during the war and after the war. But in 1947, contemplating the world around it, the American people, whatever their grievances against the foresight or lack of it of their rulers, could truthfully acquit themselves of any desire to exploit victory or to impose their will. If they preached and in a sense practiced and imposed democracy in Germany and Japan, they did so in good faith and in no spirit of revenge. If they were disappointed in their efforts, the disappointments were often taken philosophically or humorously. *The Teahouse of the August Moon* was a fable applicable in more places than Okinawa. On the whole, the results of American leadership and munificence in both Germany and Japan gratified the American people, who took possibly too complacent a view of their success as re-educators.

34 It was elsewhere that the American public suffered its great disillusionment and had fostered in it that attitude of resentful wonder at the outside world that is part of the American problem today. First of all, America was faced with the paradox not merely of ingratitude but of wrongly directed gratitude. It was not only that so many millions in France, in Italy, in Britain even, did not sufficiently appreciate what they owed to American power and generosity. It was that they felt or professed to feel more gratitude to the remote Soviet Union that had no doubt been a main force in bringing down the Nazi power but had not freed Paris or Rome from the Nazi forces or London from the daily menace of V-1 and V-2.

35 I shall certainly make no attempt to justify this error of morals and of judgment. Nor can I do more than allude to some reasons for it. All of Europe was exhausted, morally as well as physically debilitated, and full of more or less conscious resentment of the apparent prosperity and immunity of the United States. The contrast between New York and London in 1947 was dramatic enough for anyone who went to America frequently. To those who only knew of the earthly paradise by report it was humiliating, maddening or inexplicable. Or it was explicable simply. The Americans had taken the chance of the war vastly to enrich themselves. And they could only have done that at the expense of their allies. The old sullen Socialist suspicion of American capitalism revived. The contrast between the austerity of England, the gross inequalities of well-being in France and Italy, and what was rumored of the paradise over the ocean was more than human nature could bear. What the Americans had they owed to others. It was their duty, their interest to share it. Instead of being grateful for such acts of generosity as the Marshall Plan, Europeans should rather praise themselves for their magnanimity in letting the Americans do their duty! In this period I more than once recalled Napoleon's explanation of why the brothers and sisters whom he had made kings and princes were so ungrateful. "They think I have cheated them of their due share in the inheritance of our father the late King." So much of Europe felt regarding the plenty and the bounty of the United States.

36 It would be wrong to attach too much importance to this European attitude (which was far from universal) or to the natural American resentment of it. The Marshall Plan succeeded; Western Europe was saved from ruin and from communism and if the rescued were not adequately grateful or adequately conscious of the abyss from which they had been saved, the Americans were and are a pragmatic people. They had done what they set out to do and, although it would have been nice to be thanked for it, success is better than gratitude. And if the European nations by 1950 were in a position to answer back and be sassy, that was proof of the success of American policy. Like the parent of a troublesome

teen-ager, the American as taxpayer and voter felt a mixture of pride and annoyance. But pride predominated.

37 But it was not in Europe that the average American was most disappointed. It was in Asia; it may soon be in Africa. It would be absurd to attempt to allocate praise or blame for the events in China, sometimes summed up in a misleading shorthand phrase as "the loss of China." But nothing is more natural or more defensible than the spontaneous American reaction to the discovery that China had been saved from Japanese imperialism only to fall under Communist control. I have always thought that the American interest in China owed more to missionary than to economic connections; nevertheless, the interest in China was deep and genuine.

38 There were few Pacific isolationists and it can plausibly be asserted that it was not only formally but really the determination to protect the "freedom of China" that brought America into the Second Word War. Seeing China pass under Communist control, seeing the uprooting of a century of missionary effort, the quenching of a century of missionary hopes was an embittering and a blinding experience. It blinded many Americans to the fact that there are more than three Chinese for each American and no natural law determines that the United States can or could determine the fate of China. To "lose China" was to lose something that had never been possessed. Yet the sense of loss was reasonable and human, the sense of danger is not totally unreasonable now, and possibly will be much less unreasonable in the future.

39 If China is to be communized, transformed, deprived of its ancient weaknesses as well as its ancient virtues, this may be a greater event in the history of the world than even the Russian Revolution and one removing a great part of the human race from the American influence and leadership so confidently counted on in 1945. Here the American paradox is most bitter. For it was American victory, by eliminating Japanese power, that made possible the Communist victory in China. To have dropped the atomic bomb, to have risked that guilt, to produce such a result, this is irony unbearable. This is a world that no American wished to make but for which the United States must take some responsibility. If the American sense that the world is uncontrollable, not subject to reason and not necessarily moving in the direction of liberty and human betterment, has any one root it is in the great deception of China.

40 That deception was reinforced by the experience of the Korean War. To the average American, no war could be more innocent in origin, more worthy in object. Yet it was a war full of disillusionment. It involved a temporary but humiliating American defeat at the hands of those Chinese who had already inflicted a political defeat on the United States by their conquest of the Nationalists. Fought in the name of the United

Nations, it was a war whose burden fell overwhelmingly on the Americans and for most of the members of the United Nations the motto was obviously "Let Sam do it." And it was a war settled in an unsatisfactory way.

41 Americans brought up to believe in what I once called "the illusion of American omnipotence" found it painful to accept and hard to believe that a settlement could mean less than a complete American triumph. Was it for this that tens of thousands of Americans had died in Korea as, before them, hundreds of thousands had died in the Pacific? This was a world unintelligible to millions of honest men and women. It was natural that they should seek an explanation in cries of "treason." And if that was not enough, there was the further resource of seeing a world in which the United States alone did its duty, and if that world was in a bad way the fault lay entirely elsewhere.

42 Nor was this the only disillusionment. It was natural to see in the newly liberated nations children eager to come to school to the great pioneer in the cause of freedom, the great exemplar of the more abundant life. Yet everywhere eager pupils went to another school, not only in China but in other parts of Asia and Africa. The ending of the old imperialism did not necessarily give the United States a set of friendly, grateful, and admiring pupils. At most it gave the opportunity to compete in what often seemed a rigged market for the friendship and tolerance of the newly liberated peoples. It was even a shock to learn that in some liberated countries, like India, the old masters preserved in some minds more prestige than the new allies.

43 Far from finding a world ready to follow the American lead, the American people found, even in Latin America, a world that was ready to shop and bargain and hesitate as to which of the rival world leaders to follow. And even when the American people won the support or docility of the governments where the competition for adherence was keenest, it did not follow that they had won the most active elements of the population. To their horror and usually to their justified horror the American people found the tag of "imperialist" pinned to the coattails of Uncle Sam, and in the war for men's minds the American way did not always win. The old identification of liberty in the sense of freedom from foreign rule with liberty in the sense of freedom from domestic tyranny was no longer firm or even customary.

44 All over the world liberty in the first sense warred with liberty in the second, a war that was often waged to the loss of the United States, which offered not authoritarian leadership but the more complicated way to self-rule. Were the common peoples of the world so blinded by nationalist passion, so ill-equipped to work democracy, American style, that the United States must give up the old hope of being automatically the

natural leader of nations rightly struggling to be free? That there should be any question, that there should be any contest between so obviously tyrannical a system as Russian communism and the time-tried and inevitably beneficent system proclaimed to a candid world in 1776 was an affront to the spirit of '76 and to the American belief in an intelligible and manageable world.

45 And when, in addition to the too often successful competition offered by new societies that prostituted the name of freedom and democracy, there was suddenly flashed across the heavens proof that the other competition in material achievement was open too, the American whose history had been so fortunate, who until this century and until this generation, had never had to consider the limits of American power, was forced to reconsider his national situation. At the moment when mankind was on the edge of adventuring into space, the old, familiar world seemed less familiar, less homely, more in danger of self-destruction than ever. And now it could no longer be doubted by even the most obstinate that of that old, dangerous, and ill-ordered world the United States was at last and finally a part. It is a world the Americans never made but have to live in.

STUDY GUIDE

Theme and Structure

1. Brogan's theme here is the disillusionment Americans have experienced in gradually discovering that the United States is not the paradise which they had imagined it to be—and which the rest of the world was eagerly waiting to emulate. His essay falls into two parts: paragraphs 1–17, and 18–45. In the first part Brogan discusses how the American came to develop his somewhat naïve hopefulness about his position in the world. What are some of the reasons for this attitude adduced by Brogan?

2. The second part is developed by a chronological enumeration of the events that have progressively brought disillusionment to the American about the idea of inevitable progress in general and about America's messianic mission to spread that progress. List those events and indicate what was disillusioning to America in each of them.

3. Show how the author has used the idea expressed in the title of the essay as a unifying framework for his whole essay.

Suggestion for Writing

Using some of the ideas about its mission in the world attributed to the United States in this essay, write an essay of your own on the United States' involvement in Viet Nam.

THE CALL OF THE OPEN ROAD

John Keats

1 All advertisements show automobiles in unusual circumstances. They depict smiling, handsome people in evening clothes arriving in glittering hardtops beneath the portecocheres of expensive tropical saloons. A polished convertible, top down, filled with laughing young people in yachting costumes, whispers along an idealized shoreline. A ruggedly healthy Mom, Pop, Sis and Buzz smile the miles away as their strangely dustless station wagon whisks over the Rockies. Sometimes, automobiles strangely shine on pedestals; sometimes they slip through astral voids like comets. None of the advertisements show you and me in the automobile as most of us know it—that is, wedged in a fuming line of commuter traffic at 8:30 A.M., or locked in an even worse outbound line at 6 P.M.

2 A manufacturer, of course, would commit economic harakiri if he were to try to sell us a car on truthful grounds, for how could he ask anyone to pay $4,500 for a three-hundred-horsepower contraption on grounds that it would be used only two hours a day for 240 working days a year, and would at all other times—except briefly, on vacations—be parked in an expensive parking lot or sit depreciating at a curb? Would you buy such a car if it were truthfully put to you that the thing would cost you more than $9 an hour to use? No manufacturer in his right mind would plead with you to buy a luggage compartment only slightly smaller than Delaware in order that you could use part of this space just twice a year. Manufacturers know very well that the American automobile is not primarily a means of transportation and that it cannot be sold as such. Therefore, their advertisements invariably portray the automobile As Flying Carpet—as a thing to sweep us off to ineffable lotus lands—and this, we discover, is the greatest lie of all. Yet, we cannot plead surprise, because—as a friend remarked—if we now suspect that our automobiles are overblown, overpriced monstrosities built by oafs for thieves to sell to mental defectives it is only logical to expect that there is not much point in driving them, and that any place an automobile can go is probably not worth visiting. Nevertheless, the advertisements have a certain appeal, because the dream they represent once had substance. There was a time in man's memory when travel was exciting.

3 It is difficult to say just when the last shred of fun disappeared from the American highway. Some people think it was in 1927, when Henry

Ford stopped making the Model T, but other authorities put the date in the late 1930's when the first national restaurant chains spread like plague. Speculation is idle, because we must accept things as they are, and there is no question today but that family travel in America is apt to be one of life's more crashing bores. Let me wipe off the lens a bit for a quick look at two generations of the Foresight family:

4 Early in the 19th century, Abel Foresight, his wife, Hope, and their children, Prudence, Faith and Jonah, set out from Morgantown, Pennsylvania, in a wagon. They chopped through forests, crept over mountains, forded floods, shot their suppers, struggled with savages, and trusted in God and in their strength to cross an unknown continent. They were more than a year en route, but the Foresight family arrived in California with the look of eagles in their eyes. Theirs was the age of travel adventure.

5 In the summer of 1958, Roger Foresight followed the path of his longfathers across his native land.

6 "We take the car it's cheaper," he told his wife June, in the curious English of his day. "You don't see the country you take the train or fly."

7 Whereupon, Roger gripped the Deep-Dish Command Wheel of his twenty-foot-long Flite-Flo Hacienda Wagon, stirred the Jet-Boom Eight's Power Plus into life, pressed a master button that wound up all the Saf-T-Tint windows, adjusted the Koolaire to a desired temperature, pushed another button to bring the Flote-Fome seat to its proper level and distance, pressed yet another to cut in the Glyde-Ryde Dynamatic Turbo-mission, and swung away from his Cape Cod Tri-Level's Kar Porte to begin three thousand miles of driving pleasure.

8 A week later, the Foresights arrived on the opposite coast a little tired from sitting so long on foam rubber, but otherwise they were quite the same people who had left home. There was still that look of vague disappointment in their eyes, because Roger and June Foresight dwell in the tasteless, or Pablum, stage of family travel.

9 Several springs feed Roger Foresight's sense of disappointment. Even after the West was subdued and the automobile devised, there was a time when motoring was not dull and tasteless, and together with many Americans, Roger Foresight can remember it. Therefore, we can say that today's realities disappoint Foresight's memories. Next, we can say his disappointment was inevitable because Foresight was dead wrong in three major assumptions. He was wrong in imagining there might be some significant difference between New York and San Francisco, or indeed, that there might be any fundamental differences among any American cities. Oh, there are plenty of superficial differences, to be sure. San Francisco has hills and a lovely harbor and New York does not. Denver has a magnificent public park system and Chicago is simply a blot on the landscape. The point, however, is that the cultural anthropology of our cities is much

the same; the life of the average citizen of City A is very like the life of the citizen of City B because the ecology of one big town is quite like that of any other, particularly in a nation of standard brands, chain stores and national fads. Neither you, nor I, nor Roger Foresight would be able to tell whether we were in Philadelphia or New York if we joined a crowd of shoppers in Gimbels, because the shoppers in Gimbels, Philadelphia store look exactly like the shoppers in Gimbels New York store and come from the same economic classes, have the same kind of jobs and entertain much the same hopes of Eternity. No doubt there are many reasons for this situation, but one of the more massive seems to be the automobile, as we'll see in a moment. Meanwhile, allow me to suggest that Roger Foresight was also wrong in thinking he'd see more of the American continent if he drove. He was also hopelessly wrong in assuming that driving across the nation would be cheaper than flying or taking a train. Here are matters that merit investigation, so let's dispose of the easiest of them first, giving Roger Foresight the benefit of every doubt, even if he might not deserve it. Consider the matter of cost:

10 We remember the current national average operating cost of a $2,300 automobile is $.1042 per mile; thus the cost of driving the 3,030 miles between New York and San Francisco would be $315.72. Roger's Flite-Flo Hacienda Wagon is a dreamboat in the $4,500 class, and it costs a good deal more than this to run, but we're going to give Roger all the breaks and use the low average figure. He will have to drive 473 miles a day to make the trip in a week. If we can possibly imagine that he and June together can spend only $9 a day for food and only $5 a night for lodgings, it will cost them a rock-bottom $413.72 to make the trip—one way.

11 The cost of two Pullman berths—lower berths—for the same trip is $374.62, and the Foresights would be only three days in transit. Even when we consider the outrageous prices of railroad dining car meals, and the necessary tips to porters, it would be cheaper for the Foresights to take the train.

12 An airline will sell Roger two one-way tickets from New York to San Francisco for $317.70, one meal included, and the trip takes half a day.

13 If we further presume the Foresights will return, we must note that there is no round-trip saving if they drive, but that there is a substantial round-trip saving on air or rail transportation. Purely for argument's sake, let's say that driving is no strain on the Foresights, and that time is no object. They are as insensate as two bags of wool. Even if we grant this preposterous assumption, the economics of the thing indicate the Foresights are silly to drive unless, perhaps, they like to throw their money away. Some people do. In fact, we find them buying Flite-Flo Hacienda Wagons. Nevertheless, we might imagine Roger Foresight to be a little dis-

appointed to find that his trip cost him more than he had thought it would.

14 The major reason for the lackluster look in the Foresights' eyes, however, was their discovery that it is now possible to drive across the face of the nation without feeling you've been anywhere or that you've done anything. The Foresights remembered the first days of the twentieth century, when most Americans lived out their modest lives within five miles of the rumpsprung hamlets of their births. In those days, there was difference and variety in the land. Tennessee's troubadors were mercifully pent within Tennessee's forgotten hills, and did not wail and whine from every jukebox. A visible, palpable cultural distinction then existed between Philadelphia and Chicago. In 1900, a man could cross the nation and smell different smells, taste different foods, hear different accents and be cheated by different methods. Driving anywhere was almost as much of a demanding adventure as was waddling along in Abel's wagon. The hardy motorist took joy in being his own mechanic, and he was ever watchful for signs of trouble among the natives, for in those days rustics buried rakes tines-up in the dust of country lanes to puncture the tires of the devil-carts that frightened the horses.

15 As the automobile became more general, the various tumult of our native land subsided, and now that nearly everyone has at least one car, scarcely one American in fifteen lives anywhere near his birthplace, and Americans drift about their continent as easily as tumbleweeds, and with as much sense of direction or purpose. No matter. Like tumbleweeds, they may expect to find a congenial ecology wherever they go; one Howard Johnson restaurant is exactly like all the others.

16 If you fly across the nation, it is still possible to observe some variety, because you look down on a geological exhibit. The bones of the land are still apparent from ten thousand feet up. You can see rivers eating through the plains; see the mountains thrusting up from the dead shores of unknown epiric seas. At a convenient altitude, it is still possible to sense the majesty of old Abel Foresight's accomplishment; you are overwhelmed by America's space.

17 If you take the train, you have not the same Olympian perspective, but you can see more of the country than if you drive, because you rattle along miles of open landscape and you have some opportunity to look at it, for your view is not blocked by billboards and your attention is not commanded by the demands of the road.

18 The road. Ah yes, the road. Let us think of *this* together, you and I.

19 For centuries, "road" was a word of magic. Armies, gypsies, beggars, tinkers, peasants, merchants, highwaymen, scholars, minstrels and runaway apprentice boys were once found upon the road. As recently as fifty years ago, you could still build your house beside the road and be a friend to

man, because mankind passed your doors. Today, this is not so. The road belongs entirely to the automobile, and he who builds his house beside it can only watch the Fords go by, because there is no human life on the road itself. Indeed, so mechanical, so abstract, so inhuman have our roads become that American drivers never think of passing the people ahead; they think of passing the car ahead.

20 If this point seems somewhat frivolous to us, it is by no means frivolous to occasional visitors from less peppy lands where horsepower is still a word relating to the power of a horse, and where the word "road" still has connotations of Pilgrim's Progress, or of the royal road to romance. Last year, America was host to one Dan Jacobson, a South African, who expressed his sense of bewilderment to the editors of *The Reporter* magazine.

21 "The six and eight lanes of traffic are flung into swathes of tar and concrete that fill the sky in loops and curves dwarfing even the city beneath them," Mr. Jacobson wrote. "There the roofs of the cars, curved like the wing cases of beetles, flash above the concrete parapets in a hundred different colors; there are no shops there, no billboards, there are no people and nowhere for people to walk but a kind of narrow catwalk along the side of the parapet where a man can clamber to the emergency telephones if his car breaks down. There, where there is no place for a man outside his moving car, the road reaches its purest, most abstracted state—it can be used for nothing but to carry cars from one end of its giant structures to the other. The colors are black and gray; from afar it is desolate and beautiful, but unlike a natural desert, it has no peace. . . ."

22 Significantly enough, Mr. Jacobson at no point suggests that man has anything to do with the road—not even with its creation. He reflects the road's sole concession to animal life is a catwalk—but this leads only to the telephone that summons help for the broken car. Mr. Jacobson was talking about the superhighway, or Autobahn, which is the road's ultimate abstraction, serving cars, not men. As the automobile evolved from Tin Lizzie to the overblown Cleopatra's barge we see today, she demanded wider, smoother, straighter roads, and every human juice was distilled from road building in order to accommodate the desires of the automobiles. The automobiles' demands constantly multiply faster than we can build Autobahns, however, and thus traffic engineers say that the U.S. Government's plans for new superhighways to be completed by the end of 1975 are already hopelessly inadequate in terms of the number and kind of automobile Detroit expects to spew forth in the next *twelve* years. Therefore, if our automania persists, we shall ever need ever wider roads and the townless superhighway, desolate as the desert Mr. Jacobson says it is, is clearly the shape of our future. A part of Roger Foresight's transcon-

tinental journey was undertaken on such a road, and this is how it was for him:

23 His left leg kept falling to sleep because there was nothing for his left foot to do in the pushbutton Flite-Flo Hacienda Wagon. His neck grew stiff from having to hold his head fixed straight ahead as he stared down the endlessly unrolling straight strip of black tarmac. Traveling at speed, he dared not take his eyes from it. The banked, graded, militarily landscaped road was identical for all its fantastic length, and thus there was no new thing to entrance June Foresight's idle eyes. On this road, a thing as monotonous as an indoor track built for six-day bicycle races, the Foresights had no idea of miles because the scenery never changed. Thus, they kept track of time. It was so many hours from one town to another; from one service area to the next. All the service areas, with their uniform gas pumps and their identical restaurants and their identical jittery travelers, served to illustrate the proposition that America has achieved a peculiarly high degree of standardization in our time. Modern Americans that they were, it did not occur to June and Roger Foresight that there was anything odd in classifying food as a service.

24 The Foresights passed each Autobahn night in a neon-lit AAA-approved motel that was exactly like the motel of the night before and like the motel of the night to come, and thanks to television in every room, the Foresights never missed an instant of Mark Sade's coast-to-coast quiz show, *Can You Take It?* All along the everlasting monotony of the Autobahn, the same national voices beat into the Foresights' ears during the day, thanks to the miracle of the Flite-Flo's radio. Thus, Roger and June were spared the burden of having to think of something to say to each other as they hurtled across the continent, but even for souls more lost than they, a ride on the Autobahn is apt to be a journey in Limbo. No one can say it is in any way a pleasure to sit like a lump for endless hours while one speeds along in a vacuum, and no one does. Instead, the Foresights—and every other American user of Autobahns—say that *where* they want to go is far more important than the act of *going there*. This statement not only strips travel of at least half its pleasure, but it is as ironical as it is pitiful, as we will very shortly see.

25 Meanwhile, it is clear that not all American roads are Autobahns, but our secondary highways are just as devoted to the needs of the automobile. They are distinguished from Autobahns by a hardy species of anthropoid life that clings to their edges, just as weeds curiously flourish among the cindery desolation of railroad yards. Here, along the berms, are to be found the proprietors of cut-rate filling stations, the sellers of fried foods, the owners of ice-cream palaces shaped like bulldogs, the concierges of the motels that Mr. J. Edgar Hoover regards as "camps of crime

. . . little more than camouflaged brothels," the juke joints that sell knick-knacks and balsam-stuffed pillows that say For Mother on one side and Souvenir of Lake On-Wee on the other. Here are the small businessmen who have put away their masks and riding boots to set up roadside garages. Here are the stands that sell hooked rugs, cut bait and plaster garden sculpture all at once. Here are the proprietors of junkyards and the businesses of those who tow broken cars out of the way of the cars that still work. Here are the birds that pick the crocodile's teeth; the pilot fish that flit ahead of the shark; here are the practitioners of twentieth century symbiosis. Here, along the edges of America's highways, is the detritus of our century—the fields of burnt and rusting automobile carapaces; the billboards that suggest the only thing keeping you out of the voluptuous arms of a hot woman is your dreadful stench. Here are the broken beer bottles and the signs that ask you to help keep America green and the signs that strangely hope that Jesus saves. Here, in a word, is U.S. 1—perhaps from Philadelphia to Washington; from the old capital to the new.

26 The Foresights moved over these roads, too, and discovered that travel along them is merely an endless passage down an indefinitely extended unplanned Main Street. It is disheartening to admit that America generally accepted the billboards and the brothels, the ice cream and the junk long before it came to the conclusion that such a street with its innumerable entrances, exits, crossings, pull-offs, winking neon signs and varying speed limits was unsafe for the automobile and should therefore be abandoned. Yet, the fact that the cluttered two-way highway is unsafe is solely responsible for the present transition to the sterile Autobahn, and so we may say that even the last vestige of adventure—physical danger—may disappear from American motoring as our Pablum stage of travel wears on.

27 When Roger and June Foresight drove across the country, they ever felt time's winged chariot hurrying near, and thus they did not explore the only American roads that are neither boring nor blatant. In short, they did not travel our rural lanes, and it is a pity they did not, for they may never have a chance to see one again. Parochial politicians have already covered most of them with asphalt in a naked bid for the peasant vote, but until quite recently the little roads have been the quiet routes of reapers and wains, and the few automobiles to use them merely carried unsuccessful agriculturalists to the village post offices on the first of the month when the government checks arrive. Today all this is rapidly changing. The back country roads have been discovered by the rich, who go wistfully popping and bouncing over them in their little foreign cars still trying to discover the automobile's once-hinted promise of fun.

28 Unfortunately, the handwriting is on the wall. Within the next ten

years, there won't be a lane in the land that lacks its Jaguar agency, its French restaurant and branch of Abercrombie & Fitch. Next will come the middle classes, aping their betters as is their wont, but demanding wider, straighter roads for their less agile Buicks, and the French restaurants will print menus in English and serve Parker House rolls. The country-day schools will appear, and the rich will be forced once again to search for private amusement in yet another corner of the world. By this time, the lower middle classes will be pushing in, as they do and the former country lane will be well on the way to becoming the four-lane highway, lined with filling stations and leering with used car lots, connecting the housing development to the shopping center that offers plenty of everything and the best of nothing.

29 Thus we see that the smaller road, built more to the human scale, is inevitably de-humanized as the volume of traffic increases; the country lane of today is the cluttered highway of tomorrow and the abstract Autobahn of the day after. At this point, the triumph of the automobile is complete and the full attention of driver and passenger is directed to the automobile itself. From this point on, the only possible emotions available to the passengers are boredom or terror.

30 We note the Autobahn is somewhat safer for the automobile than the cluttered highway, but safety is always a relative term. It should be remembered that our automobiles are not built with safety in mind; quite the contrary; and you put your life in the automobile's trust the moment you leave your driveway, because the car was born accident-prone if not downright bloody-minded. In 1905, for instance, there were only two automobiles in the whole of the sprawling Kansas City area. Somehow they managed to find one another and collide. Since then, a national folk saying has grown up used whenever anyone wishes to cajole anyone else into a dangerous undertaking. The hazard, we say, is no greater "than crossing the street," and everyone knows what we mean. We mean to say the street is damned risky, and you have to have your wits about you to negotiate it in good health, but if you take every precaution and obey all the rules, you might just make it. Indeed, when Roger Foresight drove across America, he ran a much higher risk of disembowelment en route than did his ancestor Abel, who had to contend with the hostiles. It is possible to come to a sticky end at any moment through no fault of your own on the safest of our Autobahns, but as if determined that better roads will not reduce unduly the quality of danger, and so denude happy motoring of its one last thrill Detroit keeps on producing faster, more powerful cars and shows an equal genius in making them progressively more collapsible. I beg you to recall the not-so-hard tops.

31 Curiously enough, the increasing power and speed of the automo-

bile contains a contradiction. On the one hand, speed adds a quality of danger, but at the same time, speed helps to make auto travel even more bland, because whatever scenery there might have been between City A and City B passes faster than the passenger's eye can comprehend it, and speed requires the driver's eye to be fixed on the unrelenting road. This is why Keats' Law of Autobahn Travel says the only possible emotions are terror or boredom, depending on the individual phlegm quotient of the traveler, as influenced by speed. We state this mathematically in two formulae:

32 Let T stand for terror and IPQ for individual phlegm quotient. R stands for rate, or speed, and B for boredom. The formulae will now read: T equals IPQ times R; B equals IPQ divided by R. It will be seen that speed is the crucial factor, no matter what the IPQ.

33 These formulae most usually apply to visiting Europeans however, because the IPQ of most Americans is O. Most Americans like the Foresights, are content to work out the more familiar formula, Distance equals Rate times Time. Like the Foresights, they never think of, much less try to solve the equation in terms of Distance. They always seek Rate in order to find Time. International marriages often demonstrate conflicts of attitudes, and fortunately we have an example close at hand:

34 Muriel, an English girl, was only a few days arrived in America when her Yankee bridegroom told her they would have supper the following day with friends who lived thirty miles away. Early the following morning, Muriel began packing for the trip, selecting clothes and putting up a picnic lunch. She envisioned a pleasant outing along placid lanes. She looked forward to savoring new sights; to seeing something of the natives and of their curious customs and dress. Muriel dreamed of a picnic beside a stream at midday; of a little post-prandial nap with her love in the shade of the trees; then to taking high tea at an American inn, and ultimately arriving at their hostess' house in time to dress for a champagne supper—staying the night and returning the following day. Now, Muriel is as good at arithmetic as anyone, but it never occurred to her to think of a supper invitation in terms of D – RT. She had anticipated a civilized little holiday on the continental order, where the distance to be traveled is something to be explored and enjoyed. Therefore, she was somewhat startled when her bridegroom, used to dividing America's Distance by the automobile's Rate, slipped her the word in terms of Time. He solved the formula in his head, automatically.

35 "Say, honey," he said, "I got noos for you. It on'y takes fordy minnits to get there."

36 Now, wiser in the ways of Ammedica, Muriel understands. One does not sup in Ammedica; one eats. One does not cover distance; one

travels through time, and the sooner the better, because the distance is such a bore with nothing much to see if the billboards let you see it. Her husband always puts it thus:

37 "You wanna get there, don't you?"

38 A new veteran of America's roads, Muriel sometimes agrees with him, but most often she says, "Why don't we just stay home?"

39 We must admit Muriel has a point, the point being that there isn't much point in going to, or being in any place in America other than where you happen to find yourself at the moment, and we have the automobile to thank for this. We have seen what the automobile has done to the road, but now let's look at what it has done to our cities and to our vacation resorts. Perhaps then we will better understand Muriel's resignation and that dull look of disappointment in the Foresights' eyes.

40 On their way between New York and San Francisco, Roger and June Foresight passed through Cleveland, Chicago, Hannibal, St. Joseph, Denver, Salt Lake City, Reno and Sacramento. They could tell when they were leaving a town because little pennants began to appear on the gasoline stations at the city limits and when the Foresights next saw pennants on gas stations, they realized they were approaching another city—not a new city, mind you, but just another one.

41 Had the Foresights wished, they might have reflected that a curious kind of national square dance goes on night and day in downtown Cleveland, in downtown Denver, in downtown Anywhere, U.S.A. Stop! the lights say, and twenty million automobiles jerk to a halt. Walk! the lights say, and seventy million pedestrians obey. Go! the lights say, and twenty million automobiles lurch ahead. Necks snap, eyes pop, legs flex, lights blink, whistles blow, horns honk, fumes choke, and we call this civilization. From time to time we are asked to defend it.

42 Obviously, this civilization is exclusively designed to meet the demands of our automobiles, and since all automobiles have the same demands, all our cities are built alike. All of them tend to become as inhuman and as abstract as the Autobahn that struck poor Mr. Jacobson all of a heap.

43 It remained for *Yank*—a soldier-edited, Army-sponsored magazine—to drive the point home during World War II. Thinking to remind the brave soldier boys of Mom, Sis, and the Girl Next Door, *Yank* decided to run pictures of sundry American Main Streets. Several hundred photographs were selected, whereupon one sly editor suggested running a number of uncaptioned photographs on the same page, challenging the readers correctly to identify their home towns. The venture was a morbid success, for devil a soldier could find devil a bit of difference among the pictures, and the nasty suspicion grew that *Yank* had merely taken several snapshots of the same street full of automobiles from several minutely different an-

gles. Few believed *Yank's* answer to its puzzle was on the up-and-up.

44 If all our downtowns are somewhat surrealistic landscapes populated by automobile-dominated automatons, what can we say of the suburban housing developments which fester around the edges of these civic wounds? Here are mantraps as devoid of originality as anything that ever rolled off a Detroit assembly line. Here, too, are robot populations that are slaves to the automobiles that make the developments possible in the first place. A housing development anywhere is—in two dirty words—a car pool.

45 If in traveling from coast to coast, the Foresights had merely seen more mechanical roads, more mechanical Main Streets, more mass-produced suburbs and more mechanical people riding in machines to their mechanical tasks, we might reasonably expect them to be entitled to a little routine disappointment on discovering that New York is just a larger version of San Francisco, except for superficial, or detailed differences, particularly if they had misty memories that some kind of real difference once existed. They might have wondered, privately, if their trip had really been necessary. All this is as easy for us to see as it is discouraging, but wait—a more massive disappointment clamors for attention. Suppose the Foresights had more than seven days to spend on themselves. Let's say they floated free as disembodied spirits, seeking out those lotus lands the automobile advertisements seem to guarantee as part of the purchase price. Let us imagine the Foresights at Cape Cod.

46 On Cape Cod, the Foresights found the natives much the same as natives anywhere else in America—the Cape Codders' beady little eyes glittered through their glasses as they smiled the empty smile of commerce and made change at their cash registers. The tourists were gaudy blotches of color moving on crowded sidewalks; there was a honk of horns in the street; there was a frenzy of fat ladies in shorts and thin ladies in dirndls; a coming and going of paunchy, knock-kneed men in Bermuda shorts and polo shirts. There were up-tilted sunglasses everywhere, and shops where you could buy souvenir postcards of places you had never seen and would never visit, and other postcards that built little jests around the presence of wasps in the outhouse. Cape Cod was a flow of hot children, an ebb of exhausted mothers, a drift of people walking in between people who were taking pictures of each other. Cape Cod was waves of juke boxes, Coca-Cola, suntan lotion, high prices, sand in the shoes, twenty-three flavors of ice cream and there was one peculiar odor which, from time to time, ate through the grease smoke of the restaurants and the exhaust fumes of the automobiles. A child asked, "What's 'at funny smell?"

47 "It's the sea," his mother explained.

48 At Ausable Chasm, there was not the disquieting smell of the sea,

but a fungus-scent of damp growths in the narrow gorge, and girls seeking immortality added their names in lipstick to the thousand other names on the rocky walls. Otherwise, the Foresights found Ausable Chasm to be like Cape Cod in all significant respects, and when they drove to the top of Mount Washington, they found the same tourists, the same natives, the same indigestibles, and the same souvenir postcard a few thousand feet above sea level.

49 Of course, the Foresights could have gone to the Catskills where the planned entertainment is so well planned that nobody has a chance to be alone or to do anything but follow the leader through a round of merriment that includes wearing funny hats and blowing tinsel horns. Or, they could have gone to the Golden West, to join the fantastic line of automobiles slowly inching along the precipice of Yellowstone Canyon. Or, perhaps, they could have sought out some sylvan retreat in Minnesota, to join the hundreds of other people who were either water-skiing on the lake or throwing beer cans into it.

50 It would not matter where the Foresights drove to their vacation. The scenes everywhere are much the same, because where one automobile can go, all other automobiles *do* go, and wherever the automobile goes, the automobile's version of civilization surely follows. To be sure, there are still some vacation resorts not yet in a stage of full development, but there are none in a stage of *arrested* development.

51 Twenty years ago, the slogan, See America First, still had some point. Nowadays, the fact is that if you've seen one part of America, you've seen it all. The automobile did not put the adventure of travel within reach of the common man. Instead, *it first gave him the opportunity to make himself more and more common*, so that when he reached the point in his development where he could find leisure for travel, the lotus lands had disappeared *because he was already there.*

52 Still, it cannot be said that the common man knows this. We find him constantly trying to pretend otherwise. Who, for instance, do you think really is in that advertised hardtop that swirls to a stop beneath the porte-cochere of the expensive tropical saloon?

53 Queen Marie of Roumania?

54 No.

55 It is merely Roger and June Foresight, or perhaps even Tom and Mae Wretch, listlessly fetching up at one more deadfall—this one in Miami—there to try to escape for a few numbing hours from the fantastic boredom of aimless wandering in the automobile age. They seek surcease in the familiar national joys of tough steaks, cigarette smoke, watered drinks, insolent service, padded bills and a noisy band.

56 Man, they say, is really living it up these days.

STUDY GUIDE

Theme and Structure

1. Although this essay is entertainingly written, the author has a serious point to make about what the automobile is doing to our society. What is his point?

2. The point is much more interestingly made by relating it to the concrete experience of the Foresights. Show how the whole body of the essay from paragraphs 5–56 is organized around the progressive disappointments of this couple on their trip to California. How are paragraphs 10–13, 14–39, and 40–56 related to statements made in paragraph 9?

Tone

The author succeeds in making his devastating criticisms of the effects of the automobile in an offhand and humorous manner. This tone is partly created by his diction, for instance, when he says, in those days "Tennessee's troubadours were *mercifully pent within* Tennessee's forgotten hills, and did not *wail* and *whine* from every jukebox." The author's lightly critical attitude toward folk music is expressed by the pejorative connotations of the italicized words. This sort of evaluative connotation operates in the diction throughout the essay. Find other examples of it and show how, through this kind of diction, the author maintains a persistent critical attitude toward the "automobile culture" of America.

THE DECLINE OF THE MACHINE

John Kenneth Galbraith

1 Those who guide our worries on large issues regularly ask us to ponder man's losing competition with the machine. On the assembly lines he is being replaced by automatic machinery which is regulated and instructed by electronic controls. If the resulting product is a consumer item it has almost certainly been designed to minimize both the effort and intelligence required of its user. Not even the question of whether people will want it has been left entirely to judgment. This has been ascertained by market surveys and insured by advertising and both, perhaps, were analyzed with the aid of an electronic computer, sometimes too ambitiously called an electronic brain.

2 The tendency to dispense with men and intelligence is held to go

From John Kenneth Galbraith, *The Liberal Hour* (Boston: Houghton Mifflin Company, 1960). Reprinted by permission of the publisher.

far beyond the consumer gadgets. The unmanned missile is about to replace the old-fashioned hand-operated bomber. In the near future, according to enthusiasts, unmanned missiles will take flight to intercept other unmanned missiles which will prevent these from intercepting other automated missles. The operation will be handled under contract by IBM. If the globe were larger or the explosions smaller the prospect would be not unattractive. The machines having taken over, men would all be noncombatants. The charm of war has always been greatest for those whose role was to guide it from a certain distance.

3 These visions of the triumph of the machine can be multiplied endlessly. We do not take them quite seriously for we do not really believe that we are being replaced, and our instinct is sound. If there is a competition between man and machine, man is winning it—not for at least two centuries has his position been so strong as compared with the apparatus with which he works.

4 And the fact that this is the age of ascendant man, not triumphant machine, has practical consequences. If machines are the decisive thing, then the social arrangements by which we increase our physical plan and equipment will be of first importance. But if it is men that count, then our first concern must be with arrangements for conserving and developing personal talents. It will be these on which progress will depend. Should it happen, moreover, that for reasons of antiquated design our society does well in supplying itself with machines and badly in providing itself with highly improved manpower, there would be cause for concern. There is such cause, for that, precisely, is our situation.

5 But first, what is the evidence that men have been gaining on machines—that skill and intelligence have become more important in what we call economic progress than capital plant and equipment?

6 The change is most prominently reflected in the changed position of the owner or supplier of physical capital. For a half century he has been a man of steadily declining prestige and importance. Once it was taken for granted that ownership of an industrial enterprise—the ownership of the capital assets or a substantial share of them—gave a man a decisive voice in its direction. So it was with Ford, Carnegie, the elder Rockefeller, Commodore Vanderbilt, and John Jacob Astor. And to be a source of capital, as in the case of the elder Morgan, insured an almost equal power over the enterprise. It also insured a considerable position in the community. Indeed, it was because the provision of capital conveyed such power that the system was called capitalism.

7 Now the ownership of capital, or the capacity to supply it, accords no such power. Few large corporations are now run by their owners; those like Du Pont where, for many generations, a talented family has had a decisive influence on the enterprise it owns, are becoming a rarity. Typically

the power lies with the professional managers. These make elaborate obeisance to the stockholders. But they select the Board of Directors, which the stockholders then dutifully elect, and in equally solemn ritual the Board then selects the management that selected it. In some cases, for example the Standard Oil Company of New Jersey, once dominated by the first Rockefeller, the Board consists exclusively of managers selected by the managers who were selected by the Board.

8 There are a number of reasons for the rise of the professional manager, but by far the most important is that ownership of capital has come to count for much less than ownership of ability, knowledge, and brains. The man of ability could get the capital; the man who had capital and was devoid of other qualification had become pretty much a hopeless case. (Even to give away his money would eventually require the services of a professional.) The relatively impecunious but better-trained, more intelligent, more determined, or politically more adept managers have almost everywhere taken over. Once in office it is only rarely that the owners of capital can dislodge them.

9 Nor is this a misfortune for the companies in question. Some of the worst cases of corporate misfortune in recent times have been those in which the owners of the capital have managed to use their power to keep the professionals out. In the thirties and early forties the elder Henry Ford used his power as the sole owner of the Ford Motor Company to remain in command. It is now freely acknowledged that the company suffered severely as a result. Following his death the management was professionalized and much improved. The great merchandising house of Montgomery Ward under Sewell Avery provided a parallel example. Control and direction of a large company by a capitalist has become, indeed, a rather risky affair. He may try to do what can only be done well by a professionally qualified group of diverse and specialized talent.

10 But though it is most visible at the top, the shift in the comparative importance of men and capital is perceptible throughout the modern industrial enterprise. The procedures by which the large and successful enterprise raises funds for new plant and equipment are orderly and predictable. And, depending on circumstances, there is a considerable range of choice—earnings can be withheld, there can be resort to banks, or securities can be sold. A great deal of pompous ritual attends this process, but for the large and successful firm this signifies neither uncertainty nor difficulty but only that we have considerable respect for money and expect large sums to be handled with decent ceremony.

11 There is no similar certainty in the procedures by which even the most successful concern supplies itself with talent. It must send its emissaries to participate in the annual talent hunt, and if the most imposing

men still go to the money markets, the most eloquent go to the colleges. The bag is always uncertain and frequently inadequate. If a successful firm is contemplating a considerable expansion it will almost certainly worry more about where to find the men than where to get the money.

12 And the change is reflected in the fears and apprehensions of the community at large. We wonder whether we are investing as much as we should in physical capital; we hear that the Soviets, who in our time have largely replaced conscience as the stern small voice of duty, are doing much more. But there is more everyday concern about the state of our schools and colleges. Are they doing properly by our children? Where can we find the resources to enable them to do better? Increasingly we are wondering about the adequacy of our output of highly trained and educated people.

13 This shows itself in a very practical way. Every family knows that the automobile industry is equipped to supply it with a new car almost on a moment's notice. Such is the admirable condition of our physical plant. But it cannot be at all sure there will be a place for all the children in a good college. Even the automobile executive may wonder where he can get his boy in. Such is the contrasting state of our facilities for human development.

14 The forces back of the change in the relative position of man as compared with capital are not new. Some of them, curiously enough, are those which, at first glance, seem to suggest the ascendancy of the machine.

15 The classical trinity of productive factors were land (including natural resources), labor (broadly defined to include both physical and intellectual effort), and capital. All production was seen as resulting from the combination of these factors in one form or another and in one proportion or another. Some economists have questioned whether there was much difference between land and capital goods—both support man's efforts to produce things, and many economists have insisted on adding as a fourth factor of production entrepreneurship or the human effort which was devoted to organizing and managing the other three factors. Subject to these modifications and a few quibbles, the classical delineation of productive agents is still accepted and, indeed, is deeply imbedded in economic thought.

16 All production requires all three (or all four) factors and in this sense all are equally vital. But the importance attached to the different factors has changed remarkably in the last hundred and fifty years. At the beginning of the last century—the formative years of modern economics—land seemed peculiarly important. Population was growing. Europe and Asia seemed very crowded. The vast fertile spaces of the Americas, Australia, and Africa were but slightly appreciated. The effect of modern agricultural

techniques on production per acre was, of course, beyond view. Both Ricardo and Malthus, two of the towering figures in the history of economic ideas, concluded that, in different ways, man's fate would be largely decided by the relentless pressure of population on limited land. Labor being abundant, perhaps excessively so, it seemed far less important than land. Capital, though important, also lacked the life-and-death significance of the land supply. Land was the factor of greatest prestige.

17 As the nineteenth century passed, capital gained rapidly to a position of dominance in the trinity. The new world added enormously to the supply of land. The decisive question was its development and for this ports, steamships, roads, railroads, farmsteads, and farm equipment were needed. The land was there; the labor came almost automatically; but the more capital the greater the pace of progress.

18 This emphasis on capital was reinforced by the nature of industrial advance during the last century. It consisted not of the invention of a great number of new techniques but the spread of a relatively small number of spectacularly important ones. Thus, textile manufacture became a factory industry. Steam power was applied to manufacturing, transport, and mining to replace power from men, animals, falling water, or wind. Iron and steel became plentiful and cheap and thus available for many new uses.

19 These inventions resulted, so far as anyone could tell, from a combination of accident, inspiration, and genius. Men like James Watt, Benjamin Franklin, and Eli Whitney could not be cultivated, and while they might under some circumstances be protected by the patent office, that was about all that could be done to foster technological progress.

20 But if little could be done to stimulate inventions, much could be done about putting them to use. Savings could be stimulated by exhortations to thrift—and even more by a system of ethics and religion which assured the diligent, abstemious, and self-denying man esteem in this world and salvation in the next. Investment could be encouraged by stable government and laws which assured investors that profits would be theirs to enjoy. Looking rationally at the thing that was subject to wise policy, economists came to measure progress by the proportion of the nation's income that, each year, was saved and invested.

21 Investment in physical capital is still a prime measure of progress but it is an obsolescent one. More and more progress is coming to depend on the quality rather than the quantity of the capital equipment in use and on the intelligence and skill of those who use it.

22 There are reasonably good figures to go on. Between the early seventies of the last century and the decade 1944–53, according to calculations made under the auspices of the National Bureau of Economic Research, the net output of the American economy increased by an average of 3.5 per cent a year. Less than half of this (1.7 per cent) is explained by increases

in the supply of capital and labor.[1] The rest was the result of improvements in capital equipment—technological advance—and improvements in the working force, including, of course, its leadership and direction. The *share* in the advance attributable to technological improvement and to the improved skill and ability of workers, technicians, and managers has been increasing.

23 But both technological advance and improved skills and abilities are the product of personal development. Machines do not improve themselves; this is still the work of highly improved men. And most technological advance is now the result not of the accident of inspiration or genius but of highly purposeful effort. Once we had to wait for the accidental appearance of Edisons and Wrights. Now through education and organized effort in a laboratory or experimental shop we get something approaching the same results from much more common clay.

24 So it comes to this. We now get the larger part of our industrial growth not from more capital investment but from improvements in men and improvements brought about by highly improved men. And this process of technological advance has become fairly predictable. We get from men pretty much what we invest in them. So now in its turn, after land and after capital, labor—highly improved labor to be sure—has come to the center of the stage. Investment in personal development is therefore at least as useful as an index of progress as investment in physical capital. It could be more valuable. This is the kind of change which solemn men of self-confessed soundness of judgment will continue to resist; the familiar is always defended with much more moral fervor just before it becomes foolish.

25 What then of our practical accommodation to this new urgency of investment in personal development?

26 At first glance our position would seem to be quite good. We have been reaping large gains from the application of trained intelligence to our economic life. This is the fruit of one of the world's pioneer experiments in public education. Surely our advantage will continue.

27 We cannot be so optimistic. Until the last century learning and even literacy were the badges of privilege. They had always been reserved to the favored few. Accordingly learning was a symbol of equality—a symbol that our grandparents, determined to establish their claim to full equality, were not disposed to overlook. Hence the free elementary schools, high schools, the Land Grant College system, and the remarkable number and variety of other institutions of higher (and not excessively high) learning.

28 This system was adequate, even admirable, so long as education was

[1] These figures have been most thoughtfully interpreted by Professor Theodore Schultz to whom all who discuss these matters are in debt. See his "Investment in Man: An Economist's View," *Social Service Review*, XXXIII, No. 2, June 1959.

a socially provided service designed to insure (though it had other purposes too) rough equality of opportunity. It has ceased to be sufficient as education has become a form of investment.

29 The test of what a community should spend on a social service is what it can afford—what it believes it can spare from other forms of consumption. The test of investment, by contrast, is what will pay for itself. We apply the investment test as a matter of course to physical capital and even the commonplace terminology reflects the different attitudes; while we "invest" in physical capital, we "spend" for education.

30 The investment test is far the more generous of the two—that is to say, it sanctions much larger outlays. It implies an aggressive canvas of all possible uses of funds to see what will pay off at a profit. To find new ways of investing at a profit is to prove one's enterprise. One of the most familiar theorems of accepted economics is that, subject to some lags and irregularities, investment in physical capital will occur whenever marginal return exceeds the marginal cost; that is, whenever the return to additional investment is sufficient to cover the added cost including interest and some allowance for risk.

31 The test of what can be afforded, by contrast, invokes far more frugal attitudes. The outlay, even if it is for education, is vaguely self-indulgent. If we wish it—if we wish our children to have the prestige and satisfactions and opportunities from learning—we must measure the cost against other important alternatives. Virtue resides not in finding ways of investing more but in finding ways of spending less. The community honors the man who is identified with economy. These attitudes remain even though, as we have seen, the outlays economized may yield as large a return (perhaps larger) as those for physical capital.

32 Investment in personal development is also handicapped by the lack of a close relationship of outlay with the resulting benefit. A chemical company invests in a new plant because it knows it will get the higher earnings. If it invests in the education of a young chemist it has no similar assurance that it will get a return from its outlay. The fellow may decide to become an artist or a farmer, or he may go faithlessly to work for a competitor.

33 One can see by a simple illustration what the kind of firm relationship of cost to benefit that exists for physical capital would do for investment in personal development if it existed there. Imagine an arrangement by which promising youngsters, when halfway through high school, were indentured for life to a corporation. The corporation would then be responsible for all further education and would be assured of their services for life. Performance of the companies tomorrow, it would soon be evident, would depend on the quality of the postulant executives, scientists, and other specialists being selected and trained today. The quality of this group

would become a matter of major concern. It would be under the eye of accomplished educators. Money would start flowing into it. Investment fund managers would send scouts to seek information on its quality. If one of the larger oil companies found that the schools and colleges available for training its oncoming geologists and engineers were inadequate, it would obviously have to take steps to remedy the situation—perhaps by establishing its own. Otherwise, in a few years, it would be outclassed by the companies with better talent. One can easily imagine bond issues by backward companies to develop stronger technical echelons. The result would be a substantial and possibly an astronomical increase in outlays for personal development—all justified by the resulting profit. All this would be the result of giving the corporation a firm lien on the individual's services and thus on the return on the money it spends on him. It has such a lien on a machine; the example only makes human beings as privileged, for purposes of investment, as are machines.

34 The final reason for thinking that our arrangements for investing in personal development are deficient is that the Soviets have, technically speaking, superior ones. They begin with all resources under public control; hence, there is no problem in transferring those to be devoted to personal development from private to public use. And outlays for physical capital and those for personal development are items in the same huge budget. The returns from one type of investment can be measured against the returns from the other. There is no inherent reason why physical capital should have a preference as in our case. The result is that the U.S.S.R., by our standards still a comparatively poor country, treats its schools, research and training institutes, universities, and adult and worker education with a generosity which impresses all Western visitors. These outlays, needless to say, not old-fashioned expansion of physical capital, were decisive for launching the Sputniks and for landing their successor on the moon.

35 We cannot solve the problem of personal investment by indenturing our youngsters at a tender age to a corporation. And we should not expect the kindly corporation to rise to the rescue with large voluntary grants for education. Time has already been wasted on this notion. The problem is far too serious to be left to the conscience of those with a particular willingness to spend the stockholder's money.

36 Most likely we will solve the problem by making fuller and better use of the familiar instruments of public finance. We must see spending for personal development not as a cost but as an opportunity. Then we must make sure that we are taxing ourselves sufficiently to exploit this opportunity. That the Federal Government must play a role is elementary. It has access to fiscal resources that are inherently far greater than those of states and localities; now that education has become an investment rather than a

social service, these resources are indispensable. It is also the unit of government with responsibility for national development and growth. There is at least a likelihood that investment in personal development is a better guarantee of national power than some of our military expenditures.

37 We need also to review our attitudes toward state and local taxation. In a poor country there are sound reasons for reluctance in taxing objects of everyday consumption in order to have more public services and amenities. But we are not a poor country and personal development has become not a service but an investment. So states and localities should no longer hesitate to use sales and excise taxes (as an addition to and not as a substitute for others) to pay for schools and universities. And liberals, in particular, should not be too indignant when this is proposed.

38 There is another way of putting provision for personal development on a par with capital development that we should consider. We assume that a corporation, either by withholding from earnings or by resort to the capital market, will take responsibility for improving and expanding its own physical plant. The pressure for voluntary contributions by corporations to education reflects, no doubt, a feeling that there is a similar responsibility for personal development. Corporations are the largest employers of trained talent. They reap the rewards from employing such people. Why shouldn't they pay a part of the cost of training this talent?

39 Perhaps they should. Voluntary contributions will always be inequitable as well as inadequate. Conscience can readily be assuaged by a small contribution and the levy falls only on those with a social view of the corporation. But a special tax for education and training would encounter no similar objection. Levied as a percentage of total payroll—executive, scientific, skilled and unskilled—it would be roughly proportioned to the quantity and quality of the people employed. Thus it would be related to benefit from past investment in personal development; and it would mean that the company was assuming its rough share of the cost of replacing with improved talent the skilled workers, technicians, scientists, and executives that it employs. Initially the tax would presumably be borne in the form of higher prices by the consumers of the product. Ultimately the better talent would bring better methods, improved efficiency, and hence lower prices. It would be self-liquidating for it supports a profitable investment.

40 Corporations are now at great pains to explain that their prices must include provision for earnings sufficient to replace and expand their physical capital. This, they regularly assure their public, means that production will continue and be more efficient in the future. But, as the National Bureau figures show, we have more to gain from improving the quality of people. So a levy for this purpose would be an even better bargain.

41 Maybe there are other ways of augmenting the flow of resources into

personal development. In a society that is changing we dare not assume that we have thought the last thoughts on any such subject. For man has not retreated before the machine; rather the machine has become desperately dependent on the improvement of man. And our economy is still arranged to supply machines rather than to improve men.

STUDY GUIDE

Theme and Structure

1. Although Keats's manner in the previous essay was humorous, his idea of man's relationship to the machine, especially to the automobile, was pessimistic. Galbraith in this essay is more serious in manner, but he takes a much more optimistic view of man's relationship to the machine in general than does Keats. What is the main thematic idea of his essay?

2. Indicate the main thought divisions of the essay, and give the numbers of the paragraphs devoted to developing each of these divisions.

3. The author has made effective use of concrete examples to develop some of his ideas. Point out some instances of this device in the essay.

SECTION 6

Understanding the Hero

NOTE TO THE INSTRUCTOR: This unit is conceived as an introduction to a program of reading in the great epics of Western civilization. If we know what an age honors in its heroes, we know one of its most revealing characteristics. And since an epic, at its best, is a prolonged story of the exploits of a nation's hero told precisely to elicit admiration for that hero, the epic is one of the very best helps to an understanding of a nation or an epoch. A hero is a man to be admired; but the qualities for which he is admired shift from age to age and from culture to culture. Ruskin, in his essay on honor, tries to get at the root of this whole business of hero worship, and thinks he finds it in the spirit of self-sacrifice. But the story of Achilles in *The Iliad* is enough to show that this was not always a prime requisite for heroism. The five essays that follow Ruskin's call attention to the shifting basis of honor in the great epics from *The Iliad* to *Paradise Lost*. A careful reading of these essays may provide the student with a helpful approach to a better understanding of the central character and controlling action of each of the great epics themselves.

The epics were for the most part success stories revealing the positive ideals of a nation or culture. Even *Paradise Lost* reveals a positive heroic ideal redefined by Milton in Book IX of his epic. And perhaps Milton's poem gives a more complete picture of the human situation than do the earlier Greek and Roman epics because it takes account of the tragic fall of man. C. S. Lewis has pointed out that early epics have something of the adolescent about them—an emphasis on positive ideals without much sense of the tragic in man's life.

The Greeks, however, developed a high sense of tragedy in their drama. An interesting alternate reading program might consist of just the Greek epics and several Greek plays (*The Oresteia* by Aeschylus and *Oedipus the King* and *Antigone* by Sophocles, for instance), in which one might discover the deeper and more mature view of man that is evident in the tragedies. For such a unit the essay on "The Tragic Spirit in Modern Times" by Henry Alonzo Myers would prove helpful. In such a unit one might also want to include a modern tragedy or two such as Arthur Miller's *Death of a Salesman* or Eugene O'Neill's *Long Day's Journey into Night*.

An early start in the semester on this unit and the actual reading of the epics and tragedies will provide unlimited material for class discussion and theme subjects. For classes in which considerable time has to be spent on a review of fundamentals, it is suggested that at least the *Odyssey* be read. Perhaps the application of Ruskin's ideas to such modern works as *Death of a Salesman* or *Point of No Return* might be a more successful venture for such groups. But for the more advanced classes there could hardly be any better preparation for later work in literature, history, and art than this early experience of the ideals of Western civilization as revealed in the great epics and tragedies.

The essay by Arthur M. Schlesinger, Jr., on "The Decline of Heroes" and the *Time* essay "On the Difficulty of Being a Contemporary Hero" bring the discussion of the hero up to the contemporary scene.

THE ROOTS OF HONOR

John Ruskin

1 I have already alluded to the difference hitherto existing between regiments of men associated for purposes of violence, and for purposes of manufacture; in that the former appear capable of self-sacrifice—the latter, not; which singular fact is the real reason of the general lowness of estimate in which the profession of commerce is held, as compared with that of arms. Philosophically, it does not, at first sight, appear reasonable (many writers have endeavored to prove it unreasonable) that a peaceable and rational person whose trade is buying and selling, should be held in less honor than an unpeaceable and often irrational person whose trade is slaying. Nevertheless, the consent of mankind has always, in spite of the philosophers, given precedence to the soldier.

2 And this is right. For the soldier's trade, verily and essentially, is not slaying, but being slain. This, without well knowing its own meaning,

From "Unto This Last," *The Works*, E. T. Cook and Alexander Wedderburn (eds.) (London: George Allen, 1905), XVII, 36–42.

the world honors it for. A bravo's trade is slaying; but the world has never respected bravoes more than merchants; the reason it honors the soldier is that he holds his life at the service of the State. Reckless he may be—fond of pleasure or of adventure—all kinds of bymotives and mean impulses may have determined the choice of his profession, and may affect (to all appearance exclusively) his daily conduct in it; but our estimate of him is based on this ultimate fact—of which we are well assured—that, put him in a fortress breach, with all the pleasures of the world behind him, and only death and his duty in front of him, he will keep his face to the front; and he knows that this choice may be put him at any moment, and has beforehand taken his part—virtually takes such part continually—does, in reality, die daily.

3 Not less is the respect we pay to the lawyer and physician, founded ultimately on their self-sacrifice. Whatever the learning or acuteness of a great lawyer, our chief respect for him depends on our belief that, set in a judge's seat, he will strive to judge justly, come of it what may. Could we suppose that he would take bribes, and use his acuteness and legal knowledge to give plausibility to iniquitous decisions, no degree of intellect would win for him our respect. Nothing will win it, short of our tacit conviction that in all important acts of his life justice is first with him; his own interest, second.

4 In the case of a physician, the ground of the honor we render him is clearer still. Whatever his science, we should shrink from him in horror if we found him regard his patients merely as subjects to experiment upon; much more, if we found that, receiving bribes from persons interested in their deaths, he was using his best skill to give poison in the mask of medicine.

5 Finally, the principle holds with utmost clearness as it respects clergymen. No goodness of disposition will excuse want of science in a physician or of shrewdness in an advocate; but a clergyman, even though his power of intellect be small, is respected on the presumed ground of his unselfishness and serviceableness.

6 Now, there can be no question but that the fact, foresight, decision, and other mental powers required for the successful management of a large mercantile concern, if not such as could be compared with those of a great lawyer, general, or divine, would at least match the general conditions of mind required in the subordinate officers of a ship, or of a regiment, or in the curate of a country parish. If, therefore, all the efficient members of the so-called liberal professions are still somehow in public estimate of honor preferred before the head of a commercial firm, the reason must lie deeper than in the measurement of their powers of mind.

7 And the essential reason for such preference will be found to lie in the fact that the merchant is presumed to act always selfishly. His work may be very necessary to the community; but the motive of it is understood to be wholly personal. The merchant's first object in all his dealings must be (the public believe) to get as much for himself and leave as little to his neighbor (or customer) as possible. Enforcing this upon him, by political statute, as the necessary principle of his action; recommending it to him on all occasions, and themselves reciprocally adopting it; proclaiming vociferously, for law of the universe, that a buyer's function is to cheapen, and a seller's to cheat—the public, nevertheless, involuntarily condemn the man of commerce for his compliance with their own statement, and stamp him forever as belonging to an inferior grade of human personality.

8 This they will find, eventually, they must give up doing. They must not cease to condemn selfishness; but they will have to discover a kind of commerce which is not exclusively selfish. Or, rather, they will have to discover that there never was, or can be, any other kind of commerce; that this which they have called commerce was not commerce at all but cozening. . . . They will find that commerce is an occupation which gentlemen will every day see more need to engage in, rather than in the businesses of talking to men, or slaying them; that, in true commerce, as in true preaching, or true fighting, it is necessary to admit the idea of occasional voluntary loss—that sixpences have to be lost, as well as lives, under a sense of duty; that the market may have its martyrdoms as well as the pulpit; and trade its heroisms, as well as war.

9 May have—in the final issue, must have—and only has not had yet, because men of heroic temper have always been misguided in their youth in other fields; not recognizing what is in our days, perhaps, the most important of all fields; so that, while many a zealous person loses his life in trying to teach the form of a gospel, very few will lose a hundred pounds in showing the practice of one.

10 The fact is that people never have had clearly explained to them the true functions of a merchant with respect to other people. I should like the reader to be very clear about this.

11 Five great intellectual professions, relating to daily necessities of life, have hitherto existed—three exist necessarily, in every civilized nation:

The Soldier's profession is to *defend* it.
The Pastor's, to *teach* it.
The Physician's, to *keep it in health*.
The Lawyer's, to *enforce justice* in it.
The Merchant's, to *provide* for it.

And the duty of all these men is, on due occasion, to die for it. "On due occasion," namely:

The Soldier, rather than leave his post in battle.
The Physician, rather than leave his post in plague.
The Pastor, rather than teach falsehood.
The Lawyer, rather than countenance injustice.

The Merchant—What is *his* "due occasion" of death? It is the main question for the merchant, as for all of us. For, truly, the man who does not know when to die, does not know how to live.

12 Observe, the merchant's function (or manufacturer's, for in the broad sense in which it is here used the word must be understood to include both) is to provide for the nation. It is no more his function to get profit for himself out of that provision than it is a clergyman's function to get his stipend. The stipend is a due and necessary adjunct, but not the object, of his life, if he be a true clergyman, any more than his fee (or honorarium) is the object of life to a true physician. Neither is his fee the object of life to a true merchant. All three, if true men, have a work to be done irrespective of fee—to be done even at any cost, or for quite the contrary of fee; the pastor's function being to teach, the physician's to heal, and the merchant's, as I have said, to provide. That is to say, he has to understand to their very root the qualities of the thing he deals in, and the means of obtaining or producing it; and he has to apply all his sagacity and energy to the producing or obtaining it in perfect state, and distributing it at the cheapest possible price where it is most needed.

13 And because the production or obtaining of any commodity involves necessarily the agency of many lives and hands, the merchant becomes in the course of his business the master and governor of large masses of men in a more direct, though less confessed way, than a military officer or pastor; so that on him falls, in great part, the responsibility for the kind of life they lead; and it becomes his duty, not only to be always considering how to produce what he sells in the purest and cheapest forms, but how to make the various employments involved in the production, or transference of it, most beneficial to the men employed.

14 And as into these two functions, requiring for their right exercise the highest intelligence, as well as patience, kindness, and tact, the merchant is bound to put all his energy, so for their just discharge he is bound, as soldier or physician is bound, to give up, if need be, his life, in such way as it may be demanded of him. Two main points he has in his providing function to maintain: first, his engagements (faithfulness to engagements being the real root of all possibilities in commerce); and secondly, the per-

fectness and purity of the thing provided; so that, rather than fail in any engagement, or consent to any deterioration, adulteration, or unjust and exorbitant price of that which he provides, he is bound to meet fearlessly any form of distress, poverty, or labor, which may, through maintenance of these points, come upon him.

15 Again: in his office as governor of the men employed by him, the merchant or manufacturer is invested with a distinctly paternal authority and responsibility. In most cases, a youth entering a commercial establishment is withdrawn altogether from home influence; his master must become his father, else he has, for practical and constant help, no father at hand; in all cases the master's authority, together with the general tone and atmosphere of his business, and the character of the men with whom the youth is compelled in the course of it to associate, have more immediate and pressing weight than the home influence, and will neutralize it either for good or evil; so that the only means which the master has of doing justice to the men employed by him is to ask himself sternly whether he is dealing with such subordinate as he would with his own son, if compelled by circumstances to take such a position.

16 Supposing the captain of a frigate saw it right, or were by any chance obliged, to place his own son in the position of a common sailor; as he would then treat his son, he is bound always to treat every one of the men under him. So, also, supposing the master of a manufactory saw it right, or were by any chance obliged to place his own son in the position of an ordinary workman; as he would then treat his son, he is bound always to treat every one of his men. This is the only effective, true, or practical Rule which can be given on this point of political economy.

17 And as the captain of a ship is bound to be the last man to leave his ship in case of wreck, and to share his last crust with the sailors in case of famine, so the manufacturer, in any commercial crisis or distress, is bound to take the suffering of it with his men, and even to take more of it for himself than he allows his men to feel; as a father would in a famine, shipwreck, or battle, sacrifice himself for his son.

18 All which sounds very strange—the only real strangeness in the matter being, nevertheless, that it should so sound. For all this is true, and that not partially nor theoretically, but everlastingly and practically; all other doctrine than this respecting matters political being false in premises, absurd in deduction, and impossible in practice, consistently with any progressive state of national life; all the life which we now possess as a nation showing itself in the resolute denial and scorn, by a few strong minds and faithful hearts, of the economic principles taught to our multitudes, which principles, so far as accepted, lead straight to national destruction.

STUDY GUIDE

Theme and Structure

1. State the theme of the entire essay. In what sentence does Ruskin state the theme most exactly?

2. Write a one-paragraph *précis* of the entire essay, emphasizing by proper connectives the exact thought progression of the original.

3. Comparison and contrast figure prominently in the organization of this essay. List all the comparisons and contrasts and show how they help clarify the subject Ruskin is discussing.

Content

1. A. Do you agree that the root of the honor paid to lawyers, physicians, and pastors is their willingness to sacrifice themselves for the benefit of the community?

B. In this connection, analyze the root of the disrespect which the public feels for "shyster lawyers" and "venal physicians."

C. What does history show to be one of the chief roots of anti-clericalism?

2. A. Do you think Ruskin's concept of the functions and duties of the businessman (merchant and manufacturer) is too idealistic?

B. Ruskin wrote this essay in late nineteenth-century England. Do you think that what he says in paragraphs 6 and 7 about the attitude of the public toward the merchant and manufacturer holds today? If you think it does not, write an essay in which you give some evidence for the changed attitude and in which you give some explanation for this change.

ACHILLES, THE TYPICAL GREEK HERO

Maurice B. McNamee

1 To many modern readers, Achilles may appear to be proud, selfish, egotistical, and unbelievably stubborn, and therefore deserving of neither admiration nor sympathy. To some modern critics, on the other hand, he seems to be essentially a tragic character, who by an excess of anger and hurt pride, brings about the death of his dearest friend and of dozens of his fellow Achaeans. The Greeks themselves, for whom *The Iliad* was written, would probably have reacted to his character quite differently. So far from condemning him as overly proud or pitying him as a tragic figure, they would more probably have admired him as a rather good embodiment

of their notion of a hero. They would very likely have considered the final outcome of the poem as much a triumph for Achilles as was the victory over the suitors for Odysseus.

2 For, after all, what is the central action of *The Iliad*? In its baldest terms it is simply this. The great Achilles has been dishonored before the whole Greek host by King Agamemnon, and so important is his honor to Achilles that he is willing to sacrifice half the Greek army to reassert his superiority over the King. The details of the story are familiar. The Greek army was being decimated with a plague by the god Apollo, who was angered because Agamemnon refused to restore to her father, a priest of Apollo, the damsel Chryseis whom Agamemnon had taken to himself as part of the spoils of war. To placate the god and save his army from the plague, Agamemnon finally agrees to restore the girl to her father, but consoles himself for the loss by confiscating the damsel Briseis who had been given to Achilles as a very special gift of honor in recognition of that incomparable hero's prowess in conquering and sacking innumerable cities. Achilles would not have been so mortally offended if Agamemnon had stripped him of all the rich booty that fell to him from previous exploits, but it was a black unforgivable insult to take away this girl, who had been given to him as a special public mark of honor in recognition of his superior prowess and valor. It was tantamount to Agamemnon's saying that Achilles was inferior to him, and this was a humiliation at the hands of the King, a man whose opinion counted in the eyes of men, that the great Achilles simply could not brook. He withdrew from battle, and remained aloof until it was quite apparent to Agamemnon and the whole Greek host that without him they were helpless to save themselves from destruction at the hands of the Trojans. We are left in no possible doubt about this dominant motive of Achilles for his withdrawal from battle and for his stubborn aloofness. As he withdraws he flings this taunt at Agamemnon:

> "The day is coming when the Achaeans one and all will miss me sorely, and you in your despair will be powerless to help them as they fall in their hundreds to Hector killer of men. Then will you tear your heart out in remorse for having treated the best man in the expedition with contempt." [1]

Pleading with his goddess mother Thetis later to win over Zeus to his course, he says:

> "Persuade him, if you can, to help the Trojans, to fling the Achaeans back on their ships, to pen them in against the sea and slaughter them. That

[1] The quotations used throughout this selection are from *The Iliad*, translated by Dr. E. V. Rieu and published by Penguin Books, Ltd.

> would teach them to appreciate their King. That would make imperial Agamemnon son of Atreus realize what a fool he was to insult the noblest of them all."

Later, when the Trojans are already threatening the very ships of the Achaeans, Achilles sees it as an answer to his prayer. He remarks to Patroclus:

> "My dear prince and my heart's delight, at last I see the Achaeans gathering at my knees to abase themselves, for they are in desperate straits."

3 In this central action of the poem there is no tragic defeat for Achilles; he gets exactly what he wants and stands at the end of the poem completely victorious. In the last scene, in which we see Achilles and Agamemnon together at the funeral games for Patroclus, Achilles is friendly and even condescending towards Agamemnon. He could now afford to be, because his own superiority over the king had been completely vindicated. If we wish to see this central motivation and action of the poem as the Greeks saw it, we would do well to see it in the light of Aristotle's emphasis on the supreme importance of personal honor in the life of the hero. If we look carefully, it becomes apparent that every detail of the story, as it touches Achilles, gyrates around his quest for and insistence on his own personal honor and fame above all other values.

4 In the first place, Achilles is certainly given heroic stature in the poem. He is described as superior to everyone in the whole Greek host, Agamemnon included. With the possible exception of Telemonian Ajax, there is no one in the whole Greek army who can match him in sheer strength and physical prowess. Ajax, however, is more brawny than brainy; while Achilles has an intelligence that matches his towering strength. On the battlefield he has no peer for indomitable courage and ruthlessness. His beauty of physique is so great that it frequently reveals him to be what he is—half divine. As became the "greatest Achaean of them all," there was nothing about his circumstances that was mediocre. His armor surpassed that of all the other Achaeans, fashioned as it was by the divine hands of Hephaetus himself. His spear was so tremendous that no one except himself could wield it. It took three men to draw the tremendous bar to the gate of his enclosure, but he, of course, could flick it open or shut with one hand. And so it went. Even his horses were superior to all others. They were, in fact, also half divine; and one of them, Xanthus, had the power of speech which he used, naturally, to praise his master and lament his fated early death.

5 Achilles' preeminence is highlighted not only by the many excellent qualities that are attributed to him personally, but also by the contrasts that are drawn between him and other great characters in the story. The

central action, we have seen, is designed to demonstrate his superiority over Agamemnon. Ajax is described as mighty and devastating in combat, the greatest battler of the Achaeans, but only in the absence of Achilles. Odysseus is conceded to excel in wily counsels, or as Achilles himself puts it, "in the war of words"; but he is frequently pictured as something less than eager for the gory business of the battlefield where Achilles is most at home. Menelaus is almost the perfect example of the ambitious man as Aristotle defines him. He is mediocre in almost every respect, but is forever volunteering or ambitioning to take up challenges that are beyond his capacities, not without an eye to the glory that would be his, if he succeeded in these exploits. He has to be frequently reminded of his limitations and gently shown his place even by his brother Agamemnon. But his very mediocrity is a foil against which Achilles' superiority shines the brighter. Achilles' heroic stature also grows by contrast with even the greatest of Trojan warriors. Aeneas is described by the god Poseidon as truly magnanimous, but the old sea-god recognizes that he is simply no match for Achilles and tells him so as he snatches him from a premature death at the "man-killing" hands of Achilles.

> "Which of the gods told you to fight with the proud Achilles," Poseidon chides, "who is not only a better soldier than you but a greater favourite with the immortals? If ever you come up against that man, withdraw at once, or you will find yourself in Hades' Halls before your time. But when he is dead and gone, you can boldly play your part in the front line, for no one else on the Achaean side is going to kill you."

But the most flattering foil for Achilles' greatness, of course, is his Trojan opponent Hector. Since Achilles' is to win his greatest fame in the story by defeating Hector, Homer had to give that Trojan warrior heroic stature. In the absence of Achilles Hector is the most formidable thing on the plains of Troy. He carries everything before him. But his very preeminence and the chaos he creates in the Greek ranks only serve to augment the glory of Achilles when he rejoins the fray and defeats the redoubtable Hector. Thus both the strength and the weakness of Greek and Trojan heroes alike are made to highlight the towering superiority of "the noblest of the Achaeans."

6 Achilles himself is the last to deny this superiority; indeed, he is keenly aware of it and asserts it on every possible occasion. We have already heard him bitterly taunting Agamemnon for treating "the best man in the expedition with contempt." When he is threatening to launch his ships and sail home to Phthia, at the moment when Hector is threatening the very ships of the Greeks, he reminds Odysseus that "when he, [Achilles] took the field with the Achaeans nothing would have induced Hector to throw his men into battle at any distance from the city walls. He

came no farther than the Scaean Gate and the oak-tree, where he took me on alone one day, and was lucky to get home alive." In his conversation with his mother Thetis about going back into battle to revenge the death of his friend Patroclus, he laments that he, "the best man in all the Achaean force, the best in battle, defeated only in the war of words," has proven a broken reed to his friend. He seldom, in fact, ever refers to himself except in superlatives, and none of his auditors, human or divine, ever deny that they are justified.

7 Achilles shows this consciousness of his own superiority not only by his own statements and presumptions about himself but also by his attitude towards all his fellow Achaeans. His relationships with all of them are very much those of the magnanimous man as Aristotle later described him. With inferiors like Ajax and Odysseus, for instance, he can be quite friendly and condescending, but towards Agamemnon, the recognized leader of the whole Greek army, who has dishonored him, he is consistently haughty and insolent. Even his relationship with Patroclus fits the Aristotelian pattern. Aristotle said that the magnanimous man "must be unable to make his life revolve round another, unless it be a friend." Patroclus is such a friend. But even towards Patroclus Achilles' attitude is not entirely unselfish. He does not look on Patroclus as an equal but as a lesser version of himself in whose good qualities he sees himself reflected. So he looks upon the death of Patroclus as another insult flung by Hector at himself. Patroclus, we recall, had gone to battle in Achilles' armor, and the driving motive of Hector in slaying him is to have the honor of capturing the armor of the famed Achilles. It is not *all* an unselfish grief for his friend that so infuriates Achilles at Hector's slaying of Patroclus.

8 Achilles' personal honor, in fact, is behind almost every move, great and small, that he makes throughout the whole *Iliad*. As we have already seen, he withdrew from battle in boiling wrath because he was dishonored by Agamemnon. He remained aloof from the battlefield until, with the whole Greek army and the very ships on the brink of annihilation by the Trojans, it had become painfully apparent to Agamemnon and all the Greeks how completely dependent they were upon him for victory. His answer to the second delegation from Agamemnon makes his position and his motives perfectly clear.

> "My blood boils when I think of what happened, and the vile way in which Atreides treated me in public, like some disreputable outcast. Go now, and report my decisions. I will not think again of bloodshed and war, until Prince Hector, son of the wise Priam, reaches the huts and ships of the Myrmidons, killing Argives as he comes, and destroys the fleet by fire. I have a notion that, however furious his attack may be, Hector will be brought up short, here by my own hut and my own black ship."

In other words, he planned on waiting for the moment which would be most humiliating to Agamemnon and which would redound most to his own glory. Later, when the Trojans are already at the ships, we hear him remarking with obvious satisfaction to Patroclus:

> "My dear prince and my heart's delight, at last I see the Achaeans gathering at my knees to abase themselves, for they are in desperate straits."

Finally, persuaded by Patroclus to do something to save the ships from going up in smoke he consents to allow Patroclus to go into battle in his armor, as he gloats over the helplessness of the Achaeans without him.

> "The whole town of Troy [he says] seems to have taken heart and turned out against us. And no wonder, when they do not see the vizor of *my* helmet flashing in the foreground. They would soon take to their heels and fill the gullies with their dead, if King Agamemnon would treat me as a friend."

Achilles is confident that, if he merely sends Patroclus into the battle in his armor, the Trojans will scatter in panic. But before he allows Patroclus to go into battle to save the ships, he cautions him about just how far he is to go. He must not allow his head to be turned by success in the fray and carry on the battle against Hector by himself. That honor is to be reserved for Achilles. He is blatantly explicit on the point. His sending Patroclus is part of a maneuver to reflect credit not on Patroclus, but on himself:

> "But listen while I tell you exactly how far to go, in order to induce the whole Danaan army to value and respect me as they should and to send the lovely lady back to me, with ample compensation too. Return to me, directly you have swept the Trojans from the ships. Even if Zeus the Thunderer offers you the chance of winning glory for yourself, you must not seize it. You must not fight without *me* against those warlike Trojans —you would only make me cheaper."

And then he makes a remark which reveals the colossal proportions of his egoism, and the degree to which he puts his own glory above the welfare of his fellow Achaeans:

> "Ah, Father Zeus, Athene and Apollo, how happy I should be if not a Trojan got away alive, not one, and not an Argive either, if we two survived the massacre to pull down Troy's holy diadem of towers singlehanded."

Egoism can hardly go farther than that, but with Achilles it does.

9 Patroclus, in the event, forgets his restrictions, pursues the Trojans

to their very walls, and is slain at the hands of Hector. This enrages Achilles beyond measure; and he decides that this is the time to revenge the death of his friend and to cover himself with glory by slaying single-handed the greatest of the Trojans who until then has had the whole Greek army in rout. He is so impatient to get at the Trojans that he will not even wait for his new coat of armor. He rushes out on the plain and gives out with such blood curdling battle cries that the whole Trojan army is petrified with terror, and some of their best men commit suicide on the spot. When he finally consents to delay the combat until his goddess Mother has procured a new suit of armor for him from the forge of Hephaestus, he tells her that he is obsessed now not mainly by the thought of revenge nor with the thought of his own predestined death there on the windy plains of Troy but with the thought of the undying fame that will be his as the slayer of the matchless Hector. These are his own words:

> "I will go now and seek out Hector, the destroyer of my dearest friend. As for my death, when Zeus and the other deathless gods appoint it, let it come. . . . But for the moment, glory is my aim. I will make these Trojan women and deep-bosomed daughters of Dardanus wipe the tears from their tender cheeks with both their hands as they raise the dirge, to teach them just how long I have been absent from the war."

As a last resource, Odysseus had appealed to this very motive when he tried to persuade Achilles to get back into the battle. Achilles had already refused to accept the gift of the humbled Agamemnon, and Odysseus shrewdly couched his final appeal in these words:

> "If your hatred for Atreides, gifts and all, outweighs every other consideration, do have some pity on the rest of the Achaeans, lying dead-beat in their camp. They will honour you like a god. Indeed, you could cover yourself with glory in their eyes, for now is the time when you could get Hector himself. He fancies that he has no match among all the Danaans whom the ships brought here, and he may even venture near you, in his insensate fury."

The wily Odysseus is showing his real shrewdness in making this final appeal to Achilles' love of glory, but Achilles is not yet sure the time is ripe for reaping the fullest harvest of glory. He will not come back until he has humiliated Agamemnon to the dust. "First he must pay in kind for the bitter humiliation I endured," is his reply.

10 When Achilles finally does go into battle against Hector, blazing like a god in his new armor, it is quite apparent that his dominant motive is not "pity for the rest of the Achaeans" but rather the glory that will be his forever as the slayer of the great Hector. And he makes it clear that he does

not intend to share that glory with anyone else. When he is in pursuit of the fleeing Hector around the walls of Troy, he signals to his men

> . . . by movements of his head that they were not to shoot at the quarry, for fear that he might be forestalled and one of them might win renown by striking Hector with an arrow.

When he has finally brought Hector low with a well-aimed thrust of his spear, he taunts his victim with these words:

> "Hector, no doubt you fancied as you stripped Patroclus that you would be safe. You never thought of me: I was too far away. You were a fool. Down by the hollow ships there was a man far better than Patroclus in reserve, the man who has brought you low."

With that he deals the death blow to the prostrate Hector. Achilles' followers look in amazement at "the size and marvellous good looks of Hector," and each of them tries to steal some of Achilles' honor by thrusting his spear into the body of the mightiest of the Trojans. But Achilles reminds them that Hector had once been more formidable to them all with the words, "Hector is easier to handle now than when he set the ships on fire." Achilles, now exultant, has the Achaeans take up the body of Hector and carry it back to the ships as they sing with him this song of triumph: "We have won great glory. We have killed the noble Hector, who was treated like a god in Troy." And to savor his triumph over the great Trojan, Achilles proceeds to subject his dead body to the indignity of being dragged in the dust about the walls of Troy and the barrow of Patroclus tied to the rear of his chariot.

11 Achilles has at last attained his greatest wish, even if he has paid for it with the death of so many Achaeans, including that of his dearest friend. He has humiliated Agamemnon, who came crawling to him to save the Achaeans from destruction, and he has won imperishable glory for himself by slaying the mighty Hector. As something of an outward symbol of his truimph over Agamemnon, the gifts which the king had promised to him if he came to the aid of the Achaeans are now brought to him with all due ceremony; and they include the damsel Briseis, that special prize of honor whose confiscation had occasioned his unquenchable wrath.

12 The Achilles we see at the funeral games of Patroclus is a friendly, condescending Achilles. He abstains from entering the chariot race because his horses are grieving over the death of Patroclus, but not without reminding the contestants that on any other occasion he would win against any challengers. In any event, he has just won a much bigger contest, so he can afford to be indifferent about these much smaller stakes.

In like spirit he doubles the prize for Antilochus because Antilochus had made the complimentary remark that Odysseus is a hard man to overcome in a race—"for anyone but Achilles." He awards a prize to Agamemnon without letting him contend for it and graciously compliments him on his superior prowess as a spearsman. He can afford to be gracious even to Agamemnon now, since he has so completely vindicated his own superiority over him. But it is his own glory that remains uppermost in his mind until the last. He bids his followers construct a modest barrow for Patroclus now, but later a mighty one for himself and his friend when he has followed Patroclus into Hades. "As for his barrow," he says, "I do not ask you to construct a very large one, something that is seemly but no more. Later you can build a big and high one, you Achaeans that are left in the well-found ships when I am gone."

13 If we follow Achilles into the underworld as Homer does in *The Odyssey*, we will see that Achilles in Hades is the same old Achilles that we have come to know in *The Iliad*. When Odysseus visits the underworld, he meets the shade of Achilles there and hails him as the

> "most fortunate man that ever was or will be! For in the old days when you were on earth, we Argives honoured you as though you were a god; and now, down here, you are a mighty prince among the dead. For you, Achilles, Death should have lost his sting."

But Achilles takes a less glowing view of his present situation:

> "Put me on earth again [he says] and I would rather be a serf in the house of some landless man, with little enough for himself to live on, than king of all these dead men that have done with life."

What he is really interested in is his son on earth. Is he living up to the reputation of his celebrated father? "Did he follow me to the war and play a leading part or not?" And what about his old father? How is he now without his son to protect him? These are the interests of Achilles in Hades; and as he shouts these questions at Odysseus a spark of the old boastful Achilles flashes out for a moment:

> "If I could return [he says] for a single day to my father's house with the strength I then enjoyed, I would make those who injure him and rob him of his rights shrink in dismay before my might and my unconquerable hands."

14 About Achilles' father Odysseus knows nothing, but about his son he can be very reassuring. He is a son of whom Achilles can be proud. He gives Achilles a glowing account of the prowess of the lad. It would seem that

he gives promise of even bettering his father in one area, since Odysseus says he is bettered in debate by only the wise old Nestor and himself. Achilles lets that pass without comment, but he listens eagerly as Odysseus describes his son's prowess on the battlefield.

> "That impetuous spirit of his [says Odysseus] gave place to none, and he would sally out beyond the foremost. Many was the man he brought down in mortal combat. I could not tell you all the people he killed in battle for the Argives. . . . When we Argive captains took our places in the wooden horse Epeius made, and it rested solely with me to throw our ambush open or to keep it shut, all the other Danaan chieftains and officers were wiping the tears from their eyes and every man's legs were trembling beneath them, but not once did I see your son's fine colour change to pallor nor catch him brushing a tear from his cheek. On the contrary he begged me time and again to let him sally from the Horse and kept fumbling eagerly at his sword-hilt and his heavy spear in his keenness to fall on the Trojans."

Here was a son after the heart of the mighty Achilles himself. This news of home was a bright spot for Achilles in the darkness of the underworld.

> "The soul of Achilles, [said Odysseus] whose feet had been so fleet on earth, passed with great strides down the meadow of asphodel, rejoicing in the news I had given him of his son's renown."

To have such a son was the next best thing to being among the living himself, where he could be winning undying fame with his "unconquerable hands."

15 We catch another glimpse of Achilles in the underworld when the souls of the suitors arrive there. They find him in conversation with the shade of Agamemnon. He is condoling with the king for his inglorious death at the hands of the faithless Clytemnestra. Agamemnon agrees that Achilles' death was by far the happier one

> ". . . in Troyland far away from Argos, with the flower of the Trojan and Achaean forces falling round you in battle for your corpse. There in a whirl of dust you lay, great even in your fall, thinking no longer of charioteer's delights."

Then, after relating in great detail all the funeral honors paid to Achilles by Achaeans and gods alike, Agamemnon describes the glorious mound that was built for him.

> "We soldiers of the mighty Argive force built up a great and glorious mound, on a foreland jutting out over the broad waters of the Hellespont, so that it might be seen far out at sea by the sailors of to-day and future

> ages. Then, in the middle of the lists where the Achaean champions were to test their skill, your mother placed the magnificent prizes she had asked the gods to give. You must often have attended royal funerals yourself, when the young men strip and make ready for the games by which they honour their dead king, but the splendid prizes offered in *your* honour by the divine Thetis of the Silver Feet would have struck you as the most wonderful you had ever seen. For the gods loved you very dearly. Thus even death, Achilles, did not destroy your glory and the whole world will honour you for ever."

What satisfaction it was to be hearing all this from Agamemnon. Achilles had once been given a choice: to go home to Phthia and live to a peaceful but inglorious old age, or to remain at Troy and die an early death but gain immortal fame. He pretended for a time to have chosen home and the peaceful old age; but it was only a pretense. His real and ultimate choice was death and immortal fame on the plains of Troy. He had lived for glory; he had died for glory; and now Agamemnon was telling him that not even death had destroyed his glory. The whole world would honor him forever. That was all that Achilles had ever asked for in life.

16 It should also be noted that it is not just any kind of glory that interests Achilles. He is even willing to concede that he is worsted by Odysseus in debate, in the "war of words"; but he will yield to no one in what he considers the far more important war of swords. Nor is it just any kind of battle in which he is interested, but only one which he considers a real challenge to his superior prowess. That is why he is so anxious to reserve the combat with Hector to himself. Aristotle had observed that the magnanimous man

> . . . does not run into trifling dangers, nor is he fond of danger, because he honours few things; but he will face great dangers, and when he is in danger he is unsparing of his life, knowing that there are conditions on which life is not worth having.

This is only partly the code of Achilles. It is true that he despises small dangers as not a sufficient challenge to his superior powers, and that honor on the battlefield means more to him than life; but we have a feeling all through *The Iliad* that in Achilles we are dealing with a more primitive ideal than even that described by Aristotle. Achilles, of course, does love battle chiefly as a means of winning undying fame; but he also seems to have an unholy delight in the sheer butchery of the battlefield. He appears to be happiest when his "unconquerable hands are besmattered with gore." When he is finally ready to go into battle against the Trojans he has no time to eat himself nor does he wish to allow the weary Achaean soldiers a respite for food; his one thought is of "blood and slaughter and the groans of dying men." The following are only two from among many passages that show his delight in the bloody business of the battlefield. While Achilles is slaying Trojans right and left Tros, a young Trojan warrior clasps his knees and begs for mercy, to no avail.

> Achilles [says Homer] was not kind or tender-hearted, but a man of fierce passions; and when Tros in his eagerness to plead for mercy put his hands on his knees, he struck him in the liver with his sword. The liver came out and drenched his lap with blood. He swooned, and night descended on his eyes.

But Tros is just one among many in the slaughter:

> Achilles then went up to Mulius and struck him on the ear with his javelin, so hard that the bronze point came out at the other ear. The next was Echeclus, son of Agenor. Achilles caught him full on the head with a stroke of his hilted sword—the blood made the whole blade warm . . . Deucalion next. Achilles pierced his forearm with the bronze point of his spear, just where the sinews of the elbow are attached. Deucalion, waiting for him with his arm weighed down by the spear, looked Death in the face. Achilles struck the man's neck with his sword and sent head and helmet flying off together. The marrow welled up from the vertebrae, and the corpse lay stretched on the ground. The next quarry of Achilles was Rhigmus, the noble son of Peiros, who had come from the deep-soiled land of Thrace. He cast at him and caught him full. The bronze javelin came to rest in his lung and he tumbled from his chariot. . . . Thus Achilles ran amuck with his spear. . . . He chased his victims with the fury of a fiend, and the earth was dark with their blood. At their imperious master's will the horses of Achilles with their massive hooves trampled dead men and shields alike with no more ado than when a farmer has yoked a pair of broad-browed cattle to trample the white barley on a threshing-floor and his lowing bulls tread out the grain. The axle-tree under his chariot, and the rails that run round it, were sprayed with the blood thrown up by the horses' hooves and by the tyres. And the son of Peleus pressed on in search of glory, bespattering his unconquerable hands with gore.

We get, in all this attention to the gory, anatomical details of the battlefield a fleeting glimpse into an ideal that is not too far removed from savagery. In this glorification of the butchery of warfare as a means to personal fame we have an aspect of the Greek epic ideal which contrasts sharply with that of the Romans. But whether it is won by wily debate or by prowess on the battlefield, there is no possible doubt that personal glory is the dominant element in the primitive Greek heroic ideal, and for Achilles it is definitely glory won on the battlefield.

17 It is also important to notice that Achilles is not criticized in *The Iliad* for his stand in the matter of his personal honor. On the contrary, it is conceded by the gods and men alike that he has a genuine grievance and

has a right to demand reparation from Agamemnon. In the first place his goddess Mother, Thetis, is on his side from the beginning. Achilles asks her to persuade Zeus to help him get amends from Agamemnon.

> "Persuade him [Zeus], if you can [he begs Thetis] to help the Trojans, to fling the Achaeans back on their ships, to pen them in against the sea and slaughter them. That would teach them to appreciate their King. That would make Imperial Agamemnon son of Atreus realize what a fool he was to insult the noblest of them all."

Thetis uses her influence with Zeus and wins a promise from him to espouse the cause of her injured son.

> "Father Zeus [she pleads] . . . grant me a wish and show your favour to my son. He is already singled out for early death, and now Agamemnon King of men has affronted him. He has stolen his prize and kept her for himself. Avenge my son, Olympian Judge, and let the Trojans have the upper hand till the Achaeans pay him due respect and make him full amends."

Zeus agrees to let the Trojans have their day in order to humble Agamemnon and exalt Achilles. "Zeus had in mind," we are told in Book XIII, "a victory for the Trojans and Hector, with a view to exalting Achilles." Again when Zeus assures her that the ultimate victory will go to the Achaeans, he reminds her that for the present the Trojans will be victorious to fulfill the wishes of Achilles.

> "But in the meantime [he says] I remain hostile to the Danaans, and I will not permit any other of the immortals to come down to their assistance before the wishes of Achilles are fulfilled, in accordance with the promise I gave him (and confirmed with a nod of my head) that day when the divine Thetis put her arms around my knees and implored me to vindicate her son, the sacker of cities."

This would certainly suggest that both Thetis and Zeus considered Achilles to be right. When the sea-god, Poseidon, is trying to bestir the disheartened Achaeans to make a last-ditch stand at the ships against the Trojans, he admits that Agamemnon is to blame for their sad straits by having insulted Achilles, but he says nothing derogatory of Achilles himself. This is part of his incendiary speech:

> "Now, they [the Trojans] have left their city far behind them and are fighting by the hollow ships, all through the incompetence of our Commander-in-Chief and the slackness of the troops, who are so disgusted with their leader that they would rather die beside their fast ships than

> defend them. Yet even if the whole blame does rest with our overlord Agamemnon son of Atreus, who insulted the great runner Achilles, we have no excuse whatever for giving up the struggle."

The gods, then, either take it for granted or positively state that Achilles is in the right and Agamemnon in the wrong, and they positively intervene to help Achilles achieve his end of humiliating Agamemnon and of bringing the whole Achaean host to recognize his own superiority over their king.

18 The attitude of the gods is echoed in that of practically all the important Achaean leaders. The first criticism of Agamemnon, however, comes by way of an ironic jest from the comedian Thersites. But what he says is not all jest. He accuses Agamemnon of practically all the capital sins—greed, lust, and cowardice, and then turns on the soldiery and calls them a crowd of women.

> "As for you, my friends, poor specimens that you are, Achaean women—I cannot call you men—let us sail home by all means and leave this fellow [Agamemnon] here to fatten on his spoils and find out how completely he depends on the ranks. Why, only a little while ago he insulted Achilles, a far better man than he is. He walked off with his prize and kept her for himself. But it needs more than that to make Achilles lose his temper. He takes things lying down. Otherwise, my lord, that outrage would have been your last."

When we recall the towering rage of Achilles and the fact that if the gods had not intervened he would have killed Agamemnon on the spot, Thersites' description of Achilles as a restrained man is highly ironic. Although Thersites is cruelly cuffed into silence by Odysseus, both Odysseus and the other Achaean leaders recognize that there is much truth in what he has said and say so themselves on other occasions.

19 The first to criticize Agamemnon seriously is wise old Nestor. At a council meeting of all the Achaeans, he tells Agamemnon that he was utterly wrong in taking Briseis from Achilles.

> "We were all against it [he says] and I, for one, did my utmost to dissuade you. But your arrogant temper got the better of you and you degraded a man of highest distinction, whom the gods themselves esteem, by confiscating his prize, to your own profit. Which brings me to my point. Even at this late hour let us take steps to approach and placate him with peace offerings and a humble apology."

That leaves little doubt about where Nestor considers the rights to lie. When the revered old Phoenix is trying to persuade Achilles to rejoin the Achaeans he tells Achilles he is overly stubborn for not accepting the reparation that Agamemnon has offered to make to him. But there is no suggestion that Achilles is wrong in his fundamental attitude toward Agamemnon; on the contrary, Phoenix admits that "nobody can blame you for the resentment you have felt till now." And Odysseus, in a speech which he makes to both Agamemnon and Achilles, when the latter has finally agreed to rejoin the battle, tells Agamemnon publicly to display all the gifts he has promised Achilles to advertise his willingness to make reparation to him, to return Briseis and to swear before the whole Achaean host that he has never slept with her. All this to vindicate Achilles. Achilles is also advised to show a forgiving spirit. But the final advice goes to Agamemnon.

> "Then, as a peace offering, let him [Agamemmon] give you [Achilles] a rich banquet in his hut and so complete your vindication. And may I recommend *you*, my lord Atreides, to be more scrupulous in your future dealings? It is no disgrace for a king, when he has given offence, to come forward and repair the breach."

Odysseus, like all the rest, lays the burden of the blame on Agamemnon. Agamemnon is never advised to forgive Achilles, because fundamentally Achilles has done nothing for which he needs forgiveness. Achilles has been right, and Agamemnon has been wrong.

20 And what does Agamemnon say about all this himself. He is the very first to admit that he was utterly unjustified in his conduct towards Achilles. It is true that he explains his conduct by blaming the gods for entangling him in a coil of Ate, but that still makes Achilles' resentment justifiable. In the very first public council he admits to Nestor that in the quarrel with Achilles he was the first to lose his temper. And this is his answer to Nestor's later advice that he make a humble apology to Achilles:

> "My venerable lord, the account of my blind folly that you have given us is wholly true. Blinded I was—I do not deny it myself. The man whom Zeus has taken to his heart and honours as he does Achilles, to the point of crushing the Achaeans for his sake, is worth an army. But since I did give in to a lamentable impulse and commit this act of folly, I am willing to go back on it and propitiate him with a handsome indemnity."

Although he throws more blame on the gods in doing so, Agamemnon later repeats all this and more to Achilles himself, when the feud has ended and Achilles is girding himself to go into battle once more.

21 It is true that Achilles is criticized by several of the Achaeans for his prolonged rancor, but nobody ever denies that he has a grievance and the right to redress from Agamemnon. And almost without exception, these criticisms occur in speeches in which the speakers are trying to persuade Achilles to get back into the conflict and save the sorely pressed

Achaeans. The speakers all try to show him that he is going too far in hanging on to his grudge against Agamemnon when the king has already admitted his fault and shown himself willing to make full reparation, but they all, like Phoenix, would admit that "nobody can blame [him] for the resentment [he has] felt till now." The old man Phoenix is the first to criticize him; Odysseus does so on at least one occasion. Diomedes is quite forthright in his criticism, as is Ajax in his, and finally even his friend Patroclus on the advice of Nestor tells him he has gone too far in nursing his grudge "warping a noble nature to ignoble ends." When Achilles finally does relent, like Agamemnon, he blames his stubborn wrath on Ate, a blind power that has possessed him; but, as we have seen, he never denies that he was justified in his fundamental resentment against Agamemnon for having so dishonored him in the eyes of the Achaean host. The only mistake he ever admits to is having harbored his indignation too long; the indignation itself would to him and to his fellow Achaeans look more like a virtue than a vice. Recall, again, old Phoenix' remark: "Nobody can blame you for the resentment you have felt till now." The whole action of *The Iliad* was designed to vindicate Achilles in his resentment.

22 It would seem, then, that a careful reading of *The Iliad* justifies the conclusion that Achilles is a man whose supreme value in life and death is his own personal honor and glory. He is a man for whom the Greeks would have had more admiration than pity. Certainly they would have had for him little if any of the contempt that we feel for a proud and egotistical individual. Difficult as it may be for us in reading *The Iliad* to tolerate the arrogance of Achilles, we should try to remember that for the Greeks he, like Odysseus, would have been predominantly an epic hero whom they admired rather than a tragic one whom they pitied.

ODYSSEUS, THE UNTYPICAL GREEK HERO

W. B. Stanford

1 There is nothing freakish about Odysseus's personality in the Homeric poems. In the *Iliad* Homer endows him with the normal qualities of an Achaean hero—princely birth, good physique, strength, skill in athletics

From William B. Stanford, *The Ulysses Theme*, second edition (New York: Barnes & Noble, Inc., 1964). Reprinted by permission of the publisher.

and battle, courage, energy, and eloquence. But in most of these Odysseus is surpassed or equalled by some of his colleagues at Troy. The Atreidae and Aeacids are of more illustrious lineage. Agamemnon and Menelaus are of more impressive stature. Achilles and Ajax surpass him in strength and force of arms. Diomedes is more gallant and dashing in battle. Even in oratory he is not unrivalled.

2 The fact is, of course, that Odysseus is not the chief hero of the *Iliad*. Achilles, and after him Ajax, Hector, Diomedes, and the Atreidae, are more prominent. Not that the *Iliad* presents Odysseus as a minor hero: he has his triumphs in the council and in the assembly, on the field of battle and in the athletic contests. But his unique personality is not allowed to divert attention from the Iliad's main themes, the wrath of Achilles and the death of Hector. On the other hand, in the Odyssey he, "the man of many turns," is the main theme, and his personal qualities become specially luminous against the sordidness of his environment, as he makes his way among foolish shipmates, ruthless monsters, and greedy usurpers. Yet here, too, Odysseus meets his equal at time. Eumaeus the swineherd shows a loyalty and gentle courtesy quite as fine as his, and Penelope is wily enough to outwit him in their final recognition scene.

3 By endowing Odysseus with a share of the normal heroic qualities Homer avoided any suggestion that he was an eccentric figure or a narrowly limited type. But at the same time Homer, especially in the *Iliad*, skilfully succeeded in distinguishing Odysseus by slight deviations from the norm in almost every heroic feature. In his ancestry there was the unique Autolycan element. In physique he had the unusually short legs and long torso described by Antenor and Helen. He reminded Helen of a sturdy ram, she said, as he marshalled the Achaean ranks. Any hint of the ludicrous in this comparison is removed by Antenor's subsequent description of Odysseus's imposing presence. But there is something a little unaristocratic, or at least non-Achaean, in this portrait, contrasting with the tall, long-limbed stature of the other heroes. Napoleon would have looked like that beside Wellington; or Cuchulain, that "short, dark man," among the taller champions of the Red Branch Knights. Possibly Homer meant to imply something more than a personal peculiarity here. It may be intended as an indication of some racial difference between Odysseus and the other Achaeans. Perhaps—but it is a pure guess—Homer regarded Odysseus as being partly a survival of the pre-Greek stock in Greece, an "Aegean" or "Mediterranean" type. At any rate, the physical difference serves to mark Odysseus out as exceptional, without giving an impression of ugliness, oddity, or deformity.

4 One finds the same distinction in a quite different kind of trait—in Odysseus's unusually frank and realistic remarks on the importance of food in human life. All the Homeric heroes were hearty eaters and drinkers. But,

whether by accident or convention, none of them except Odysseus had anything notable to say about eating. Perhaps it was regarded as a plebeian subject, unfit for high-born Achaeans; or perhaps they simply were not interested in it as a subject for conversation. It was typical of the average Homeric hero that he was prepared on occasion to ignore the need for food, both for himself and for others. The contrast with Odysseus's attitude is well illustrated in a scene between him and Achilles in *Iliad* Nineteen. Achilles, now equipped with new armour and ready for battle, is impatient to launch a general attack against the Trojans to take vengeance for Patroclus's death. Odysseus objects. The Greek soldiers have been kept awake all night in lamenting Patroclus and in preparing his body for burial. The Trojans, on the contrary, have been able to enjoy a quiet supper and a night's rest. Odysseus, not being blinded by personal feeling like Achilles, knows that unless soldiers get a good meal first they will not be able to fight all day: even if they are eager to continue the battle, "yet their limbs are treacherously weighed down as hunger and thirst overtake them, and their knees fail them as they go." There is both compassionate understanding and Napoleonic common sense here: the spirit may be willing, but the flesh is weak; an army marches on its stomach. Odysseus adds some further remarks on the strengthening and cheering effect of food and wine, and ends by demanding that the army should have a full meal before being ordered to attack.

5 Achilles's reply to Odysseus's reasonable objection is characteristic: "*You* go and busy yourselves with food: *I* shall not touch a morsel until Patroclus is avenged. And, let me tell you, if I were in supreme command, the whole army would have to fight fasting, too, till sunset. Then, with vengeance achieved, we should have a great supper." What is one to call such arrogant confidence as this—with no thought of fatigue or death, no consideration for himself or for others? Is it heroic, or is it schoolboyish? Is it superb singleness of purpose or callow rashness? Odysseus in his reply deftly and gently suggests that youthful heedlessness is partly, at least, to blame. Addressing Achilles with great deference as "Much the mightiest of the Achaeans" he admits his own inferiority to him in martial valour. But he claims definite superiority in thinking things out. Then after an appeal to Achilles to listen patiently for a moment (Odysseus clearly wants to avoid provoking Achilles's wrath again in any way: but he insists on making his point about the need for food), he emphasizes the danger of fatigue in war, and mildly ridicules Achilles's notion that fasting is a good way for warriors to mourn those slain in battle. Bury the dead with pitiless heart, bewail them for a day, yes—but those who survive must eat to get energy for punishing the enemy. Odysseus is trying to persuade Achilles to eat with the others. If Achilles fights fasting against a well-fed Hector, even Achilles may be conquered. Odysseus's arguments fail, as in the Embassy

scene, to overcome Achilles's passionate resolve. But, significantly, Athene intervenes later, at Zeus's request, and feeds Achilles with nectar and ambrosia "so that," the poet remarks, "joyless hunger should not reach his knees." Thus obliquely Homer, Athene, and Zeus agree with Odysseus's advice.

6 But the typical Homeric hero would probably have admired Achilles's intransigence more than Odysseus's more practical policy. One does in fact find an indication elsewhere in the *Iliad* that Odysseus had already got a reputation for being too much interested in the pleasures of eating. In the *Iliad* Agamemnon accuses Odysseus and the Athenian Menestheus of being quick to hear invitations to a feast, but slow to answer the call to arms. Odysseus emphatically denies any reluctance to join the fight, but he passes over the accusation of unusual alacrity in coming to feasts. Probably he thought it beneath contempt. Yet, as in Agamemnon's accompanying accusation of evil deceitfulness, it may well be that Homer intends us to catch a glimpse here of a general tendency to regard Odysseus as rather more partial to good fare than a hero should have been.

7 This is uncertain. But there is no uncertainty about the attitude of post-Homeric writers. Attic comedians, fourth-century philosophers, Alexandrian critics, late classical chroniclers, agree in accusing Odysseus of greed and gluttony. They based their slanders chiefly on some of his actions and remarks in the *Odyssey* which, considered out of their contexts, certainly do give a bad impression. Thus in the *Odyssey*, Book 6, Odysseus asks Alcinous to let him go on with his supper without interruption, remarking that there is no more shameful compulsion than that of the "abominable belly" which compels even a mourner to eat and forget his grief for a while. In Book 9, after the Phaeacians have given him a splendid banquet, Odysseus pronounces that he knows of no more beautiful consummation in life than a feast with good food, good wine, good song, and general good cheer. Later, after his arrival in Ithaca, when still in his beggar's disguise, Odysseus returns to the theme of hunger and appetite. He tells Eumaeus that it is for the sake of "the accursed belly" that vagabonds are compelled to suffer all the hardships of wandering from place to place. Later he tells Eumaeus again that in his opinion it is impossible to conceal the "accursed belly" when it is in its full fury: it brings many evils to men, and for its sake men sail the barren seas to attack their enemies. Soon afterwards he attributes a violent assault by Antinous to the promptings of his "baneful accursed belly." In the following book he pretends that he wants to attack the rival beggar, Irus, at the behest of "the evil-working belly," but repudiates a suggestion by a Suitor that he was good for nothing but gross eating.

8 If one remembers that no other hero in the *Iliad,* nor any Homeric

heroine in either poem, even uses the word for "belly" and still less discusses its effects, it is clear that Odysseus is an untypical hero in this respect. And it is obvious how easy it was for comic writers to portray him as a glutton, courtly critics as a crudely indelicate eater, and philosophers as a confirmed voluptuary, by concentrating on a few passages out of their contexts. Thus Plato was shocked at Odysseus's praise of banquets, as being one of the finest "consummations" in life. But surely the effusive remarks of an after-dinner speaker at a royal banquet are not to be judged as a solemn philosophical pronouncement. Besides, should not Odysseus's more sober aphorisms on the harmful effects of appetite in human life be weighed against this? And should it not have been remembered to Odysseus's credit how he had rejected the temptation of the Lotus-fruit and had resolutely held out against eating the Cattle of the Sun? When he eats "greedily" after his reception in Alcinous's palace, should we not bear in mind that (apart from a snack from the remains of Nausicaa's picnic in Book Six) he had not eaten for three days and had suffered terrible physical and mental agonies in Poseidon's long storm? Indeed, he had shown supreme self-control during his first supplication to Nausicaa: he had never mentioned food, but modestly asked only for a scrap of clothing and for information about the city. One almost loses patience with armchair critics who censure the conduct of a ravenous shipwrecked mariner for not conforming with the court etiquette of Alexandria or Versailles, and with moralists who demand the scruples of the confessional in the speeches of the banqueting-hall.

9 Odysseus's remarks on food in the second half of the *Odyssey* were less criticized, because he was obviously playing up to his rôle as a beggar in all of them. Further, as the Cynics noticed, he was a philosophical beggar. He showed that he understood the effects of appetite on men in general: how it drives men to war as well as to trade; how it moves the languid fingers of the courtier as well as the clutching fists of the starveling outcast. Yet he never suggested, as the more cynical Cynics did, that the belly was lord of all, and that he and his dog Argos were equally its slaves. He simply accepted it as one of the inescapable elemental forces in human life. Heroes like Agamemnon, Ajax, and Achilles, who had, as far as we know, never been compulsorily deprived of food in their lives, could nonchalantly disregard its demands. But Odysseus, by the time of his return to Ithaca, had become painfully familiar with the effects of involuntary hunger. Homer himself, if he was a bard wandering from audience to audience "for the sake of the accursed belly," may well have made Odysseus his own spokesman here. He, too, if we can deduce his personal feelings from the vivid description of the blind bard Demodocus in the *Odyssey*, Book

8, appreciated the comfort of having a basket of food and a cup of wine within reach to take "whenever his spirit prompted him."

10 The contrast here between the conventional hero's insouciance, or reticence, on the subject of food and Odysseus's frequent attention to it is one of the best illustrations of Odysseus's unconventionality as a hero. But Homer, perhaps for fear that his less philosophical hearer might fail to appreciate this kind of example, also exemplified Odysseus's uniqueness in a small matter that all warriors would notice. It is frequently emphasized in the *Odyssey* (and also mentioned in *Iliad*, Ten) that Odysseus had unusual skill as an archer. His triumph over the Suitors at the end of the *Odyssey* depended on this. But only a few, and those not the most illustrious, of the other heroes at Troy show any interest in the use of the bow. Indeed, there are some indications that archery was despised as plebeian or unmanly, much as a medieval knight of the sword and lance scorned to assail another knight with arrows. Perhaps Odysseus was merely old fashioned in his military technique. Or perhaps it was because the plot of the *Odyssey* demanded a triumph by means of the bow. But the trait does also serve to distinguish him from the other chief heroes. Another feature is far more peculiar. It is twice mentioned in the *Odyssey* that Odysseus possessed, and so he presumably used, poisoned arrows. This, however, like the Autolycan ancestry, is never referred to in the *Iliad*.

11 Though Odysseus's Homeric speeches were the admiration of every age of classical rhetoric, their excellence is not that of an orator among tongue-tied men. Oratory was a recognized part of heroic training. Thus in the Embassy scene Achilles's reply is fully as powerful and eloquent as Odysseus's pleadings. At times, too, Nestor's speeches in council are as wise and cogent as Odysseus's. The difference is not one of skill. It lies more in the fact that, when the other heroes speak, their minds are obsessed with conventions and prerogatives or weakened by passion and self-concern. Achilles's wrath and Nestor's tendency to guarrulous reminiscences tend to make their orations more effective as expressions of prejudices and personal feelings than as instruments of policy. In contrast, Odysseus's speeches are strictly functional, as a rule, when he shows passion or introduces a personal touch it is almost always because it will help to achieve his aim—to quell Thersites and to rebuke the wavering Agamemnon or an insolent prince of Phaeacia. Those who consider passionate self-esteem an essential quality of the genuine heroic type may find this kind of self-possession mean or machiavellian. But, as Sophocles indicates in his *Ajax*, it is the faculty that maintains justice and humanity among passionate men.

12 Besides this functional difference between Odysseus's speeches and those of other heroes, Homer signalizes his oratory by a peculiar personal

trait. In Antenor's speech, as already mentioned, there is a description of Odysseus's curious habitual pose before beginning an important speech. He would stand with his eyes fixed on the ground, his body and gestures stiff "like an ignorant fellow's." His voice, Antenor adds, was of great power. But he seems to have controlled this Gladstonian organ with the deftness of a Disraeli: his words came smoothly, lightly, continuously, flake after flake like falling snow—perhaps in the quiet, level tone characteristic of adepts in the art of plausibility. The general effect, we are told, was overwhelming. Homer corroborates this impression in several scenes in the *Odyssey*, where he describes how Odysseus could hold an audience spellbound "like a skilled bard." Homer could hardly have paid a higher tribute to his oratory. Once again he identifies Odysseus's powers with his own.

13 In the later tradition Odysseus was often accused of cowardice. The charge was based less on incidents mentioned by Homer than on others first recorded in the post-Homeric tradition, Odysseus's attempt to evade conscription, for example, and in later versions of his conduct with Palamedes and Philoctetes. There is nothing of that kind in the Homeric poems. But one ambiguous incident in *Iliad* Eight left a shadow on his reputation for courage. The circumstances are these. A general rout of the Achaeans has begun. Agamemnon, the two Ajaxes, and Idomeneus retreat rapidly. Nestor is left behind in grave danger. Hector rushes forward to cut him down. Diomedes sees the danger and calls to Odysseus for help in rescuing the old king. "But," Homer records, "Odysseus did not hear (or listen to) his call, and sped on to the Achaean ships." The crucial verb is capable of two interpretations. It was left open to Odysseus's defenders in post-Homeric controversies to argue that Odysseus had simply not heard Diomedes's cry in the confusion of the general retreat. But his detractors could take it as a deliberate ignoring of a comrade's cry for help. Homer's own intention is hidden in the ambiguity. However, no matter what he meant here, he soon makes it clear that none of his heroes attached any blame to Odysseus for his conduct. On the contrary, Odysseus's prestige is at its highest in the next three books.

14 If one considers the whole of Odysseus's career, a general accusation of cowardice is plainly absurd. In *Iliad* Eleven, he stands valorously alone against the whole Trojan host. His bravery in the Doloneia is incontestable. Similarly it took the highest courage to vanquish the Cyclops, to resist Scylla, to overthrow the horde of Suitors. Yet Homer does seem to hint occasionally, not at cowardice, but at a kind of tension between prudence and boldness. Thus in Odysseus's brief spell as supreme champion of the Greeks in *Iliad* Eleven, he pauses for a moment to wonder whether it would not be wiser to retreat with the rest. He immediately reminds himself of his heroic duty, and, with a touch of fatalism, unusual in him, fights on. There is obviously no cowardice in this. On the contrary, the man who

fully foresees danger and then goes on to meet it is more truly courageous than an insensate Ajax or a furious Achilles. . . .

15 A commentator on Euripides's version of the Cyclops incident has seen something of a Hamletesque figure in Odysseus as portrayed there. This was possible in the atmosphere of the late fifth century. But Homer's Odysseus is obviously no indecisive princeling sicklied o'er with the pale cast of thought. His decisive boldness is made clear both at the beginning of the *Iliad* in his handling of the Thersites affair, and at the outset of his Odyssean adventures when he sacks Ismarus like any Elizabethan buccaneer or Spanish conquistador. He is "the great-hearted," "the sacker of cities," as well as the prudent and resourceful Odysseus. Yet in both these bold deeds his prudence is not entirely in abeyance. While he faces Thersites uncompromisingly, he coaxes, amuses, and flatters the other Greeks. Again in the sack of Ismarus he orders a withdrawal as soon as a counter-attack seems likely. His comrades refuse, with disastrous results. Odysseus calls them "great fools" for not obeying his prudent command. But when he first gave it, they, for their part, may well have thought his prudence was mere timidity.

16 The fact is that, even though no real cowardice was involved, Odysseus's gift for anticipating dangers and his readiness to avoid them when it best served his purpose, did separate him from the normal hero of his time. Whether one admires it or not, a certain mulish stubbornness in the manner of Ajax, a reckless *élan* like that of Diomedes, a readiness to let everything be turned upside down for the sake of some point of honour in the manner of Achilles, was more characteristic of the early heroic temperament than a prudent resourcefulness. When the typical hero found his path to fame and glory blocked, his instinct was to batter his own or someone else's head against the obstacle until something broke. The gentle Hector and the tough Ajax were alike in this intransigence. Odysseus was no less determined to gain his purpose; but he was far less intransigent. He was prepared to undermine an obstacle or to look for another path, to imitate the mole or the fox rather than the rhinoceros.

17 In the later tradition, admirers of the simpler, prouder kind of hero will despise this quality, calling it cowardly or opportunistic. Homer suggests no such disapproval. On the contrary the *Odyssey* implies that some such resourcefulness is necessary to overcome the trials of human life in general. Almost all Homer's more intransigent heroes die unhappily, Agamemnon murdered by his wife, Ajax killed by his own hand, Achilles slain by a cowardly arrow. Odysseus, like Nestor and Menelaus, returns home at last to live in peace and prosperity.

18 Odysseus was also the "much-enduring" man. Among the other Homeric heroes only Nestor, whose life had extended over three normal generations, shared this epithet with him. Why? After all, many of the

rest showed great endurance in battle. The answer seems to lie in a special implication in Homer's use of epithets in *poly*-meaning "much." As has been suggested elsewhere, it seems to imply variety rather than degree, especially in its active compounds. The other heroes were "much-enduring" in their own special forte, namely, fighting. But Odysseus and Nestor were men who had shown their endurance in an unusual variety of circumstances: Nestor because of his abnormally long life, Odysseus because of his enterprising nature. Here once again a clash between Odysseus's qualities and the typical heroic temperament emerges. Ajax or Achilles would never have been willing to undergo some of Odysseus's experiences—his three adventures in beggar's disguise, for instance, and his ignominious escape from the Cyclops's cave by hanging under a ram's belly (which was a kind of Trojan Horse stratagem in reverse). In the later tradition Odysseus is accused of ignobleness, even cowardice, for his readiness to employ disguise or stealth when necessary to achieve his purpose. Undoubtedly one can detect an element of Autolycanism here. But what was often forgotten was that these various examples of combined resourcefulness and endurance were generally used *pro bono publico*. . . .

19 All these deviations from the heroic norm are exemplified in the *Iliad* as well as in the *Odyssey*. The next quality to be considered has little or no scope in the restricted Iliadic *milieu*. It needs the more expansive background of the *Odyssey*. It is a quality that points away from the older Heroic Age with its code of static conventions and prerogatives, and on to a coming era, the era of Ionian exploration and speculation. This is Odysseus's desire for fresh knowledge. Homer does not emphasize it. But it can be seen plainly at work in two of the most famous of Odysseus's Odyssean exploits. It becomes the master passion of his whole personality in the post-classical tradition, notably in Dante, Tennyson, Arturo Graf, and Kazantzakis.

20 This eagerness to learn more about God, man, and nature is the most characteristic feature of the whole Greek tradition. To quote a recent commentator on Dante's conception of Ulysses:

> To be a Greek was to seek to know; to know the primordial substance of matter, to know the meaning of number, to know the world as a rational whole. In no spirit of paradox one may say that Euclid is the most typical Greek: he would fain know to the bottom, and know as a rational system, the laws of the measurement of the earth. . . . No doubt the Greek genius means many things. To one school . . . it means an aesthetic ideal. . . . To others, however, it means an austere thing, which delights in logic and mathematics; which continually wondering and always inquisitive, is driven by its wonder into philosophy, and into inquiry about the why and wherefore, the whence and whither, of tragedy, of the State, indeed, of all things.

This eagerness to learn is not, of course, entirely a Greek quality. Every child, scholar, and scientist, shares it. But it can hardly be denied that the Greeks were endowed more richly with intellectual curiosity than any other ancient people. More conservative cultures like the Egyptian and the Roman judged the Greek spirit of experiment and inquiry either childlike or dangerous. But, for good and ill, it has been the strongest force in the development of modern European civilization and science.

21 Odysseus is alone among Homer's heroes in displaying this intellectual curiosity strongly. There is an obvious reason for this. A spirit of inquiry would naturally get more stimulus from the unexplored territories of Odysseus's fabulous wanderings than from the conventional environment of the *Iliad*. But it was hardly accidental that Odysseus should have had these special opportunities for acquiring fresh knowledge. To him that hath shall be given: adventures are to the adventurous. One may well doubt whether an Ajax or a Nestor would have shown as much alert curiosity even in the cave of the Cyclops or near the island of the Sirens if they had been there instead of Odysseus. Odysseus's personality and exploits are indivisible: he has curious adventures because he is Odysseus, and he is Odysseus because he has curious adventures. Set another hero in Circe's palace or in Phaeacia and you may have some story like *Innocents Abroad*, or a *Childe Harold's Pilgrimage*, or an *Aeneid*, but not an *Odyssey*.

22 Odysseus's desire to know is most clearly illustrated in the episodes with the Cyclops and the Sirens. He himself asserts that his original motive for landing on the Cyclops's island was to see whether its unknown inhabitants were "violent, savage and lawless, or else hospitable men with god-fearing mind"—almost as if, in modern terms, he wanted to do some anthropological research. It is more the motive of a Malinowski approaching the Trobriand Islands, than of a pirate or a conquistador. But his crew did not share this zeal for knowledge. When they entered the Cyclops's cave, the Companions felt a presentiment of danger and begged him to withdraw. Odysseus refused, still eager to see what the giant was like. In describing the consequences Odysseus admits his folly here in the strongest words of self-denunciation that he ever uses (*Od.* 9). As a result of his imprudence six of his companions were eaten alive. It becomes clear later, in the Sirens incident, when Odysseus meets a similar temptation to dangerous knowledge, that he had learned a lesson from his rash curiosity, for he takes great care to prevent any danger to his companions from hearing their deadly song.

23 But Odysseus's motives in the Cyclops episode were not unmixed. He admits that his second reason for wanting to meet the ogre was a hope of extracting some guest-gifts from him—acquisitiveness as well as inquisitiveness. The post-Homeric tradition was inclined to censure Odysseus for

unheroic cupidity here and elsewhere. But other Homeric heroes were quite as eager to receive gifts as he. It was a normal part of heroic etiquette; and in general the Greeks always had a flair for trade as well as for science. Odysseus's fault lay not in his hope of getting gifts but in his allowing that hope (combined with curiosity) to endanger the lives of his companions. Homer left it to others to draw a moral. . . .

24 Odysseus's intellectual curiosity is presented in a much purer light in his encounter with the Sirens. Here no greed for gain, or indifference to his companions' safety, intrudes. Circe (who in Athene's absence takes her place for a while in advising Odysseus) has warned Odysseus of the Sirens' fatal attractions, telling him of "the great heap of men rotting on their bones" which lies in the flowery meadow beside them. Better not to hear their seductive song at all; but if he, Odysseus cannot resist a desire to hear it—and Circe knows Odysseus well enough to expect that he cannot resist it—he must fill his comrades' ears with wax and have himself bound tightly to the mast.

25 What happens in the actual encounter became one of the most famous stories in European literature and a rich source of allegorical and symbolical interpretations. Its significance for the present study lies in the nature of the Sirens' temptation. This was not based on any amorous enticements. Instead the Sirens offered information about the Trojan war and knowledge of "whatever has happened on the wide, fertile earth." To put it in modern jargon, the Sirens guaranteed to supply a global news-service to their clients, an almost irresistible attraction to the typical Greek whose chief delight, as observed in the Acts of the Apostles (xvii. 21) was "to tell or to hear some new thing."

26 As Homer describes the incident, the attractions of the Sirens were primarily intellectual. Merely sensual pleasures would not, Homer implies (and Cicero later insists), have allured him so strongly. He had resisted the temptation to taste of the fruit of the Lotus. But one must not overlook, with Cicero, the effect of their melodious song and their unrivalled voices. Music for the Greeks was the most moving of the arts. Besides, as Montaigne observes in his essay on *Glory*, there was a subtle touch of flattery in their first words:

> Deca vers nous, deca, O treslouable, Ulysse,
> Et le plus grand honneur dont la Grece fleurisse.

And perhaps their subtlest flattery was in recognizing Odysseus's calibre at once and in appealing only to his intellect. If an Agamemnon or a Menelaus had been in his place, they might have changed their tune. . . .

27 It might rashly be concluded from the preceding analysis that Homer's Odysseus was a man distracted by psychological conflicts and distressed by social tensions. The general impression derived from the Homeric poems suggests nothing of the kind. The inner and outer tensions are skillfully implied, but the total portrait is that of a man well integrated both in his own temperament and with his environment. As Athene emphasized, he was essentially "self-possessed," fully able to control conflicting passions and motives. His psychological tensions never reach a breaking-point. They serve rather to give him his dynamic force. As a result his purposefulness is like an arrow shot from a well-strung bow, and his energy has the tirelessness of coiled springs. Resilience, elasticity, concentration, these are the qualities that maintain his temperamental balance. In contrast the Ajax-like hero was superficially firm and strong. His code of conduct and his heroic pride encased his heart like archaic armour. Once this psychological carapace was pierced by some violent shock the inner parts were as soft as any crustacean's. Odysseus's strength and self-possession did not depend on any outer armour. He could be as firm and enduring in the role of a beggar or in the cave of a Cyclops as in full battle-dress at Troy. This was the quality that the Cynic and Stoic philosophers were most to admire later.

28 Such was his inner harmony and strength. His conduct in matters of major importance shows a similar purposeful integrity. He had a remarkable power of taking the long view, of seeing actions in their widest context, of disciplining himself to the main purpose in hand. Thus while other heroes at Troy are squabbling like children over questions of honour and precedence, Odysseus presses on steadily towards victory. And why? Not, Homer implies, for the sake of triumph and plunder, but in order to return to his beloved Ithaca as soon as possible. Here Odysseus's efforts for the Greek cause are integrated with his fundamental love of home; *pro bono publico* is ultimately *pro domo sua.* Similarly his loyalty to the Companions during the fabulous voyages, and his patience with their infuriating alternations of rashness and timidity, were part of the same enlightened egotism: he needed a crew to sail his ship home. His love for Penelope, too, was, as has been suggested already, not based entirely on *eros* or *agape,* but also contained that *philia,* that attachment to one's normal and natural social environment which underlies so much of Greek happiness. And his piety is the piety of one who wishes to keep on good terms with the gods.

29 Such mixed motives may seem impure or ignoble to those who take their ideals from self-sacrificing patriotism, or from self-effacing saintliness, or from self-forgetting romanticism. But these are post-Homeric concepts. Within the context of the Heroic Age and perhaps of the Homeric Age, too, this identification of one's own best interests with the general welfare of one's kith, kin, and comrades, with one's *philoi* in fact, was a saving

grace for both the individual and society. All the Homeric heroes are egotists; but Odysseus's egotism has sent its roots out more widely into his personal environment than that of Agamemnon, Achilles, or Ajax.

30 One other aspect of Odysseus's Homeric character needs to be kept in mind at the last. In a way it is the most important of all for the development of the tradition. This is the fundamental ambiguity of his essential qualities. We have seen how prudence may decline towards timidity, tactfulness towards a blameworthy *suppressio veri*, serviceability towards servility, and so on. The ambiguity lies both in the qualities themselves and in the attitudes of others towards them. Throughout the later tradition this ambiguity in Odysseus's nature and in his reputation will vacillate between good and bad, between credit and infamy. Odysseus's personality and reputation at best are poised, as it were, on a narrow edge between Aristotelian faults of excess and deficiency. Poised between rashness and timorousness, he is prudently brave; poised between rudeness and obsequiousness he is "civilized"; poised between stupidity and overcleverness he, at his best, is wise.

AENEAS, THE TYPICAL ROMAN

C. M. Bowra

1 Virgil was not the first to write the epic of Rome. In the third century B.C. Naevius had used the old Saturnian measure for his *Punic War* and in the next century Ennius' *Annals* traced the Roman story from Romulus to his own day. The first of these poems must have had many similarities to oral epic or even to ballad; the second, despite its use of the hexameter and many effective adaptations of the Homeric manner, was built on the annalistic plan which is always liable to appear when poetry annexes history. Virgil knew both works, and his own poem must have been meant to supersede them and to give in a more satisfactory form the truth about Rome as it had been revealed to his own generation. To do this he adopted a remarkable method. He abandoned the annalistic scheme and instead of versifying history presented the Roman character and destiny through a poem about a legendary and largely imaginary past. His concern was less

From *From Virgil to Milton* (London: Macmillan & Company, Ltd., 1945). Used with permission of Macmillan & Co., Ltd., The Macmillan Co. of Canada, Ltd., and St. Martin's Press, Inc., pp. 33–85.

with historical events than with their meaning, less with Rome at this or at that time than as it was from the beginning and for ever, less with individual Romans than with a single, symbolical hero who stands for the qualities and the experience which are typically Roman. By skilful literary devices, such as prophecies spoken by gods or visions seen in Elysium or scenes depicted on works of art, Virgil links up the mythical past with recorded history and his own time. But such excursions are exceptional and take up less than 300 lines in a total of nearly 10,000. The main action of the *Aeneid* takes place some three hundred years before the foundation of Rome; the leading hero and his followers are not Romans nor even Italians but Trojans whose ancestral connection with Italy is dim and remote; much of the action takes place outside Italy, and when it moves there, is confined to a small area around the Tiber; Aeneas himself is a homeless wanderer who asks for no more than a few acres for himself and his company. This remote past is connected with the present by many ingenious ties. The Trojan heroes are the ancestors of famous Roman families and bear names honoured in Roman history; their ceremonies, their habits, their games, forecast what are later to be characteristic of Rome; they touch at places familiar to every Roman; into their story local legends and traditions are woven; the gods who support and sustain them are those whose cults formed the official religion of the Roman people. And more significant than these external connections are the Roman spirit, virtues, and outlook which the Trojans display. The difficulties encountered by these first ancestors, their relations to the gods, their emotions and their ideals, their family loyalties, their behaviour in peace and war, their attitude to the divine task laid upon them, are somehow typical and representative of the Romans as they were believed to have always been. Virgil is less concerned with origins than with a permanent reality as it was displayed from the first and is still being displayed in his own time.

2 Such a plan and such a purpose demanded a new kind of poetry, and when we turn from the *Iliad* to the *Aeneid*, it is clear that the whole outlook is different and that Virgil has a new vision of human nature and of heroic virtue. Homer concentrates on individuals and their destinies. The dooms of Achilles and Hector dominate his design; their characters determine the action. But from the start Virgil shows that his special concern is the destiny not of a man but of a nation, not of Aeneas but of Rome. Though he opens with "Arms and the man" and suggests that his hero is another Achilles or Odysseus, he has, before his first paragraph is finished, shown that he reaches beyond Aeneas to the long history that followed from him:

> whence came the Latin race,
> The Alban sires and lofty walls of Rome.

Soon afterwards, when he has noted the obstacles which the Trojans meet in their wanderings, he again ends a period on a similar note:

> So vast a task to found the Roman race.

Then, when Venus complains that her son, Aeneas, is unjustly treated, Jupiter replies not only by promising that all will be well with Aeneas but by giving a prophetic sketch of Roman history to Julius Caesar. The reward which the ancestor of the Roman race is to receive is much more than his own success or glory, more even than his settlement in Italy; it is the assurance of Rome's destiny, of universal and unending dominion:

> To them I give no bounds in space or time
> But empire without end.

At the outset Virgil shows what kind of destiny is the subject of his poem. The wanderings and sufferings and ultimate success of Aeneas and his followers are but a preliminary and a preparation for a much vaster theme. It was with reason that Petronius, like Tennyson, called the poet "Roman Virgil."

3 The fundamental theme of the *Aeneid* is the destiny of Rome as it was revealed in this mythical dawn of history before Rome itself existed. This destiny is presented in the person of Aeneas who not only struggles and suffers for the Rome that is to be but is already a typical Roman. If his individual fortune is subordinate to the fortune of Rome, his character shows what Romans are. He is Virgil's hero in a new kind of heroic poem, and in him we see how different Virgil's epic vision is from Homer's. Aeneas is Virgil's own creation, conceived with the special purpose of showing what a Roman hero is. Unlike Homer, Virgil owes little in his hero's character to tradition. Whereas Homer had to conform to established notions and make his Achilles "swift of foot," his Agamemnon "king of men" and his Odysseus "of many wiles," Virgil was bound by no such obligations. He could find his characters where he chose and shape them to suit his own purpose. His Aeneas owes something to Homeric precedent in being a great warrior and a devout servant of the gods, but he has taken on a new personality and is the true child of Virgil's brooding meditation and imaginative vision. The persons of the *Aeneid* are created and fashioned for a special purpose. They contribute to the main design, and everything that they say or do may be considered in the light of Rome's destiny. For this reason it is wrong to treat them as if they were dramatic characters like Homer's. They are more, and they are less. They are more, because they stand for something outside themselves, for something typically and essentially Roman; they are types, examples, symbols. And

they are less, because any typical character will lack the lineaments and idiosyncrasies, the personal appeal and the intimate claims, of a character who is created for his own sake and for the poet's pleasure in him. . . .

4 Against the imperfect types of Turnus and Dido Virgil had to set his own reformed and Roman ideal of manhood. His task was indeed difficult. He had to create a man who should on the one hand be comparable to the noblest Homeric heroes in such universally honoured qualities as courage and endurance and on the other hand should present in himself the qualities which the Augustan age admired beyond all others but which had meant nothing to Homer. Virgil's treatment of Dido and Turnus shows that his new hero could not be ruled by the self-assertive spirit and cult of honour which inspired the heroic outlook; he must be based on some other principle more suited to an age of peace and order. But if he was to rival Achilles and Odysseus, he must be a great man and ruler of men. Virgil had to present a hero who appealed both by his greatness and by his goodness, by his superior gifts and by his Roman *virtus*. On the one hand he must be a fitting member of the heroic age to which legend assigned him, and on the other he must represent in its fullness and variety the new idea of manhood which Augustus advocated and proclaimed as characteristically Roman. The result was Aeneas, a character so compounded of different elements that he has often been derided even by those who love Virgil. Yet to him Virgil gave his deepest meditations and some of his finest poetry. To understand him we must try to recapture some of the ideas and sentiments of the Augustan age.

5 Aeneas comes from Homer, and in the *Aeneid* he is presented as a great warrior who is almost the equal of Hector. To him Hector appears after death, as to his legitimate successor in the defence of Troy. Andromache associates him with Hector when she asks if the boy Ascanius has the courage and the spirit of his father Aeneas and his uncle Hector. Aeneas' fame has spread through the whole world, and Dido knows all about him before she sees him, while in Italy Pallas is amazed that so renowned a man should appear before him on the Tiber. He has the heroic qualities of divine blood, prowess in war, personal beauty, and power to command men. But he has something more than this. His essential quality, as his distinguishing epithet of *pius* shows, is his *pietas*, his devotion to the gods and to all their demands. When Iloneus speaks of him to Dido, he shows the combination of qualities in Aeneas:

> A king we had, Aeneas: none more just,
> More righteous, more renowned in war and arms.

Aeneas is not only a great soldier; he is a good man. So to some degree, Homer had made him when he told of his many sacrifices to Poseidon, but

Virgil enlarges the concept of this goodness until it covers much more than the performance of religious rites. Aeneas' *pietas* is shown in his devotion to his country, to his father, to his wife, to his child, to his followers and above all to the many duties and the special task which the gods lay on him. He is *pius* because he does what a good man should. The epithet which Virgil gives him is unlike the epithets which Homer gives to his heroes. For while these denote physical characteristics or qualities useful in war, *pius* indicates a spiritual quality which has nothing to do with war and is specially concerned with the relations between Aeneas and the gods. Thus at the start Virgil's hero is set in a different order of things and claims a different kind of attention. In this unprecedented epithet for an epic hero and in all that it implies is the clue to Virgil's conception of Aeneas.

6 Aeneas is *pius*, but he is not a perfect and ideal man throughout the poem. The indignation which he has excited in more than one critic for his obvious faults shows not that Virgil's idea of goodness was singularly unlike our own but that he chose to show a good man in the making and the means by which he is made. To understand Aeneas we must understand the scheme by which Virgil presents him, a scheme based on the moral views of the Augustan age but modified by Virgil's own beliefs and admirations. The clue to Aeneas is that he is built on a Stoic plan. St. Augustine hints at this when he touches on Aeneas' treatment of Dido and treats it as being typically Stoic because while he sheds tears for her, his purpose is not shaken by her sufferings:

> His mind unmoved, his tears fall down in vain.

It is not certain that St. Augustine interprets the line correctly, but his main conclusion is right. Aeneas has undeniably something Stoic about him which accounts for the alleged paradoxes and contradictions of his character. There is nothing strange in this. In the moral reforms which Augustus preached and planned a revived Stoicism took a prominent place. It breathes through the patriotic odes of Horace, and it survived through the first two centuries A.D. Originally Stoicism was a creed to meet the horrors of an age in which there was no political or personal security. Against this disorder it set the citadel of a man's soul in which he could live at peace with himself and with the universe and by subduing his emotions be undismayed at whatever might happen. The Augustan Romans took over this creed and gave it a new reference. It suited them because it disapproved of self-assertion and ambition and laid great emphasis on social duties. It was well suited to an age which hoped to recover from the excesses of unfettered individualism. The quiet, self-denying, self-sacrificing citizen who was prepared to do what he was told was a type dear to Augustus. Virgil knew the theory and the doctrine, and though in his youth he had leaned towards Epicurus, he was deeply affected by them. . . .

7 In his relations with Dido Aeneas fails though not quite in the way that modern critics find so deplorable. What is wrong is not his desertion of her, which is ordered by the gods and necessary for the fulfilment of his task in Italy, but his surrender in the first place to her love and his subsequent neglect of his real duty which lies away from Carthage. Virgil does not show clearly what Aeneas' motives are; they seem at least not to be love for Dido, for whom he shows little more than grateful affection. But of his fault there is no question; it is neglect and forgetfulness of duty. Mercury, sent by Jupiter, makes it quite clear:

> Forgetful of thy realm and fate!

This forgetfulness, due perhaps to sloth and love of ease, is a kind of intemperance, a failure in moderation, a state of false pleasure in which a temporary advantage is mistaken for a real good. Aeneas' duty, as Mercury tells him, is owed to his son, and he must do it. This is precisely what he tells Dido, and though her furious reception of his defence makes it look feeble, it is all that he can say, and it is right. Nor would it perhaps have seemed so weak to a Roman. For his duty is concerned with the foundation of Rome, and it cannot be right to set a woman's feelings before that destiny. Aeneas is fond of Dido and feels pity for her, but his conscience is stronger than his emotions and wins in the end. When he leaves her, he acts as a Stoic should, and undoes, so far as he can, the evil which he has committed by allowing himself to forget his task in her company.

8 In Book V Aeneas is faced with another crisis. During the Funeral Games of his father, the women of his company, stirred up by Juno's agent, begin to burn his ships with the purpose of keeping him in Sicily. Aeneas sees the havoc that they have started and prays to Jupiter to stop it. Jupiter sends rain and the fire is quenched. But even after this display of divine help, Aeneas is full of misgivings:

> But prince Aeneas, by that sad mischance
> Sore stricken, rolls the burden of his thoughts
> This way and that. There should he make his home,
> Heedless of fate, or grasp Italian shores?

It seems almost incredible that Aeneas should at this juncture think of abandoning his quest. Yet he does, and it shows how deeply his emotions still rule him. The catastrophe of the burned ships has filled him with such despair that for the moment he ceases to believe in his destiny. Fortunately he is saved by the old sailor Nautes, who not only gives him sensible advice about leaving the women in Sicily and sailing with the rest of his company, but sums up the situation in a way that must have appealed to every Roman conscience:

> Go, goddess' son, where fate drives—back or on.
> Endurance conquers fortune, come what may.

The fate which Aeneas should follow is the destiny which the gods have given him, and he should be master enough of himself to know this. Nautes brings him to his senses, and when this advice is fortified by words from the spirit of Anchises, Aeneas recovers his confidence and sets sail for Italy. He never again allows his feelings to *obscure* his knowledge of his duty.

9 Once he lands in Italy Aeneas is a new man. He makes no more mistakes, and always does what is right in the circumstances. He is never again assailed by doubt or despair; his only hesitations are about the right means to the known end, and these after due consideration he finds. . . . When Aeneas touches the fated soil of Italy, he has learned his lessons and found that self-control and wisdom which the Stoics regarded as the mark of a good man. His earlier adventures and mistakes have not been in vain. For they have made him surer of himself and more confident of the divine destiny which leads him.

10 The Stoic ideas which inform Virgil's conception of Aeneas' ordeal and development persist to some degree in the later books of the *Aeneid*, but with a different purpose. Aeneas is the just and wise prince, and he must not act unjustly, particularly in such important matters as peace and war, about which the Augustan age had been taught by bitter experience to hold strong views. Aeneas is very like an invader, and he lives in a heroic past, but he must not be allowed to make war as Homer's heroes make it, simply to indulge his own desire for glory. For this reason Virgil makes Aeneas face war with a consciousness of grave responsibilities and of nice distinctions between moral issues. Just as Cicero says that the only right reason for declaring war is that "life may be lived in peace without wrong," so Virgil is careful to put Aeneas in the right when war is forced upon him by the Latins. Earlier versions of the story said that the Trojans began the attack and were resisted by the Latins; Virgil reverses the situation and makes Aeneas do everything to secure his aims by peaceful negotiations. His envoy makes the most modest demands of King Latinus, and the king is perfectly willing to accede to them. When war is begun by the Latins, Aeneas conducts it in the spirit which Cicero advocates, "that nothing should be sought but peace." Even after the aggression of the Latins, Aeneas tells their envoys, who ask for leave to bury the dead, that he is willing to grant much more than that:

> Peace for the dead and slain in war you ask.
> I'd grant it gladly to the living too.

When the truce is broken, his chief thought is to have it restored. He tries to avert a general slaughter and offers to settle the issue by a single combat between himself and Turnus. He cries out to the excited armies:

> Oh stay your wrath! The pact is made, and all
> The rules are fixt. My right to fight alone!

In this we hear the spirit of the Augustan age as its master proclaimed it when he said that he himself had never made war "without just and necessary reasons" and that he always pardoned his enemies when the general safety allowed. Such an attitude towards war bears no resemblance to anything heroic or Homeric. War had become an evil which may be undertaken only when there is no alternative, and it must be conducted in a spirit of chivalry and clemency.

11 Though Aeneas is built largely on a Stoic plan and conforms in some important respects to the Stoic ideal of the wise man, he is not only this. He has other qualities which lie outside the Stoic purview and are even hostile to it. This is not hard to understand. The Stoic ideal, interesting though it is as an attempt to set a man above his troubles and his failings and to provide him with a feeling of security in a disordered society, failed to conquer mankind because it denied the worth of much that the human heart thinks holy and will not willingly forgo. St. Augustine was not alone in feeling that the Stoics were inhuman in their attempt to suppress all emotions, no matter how reputable. Many other men felt that such an exaltation of reason is wrong in so far as it dries up the natural springs of many excellent actions. Though Virgil used Stoic conceptions for the development of Aeneas' character, his warm-hearted, compassionate temperament was not satisfied with an ordeal so cold and so remote. If Stoicism provides a scheme by which Aeneas is tested and matured, it does not explain much else in him. Aeneas, with all his faults and contradictions, is essentially a creature of emotions. It is true that at first these are the cause of his failures and may be condemned, but Virgil did not believe that his ideal Roman should lack emotions altogether. His confident Aeneas of the later books is still highly emotional, but his emotions are now in harmony with his appointed purpose and help in his pursuit of it.

12 The most important of these divagations from the Stoic norm is the part played by pity in the character of Aeneas. For many readers this is the most Virgilian of all qualities, the most typical and most essential feature of the *Aeneid*. When Aeneas sees the episodes of the Trojan War depicted in stone at Carthage, he utters the famous words which have so often been quoted as the centre of Virgil's outlook and message:

> Here praise has its rewards,
> Fortune its tears, and man's fate stirs the heart.

The words do not mean all that is sometimes claimed for them; they are certainly not a declaration that human life is nothing but tears. But they show that Aeneas on arriving in a strange- land feels that here too is not only the glory but the pathos of life. In his mind the two are equally important, and such a view is far removed from Stoic detachment. The same quality comes out when Aeneas sees the ghosts of the unburied dead wandering in the underworld and halts his steps:

> With thought and pity for their unjust lot.

He allows his compassion here to assert itself at the expense of a divine ordinance and to criticize the government of the universe. No correct Stoic would dream of doing such a thing, and it shows how strong pity is in Aeneas and what importance Virgil attaches to it. . . .

13 More surprising than Aeneas' outbursts of pity are his outbursts of anger and fury, which continue after he has arrived in Italy and are evidently essential to his mature personality. The Stoics would have disapproved of them without qualification. They defined anger as the desire for revenge and thought it odious because it makes deliberate and considered action impossible. Seneca says that it is the result not of goodness but of weakness, often frivolous or flippant, and that any good it may do in the way of punishment or correction can be better done from a sense of duty. Even Marcus Aurelius, who in many ways resembles Aeneas and seems to enbody the ideal Roman in his historical self, condemns anger with majestic austerity. In anger, he says, the soul wrongs itself; it is senseless against wrongdoers because they act unwillingly through ignorance, and it is not a proper function of man. Yet Virgil made anger part of Aeneas' character and a potent force in his warlike doings. It rises at the death of Pallas and takes the form of a violent desire to punish Turnus, though for a time it is exercised at the expense of others like Magus, Tarquitus and Lucagus, who do not share Turnus' responsibility for killing Pallas. In the second part of Book X Aeneas is driven by wild fury against all his opponents. He takes the four sons of Sulmo to be a human sacrifice at Pallas' pyre, and not all the admiration of Donatus—"how great Aeneas' virtue is shown to be, how great his devotion in honouring the memory of the dead"—can make us feel that he is acting humanly or even rationally. When Magus makes a pitiful appeal for mercy, Aeneas refuses with heartless irony and tells him that his death is demanded by the dead Anchises and the boy Iulus. He throws Tarquitus to the fishes and denies him the decencies of burial with the derisive taunt that his mother will not bury him nor lay his limbs in the ancestral tomb. . . .

14 The combination of such qualities in a single hero demands some explanation. It is sometimes said that in it Virgil modelled Aeneas on Achilles and did not reconcile the obvious discords. It is true that these episodes have their parallels in the furious revenge which Achilles exacts for the death of Patroclus. But if so, Virgil has failed to make his hero convincing or consistent. These outbursts of heroic fury ill suit the exponent of Roman virtues with his strong distaste for war. But another explanation is possible. Virgil liked and admired Augustus, and at the same time knew that Augustus' dominion was based on force. In his youth he had risen to power by a series of violent acts, which he justified as the vengeance for the death of Julius. Legends had gathered round this vengeance and portrayed Augustus as moved by violent and angry feelings. They may not be true, but they were circulated and known and had become part of Augustus' myth. After Philippi Augustus was said to have behaved much as Aeneas behaves after the death of Pallas. Aeneas refuses burial to Tarquitus and tells him that the birds and fishes will lick his wounds; when a dying man asked Augustus for burial, he said that the birds would soon settle that question. Aeneas is so angry that no appeal to the names of his father and his son moves him to spare Lucagus; Augustus is said to have made a father play a game with his sons to decide which should live and then looked on while both were killed. Aeneas sacrifices the sons of Sulmo at Pallas' pyre; Augustus was said to have sacrificed three hundred prisoners of war after Perusia on the Ides of March at the altar of Julius. Whether these tales are true or not, Augustus undoubtedly took a fierce revenge for the murder of his adopted father, and it is possible that Virgil modelled Aeneas' revenge for Pallas on it. He seems to have felt that there are times when it is right even for a compassionate man like Aeneas to lose control of himself and to be carried away by anger. This anger is thought to be good not only in its cause but in its results. It helps Aeneas to secure his destiny and to overcome those who resist it. Normally considerate and compassionate, he is slow to anger, but some things so shock him that they awake it, and, when it comes, it is terrible. At the back of his mind Virgil seems to have had a conception of a great man whose natural instincts are all for reason and agreement, but who, when he finds that these are useless, shows how powerful his passions can be. Aeneas, who has to subdue so much of himself, has also at times to subdue his gentler feelings and to allow full liberty to more primitive elements which are normally alien to him.

15 Virgil has put so much into Aeneas that he has hardly made him a living man. But though he lacks human solidity, he is important as an ideal and a symbol. So far from acting for his own pleasure or glory, he does what the gods demand of him. In the performance of this duty he finds little happiness. He would rather at times give up his task, and he envies the

Trojans who have settled in Sicily and have no such labours as his. His stay in Carthage shows how easily his natural instincts can conquer his sense of duty, and there is a pathetic sincerity in his words to Dido:

> I seek not Italy by choice.

He takes no pride in his adventures, no satisfaction in their successful conclusion. His whole life is dictated by the gods. They tell him what to do and make him do it, and he obeys in an uncomplaining but certainly not a joyful spirit of acceptance. He is aptly symbolised by Virgil's picture of him shouldering the great shield on which Vulcan has depicted the deeds of his descendents:

> His shoulder bears his grandson's fame and fate.

On Aeneas the whole burden of Rome seems to lie, and it is not surprising that he lacks the instinctive vigour and vitality of Homer's heroes. The new world which Virgil sought to interpret needed men like this, not heroes like Turnus whose individual ambitions lead to destruction. . . .

16 In the *Aeneid* Virgil presented a new ideal of heroism and showed in what fields it could be exercised. The essence of his conception is that a man's *virtus* is shown less in battle and physical danger than in the defeat of his own weaknesses. The chief obstacles which Aeneas finds are in himself, and his greatest victories are when he triumphs over them. Even in battle his highest moments are when he sees past the fury of the fight to some higher end of unity and harmony. Conversely, Dido and Turnus fail because, despite their innate nobility and strength of will, they give in to their passions and desires. Virgil's idea of heroism is quite different from Homer's because it depends much less on physical gifts than on moral strength and is displayed not merely in battle but in many departments of life. Moreover, Homer's heroes never question the worth of the glory which they seek, but Aeneas, hampered by doubts and misgivings, is unsure not only about his glory but about his whole destiny. This uncertainty is one of his greatest trials, and he shows his worth by pursuing his task despite all his doubts about it. His success is all the greater because it is won largely in spite of his own human feelings. In him Virgil displays what man really is, a creature uncertain of his place in the universe and of the goal to which he moves. To the distrustful and uncertain Augustan age this conception came with the urgency of truth, and Virgil's immediate and lasting success was due to his having found an answer to the spiritual needs of his time. In the vision of Rome he presented an ideal strong enough to win the devotion of his contemporaries, and in his belief in sacrifice and suffering he prepared the way across the centuries to those like Marcus Aurelius and

St. Augustine who asked that men should live and die for an ideal city greater and more truly universal than Rome. Once Virgil had opened up a new vision of human worth and recast the heroic ideal in a new mould, he set an example which later poets could not but follow. They might not accept his interpretation of human destiny in all its details, but they felt that he had marked out the main lines for epic poetry and that any new heroic ideal must take account of what he said.

BEOWULF AND THE HEROIC AGE

R. W. Chambers

1 What is remarkable about the Old English religious poetry (and the Old Saxon which was imitated from it) is this: that the metre, tricks of style, even the very ethical standpoint of the old war-songs are all pressed into the service of the Christian religion with a magnificent recklessness:

> Whither shall we go, if we betray thee, lordless, sad in mood, worthless, our virtue gone? In every land shall we be hated, despised among the folk, when the children of men, the valiant ones, make reckoning which of them ever best served his lord at the war, when on the field of battle hand and shield endured hardship in the struggle, smitten by the sword.

2 It is with these words that, in the Old English *Andreas,* the disciples of St. Andrew refuse to desert their master when bound on a rather desperate missionary journey to the land of the cannibals.

3 Now it seems clear that *Beowulf* was written under the influence of this vernacular Christian poetry. It may have been inspired by lost works of Caedmon and of Aldhelm. At any rate, there are striking points of verbal resemblance between *Beowulf* and the Christian poems of the school of Caedmon. And the whole spirit of *Beowulf* is Christian. It looks as if some man, by no means convinced that there is nothing "in common between Ingeld and Christ," had set to work to write a poem which should bring in the great heroes of Germanic minstrelsy, Ingeld and Froda, Hrothgar and Hrothulf, Siegmund and Heremod, Offa and Scyld. But the poet is careful to avoid anything incompatible with the Christian faith and morals. He goes further, and, after the manner of the Aldhelm, "works in words of Scripture among the more amusing matter.". . .

From *Man's Unconquerable Mind* (London: Jonathan Cape, Ltd., 1939), pp. 61–68.

4 In *Beowulf* the combination of Christian and heathen elements, though sometimes incongruous, is certainly better harmonized than in the passage from the *Andreas,* quoted above. The scholars of a generation ago were chiefly interested in trying to strip off the Christian element in *Beowulf*—the work, as they believed, of monkish interpolators and revisers. Thus they hoped to be able to disentangle the original heathen lays from which they believed that *Beowulf* had been pieced together. Here and there a stalwart scholar can still be discovered engaged on this labour. But most students have long ago abandoned the attempt, and have come to agree that "the Christian elements are, almost without exception, so deeply ingrained in the very fabric of the poem that they cannot be explained away as the work of a reviser or later interpolator. Whilst the episodes are all but free from these modern influences, the main story has been thoroughly imbued with the spirit of Christianity.". . .

5 A study of *Beowulf* can also be made to throw new light upon the study of Homer. For in both we have a picture of society in its Heroic Age. The society of *Beowulf* is in many respects cruder and less developed, just as the hall of Hrothgar is a less elaborate thing than the hall of Odysseus. But there is a fundamental likeness in the life depicted.

6 Now in Anglo-Saxon England this Heroic Age was brought into contact with Christianity, and with all the civilization of the Mediteranean which came to England with Christianity. It is just this which makes the Seventh Century in England so exciting an epoch. Christian gentleness, working upon the passions of the Heroic Age, produces at once a type which is the rough outline of what later becomes the medieval ideal of the knight, or the modern ideal of the gentleman.

7 In the Heroic Age, elementary passions are still very near the surface. This causes the tension in the twenty-fourth *Iliad*. In spite of the command of Zeus, in spite of the laws of hospitality, there is always the possibility that the wrath of Achilles may overmaster him, and that he may slay Priam within his hut. And the history of Europe during the incursions of the Germanic barbarians tells of many a deed as grizzly as that to which Achilles feared that he might, despite himself, be driven.

8 In the epoch of *Beowulf*, an Heroic Age more wild and primitive than that of Greece is brought into touch with Christendom, with the Sermon on the Mount, with Catholic theology and ideas of Heaven and Hell. We see the difference if we compare the wilder things—the folktale element—in *Beowulf* with the wilder things in Homer. Take for example the tale of Odysseus and the Cyclops—the No-Man trick. Odysseus is struggling with a monstrous and wicked foe, but he is not exactly thought of as struggling with the powers of darkness. Polyphemus, by devouring his guests, acts in a way which is hateful to Zeus and the other gods: yet the Cyclops is himself godbegotten and under divine protection, and the fact

that Odysseus has maimed him is a wrong which Poseidon is slow to forgive.

9 But the gigantic foes whom Beowulf has to meet are identified with the foes of God. Grendel is constantly referred to in language which is meant to recall the powers of darkness with which Christian men felt themselves to be encompasssed: "Inmate of Hell," "adversary of God," "offspring of Cain," "enemy of mankind." Consequently, the matter of the main story of *Beowulf*, monstrous as it is, is not so far removed from common medieval experience as it seems to us to be from our own. It was believed that Alcuin as a boy had been beset by devils because he neglected divine service in order to read Virgil. Grendel resembles the fiends of the pit who were always in ambush to waylay a righteous man. And so Beowulf, for all that he moves in the world of the primitive Heroic Age of the Germans, nevertheless is almost a Christian knight. If Spenser had known *Beowulf*, he would have found a hero much nearer to his Red Cross Knight than Achilles or Odysseus. The long sermon on humility, which Hrothgar preaches to Beowulf after his victory, is as appropriate as the penance in the House of Holiness which the Red Cross Knight has to undergo.

10 *Beowulf*, then, has this added claim on our attention. Here we find the character of the Christian hero, the medieval knight, emerging from the turmoil of the Germanic Heroic Age. Not but what many of Beowulf's virtues can be traced back to that Heroic Age. For example, Beowulf's loyalty, when he refuses to take the throne at the expense of his young cousin Heardred, is a part of the Teutonic code of honour, though a part often not put into practice. But the emphasis placed upon gentleness, humility, and judgment to come is a thing in which we can trace the influence of the new faith. In his dying speeches, Beowulf rejoices that he has sought no cunning hatreds, nor sworn oaths unrighteously: "For all this may I have joy, though sick with deadly wounds, that the Ruler of men may not charge me with the slaughter of kinsfolk." And he thanks the Lord of all, the King of glory, that he has been able to win such treasure for his people. And so the poem ends:

> So did the people of the Geatas, his hearth-companions, bewail the fall of their lord: they said that he was a mighty king, the mildest and gentlest of men, most kind to his people, and the most desirous of praise.

11 It was with reason that Professor Earle quoted the words of Sir Ector de Maris over Lancelot dead as being "like an expression of these closing lines of the *Beowulf*":

> And now I dare say, said Sir Ector, thou, Sir Launcelot, there thou liest, that thou were never matched of earthy knight's hand; and thou were the

> courteoust knight that ever bare shield; and thou were the truest friend to thy lover that ever bestrad horse: and thou were the truest lover of a sinful man that ever loved woman: and thou were the kindest man that ever struck with sword: and thou were the goodliest person that ever came among press of knights; and thou was the meekest man and the gentlest that ever ate in hall among ladies: and thou were the sternest knight to thy mortal foe that ever put spear to the test.

12 And the stories told by Bede are enough to prove that the combination in Beowulf of valour with mildness and gentleness is no mere idealization. Seventh-Century England *did* produce men of that type, as can be proved from many of Bede's stories, such as that of Oswin, King of Deira.

13 Many different standards and ideals were brought into contact in England in the Seventh Century and the generations following: the civilization of Rome, the loyalties and the violence of the Germanic Heroic Age, the teaching of Christianity. We see these things combining, in different ways, in the historical record of Bede, in *Beowulf*, in the Old English poetry dealing with definitely Christian topics. The elements are, as yet, not perfectly fused: from their combination the civilization and ethics of modern Europe were to grow in the fullness of time.

MILTON'S SATAN, A HERO IN REVERSE

C. S. Lewis

1 Before considering the character of Milton's Satan it may be desirable to remove an ambiguity by noticing that Jane Austen's Miss Bates could be described either as a very entertaining or a very tedious person. If we said the first, we should mean that the author's portrait of her entertains us while we read; if we said the second, we should mean that it does so by being the portrait of a person whom the other people in *Emma* find tedious and whose like we also should find tedious in real life. For it is a very old critical discovery that the imitation in art of unpleasing objects may be a pleasing imitation. In the same way, the proposition that Milton's Satan is a magnificent character may bear two senses. It may mean that Milton's presentation of him is a magnificent poetical achievement

From A *Preface to Paradise Lost* (London: Oxford University Press, 1952), pp. 92–100. Reprinted by permission of Oxford University Press.

which engages the attention and excites the admiration of the reader. On the other hand, it may mean that the real being (if any) whom Milton is depicting, or any real being like Satan if there were one, or a real human being in so far as he resembles Milton's Satan, is or ought to be an object of admiration and sympathy, conscious or unconscious, on the part of the poet or his readers or both. The first, so far as I know, has never till modern times been denied; the second, never affirmed before the times of Blake and Shelley—for when Dryden said that Satan was Milton's "hero" he meant something quite different. It is, in my opinion, wholly erroneous. In saying this I have, however, trespassed beyond the bounds of purely literary criticism. In what follows, therefore, I shall not labour directly to convert those who admire Satan, but only to make a little clearer what it is they are admiring. That Milton could not have shared their admiration will then, I hope, need no argument.

2 The main difficulty is that any real exposition of the Satanic character and the Satanic predicament is likely to provoke the question "Do you, then, regard *Paradise Lost* as a comic poem?" To this I answer, No; but only those will fully understand it who see that it might have been a comic poem. Milton has chosen to treat the Satanic predicament in the epic form and has therefore subordinated the absurdity of Satan to the misery which he suffers and inflicts. Another author, Meredith, has treated it as comedy with consequent subordination of its tragic elements. But *The Egoist* remains, none the less, a pendant to *Paradise Lost*, and just as Meredith cannot exclude all pathos from Sir Willoughby, so Milton cannot exclude all absurdity from Satan, and does not even wish to do so. That is the explanation of the Divine laughter in *Paradise Lost* which has offended some readers. There is a real offence in it because Milton has imprudently made his Divine Persons so anthropomorphic that their laughter arouses legitimately hostile reactions in us—as though we were dealing with an ordinary conflict of wills in which the winner ought not to ridicule the loser. But it is a mistake to demand that Satan, any more than Sir Willoughby, should be able to rant and posture through the whole universe without, sooner or later, awaking the comic spirit. The whole nature of reality would have to be altered in order to give him such immunity, and it is not alterable. At that precise point where Satan or Sir Willoughby meets something real, laughter *must* arise, just as steam must when water meets fire. And no one was less likely than Milton to be ignorant of this necessity. We know from his prose works that he believed everything detestable to be, in the long run, also ridiculous; and mere Christianity commits every Christian to believing that "the Devil is (in the long run) an ass."

3 What the Satanic predicament consists in is made clear, as Mr. Williams points out, by Satan himself. On his own showing he is suffering from

a "sense of injur'd merit" (I, 98). This is a well known state of mind which we can all study in domestic animals, children, filmstars, politicians, or minor poets; and perhaps nearer home. Many critics have a curious partiality for it in literature, but I do not know that any one admires it in life. When it appears, unable to hurt, in a jealous dog or a spoiled child, it is usually laughed at. When it appears armed with the force of millions on the political stage, it escapes ridicule only by being more mischievous. And the cause from which the Sense of Injured Merit arose in Satan's mind—once more I follow Mr. Williams—is also clear. "He thought himself impaired" (V, 662). He thought himself impaired because Messiah had been pronounced Head of the Angels. These are the "wrongs" which Shelley described as "beyond measure." A being superior to himself in kind, by whom he himself had been created—a being far above him in the natural hierarchy—had been preferred to him in honour by an authority whose right to do so was not disputable, and in a fashion which, as Abdiel points out, constituted a compliment to the angels rather than a slight (V, 823–843). No one had in fact done anything to Satan; he was not hungry, nor overtasked, nor removed from his place, nor shunned, nor hated—he only thought himself impaired. In the midst of a world of light and love, of song and feast and dance, he could find nothing to think of more interesting than his own prestige. And his own prestige, it must be noted, had and could have no other grounds than those which he refused to admit for the superior prestige of Messiah. Superiority in kind, or Divine appointment, or both—on what else could his own exalted position depend? Hence his revolt is entangled in contradictions from the very outset, and he cannot even raise the banner of liberty and equality without admitting in a tell-tale parenthesis that "Orders and Degrees Jarr not with liberty" (V, 789). He wants hierarchy and does not want hierarchy. Throughout the poem he is engaged in sawing off the branch he is sitting on, not only in the quasi-political sense already indicated, but in a deeper sense still, since a creature revolting against a creator is revolting against the source of his own powers—including even his power to revolt. Hence the strife is most accurately described as "Heav'n ruining from Heav'n" (VI, 868), for only in so far as he also is "Heaven"—diseased, perverted, twisted, but still a native of Heaven—does Satan exist at all. It is like the scent of a flower trying to destroy the flower. As a consequence the same rebellion which means misery for the feelings and corruption for the will, means Nonsense for the intellect.

4 Mr. Williams has reminded us in unforgettable words that "Hell is inaccurate," and has drawn attention to the fact that Satan lies about every subject he mentions in *Paradise Lost*. But I do not know whether we can distinguish his conscious lies from the blindness which he has almost willingly imposed on himself. When, at the very beginning of his

insurrection, he tells Beelzebub that Messiah is going to make a tour "through all the Hierarchies . . . and give Laws" (V, 688–690) I suppose he may still know that he is lying; and similarly when he tells his followers that "all this haste of midnight march" (V, 774) had been ordered in honour of their new "Head." But when in Book I he claims that the "terror of his arm" had put God in doubt of "his empire," I am not quite certain. It is, of course, mere folly. There never had been any war between Satan and God, only between Satan and Michael; but it is possible that he now believes his own propaganda. When in Book X he makes to his peers the useless boast that Chaos had attempted to oppose his journey "protesting Fate supreame" (480) he may really, by then, have persuaded himself that this was true; for far earlier in his career he has become more a Lie than a Liar, a personified self-contradiction.

5 This doom of Nonsense—almost, in Pope's sense, of Dulness—is brought out in two scenes. The first is his debate with Abdiel in Book V. Here Satan attempts to maintain the heresy which is at the root of his whole predicament—the doctrine that he is a self-existent being, not a derived being, a creature. Now, of course, the property of a self-existent being is that it can understand its own existence; it is *causa sui*. The quality of a created being is that it just finds itself existing, it knows not how nor why. Yet at the same time, if a creature is silly enough to try to prove that it was not created, what is more natural than for it to say, "Well I wasn't there to see it being done?" Yet what more futile, since in thus admitting ignorance of its own beginnings it proves that those beginnings lay outside itself? Satan falls instantly into this trap (850 *et seq.*)—as indeed he cannot help doing—and produces as proof of his self-existence what is really its disproof. But even this is not Nonsensc enough. Uneasily shifting on the bed of Nonsense which he has made for himself, he then throws out the happy idea that "fatal course" really produced him, and finally, with a triumphant air, the theory that he sprouted from the soil like a vegetable. Thus in twenty lines, the being too proud to admit derivation from God, has come to rejoice in believing that he "just grew" like Topsy or a turnip. The second passage is his speech from the throne in Book II. The blindness here displayed reminds one of Napoleon's utterance after his fall, "I wonder what Wellington will do now?—he will never be content to become a private citizen again." Just as Napoleon was incapable of conceiving, I do not say the virtues, but even the temptations, of an ordinarily honest man in a tolerably stable commonwealth, so Satan in this speech shows complete inability to conceive any state of mind but the infernal. His argument assumes as axiomatic that in any world where there is any good to be envied, subjects will envy their sovereign. The only exception is Hell, for there, since there is no good to be had, the sovereign cannot have more of it, and therefore cannot be envied. Hence he con-

cludes that the infernal monarchy has a stability which the celestial lacks. That the obedient angels might love to obey is an idea which cannot cross his mind even as a hypothesis. But even within this invincible ignorance contradiction breaks out; for Satan makes this ludicrous proposition a reason for hoping ultimate victory. He does not, apparently, notice that every approach to victory must take away the grounds on which victory is hoped. A stability based on perfect misery, and therefore diminishing with each alleviation of that misery, is held out as something likely to assist in removing the misery altogether (II, 11–43).

6 What we see in Satan is the horrible co-existence of a subtle and incessant intellectual activity with an incapacity to understand anything. This doom he has brought upon himself; in order to avoid seeing one thing he has, almost voluntarily, incapacitated himself from seeing at all. And thus, throughout the poem, all his torments come, in a sense, at his own bidding, and the Divine judgement might have been expressed in the words "*thy* will be done." He says "Evil be thou my good" (which includes "Nonsense be thou my sense") and his prayer is granted. It is by his own will that he revolts; but not by his own will that Revolt itself tears its way in agony out of his head and becomes a being separable from himself, capable of enchanting him (II, 749–766) and bearing him unexpected and unwelcome progeny. By his own will he becomes a serpent in Book IX; in Book X he is a serpent whether he will or no. This progressive degradation, of which he himself is vividly aware, is carefully marked in the poem. He begins by fighting for "liberty," however misconceived; but almost at once sinks to fighting for "Honour, Dominion, glorie, and renoune" (VI, 422). Defeated in this, he sinks to that great design which makes the main subject of the poem—the design of ruining two creatures who had never done him any harm, no longer in the serious hope of victory, but only to annoy the Enemy whom he cannot directly attack. (The coward in Beaumont and Fletcher's play, not daring to fight a duel, decided to go home and beat his servants.) This brings him as a spy into the universe, and soon not even a political spy, but a mere peeping Tom leering and writhing in prurience as he overlooks the privacy of two lovers, and there described, almost for the first time in the poem, not as the fallen Archangel or Hell's dread Emperor, but simply as "the Devil" (IV, 502)—the salacious grotesque, half bogey and half buffoon, of popular tradition. From hero to general, from general to politician, from politician to secret service agent, and thence to a thing that peers in at bedroom or bathroom windows, and thence to a toad, and finally to a snake—such is the progress of Satan. This progress, misunderstood, has given rise to the belief that Milton began by making Satan more glorious than he intended and then, too late, attempted to rectify the error. But such an unerring picture of the "sense of injured merit" in its actual operations upon character cannot

have come about by blundering and accident. We need not doubt that it was the poet's intention to be fair to evil, to give it a run for its money—to show it *first* at the height, with all its rants and melodrama and "God-like imitated state" about it, and *then* to trace what actually becomes of such self-intoxication when it encounters reality. Fortunately we happen to know that the terrible soliloquy in Book IV (32–113) was conceived and in part composed before the first two books. It was from this conception that Milton started and when he put the most specious aspects of Satan at the very beginning of his poem he was relying on two predispositions in the minds of his readers, which in that age, would have guarded them from our later misunderstanding. Men still believed that there really was such a person as Satan, and that he was a liar. The poet did not foresee that his work would one day meet the disarming simplicity of critics who take for gospel things said by the father of falsehood in public speeches to his troops.

7 It remains, of course, true that Satan is the best drawn of Milton's characters. The reason is not hard to find. Of the major characters whom Milton attempted he is incomparably the easiest to draw. Set a hundred poets to tell the same story and in ninety of the resulting poems Satan will be the best character. In all but a few writers the "good" characters are the least successful, and every one who has ever tried to make even the humblest story ought to know why. To make a character worse than oneself it is only necessary to release imaginatively from control some of the bad passions which, in real life, are always straining at the leash; the Satan, the Iago, the Becky Sharp, within each of us, is always there and only too ready, the moment the leash is slipped, to come out and have in our books that holiday we try to deny them in our lives. But if you try to draw a character better than yourself, all you can do is to take the best moments you have had and to imagine them prolonged and more consistently embodied in action. But the real high virtues which we do not possess at all, we cannot depict except in a purely external fashion. We do not really know what it feels like to be a man much better than ourselves. His whole inner landscape is one we have never seen, and when we guess it we blunder. It is in their "good" characters that novelists make, unawares, the most shocking self-revelations. Heaven understands Hell and Hell does not understand Heaven, and all of us, in our measure, share the Satanic, or at least the Napoleonic, blindness. To project ourselves into a wicked character, we have only to stop doing something, and something that we are already tired of doing; to project ourselves into a good one we have to do what we cannot and become what we are not. Hence all that is said about Milton's "sympathy" with Satan, his expression in Satan of his own pride, malice, folly, misery, and lust, is true in a sense, but not in a

sense peculiar to Milton. The Satan in Milton enables him to draw the character well just as the Satan in us enables us to receive it. Not as Milton, but as man, he has trodden the burning marl, pursued vain war with heaven, and turned aside with leer malign. A fallen man *is* very like a fallen angel. That, indeed, is one of the things which prevents the Satanic predicament from becoming comic. It is too near us; and doubtless Milton expected all readers to perceive that in the long run either the Satanic predicament or else the delighted obedience of Messiah, of Abdiel, of Adam, and of Eve, must be their own. It is therefore right to say that Milton has put much of himself into Satan; but it is unwarrantable to conclude that he was pleased with that part of himself or expected us to be pleased. Because he was, like the rest of us, damnable, it does not follow that he was, like Satan, damned.

8 Yet even the "good" characters in *Paradise Lost* are not so unsuccessful that a man who takes the poem seriously will doubt whether, in real life, Adam or Satan would be the better company. Observe their conversation. Adam talks about God, the Forbidden Tree, sleep, the difference between beast and man, his plans for the morrow, the stars, and the angels. He discusses dreams and clouds, the sun, the moon, and the planets, the winds, and the birds. He relates his own creation and celebrates the beauty and majesty of Eve. Now listen to Satan: in Book I at line 83 he starts to address Beelzebub; by line 94 he is stating his own position and telling Beelzebub about his "fixt mind" and "injured merit." At line 241 he starts off again, this time to give his impressions of Hell: by line 252 he is stating his own position and assuring us (untruly) that he is "still the same." At line 622 he begins to harangue his followers; by line 635 he is drawing attention to the excellence of his public conduct. Book II opens with his speech from the throne; before we have had eight lines he is lecturing the assembly on his right to leadership. He meets Sin—and states his position. He sees the Sun; it makes him think of his own position. He spies on the human lovers; and states his position. In Book IX he journeys round the whole earth; it reminds him of his own position. The point need not be laboured. Adam, though locally confined to a small park on a small planet, has interests that embrace "all the choir of heaven and all the furniture of earth." Satan has been in the Heaven of Heavens and in the abyss of Hell, and surveyed all that lies between them, and in that whole immensity has found only one thing that interests Satan. It may be said that Adam's situation made it easier for him, than for Satan, to let his mind roam. But that is just the point. Satan's monomaniac concern with himself and his supposed rights and wrongs is a necessity of the Satanic predicament. Certainly, he has no choice. He has chosen to have no choice. He has wished to "be himself," and to be in himself and for himself, and his wish

has been granted. The Hell he carries with him is, in one sense, a Hell of infinite boredom. Satan, like Miss Bates, is interesting to read about; but Milton makes plain the blank uninterestingness of *being* Satan.

9 To admire Satan, then, is to give one's vote not only for a world of misery, but also for a world of lies and propaganda, of wishful thinking, of incessant autobiography. Yet the choice is possible. Hardly a day passes without some slight movement towards it in each one of us. That is what makes *Paradise Lost* so serious a poem. The thing is possible, and the exposure of it is resented. Where *Paradise Lost* is not loved, it is deeply hated. As Keats said more rightly than he knew, "there is death" in Milton. We have all skirted the Satanic island closely enough to have motives for wishing to evade the full impact of the poem. For, I repeat, the thing is possible; and after a certain point it is prized. Sir Willoughby may be unhappy, but he *wants* to go on being Sir Willoughby. Satan *wants* to go on being Satan. That is the real meaning of his choice "Better to reign in Hell, than serve in Heav'n." Some, to the very end, will think this a fine thing to say; others will think that it fails to be roaring farce only because it spells agony. On the level of literary criticism the matter cannot be argued further. Each to his taste.

THE TRAGIC SPIRIT IN MODERN TIMES

Henry Alonzo Myers

1 What is the tragic spirit? As an introduction to my answer, I shall quote two short poems on pain and suffering. The first is a translation from Sappho by W. S. Landor:

> Mother, I cannot mind my wheel;
> My fingers ache, my lips are dry;
> Oh! if you felt the pain I feel!
> But oh! who ever felt as I!

2 The second, entitled "The Mystery of Pain," is by Emily Dickinson:

> Pain has an element of blank;
> It cannot recollect

When it began, or if there were
A day when it was not.
It has no future but itself,
Its infinite realms contain
Its past, enlightened to perceive
New periods of pain.[1]

3 One reason why these two lyrics are memorable is that they remind us of an important aspect of suffering and pain, namely, of the sufferer's loneliness, of his feeling of complete isolation from his fellows. Sappho's poem reveals the sufferer's craving for sympathetic understanding and his despairing conviction that no one else can understand because no one else has ever suffered as he suffers. When we read Sappho's poem in a carefree moment, we may smile a bit at human nature because we know the answer to the question. "But oh! who ever felt as I!" The answer is, of course, everyone—without exception. To an actual sufferer, however, we would, if we could, answer the question as convincingly and gently as possible. We would offer the consolation and relief that come to the sufferer who knows that his suffering is a meaningful bond uniting him with his fellows, and not a void separating him from them. Indeed, to answer the sufferer, we would, if we could, be tragic poets.

4 The second poem is more intellectual and possibly less touching, but it has the merit of turning into explicit statement the sufferer's sense that he is cut off, not only from his fellows, but also from the past and the future. "Pain," says Emily, "cannot recollect / When it began, or if there were / A day when it was not. / It has no future but itself."

5 For the sufferer who cannot escape from the insulated awareness of his own pain, there can be no significant pattern evident in the ever-flowing now of experience. Living in a void without memory or hope, he cannot discover meaning or purpose in his being. Pain truly has an intensity which makes the sufferer forget its context, and experienced or considered by itself, it has a singleness, a uniqueness, which precludes intelligibility.

6 These two poems deserve to live, but neither has even the smallest place in the world's tragic literature. Lyric poetry is subjective and intensive: it is most effective when it does all that words can do to represent a single mood, feeling, or value. Tragic poetry is universal: at its best, it represents the sum total of all possible feelings, moods, and values. Sappho and Emily Dickinson deepen our understanding of suffering as a single, separate phenomenon, and of its power to cut us off from our fellow men and from the cosmos. Such a revelation of the nature of suffering is an indispensable part of tragic poetry, but it is only a part. Sophocles and Shake-

[1] Reprinted by permission of the publishers and the Trustees of Amherst College from Thomas H. Johnson, Editor, *The Poems of Emily Dickinson*, Cambridge, Mass.: The Belknap Press of Harvard University Press, Copyright 1951, 1955, by The President and Fellows of Harvard College.

speare show us the sufferings of individuals, but they achieve their tragic effects by presenting the individual sufferer as a representative of mankind and by showing us the justice which brings to every man equal measures of sufferings and joy.

7 Although Emily Dickinson wrote in the nineteenth century and Sappho more than twenty-five hundred years ago, their two poems seem quite modern in substance and spirit. Our own age—modern times—has thus far shown an acute awareness of pain as an isolated phenomenon, an awareness which characterizes its chief contributions in literature and criticism. Our modern world has been repeatedly described as a wasteland; our age is pleased to think of itself as peculiarly the Age of Anxiety; we have mourned over a lost generation; we have elaborated the theory that the artist is a sick man whose function is either to reveal his own frustration or to mirror faithfully the sufferings of a sick society.

8 These themes do not exhaust the wealth and variety of contemporary literature and criticism. Their supporters have, however, succeeded in making them seem to be the especially modern themes. One finds, therefore, in our climate of opinion a widespread assumption which reminds us of Sappho's "But oh! who ever felt as I!" and a resulting state of mind parallel to Emily Dickinson's observation that "pain . . . cannot recollect when it began" and "has no future but itself." The widespread assumption is that, because of his deep and unsoothed wounds, modern man is unique: other men in other times may have suffered as he has suffered, but they had remedies and consolations which we supposedly have lost. The resulting state of mind can be described as a kind of temporal provincialism. Believing himself unique, modern man is too often interested only in modern ideas and modern books, particularly those which faithfully portray his plight. He thinks of the great writers of the past as being great because they had something to say to the men of their own times, and not because they have something to say to him. He can appreciate only those writers who confirm his belief that modern man is unique.

9 Understandably enough, in an age preoccupied with suffering as a single, separate phenomenon, the words tragedy and tragic are commonly misused. To journalists tragedy is a synonym for disaster, calamity, or catastrophe, and tragic a synonym for disastrous, calamitous, and catastrophic. A flood washes away a dam; a drought brings on a famine; an airplane flight ends in a crash landing—such is the nature of tragedy and the tragic to modern journalists; the more unexpected, the more inexplicable the disaster, the greater is the tragedy. In common usage, then, the word tragic has acquired a meaning which is the exact opposite of the meaning it must have had for Aeschylus, who above all else sought to make suffering bearable by making it intelligible.

10 Modern reviewers, moreover, in applying the words tragedy and

tragic to current books commonly have in mind the popular rather than the original usage; a book is profound and tragic if it shows an individual living a life without meaning, or if it portrays the disintegration of contemporary civilization, or if, in the eyes of the author or of his hero, reality is a chaos instead of a cosmos.

11 The masterpieces of Sophocles and Shakespeare represent disasters as sensational and shocking as any so-called tragedy in modern life: the misfortunes of Oedipus, who blinds himself in an agony of grief when he discovers that he has murdered his father and married his own mother, or of Othello, who kills himself when he discovers the innocence of Desdemona, would be reported, if they were actual events, under headlines on the front pages of most newspapers. In *Oedipus the King* and in *Othello*, however, we find much more than the meaningless evil which confronts us in the report of an actual disaster. The disaster which overtakes the Sophoclean or Shakespearean hero is not presented to us as a single, shocking fact, meaningless in its isolation from other facts, but as a link in an intelligible chain of events. This chain of events reveals links between the fate of the hero and his character and between his prosperity and his adversity, and it furnishes us with the evidence which enables us to find in the worst evils that can afflict men proof that in human affairs an intelligible order prevails.

12 Since it is positive and affirmative, great tragic poetry satisfies our deepest rational and moral inclinations. As rational beings, we are always looking for patterns, for order, for meaning, in experience; as moral beings, we can be satisfied only by discovering in the realm of good and evil the special kind of pattern or order which we call justice. Tragedy reconciles us to evil by showing us that it is not a single, separate phenomenon but one side of change of fortune, and makes us feel that the change of fortune of a representative man is just.

13 Melodrama, it must be admitted, also satisfies our rational and moral nature: it too presents an order which is just. The inadequacy of melodrama arises from the fact that the just order which it represents will not stand the test of critical judgment. The first premise of melodrama distorts the facts of life. Men, we know, are neither angels nor devils. When we know only the good side of someone and know nothing of his weaknesses, we rightly think of him as being a bit too good for this world. And when, forgetting our better understanding of human nature, we think that someone has for his object in life a goal which he knows to be evil and evil only —as Mephistopheles has for his goal the downfall of Faust—we correctly think of him as diabolical. If such a person did live on earth, he would be a devil, not a man.

14 The conclusion of melodrama, which follows inescapably from its first premise, is also false to the facts as we know them. Poetic justice is

more often the exception than the rule; indeed we call it "poetic" justice because we have found it oftener in literature than in life. Sometimes, it is true, the innocent are rewarded and the guilty punished; more often the innocent and the guilty escape together or are punished together, as in war; sometimes the innocent suffer while the guilty go free.

15 No one has ever questioned the superiority of tragedy over melodrama. All who have known and enjoyed both testify that tragedy is greater and more effective because it presents a more convincing picture of man and of the relation between his grief and his gladness.

16 Tragic insight offers us a mean between all melodramatic extremes —between the extremes of optimism and pessimism, between the extremes of fatalism and utopianism, and between the view that man is naturally good and the view that he is inherently depraved.

17 The tragic artist is neither optimist nor pessimist: he represents good and evil as eternally necessary aspects of experience, and the relation between them as just. Change of fortune is the condition of man's destiny on earth; no man can hope to be happy and happy only; no man need fear that he may sink into endless misery. To the tragic poet man is like the sunflower. It is the nature of the sunflower to turn toward the sun, but it is its destiny to live half in sunshine, half in shadow. Similarly, it is the nature of man to seek happiness, but it is his destiny to suffer as well as to enjoy.

18 Tragedy reminds the utopian that suffering and all forms of evil are always with us—that change of fortune is the fundamental and inevitable condition of our experience. Whoever seeks to evade this inevitable condition merely hastens its fulfillment. Perhaps that is why, in an age dedicated to the task of bringing to all freedom from fear and insecurity, we are all so fearful and insecure. Certainly, by tragic irony, the utopian hopes of man are today closer to reversal than to realization.

19 On the other hand, tragedy reminds the fatalist that man can get what he wants—if he is willing to pay the price. Although he pays a heavy price for success, the tragic hero does reach his goal. Oedipus finds the unknown murderer; Orestes and Hamlet punish the murderers of their fathers; Medea crushes Jason; Tamburlaine conquers kingdoms and empires; Doctor Faustus has his four and twenty years, and Faust his fair moment; Romeo is united with Juliet in life and in death; Lear has ample proof of Cordelia's love, as does Othello of Desdemona's; Everyman is saved; Samson destroys the Philistines; Solness climbs the tower; Ahab hurls the harpoon at Moby Dick. Tragedy is not a spectacle of futility and frustration; it is a demonstration of the universal moral law: man gets what he pays for, and pays for what he gets.

20 The tragic view of man's moral capacities is again a mean between two extreme views. The tragic hero—the representative man—is neither eminently virtuous nor totally depraved. He has equal capacities for good

and for evil; he is free to choose between a good deed and wrongdoing, and is responsible for his choice.

21 These are the main features of the tragic spirit. It lifts us above self-pity and reconciles us to suffering by showing that evil is a necessary part of the intelligible and just order of our experience. It lifts us above the divisive spirit of melodrama by showing that men are neither naturally good nor inherently evil. It saves us from the pitfalls of utopianism and fatalism. It teaches moderation by showing that the way of the extremist is short, but at the same time it shows the man of principle that an uncompromising stand is not without its just compensations. And most important, it teaches us that all men are united in the kinship of a common fate, that all are destined to suffer and enjoy, each according to his capacity.

22 Since the tragic spirit lifts us out of the mood of disillusion, some of the tenets designed to preserve and justify this mood imply that in modern times the tragic vision is either an impossibility or itself an illusion.

23 The fact that we have produced no great contemporary tragedy—no picture of modern man which shows him as a glorious being, capable of reaching the heights and the depths and capable of discovering in his experience a meaning which justifies it—is proof, we have often been told, that the times are out of joint, that civilization is disintegrating, and that man in our age, in comparison with man in the great ages of Sophocles and Shakespeare, is enfeebled in spirit. The assumption behind this oft-repeated assertion seems to be that tragic poets in other ages have been able, without seeming to be ridiculous, to sketch their ideal tragic heroes from contemporary life. Is this true? Certainly not of the Greeks. The glorious company of Greek tragic heroes whom we know—Prometheus, Agamemnon, Orestes, Electra, Oedipus, Antigone, Medea, Hippolytus—were all legendary figures. Certainly it is not true of Shakespeare. His tragic heroes and plots are all drawn from the past, often the dim and legendary past—King Lear, Macbeth—and often from distant places—Caesar, Anthony and Cleopatra, Romeo, Othello, Hamlet. Nor true of Marlowe—Tamburlaine, Doctor Faustus, Edward II. Nor of Milton—Samson Agonistes. Nor of Goethe—Faust. Nor of French classical tragedy. Indeed, not until we come to Ibsen do we find a dramatist who repeatedly attempts to demonstrate the conditions of our destiny with models drawn from contemporary life.

24 One reason why the poets have either consciously or instinctively turned to the past in their search for heroes suitable for tragedy is that, to be dramatically most effective, the hero must be a person of some consequence, and yet must be a man like ourselves, and neither eminently virtuous like the hero of melodrama, nor altogether vicious like the melodramatic villain. To find such a person in contemporary society in any age is indeed difficult, not because they do not exist but because we cannot view

them without partisan bias. Men of consequence live in every age, and every man is a man like ourselves. But in a world of different factions, parties, sects, faiths, and nations, the contemporary hero in any age always has followers, who through partisanship are blind to his faults, and enemies, who are equally blind to his virtues. The saint is only a fool to the village atheist. And even after almost a century the birthday of Abraham Lincoln, who saved the American Union and freed the slaves, is ignored in the states which formed the vanquished Confederacy, which celebrate instead the birthdays of Jefferson Davis and of General Robert E. Lee.

25 Whether anyone has ever succeeded in writing a great tragedy with a contemporary hero is a matter of opinion. I have already praised *Moby Dick* as a tragic masterpiece. Ibsen's celebrated *Ghosts* presents a one-sided naturalistic picture rather than a tragedy; we see Oswald, never as a free and responsible man like ourselves but always as determined by past events, not as a man but as a mere ghost of the past. The plots of *Hedda Gabler* and *The Master Builder* are Sophoclean in their artful combinations of changes of fortune with reversals and discoveries, but their central figures are too cold and self-centered, too small-souled, to be fully acceptable as human beings like ourselves, a defect which can be attributed to Ibsen's limitations as an artist rather than to any loss in stature by modern man. Eugene O'Neill is more gifted with tragic insight than any other modern writer, and in *Beyond the Horizon* and *The Great God Brown* he has come close, and in *The Emperor Jones* even closer, to success in the attempt to invest figures drawn from contemporary life with tragic dignity. But although his best plays are poetic and tragic in other respects, their weakness in diction is a serious defect. Euripides is said to have been the most quoted writer in antiquity; Shakespeare has enriched the English language; but we never meet a man who can quote a line from O'Neill. Whether any other modern writer has succeeded in finding in contemporary life the model for a great tragic hero is also a matter of opinion. One point, however, is a matter of fact, not of opinion. It is not our age which alone has failed to write contemporary tragedy.

26 Further, the fact that our age has not produced an artist in tragedy to rival Sophocles and Shakespeare is no proof that the human spirit is becoming enfeebled. The thirteenth century and the eighteenth century were great ages, but they produced no rivals to Sophocles and Shakespeare. In every mountain range only a few peaks can stand out as highest; the best in every activity are, by definition, best because they are better than others; and they are necessarily rare. Between Sophocles and Shakespeare a period of some twenty-one hundred years elapsed; and since Shakespeare died only three hundred years ago, we can wait another eighteen hundred years before we need worry about the decline of the human spirit.

27 If we Americans search our civilization for an ideal tragic hero, we

cannot find him in literature; we must turn to life itself, and even there we can find, I think, only one—Abraham Lincoln.

28 Lincoln had artistic gifts of the highest order and an unsurpassed comic and tragic insight into the absurdities and depths of human nature. His less-gifted contemporaries could never understand how the Lincoln of the droll stories and politically effective witticisms could be the same man as the author of the Gettysburg and Second Inaugural addresses. As Carl Sandburg brilliantly remarks, limited and conventional worthies could never understand "the wriggling in one human frame of Hamlet and Falstaff." In an older community Lincoln might well have become a great comic and tragic poet. The frontier drove him, as a matter of course, into public speaking and politics, the only arts it could afford. His mastery of the art of politics equaled that of Sophocles and of Shakespeare in the theatre.

29 As President, Lincoln consciously aimed to leave the nation a solemn reminder of its historic meaning, a testament of faith worthy of a place beside the Declaration of Independence. In the Gettysburg Address he succeeded. But he rightly regarded the Second Inaugural Address as his own best accomplishment. In it he reveals his full stature as a perfect tragic hero and views the terrible Civil War with supreme tragic insight.

30 The address was delivered in March, 1865, at the beginning of his second term as President and about six weeks before his death. At the time, victory for the North seemed to be in sight, but in an uncertain world, it was not certain.

31 Lincoln's Second Inaugural is in length only a wonderful soliloquy, filled with tragic insight, but the hero and the occasion give it adequate magnitude. In it the hero reveals all his qualities: his strength of purpose, his depth and breadth of feeling, his ability to penetrate to the central meaning of events. First, let us remember his unyielding will, the fundamental intensity of the hero. "With firmness in the right, as God gives us to see the right," he tells us, "let us strive on to finish the work we are in." The "work" he refers to is the prosecution of the war, at first fought to preserve the Union, and now, two years after his Emancipation Proclamation, being fought also to abolish African slavery. Next we should notice the depth and range of his feeling. Although he is himself the central actor in the drama, although he has been vilified and threatened with death, and although he is each day tormented by the necessity of making decisions which go against the grain of a kindly man, he gives no thought to himself except insofar as he is one of the people for whom he grieves. And the people for whom he grieves are not the people of the North alone: "this terrible war," "this mighty scourge of war," has been given to both North and South. And finally, with his tragic insight, what does he see? Does he see only suffering—chance and meaningless? He sees a tragic justice in

events—not a melodramatic justice, with deserved victory for virtuous Northerners and deserved defeat for vicious Southerners. He sees a nation, with all its people, North and South, a nation which in its Declaration of Independence had published its faith in human equality to all the world, punished for its failure to live up to its faith.

> Fondly do we hope—fervently do we pray—that this mighty scourge of war may speedily pass away. Yet, if God wills that it continue until all the wealth piled by the bondsman's two hundred and fifty years of unrequited toil shall be sunk, and until every drop of blood drawn with the lash shall be paid by another drawn with the sword, as was said three thousand years ago, so still it must be said, "The judgments of the Lord are true and righteous altogether."

And with this vision of justice fulfilled through mutual suffering, he can look forward to reconciliation and peace.

> With malice toward none; with charity for all; with firmness in the right, as God gives us to see the right, let us strive on to finish the work we are in; to bind up the nation's wounds; to care for him who shall have borne the battle and for his widow, and his orphan—to do all which may achieve and cherish a just and a lasting peace, among ourselves, and with all nations.

32 Here, for once, life outdoes art: not only Ahab, but even Oedipus and Hamlet are outmatched. But no, on second thought, art had its share in the shaping of this hero and this occasion. Abraham Lincoln was himself a supreme artist. As a self-made man, through fidelity to principle he shaped himself into the ideal hero; and if we see in the great Civil War a step in the moral perfection of man rather than a meaningless collision of forces, we are, first of all, indebted to his fidelity to principle and to his tragic vision.

33 On a world-wide scale, this age is like the age of Abraham Lincoln, who said in 1858, three years before the Civil War:

> "A house divided against itself cannot stand." I believe this government cannot endure permanently half slave and half free. I do not expect the Union to be dissolved—I do not expect the house to fall—but I do expect it will cease to be divided. It will become all one thing, or all the other.

His words proved to be altogether prophetic; and it may well be that they fortell the course of events in a world divided now between freedom and slavery, just as they foretold the course of events in the United States a hundred years ago.

34 Our age is neither better nor worse than any other age. The life of

man—caught, like the heart of Gloucester, " 'twixt two extremes of passion, joy and grief," and often "alack! too weak the conflict to support"—is always tragic, in all times and all places. But this age, the age of the World Wars, is different from other and more serene ages in the degree of its intensity. It is a heroic age. Like the whalers on the *Pequod*, we are carried away by the iron will of the Ahabs who propose either to make us swallow their prescriptions or to liquidate us. Like Abraham Lincoln, the ordinary man in modern times is often obliged, against his desires, to be an extremist—to play the part of a tragic hero. As tragedy shows us, the conditions of human destiny are universal, and justice prevails in the lives of ordinary men as it prevails in the lives of heroes; but men should have the choice between the heroic and the ordinary, between intensity and duration. We, who would choose the little ups and downs of peace, are in danger of having war with its spectacular changes of fortune thrust upon us.

35 Like Abraham Lincoln, "fondly do we hope" that the world will become all free, and that freedom will come through the triumph of wisdom on both sides rather than through the judgment of war. If we are to realize our hopes, we need all the understanding and patience which tragic insight can furnish. We cannot meet the challenge of the times if we are sunk in a mood of disillusion and self-pity. We need to be lifted above the melodramatic mood which the spirit of war has brought, with the aid of demagogues, into our politics and our daily lives. Much as we disagree with their principles and condemn their methods, we must always see the people on the other side of any question, at home or abroad, not as melodramatic villains, but as men like ourselves, who seek the good as they see it, even though their clouded judgment and passions may bring about their downfall and involve us in their ruin.

36 And if war comes, as it came for Abraham Lincoln—if we are driven against our desires, as he was driven against his desires, to defend with the sword the union of free states and the dignity and freedom of the individual human being—then we shall have even greater need for the tragic wisdom which can find the significance of terrible events, which can assure us that fidelity to duty has its rewards, and which alone can use the common suffering of both sides in war as the means to their eventual understanding and reconciliation.

37 For the tragic spirit was the highest achievement of Athenian democracy; through Abraham Lincoln it ennobled this Republic at the time of its first great trial; and it alone can bring about that union of hearts which Alexander the Great once prayed for as a means of uniting Macedonians and Persians, and which must come if ever the sharers of a common fate are to be united in a worldwide society.

38 In modern times we are reaching the end of a long period during

which an optimistic faith in progress-to-happiness on earth has prevailed. The popular faith in progress was a great illusion; many good things, it must be admitted, came from it; and in spite of the sufferings of modern man in war and revolution—in spite of the tragic reversal whereby we seem more likely to turn earth into a hell than into a heaven—the old illusion dies hard. As both statesmen and demagogues know, many men in modern times, as yet unable to find a satisfactory substitute, still cling to the old popular faith.

39 Until recently our age has been too much under the spell of the great illusion of progress to discover the tragic vision. Our age has been too busy in its search for joy-without-sorrow to spare more than an occasional Melville to tell our tragic story, and too busy to heed it when it is told.

40 The ablest of our poets and critics have discovered the inadequacies of this faith and, in trying to come to terms with the stubborn fact that evil is an ever-present aspect of experience, have reached at least a partial understanding of the meaning of tragedy. The American critic, F. O. Matthiessen, for example, stressed the development of tragic insight from Baudelaire to Yeats and Eliot, showing the reaction by critics and poets against a groundless optimism and ending in the beginnings of tragic insight.

41 But the majority of writers and critics who have lost the popular faith in progress-to-happiness on earth have found nothing to replace it; they think of suffering as a single, separate phenomenon, and of modern man as unique, or almost unique, in his sufferings; they have lost the great illusion only to lapse into an empty and negative state of disillusion. Disillusion is the most overworked word in modern writing, both critical and creative, so that two forms of the word are needed to carry the burden. Some prefer disillusion; other prefer disillusionment, which may be a stronger form, meaning complete, permanent, and militant disillusion.

42 Since we have all lost some illusion, we can sympathize with the mood of disillusion. And since we have all suffered, we know that it is human—all too human—for the sufferer to cry out, "But oh! who ever felt as I," and to feel cut off from his fellow men, past, present, and future. But in modern times we have witnessed the hardening of the mood of disillusion into a creed, with tenets which have, after thirty years of overuse, become venerable clichés.

43 Because the creed of disillusion is only a rationalization intended to justify this hardening of an understandable temporary mood into a permanent attitude toward life, the arguments supporting its tenets are certain to be merely specious. Their disproof is not enough, however, to cure the ailment. Disillusion is an emotional as well as an intellectual state of being: what is needed is a view of life which touches the feelings as well as

the mind and which has the power to lift the viewer out of the narrow swamp of self-pity and on to the broad and healthy plains of a sympathy directed toward all men. What is needed is a remedy which will first make the disillusioned soul see and feel, as Matthiessen, Eliot, and Yeats have seen and felt, that "there is no such thing as good unless there is also evil, or evil unless there is good" and which at last will make him see and feel, as Sophocles and Shakespeare have seen and felt, that the rise and fall of a representative man is the symbol of a justice which universally prevails.

44 Tragic poetry, with its magnificent appeal to both feelings and mind, has this power—if we take it seriously. And why should we not take seriously an art which has brought deep satisfaction to many generations of audiences and readers, and which has never failed to win from perceptive and intelligent critics the tribute which belongs to the highest of the arts—the art which best reveals the full possibilities of human insight?

45 We can understand why anyone under the spell of the great illusion of progress must reject the tragic vision. As views of life, utopianism and tragic wisdom are incompatible. But the disillusioned soul—he who has lost faith in romantic optimism—is seemingly well prepared for the realism of the tragic poet, who through his courageous recognition of the worst succeeds in showing that the worst is the counterpart and proof of the best.

46 Here, however, we come upon the deepest resistance of the disillusioned soul to a disturbance of his mood and upon the tenet of his creed which is most difficult to answer. All visions of order and justice in the universe, he maintains, are illusions. Tragedy is realistic when it is seen only as a spectacle of suffering, but when we derive from it a sense of reconciliation, we are being lulled by a splendidly effective trick, whereby the artist imposes his own sense of form on the formless.

47 This argument, if valid, cuts both ways: if we apply it to the tragic poets, we must also apply it to the prophets of disillusion. For if all creative pictures of life are merely subjective, does it not follow that the disillusioned writer's picture of life is not, as his admiring reviewers maintain, a faithful mirroring of the inevitable frustration of man in a disintegrating society and a meaningless universe, but only a faithful mirroring of the futility of his own emotional attitude and of the chaos and incoherence of his own mind?

48 If such is the nature of creative art—if men are altogether cut off from knowledge of the meaning of human values and must live together by the flickering light of opinions dictated by different temperaments and intellectual capacities—whose company shall we prefer, whose light shall we choose? The tragic poet's or the disillusioned writer's? The disillusioned writer tempts us to indulge in self-pity by confirming the defeatism of those dark moments in which we can find neither rhyme nor reason in

events; the tragic poet encourages us to drown self-pity in universal sympathy. If we were confronted with a choice on these terms, I think we would say, "All honor to the tragic poet, who reminds us of the best that is in us, even if he cannot prove to us that his vision is the order of the universe."

49 Does life itself provide the pattern for tragedy, or is life itself, apart from the tragic artist's vision, formless and unintelligible? Are change of fortune, reversal, discovery, irony, and incidents in a necessary sequence faithful reproductions of the fundamental forms of experience, or are they merely artistic inventions, whereby the tragic poet imposes his own sense of form upon the formless, his own meaning upon the meaningless, his own vision of order and justice upon chance and chaos?

50 Aristotle believed that the poet finds his forms and patterns in life itself: "Tragedy," he said, "is an imitation of an action." Furthermore, he believed that the poet discovers universal forms and patterns: "Poetry," he said, "is higher and more philosophical than history, for poetry stresses the universal, whereas history stresses the particular." Others have disagreed with Aristotle. Nietzsche reached the conclusion, derived partly from Schopenhauer's pessimism, partly from his own study of Greek tragedy, that only as an aesthetic phenomenon is life eternally justified.

51 Although we have seen in the past few years a growing appreciation of the tragic spirit and vision, and although we may live to see a great new age of poetic and tragic drama, we must assume that our contemporaries who feel isolated from their fellow men, and from the past and the future, find in tragedy at best only an effective artistic illusion, and not an accurate description of the life of man in modern times.

52 I cannot agree either with Nietzsche, or with our contemporaries who believe that the tragic view of life is at best an illusion. I agree with Aristotle that the tragic poet finds his forms and patterns in life itself, in experiences common to all; and since I do not share Aristotle's desire to exclude the poets from the realm of reason, I find in tragic poetry the important view of life which he ignored.

53 Without appealing to supernatural faith—an appeal which the disillusioned writer would reject—I think it can be shown that the tragic poet's vision, though limited, is real and not an illusion, and that the great scientist and the great tragic poet are equally reliable reporters—one of the events in the physical world, the other of man's joys and sorrows, his change of fortune. Tragic poetry is not the only source of wisdom concerning values, nor can it provide us, on many important points, with more than fancies something like the truth, but the tragic view of life is something more than a splendid illusion, and it still has the power, if properly appreciated, to deprive pain of some of the sharp edges which Sappho and Emily Dickinson describe.

THE DECLINE OF HEROES

Arthur M. Schlesinger, Jr.

1 Ours is an age without heroes—and, when we say this, we suddenly realize how spectacularly the world has changed in a generation. Most of us grew up in a time of towering personalities. For better or for worse, great men seemed to dominate our lives and shape our destiny. In the United States we had Theodore Roosevelt, Woodrow Wilson, Franklin Roosevelt. In Great Britain, there were Lloyd George and Winston Churchill. In other lands, there were Lenin, Stalin, Hitler, Mussolini, Clemenceau, Gandhi, Kemal, Sun Yat-sen. Outside of politics there were Einstein, Freud, Keynes. Some of these great men influenced the world for good, others for evil; but, whether for good or for evil, the fact that each had not died at birth made a difference, one believed, to everyone who lived after them.

2 Today no one bestrides our narrow world like a colossus; we have no giants who play roles which one can imagine no one else playing in their stead. There are a few figures on the margin of uniqueness, perhaps: Adenauer, Nehru, Tito, De Gaulle, Chiang Kai-shek, Mao Tse-tung. But there seem to be none in the epic style of those mighty figures of our recent past who seized history with both hands and gave it an imprint, even a direction, which it otherwise might not have had. As De Gaulle himself remarked on hearing of Stalin's death, "The age of giants is over." Whatever one thought, whether one admired or detested Roosevelt or Churchill, Stalin or Hitler, one nevertheless felt the sheer weight of such personalities on one's own existence. We feel no comparable pressures today. Our own President, with all his pleasant qualities, has more or less explicitly renounced any desire to impress his own views on history. The Macmillans, Khrushchevs and Gronchis have measurably less specific gravity than their predecessors. Other men could be in their places as leaders of America or Britain or Russia or Italy without any change in the course of history. Why ours should thus be an age without heroes, and whether this condition is good or bad for us and for civilization, are topics worthy of investigation.

3 Why have giants vanished from our midst? One must never neglect the role of accident in history; and accident no doubt plays a part here. But too many accidents of the same sort cease to be wholly accidental. One must inquire further. Why should our age not only be without great men but even seem actively hostile to them? Surely one reason we have so few

heroes now is precisely that we had so many a generation ago. Greatness is hard for common humanity to bear. As Emerson said, "Heroism means difficulty, postponement of praise, postponement of ease, introduction of the world into the private apartment, introduction of eternity into the hours measured by the sitting-room clock." A world of heroes keeps people from living their own private lives.

4 Moreover, great men live dangerously. They introduce extremes into existence—extremes of good, extremes of evil—and ordinary men after a time flinch from the ultimates and yearn for undemanding security. The Second World War was the climax of an epoch of living dangerously. It is no surprise that it precipitated a universal revulsion against greatness. The war itself destroyed Hitler and Mussolini. And the architects of victory were hardly longer-lived. After the war, the British repudiated Churchill, and the Americans (with the adoption of the 22nd Amendment), Roosevelt. In due course, the French repudiated De Gaulle (they later repented, but it took the threat of civil war to bring him back); the Chinese, Chiang Kai-shek; and the Russians, Stalin. Khrushchev, in toppling Stalin from his pedestal, pronounced the general verdict against the uncommon man: the modern world, he said, had no use for the "cult of the individual." And, indeed, carried to the excesses to which the worshipers of Hitler and Stalin carried it, even to the much milder degree to which admirers of Roosevelt and Churchill sometimes carried it, the cult of the individual was dangerous. No man is infallible, and every man needs to be reminded of this on occasion. Still, our age has gone further than this—it objects not just to hero worship but to heroes. The century of the common man has come into its own.

5 This term, "common man," suggests the deeper problem. There is more involved than simply a dismissal of those colossi whom the world identified with a season of blood and agony. The common man has always regarded the great man with mixed feelings—resentment as well as admiration, hatred as well as love. The Athenian who refused to vote for Aristides because he was so tired of hearing him called "the Just" expressed a natural reaction. Great men make small men aware of their smallness. Rancor is one of the unavowed but potent emotions of politics; and one must never forget that the envy of the have-nots can be quite as consuming when the haves have character or intelligence as it is when they have merely material possessions.

6 Modern democracy inadvertently gave envy new scope. While the purpose of democracy was to give everyone a fair chance to rise, its method enabled rancorous men to invoke "equality" as an excuse for keeping all down to their own level. "I attribute the small number of distinguished men in political life," wrote Alexis de Tocqueville after visiting the United States in the 1830's, "to the ever-increasing despotism of the ma-

jority. . . . The power of the majority is so absolute and irresistible that one must give up one's rights as a citizen and almost abjure one's qualities as a human being, if one intends to stray from the track which it prescribes." James Bryce even titled a chapter in his *American Commonwealth*, Why Great Men Are Not Chosen President.

7 History has shown these prophets unduly pessimistic. Distinguished men do enter American politics; great men have been chosen President. Democracy demonstrates a capability for heroic leadership quite as much as it does a tendency toward mediocrity. Yet Tocqueville and the others were correct enough in detecting the dislike of great men as a permanent potentiality in a democracy. And the evolution of industrial society appears to have given this sentiment new force. More and more of us live and work within great organizations; an influential book has already signaled out the organization man as the American of the future. The bureaucratization of American life, the decline of the working class, the growth of the white-collar class, the rise of suburbia—all this has meant the increasing homogeneity of American society. Though we continue to speak of ourselves as rugged individualists, our actual life has grown more and more collective and anonymous. As a Monsanto Chemical film put it, showing a group of technicians at work in a laboratory: "No geniuses here; just a bunch of average Americans working together." Our ideal is increasingly smooth absorption into the group rather than self-realization in the old-fashioned, strong-minded, don't-give-a-damn sense. Where does the great man fit into our homogenized society?

8 "The greatness of England is now all collective," John Stuart Mill wrote a century ago: "individually small, we only appear capable of anything great by our habit of combining." He might have been writing about contemporary America; but where we Americans are inclined to rejoice over the superiority of the "team," Mill added somberly, "It was men of another stamp than this that made England what it has been; and men of another stamp will be needed to prevent its decline."

9 But was Mill right? Do individuals really have impact on history? A powerful school of philosophers has denied any importance at all to great men. Such thinkers reject heroes as a childish hangover from the days when men ascribed everything to the action of gods. History, they assert, is not made by men, but by inexorable forces or irrevocable laws: if these forces or laws do not manifest themselves through one individual, they will do so through another. What has happened already has comprehensively and absolutely decided what will happen in the future. "If there is a single human action due to free will," wrote Tolstoi, "no historical law exists, and no conception of historical events can be formed." If all this is so, obviously the presence or absence of any particular "hero" at any particular time cannot make the slightest difference.

10 This view of history is a form of fatalistic determinism; and Tolstoi's *War and Peace* offers one of its most eloquent statements. Why, Tolstoi asked, did millions of men in the time of Napoleon, repudiating their common sense and their human feelings, move from west to east, slaughtering their fellows? The answers provided by historians seemed to him hopelessly superficial. His own answer was: "The war was bound to happen simply because it was bound to happen"; all previous history predetermined it. Where did this leave the great men? In Tolstoi's view, they were the most deluded figures of all. Great men, he said, "are but the labels that serve to give a name to an event and, like labels, they have the least possible connection with the event itself." The greater the man, "the more conspicuous is the inevitability and predestination of every act he commits." The hero, said Tolstoi, "is the slave of history."

11 There are many forms of historical fatalism. Toynbee and Spengler, with their theory of the inexorable growth and decay of civilizations, represent one form. The Marxists, with their theory that changes in the modes of production control the course of history, represent another. When Khrushchev denounced the practice of making "a hero" out of "a particular leader" and condemned the cult of the individual as "alien to the spirit of Marxism-Leninism," he was speaking the true spirit of his faith. And Marxism is not the only form of economic determinism; there are also, for example, economic determinists of the laissez-faire school who believe that all civilization is dependent on rigid adherence to a certain theory of the sacredness of private property.

12 Fatalists differ greatly among themselves. But, however much they differ, they unite in the conclusion that the individual plays no role of his own in history. If they are right, then nothing could matter less whether or not this is an age without heroes.

13 But they are not right. The philosophy of historical fatalism rests on serious fallacies. For one thing, it supposes that, because a thing happens, it had to happen. But causation is one matter; predestination another. The construction of a causal explanation after an event merely renders that event in some sense intelligible. It does not in the least show that this particular event, and no other, had to take place; that nothing else could possibly have occurred in its stead. The serious test of the fatalist case must be applied before the event. The only conclusive proof of fatalism would lie in the accurate prediction of events that have not yet happened. And to say, with Tolstoi, that all prior history predetermines everything that follows is to say nothing at all. It is to produce an explanation which applies equally to everything—and thus becomes so vague and limitless as to explain nothing.

14 Fatalism raises other difficulties. Thus it imputes reality to mystical historical "forces"—class, race, nation, the will of the people, the spirit of

the times, history itself. But there are no such forces. They are merely abstractions or metaphors with no existence except in the mind of the beholder. The only evidence for them is deduction from the behavior of individuals. It is therefore the individual who constitutes the basic unit of history. And, while no individual can be wholly free—and, indeed, recent discoveries of the manifold ways in which we are unconsciously conditioned should constitute a salutary check on human vanity—one must assume the reality of an area of free choice until that assumption is challenged, not by metaphysical affirmation, but by verifiable proof—that is, consistently accurate prediction of the future.

15 Fatalism, moreover, is incompatible with human psychology and human morality. Anyone who rigorously accepted a deterministic view of life, for example, would have to abandon all notions of human responsibility, since it is manifestly unfair to praise or punish people for acts which are by definition beyond their control. But such fatalism is belied by the assumption of free choice which underlies every move we make, every word we utter, every thought we think. As Sir Isaiah Berlin observes of determinism, "If we begin to take it seriously, then, indeed, the changes in our language, our moral notions, our attitudes toward one another, our views of history, of society and of everything else will be too profound to be even adumbrated." We can no more imagine what the universe of the consistent determinist would be like than we can imagine what it would be like to live in a world without time or one with seventeen-dimensional space.

16 For the historian concerned with concrete interpretation of actual events, he can easily demonstrate the futility of fatalism by trying to apply it to specific historical episodes. According to the extreme determinist view, no particular individual can make the slightest difference. As slaves of history, all individuals are, so to speak, interchangeable parts. If Napoleon had not led his armies across Europe, Tolstoi implies, someone else would have. William James, combating this philosophic fatalism, once asked the determinists whether they really believed "the convergence of sociological pressures to have so impinged on Stratford on Avon about April 23, 1564, that a W. Shakespeare, with all his mental peculiarities, had to be born there." And did they further believe, James continued, that "if the aforesaid W. Shakespeare had died of cholera infantum, another mother at Stratford on Avon would needs have engendered a duplicate copy of him to restore the sociologic equilibrium?" Who could believe such stuff? Yet, if the determinists do not mean exactly this, how can they read the individual out of history?

17 In December, 1931, a British politician, crossing Fifth Avenue in New York between 76th and 77th streets around ten-thirty at night, was knocked down and gravely injured by an automobile. Fourteen months later an American politician, sitting in an open car in Miami, Florida, was

fired on by an assassin; a man standing beside him was killed. Would the next two decades of history have been the same had Contasini's car killed Winston Churchill in 1931 and Zangara's bullets killed Franklin Roosevelt in 1933? Suppose, in addition, that Adolf Hitler had been killed in the street fighting during the Munich *Putsch* of 1923, and Lenin and Mussolini had died at birth. Where would our century be now?

18 Individuals, of course, must operate within limits. They cannot do everything. They cannot, for example, propel history into directions for which the environment and the human material are not prepared: no genius, however heroic, could have brought television to ancient Troy. Yet, as Sidney Hook has convincingly argued in his thoughtful book, *The Hero in History*, great men can count decisively "where the historical situation permits of major alternative paths of development."

19 This argument between fatalism and heroism is not one in which there is a lot to be said on both sides. The issue is far too sharp to be straddled. Either history is rigidly determined and foreordained, in which case individual striving does not matter; or it is not, in which case there is an essential role for the hero. Analysis of concrete episodes suggests that history is, within limits, open and unfinished; that men have lived who did what no substitute could ever have done; that their intervention set history on one path rather than another. If this is so, the old maxim, "There are no indispensable men," would seem another amiable fallacy. There is, then, a case for heroes.

20 To say that there is a case for heroes is not to say that there is a case for hero worship. The surrender of decision, the unquestioning submission to leadership, the prostration of the average man before the Great Man—these are the diseases of heroism, and they are fatal to human dignity. But, if carried too far, hero worship generates its own antidote. "Every hero," said Emerson, "becomes a bore at last." And we need not go too far. History amply shows that it is possible to have heroes without turning them into gods.

21 And history shows, too, that, when a society, in flight from hero worship, decides to do without great men at all, it gets into troubles of its own. Our contemporary American society, for example, has little use for the individualist. Individualism implies dissent from the group; dissent implies conflict; and conflict suddenly seems divisive, un-American and generally unbearable. Our greatest new industry is evidently the production of techniques to eliminate conflict, from positive thoughts through public relations to psychoanalysis, applied everywhere from the couch to the pulpit. Our national aspiration has become peace of mind, peace of soul. The symptomatic drug of our age is the tranquilizer. "Togetherness" is the banner under which we march into the brave new world.

22 Obviously society has had to evolve collective institutions to cope

with problems that have grown increasingly complex and concentrated. But the collective approach can be overdone. If Khrushchev worried because his collectivist society developed a cult of the individual, maybe we Americans should start worrying as our so-called individualist society develops a cult of the group. We instinctively suppose that the tough questions will be solved by an interfaith conference or an interdisciplinary research team or an interdepartmental committee or an assembly of wise men meeting at Arden House. But are not these group tactics essentially means by which individuals hedge their bets and distribute their responsibilities? And do they not nearly always result in the dilution of insight and the triumph of mish-mash? If we are to survive, we must have ideas, vision, courage. These things are rarely produced by committees. Everything that matters in our intellectual and moral life begins with an individual confronting his own mind and conscience in a room by himself.

23 A bland society will never be creative. "The amount of eccentricity in a society," said John Stuart Mill, "has generally been proportional to the amount of genius, mental vigor and moral courage it contained. That so few now dare to be eccentric marks the chief danger of the time." If this condition frightened Mill in Victorian England, it should frighten us much more. For our national apotheosis of the group means that we systematically lop off the eccentrics, the originals, the proud, imaginative, lonely people from whom new ideas come. What began as a recoil from hero worship ends as a conspiracy against creativity. If worship of great men brings us to perdition by one path, flight from great men brings us there just as surely by another. When we do not admire great men, then our instinct for admiration is likely to end by settling on ourselves. The one thing worse for democracy than hero worship is self-worship.

24 A free society cannot get along without heroes, because they are the most vivid means of exhibiting the power of free men. The hero exposes to all mankind unsuspected possibilities of conception, unimagined resources of strength. "The appearance of a great man," wrote Emerson, "draws a new circle outside of our largest orbit and surprises and commands us." Carlyle likened ordinary, lethargic times, with their unbelief and perplexity, to dry, dead fuel, waiting for the lightning out of heaven to kindle it. "The great man, with his free force direct out of God's own hand, is the lightning. . . . The rest of men waited for him like fuel, and then they too would flame."

25 Great men enable us to rise to our own highest potentialities. They nerve lesser men to disregard the world and trust to their own deepest instinct. "In picking out from history our heroes," said William James, "each one of us may best fortify and inspire what creative energy may lie in his own soul. This is the last justification of hero worship." Which one of us has not gained fortitude and faith from the incarnation of ideals in men,

from the wisdom of Socrates, from the wondrous creativity of Shakespeare, from the strength of Washington, from the compassion of Lincoln, and above all perhaps, from the life and the death of Jesus? "We feed on genius," said Emerson. "Great men exist that there may be greater men."

26 Yet this may be only the smaller part of their service. Great men have another and larger role—to affirm human freedom against the supposed inevitabilities of history. The first hero was Prometheus, who defied the gods and thus asserted the independence and autonomy of man against all determinism. Zeus punished Prometheus, chaining him to a rock and encouraging a vulture to pluck at his vitals.

27 Ever since, man, like Prometheus, has warred against history. It has always been a bitter and remorseless fight; for the heavy weight of human inertia lies with fatalism. It takes a man of exceptional vision and strength and will—it takes, in short, a hero—to try to wrench history from what lesser men consider its preconceived path. And often history tortures the hero in the process, chains him to a rock and exposes him to the vulture. Yet, in the model of Prometheus, man can still hold his own against the gods. Brave men earn the right to shape their own destiny.

28 An age without great men is one which acquiesces in the drift of history. Such acquiescence is easy and seductive; the great appeal of fatalism, indeed, is as a refuge from the terror of responsibility. Where a belief in great men insistently reminds us that individuals can make a difference, fatalism reassures us that they can't. It thereby blesses our weakness and extenuates our failure. Fatalism, in Berlin's phrase, is "one of the great alibis" of history.

29 Let us not be complacent about our supposed capacity to get along without great men. If our society has lost its wish for heroes and its ability to produce them, it may well turn out to have lost everything else as well.

ON THE DIFFICULTY OF BEING A CONTEMPORARY HERO

A *Time* Essay

1 "A hero cannot be a hero unless in a heroic world," observed Nathaniel Hawthorne, who thought even in 1850 that America's world had turned unheroic. Thomas Carlyle felt that "Ballot-boxes and Electoral suf-

From *Time* (June 24, 1966), pp. 32–33. Reprinted by permission of *Time*, The Weekly Newsmagazine.

frages" might prove a fatal threat to heroes. Americans today find heroism daily in Viet Nam and high courage in a thousand situations, from space to civil rights. And yet there is a widespread feeling that the leap of imagination that makes heroes and the generosity of spirit that acknowledges them are disappearing. Can there be real heroes in a time of the computer and the committee decision?

2 In the heyday of the hero, history was a game with few players, and a single man could more readily change it all. The Greeks were losing the Trojan war until Achilles was coaxed from his tent. Horatius defended Rome's bridge with only two friends, and even as late as 1528, Pizarro could overthrow the mighty Inca civilization with only 167 men—less than the number commanded by Captain William Carpenter in that recent local battle in Viet Nam. Now with a cast of many thousands or millions, each leader heads only a segment, and decision is often a synthesis of the opinions of many herolings. Where there are too many heroes, there may be none in the end, for the essence of heroism is singularity. Lindbergh is perhaps the greatest of all American heroes, a machine-borne Icarus who did not fall. The astronauts are his heirs and yet they are already submerged in team heroism. First there was Alan Shepard, who was succeeded by the engaging John Glenn, and then Edward White was the first American to walk in space, and then . . . By now few people can remember all the names. But the astronaut remains truly heroic as a composite figure.

3 The classic heroes, in the words of U.C.L.A.'s late Historian Dixon Wecter, "were taller by a head than any of their tribesmen, could cut iron with their swords, throw the bar farther or wind the horn louder than their fellows—Achilles and Ulysses, Siegfried and Roland, Beowulf and Richard the Lionhearted." Their latter-day American equivalents might be Douglas MacArthur, reconquering the Pacific, true to his vow, "I shall return," and Ike Eisenhower, commanding the massed D-day armies or winning his sweeping 1952 election victory. But it is difficult to imagine Beowulf getting only ten nominating votes as Republican candidate for President (which is what happened to MacArthur), or Roland trying to govern with benign passivity (which is what Ike did during much of his White House tenure).

4 With modern communications, mythmaking, which is essential to heromaking, is far more difficult. The democratic press exposes leaders to a relentless scrutiny that no putative hero of the past had to survive. Alexander the Great was able to achieve hero status by his own declaration that he was descended from Zeus, and his far-off conquests were known to Macedonian peasants only by a crying in the market—the more magical because it was imprecise. If he slapped a soldier in the face or picked up a beagle by the ears, they might never have known.

5 The hero's metaphysical underpinnings have been giving way for centuries. Professor George M. Harper of the University of North Carolina points out that "the Greek and Shakespearean concept of the hero as an essentially noble man created in the image of his Creator and sharing his attributes is no longer possible." The decline began, Harper suggests, with Copernicus and Galileo, who demonstrated that the earth was not the center of the universe and that man is therefore not the center of creation. Darwin described man as a pawn of evolution, Freud as a puppet of the unconscious, Marx and other determinists as a prisoner of an abstraction called history. "Show our critics a great man, a Luther for example," complained Carlyle. "He was the 'creature of the Time,' they say; the Time called him forth, the Time did everything, he nothing."

6 In recent decades, talk of heroes seemed to carry overtones of tyranny, of Nazism's "supermen." In socialist mythology, the masses, not the individual, were regarded as heroic. In literature, the non-hero took over. He thrives in the U.S. today in the hands of such writers as Saul Bellow—whose Herzog has his great moment at the end of the book when he manages to summon enough strength to tell his cleaning woman to sweep the kitchen. Other literary "heroes" are fall guys, incipient madmen, badgered Everymen, victims. Their motto, says Daniel Aaron, professor of English at Smith, seems to be, "Call me schlemiel." In more mundane life, there is much revulsion against the pose, if not the reality, of heroism. "Ya wanna be a hero?" is a mockery, not a compliment.

7 In spite of all that, the U.S. still has its heroes—though they are different from those of any other society.

8 There is today no agreed definition of what a hero is. Philosopher Sidney Hook defines a hero as an "eventmaking" man who changes history, like Churchill or Lenin, as distinct from the merely "eventful" man, like Lyndon Johnson (so far) or Charles de Gaulle. "De Gaulle would be an eventmaking man," says Hook, "if he had the power." Yet there are many heroes who did not change events, or who had heroism thrust upon them through accident.

9 Another valid definition of a hero is "a person regarded as a model." In *The Natural*, Novelist Bernard Malamud has one character explain: "Without heroes we're all plain people and don't know how far we can go . . . It's their function to be the best." But excellence is not enough to make a hero, nor is willingness to challenge the odds; those qualities may merely add up to leadership. "Heroism should not be confused with strength and success," says Author John Updike. "Our concept of the hero must be humanized to include the ideas of sacrifice and death, even of failure." The hero also must touch people's emotions. In modern jargon, that means someone who "turns people on."

10 U.S. Presidents should be hero material, but not too many have turned people on. America's most unequivocal hero, if somewhat dutifully admired, is George Washington, who has the built-in title of father of his country. Far more beloved is Lincoln—perhaps because he was ugly, because he was born poor, because he was funny, but most of all because he carried doubts and uncertainties in the lines of his face but still was able to make great decisions.

11 Beyond these, the U.S. has been sparing in awarding even part-time hero status to its Presidents. Andrew Jackson probably makes it, though more because he was Old Hickory "who brought the people into the White House" than because he was the victor of New Orleans. Teddy Roosevelt may have changed the course of human events less significantly than Woodrow Wilson, who led the U.S. into World War I. But Teddy's robust vigor captured the American imagination, while there lingered about Wilson, even in his martyrdom, a distressing air of the austere schoolmaster.

12 With increasing sophistication, Americans no longer seem impressed with a born-in-a-log-cabin background. Franklin D. Roosevelt and John F. Kennedy were born to wealth and flaunted shamelessly expensive tastes (while no one was much interested in Nixon's poor-boy origin). Roosevelt demonstrated a characteristic of the classic hero, who, according to Historian Wecter, "envisages his era as a crisis, a drama of good versus evil, and himself as the man of destiny. In a sense, he must be a hero to himself before he can command that worship in others." Kennedy's record is mixed, and the assassin's bullet cut it short before it was completed. But he, too, was a hero to himself. Visibly and with eloquence, he embodied the hope of a new start. His looks and his style, the glamour of his wife and his clan permanently enshrined him as the most romantic of U.S. Presidents.

13 It says something about the national character that Americans have always had only tempered admiration for the men of strictly military exploits. John Paul Jones and Farragut rise from the history books as authors of heroic slogans, but hardly as full-fledged heroes. Besides, there is a strong prejudice in favor of the gallant loser and the persistent defender of a lost cause. Lee and Stonewall Jackson outrank Ulysses S. Grant. World War I produced no military heroes unless it was Sergeant York, a man of peace reacting to pressure. World War II and after showed a growing sophistication in American taste in war heroes. The dashing George Patton was ranked well behind the judicious men of wide responsibility such as Eisenhower, Bradley, Marshall.

14 Heroes are not only soldiers, but champions of political causes. Among the most conspicuous champions today are the fighters for civil rights, and perhaps posterity will find a degree of heroism in that quiet

man, Earl Warren, who wrote the historic decision striking down separate-but-equal education. But heroism requires panache, which makes Martin Luther King a more vivid current hero.

15 American hero worship is not necessarily nationalistic. Most Americans acknowledge Churchill as one of their greatest heroes, not only because he forged blood, toil, tears and sweat into victory, but because he seemed to embody, like a noble caricature, all the legendary qualities of the English. Not that pugnacity is essential. Americans see Pope John XXIII as a hero because he exuded love and managed to combine the saintly with the jolly. Many Americans would also accord the status of saint-hero to Albert Schweitzer, because they cherish the sentimental picture of the man who gave up the world in order to do good works in a dark corner of the globe. But Schweitzer perhaps lived too long. "Every hero becomes a bore at last," said Emerson.

16 In another context, giving up the world is an achievement to which Americans are profoundly drawn. All the great Western heroes from Daniel Boone on are revered and envied not merely for physical prowess but for attaining a free life, unfettered by civilization's rules. Today, the hero must find his niche very much inside civilization, and he will probably belong to the ranks of the specialist heroes. No intellectual can be a hero to those who don't read (except in France), nor any baseball player to a man who never goes to a game. But they have a common denominator—they expand the sense of human capability.

17 Athletes have traditionally been heroes in the human imagination. Men still dream of themselves as Samson, tearing down the temple around the mocking ears, or as Lancelot, cutting down all challengers and incidentally winning the lady. But the commercialization of athletics and pervasive publicity have altered the image of the "parfit knight."

18 Babe Ruth survived as a hero largely because his young admirers never realized that his private life was pretty disheveled. Today's sports hero is more widely known, but loses glamour when seen combing greasy kid stuff out of his hair. Americans like their heroes earthy, whether it is Ted Williams or Casey Stengel—but he must not be too loutish. Jackie Robinson is elected because he displayed grace under the pressure of breaking the color bar in baseball. Still, the arena is crowded; so many good athletes are on view that heroes, as distinct from mere record breakers, are scarce.

19 The U.S.'s newest heroes are scientists. Though inventors such as Eli Whitney, Edison or Bell have long been acknowledged, only Einstein among the pure scientists held a place in the U.S. consciousness until World War II. Today the roster would be long, studded with such names as Teller, Oppenheimer and Waksman. Another set of latter-day heroes are physicians, whose list would include Drs. Fleming, DeBakey, Salk

and Paul Dudley White. Among businessmen, only Henry Ford has achieved anything like heroic dimensions, although such magnates as Astor and Carnegie were heroes to their day. The values of commerce, no matter how much they may accomplish, are the antithesis of the traditional values of glory.

20 Does the U.S. need heroes? Not in the sense of the man on the white horse who will take care of everything. To the uncertain, sheer conviction—right or wrong—is a kind of relief. This is what makes "herocs" out of the Hitlers, the Stalins, and even the Joe McCarthys. Adlai Stevenson, who is a hero of the intellectuals, knew the difference. Reaching back to Cicero in comparing himself to Jack Kennedy, he noted ruefully, "When Cicero had finished speaking, the people said, 'How well he spoke'—but when Demosthenes had finished speaking, the people said, 'Let us march.' " Heroes may be wrong, but they must be sure.

21 Even the U.S.'s most sacrosanct heroes have a relation to American life that is not quite equivalent to other nations' heroes. Britain's Wellington, France's Napoleon, Russia's Peter the Great are national heroes, who specifically did something for the greater glory of the nation and can be claimed by no other country. But the U.S.'s Washington and Lincoln, Wilson and Kennedy are celebrated for the ideals they championed. They reaffirm the American idea of itself as a nation dedicated not to power but to ideals. In that sense, the U.S. needs heroes more than ever.

22 One sign of the need comes from the young who are indeed looking for heroes. The seriousness of the search is only underlined by the weird pseudo heroes whom some have discovered, ranging from Bob Dylan, the long-playing minstrel of social protest, to the Beatles, who demonstrated a way to shock their elders and still be innocent.

23 The need for heroes is also seen in the widespread rejection of the literary anti-hero. He is kept alive only because "people who can't manage their own lives identify with him," says Joseph Campbell, professor of literature at Sarah Lawrence. The anti-hero, suggests Campbell, is a disease of New York, "a city which is a psychological calamity and which has no connection with the land America." In a very real way, the land America prefers Humphrey Bogart and James Bond. Bogart demonstrates the belief that a man can be tough but tender, ugly but sexy. The Bond syndrome suggests a yearning for the old-fashioned action hero, free from conventional fetters. Says Sociologist Marshall Fishwick of the University of Delaware: "The playboy is a cowboy who has just discovered woman."

24 On the personal level, there may be a distaste for "getting involved," and the story of people standing by passively while someone is being beaten up has become almost a newspaper cliché. But for every such incident, there are a series of uncelebrated acts of bravery performed to help others or to defend the right. Psychiatrists are apt to point out that such

spontaneous heroes may be motivated only by suppressed anxiety or a desire for violent action. The soldier who flings himself on a grenade is simply reacting to a "subconscious impulse toward self-destruction" or because "identification with the group supersedes his own ego." It seems a singularly graceless way of defining an impulse that still stirs human hearts: "Greater love hath no man than this, that a man lay down his life for his friends."

25 The ultimate hero is the democratic process itself, which is bigger than any individual. This may cut down heroes. But it can also inspire an increment of effort that can make a hero out of many a man who was born in obscurity and never suspected his own strength.

26 It is a process that also gives American heroism, once achieved, a special status. For despite the glib techniques of image-building, the American chooses his heroes only in a final stubborness of spirit that resists campaign posters, opinion polls, or cocktail harangues. It is an act that differentiates Americans from other people in other times, who may have felt that their heroes had already become heroes without consultation. The American has a sense of electing his own heroes—a vote freely given that can also be freely withdrawn. Without advice and consent, there are no heroes.

PART II

Understanding the Patterns of Literature

SECTION 7

Understanding the Patterns of Art, Literature, and Music

POETIC PEOPLE

Max Eastman

1 A simple experiment will distinguish two types of human nature. Gather a throng of people and pour them into a ferryboat. By the time the boat has swung into the river you will find that a certain proportion have taken the trouble to climb upstairs, in order to be out on deck and see what is to be seen as they cross over. The rest have settled indoors, to think what they will do upon reaching the other side, or perhaps to lose themselves in apathy or tobacco smoke. But leaving out those apathetic, or addicted to a single enjoyment, we may divide all the alert passengers on the boat into two classes—those who are interested in crossing the river, and those who are merely interested in getting across. And we may divide all the people on the earth, or all the moods of people, in the same way. Some of them are chiefly occupied with attaining ends, and some with receiving experiences. The distinction of the two will be more marked when we name the first kind practical, and the second poetic, for common knowledge recognizes that a person poetic or in a poetic mood is impractical, and a practical person is intolerant of poetry.

2 We can see the force of this intolerance too, and how deeply it is justified, if we make clear to our minds just what it means to be practical, and what a great thing it is. It means to be controlled in your doings by the con-

sideration of ends yet unattained. The practical man is never distracted by things, or aspects of things, which have no bearing on his purpose, but ever seizing the significant, he moves with a single mind and a single emotion toward the goal. And even when the goal is achieved you will hardly see him pause to rejoice in it; he is already on his way to another achievement. For that is the irony of his nature. His joy is not in any conquest or destination, but his joy is in going toward it. To which joy he adds the pleasure of being praised as a practical man, and a man who will arrive.

3 In a more usual sense, perhaps, a practical man is a man occupied with attaining certain ends that people consider important. He must stick pretty close to the business of feeding and preserving life. Nourishment and shelter, money-making, maintaining respectability, and if possible a family—these are the things that give its common meaning to the word practical. An acute regard for such features of the scenery, and the universe, as contribute or can be made to contribute to these ends, and a systematic neglect of all other features, are the traits of mind which this word popularly suggests. And it is because of the vital importance of these things to almost all people that the word "practical" is a eulogy, and is able to be so scornful of the word "poetic."

4 "It is an earnest thing to be alive in this world. With competition, with war, with disease and poverty and oppression, misfortune and death on-coming, who but fools will give serious attention to what is not significant to the business?"

5 "Yes, but what is the *use* of being alive in the world, if life is so oppressive in its moral character that we must always be busy getting somewhere, and never simply realizing where we are? What were the value of your eternal achieving, if we were not here on our holiday to appreciate among other things, some of the things you have achieved?"

6 Thus, if we could discover a purely poetic and a purely practical person, might they reason together. But we cannot discover anything so satisfactory to our definitions, and therefore let us conclude the discussion of the difference between them. It has led us to our own end—a clearer understanding of the nature of poetic people, and of all people when they are in a poetic mind. They are lovers of the qualities of things. They are not engaged, as the learned say that all life is, in becoming adjusted to an environment, but they are engaged in becoming acquainted with it. They are possessed by the impulse to realize, an impulse as deep, and arbitrary, and unexpected as that will to live which lies at the bottom of all explanations. It seems but the manifestation, indeed, of that will itself in a concrete and positive form. It is a wish to experience life and the world. That is the essence of the poetic temper. . . .

7 It would be foolish, however, to question whether or not the poetic are capable of purposeful achievement, and the practical capable of intense

experience, for we are all, except those lost in apathy, in some degree both poetic and practical. The example of the hero Aeschylus (poet and efficient soldier at Marathon) proves that it is possible for a man, who can think clearly and command the differences that lie within him, to be both poetic and practical in a high degree.

8 If we could but free our minds from a contamination with certain modern people who teach themselves that they are presided over by a pretty demon called an Artistic Temperament, we should not only cease cherishing by suggestion the tickle-brain condition into which they decay, but we should have ourselves a sounder estimate of the place and dignity of the poetic. It is not an attribute of special, exotic, or disordered types, but a universal quality of our nature. No live man is without an arbitrary passion for some experience. Indeed, the defect of many of those most scornful of poetry is not that they are strong in the practical life, but that the attachment to some single state of being has got the better of them. There are fifty thousand morphine-takers in Paris, and all over the face of the earth how many million chewers, and breathers, and swallowers of what, far from being of practical value, is both costly and deleterious, bearing unconscious witness to the poetry of human nature.

9 The greatly poetic differ from them only in the healthy varieties of their loves, prevailing everywhere and always. They are those who live variously as well as vividly in the present. This alone distinguishes them from all those excluded by our experiment at the beginning, who confine their enjoyment to smoking while they are crossing the river. They are not without realization. But it is only the poetic who make the innumerable intimate acquaintances that are to be made, who welcome all living qualities and perfect them, and finally perhaps, in a supreme moment of morning sunshine and mist over the city, realize what we may call the essence of crossing a ferry.

STUDY GUIDE

Word Study

1. A. Look up the etymology of the following words: *apathy* and *addicted* (paragraph 1), *aspect* (paragraph 2), *eulogy* (paragraph 3), and *arbitrary* (paragraph 8).

B. What is the root meaning of *practical* and *poetic?* Show how the root meanings of these words are connected with what Eastman says about the practical and poetic character.

2. A. Look up the exact meaning of *irony* (paragraph 2). Distinguish clearly between *irony, sarcasm, paradox, humor,* and *satire.*

B. Look up the exact meaning of *exotic, deleterious, essence.*

Effective Diction

1. Comment on the following phrases as examples of a personal use of language: *addicted to a single enjoyment* (paragraph 1) and *an acute regard* and *a systematic neglect* (paragraph 3).

2. Comment on the effectiveness of the following verbs through their connotation: *gather, pour, swung, climb,* and *settled* (paragraph 1), and *adjusted* and *acquainted* (paragraph 6).

3. In the first paragraph there are two *sustained images* (a simile or metaphor sustained throughout a passage). One is expressed; the other is only implied. State what they are, and show how they are sustained throughout the passage. (The key to the implied comparison is a word in the opening sentence of paragraph 1.) Show how these comparisons add interest to the passage.

4. An author will reveal his own attitude (like or dislike) toward the subject with which he is dealing by the pleasant or unpleasant connotations of the words or figures he uses in discussing it. With this in mind, cite evidence from paragraph 8, sentences 1 and 2, to show what Eastman's attitude toward the "Artistic Temperament" is.

The Rhetoric of the Paragraph

1. Pick out the topic sentence in paragraphs 1, 2, 3, 6, 8, and 9, and be ready to show how the other sentences in these paragraphs are related to the topic sentences.

2. What method of paragraph development is employed in paragraphs 2, 3, 8, and 9?

3. Make a topical outline of the division of people indicated in the first paragraph. Which of these divisions of people does Eastman discuss in the rest of the selection?

4. A. Indicate how the transitions are made from paragraphs 1 to 2, 2 to 3, 5 to 6, and 8 to 9.

B. There seem to be no connecting links between paragraphs 3 and 4 and between 4 and 5. Can you justify their absence?

Content

1. What is the main point that Eastman is trying to make in this entire passage? Point out the sentence in which you think he most clearly expresses that point.

2. How are the following two pairs of phrases related to the root meanings of *practical* and *poetic: interested in crossing the river* and *interested in getting across;* and *occupied with attaining ends* and *occupied with receiving experiences?*

3. Show how the phrase *with a single mind and a single emotion* highlights the dominant characteristic of the practical man.

4. Recalling the definitions of *irony* and *practical,* show why the practical man's taking joy in going toward a goal rather than in arriving at it is ironic.

5. Does Eastman believe that the poetic and the practical character as he describes them in paragraphs 1, 2, and 3, and represents them as speaking in paragraphs 4 and 5 actually exist? Answer this question in Eastman's own words.

6. Eastman says that the poetic instinct of the "wish to experience life and the world" is "a universal instinct of our nature." Can you cite proof for this from your own observation?

7. How do the fifty thousand morphine-takers in Paris "bear witness to the poetry in human nature"?

USELESS BEAUTY AND UNSELFISH ART

Jaime Castiello

1 Beauty as such is certainly the most useless of all useless things. This may sound like a paradox, but it is really an obvious, though much forgotten, truth. The proof is very easy. Take away the beauty from any useful thing whatever, and it keeps on being as useful as it was before. Churches need not be Romanesque or Gothic or Baroque in order to harbor us and protect us against the sun, rain, and noise. They need only be a shelter. As for their form, it can be as simple as that of a barn. It is the same with furniture. Take away from it all proportion, grace, and nobility of line, and it will still be useful; chairs and beds and tables will still continue to support that which they are supposed to support. The same could be said of cities: nothing whatever would happen to a community if its parks and gardens were not trimmed into beautiful patterns, but were allowed to grow wild. Trimmed or not, shrubs and trees would still go on refreshing the air and pumping oxygen into the atmosphere at night. As for pictures and statues and such things, whose very nature it is to beautify: if they were all to disappear from the world, houses would still go on sheltering, trains running, elevators ascending, and restaurants cooking meals.

2 Nor can it be claimed that beauty is at least useful for the intellect and the will. That could be said of truth and goodness. Possession of the truth through knowledge is equivalent to power, as Bacon knew so well, and modern scientists, of the pragmatist school, are never tired of preaching. Think of the power which the knowledge of electricity has given man. And in the sphere of the will, it is goodness which is useful and is loved because it is convenient for us and makes us capable of attaining our human end. But as for beauty as such, even in the intellectual and moral

From "Creative Power," *A Humane Psychology of Education* (New York: Sheed & Ward, Inc., 1936), pp. 53–56, 93.

order it is completely useless. When the truth and goodness of a thing have been considered, we have done with utility as such. Even for the intellect and the will beauty is a perfectly useless thing.

3 Yet there are and always have been men who, even at the cost of heroic sacrifices, have dedicated their whole lives to this utterly useless thing. There is no better example than that of the late Vincent van Gogh, whose works have so captivated our times: sunflowers saturated with an almost uncanny glow of dazzling light; kindly, wistful, ugly faces; interiors flaming with colors of strong, sharp, almost three-dimensional relief. Son of a well-to-do-family, Vincent van Gogh gave up a comfortable living in order to create useless beauty. Of course, he sold his paintings and even got money for them. His entire production brought him the sum of $129 in the whole course of his miserable existence. A single picture of his was sold, after his death, for $85,000. It is clear then that Vincent van Gogh did not paint for money.

4 Van Gogh's, moreover, is not an isolated case. Chopin preferred to go hungry, risking his poor health, rather than spend the little energy he had in lucrative concert work. Whatever energy he had, however, he employed in composition, which was not lucrative, made him very uncomfortable, and exhausted his consumptive body. Beethoven renounced marriage in order to consecrate himself to music. His is the admirable saying that the creative artist "must hew out of himself." As for his life, it was one of poverty and intense solitude, of great moral anguish, and tremendous, racking mental effort, all for the sake of that perfectly useless thing: beauty.

5 There is no need to multiply such proofs or to back up the underlying conclusions with the testimony of such keen, introspective minds as St. Thomas, Kant, Schelling, or Hegel. There is no need to draw upon authority or philosophical principles, but upon hard facts and experience. And this experience and these facts all point to the following conclusions: first of all, that beauty, in itself and considered as such, is essentially useless; secondly that, precisely because it is useless and can never be used as a means for anything else, beauty is loved exclusively for its own sake, and is, therefore, in a very real sense, an absolute, an imitation of God's own absolute value; thirdly, and consequently, that the human urge after beauty, which we call creative action, is not a selfish urge, but essentially selfless.

6 These are significant conclusions, for they show up one important difference between instinct and creative power. The nature of instinct is "to take"; that of art is "to give." Instinct exists for the preservation of the individual or the species. Think of the function of hunger and sex, of rage and fear, for example. Art does nothing for the preservation of the individual or the species. The work of art is a gift, made for the sake of the gift, because

it is beautiful and worthy of existence. Creative action, then, is the very opposite of "bartering," "exchanging," "earning," "winning," "getting something out of," "go getting." It is, on the contrary, a "communication," and "endowing," a free, spontaneous, and absolutely disinterested "giving."...

7 The moment a man starts to beautify something, in that very instant he has ceased to be selfish. He is giving without receiving. He is considering the thing which he is moulding not as useful, but as lovable in itself and therefore worth beautifying.

8 It is not only the great artists who beautify that which they touch. All men have it in them to beautify anything somewhat; more or less according to their inborn capacity. The coarse person uses things. He has nothing to give; he only grabs and takes. The humane personality gives to everything he does a finish, a touch of perfection which are a joy to himself, and to all those who live with him. He cares for his own person, for his own mind, for what he writes and says, for his home and his garden, for his friends, and for the land in which he lives. He wants to give everything something of himself. . . . He loves, and he is, therefore, unselfish. . . . The cult of the beautiful, when carried out in a healthy, virile way, is the most social of all training. It is a training for unselfishness.

STUDY GUIDE

Word Study

Look up the exact meaning of the following words: *paradox* (paragraph 1), *pragmatist* (paragraph 2), *isolated* and *lucrative* (paragraph 4), *absolute* (paragraph 5), *instinct* (paragraph 6), and *humane* and *cult* (paragraph 8).

Thought Structure and Paragraph Development

1. A. What is the central idea developed in this selection?

B. What is the method of proof employed throughout the passage? Where in the passage does the author expressly remind the reader that he is following this method of proof?

2. Select what you consider to be the topic sentence of each paragraph in the selection and be ready to show how the other sentences in the paragraphs are related to the topic sentences.

3. Indicate the method of paragraph development employed in each paragraph in the selection.

4. Can you suggest a reason for beginning a new paragraph with the last sentence in paragraph 1?

Content

1. In how many ways can you relate the general contents of this passage with Eastman's discussion of the practical and poetic character?

2. A. In what sense is Castiello employing *useful* in this passage?

B. Is there any relation between *utility* as Castiello uses the term here and the *pragmatist* to whom he refers in paragraph 2, sentence 3?

C. Is there any relation between a *pragmatist* and the *practical man* as Eastman defines him?

3. A. Show how the author proceeds from the generic to the more specific in paragraph 1, sentences 5–7, 8 and 9, and 10 and 11.

B. What is the principle of order in speaking of Romanesque, Gothic, and Baroque churches in paragraph 1, sentence 5?

4. A. Comment on the effectiveness of the words *saturated, uncanny glow, dazzling light*, and *flaming* to suggest the quality of light and color in van Gogh's paintings.

B. What does the author suggest about the inclusiveness of van Gogh's paintings in their human subject matter by the phrase *kindly, wistful, ugly faces?*

5. Point out the irony in the last three sentences of paragraph 3.

6. A. What is implied by the statement in the first sentence of paragraph 5 that "there is no need to multiply such proofs"?

B. What is the difference between the proof the author has been giving thus far and that which he indicates he could give if he chose from the "introspective minds of St. Thomas, Kant, Schelling, or Hegel"?

C. What is *introspection*? Is it a valid source of proof?

D. Discuss the difference between authority, philosophical principles, and experience as sources of knowledge. Prove that we use all three of them in our everyday experience.

7. A. What is the opposite of an absolute value?

B. What are the *facts* from which the conclusions listed in paragraph 5, sentence 3 follow?

8. A. What is the relation between *creative action* (paragraph 5, sentence 3) and *art* (paragraph 6, sentence 2)?

B. Using the examples of instinct cited by the author (*hunger, sex, fear*), show that they do function for the preservation of the individual or the species.

C. In what sense is it true to say that art does nothing for the preservation of the individual or the species?

9. A. Write a series of *because* clauses in which you give the reason why creative action is the opposite of bartering, exchanging, earning, winning, getting something out of, go getting.

B. Which of these words would best apply to Eastman's practical man?

C. Why does *endowing* well characterize creative action as Castiello is defining it here?

BEAUTY IN ART AND INTELLECTUAL PURSUITS

E. F. Caldin

1 Beauty in a general sense is closely connected with truth and goodness, and perhaps we may say that anything (a tree, a person, a theorem, a poem) is beautiful in so far as its truth and goodness lay it open to our minds, so that we can grasp its form intuitively. A friend is beautiful to us —more beautiful than, say, a stone—because we have a certain knowledge of his character, and rejoice in it. We know him as a unity, a person—not exhaustively but yet not merely as a series of episodes or aspects or appearances. And we know him, not merely by discursive reasoning—comparing, contracting, discussing, abstracting—but also by some measure of intuition, sympathy, assimilation, insight. For instance, we do not argue that on certain occasions in the past he has been found reliable and so there is a certain likelihood that he will not let us down tomorrow; we simply trust him, on the ground that we know his character. It is this intuitive knowledge of a lovable being that constitutes the perception of beauty. It is not an affair of the senses and emotions only, but of insight and love as well. I do not deny that emotion plays a part in the experience of beauty, but suggest that it is secondary; it is the intuition that is primary and is the root cause of the joy. Nor do I deny the contribution of purely sensuous delight, but hold that though itself good it is relatively unimportant except in relation to the vision it serves. Beauty, then, is one kind of good, arising from one kind of knowledge; it is intimately connected with goodness and truth.

2 It follows that beauty depends on form—unity, order, pattern, design. For a thing is both more knowable and more lovable the more developed is its form. A friend is more beautiful than a kitten, a kitten more than a pebble. Beauty increases as we go up the scale of existence—inanimate, animate, human. Now it is in respect of form that these levels of existance differ from one another. The material is the same for all—the same set of chemical elements, the same set of physical laws; but the forms are different. The form of the man is a rational soul and so higher than that of the organism, which in turn is capable of spontaneous growth, development, and reproduction and so is higher than that of inanimate nature. And the higher form is at once more knowable and more lovable; and since it is more open to our minds, and since when intuited it gives us the more de-

Reproduced from *The Power and Limits of Science* (E. F. Caldin) by permission of the author and publishers (Chapman & Hall) 1949, pp. 121–126.

light, it is also more beautiful. It is by degrees of form, then, that we can assess beauty.

3 We may inquire, then, what account can be given on these principles of beauty in painting, in sculpture, in poetry. These arts, I shall assume, are concerned with *significant* forms. The form of a work of art is distilled from the artist's experience in order to convey an intuitive vision of some reality; some person, situation, mood, or occasion. The "outer" form of the work and the "inner" form of what is represented are both important. What delights us at first sight in a painting is the intuitive knowledge of its outer form. The prima facie beauty of a painting is not the beauty of what it represents; it has an independent beauty, related to the joy of seeing something as a whole, of reaching intuitive knowledge; the mind rejoices in the free movement of the intuition, in the relief from ratiocination. The artist has solved a problem in line, colour, and composition; he has not merely copied; he has selected, emphasised, concentrated; he has made something that is visibly a unity, and a delightful unity. If now the outer form is significant of a beloved reality, we are the more delighted, because of the further beauty that we touch through the work of art—the inner form revealed by means of the outer form; for instance, the character revealed by a portrait. We find a portrait beautiful because in it we see, condensed into one form, the whole complex of a character, a human life. If the character is beloved, too, we are the more delighted with this fresh beauty revealed and intuited through art. Raphael's *Madonna in the Meadow* is a superb piece of painting, and it would still be magnificent if we knew nothing of the people represented in it. But since we do know the tender relation of son and mother, the sight of the picture conveys far more than a lovely whole of colour; it gives a vision in the mind's eye of something that we love and delight in contemplating.

> O! how much more doth beauty beauteous seem
> By that sweet ornament which truth doth give!

4 Again, if we go to a performance of Shakespeare's *Henry the Fifth* we see, unrolled before our intuition rather than our reason, the epitome of a vast variety of human life, brought into unity by plot and characters, so that we cannot but admire the play as a play. And in so far as the reality represented is itself beautiful, we are the more delighted; whether we merely enjoy the vigorous Elizabethan world-picture that the play exhibits, or whether we admire besides the truth of its valuations of honour, courage, and kingship.

5 A work of art, then—a significant form—opens to us both its own beauty and that of the reality it represents; the outer form is significant of the inner form. Evidently the work of art will be the greater, the greater the

range and depth of the experience drawn upon. We all think the *Divine Comedy* a greater poem than some slight lyric that may nevertheless be as adequate technically to its tiny theme as Dante's poem is to his mighty one. The poem (or the portrait, or the sculpture) is the greater, moreover, the more the outer form is adequate to the reality represented. It should be transparent, should reveal to our intuition the form of the reality that it expresses. Compare the familiar doggerel:

Twinkle twinkle, little star,
How I wonder what you are!
Up above the world so high
Like a diamond in the sky,

with a passage from Shelley's *Prometheus Unbound*:

The point of one white star is quivering still
Deep in the orange light of widening morn
Beyond the purple mountains: through a chasm
Of wind-divided mist the darker lake
reflects it: now it wanes: it gleams again
As the waves fade, and as the burning threads
Of woven cloud unravel in pale air . . .

Each passage is inspired by the sight of a star, but while the second brings a superb scene vividly before us, the first makes even the night sky seem trivial.

6 Further, in proportion to the reality represented, the outer form must have a unified complexity, an ordered richness, a variety in unity. The power of Shakespeare's sonnets, or of "metaphysical" poetry, for example, is surely due to the great range of experience concentrated into one of those vivid poems, allied with the corresponding wealth of phrase and with the close-knit structure. The richer the diversity, and the closer the unification, the more do we find beauty in such a work. Here, for instance, in Shakespeare's Sonnet XIX, is unity in diversity exemplified in an amalgam of nature, mythology, and human love, mutability and immortality, supplication and defiance:

Devouring Time, blunt thou the lion's paws,
And make the earth devour her own sweet brood;
Pluck the keen teeth from the fierce tiger's jaws,
And burn the long-liv'd phoenix in her blood;
Make glad and sorry seasons as thou fleets,
And do whate'er thou wilt, swift-footed Time,
To the wide world and all her fading sweets;
But I forbid thee one most heinous crime:
O! carve not with thy hours my love's fair brow,

Nor draw no lines there with thine antique pen;
Him in thy course untainted do allow
For beauty's pattern to succeeding men.
  Yet do thy worst, old Time: despite thy wrong,
  My love shall in my verse ever live young.

And here is a poem of George Herbert's which perhaps is even more successful, because the appeal to sense, imagination, and memory is as vivid, the form at least as balanced and compact, and the thought more realist, feeding the mind as well as the fancy:

Sweet day, so cool, so calm, so bright—
  The bridal of the earth and sky;
The dew shall weep thy fall to-night
  For thou must die.

Sweet rose, whose hue angry and brave
  Bids the rash gazer wipe his eye,
Thy root is ever in its grave
  And thou must die.

Sweet spring, full of sweet days and roses,
  A box where sweets compacted lie,
My music shows ye have your closes
  And all must die.

Only a sweet and virtuous soul,
  Like seasoned timber, never gives;
But though the whole world turn to coal,
  Then chiefly lives.

7 Now I do not say that unity in diversity is the whole of beauty; but it is the element common to beauty in art and literature and to beauty in intellectual pursuits. It gives us the clue to beauty in philosophy and mathematics, and it is the characteristic by which we can best assess it. Mathematics lends us a simple example. A table of integrals is less beautiful than an elegant mathematical theorem, because our minds can seize the theorem as a whole, but not the collections of integrals, which has no logical unity. A system of such theorems subsumed under some general principle, or still more an ordered treatment of a whole branch of the subject (such as the integral calculus), has a still fuller beauty, because of its richer variety-in-unity. In philosophy, again, we may find a beauty in great metaphysics that is lacking in the work of one who confines himself to mathematical logic.

8 The key, then, is variety-in-unity in the human construction, agreeing with the form of what it represents. Accordingly we can assess intellectual beauty in terms of form, and form in terms of unified variety.

STUDY GUIDE

Word Study

1. With the help of your dictionary distinguish between *intuition* and *discursive reasoning* as they are used in paragraph 1. Is the *ratiocination* mentioned in paragraph 3 the same as *discursive reasoning?*

2. Is there any dictionary definition of the word *form* that fits the author's use of the term in paragraph 2?

Content

1. Very fundamental to the understanding of this discussion of beauty is a clear idea of the various meanings of the word *form* as it is employed by the author.

A. In one case it is synonymous with external shape, visible design, and pattern. This is what the author calls outer form. Point out all the places in which the word is used in this sense in the passage.

B. In other cases the word *form* is employed in the passage as not identical with external pattern but rather with the internal meaning or reality that the visible pattern or form signifies. This is what the author means by significant or inner form. Point out all the places in the essay in which the word *form* is used with this meaning.

2. To get at some of the elements that go into the pleasure experienced in the beauty of external "form" or pattern, the following exercise might prove useful. Analyze carefully what it is that makes it possible to apprehend Figure 1 quickly and pleasurably as a unity, while it is not possible to experience a like pleasure in contemplating Figure 2.

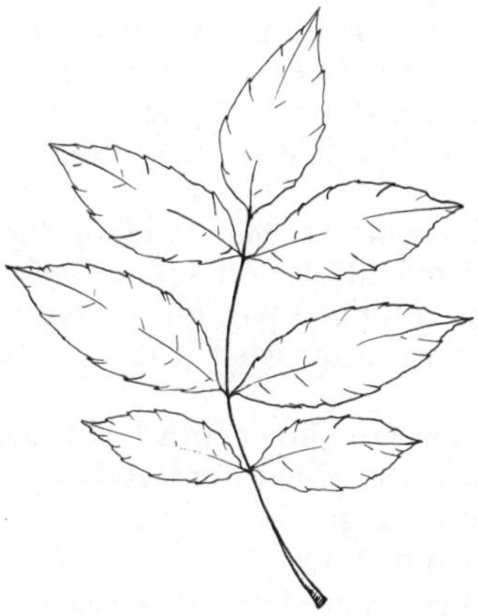

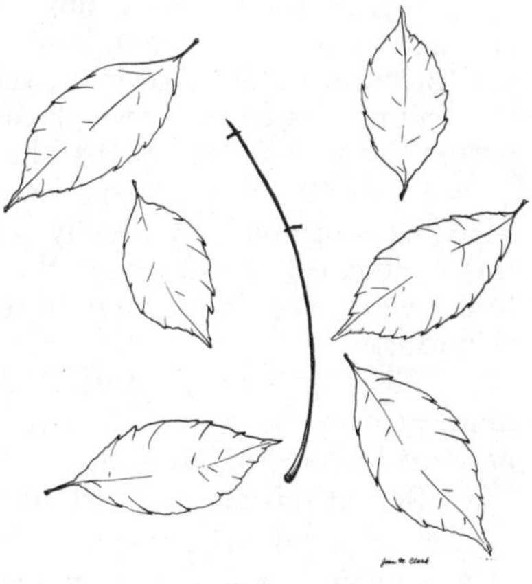

In making this analysis consider the contribution that the element of rhythm or regular repetition has in creating the recognizable pattern in Figure 1 and how the lack of this regular repetition results in no unity at all in Figure 2.

This regular repetition, here, as in all good design, gives us the pleasure of recognition—the joy people take in recognizing a repeated pattern once it is established.

Equally evident, in Figure 1, is the second principle of aesthetic pleasure, the principle of variation, which provides the pleasure of surprise. Analyze carefully the several ways in which this principle is illustrated in the design of the leaf frond in Figure 1. Without this variety, a design, whether in nature or in art, becomes monotonous. Think, for instance, of the several reasons why a leaf frond a mile long made up of pairs of leaves exactly the same size would be less pleasing than the one reproduced in Figure 1.

What does the stem contribute to the creation of a unified pattern in Figure 1?

This combination of regularly repeated and subtly varied details creates a visual pattern which provides both the pleasures of recognition and surprise—the pleasures experienced in outer pattern or form everywhere. This is separate from the added pleasure that the same pattern can provide as a significant form, enabling me to recognize it, through its very special shape, as an ash rather than a hickory or walnut frond. In other words a visual form or pattern can signify or represent an "inner" form or meaning which is distinct from its actual visual appearance. The greater and more important that inner reality is, the greater can be the pleasure in recognizing it in the visual pattern that incarnates it. This is what the author means in paragraph 2 when he says: "A thing is both more knowable and more lovable the more developed is its form [inner form or being]. A friend is more beautiful than a kitten, a kitten more than a pebble. Beauty increases as we go up the scale of existence—inanimate, animate, human."

Find other examples of visual pattern in natural objects and analyze carefully the elements of pleasurable design that are exemplified in their outer form or pattern.

3. The principles of unity amidst variety, or repetition and variation, analyzed above in an example of a beautiful object in nature, will be discoverable in beautiful art objects as well. The author suggests some applications of these principles in the areas of painting and poetry. It might be rewarding to pursue the analysis farther than he does.

A. Get a good colored reproduction of Raphael's *Madonna in the Meadow*, and analyze carefully how, by a regular repetition and subtle variation of line, color, and shapes the artist has created a unified pattern (or outer form) which is quite pleasing to the eye even independent of what it represents or means.

Then try to arrive at what idea of the Madonna (the inner form) is communicated in the picture, and try to determine how the visual lines and color patterns help to communicate that inner form or meaning.

Repeat this exercise with other representational pictures.

B. Make the same kind of analysis of the "outer" form or pattern of a nonobjective painting by a painter like Mondrian. Do you think such a painting can have or is intended to have an inner form or meaning? Whatever your thoughts in the matter are, be ready to discuss and illustrate them.

4. A. Can you suggest how the principles of unity amidst variety or repetition and variation are exemplified in a work of literature like an epic or a play?

B. What would be the chief unifying principle of a poem like those quoted by the author?

5. A. What would be the outer form or pattern of the poems quoted in the essay?

B. What would be their inner form?

6. If what the author has said by way of a partial analysis of the principles of beauty is valid, why is he correct in seeing more beauty in a mathematical theorem than in a table of integrals? Why more beauty in a great metaphysics than in mere mathematical logic?

THE TESTIMONY OF MODERN ART

William Barrett

1 Anyone who attempts to gain a unified understanding of modern art as a whole is bound to suffer the uncomfortable sensation of having fallen into a thicket of brambles. We ourselves are involved in the subject, and we can hardly achieve the detachment of the historian a few centuries hence. Modern art still provokes violent controversy, even after it has been on the scene a good half century and names like Picasso and Joyce have become almost household words. The Philistine still finds it shocking, scandalous, and foolish; and there is always a case to be made for the Philistine, and surely for the Philistine in ourselves without whom we could not carry on the drab business of ordinary living. Indeed, from the point of view we are taking here, the Philistine attitude, particularly in its irritation, may be just as revelatory historically as any other. But it is a case not only of the Philistine; sensitive observers still exist—directors of museums, connoisseurs, and historians—who find in modern art a disastrous falling away from the excellence of the art of the past. In a sense, all this controversy is pointless; so much of it has to do with the eventual historical rating of our own period, which is something we cannot even forsee. The century from Manet to Matisse may figure in future art histories as a period of impoverishment and decline, whose works cannot stand beside those of the old masters; or it may figure as a period of such abundant creativity that it can be matched only by the Renaissance during the fifteenth century. My own personal prejudice is toward the latter judgment, but I have no way of proving it; and such speculation, in any case, does not enter into my own experience of this art. We have simply got to give up the attempt to assess

ourselves for posterity; the men of the future will form their own opinion without our help. What we so self-consciously call "modern art," after all, is nothing more nor less than the art of this time, *our* art; there is no other today. If we could have a different art, or a better, we would have it. As it is, we are lucky in this period to have any art at all. The Philistine rebukes the artist for being willful, as if all of modern art were a deliberate conspiracy against him, the viewer; the artist can hardly hope to make this man understand that art is not a mere matter of conscious will and conscious contrivance, and that the artist, by changing his ideas (even by adopting the Philistine's), will not become a different person living at a different time and place. In the end the only authentic art is that which has about it the power of inevitability.

2 Nevertheless, the controversy, irritation, and bafflement to which modern art gives rise does not provide us a very effective handle with which to take hold of it. Irritation usually arises when something touches a sore spot in ourselves, which most of the time we would like desperately to hide; rarely if ever does the fault lie totally with the provoking object. Modern art touches a sore spot, or several sore spots, in the ordinary citizen of which he is totally unaware. The more irritated he becomes at modern art the more he betrays the fact that he himself, and his civilization, are implicated in what the artist shows him. The ordinary citizen objects to modern art because it is difficult and obscure. Is it so certain that the world the ordinary citizen takes for granted, the values upon which his civilization rests are so clear, either to him or in themselves? Sometimes the artist's image is very clear (in general, modern art is *simpler* than academic art), but it goes against the grain of the ordinary man because secretly he understands its intent all too well; and besides, he has already limited "understanding" to the habitual pigeonholes into which he slips every experience. The ordinary man is uncomfortable, angry, or derisive before the dislocation of forms in modern art, before its bold distortions, or arbitrary manipulations of objects. The painter puts three or more eyes in the face, or several noses, or twists and elongates the body at the expense of photographic resemblance in order to build up his own inner image. Has the contrary attitude of strict and literal attachment to objects succeeded in resolving all the anxieties of the ordinary man, and has not in fact the rampant extroversion of modern civilization brought it to the brink of the abyss? Finally, the ordinary man—and in this respect the ordinary man is joined by the learned and sensitive traditionalist in art—objects to the content of modern art: it is too bare and bleak, too negative or "nihilistic," too shocking or scandalous; it dishes out unpalatable truths. But have the traditional ideals worked so well in this century that we can afford to neglect the unpalatable truths about human life that those ideals have chosen to ignore? Does the aesthete who extols the greatness of the past

as an argument against modern art have any idea of how pallid his own response to, say, the Virgin of Chartres appears beside the medieval man's response? Or that his own aestheticism, however cultured, is in fact a form of sentimentality—since sentimentality, at bottom, is nothing but false feeling, feeling that is untrue to its object, whether by being excessive or watered down?

3 In a famous passage in *A Farewell to Arms* Ernest Hemingway writes:

> I was always embarrassed by the words sacred, glorious, and sacrifice and the expression in vain. We had heard them, sometimes standing in the rain almost out of earshot, so that only the shouted words came through, and had read them, on proclamations that were slapped up by billposters over other proclamations, now for a long time, and I had seen nothing sacred, and the things that were glorious had no glory and the sacrifices were like the stockyards at Chicago if nothing was done with the meat except to bury it. There were many words that you could not stand to hear and finally only the names of places had dignity. Certain numbers were the same way and certain dates and these with the names of places were all you could say and have them mean anything. Abstract words such as glory, honor, courage, or hallow were obscene beside the concrete names of villages, the numbers of roads, the names of rivers, the numbers of regiments and the dates.

For a whole generation that was the great statement of protest against the butchery of the First World War. But it has a greater historical significance than that: it can be taken as a kind of manifesto of modern art and literature, an incitement to break through empty abstractions of whatever kind, to destroy sentimentality even if the real feelings exposed should appear humble and impoverished—the names of places and dates; and even if in stripping himself naked the artist seems to be left with Nothing. Modern art thus begins, and sometimes ends, as a confession of spiritual poverty. That is its greatness and its triumph, but also the needle it jabs into the Philistine's sore spot, for the last thing he wants to be reminded of is his spiritual poverty. In fact, his greatest poverty is not to know how impoverished he is, and so long as he mouths the empty ideals or religious phrases of the past he is but as tinkling brass. In matters of the spirit, poverty and riches are sometimes closer than identical twins: the man who struts with borrowed feathers may be poor as a church mouse within, while a work that seems stark and bleak can, if genuine, speak with all the inexhaustible richness of the world. The triumph of Hemingway's style is its ability to break through abstractions to see what it is one really senses and feels. When the modern sculptor disdains the pomp of marble and uses industrial materials, steel wire, or bolts, or even rejected materials like old board, rope, or nails, he is perhaps showing himself to be impoverished next to the heroic grandeur of a Michelangelo, but he is also bringing us back to the inexhaustible brute world that surrounds us. Sometimes the confession of poverty takes a violent and aggressive tone, as when the Dadaists drew a mustache on the Mona Lisa. Dada itself, like Hemingway, came out of the revolt against the First World War, and despite its clowning must now be regarded as one of the *valid* eruptions of the irrational in this century. The generation of the First World War could hardly be expected to view Western culture as sacrosanct, since they perceived—and rightly—that it was bound up with the civilization that had ended in that ghastly butchery. Better then to reject the trappings of that culture, even art itself, if that would leave one a little more honest in ones nakedness. To discover one's own spiritual poverty is to achieve a positive conquest by the spirit.

4 Modern art has been an immense movement toward the destruction of forms—of received and traditional forms. The positive side of this has been an immense expansion of the possibilities of art and an almost greedy acquisition of new forms from all over the globe. Around 1900 French painters became interested in African sculpture. (The introduction of Japanese prints into Europe in the nineteenth century had already brought with it a profound shift in the sensibility of Western painters.) And these borrowings were only the beginning: by now we have become accustomed to painters and sculptors drawing their forms from Oriental and primitive art of every culture. This century in art, André Malraux has said, will go down in history not as the period of abstract art but as the period in which all the art of the past, and from every quarter of the globe, became available to the painter and sculptor, and through them became a part of our modern taste. Certainly, we can no longer look upon the canon of Western art—Greco-Roman art as revived, extended, and graced by the Renaissance—as *the* tradition in art, or even any longer as distinctly and uniquely *ours*. That canon is in fact only one tradition among many, and indeed in its strict adherence to representational form is rather the exception in the whole gallery of *human* art. Such an extension of the resources of the past, for the modern artist, implies a different and more comprehensive understanding of the term "human" itself: a Sumerian figure of a fertility goddess is as "human" to us as a Greek Aphrodite. When the sensibility of an age can accommodate the alien "inhuman" forms of primitive art side by side with the classic "human" figures of Greece or the Renaissance, it should be obvious that the attitude toward man that we call classical humanism—which is the intellectual expression of the spirit that informs the classical canon of Western art—has also gone by the boards. This is an historical fact the most immediate evidence of which is the whole body of modern art itself. Even if existential philosophy had

not been formulated, we would know from modern art that a new and radical conception of man was at work in this period.

5 It would be a mistake to construe this breaking out on the part of Western artists from the confinement of what had been their tradition as mere expansion or a spiritually imperialistic act of acquisition. It is not simply an external and quantitative change in the number of forms the artist can assimilate, it is also, and more profoundly, an internal and qualitative change in the spirit with which the artist appropriates these forms. This breaking out of the tradition is in fact also a breakdown within the Western tradition. On this point the artistic conservative who rejects modern art, seeing it as a scandal and a departure from the tradition, sees rightly, however he may turn what he sees to his own purposes. That Western painters and sculptors have in this century gone outside their own tradition to nourish themselves on the art of the rest of the world—Oriental, African, Melanesian—signifies that what we have known as *the* tradition is no longer able to nourish its most creative members: the confining mold of this tradition has broken, under pressures both from within and without. It would be possible to avoid this painful conclusion, and to dismiss this group of artists as mere irresponsibles, and skillful renegades from the tradition, if there were any artists of comparable achievement whose work the anti-modernist could set over against theirs. But what is equally sure—and this negative evidence is strong or even stronger on the side of the moderns—is that the academic art of this period is as dead as mutton. It excites no one, depresses no one, and does not even really soothe anyone. It simply does not live; it is outside the time.

6 If we turn to the internal and formal characteristics of modern art, without reference to its external inspirations in African or primitive or Oriental art, we find the same indications of a radical transformation of the Western spirit. Cubism is the classicism of modern art: that is, the one formally perfected style which modern art has elaborated and from which all modern abstract art that is valid has derived. A great deal of nonsense has been written about the creation of Cubism, connecting it with relativity physics, psychoanalysis, and heaven knows how many other complex and remote things. The fact is that the painters who created Cubism were creating paintings and nothing else—certainly they were not dealing in ideologies. Cubism evolved in a succession of perfectly logical steps out of previous stages of painting, out of the Impressionist and Cézanne, and it raised a series of pictorial problems that had to be solved within the medium of painting and by painters working strictly as painters—that is, upon the visual image as such.

7 Yet a great formal style in painting has never been created that did not draw upon the depths of the human spirit, and that did not, in its new-

ness, express a fresh mutation of the human spirit. Cubism achieved a radical flattening of space by insisting on the two-dimensional fact of the canvas. This flattening out of space would seem not to be a negligible fact historically if we reflect that when, once before in history, such a development occurred but in the opposite direction—when the flatness of the Gothic or primitive painters passed over into the solidity, perspective, and three-dimensional style of early Renaissance painting—it was a mark that man was turning outward, into space, after the long period of introspection of the Middle Ages. Western man moved out into space in his painting, in the fourteenth century, before he set forth into actual physical space in the age of exploration that was to follow. Thus painting was prophetic of the new turn of the human spirit which was eventually to find expression in the conquest of the whole globe. Have we the right, then, to suggest that the flattening of painting in our own century portends a turning inward of the human spirit, or at any rate a turning away from that outer world of space which has hitherto been the ultimate arena of Western man's extroversion? With Cubism begins that process of detachment from the object which has become the hallmark of modern art. Even though Cubism is a classical and formal style, the artist nevertheless asserts his own subjectivity by the freedom with which he cuts up and dislocates objects—bottles, pitchers, guitars—as it pleases him for the sake of the picture, which is now no longer held up to us as a representation of those objects but as a visual image with its own independent value alongside that of nature. The subjectivity that is generally present in modern art is a psychological compensation for, sometimes a violent revolt against, the gigantic externalization of life within modern society. The world pictured by the modern artist is, like the world meditated upon by the existential philosopher, a world where man is a stranger.

8 When mankind no longer lives spontaneously turned toward God or the supersensible world—when, to echo the words of Yeats, the ladder is gone by which we would climb to a higher reality—the artist too must stand face to face with a flat and inexplicable world. This shows itself even in the formal structures of modern art. Where the movement of the spirit is no longer vertical but only horizontal, the climactic elements in art are in general leveled out, flattened. The flattening of pictorial space that is achieved in Cubism is not an isolated fact, true only of painting, but is paralleled by similar changes in literary techniques. There is a general process of flattening, three chief aspects of which may be noted:

9 (1) *The flattening out of all planes* upon the plane of the picture. Near and far are pushed together. So in certain works of modern literature time, instead of space, is flattened out upon one plane. Past and present are represented as occurring simultaneously, upon a single plane of time. James Joyce's *Ulysses*, T. S. Eliot's *The Waste Land*, and Ezra Pound's

Cantos are examples; and perhaps the most powerful use of the device was made by Faulkner in his early novel *The Sound and the Fury*.

10 (2) More important perhaps is *the flattening out of climaxes*, which occurs both in painting and literature. In traditional Western painting there is a central subject, located at or near the center of the picture, and the surrounding space in the picture is subordinate to this. In a portrait the figure is placed near the center, and the background becomes secondary to it, something to be blended as harmoniously as possible with the figure. Cubism abolished this idea of the pictorial climax: the whole space of the picture became of equal importance. Negative spaces (in which there are no objects) are as important as positive spaces (the contours of physical objects). If a human figure is treated, it may be broken up and distributed over various parts of the canvas. Formally speaking, the spirit of this art is anticlimactic.

11 When we turn to observe this same deflation or flattening of climaxes in literature, the broader human and philosophic questions involved become much clearer. The classical tradition in literature, deriving from Aristotle's *Poetics*, tells us that a drama (and consequently any other literary work) must have a beginning, middle, and end. The action begins at a certain point, rises toward a climax, and then falls to a denouement. One can diagram a classical plot of this kind by means of a triangle whose apex represents the climax with which everything in the play has some logical and necessary connection. The author subordinates himself to the requirements of logic, necessity, probability. His structure must be an intelligible whole in which each part develops logically out of what went before. If our existence itself is never quite like this, no matter; art is a selection from life, and the poet is required to be selective. However it is important to note that this canon of intelligible literary structure—beginning, middle, and end, with a well-defined climax—arose in a culture in which the universe too was believed to be an ordered structure, a rational and intelligible whole.

12 What happens if we try to apply this classical Aristotelian canon to a modern work like Joyce's *Ulysses*, 734 pages of power and dullness, beauty and sordidness, comedy and pathos, where the movement is always horizontal, never ascending toward any crisis, and where we detect not the shadow of anything like a climax, in the traditional sense of that term? If Joyce's had been a disordered mind, we could dismiss all this as a sprawling chaos; but he was in fact an artist in superb control of his material, so that the disorder has to be attributed to his material, to life itself. It is, in fact, the banal gritty thing that we live that Joyce gives us, in comparison with which most other fiction is indeed fiction. This world is dense, opaque, unintelligible; that is the datum from which the modern artist always starts. The formal dictates of the well-made play or the well-made novel,

which were the logical outcome of thoroughly rational preconceptions about reality, we can no longer hold to when we become attentive "to the things themselves," to the facts, to existence in the mode in which we do exist. If our epoch still held to the idea, as Western man once did, that the whole of reality is a system in which each detail providentially and rationally is subordinated to others and ultimately to the whole itself, we could demand of the artist that his form imitate this idea of reality, and give us coherence, logic, and the picture of a world with no loose ends. But to make such a demand nowadays is worse than an impertinence: it is a travesty upon the historical being of the artist.

13 Even where the writer has more of a story, in the traditional sense, to tell, he may prefer not to tell it in the traditional way. In *The Sound and the Fury* Faulkner has much more of a novelistic narrative than Joyce in *Ulysses*—the decline of a family, a suicide, the elopement of a girl, and so on—but he chooses not to present these events in the form of the well-made novel. And the choice is wise, for the power of the novel is increased immeasurably thereby. The brute, irrational, given quality of the world comes through so strongly in Faulkner's peculiar technique that he actually shows, and does not merely state, the meaning of the quotation from which his title is derived:

> [*Life*] *is a tale,*
> *Told by an idiot, full of sound and fury,*
> *Signifying nothing.*

Shakespeare places these lines in the context of a fairly well-made tragedy in which evil is destroyed and good triumphs; but Faulkner shows us the world of which Shakespeare's statement would be true: a world opaque, dense, and irrational, that could not have existed for Shakespeare, close as he was still to medieval Christianity. Even where a purposeful human action is planned, in the novel, and the necessary steps taken to carry it through—as in the section on the day Quentin Compson commits suicide—what really happens has little to do with the traditional order, logic, sequence of events that normally accompany such an action. The day described shows us not the abstraction "Quentin Compson commits suicide" but, as the author turns his own and his reader's eye "to the things themselves," a process far more concrete and contingent: a sparrow chirps at the window, a watch breaks, the hero gets entangled in a perfectly absurd melee with a little runaway girl, there is a fist fight, etc.; and underneath all this is, but never mentioned, the slow blind surge moving forward like an underground river toward the sea, of a man's going to his death. This section, and the book itself, is a masterpiece, perhaps as great as anything yet written by an American; and is to be recommended to anyone who wants to know the concrete feel of that world with which in his thinking the existential philosopher has to deal.

14 In the course of the brute random flow of detail that is that last day of his life, Quentin Compson breaks the crystal of his watch. He twists off the two hands and thereafter, throughout the day, the watch continues to tick loudly but cannot, with its faceless dial, indicate the time. Faulkner could not have hit on a better image to convey the sense of time which permeates the whole book. The normal reckonable sequence of time—one moment after another—has been broken, has disappeared; but as the watch pounds on, time is all the more urgent and real for Quentin Compson. He cannot escape time, he is in it, it is the time of his fate and his decision; and the watch has no hands to reassure him of that normal, calculable progression of minutes and hours in which our ordinary day-to-day life is passed. Time is no longer a reckonable sequence, then, for him, but an inexhaustible inescapable presence. We are close here—as we shall see later—to the thought of Heidegger. (Faulkner certainly never read Heidegger; he may never even have heard of him. So much the better; for the testimony of the artist, the poet, is all the more valid when it is not contaminated by any intellectual preconceptions.) Real time, the time that makes up the dramatic substance of our life, is something deeper and more primordial than watches, clocks, and calendars. Time is the dense medium in which Faulkner's characters move about as if dragging their feet through water: it is their substance or Being, as Heidegger would put it. The abolition of clock time does not mean a retreat into the world of the timeless; quite the contrary: the timeless world, the eternal, has disappeared from the horizon of the modern writer as it has from the horizon of modern Existentialists like Sartre and Heidegger, and from the horizon of our own everyday life; and time thereby becomes all the more inexorable and absolute a reality. The temporal is the horizon of modern man, as the eternal was the horizon of the man of the Middle Ages. That modern writers have been so preoccupied with the reality of time, handling it with radically new techniques and from radically new points of view, is evidence that the philosophers in our age who have attempted a new understanding of time are responding to the same hidden historical concerns, and are not merely elaborating some new conceptual novelty out of their heads.

15 These details about art, it should be apparent to the reader, are not dragged in by the heels. Nor are they the elaborate constructions which it has become the critical fashion in this country to force upon works of art. On the contrary, the features we have mentioned lie open and accessible—on the very surface, so to speak, of the works of art themselves; and to see them requires only that we take art seriously, which means to take it as a revelation: a revelation of its time and of the being of man, and of the two together, the being of man in his time.

16 No beginning, middle, end—such is the structureless structure that some modern literary works struggle toward; and analogously in painting, no clearly demarcated foreground, middleground, and background. To the traditionalist, immersed in the classical Western tradition, all this will appear negative, purely destructive. But if we do not keep our gaze narrowly riveted on the tradition of the West (and in any case this classical canon is only one of the traditions that have arisen in the course of the whole history of the West), we find that these requirements of logical and rational form do not hold for other traditions of art in other cultures. Oriental art, for example, is much more formless, organic, and sprawling than classical Western art. It has form, but a different form from that of the West. Why is this? The question is not a trivial one; it is perhaps as profound as any the West can ask these days, for this difference in art is not mere happenstance but the inevitable concomitant of a different attitude toward the world.

17 One of the best indications of this peculiar (to us) sense of artistic form among Orientals is given by E. M. Forster in his novel *A Passage to India.* A mixed group, English and Indians, are at tea, and Professor Godbole, a Hindu, has been asked to sing, but has let the occasion go by; then, as all are leaving, the Hindu says, "I may sing now," quite unexpectedly. (This unexpectedness is significant, for the song is not to be given a formal setting, but to drop upon their ears as casually and contingently as life itself.) Forster's description of the song makes our point so beautifully that it is worth quoting in its entirety:

> His thin voice rose, and gave out one sound after another. At times there seemed rhythm, at times there was the illusion of a Western melody. But the ear, baffled repeatedly, soon lost any clue, and wandered in a maze of noises, none harsh or unpleasant, none intelligible. It was the song of an unknown bird. Only the servants understood it. They began to whisper to one another. The man who was gathering water chestnuts came naked out of the tank, his lips parted with delight, disclosing his scarlet tongue. The sounds continued and ceased after a few moments as casually as they had begun—apparently half through a bar, and upon the subdominant.[2]

The song begins, goes on, suddenly stops; but there is not the least trace of an Aristotelian beginning, middle, or end. Compare Godbole's song with the structure of an aria from an Italian opera. In the latter we have a beginning, a development through certain predictable phases toward the inevitable climax of the high note, and then the falling away or denouement, tying up the whole thing in a neat package: here is Aristotelian and rational

[2] From *A Passage to India* by E. M. Forster. Reprinted by permission of Harcourt, Brace & World, Inc.

form in music. But the Oriental song baffles the ear of the Westerner; it appears unintelligible. The reason is that the Westerner demands (or, let us say, used to demand) an intelligibility that the Easterner does not. If the Westerner finds the Oriental music "meaningless," the Oriental might very well reply that this is the meaninglessness of nature itself which goes on endlessly without beginning, middle, or end.

18 The real reason for the difference between the sense of artistic form in the East and in the West is thus ultimately a difference in philosophic outlook. Since the Greeks, Western man has believed that Being, all Being, is intelligible, that there is a reason for everything (at least, the central tradition that runs from Aristotle through St. Thomas Aquinas into the beginning of the modern period has held this), and that the cosmos is, finally, intelligible. The Oriental, on the other hand, has accepted his existence within a universe that would appear to be meaningless, to the rational Western mind, and has lived with this meaninglessness. Hence the artistic form that seems natural to the Oriental is one that is just as formless or formal, as irrational, as life itself. That the Western artist now finds his own inherited classical form unconvincing and indeed almot intolerable is because of a profound change in his total attitude toward the world—a change that is no less true even when the artist himself has not been able to bring it to conceptual expression. The final intelligibility of the world is no longer accepted. Our existence, as we know it, is no longer transparent and understandable by reason, bound together into a tight, coherent structure. The world that we are shown in the work of the modern painters and writers is opaque and dense. Their vision is not inspired primarily by intellectual premises; it is a spontaneous revelation of the kind of which perhaps only art is capable: it shows us where we stand, whether or not we choose to understand it. If we really open ourselves to the experience of two works of art as widely separated in time as Dante's *Divine Comedy* and Faulkner's *The Sound and the Fury*, the distance that Western man has traveled in the intervening centuries is revealed to us more clearly than through any number of abstract arguments. And the road that has been traveled is irreversible.

19 (3) The last and most important aspect of what we have called the process of flattening in modern art is *the flattening out of values*. To understand this one can begin at the simplest level in painting, where it means merely that large and small objects are treated as of equal value. Cézanne paints apples with the same passionate concentration as he paints mountains, and each apple is as monumental as a mountain. Indeed, in some of Cézanne's still lifes, if one covers up all of the picture except a certain patch of folded tablecloth, one might very well be looking at the planes and peaks of his Mont St. Victoire. For Cézanne the painting dictates its own values: little and big, high and low, sublime and ordinary outside the paint-

ing are of equal importance if in a given painting they play the same plastic role.

20 Now all this is quite contrary to the great tradition of Western art, which distinguishes sharply between the sublime and the banal and requires that the highest art treat the most sublime subjects. The mind of the West has always been hierarchical: the cosmos has been understood as a great chain of Being, from highest to lowest, which has at the same time operated as a scale of values, from lowest to highest. Painters were expected to portray the sublime scenes from the Gospel, great battles, or noble personages. The beginning of genre painting in the seventeenth century was the first step toward what we now think of as modern painting, but it was not until the present century that the reversal of Western Values was really accomplished. By now, the hierarchical scheme has been abolished altogether. Following Cézanne, the Cubists took as subjects for their most monumental paintings ordinary objects like tables, bottles, glasses, guitars. Now the painter dispenses with objects altogether: the colored shape on his canvas is itself an absolute reality, perhaps more so than the imaginary scene, the great battle, which in a traditional canvas it might serve to depict. Thus we arrive at last at *l'art brut* (raw, crude, or brute art), which seeks to abolish not only the ironclad distinction between the sublime and the banal but that between the beautiful and the ugly as well. Says the painter Dubuffet, one of the more interesting cultivators of this style:

> The idea that there are beautiful objects and ugly objects, people endowed with beauty and others who cannot claim it, has surely no other foundation than convention—old poppycock—and I declare that convention unhealthy. . . . People have seen that I intend to sweep away everything we have been taught to consider—without question—as grace and beauty; but have overlooked my work to substitute another and vaster beauty, touching all objects and beings, not excluding the most despised—and because of that, all the more exhilarating. . . . I would like people to look at my work as an enterprise for the rehabilitation of scorned values, and, in any case, make no mistake, a work of ardent celebration. . . .
>
> I am convinced that any table can be for each of us a landscape as inexhaustible as the whole Andes range. . . .
>
> I am struck by the high value, for a man, of a simple permanent fact, like the miserable vista on which the window of his room opens daily, that comes, with the passing of time, to have an important role in his life. I often think that the highest destination at which a painting can aim is to take on that function in someone's life.[3]

[3] From "Landscaped Tables, Landscapes of the Mind" by Jean Dubuffet, published by the Pierre Matisse Gallery. Reprinted by permission of the author and publisher.

21 Such ideas seem scandalous to the Western traditionalist; they undermine the time-honored canon of beauty, countenance the most disorderly elements in existence, and strike against art itself. Yet they are ideas that might be easily understood by an Oriental. For the Oriental, opposites have never been put into separate watertight compartments as with the Westerner: as it is above, so it is below, in the East; the small is equal to the great, for amid the endless expanse of countless universes, each individual universe is as but a grain of sand on the shores of the Ganges, and a grain of sand is the equal of a universe. The lotus bloom in the mud; and generally the Oriental is as willing, in his indifference, to accept the ugly dross of existence as he is its beauty, where the Westerner might very well gag at the taste. We are not concerned here with the question of whether the West is now moving toward forms of thinking and feeling that are closer to what were once those of the East. What is of concern to the philosopher is the fact that here, in art, we find so many signs of a break with the Western tradition, or at least with what had been thought to be *the* Western tradition; the philosopher must occupy himself with this break if he is to recast the meaning of this tradition.

22 The deflation, or flattening out, of values in Western art does not necessarily indicate an ethical nihilism. Quite the contrary; in opening our eyes to the rejected elements of existence, art may lead us to a more complete and less artificial celebration of the world. In literature, again, the crucial example is Joyce's *Ulysses.* It was not a literary critic but a psychologist, C. G. Jung, who perceived that this book was non-Western in spirit; he sees it as Oriental to such an extent that he recommends it as a much-needed bible to the white-skinned races. For *Ulysses* breaks with the whole tradition of Western sensibility and Western aesthetics in showing each small object of Bloom's day—even the objects in his pocket, like a cake of soap—as capable at certain moments of taking on a transcendental importance—or in being, at any rate, equal in value to those objects to which men usually attribute transcendental importance. Each grain of sand, Joyce seems to be saying (as the Oriental says), reflects the whole universe—and the Irish writer was not in the least a mystic; he simply takes experience as it comes, in the course of the single day he depicts in the novel. Any such break with tradition, where a serious reversal of values is involved, is of course dangerous, for the artist runs the risk of losing the safeguards that the experience of the past has erected for him. A good deal of modern art has clearly succumbed to this danger, and the result is disorder in the art and the artist; but the danger is the price that must be paid for any step forward by the human spirit.

23 We have seen thus far that modern art, in its formal and structural qualities, is an art of breakdown and bold innovation, the expression of an

epoch in which the accepted structures and norms of Western civilization are either in a state of dissolution or at least stand in question. But now, what about the content of this art? What does this content tell us about man? In what ways does it compel the philosopher to recast his traditional concept of man?

24 *Every age projects its own image of man into its art.* The whole history of art confirms this proposition, indeed this history is itself but a succession of images of man. A Greek figure is not just a shape in stone but the image of man in the light of which the Greeks lived. If you compare, feature by feature, the bust of a Roman patrician with the head of a medieval saint—as André Malraux has done with a spectacularly sharp eye in his *Voices of Silence*—you cannot account in formal terms for the difference between them: the two heads stare at each other and cancel each other out; they give us two different images of the destiny and possibilities of being a man. The Roman head shows us the face of the *imperium*, of power and empire, the Christian the face of the Incarnation, the humility of the earthly transfigured by the Divine. If we knew nothing at all about Taoism, we could still reconstruct from Chinese Sung painting what the Taoist felt about man and nature. And so it goes. Whenever a civilization has lived in terms of a certain image of man, we can see this image in its art; sometimes the image is present even when it was never articulated in thought, the artist in this way anticipating the philosopher. With primitive or prehumanist art it is another matter; here we are presented with images that are much more primordial and abstract, and we are not able to discern in them the features of man. In those primitive cultures humanism had not yet come into existence. Man was still too close to his totem animal. Yet even in this art if we will, we can see the image—or non-image—of man in the light of which the primitives lived, in the archetypal images from which man's own individuated features have not yet emerged.

25 And now, what about modern art? What image of man do we find in it?

26 It is very suggestive that modern artists have discovered primitive art to be valid for them and have found a strange kinship with its forms. To be sure, when the modern artist uses primitive motifs, they mean for him something altogether different from what they meant for the primitive. One cannot undo thirty centuries of civilization. Nevertheless, the extraordinarily vital attraction which primitive art now has for us is of no little significance. The tradition of Western humanism has faltered, become questionable; we are not so sure any more that we know what man is, and we do know in this century what blind forces can disturb or destroy his so-called humanity. Hence we respond to the archetypal images of prehumanist man, more abstract and impersonal than the features of man as we know him.

27 The one thing that is not clear in modern art is its image of man. We can select a figure from Greek art, from the Renaissance, or the Middle Ages and say with some certainty, "That is the image of man as the Greek, the medieval, or Renaissance man conceived him." I do not think we can find any comparably clear-cut image of man amid the bewildering thicket of modern art. And this is not because we are too close to the period, as yet, to stand back and make such a selection. Rather, the variety of images is too great and too contradictory to coalesce into any single shape or form. May the reason why modern art offers us no clear-cut image of man not be that it already knows—whether or not it has brought this knowledge to conceptual expression—that man is a creature who transcends any image because he has no fixed essence or nature, as a stone or tree have?

28 A good deal of modern art has been concerned, in any case, simply with the destruction of the traditional image of man. Man is laid bare; more than that, he is flayed, cut up into bits, and his members strewn everywhere, like those of Osiris, with the reassembling of these scattered parts not even promised but only dumbly waited for. Our novels are increasingly concerned with the figure of the faceless and anonymous hero, who is at once everyman and nobody. Perhaps, again, it is Joyce who began this process of dissection, and he can even evoke an echo of prehumanist art in the incident of Odysseus' encounter with the blind giant Polyphemus, in which the Greek hero calls himself *ou tis*, Noman, the man without an identity. In the novels of Franz Kafka the hero is a cipher, an initial; a cipher, to be sure, with an overwhelming passion to find out his individual place and responsibility—things which are not given to him *a priori* and which he dies without ever finding out. The existence of this cipher who does not discover his own meaning is marginal, in the sense that he is always beyond the boundary of what is secure, stable meaningful, ordained. Modern literature tends to be a literature of "extreme situations," to use Jaspers' expression. It shows us man at the end of his tether, cut off from the consolations of all that seems so solid and earthly in the daily round of life—that seems so as long as this round is accepted without question.

29 Naturally enough, this faceless hero is everywhere exposed to Nothingness. When by chance or fate, we fall into an extreme situation—one, that is, on the far side of what is normal, routine, accepted, traditional, safeguarded—we are threatened by the void. The solidity of the so-called real world evaporates under the pressure of our situation. Our being reveals itself as much more porous, much less substantial than we had thought it—it is like those cryptic human figures in modern sculpture that are full of holes or gaps. Nothingness has, in fact, become one of the chief themes in modern art and literature, whether it is directly named as such or merely drifts through the work as the ambiance in which the human figures live, move, and have their being. We are reminded of the elongated and

attenuated figures of the sculptor Giacometti, figures that seem to be invaded by the surrounding void. "*Some live in it and never know it,*" writes Hemingway in the story "A Clean, Well-Lighted Place," which presents in its six or seven pages a vision of Nothing that is perhaps as powerful as any in modern art, and he continues, "*It was all a nothing, and man is a nothing too.*" The example of Hemingway is valuable here, for he is not an artist inspired by intellectual themes; quite the contrary, he is a reporter and a poet intent on reporting what it is he really sees in experience, and what he has seen and reports to us in this story is the Nothing that sometimes rises up before the eyes of human beings. A story by Sartre on the same subject would be much more suspect to us: we would have reason to believe that Existentialist writer was loading the dice intellectually, reporting on experience out of a previous philosophical commitment. But to reject Hemingway's vision of the Nothing, of Nothingness, might well be to close our eyes to our own experience.

30 It is worth emphasizing, once again, that the vision of Nothingness with which modern art presents us does express a real encounter, one that is part of the historical destiny of the time. Creative artists do not produce such a vision out of nowhere. Nor in general do audiences or readers fail to respond to it. When a play *Waiting for Godot*, by an Irish disciple of Joyce's, Samuel Beckett—a play in which Nothingness circulates through every line from beginning to end—runs for more than sixteen months to packed houses in the capitals of Europe, we can only conclude that something is at work in the European mind against which its traditions cannot wholly guard it and which it will have to live through to the bitter end. Surely the audience at Beckett's play recognized something of its own experience in what it saw on the stage, some echo, however, veiled, of its own emptiness and, in Heidegger's phrase, its "waiting for God." It is not only stuffy and pompous of the Philistine to reject these responses in artist and in audience, but dangerously unintelligent, for he loses thereby the chance of finding out where he himself stands historically.

31 An epoch, as we have seen, reveals itself in its religion, its social forms, but perhaps most profoundly or, at any rate, lucidly in its art. Through modern art our time reveals itself to itself, or at least to those persons who are willing to look at their own age dispassionately and without the blindness of preconceptions, in the looking glass of its art. In our epoch existential philosophy has appeared as an intellectual expression of the time, and this philosophy exhibits numerous points of contact with modern art. The more closely we examine the two together, the stronger becomes the impression that existential philosophy is the authentic intellectual expression of our time, as modern art is the expression of the time in terms of image and intuition.

32 Not only do the two treat similar themes, but both start off from

the sense of crisis and of a break in the Western tradition. Modern art has discarded the traditional assumptions of rational form. The modern artist sees man not as the rational animal, in the sense handed down to the West by the Greeks, but as something else. Reality, too, reveals itself to the artist not as the Great Chain of Being, which the tradition of Western rationalism had declared intelligible down to its smallest link and in its totality, but as much more refractory: as opaque, dense, concrete, and in the end inexplicable. At the limits of reason one comes face to face with the meaningless; and the artist today shows us the absurd, the inexplicable, the meaningless in our daily life.

33 This break with the Western tradition imbues both philosophy and art with the sense that everything is questionable, problematic. Our time, said Max Scheler, is the first in which man has become thoroughly and completely problematic to himself. Hence the themes that obsess both modern art and existential philosophy are the alienation and strangeness of man in his world; the contradictoriness, feebleness, and contingency of human existence; the central and overwhelming reality of time for man who has lost his anchorage in the eternal.

34 The testimony art brings to these themes is all the more convincing in that it is spontaneous; it does not spring from ideas or from any intellectual program. That modern art which is most successful and powerful moves us because we see in it the artist subordinate (as must always be the case in art) to his vision. And since we recognize that man's being is historical through and through, we must take this vision of modern art as a sign that the image of man which has been at the center of our tradition till now must be re-evaluated and recast.

35 There is a painful irony in the new image of man that is emerging, however fragmentarily, from the art of our time. An observer from another planet might well be struck by the disparity between the enormous power which our age has concentrated in its external life and the inner poverty which our art seeks to expose to view. This is, after all, the age that has discovered and harnessed atomic energy, that has made airplanes that fly faster than the sun, and that will, in a few years (perhaps in a few months), have atomic-powered planes which can fly through outer space and not need to return to mother earth for weeks. What cannot man do! He has greater power now than Prometheus or Icarus or any of those daring mythical heroes who were later to succumb to the disaster of pride. But if an observer from Mars were to turn his attention from these external appurtenances of power to the shape of man as revealed in our novels, plays, painting, and sculpture, he would find there a creature full of holes and gaps, faceless, riddled with doubts and negations, starkly finite.

36 However disconcerting this violent contrast between power and impoverishment, there is something a little consoling in it for anyone who is

intimidated by excessive material power, as there is in learning that a dictator is a drunkard or marked by some other ordinary failing which makes him seem a trifle more human. If we are to redeem any part of our world from the brute march of power, we may have to begin as modern art does by exalting some of the humble and dirty little corners of existence. On another level, however, this violent contrasting is frightening, for it represents a dangerous lagging of man behind his own works; and in this lag lies the terror of the atomic bomb which hangs over us like impending night. Here surely the ordinary man begins to catch a fleeting glimpse of that Nothingness which both artist and philosopher have begun in our time to take seriously. The bomb reveals the dreadful and total contingency of human existence. Existentialism is the philosophy of the atomic age.

STUDY GUIDE

Theme and Structure

1. Barrett is saying in this essay that modern art has some very revealing testimony to give about modern man and modern society. Write a paragraph in which you summarize the chief points that modern art reveals about modern man and society.

2. The main thought divisions of the essay are paragraphs 1–5, 6–22, and 23–30. Paragraphs 31–36 serve as a summary and conclusion. Write a sentence outline of the first three parts in which you indicate what Barrett says about the aspects of modern art discussed in each of these divisions. What are his conclusions in the essay?

3. Barrett clarifies the nature of modern art by many contrasts. List some of the contrasts he employs and indicate what each of them tells about modern art.

4. The essay is also admirable for its constant use of concrete illustrations to clarify the points being made. List some of the most effective examples and state how they help to enlarge and deepen the reader's understanding of modern art.

Content

1. Reread Troisfontaines' essay on existentialism and then write a paper in which you show how Troisfontaines would partly agree and partly disagree with Barrett's insistence that existentialism, like modern art, is the authentic expression of our time. What do the two discussions of existentialism have in common? How do they differ?

2. What is the irony in the modern human situation discussed in the conclusion of the essay? Write a paper in which you enlarge on the *outer power* and *inward weakness* of modern man as he reveals himself in modern science and art.

3. Look up the word *Philistine* in your dictionary. Which of its meanings is relevant to Barrett's use of the term at the beginning of the essay?

4. Look up in the dictionary or in an art history or encyclopedia the

meaning of *dadaism* and *cubism*. What does Barrett see in each of these forms of art that reveals special facets of the modern human situation?

5. After studying the entire essay, discuss what is appropriate about Barrett's opening simile that attempting to gain a unified understanding of modern art as a whole is like the uncomfortable sensation "of having fallen into a thicket of brambles."

6. If the vision presented by modern art and literature is as empty and confused as Barrett suggests, what advantage is there in reading or observing it? Does Barrett himself state the advantage of doing so?

HOW WE LISTEN

Aaron Copland

1 We all listen to music according to our separate capacities. But, for the sake of analysis, the whole listening process may become clearer if we break it up into its component parts, so to speak. In a certain sense we all listen to music on three separate planes. For lack of a better terminology, one might name these: (1) the sensuous plane, (2) the expressive plane, (3) the sheerly musical plane. The only advantage to be gained from mechanically splitting up the listening process into these hypothetical planes is the clearer view to be had of the way in which we listen.

2 The simplest way of listening to music is to listen for the sheer pleasure of the musical sound itself. That is the sensuous plane. It is the plane on which we hear music without thinking, without considering it in any way. One turns on the radio while doing something else and absent-mindedly bathes in the sound. A kind of brainless but attractive state of mind is engendered by the mere sound appeal of the music.

3 You may be sitting in a room reading this book. Imagine one note struck on the piano. Immediately that one note is enough to change the atmosphere of the room—proving that the sound element in music is a powerful and mysterious agent, which it would be foolish to deride or belittle.

4 The surprising thing is that many people who consider themselves qualified music lovers abuse that plane in listening. They go to concerts in order to lose themselves. They use music as a consolation or an escape. They enter an ideal world where one doesn't have to think of the realities of everyday life. Of course they aren't thinking about the music either.

Music allows them to leave it, and they go off to a place to dream, dreaming because of and apropos of the music yet never quite listening to it.

5 Yes, the sound appeal of music is a potent and primitive force, but you must not allow it to usurp a disproportionate share of your interest. The sensuous plane is an important one in music, a very important one, but it does not constitute the whole story.

6 There is no need to digress further on the sensuous plane. Its appeal to every normal human being is self-evident. There is, however, such a thing as becoming more sensitive to the different kinds of sound stuff as used by various composers. For all composers do not use that sound stuff in the same way. Don't get the idea that the value of music is commensurate with its sensuous appeal or that the loveliest sounding music is made by the greatest composer. If that were so, Ravel would be a greater creator than Beethoven. The point is that the sound element varies with each composer, that his usage of sound forms an integral part of his style and must be taken into account when listening. The reader can see, therefore, that a more conscious approach is valuable even on this primary plane of music listening.

7 The second plane on which music exists is what I have called the expressive one. Here, immediately, we tread on controversial ground. Composers have a way of shying away from any discussion of music's expressive side. Did not Stravinsky himself proclaim that his music was an "object," a "thing," with a life of its own, and with no other meaning than its own purely musical existence? This intransigent attitude of Stravinsky's may be due to the fact that so many people have tried to read different meanings into so many pieces. Heaven knows it is difficult enough to say precisely what it is that a piece of music means, to say it definitely, to say it finally so that everyone is satisfied with your explanation. But that should not lead one to the other extreme of denying to music the right to be "expressive."

8 My own belief is that all music has an expressive power, some more and some less, but that all music has a certain meaning behind the notes and that that meaning behind the notes constitutes, after all, what the piece is saying, what the piece is about. This whole problem can be stated quite simply by asking, "Is there a meaning to music?" My answer to that would be, "Yes." And "Can you state in so many words what the meaning is?" My answer to that would be, "No." Therein lies the difficulty.

9 Simple-minded souls will never be satisfied with the answer to the second of these questions. They always want music to have a meaning, and the more concrete it is the better they like it. The more the music reminds them of a train, a storm, a funeral, or any other familiar conception the more expressive it appears to be to them. This popular idea of music's meaning—stimulated and abetted by the usual run of musical commenta-

tor—should be discouraged wherever and whenever it is met. One timid lady once confessed to me that she suspected something seriously lacking in her appreciation of music because of her inability to connect it with anything definite. That is getting the whole thing backward, of course.

10 Still, the question remains, How close should the intelligent music lover wish to come to pinning a definite meaning to any particular work? No closer than a general concept, I should say. Music expresses, at different moments, serenity or exuberance, regret or triumph, fury or delight. It expresses each of these moods, and many others, in a numberless variety of subtle shadings and differences. It may even express a state of meaning for which there exists no adequate word in any language. In that case, musicians often like to say that it has only a purely musical meaning. They sometimes go farther and say that *all* music has only a purely musical meaning. What they really mean is that no appropriate word can be found to express the music's meaning and that, even if it could, they do not feel the need of finding it.

11 But whatever the professional musician may hold, most musical novices still search for specific words with which to pin down their musical reactions. That is why they always find Tchaikovsky easier to "understand" than Beethoven. In the first place, it is easier to pin a meaning-word on a Tchaikovsky piece than on a Beethoven one. Much easier. Moreover, with the Russian composer, every time you come back to a piece of his it almost always says the same thing to you, whereas with Beethoven it is often quite difficult to put your finger right on what he is saying. And any musician will tell you that that is why Beethoven is the greater composer. Because music which always says the same thing to you will necessarily soon become dull music, but music whose meaning is slightly different with each hearing has a greater chance of remaining alive.

12 Listen, if you can, to the forty-eight fugue themes of Bach's *Well Tempered Clavichord*. Listen to each theme, one after another. You will soon realize that each theme mirrors a different world of feeling. You will also soon realize that the more beautiful a theme seems to you the harder it is to find any word that will describe it to your complete satisfaction. Yes, you will certainly know whether it is a gay theme or a sad one. You will be able, in other words, in your own mind, to draw a frame of emotional feeling around your theme. Now study the sad one a little closer. Try to pin down the exact quality of its sadness. Is it pessimistically sad or resignedly sad; is it fatefully sad or smilingly sad?

13 Let us suppose that you are fortunate and can describe to your own satisfaction in so many words the exact meaning of your chosen theme. There is still no guarantee that anyone else will be satisfied. Nor need they be. The important thing is that each one feel for himself the specific expressive quality of a theme or, similarly, an entire piece of music. And if

it is a great work of art, don't expect it to mean exactly the same thing to you each time you return to it.

14 Themes or pieces need not express only one emotion, of course. Take such a theme as the first main one of the *Ninth Symphony*, for example. It is clearly made up of different elements. It does not say only one thing. Yet anyone hearing it immediately gets a feeling of strength, a feeling of power. It isn't a power that comes simply because the theme is played loudly. It is a power inherent in the theme itself. The extraordinary strength and vigor of the theme results in the listener's receiving an impression that a forceful statement has been made. But one should never try to boil it down to "the fateful hammer of life," etc. That is where the trouble begins. The musician, in his exasperation, says it means nothing but the notes themselves, whereas the nonprofessional is only too anxious to hang on to any explanation that gives him the illusion of getting closer to the music's meaning.

15 Now, perhaps, the reader will know better what I mean when I say that music does have an expressive meaning but that we cannot say in so many words what that meaning is.

16 The third plane on which music exists is the sheerly musical plane. Besides the pleasurable sound of music and the expressive feeling that it gives off, music does exist in terms of the notes themselves and of their manipulation. Most listeners are not sufficiently conscious of this third plane. It will be largely the business of this book to make them more aware of music on this plane.

17 Professional musicians, on the other hand, are, if anything, too conscious of the mere notes themselves. They often fall into the error of becoming so engrossed with their arpeggios and staccatos that they forget the deeper aspects of the music they are performing. But from the layman's standpoint, it is not so much a matter of getting over bad habits on the sheerly musical plane as of increasing one's awareness of what is going on, in so far as the notes are concerned.

18 When the man in the street listens to the "notes themselves" with any degree of concentration, he is most likely to make some mention of the melody. Either he hears a pretty melody or he does not, and he generally lets it go at that. Rhythm is likely to gain his attention next, particularly if it seems exciting. But harmony and tone color are generally taken for granted, if they are thought of consciously at all. As for music's having a definite form of some kind, that idea seems never to have occurred to him.

19 It is very important for all of us to become more alive to music on its sheerly musical plane. After all, an actual musical material is being used. The intelligent listener must be prepared to increase his awareness of the musical material and what happens to it. He must hear the melodies, the

rhythms, the harmonies, the tone colors in a more conscious fashion. But above all he must, in order to follow the line of the composer's thought, know something of the principles of musical form. Listening to all of these elements is listening on the sheerly musical plane.

20 Let me repeat that I have split up mechanically the three separate planes on which we listen merely for the sake of greater clarity. Actually, we never listen to one or the other of these planes. What we do is to correlate them—listening in all three ways at the same time. It takes no mental effort, for we do it instinctively.

21 Perhaps an analogy with what happens to us when we visit the theater will make this instinctive correlation clearer. In the theater, you are aware of the actors and actresses, costumes and sets, sounds and movements. All these give one the sense that the theater is a pleasant place to be in. They constitute the sensuous plane in our theatrical reactions.

22 The expressive plane in the theater would be derived from the feeling that you get from what is happening on the stage. You are moved to pity, excitement, or gayety. It is this general feeling, generated aside from the particular words being spoken, a certain emotional something which exists on the stage, that is analogous to the expressive quality in music.

23 The plot and plot development is equivalent to our sheerly musical plane. The playwright creates and develops a character in just the same way that a composer creates and develops a theme. According to the degree of your awareness of the way in which the artist in either field handles his material will you become a more intelligent listener.

24 It is easy enough to see that the theatergoer never is conscious of any of these elements separately. He is aware of them all at the same time. The same is true of music listening. We simultaneously and without thinking listen on all three planes.

25 In a sense, the ideal listener is both inside and outside the music at the moment, judging it and enjoying it, wishing it would go one way and watching it go another—almost like the composer at the moment he composes it; because in order to write his music, the composer must also be inside and outside his music, carried away by it and yet coldly critical of it. A subjective and objective attitude is implied in both creating and listening to music.

26 What the reader should strive for, then, is a more *active* kind of listening. Whether you listen to Mozart or Duke Ellington, you can deepen your understanding of music only by being a more conscious and aware listener—not someone who is just listening, but someone who is listening *for* something.

STUDY GUIDE

Theme and Structure

1. To write a good piece of expository prose, an author must be keenly aware of the public for whom he is writing. For whom is Copland writing this essay—a general audience or a group of sophisticated musicians? How do you know for whom he is writing from the essay itself? From its structure? Its diction? Its allusions and comparisons?

2. *Divide et impera* ("Divide and conquer") reads the old proverb. That holds for a successful expository essay as well as for a successful government. In paragraph 1, Copland divides the subject of listening into three parts and then develops each of these parts in three successive sections of his essay: paragraphs 2–6, 7–15, and 16–19. What does he discuss in each of these parts? Where has he stated that he is conscious of artificially dividing his subject for expository purposes?

3. These separate ways of listening in practice, Copland says, are actually experienced simultaneously. He develops this idea through an analogy. What is it? How does it parallel the three elements in musical listening?

4. Actually Copland works out an extended definition of the three kinds of musical listening. From his extended definition write a more concise definition of each of the three kinds of listening.

5. Paragraphs 25 and 26 function as a conclusion to this well-organized essay. What is Copland's conclusion? What does he mean by saying that the ideal listener must be both inside and outside the music to which he is listening?

6. From what you have learned in previous essays about art and ways of looking at it, plan and write an essay, built on the pattern of this one, entitled "How We Look at Art."

COMMUNICATION THROUGH LITERATURE

John Henry Newman

1 Literature, from the derivation of the word, implies writing, not speaking; this, however, arises from the circumstances of the copiousness, variety, and public circulation of the matters of which it consists. What is spoken cannot outrun the range of the speaker's voice, and perishes in the uttering. When words are in demand to express a long course of thought, when they have to be conveyed to the ends of the earth, or perpetuated for the benefit of posterity, they must be written down, that is, reduced to the

Reprinted from John Henry Newman, *The Idea of a University* (1873).

shape of literature; still, properly speaking, the terms by which we denote this characteristic gift of man belong to its exhibition by means of the voice, not of handwriting. It addresses itself, in its primary idea, to the ear, not to the eye. We call it the power of speech, we call it language, that is, the use of the tongue; and, even when we write, we still keep in mind what was its original instrument, for we use freely such terms in our books as "saying," "speaking," "telling," "talking," "calling"; we use the terms "phraseology" and "diction," as if we were still addressing ourselves to the ear.

2 Now I insist on this, because it shows that speech, and therefore literature, which is its permanent record, is essentially a personal work. It is not some production or result, attained by the partnership of several persons, or by machinery, or by any natural process, but in its very idea it proceeds, and must proceed, from some one given individual. Two persons cannot be the authors of the sounds which strike our ear; and, as they cannot be speaking one and the same speech, neither can they be writing one and the same lecture or disclosure—which must certainly belong to some one person or other, and is the expression of that one person's ideas and feelings—ideas and feelings personal to himself, though others may have parallel and similar ones—proper to himself, in the same sense as his voice, his air, his countenance, his carriage, and his action, are personal. In other words, literature expresses, not objective truth, as it is called, but subjective; not things, but thoughts.

3 Now this doctrine will become clearer by considering another use of words, which does relate to objective truth, or to things; which relates to matters, not personal, not subjective to the individual, but which, even were there no individual man in the whole world to know them or to talk about them, would exist still. Such objects become the matter of science, and words indeed are used to express them; but such words are rather symbols than language; and however many we use, and however we may perpetuate them by writing, we never could make any kind of literature out of them, or call them by that name. Such, for instance, would be Euclid's Elements; they relate to truths universal and external; they are not mere thoughts, but things; they exist in themselves, not by virtue of our understanding them, not in dependence upon our will, but in what is called the nature of *things*, or at least on conditions external to us. The words, then, in which they are set forth are not language, speech, literature, but rather, as I have said, symbols. And, as a proof of it, you will recollect that it is possible, nay usual, to set forth the propositions of Euclid in algebraical notation, which, as all would admit, has nothing to do with literature. What is true of mathematics is true also of every study, so far forth as it is scientific; it makes use of words as the mere vehicle of things, and is thereby withdrawn from the province of literature. Thus meta-

physics, ethics, law, politics, economy, chemistry, theology cease to be literature in the same degree as they are capable of a severe scientific treament. . . . However, law or natural history has before now been treated by an author with so much of colouring derived from his own mind as to become a sort of literature; this is especially seen in the instance of theology, when it takes the shape of pulpit eloquence. It is seen in historical composition, which becomes a mere specimen of chronology, or a chronicle, when divested of the philosophy, the skill, or the party and personal feelings of the particular writer. Science, then, has to do with things, literature with thoughts; science is universal, literature is personal; science uses words merely as symbols, but literature uses language in its full compass, as including phraseology, idiom, style, composition, rhythm, eloquence.

4 Let us then put aside the scientific use of words, when we are to speak of language and literature. Literature is the personal use or exercise of language. That this is so is further proved from the fact that one author uses it so differently from another. Language itself in its very origination would seem to be traceable to individuals. Their peculiarities have given it its character. We are often able in fact to trace particular phrases or idioms to individuals; we know the history of their rise. Slang surely, as it is called, comes of, and breathes of the personal. The connection between the force of words in particular languages and the habits and sentiment of the nations speaking them has often been pointed out. And, while the many use language as they find it, the man of genius uses it indeed, but subjects it withal to his own peculiarities. The throng and succession of ideas, thoughts, feelings, imaginations, aspirations, which pass within him, the abstractions, the juxtapositions, the comparisons, the discriminations, the conceptions, which are so original to him, his views of external things, his judgments upon life, manners, and history, the exercises of his wit, of his humour, of his depth, of his sagacity, all these innumerable and incessant creations, the very pulsation and throbbing of his intellect, does he image forth, to all does he give utterance, in a corresponding language, which is as multiform as this inward mental action itself and analogous to it, and which is the faithful expression of his intense personality, attending on his inward world of thought as its very shadow; so that we might as well say that one man's shadow is another's as that the style of a really gifted mind can belong to any but himself. It follows him about *as* a shadow. His thought and feeling are personal, and so his language is personal.

5 Thought and speech are inseparable from each other. Matter and expression are parts of one; style is a thinking out into language. This is what I have been laying down, and this is literature; not *things*, not the verbal symbols of things; not on the other hand mere *words*; but thoughts expressed in language. Call to mind, Gentlemen, the meaning of the Greek word which expresses this special prerogative of man over the feeble intelligence of the inferior animals. It is called logos. What does logos mean? It

stands both for reason and for speech, and it is difficult to say which it means more properly. It means both at once. Why? Because really they cannot be divided; because they are in a true sense one. When we can separate light and illumination, life and motion, the convex and the concave of a curve, then will it be possible for thought to tread speech under foot, and to hope to do without it—then will it be conceivable that the vigorous and fertile intellect should renounce its own double, its instrument of expression, and the channel of its speculations and emotions. . . .

6 By literature, then, is meant the expression of thought in language; where by "thought" I mean ideas, feelings, views, reasonings, and other operations of the human mind. And the art of letters is the method by which a speaker or writer brings out in words, worthy of his subject, and sufficient for his audience or readers, the thoughts which impress him. Literature, then, is of a personal character; it consists in the enunciations and teachings of those who have a right to speak as representatives of their kind, and in whose words their brethren find an interpretation of their sentiments, a record of their own experience, and a suggestion for their own judgments.

7 A great author is not one who merely has a wealth of words, whether in prose or in verse, and can, as it were, turn on at his will any number of splendid phrases and swelling sentences; but he is one who has something to say and knows how to say it. I do not claim for him, as such, any great depth of thought, or breadth of view, or philosophy, or sagacity, or knowledge of human nature, or experience of human life, though these additional gifts he may have, and the more he has of them the greater he is; but I ascribe to him, as his characteristic gift, in a large sense the faculty of expression. He is master of the two-fold *logos*, the thought and the word, distinct, but inseparable from each other. He may, if so be, elaborate his compositions, or he may pour out his improvisations; but, in either case, he has but one aim, which he keeps steadily before him, and is conscientious and single-minded in fulfilling. That aim is to give forth what he has within him; and, from his very earnestness, it comes to pass that, whatever be the splendor of his diction or the harmony of his periods, he has within him the charm of an incommunicable simplicity. Whatever be his subject, high or low, he treats it suitably and for its own sake. His page is the lucid mirror of his mind and life. . . .

8 The great author writes passionately, because he feels keenly; forcibly, because he conceives vividly; he sees too clearly to be vague; he is too serious to be otiose; he can analyze his subject, and therefore he is rich; he embraces it as a whole and in all its parts, and therefore he is consistent; he has a firm hold of it, and therefore he is luminous. When his imagination wells up, it overflows in ornament; when his heart is touched, it thrills along his verse. He has always the right word for the right idea, and never a word too much. If he is brief, it is because few words will suffice;

when he is lavish of them, still each word has its mark, and aids, not embarrasses, the vigorous march of his elocution. He expresses what all feel, but all cannot say; and his sayings pass into proverbs among his people, and his phrases become house-hold words and idioms of their daily speech, which is tessellated with the rich fragments of his language, as we see in foreign lands the marbles of Roman grandeur worked into the walls and pavements of modern palaces.

9 If then the power of speech is a gift as great as any that can be named; if the origin of language is by many philosophers even considered to be nothing short of divine; if by means of words the secrets of the heart are brought to light, pain of soul is relieved, hidden grief is carried off, sympathy conveyed, counsel imparted, experience recorded, and wisdom perpetuated—if by great authors the many are drawn up into unity, national character is fixed, a people speaks, the past and the future, the East and the West are brought into communication with each other—if such men are, in a word, the spokesmen and prophets of the human family, it will not answer to make light of literature or to neglect its study. Rather we may be sure that, in proportion as we master it in whatever language, and imbibe its spirit, we shall ourselves become in our own measure the ministers of like benefits to others, be they many or few, be they in the obscurer or the more distinguished walks of life, who are united to us by social ties, and are within the sphere of our personal influence.

STUDY GUIDE

The Rhetoric of the Sentence

Study the rhetorical effectiveness of paragraphs 4, 5, 8, and 9. Be able to show in how far the effectiveness of these four paragraphs is the result of the type of sentence employed (long, short; simple, compound, complex; loose, periodic). Are the types of sentences Newman employs in these paragraphs appropriate to the ideas he is expressing in them? If so, show why.

Method of Development

What method of paragraph development does Newman employ in 1, 3, and 4?

Order

What order does Newman follow in arranging the substance of his paragraph in the paragraphs listed below (from less to greater, climactic; from familiar to unfamiliar; from general to particular, deductive; from particular to general, inductive)? The paragraphs: 3, 4, and 6.

Transitions

1. A. In paragraphs 2, 3, and 4 underline every connective (repeated words: reference words; pronouns or demonstrative adjectives; transitional ex-

pressions) which link sentence to sentence. Be ready to state to what each of these connectives points back in previous sentences or paragraphs.

B. Study the first and last sentences of the first five paragraphs, and be ready to show how Newman has made the transition from one paragraph to the next.

Content

1. Newman says in paragraph 4 that "literature is the *personal* use of *language*." Restate in your own words and in complete sentences every item in the paragraph which Newman mentions as proof of his statement, and be ready to explain why each of these items proves his point.

2. In paragraph 5 Newman says that "thought and speech are inseparable from each other." In the course of the paragraph he restates that idea several times. See how many individual words and phrases you can find in the paragraph that are synonymous with "thought" and "speech" in the first sentence. List them in parallel columns.

3. From a careful reading of paragraphs 6 and 7 restate in your own words:

A. Newman's definition of literature.

B. What Newman conceives to be the purpose of a great author in writing.

4. Make a list of all the advantages to be derived from the study of literature mentioned by Newman in paragraph 9. Using this list write a paragraph of your own directed to a younger brother or sister in which you try to make him or her see one of the advantages to be derived from the study of literature.

5. With Newman's definition of literature as the "personal use of language" in mind, explain why the telephone book and the mathematics textbook are not literature.

6. Make a selection from your current reading which you consider to be literary, and state in your own words what is personal about the author's choice of language.

POETRY FOR THE PERFECTLY PRACTICAL MAN

John Unterecker

1 I am out to sell poetry to people who don't read it, who don't like it, who don't want their children to read it, and who, especially, don't want their friends and business associates to think they read it. I want not only to persuade them to read poems but as well to transform them into a band

Reprinted from The Columbia University *Forum*, Winter 1959, Vol. II, No. 2.

of missionary spirits who, suspending poems on every shining television aerial, will convert the American landscape into a forest leafing out in literature.

2 I have no illusions, of course, as to the possibilities of my succeeding in this project. It is a very idle dream. Most of us, by and large, give considerable lip service to poetry, and lip service seldom if ever brings poetry to the lip. We (properly) deplore the Russian treatment of Boris Pasternak, and we (improperly) congratulate ourselves that a Pasternak in America would never be subjected to such shabby treatment. We keep the anthology of poetry we always intend to read in some handy place—the guest room, usually. And we frequently regret, publicly, that we have just never had time to learn to appreciate poetry (thus assuring the world that we're on its side, that it has nothing to fear from us). Comforted by our virtuous attitudes, we're able to experience the joy of doing our cultural bit without struggling through the words on the page.

3 And yet the words on the page have value. In escaping them we escape, perhaps, a kind of fullness we can experience in no other place.

4 For the fact of the matter is that all the slogans we believe in and therefore ignore are right. Intellectual and artistic freedom *is* the great Western achievement we have claimed it to be. In making the uninhibited exploration of the word every man's right, we have, in fact, loosened the shackles of ignorance, prejudice, and fear. And in creating a society in which some leisure is available to that man we have made possible the great dream of the nineteenth century: a citizenry released by the machine to pursue those cultural objectives which make life not only bearable but valued. The arts, which in the past have opened the eyes of only those men lucky enough to be born to a leisured class (artists themselves, of course, are classless creatures), are now at last within reach of the man in the street.

5 And yet we in America are not—as Robert Brustein pointed out in a recent *Forum* ["The Theatre Is Losing Its Minds"; Fall 1958]—conspicuous for our intelligent interest in the theatre. Nor is the theatre we attend conspicuous for its quality. Serious new music languishes in America. Try, for example, to assemble an audience for a program of contemporary chamber music. And poetry perishes.

6 How did we get this way? How can we evolve toward a happier condition?

7 Though how we got this way is a far more complicated story than the oversimplification I am about to offer, involved in it, at least, are the very machines that liberated us, the ones that created so much leisure. For as they created leisure they helped remove man from the sort of "organic" activities which had in earlier times given him the illusion that his little contribution helped establish the order of an essentially ordered world.

The potter had made a whole thing, a shaped object from the blob of clay he wedged, whirled, and fired into form. The baker had measured out flour, milk and salt, stirred the mess himself, shaped loaves, baked and sold them. These men, though only in the broadest sense artists, experienced the artist's shaping function. Participants in ordering their world, they were able to watch an entire progression from disorder to order take place under their hands. And, adjusted to order, they were able to value those arts they *did* experience.

8 The individual farmer, cabinetmaker, tinsmith, blacksmith of the nineteenth century was a survivor of the earlier system of relatively personal production, and each of those survivors retained some real measure of creative activity. Farmer, cabinetmaker, tinsmith, blacksmith held out longest against the tide; but in our time we have seen them, like most of us, go under to the powers of corporate efficiency. And not in America only. In England, France, Russia—in every successful industrialized state—the person has lost contact with total processes. Almost always he fabricates a part, seldom a whole.

9 Even in education, departmentalized for efficiency, it is more and more difficult for the whole man to shape the mind of the whole man of the next generation. Rolled from impersonal class to impersonal class or polished by the glittering mechanical marvel of educational television, the modern student finds himself machined to a well-rounded intellectual billiard ball.

10 And these triumphs of the machine are, I think most of us would agree, not only economically imperative (we have to be efficient in order to feed, clothe, and house the world's huge, growing, gobbling population) but also inevitable.

11 At the same time that organic work activity was being replaced by necessary industrial fragmentation (the cabinetmakers replaced by sanders, gluers, and varnishers and each of these in turn by button pushers), depersonalized states and—at least in some places—depersonalized religions began to emerge. Compartmentalized, isolated from order in his amusement, much of his education, most of his work, frightened by the huge uncontrollable disorders about him (and by the powers of total destruction which lie at last in his hands), twentieth-century man seeks not happiness but distractions. It is no wonder that he buries his head in the Great American Comic Book.

12 And yet, in spite of everything that has contributed to his feeling that he is only a meaningless part of a meaningless world, man is essentially the systematizer that he has always been. His happiness is still the struggle for form, the construction of images of order from the apparent chaos which surrounds him. Not often, but occasionally, he has the craftsman's sense of design. Happiness can come from the invention of a master form

letter that will be good for all nonsense inquiries. The scientist—though he may incidentally discover the most efficient device to finish us off—still pursues principles of order. Architect, engineer, executive still struggle to give shape to things and, keeping chaos from the door, find moments of joy. Perhaps joy comes even to advertising copy writers and those poets, gone over to nightmare, who compose singing commercials for otherwise reputable products, which—their brand name hammered home—some of us have learned scrupulously to avoid.

13 That many of us really do try to escape from the fragmentation in which we seem to be caught is attested not only by the astonishing popularity of adult education courses but by the even more astonishing sale of how-to-do-it books. We really do want to understand philosophy, music, painting, and poetry. We attend thousands of lectures. We consume—or at least buy—hundreds of thousands of books that tell us how to read philosophy, how to listen to music, how to paint and how to look at paintings, how to read poetry and how to choose poets to read.

14 In this welter of educational opportunity, most of us, for perfectly good reasons, never get to examine philosophies, never attend concerts, never go to art galleries, never read poems. Timid, knowing what we don't know, sure only of our ignorance and our inability to understand the self-help books, we conclude either that the arts are beyond us or that the opinions of the critics are safe substitutes for paintings, quartets, or poems.

15 If we successfully delude ourselves in either of these ways, we are, of course, doomed. We are also, of course, wrong. For no critic, present company included, is a safe substitute for anything, let alone a work of art. The critic's only function is to lead the audience to the work or to point up (to an audience that is in the presence of the work) some of the elements that make it operate. He can hardly do anything else of real value. And the man who—with or without critic—subjects himself to the work of art, who stares long enough at it, almost always experiences it exactly as it should be experienced. (If he hears, say, a Yeats poem as often as he hears the average singing commercial, he can scarcely avoid "getting" the poem. He may also, perhaps, come to admire its order quite as much as he may come to detest the commercial's disorder.)

16 And now, at last, I have worked around to the selling point. It is here that I mount the soapbox. It is here that I want to make my pitch for poetry.

17 For poetry, among the arts, has certain very real advantages. Like the "book bar" I saw displayed this morning in the window of the local liquor store ("Closed, it's a handsome volume you'll be proud to display on your desk, bookshelf, or end table. Open it's a handy container for two full fifths of your favorite liquor!"), poetry is portable, potent, and practical. Unlike most of the arts, it can be dragged about easily from place to

place. It can be consulted in spare moments. It can be sampled privately. (It can, even, be a secret vice.)

18 For the reader who has always wanted to read poetry but has never quite known how to go about it, I have a few very practical suggestions.

19 In the first place, he should begin with the poetry itself. No self-help book is as good for the novice as a book of poems. *After* one is fairly well acquainted with an author, one can very profitably go on to sample critical opinion, explications, etc. Criticism can function, and function well, during the reader's second trip through an author. But on the first round it is all too often deadly. It is, after all, almost always intended to make difficult matter clear. But if one reads it before the poetry, one inevitably gets the mistaken impression that nearly all of the poems are well-nigh impenetrable.

20 For a beginner, one volume of poetry should do—preferably not an anthology. (The "book bar" analogy holds here too: casually mixed poets—say, Allen Ginsberg, Wordsworth, Dylan Thomas, and Pope—are no more palatable than a cocktail compounded from absinth, beer, champagne and sherry.) Ideally the first book should be a Collected Works. There is a real advantage in being able to see a writer's full development from start to finish. Not only is each poem clearer in the context of the neighbors it started out with, but a second wholeness, the sort of unity a life necessarily imposes on a lifetime's work, begins to appear to the diligent reader, the one who does not pick and choose but who reads carefully through a volume in the way the author intended him to read through it. If my notion is correct that the source of much modern anguish is a sense of disorder, this sort of chronological approch to a writer should give many readers pleasure. For they will be able to apprehend not only the little ordered worlds that the individual poems are but also the larger ordered world that the body of work becomes and, beyond that, the organic thing, the organizer, the poet himself.

21 My second recommendation is that the reader give the poems a chance to work on him. No poem, as I've already suggested, gives up everything on a first reading; some give up very little. If he plans to spend about as much time reading *back* as he does reading forward, the reader will have a much better chance of liking both the poems he is looking at and poetry in general. Getting used to a poem in the way one gets used to a popular song—by casual repetition half a dozen times, say, in a month—is a very satisfactory system. Here, a little strategy is helpful. The housewife interested in finding out what T. S. Eliot is doing might very well want to secrete his *Collected Poems* among her cookbooks, or, if she eats breakfast after the rest of the family is out of the way or before they arrive, put it perhaps among the cold cereals. (With what delight, in that setting, she would come upon Eliot's "A Cooking Egg"!)Or the busy executive could

take the two bottles *out* of the portable "book bar," substitute in their place Yeats' *Collected Poems*, and, without arising, be able inconspicuously to go to Innisfree. My point is, of course, that the book of poems has to come out of the guest room. It has to be readily available. I know one man who, immersed in a bathtub, has made his way through all of John Donne and most of Blake.

22 My third recommendation is that one go to poetry for what it can give and not for what it cannot. Poems may incidentally inspire readers to all sorts of deeds, but, by and large, poems—unlike essays of this sort—are not primarily propagandistic. The poet may be trying to inspire, and inspiration may come of his efforts; but his primary purpose almost always is to assemble the organized thing that a poem is. The "message" is part of poetry, but it is only a part. Like rhymes, rhythms, metaphors, images, symbols, repeated words—all the other materials of poetry—themes help hold the whole business together. They are not, however, the normal poem's reason for being. If we visualize the poem as a kind of an architectural unit, a framework compounded from various kinds of tensions (rhyme and rhythm, for instance, lacing together a structure of sound; definable themes and a paraphrasable prose sense shaping the outward thrust of metaphor and symbol) we may better be able to see it for what it is.

23 More simply yet, all I am really saying is that the poem ought to be approached as a work of art, a structured thing, a shape. That does not mean that we do not have to worry about what the poem is saying. Of course, we have to. But it does mean that we must not for a moment assume that what the poem is saying *is* the poem. (The dog says "Arf" but "Arf" is not the dog.) The thing that ultimately satisfies us in a work of art is not its subject matter but the way that subject matter is decked out: the balances that make any painting, building, poem, trio an organic whole.

24 If we can apprehend the work of art as a totality—by looking at it long enough, often enough, carefully enough—it will give us the satisfaction that only whole things can give us. It will remind us of order. It will remind us that man, for all the chaos he creates, shapes too. It will—in offering design—provide the sort of image that can bring to our eyes, focused so long on fragmented things, essential constructions to set against the rubble landscape of our world.

STUDY GUIDE

Theme, Structure, and Tone

1. The author introduces his subject and announces his purpose in the first part of the essay (paragraphs 1–5). What are they?

2. The two concerns of the body of the essay are formulated in questions in paragraph 6. The first question is answered in paragraphs 7–11. What method of rhetorical development is employed in these paragraphs?

3. The second question is answered in the rest of the essay. The general answer is found in paragraphs 12 and 13 and the specific answer as it touches poetry in paragraphs 16–24. What is the answer? How has the author prepared his readers for the point he wishes to make about poetry in paragraph 16?

4. The tone of this essay is set in paragraph 1 by such clauses and phrases as *I am out to sell poetry, band of missionary spirits,* and *convert the landscape into a forest leafing out in literature*. How would you define the tone? Point out other elements of diction in the essay that sustain that tone.

5. The position taken up by Unterecker in the last part of the essay as regards art and the human situation is very different from that of Barrett in "The Testimony of Modern Art." What is the difference? Find statements in each essay that very clearly reveal that difference. You might write a paper in which you compare and contrast the views of the two men.

6. Unterecker's view of man and literature is more hopeful than that of Barrett. On what is his hope based? How can a reading of poetry help realize that hope? How can it serve as an antidote to the chaos and meaninglessness so much stressed by Barrett as part of the modern scene?

7. The instructor might have each of the students work on a volume of one poet's work during the year. The poet's biography might be written up in a biographical essay, and eventually an essay might be written about some of the poet's favorite ideas and manners of expression revealed through a year's familiarity with his work.

THE ANALYST'S COUCH AND THE CREATIVE MIND

Roger Burlingame

1 I have not called myself an artist though in much of my writing I have worked with artist's materials and in the artist's framework. I believe, therefore, that I have what is known as a creative mind and though circumstances have not always permitted it, I like to write from the inside out. And, from my own long and kaleidoscopic experience and from the experiences of some true artists whom I have known closely I am convinced that, however much good it may do the business executive, the physician, the politician, or the housewife, the psychoanalyst's couch is not for the creative mind. In testimony I offer case history.

2 If, for instance, the theses of the psychiatrists and psychoanalysts are

Reprinted from *Harper's Magazine* (May 1959).

applicable to me, I should be, if not a gibbering idiot, at least a model of chronic maladjustment. According to late theory, my parents—indeed my entire family including my Irish Nanny—did everything wrong from the moment the doctor shook the breath into me.

3 First of all, I was an afterthought. I came along eleven years after my parents had apparently decided that enough was enough. Later, when it was supposed that I could understand such things, I was told that I was planned and I believe it. A year or so before my birth, the family's economic condition improved and this, added to Mother's nostalgia for babies, moved the uninstructed parental minds toward the belated impulse. And, in those primitive days, insufficient exploration had not yet proved how dangerous afterthoughts can be—especially when the progenitors are past forty.

4 During the fateful years zero to five, my nurse indoctrinated me with every variety of morbid fancy. She had, for example, a passion for funerals. Often when she took me walking in the city she would detect a funeral blocks away and seizing me by the hand would run me breathlessly to the scene so that she could count the carriages behind the hearse. I became so fascinated with the pomp of death that once, when asked what I wanted for Christmas, I replied a toy cemetery, please, complete with plumed hearse, corpse, and practicable coffin.

5 Nanny also exploited my precarious constitution. Born in what was known as "the grippe year," I was frequently on the threshold of death, from which I was saved by a series of miracles. In the intervals between the crises, Nanny surrounded me with fears. Everything that I must not do I must not do "for fear" of the consequences: bronchial pneumonia, for example, if I went out in the rain. Nanny was entranced by the long names of diseases and I too grew to mouth and love their resonant beauty. Starting with the sonorous "pneumonia," my sallies into the poetry of medicine have led me into rapture over the rhythm and melody of "insomnia," "arteriosclerosis," and, best of all, "electrocardiogram."

6 The "sentence of silence" so abundantly condemned in the paleo-Freudian days was strictly imposed upon me. Every scrap of information about sex was withheld from me notwithstanding my insistent questioning and the fact that my mind was, from my first consciousness, profoundly occupied with the subject.

7 Far from the teachings of "progressive" up-bringing, my behavior was geared to a set of absolutes. Reason rarely intervened between me and parental authority. I did things because they were right and they were right because Mother or Father or my grown-up brother or sisters or Holy Scripture said so. (Nanny also got in on this act.) In my consciousness, moral relativity was a stranger though I know now that it governed much of my father's thinking.

8 Finally, my strenuous religious training brought me into a vivid and daily awareness of sin. I don't think the reality of sin would have impinged much upon Mother's clean and extrovert mind except that her prayer book was so jam-packed with it. But to me the abstraction inherent in all the resounding Anglican prayers was troubling indeed and, in my introspective hours, as I grew older, I even became fearful that I might have sinned without knowing it. On my knees in church, my small head buried in my folded arms, I sometimes put the question to my Maker but I was never quite sure of any response.

9 My earliest memory is of weaving my way through a forest of legs. Unlike most children, I had five parents instead of two. All—even my still adolescent sister—had equal authority, at least when the others weren't around. They could all say Don't to me and they all did. Sometimes there were jurisdictional disputes conducted in whispers which I heard or in French which I understood. I hugely enjoyed the conflicts between my sisters, sometimes involving slammed doors or ending with that final thrust, "All right for you," which was so popular in those days among the young.

10 The only time no one said Don't to me was when I was sick. Then they hovered silently near my bedside so imbued with the belief that I was going to die, I wonder they did not kill me with their thoughts. I did, indeed, sometimes suspect the incidence of my demise. I was deeply impressed by that macabre prayer they used to teach children to say:

> If I should die before I wake
> I pray the Lord my soul to take . . .

I could see the Lord's hand coming through the darkness and grabbing my small soul. I then thought myself into a white coffin with my disembodied spirit hovering over my bereaved family and happily observing their tears.

11 When it wasn't too painful, I really enjoyed being sick. To lie in a darkened room with Mother's countless petticoats rustling about and a fragrant inhalant cooking over an alcohol lamp was quite pleasurable. I liked the taste of the paregoric—the universal remedy for everything that could not be cured by castor oil—the frequent doses of which, by another miracle, I survived. Nanny, in these times, was relegated to the background and Mother took full charge. Is it surprising, then, that I acquired that most devastating of all fixations for the growing male, a "silver cord" attachment?

12 Could a combination of Doctors Freud, Jung, and Adler—not to mention John Dewey and the progressive educationeers—imagine a more blighting background? Yet I have eluded breakdown, compulsive criminality, perversion, and the Death Wish. I have spasms of self-pity but so do my younger acquaintances whose psychiatrists are just around the corner.

My suicidal impulses are rare and fleeting—subject to diversion by almost any bright object. Rape, homosexuality, and sadism have appeared interesting but not compelling. My impulses toward murder have usually had rational motivation. It is true that I often treat my wife with extreme mental cruelty but so do the graduates of the progressive schools.

13 I take no credit for having licked, with my heroic character, all of the grim conditioners I have described. Indeed, I have never wanted to lick them. On the contrary, I exult in every one. Far from frustrating me they have been largely responsible for every worthy thing I have done.

14 Take, for example, the reticence about the so-called facts of life. The silence was highly stimulating to what I like to think was my incipiently creative mind. Had I been told, I should have been deprived of the delight as well as the constructive exercise of discovering them for myself. Does the child from whom nothing is hidden get more fun out of life? Will the creativeness of new generations be enhanced by absence of mystery? Is the imaginative child whose stories are all told him on the television screen any better equipped than one who devises his own plots and people, albeit with a certain creative agony? No; I cherish the secrecy to which I was so early introduced and I have practiced it happily.

15 What I have withheld has given me more joy than what I have expressed because it has helped build a storehouse, a potential of great pregnancy. Secret after secret I can now give birth to in sublime pain. The confessional to priest or analyst is abhorrent to me. If you keep your hopes or fears, your chimeras, the tantrums of your conscience inside you, you can still make use of them; told, they leave you empty, sterile and impotent. Confession, except in creation, is exceedingly bad for the creative soul.

16 And how about the other mental and emotional ingredients of my child life? To the artist, morbid thought is a pigment. To be there ready at any moment to be dipped into for the creation of a painting or a story it must be squeezed early on the palette of the child's mind. If the child is an incipient artist, it will not stand there alone. Brighter colors will probably be juxtaposed. The child need not be preoccupied by morbid thought but if he is to be an artist he must be aware of its existence. It is cruel to protect an imaginative child from the sense of death or the taste of grief. To an artist a Nanny with her funerals may be immensely useful.

17 Nor are the feminine pressures hurtful to the male artist. If he is a novelist he must be, in himself, man, woman, and child. The mother who runs frightened by the shadows of Oedipus had better consider carefully whether her son is a potential artist or bond broker.

18 As to the unreasoned dicta about right and wrong, these established a code like the multiplication table which catches you up when you make

a mistake. Yet it may also, to change the metaphor, be a springboard from which to take off. Of course I have departed from some of the formulas but how could I have departed if there was nothing to depart from? The shore you leave stays in your mind however far you swim away, but how about the child who has known no shore, who has been taken out in a boat in the dark and dropped into an unbounded sea?

19 There is a truism which says you must know the rules in order to break them, and who breaks more rules than the writer unless it be the painter or composer?

20 I have left behind most of the religious concepts that were so important to my mother and I have sometimes said that my strict religious bringing up threw me, on maturity, into agnosticism, yet in my heart, I also value that memory. Once the sin ingredient evaporated there was a residue of beauty. My doubts about a personal God cannot filter that out. But how constructive that knowledge of faith, of the faith of others if not my own, of the intellectual fact of God, however skeptical I may be of his tangible existence! The best book by far that I ever wrote was based on what I heard in those solemn hours when Mother prepared me for confirmation.

21 I once knew a true artist—a painter of transcendent talent—who had been brought up on an austere New England farm, a desire-under-the-elms sort of place where morbid thought abounded. His own ran to cows. For hours, as a child, he would sit on a fence and reflect on the sufferings of cows. The cow, to him, was a symbol of exploited femininity; her entire existence was by necessity dedicated to being a female. She was bred, gave birth, and began to nurse her child; then both child and milk were stolen from her. When the milk stopped, the whole sad sequence was repeated. What my friend supposed to be the other enterprises in which the cow might have engaged had she been relieved of the urgency imposed upon her was never quite clear to me or perhaps to him; the point was that the grief about the cows developed into other griefs as he matured and he became, so he said, an exceedingly unhappy man. Yet all this time he was painting pictures which were the wonder of the art world. Everything he did had the nostalgic trace essential to any real work of art.

22 One day he heard about a Swiss psychoanalyst who could treat those grim neuroses which were a legacy from a morbid childhood. So he laid his painting aside and spent a year in Zurich. I had lunch with him the day after he returned. "I am," he said, "completely happy. The nightmares are gone. I can look back on my obsessions and laugh at them. My slate has been washed clean."

23 Unfortunately his palette had also been washed clean. From that moment his pictures were commonplace or pretty. He lost his place in the top rank. Perhaps he would have been restored in time because I am in-

clined to believe that a true artist is, in the long run, indestructible, but not until he had put back some of the things that the doctor had erased. For that he died too soon.

24 But this is only one story. I could tell others as true and as sad of men and women who have confessed too much. Some have survived because, once on the couch, they have instinctively kicked and screamed or slyly, with tongue in check, defrauded their expensive doctor.

25 I am far from believing that there is pain in all creativity; I have touched the fringe often enough to be aware of its joys—even when they are merely the joys of cool sweat after fever, but I am certain that therapy designed to eliminate suffering from the creative mind is more often destructive than otherwise. I think certain honest analysts have become aware of this. At least two of them who are more interested in the truth than in their bank accounts told me that certain artists have so resisted the treatment—as if they were being robbed—that the doctors have had to abandon the cases.

26 Now if all this be true, why is it that psychoanalysis may still be good for the industrial executive, the lawyer, the government worker, or the secretary of the woman's club? It is, I think, because these people have no machinery for sublimating their childhood "disasters." They cannot *use* their traumas as the painter, the writer, or the composer may. Use is the great anodyne for these wounds. The use may be painful, but when the chagrin is painted or written it is often gone or its combination with its product mellows it. At any rate something has resulted, the rotary motion has ceased, a tangent has been struck. The frustration has been embodied in something which may partake of immortality; at least it may transfer the artist's hurt to the multitude of those who see or read it. A neurosis is better expressed, I think, than confessed.

27 But it has now become fashionable to turn adolescents or even children—whose talents may still be unsuspected—over to persons who practice under the general name of psychiatrist. "Send her to a psychiatrist," or, "Let Doctor X see him," say parents at the drop of a tantrum. In many cases neither parent nor child knows what creative potentials may be in Dick's or Mary's make-up.

28 My advice to parents would be: Try to find out if your child has leanings toward graphic or literary or musical creation before you call in the doctor. And to the doctor, I would say, impertinently, make sure you are not removing something valuable in your attempt to ease your patient's pain or his family's inconvenience. If you detect a foreshadowing of the art that may come, forego your fee and send the patient home. Usually even the child, if he be an embryonic artist, will quickly show his allergy to the analyst's methods.

29 In days past, there was a synthetic treatment of non-creative patients

which was known as occupational therapy. This is still practiced, I believe, in the rehabilitation of mentally wounded veterans and in various old-fashioned establishments. Here, patients are made to express their troubles in some medium of art if it be only a string of beads. This, I am told, is looked down upon by "modern" practitioners. Yet does it not suggest that the man or woman dedicated—one might almost say addicted—to some all-absorbing creative endeavor is in little danger from his neurosis and, perhaps, even cannot do without it?

STUDY GUIDE

Theme, Structure, and Tone

1. The thematic idea of this essay is stated both in the introductory paragraph and in the conclusion section (paragraphs 26–29). What is it?

2. The thesis idea is developed by a double enumeration (paragraphs 2–11 and 12–20). What is enumerated in each of these sections and how do the enumerations relate to the idea the author is attempting to prove?

3. The main proof is based on the author's personal experience. Where in the essay is this proof augmented by the experience of another individual?

4. Although the writer is evidently convinced of the truth of his position, he presents his ideas in a lightly humorous manner. This tone is first introduced in the second paragraph by such expressions as "I should be, if not a *gibbering idiot,* at least a *model of chronic maladjustment.*" Point out other examples of diction that sustain that tone throughout the essay.

A HOPE FOR LITERATURE

Chad Walsh

1 That literature will continue to be created, so long as there are men to create it, I am certain. In a time of utter catastrophe it might dwindle to the village bard and storyteller and be transmitted by word of mouth, but it would not cease. Its continuance is not the question. The question is whether it will be any good.

2 I shall confine myself to the English-speaking world, and shall not try to peer into the future more than a generation or two. With this lim-

ited perspective, my surmise is that which is suggested by the title of this chapter. There is hope for literature—if, and if, and if. . . .

3 Great literature seems to require a major talent living at a time suitable for its particular kind of genius. There have been centuries when these double conditions were apparently not met. The specialist happily immerses himself in the literature of fifteenth-century England, but what is there for the general cultivated reader except Malory and the Scotch Chaucerians? Between the twin heights of Chaucer and the Elizabethans, there is a low valley of humility. Possibly we are wandering toward such a valley now, or are already in one. I do not believe we are, but the point can be debated.

4 Literary geniuses are born, not produced. But the time of their birth can be favorable or unfavorable. If Shakespeare had lived three centuries earlier he might have been the greatest writer of rhymed romances, but it is difficult to believe he would have found in them the same scope that the theater offered. His birth was perfectly timed by the Muse, by the gods, by God, or by chance. When he grew to manhood the ground had been cleared for a mature theater. He did not have to invent blank verse or the five-act form; he had only to perfect them. The audience was already at hand. And the social and psychological state of London was just right. The Middle Ages, with their sense of human and divine hierarchy and an undergirding and overarching moral structure to morality, were still in the blood and bone of men. But restless doubts and questions were shaking the old implicit assumptions. There was just the right tension between the tried-and-true assumptions of an ageless, organic society and the thrust of new individualism and gnawing doubts, to enliven and complicate and loosen the old certainties but not destroy them.

5 Shakespeare had an audience whose responses he could predict, for he shared the attitudes that engendered the responses. But it was not an audience made dull and sodden by unchallenged faith in the inherited beliefs and patterns of living. The audience was part of a society in which men were beginning to stride, often more than life-size, shaking every wall erected by man or God. It was a society that produced real Macbeths and still believed, or wanted to believe, that the avenger would always be sent by the very nature of things, to restore the divine ordering of relationships.

6 Dostoevski had the same good fortune. After his youthful flirtation with advanced thought, he became a staunch disciple of the established order of Tsar, Orthodox Church, and the Slavic mission. All around him the old ties were being eroded by new ideas, but the masses were still faithful to a way of life that seemed an outcropping of the divine will. The same tensions were in nineteenth-century Russia as in Shakespearean England. Dostoevski knew well how to use them in novels that are the nearest prose parallel to the poetic tragedies of Shakespeare.

7 I take it that the Greek playwrights enjoyed circumstances somewhat similar. They had a public still living in a traditional and largely unexamined pattern of life, but the winds of modernity were blowing, and the old assumptions were no longer impregnable. The cultural situation into which Shakespeare, Dostoevski, or the Greek dramatists were born is not, however, the only kind that can be favorable to a major talent. Dante lived when the Middle Ages were crystalizing into their classical form; he was the younger contemporary of that great systematizer and exponent of the newest intellectual trends, Thomas Aquinas. Dante was in the position of a Soviet writer who feels himself part of the "coming thing," and can set his imagination to work exploring and presenting it. He had the joy of being, in his highly individual way, part of the wave of the future.

8 But what of Homer? His two epics—if he wrote them—are retrospective works, composed several centuries after the events they purport to chronicle. They are his *Gone with the Wind*, except that he sings the winning side. He lived in a time of breakdown and confused turmoil, when the past seemed a golden age of heroism and splendor, fit to be celebrated in ringing hexameters if hardly to be emulated. In this feeling for the past, Homer was one with his public. It looked backward to Achilles as the Dark Ages did to the fabulous Caesar and Alexander.

9 So far I have mentioned writers who stood inside their society rather than taking a vantage point outside it. Any quarrel they had with society was distinctly a family altercation. Dante advanced sharp views on many religious and political matters, but these were shared by many of his nonpoetic contemporaries. Shakespeare was, if anything, something of a conservative, even a "reactionary," to use the modern jargon. As far as we can judge, he loved queen, country, and the inherited social system as simply as any British regimental commander of the nineteenth century. He was no Jacobin, no leveler, no one out to remake the world that he observed with such unswerving accuracy.

10 At times a writer seems to draw strength from a lover's quarrel with his society. This I take to have been the case with Faulkner. Moving through an archaic world, at once benighted and yet possessing a depth of sensibility and relationship lost by most of the urbanized, industrialized, and rationalized North, he was fiercely Southern to the outside world and an *enfant terrible* to his fellow Southerners. One can perceive how flattened out his work would be if he had been merely the complacent Southerner or equally if he had chosen the position of the Southern expatriate who parrots the shallow certainties of Northern liberalism and loses all rooted relationship with the nuances of a society in which men still live by organic relationship rather than by the casual and cold bonds of the voluntary, social contract.

11 But what of the writer—and he is popularly supposed to be the norm

—who is "alienated" from his society and writes in isolation from it? He is harder to find than one expects. Where he exists at all, he occurs chiefly in the nineteenth and twentieth centuries and appears to be the by-product of those great events and intellectual movements that have dissolved the old social ties and thrown the individual back upon his aloneness. The industrial revolution, replacing the rising and setting sun with the time and motion studies; the contractual relationship between employer and employee, instead of the inherited obligations of a feudal world; the weakening of the Christian creed and code and its replacement by nothing much; the rise of science and its inherent inability to supply the certainties that religion and custom once bequeathed from generation to generation—all these things, and many more, have left society a thing so little viable that the writer has scarcely known whether anything is left to be either accepted or rejected. Add to this the fact that all men have become specialists; the writer is regarded as one specialist among others. And specialists have not found the Esperanto that will permit them to communicate across the boundary lines of their specialties. Meanwhile, a low-level ordering of values has offered a kind of consensus—material possessions, gadgets, security, peace of mind—that hardly calls for strident rejection, since there is so little in it to tempt a perceptive and sensitive writer.

12 What I have just said applies more particularly to Great Britain, the southern United States, and parts of New England. In most of America there were from the start only traces and vestiges of the kind of organic society, ultimately feudal in its roots, that I have been describing. But its psychological equivalent was supplied in many ways by the frontier, which at its best called forth a society at once organic and equalitarian to meet its implacable demands. The passing of the frontier and its replacement by the assembly line and the public relations office have done things to America of which we are yet only dimly aware, though I think our psychiatrists could speak on this point. We are haunted by national memories of heroic achievements, of bitter challenges triumphantly surmounted. Meanwhile we punch the time clock or write copy for magazine advertisements and television commercials. Each year residential mobility increases, so that the colleges are filled with young people who have never lived five years in one community. No wonder there is a depersonalization of relationships. In the spawning suburbs one sees the desperate attempt to create a sense of organic community by committees within committees, planned playfulness, and that trinitarian cluster of institutions to bring people together: the Church, the country club, and the Parent-Teachers Association. I read recently in the *Milwaukee Journal* of a new housing development that intended to embody the values of "village life." The promoter promises: "The management also would help establish a way of life in the village by having a sociologist plan the leisure time for interested tenants. . . .

There would be dances, entertainments, educational lectures, card parties, etc."

13 One wishes the promoter success, but doubts that he will have it. At any rate, the crumbling of many certainties and patterns of life has left society a vaguer and more confusing milieu than it used to be. Some writers have reacted by trying to hasten the process. Others have psychologically pulled away and created a private world.

14 Certainly many nineteenth- and twentieth-century writers have felt themselves out of step with Victorianism and its attenuated survivals. Thomas Hardy set himself in opposition to the rigid certainties of the late nineteenth century. Theodore Dreiser proclaimed a world in which man, no longer the sinful yet glorious image of God, was the blind plaything of "chemisms." Sinclair Lewis (though with more than a touch of the lover's quarrel) put the business and professional world of America under a microscope that magnified its great, open spaces. James Joyce dissolved and reformed the language of a dissolving world. As for the poets, they have found patterns of meaning where they could. Robinson Jeffers took to the hawk and the rock and the dark, unloving God of natural processes. William Butler Yeats constructed his own mythology from eclectically borrowed materials. Robert Frost found in archaic rural New England a set of assumptions still viable for poetry. T. S. Eliot turned to orthodox Christianity, a decision almost as bizarre for his time as the current preoccupation of the "beats" with Zen Buddhism. In short, finding little meaningful order in society at large, the poets have found or created a local or private order, and thus have been enabled to write.

15 All these instances involve rejection of a sort. But one must bring in the qualifying terms. The writer who seems to be rejecting his society may actually be expressing the half-formed conviction of a minority which tomorrow will be the majority. He may be the first bomb thrower of the successful revolution. When Wordsworth and Coleridge led their early readers away from the geometrically planned gardens of eithteenth-century reason, to explore the cottages of peasants, the uncharted wildernesses by land and sea, and the inner world of the heart, they were not alone. They were the pioneers of a new sensibility, everywhere in the air, which lacked only the poetic voices that would give it words and power. Similarly, Hardy and Dreiser did not march as solitary rebels against Queen Victoria; rather, they composed the battle hymns that modern man, convinced man is "nothing but," mumbles today off key. Once Eugene O'Neill seemed very far out when he translated Freud into the tortured figures of his stage; today every college student can psychoanalyze himself and his roommate without having read a word of Freud. Or can one really say that the Zen-reading, beard-growing beatniks are solitary figures? They represent a subculture, a society within society. It is a world of conscious rebels, but

within that world there are strict norms and traditions. One recalls the *New Yorker* cartoon of the man reading a copy of *Time* in a beatnik restaurant; the waiter apologetically requests him to leave.

16 The case of the atheist existentialist writers is particularly illuminating. They express man's agonizing sense of aloneness in a world where God is dead, and society is just one solitary figure after another, bumbling around in the darkened confusion that Matthew Arnold accurately portrayed and depicted. But to picture such a world is not a retreat from society; rather, it is an attempt to understand it. The physician who says, "I'm afraid it looks like cancer," is a realist, not an escapist. And it is noteworthy that a strong moral passion often infuses the books of the existentialists; they will not let man use his solitariness as an excuse for inner or outer anarchy. He is sternly commanded to create his own world, but that world inescapably involves others through his decisions. He is not permitted the pretense that he is the innocent plaything of impersonal forces.

17 All that I have so far said is a prelude to three conclusions. Great literature seems to involve, most often, three preconditions: (1) The birth of a literary genius. Since this cannot be brought about by any act of will or marvel of scientific manipulation, I shall say little more about it. At least, if a Shakespeare could be born into a nation of five million, there is the statistical hope that geniuses will continue to enter our teeming world. (2) A society with attitudes, values, and beliefs that are interesting and significant enough for the writer to embrace them, reject them angrily, or enter into a lover's quarrel with them. (3)An angle of vision, a way of looking at things, which the writer may share with society or which may be his supreme act of defiance. In any case, it gives him a means of ordering his observation and experience, so that he can make sense (and this includes aesthetic sense) of it.

18 Precondition (2) demands guesswork. I think it likely that during the next couple of generations the English-speaking world will not change beyond recognition its attitudes and implicit assumptions. A diffused Christianity and generalized religiosity will continue widespread, if often confusingly blended in the United States with "the religion of democracy" and "Amercanism"—whatever one means by that; and alloyed with the values of "The Establishment" in Great Britain. For the greater number of persons, it is likely to be a Christianity without cutting edges, blandly tolerant not from charity but from ignorance of doctrine; a religion of comfort and psychological gimmicks rather than a revelation centering about salvation, sanctity, a Cross, and an empty tomb. Even diluted and diffused, Christianity is not to be despised. Diffused Christianity grows sweeter fruits than diffused fascism or diffused *laissez-faire*. But I question whether this mild and vague faith produces a society with which the writer can have either a passionate love affair or a bitter quarrel. It is too soft and

rubbery; he can't sink his teeth into it. Certainly, very few writers will find this bland, adulterated Christianity adequate for *themselves*. They need something starker, more categorical, if they are to have a vantage point from which they can view the world about them, whatever that world may be.

19 If the prediction I have hazarded is at all correct, I expect to see another, complementary movement, not important in numbers but important in every other way. There are already some indications of it. Christianity is beginning to develop a core, an inner group. This consists of those Christians who are not content with the nebulous and undemanding faith that is offered in painless potions. Movements such as that centered in the Iona community are one indication of what I mean; The Quaker community at Pendle Hill is another. In most parishes one can find what is, in effect, an inner circle—much as the phrase is repulsive. By inner circle I mean not those who are the "pillars of the Church" and frequently its lay popes, holding the minister in subjugation, but rather the persons who take Christianity seriously by studying it, by constant prayer, and by specific efforts to do the concrete things that make the faith a weekday reality. These various tendencies may never become united in any sort of "third order"—it could be best that they do not—but they point, spiritually and psychologically, in that direction. Christians who mean business are a Church within the Church; they are Christian colonies in a society so vaguely Christian that the word has only a minimal meaning.

20 A writer of the near future, as now, will see around him a world that cannot be neatly schematized. He will observe many people living, apparently, for the proverbial television sets and split-level houses, for security and social standing, for a healthy and happy sex life, for protection against the lowering Communists. But if this is all he sees, he will be a superficial observer. Almost always there is a wistfulness. There is the diffused sense of anxiety, at times of futility, the wish to believe "there is really something beyond all this." Here and there the observer will see people who know precisely what the "something" is. The well-instructed and dedicated Marxist is not given to gentle wistfulness. The scientific humanist has a philosophy and a program of action. And the religious person, who takes his religion with life-and-death seriousness, will also know where he stands.

21 The one safe prediction seems to be that for some decades, at the very least, society will probably continue to be as blurred and confusing as it now is. Perhaps here and there, little islands of meaning will rise and take definite shape from the murky seas of vagueness. Marxism, scientific humanism, authentic Christianity—they may become more sharply defined, as scattered individuals find in them the key to making sense of life, and as such individuals discover one another.

22 What I have so far said is based on the unprovable assumption that the Cold War will continue, without substantial changes in the power positions of the two great systems. If Khrushchev should turn out to be a better prophet than I, and our grandchildren happily live under a system imported from the USSR, then the writer would find his task either enormously simplified or made impossible. He could throw himself into the new world being created all around him and become its bard and laureate, or—if he were out of sympathy with it—oppose it as long as he could and then fall silent. He would in either case at least have about him a society lacking the ambiguities that today so often make the writer feel he is touching a shapeless lump of wet clay.

23 I shall assume that Khrushchev is wrong. If so, we need to look now at the writer, living in a society whose values, attitudes, and beliefs are vague, fluctuating, and often trivial. Can he possibly find on one of the "islands" the vantage point from which he can make sense of his experience and observations?

24 Precondition (3) implies that a writer must acquire a pair of eyes through which he can view everything. But this figure of speech is too superficial. The writer needs to find meaning and significant order not merely in what he sees but in himself—in what he is and what he does. The first thing to be liberated into meaningful order is himself and his life. In trying to find meaning for himself, he is simultaneously seeking a meaningful way of relating himself to society, even though—in some cases—his relationship will appear to be that of the detached observer, chronicler, and interpreter.

25 We are born with physical eyes but we acquire metaphorical eyes. These give us our patterns of understanding: the key ideas and emotions by which we organize what we experience and observe, and make some sense of it. The metaphorical eyes are, in short, our philosophies, religions, and ideologies. These may be conscious and explicit or almost entirely unconscious and implicit.

26 One pair of metaphorical eyes is what I shall call, for lack of any more precise term, "naturalism." man is "nothing but." He is a curiously developed and specialized animal; he builds temples and organizes symphony orchestras, and he makes of sex a ritual and an art. He lacks the charming and direct common sense of the other animals. But after the qualifying phrases have been conceded, man is still nothing but an animal. He bears no image of God; there are no angels for him to rival, and no real devils to tempt him. He is simply an animal that evolved in a direction as odd as that of the duckbilled platypus.

27 Naturalism can produce significant literature. Some of Zola's novels still have a massive impact that the reader cannot evade. Whether it can produce a literature of the greatest heights and depths, I question. One

does not compose a *Divine Comedy* or a *King Lear* about dachshunds, not even about anthropoids that wear tuxedos or blue jeans. Mankind, viewed through the eyes of naturalism, is diminished and flattened. The words damnation and salvation lose their sharp meaning. It is hard to think of a hell or heaven for even the most highly developed "mere animals." Naturalism makes the human drama duller. No longer is the visible scene a battleground between the invisible Devil and the invisible God; the landscape ceases to be one of bottomless abysses of the spirit and soaring Everests. It becomes a flattened plain or teeming jungle. One need not be a Christian to recognize all this. Sophocles knew it perfectly well. Naturalism may or may not be "true" but, if it is taken as a complete way of viewing man, it makes him less complex, less fascinating, less memorable than he once appeared. In actual practice, as one would expect, the naturalistic writers have dealt with the instincts, impulses, passions, and in general the "animal-like" side of man, and have shown considerable embarrassment when confronted by his capacity for self-transcendence and altruistic nobility. At the same time—and this is a striking thing—many of the naturalistic writers, such as Zola, Dreiser, and Crane, have been aflame with a zeal for justice which to the observer's puzzled eye seems to come from some mysterious source altogether outside the naturalistic world view.

28 I have been speaking of naturalism in its old-fashioned, simplistic form. Indeed, its origin is closely linked with the partially outmoded science of the nineteenth century, a time when scientific certainties had a pat assurance they have not lost. Many of the modern scientists, such as Julian Huxley, now offer a considerably more subtle and adequate view, conveniently called scientific humanism. This is an effort to see in the scientific outlook a basis for man's finest intuitions and what could be called his spiritual character. Scientific humanism is not reductionist; it does not fall into the genetic fallacy. True, it refuses to leap back into the bosom or brain of any recognizable God, but it discovers in the life process, indeed in matter, a quality that is potentially spiritual from the beginning. Evolution becomes a progressive unfolding of the possibilities latent in a speck of dust. Man's arts, ethics, and even his religions are not accidental freaks in the history of a strange animal, but rather the line of development toward the full actualization of what has always been latent in the universe. The scientific humanist does not say "nothing but." His thought is really teleological, though he posits no traditional God as the goad toward the ultimate goal, and the goal is not one miraculously revealed in advance, but rather one to be discovered and created in the course of man's continuing evolution—an evolution that is decreasingly biological, and increasingly social, psychological, and ethical.

29 To an author, this pair of eyes reveals a much more interesting landscape than the eyes of simple naturalism permit him to see. He can look at

a man such as Schweitzer and see in him, not a biological curiosity, but a person who is in the mainstream of the long epic from "lifeless matter" to the finest flowering of the spirit. Shakespeare is not a biological sport but a major means by which life in its unfolding has come to know itself.

30 Scientific humanism permits one to take the human story seriously and to recognize in it a beauty and a poignant grandeur. It is, from the Christian's viewpoint, an impressive attempt to put scientific foundations under very much of what the Christian has always believed for reasons other than science. The writer whose metaphorical eyes are those of scientific humanism will not be forced into reinterpreting human motivations so as to make them acceptable to the chimpanzee or lemur. Rather, he will look with something of the eyes of a St. Francis at all furred and feathered things, seeing in them the dawning hints of the progressive revelation of cosmic meaning—which, on this planet at least, has its standard-bearer in man.

31 Does a writer find anything lacking in scientific humanism? I am not referring to its ultimate truth or falsehood. Certainly it is a creed that demands an act of faith as great as that of the theistic religions. To see a Mozart latent in a handful of dust is as daring a leap of faith as to see God breathing upon a handful of dust. But the question is a different one. Can scientific humanism offer the writer a pair of eyes through which he can observe every scene (including his own inner landscape) and make sense of it?

32 It will open many more doors than mere naturalism. Where it fails, I think, is in lack of inwardness. There is something once-born, healthy-minded, about scientific humanism. It has a well-scrubbed quality, handsome teeth gleaming in an optimistic smile. It seems to be saying, "Buck up, the great human adventure is just beginning." Its buoyancy is exhilarating to the man who feels himself fit and ready to march forward with his fellows down the evolutionary highway. It cannot say much to the Kierkegaards of this world nor to the man whose advanced state of cancer prevents him from marching. Scientific humanism holds forth glowing landscapes for that collectivity, mankind, but so far as I can see it has little to say to solitary man, particularly solitary man in his incommunicable abysses and heights. The focus on the broader pattern and drama is just the opposite of the vision of most writers. To them, Tom, Dick, and Harry, Oedipus and Othello, have always been more interesting than mankind.

33 Speaking still and always from a writer's point of view, scientific humanism is weak where existentialism is strong. It is faithful to the intuition that we are part of a blundering but always marching army of fellow pilgrims trying to find the half-guessed shrine that is the goal of our drama. It is too healthy-minded for the tormented solitary, alone with his own consciousness. And part of mankind's evolution is the gift or curse of experiencing this aloneness and forlornness. Existentialism, for its part,

is a solitary awareness reaching out in an agony of yearning to make contact with other imprisoned centers of consciousness.

34 I have so far mentioned Marxism only in passing. This is because, for the moment, it is a minor alternative with most English-speaking writers. The reasons for this are as much historical as theoretical. The enchantment with Marxism that enlivened and bedeviled the 1930's has been shattered by the harsh actualities of the Communist development in the USSR. Stalin, the purge trials, and the fading of Utopia as the commissars began to organize it, have resulted in widespread disillusionment among Western intellectuals who greeted the mild welfare state with approval but resisted a doctrinaire attempt to impose an ideology on all human activities. The cold war, calling into play the simplest emotions of fear and national self-concern, has made it still more difficult for writers to find in Marxism, at least of the Soviet variety, the metaphorical extra pair of eyes.

35 If the writers of the 1930's overrated Marxism, both as a world-view and a program for action, those of the 1960's underrate it. There must be something emotionally and intellectually compelling in a creed that has won a third of the world—and not wholly by force of arms and sly deceit. Marxism is a peculiarly potent amalgam of Old Testament prophecy, the apocalyptic hope, Hegel, and nineteenth-century science. It offers a view of history that makes some sense, at least, of humanity's dark agonies and dark deeds, as well as its creative achievements; it combines the conviction of inevitable fulfillment (found in a gentle form in the doctrine of inevitable progress) with a social passion that has unmistakable Biblical roots. A writer who is looking for some way to make sense of his observations will find in Marxism some very keen tools to be used in analysis. But he will find an additional thing. No more than Christianity does Marxism invite the writer or anyone else to use it merely as a pair of eyes. It professes to be the way, the truth, and the life; it is a call to action and commitment. It says, "Follow me, and be a part of the vanguard of history's movement forward, a movement that will reach its goal with you or without you." This commandment has a curiously Biblical ring.

36 Is Marxism, then, adequate to the needs of the writer? No, not finally. It also is too simple and too healthy minded. It lacks inwardness. In Russian painting, it produces the ruddy-cheeked peasant rejoicing at tractors. But a peasant can also mourn the scorn of the girl he loves, the death of his child, the coming of old age, the breakdown of understanding between friends. He can have purely private ecstasies that do not seem to serve a social purpose. Finally, the triumphant sweep of history is small consolation to the man who is assured that he will be dead, really dead, and never see the earthly paradise. The degree of disinterested idealism to which he is summoned is impressive, noble, and murderous to the very roots of his being.

37 Marxism explains much. It explains too much. It is too simple.

And it demands too much. We have seen in the USSR how writers are constantly probing the ideological walls, hoping to find a chink here and there. Being writers, and therefore men with a more than normal sensitivity, they perceive—consciously or unconsciously—that there are vast continents of human experience and yearning that simply have no significant point of contact with economics, production, and the unrolling of makind's broad history.

38 It is significant that the decline in Marxist influence among English-speaking intellectuals has been paralleled by the rise of Oriental religion as a live option. The various strands of Hinduism and Buddhism that are packed for export all have in common an inwardness, and a relatively minor preoccupation with those events that loom blackest in the daily newspapers. When the individual is urged to lose himself, it is not to history, to the masses, to the economic process, or to the movement, but rather to the unconditioned Ultimate (words falter here) which, he is likely to be told, is akin to, or identical with, the deepest level of his own being. Thus in losing himself he finds himself.

39 It is perilous and also unfair to attempt any vast generalizations about the influence of the Oriental religions and philosophies on current and future Western literature. These faiths are not monochrome, and one must reckon also with Western misunderstanding, as well as understanding, of them. But one assertion seems safe. The inwardness that is lacking in Marxim is found in them. In a way, however, it is a provisional or momentary inwardness, if by inwardness one is thinking of individuality and sense of identity. The general imperative of imported Orientalism is—through individuality and then beyond it—back to the All. Liberation is escape from the nagging demands of the ego and the discovery that the most profound level of the spirit is one with the Ultimate. The logical upshot of this kind of religion is prayer, meditation, silence, and union with the Ultimate. History cannot have the same meaning that it does for the Jew, the Christian, or the Marxist. If all things are ultimately one, the diversity of the passing scene and the excitement and terror of the momentary abysses and heights of history is a secondary thing. In short, Oriental religion at least as it is understood by the West, devalues the sense of individuality and the significance of history. In doing this, it partially devalues the usual function of the writer.

40 Some writers have discovered, and I think more will discover, that Christianity offers them the best pair of eyes. This is not the main reason for being a Christian—one should not worship Christ merely in order to write a *Hamlet*—but the discovery remains valid. To change the metaphor, the Christian lives in the roomiest house that seems to be available. The writer who becomes a Christian discovers that he has only his negations to lose. The affirmations that other faiths make, he can mostly second—with appropriate footnotes, of course. Their negations he must deny.

41 He can agree with the old-fashioned naturalism that man is an animal, but he cannot add "nothing but." He must rather add "plus." With the scientific humanist he has much in common, but his act of faith is a milder one, for he posits an intelligent and loving Will that wooed the miraculous dust and guided it until it became Michelangelo. He also sees a bigger place for individuality and the intractable oneness of the individual (thanks to God) than scientific humanism, engrossed with the collective march down the highway of evolution, easily accords. He has a view that makes room for neurosis as well as mental health, for crosses as well as schools and art museums.

42 With the Marxist, the Christian has much in common, more than with the traditional Hindu. He believes that history has meaning (though the full revelation of that meaning is not wholly boxed in by history); that the most grubby details of daily life, such as banking systems and modes of production, are to be taken with all seriousness; that the quest for justice here and now is the essence and evidence of enlightenment. But again, the Christian must negate the negations. He negates the atheism of Marx, and he negates the naive insistence that productive processes are always primary and "culture" is always an epiphenomenon. It must be quickly added that he negates this latter not by an equally false idealism, which would contend that disembodied ideas incarnate themselves in factories and counting houses, but rather by seeing all of man's activities as a broken and sometimes demonic—but occasionally magnificent—reflection of the image he bears within him. Neither "matter" nor "mind" is primary. God is.

43 At any rate, with the Marxist the Christian finds enduring and exciting meaning in the making of goods, the distribution, and the development of new processes—but his ultimate lies as much beyond these human achievements as it lies beyond the finest performance of *Oedipus Rex*. Christianity supplies a real ultimate, not a deification of history and process; it also gives the individual whereon to stand. His destiny is inseparably linked with the total, ongoing spectacle, and yet not wholly. God saves men one by one. One by one, at the last, we find whether we have accepted salvation.

44 I have mentioned the increasing influence of Oriental thought. I expect this to continue and grow. A Christianity worn threadbare by sterile moralism, old truths somehow shriveled into platitudes and clichés, and psychology dressed up in the faded finery of Christian theology, lacks the power to grip, heal, and illumine. To the Westerner, there is something crisp and clean about a religion from far away, one with great spiritual and psychological subtlety, one that restores his inwardness and leads him beyond it. And yet—one must make these judgments with all possible humility, but still make them—I am convinced that the various Oriental varieties of the "perennial philosophy" will not long provide, for many writers, the firm island of meaning on which they can plant their solid feet

and make sense of their own lives and of what they observe. Too much is left out. If everything is somehow a part of the All, and the All is what matters, then why write novels? Unless the passing scene has some meaning in its diversity and perverse insistence on being what it is and not something else; if the passing scene is a half-illusory pageant, marking the retreat from the All and the return to the All—then it is hardly a fit object for prolonged identification or agonized and loving study. I am more likely to write a poem about a bluebird when it is intractably a bluebird; less likely if I consider it a pale reflection of the eternal, metaphysical, and invisible bluebird; least likely of all, if the bluebird appears to me as a momentary and insignificant aberration from the unity of all things. Nor do I see how the passion for social justice can be as deeply anchored in a religion that takes the material world and history lightly, as in one that regards history as the theater, here and now, of duty, love, salvation, and damnation. Marxism is too materialistic, and most Oriental religion seems too spiritual. Christianity, by its doctrines of creation and providence and by its sacramental mode of experience, manages to be both fiercely materialistic and fiercely spiritual. Again, it negates only the negations.

45 I need hardly point out the great amount of agreement between existentialism, even in its atheist varieties, and Christianity. There is the same sense of the uniqueness, and the aloneness of the individual, and there is the same inescapable necessity of making choices. But where existentialism can offer little way out, other than responsibly creating one's world (as though Adam had not already named all the animals!), Christianity assumes a world that already exists, a dimension of meaning whose center is God, and holds forth the hope that entrance into this world—now, this minute—can unite our separate lonelinesses into a communion that does no violence to any man's unique selfhood.

46 I come back to my prediction. I think a fair number of writers may turn to Christianity. They will do this, in most instances, after a process of trial and error, much of it unconscious—in an effort not so much to write better as to find meaning in their own lives. With writers, of course, these two yearnings cannot be neatly separated. They will often come to Christianity reluctantly and with a hangdog feeling, having experimented with many alternatives and discovering at some point that each alternative makes them say *no* to some experience or observation which they know in their bones to be meaningful.

47 Christianity is not an easy religion for the person who wants sheer logic. It is full of odd twists and paradoxes that do violence to logic and even to ordinary morality, but which ring oddly true. The mathematical absurdity of the Trinity leaves any theologian stammering when he tries to explain it to an intelligent (or stupid) university student, yet it tallies with actual religious experience. The assertion that the last shall be first out-

rages ordinary morality and justice, yet it is not alien to the deepest perceptions of a sensitive participant in life. The Hindu doctrine of Karma is a plausible way of viewing cause-and-effect in the moral life, but Christianity cuts violently across the rational diagram with a God who breaks the cycle of Karma by shouldering his way to the Cross and bearing on his shoulders the consequences of men's sins. And so it goes. The Christian faith has about it something of the off-beat, compelling quality that one finds in a very great writer, who knows how to break the ordinary rules of writing, and in breaking them fulfills them. It is like the violent liberties that Shakespeare takes with iambic pentameter in his plays. There the lord of all metrical feet affirms them by remembering them or forgetting them for a time: blank verse is made for Shakespeare, not Shakespeare for blank verse. Or it is like Shakespeare writing *Hamlet*, a play that has everything wrong with it from a formal viewpoint and is also the play that haunts mankind more than any other. In Christianity, man's neat schematizations of the moral and spiritual life must be broken and reshaped by God. And God has done this in Christ.

48 Ordinary life is full of similar odd twists, absurdities, and paradoxes. A man who falls five hundred feet from an airplane almost certainly dies, but he *may* land in a snowdrift and live. Architects who are failures at fifty usually remain failures, but sometimes they live to be a glory and an abiding influence. The best seller is forgotten; the book written by an obscure crank comes out in paperbacks a century later. Nations that are mortal enemies turn into allies. A chaste, water-drinking, and honest mayor can leave his city in worse shape than he found it; whereas his philandering, gin-guzzling, pocket-lining successor may build symphony halls, attract industry, and find ways to reduce juvenile delinquency. The unpredictability and downright ironic irrationality of real life seems more akin to the paradoxes of the Christian faith than to the more strictly rational assertions of most of the competitive religions and ideologies. Of these, only existentialism seems to have the same respect for the absurd.

49 What advantages are there for a writer in being a Christian? I am speaking now of advantages to him *as writer*, not *as man*. In the first place, it gives him whereon to stand, an ordering of his own personal life that makes intellectual and emotional sense. It also gives him a perspective on his work as a writer. He can honestly see himself as a kind of earthly assistant to God (so can the carpenter), carrying on the delegated work of creation, making the fullness of creation fuller. At the same time, he is saved from the romantic tendency toward idolatry. Art is not religion. A writer is not a god or godling. There is wisdom and illumination but not salvation in a sonnet. Thus the work of any writer is set in proper proportion. Just as a husband and wife have a deeper marriage if they see their love as a human reflection of God's love, but do not make gods of each

other, and do not equate the ceremonies of the marriage-bed with the love upon the Cross, so an author writes better (for the inner setting of his work is founded on true relationships) if he gives himself to his work in a spirit of deadly serious playfulness and does not pretend to himself and others that he is a temple builder and the high priest and divinity of the temple.

50 Christianity offers also to the writer, as it does to every man, a community. In the earlier part of this chapter I suggested that the old organic communities are visibly dissolving. I do not think this process can be reversed. Perhaps it should not be. In the organic communities, the individual was born into a world of inescapable relationships and duties. As the organic community crumbles into the vague society of the social contract and voluntary relationships, there is a gain in freedom. One must select, one must take the initiative to establish relationships, rather than merely inherit them. New dimensions of liberty—frightening, it is true—are opened up. In terror at their new freedom, men hastily erect clumsy substitutes for the old organic bonds: they invent ideologies and stage mass rallies; they organize interlocking committees and hire sociologists to create an ersatz togetherness. But a Communist rally or a community square dance planned by a committee with sociological goals in mind is not the same thing as the old organic community, which was like an extended family. One can be as lonely in a planned demonstration or a community-sponsored fun night as in a solitary cell.

51 Angels or demons with flaming swords bar the way back. The Church offers a way forward, beyond mere individualism, beyond mere organization. It is a voluntary community of those who have caught some glimmering of what God means in Christ and how Christ unites all who accept the Accepter. Thus in the Church, at its best, there is both the flowering of individuality and also the sense of belonging, of being accepted, of forgiving, of being forgiven, of loving and being loved.

52 Admittedly, the average parish church does not bear much visible resemblance to the community of voluntary love and acceptance and mutual responsibility that I have briefly sketched. It is too much like the world about it. It bears traces of the old organic society, now in decay; it is sometimes an anarchy of solitary individuals who come together and worship as though each were in a lonely, separate room; or at times it feverishly generates a synthetic sense of community by activities, activities, and activities. Those who have the peculiarly Christian sense of community are likely to be a minority, a kind of third order of *ecclesia in ecclesia*. Thus it may be that the writer will find his "community" not so much in the parish church as in that "scattered brotherhood" of persons whom he meets here and there, comes to know, and in whom he finds a hint of what it means to be centered in Christ and therefore members one of another.

53 Any genuine community, whether localized or diffused, is a home. Living in it, drawing strength from it, the writer can move back and forth into the surrounding and interpenetrating world, and yet always have solid ground under his feet. Paradoxically, the firmer his sense of community, the less fearfully he will throw himself into society as a whole. He will be enabled to love it more, to study it with more compassion and interest, for he will not be afraid of absorption and destruction by it. And, yet another paradox, he will find strong evidence that in the apparently non-Christian or very vaguely Christian society, the secret Christ is at work. The scattered brotherhood will come to include, for him, men and women who do not recognize the Master they nevertheless serve.

54 Most of the gifts I have so far mentioned are those equally precious to the housewife, the business executive, and the writer. But there are some gifts that are especially valuable to the writer. The poet, for instance, is reassured that his preoccupation with sensory observations is not a frivolous study of *maya*. Things are real; they are real because God made them; and, because he made them, they are important and worthy of study and even a proper portion of love. Not only did God make things. He built us so that we perceive them as much through our animal senses as our minds; the mind must turn to the senses to have something to feed upon. The color and smell of a rose are not irrelevant or illusory. We were constructed so that we come into communion with the rose through its color, fragrance, and the thorns that scratch. Compared to the rose that the senses perceive, the rose of the botanist—still more the rose of the physicist—is a construct or abstraction, true in its own way, but not the rose that we are built to admire and love.

55 The novelist and playwright receive the assurance that man's social and psychological life and his entire historical existence are meaningful. History becomes part of a cosmic drama, reaching backward to the moment outside of time when the command. "Let there be," was spoken into the void, leading forward toward a culmination that is destined but not compelled; a culmination that by some mysterious paradox lies both inside and outside history and calls forth man's deepest freedom in working with what will surely come to pass.

56 There is another gift that Christianity bestows. In some systems of thought, diversity dissolves into a totality of one kind or another. Sciences move steadily toward mathematics as the All. Hindu thought, so far as I understand it, has no meaningful place for diversity. The teeming variety of this earth is a strange and passing thing, eventually to be merged once more with the All. To Christian eyes, diversity is a good thing in itself, for God made diversity. He did not create "trees"; he created pines, oaks, and ginkgoes. The animals are as fantastically varied as the impish drawings of a surrealist. The temperaments of men are as varied as the forms of animals.

Christianity aims not at the bypassing of individuality and absorption back into the All, but at fulfillment and redemption of the individual. Salvation is not absorption but relationship. If Hamlet and Lear are both in heaven, it is not because they have become indistinguishable nor because they have lost individual consciousness and are now merged as raindrops in the ocean of God. No, each is more himself than ever, but each self is a redeemed self, oriented to turn with love to God and his creatures. In sum, Christianity is concerned with the fulfillment of personality, not its negation. We are called to be sons of God, and a son is not his father. A novelist is not being frivolous when he takes his characters seriously.

57 Another way in which Christian eyes aid the writer is simply that he can make greater sense of the towering heights and dizzy abysses of the human drama. He does not have to explain them away. He need not elucidate Hitler as a throwback to the anthropoids or St. Francis as a complex manifestation of the herd instinct. He sees in man both the angels and the demons at work, as well as the simpler imperatives of the animal nature. And he observes, and experiences, a drama with eternal stakes. The stakes are not merely the welfare or destruction of society, but the drama of individual damnation and salvation. It is a drama with no foregone conclusions. In real life, as in a good novel, the spectator is kept guessing up to the end.

58 So much for some of the special gifts and graces that a writer can receive when his eyes are baptized. His faith is no substitute for talent, for genius. But if he has that, the new eyes can aid him in seeing more, understanding more, saying more.

59 But to whom shall he say it? Is the Christian writer of the near future doomed to be an esoteric, coterie figure, speaking only to those who share his pair of eyes? It is possible that this is the case, but I am hopeful that he can reach many others. If it is true that the soul is *naturaliter christiana*, Christian insight should not be without response among non-Christians. Many an agnostic is deeply moved by Dante; there is Graham Greene, whose novels are meaningful to thousands who reject his theology. If the Christian faith provides the roomiest dwelling; if Christian eyes can see more and see it more exactly, it should follow that the truth a Christian writer can portray will somehow get through, because it will ring true even in men who consciously reject the faith that offers the new eyes.

60 I could be mistaken in this. It may be that for the next few generations the Christian writer is condemned to write for a coterie. This is more likely to happen with the playwright than anyone else. He requires a certain community of reaction. The people sitting in the theater need to have enough in common so that they will respond with some unanimity to the play. If their assumptions and ingrained attitudes are too different, it may be impossible to arouse the spontaneous symphony of individual responses that great plays call forth when there is common ground between play-

wright and audience. Conceivably, the Christian playwright may have to develop his own audience in Church circles. I do not believe this is the case, but it could be so.

61 The case of the novelist and the poet is more hopeful. Except for public readings of poetry (almost a form of drama) these two types of literature are read by individuals in their solitude. There is not the necessity to arouse a group response. A man reading a novel or a poem can mull it over, let it sink in, and respond to it at his own speed. If the soul is Christian by nature, it can take its time and slowly grasp whatever insight is offered.

62 At this point I have the uneasy feeling that some readers may assume I expect Christian writers to produce "Christian literature." If by that they mean books in which such words as God, Christ, soul, etc., frequently occur; or books dealing with Church life, ministers, devout souls, etc.—they are mistaken. The Christian writer does not necessarily deal directly with anything that would be labeled "Christian." His plots and characters may be precisely those one would find in a naturalistic or existentialist novel. The difference is much more subtle and more important. It is again the angle of vision, the nuances that a different pair of eyes can yield, a way of understanding, not subject matter.

63 I have tried to state the "hope for literature" in modest and tentative terms. One must not claim too much nor hope too much. If there is to be a great literature, it will come about first of all because great talents arise. In the future, as in the past, many of these may be non-Christians. Their insights will often be more probing than those of devout but less gifted Christian authors. In a sense, a real sense, they may write books more radically "Christian" than many Christians have the skill to write.

64 But, for Christian and non-Christian alike, this is a world moving into a period when all foundations are increasingly shaken and new foundations are perhaps being built without our quite knowing the building material we are using. Science, for good or evil—that is our choice—is doubling and redoubling the wager. The old dream of world brotherhood is becoming a possibility, a mirage, an absolute necessity, all simultaneously. Mankind is called upon to achieve the impossible or perish. The nineteenth-century world order, as hierarchical with its distinction of "civilized" and "primitive" nations as the social hierarchy of the Middle Ages, is dissolving in fire, blood, and strident shouts for equality and dignity, in tongues only recently reduced to alphabetical form. Meanwhile, the space vehicles are probing the heavens, and who knows what adventures of the spirit lie barely beyond tomorrow's newspaper, when the first contact is made with intelligences independent of our parochial earth? Closer to home, all the advances of science make a human being more a marvel, more an impenetrable mystery, than ever before. The final frontier is ourselves.

65 It could be another Elizabethan age, a century of outer and inner explorations, while everywhere the relations among men and between men and whatever they call God are being reordered. Like the Elizabethan age, it is already a time dominated by voices of pessimism, at the very moment when men are acting with frantic energy and, for good or evil, are doing mighty deeds.

66 Writers will continue to write. They will have much to write about. It may be that the Christian faith will help some of them to see more, see it more truly. This is a hope, not a certainty, but when was hope ever the name for a sure thing?

STUDY GUIDE

Theme and Structure

1. In paragraph 1, Walsh states that as long as there are human beings there will always be literature. The question he raises is what hopes there are for its being any good. What is his answer? What conditions does he envision as necessary for a great literature?

2. The essay has two introductory paragraphs and two concluding ones. Draw up a sentence outline in which you show what Walsh does to develop his idea that there is a hope for great literature in the future. Observe the following thought divisions: paragraphs 3–16, 17–58, 59–61, and 62.

3. What are the three possible attitudes of a writer toward the society in and about which he writes discussed by Walsh in paragraphs 3–16? What great writers does he cite to illustrate these various attitudes?

4. What are the various "sets of eyes" (exclusive of Christianity) with which a writer may look at the world described in the third precondition of a great literature? What are the advantages and limitations of each?

5. Walsh says in paragraph 40 that Christianity offers writers "the best pair of eyes," and that the Christian lives in "the roomiest house that seems to be available." In an earlier part of the essay he explained the Christianity that he considers might be helpful to the writer (paragraph 19). What is it? What advantages does he suggest that the Christian writer of talent might have over his non-Christian confrere (see paragraphs 49–58)?

6. In paragraph 24, Walsh says that a writer must find "meaning and significant order not merely in what he sees but in himself." How does this idea relate to Barrett's description of the artist's situation in the modern world? Is there any way of reconciling the views of Walsh and Barrett? You might write a paper in which you try to reconcile these two views. In it you would want to show, among other things, what value there is in an artist's expression on his own inner emptiness and of a meaningless world.

SECTION **8**

Understanding the Essay

A NOTE ON THE ESSAY

Carl Van Doren

1 The sonnet has a standard form very much as a man has. Leave off the sestet of your sonnet and you do about what a god does when he leaves the legs off a man. The drama has a standard form very much as a rendezvous has. Write a drama in which no spark is exchanged between the audience and the action, and you have done what fate does when it keeps lovers from their meetings. The novel has a standard form very much as a road has. You may set out anywhere you like and go wherever you please, at any gait, but you must go somewhere, or you have made what is no more a novel than some engineer's road would be a road if it had neither beginning, end, nor direction. But the essay! It may be of any length, breadth, depth, weight, density, color, savor, odor, appearance importance, value, or uselessness which you can or will give it. . . . It differs from a letter by being written to more—happily a great many more—than one person. It differs from talk chiefly by being written at all.

2 Having to obey no regulations as to form, the essay is very free to choose its matter. The sonnet, by reason of its form, tends to deal with solemn and not with gay themes. The drama, for the same reason, tends to look for intense and not for casual incidents. The novel tends to feel that it must carry a considerable amount of human life on its back. The essay may be as fastidious as a collector of carved emeralds or as open-minded as a garbage-gatherer. Nothing human, as the platitude says, is alien to it. The essay, however, goes beyond the platitude and dares to choose matter from

Originally printed in *The New Pearson's*. Reprinted by permission of the author.

numerous non-human sources. Think of the naturalists and their essays. Think, further, of the range of topics for essayists at large. Theodore Roosevelt in an essay urges the strenuous life; Max Beerbohm in an essay defends cosmetics. De Quincey expounds the fine art of murder, Thoreau the pleasures of economy, William Law the blisses of prayer, Hudson the sense of smell in men and in animals, Schopenhauer the ugliness of women, Bacon the advantages of a garden, Plutarch the traits of curiosity, and A. C. Benson the felicity of having nothing much in the mind. All, in fact, an essayist needs to start with is something, anything, to say. He gets up each morning and finds the world spread out before him, as the world was spread out before Adam and Eve the day they left paradise. With the cosmos, past, present, and future, to pick from, the essayist goes to work. If he finds a topic good enough he may write a good essay, no matter how he writes it.

3 He may. There is still, however, the question of his manner. Thousands of dull men have written millions of true things which no one but their proof-readers, wives, or pupils ever read. . . . Competition in such affairs is free and endless. The only law which gives an essayist a right to his material is the law which rules that the best man wins. The law does not say in what fashion he must be best. Any fashion will do. Let him be more sententious, like Bacon; or more harmonious, like Sir Thomas Browne; or more elegant, like Addison; or more direct, like Swift; or more hearty, like Fielding; or more whimsical, like Lamb; or more impassioned, like Hazlitt; or more encouraging, like Emerson; or more Olympian, like Arnold; or more funny, like Mark Twain; or more musical, like Pater; or more impish, like Max Beerbohm; or more devastating, like Mencken. Let the essayist be any of these things and he may have a copyright till someone takes it away from him. What matters is the manner. If he has good matter, he *may* write a good essay; if he has a good manner he probably *will* write a good essay.

4 An essay is a communication. If the subject of the discourse were the whole affair, it would be enough for the essayist to be an adequate conduit. If the manner were the whole affair, any versatile fellow might try all the manners and have a universal triumph. But back of matter and manner both lies the item which is really significant. The person who communicates anything in any way must be a person. His truth must have a tone; his speech must have a rhythm which are his and solely his. His knowledge or opinions must have lain long enough inside him to have taken root there; and, when they come away, they must bring some of the soil clinging to them. They must, too, have been shaped by that soil—as plants are which grow in cellars, on housetops, on hillsides, in the wide fields, under shade in forests. Many kinds of men, many kinds of essays! Important essays come from important men.

STUDY GUIDE

1. Carl Van Doren's purpose in this selection is to give an informal definition of the essay. Every definition must give a positive statement about the thing being defined which tells what it is and which enables the reader to distinguish it from other similar objects.

A. Using what Van Doren says here, try to draw up a simple definition of the essay. Be sure to include in your definition the purpose, the subject matter, and the tone or manner of the essay.

B. State how an essay differs in subject matter and form from a sonnet, a drama, and a novel.

2. Show how what Van Doren says about the essay in paragraph 4 is related to what Newman says about all literature in his "Communication through Literature."

3. What methods of paragraph development are employed in paragraph 1?

4. Cite and discuss the effectiveness of the figures (similes and metaphors) used in the following sentences: paragraph 1, sentences 2, 3, and 5; paragraph 2, sentence 5; and paragraph 4, sentences 2, 7, and 8.

5. A. Show how the breadth of subject matter open to the essayist is suggested by concrete examples cited in paragraph 2, sentences 8–12.

B. Using essays that you have read, draw up a similar illustrative list of your own.

6. Show how the variety of tone or manner which characterizes the essay as a literary type is illustrated by the concrete examples cited in paragraph 3, sentence 8.

Francis Bacon (1561–1626)

Francis Bacon is credited with introducing the essay into English literature. The philosopher Montaigne had already developed the genre in French. There had been collections of disparate aphorisms on various topics all through the Middle Ages. Montaigne's *essais*—"attempts"' or tentative observations—differed from the medieval commonplace books in containing more of the author's own observations on the various topics. But even Montaigne's essays were not logical or rhetorical developments of their topics.

Bacon's essays, in the 1597 edition, were related to the commonplace tradition. They were little more than a collection of disparate aphoristic statements on the given topics. It was not that Bacon was unfamiliar with the methods of rhetorical development. He shows a complete awareness of the traditional rhetoric in both theory and practice in his *Advancement of Learning;* actually the first book is built on the pattern of a complete classical oration. It was rather that he envisioned a different purpose and audience for his early essays. On occasions when ethical or scientific observation was in order, he felt that disparate aphorisms were more appropriate than a style fully developed by examples, contrast, comparison, the citation of authority, and so on. This latter rhetorical method of development he considered necessary when the writer had a popular audience in mind. Bacon himself did not have such an audience in mind for the first edition of his essays (here exemplified by "Of Studies" in the 1597 version), and hence the first edition of the *Essays* is little more than a collection of disparate aphorisms on their topics. In later editions, when he began to think of a popular audience, he did slightly augment the original essays with examples and comparisons (see the additions made to "Of Studies" in the 1625 version). And essays on new subjects written from the first for this popular audience were composed in the traditional rhetorical manner—logically divided and augmented by concrete examples, comparisons and contrasts, the citation of authorities, and so forth. (See the 1612 essay "Of Friendship.") Here we have a fully developed essay on the topic rather than a mere collection of aphoristic statements about it.

OF STUDIES

Francis Bacon

(1597 version)	(1625 version)
1 Studies serve for pastimes, for ornaments and for abilities. Their chief use for pastime is in privateness and retiring; for ornament is in discourse, and for ability is in judgment. For expert men can execute, but learned men are fittest to judge or censure.	1 Studies serve for delight, for ornament, and for ability. Their chief use for delight, is in privateness and retiring; for ornament, is in discourse; and for ability, is in the judgment and disposition of business. For expert men can execute, and perhaps judge of particulars, one by one; but the general counsels, and the plots, and marshalling of affairs, come best from those that are learned.
2 To spend too much time in them is sloth; to use them too much for ornament is affectation; to make judgement wholly by their rules, is the humor of a scholar.	2 To spend too much time in studies, is sloth; to use them too much for ornament, is affectation; to make judgment wholly by their rules is the humor of a scholar.

3 They perfect nature, and are perfected by experience.

3 They perfect nature, and are perfected by experience: For natural abilities, are like natural plants, that need pruning by study: and studies themselves, do give forth directions too much at large, except they be bounded in by experience.

4 Crafty men condemn them, simple men admire them, wise men use them: For they teach not their own use, but that is a wisdom without them: and above them won by observation.

4 Crafty men condemn studies; simple men admire them; and wise men use them: For they teach not their own use; but that is a wisdom without them, and above them, won by observation.

5 Read not to contradict, nor to believe, but to weigh and consider.

5 Read not to contradict, and confute; nor to believe and take for granted; nor to find talk and discourse; but to weigh and consider.

6 Some books are to be tasted, others to be swallowed, and some few to be chewed and digested: that is, some books are to be read only in parts; others to be read, but cursorily, and some few to be read wholly and with diligence and attention.

6 Some books are to be tasted, others to be swallowed, and some few to be chewed and digested: that is, some books are to be read only in parts; others to be read but not curiously; and some few to be read wholly, and with diligence and attention. Some books also may be read by deputy, and extracts made of them by others: but that would be, only in the less important arguments, and the meaner sort of books: else distilled books, are like common distilled waters, flashy things.

7 Reading maketh a full man, conference a ready man, and writing an exact man. And therefore if a man write little, he had need have a great memory, if he confer little, he had need have a present wit, and if he read little, he had need have much cunning, to seem to know that he doth not.

7 Reading maketh a full man; conference a ready man; and writing an exact man. And therefore, if a man write little, he had need have a great memory; if he confer little, he had need have a present wit; and if he read little, he had need have much cunning, to seem to know that, he doth not.

8 Histories make men wise, poets witty: the mathematics subtle, natural philosophy deep: moral grave, logic and rhetoric able to contend.

8 Histories make men wise, poets witty; the mathematics subtle, natural philosophy deep; moral grave; logic and rhetoric able to contend. *Abeunt studia in mores.*[1] Nay there is no stond or impediment in the wit, but may be wrought out by fit studies: Like as diseases of the body, may have appropriate exercises. Bowling is good for the stone and reines; shooting for the lungs and breast; gentle walking for the stomach; riding for the head; and the like. So if a man's wit be wandering, let him study the mathematics; for in demonstrations, if his wit be called away never so little, he must begin again. If his wit be not apt to distinguish or find differences, let him study the schoolmen; for they are *cymini sectores.*[2] If he be not apt to beat over matters, and to call up one thing, to prove and illustrate another, let him study the lawyers' cases: so every defect of the mind, may have a special receit.

OF FRIENDSHIP

Francis Bacon

1 There is no greater desert or wilderness than to be without true friends. For without friendship, society is but meeting. And as it is certain, that in bodies inanimate, union strengtheneth any natural motion, and weakeneth any violent motion; so amongst men, friendship multiplieth joys, and divideth griefs. Therefore whosoever wanteth fortitude, let him worship friendship. For the yoke of friendship maketh the yoke of fortune

[1] Studies find their completion in manners or morals.—*Ed.*
[2] Dividers of cumin seed, that is, hairsplitters.—*Ed.*

more light. There be some whose lives are, as if they perpetually played upon a stage, disguised to all others, open only to themselves. But perpetual dissimulation is painful; and he that is all fortune, and no nature is an exquisite hireling. Live not in continual smother, but take some friends with whom to communicate. It will unfold thy understanding; it will evaporate thy affections; it will prepare thy business. A man may keep a corner of his mind from his friend, and it be but to witness to himself, that it is not upon facility, but upon true use of friendship that he imparteth himself. Want of true friends, as it is the reward of perfidious natures; so is it an imposition upon great fortunes. The one deserve it, the other cannot scape it. And therefore it is good to retain sincerity, and to put it into the reckoning of ambition, that the higher one goeth, the fewer true friends he shall have. Perfection of friendship, is but a speculation. It is friendship, when a man can say to himself, I love this man without respect of utility. I am open hearted to him, I single him from the generality of those with whom I live; I make him a portion of my own wishes.

2 It had been hard for him that spake it to have put more truth and untruth together in few words, than in that speech, "Whosoever is delighted in solitude is either a wild beast or a god." For it is most true that a natural and secret hatred and aversation towards society in any man, hath somewhat of the savage beast; but it is most untrue that it should have any character at all of the divine nature; except it proceed, not out of a pleasure in solitude, but out of a love and desire to sequester a man's self for a higher conversation: such as is found to have been falsely and feignedly in some of the heathen; as Epimenides the Candian, Numa the Roman, Empedocles the Sicilian, and Apollonius of Tyana; and truly and really in divers of the ancient hermits and holy fathers of the church. But little do men perceive what solitude is, and how far it extendeth. For a crowd is not company; and faces are but a gallery of pictures; and talk but a tinkling cymbal, where there is no love. The latin adage meeteth with it a little: *Magna civitas, magna solitudo*;[1] because in a great town friends are scattered; so that there is not that fellowship, for the most part, which is in less neighborhoods. But we may go further, and affirm most truly that it is a mere and miserable solitude to want true friends; without which the world is but a wilderness; and even in this sense also of solitude, whosoever in the frame of his nature and affections is unfit for friendship, he taketh it of the beast, and not from humanity.

3 A principal fruit of friendship is the ease and discharge of the fulness and swellings of the heart, which passions of all kinds do cause and induce. We know diseases of stoppings and suffocations are the most dangerous in the body; and it is not much otherwise in the mind; you may take

[1] A great city is a great solitude.—*Ed.*

sarza to open the liver, steel to open the spleen, flower of sulphur for the lungs, castoreum for the brain; but no receipt openeth the heart, but a true friend; to whom you may impart griefs, joys, fears, hopes, suspicions, counsels, and whatsoever lieth upon the heart to oppress it, in a kind of civil shrift or confession.

4 It is a strange thing to observe how high a rate great kings and monarchs do set upon this fruit of friendship whereof we speak: so great, as they purchase it many times at the hazard of their own safety and greatness. For princes, in regard of the distance of their fortune from that of their subjects and servants, cannot gather this fruit, except (to make themselves capable thereof) they raise some persons to be as it were companions and almost equals to themselves, which many times sorteth to inconvenience. The modern languages give unto such persons the name of favorites, or privadoes; as if it were matter of grace, or conversation. But the Roman name attaineth the true use and cause thereof, naming them *participes curarum;* [2] for it is that which tieth the knot. And we see plainly that this hath been done, not by weak and passionate princes only, but by the wisest and most politic that ever reigned; who have often-times joined to themselves some of their servants; whom both themselves have called friends, and allowed others likewise to call them in the same manner; using the word which is received between private men.

5 L. Sylla, when he commanded Rome, raised Pompey (after surnamed the Great) to that height, that Pompey vaunted himself for Sylla's overmatch. For when he had carried the consulship for a friend of his, against the pursuit of Sylla, and that Sylla did a little resent thereat, and began to speak great, Pompey turned upon him again, and in effect bade him be quiet; *for that more men adored the sun rising than the sun setting.* With Julius Caesar, Decimus Brutus had obtained that interest, as he set him down in his testament for heir in remainder after his nephew. And this was the man that had power with him to draw him forth to his death. For when Caesar would have discharged the senate, in regard of some ill presages, and specially a dream of Calpurnia; this man lifted him gently by the arm out of his chair, telling him he hoped he would not dismiss the senate till his wife had dreamt a better dream. And it seemeth his favor was so great, as Antonius, in a letter which is recited *verbatim* in one of Cicero's Philippics, calleth him *venefica, witch;* as if he had enchanted Caesar. Augustus raised Agrippa (though of mean birth) to that height, as when he consulted with Maecenas about the marriage of his daughter Julia, Maecenas took the liberty to tell him, that he must either marry his daughter to Agrippa, or take away his life: there was no third way, he had made him so great. With Tiberius Caesar, Sejanus had ascended to that height, as they

[2] Sharers of burdens.—*Ed.*

two were termed and reckoned as a pair of friends. Tiberius in a letter to him saith, *haec pro amicitia nostra non occultavi*[3] and the whole senate dedicated an altar to Friendship, as to a goddess, in respect of the great dearness of friendship between them two. The like or more was between Septimius Severus and Plautianus. For he forced his eldest son to marry the daughter of Plautianus; and would often maintain Plautianus in doing affronts to his son; and did write also in a letter to the senate, by these words: "I love the man so well, as I wish he may over-live me." Now if these princes had been as a Trajan or a Marcus Aurelius, a man might have thought that this had proceeded of an abundant goodness of nature; but being men so wise, of such strength and severity of mind, and so extreme lovers of themselves, as all these were, it proveth most plainly that they found their own felicity (though as great as ever happened to mortal men) but as an half piece, except they mought have a friend to make it entire; and yet, which is more, they were princes that had wives, sons, nephews; and yet all these could not supply the comfort of friendship.

6 It is not to be forgotten what Comineus observeth of his first master, Duke Charles the Hardy; namely, that he would communicate his secrets with none; and least of all, those secrets which troubled him most. Whereupon he goeth on and saith that towards his latter time *that closeness did impair and a little perish his understanding*. Surely Comineus mought have made the same judgment also, if it had pleased him, of his second master Lewis the Eleventh, whose closeness was indeed his tormentor. The parable of Pythagoras is dark, but true; *Cor ne edito:* Eat not the heart. Certainly, if a man would give it a hard phrase, those that want friends to open themselves unto are cannibals of their own hearts. But one thing is most admirable (wherewith I will conclude this first fruit of friendship), which is, that this communicating of a man's self to his friend works two contrary effects; for it redoubleth joys, and cutteth griefs in halfs. For there is no man that imparteth his joys to his friend, but he joyeth the more; and no man that imparteth his griefs to his friend, but he grieveth the less. So that it is in truth of operation upon a man's mind, of like virtue as the alchemists use to attribute to their stone for man's body; that it worketh all contrary effects, but still to the good and benefit of nature. But yet without praying in aid of alchemists, there is a manifest image of this in the ordinary course of nature. For in bodies, union strengtheneth and cherisheth any natural action; and on the other side weakeneth and dulleth any violent impression; and even so it is of minds.

7 The second fruit of friendship is healthful and sovereign for the understanding, as the first is for the affections. For friendship maketh indeed a fair day in the affections, from storm and tempests; but it maketh day-

[3] For the sake of friendship I have not concealed these things from you.—*Ed.*

light in the understanding, out of darkness and confusion of thoughts. Neither is this to be understood only of faithful counsel, which a man receiveth from his friend; but before you come to that, certain it is that whosoever hath his mind fraught with many thoughts, his wits and understanding do clarify and break up, in the communicating and discoursing with another; he tosseth his thoughts more easily; he marshalleth them more orderly; he seeth how they look when they are turned into words; finally, he waxeth wiser than himself; and that more by an hour's discourse than by a day's meditation. It was well said by Themistocles to the king of Persia, "That speech was like cloth of Arras, opened and put abroad; whereby the imagery doth appear in figure; whereas in thoughts they lie but as in packs." Neither is the second fruit of friendship, in opening the understanding, restrained only to such friends as are able to give a man counsel (they indeed are best), but even without that, a man learneth of himself, and bringeth his own thoughts to light, and whetteth his wits as against a stone, which itself cuts not. In a word, a man were better relate himself to a statua or picture, than to suffer his thoughts to pass in smother.

8 Add now, to make this second fruit of friendship complete, that other point which lieth more open and falleth within vulgar observation; which is faithful counsel from a friend. Heraclitus saith well in one of his enigmas, "dry light is ever the best." And certain it is, that the light that a man receiveth by counsel from another, is drier and purer than that which cometh from his own understanding and judgment; which is ever infused and drenched in his affections and customs. So as there is as much difference between the counsel that a friend giveth, and that a man giveth himself, as there is between the counsel of a friend and of a flatterer. For there is no such flatterer as is a man's self; and there is no such remedy against flattery of a man's self, as the liberty of a friend. Counsel is of two sorts: the one concerning manner, the other concerning business. For the first, the best preservative to keep the mind in health is the faithful admonition of a friend. The calling of a man's self to a strict account is a medicine, sometime, too piercing and corrosive. Reading good books of morality is a little flat and dead. Observing our faults in others is sometimes improper for our case. But the best receipt (best, I say, to work, and best to take) is the admonition of a friend. It is a strange thing to behold what gross errors and extreme absurdities many (especially of the greater sort) do commit, for want of a friend to tell them of them; to the great damage both of their fame and fortune: for, as St. James saith, they are as men "that look sometimes into a glass, and presently forget their own shape and favor." As for business, a man may think, if he will, that two eyes see no more than one; or that a gamester seeth always more than a looker-on; or that a man in anger is as wise as he that hath said over the four and twenty letters; or that a musket may be shot off as well upon the arm as upon a rest; and such

other fond and high imaginations, to think himself all in all. But when all is done, the help of good counsel is that which setteth business straight. And if any man think that he will take counsel, but it shall be by pieces; asking counsel in one business of one man, and in another business of another man; it is well, (that is to say, better perhaps than if he asked none at all;) but he runneth two dangers: one, that he shall not be faithfully counselled; for it is a rare thing, except it be from a perfect and entire friend, to have counsel given, but such as shall be bowed and crooked to some ends which he hath that giveth it. The other, that he shall have counsel given, hurtful and unsafe, (though with good meaning) and mixed partly of mischief and partly of remedy; even as if you would call a physician that is thought good for the cure of the disease you complain of, but is unacquainted with your body; and therefore may put you in way for a present cure, but overthroweth your health in some other kind; and so cure the disease and kill the patient. But a friend that is wholly acquainted with a man's estate will beware, by furthering any present business, how he dasheth upon other inconvenience. And therefore rest not upon scattered counsels; they will rather distract and mislead, than settle and direct.

9 After these two noble fruits of friendship, (peace in the affections, and support of the judgment,) followeth the last fruit; which is like the pomegranate, full of many kernels; I mean aid and bearing a part in all actions and occasions. Here the best way to represent to life the manifold use of friendship, is to cast and see how many things there are which a man cannot do himself; and then it will appear that it was a sparing speech of the ancients, to say, "that a friend is another himself"; for that a friend is far more than himself. Men have their time, and die many times in desire of some things which they principally take to heart; the bestowing of a child, the finishing of a work, or the like. If a man have a true friend, he may rest almost secure that the care of those things will continue after him. So that a man hath, as it were, two lives in his desires. A man hath a body, and that body is confined to a place; but where friendship is, all offices of life are as it were granted to him and his deputy. For he may exercise them by his friend. How many things are there which a man cannot, with any face or comeliness, say or do himself? A man can scarce allege his own merits with modesty, much less extol them; a man cannot sometimes brook to supplicate or beg; and a number of the like. But all these things are graceful in a friend's mouth, which are blushing in a man's own. So again, a man's person hath many proper relations which he cannot put off. A man cannot speak to his son but as a father; to his wife but as a husband; to his enemy but upon terms; whereas a friend may speak as the case requires, and not as it sorteth with the person. But to enumerate these things were endless; I have given the rule, where a man cannot fitly play his own part; if he have not a friend, he may quit the stage.

STUDY GUIDE

1. In these selections by Francis Bacon the essay form can be seen evolving from a collection of aphoristic statements on a topic into a more logically and rhetorically developed whole. Study carefully the nature of the additions made in the 1625 version of the essay "Of Studies." Why do they suggest a more popular audience?

2. The essay "Of Friendship" falls into logical divisions—paragraphs 1 and 2 and 3–9. What topic is Bacon concerned with in each of these divisions?

3. What methods of rhetorical development does he employ in each of these parts?

4. In contrast to the early essay "Of Studies," Bacon's later essay "Of Friendship" has connectives to guide readers from one part to the next. What are they?

Joseph Addison (1672–1719)

Bacon introduced the essay into English literature, but Joseph Addison and Richard Steele, in the *Tatler* and *Spectator* papers, gave the informal essay the characteristics it has retained from their day to our own. In structure their essays are loose and meandering, and in tone, personal, whimsical, urbane, and sometimes lightly satirical. Addison's own essays fall into two main groups: One of them is a fairly serious treatment of broad subjects like marriage, death, education, and politics; and the other, a lightly satirical treatment of the foibles and follies of mankind. "Westminster Abbey" is an example of Addison's treatment of a serious subject, and "On Pedants" is an example of his lighter style.

ON PEDANTS

Joseph Addison

1 My friend Will Honeycomb values himself very much upon what he calls the knowledge of mankind, which has cost him many disasters in his youth; for Will reckons every misfortune that he has met with among the

Reprinted from *The Spectator*, No. 105.

women, and every rencounter among the men, as parts of his education; and fancies he should never have been the man he is, had he not broke windows, knocked down constables, disturbed honest people with his midnight serenades, and beat up a lewd woman's quarters, when he was a young fellow. The engaging in adventures of this nature Will calls the studying of mankind; and terms this knowledge of the town, the knowledge of the world. Will ingeniously confesses, that for half his life his head ached every morning with reading of men over-night; and at present comforts himself under certain pains which he endures from time to time, that without them he could not have been acquainted with the gallantries of the age. This Will looks upon as the learning of a gentleman, and regards all other kind of science as the accomplishments of one whom he calls a scholar, a bookish man, or a philosopher.

2 For these reasons Will shines in mixed company, where he has the discretion not to go out of his depth, and has often a certain way of making his real ignorance appear a seeming one. Our club however has frequently caught him tripping, at which times they never spare him. For as Will often insults us with the knowledge of the town, we sometimes take our revenge upon him by our knowledge of books.

3 He was last week producing two or three letters which he writ in his youth to a coquette lady. The raillery of them was natural, and well enough for a mere man of the town; but very unluckily, several of the words were wrong spelt. Will laughed this off at first as well as he could; but finding himself pushed on all sides, and especially by the Templar, he told us with a little passion, that he never liked pedantry in spelling, and that he spelt like a gentleman and not like a scholar. Upon this Will had recourse to his old topic of showing the narrow-spiritedness, the pride, and ignorance of pedants; which he carried so far, that, upon my retiring to my lodgings, I could not forbear throwing together such reflections as occurred to me upon that subject.

4 A man who has been brought up among books, and is able to talk of nothing else, is a very indifferent companion, and what we call a pedant. But methinks, we should enlarge the title, and give it every one that does not know how to think out of his profession and particular way of life.

5 What is a greater pedant than a mere man of the town? Bar him the play-houses, a catalogue of the reigning beauties, and an account of a few fashionable distempers that have befallen him, and you strike him dumb. How many a pretty gentleman's knowledge lies all within the verge of the court? He will tell you the names of the principal favourites, repeat the shrewd sayings of a man of quality, whisper an intrigue that is not yet blown upon by common fame; or, if the sphere of his observations is a little

larger than ordinary, will perhaps enter into all the incidents, turns, and revolutions in a game of *ombre*. When he has gone thus far, he has shown you the whole circle of his accomplishments, his parts are drained, and he is disabled from any farther conversation. What are these but rank pedants? and yet these are the men who value themselves most on their exemption from the pedantry of colleges.

6 I might here mention the military pedant who always talks in a camp, and in storming towns, making lodgments and fighting battles from one end of the year to the other. Every thing he speaks smells of gunpowder; if you take away his artillery from him, he has not a word to say for himself. I might likewise mention the law pedant, that is perpetually putting cases, repeating the transactions of Westminster-hall, wrangling with you upon the most indifferent circumstances of life, and not to be convinced of the distance of a place, or of the most trivial point in conversation, but by dint of argument. The state pedant is wrapt up in news, and lost in politics. If you mention either of the kings of Spain or Poland, he talks very notably; but if you go out of the Gazette, you drop him. In short, a mere courtier, a mere soldier, a mere scholar, a mere any thing, is an insipid pedantic character, and equally ridiculous.

7 Of all the species of pedants, which I have mentioned, the book pedant is much the most supportable; he has at least an exercised understanding, and a head which is full though confused, so that a man who converses with him may often receive from him hints of things that are worth knowing, and what he may possibly turn to his own advantage, though they are of little use to the owner. The worst kind of pedants among learned men are such as are naturally endued with a very small share of common sense, and have read a great number of books without taste or distinction.

8 The truth of it is, learning, like travelling, and all other methods of improvement, as it finishes good sense, so it makes a silly man ten thousand times more insufferable, by supplying variety of matter to his impertinence, and giving him an opportunity of abounding in absurdities.

9 Shallow pedants cry up one another much more than men of solid and useful learning. To read the titles they give an editor, or collator of a manuscript, you would take him for the glory of the commonwealth of letters, and the wonder of his age, when perhaps upon examination you find that he has only rectified a Greek particle, or laid out a whole sentence in proper commas.

10 They are obliged indeed to be thus lavish of their praises, that they may keep one another in countenance; and it is no wonder if a great deal of knowledge, which is not capable of making a man wise, has a natural tendency to make him vain and arrogant.

STUDY GUIDE

1. Joseph Addison says in paragraph 3 that he *threw together* these thoughts on the pedant after an experience with Will Honeycomb at the Club. This somewhat describes the casual order or structure of an informal essay. Show how this essay wanders from one topic to another in the order that the ideas seem to be suggested to the writer.
2. What is the dictionary definition of a pedant? Where does Addison take account of the ordinary meaning of the term in the essay?
3. Addison, however, defines a pedant in such a way as to include Will Honeycomb in the term. What is this definition?
4. What is Addison's attitude toward Will? Laudatory? Ironical? Satirical? Critical? Give evidence for your answer from the diction of the text.

WESTMINSTER ABBEY

Joseph Addison

1 When I am in a serious humor, I very often walk by myself in Westminster Abbey; where the gloominess of the place, and the use to which it is applied, with the solemnity of the building, and the condition of the people who lie in it, are apt to fill the mind with a kind of melancholy, or rather thoughtfulness, that is not disagreeable. I yesterday passed a whole afternoon in the churchyard, the cloisters, and the church, amusing myself with the tombstones and inscriptions that I met with in those several regions of the dead. Most of them recorded nothing else of the buried person, but that he was born upon one day and died upon another: the whole history of his life being comprehended in those two circumstances, that are common to all mankind. I could not but look upon these registers of existence, whether of brass or marble, as a kind of satire upon the departed persons; who had left no other memorial of them, but that they were born and that they died. They put me in mind of several persons mentioned in the battles of heroic poems, who have sounding names given them, for no other reason but that they may be killed, and are celebrated for nothing but being knocked on the head.

> Γλαῦκόν τε Μέδοντά τε θερσίλοχόν τε—HOMER
>
> Glaucumque, Medontaque, Thersilochumque—VIRGIL [1]

Reprinted from *The Spectator*, No. 26.

[1] Glaucus, Medon, and Thersilochus are names of Greek heroes slain in the Trojan War.—*Ed.*

2 The life of these men is finely described in Holy Writ by "the path of an arrow," which is immediately closed up and lost.

3 Upon my going into the church, I entertained myself with the digging of a grave; and saw in every shovelful of it that was thrown up, the fragment of a bone or skull intermixed with a kind of fresh moldering earth that some time or other had a place in the composition of a human body. Upon this I began to consider with myself what innumerable multitudes of people lay confused together under the pavement of that ancient cathedral; how men and women, friends and enemies, priests and soldiers, monks and prebendaries, were crumbled amongst one another and blended together in the same common mass; how beauty, strength, and youth, with old age, weakness, and deformity, lay undistinguished in the same promiscuous heap of matter.

4 After having thus surveyed this great magazine of mortality, as it were, in the lump, I examined it more particularly by the accounts which I found on several of the monuments which are raised in every quarter of that ancient fabric. Some of them were covered with such extravagant epitaphs that, if it were possible for the dead person to be acquainted with them, he would blush at the praises which his friends have bestowed upon him. There are others so excessively modest that they deliver the character of the person departed in Greek or Hebrew, and by that means are not understood once in a twelve-month. In the poetical quarter, I found there were poets who had no monuments, and monuments which had no poets. I observed, indeed, that the present war had filled the church with many of these uninhabited monuments, which had been erected to the memory of persons whose bodies were perhaps buried in the plains of Blenheim, or in the bosom of the ocean.

5 I could not but be very much delighted with several modern epitaphs, which are written with great elegance of expression and justness of thought, and therefore do honor to the living as well as to the dead. As a foreigner is very apt to conceive an idea of the ignorance or politeness of a nation from the turn of their public monuments and inscriptions, they should be submitted to the perusal of men of learning and genius before they are put in execution. Sir Cloudesly Shovel's monument has very often given me great offense: instead of the brave rough English Admiral, which was the distinguishing character of that plain gallant man, he is represented on his tomb by the figure of a beau, dressed in a long periwig, and reposing himself upon velvet cushions under a canopy of state. The inscription is answerable to the monument; for instead of celebrating the many remarkable actions he had performed in the service of his country, it acquaints us only with the manner of his death, in which it was impossible for him to reap any honor. The Dutch, whom we are apt to despise for want of genius, show an infinitely greater taste of antiquity and politeness in their buildings and works of this nature than what we meet with in those of our own

country. The monuments of their admirals, which have been erected at the public expense, represent them like themselves; and are adorned with rostral crowns and naval ornaments, with beautiful festoons of sea-weed, shells, and coral.

6 But to return to our subject. I have left the repository of our English kings for the contemplation of another day, when I shall find my mind disposed for so serious an amusement. I know that entertainments of this nature are apt to raise dark and dismal thoughts in timorous minds and gloomy imaginations; but for my own part, though I am always serious, I do not know what it is to be melancholy; and can therefore take a view of nature in her deep and solemn scenes, with the same pleasure as in her most gay and delightful ones. By this means I can improve myself with those objects which others consider with terror. When I look upon the tombs of the great, every emotion of envy dies in me; when I read the epitaphs of the beautiful, every inordinate desire goes out; when I meet with the grief of parents upon a tombstone, my heart melts with compassion; when I see the tomb of the parents themselves, I consider the vanity of grieving for those whom we must quickly follow: when I see kings lying by those who deposed them, when I consider rival wits placed side by side, or the holy men that divided the world with their contests and disputes, I reflect with sorrow and astonishment on the little competitions, factions, and debates of mankind. When I read the several dates of the tombs, of some that died yesterday, and some six hundred years ago, I consider that great day when we shall all of us be contemporaries, and make our appearance together.

STUDY GUIDE

1. This piece is an example of the more serious and meditative type of Addisonian essay. But it is almost as loosely organized as the essay "On Pedants." What is the central idea that gives some kind of unity to the meandering details?
2. Show how the last two sentences function somewhat as a summary that pulls together the loosely organized details of the essay.
3. Write a similar personal essay of your own occasioned by the visit to a cemetery or an historical museum.

Jonathan Swift (1667–1745)

Swift was in every possible way a sharp contrast to Addison. Where Addison was only lightly satirical, Swift was generally very sharply so; and where Addison was loose and meandering in structure, Swift was most often tightly organized and highly structured. In fact, the structure of many of Swift's writings was based on the highly developed rhetorical pattern of the classical oration. It is the assimilation of that pattern into his works that helped develop a sense of logical structure in the formal essay in English and in serious expository and argumentative writing in general. The evidence of that influence is perhaps most clearly discerned in the structure of his essay "A Modest Proposal." Part of the irony of this highly ironic work resides in the fact that the monstrous proposal Swift is making is presented within the logical framework of a classical oration. He is implying that what he is proposing is no more monstrous than what the English are actually doing to the Irish and defending with all sorts of specious argumentation.

A MODEST PROPOSAL

For preventing the children of poor people in Ireland from being a burden to their parents or country, and for making them beneficial to the public

Jonathan Swift

1 It is a melancholy object to those who walk through this great town or travel in the country, when they see the streets, the roads, and cabin doors, crowded with beggars of the female sex, followed by three, four, or six children, all in rags and importuning every passenger for an alms. These mothers, instead of being able to work for their honest livelihood, are forced to employ all their time in strolling to beg sustenance for their helpless infants: who as they grow up either turn thieves for want of work, or leave their dear native country to fight for the pretender in Spain, or sell themselves to the Barbadoes.

2 I think it is agreed by all parties that this prodigious number of children in the arms, or on the backs, or at the heels of their mothers, and frequently of their fathers, is in the present deplorable state of the kingdom a very great additional grievance; and, therefore, whoever could find out a fair, cheap, and easy method of making these children sound, useful members of the commonwealth, would deserve so well of the public as to have his statue set up for a preserver of the nation.

3 But my intention is very far from being confined to provide only for

Reprinted from a pamphlet first published in 1729.

the children of professed beggars; it is of a much greater extent, and shall take in the whole number of infants at a certain age who are born of parents in effect as little able to support them as those who demand our charity in the streets.

4 As to my own part, having turned my thoughts for many years upon this important subject, and maturely weighed the several schemes of our projectors, I have always found them grossly mistaken in their computation. It is true, a child just dropped from its dam may be supported by her milk for a solar year, with little other nourishment; at most not above the value of 2s., which the mother may certainly get, or the value in scraps, by her lawful occupation of begging; and it is exactly at one year old that I propose to provide for them in such a manner as instead of being a charge upon their parents or the parish, or wanting food and raiment for the rest of their lives, they shall on the contrary contribute to the feeding, and partly to the clothing, of many thousands.

5 There is likewise another great advantage in my scheme, that it will prevent those voluntary abortions, and that horrid practice of women murdering their bastard children, alas! too frequent among us! sacrificing the poor innocent babes I doubt more to avoid the expense than the shame, which would move tears and pity in the most savage and inhuman breast.

6 The number of souls in this kingdom being usually reckoned one million and a half, of these I calculate there may be about 200,000 couple whose wives are breeders; from which number I subtract 30,000 couple who are able to maintain their own children (although I apprehend there cannot be so many, under the present distresses of the kingdom); but this being granted, there will remain 170,000 breeders. I again subtract 50,000 for those women who miscarry, or whose children die by accident or disease within the year. There only remains 120,000 children of poor parents annually born. The question therefore is, how this number shall be reared and provided for? which, as I have already said, under the present situation of affairs, is utterly impossible by all the methods hitherto proposed. For we can neither employ them in handicraft or agriculture; we neither build houses (I mean in the country) nor cultivate land; they can very seldom pick up a livelihood by stealing, till they arrive at six years old, except where they are of towardly parts; although I confess they learn the rudiments much earlier; during which time, they can however be properly looked upon only as probationers; as I have been informed by a principal gentleman in the country of Cavan, who protested to me that he never knew above one or two instances under the age of six, even in a part of the kingdom so renowned for the quickest proficiency in that art.

7 I am assured by our merchants, that a boy or a girl before twelve years old is no saleable commodity; and even when they come to this age

they will not yield above 3*l.* or 3*l.* 2*s.* 6*d.* at most on the exchange; which cannot turn to account either to the parents or kingdom, the charge of nutriment and rags having been at least four times that value.

8 I shall now therefore humbly propose my own thoughts, which I hope will not be liable to the least objection.

9 I have been assured by a very knowing American of my acquaintance in London, that a young healthy child well nursed is at a year old a most delicious, nourishing, and wholesome food, whether stewed, roasted, baked, or boiled; and I make no doubt that it will equally serve in a fricassee or a ragout.

10 I do therefore humbly offer it to public consideration that of the 120,000 children already computed, 20,000 may be reserved for breed, whereof only one-fourth part to be males; which is more than we allow to sheep, black cattle, or swine; and my reason is, that these children are seldom the fruits of marriage, a circumstance not much regarded by our savages, therefore one male will be sufficient to serve four females. That the remaining 100,000 may, at a year old, be offered in sale to the persons of quality and fortune through the kingdom; always advising the mother to let them suck plentifully in the last month, so as to render them plump and fat for a good table. A child will make two dishes at an entertainment for friends; and when the family dines alone, the fore or hind quarter will make a reasonable dish, and seasoned with a little pepper or salt will be very good boiled on the fourth day, especially in winter.

11 I have reckoned upon a medium that a child just born will weigh 12 pounds, and in a solar year, if tolerably nursed, will increase to 28 pounds.

12 I grant this food will be somewhat dear, and therefore very proper for landlords, who, as they have already devoured most of the parents, seem to have the best title to the children.

13 Infant's flesh will be in season throughout the year, but more plentifully in March, and a little before and after: for we are told by a grave author, an eminent French physician, that fish being a prolific diet, there are more children born in Roman Catholic countries about nine months after Lent, the markets will be more glutted than usual, because the number of popish infants is at least three to one in this kingdom: and therefore it will have the other collateral advantage, by lessening the number of papists among us.

14 I have already computed the charge of nursing a beggar's child (in which list I reckon all cottagers, laborers, and four-fifths of the farmers) to be about 2*s.* per annum, rags included; and I believe no gentleman would repine to give 10*s.* for the carcass of a good fat child, which, as I have said, will make four dishes of excellent nutritive meat, when he has only some particular friend or his own family to dine with him. Thus the squire will learn to be a good landlord, and grow popular among the tenants; the

mother will have 8s. net profit, and be fit for work till she produces another child.

15 Those who are more thrifty (as I must confess the times require) may flay the carcass; the skin of which artificially dressed will make admirable gloves for ladies, and summer boots for fine gentlemen.

16 As to our city of Dublin, shambles may be appointed for this purpose in the most convenient parts of it, and butchers we may be assured will not be wanting; although I rather recommend buying the children alive, and dressing them hot from the knife as we do roasting pigs.

17 A very worthy person, a true lover of his country, and whose virtues I highly esteem, was lately pleased in discoursing on this matter to offer a refinement upon my scheme. He said that many gentlemen of this kingdom, having of late destroyed their deer, he conceived that the want of venison might be well supplied by the bodies of young lads and maidens, not exceeding fourteen years of age nor under twelve; so great a number of both sexes in every country being now ready to starve for want of work and service; and these to be disposed of by their parents, if alive, or otherwise by their nearest relations. But with due deference to so excellent a friend and so deserving a patriot, I cannot be altogether in his sentiments; for as to the males, my American acquaintance assured me, from frequent experience that their flesh was generally tough and lean, like that of our schoolboys by continual exercise, and their taste disagreeable; and to fatten them would not answer the charge. Then as to the females, it would, I think, with humble submission be a loss to the public, because they soon would become breeders themselves: and besides, it is not improbable that some scrupulous people might be apt to censure such a practice (although indeed very unjustly), as a little bordering upon cruelty; which, I confess, has always been with me the strongest objection against any project, how well soever intended.

18 But in order to justify my friend, he confessed that this expedient was put into his head by the famous Psalmanazar, a native of the island Formosa, who came from thence to London about twenty years ago: and in conversation told my friend, that in his country when any young person happened to be put to death, the executioner sold the carcass to persons of quality as a prime dainty; and that in his time the body of a plump girl of fifteen, who was crucified for an attempt to poison the emperor, was sold to his imperial majesty's prime minister of state, and other great mandarins of the court, in joints from the gibbet, at 400 crowns. Neither indeed can I deny, that if the same use were made of several plump young girls in this town, who without one single groat to their fortunes cannot stir abroad without a chair, and appear at playhouse and assemblies in foreign fineries which they never will pay for, the kingdom would not be worse.

19 Some persons of a desponding spirit are in great concern about the

vast number of poor people, who are aged, diseased, or maimed, and I have been desired to employ my thoughts what course may be taken to ease the nation of so grievous an encumbrance. But I am not in the least pain upon that matter, because it is very well known that they are every day dying and rotting by cold and famine, and filth and vermin, as fast as can be reasonably expected. And as to the young laborers, they are now in as hopeful a condition; they cannot get work, and consequently pine away for want of nourishment, to a degree that if at any time they are accidentally hired to common labor, they have not strength to perform it; and thus the country and themselves are happily delivered from the evils to come.

20 I have too long digressed, and therefore shall return to my subject. I think the advantages by the proposal which I have made are obvious and many, as well as of the highest importance.

21 For the first, as I have already observed, it would greatly lessen the number of papists, with whom we are yearly overrun, being the principal breeders of the nation as well as our most dangerous enemies; and who stay at home on purpose to deliver the kingdom to the Pretender, hoping to take their advantage by the absence of so many good protestants, who have chosen rather to leave their country than stay at home and pay tithes against their conscience to an episcopal curate.

22 Secondly, The poor tenants will have something valuable of their own, which by law may be made liable to distress and help to pay their landlord's rent, their corn and cattle being already seized, and money a thing unknown.

23 Thirdly, Whereas the maintenance of 100,000 children, from two years old and upward, cannot be computed at less than 10*s.* a-piece per annum, the nation's stock will be thereby increased £50,000 per annum, beside the profit of a new dish introduced to the tables of all gentlemen of fortune in the kingdom who have any refinement in taste. And the money will circulate among ourselves, the goods being entirely of our own growth and manufacture.

24 Fourthly, The constant breeders, beside the gain of 8*s.* sterling per annum by the sale of their children, will be rid of the charge of maintaining them after the first year.

25 Fifthly, This food would likewise bring great custom to taverns; where the vintners will certainly be so prudent as to procure the best receipts for dressing it to perfection, and consequently have their houses frequented by all the fine gentlemen, who justly value themselves upon their knowledge in good eating: and a skilful cook, who understands how to oblige his guests, will contrive to make it as expensive as they please.

26 Sixthly, This would be a great inducement to marriage, which all wise nations have either encouraged by rewards or enforced by laws and penalties. It would increase the care and tendencies of mothers toward

their children, when they were sure of a settlement for life to the poor babes, provided in some sort by the public, to their annual profit instead of expense. We should see an honest emulation among the married women, which of them could bring the fattest child to the market. Men would become as fond of their wives during the time of their pregnancy as they are now of their mares in foal, their cows in calf, their sows when they are ready to farrow; nor offer to beat or kick them (as is too frequent a practice) for fear of a miscarriage.

27 Many other advantages might be enumerated. For instance, the addition of some thousand carcasses in our exportation of barreled beef, the propagation of swine's flesh, and improvement in the art of making good bacon, so much wanted among us by the great destruction of pigs, too frequent at our table: which are no way comparable in taste or magnificence to a well-grown, fat, yearling child, which roasted whole will make a considerable figure at a lord mayor's feast or any other public entertainment. But this and many others I omit, being studious of brevity.

28 Supposing that 1000 families in this city would be constant customers for infants' flesh, beside others who might have it at merry-meetings, particularly at weddings and christenings, I compute that Dublin would take off annually about 20,000 carcasses; and the rest of the kingdom (where probably they will be sold somewhat cheaper) the remaining 80,000.

29 I can think of no one objection that will possibly be raised against this proposal, unless it should be urged that the number of people will be thereby much lessened in the kingdom. This I freely own, and it was indeed one principal design in offering it to the world. I desire the reader will observe, that I calculate my remedy for this one individual kingdom of Ireland and for no other that ever was, is, or I think ever can be upon earth. Therefore let no man talk to me of other expedients: of taxing our absentees at 5*s.* a pound: of using neither clothes nor household furniture except what is of our own growth and manufacture: of utterly rejecting the materials and instruments that promote foreign luxury: of curing the expensiveness of pride, vanity, idleness, and gaming in our women: of introducing a vein of parsimony, prudence, and temperance: of learning to love our country, in the want of which we differ even from LAPLANDERS and the inhabitants of TOPINAMBOO: of quitting our animosities and factions, nor acting any longer like the Jews, who were murdering one another at the very moment their city was taken: of being a little cautious not to sell our country and conscience for nothing: of teaching landlords to have at least one degree of mercy toward their tenants: lastly, of putting a spirit of honesty, industry, and skill into our shopkeepers; who, if a resolution could now be taken to buy only our native goods, would immediately unite to cheat and exact upon us in the price, the measure, and the good-

ness, nor could ever yet be brought to make one fair proposal of just dealing, though often and earnestly invited to it.

30 Therefore I repeat, let no man talk to me of these and the like expedients, till he has at least some glimpses of hope that there will be ever some hearty and sincere attempt to put them in practice.

31 But as to myself, having been wearied out for many years with offering vain, idle, visionary thoughts, and at length utterly despairing of success, I fortunately fell upon this proposal; which, as it is wholly new, so it has something solid and real, of no expense and little trouble, full in our own power, and whereby we can incur no danger in disobliging ENGLAND. For this kind of commodity will not bear exportation, the flesh being of too tender a consistence to admit a long continuance in salt, although perhaps I could name a country which would be glad to eat up our whole nation without it.

32 After all, I am not so violently bent upon my own opinion as to reject any offer proposed by wise men, which shall be found equally innocent, cheap, easy, and effectual. But before something of that kind shall be advanced in contradiction to my scheme, and offering a better, I desire the author or authors will be pleased maturely to consider two points. First, as things now stand, how they will be able to find food and raiment for 100,000 useless mouths and backs. And secondly, there being a round million of creatures in human figure throughout this kingdom, whose whole subsistence put into a common stock would leave them in debt 2,000,000*l.* sterling, adding those who are beggars by profession to the bulk of farmers, cottagers and laborers, with the wives and children who are beggars in effect; I desire those politicians who dislike my overture, and may perhaps be so bold as to attempt an answer, that they will first ask the parents of these mortals, whether they would not at this day think it a great happiness to have been sold for food at a year old in the manner I prescribe, and thereby have avoided such a perpetual scene of misfortunes as they have since gone through by the oppression of landlords, the impossibility of paying rent without money or trade, the want of common sustenance, with neither house nor clothes to cover them from the inclemencies of the weather, and the most inevitable prospect of entailing the like or greater miseries upon their breed for ever.

33 I profess, in the sincerity of my heart, that I have not the least personal interest in endeavoring to promote this necessary work, having no other motive than the public good of my country, but advancing our trade, providing for infants, relieving the poor, and giving some pleasure to the rich. I have no children by which I can propose to get a single penny; the youngest being nine years old, and my wife past child-bearing.

STUDY GUIDE

1. The parts of a classical oration are very consciously employed by Swift in "A Modest Proposal": the *exordium*, or introduction, which states the subject and builds the good character of the speaker (paragraphs 1–7); the *narration*, which makes a preliminary statement of the proposal and prepares for the proof (paragraphs 8–16); a *digression*, which frequently deals with material parallel to the main topic (paragraphs 17–19); the formal proof (paragraphs 20–28); the *refutation*, which answers the objections (paragraphs 29 and 30); and the *peroration* (paragraphs 31–33), which sums up the main points of the whole and further bolsters up the good intentions of the speaker. Draw up an outline in which you indicate how "A Modest Proposal" fulfills these functions of each of these parts of a classical oration.

2. This essay is a supreme example of irony. Part of the ironic effect is achieved by using the rhetorical figure of *diminution*, in which by a shift of diction the subject being discussed is gradually reduced in importance. Here the Irish peasants are reduced from human beings, to animals, to food. Indicate several places in the essay where this occurs.

3. Part of the ironic effect is also achieved by the pretence that the "modest" proposal (actually a monstrous one) is bolstered up by all sorts of statistical evidence. Point out instances of this in the essay.

4. Although the essay is really intense in its feeling, there is an attempt to keep its expression relatively unemotional. As a result, there are few emotionally connotative sentences (questions, exclamations, imperatives). What form of sentence predominates in the essay? How does this contribute to the apparently scientific tone of the piece?

Charles Lamb (1775–1834)

Of all the writers of the informal essay in the English language, Charles Lamb perhaps best realized its potentialities. His interest in the fanciful and the whimsical made the loose structure of the informal essay a natural medium for him. He led a rather uneventful life as an accountant for the East India Company. But perhaps it was this very existence somewhat off center from the main literary events of his age that gave him the fresh, personal, and semihumorous approach to everything he touches in his essays. He is not concerned with world-shaking events, but ordinary things like a card game, old china, poor relations, and chimney sweeps take on great significance when they are seen through Lamb's eyes. Sometimes he can strike a wistful note that becomes very personal, as in his "Dream Children." This essay takes on added significance if the reader knows that he never had any children of his own because he had sacrificed the happiness of marriage to take care of his sister. One of his best known and perennially charming essays is "A Dissertation upon Roast Pig," in which his characteristic imagination and whimsy show at their best.

A DISSERTATION UPON ROAST PIG

Charles Lamb

1 Mankind, says a Chinese manuscript, which my friend M. was obliging enough to read and explain to me, for the first seventy thousand ages ate their meat raw, clawing or biting it from the living animal, just as they do in Abyssinia to this day. This period is not obscurely hinted at by their great Confucius in the second chapter of his *Mundane Mutations*, where he designates a kind of golden age by the term Cho-fang, literally the Cooks' Holiday. The manuscript goes on to say, that the art of roasting, or rather broiling (which I take to be the elder brother) was accidentally discovered in the manner following. The swineherd, Ho-ti, having gone out into the woods one morning, as his manner was, to collect mast for his hogs, left his cottage in the care of his eldest son Bo-bo, a great lubberly boy, who being fond of playing with fire, as younkers of his age commonly are, let some sparks escape into a bundle of straw, which kindling quickly, spread the conflagration over every part of their poor mansion till it was reduced to ashes. Together with the cottage (a sorry antediluvian makeshift of a building, you may think it), what was of much more importance, a fine litter of new-farrowed pigs, no less than nine in number, perished. China pigs have been esteemed a luxury all over the East from the remotest periods that we read of. Bo-bo was in the utmost consternation, as you may think, not so much for the sake of the tenement, which his father and he could easily build up again with a few dry branches, and the labor of an hour or two, at any time, as for the loss of the pigs. While he was thinking what he should say to his father, and wringing his hands over the smoking remnants of one of those untimely sufferers, an odor assailed his nostrils, unlike any scent which he had before experienced. What could it proceed from?—not from the burnt cottage—he had smelt that smell before—indeed this was by no means the first accident of the kind which had occurred through the negligence of this unlucky young fire-brand. Much less did it resemble that of any known herb, weed or flower. A premonitory moisten-

Reprinted from Charles Lamb, *The Essays of Elia* (1823).

ing at the same time overflowed his nether lip. He knew not what to think. He next stooped down to feel the pig, if there were any signs of life in it. He burnt his fingers, and to cool them he applied them in his booby fashion to his mouth. Some of the crumbs of the scorched skin had come away with his fingers, and for the first time in his life (in the world's life, indeed, for before him no man had known it) he tasted—*crackling.* Again he felt and fumbled at the pig. It did not burn him so much now, still he licked his fingers from a sort of habit. The truth at length broke into his slow understanding, that it was the pig that smelt so, and the pig that tasted so delicious; and, surrendering himself up to the new-born pleasure, he fell to tearing up whole handfuls of the scorched skin with the flesh next it, and was cramming it down his throat in his beastly fashion, when his sire entered amid the smoking rafters, armed with retributory cudgel, and finding how affairs stood, began to rain blows upon the young rogue's shoulders, as thick as hail-stones, which Bo-bo heeded not any more than if they had been flies. The tickling pleasure, which he experienced in his lower regions, had rendered him quite callous to any inconveniences he might feel in those remote quarters. His father might lay on, but he could not beat him from his pig, till he had fairly made an end of it, when, becoming a little more sensible of his situation, something like the following dialogue ensued.

2 "You graceless whelp, what have you got there devouring? Is it not enough that you have burnt me down three houses with your dog's tricks, and be hanged to you, but you must be eating fire, and I know not what—what have you got there, I say?"

3 "O father, the pig, the pig, do come and taste how nice the burnt pig eats."

4 The ears of Ho-ti tingled with horror. He cursed his son, and he cursed himself that ever he should beget a son that should eat burnt pig.

5 Bo-bo, whose scent was wonderfully sharpened since morning, soon raked out another pig, and fairly rending it asunder, thrust the lesser half by main force into the fists of Ho-ti, still shouting out "Eat, eat, eat the burnt pig, father, only taste—O Lord,"—with such-like barbarous ejaculations, cramming all the while as if he would choke.

6 Hoti trembled in every joint while he grasped the abominable thing, wavering whether he should not put his son to death for an unnatural young monster, when the crackling scorching his fingers, as it had done his son's, and applying the same remedy to them, he in his turn tasted some of its flavour, which, make what sour mouths he would for a pretence, proved not altogether displeasing to him. In conclusion (for the manuscript here is a little tedious) both father and son fairly sat down to the mess, and never left off till they had despatched all that remained of the litter.

7 Bo-bo was strictly enjoined not to let the secret escape, for the neighbors would certainly have stoned them for a couple of abominable wretches, who could think of improving upon the good meat which God had sent them. Nevertheless, strange stories got about. It was observed that Ho-ti's cottage was burnt down now more frequently than ever. Nothing but fires from this time forward. Some would break out in broad day, others in the night-time. As often as the sow farrowed, so sure was the house of Ho-ti to be in a blaze; and Ho-ti himself, which was the more remarkable, instead of chastising his son, seemed to grow more indulgent to him than ever. At length they were watched, the terrible mystery discovered, and father and son summoned to take their trial at Pekin, then an inconsiderable assize town. Evidence was given, the obnoxious food itself produced in court, and verdict about to be pronounced, when the foreman of the jury begged that some of the burnt pig, of which the culprits stood accused, might be handed into the box. He handled it, and they all handled it, and burning their fingers, as Bo-bo and his father had done before them, and nature prompting to each of them the same remedy, against the face of all the facts, and the clearest charge which judge had ever given—to the surprise of the whole court, townfolk, strangers, reporters, and all present—without leaving the box, or any manner of consultation whatever, they brought in a simultaneous verdict of Not Guilty.

8 The judge, who was a shrewd fellow, winked at the manifest iniquity of the decision: and, when the court was dismissed, went privily, and bought up all the pigs that could be had for love or money. In a few days his Lordship's town house was observed to be on fire. The thing took wing, and now there was nothing to be seen but fires in every direction. Fuel and pigs grew enormously dear all over the district. The insurance offices one and all shut up shop. People built slighter and slighter every day, until it was feared that the very science of architecture would in no long time be lost to the world. Thus this custom of firing houses continued, till in process of time, says my manuscript, a sage arose, like our Locke, who made a discovery, that the flesh of swine, or indeed of any other animal, might be cooked (*burnt*, as they called it) without the necessity of consuming a whole house to dress it. Then first began the rude form of a gridiron. Roasting by the string, or spit, came in a century or two later; I forget in whose dynasty. By such slow degrees, concludes the manuscript, do the most useful and seemingly the most obvious arts, make their way among mankind.

9 Without placing too implicit faith in the account above given, it must be agreed, that if a worthy pretext for so dangerous an experiment as setting houses on fire (especially in these days) could be assigned in favour of any culinary object, that pretext and excuse might be found in ROAST PIG.

10 Of all the delicacies in the whole *mundus edibilis,*[1] I will maintain it to be the most delicate—*princeps obsoniorum.*[2]

11 I speak not of your grown porkers—things between pig and pork—those hobbydehoys—but a young and tender suckling—under a moon old—guiltless as yet of the sty—with no original speck of the *amor immunditiae,*[3] the hereditary failing of the first parent, yet manifest—his voice as yet not broken, but something between a childish treble, and a grumble—the mild forerunner, or *praeludium,* of a grunt.

12 *He must be roasted.* I am not ignorant that our ancestors ate them seethed, or boiled—but what a sacrifice of the exterior tegument!

13 There is no flavour comparable, I will contend, to that of the crisp, tawny, well-watched, not over-roasted, *crackling,* as it is well called—the very teeth are invited to their share of the pleasure at this banquet in overcoming the coy, brittle resistance—with the adhesive oleaginous—O call it not fat—but an indefinable sweetness growing up to it—the tender blossoming of fat—fat cropped in the bud—taken in the shoot—in the first innocence—the cream and quintessence of the child-pig's yet pure food—the lean, no lean, but a kind of animal manna—or, rather, fat and lean (if it must be so) blended and running into each other, that both together make but one ambrosian result, or common substance.

14 Behold him, while he is doing—it seemeth rather a refreshing warmth, than a scorching heat, that he is so passive to. How equably he twirleth round the string!—Now he is just done. To see the extreme sensibility of that tender age, he hath wept out his pretty eyes—radiant jellies—shooting stars—

15 See him in the dish, his second cradle, how meek he lieth!—wouldst thou have had this innocent grow up to the grossness and indocility which too often accompany maturer swinehood? Ten to one he would have proved a glutton, a sloven, an obstinate, disagreeable animal—wallowing in all manner of filthy conversation—from these sins he is happily snatched away—

> Ere sin could blight, or sorrow fade,
> Death came with timely care—

his memory is odoriferous—no clown curseth, while his stomach half rejecteth, the rank bacon—no coal heaver bolteth him in reeking sausages—he hath a fair sepulchre in the grateful stomach of the judicious epicure—and for such a tomb might be content to die.

[1] A world of eatables.—*Ed.*
[2] Chief of delicacies.—*Ed.*
[3] Love of filth.—*Ed.*

16 He is the best of sapours. Pine-apple is great. She is indeed almost too transcendent—a delight, if not sinful, yet so like to sinning, that really a tender-conscienced person would do well to pause—too ravishing for mortal taste, she woundeth and excoriateth the lips that approach her—like lovers' kisses, she biteth—she is a pleasure bordering on pain from the fierceness and insanity of her relish—but she stoppeth at the palate—she meddleth not with the appetite—and the coarsest hunger might barter her consistently for a mutton chop.

17 Pig—let me speak his praise—is no less provocative of the appetite, than he is satisfactory to the criticalness of the censorious palate. The strong man may batten on him, and the weakling refuseth not his mild juices.

18 Unlike to mankind's mixed characters, a bundle of virtues and vices, inexplicably intertwisted, and not to be unravelled without hazard, he is good throughout. No part of him is better or worse than another. He helpeth, as far as his little means extend, all around. He is the least envious of banquets. He is all neighbours' fare.

19 I am one of those who freely and ungrudgingly impart a share of the good things of this life which fall to their lot (few as mine are in this kind), to a friend. I protest I take as great an interest in my friend's pleasures, his relishes, and proper satisfactions, as in mine own. "Presents," I often say, "endear Absents." Hares, pheasants, partridges, snipes, barn-door chicken (those "tame villatic fowl"), capons, plovers, brawn, barrels of oysters, I dispense as freely as I receive them. I love to taste them, as it were, upon the tongue of my friend. But a stop must be put somewhere. One would not, like Lear, "give everything." I make my stand upon pig. Methinks it is an ingratitude to the Giver of all good flavours, to extra-domiciliate, or send out of the house, slightingly, (under pretext of friendship, or I know not what) a blessing so particularly adapted, predestined, I may say, to my individual palate.—It argues an insensibility.

20 I remember a touch of conscience in this kind at school. My good old aunt, who never parted from me at the end of a holiday without stuffing a sweet-meat, or some nice thing, into my pocket, had dismissed me one evening with a smoking plum-cake, fresh from the oven. In my way to school (it was over London bridge) a grey headed old beggar saluted me (I have no doubt at this time of day that he was a counterfeit). I had no pence to console him with, and in the vanity of self-denial, and the very coxcombry of charity, school-boy-like, I made him a present of—the whole cake! I walked on a little, buoyed up, as one is on such occasions, with a sweet soothing of self-satisfaction; but before I had got to the end of the bridge, my better feelings returned, and I burst into tears, thinking how ungrateful I had been to my good aunt, to go and give her good gift away to a

stranger, that I had never seen before, and who might be a bad man for aught I knew: and then I thought of the pleasure my aunt would be taking in thinking that I—I myself, and not another—would eat her nice cake—and what should I say to her the next time I saw her—how naughty I was to part with her pretty present—and the odor of that spicy cake came back upon my recollection, and the pleasure and the curiosity I had taken in seeing her make it, and her joy when she sent it to the oven, and how disappointed she would feel that I had never had a bit of it in my mouth at last—and I blamed my impertinent spirit of alms-giving, and out-of-place hypocrisy of goodness, and above all I wished never to see the face again of that insidious, good-for-nothing, old grey impostor.

21 Our ancestors were nice in their method of sacrificing these tender victims. We read of pigs whipped to death with something of a shock, as we hear of any other obsolete custom. The age of discipline is gone by, or it would be curious to inquire (in a philosophical light merely) what effect this process might have towards intenerating and dulcifying a substance, naturally so mild and dulcet as the flesh of young pigs. It looks like refining a violet. Yet we should be cautious, while we condemn the inhumanity, how we censure the wisdom of the practice. It might impart a gusto—

22 I remember an hypothesis, argued upon by the young students, when I was at St. Omer's, and maintained with much learning and pleasantry on both sides, "whether, supposing that the flavour of a pig who obtained his death by whipping (*per flagellationem extremam* [4]) superadded a pleasure upon the palate of a man more intense than any possible suffering we can conceive in the animal, is man justified in using that method of putting the animal to death?" I forget the decision.

23 His sauce should be considered. Decidedly, a few bread crumbs, done up with his liver and brains, and a dash of mild sage. But, banish, dear Mrs. Cook, I beseech you, the whole onion tribe. Barbecue your whole hogs to your palate, steep them in shalots, stuff them out with plantations of the rank and guilty garlic; you cannot poison them, or make them stronger than they are—but consider, he is a weakling—a flower.

STUDY GUIDE

1. Part of the humor of this essay is created by the sustained incongruity of presenting this obviously absurd explanation of the origin of roast pig as if it were a factual report or dissertation. What device does Lamb use at the

[4] By excessive flogging.—*Ed.*

opening of the essay to create the impression that he is giving us a report of an actual historical event?

2. Although an informal essay seems to have no clearly discernible structure, it is not completely structureless. There are recognizable parts in this essay: paragraphs 1–6, 8 and 9, 10–18, 19 and 20, and 21–23. With what is Lamb concerned in each of them?

3. Why is the shift from largely declarative to exclamatory and imperative sentences in paragraphs 10–18 particularly appropriate?

John Henry Newman (1801–1890)

The Romantic interest in the feelings and sentiments of the individual made the informal essay the natural vehicle for such writers of the early nineteenth century as Hazlitt, De Quincey, Hunt, and Lamb. But in the later part of the century the problems engaging the minds of the great thinkers and writers of the Victorian age were too momentous to find expression in the loose and whimsical style of the informal essay. It was the more logically structured formal essay that was used by Macaulay, Mill, Arnold, Ruskin, Carlyle, and Newman.

Of all these writers, John Henry Newman was perhaps the greatest master of the formal essay. Both his training and circumstances inclined him to write in a formal rhetorical manner. He was educated at Oxford University in the whole rhetorical tradition and very much admired the style of Cicero, the greatest rhetorician of them all. In addition, the circumstances of Newman's life—his position in the Oxford movement before his conversion to Catholicism; the attack of Charles Kingsley on his sincerity, which occasioned his *Apologia pro vita sua;* and his criticism of the exaggerated educational and philosophical positions of writers like Macaulay, Mill, and Locke, which occasioned his *Idea of a University* and other works—almost demanded the rhetorical and argumentative patterning of his responses. Newman's writing illustrates some of the best qualities of persuasive, Ciceronian prose. Its frequent use of rotund, periodic sentences may not recommend it to modern readers, who favor a simpler manner, but readers today still have much to learn from the well-structured writing of Newman and other Victorian writers.

"What Is a University?"shows how well Newman understood some of the rhetorical methods of development that have been discussed in previous essays in this book.

WHAT IS A UNIVERSITY?

John Henry Newman

1 If I were asked to describe as briefly and popularly as I could, what a University was, I should draw my answer from its ancient designation of a *Studium Generale*, or "School of University Learning." This description implies the assemblage of strangers from all parts in one spot;—*from all parts*; else, how will you find professors and students for every department of knowledge? and *in one spot*; else, how can there be any school at all? Accordingly, in its simple and rudimental form, it is a school of knowledge of every kind, consisting of teachers and learners from every quarter. Many things are requisite to complete and satisfy the idea embodied in this description; but such as this a University seems to be in its essence, a place for the communication and circulation of thought, by means of personal intercourse, through a wide extent of country.

2 There is nothing far-fetched or unreasonable in the idea thus presented to us; and if this be a University, then a University does but contemplate a necessity of our nature, and is but one specimen in a particular medium, out of many which might be adduced in others, of a provision for that necessity. Mutual education, in a large sense of the word, is one of the great and incessant occupations of human society, carried on partly with set purpose, and partly not. One generation forms another; and the existing generation is ever acting and reacting upon itself in the persons of its individual members. Now, in this process, books, I need scarcely say, that is, the *litera scripta*,[1] are one special instrument. It is true; and emphatically so in this age. Considering the prodigious powers of the press, and how they are developed at this time in the never-intermitting issue of periodicals, tracts, pamphlets, works in series, and light literature, we must allow there never was a time which promised fairer for dispensing with every other means of information and instruction. What can we want more, you will say, for the intellectual education of the whole man, and for every man, than so exuberant and diversified and persistent a promulgation of all kinds of knowledge? Why, you will ask, need we go up to knowledge, when knowledge comes down to us? The Sibyl wrote her prophecies upon the leaves of the forest, and wasted them; but here such careless profusion might be prudently indulged, for it can be afforded without loss, in consequence of the almost fabulous fecundity of the instrument which these latter ages have invented. We have sermons in stones, and books in the

Reprinted from John Henry Newman, *The Idea of a University* (1873).

[1] The written word.—*Ed.*

running brooks; works larger and more comprehensive than those which have gained for ancients an immortality, issue forth every morning, and are projected onwards to the ends of the earth at the rate of hundreds of miles a day. Our seats are strewed, our pavements are powdered, with swarms of little tracts; and the very bricks of our city walls preach wisdom, by informing us by their placards where we can at once cheaply purchase it.

3 I allow all this, and much more; such certainly is our popular education, and its effects are remarkable. Nevertheless, after all, even in this age, whenever men are really serious about getting what, in the language of trade, is called "a good article," when they aim at something precise, something refined, something really luminous, something really large, something choice, they go to another market; they avail themselves, in some shape or other, of the rival method, the ancient method, of oral instruction, of present communication between man and man, of teachers instead of learning, of the personal influence of a master, and the humble initiation of a disciple, and, in consequence, of great centres of pilgrimage and throng, which such a method of education necessarily involves. This, I think, will be found to hold good in all those departments or aspects of society, which possess an interest sufficient to bind men together, or to constitute what is called "a world." It holds in the political world, and in the high world, and in the religious world; and it holds also in the literary and scientific world.

4 If the actions of men may be taken as any test of their convictions, then we have reason for saying this, viz.: that the province and the inestimable benefit of the *litera scripta* is that of being a record of truth, and an authority of appeal, and an instrument of teaching in the hands of a teacher; but that, if we wish to become exact and fully furnished in any branch of knowledge which is diversified and complicated, we must consult the living man and listen to his living voice. I am not bound to investigate the cause of this, and anything I may say will, I am conscious, be short of its full analysis;—perhaps we may suggest, that no books can get through the number of minute questions which it is possible to ask on any extended subject, or can hit upon the very difficulties which are severally felt by each reader in succession. Or again, that no book can convey the special spirit and delicate peculiarities of its subject with that rapidity and certainty which attend on the sympathy of mind with mind, through the eyes, the look, the accent, and the manner, in casual expressions thrown off at the moment, and the unstudied turns of familiar conversation. But I am already dwelling too long on what is but an incidental portion of my main subject. Whatever be the cause, the fact is undeniable. The general principles of any study you may learn by books at home; but the detail, the colour, the tone, the air, the life which makes it live in us, you must catch all these from those in whom it lives already. You must imitate the

student in French or German, who is not content with his grammar, but goes to Paris or Dresden: you must take example from the young artist, who aspires to visit the great Masters in Florence and in Rome. Till we have discovered some intellectual daguerreotype, which takes off the course of thought, and the form, lineaments, and features of truth, as completely and minutely, as the optical instrument reproduces the sensible object, we must come to the teachers of wisdom to learn wisdom, we must repair to the fountain, and drink there. Portions of it may go from thence to the ends of the earth by means of books; but the fulness is in one place alone. It is in such assemblages and congregations of intellect that books themselves, the masterpieces of human genius, are written, or at least originated.

5 The principle on which I have been insisting is so obvious, and instances in point are so ready, that I should think it tiresome to proceed with the subject, except that one or two illustrations may serve to explain my own language about it, which may not have done justice to the doctrine which it has been intended to enforce.

6 For instance, the polished manners and high-bred bearing which are so difficult of attainment, and so strictly personal when attained,—which are so much admired in society, from society are acquired. All that goes to constitute a gentleman,—the carriage, gait, address, gestures, voice; the ease, the self-possession, the courtesy, the power of conversing, the talent of not offending; the lofty principle, the delicacy of thought, the happiness of expression, the taste and propriety, the generosity and forbearance, the candour and consideration, the openness of hand;—these qualities, some of them come by nature, some of them may be found in any rank, some of them are a direct precept of Christianity; but the full assemblage of them, bound up in the unity of an individual character, do we expect they can be learned from books? are they not necessarily acquired, where they are to be found, in high society? The very nature of the case leads us to say so; you cannot fence without an antagonist, nor challenge all comers in disputation before you have supported a thesis; and in like manner, it stands to reason, you cannot learn to converse till you have the world to converse with; you cannot unlearn your natural bashfulness, or awkwardness, or stiffness, or other besetting deformity, till you serve your time in some school of manners. Well, and is it not so in matter of fact? The metropolis, the court, the great houses of the land, are the centres to which at stated times the country comes up, as to shrines of refinement and good taste; and then in due time the country goes back again home, enriched with a portion of the social accomplishments, which those very visits serve to call out and heighten in the gracious dispensers of them. We are unable to conceive how the "gentleman-like" can otherwise be maintained; and maintained in this way it is.

7 And now a second instance: and here, too, I am going to speak without personal experience of the subject I am introducing. I admit I have not been in Parliament, any more than I have figured in the *beau monde;* yet I cannot but think that statesmanship, as well as high breeding, is learned, not by books, but in certain centres of education. If it be not presumption to say so, Parliament puts a clever man *au courant* with politics and affairs of state in a way surprising to himself. A member of the Legislature, if tolerably observant, begins to see things with new eyes, even though his views undergo no change. Words have a meaning now, and ideas a reality, such as they had not before. He hears a vast deal in public speeches and private conversation, which is never put into print. The bearings of measures and events, the action of parties, and the persons of friends and enemies, are brought out to the man who is in the midst of them with a distinctness, which the most diligent perusal of newspapers will fail to impart to them. It is access to the fountainheads of political wisdom and experience, it is daily intercourse, of one kind or another, with the multitude who go up to them, it is familiarity with business, it is access to the contributions of fact and opinion thrown together by many witnesses from many quarters, which does this for him. However, I need not account for a fact, to which it is sufficient to appeal; that the Houses of Parliament and the atmosphere around them are a sort of University of politics.

8 As regards the world of science, we find a remarkable instance of the principle which I am illustrating, in the periodical meetings for its advance, which have arisen in the course of the last twenty years, such as the British Association. Such gatherings would to many persons appear at first sight simply preposterous. Above all subjects of study, Science is conveyed, is propagated, by books, or by private teaching; experiments and investigations are conducted in silence; discoveries are made in solitude. What have philosophers to do with festive celebrities, and panegyrical solemnities with mathematical and physical truth? Yet on a closer attention to the subject, it is found that not even scientific thought can dispense with the suggestions, the instruction, the stimulus, the sympathy, the intercourse with mankind on a large scale, which such meetings secure. A fine time of year is chosen, when days are long, skies are bright, the earth smiles, and all nature rejoices; a city or town is taken by turns, of ancient name or modern opulence, where buildings are spacious and hospitality hearty. The novelty of place and circumstance, the excitement of strange, or the refreshment of well-known faces, the majesty of rank or of genius, the amiable charities of men pleased both with themselves and with each other; the elevated spirits, the circulation of thought, the curiosity; the morning sections, the outdoor exercise, the well-furnished, well-earned board, the not ungraceful hilarity, the evening circle; the brilliant lecture,

the discussions or collisions or guesses of great men one with another, the narratives of scientific processes, of hopes, disappointments, conflicts, and successes, the splendid eulogistic orations; these and the like constituents of the annual celebration are considered to do something real and substantial for the advance of knowledge which can be done in no other way. Of course they can but be occasional; they answer to the annual Act or Commencement, or Commemoration, of a University, not to its ordinary condition; but they are of a University nature; and I can well believe in their utility. They issue in the promotion of a certain living and, as it were, bodily communication of knowledge from one to another, of a general interchange of ideas, and a comparison and adjustment of science with science, of an enlargement of mind, intellectual and social, of an ardent love of the particular study, which may be chosen by each individual, and a noble devotion to its interests.

9 Such meetings, I repeat, are but periodical, and only partially represent the idea of a University. The bustle and whirl which are their usual concomitants, are in ill keeping with the order and gravity of earnest intellectual education. We desiderate means of instruction which involve no interruption of our ordinary habits; nor need we seek it long, for the natural course of things brings it about, while we debate over it. In every great country, the metropolis itself becomes a sort of necessary University, whether we will or no. As the chief city is the seat of the court, of high society, of politics, and of law, so as a matter of course is it the seat of letters also; and at this time, for a long term of years, London and Paris are in fact and in operation Universities, though in Paris its famous University is no more, and in London a University scarcely exists except as a board of administration.[2] The newspapers, magazines, reviews, journals, and periodicals of all kinds, the publishing trade, the libraries, museums, and academies there found, the learned and scientific societies, necessarily invest it with the functions of a University; and that atmosphere of intellect, which in a former age hung over Oxford or Bologna or Salamanca, has, with the change of times, moved away to the centre of civil government. Thither come up youths from all parts of the country, the students of law, medicine, and the fine arts, and the *employés* and *attachés* of literature. There they live, as chance determines; and they are satisfied with their temporary home, for they find in it all that was promised to them there. They have not come in vain, as far as their own object in coming is concerned. They have not learned any particular religion, but they have learned their own particular profession well. They have, moreover, become acquainted with the

[2] London University was founded in 1827, and incorporated by royal charter in 1836. There was much opposition to it at first, and hence the University of London was for several decades little more than a body with examining functions and degree-giving powers.

habits, manners, and opinions of their place of sojourn, and done their part in maintaining the tradition of them. We cannot then be without virtual Universities; a metropolis is such: the simple question is, whether the education sought and given should be based on principle, formed upon rule, directed to the highest ends, or left to the random succession of masters and schools, one after another, with a melancholy waste of thought and an extreme hazard of truth.

10 Religious teaching itself affords us an illustration of our subject to a certain point. It does not, indeed, seat itself merely in centres of the world; this is impossible from the nature of the case. It is intended for the many, not the few; its subject-matter is truth necessary for us, not truth recondite and rare; but it concurs in the principle of a University so far as this, that its great instrument, or rather organ, has ever been that which nature prescribes in all education, the personal presence of a teacher, or, in theological language, Oral Tradition. It is the living voice, the breathing form, the expressive countenance, which preaches, which catechises. Truth, a subtle, invisible, manifold spirit, is poured into the mind of the scholar by his eyes and ears, through his affections, imagination, and reason; it is poured into his mind and is sealed up there in perpetuity by propounding and repeating it, by questioning and requestioning, by correcting and explaining, by progressing and then recurring to first principles, by all those ways which are implied in the word "catechising." In the first ages, it was a work of long time; months, sometimes years, were devoted to the arduous task of disabusing the mind of the incipient Christian of its pagan errors, and of moulding it upon the Christian faith. The Scriptures, indeed, were at hand for the study of those who could avail themselves of them; but St. Irenæus does hesitate to speak of whole races, who had been converted to Christianity, without being able to read them. To be unable to read or write was in those times no evidence of want of learning: the hermits of the deserts were, in this sense of the word, illiterate; yet the great St. Anthony, though he knew not letters, was a match in disputation for the learned philosophers who came to try him. Didymus again, the great Alexandrian theologian, was blind. The ancient discipline, called the *Disciplina Arcani*,[3] involved the same principle. The more sacred doctrines of Revelation were not committed to books but passed on by successive tradition. The teaching on the Blessed Trinity and the Eucharist appears to have been so handed down for some hundred years; and when at length reduced to writing, it has filled many folios, yet has not been exhausted.

11 But I have said more than enough in illustration; I end as I began;—a University is a place of concourse, whither students come from every quarter for every kind of knowledge. You cannot have the best of every

[3] The Discipline of the Secret.—*Ed.*

kind everywhere; you must go to some great city or emporium for it. There you have all the choicest productions of nature and art all together, which you find each in its own separate place elsewhere. All the riches of the land, and of the earth, are carried up thither; there are the best markets, and there the best workmen. It is the centre of trade, the supreme court of fashion, the umpire of rival talents, and the standard of things rare and precious. It is the place for seeing galleries of first-rate pictures, and for hearing wonderful voices and performers of transcendent skill. It is the place for great preachers, great orators, great nobles, great statesmen. In the nature of things, greatness and unity go together; excellence implies a centre. And such, for the third or fourth time, is a University; I hope I do not weary out the reader by repeating it. It is the place to which a thousand schools make contributions; in which the intellect may safely range and speculate, sure to find its equal in some antagonist activity, and its judge in the tribunal of truth. It is a place where inquiry is pushed forward, and discoveries verified and perfected, and rashness rendered innocuous, and error exposed, by the collision of mind with mind, and knowledge with knowledge. It is the place where the professor becomes eloquent, and is a missionary and a preacher, displaying his science in its most complete and most winning form, pouring it forth with the zeal of enthusiasm, and lighting up his own love of it in the breasts of his hearers. It is the place where the catechist makes good his ground as he goes, treading in the truth day by day into the ready memory, and wedging and tightening it into the expanding reason. It is a place which wins the admiration of the young by its celebrity, kindles the affections of the middle-aged by its beauty, and rivets the fidelity of the old by its associations. It is a seat of wisdom, a light of the world, a minister of the faith, an Alma Mater of the rising generation. It is this and a great deal more, and demands a somewhat better head and hand than mine to describe it well.

STUDY GUIDE

Theme, Structure, and Tone

1. Newman made very good use in his writings of the traditional methods of rhetorical development. This essay is developed by definition, by illustration, and by analogy. Indicate the parts of the essay that are developed by each of these methods. Which method is used most extensively?

2. The last paragraph is a summary statement of the idea developed in the whole essay. Show how Newman has used parallel sentence structure in it to express this summary statement effectively.

3. This essay was actually a lecture delivered to the faculty of the new Catholic University in Dublin. What elements of its style show that it was meant for oral delivery?

4. Newman says here that a multiplicity of printed books does not make the living teacher obsolete. What arguments does he give for this? Do you think the modern technological communications devices (radio, television, motion pictures, computers) make him obsolete? Do these modern devices somewhat change his function? Write an essay of your own in which you discuss this problem.

Ralph Waldo Emerson (1803–1882)

Ralph Waldo Emerson was one of the most influential philosophers and writers in the New England Transcendentalist movement. He achieved some distinction as a poet, but he is chiefly known as an essayist. Many of his longer essays, such as "Nature," express aspects of his Transcendentalist philosophy. One of them, "The American Scholar," is a declaration of independence from European influence on American culture and writing. But Emerson himself was indebted to Europe for much of his thought and style. The stylists who most influenced him were the Senecan writers with their curt and staccato rhythms. Emerson's essays, his shorter ones particularly, read like the early essays of Bacon and those of Montaigne. They do not progress logically but are made up of a succession of aphoristic sentences which throw flashes of light on the topic being discussed but do not really advance it logically. The separate curt sentences, however, often frame a striking thought memorably. "Gifts" is a good example of this Senecan or Stoic manner.

GIFTS

Ralph Waldo Emerson

Gifts of one who loved me—
'T was high time they came;
When he ceased to love me,
Time they stopped for shame.

1 It is said that the world is in a state of bankruptcy; that the world owes the world more than the world can pay, and ought to go into chancery

Reprinted from Ralph Waldo Emerson, *Essays, Second Series* (1844).

and be sold. I do not think this general insolvency, which involves in some sort all the population, to be the reason of the difficulty experienced at Christmas and New Year and other times, in bestowing gifts; since it is always so pleasant to be generous, though very vexatious to pay debts. But the impediment lies in the choosing. If at any time it comes into my head that a present is due from me to somebody, I am puzzled what to give, until the opportunity is gone. Flowers and fruits are always fit presents; flowers, because they are a proud assertion that a ray of beauty outvalues all the utilities of the world. These gay natures contrast with the somewhat stern countenance of ordinary nature: they are like music heard out of a work-house. Nature does not cocker us; we are children, not pets; she is not fond; everything is dealt to us without fear or favor, after severe universal laws. Yet these delicate flowers look like the frolic and interference of love and beauty. Men used to tell us that we love flattery even though we are not deceived by it, because it shows that we are of importance enough to be courted. Something like that pleasure, the flowers give us: what am I to whom these sweet hints are addressed? Fruits are acceptable gifts, because they are the flower of commodities, and admit of fantastic values being attached to them. If a man should send to me to come a hundred miles to visit him and should set before me a basket of fine summer-fruit, I should think there was some proportion between the labor and the reward.

2 For common gifts, necessity makes pertinences and beauty every day, and one is glad when an imperative leaves him no option; since if the man at the door have no shoes, you have not to consider whether you could procure him a paint-box. And as it is always pleasing to see a man eat bread, or drink water, in the house or out of doors, so it is always a great satisfaction to supply these first wants. Necessity does everything well. In our condition of universal dependence it seems heroic to let the petitioner be the judge of his necessity, and to give all that is asked, though at great inconvenience. If it be a fantastic desire, it is better to leave to others the office of punishing him. I can think of many parts I should prefer playing to that of the Furies. Next to things of necessity, the rule for a gift, which one of my friends prescribed, is that we might convey to some person that which properly belonged to his character, and was easily associated with him in thought. But our tokens of compliment and love are for the most part barbarous. Rings and other jewels are not gifts, but apologies for gifts. The only gift is a portion of thyself. Thou must bleed for me. Therefore the poet brings his poem; the shepherd, his lamb; the farmer, corn; the miner, a gem; the sailor, coral and shells; the painter, his picture; the girl, a handkerchief of her own sewing. This is right and pleasing, for it restores society in so far to the primary basis, when a man's biography is conveyed in his gift, and every man's wealth is an index of his merit. But it is a cold lifeless business when you go to the shop to buy me something which does not

represent your life and talent, but a goldsmith's. This is fit for kings, and rich men who represent kings, and a false state of property, to make presents of gold and silver stuffs, as a kind of symbolical sin-offering, or payment of blackmail.

3 The law of benefits is a difficult channel, which requires careful sailing, or rude boats. It is not the office of a man to receive gifts. How dare you give them? We wish to be self-sustained. We do not quite forgive a giver. The hand that feeds us is in some danger of being bitten. We can receive anything from love, for that is a way of receiving it from ourselves; but not from any one who assumes to bestow. We sometimes hate the meat which we eat, because there seems something of degrading dependence in living by it:

> Brother, if Jove to thee a present make,
> Take heed that from his hands thou nothing take.

We ask the whole. Nothing less will content us. We arraign society if it do not give us, besides earth and fire and water, opportunity, love, reverence and objects of veneration.

4 He is a good man who can receive a gift well. We are either glad or sorry at a gift, and both emotions are unbecoming. Some violence I think is done, some degradation borne, when I rejoice or grieve at a gift. I am sorry when my independence is invaded, or when a gift comes from such as do not know my spirit, and so the act is not supported; and if the gift pleases me overmuch, then I should be ashamed that the donor should read my heart, and see that I love his commodity, and not him. The gift, to be true, must be the flowing of the giver unto me, correspondent to my flowing unto him. When the waters are at level, then my goods pass to him, and his to me. All his are mine, all mine his. I say to him, How can you give me this pot of oil or this flagon of wine when all your oil and wine is mine, which belief of mine this gift seems to deny? Hence the fitness of beautiful, not useful things, for gifts. This giving is flat usurpation, and therefore when the beneficiary is ungrateful, as all beneficiaries hate all Timons, not at all considering the value of the gift but looking back to the greater store it was taken from—I rather sympathize with the beneficiary than with the anger of my lord Timon. For the expectation of gratitude is mean, and is continually punished by the total insensibility of the obliged person. It is a great happiness to get off without injury and heartburning from one who has had the ill-luck to be served by you. It is a very onerous business, this of being served, and the debtor naturally wishes to give you a slap. A golden text for these gentlemen is that which I so admire in the Buddhist, who never thanks, and who says, "Do not flatter your benefactors."

5 The reason of these discords I conceive to be that there is no commensurability between a man and any gift. You cannot give anything to a

magnanimous person. After you have served him he at once puts you in debt by his magnanimity. The service a man renders his friend is trivial and selfish compared with the service he knows his friend stood in readiness to yield him, alike before he had begun to serve his friend, and now also. Compared with that good-will I bear my friend, the benefit it is in my power to render him seems small. Besides, our action on each other, good as well as evil, is so incidental and at random that we can seldom hear the acknowledgments of any person who would thank us for a benefit, without some shame and humiliation. We can rarely strike a direct stroke, but must be content with an oblique one; we seldom have the satisfaction of yielding a direct benefit which is directly received. But rectitude scatters favors on every side without knowing it, and receives with wonder the thanks of all people.

6 I fear to breathe any treason against the majesty of love, which is the genius and god of gifts, and to whom we must not affect to prescribe. Let him give kingdoms of flower-leaves indifferently. There are persons from whom we always expect fairy-tokens; let us not cease to expect them. This is prerogative, and not to be limited by our municipal rules. For the rest, I like to see that we cannot be bought and sold. The best of hospitality and of generosity is also not in the will, but in fate. I find that I am not much to you; you do not need me; you do not feel me; then am I thrust out of doors, though you proffer me house and lands. No services are of any value, but only likeness. When I have attempted to join myself to others by services, it proved an intellectual trick—no more. They eat your service like apples, and leave you out. But love them, and they feel you and delight in you all the time.

STUDY GUIDE

1. Morris Croll has said that a paragraph or essay composed in the curt, baroque or Senecan manner does not progress logically but resembles the flashes of light cast from a cut gem slowly turned on a standard. Apply this notion to the successive sentences in any one paragraph of this essay.

2. Single out particularly striking aphoristic statements in Emerson's essay.

Henry Adams (1838–1918)

Henry Adams brought to his writing an inheritance of the best that New England culture had to offer. Although he revolted against the restrictive spirit of this culture, he was greatly indebted to it for his sense of high seriousness and good taste. Ironically, Adams did not look upon himself as a man of letters but as an historian. His achievement as an historian was, indeed, of the highest caliber. His nine-volume *History of the United States of America during the Administrations of Jefferson and Madison* has sometimes been ranked with Gibbon's *The Decline and Fall of the Roman Empire*. Some of his literary works were at first circulated only among friends, and they were published only after his death, when they became widely known. But it is the *Mont Saint Michel and Chartres* and his autobiography *The Education of Henry Adams* that have won him a secure place in the history of American letters. Ernest Samuels has remarked that "the most unstinted praise has gone to the *Chartres,* whatever cavils it may deserve for its romantic distortions of life in the Middle Ages and for its highly unorthodox theology. The Virgin of his creation is undoubtedly one of the remarkable heroines of literature." Henry Adams wrote innumerable essays for American journals during his life time, but it is upon the *Chartres* and the *Education* that his reputation as an essayist chiefly rests.

THE VIRGIN OF CHARTRES

Henry Adams

1 We must take ten minutes to accustom our eyes to the light, and we had better use them to seek the reason why we come to Chartres rather than to Rheims or Amiens or Bourges, for the cathedral that fills our ideal. The truth is, there are several reasons; there generally are, for doing the things we like; and after you have studied Chartres to the ground, and got your reasons settled, you will never find an antiquarian to agree with you; the architects will probably listen to you with contempt; and even these excellent priests, whose kindness is great, whose patience is heavenly, and whose good opinion you would so gladly gain, will turn from you with pain, if not with horror. The Gothic is singular in this; one seems easily at home in the Renaissance; one is not too strange in the Byzantine; as for the Roman, it is ourselves; and we could walk blindfolded through every chink and cranny of the Greek mind; all these styles seem modern, when we come close to them; but the Gothic gets away. No two men think alike about it, and no woman agrees with either man. The Chruch itself never agreed about it, and the architects agree even less than the priests. To most minds

it casts too many shadows; it wraps itself in mystery; and when people talk of mystery, they commonly mean fear. To others, the Gothic seems hoary with age and decrepitude, and its shadows mean death. What is curious to watch is the fanatical conviction of the Gothic enthusiast, to whom the twelfth century means exuberant youth, the eternal child of Wordsworth, over whom its immortality broods like the day; it is so simple and yet so complicated; it sees so much and so little; it loves so many toys and cares for so few necessities; its youth is so young, its age so old, and its youthful yearning for old thought is so disconcerting, like the mysterious senility of the baby that

> Deaf and silent, reads the eternal deep
> Haunted forever by the eternal mind.[1]

One need not take it more seriously than one takes the baby itself. Our amusement is to play with it, and to catch its meaning in its smile; and whatever Chartres may be now, when young it was a smile. To the Church, no doubt, its cathedral here has a fixed and administrative meaning, which is the same as that of every other bishop's seat and with which we have nothing whatever to do. To us, it is a child's fancy; a toyhouse to please the Queen of Heaven—to please her so much that she would be happy in it—to charm her till she smiled.

2 The Queen Mother was as majestic as you like; she was absolute; she could be stern; she was not above being angry; but she was still a woman, who loved grace, beauty, ornament—her toilette, robes, jewels;—who considered the arrangements of her palace with attention, and liked both light and colour; who kept a keen eye on her Court, and exacted prompt and willing obedience from king and archbishops as well as from beggars and drunken priests. She protected her friends and punished her enemies. She required space, beyond what was known in the Courts of kings, because she was liable at all times to have ten thousand people begging her for favours—most inconsistent with law—and deaf to refusal. She was extremely sensitive to neglect, to disagreeable impressions, to want of intelligence in her surroundings. She was the greatest artist, as she was the greatest philosopher and musician and theologist, that ever lived on earth, except her Son, Who, at Chartres, is still an Infant under her guardianship. Her taste was infallible; her sentence eternally final. This church was built for her in this spirit of simple-minded, practical, utilitarian faith—in this singleness of thought, exactly as a little girl sets up a doll-house for her favourite blonde doll. Unless you can go back to your dolls, you are out of place here. If you can go back to them, and get rid for one small hour of the weight of custom, you shall see Chartres in glory.

3 The palaces of earthly queens were hovels compared with these

[1] William Wordsworth, "Intimations of Immortality," viii.—*Ed.*

palaces of the Queen of Heaven at Chartres, Paris, Laon, Noyon, Rheims, Amiens, Rouen, Bayeux, Coutances—a list that might be stretched into a volume. The nearest approach we have made to a palace was the Merveille at Mont-Saint-Michel, but no Queen had a palace equal to that. The Merveille was built, or designed, about the year 1200; toward the year 1500, Louis XI built a great castle at Loches in Touraine, and there Queen Anne de Bretagne had apartments which still exist, and which we will visit. At Blois you shall see the residence which served for Catherine de Medicis till her death in 1589. Anne de Bretagne was trebly queen, and Catherine de Medicis took her standard of comfort from the luxury of Florence. At Versailles you can see the apartments which the queens of the Bourbon line occupied through their century of magnificence. All put together, and then trebled in importance, could not rival the splendour of any single cathedral dedicated to Queen Mary in the thirteenth century; and of them all, Chartres was built to be peculiarly and exceptionally her delight.

4 One has grown so used to this sort of loose comparison, this reckless waste of words, that one no longer adopts an idea unless it is driven in with hammers of statistics and columns of figures. With the irritating demand for literal exactness and perfectly straight lines which lights up every truly American eye, you will certainly ask when this exaltation of Mary began, and unless you get the dates, you will doubt the facts. It is your own fault if they are tiresome; you might easily read them all in the "Iconographie de la Sainte Vierge," by M. Rohault de Fleury, published in 1878. You can start at Byzantium with the Empress Helena in 326, or with the Council of Ephesus in 431. You will find the Virgin acting as the patron saint of Constantinople and of the Imperial residence, under as many names as Artemis or Aphrodite had borne. As Godmother (θεομητηρ), Deipara[2] (θεοτοκος), Pathfinder (ʻΟδηγητρια), she was the chief favourite of the Eastern Empire, and her picture was carried at the head of every procession and hung on the wall of every hut and hovel, as it is still wherever the Greek Church goes. In the year 610, when Heraclius sailed from Carthage to dethrone Phocas at Constantinople, his ships carried the image of the Virgin at their mastheads. In 1143, just before the flèche on the Chartres clocher was begun, the Basileus John Comnenus died, and so devoted was he to the Virgin that, on a triumphal entry into Constantinople, he put the image of the Mother of God in his chariot, while he himself walked. In the Western Church the Virgin had always been highly honoured, but it was not until the crusades that she began to overshadow the Trinity itself. Then her miracles became more frequent and her shrines more frequented, so that Chartres, soon after 1100, was rich enough to build its western portal with Byzantine splendour. A proof of the new outburst can be read

[2] God-bearer or Mother of God.—*Ed.*

in the story of Citeaux. For us, Citeaux means Saint Bernard, who joined the Order in 1112, and 1115 founded his Abbey of Clairvaux in the territory of Troyes. In him, the religious emotion of the half-century between the first and second crusades (1095–1145) centred as in no one else. He was a French precursor of Saint Francis of Assisi who lived a century later. If we were to plunge into the story of Citeaux and Saint Bernard we should never escape, for Saint Bernard incarnates what we are trying to understand, and his mind is further from us than the architecture. You would lose hold of everything actual, if you could comprehend in its contradictions the strange mixture of passion and caution, the austerity, the self-abandonment, the vehemence, the restraint, the love, the hate, the miracles, and the scepticism of Saint Bernard. The Cistercian Order, which was founded in 1098, from the first put all its churches under the special protection of the Virgin, and Saint Bernard in his time was regarded as the apple of the Virgin's eye. Tradition as old as the twelfth century, which long afterwards gave to Murillo the subject of a famous painting, told that once, when he was reciting before her statue the "Ave Maris Stella," and came to the words, "Monstra te esse Matrem," [3] the image, pressing its breast, dropped on the lips of her servant three drops of the milk which had nourished the Saviour. The same miracle, in various forms, was told of many other persons, both saints and sinners; but it made so much impression on the mind of the age that, in the fourteenth century, Dante, seeking in Paradise for some official introduction to the foot of the Throne, found no intercessor with the Queen of Heaven more potent than Saint Bernard. You can still read Bernard's hymns to the Virgin, and even his sermons, if you like. To him she was the great mediator. In the eyes of a culpable humanity, Christ was too sublime, too terrible, too just, but not even the weakest human frailty could fear to approach his Mother. Her attribute was humility; her love and pity were infinite. "Let him deny your mercy who can say that he has ever asked it in vain."

5 Saint Bernard was emotional and to a certain degree mystical, like Adam de Saint-Victor, whose hymns were equally famous, but the emotional saints and mystical poets were not by any means allowed to establish exclusive rights to the Virgin's favour. Abélard was as devoted as they were, and wrote hymns as well. Philosophy claimed her, and Albert the Great, the head of scholasticism, the teacher of Thomas Aquinas, decided in her favour the question: "Whether the Blessed Virgin possessed perfectly the seven liberal arts." The Church at Chartres had decided it a hundred years before by putting the seven liberal arts next her throne, with Aristotle himself to witness; but Albertus gave the reason: "I hold that she did, for it is written, 'Wisdom has built herself a house, and has sculptured

[3] Show that you are a Mother.—*Ed.*

seven columns.' That house is the blessed Virgin; the seven columns are the seven liberal arts. Mary, therefore, had perfect mastery of science." Naturally she had also perfect mastery of economics, and most of her great churches were built in economic centres. The guilds were, if possible, more devoted to her than the monks; the bourgeoisie of Paris, Rouen, Amiens, Laon, spent money by millions to gain her favour. Most surprising of all, the great military class was perhaps the most vociferous. Of all inappropriate haunts for the gentle, courteous, pitying Mary, a field of battle seems to be the worst, if not distinctly blasphemous; yet the greatest French warriors insisted on her leading them into battle, and in the actual mêlée when men were killing each other, on every battlefield in Europe, for at least five hundred years, Mary was present, leading both sides. The battle-cry of the famous Constable du Guesclin was "Notre-Dame-Guesclin"; "Notre-Dame-Coucy" was the cry of the great Sires de Coucy; "Notre-Dame-Auxerre"; "Notre-Dame-Sancerre"; "Notre-Dame-Hainault"; "Notre-Dame-Gueldres"; Notre-Dame-Bourbon"; "Notre-Dame-Bearn";—all well-known battle-cries. The King's own battle at one time cried, "Notre-Dame-Saint-Denis-Montjoie"; the Dukes of Burgundy cried, "Notre-Dame-Bourgogne"; and even the soldiers of the Pope were said to cry, "Notre-Dame-Saint-Pierre."

6 The measure of this devotion, which proves to any religious American mind, beyond possible cavil, its serious and practical reality, is the money it cost. According to statistics, in the single century between 1170 and 1270, the French built eighty cathedrals and nearly five hundred churches of the cathedral class, which would have cost, according to an estimate made in 1840, more than five thousand millions to replace. Five thousand million francs is a thousand million dollars, and this covered only the great churches of a single century. The same scale of expenditure had been going on since the year 1000, and almost every parish in France had rebuilt its church in stone; to this day France is strewn with the ruins of this architecture, and yet the still preserved churches of the eleventh and twelfth centuries, among the churches that belong to the Romanesque and Transition period, are numbered by hundreds until they reach well into the thousands. The share of this capital which was—if one may use a commercial figure—invested in the Virgin cannot be fixed, any more than the total sum given to religious objects between 1000 and 1300; but in a spiritual and artistic sense, it was almost the whole, and expressed an intensity of conviction never again reached by any passion, whether of religion, of loyalty, of patriotism, or of wealth; perhaps never even paralleled by any single economic effort except in war. Nearly every great church of the twelfth and thirteenth centuries belonged to Mary, until in France one asks for the church of Notre Dame as though it meant cathedral; but, not satisfied with this, she contracted the habit of requiring in all churches a chapel of her own, called in English the "Lady Chapel,"

which was apt to be as large as the church but was always meant to be handsomer; and there, behind the high altar, in her own private apartment, Mary sat, receiving her innumerable suppliants, and ready at any moment to step upon the high altar itself to support the tottering authority of the local saint.

7 Expenditure like this rests invariably on an economic idea. Just as the French of the nineteenth century invested their surplus capital in a railway system in the belief that they would make money by it in this life, in the thirteenth they trusted their money to the Queen of Heaven because of their belief in her power to repay it with interest in the life to come. The investment was based on the power of Mary as Queen rather than on any orthodox church conception of the Virgin's legitimate station. Papal Rome never greatly loved Byzantine empresses or French queens. The Virgin of Chartres was never wholly sympathetic to the Roman Curia. To this day the Church writers—like the Abbé Bulteau or M. Rohault de Fleury—are singularly shy of the true Virgin of majesty, whether at Chartres or at Byzantium or wherever she is seen. The fathers Martin and Cahier at Bourges alone felt her true value. Had the Church controlled her, the Virgin would perhaps have remained prostrate at the foot of the Cross. Dragged by a Byzantine Court, backed by popular insistence and impelled by overpowering self-interest, the Church accepted the Virgin throned and crowned, seated by Christ, the Judge throned and crowned; but even this did not wholly satisfy the French of the thirteenth century who seemed bent on absorbing Christ in His Mother, and making the Mother the Church, and Christ the Symbol.

8 The Church had crowned and enthroned her almost from the beginning, and could not have dethroned her it if would. In all Christian art—sculpture or mosaic, painting or poetry—the Virgin's rank was expressly asserted. Saint Bernard, like John Comnenus, and probably at the same time (1120–40), chanted hymns to the Virgin as Queen:

O salutaris Virgo Stella Maris
Generans prolem, Aequitatis solem,
Lucis auctorem, Retinens pudorem,
Suscipe laudem!

Celi Regina Per quam medicina
Datur aegrotis, Gratia devotis,
Gaudium moestis, Mundo lux coelestis,
Spesque salutis;

Aula regalis, Virgo specialis,
Posce medelam Nobis et tutelam,
Suscipe vota, Precibusque cuncta
Pelle molesta!

O saviour Virgin, Star of Sea,
Who bore for child the Son of Justice,
The source of Light, Virgin always
Hear our praise!

Queen of Heaven who have given
Medicine to the sick, Grace to the devout,
Joy to the sad, Heaven's light to the world
And hope of salvation;

Court royal, Virgin typical,
Grant us cure and guard,
Accept our vows, and by prayers
Drive all griefs away!

9 As the lyrical poet of the twelfth century, Adam de Saint-Victor seems to have held rank higher if possible than that of Saint Bernard, and his hymns on the Virgin are certainly quite as emphatic an assertion of her majesty:

Imperatrix supernorum!
Superatrix infernorum!
Eligenda via coeli,
Retinenda spe fideli,
Separatos a te longe
Revocatos ad te junge
Tuorum collegio!

Empress of the highest,
Mistress over the lowest,
Chosen path of Heaven,
Held fast by faithful hope,
Those separated from you far,
Recalled to you, unite
In your fold!

10 To delight in the childish jingle of the mediaeval Latin is a sign of a futile mind, no doubt, and I beg pardon of you and of the Church for wasting your precious summer day on poetry which was regarded as mystical in its age and which now sounds like a nursery rhyme; but a verse or two of Adam's hymn on the Assumption of the Virgin completes the record of her rank, and goes to complete also the documentary proof of her majesty at Chartres:

Salve, Mater Salvatoris!
Vas electum! Vas honoris!
Vas coelestis Gratiae!

Ab aeterno Vas provisum!
Vas insigne! Vas excisum
    Manu sapientiae!

Salve, Mater pietatis,
Et totius Trinitatis
    Nobile Triclinium!
Verbi tamen incarnati
Speciale majestati
    Praeparans hospitium!

O Maria! Stella maris!
Dignitate singularis,
Super omnes ordinaris
    Ordines coelestium!
In superno sita poli
Nos commenda tuae proli,
Ne terrores sive doli
    Nos supplantent hostium!

Mother of our Saviour, hail!
Chosen vessel! Sacred Grail!
    Font of celestial grace!
From eternity forethought!
By the hand of Wisdom wrought!
    Precious, faultless Vase!

Hail, Mother of Divinity!
Hail, Temple of the Trinity!
    Home of the Triune God!
In whom the Incarnate Word had birth,
The King! to whom you gave on earth
    Imperial abode.

Oh, Maria! Constellation!
Inspiration! Elevation!
Rule and Law and Ordination
    Of the angels' host!
Highest height of God's Creation,
Pray your Son's commiseration,
Lest, by fear or fraud, salvation
    For our souls be lost!

11 Constantly—one might better say at once, officially, she was addressed in these terms of supreme majesty: "Imperatrix supernorum!" "Coeli Regina!" "Aula regalis!" [4] but the twelfth century seemed determined to carry the idea out to its logical conclusion in defiance of dogma. Not only was the Son absorbed in the Mother, or represented as under her

[4] Empress of the highest, Queen of Heaven, Regal Power.—*Ed.*

guardianship, but the Father fared no better, and the Holy Ghost followed. The poets regarded the Virgin as the "Templum Trinitatis"; "totius Trinitatis nobile Triclinium."[5] She was the refectory of the Trinity—the "Triclinium"—because the refectory was the largest room and contained the whole of the members, and was divided in three parts by two rows of columns. She was the "Templum Trinitatis," and Church itself, with its triple aisle. The Trinity was absorbed in her.

12 This is a delicate subject in the Church, and you must feel it with delicacy, without brutally insisting on its necessary contradictions. All theology and all philosophy are full of contradictions quite as flagrant and far less sympathetic. This particular variety of religious faith is simply human, and has made its appearance in one form or another in nearly all religions; but though the twelfth century carried it to an extreme, and at Chartres you see it in its most charming expression, we have got always to make allowances for what was going on beneath the surface in men's minds, consciously or unconsciously, and for the latent scepticism which lurks behind all faith. The Church itself never quite accepted the full claims of what was called Mariolatry. One may be sure, too, that the bourgeois capitalist and the student of the schools, each from his own point of view, watched the Virgin with anxious interest. The bourgeois had put an enormous share of his capital into what was in fact an economical speculation, not unlike the South Sea Scheme, or the railway system of our own time; except that in one case the energy was devoted to shortening the road to Heaven; in the other, to shortening the road to Paris; but no serious schoolman could have felt entirely convinced that God would enter into a business partnership with man, to establish a sort of joint-stock society for altering the operation of divine and universal laws. The bourgeois cared little for the philosophical doubt if the economical result proved to be good, but he watched this result with his usual practical sagacity, and required an experience of only about three generations (1200–1300) to satisfy himself that relics were not certain in their effects; that the Saints were not always able or willing to help; that Mary herself could not certainly be bought or bribed; that prayer without money seemed to be quite as efficacious as prayer with money; and that neither the road to Heaven nor Heaven itself had been made surer or brought nearer by an investment of capital which amounted to the best part of the wealth of France. Economically speaking, he became satisfied that his enormous money-investment had proved to be an almost total loss, and the reaction on his mind was as violent as the emotion. For three hundred years it prostrated France. The efforts of the bourgeoisie and the peasantry to recover their property, so far as it was recoverable, have

[5] Temple of the Trinity, Noble refectory of the whole Trinity.—*Ed.*

lasted to the present day and we had best take care not to get mixed in those passions.

13 If you are to get the full enjoyment of Chartres, you must, for the time, believe in Mary as Bernard and Adam did, and feel her presence as the architects did, in every stone they placed, and every touch they chiselled. You must try first to rid your mind of the traditional idea that the Gothic is an intentional expression of religious gloom. The necessity for light was the motive of the Gothic architects. They needed light and always more light, until they sacrificed safety and common sense in trying to get it. They converted their walls into windows, raised their vaults, diminished their piers, until their churches could no longer stand. You will see the limits at Beauvais; at Chartres we have not got so far, but even here, in places where the Virgin wanted it—as above the high altar—the architect has taken all the light there was to take. For the same reason, fenestration became the most important part of the Gothic architect's work, and at Chartres was uncommonly interesting because the architect was obliged to design a new system, which should at the same time satisfy the laws of construction and the taste and imagination of Mary. No doubt the first command of the Queen of Heaven was for light, but the second, at least equally imperative, was for colour. Any earthly queen, even though she were not Byzantine in taste, loved colour; and the truest of queens—the only true Queen of Queens—had richer and finer taste in colour than the queens of fifty earthly kingdoms, as you will see when we come to the immense effort to gratify her in the glass of her windows. Illusion for illusion—granting for the moment that Mary was an illusion—the Virgin Mother in this instance repaid to her worshippers a larger return for their money than the capitalist has ever been able to get, at least in this world, from any other illusion of wealth which he has tried to make a source of pleasure and profit.

14 The next point on which Mary evidently insisted was the arrangement for her private apartments, the apse, as distinguished from her throne-room, the choir; both being quite distinct from the hall, or reception-room of the public, which was the nave with its enlargement in the transepts. This arrangement marks the distinction between churches built as shrines for the deity and churches built as halls of worship for the public. The difference is chiefly in the apse, and the apse of Chartres is the most interesting of all apses from this point of view.

15 The Virgin required chiefly these three things, or, if you like, these four: space, light, convenience; and colour decoration to unite and harmonize the whole. This concerns the interior; on the exterior she required statuary, and the only complete system of decorative sculpture that existed seems to belong to her churches: Paris, Rheims, Amiens, and Chartres. Mary required all this magnificence at Chartres for herself alone, not for

the public. As far as one can see into the spirit of the builders, Chartres was exclusively intended for the Virgin, as the Temple of Abydos was intended for Osiris. The wants of man, beyond a mere roofcover, and perhaps space to some degree, enter to no very great extent into the problem of Chartres. Man came to render homage or to ask favours. The Queen received him in her palace, where she alone was at home, and alone gave commands.

16 The artist's second thought was to exclude from his work everything that could displease Mary; and since Mary differed from living queens only in infinitely greater majesty and refinement, the artist could admit only what pleased the actual taste of the great ladies who dictated taste at the Courts of France and England, which surrounded the little Court of the Counts of Chartres. What they were—these women of the twelfth and thirteenth centuries—we shall have to see or seek in other directions; but Chartres is perhaps the most magnificent and permanent monument they left of their taste, and we can begin here with learning certain things which they were not.

17 In the first place, they were not in the least vague, dreamy, or mystical in a modern sense;—far from it! They seemed anxious only to throw the mysteries into a blaze of light; not so much physical, perhaps—since they, like all women, liked moderate shadow for their toilettes—but luminous in the sense of faith. There is nothing about Chartres that you would think mystical, who know your Lohengrin, Siegfried, and Parsifal. If you care to make a study of the whole literature of the subject, read M. Mâle's "Art Religieux du XIIIe Siècle en France," and use it for a guide-book. Here you need only note how symbolic and how simple the sculpture is, on the portals and porches. Even what seems a grotesque or an abstract idea is no more than the simplest child's personification. On the walls you may have noticed the *Ane qui vielle*—the ass playing the lyre; and on all the old churches you can see "bestiaries," as they were called, of fabulous animals, symbolic or not; but the symbolism is as simple as the realism of the oxen at Laon. It gave play to the artist in his effort for variety of decoration, and it amused the people—probably the Virgin also was not above being amused;—now and then it seems about to suggest what you would call an esoteric meaning, that is to say, a meaning which each one of us can consider private property reserved for our own amusement, and from which the public is excluded; yet, in truth, in the Virgin's churches the public is never excluded, but invited. The Virgin even had the additional charm to the public that she was popularly supposed to have no very marked fancy for priests as such; she was a queen, a woman, and a mother, functions, all, which priests could not perform. Accordingly, she seems to have had little taste for mysteries of any sort, and even the symbols that seem most mysterious were clear to every old peasant-woman in her church. The most

pleasing and promising of them all is the woman's figure you saw on the front of the cathedral in Paris; her eyes bandaged; her head bent down; her crown falling; without cloak or royal robe; holding in her hand a guidon or banner with its staff broken in more than one place. On the opposite pier stands another woman, with royal mantle, erect and commanding. The symbol is so graceful that one is quite eager to know its meaning; but every child in the Middle Ages would have instantly told you that the woman with the falling crown meant only the Jewish Synagogue, as the one with the royal robe meant the Church of Christ.

18 Another matter for which the female taste seemed not much to care was theology in the metaphysical sense. Mary troubled herself little about theology except when she retired into the south transept with Pierre de Dreux.[6] Even there one finds little said about the Trinity, always the most metaphysical subtlety of the Church. Indeed, you might find much amusement here in searching the cathedral for any distinct expression at all of the Trinity as a dogma recognized by Mary. One cannot take seriously the idea that the three doors, the three portals, and the three aisles express the Trinity, because, in the first place, there was no rule about it; churches might have what portals and aisles they pleased; both Paris and Bourges have five; the doors themselves are not allotted to the three members of the Trinity, nor are the portals; while another more serious objection is that the side doors and aisles are not of equal importance with the central, but mere adjuncts and dependencies, so that the architect who had misled the ignorant public into accepting so black a heresy would have deserved the stake, and would probably have gone to it. Even this suggestion of trinity is wanting in the transepts, which have only one aisle, and in the choir, which has five, as well as five or seven chapels, and, as far as an ignorant mind can penetrate, no triplets whatever. Occasionally, no doubt, you will discover in some sculpture or window, a symbol of the Trinity, but this discovery itself amounts to an admission of its absence as a controlling idea, for the ordinary worshipper must have been at least as blind as we are, and to him, as to us, it would have seemed a wholly subordinate detail. Even if the Trinity, too, is anywhere expressed, you will hardly find here an attempt to explain its metaphysical meaning—not even a mystic triangle.

19 The church is wholly given up to the Mother and the Son. The Father seldom appears; the Holy Ghost still more rarely. At least, this is the impression made on an ordinary visitor who has no motive to be orthodox; and it must have been the same with the thirteenth-century worshipper who came here with his mind absorbed in the perfections of Mary. Chartres represents, not the Trinity, but the identity of the Mother and Son. The Son represents the Trinity, which is thus absorbed in the Mother. The idea

[6] Pierre de Dreux, Duke of Brittany, built the south porch of Chartres.—*Ed.*

is not orthodox, but this is no affair of ours. The Church watches over its own.

20 The Virgin's wants and tastes, positive and negative, ought now to be clear enough to enable you to feel the artist's sincerity in trying to satisfy them; but first you have still to convince yourselves of the people's sincerity in employing the artists. The point is the easiest of all, for the evidence is express. In the year 1145 when the old flèche was begun—the year before Saint Bernard preached the second crusade at Vézelay—Abbot Haimon, of Saint-Pierre-sur-Dives in Normandy, wrote to the monks of Tutbury Abbey in England a famous letter to tell of the great work which the Virgin was doing in France and which began at the Church of Chartres. "Hujus sacrae institutionis ritus apud Carnotensem ecclesiam est inchoatus." [7] From Chartres it had spread through Normandy, where it produced among other things the beautiful spire which we saw at Saint-Pierre-sur-Dives. "Postremo per totam fere Normanniam longe lateque convaluit ac loca per singula Matri misericordiae dicta praecipue occupavit." [8] The movement affected especially the places devoted to Mary, but ran through all Normandy, far and wide. Of all Mary's miracles, the best attested, next to the preservation of her church, is the building of it; not so much because it surprises us as because it surprised even more the people of the time and the men who were its instruments. Such deep popular movements are always surprising, and at Chartres the miracle seems to have occurred three times, coinciding more or less with the dates of the crusades, and taking the organization of a crusade, as Archbishop Hugo of Rouen described it in a letter to Bishop Thierry of Amiens. The most interesting part of this letter is the evident astonishment of the writer, who might be talking to us today, so modern is he:

> The inhabitants of Chartres have combined to aid in the construction of their church by transporting the materials; our Lord has rewarded their humble zeal by miracles which have roused the Normans to imitate the piety of their neighbours. . . . Since then the faithful of our diocese and of other neighbouring regions have formed associations for the same object; they admit no one into their company unless he has been to confession, has renounced enmities and revenges, and has reconciled himself with his enemies. That done, they elect a chief, under whose direction they conduct their waggons in silence and with humility.

21 The quarries at Berchhéres-l'Evêque are about five miles from Chartres. The stone is excessively hard, and was cut in blocks of considerable

[7] The observance of this holy rite as begun at Chartres cathedral.—*Ed.*

[8] Afterwards it spread far and wide throughout Normandy and particularly affected those places dedicated to the mercy of Mary.—*Ed.*

size, as you can see for yourselves; blocks which required great effort to transport and lay in place. The work was done with feverish rapidity, as it still shows, but it is the solidest building of the age, and without a sign of weakness yet. The Abbot told, with more surprise than pride, of the spirit which was built into the cathedral with the stone:

> Who has ever seen!—Who has ever heard tell, in times past, that powerful princes of the world, that men brought up in honour and in wealth, that nobles, men and women, have bent their proud and haughty necks to the harness of carts, and that, like beasts of burden, they have dragged to the abode of Christ these waggons, loaded with wines, grains, oil, stone, wood, and all that is necessary for the wants of life, or for the construction of the church? But while they draw these burdens, there is one thing admirable to observe; it is that often when a thousand persons and more are attached to the chariots—so great is the difficulty—yet they march in such silence that not a murmur is heard, and truly if one did not see the thing with one's eyes, one might believe that among such a multitude there was hardly a person present. When they halt on the road, nothing is heard but the confession of sins, and pure and suppliant prayer to God to obtain pardon. At the voice of the priests who exhort their hearts to peace, they forget all hatred, discord is thrown far aside, debts are remitted, the unity of hearts is established.
>
> But if any one is so far advanced in evil as to be unwilling to pardon an offender, or if he rejects the counsel of the priest who has piously advised him, his offering is instantly thrown from the waggon as impure, and he himself ignominiously and shamefully excluded from the society of the holy. There one sees the priests who preside over each chariot exhort every one to penitence, to confession of faults, to the resolution of better life! There one sees old people, young people, little children, calling on the Lord with a suppliant voice, and uttering to Him, from the depth of the heart, sobs and sighs with words of glory and praise! After the people, warned by the sound of trumpets and the sight of banners, have resumed their road, the march is made with such ease that no obstacle can retard it. . . . When they have reached the church they arrange the waggons about it like a spiritual camp, and during the whole night they celebrate the watch by hymns and canticles. On each waggon they light tapers and lamps; they place there the infirm and sick, and bring them the precious relics of the Saints for their relief. Afterwards the priests and clerics close the ceremony by processions which the people follow with devout heart, imploring the clemency of the Lord and of his Blessed Mother for the recovery of the sick.

22 Of course, the Virgin was actually and constantly present during all this labour, and gave her assistance to it, but you would get no light on the architecture from listening to an account of her miracles, nor do they heighten the effect of popular faith. Without the conviction of her personal presence, men would not have been inspired; but, to us, it is rather

the inspiration of the art which proves the Virgin's presence, and we can better see the conviction of it in the work than in the words. Every day, as the work went on, the Virgin was present, directing the architects, and it is in this direction that we are going to study, if you have now got a realizing sense of what it meant. Without this sense, the church is dead. Most persons of a deeply religious nature would tell you emphatically that nine churches out of ten actually were dead-born, after the thirteenth century, and that church architecture became a pure matter of mechanism and mathematics; but that is a question for you to decide when you come to it; and the pleasure consists not in seeing the death, but in feeling the life.

23 Now let us look about!

STUDY GUIDE

Theme and Structure

1. In the introductory note on Henry Adams, his biographer, Ernest Samuels, was quoted as saying that "the Virgin of his creation is undoubtedly one of the remarkable heroines of literature." Show how she is made the heroine of Chartres Cathedral in this passage.

2. Write a paragraph that you develop by multiple examples from the text, showing how each successive topic in this passage is presented from the Virgin's point of view and is somehow related to her.

3. What are the methods of paragraph development employed by Adams in paragraphs 3 and 4?

4. Write out the first sentence of paragraph 2 in *sense lines* to show how Adams has used parallel structure to good effect there. Find other sentences exemplifying effective parallelism in the essay and write them out in sense lines.

Clifton Fadiman (1904–)

Clifton Fadiman first became known to a large audience for his radio program "Information, Please!" But he has been a steady contributor of articles to magazines and newspapers since he was twenty. Fadiman was the book editor of *The New Yorker* from 1933 to 1943. He writes a regular column for *Holiday* magazine and is a member of the selection committee for the Book-of-the-Month Club. Readers have come to know him well for his intelligent and sensitive book reviews. His writings and his appearances on radio and television have given Fadiman a reputation for a sophisticated sense of humor. That quality is well illustrated in the following essay.

TRIBUTE TO THE CIGAR

Clifton Fadiman

1 This essay really began some years ago in a Pennsylvania Railroad dining car. It was inspired by a meal entirely up to the Pennsylvania's usual standard. Every pressure of the fork produced from the cheese omelet a mysterious gray whey. The potatoes were less mashed than crestfallen. Over the vivid peas and carrots I swear there glimmered a sign: DON'T EAT ME. The apple pie, thoughtfully placed on a dish too small for it, consisted of half an ancient apple, quartered and thrust into a coffin of unabashed dough. The milk had been carefully warmed to galley temperature. I ordered a liqueur. Its mineral oil content was generous. A wine fly appeared, fell into it, sensibly expired: doubtless a gourmet. I finished the meal. And nearly vice versa.

2 Then I remembered. Waving aside the luciferous steward (all dining-car stewards must pass a short course in how to light a cigar improperly), I opened my cigar case. Five puffs, and life again held out its rosy arms. Paradisal contrast: the integrity of fine tobacco erased from my mind the degeneracy of the railroad cuisine. I contemplated Mr. Upmann's slim brunettes; selected one; and, as with the Ancient Mariner,

> A spring of love gushed from my heart,
> And I blessed them unaware.

There and then I vowed that some day, using the poor currency of words, I would try to repay my debt to what Thackeray has called "a kind companion, a gentle stimulant, an amiable anodyne, a cementer of friendship."

3 Let me make my position clear. With respect to cigars I stand far to the right of Louis XIV. Class distinctions must be observed. At the bottom one finds the ordinary American commercial cigar. This may be made of domestic leaf (sometimes with a Havana wrapper); or of cheap Cuban tobacco; or may be variously blended. Some of these cigars are honest commoners. Others represent a sinister underworld, bringing to mind the box of cigars Robert Burdette, a forgotten American humorist, won on an election bet. After lighting a sample, he pointed it at a dog. The dog turned to stone.

4 Above the proletariat stands the bourgeoisie, middle-class cigars with acceptable but hardly complex virtues of their own. I have enjoyed some from Holland, from Jamaica and lately from the Canary Islands, where the

Reprinted from *Holiday* (September 1962).

temporarily exiled makers of the Upmann and Monte Cristo brands are offering Don Miguels in the, to my taste, superior dark English Market Selection wrappers. These latter, as I understand it, are grown from the best Havana seed. Unfortunately the decisive factor seems to be less the seed than the soil in which the plant is nourished.

5 Finally there are the true aristocrats rolled in Havana from leaf grown exclusively within the twenty-five square miles of Cuba known as the Vuelta Abajo. Expensive, subtle, magisterial, they are to the common "smoke" as a perfect Latour is to a gross Algerian wine. When I speak of cigars I mean only these—the Upmanns, the Por Larrañagas, the Ramón Allones, the Monte Cristos, the Hoyo de Monterreys, the Partagás and a few others.

6 Should the intolerable Castro continue to be tolerated by his gulled people, such cigars will gradually disappear from the American market. One will have to travel to Europe or Canada to smoke them. The consequence will be a slow degeneration of taste. In the end our taste buds will have forgotten what a good cigar is. Then technology will doubtless step in with a synthetic triumph. Perhaps cigars will be made, like Captain Nemo's in *20,000 Leagues Under the Sea,* from nicotine-rich seaweed. "Man and cigars," wrote James Russell Lowell, "decline together."

7 But let us puff away such gloomy thoughts. For the moment it is still possible to smoke well. And this year particularly should be one of unrestrained celebration, indeed of tobacchanalia, for, by a happy accident of chronology, it marks the two hundredth birthday of the cigar in the United States. It was in 1762 that Gen. Israel Putnam returned to the Massachusetts Bay Colony from a British campaign in Cuba, accompanied by three donkeys laden with Havanas. If Old King Cole is properly the saint of pipe smokers, Old Put would seem to be the patron saint of cigar smokers in our native land. A deep reverence to him and his trio of beautifully burdened asses.

8 Now for my credo. A good cigar being a spiritual affair, to light one is to produce an interior illumination. Following this credo, herewith a fancy theory. In neolithic days our brutish ancestors doubtless discovered that a club was a comforting thing to carry around even during intervals of nonuse. Ever since, the male of the species—for this would appear to be a more or less sex-linked characteristic—has derived an illogical pleasure from the habitual idle manipulation of some inanimate object: a penknife, a stick, a cane, a quizzing glass, prayer beads, even a jingling ring of keys or a few coins. Theodore Dreiser kept knotting and pulling away at a large silk handkerchief. The ashplant was part of Stephen Dedalus.

9 I am aware of the Freudian explanation. I prefer one no less airily unprovable. I believe that the male's addiction to these handleable pieces of

inorganic matter stems from his desire to mitigate a feeling that he is alone in the world. His stick is not only an extension of himself, it is a kind of other self.

10 Now, far subtler than the stick and vastly more satisfying for the purpose is the cigar. As for the smoke of democracy, the cigarette, I view it as a kind of machine, quite proper to an age of neurosis, speed and efficiency. The cigar is an agent of spiritual deceleration, whereas the cigarette, whose main attraction lies in its almost instantaneous combustibility, functions as the appropriate recreation of technological man (and woman). To list it among genuinely human pleasures, as Oscar Wilde did, seems at least questionable. As for the pipe, I hold it in theoretical esteem, but confess that it is not sib to my temperament. I might strengthen my position by invoking the authority of Lord Byron, who in his poem *The Island* thus praises tobacco:

> Divine in hookas, glorious in a pipe,
> When tipp'd with amber, mellow, rich, and ripe;
> Like other charmers, wooing the caress
> More dazzlingly when daring in full dress;
> Yet thy true lovers more admire by far
> Thy naked beauties—Give me a cigar!

11 My favored naked beauty (though it is getting harder to come by) is a long, thin panatela called Upmann 240. As I am, alas, neither long nor thin, my preference for the shape must be compensatory. Borrowing in fancy my cigar's physical charms I feel a brief attenuation and etheralization. (The great Churchill, a short man, smokes cigars that are enormous, in fact cigargantuan.)

12 Back to my theory. In the course of the many years that I have spent in the practice of one-Upmanship, my cigar has developed talismanic powers. Of these the most useful is its capacity to blunt, to deaden my sorrowful sense that, no matter what John Donne says, I am an island. Cigar in hand, I become one of a fellowship.

13 You say that I am using my cigar, as others do candy, for consolation? Granted. I need consolation, I insist on having consolation and I am made uneasy by men so formed that they can do without consolation. There *are* some able to live exclusively off the fat of their own souls, and they are usually non-smokers. Bernard Shaw's real social life was passed among ideas, and he was a fanatical hater of cigars. And Thoreau: how natural for a professional hermit to speak of "the barrooms of Massachusetts, where the full-grown are not weaned from savage and filthy habits—still sucking a cigar." One is not surprised to find men with towering egos—Goethe, Ruskin,

Hitler—anti-cigar. On the other hand, one of the fine characters in history, Robert E. Lee, never smoked. Still, it was Grant who won the war.[1]

14 Yes, I am weak. I need my cigar. To select an elegant dark prince from a box housing, unlike Pandora's, no evils; to V-clip his head tenderly; to release his imprisoned aromatic virtues with the aid of a careful match —never the monstrous lighter; to use each of his twenty minutes of life to pleasure my fingers, eyes, nose, lips, taste buds: these ritual gestures, unstaleable by repetition, act as protective devices; magical stratagems of de-isolation. Like any savage, I lapse into animism: a roll of dead weeds becomes a kind of living thing, an ever-recognizable, reliable, sympathetic companion. Though his conversation be but blue-gray smoke, how light it is, how airy, how well-bred. Few though my fancies, without him they would be fewer still. I draw him in, he draws me out.

> When men are calling names and making faces,
> And all the world's ajangle and ajar,
> I meditate on interstellar spaces
> And smoke a mild seegar.

15 So in happier days wrote Bert Leston Taylor. And for over four hundred years men of intellect have been of his persuasion. Indeed, when I consider what a quantity of noble thought was actually generated in the era preceding the mid-16th Century, when tobacco was introduced into Europe, I am lost in amazement.

16 True, there have been some anti-cigar men notable for their brains. I have already cited those self-mortifiers, Shaw and Thoreau; and I cannot conceive Gandhi with a cheroot. There was Balzac, who drank ten thousand cups of coffee and died of them, but who was once made drunk by a single cigar. There was Horace Greeley with his testy description of a cigar as having "a fire at one end and a fool at the other."

17 Think, however, of the contrary evidence. Who can tell how much of *Huckleberry Finn* was traced by the lighted end of Mark Twain's cigar, how much of his humor came out of his humidor? A *harem of dusky beauties, fifty tied in a string,* inspired Kipling's *The Betrothed,* that classic paean to his beloved Larrañagas and Henry Clays. Although as matters have turned out, I wish he had been compelled to smoke cigarettes, it remains an historical fact that without a cigar Karl Marx could not think. Among our Pres-

[1] I admit that the logic of this argument is on a par with that of the Cuban National Commission for the Propaganda and Defense of Havana Tobacco, which notes triumphantly that since the discovery of the tobacco plant the span of human life has doubled.

idents, which possessed the most philosophical intellect? John Quincy Adams. What did he smoke? Cigars. Ten cigars per day was the ration of the great Finnish composer Sibelius. The electrical wizard Charles Proteus Steinmetz, starting work for General Electric and finding in his office a NO SMOKING sign, left a note reading, "No Smoking—No Steinmetz." (He smoked, I regret to say, proletarian cigars.)

18 I could extend this list indefinitely—Byron, Thomas Hood, Thackeray, the newspaper genius E. W. Scripps with his touching last words, "Too many cigars this evening, I guess." Should such shining intellects fail to impress, I offer you and the John Birch Society John L. Sullivan's splendid utterance, "An American ought to smoke cigars." And, if you still remain unconvinced, allow me to state that the very composition of these profound reflections was aided by the decomposition of forty-seven cigars.

19 The cigar, however, is not merely the adjunct of solitary meditation. It is a social lubricant. The Chinese call tobacco "the herb of amiability," and of this herb surely the cigar represents the most refined form.[2] No conversation, unless among the mentally retarded, could ever base itself on preferences in cigarettes. One might as well discuss preferences in four-cent stamps.

20 But cigars are so varied and multiform, so subtle an extension of the smoker's personality, that they become, shall we say, of consuming interest, and constitute a natural foundation for good talk. When one cigar smoker encounters another, he feels a slight but marked sense of fraternity. There comes to mind the remark of Sydney Smith, the early 19th Century clergyman and wit: "Madam, I have been looking for a person who disliked gravy all my life; let us swear eternal friendship."

21 And then one recalls the most moving tribute ever paid to the cigar's power to advance the brotherhood of man, G. K. Chesterton's "Dedication" to his life-long friend, E. C. Bentley:

> He was, through boyhood's storm and shower,
> My best, my dearest friend;
> We wore one hat, smoked one cigar
> One standing at each end.

22 But when two men, their cigar cases wistfully nestling in their pockets, are warned by their dinner-party hostess that only cigarettes are licit,

[2] Just as chewing tobacco represents its coarsest. In this connection I invite the reader's attention to the remarkable phrasing of a sentence drawn from a 1918 decision of the Supreme Court of Mississippi: "We can imagine no reason why, with ordinary care, human toes couldn't be left out of chewing tobacco, and if toes are found in chewing tobacco, it seems to us that somebody has been very careless."

they can do nothing beyond sharing each other's mute misery. Hence the dying out of the postprandial separation of the sexes is a body blow to cigar smokers, as well as to conversation in general. All of which brings us to the question of cigars versus the fair sex. Shall we join the ladies?

23 I have before me the answers to a questionnaire about cigars filled out by a sampling of young businesswomen. No doubt about it: almost all the interviewees disliked cigars. Reasons: (1) the odor itself; (2) the odor's clinging affection for furnishings and draperies; (3) the unpleasantness of chewed cigar ends, whether framed by mouth or ash tray; (4) the unattractive look of men busy smoking cigars. To the question, *Does your boy friend smoke cigars?* most answered: *No, thank God.* (One young lady replied: *Wish I had a boy friend.*)

24 The female indictment admittedly has a certain justice. Adherence by cigar smokers to a code of etiquette can blunt its edge, but probably not completely dispose of it. We should of course never chew a cigar but handle it as elegantly as we can; dispose of stubs at once, via a discreet toilet flush; and (quite impractical, but really the heart of the matter) smoke only good, that is, expensive cigars.

25 Vance Packard in *The Hidden Persuaders* cites the findings of a Chicago advertising agency to the effect that men *like* to smoke cigars in front of women *because* it is objectionable, as an aggressive assertion of their masculinity. To which I would reply, as Sir Winston Churchill did to a suggestion that displeased him, "The answer is in the plural and they bounce."

26 I place no more faith in the notion that cigars are a virility symbol than I do in the equally half-baked idea that cigar-smoking is an adult substitute for thumb-sucking. Cigars would be smoked if men had no thumbs, and you may quote me similarly with respect to the virility theory.

27 The only truly effective solution of the problem of female antagonism is for the ladies themselves to turn to cigar-smoking. This I strongly favor even if it should be demonstrated that no link exists binding cigarette-smoking to cancer. There is nothing intrinsically absurd about the idea. Much (though, as I admit, not all) feminine resistance stems from traditional social myths, such as the notion that cigars go with crooked politicians, bloated capitalists, fat men and vulgarians (T. S. Eliot's "Bleistein with a cigar"). Some of the dislike, I believe, turns on unconscious sexual jealousy, for a cigar (unlike a cigarette) is, as I have said, a beloved companion, and therefore cigar-smoking is to a degree a form of visible adultery. (Does this explain why many women who reluctantly tolerate a cigar in the drawing room ban it fiercely from the bedroom? Probably not.)

28 All these resistances would disappear if women could be induced to smoke cigars. They do and have long done so in many non-Anglo-Saxon

countries, and even in Nordic lands, such as Denmark. As a matter of fact, during the heyday of the cigar in England, say from 1815 to 1850, many ladies were devotees of small cigars called Queens. I admit, however, that the preponderance of Victorian female opposition was so crushing that husbands would stealthily crouch in the fireplace, like guilty criminals, and exhale up the chimney. There is a pathetic record of Dickens smoking a cigar "after dinner when I am alone."

29 Still, women of the most impeccable background have been confirmed cigar smokers. In his delightful *Sublime Tobacco* Compton Mackenzie tells us that the first woman he ever saw smoking a cigar (this would have been around 1907) was Mrs. Bernard Berenson. The wife of the great art scholar was not only the sister of the elegant Logan Pearsall Smith but also a Quakeress. One cannot demand more respectability than that. During part of the 19th Century the head of English aristocratic society in Florence was Lady Orford, who chain-smoked black cigars during her weekly salon, from ten at night to four in the morning. Then there is always Amy Lowell, whose antecedents cannot be faulted. One of the most agreeable sights I have ever witnessed was that of the beautiful and distinguished actress, Leueen MacGrath, gracefully puffing away on a full Havana. Perhaps we can start the ball rolling by persuading Mrs. Kennedy to join her cigar-smoking husband. After all, Mrs. Andrew Jackson and Mrs. Zachary Taylor both smoked pipes.

30 What we need from the ladies is a more sensitive feeling for the poetry, even the romance of cigar smoke. It is in Chapter 23 of *Jane Eyre* that the heroine, pacing the garden of Mr. Rochester's house at dusk, recognizes "a subtle, well-known scent—that of a cigar." She steals into the orchard, but Mr. Rochester has followed her, for to the evening scents of sweet-briar and jasmine and other shrubs and flowers is added still another. "I know it well—it is Mr. Rochester's cigar." There, ladies, you have the proper attitude.

31 I realize that I have not even begun to pay just tribute to the cigar on its bicentennial birthday. I have not mentioned the post-breakfast cigar, which starts the day with joy and serenity. Or the utility of the cigar on a long, solitary motor trip, when the continued lighting of pipe or cigarette is always an irritation. Or the perfect correspondence between cigar-smoking and book-reading. I have not even told you that cigar ashes, mixed with camphorated chalk, will make a good tooth powder—but then, few people care for the taste of camphorated chalk. Nor have I stressed the harmlessness, the safety of cigar-smoking. We do have one record of a cigar setting alight the beard of a patriarchal Jew and causing his death by suffocation. He was, however, 109 years of age at the time of conflagration.

32 Finally, should this imperfect vindication of the cigar appear to need

bolstering by a higher authority, I refer you to Marc Connelly's reverent *The Green Pastures*, where De Lawd makes his stage entry smoking a large, a black, a fragrant, a transcendental cigar.

STUDY GUIDE

Theme, Structure, and Tone

1. The tone of this essay is lightly humorous. All humor is based on incongruity. Part of the incongruity here consists in the structure of the essay. It is built partly as a *defense* or *vindication* of the cigar against its detractors (see the statement in the last paragraph) but mostly as a *laudatory tribute* to the cigar on the occasion of its two hundredth birthday in the United States. Show how these two elements enter into the structure of the essay and how they create something of a mock-serious tone.

2. The humorous tone is set in the very first paragraph in the description of the dining-car meal. Point out details of this description that create this tone. But the humor of the first paragraph is more pointed and critical than that of the rest of the essay. Why does the author begin with this more negative type of humorous situation?

3. Show where the author has used methods of proof ordinarily found in serious orations of defense or laudatory speeches: multiple concrete examples that build into a kind of inductive proof, citation of authorities, contrasts, and so on.

4. What special aspect of cigar smoking is developed in paragraphs 23–30?

5. What method of rhetorical development is employed in paragraphs 28 and 29?

Ronald Knox (1888–1957)

Ronald Knox had much in common with Newman. He was the son of the Anglican Bishop of Manchester, attended Eton and Oxford University, received Anglican orders, and was converted to Catholicism in 1917. He was made Catholic chaplain at Oxford in 1925, a post from which he retired in 1939 to begin a new translation of the Vulgate. His translation is one of the most readable of the modern versions of Scripture. Knox contributed voluminously to many magazines all though his life, and many of these articles were later published as collections of essays. His essays are remarkable for their urbanity, exuberance, and light-hearted satire—all qualities evident in the essay on "The Stupidity of Animals."

THE STUPIDITY OF ANIMALS

Ronald Knox

1 There was a letter the other day in one of these morning papers under the title "Do dogs dream?" It was a very brief communication, and I judged (from all my experience of people who have the itch for epistolography) that it must have been an excerpt from a much longer document. Possibly the writer would have made his meaning clearer if he had been allowed more space; one can only guess.

2 The problem whether dogs dream might be the subject of endless controversy, because for practical purposes they never wake. They never come down to breakfast and tell us what they have been dreaming about. A psychoanalyst might say that dogs dream, because he is quite prepared to tell you that you have been dreaming when you know perfectly well that you haven't. But we others can only say that dogs when they are asleep sometimes go through the same motions as people go through in their sleep and then tell us when they wake up that they have been dreaming (that sentence takes some parsing), and that's all there is to it. "Hunting in his sleep," we say, but how do we know it is not a matter of digestion?

3 Be that as it may, this epistolographer went one better by asserting that this dog laughed in his sleep. Just like that. It may have been one of these humorists who try it on to see whether they can catch the sub-editor napping. I am afraid it is far more likely to have been a genuine case of dogmania. There was no note put in to explain whether this dog was in the habit of laughing during its waking moments, and there was no accompanying portrait to show how the dog did it. How does a dog laugh? According to King David, it is possible to grin like a dog, but that only means that when a man grins he shows his teeth like a dog. I have seen a dog show his teeth, but it never suggested to me that the dog was amused: the laughter, if laughter it was, was not infectious. Who does not know that the best-drawn animals cease to look like animals at all the moment they are represented as laughing? Well, there is the hyena, and there is the laughing jackass. But is the hyena really amused? It is terrible to think what a lot of funny thoughts must pass through its mind, all unbidden by outward circumstances, only to be lost to posterity.

4 Mr. Chesterton's new book, "The Everlasting Man," has some excellent thoughts on the absoluteness of the difference between animals and

From Ronald Knox, *An Open-air Pulpit* (London: Constable & Company, 1926), pp. 101–106. Reprinted by permission of A. P. Watt & Son, trustees for the Estate of Ronald Knox.

men. Undeterred by the hyena, he claims laughter as one of man's characteristic privileges. The difference, he says, between a man and a monkey is not that a man draws better than a monkey, but that a man does draw, however badly, whereas a monkey does not draw at all. Again one might distinguish; a monkey does draw, no doubt, if it imitates a man drawing, but it does not notice whether its pencil has a lead in or not; and if anything emerges from the process, it is doubtful if even a futurist critic would be able to praise it as a work of genius.

5 Humor and art are extreme instances of the difference, since each springs essentially from the reflective principle in man. The old-fashioned philosophers put the thing more simply by saying that man has intelligence and the brutes have not. And that is, of course, the assumption which underlies all the good animal books which have ever been written, from the Batracho-myomachia to Uncle Remus and "the Wind in the Willows." It is funny to make animals talk and think only because we know that as a matter of fact they don't talk and don't think.

6 Perhaps they are right not to. There is a great deal to be said for not talking; and, to judge by the quotations Dr. Sheen has collected in his new book, "God and Intelligence," the philosophers nowadays are coming to the conclusion that it is rather a mistake to think. "For my part," wrote William James, "I have found myself compelled to give up logic." Why such philosophers are allowed to keep their chairs it is hard to understand; it is as if a doctor should turn Christian Scientist. But, granted that the intellect is on the whole a thing to be discouraged, it still does divide us from the beasts. We have not yet managed to live it down altogether. Strap-hanging has not yet quite reduced us to that life of mere prehensility which would make us one with our putative ancestors at the Zoo; we have not quite acquired the happy disposition of the jackass, which can laugh when there is no joke at all. This degrading handicap, intelligence, still distinguishes the sons of men.

7 The beasts haven't got it, and we know they haven't got it; no need to discuss here whether they are the better or the worse off. I have thought sometimes that dogs are sorry they have no souls and cats are glad they have no souls. Or, rather, I have said it, but I have not thought it; obviously it is nonsense. What is so baffling is that people will go on telling you stories about their dogs and cats which conclusively prove that their dogs and cats possess intelligence without seeming to see that in that case the whole of our views of life must be entirely revised. If a dog has intelligence, presumably it has a soul, and, if it has a soul, are we not committing murder when we shoot it in its old age? If a dog really "understands every word you say," are you always careful to turn it out of the room before one of these smoking-room stories is told? If a dog is really "the best friend you have," why don't you let it kill the chickens? Until the philosophers have succeeded in providing us with a cheap substitute for intelligence, may we not

as well use our intelligence when we talk about animals, and get rid of all this metaphorical nonsense?

8 No; don't write to me and deluge me with stories of calculating horses and learned pigs, and the tricks monkeys have been taught to do in the music-halls. Anybody can tell those stories. I myself once gave, by mistake, a bent coin to the elephant to put into the cent machine. When nothing happened the elephant first patted the machine in the stomach with its trunk, and then, with a still better inspiration, curled up its trunk and blew down the slot. I have often told this story and always been called a liar, so that I am beginning to doubt it myself, but I know that it really happened. In any case, it is no more extraordinary than plenty of things which do happen. Anyhow, it is my story, and I refuse to admit that the elephant in my story showed intelligence. It didn't think to itself, "Let us see, what will be the best way of preventing this young gentleman feeling that he has been defrauded? Perhaps the machine wants oiling and is working badly; let us see whether a little pressure will have a good effect." What it did show was sagacity—an uncanny instinct for doing what looked like the right thing.

9 The *sagacity* of animals is extraordinary, but it is something quite different from intelligence. A pigeon can find its way home to a place from which it has been transported in a basket; put an intelligent aviator in a basket and see whether he can find his way home without directions. A Welsh collie can do the most amazing feats in rounding up sheep, but not by intelligence; if intelligence were the quality needed, a Welsh collier would be able to do it still better. Animal sagacity is far more like that extraordinary aplomb which sometimes inspires the acrobatic feats of the hopelessly drunk: a sort of instinct which comes from nowhere—you might even guess that it comes from not being burdened with an intelligence.

10 What I want to do is to make a collection of stories which illustrate the stupidity of animals. Look at the dog which goes on barking its teeth out at you as long as it is chained up, even when you are walking with its owner, and then comes up and licks your hand the moment its chain is slipped! Obviously, it has not begun on the path of intelligence, for it has not learned to make any distinction between subject and object. If it had ceased to regard me as an enemy when I took off my dog-collar, it might have been anticlericalism. But ceasing to regard *me* as an enemy because *it* has not a collar on is sheer absence of the intellectual faculty. Look at the way a bird goes on flying with its nose against the window, and apparently expecting that sooner or later it will get out! That is not mere defect of sight; a man restrained by a totally invisible obstacle would draw back and take a kick at it; the bird, being unable to perceive the glass, is equally unable to conceive it. I wish one of these daily papers would offer a prize for the best stories of animal unintelligence.

11 I am sorry to have wasted so much time over the obvious but why

will people refuse to see that it is obvious? Why will everybody assert that his dog has an intellect, still more her dog, without noticing the anomaly that no other animal has?

STUDY GUIDE

Word Study

1. The author has invented the following two words: "epistolographer" and "dogmania" (paragraph 3), which mean "letter writer" and "dog-madness." What kind of person is connoted by the invented terms which the equivalents given above do not suggest? How does the idea of an "itch" for epistolography (paragraph 1) intensify the connotation of epistolography?

2. Look up the exact meaning of the following terms: *prehensility* and *putative* (paragraph 6); *collier* and *aplomb* (paragraph 9); and *anomaly* (paragraph 11).

3. A. With the help of your dictionary distinguish among *sagacity, instinct,* and *intelligence* (paragraph 9).

B. Does the author use any of the dictionary meanings of the word *sagacity*? Does he tell us what he means by the term?

4. What is the distinction the author is making between *perceive* and *conceive* paragraph 10, sentence 7? Why do animals perceive but not conceive an object?

Subject Matter, Theme, and Tone

Both the subject matter and theme of this essay are stated in the title. The author is talking about animals and saying that they are stupid, which is the same as saying that they have no intelligence.

1. What does the author say prompted him to write this essay? Similar items are constantly appearing in our newspapers and magazines. Find some.

2. What two fundamental points about animals does Knox emphasize in the essay to remind his readers of the unintelligence of animals?

3. This essay is *satirical.* The author wants to point up the essential nonsense of talking about the intelligence of animals. He reminds us that our common sense tells us that it is really ridiculous to talk about animals thinking or laughing or dreaming or doing any of the things that are specifically human. Beast fables and Walt Disney movies are always funny precisely because we recognize the incongruity of representing animals as thinking and talking.

In this essay Knox makes statements that call attention to our instinctive recognition of the *incongruity* of thinking about animals as intelligent. Show how the following statements make readers see this incongruity: paragraph 2, sentences 1 and 2; paragraph 3, sentences 5–9; paragraph 4, sentences 3 and 4; and paragraph 7, sentences 5–8.

4. One of the most artistic and effective instruments of good satire is *irony*. Irony is a tongue-in-cheek statement in which you say the exact opposite of what you mean. It is easy enough to detect irony in oral discourse because the tone of the voice can reveal the fact that the speaker means the opposite of what he is saying. To detect irony in the written word is more difficult and therefore a good test of intelligence. Context and the intention of the whole

passage must tell you the real meaning of an ironic statement. Pick out all the ironic statements in paragraph 6, sentences 5–8, and explain what the author means by them.

5. Besides irony of statement, there is such a thing as *irony of situation,* in which the actual situation is the opposite of what is demanded in the circumstances. For example, it would be an ironic situation for a doctor accidentally to kill the patient whose life he is endeavoring to save.

What is ironic (paragraph 6, sentences 2–4) in the situation of a philosopher concluding that it is a mistake to think and of a doctor becoming a Christian Scientist?

Edwyn Brooks White (1899–)

Like Addison, E. B. White has been something of a spectator of life, looking on from a distance and commenting on what he sees in a gently ironic and satiric manner. For more than a decade he wrote "The Talk of the Town" in *The New Yorker,* and he still writes the column "One Man's Meat" in *Harper's Magazine.* For many years White has lived in retirement on a farm in Brooklin, Maine, where he combines farm work and writing. There is a down-to-earth quality in his writing that probably derives in part from his closeness to nature and rural life. His style is highly personal, always lightly humorous and ironic but never bitterly satiric. Perhaps better than any other modern writer, White embodies the spirit of the informal eassy that derives from Addison and Lamb.

DEATH OF A PIG

E. B. White

1 I spent several days and nights in mid-September with an ailing pig and I feel driven to account for this stretch of time, more particularly since the pig died at last, and I lived, and things might easily have gone the other way round and none left to do the accounting. Even now, so close to the event, I cannot recall the hours sharply and am not ready to say whether

death came on the third night or the fourth night. This uncertainty afflicts me with a sense of personal deterioration; if I were in decent health I would know how many nights I had sat up with a pig.

2 The scheme of buying a spring pig in blossomtime, feeding it through summer and fall, and butchering it when the solid cold weather arrives, is a familiar scheme to me and follows an antique pattern. It is a tragedy enacted on most farms with perfect fidelity to the original script. The murder, being premeditated, is in the first degree but is quick and skillful, and the smoked bacon and ham provide a ceremonial ending whose fitness is seldom questioned.

3 Once in a while something slips—one of the actors goes up in his lines and the whole performance stumbles and halts. My pig simply failed to show up for a meal. The alarm spread rapidly. The classic outline of the tragedy was lost. I found myself cast suddenly in the role of pig's friend and physician—a farcical character with an enema bag for a prop. I had a presentiment, the very first afternoon, that the play would never regain its balance and that my sympathies were now wholly with the pig. This was slapstick—the sort of dramatic treatment that instantly appealed to my old dachshund, Fred, who joined the vigil, held the bag, and, when all was over, presided at the interment. When we slid the body into the grave, we both were shaken to the core. The loss we felt was not the loss of ham but the loss of pig. He had evidently become precious to me, not that he represented a distant nourishment in a hungry time, but that he had suffered in a suffering world. But I'm running ahead of my story and shall have to go back.

4 My pigpen is at the bottom of an old orchard below the house. The pigs I have raised have lived in a faded building that once was an icehouse. There is a pleasant yard to move about in, shaded by an apple tree that overhangs the low rail fence. A pig couldn't ask for anything better—or none has, at any rate. The sawdust in the icehouse makes a comfortable bottom in which to root, and a warm bed. This sawdust, however, came under suspicion when the pig took sick. One of my neighbors said he thought the pig would have done better on new ground—the same principle that applies in planting potatoes. He said there might be something unhealthy about that sawdust, that he never thought well of sawdust.

5 It was about four o'clock in the afternoon when I first noticed that there was something wrong with the pig. He failed to appear at the trough for his supper, and when a pig (or a child) refuses supper a chill wave of fear runs through any household, or ice-household. After examining my pig, who was stretched out in the sawdust inside the building, I went to the phone and cranked it four times. Mr. Dameron answered. "What's good for a sick pig?" I asked. (There is never any identification needed on a country phone; the person on the other end knows who is talking by the sound of the voice and by the character of the question.)

6 "I don't know, I never had a sick pig," said Mr. Dameron, "but I can find out quick enough. You hang up and I'll call Henry."

7 Mr. Dameron was back on the line again in five minutes. "Henry says roll him over on his back and give him two ounces of castor oil or sweet oil, and if that doesn't do the trick give him an injection of soapy water. He says he's almost sure the pig's plugged up, and even if he's wrong, it can't do any harm."

8 I thanked Mr. Dameron. I didn't go right down to the pig, though. I sank into a chair and sat still for a few minutes to think about my troubles, and then I got up and went to the barn, catching up on some odds and ends that needed tending to. Unconsciously I held off, for an hour, the deed by which I would officially recognize the collapse of the performance of raising a pig; I wanted no interruption in the regularity of feeding, the steadiness of growth, the even succession of days. I wanted no interruption, wanted no oil, no deviation. I just wanted to keep on raising a pig, full meal after full meal, spring into summer into fall. I didn't even know whether there were two ounces of castor oil on the place.

9 Shortly after five o'clock I remembered that we had been invited out to dinner that night and realized that if I were to dose a pig there was no time to lose. The dinner date seemed a familiar conflict: I move in a desultory society and often a week or two will roll by without my going to anybody's house to dinner or anyone's coming to mine, but when an occasion does arise, and I am summoned, something usually turns up (an hour or two in advance) to make all human intercourse seem vastly inappropriate. I have come to believe that there is in hostesses a special power of divination, and that they deliberately arrange dinners to coincide with pig failure or some other sort of failure. At any rate, it was after five o'clock and I knew I could put off no longer the evil hour.

10 When my son and I arrived at the pigyard, armed with a small bottle of castor oil and a length of clothesline, the pig had emerged from his house and was standing in the middle of his yard, listlessly. He gave us a slim greeting. I could see that he felt uncomfortable and uncertain. I had brought the clothesline thinking I'd have to tie him (the pig weighed more than a hundred pounds) but we never used it. My son reached down, grabbed both front legs, upset him quickly, and when he opened his mouth to scream I turned the oil into his throat—a pink, corrugated area I had never seen before. I had just time to read the label while the neck of the bottle was in his mouth. It said Puretest. The screams, slightly muffled by oil, were pitched in the hysterically high range of pig-sound, as though torture were being carried out, but they didn't last long: it was all over rather suddenly, and, his legs released, the pig righted himself.

11 In the upset position the corners of his mouth had been turned down, giving him a frowning expression. Back on his feet again, he regained

the set smile that a pig wears even in sickness. He stood his ground, sucking slightly at the residue of oil; a few drops leaked out of his lips while his wicked eyes, shaded by their coy little lashes, turned on me in disgust and hatred. I scratched him gently with oily fingers and he remained quiet, as though trying to recall the satisfaction of being scratched when in health, and seeming to rehearse in his mind the indignity to which he had just been subjected. I noticed, as I stood there, four or five small dark spots on his back near the tail end, reddish brown in color, each about the size of a housefly. I could not make out what they were. They did not look troublesome but at the same time they did not look like mere surface bruises or chafe marks. Rather they seemed blemishes of internal origin. His stiff white bristles almost completely hid them and I had to part the bristles with my fingers to get a good look.

12 Several hours later, a few minutes before midnight, having dined well and at someone else's expense, I returned to the pighouse with a flashlight. The patient was asleep. Kneeling, I felt his ears (as you might put your hand on the forehead of a child) and they seemed cool, and then with the light made a careful examination of the yard and the house for sign that the oil had worked. I found none and went to bed.

13 We had been having an unseasonable spell of weather—hot, close days, with the fog shutting in every night, scaling for a few hours in midday, then creeping back again at dark, drifting in first over the trees on the point, then suddenly blowing across the fields, blotting out the world and taking possession of houses, men, and animals. Everyone kept hoping for a break, but the break failed to come. Next day was another hot one. I visited the pig before breakfast and tried to tempt him with a little milk in his trough. He just stared at it, while I made a sucking sound through my teeth to remind him of past pleasures of the feast. With very small, timid pigs, weanlings, this ruse is often quite successful and will encourage them to eat; but with a large, sick pig the ruse is senseless and the sound I made must have made him feel, if anything, more miserable. He not only did not crave food, he felt a positive revulsion to it. I found a place under the apple tree where he had vomited in the night.

14 At this point, although a depression had settled over me, I didn't suppose that I was going to lose my pig. From the lustiness of a healthy pig a man derives a feeling of personal lustiness; the stuff that goes into the trough and is received with such enthusiasm is an earnest of some later feast of his own, and when this suddenly comes to an end and the food lies stale and untouched, souring in the sun, the pig's imbalance becomes the man's, vicariously, and life seems insecure, displaced, transitory.

15 As my own spirits declined, along with the pig's, the spirits of my vile old dachshund rose. The frequency of our trips down the footpath through the orchard to the pigyard delighted him, although he suffers greatly from

arthritis, moves with difficulty, and would be bedridden if he could find anyone willing to serve him meals on a tray.

16 He never missed a chance to visit the pig with me, and he made many professional calls on his own. You could see him down there at all hours, his white face parting the grass along the fence as he wobbled and stumbled about, his stethoscope dangling—a happy quack, writing his villainous prescriptions and grinning his corrosive grin. When the enema bag appeared, and the bucket of warm suds, his happiness was complete, and he managed to squeeze his enormous body between the two lowest rails of the yard and then assumed full charge of the irrigation. Once, when I lowered the bag to check the flow, he reached in and hurriedly drank a few mouthfuls of the suds to test their potency. I have noticed that Fred will feverishly consume any substance that is associated with trouble—the bitter flavor is to his liking. When the bag was above reach, he concentrated on the pig and was everywhere at once, a tower of strength and inconvenience. The pig, curiously enough, stood rather quietly through this colonic carnival, and the enema, though ineffective, was not as difficult as I had anticipated.

17 I discovered, though, that once having given a pig an enema there is no turning back, no chance of resuming one of life's more stereotyped roles. The pig's lot and mine were inextricably bound now, as though the rubber tube were the silver cord. From then until the time of his death I held the pig steadily in the bowl of my mind; the task of trying to deliver him from his misery became a strong obsession. His suffering soon became the embodiment of all earthly wretchedness. Along toward the end of the afternoon, defeated in physicking, I phoned the veterinary twenty miles away and placed the case formally in his hands. He was full of questions, and when I casually mentioned the dark spots on the pig's back, his voice changed its tone.

18 "I don't want to scare you," he said, "but when there are spots, erysipelas has to be considered."

19 Together we considered erysipelas, with frequent interruptions from the telephone operator, who wasn't sure the connection had been established.

20 "If a pig has erysipelas can he give it to a person?" I asked.

21 "Yes, he can," replied the vet.

22 "Have they answered?" asked the operator.

23 "Yes, they have," I said. Then I addressed the vet again. "You better come over here and examine this pig right away."

24 "I can't come myself," said the vet, "but McFarland can come this evening if that's all right. Mac knows more about pigs than I do anyway. You needn't worry too much about the spots. To indicate erysipelas they would have to be deep hemorrhagic infarcts."

25 "Deep hemorrhagic what" I asked.

26 "Infarcts," said the vet.

27 "Have they answered?" asked the operator.

28 "Well," I said, "I don't know what you'd call these spots, except they're about the size of a housefly. If the pig has erysipelas I guess I have it, too, by this time, because we've been very close lately."

29 "McFarland will be over," said the vet.

30 I hung up. My throat felt dry and I went to the cupboard and got a bottle of whiskey. Deep hemorrhagic infarcts—the phrase began fastening its hooks in my head. I had assumed that there could be nothing much wrong with a pig during the months it was being groomed for murder; my confidence in the essential health and endurance of pigs had been strong and deep, particularly in the health of pigs that belonged to me and that were part of my proud scheme. The awakening had been violent and I minded it all the more because I knew that what could be true of my pig could be true also of the rest of my tidy world. I tried to put this distasteful idea from me, but it kept recurring. I took a short drink of the whiskey and then, although I wanted to go down to the yard and look for fresh signs, I was scared to. I was certain I had erysipelas.

31 It was long after dark and the supper dishes had been put away when a car drove in and McFarland got out. He had a girl with him. I could just make her out in the darkness—she seemed young and pretty. "This is Miss Owen," he said. "We've been having a picnic supper on the shore, that's why I'm late."

32 McFarland stood in the driveway and stripped off his jacket, then his shirt. His stock arms and capable hands showed up in my flashlight's gleam as I helped him find his coverall and get zipped up. The rear seat of his car contained an astonishing amount of paraphernalia, which he soon overhauled, selecting a chain, a syringe, a bottle of oil, a rubber tube, and some other things I couldn't identify. Miss Owen said she'd go along with us and see the pig. I led the way down the warm slope of the orchard, my light picking out the path for them, and we all three climbed the fence, entered the pighouse, and squatted by the pig while McFarland took a rectal reading. My flashlight picked up the glitter of an engagement ring on the girl's hand.

33 "No elevation," said McFarland, twisting the thermometer in the light. "You needn't worry about erysipelas." He ran his hand slowly over the pig's stomach and at one point the pig cried out in pain.

34 "Poor piggledy-wiggledy!" said Miss Owen.

35 The treatment I had been giving the pig for two days was then repeated, somewhat more expertly, by the doctor, Miss Owen and I handing him things as he needed them—holding the chain that he had looped around the pig's upper jaw, holding the syringe, holding the bottle stopper,

the end of the tube, all of us working in darkness and in comfort, working with the instinctive teamwork induced by emergency conditions, the pig unprotesting, the house shadowy, protecting, intimate. I went to bed tired but with a feeling of relief that I had turned over part of the responsibility of the case to a licensed doctor. I was beginning to think, though, that the pig was not going to live.

36 He died twenty-four hours later, or it might have been forty-eight—there is a blur in time here, and I may have lost or picked up a day in the telling and the pig one in the dying. At intervals during the last day I took cool fresh water down to him and at such times as he found the strength to get to his feet he would stand with head in the pail and snuffle his snout around. He drank a few sips but no more; yet it seemed to comfort him to dip his nose in water and bobble it about, sucking in and blowing out through his teeth. Much of the time, now, he lay indoors half buried in sawdust. Once, near the last, while I was attending him I saw him try to make a bed for himself but he lacked the strength, and when he set his snout into the dust he was unable to plow even the little furrow he needed to lie down in.

37 He came out of the house to die. When I went down, before going to bed, he lay stretched in the yard a few feet from the door. I knelt, saw that he was dead, and left him there: his face had a mild look, expressive neither of deep peace nor of deep suffering, although I think he had suffered a good deal. I went back up to the house and to bed, and cried internally—deep hemorrhagic intears. I didn't wake till nearly eight the next morning, and when I looked out the open window the grave was already being dug, down beyond the dump under a wild apple. I could hear the spade strike against the small rocks that blocked the way. Never send to know for whom the grave is dug, I said to myself, it's dug for thee. Fred, I well knew, was supervising the work of digging, so I ate breakfast slowly.

38 It was a Saturday morning. The thicket in which I found the grave-diggers at work was dark and warm, the sky overcast. Here, among alders and young hackmatacks, at the foot of the apple tree, Lennie had dug a beautiful hole, five feet long, three feet wide, three feet deep. He was standing in it, removing the last spadefuls of earth while Fred patrolled the brink in simple but impressive circles, disturbing the loose earth of the mound so that it trickled back in. There had been no rain in weeks and the soil, even three feet down, was dry and powdery. As I stood and stared, an enormous earthworm which had been partially exposed by the spade at the bottom dug itself deeper and made a slow withdrawal, seeking even remoter moistures at even lonelier depths. And just as Lennie stepped out and rested his spade against the tree and lit a cigarette, a small green

apple separated itself from a branch overhead and fell into the hole. Everything about this last scene seemed overwritten—the dismal sky, the shabby woods, the imminence of rain, the worm (legendary bedfellow of the dead), the apple (conventional garnish of a pig).

39 But even so, there was a directness and dispatch about animal burial, I thought, that made it a more decent affair than human burial: there was no stopover in the undertaker's foul parlor, no wreath nor spray; and when we hitched a line to the pig's hind legs and dragged him swiftly from his yard, throwing our weight into the harness and leaving a wake of crushed grass and smoothed rubble over the dump, ours was a businesslike procession, with Fred, the dishonorable pallbearer, staggering along in the rear, his perverse bereavement showing in every seam in his face; and the post mortem performed handily and swiftly right at the edge of the grave, so that the inwards that had caused the pig's death preceded him into the ground and he lay at last resting squarely on the cause of his own undoing.

40 I threw in the first shovelful, and then we worked rapidly and without talk, until the job was complete. I picked up the rope, made it fast to Fred's collar (he is a notorious ghoul), and we all three filed back up the path to the house, Fred bringing up the rear and holding back every inch of the way, feigning unusual stiffness. I noticed that although he weighed far less than the pig, he was harder to drag, being possessed of the vital spark.

41 The news of the death of my pig travelled fast and far, and I received many expressions of sympathy from friends and neighbors, for no one took the event lightly and the premature expiration of a pig is, I soon discovered, a departure which the community marks solemnly on its calendar, a sorrow in which it feels fully involved. I have written this account in penitence and in grief, as a man who failed to raise his pig, and to explain my deviation from the classic course of so many raised pigs. The grave in the woods is unmarked, but Fred can direct the mourner to it unerringly and with immense good will, and I know he and I shall often revisit it, singly and together, in seasons of reflection and despair, on flagless memorial days of our own choosing.

STUDY GUIDE

Structure and Tone

1. The essay is constructed in two parts: paragraphs 1–3 and 4–41. In the first part White tells the whole story of the death of the pig briefly, and then in the second part he goes back and retells it at length detail by detail. The humorous tone of the essay is created in the first part by the incongruity

of talking about the life and death of a pig in *human* terms. The pig, bought in blossomtime, was, in the regular course of events, destined for a *tragic* end—a *premeditated, first-degree murder* to provide the table with smoked bacon. But in this case the *play* does not work out according to the script. An *actor* slips up, and the *performance stumbles and halts*. The writer's pig takes sick—and he finds himself *cast in the role* of the pig's friend and physician—a farcical character with an *enema bag*. He is no longer a potential murderer of the pig; his sympathies are wholly with the pig. The sympathy continues all through the illness until at the pig's demise the writer and Fred, his sympathetic dachshund, preside at the *interment*. By the end of the first part White has established the incongruity of the situation—his transformation into a nurse and physician of a pig who really cares for the pig as a pig and not potential ham.

This humorous situation established in the first three paragraphs is sustained throughout the longer second part of the essay with fewer details. Point out the details that sustain the author's incongruous situation.

2. A similar humorous effect is achieved by the incongruity of giving human traits to Fred, the dachshund, throughout the essay. Point out the details of diction by which this effect is achieved.

3. Behind the humor of the essay there are revealed some very human traits of the author and his neighbors. What are some of them? Where are they revealed in the essay?

Mary McCarthy (1912–)

Mary McCarthy has gained a reputation as a writer of both fiction and critical and informal essays. In both areas she has developed a very personal and direct style that gives her writing verve and punch. Her background, perhaps, explains some of the sharpness and ultracritical tone that sometimes marks her writings. Her parents died when she was only six years old, and she and her brothers were shifted from one set of foster parents to another among the relatives on both sides of her family. She seems to have lost her faith as a schoolgirl in Tacoma, Washington, but as in the case of James Joyce, her early acquaintance with Catholicism has made her sensitive to many things in her environment that she might otherwise have missed. Her partly Jewish background, to which she refers in the essay reproduced here, has also added to the tenseness of her human situation, but it has undoubtedly widened her sensitivities as a person. Much of the complexity of her own personal situation, as well as her superior intelligence and good common sense, is evident in "Settling the Colonel's Hash."

SETTLING THE COLONEL'S HASH

Mary McCarthy

1 Seven years ago, when I taught in a progressive college, I had a pretty girl student in one of my classes who wanted to be a short-story writer. She was not studying writing with me, but she knew that I sometimes wrote short stories, and one day, breathless and glowing, she came up to me in the hall, to tell me that she had just written a story that her writing teacher, a Mr. Converse, was terribly excited about. "He thinks it's wonderful," she said, "and he's going to help me fix it up for publication."

2 I asked what the story was about; the girl was a rather simple being who loved clothes and dates. Her answer had a deprecating tone. It was just about a girl (herself) and some sailors she had met on the train. But then her face, which looked perturbed for a moment, gladdened.

3 "Mr. Converse is going over it with me and we're going to put in the symbols."

4 Another girl in the same college, when asked by us in her sophomore orals why she read novels (one of the pseudo-profound questions that ought never to be put) answered in a defensive flurry: "Well, *of course* I don't read them to find out what happens to the hero."

5 At the time, I thought these notions were peculiar to progressive education: it was old-fashioned or regressive to read a novel to find out what happens to the hero or to have a mere experience empty of symbolic pointers. But I now discover that this attitude is quite general, and that readers and students all over the country are in a state of apprehension, lest they read a book or story literally and miss the presence of a symbol. And like everything in America, this search for meanings has become a socially competitive enterprise; the best reader is the one who detects the most symbols in a given stretch of prose. And the benighted reader who fails to find any symbols humbly assents when they are pointed out to him; he accepts his mortification.

6 I had no idea how far this process had gone until last spring, when I began to get responses to a story I had published in *Harper's*. I say "story" because that was what it was called by *Harper's*. I myself would not know quite what to call it; it was a piece of reporting or a fragment of autobiography—an account of my meeting with an anti-Semitic army colonel. It began in the club car of a train going to St. Louis; I was wearing an apple-green shirtwaist and a dark-green skirt and pink earrings; we got into an

argument about the Jews. The colonel was a rather dapper, flashy kind of Irish-American with a worldly blue eye; he took me, he said, for a sculptress, which made me feel, to my horror, that I looked Bohemian and therefore rather suspect. He was full of the usual profound clichés that anti-Semites air, like original epigrams, about the Jews: that he could tell a Jew, that they were different from other people, that you couldn't trust them in business, that some of his best friends were Jews, that he distinguished between a Jew and a kike, and finally but, of course, he didn't agree with Hitler: Hitler went too far; the Jews were human beings.

7 All the time we talked, and I defended the Jews, he was trying to get my angle, as he called it; he thought it was abnormal for anybody who wasn't Jewish not to feel as he did. As a matter of fact, I have a Jewish grandmother, but I decided to keep this news to myself: I did not want the colonel to think that I had any interested reason for speaking on behalf of the Jews, that is, that I was prejudiced. In the end, though, I got my comeuppance. Just as we were parting, the colonel asked me my married name, which is Broadwater, and the whole mystery was cleared up for him, instantly; he supposed I was married to a Jew and that the name was spelled B-r-o-d-w-a-t-e-r. I did not try to enlighten him; I let him think what he wanted; in a certain sense, he was right; he had unearthed my Jewish grandmother or her equivalent. There were a few details that I must mention to make the next part clear: in my car, there were two nuns, whom I talked to as a distraction from the colonel and the moral problems he raised. He and I finally had lunch together in the St. Louis railroad station, where we continued the discussion. It was a very hot day. I had a sandwich; he had roast-beef hash. We both had an old-fashioned.

8 The whole point of this "story" was that it really happened; it is written in the first person; I speak of myself in my own name, McCarthy; at the end, I mention my husband's name, Broadwater. When I was thinking about writing the story, I decided not to treat it fictionally; the chief interest, I felt, lay in the fact that it happened, in real life, last summer, to the writer herself, who was a good deal at fault in the incident. I wanted to embarrass myself and, if possible, the reader too.

9 Yet, strangely enough, many of my readers preferred to think of this account as fiction. I still meet people who ask me, confidentially, "That story of yours about the colonel—was it really true?" It seemed to them perfectly natural that I would write a fabrication, in which I figured under my own name, and sign it, though in my eyes this would be like perjuring yourself in court or forging checks. Shortly after the "story" was published, I got a kindly letter from a man in Mexico, in which he criticized the menu from an artistic point of view: he thought salads would be better for hot weather and it would be more in character for the narrator-heroine to have a martini. I did not answer the letter, though I was moved to, because I

had the sense that he would not understand the distinction between what *ought* to have happened and what *did happen*.

10 Then in April I got another letter, from an English teacher in a small college in the Middle West, that reduced me to despair. I am going to cite it at length.

11 "My students in freshman English chose to analyze your story, 'Artists in Uniform,' from the March issue of *Harper's*. For a week I heard oral discussions on it and then the students wrote critical analyses. In so far as it is possible, I stayed out of their discussions, encouraging them to read the story closely with your intentions as a guide to their understanding. Although some of them insisted that the story has no other level than the realistic one, most of them decided it has symbolic overtones.

12 "The question is: how closely do you want the symbols labeled? They wrestled with the nuns, the author's two shades of green with pink accents, with the 'materialistic godlessness' of the colonel. . . . A surprising number wanted exact symbols; for example, they searched for the significance of the colonel's eating hash and the author eating a sandwich. . . . From my standpoint, the story was an entirely satisfactory springboard for understanding the various shades of prejudice, for seeing how much of the artist goes into his painting. If it is any satisfaction to you, our campus was alive with discussions about 'Artists in Uniform.' We liked the story and we thought it amazing that an author could succeed in making readers dislike the author—for a purpose, of course!"

13 I probably should have answered this letter, but I did not. The gulf seemed to me too wide. I could not applaud the backward students who insisted that the story has no other level than the realistic one without giving offense to their teacher, who was evidently a well-meaning person. But I shall try now to address a reply, not to this teacher and her unfortunate class, but to a whole school of misunderstanding. There were no symbols in this story; there was no deeper level. The nuns were in the story because they were on the train; the contrasting greens were the dress I happened to be wearing; the colonel had hash because he had hash; materialistic godlessness meant just what it means when a priest thunders it from the pulpit—the phrase, for the first time, had meaning for me as I watched and listened to the colonel.

14 But to clarify the misunderstanding, one must go a little further and try to see what a literary symbol is. Now in one sense, the colonel's hash and my sandwich can be regarded as symbols; that is, they typify the colonel's food tastes and mine. (The man in Mexico had different food tastes which he wished to interpose into our reality.) The hash and the sandwich might even be said to show something very obvious about our characters and bringing-up, or about our sexes; I was a woman, he was a man.

And though on another day I might have ordered hash myself, that day I did not, because the colonel and I, in our disagreement, were polarizing each other.

15 The hash and the sandwich, then, could be regarded as symbols of our disagreement, almost conscious symbols. And underneath our discussion of the Jews, there was a thin sexual current running, as there always is in such random encounters or pickups (for they have a strong suggestion of the illicit). The fact that I ordered something conventionally feminine and he ordered something conventionally masculine represented, no doubt, our awareness of a sexual possibility; even though I was not attracted to the colonel, nor he to me, the circumstances of our meeting made us define ourselves as a woman and a man.

16 The sandwich and the hash were our provisional, *ad hoc* symbols of ourselves. But in this sense all human actions are symbolic because they represent the person who does them. If the colonel had ordered a fruit salad with whipped cream, this too would have represented him in some way; given his other traits, it would have pointed to a complexity in his character that the hash did not suggest.

17 In the same way, the contrasting greens of my dress were a symbol of my taste in clothes and hence representative of me—all too representative, I suddenly saw, in the club car, when I got an "artistic" image of myself flashed back at me from the men's eyes. I had no wish to stylize myself as an artist, that is, to parade about as a symbol of flamboyant unconventionality, but apparently I had done so unwittingly when I picked those colors off a rack, under the impression that they suited me or "expressed my personality" as salesladies say.

18 My dress, then, was a symbol of the perplexity I found myself in with the colonel; I did not want to be categorized as a member of a peculiar minority—an artist or a Jew; but brute fate and the colonel kept resolutely cramming me into both those uncomfortable pigeonholes. I wished to be regarded as ordinary or rather as universal, to be anybody and therefore everybody (that is, in one sense, I wanted to be on the colonel's side, majestically above minorities); but every time the colonel looked at my dress and me in it with my pink earrings I shrank to minority status, and felt the dress in the heat shriveling me, like the shirt of Nessus, the centaur, that consumed Hercules.

19 But this is not what the students meant when they wanted the symbols "labeled." They were searching for a more recondite significance than that afforded by the trite symbolism of ordinary life, in which a dress is a social badge. They supposed that I was engaging in literary or artificial symbolism, which would lead the reader out of the confines of reality into the vast fairy tale of myth, in which the color green would have an emble-

matic meaning (or did the two greens signify for them what the teacher calls "shades" of prejudice), and the colonel's hash, I imagine, would be some sort of Eucharistic mincemeat.

20 Apparently, the presence of the nuns assured them there were overtones of theology; it did not occur to them (a) that the nuns were there because pairs of nuns are a standardized feature of summer Pullman travel, like crying babies, and perspiring businessmen in the club car, and (b) that if I thought the nuns worth mentioning, it was also because of something very simple and directly relevant; the nuns and the colonel and I all had something in common—we had all at one time been Catholics—and I was seeking common ground with the colonel, from which to turn and attack his position.

21 In any account of reality, even a televised one, which comes closest to being a literal transcript or replay, some details are left out as irrelevant (though nothing is really irrelevant). The details that are not eliminated have to stand as symbols of the whole, like stenographic signs, and of course there is an art of selection, even in a newspaper account: the writer, if he has any ability, is looking for the revealing detail that will sum up the picture for the reader in a flash of recognition.

22 But the art of abridgment and condensation, which is familiar to anybody who tries to relate an anecdote, or give a direction—the art of natural symbolism, which is at the basis of speech and all representation—has at bottom a centripetal intention. It hovers over an object, and event, or series of events and tries to declare what it is. Analogy (that is, comparison to other objects) is inevitably onc of its methods. "The weather was soupy," i.e., like soup. "He wedged his way in," i.e., he had to enter, thin edge first, as a wedge enters, and so on. All this is obvious. But these metaphorical aids to communication are a far cry from literary symbolism, as taught in the schools and practiced by certain fashionable writers. Literary symbolism is centrifugal and flees from the object, the event, into the incorporeal distance, where concepts are taken for substance and floating ideas and archetypes assume a hieratic authority.

23 In this dream-forest, symbols become arbitrary; all counters are interchangeable; anything can stand for anything else. The colonel's hash can be a Eucharist or a cannibal feast or the banquet of Atreus, or all three, so long as the actual dish set before the actual man is disparaged. What is depressing about this insistent symbolization is the fact that while it claims to lead to the infinite, it quickly reaches very finite limits—there are only so many myths on record, and once you have got through Bulfinch, the Scandinavian, and the Indian, there is not much left. And if all stories reduce themselves to myth and symbol, qualitative differences vanish, and there is only a single, monotonous story.

24 American fiction of the symbolist school demonstrates this mournful

truth, without precisely intending to. A few years ago, when the mode was at its height, chic novels and stories fell into three classes: those which had a Greek myth for their framework, which the reader was supposed to detect, like finding the faces in the clouds in old newspaper puzzle contests; those which had symbolic modern figures, dwarfs, hermaphrodites, and cripples, illustrating maiming and loneliness; and those which contained symbolic animals, cougars, wild cats, and monkeys. One young novelist, a product of the Princeton school of symbolism, had all three elements going at once, like the ringmaster of a three-ring circus, with the freaks, the animals, and the statues.

25 The quest for symbolic referents had as its object, of course, the deepening of the writer's subject and the reader's awareness. But the result was paradoxical. At the very moment when American writing was penetrated by the symbolic urge, it ceased to be able to create symbols of its own. Babbitt, I suppose, was the last important symbol to be created by an American writer; he gave his name to a type that henceforth would be recognizable to everybody. He passed into the language. The same thing could be said, perhaps, though to a lesser degree, of Caldwell's Tobacco Road, Eliot's Prufrock, and possibly of Faulkner's Snopeses. The discovery of new symbols is not the only function of a writer, but the writer who cares about this must be fascinated by reality itself, as a butterfly collector is fascinated by the glimpse of a new specimen. Such a specimen was Mme. Bovary or M. Homais or M. de Charlus or Jupien; these specimens were precious to their discoverers, not because they repeated an age-old pattern but because their markings were new. Once the specimen has been described, the public instantly spots other examples of the kind, and the world seems suddenly full of Babbitts and Charluses, where none had been noted before.

26 A different matter was Joyce's Mr. Bloom. Mr. Bloom can be called a symbol of eternal recurrence—the wandering Jew, Ulysses the voyager—but he is a symbol thickly incarnate, fleshed out in a Dublin advertising canvasser. He is not *like* Ulysses or vaguely suggestive of Ulysses; he is Ulysses, circa 1905. Joyce evidently believed in a cyclical theory of history, in which everything repeated itself; he also subscribed in youth to the doctrine that declares that the Host, a piece of bread, is also God's body and blood. How it can be both things at the same time, transubstantially, is a mystery, and Mr. Bloom is just such a mystery: Ulysses in the visible appearance of a Dublin advertising canvasser.

27 Mr. Bloom is not a symbol of Ulysses, but Ulysses-Bloom together, one and indivisible, symbolize or rather demonstrate eternal recurrence. I hope I make myself clear. The point is transubstantiation: Bloom and Ulysses are transfused into each other and neither reality is diminished. Both realities are locked together, like the protons and neutrons of an atom.

Finnegans Wake is a still more ambitious attempt to create a fusion, this time a myriad fusion, and to exemplify the mystery of how a thing can be itself and at the same time be something else. The world is many and it is also one.

28 But the clarity and tension of Joyce's thought brought him closer in a way to the strictness of allegory than to the diffuse practices of latter-day symbolists. In Joyce, the equivalences and analogies are very sharp and distinct, as in a pun, and the real world is almost querulously audible, like the voices of the washerwomen on the Liffey that come into Earwicker's dream. But this is not true of Joyce's imitators or of the imitators of his imitators, for whom reality is only a shadowy pretext for the introduction of a whole *corps de ballet* of dancing symbols in mythic draperies and animal skins.

29 Let me make a distinction. There are some great writers, like Joyce or Melville, who have consciously introduced symbolic elements into their work; and there are great writers who have written fables or allegories. In both cases, the writer makes it quite clear to the reader how he is to be read; only an idiot would take *Pilgrim's Progress* for a realistic story, and even a young boy, reading *Moby Dick*, realizes that there is something more than whale-fishing here, though he may not be able to name what it is. But the great body of fiction contains only what I have called natural symbolism, in which selected events represent or typify a problem, a kind of society or psychology, a philosophical theory, in the same way that they do in real life. What happens to the hero becomes of the highest importance. This symbolism needs no abstruse interpretation, and abstruse interpretation will only lead the reader away from the reality that the writer is trying to press on his attention.

30 I shall give an example or two of what I mean by natural symbolism and I shall begin with a rather florid one: Henry James' *The Golden Bowl*. This is the story of a rich American girl who collects European objects. One of these objects is a husband, Prince Amerigo, who proves to be unfaithful. Early in the story, there is a visit to an antique shop in which the Prince picks out a gold bowl for his fiancée and finds, to his annoyance, that it is cracked. It is not hard to see that the cracked bowl is a symbol, both of the Prince himself, who is a valuable antique but a little flawed, morally, and also of the marriage, which represents an act of acquisition or purchase on the part of the heroine and her father. If the reader should fail to notice the analogy, James calls his attention to it in the title.

31 I myself would not regard this symbol as necessary to this particular history; it seems to me, rather, an ornament of the kind that was fashionable in the architecture and interior decoration of the period, like stylized sheaves of corn or palms on the façade of a house. Nevertheless, it is handsome and has an obvious appropriateness to the theme. It introduces the reader into the Gilded Age attitudes of the novel. I think there is also a

scriptural echo in the title that conveys the idea of punishment. But having seen and felt the weight of meaning that James put into this symbol, one must not be tempted to press further and look at the bowl as a female sex symbol, a chalice, a Holy Grail, and so on; a book is not a pious excuse for reciting a litany of associations.

32 My second example is from Tolstoy's *Anna Karenina.* Toward the beginning of the novel, Anna meets the man who will be her lover, Vronsky, on the Moscow-St. Petersburg express; as they meet, there has been an accident; a workman has been killed by the train. This is the beginning of Anna's doom, which is completed when she throws herself under a train and is killed; and the last we see of Vronsky is in a train, with a toothache; he is off to the wars. The train is necessary to the plot of the novel, and I believe it is also symbolic, both of the iron forces of material progress that Tolstoy hated so and that played a part in Anna's moral destruction, and also of those iron laws of necessity and consequence that govern human action when it remains on the sensual level.

33 One can read the whole novel, however, without being conscious that the train is a symbol; we do not have to "interpret" to feel the import of doom and loneliness in the train's whistle—the same import we ourselves can feel when we hear a train whistle blow in the country, even today. Tolstoy was a deeper artist than James, and we cannot be sure that the train was a conscious device with him. The appropriateness to Anna's history may have been only a *felt* appropriateness; everything in Tolstoy has such a supreme naturalness that one shrinks from attributing contrivance to him, as if it were a sort of fraud. Yet he worked very hard on his novels —I forget how many times Countess Tolstoy copied out *War and Peace* by hand.

34 The impression one gets from his diaries is that he wrote by ear; he speaks repeatedly, even as an old man, of having to start a story over again because he has the wrong tone, and I suspect that he did not think of the train as a symbol but that it sounded "right" to him, because it was, in that day, an almost fearsome emblem of ruthless and impersonal force, not only to a writer of genius but to the poorest peasant in the fields. And in Tolstoy's case I think it would be impossible, even for the most fanciful critic, to extricate the train from the novel and try to make it say something that the novel itself does not say directly. Every detail in Tolstoy has an almost cruel and viselike meaningfulness and truth to itself that make it tautological to talk of symbolism; he was a moralist and to him the tiniest action, even the curiosities of physical appearance, Vronsky's bald spot, the small white hands of Prince Andrei, told a moral tale.

35 It is now considered very old-fashioned and tasteless to speak of an author's "philosophy of life" as something that can be harvested from his work. Actually, most of the great authors did have a "philosophy of life"

which they were eager to communicate to the public; this was one of their motives for writing. And to disentangle a moral philosophy from a work that evidently contains one is far less damaging to the author's purpose and the integrity of his art than to violate his imagery by symbol-hunting, as though reading a novel were a sort of paperchase.

36 The images of a novel or a story belong, as it were, to a family, very closely knit and inseparable from each other; the parent "idea" of a story or a novel generates events and images all bearing a strong family resemblance. And to understand a story or a novel, you must look for the parent "idea," which is usually in plain view, if you read quite carefully and literally what the author says.

37 I will go back, for a moment, to my own story, to show how this can be done. Clearly, it is about the Jewish question, for that is what the people are talking about. It also seems to be about artists, since the title is "Artists in Uniform." Then there must be some relation between artists and Jews. What is it? They are both minorities that other people claim to be able to recognize by their appearance. But artists and Jews do not care for this categorization; they want to be universal, that is, like everybody else. They do not want to wear their destiny as a badge, as the soldier wears his uniform. But this aim is really hopeless, for life has formed them as Jews or artists, in a way that immediately betrays them to the majority they are trying to melt into. In my conversation with the colonel, I was endeavoring to play a double game. I was trying to force him into a minority by treating anti-Semitism as an aberration, which, in fact, I believe it is. On his side, the colonel resisted this attempt and tried to show that anti-Semitism was normal, and he was normal, while I was the queer one. He declined to be categorized as anti-Semite; he regarded himself as an independent thinker, who by a happy chance thought the same as everybody else.

38 I imagined I had a card up my sleeve, I had guessed that the colonel was Irish (i.e., that he belonged to a minority) and presumed that he was a Catholic. I did not see how he could possibly guess that I, with my Irish name and Irish appearance, had a Jewish grandmother in the background. Therefore when I found I had not convinced him by reasoning, I played my last card; I told him that the Church, his Church, forbade anti-Semitism. I went even further; I implied that God forbade it, though I had no right to do this, since I did not believe in God, but was only using Him as a whip to crack over the colonel, to make him feel humble and inferior, a raw Irish Catholic lad under discipline. But the colonel, it turned out, did not believe in God, either, and I lost. And since, in a sense, I had been cheating all along in this game we were playing, I had to concede the colonel a sort of moral victory in the end; I let him think that my husband was Jewish and that that "explained" everything satisfactorily.

39 Now there are a number of morals or meanings in this little tale, starting with the simple one: don't talk to strangers on a train. The chief moral or meaning (what I learned, in other words, from this experience) was this: you cannot be a universal unless you accept the fact that you are a singular, that is, a Jew or an artist or what-have-you. What the colonel and I were discussing, and at the same time illustrating and enacting, was the definition of a human being. I was trying to be something better than a human being; I was trying to be the voice of pure reason; and pride went before a fall. The colonel, without trying, was being something worse than a human being, and somehow we found ourselves on the same plane—facing each other, like mutually repellent twins. Or, put in another way: it is dangerous to be drawn into discussions of the Jews with anti-Semites: you delude yourself that you are spreading light, but you are really sinking into muck; if you endeavor to be dispassionate, you are really claiming for yourself a privileged position, a little mountain top, from which you look down, impartially, on both the Jews and the colonel.

40 Anti-Semitism is a horrible disease from which nobody is immune, and it has a kind of evil fascination that makes an enlightened person draw near the source of infection, supposedly in a scientific spirit, but really to sniff the vapors and dally with the possibility. The enlightened person who lunches with the colonel in order, as she tells herself, to improve him, is cheating herself, having her cake and eating it. This attempted cheat, on my part, was related to the question of the artist and the green dress; I wanted to be an artist but not to pay the price of looking like one, just as I was willing to have Jewish blood but not willing to show it, where it would cost me something—the loss of superiority in an argument.

41 These meanings are all there, quite patent, to anyone who consents to look *into* the story. They were *in* the experience itself, waiting to be found and considered. I did not perceive them all at the time the experience was happening; otherwise, it would not have taken place, in all probability—I should have given the colonel a wide berth. But when I went back over the experience, in order to write it, I came upon these meanings, protruding at me, as it were, from the details of the occasion. I put in the green dress and my mortification over it because they were part of the truth, just as it had occurred, but I did not see how they were related to the general question of anti-Semitism and my grandmother until they *showed* me their relation in the course of writing.

42 Every short story, at least for me, is a little act of discovery. A cluster of details presents itself to my scrutiny, like a mystery that I will understand in the course of writing or sometimes not fully until afterward, when, if I have been honest and listened to these details carefully, I will find that they are connected and that there is a coherent pattern. This pattern is *in*

experience itself; you do not impose it from the outside and if you try to, you will find that the story is taking the wrong tack, dribbling away from you into artificiality or inconsequence. A story that you do not learn something from while you are writing it, that does not illuminate something for you, is dead, finished before you started it. The "idea" of a story is implicit in it, on the one hand; on the other hand, it is always ahead of the writer, like a form dimly discerned in the distance; he is working *toward* the "idea."

43 It can sometimes happen that you begin a story thinking that you know the "idea" of it and find, when you are finished, that you have said something quite different and utterly unexpected to you. Most writers have been haunted all their lives by the "idea" of a story or a novel that they think they want to write and see very clearly: Tolstoy always wanted to write a novel about the Decembrists and instead, almost against his will, wrote *War and Peace*; Henry James thought he wanted to write a novel about Napoleon. Probably these ideas for novels were too set in their creators' minds to inspire creative discovery.

44 In any work that is truly creative, I believe, the writer cannot be omniscient in advance about the effects that he proposes to produce. The suspense in a novel is not only in the reader, but in the novelist himself, who is intensely curious too about what will happen to the hero. Jane Austen may know in a general way that Emma will marry Mr. Knightley in the end (the reader knows this too, as a matter of fact); the suspense for the author lies in the how, in the twists and turns of circumstance, waiting but as yet unknown, that will bring the consummation about. Hence, I would say to the student of writing that outlines, patterns, arrangements of symbols may have a certain usefulness at the outset for some kinds of minds, but in the end they will have to be scrapped. If the story does not contradict the outline, overrun the pattern, break the symbols, like an insurrection against authority, it is surely a stillbirth. The natural symbolism of reality has more messages to communicate than the dry Morse code of the disengaged mind.

45 The tree of life, said Hegel, is greener than the tree of thought; I have quoted this before but I cannot forbear from citing it again in this context. This is not an incitement to mindlessness or an endorsement of realism in the short story (there are several kinds of reality, including interior reality); it means only that the writer must be, first of all, a listener and observer, who can pay attention to reality, like an obedient pupil, and who is willing, always, to be surprised by the messages reality is sending through to him. And if he gets the messages correctly he will not have to go back and put in the symbols; he will find that the symbols are there, staring at him significantly from the commonplace.

STUDY GUIDE

Theme and Structure

1. State as simply as you can the idea about symbolism that Mary McCarthy is trying to explain in this essay.
2. What has the title of the essay to do with the author's main idea about symbolism?
3. The author makes a distinction between a natural symbol growing out of the real material of a story and a literary or artificial symbol. What does she mean by a natural symbol? What concrete examples does she give to illustrate what she means by it?
4. What does she mean by saying that natural symbolism is *centripetal* and artificial symbolism *centrifugal?* Look up the exact meaning of these terms themselves and then analyze the author's use of them in paragraph 21.
5. The essay begins with an introduction, paragraphs 1–7, and concludes in paragraphs 42–45. Show how the author has led up to and actually introduced her subject of symbolism in literature in her introduction. What connection has the concluding discussion on the writing of a short story with the general subject of natural symbolism? Does the author advert in her conclusion to the anecdote with which she introduced her essay?
6. How would you divide the main part of the essay—paragraphs 8–41? Indicate what each of the divisions that you point out does to develop the author's idea of symbolism.
7. How does Mary McCarthy's idea of symbolism compare with that expressed by Bellow in his essay "Deep Readers of the World, Beware!"
8. What are some of the common elements of all prejudice that Mary McCarthy's experience with the colonel illustrates?

James Baldwin (1924–   )

James Baldwin is unquestionably one of the most talented Negro writers in America today. His novels *Go Tell It on the Mountain* and *Another Country* reveal him as a master of creative fiction, but he is equally well known for the new life he has given the essay form. Many of his essays have appeared in the *Partisan Review* and other magazines. He has published collections of them under the titles of *Notes of a Native Son, Nobody Knows My Name,* and *The Fire Next Time.* Their moving and competent style have done much to acquaint the reading public with what it means to be a Negro in this country.

FIFTH AVENUE, UPTOWN

A Letter from Harlem

James Baldwin

1 There is a housing project standing now where the house in which we grew up once stood, and one of those stunted city trees is snarling where our doorway used to be. This is on the rehabilitated side of the avenue. The other side of the avenue—for progress takes time—has not been rehabilitated yet and it looks exactly as it looked in the days when we sat with our noses pressed against the windowpane, longing to be allowed to go "across the street." The grocery store which gave us credit is still there, and there can be no doubt that it is still giving credit. The people in the project certainly need it—far more, indeed, than they ever needed the project. The last time I passed by, the Jewish proprietor was still standing among his shelves, looking sadder and heavier but scarcely any older. Farther down the block stands the shoe-repair store in which our shoes were repaired until reparation became impossible and in which, then, we bought all our "new" ones. The Negro proprietor is still in the window, head down, working at the leather.

2 These two, I image, could tell a long tale if they would (perhaps they would be glad to if they could), having watched so many, for so long, struggling in the fishhooks, the barbed wire, of this avenue.

3 The avenue is elsewhere the renowned and elegant Fifth. The area I am describing, which, in today's gang parlance, would be called "the turf," is bounded by Lenox Avenue on the west, the Harlem River on the east, 135th Street on the north, and 130th Street on the south. We never lived beyond these boundaries; this is where we grew up. Walking along 145th Street—for example—familiar as it is, and similar, does not have the same impact because I do not know any of the people on the block. But when I turn east on 131st Street and Lenox Avenue, there is first a soda-pop joint, then a shoeshine "parlor," then a grocery store, then a dry cleaners', then the houses. All along the street there are people who watched me grow up, people who grew up with me, people I watched grow up along with my brothers and sisters; and, sometimes in my arms, sometimes underfoot, sometimes at my shoulder—or on it—their children, a riot, a forest of children, who include my nieces and nephews.

4 When we reach the end of this long block, we find ourselves on wide,

Reprinted from James Baldwin, *Nobody Knows My Name* (New York: The Dial Press, Inc., 1961) by permission of Robert Lantz.

filthy, hostile Fifth Avenue, facing that project which hangs over the avenue like a monument to the folly, and the cowardice, of good intentions. All along the block, for anyone who knows it, are immense human gaps, like craters. These gaps are not created merely by those who have moved away, inevitably into some other ghetto; or by those who have risen, almost always into a greater capacity for self-loathing and self-delusion; or yet by those who, by whatever means—World War II, the Korean war, a policeman's gun or billy, a gang war, a brawl, madness, an overdose of heroin, or simply, unnatural exhaustion—are dead. I am talking about those who are left, and I am talking principally about the young. What are they doing? Well, some, a minority, are fanatical churchgoers, members of the more extreme of the Holy Roller sects. Many, many more are "moslems," by affiliation or sympathy, that is to say that they are united by nothing more—and nothing less—than a hatred of the white world and all its works. They are present, for example, at every Buy Black street-corner meeting—meetings in which the speaker urges his hearers to cease trading with white men and establish a separate economy. Neither the speaker nor his hearers can possibly do this, of course, since Negroes do not own General Motors or RCA or the A & P, nor, indeed, do they own more than a wholly insufficient fraction of anything else in Harlem (those who *do* own anything are more interested in their profits than in their fellows). But these meetings nevertheless keep alive in the participators a certain pride of bitterness without which, however futile this bitterness may be, they could scarcely remain alive at all. Many have given up. They stay home and watch the TV screen, living on the earnings of their parents, cousins, brothers, or uncles, and only leave the house to go to the movies or to the nearest bar. "How're you making it?" one may ask, running into them along the block, or in the bar. "Oh, I'm TV-ing it"; with the saddest, sweetest, most shamefaced of smiles, and from a great distance. This distance one is compelled to respect; anyone who has traveled so far will not easily be dragged again into the world. There are further retreats, of course, than the TV screen or the bar. There are those who are simply sitting on their stoops, "stoned," animated for a moment only, and hideously, by the approach of someone who may lend them the money for a "fix." Or by the approach of someone from whom they can purchase it, one of the shrewd ones, on the way to prison or just coming out.

5 And the others, who have avoided all of these deaths, get up in the morning and go downtown to meet "the man." They work in the white man's world all day and come home in the evening to this fetid block. They struggle to instill in their children some private sense of honor or dignity which will help the child to survive. This means, of course, that they must struggle, stolidly, incessantly, to keep this sense alive in themselves, in spite of the insults, the indifference, and the cruelty they are

certain to encounter in their working day. They patiently browbeat the landlord into fixing the heat, the plaster, the plumbing; this demands prodigious patience; nor is patience usually enough. In trying to make their hovels habitable, they are perpetually throwing good money after bad. Such frustration, so long endured, is driving many strong, admirable men and women whose only crime is color to the very gates of paranoia.

6 One remembers them from another time—playing handball in the playground, going to church, wondering if they were going to be promoted at school. One remembers them going off to war—gladly, to escape this block. One remembers their return. Perhaps one remembers their wedding day. And one sees where the girl is now—vainly looking for salvation from some other embittered, trussed, and struggling boy—and sees the all-but-abandoned children in the streets.

7 Now I am perfectly aware that there are other slums in which white men are fighting for their lives, and mainly losing. I know that blood is also flowing through those streets and that the human damage there is incalculable. People are continually pointing out to me the wretchedness of white people in order to console me for the wretchedness of blacks. But an itemized account of the American failure does not console me and it should not console anyone else. That hundreds of thousands of white people are living, in effect, no better than the "niggers" is not a fact to be regarded with complacency. The social and moral bankruptcy suggested by this fact is of the bitterest, most terrifying kind.

8 The people, however, who believe that this democratic anguish has some consoling value are always pointing out that So-and-So, white, and So-and-So, black, rose from the slums into the big time. The existence—the public existence—of say, Frank Sinatra and Sammy Davis, Jr. proves to them that America is still the land of opportunity and that inequalities vanish before the determined will. It proves nothing of the sort. The determined will is rare—at the moment, in this country, it is unspeakably rare—and the inequalities suffered by the many are in no way justified by the rise of a few. A few have always risen—in every country, every era, and in the teeth of regimes which can by no stretch of the imagination be thought of as free. Not all of these people, it is worth remembering, left the world better than they found it. The determined will is rare, but it is not invariably benevolent. Furthermore, the American equation of success with the big time reveals an awful disrespect for human life and human achievement. This equation has placed our cities among the most dangerous in the world and has placed our youth among the most empty and most bewildered. The situation of our youth is not mysterious. Children have never been very good at listening to their elders, but they have never failed to imitate them. They must, they have no other models. That is exactly

what our children are doing. They are imitating our immorality, our disrespect for the pain of others.

9 All other slum dwellers, when the bank account permits it, can move out of the slum and vanish altogether from the eye of persecution. No Negro in this country has ever made that much money and it will be a long time before any Negro does. The Negroes in Harlem, who have no money, spend what they have on such gimcracks as they are sold. These include "wider" TV screens, more "faithful" hi-fi sets, more "powerful" cars, all of which, of course, are obsolete long before they are paid for. Anyone who has ever struggled with poverty knows how extremely expensive it is to be poor; and if one is a member of a captive population, economically speaking, one's feet have simply been placed on the treadmill forever. One is victimized, economically, in a thousand ways—rent, for example, or car insurance. Go shopping one day in Harlem—for anything—and compare Harlem prices and quality with those downtown.

10 The people who have managed to get off this block have only got as far as a more respectable ghetto. This respectable ghetto does not even have the advantages of the disreputable one—friends, neighbors, a familiar church, and friendly tradesmen; and it is not, moreover, in the nature of any ghetto to remain respectable long. Every Sunday, people who have left the block take the lonely ride back, dragging their increasingly discontented children with them. They spend the day talking, not always with words, about the trouble they've seen and the trouble—one must watch their eyes as they watch their children—they are only too likely to see. For children do not like ghettos. It takes them nearly no time to discover exactly why they are there.

11 The projects in Harlem are hated. They are hated almost as much as policemen, and this is saying a great deal. And they are hated for the same reason: both reveal, unbearably, the real attitude of the white world, no matter how many liberal speeches are made, no matter how many lofty editorials are written, no matter how many civil-rights commissions are set up.

12 The projects are hideous, of course, there being a law, apparently respected throughout the world, that popular housing shall be as cheerless as a prison. They are lumped all over Harlem, colorless, bleak, high, and revolting. The wide windows look out on Harlem's invincible and indescribable squalor: the Park Avenue railroad tracks, around which, about forty years ago, the present dark community began; the unrehabilitated houses, bowed down, it would seem, under the great weight of frustration and bitterness they contain; the dark, the ominous schoolhouses from which the child may emerge maimed, blinded, hooked, or enraged for life; and the churches, churches, block upon block of churches, niched in the walls like cannon in the walls of a fortress. Even if the administration of the proj-

ects were not so insanely humiliating (for example: one must report raises in salary to the management, which will then eat up the profit by raising one's rent; the management has the right to know who is staying in your apartment; the management can ask you to leave, at their discretion), the projects would still be hated because they are an insult to the meanest intelligence.

13 Harlem got its first private project, Riverton [1]—which is now, naturally, a slum—about twelve years ago because at that time Negroes were not allowed to live in Stuyvesant Town. Harlem watched Riverton go up, therefore, in the most violent bitterness of spirit, and hated it long before the builders arrived. They began hating it at about the time people began moving out of their condemned houses to make room for this additional proof of how thoroughly the white world despised them. And they had scarcely moved in, naturally, before they began smashing windows, defacing walls, urinating in the elevators, and fornicating in the playgrounds. Liberals, both white and black, were appalled at the spectacle. I was appalled by the liberal innocence—or cynicism, which comes out in practice as much the same thing. Other people were delighted to be able to point to proof positive that nothing could be done to better the lot of the colored people. They were, and are, right in one respect: that nothing can be done as long as they are treated like colored people. The people in Harlem know they are living there because white people do not think they are good enough to live anywhere else. No amount of "improvement" can sweeten this fact. Whatever money is now being earmarked to improve this, or any other ghetto, might as well be burnt. A ghetto can be improved in one way only: out of existence.

14 Similarly, the only way to police a ghetto is to be oppressive. None of the Police Commissioner's men, even with the best will in the world, have any way of understanding the lives led by the people they swagger about in twos and threes controlling. Their very presence is an insult, and it would be, even if they spent their entire day feeding gumdrops to children. They represent the force of the white world, and that world's real intentions are, simply, for that world's criminal profit and ease, to keep the black man corraled up here, in his place. The badge, the gun in the holster, and the swinging club make vivid what will happen should his rebellion be-

[1] The inhabitants of Riverton were much embittered by this description; they have, apparently, forgotten how their project came into being; and have repeatedly informed me that I cannot possibly be referring to Riverton, but to another housing project which is directly across the street. It is quite clear, I think, that I have no interest in accusing any individuals or families of the depredations herein described: but neither can I deny the evidence of my own eyes. Nor do I blame anyone in Harlem for making the best of a dreadful bargain. But anyone who lives in Harlem and imagines that he has *not* struck this bargain, or that what he takes to be his status (in whose eyes?) protects him against the common pain, demoralization, and danger, is simply self deluded.

come overt. Rare, indeed, is the Harlem citizen, from the most circumspect church member to the most shiftless adolescent, who does not have a long tale to tell of police incompetence, injustice, or brutality. I myself have witnessed and endured it more than once. The businessmen and racketeers also have a story. And so do the prostitutes. (And this is not, perhaps, the place to duscuss Harlem's very complex attitude toward black policemen, nor the reasons, according to Harlem, that they are nearly all downtown.)

15 It is hard, on the other hand, to blame the policeman, blank, good-natured, thoughtless, and insuperably innocent, for being such a perfect representative of the people he serves. He, too, believes in good intentions and is astounded and offended when they are not taken for the deed. He has never, himself, done anything for which to be hated—which of us has? —and yet he is facing, daily and nightly, people who would gladly see him dead, and he knows it. There is no way for him not to know it: there are few things under heaven more unnerving than the silent, accumulating contempt and hatred of a people. He moves through Harlem, therefore, like an occupying soldier in a bitterly hostile country; which is precisely what, and where, he is, and is the reason he walks in twos and threes. And he is not the only one who knows why he is always in company: the people who are watching him know why, too. Any street meeting, sacred or secular, which he and his colleagues uneasily cover has as its explicit or implicit burden the cruelty and injustice, of the white domination. And these days, of course, in terms increasingly vivid and jubilant, it speaks of the end of that domination. The white policeman standing on a Harlem street corner finds himself at the very center of the revolution now occurring in the world. He is not prepared for it—naturally, nobody is—and, what is possibly much more to the point, he is exposed, as few white people are, to the anguish of the black people around him. Even if he is gifted with the merest mustard grain of imagination, something must seep in. He cannot avoid observing that some of the children, in spite of their color, remind him of children he has known and loved, perhaps even of his own children. He knows that he certainly does not want *his* children living this way. He can retreat from his uneasiness in only one direction: into a callousness which very shortly becomes second nature. He becomes more callous, the population become more hostile, the situation grows more tense, and the police force is increased. One day, to everyone's astonishment, someone drops a match in the powder keg and everything blows up. Before the dust has settled or the blood congealed, editorials, speeches, and civil-rights commissions are loud in the land, demanding to know what happened. What happened is that Negroes want to be treated like men.

16 *Negroes want to be treated like men:* a perfectly straightforward statement, containing only seven words. People who have mastered Kant, Hegel, Shakespeare, Marx, Freud, and the Bible find this statement utterly

impenetrable. The idea seems to threaten profound, barely conscious assumptions. A kind of panic paralyzes their features, as though they found themselves trapped on the edge of a steep place. I once tried to describe to a very well-known American intellectual the conditions among Negroes in the South. My recital disturbed him and made him indignant; and he asked me in perfect innocence, "Why don't all the Negroes in the South move North?" I tried to explain what *has* happened, unfailingly, whenever a significant body of Negroes move North. They do not escape Jim Crow: they merely encounter another, not-less-deadly variety. They do not move to Chicago, they move to the South Side; they do not move to New York, they move to Harlem. The pressure within the ghetto causes the ghetto walls to expand, and this expansion is always violent. White people hold the line as long as they can, and in as many ways as they can, from verbal intimidation to physical violence. But inevitably the border which has divided the ghetto from the rest of the world falls into the hands of the ghetto. The white people fall back bitterly before the black horde; the landlords make a tidy profit by raising the rent, chopping up the rooms, and all but dispensing with the upkeep; and what has once been a neighborhood turns into a "turf." This is precisely what happened when the Puerto Ricans arrived in their thousands—and the bitterness thus caused is, as I write, being fought out all up and down those streets.

17 Northerners indulge in an extremely dangerous luxury. They seem to feel that because they fought on the right side during the Civil War, and won, they have earned the right merely to deplore what is going on in the South, without taking any responsibility for it; and that they can ignore what is happening in Northern cities because what is happening in Little Rock or Birmingham is worse. Well, in the first place, it is not possible for anyone who has not endured both to know which is "worse." I know Negroes who prefer the South and white Southerners, because "At least there, you haven't got to play any guessing games!" The guessing games referred to have driven more than one Negro into the narcotics ward, the madhouse, or the river. I know another Negro, a man very dear to me, who says, with conviction and with truth, "The spirit of the South is the spirit of America." He was born in the North and did his military training in the South. He did not, as far as I can gather, find the South "worse"; he found it, if anything, all too familiar. In the second place, though, even if Birmingham *is* worse, no doubt Johannesburg, South Africa, beats it by several miles and Buchenwald was one of the worst things that ever happened in the entire history of the world. The world has never lacked for horrifying examples; but I do not believe that these examples are meant to be used as justification for our own crimes. This perpetual justification empties the heart of all human feeling. The emptier our hearts become the greater will be our crimes. Thirdly, the South is not merely an embarrassingly backward

region, but a part of this country, and what happens there concerns every one of us.

18 As far as the color problem is concerned, there is but one great difference between the Southern white and the Northerner: the Southerner remembers, historically and in his own psyche, a kind of Eden in which he loved black people and they loved him. Historically, the flaming sword laid across this Eden is the Civil War. Personally, it is the Southerner's sexual coming of age, when, without any warning, unbreakable taboos are set up between himself and his past. Everything, thereafter, is permitted him except the love he remembers and has never ceased to need. The resulting, indescribable torment affects every Southern mind and is the basis of the Southern hysteria.

19 None of this is true for the Northerner. Negroes represent nothing to him personally, except, perhaps, the dangers of carnality. He never sees Negroes. Southerners see them all the time. Northerners never think about them whereas Southerners are never really thinking of anything else. Negroes are, therefore, ignored in the North and are under surveillance in the South, and suffer hideously in both places. Neither the Southerner nor the Northerner is able to look on the Negro simply as a man. It seems to be indispensable to the national self-esteem that the Negro bc considered either as a kind of ward (in which case we are told how many Negroes, comparatively, bought Cadillacs last year and how few, comparatively, were lynched), or as a victim (in which case we are promised that he will never vote in our assemblies or go to school with our kids). They are two side of the same coin and the South will not change—*cannot* change—until the North changes. The country will not change until it reexamines itself and discovers what it really means by freedom. In the meantime, generations keep being born, bitterness is increased by incompetence, pride, and folly, and the world shrinks around us.

20 It is a terrible, an inexorable, law that one cannot deny the humanity of another without diminishing one's own: in the face of one's victim, one sees oneself. Walk through the streets of Harlem and see what we, this nation, have become.

STUDY GUIDE

Tone

1. James Baldwin is one of the most powerful writers in the civil-rights movement in America today. He reveals a sharp, critical intelligence in everything he writes and an intense personal feeling. But he never allows this feeling to get out of hand. He exercises classical economy and restraint in his expression, which makes his indictment of the white man's treatment of the Negro all the more telling. Part of this control is revealed in his mastery of

the English sentence. Study his effective use of the *compound predicate, cumulative modifiers,* and *multiple appositives* to intensify his expression.

2. But perhaps the most striking characteristic of Baldwin's style—and one which contributes to both the great economy and emotional intensity of his expression—is his genius for the well-chosen metaphor or simile. It is this which most definitely creates the intensely critical but emotionally controlled tone of his writing. It would be well to discuss in detail the effect—in their context—of such statements and phrases as the following: "One of those stunted city trees is *snarling* where our doorway used to be . . ." (paragraph 1); ". . . having watched so many, for so long, struggling *in the fishooks,* the *barbed wire,* of this avenue" (paragraph 2); "a *riot,* a *forest* of children" (paragraph 3); "All along the block . . . are immense human gaps, like *craters*" (paragraph 4); "churches, niched in the walls *like cannon in the walls of a fortress*" (paragraph 12); "He [the policeman] moves through Harlem . . . *like an occupying soldier in a bitterly hostile country*" and "One day . . . someone *drops a match in the powder keg* and *everything blows up*" (paragraph 15); "A kind of panic paralyzes their features [those who have been told that Negroes want to be treated like men], as though they found themselves trapped on the edge of a steep place" (paragraph 16).

Joseph Wood Krutch (1893–)

Joseph Wood Krutch is a well-known critic, essayist, and teacher. Particularly noteworthy is his drama criticism contributed for years to *The Nation.* But he has not confined himself to the dramatic and literary scene. Krutch has written on many social, political, and scientific subjects and has become known as something of a pessimist in his views. But he has the happy facility of making any subject come alive because he writes concretely and not in mere abstractions. In "No Essays, Please!" he is lamenting the unpopularity of the familiar essay, but actually his own writing has done much to keep alive an interest in the genre.

NO ESSAYS, PLEASE!

Joseph Wood Krutch

1 Every now and then someone regrets publicly the passing of the familiar essay. Perhaps such regretters are usually in possession of a recent rejection slip; in any event there are not enough of them to impress editors.

Reprinted from the *Saturday Review* (March 10, 1951) by permission of the author and publisher.

The very word "essay" has fallen into such disfavor that it is avoided with horror, and anything which is not fiction is usually called either an "article," a "story," or just "a piece." When *The Atlantic Monthly*, once the last refuge of a dying tradition, now finds it advisable to go in for such "articles," as its recent "What Night Playing Has Done to Baseball" it is obvious that not merely the genteel tradition but a whole literary form is dead.

2 I am sure that the books on how to become a writer in ten easy lessons have been stressing this fact for a long time now. If *I* were writing such a book I certainly should, and I think that I could give some very practical advice. To begin with I should say something like the following:

3 Suppose that you have drawn a subject out of your mental box and you find that it is "Fish." Now if you were living in the time of Henry Van Dyke and Thomas Bailey Aldrich your best lead would be: "Many of my friends are ardent disciples of Isaac Walton." That would have had the appropriate personal touch and the requisite not too recondite literary allusion. But today of course no live-wire editor would read any further, not because this sounds like a dull familiar essay but simply because it sounds like *a* familiar essay. But "Fish" is still a perfectly usable subject provided you remember that salable non-fiction "pieces" almost invariably fall into one of three categories: the factual, the polemic, and what we now call—though I don't know why we have to deviate into French—*reportage*.

4 If you decide to be factual a good beginning would be: "Four million trout flies were manufactured last year by the three leading sports-supply houses." That is the sort of thing which makes almost any editor sit up and take notice. But it is no better than certain other possible beginnings. The polemic article ought to start: "Despite all the efforts of our department of wild life conservation, the number of game fish in American lakes and streams continues to decline steadily." Probably this kind of beginning to this kind of article is best of all because it sounds alarming and because nowadays (and for understandable reasons) whatever sounds alarming is generally taken to be true. However, if you want to go in for the trickier *reportage* start off with a sentence something like this: " 'Cap' Bill Hanks, a lean, silent, wryly humorous down-Easterner, probably knows more about the strange habits of the American fisherman than any man alive."

5 Of course, no one will ever inquire where you got your statistics about the trout flies, whether the fish population really is declining, or whether "Cap" Bill Hanks really exists. In fact, one of the best and lengthiest "Profiles" *The New Yorker* ever ran turned out to be about a "character" at the Fulton Fishmarket who didn't. Whatever looks like official fact or on-the-spot reporting is taken at face value and will be widely quoted. The important thing is that the editor first and the reader afterwards shall get the feeling that what he is being offered is not mere

literature but the real low-down on something or other—whether that something or other is or is not anything he cares much about.

6 Fling your facts around, never qualify anything (qualifications arouse distrust), and adopt an air of jolly omniscience. Remember that "essays" are written by introverts, "articles" by extroverts, and that the reader is going to resent anything which comes between him and that low-down which it is your principal function to supply. "Personalities," the more eccentric the better, are fine subjects for *reportage*. Manufacture or get hold of a good one and you may be able to do a "profile." But no one wants any personality to show in the magazine writer, whose business it is to be all-knowing, shrewd, and detached almost to the point of non-existence. This means, of course, that your style should have no quality which belongs to you, only the qualities appropriate to the magazine for which you are writing. The most successful of all the magazines functioning in America today seldom print anything which is not anonymous and apparently owe a considerable part of their success to the fact that nearly everything which appears in them achieves the manner of *Life*, *Time*, or *Fortune*, as the case may be, but never by any chance any characteristic which would enable the most sensitive analyst of style to discover who had written it.

7 The ideal is obviously a kind of writing which seems to have been produced not by a man but by some sort of electronic machine. Perhaps in time it will actually be produced that way, since such machines now solve differential equations and that is harder to do than to write the average magazine article. Probably if Vannevar Bush were to put his mind to the problem he could replace the whole interminable list of editors, assistant editors, and research assistants employed by the Luce publications with a contraption less elaborate than that now used to calculate the trajectory of a rocket. Meanwhile the general effect of mechanical impersonality can be achieved by a system of collaboration in the course of which such personalities as the individual collaborators may have are made to cancel one another out.

8 This system works best when these collaborators are divided into two groups called respectively "researchers" and "writers"—or, in other words, those who know something but don't write and those who don't know anything but do. This assures at the very outset that the actual writers shall have no dangerous interest in or even relation to what they write and that any individuality of approach which might tend to manifest itself in one of them will be canceled out by the others. If you then pass the end-result through the hands of one or more senior editors for further regularization you will obviously get finally something from which every trace of what might be called handwork has disappeared. One might suppose that the criticism of the arts would be a department in which some trace of

individuality would still be considered desirable, but I am reliably informed that at least at one time (and for all I know still) it was the custom to send an "editor" along with the movie critic to see every film so that this editor could tell the critic whether or not the film should be reviewed. This disposed of the possibility that the review might in some way reflect the critic's taste.

9 Obviously, few publications can afford the elaborate machinery which the Luce organization has set up. However, a great many strive to achieve something of the same effect by simpler means, and they expect their contributors to cooperate by recognizing the ideal and by coming as close to the realization of it as is possible for an individual to come. The circulations achieved by these publications seem to indicate how wise from one point of view their policy is. Those which still permit or even encourage a certain amount of individuality in their writers—even those which still offer a certain amount of non-fiction which is to some extent personal and reflective as opposed to the factual and the bleakly expository—must content themselves with relatively small circulations. Moreover, since they also print a good deal of the other sort of thing they create the suspicion that they survive in spite of rather than because of their limited hospitality to the man-made as opposed to the machine-made article.

10 No doubt the kind of essay which *The Atlantic* and the old *Century* once went in for died of anemia. It came to represent the genteel tradition at its feeblest. No one need be surprised that it did not survive. But what is significant is the fact that, whereas the genteel novel was succeeded by novels of a different sort and genteel poetry by poetry in a different manner, the familiar essay died without issue, so that what disappeared was a once important literary form for which changed times found no use. And the result is that there disappeared with it the best opportunity to consider in an effective way an area of human interest.

11 Because the "article" is impersonal it can deal only with subjects which exist in an impersonal realm. If its subject is not ominous, usually it must be desperately trivial; and just as the best-selling books are likely to have for title either something like "The World in Crisis" or "My Grandmother Did a Strip Tease," so the magazine articles which are not heavy are very likely to be inconsequential. I doubt that anyone was ever quite as eccentric as almost every subject of a *New Yorker* "Profile" is made to seem; but if a topic cannot be made "devastating" the next best thing is "fabulous."

12 Perhaps what disappeared with the familiar essay was not merely a form, not merely even an attitude, but a whole subect matter. For the familiar essay affords what is probably the best method of discussing those subjects which are neither obviously momentous nor merely silly. And,

since no really good life is composed exclusively of problems and farce, either the reading of most people today does not actually concern itself with some of the most important aspects of their lives or those lives are impoverished to a degree which the members of any really civilized society would find it difficult to understand. Just as genuine conversation—by which I mean something distinguishable from disputation, lamentation, and joke-telling—has tended to disappear from social gatherings, so anything comparable to it has tended to disappear from the printed page. By no means all of the Most-of-My-Friends essays caught it. But the best of them caught something which nowadays hardly gets into print at all.

13 Somehow we have got into the habit of assuming that even the so-called "human problems" are best discussed in terms as inhuman as possible. Just how one can profitably consider dispassionately so passionate a creature as man I do not know, but that seems to be the enterprise to which we have committed ourselves. The magazines are full of articles dealing statistically with, for example, the alleged failure or success of marriage. Lawyers discuss the law, sociologists publish statistics, and psychologists discuss case histories. Those are the methods by which we deal with the behavior of animals since animals can't talk. But men can—or at least once could—communicate, and one man's "familiar essay" on love and marriage might get closer to some all-important realities than any number of "studies" could.

14 No one is, to take another example, naive enough to suppose that all the current discussions of the welfare state are actually as "objective" as most of them pretend to be. Personal tastes, even simple self-interest, obviously influence most of them but only insofar as they introduce distortions between the lines. Everybody who writes for or against the competitive society tries to write as though he did not live in it, had had no personal experience of what living in it is like, and was dealing only with a question in which he had no personal interest. This is the way one talks about how to keep bees or raise the Black Angus. It is not the way either the bees or the Black Angus would discuss the good life as it affected them, and it is a singularly unrealistic way of considering anything which would affect us. Even the objective studies would be better and more objective if their authors permitted themselves freely to express elsewhere their "familiar" reaction to conditions and prospects instead of working in these feelings disguised as logical argument or scientific deduction.

15 All the sciences which deal with man have a tendency to depersonalize him for the simple reason that they tend to disregard everything which a particular science cannot deal with. Just as medicine confessedly deals with the physical man and economics confessedly deals not with Man but with the simplification officially designated as The Economic Man, so psychiatry deals with a fictitious man of whom there would be nothing

more to be said if he were "normal," and one branch of psychology deals with what might be called the I.Q. man whose only significant aspect is his ability to solve puzzles.

16 Literature is the only thing which deals with the whole complex phenomenon at once, and if all literature were to cease to exist the result would probably be that in the end whatever is not considered by one or another of the sciences would no longer be taken into account at all and would perhaps almost cease to exist. Then Man would no longer be—or at least no longer be observed to be—anything different from the mechanical sum of the Economic man, the I.Q. man, and the other partial men with whom the various partial sciences deal. Faced with that prospect we may well look with dismay at the disappearance of any usable literary form and wonder whether or not we have now entered upon a stage during which man's lingering but still complex individuality finds itself more and more completely deprived of the opportunity not only to express itself in living but even to discover corresponding individualities revealing themselves in the spoken or the written word.

17 That the situation could be radically altered by the cultivation of the familiar essay I am hardly prepared to maintain. Its disappearance is only a minor symptom. Or perhaps it is just a little bit more than that. At least there are a number of subjects which might profitably be discussed by fewer experts and more human beings. They might achieve a different kind of understanding of certain problems and they might lead to more humanly acceptable conclusions. "Most of my friends seem to feel that . . ."

SECTION 9

Understanding the Oration

THE SIXTH OF OCTOBER, 1789

Edmund Burke

1 This king, to say no more of him, and this queen,[1] and their infant children (who once would have been the pride and hope of a great and generous people) were then forced to abandon the sanctuary of the most splendid palace in the world, which they left swimming in blood, polluted by massacre, and strewed with scattered limbs and mutilated carcases. Thence they were conducted into the capital of their kingdom. Two had been selected from the unprovoked, unresisted, promiscuous slaughter, which was made of the gentlemen of birth and family who composed the king's body guard. These two gentlemen, with all the parade of an execution of justice, were cruelly and publicly dragged to the block, and beheaded in the great court of the palace. Their heads were stuck upon spears, and led the procession; whilst the royal captives who followed in the train were slowly moved along, amidst the horrid yells, and shrilling screams, and frantic dances, and infamous contumelies, and all the unutterable abominations of the furies of hell, in the abused shape of the vilest of women. After they had been made to taste, drop by drop, more than the bitterness of death, in the slow torture of a journey of twelve miles, protracted to six hours, they were, under a guard, composed of those very soldiers who had thus conducted them through this famous triumph, lodged in one of the old palaces of Paris now converted into a bastile for kings.

Reprinted from Edmund Burke, *Reflections on the Revolution in France* (1790).

[1] Louis XVI of France and Marie Antoinette.—*Ed.*

2 Is this a triumph to be consecrated at altars? to be commended with grateful thanksgiving? to be offered to the divine humanity with fervent prayer and enthusiastic ejaculation?—These Theban and Thracian orgies, acted in France, and applauded only in the old Jewry,[2] I assure you, kindle prophetic enthusiasm in the minds but of very few people in this kingdom: although a saint and apostle, who may have revelations of his own, and who has so completely vanquished all the mean superstitions of the heart, may incline to think it pious and decorous to compare it with the entrance into the world of the Prince of Peace, proclaimed in a holy temple by a venerable sage, and not long before not worse announced by the voice of angels to the quiet innocence of shepherds.

3 At first I was at a loss to account for this fit of unguarded transport. I knew, indeed, that the sufferings of monarchs make a delicious repast to some sort of palates. There were reflections which might serve to keep this appetite within some bounds of temperance. But when I took one circumstance into my consideration, I was obliged to confess, that much allowance ought to be made for the society, and that the temptation was too strong for common discretion; I mean, the circumstance of the Io Paean of the triumph, the animating cry which called "for *all* the BISHOPS to be hanged on the lamp-posts," might well have brought forth a burst of enthusiasm on the foreseen consequences of this happy day. I allow to so much enthusiasm some little deviation from prudence. I allow this prophet to break forth into hymns of joy and thanksgiving on an event which appears like the precursor of the Millennium, and the projected fifth monarchy, in the destruction of all church establishments. There was, however, (as in all human affairs there is,) in the midst of this joy, something to exercise the patience of these worthy gentlemen, and to try the long-suffering of their faith. The actual murder of the king and queen, and their child, was wanting to the other auspicious circumstances of this "*beautiful day*." The actual murder of the bishops, though called for by so many holy ejaculations, was also wanting. A group of regicide and sacrilegious slaughter, was indeed boldly sketched, but it was only sketched. It unhappily was left unfinished, in this great history-piece of the massacre of innocents. What hardy pencil of a great master, from the school of the rights of men, will finish it, is to be seen hereafter. The age has not yet the complete benefit of that diffusion of knowledge that has undermined superstition and error; and the king of France wants another object or two to consign to oblivion, in consideration of all the good which is to arise from his own sufferings, and the patriotic crimes of an enlightened age.

4 Although this work of our new light and knowledge did not go to the

[2] Dr. Richard Price, a Unitarian minister, had made a speech in a section of London called the Old Jewry, in which he defended the Revolution.—*Ed.*

length that in all probability it was intended it should be carried, yet I must think that such treatment of any human creatures must be shocking to any but those who are made for accomplishing revolutions. But I cannot stop here. Influenced by the inborn feelings of my nature, and not being illuminated by a single ray of this new-sprung modern light, I confess to you, Sir, that the exalted rank of the persons suffering, and particularly the sex, the beauty, and the amiable qualities of the descendant of so many kings and emperors, with the tender age of royal infants, insensible only through infancy and innocence of the cruel outrages to which their parents were exposed, instead of being a subject of exultation, adds not a little to my sensibility on that most melancholy occasion.

5 I hear that the august person, who was the principal object of our preacher's triumph, though he supported himself, felt much on that shameful occasion. As a man, it became him to feel for his wife and his children, and the faithful guards of his person, that were massacred in cold blood about him; as a prince, it became him to feel for the strange and frightful transformation of his civilized subjects, and to be more grieved for them than solicitous for himself. It derogates little from his fortitude, while it adds infinitely to the honor of his humanity. I am very sorry to say it, very sorry indeed, that such personages are in a situation in which it is not becoming in us to praise the virtues of the great.

6 I hear, and I rejoice to hear, that the great lady, the other object of the triumph, has borne that day, (one is interested that beings made for suffering should suffer well), and that she bears all the succeeding days, that she bears the imprisonment of her husband, and her captivity, and the exile of her friends, and the insulting adulation of addresses, and the whole weight of her accumulated wrongs, with a serene patience, in a manner suited to her rank and race, and becoming the offspring of a sovereign distinguished for her piety and her courage; that, like her, she has lofty sentiments; that she feels with the dignity of a Roman matron; that in the last extremity she will save herself from the last disgrace; and that, if she must fall, she will fall by no ignoble hand.

7 It is now sixteen or seventeen years since I saw the queen of France, then the dauphiness, at Versailles; and surely never lighted on this orb, which she hardly seemed to touch, a more delightful vision. I saw her just above the horizon, decorating and cheering the elevated sphere she just began to move in—glittering like the morning-star, full of life, and splendor, and joy. Oh! what a revolution! and what a heart must I have to contemplate without emotion that elevation and that fall! Little did I dream when she added titles of veneration to those of enthusiastic, distant, respectful love, that she should ever be obliged to carry the sharp antidote against disgrace concealed in that bosom; little did I dream that I should have lived to see such disasters fallen upon her in a nation of gallant men,

in a nation of men of honor, and of cavaliers. I thought ten thousand swords must have leaped from their scabbards to avenge even a look that threatened her with insult. But the age of chivalry is gone. That of sophisters, economists, and calculators, has succeeded; and the glory of Europe is extinguished for ever. Never, never more shall we behold that generous loyalty to rank and sex, that proud submission, that dignified obedience, that subordination of the heart, which kept alive, even in servitude itself, the spirit of an exalted freedom. The unbought grace of life, the cheap defense of nations, the nurse of manly sentiment and heroic enterprise, is gone! It is gone, that sensibility of principle, that chastity of honor, which felt a stain like a wound, which inspired courage whilst it mitigated ferocity, which ennobled whatever it touched, and under which vice itself lost half its evil, by losing all its grossness.

8 This mixed system of opinion and sentiment had its origin in the ancient chivalry; and the principle, though varied in its appearance by the varying state of human affairs, subsisted and influenced through a long succession of generations, even to the time we live in. If it should ever be totally extinguished, the loss I fear will be great. It is this which has given its character to modern Europe. It is this which has distinguished it under all its forms of government, and distinguished it to its advantage, from the states of Asia, and possibly from those states which flourished in the most brilliant periods of the antique world. It was this, which, without confounding ranks, had produced a noble equality, and handed it down through all the gradations of social life. It was this opinion which mitigated kings into companions, and raised private men to be fellows with kings. Without force or opposition, it subdued the fierceness of pride and power; it obliged sovereigns to submit to the soft collar of social esteem, compelled stern authority to submit to elegance, and gave a dominating vanquisher of laws to be subdued by manners.

9 But now all is to be changed. All the pleasing illusions, which made power gentle and obedience liberal, which harmonized the different shades of life and which, by a bland assimilation, incorporated into politics the sentiments which beautify and soften private society, are to be dissolved by this new conquering empire of light and reason. All the decent drapery of life is to be rudely torn off. All the superadded ideas, furnished from the wardrobe of a moral imagination, which the heart owns, and the understanding ratifies, as necessary to cover the defects of our naked, shivering nature, and to raise it to dignity in our own estimation, are to be exploded as a ridiculous, absurd, and antiquated fashion.

10 On this scheme of things, a king is but a man, a queen is but a woman; a woman is but an animal, and an animal not of the highest order. All homage paid to the sex in general as such, and without distinct views, is to be regarded as romance and folly. Regicide and parricide and sacri-

lege are but fictions of superstition, corrupting jurisprudence by destroying its simplicity. The murder of a king, or a queen, or a bishop, or a father are only common homicide; and if the people are by any chance, or in any way, gainers by it, a sort of homicide much the most pardonable, and into which we ought not to make too severe a scrutiny.

11 On the scheme of this barbarous philosophy, which is the offspring of cold hearts and muddy understandings, and which is as void of solid wisdom as it is destitute of all taste and elegance, laws are to be supported only by their own terrors, and by the concern which each individual may find in them from his own private speculations, or can spare to them from his own private interests. In the groves of *their* academy, at the end of every vista, you see nothing but the gallows. Nothing is left which engages the affections on the part of the commonwealth. On the principles of this mechanic philosophy, our institutions can never be embodied, if I may use the expression, in persons, so as to create in us love, veneration, admiration, or attachment. But that sort of reason which banishes the affections is incapable of filling their place. These public affections, combined with manners, are required sometimes as supplements, sometimes as correctives, always as aids to law. The precept given by a wise man, as well as a great critic, for the construction of poems, is equally true as to states: *Non satis est pulchra esse poemata, dulcia sunto.*[3] There ought to be a system of manners in every nation, which a well-formed mind would be disposed to relish. To make us love our country, our country ought to be lovely.

12 But power, of some kind or other, will survive the shock in which manners and opinions perish; and it will find other and worse means for its support. The usurpation which, in order to subvert ancient institutions, has destroyed ancient principles, will hold power by arts similar to those by which it has acquired it. When the old feudal and chivalrous spirit of *fealty*, which, by freeing kings from fear, freed both kings and subjects from the precautions of tyranny, shall be extinct in the minds of men, plots and assassinations will be anticipated by preventive murder and preventive confiscation, and that long roll of grim and bloody maxims, which form the political code of all power, not standing on its own honor, and the honor of those who are to obey it. Kings will be tyrants from policy, when subjects are rebels from principle.

13 When ancient opinions and rules of life are taken away, the loss cannot possibly be estimated. From that moment we have no compass to govern us; nor can we know distinctly to what port we steer. Europe, undoubtedly, taken in a mass, was in a flourishing condition the day on which your Revolution was completed. How much of that prosperous

[3] It is not enough that poems be merely beautiful; let them also be delightful.—*Horace.*

state was owing to the spirit of our old manners and opinions is not easy to say; but as such causes cannot be indifferent in their operation, we must presume, that, on the whole, their operation was beneficial.

14 We are but too apt to consider things in the state in which we find them, without sufficiently adverting to the causes by which they have been produced, and possibly may be upheld. Nothing is more certain, than that our manners, our civilization, and all the good things which are connected with manners, and with civilization, have, in this European world of ours, depended for ages upon two principles; and were indeed the result of both combined; I mean the spirit of a gentleman, and the spirit of religion. The nobility and the clergy, the one by profession, the other by patronage, kept learning in existence, even in the midst of arms and confusions, and whilst governments were rather in their causes, than formed. Learning paid back what it received to nobility and to priesthood; and paid it with usury, by enlarging their ideas, and by furnishing their minds. Happy if they had all continued to know their indissoluble union, and their proper place! Happy if learning, not debauched by ambition, had been satisfied to continue the instructor, and not aspired to be the master! Along with its natural protectors and guardians, learning will be cast into the mire, and trodden down under the hoofs of a swinish multitude.

15 If, as I suspect, modern letters owe more than they are always willing to own to ancient manners, so do other interests which we value full as much as they are worth. Even commerce, and trade, and manufacture, the gods of our economical politicians, are themselves perhaps but creatures; are themselves but effects, which, as first causes, we choose to worship. They certainly grew under the same shade in which learning flourished. They too may decay with their natural protecting principles. With you, for the present at least, they all threaten to disappear together. Where trade and manufactures are wanting to a people, and the spirit of nobility and religion remains, sentiment supplies, and not always ill supplies, their place; but if commerce and the arts should be lost in an experiment to try how well a state may stand without these old fundamental principles, what sort of a thing must be a nation of gross, stupid, ferocious, and, at the same time, poor and sordid barbarians, destitute of religion, honor, or manly pride, possessing nothing at present, and hoping for nothing hereafter?

16 I wish you may not be going fast, and by the shortest cut, to that horrible and disgustful situation. Already, there appears a poverty of conception, a coarseness and vulgarity in all the proceedings of the assembly and of all their instructors. Their liberty is not liberal. Their science is presumptuous ignorance. Their humanity is savage and brutal.

17 It is not clear, whether in England we learned those grand and decorous principles, and manners, of which considerable traces yet remain, from you, or whether you took them from us. But to you, I think, we trace them

best. You seem to me to be—*gentis incunabula nostrae.*[4] France has always more or less influenced manners in England: and when your fountain is choked up and polluted, the stream will not run long, or not run clear, with us, or perhaps with any nation. This gives all Europe, in my opinion, but too close and connected a concern in what is done in France. Excuse me, therefore, if I have dwelt too long on the atrocious spectacle of the 6th of October, 1789, or have given too much scope to the reflections which have arisen in my mind on occasion of the most important of all revolutions, which may be dated from that day, I mean a revolution in sentiments, manners, and moral opinions. As things now stand, with everything respectable destroyed without us, and an attempt to destroy within us every principle of respect, one is almost forced to apologize for harboring the common feelings of men.

STUDY GUIDE

1. The *formal oration* is no longer a very popular literary genre, but, as pointed out in connection with "A Modest Proposal," it did have a great influence in developing a sense of structure in English writing. Its influence is easily detected in nineteenth-century writers like Macaulay, Arnold, and Newman. Edmund Burke, who wrote at the very end of the eighteenth century, was one of the greatest masters of the oratorical style in English. Several of Burke's orations, and particularly his "On Conciliation with the Colonies," were written on the pattern of the classical oration, and all of his writings show the effect of the traditional oratorical style. This is especially true of sections of his "Reflections on the Revolution in France." In the selection reproduced here Burke is lamenting the passing of royalty and the old aristocracy. It is partly a defense of the idea of a monarchy and an aristocracy and partly a laudatory speech, or *encomium,* on Marie Antoinette. The oratorical quality of the passage is evident in the smooth-flowing rotundity of the sentence structure. Many of the sentences are periodic, which is partly responsible for its emotional intensity. Check on the number of periodic sentences in the passage and study their effect in building the emotional intensity and sense of suspense.

2. In any style that is chiefly aural in its appeal, as oratory is, there is bound to be a great deal of repetition and parallelism in sentence structure. This is helpful to the audience, which must catch what is said on the fly. The repeated structural patterns allow successive ideas to slide into the audience's consciousness on the same wavelength. A shift of structure would make comprehension more difficult. This repetition shows in repeated words, in accumulated appositives, in compound predicates, in phrases in parallel grammatical structure, and in whole sentences that are constructed in a similar pattern. Note, for instance, the repeated sentence pattern in paragraph 8 created by the repetition of "It is this . . ." at the beginning of successive sentences. Try to find examples of each of the kinds of repetition enumerated

[4] The cradle of our race.—*Virgil.*

above in the selection and show how they contribute to the swelling rhythm of the style.

3. One of the dangers of an oratorical style is that the audience can be swept along on an emotional wave through the very rhythm of the language without thinking very much about what is being said. The speaker or writer, too, can allow himself to be carried away by his emotions rather than by logic. Newman felt that this has happened to Burke in this passage. Can you point out instances where the appeal is overly emotional at the expense of history and ethics?

4. There is no doubt whatever where Burke's sympathies lie in the passage. He shows his admiration for aristocratic values and his antipathy towards the new bourgeois revolution by the diction he employs. Words create values (good or bad) through their connotations. Note, for instance, the pejorative connotation of the italicized words and phrases in the following sentence: "Their heads were stuck upon spears, and led the procession; whilst the royal captives who followed in the train were slowly moved along, amidst the *horrid yells,* and *shrilling screams,* and *frantic dances,* and *infamous contumelies,* and all the *unutterable abominations of the furies of hell,* in the *abused shape of the vilest of women.*" And, on the other hand, note the favorable connotation of the italicized words in the following sentences: "It is now sixteen or seventeen years since I saw the queen of France, then the dauphiness, at Versailles; and surely never *lighted on this orb, which she hardly seemed to touch, a more delightful vision.* I saw her *just above the horizon, decorating and cheering the elevated sphere she just began to move in—glittering like the morning-star, full of life, and splendor, and joy.*" Find other examples of diction in the passage that create a bad atmosphere around the group the audience is expected to dislike and a good atmosphere around those it is expected to like.

ADDRESS AT THE DEDICATION OF THE GETTYSBURG NATIONAL CEMETERY

Abraham Lincoln

1 Four score and seven years ago our fathers brought forth on this continent, a new nation, conceived in Liberty, and dedicated to the proposition that all men are created equal.

2 Now we are engaged in a great civil war; testing whether that nation, or any nation so conceived and so dedicated, can long endure. We are met on a great battlefield of that war. We have come to dedicate a portion of that field as a final resting-place for those who here gave their lives that that nation might live. It is altogether fitting and proper that we should do this.

Delivered at Gettysburg, Pennsylvania, November 19, 1863.

3 But, in a larger sense, we cannot dedicate—we cannot consecrate—we cannot hallow—this ground. The brave men, living and dead, who struggled here have consecrated it, far above our poor power to add or detract. The world will little note, nor long remember, what we say here, but it can never forget what they did here. It is for us the living, rather, to be dedicated here to the unfinished work which they who fought here have thus far so nobly advanced. It is rather for us to be here dedicated to the great task remaining before us—that from these honored dead we take increased devotion to that cause for which they gave the last full measure of devotion; that we here highly resolve that these dead shall not have died in vain; that this nation, under God, shall have a new birth of freedom; and that government of the people, by the people, for the people, shall not perish from the earth.

STUDY GUIDE

1. In contrast to the flowing Ciceronian style of Burke, Lincoln's address sounds Senecan in its curt and terse expression. Yet it, too, has some of the structure and style of an oration. Huntington Brown, professor of English literature at the University of Minnesota, calls it a lay sermon. The opening sentence, Brown says, "is something like a text."[1] Show how the sentences and paragraphs that follow develop the idea expressed in that opening sentence.

2. The address is really bound together by the rhetorical *schemata verborum* (repetative sound patterns): repeated words, and repeated phrases and clauses. Show how this element of repetition does create a sense of continuity and climax in the address.

THE RETREAT FROM FLANDERS

Winston Churchill

1 From the moment when the defenses at Sedan on the Meuse were broken at the end of the second week in May only a rapid retreat to Amiens and the south could have saved the British-French armies who had entered Belgium at the appeal of the Belgian King.

2 This strategic fact was not immediately realized. The French High

Delivered before the House of Commons, London, England, June 4, 1940. Reprinted from *Vital Speeches of the Day*, Vol. VI, pp. 516–519, by permission.

[1] Huntington Brown, *Prose Styles, Five Primary Types* (Minneapolis: University of Minnesota Press, 1966), p. 52.

Command hoped it would be able to close the gap. The armies of the north were under their orders. Moreover, a retirement of that kind would have involved almost certainly the destruction of a fine Belgian Army of twenty divisions and abandonment of the whole of Belgium.

3 Therefore, when the force and scope of the German penetration was realized and when the new French Generalissimo, General [Maxime] Weygand, assumed command in place of General Gamelin, an effort was made by the French and British Armies in Belgium to keep holding the right hand of the Belgians and give their own right hand to the newly created French Army which was to advance across the Somme in great strength.

4 However, the German eruption swept like a sharp scythe south of Amiens to the rear of the armies in the north—eight or nine armored divisions, each with about 400 armored vehicles of different kinds divisible into small self-contained units.

5 This force cut off all communications between us and the main French Army. It severed our communications for food and ammunition. It ran first through Amiens, afterward through Abbeville, and it shore its way up the coast to Boulogne and Calais, almost to Dunkerque.

6 Behind this armored and mechanized onslaught came a number of German divisions in lorries, and behind them, again, plodded comparatively slowly the dull, brute mass of the ordinary German Army and German people, always ready to be led to the trampling down in other lands of liberties and comforts they never have known in their own.

7 I said this armored scythe stroke almost reached Dunkerque—almost but not quite. Boulogne and Calais were scenes of desperate fighting. The guards defended Boulogne for a while and were then withdrawn by orders from this country.

8 The rifle brigade of the Sixtieth Rifles (Queen Victoria's Rifles), with a battalion of British tanks and 1,000 Frenchmen, in all about 4,000 strong, defended Calais to the last. The British brigadier was given an hour to surrender. He spurned the offer. Four days of intense street fighting passed before the silence reigned in Calais which marked the end of a memorable resistance.

9 Only thirty unwounded survivors were brought off by the navy, and we do not know the fate of their comrades. Their sacrifice was not, however, in vain. At least two armored divisions which otherwise would have been turned against the B. E. F. had to be sent to overcome them. They have added another page to the glories of the light division.

10 The time gained enabled the Gravelines water line to be flooded and held by French troops. Thus the port of Dunkerque was held open. When it was found impossible for the armies of the north to reopen their communications through Amiens with the main French armies, only one choice remained. It seemed, indeed, a forlorn hope. The Belgian and

French armies were almost surrounded. Their sole line of retreat was to a single port and its neighboring beaches. They were pressed on every side by heavy attacks and were far outnumbered in the air.

11 When a week ago today I asked the House to fix this afternoon for the occasion of a statement, I feared it would be my hard lot to announce from this box the greatest military disaster of our long history.

12 I thought, and there were good judges who agreed with me, that perhaps 20,000 or 30,000 men might be re-embarked, but it certainly seemed that the whole French First Army and the whole B. E. F., north of the Amiens-Abbeville gap would be broken up in open field or else have to capitulate for lack of food and ammunition.

13 These were the hard and heavy tidings I called on the House and nation to prepare themselves for.

14 The whole root and core and brain of the British Army, around which and upon which we were building and are able to build the great British armies of later years, seemed due to perish upon the field. That was the prospect a week ago, but another blow which might have proved final was still to fall upon us.

15 The King of the Belgians called upon us to come to his aid. Had not this ruler and his government severed themselves from the Allies who rescued their country from extinction in the late war, and had they not sought refuge in what has been proved to be fatal neutrality, then the French and British armies at the outset might well have saved not only Belgium but perhaps even Holland.

16 At the last moment, when Belgium was already invaded, King Leopold called upon us to come to his aid, and even at the last moment we came. He and his brave and efficient army of nearly half a million strong guarded our eastern flank; this kept open our only retreat to the sea.

17 Suddenly, without any prior consultation and with the least possible notice, without the advice of his ministers and on his own personal act, he sent a plenipotentiary to the German Command surrendering his army and exposing our flank and the means of retreat.

18 I asked the House a week ago to suspend its judgment because the facts were not clear. I do not think there is now any reason why we should not form our own opinions upon this pitiful episode. The surrender of the Belgian Army compelled the British Army at the shortest notice to cover a flank to the sea of more than thirty miles' length which otherwise would have been cut off.

19 In doing this and closing this flank, contact was lost inevitably between the British and two of three corps forming the First French Army who were then further from the coast than we were. It seemed impossible that large numbers of Allied troops could reach the coast. The enemy

attacked on all sides in great strength and fierceness, and their main power, air force, was thrown into the battle.

20 The enemy began to fire cannon along the beaches by which alone shipping could approach or depart. They sowed magnetic mines in the channels and seas and sent repeated waves of hostile aircraft, sometimes more than 100 strong, to cast bombs on a single pier that remained and on the sand dunes.

21 Their U-boats, one of which was sunk, and motor launches took their toll of the vast traffic which now began. For four or five days the intense struggle raged. All armored divisions, or what was left of them, together with great masses of German infantry and artillery, hurled themselves on the ever narrowing and contracting appendix within which the British and French armies fought.

22 Meanwhile the Royal Navy, with the willing help of countless merchant seamen and a host of volunteers, strained every nerve and every effort and every craft to embark the British and Allied troops.

23 Over 220 light warships and more than 650 other vessels were engaged. They had to approach this difficult coast, often in adverse weather, under an almost ceaseless hail of bombs and increasing concentration of artillery fire. Nor were the seas themselves free from mines and torpedoes.

24 It was in conditions such as these that our men carried on with little or no rest for days and nights, moving troops across dangerous waters and bringing with them always the men whom they had rescued. The numbers they brought back are the measure of their devotion and their courage.

25 Hospital ships, which were plainly marked, were the special target for Nazi bombs, but the men and women aboard them never faltered in their duty.

26 Meanwhile the R. A. F., who already had been intervening in the battle so far as its range would allow it to go from home bases, now used a part of its main metropolitan fighter strength to strike at German bombers.

27 The struggle was protracted and fierce. Suddenly the scene has cleared. The crash and thunder has momentarily, but only for the moment, died away. The miracle of deliverance achieved by the valor and perseverance, perfect discipline, faultless service, skill and unconquerable vitality is a manifesto to us all.

28 The enemy was hurled back by the British and French troops. He was so roughly handled that he dare not molest their departure seriously. The air force decisively defeated the main strength of the German Air Force and inflicted on them a loss of at least four to one.

29 The navy, using nearly 1,000 ships of all kinds, carried over 335,000 men, French and British, from the jaws of death back to their native land and to the tasks which lie immediately before them.

30 We must be very careful not to assign to this deliverance attributes of a victory. Wars are not won by evacuations, but there was a victory inside this deliverance which must be noted.

31 Many of our soldiers coming back have not seen the air force at work. They only saw the bombers which escaped their protective attack. This was a great trial of strength between the British and German Air Forces.

32 Can you conceive of a greater objective for the power of Germany in the air than to make all evacuations from these beaches impossible and to sink all of the ships, numbering almost 1,000? Could there have been an incentive of greater military importance and significance to the whole purpose of the war?

33 They tried hard and were beaten back. They were frustrated in their task; we have got the armies away and they have paid fourfold for any losses sustained. Very large formations of German airplanes were turned on several occasions from the attack by a quarter their number of R. A. F. planes and dispersed in different directions. Twelve airplanes have been hunted by two. One airplane was driven into the water and cast away by the charge of a British airplane which had no more ammunition.

34 All of our types and our pilots have been vindicated. The Hurricane, Spitfire and Defiance have been vindicated. When I consider how much greater would be our advantage in defending the air above this island against overseas attacks, I find in these facts a sure basis on which practical and reassuring thoughts may rest, and I will pay my tribute to these young airmen.

35 May it not be that the cause of civilization itself will be defended by the skill and devotion of a few thousand airmen? There never has been, I suppose, in all the history of the world such opportunity for youth.

36 The Knights of the Round Table and the Crusaders have fallen back into distant days, not only distant but prosaic; but these young men are going forth every morning, going forth holding in their hands an instrument of colossal shattering power, of whom it may be said that every morn brought forth a noble chance and every chance brought forth a noble deed. These young men deserve our gratitude, as all brave men who in so many ways and so many occasions are ready and will continue to be ready to give their life and their all to their native land.

37 I return to the army. In a long series of very fierce battles, now on this front, now on that, fighting on three fronts at once, battles fought by two or three divisions against an equal or sometimes larger number of the enemy, and fought very fiercely on old ground so many of us knew so well, our losses in men exceed 30,000 in killed, wounded and missing. I take this occasion for expressing the sympathy of the House with those who have suffered bereavement or are still anxious.

38 The President of the Board of Trade (Sir Andrew Duncan) is not here today. His son has been killed, and many here have felt private affliction of the sharpest form, but I would say about the missing—we have had a large number of wounded come home safely to this country—there may be very many reported missing who will come back home some day.

39 In the confusion of departure it is inevitable that many should be cut off. Against this loss of over 30,000 men we may set the far heavier loss certainly inflicted on the enemy, but our losses in material are enormous. We have perhaps lost one-third of the men we lost in the opening days of the battle on March 21, 1918, but we have lost nearly as many guns—nearly 1,000—and all our transport and all the armored vehicles that were with the army of the north.

40 These losses will impose further delay on the expansion of our military strength. That expansion has not been proceeding as fast as we had hoped. The best of all we had to give has been given to the B. E. F., and although they had not the number of tanks and some articles of equipment which were desirable they were a very well and finely equipped army. They had the first fruits of all our industry had to give. That has gone and now here is further delay.

41 How long it will be, how long it will last depends upon the exertions which we make on this island. An effort, the like of which has never been seen in our records, is now being made. Work is proceeding night and day, Sundays and week days. Capital and labor have cast aside their interests, rights and customs and put everything into the common stock. Already the flow of munitions has leaped forward. There is no reason why we should not in a few months overtake the sudden and serious loss that has come upon us without retarding the development of our general program.

42 Nevertheless, our thankfulness at the escape of our army with so many men, and the thankfulness of their loved ones, who passed through an agonizing week, must not blind us to the fact that what happened in France and Belgium is a colossal military disaster.

43 The French Army has been weakened, the Belgian Army has been lost and a large part of those fortified lines upon which so much faith was reposed has gone, and many valuable mining districts and factories have passed into the enemy's possession.

44 The whole of the Channel ports are in his hands, with all the strategic consequences that follow from that, and we must expect another blow to be struck almost immediately at us or at France.

45 We were told that Hitler has plans for invading the British Isles. This has often been thought of before. When Napoleon lay at Boulogne for a year with his flat-bottomed boats and his Grand Army, some one told him there were bitter weeds in England. There certainly were and a good many more of them have since been returned. The whole question of defense

against invasion is powerfully affected by the fact that we have for the time being in this island incomparably more military forces than we had in the last war. But this will not continue. We shall not be content with a defensive war. We have our duty to our Allies.

46 We have to reconstitute and build up the B. E. F. once again under its gallant Commander in Chief, Lord Gort. All this is en train. But now I feel we must put our defense in this island into such a high state of organization that the fewest possible numbers will be required to give effectual security and that the largest possible potential offensive effort may be released.

47 On this we are now engaged. It would be very convenient to enter upon this subject in secret sessions. The government would not necessarily be able to reveal any great military secrets, but we should like to have our discussions free and without the restraint imposed by the fact that they would be read the next day by the enemy.

48 The government would benefit by the views expressed by the House. I understand that some request is to be made on this subject, which will be readily acceded to by the government. We have found it necessary to take measures of increasing stringency, not only against enemy aliens and suspicious characters of other nationalities but also against British subjects who may become a danger or a nuisance should the war be transported to the United Kingdom.

49 I know there are a great many people affected by the orders which we have made who are passionate enemies of Nazi Germany. I am very sorry for them, but we cannot, under the present circumstances, draw all the distinctions we should like to do. If parachute landings were attempted and fierce fights followed, those unfortunate people would be far better out of the way for their own sake as well as ours.

50 There is, however, another class for which I feel not the slightest sympathy. Parliament has given us powers to put down fifth column activities with the strongest hand, and we shall use those powers subject to the supervision and correction of the House without hesitation until we are satisfied and more than satisfied that this malignancy in our midst has been effectually stamped out.

51 Turning once again to the question of invasion, there has, I will observe, never been a period in all those long centuries of which we boast when an absolute guarantee against invasion, still less against serious raids, could have been given to our people. In the days of Napoleon the same wind which might have carried his transports across the Channel might have driven away a blockading fleet. There is always the chance, and it is that chance which has excited and befooled the imaginations of many continental tyrants.

52 We are assured that novel methods will be adopted, and when we

see the originality, malice and ingenuity of aggression which our enemy displays we may certainly prepare ourselves for every kind of novel stratagem and every kind of brutal and treacherous manoeuvre. I think no idea is so outlandish that it should not be considered and viewed with a watchful, but at the same time steady, eye.

53 We must never forget the solid assurances of sea power and those which belong to air power if they can be locally exercised. I have myself full confidence that if all do their duty and if the best arrangements are made, as they are being made, we shall prove ourselves once again able to defend our island home, ride out the storms of war and outlive the menace of tyranny, if necessary, for years, if necessary, alone.

54 At any rate, that is what we are going to try to do. That is the resolve of His Majesty's Government, every man of them. That is the will of Parliament and the nation. The British Empire and the French Republic, linked together in their cause and their need, will defend to the death their native soils, aiding each other like good comrades to the utmost of their strength, even though a large tract of Europe and many old and famous States have fallen or may fall into the grip of the Gestapo and all the odious apparatus of Nazi rule.

55 We shall not flag nor fail. We shall go on to the end. We shall fight in France and on the seas and oceans; we shall fight with growing confidence and growing strength in the air. We shall defend our island whatever the cost may be; we shall fight on beaches, landing grounds, in fields, in streets and on the hills. We shall never surrender and even if, which I do not for the moment believe, this island or a large part of it were subjugated and starving, then our empire beyond the seas, armed and guarded by the British Fleet, will carry on the struggle until in God's good time the New World, with all its power and might, sets forth to the liberation and rescue of the Old.

STUDY GUIDE

1. This address was delivered by Winston Churchill before the House of Commons on June 4, 1940, after the famous evacuation at Dunkirk. It is a straightforward but moving report of the heroic operation to save the troops, rising to an eloquent appeal for cooperation in resisting the Nazis. The narration of the dramatic events of this evacuation occupy paragraphs 1–44. Within this larger division, paragraphs 30–36 are a tribute to the action of the British Air Corps, and paragraphs 45–55 bring the address to the climactic appeal for resistance to Hitler's planned invasion.

2. Charles McLaughlin analyzes the strategy of Churchill in this speech. McLaughlin writes:

> By a bold plunge into the realities of the case, he wins the confidence of his audience in the honesty of his intentions and through his masterly account of the campaign he provides them with a way of coming to terms with the chaotic experiences of the week of crisis. But more importantly, the narration, in its impersonal seeming account of causes, fixes the blame for the disaster on the French High Command and on the unexpected surrender of the Belgian army. Again, by means of the narrative technique, Churchill artfully plays with the audience's expectations, for he takes opportunity to contrast the terrible expectations that confronted the British as the crisis neared ["I feared it would be my hard lot to announce the greatest military disaster in our long history"] with the actual outcome, thereby making the evacuation seem almost to be a glorious achievement. After having cleared the British leadership from blame and having placed a new assessment upon retreat, Churchill addresses himself to the immediate future. In the second part of the speech, he brilliantly plays upon the opposite spurs to human action—fear and hope. On the one side he dramatically depicts the terrible invasion threat under which England lay after Dunkirk and, on the other, he surveys with confidence the English capacity to withdraw the threat.[1]

Trace through in detail how Churchill achieves these effects in the narrative part of the address.

3. Paragraph 55 is the much quoted peroration of this Dunkirk speech. Show how much of its force and emotional climax is achieved through the repetition of parallel sentence structure.

INAUGURAL ADDRESS

John F. Kennedy

My Fellow Citizens:

1 We observe today not a victory of party but a celebration of freedom —symbolizing an end as well as a beginning—signifying renewal as well as change. For I have sworn before you and Almighty God the same solemn oath our forebears prescribed nearly a century and three quarters ago.

2 The world is very different now. For man holds in his mortal hands the power to abolish all form of human poverty and to abolish all form of human life. And, yet, the same revolutionary beliefs for which our forebears fought are still at issue around the globe—the belief that the rights

Delivered at the United States Capitol, Washington, D.C., January 30, 1961.

[1] Charles McLaughlin, "Inside the Serious Essay," in *Using Prose*, Donald W. Lee and William T. Moynihan, eds. (New York: Dodd, Mead & Company, Inc., 1961), pp. 180–181.

of man come not from the generosity of the state but from the hand of God.

3 We dare not forget today that we are the heirs of that first revolution. Let the word go forth from this time and place, to friend and foe alike, that the torch has been passed to a new generation of Americans—born in this century, tempered by war, disciplined by a cold and bitter peace, proud of our ancient heritage—and unwilling to witness or permit the slow undoing of those human rights to which this nation has always been committed, and to which we are committed today.

4 Let every nation know, whether it wish us well or ill, that we shall pay any price, bear any burden, meet any hardship, support any friend or oppose any foe in order to assure the survival and success of liberty.

5 This much we pledge—and more.

6 To those old Allies whose cultural and spiritual origins we share, we pledge the loyalty of faithful friends. United, there is little we cannot do in a host of new co-operative ventures. Divided, there is little we can do—for we dare not meet a powerful challenge at odds and split asunder.

7 To those new states whom we now welcome to the ranks of the free, we pledge our word that one form of colonial control shall not have passed merely to be replaced by a far more iron tyranny. We shall not always expect to find them supporting our every view. But we shall always hope to find them strongly supporting their own freedom—and to remember that, in the past, those who foolishly sought to find power by riding on the tiger's back inevitably ended up inside.

8 To those peoples in the huts and villages of half the globe struggling to break the bonds of mass misery, we pledge our best efforts to help them help themselves, for whatever period is required—not because the Communists are doing it, not because we seek their votes, but because it is right. If the free society cannot help the many who are poor, it can never save the few who are rich.

9 To our sister republics south of our border, we offer a special pledge—to convert our good words into good deeds—in a new alliance for progress—to assist free men and free Governments in casting off the chains of poverty. But this peaceful revolution of hope cannot become the prey of hostile powers. Let all our neighbors know that we shall join with them to oppose aggression or subversion anywhere in the Americas. And let every other power know that this Hemisphere intends to remain the master of its own house.

10 To that world assembly of sovereign states, the United Nations, our last best hope in an age where the instruments of war have far outpaced the instruments of peace, we renew our pledge of support—to prevent its becoming merely a forum for invective—to strengthen its shield of the new and the weak—and to enlarge the area to which its writ may run.

11 Finally, to those nations who would make themselves our adversary, we offer not a pledge but a request: that both sides begin anew the quest for peace, before the dark powers of destruction unleashed by science engulf all humanity in planned or accidental self-destruction.

12 We dare not tempt them with weakness. For only when our arms are sufficient beyond doubt can we be certain beyond doubt that they will never be employed.

13 But neither can two great and powerful groups of nations take comfort from their present course—both sides overburdened by the cost of modern weapons, both rightly alarmed by the steady spread of the deadly atom, yet both racing to alter that uncertain balance of terror that stays the hand of mankind's final war.

14 So let us begin anew—remembering on both sides that civility is not a sign of weakness and sincerity is always subject to proof. Let us never negotiate out of fear. But let us never fear to negotiate.

15 Let both sides explore what problems unite us instead of belaboring the problems that divide us.

16 Let both sides, for the first time, formulate serious and precise proposals for the inspection and control of arms—and bring the absolute power to destroy other nations under the absolute control of all nations.

17 Let both sides join to invoke the wonders of science instead of its terrors. Together let us explore the stars, conquer the deserts, eradicate disease, tap the ocean depths and encourage the arts and commerce.

18 Let both sides unite to heed in all corners of the earth the command of Isaiah—to "undo the heavy burdens . . . (and) let the oppressed go free."

19 And if a beachhead of co-operation can be made in the jungles of suspicion, let both sides join in the next task: creating, not a new balance of power, but a new world of law, where the strong are just and the weak secure and the peace preserved forever.

20 All this will not be finished in the first 100 days. Nor will it be finished in the first 1,000 days, nor in the life of this Administration, nor even perhaps in our lifetime on this planet. But let us begin.

21 In your hands, my fellow citizens, more than in mine, will rest the final success or failure of our course. Since this country was founded, each generation has been summoned to give testimony to its national loyalty. The graves of young Americans who answered that call encircle the globe.

22 Now the trumpet summons us again—not as a call to bear arms, though arms we need—not as a call to battle, though embattled we are—but a call to bear the burden of a long twilight struggle, year in and year out, "rejoicing in hope, patient in tribulation"—a struggle against the common enemies of man: tyranny, poverty, disease and war itself.

23 Can we forge against these enemies a grand and global alliance, north and south, east and west, that can assure a more fruitful life for all mankind? Will you join in that historic effort?

24 In the long history of the world, only a few generations have been granted the role of defending freedom in its hour of maximum danger. I do not shrink from this responsibility—I welcome it. I do not believe that any of us would exchange places with any other people or any other generation. The energy, the faith and the devotion which we bring to this endeavor will light our country and all who serve it—and the glow from that fire can truly light the world.

25 And so, my fellow Americans: Ask not what your country will do for you—ask what you can do for your country.

26 My fellow citizens of the world: Ask not what America will do for you, but what together we can do for the freedom of man.

27 Finally, whether you are citizens of America or of the world, ask of us the same high standards of strength and sacrifice that we shall ask of you. With a good conscience our only sure reward, with history the final judge of our deeds, let us go forth to lead the land we love, asking His blessing and His help, but knowing that here on earth God's work must truly be our own.

STUDY GUIDE

1. Kennedy's inaugural address forms an interesting thematic contrast with the selection from Burke. Burke was pleading for the retention of an aristocracy. For what is Kennedy pleading?

2. Burke's appeal was highly emotional; while Kennedy's appeal is serious and intense, it is more restrained and reasoned. How does this different tone show in the structure of his sentences?

3. *Time* described the style of the speech as "lean and lucid." Do you agree that those terms accurately characterize it? If so, why?

4. The style at times approaches the antithetical style of the eighteenth century. Paragraph 2 provides an example: "For man holds in his mortal hands the power *to abolish all form of human poverty* and *to abolish all form of human life*." Find other examples of such antithetical statements.

5. Although the style in sentence structure may be called lean, that does not mean that it is colorless or without metaphor. For example, paragraph 7 concludes with the witty reminder that ". . . in the past, those who foolishly sought to find power by riding on the tiger's back inevitably ended up inside." Restate what the President was saying here unmetaphorically and then indicate what was gained in expressiveness by the metaphorical statement. Find other examples of metaphor in the address.

TRAINED INTELLIGENCE—THE NATION'S GREATEST WEAPON

Adlai E. Stevenson

1 Nietzsche said that women were God's second mistake. And I say that Radcliffe is my third mistake. I made a commencement address at Vassar College one time, and wisely concluded that I would never make that mistake again. But I did. The next time it was Smith; and once more I wisely concluded never to face all those disconcerting, lovely young faces again. And here I am, as uncomfortable as I look, making the same mistake for a third time—and of all places at Radcliffe which is such a luminous and pretty part of the boundless intellectual galaxy of Harvard.

2 I've been wondering *why* I make this foolhardy mistake again and again. Perhaps, like the ancient Greeks, I am so desperate for learning that I even turn to lecturing to acquire it. Or is it, as Dr. Johnson wrote, that one of the last things we men are willing to give up, even in advanced age, is the supposition that we have something to say of interest to the opposite sex? But, of course, it's neither. I'm just an old man who can't say no—to President Bunting and certain charming young ladies of my acquaintance.

3 Do you, by the way, know the difference between a beautiful woman and a charming one? A beauty is a woman you notice; a charmer is one who notices *you!*

4 I hope you are all going to be charming today, because my assignment is to talk to you for awhile, and yours is to listen to me. I trust we will both finish our work at the same time.

5 In previous appearances at women's colleges, my solemn remarks were addressed to women specifically—about the place of educated women in our society; about bringing up children in a neurotic world; about the conflict between the office desk and the kitchen sink. After listening to my highly instructive addresses I came to the enlightened conclusion that women would not be truly emancipated until commencement speakers ignored the fact that they were women, and directed their remarks to graduating students who happened to be women and not to women who happened to be graduating.

6 So, like most of my decisions, I shall of course ignore it and talk to you as women.

7 I proceed at once, then, to the central question. The question is whether the wonderfully diverse and gifted assemblage of humans on this

Delivered at Radcliffe College, Cambridge, Massachusetts, June 12, 1963. Reprinted from *Vital Speeches of the Day*, Vol. XXIX, pp. 581–584, by permission.

earth really know how to operate a civilization. Survival is still an open question—not because of environmental hazards, but because of the workings of the human mind. And day by day the problem grows more complex.

8 However, there is something even more difficult—something even more essential—than comprehending the great complexities. And that is comprehending the great simplicities.

9 Let me mention only a few. The first is that human ingenuity has shot far ahead of human responsibility. The destructive intelligence has far outstripped the moral imagination. We have created the engines of world annihilation long before we have given sustained thought to the mechanisms of control, let alone mastered them.

10 Another simplicity is that this world exists for people before it exists for anything else—whether we are talking about ideologies or politics or economics. It exists for people ahead of nations, notions, machines, schemes, or systems.

11 Therefore, this world must be made safe for people. And it must be made fit for people.

12 And a third great simplicity is that each of us is born with a capacity for growth—not just physical growth but growth of the ability to think, to create works of beauty, to live freely and wondrously, and to add to the lives of others.

13 And that is where you come in. For nowadays trained intelligence is the nation's greatest weapon in the battle for a world fit for people and safe for people. We can no longer be content—in the old Ivy League-Oxbridge tradition—to educate a few supremely well. We have to educate every citizen capable of intellectual development. We have to cherish and expand every "erg" of brain power our society can uncover. Our gravest social evils now spring from the neglect of training and opportunity. One thinks of the immature adolescents in our big cities, often from colored families, who are flung skill-less on a labor market which is hungry only for skills. Our greatest social opportunities—in every field of research and discovery—spring, on the contrary, from the scale of the investment we are prepared to make in minds. Some economists are ready to argue that perhaps 60 per cent of our gains in output and productivity over the last fifty years can be traced back not to physical capital—in plant and tools—but to mental investment in quick brains and visionary imagination.

14 But I believe the need for trained minds extends far beyond the limits of economic life. The forces of science and technology have made the world one, abolished space, given us instant communication, brought the world's leaders into our homes and showed us all the cultures of our shrinking globe co-existing with our own in a familiarity we might not have felt for even the next county a hundred years back.

15 In such a transformed environment, we cannot rely on tradition or

habit or what has been called the "conventional wisdom." We can rely on only the rational response of trained minds—minds that can discern facts and judge outcomes, minds sufficiently informed of the lessons of the past to know when, say, an analogy from Thucydides makes sense in the modern context and when it does not, minds disinterested enough to distinguish between a prejudice and a principle, minds steady enough to weigh risks and imaginative enough to take them. Genius consists in anticipating events and knowing how to accelerate or prevent them.

16 At any time of great social upheaval—and no age has undergone such changes as our own—profound emotions, above all the emotion of fear, are unleashed. There always seems to be so much to lose when changes are proposed—even though more will be lost if the changes are not accomplished.

17 In the summer before the French Revolution, all of France was, it seems, gripped by a deep malaise, and underlying panic to which contemporaries gave the name of *la grande Peur*—the great Fear. In our own country, where vast social transformations, especially in the relations between the races, have to be achieved, you will find, too, a fringe of hate and fear mongers who appeal to panic, ignorance and suspicion.

18 Again, I ask, with what can we combat these panic reactions except with steady intelligence in command of the facts, with the moderation that comes from knowledge, with the freedom that springs from objectivity? Today, as always, it is the truth that makes us free. But how, in this confused and confusing world, can we recognize the truth and adhere to it unless we have the tools for truth-seeking—a critical faculty, a certain humility in face of the facts, the coolness and disinterest which comes from habits of study, concentration and judgment? A mind clear of cant, a mind that "is not passion's slave," is *not* the natural state of our grasping egos; it is something we have to achieve, and it is something which it is the proudest aim of education to produce.

19 So, I repeat, for all who love the human city and wish to see its commerce proceed in dignity and peace, commencement day is or should be a day of rejoicing. And indeed, as I look about, I do rejoice. For Radcliffe is about to launch another task force of intelligent and disciplined good will. And we can take comfort from the fact that one of the truly revolutionary consequences of modern science is that the great majority of you here today will be alive and effective some fifty years hence—yielding a steady return in terms of good sense, good work and calm and rational influence.

20 When, on Commencement Day, a man looks forward to his unfolding future, he is unlikely to see, as it were built into it, any marked discontinuity. He will change jobs and places, no doubt, but probably remain broadly within his chosen calling, advancing in it with what skill and industry he has, establishing his family and his reputation, and hopefully end-

ing as Chairman of the Board. Of course, there are exceptions. I, for one, can guarantee that there are few discontinuities as marked as those of politics and public affairs.

21 But for most women there is a large and obvious "discontinuity" to be faced—by most of you, I suspect, fairly soon—and that is to be married and raise a family. Then—in our servantless society—will follow some years in which the life of the mind will co-exist, with some difficulty, with the life of the diaper and the kitchen sink. From the kind of work pursued in the Greek ideal of the academy, you proceed to the work which in the Greek definition is the work of the slave. For the Greeks, the servile quality of domestic work lay precisely in its recurrent rhythm—meal after meal, bed-making after bed-making, washing day after washing day.

22 Is this, then, the parabola of your future—from scholar to slave? The contrast is too savage, no doubt, but the dilemma is one on which we must reflect.

23 Let us put into the balance first all the obvious, unquestionable joys and rewards of family life—love, companionship, the excitement of unfolding young minds, the satisfactions of dreary work well done. And in our democratic society where politics are in large measure a "do-it-yourself" job, much community action depends upon voluntary work and many housewives will be able to make their contribution as educated citizens, too.

24 So, I do not suggest in our free, open society that women's home is her prison. On the contrary, it will be for many of you the proud center of a rich and satisfying life.

25 And yet my doubts persist. It is partly a social concern. Fifty per cent of our brains are locked up on the female side. (Perhaps your estimate is even higher!) Can we afford to waste a large percentage of this intellectual power? Can we afford not to use it in the sciences, in the professions?

26 It is also an individual problem. Many women *are* content with the domestic role. But some are not. And since, with women as with men, brain power comes not as an evenly distributed mental quota but often in large patchy concentrations, it is often where the talents are highest that the frustration is greatest, too. Social and individual waste reach a peak when the young woman who has it in her to be, say, a brilliant atomic physicist, or a pioneering sociologist, or an historian of formidable insight finds herself in front of the dishes and the diapers. The case may be exceptional. But surely in a free society we must never let the tyranny of the normal trample down the supreme contribution of the unique.

27 Another problem, as I have said, is that today a woman of forty is still young. She has thirty years or more of active life ahead of her. Is there not here again a factor of waste if, after ten or twenty years of housework, re-entry into active professional, civic or academic life is not available?

28 Marietta Tree describes it as "the dilemma in which the woman of the West frequently finds herself; her children grown, her life span longer, her tastes whetted by her education—unhappiness and dissatisfaction are all too often her lot at a time when the challenges and the achievements of the 20th Century should occupy her interest and her being."

29 In a world still very largely run by men, you will not find many ready-made answers to these questions—even though they are urgent for you and should be urgent for all of us. Men, clearly, have had some difficulty in making up their minds about women and their role: Freud remarked that after 30 years of research into the feminine soul, he still could not answer the great question: What do women want? Some philosophers dismiss you as a "second sex," inferior, says Schopenhauer, in every respect to the first. Lord Chesterfield was not alone in thinking women "only children of a larger growth" and relegated these creatures without "solid reasoning or good sense" to the kitchen or the boudoir. And we all know the restricted sphere of influence Bismark allotted you in children, kitchen and church. But I like best Maeterlinck's observation—that woman is mysterious—like everyone else!

30 You have, of course, had noble defenders too—Plato, John Stuart Mill, Erasmus, Darwin, Shelley. One of the most unequivocal recent statements in favor of removing all irrational restraints upon your capacities came from that remarkable man, Pope John XXIII.

31 Certainly our Western tradition has never denied you souls—as did the ancient world—or made your total segregation an essential foundation of the social order. But contemporary reactions to the role of women in our society remain ambiguous, and, as a result, women often lack a clear, confident picture of their status and even their identity, and for some this uncertainty reaches a tragic pitch of frustration.

32 Nor do some of the impersonal forces in our society help to clarify the issue. When were women so bombarded with the suggestion that their success depends upon the right mascara on the eyelash and the right beguiling whiff of irresistible perfume? The aspect of glamor, of allure, of conquest screams at you from a million color ads and television screens. Influenced by these hosts of persuaders, you could come to believe that your rating as a woman, as a wife, as a mother depended on the sheen of your hair, the softness of your hands, your ability to do fifty hot, vexing, repetitive jobs, and emerge looking like Jackie Kennedy or Princess Grace.

33 I remember one of those masterly Thurber drawings portraying his furiously funny view of the war between the sexes. A shapeless Thurber male leans aggressively over the back of a sofa at a startled and equally shapeless Thurber female. "Where," he hisses at her, "where did you get those great brown eyes and that tiny mind?" Can you have such perpetual insistence upon those aspects of women which are determined by her sex,

and not diminish in some degree her other attributes—intellectual power, executive ability, common sense, mature wisdom?

34 Her image can be moulded in other ways, too. "A woman preaching," said the great Johnson, "is like a dog on its hind legs. It is not that she does it well. The remarkable thing is that she does it at all." It is frustrating, it is humiliating, it can be destructive of ease and confidence if women have to feel like dogs on their hind legs whenever they leave the domestic haven to which so much of the folk thought of our society assigns them.

35 None of all this should, however, discourage you. Many great social transformations have occurred *against* the grain of accepted thought and practice, and if society is slow to realize how much it loses by this potential stifling and inhibiting of half its brain power, there is a good deal that can be done to speed up the recognition. Radcliffe is the sponsor of one such approach in your Institute for Independent Study, at which women receive fellowships to enable them to carry on their scholastic and professional interests part-time to prepare themselves for greater participation in the post-domestic years.

36 I would hope to see every university in America provided with similar institutes, so that no woman graduate need be out of reach of what, I imagine, she chiefly needs—a center for continuing work, for encouragement, for contact, for the exchange of ideas, for guidance and stimulus and, where feasible, for assistance, at the right stage, in making her return or her entry to professional and academic life.

37 In devising institutes for retraining in fashioning tax patterns which encourage both continuous and post-domestic professional life in reconsidering problems of responsibility and promotion, we have to use genuine social inventiveness, and with institutes such as yours—and with others of similar intent—an initiative of first class importance has been taken.

38 Society could help more than it does to give its women citizens the fullest sense of participation. Yet I believe that for men and women alike the fundamental liberations, the genuine experiences of equality, depend not only upon the opportunities—or disabilities—society offers, but also on the reactions and beliefs of the human beings involved. Confusion of roles, problems of identity have their origins in divided and uncertain minds, and there are ways, I think, in which all of us, as members of this strange, varied, immensely talented yet sometimes delinquent human family, can confront the future with some hope of making better sense of the years ahead.

39 In what I have to say now—do not be perturbed, this *is* the peroration—I confess that I have been profoundly influenced by a great and noble woman whose friendship was one of the exhilarating rewards of a political career in which the rewards were not, shall we say, the most

notable feature. Since Eleanor Roosevelt's death last year, I have reflected often on what made up the peculiar quality of her greatness. And I can only conclude that it was the absolute quality of her disinterestedness. She did everything because it was worth doing. She did nothing because it would help to enhance her own role. Of that she seemed simply to be unconscious. Work was there. Work had to be done. And it would require all the energy and concentration of which she was capable. But the fact that Eleanor Roosevelt was doing it interested her not at all.

40 I have never known her equal for objectivity, for unbiased judgment, for a sort of divine fairness and simplicity which sprang from the fact that she never felt her own interests or status or reputation to be involved in her activities. And perhaps for all of us who aspire to that most satisfactory form of equality—parity of esteem, equality of respect—the lesson of Eleanor Roosevelt's greatness was her lack of personal, prideful involvement in the work which came her way.

41 I recall the beguiling statement of an 18th century lady, who remarked that she did not find the Doge's garden so remarkable as the fact that *she* was sitting in it. For Eleanor Roosevelt, what *she* did, what *her* role might be, how people thought of *her*, *her* image, *her* repute—all this meant nothing. The work to be done meant all.

42 So this is the thought that I would leave with you as you start to play all the various parts which life will bring you—do them all if you can for the sake of the work, do them as little as possible for the sake of yourself. Resist those obsessive commercial voices. Be indifferent—if possible—to any limited view of your part in society. See your life as a whole, with times, no doubt, of concentrated domesticity, with times beyond when you will have leisure and energy and experience for work in the human city.

43 All these forms of work and dedication will be fruitful, will support your self-respect and give you tranquility, if they are done with self-forgetfulness because they are good in themselves. None of them, on the contrary, will release you if you are imprisoned in a narrow, inward-looking self and see them as means of *self* expression, *self* fulfilment, and heaven knows what other confusions of purpose and integrity.

44 That this mood of detachment is more difficult for women than for men in our society, I do not doubt. If people constantly exclaim that you as a woman are doing this or that, your role, not the work in hand, can appear the main objective. But never doubt one thing. The more the work is done for its own sake, the more it imposes its own respect. The more objective and disinterested your efforts, the more rapidly shall we all—men and women alike—reach that condition for which a famous English woman pleaded so eloquently when she wrote: "Let us consider women in the grand light of human creatures, who in common with men are placed on earth to unfold their faculties."

45 May every one of you stand beside us males, not as the classical helpmeet one step behind, but shoulder to shoulder, "in the grand light of human creatures."

STUDY GUIDE

1. This commencement address by Adlai Stevenson has considerably more structure than most speeches of this type. It begins with a *proemium* (paragraph 1–6) and ends with a *peroration* announced by the speaker himself (paragraphs 39–45). The body of the address falls into two main thought divisions (paragraphs 7–19 and 20–38). How does the speaker develop a favorable attitude in his audience and work up to his main topic in the proemium?

2. What is his main topic? Where does Stevenson come closest to stating it in the first part of the body of the essay? What connection has the subject of the second part (paragraphs 20–38) with the main topic?

3. How is the discussion of Eleanor Roosevelt related to the main topic? Why does it serve as an appropriate peroration for a commencement address to this audience?

4. As usual in a talk by Adlai Stevenson this address is enlivened by a delicate sense of humor. Point out several examples of it. Is the humor used just for relief, or does it sometimes add force to the point the speaker is making?

5. Stevenson showed part of his intellectual interests by the frequent literary and historical allusions in his talks. Point out several examples of allusions in this speech and indicate what they add to the force of what the speaker is saying.

6. In this unit on the oration you have encountered five very different men. Write an essay in which you try to express what each one of them has revealed about themselves in their speeches.

SECTION **10**

Understanding Description

THE SEEING EYE

John Ruskin

It is a strange thing how little in general people know about the sky. It is the part of creation in which nature has done more for the sake of pleasing man, more for the sole and evident purpose of talking to him and teaching him, than in any other part of her works, and it is just the part in which we least attend her. There are not many of her other works in which some more material or essential purpose than the mere pleasing of man is not answered by every part of their organization; but every essential purpose of the sky might, as far as we know, be answered if once in three days, or thereabouts, a great ugly, black raincloud were brought up over the blue, and everything well watered, and so all left blue again till next time, with perhaps a film of morning and evening mist for dew. And instead of this there is not a moment of any day of our lives when nature is not producing scene after scene, picture after picture, glory after glory, and working still upon such exquisite and constant principles of the most perfect beauty that it is quite certain it is all done for us and intended for our perpetual pleasure. And every man, wherever placed, however far from other sources of interest or beauty, has this doing for him constantly. The noblest scenes of the earth can be seen and known but by few; it is not intended that man should live always in the midst of them; he injures them by his presence; he ceases to feel them if he be always with them; but the sky is for all; bright as it is, it is not

Too bright or good
For human nature's daily food;

Reprinted from John Ruskin, *Modern Painters,* Vol. I (1843).

it is fitted in all its functions for the perpetual comfort and exalting of the heart, for soothing it and purifying it from dross and dust. Sometimes gentle, sometimes capricious, sometimes awful, never the same for two minutes together, almost human in its passions, almost spiritual in its tenderness almost divine in its infinity, its appeal to what is immortal in us is as distinct as its ministry of chastisement or blessing to what is mortal is essential. And yet we never attend to it, we never make it a subject of thought, but as it has to do with our animal sensations: we look upon all by which it speaks to us more clearly than to brutes, upon all which bears witness to the intention of the Supreme that we are to receive more from the covering vault than the light and the dew which we share with the weed and the worm, only as a succession of meaningless and monotonous accidents, too common and too vain to be worth a moment of watchfulness or a glance of admiration. If in our moments of utter idleness and insipidity we turn to the sky as a last resource, which of its phenomena do we speak of? One says it has been wet; and another, it has been windy; and another, it has been warm. Who, among the whole chattering crowd, can tell me of the forms and the precipices of the chain of tall white mountains that girded the horizon at noon yesterday? Who saw the narrow sunbeam that came out of the south and smote upon their summits until they melted and mouldered away in a dust of blue rain? Who saw the dance of the dead clouds when the sunlight left them last-night and the west wind blew them before it like withered leaves? All has passed, unregretted as unseen; or if the apathy be ever shaken off, even for an instant, it is only by what is gross or what is extraordinary; and yet it is not in the broad and fierce manifestations of the elemental energies, not in the clash of the hail nor the drift of the whirlwind, that the highest characters of the sublime are developed. God is not in the earthquake nor in the fire, but in the still, small voice. They are but the blunt and low faculties of our nature which can only be addressed through lampblack and lightning. It is in quiet and subdued passages of unobtrusive majesty, the deep and the calm and the perpetual; that which must be sought ere it is seen, and loved ere it is understood; things which the angels work out for us daily and yet vary eternally, which are to be found always yet each found but once; it is through these that the lesson of devotion is chiefly taught, and the blessing of beauty given. These are what the artist of highest aim must study; it is these, by the combination of which his ideal is to be created; these of which so little notice is ordinarily taken by common observers that I fully believe, little as people in general are concerned with art, more of their ideas of sky are derived from pictures than from reality, and that if we would examine the conception formed in the minds of most educated persons when we talk of clouds, it would frequently be found composed of fragments of blue and white reminiscences of the old masters.

STUDY GUIDE

The Fundamental Meaning of the Passage

What does the passage have to say?

A. The first step in a good analysis is to determine what in general the author says in the entire passage. What is the main point that Ruskin is trying to make in this entire selection? State it briefly in one sentence. Where does Ruskin come closest to expressing this main point himself?

B. How is the discussion of the sky related to this central point of the passage?

C. To satisfy yourself on what is said in any passage you must have some idea of its organization. This passage is all written in one paragraph, but there are six definite phases in the development of the central topic which might form the basis for a division of the selection into six separate paragraphs. If it were so divided, what would be the topic sentences of these separate paragraphs?

D. To be certain that you have grasped the correct fundamental meaning of a passage, you must be sure that you understand the denotation of all the words in the passage and the connotation of the most important ones. What is the exact meaning of the following words in this passage: *capricious* (sentence 7), *insipidity* and *phenomena* (sentence 9), *apathy, gross, sublime* (sentence 14), *lampblack* (sentence 16), and *unobtrusive* (sentence 17)?

What meaning is communicated to the reader by the connotation of the following phrases: "ugly, black rain-cloud" (sentence 3), "light and dew" and "weed and worm" (sentence 8), "Clash of the hail" and "drift of the whirlwind" (sentence 14), and "lampblack and lightning" (sentence 16)?

To emphasize how much meaning is communicated by the connotation of the preceding phrases, substitute other words that would express the same fundamental idea but with less connotation. For example, instead of "weed and worm" the author might have said with far less fullness of meaning, "plants and animals." What meaning does "weed and worm" communicate that "plants and animals" would not?

The Tone of the Passage

For whom is the passage written? What is the author's attitude toward his audience?

A. Another question that must be settled in the analysis of a passage is the audience for whom it was written. This should be determined largely by the internal evidence of the vocabulary, sentence structure, figures of speech, and allusions.

Try to determine the group or groups of people in nineteenth-century England for whom you think Ruskin was writing this passage. Was it the leisured middle class, or the laborers in factory towns, or both? Cite specific evidence for your conclusions from the vocabulary, allusions, and the like, of the passage itself.

B. Once you have decided for whom the author wrote this passage, try to determine (again from the evidence of specific words and phrases) what his attitude toward his audience is. Is he critical of it, sympathetic with it, and so on? The attitude of the author toward his readers determines the tone that he adopts in writing a passage. (Note: The word *tone* has been used elsewhere in this book to cover the attitude of an author towards both his audience and his subject matter. In this study guide, however, it is useful to follow the distinction of the critic I. A. Richards between *tone*, or the attitude of the author toward his audience, and *feeling*, which is the attitude of the author toward his subject matter.)

The Feeling of the Passage

How does the author feel toward his subject matter?

In the first step of your analysis you have determined the general subject matter of the passage. Here you are to attempt to settle what the personal attitude (feeling) of the author toward his subject matter is and what attitude he wishes his audience to take toward it. These are largely determined by studying the connotations (pleasant or unpleasant) of individual words and figures that the author associates with his subject. Because connotation creates values (good or bad), a predominance of pleasant connotations associated with an author's subject matter would indicate that he likes it and wants his audience to like it, whereas a predominance of unpleasant associations would indicate the exact opposite.

With this in mind study the connotation of important words in this passage sentence by sentence, and on the basis of the evidence you gather in this way, state what you think the feeling of the author is toward his subject matter.

The Intention of the Author

Why did the author write this passage?

In artistic prose writing there are various general purposes that may govern a writer: He may wish to communicate an idea clearly and effectively, and then he writes literary exposition; he may wish to persuade an audience to accept his views or feelings about a certain topic, and then he writes rhetorical or oratorical prose; or he may wish to communicate a full human experience (involving intellect, senses, and emotions), and then he writes imaginative description. It is important to decide which of these general purposes is guiding a writer when we are analyzing any concrete specimen of his writing, because, as he has one purpose or the other in mind, he will employ the techniques of the literary artist quite differently. If the clarification of an idea in expository prose is his purpose, he will use concrete words, words rich in connotation, and figures of speech only in so far as they really clarify his idea (any further use of them in expository prose is apt to be distracting and inartistic). If persuading an audience to accept his ideas and attitudes is his purpose, he will use these same devices (especially connotation) and others to bring his audience to think and feel as he himself thinks and feels about the subject. If, finally, the communication and recreation of a full, human experience is his purpose, he will use concrete, connotative, and figurative language much more generously than does either the writer of expository or oratorical prose, in order to enable his reader to share his experience: to make him think about the object as he does; to enable him to see, hear, touch, and even smell and taste it, through the power of his imagination, in somewhat the same way as he has sensed it; and to make him feel about this experience as the author himself feels about it.

Literary Exposition: Nearly all the selections that have been studied so far are examples of literary exposition in which the various authors set out to clarify ideas. This passage of Ruskin is also, with the exception of sentences 11–13, an example of literary exposition. Ruskin's chief purpose is to clarify and develop an idea—the idea you have tried to incorporate into your answer to the question: What is Ruskin writing about? (1) Does his use of concrete language in the passage in general help to clarify his idea? Point out specific examples. (2) Is his idea clarified in any instances by words that are rich in connotation? If you think so, point out some examples. (3) In the passage as a whole there are very few figures. Can you suggest why? Does the personification in sentences 7 and 8 help to clarify the main point of the selection?

Imaginative Description: In sentences 11–13, Ruskin shifts from the purpose and manner of the writer of literary, expository prose to the purpose and manner of a writer of imaginative description. He is no longer trying to clarify an idea but is attempting to bring his reader to see the beauty of the clouds as he sees them. Hence, in contrast to the meagre figurative language in the rest of the passage, these lines are full of figures, concrete language, and connotative words and phrases.

Write a detailed commentary on these three sentences in which you show as fully as you can how Ruskin has, through concrete language, connotative words and phrases (especially verbs), and a wealth of figures, enabled his readers to *see* the definite progression and pattern of specific cloud formations (their size, shape, color, motion, and changes) from noon until after sunset.

Besides these very general purposes of clarifying ideas, persuading an audience to one's own opinions, or communicating an experience, any one of dozens of other more particular and specific purposes may motivate a writer. He may wish to satirize a specific subject or audience; he may wish to criticize or praise someone or something; he may wish to interest a specific audience in a definite mode of action; and so on. Once the subject matter, the audience, and the attitude of the author toward subject matter and audience have been determined it is possible to determine what the more precise purposes are.

You have decided the audience for whom the author wrote this passage. Can you now determine what his precise purposes were in writing it for this audience? Did he wish to satirize someone or something? Did he wish to persuade someone to a definite course of action? If so, whom did he wish to persuade? To what? Do not neglect sentence 18 in answering this question, but do not be satisfied either that it contains the whole answer.

THE BEAUTY AND MYSTERY OF STONEHENGE

Howard Fast

1 It was a gray-silver day—which is something specifically English. It was neither raining nor sunny, but the sky was pearl and laced with sunshine one moment, sunless the next, and the rain came in short bursts like

fine spray. On Salisbury Plain, the rain stopped, and a soft, cold wind blew. The plain offered an immensity that was an illusion, but an illusion never dispelled. In the distance, clouds piled up and here and there a thin black windbreak of trees or a clump of thicket—otherwise nothing. No dog or cat or man or car. It was the time of the day and the moment, yet here in the midst of the most populated area of one of the most heavily populated lands on earth was this great stretch of emptiness.

2 We were only a few miles from Stonehenge now, and already we had begun to feel the aura of the place—that indefinable sense that so many others had mentioned.

3 We parked our car. The British national monument people, who are a part of the Ministry of Public Buildings and Works, have been scrupulously careful to do nothing that would lessen the impact of the circle of stones standing alone in the immensity of Salisbury Plain. The parking lot is in a fold of the ground, almost out of sight. Rest rooms are underground. You come to Stonehenge, and it still stands alone as it has stood for so long. You walk up to it—and you become a part of it. It is a very strange place indeed.

4 Technically speaking, Stonehenge is a cluster of dolmens—*dolmen* being a Cornish word that means holestone, namely any large stone upended and fixed in a hole in the ground. There are dolmens of one sort or another all over southern England and much of Western Europe. For the most part these dolmens, wherever they occur, are oblong slabs of stone, one end of which is set in a hole. Occasionally, they are finished stones; more often, they remain in their natural state and were chosen for their shape and symmetry.

5 All dolmens are related, perhaps through religion or magic, perhaps as the work of one people. We do not know just how, but this we do know: that Stonehenge is unlike any other group of dolmens in the world. It consists of dolmens, yet it is not another dolmen cluster; it is related to the people who created the other dolmens—yet it is different from all other dolmens, and among its many other qualities, it has become one of the most enticing mysteries on earth.

6 From the air, you would see it was a great circular dish about 100 yards in diameter. In the center, about 30 yards, a broken circle of giant stones; outside the stones, meadow; then an earthworks, grass grown; and then a wide ditch. There is a break in the ditch where the entrance-road crosses it, and there is a big stone, fallen and called the slaughter-stone, although in all probability no slaughter was ever done upon it. Once, it was part of the entrance, the gateway to whatever Stonehenge was.

7 It is the inner circle of big stones that we think of when we say Stonehenge, and that is certainly the most dramatic part of the ancient ruin. This is called the Sarsen Circle, the stones that constitute it being of sarsen, a type of sandstone found on the Marlborough Downs, not very far

to the north of Stonehenge. Originally, there were thirty of these great stones, standing upright to make the circle, and these were capped with thirty lintels, hardly smaller than the uprights. These thirty upright stones averaged about 25 tons each in weight, but within the ring were ten more upright stones, these also sarsen, and each of these almost twice as heavy as the 25-ton circlestones. The ten inner stones were arranged in a sort of horseshoe shape, every two uprights capped with a massive lintel.

8 Between this inner horseshoe-shaped arrangement and the outer circle of sarsen stones, there was originally a circle of sixty bluestones. Smaller than the sarsen stones, the bluestones were nevertheless substantial—each of them weighed between 11,000 and 14,000 pounds. Another circle of nineteen bluestones made an inner horseshoe, within the sarsen horseshoe.

9 Just inside the earthen bank that makes the larger circle of 100 yards, there are fifty-six pits or potholes set in a ring. They are called the Aubrey Holes after their discoverer, John Aubrey, and they are marked out in white chalk, and just what they are or were no one really knows; but they are the most fruitful source of speculation.

10 Such was the original construction of Stonehenge. There is enough left today to make it worth going a long way to look at. Seen from a certain angle, where four of the 25-ton standing sarsen stones still support three matched lintels, one can evoke Stonehenge as it was in the beginning, some 3,000 years ago; one can form the structure again, reconstitute it in the mind's eye, and partake of it. And that is the essence of Stonehenge—that one does not simply look at it; one partakes of it, recognizes it, and knows why it is there without knowing at all.

11 It means nothing to say that Stonehenge was a temple used for religious purposes, for when it was built, there was no separation between man and his religion and his life and work. All were one. It was once thought that Stonehenge was a Druid temple, used for strange rites and human sacrifice, but the people who built Stonehenge were long dead and gone when the Druids first came upon the scene.

12 As to who built Stonehenge, there, too, all the authorities are less than specific. Out of any book on Stonehenge, you will find a listing of prehistoric people who inhabited that part of England, down through the centuries from 4,500 years ago listed as: "Native Hunters," "Windmill Hill People," "Tomb Builders," "The Beaker Folk," etc. This is simply a historical calendar. Those who built Stonehenge left only Stonehenge and some barrows and dolmens, no history or record or explanation.

13 In the world of ancient man religion was something quite different than it is today. It was not a thing for Sunday, church, holy days, or re-

spectability; or a matter of faith or sin or forgiveness. It was something else that we have forgotten—the interrelationship of man and the universe —the beat of the universe and man's response to it. Stonehenge is a measure of this beat, an instrument, a tool, a vast clock. Not a clock of minutes and hours to mark off an indecent race with time, but a clock of days and months, of seasons and years.

14 This notion has been raised and abandoned many times. I cannot abandon it, because it makes sense. If Stonehenge is a clock, then obviously it is a sun clock, and as with all sun clocks, the position of its axis holds the key to it. We are not absolutely certain when Stonehenge took its present form, but in the band of years that would make a good guess, it was constructed so that its axis would point to the sunset on the evening of the summer solstice, or the longest day of the year. From this, it is commonly deduced by various writers about Stonehenge that its builders were sun worshipers; and here again is the confusion of today's religion with ancient religion. There is no real evidence that they were sun worshipers, but sun worship is a tag to which we have attached our own meaning. The sun was a part of ancient religion, but so were many other things; and in terms of Stonehenge, there are many other factors besides sun worship.

15 What was the purpose and meaning of the fifty-six potholes that surrounded the stonework just inside the five-foot-high mound? These could have comprised an intricate system of measuring the year. A British investigator sees them as a sort of primitive calculating machine, and another British writer on the subject insists that they are a calendar. Why the circle of bluestones inside the circle of sarsen stones? The large sarsen stones were hauled only 20 miles over the gentle slopes of Salisbury Plain, but the smaller bluestones—the eighty weighing between 11,000 and 14,000 pounds each—were brought to Stonehenge from the Prescelly Mountains in Southwestern Wales.

16 Here, on a high, bare peak called Carn Meini, are the great outcroppings of dolerite where the bluestones were found, and from Carn Meini to Stonehenge—by water and land as the stones must have come—is a distance of almost 200 miles. I have been over all this land and I have observed the possible routes, and the task of bringing the eighty stones. from Wales to Salisbury Plain staggers the imagination. And why? Why did thousands of men labor for months and years, build sledges and rafts, cut roads to bring these heavy stones over such a difficult distance?

17 There are two ways of looking at ancient man. Colored by our own racial prejudices, by all the lies and nonsense we have absorbed about primitive people in our own historic time, we can look back on ancient man as a sort of superstitious savage who acted senselessly and blindly and

did nothing very much that made sense in our own scientific and pseudo-scientific terms. On the other hand, we can regard ancient man objectively, observe how well he organized his own society, consider the longevity of his civilizations, examine his skill as architect and engineer and artist, and come to the conclusion that he was quite a fellow—with a great deal that we have lost, not only in terms of his knowledge of the world, but in terms of his knowledge of himself and his relationship to the universe.

18 It was in this latter sense that Stonehenge was built, a precise engineering achievement constructed primarily out of two sizes of stone and two kinds of stone. Not only were the bluestones smaller than the sarsen stones, but they did not have to be cut to shape and size. In the outcroppings on Carn Meini, hundreds of them lay waiting, split by nature into perfect size.

19 But size for what? For what is that size the perfect size?

20 Again we return to the religious interpretation that stops all thinking about Stonehenge. Certainly Stonehenge was connected with the religious practices of the people who built it—just as a computer is connected with the social and industrial life of our own society. We need computers for our own social ends; and the people who built Stonehenge needed it for their social ends. Religion could not be separated from their social life and needs.

21 They needed a machine—a great unwieldy machine—but they needed it sufficiently to spend enormous collective effort to make it. There were certain specifications for this machine. It began with a circle 300 feet in diameter. They had to dig a ditch and raise a circular barrow five feet high. Then they had to lay out fifty-six marks and dig fifty-six holes. Then they had to erect a circle of great stones, shape them, and connect them with a circular roof of lintels. Within this, they required a second circle of smaller stones—some sixty of them—and now they faced a difficult choice. They were engaged in a stupendous project and they possessed only the most primitive and inefficient tools. Should they attempt to cut sarsen sandstone to the size they needed? Or should they attempt to locate another quarry of a different type of stone that would perhaps lessen their labor very considerably?

22 They must have covered all of southern England and Wales in their search, and they must have weighed many possibilities before they decided to transport the bluestone from Wales to Salisbury. They made the decision because it was the best and quickest way to get what they were after, but they must have desperately needed whatever they were after. They were building a machine of sorts—a calculator, a calendar, a bridge for their dreams or a new doorway into the unknown. But they were not building a senseless tribute to superstition. That is the main thing.

23 As to who they were, what they were, and what was their way of

life—this we can only surmise. In some ways they were a very primitive people, in other ways they were not. They had a door open to the world. Otherwise they could never have built Stonehenge. Knowledge never comes to maturity in one culture; it is always the result of an interchange among peoples and cultures.

24 Stonehenge is superbly planned and executed architecture. There is the essence of its difference from all other dolmens in the British Isles and in Europe, and there is the key to a solution of its mystery. Who was the architect who built it?

25 Anyone who has seen a picture of the Lion Gate in the ruins of Mycenae in Greece will immediately note the similarity between the handling of these huge stones and the stones at Stonehenge, and the parallel can be continued by comparison with Agamemnon's ancient city walls. Take this together with a minor but unexplained mystery of Stonehenge, a number of Mycenaen axheads and daggers etched in the side of certain of the dolmens, and a delightful area for speculation opens.

26 The dagger and axhead marks are almost the signature of Greek civilization of the time. It was a time when Greek many-oared ships plied the Mediterranean from end to end, the time of the Homeric tales, the fall of Troy, the battles of heroes, a time of the individual. It was also a time of image-breaking, frontier-breaking, opening doors and expanding knowledge.

27 In this time, a Greek architect could have come to Britain. He must have found the people of Stonehenge engaging and rewarding, for he fell into the spirit of what they needed. Was he young or old? Did he die there in Britain or did he sail away with the memory of what he had created? And what were his feelings as he took the techniques learned in the building of palaces and city walls and turned them to the engineering of the strange sun clock and computer? How did he organize the job? Where were the hundreds and even thousands of workmen found? Interesting questions that cannot ever be answered.

STUDY GUIDE

Structure

1. The author of this essay attempts to suggest what the function of Stonehenge was. But he does it largely by a detailed description of what a tourist actually sees at Stonehenge on Salisbury Plain. The essay might be divided as follows: paragraphs 1–3, 4–10, 11–22, and 23–27. With what does each of these divisions deal? How is description involved in each of them?

2. In the first section (paragraphs 1–3) the author attempts to give the reader a general impression of the mysterious loneliness and beauty of Stonehenge on a typically over cast English day. At the same time it is made clear

that the author, Howard Fast, is attracted by the scene. He achieves this double effect by well-chosen descriptive detail. Show how this double impression is accomplished by the following expression: "gray-silver day"; "the sky was pearl, and laced with sunshine one moment, sunless the next"; "the rain came in bursts, like a fine spray"; "a soft, cold wind blew"; and "the aura of the place." Contrast the impression that would be communicated, for instance, if the following expressions were substituted for those of the author: "gray-leaden day"; "the sky was steely, and pierced with sunshine one moment, sunless the next"; "the rain came in bursts, like a cold shower"; "a sharp, cold wind blew"; and "the eerie atmosphere of the place"?

3. Discuss the metaphor used in paragraph 6 to enable the reader to see the over all shape of the Stonehenge ensemble.

4. To serve its purpose of enabling a reader to reconstruct a scene that he may never have experienced directly, a description must be orderly and exact. Show how the details supplied in paragraphs 4–10 would enable a reader to do a perspective drawing of Stonehenge or a painting of the whole Salisbury Plain in color.

5. What is the author's suggested explanation of Stonehenge? What evidence does he give for this suggestion? Where in the essay is this suggestion put forward?

6. Select some interesting place you have visited and describe it in detail for a reader who has not seen it. Try to follow the manner of the first part of this essay.

A RIVER

Anne Morrow Lindbergh

1 Our first sign of China was indicative of the immensity of the country we were going to. It was an unexpected sign, for flying over the Yellow Sea from Japan, we were looking for land on the horizon ahead, perhaps even the outline of mountains like the horizon behind us. But long before the darker blue of solid land began to rise above the shifting blue of the sea, China came out to meet us. We were aware of a difference in color between the water in front of us and the water behind us, a sharp line of demarcation where brown waves met blue. Mud from the Yangtze River darkened the sea for miles ahead. We were approaching China.

2 What a river this must be to make itself felt so far out from land, to so impress its personality on its overlord, the sea. I made obeisance to it in my mind, for I felt in the presence of a great monarch. And I was not mistaken. The Yangtze River, as we followed its smooth course up

through the immense stretches of flat farm land of coastal China, was one of those rivers which give the impression of being the only true and permanent rulers of the earth.

3 Rivers perhaps are the only physical features of the world that are at their best from the air. Mountain ranges, no longer seen in profile, dwarf to anthills; seas lose their horizons; lakes have no longer depth but look like bright pennies on the earth's surface; forests become a thin impermanent film, a moss on the top of a wet stone, easily rubbed off. But rivers, which from the ground one usually sees only in cross sections, like a small sample of ribbon—rivers stretch out serenely ahead as far as the eye can reach. Rivers are seen in their true stature.

4 They tumble down mountain sides; they meander through flat farm lands. Valleys trail them; cities ride them; farms cling to them; roads and railroad tracks run after them—and they remain, permanent, possessive. Next to them, man's gleaming cement roads which he has built with such care look fragile as paper streamers thrown over the hills, easily blown away. Even the railroads seem only scratched in with a penknife. But rivers have carved their way over the earth's face for centuries and they will stay.

5 We have seen the Susquehanna cutting across the Allegheny ridges, and have followed the Mississippi, carrying half a continent of farms magnificently on its far-reaching banks. We have watched the Rio Grande ride like a plumed serpent through the sandy wastes of the Southwest (golden sand bars streaked with water, like feathers from the air); and the innocent trickle of the Colorado River, gleaming incongruously at the bottom of a gigantic crack in the earth's face. "That little silver thread made the Grand Canyon?" one asks. "Impossible!"

6 We have a great respect for rivers, and usually they are kind to fliers. Sometimes it is just the exchange of a nod between travelers journeying over the same country. From Kansas City to St. Louis, there is the Missouri. It curls off in smooth circles to our right. We do not follow its course, but see it gleaming ahead in patches on the curves, like a skipping stone, coming up again and again—a line, a curve, a golden S, glinting, disappearing, glinting. What pleasure at rediscovery, like a recurring melody in music.

7 Sometimes, though, it is more than that. It is a hand in the dark. How many times, flying over nameless stretches in the West, some river has proved an incontestable landmark. "The Cimarron—good! We've crossed the line then—we're in Oklahoma—" And at night, when the whole universe seems a bowl of darkness uniformly starred top to bottom, gradually as one's eyes become accustomed to the dark there is that line, that demarcation, a difference in consistency in the substance below—something that holds light reflections—"a river—the Ohio!"

8 There are rivers that have cut a way for us through a mountain ridge, tunnels under the fog that one can pass through safely, like the Delaware Water Gap. And there are nameless rivers, too, often too small to be shown on our maps, that have led us over a pass in the mountains. Following a ravine up one side of a mountain range, a river below always there to lead us back to the valley we have just left behind. Then for a while we lose it and fight over a nameless territory, lakes and forests on the top of a pass. And again we pick up the silver trail, a river dashing over bowlders in the opposite direction—west. We have crossed the divide; we are over.

9 This time we were to see the river not as a friend, but as an enemy; not at peace, but in revolt. We were to see it in flood, destroying the fertile plains it had once made, breaking dykes, carrying away villages, and covering valleys. We were to see it, a huge lake smiling catlike, horribly calm and complacent, over the destroyed fields and homes of millions of people; and again, an angry sea, its muddy waves battering down houses; or a turbulent stream spouting through a break in the dykes. And always in the center of the wide area of destruction was that roaring torrent, darker and more turbulent than the rest, the very heart of the river gone mad with power, carrying all in front of it; houses, trees, boats, live stock, and coffins—inevitably swept along out to sea.

10 The yellow waters of the Yangtze surrounded our short weeks in China. They led us into the country and held us there in our attempt to chart the extent of their damage. For our plane was the only one in China which had enough range to survey the outer limits of the floods. It was the Yangtze River we followed up and down its swollen course. And it was the Yangtze River in the end which took us out of China.

STUDY GUIDE

Thought Structure

1. Show how the description of the Yangtze River as seen from the air forms the framework into which the bird's-eye view of rivers in general fits.

2. Give the topic sentence of each paragraph in the essay and state what method of paragraph development is used in each.

Diction and Imagery

Frequently, seeing a familiar object from a fresh or unexpected point of view impresses us with features of the object we had never noticed before. In this essay, Mrs. Lindbergh tries to make us *see* rivers as they appear from a plane. She, therefore, chooses her diction and imagery to enable us to see them as they appear from aloft whether we have ever actually seen them from that vantage point or not.

1. Pick out the phrases and images (similes or metaphors) in paragraph

3 which best enable us to see what the different types of terrain look like from the air.

2. Comment on the effectiveness of every verb in paragraph 4 for connoting specific action and for summoning up an accurate picture to the imagination. Why, for instance, are valleys said to *trail* rivers, and cities to *ride* them? Remember that you are seeing all this from the air.

3. The author herself explains the image which she uses in paragraph 5, sentence 2, to enable us to see what the Rio Grande looks like from a plane. Make a similar explanation of the image used in paragraph 5, sentence 3, for the Colorado River in the Grand Canyon. Why does it gleam *incongruously?*

4. Analyze the propriety of the images used in paragraph 6, sentence 5, to help us sense what a curving river looks like from a plane flying in a direct course above it. Do the same for the images in paragraph 7, sentences 2 and 6.

Suggestion for Writing

Select some familiar scene or object which you have seen at some time or other from an unusual viewpoint, and then try to describe the impression it made on you from that viewpoint as vividly and concretely as Mrs. Lindbergh here describes rivers as they appear from the air.

A BESSEMER BLOWS AT ALIQUIPPA

Stewart H. Holbrook

1 It was dusk, and we stood looking down into a valley that often knew the night but never day. Smoke poured from a few of the scores of stacks below us, and when the wind rose a bit a mild warm shower of cinders fell where we stood. They were light cinders, falling silently like so much tarnished snow.

2 One was conscious of more smoke than could be seen coming from the stacks. I actually felt that smoke was everywhere in the valley, and on the hills, too—an all-prevailing smoke, not black, not white, simply a haze that clouded everything from a fly to a building and left nothing in true perspective.

3 There it was below us, Aliquippa in western Pennsylvania, at work under a smoky moon.

4 Aliquippa is a mighty enough steel town in a region that knows steel and little else. I looked down at it through the enveloping haze and knew that the place held secrets that neither the sun nor the moon ever dis-

From *Iron Brew* (New York: The Macmillan Company, 1939), pp. 1–4.

covered. Even its vast noises seemed muted, here on the hill. Only a dull rumbling, rising and falling on the breeze, remained of the accumulated sound of ten thousand men working and sweating in a madhouse that thundered until it shook the walls around them.

5 But the eye told better of doings in the valley. Now the haze was streaked with bursts of flame, with billows of smoke, and again with small volcanoes of orange and yellow sparks. I thought of Aliquippa as an old man sitting there in the gloom of the valley, sullenly smoking his pipe in the evening: a moody old man, given to expressing visibly his fits of silent temper. When he thought of something long past that made him seethe, he puffed furiously, and the sparks came.

6 Suddenly, as if the smoke and sparks and streaks of fire had been but a mere kindling of it, the whole valley blazed with a lurid glow—not lightning, not heavy artillery, nor yet a flame thrower, but all three together. One saw the stacks plainly now, stark black silhouettes against a background of red and yellow. . . . The old man and his pipe had gone wholly mad.

7 That, said my friend, is a Bessemer in blow.

8 We went down into the murky lowland and into the steel plant, a place that took in more acres within its high fence than do most farms. Cinders were thicker here, and heavier. The noise was such as to to discourage talk. Men spoke with their fingers, their hands, their arms.

9 On and on we walked, past the glittering coke ovens that winked with eight hundred eyes, past the furnaces muttering over their nightly fare of Mesabi ore, and on to the hulking Bessemer shed. Its outside was lost in gloom. Inside was a scene to stop the late Dante Alighieri dead in his tracks.

10 Here were three tall Bessemer converters in a row. How a Bessemer looks to a veteran steelworker's eye, I don't know. To a layman it looks like the egg of a roc, that fabulous bird which was said to have borne off the biggest elephant in its flight. A roc's egg with one end cut off and gaping. It is a container of brick and riveted steel, twice as tall as the tallest man and supported near its middle on axles. It is set high up on a groundwork of brick. Into this caldron goes molten ore, fifty thousand pounds at a time. Through the iron is blown cold air—oxygen forced through the hot metal with the power of a giant's breath. Out of the egg, in good time, comes steel. It is little short of pure magic.

11 One of the converters was in blow as we entered the shed. Tilted almost but not quite straight up, the mouth of it belched flame like a cannon built for the gods. It was a terrifying sight, and hypnotic. I didn't want to look elsewhere, to turn my eyes from that leaping flame which towered thirty, perhaps forty, feet above the converter.

12 The roar was literally deafening; and little wonder, for here was a cyclone attacking a furnace in a brief but titanic struggle, a meeting in

battle of carbon and oxygen, cleverly arranged by the sweating gnomes whose red-faces appeared white in the Bessemer's glow. Both carbon and oxygen would lose, each consuming the other, and men would be the winners by twenty-five tons of bright new steel.

13 The roaring continued. The red fire changed to violet, indescribably beautiful, then to orange, to yellow, and finally to white, when it soon faded. "Drop," the boys call it. I saw the great vessel rock uneasily on its rack, moved with unseen levers by an unseen workman. A locomotive pushed a car close under. On the car was a big ladle. The hellish brew was done.

14 Slowly the converter tilted over, and from its maw came a flow of seething liquid metal—Bessemer steel. A Niagara of fire spilled out, pouring into the waiting ladle, and sixty feet away the heat was too much for comfort. A cascade of sparks rolled out and over, a sort of spray for this cataract, and it seemed everything in the shed danced with light.

15 Steel was being born in a light so blinding that one must wear dark glasses to look on it long. It was a dreadful birth. The pygmy men who ran about on the floor seemed entirely too puny to cope with such a thing. One preferred subconsciously to trust in the tall shadows on the walls, for the weird towering shapes looked more in character for this business.

16 In perhaps five minutes the ladle was filled with the running fire. The bell on the locomotive rang. The ladle was pulled away, out into the darkness of the yard, and a sudden deep gloom settled down in the Bessemer shed. The devil's pouring was over.

17 It is the most gorgeous, the most startling show that any industry can muster, a spectacle to make old Vulcan's heart beat faster, enough to awe a mortal. No camera has ever caught a Bessemer's full grim majesty, and no poet has yet sung its splendor.

STUDY GUIDE

Thought Structure

1. There are three parts to this descriptive essay. What are they? What is described in each of them?

2. The point of view shifts in the course of the essay. What is the point of view in each part? Is it the point of view or the object viewed that changes between the first and second parts?

Diction and Imagery

1. There are some verbs with vivid and powerful connotations in this descriptive essay. Select and comment upon the ten which you think most effective.

2. Analyze the effectiveness for descriptive purposes of the similes and

metaphors used in paragraph 1, sentences 2 and 3; paragraph 5, sentence 3; paragraph 10, sentence 3; paragraph 11, sentence 2; paragraph 12, sentence 1; paragraph 13, sentence 7; and paragraph 14, sentences 2 and 3.

3. Show why the literary allusions made in paragraphs 9 and 17 are particularly well suited to the inferno of molten iron being described there.

4. Show how carefully the author has chosen specific words and comparisons in paragraph 10 to make us see what a Bessemer looks like.

5. In this description the author is trying to communicate to us the awesome, semimagical, and even hellish impression which the sight of a Bessemer in blow in the murky night had on him. To build up that impression he had to select his diction carefully and consistently throughout his essay. Go through the entire essay and indicate every word or phrase which helps to create this impression of almost preternatural forces at work.

Suggestion for Writing

Select a process with which you are familiar, determine the general impression it made on you, and then try to communicate that impression to your reader as vividly as Holbrook describes a Bessemer in blow.

DAWN OVER ZERO

William L. Laurence

1 The Atomic Age began at exactly 5:30 mountain war time on the morning of July 16, 1945, on a stretch of semi-desert land about fifty air-line miles from Alamogordo, New Mexico, just a few minutes before the dawn of a new day on that part of the earth. At that great moment in history, ranking with the moment when man first put fire to work for him, the vast energy locked within the heart of the atoms of matter was released for the first time in a burst of flame such as had never before been seen on this planet, illuminating earth and sky, for a brief span that seemed eternal, with the light of many super-suns.

2 The elemental flame, first fire ever made on earth that did not have its origin in the sun, came from the explosion of the first atomic bomb. It was a full-dress rehearsal preparatory to dropping the bomb over Hiroshima and Nagasaki—and other Japanese military targets, had Japan refused to accept the Potsdam Declaration for her surrender.

3 The rehearsal marked the climax in the penultimate act of one of the greatest dramas in our history and the history of civilized man—a drama

From *Dawn over Zero* by William L. Laurence, published by Alfred A. Knopf, New York, 1946.

in which our scientists, under the direction of the Army Corps of Engineers, were working against time to create an atomic bomb ahead of our German enemy. The collapse of Germany marked the end of the first act of this drama. The successful completion of our task, in the greatest challenge by man to nature so far, brought down the curtain on the second act. The grand finale came three weeks afterward in the skies over Japan, with a swift descent of the curtain on the greatest war in history.

4 The atomic flash in New Mexico came as a great affirmation to the prodigious labors of our scientists during the past four years. It came as the affirmative answer to the until then unanswered question: "Will it work?"

5 With the flash came a delayed roll of mighty thunder, heard, just as the flash was seen, for hundreds of miles. The roar echoed and reverberated from the distant hills and the Sierra Oscuro range near by, sounding as though it came from some supremundane source as well as from the bowls of the earth. The hills said yes and the mountains chimed in yes. It was as if the earth had spoken and the suddenly iridescent clouds and sky had joined in one affirmative answer. Atomic energy—yes. It was like the grand finale of a mighty symphony of the elements, fascinating and terrifying, uplifting and crushing, ominous, devastating, full of great promise and great forebodings.

6 I watched the birth of the era of atomic power from the slope of a hill in the desert land of New Mexico, on the north-western corner of the Alamogordo Air Base, about 125 miles southeast of Albuquerque. The hill, named Compania Hill for the occasion, was twenty miles to the northwest of Zero, the code name given to the spot chosen for the atomic bomb test. The area embracing Zero and Compania Hill, twenty-four miles long and eighteen miles wide, had the code name Trinity.

7 I joined a caravan of three busses, three automobiles, and a truck carrying radio equipment at 11 P.M. on Sunday, July 15, at Albuquerque. There were about ninety of us in that strange caravan, traveling silently and in the utmost secrecy through the night on probably as unusual an adventure as any in our day. With the exception of myself the caravan consisted of scientists from the highly secret atomic bomb research and development center in the mesas and canyons of New Mexico, twenty-five miles northwest of Santa Fe, where we solved the secret of translating the fabulous energy of the atom into the mightiest weapon ever made by man. It was from there that the caravan set out at 5:30 that Sunday afternoon for its destination, 212 miles to the South.

8 The caravan wound its way slowly over the tortuous roads overlooking the precipitous canyons of northern New Mexico, passing through Espangnola, Santa Fe, and Bernalillo, arriving at Albuquerque at about 10 P.M. Here it was joined by Sir James Chadwick, who won the Nobel

Prize and knighthood for his discovery of the neutron, the key that unlocks the atom; Professor Ernest O. Lawrence of the University of California, master atom-smasher, who won the Nobel Prize for his discovery of the cyclotron; Professor Edwin M. McMillan, also of the University of California, one of the discoverers of plutonium, the new atomic bomb center, who, like me, had arrived during the afternoon.

9 The night was dark with black clouds, and not a star could be seen. Occasionally a bolt of lightning would rend the sky and reveal for an instant the flat semi-desert landscape, rich with historic lore of past adventure. We rolled along on U.S. Highway 85, running between Albuquerque and El Paso, through sleeping ancient Spanish-American towns, their windows dark, their streets deserted—towns with music in their names, Los Lunas, Belen, Bernardo, Alamillo, Socorro, San Antonio. At San Antonio we turned east and crossed "the bridge on the Rio Grande with the detour in the middle of it." From there we traveled ten and one half miles eastward on U.S. Highway 380, and then turned south on a specially built dirt road, running for twenty-five miles to the base camp at Trinity.

10 The end of our trail was reached after we had covered about five and one fifth miles on the dirt road. Here we saw the first signs of life since leaving Albuquerque about three hours earlier, a line of silent men dressed in helmets. A little farther on, a detachment of military police examined our special credentials. We got out of the busses and looked around us. The night was still pitch-black save for an occasional flash of lightning in the eastern sky, outlining for a brief instant the Sierra Oscuro Range directly ahead of us. We were in the middle of the New Mexico desert, miles away from nowhere, with hardly a sign of life, not even a blinking light on the distant horizon. This was to be our caravansary until the zero hour.

11 From a distance to the southeast the beam of a searchlight probed the clouds. This gave us our first sense of orientation. The bomb-test site, Zero, was a little to the left of the searchlight beam, twenty miles away. With the darkness and the waiting in the chill of the desert the tension became almost unendurable.

12 We gathered in a circle to listen to directions on what we were to do at the time of the test, directions read aloud by the light of a flashlight:

13 At a short signal of the siren at minus five minutes to zero, "all personnel whose duties did not specifically require otherwise" were to prepare "a suitable place to lie down on." At a long signal of the siren at minus two minutes to zero, "all personnel whose duties did not specifically require otherwise" were to "lie prone on the ground immediately, the face and eyes directed toward the ground and with the head away from Zero. Do not watch for the flash directly," the directions read, "but turn

over after it has occurred and watch the cloud. Stay on the ground until the blast wave has passed (two minutes). At two short blasts of the siren, indicating the passing of all hazard from light and blast, all personnel will prepare to leave as soon as possible.

14 "The hazard from blast is reduced by lying down on the ground in such a manner that flying rocks, glass, and other objects do not intervene between the source of blast and the individual. Open all car windows.

15 "The hazard from light injury to eyes is reduced by shielding the closed eyes with the bended arms and lying face down on the ground. If the first flash is viewed a 'blind spot' may prevent your seeing the rest of the show.

16 "The hazard from ultraviolet light injuries to the skin is best overcome by wearing long trousers and shirts with long sleeves."

17 David Dow, assistant to the scientific director of the Atomic Bomb Development Center, handed each of us a flat piece of colored glass such as is used by arc welders to shield their eyes. Dr. Edward Teller of George Washington University cautioned us against sunburn. Someone produced sunburn lotion and passed it around. It was an eerie sight to see a number of our highest-ranking scientists seriously rubbing sunburn lotion on their faces and hands in the pitch-blackness of the night, twenty miles away from the expected flash. These were the men who, more than anybody else, knew the potentialities of atomic energy on the loose. It gave one an inkling of their confidence in their handiwork.

18 The bomb was set on a structural steel tower one hundred feet high. Ten miles away to the southwest was the Base Camp. This was G.H.Q. for the scientific high command, of which Professor Kenneth T. Bainbridge of Harvard University was field commander. Here were erected barracks to serve as living-quarters for the scientists, a mess hall, a commissary, a post exchange, and other buildings. Here the vanguard of the atomists, headed by Professor J. R. Oppenheimer of the University of California, scientific director of the Atomic Bomb Project, lived like soldiers at the front, supervising the enormously complicated details involved in the epoch-making tests.

19 Here early that Sunday afternoon gathered Major General Leslie R. Groves, commander in chief of the Atomic Bomb Project; Brigadier General T. F. Farrell, hero of World War I, General Grove's deputy; Professor Enrico Fermi, Nobel Prize winner and one of the leaders in the project; President James Bryant Conant of Harvard; Dr. Vannevar Bush, director of the Office of Scientific Research and Development; Dean Richard C. Tolman of the California Institute of Technology; Professor R. F. Bacher of Cornell; Colonel Stafford L. Warren, University of Rochester radiologist; and about a hundred and fifty other leaders in the atomic bomb program.

20 At the Base Camp was a dry, abandoned reservoir, about five hundred feet square, surrounded by a mound of earth about eight feet high. Within this mound bulldozers dug a series of slit trenches, each about three feet deep, seven feet wide, and twenty-five feet long. At a command over the radio at zero minus one minute all observers at Base Camp lay down in their assigned trenches, "face and eyes directed toward the ground with the head away from Zero." But most of us on Compania Hill remained on our feet.

21 Three other posts had been established, south, north, and west of Zero, each at a distance of 10,000 yards (5.7 miles). These were known, respectively as South-10,000, North-10,000 and West-10,000 or S-10 N-10, and W-10. Here the shelters were much more elaborate—wooden structures, their walls reinforced by cement, buried under a massive layer of earth.

22 S-10 was the control center. Here Professor Oppenheimer, as scientific commander in chief, and his field commander, Professor Bainbridge, issued orders and synchronized the activities of the other sites. Here the signal was given and a complex of mechanisms was set in motion that resulted in the greatest burst of energy ever released by man on earth up to that time. No switch was pulled, no button pressed, to light this first cosmic fire on this planet.

23 At forty-five seconds to zero, set for 5:30 o'clock, young Dr. Joseph L. McKibben of the University of California, at a signal from Professor Bainbridge, activated a master robot that set off a series of other robots, until, at last, stratcgically spaced electrons moved to the proper place at the proper split second.

24 Forty-five seconds passed and the moment was zero.

25 Meanwhile at our observation post on Compania Hill the atmosphere had grown tenser as the zero hour approached. We had spent the first part of our stay eating an early morning picnic breakfast that we had taken along with us. It had grown cold in the desert, and many of us, lightly clad, shivered. Occasionally a drizzle came down, and the intermittent flashes of lightning made us turn apprehensive glances toward Zero. We had had some disturbing reports that the test might be called off because of the weather. The radio we had brought with us for communication with Base Camp kept going out of order, and when we had finally repaired it some blatant band would drown out the news we wanted to hear. We knew there were two specially equipped B-29 Superfortresses high over head to make observations and recordings in the upper atmosphere, but we could neither see nor hear them. We kept gazing through the blackness.

26 Suddenly, at 5:29.50, as we stood huddled around our radio, we heard a voice ringing through the darkness, sounding as though it had come

from above the clouds: "Zero minus ten seconds!" A green flare flashed out through the clouds, descended slowly, opened, grew dim, and vanished into the darkness.

27 The voice from the clouds boomed out again: "Zero minus three seconds!" Another green flare came down. Silence reigned over the desert. We kept moving in small groups in the direction of Zero. From the east came the first faint signs of dawn.

28 And just at that instant there rose from the bowels of the earth a light not of this world, the light of many suns in one. It was a sunrise such as the world had never seen, a great green super-sun climbing in a fraction of a second to a height of more than eight thousand feet, rising even higher until it touched the clouds, lighting up earth and sky all around with a dazzling luminosity.

29 Up it went, a great ball of fire about a mile in diameter, changing colors as it kept shooting upward, from deep purple to orange, expanding, growing bigger, rising as it expanded, an elemental force freed from its bonds after being chained for billions of years. For a fleeting instant the color was unearthly green such as one sees only in the corona of the sun during a total eclipse. It was as though the earth had opened and the skies had split. One felt as though one were present at the moment of creation when God said: "Let there be light."

30 To another observer, Professor George B. Kistiakowsky of Harvard, the spectacle was "the nearest thing to doomsday that one could possibly imagine. I am sure," he said, "that at the end of the world—in the last millisecond of the earth's existence—the last man will see what we have just seen!"

31 A great cloud rose from the ground and followed the trail of the great sun. At first it was a giant column, which soon took the shape of a supramundane mushroom. For a fleeting instant it took the form of the Statue of Liberty magnified many times. Up it went, higher, higher, a giant mountain born in a few seconds instead of millions of years, quivering convulsively. It touched the multicolored clouds, pushed its summit through them, kept rising until it reached a height of 41,000 feet, 12,000 feet higher than the earth's highest mountain.

32 All through this very short but extremely long time-interval not a sound was heard. I could see the silhouettes of human forms motionless in little groups, like desert plants in the dark. The new-born mountain in the distance, a giant among the pygmies of the Sierra Oscuro Range, stood leaning at an angle against the clouds, a vibrant volcano spouting fire to the sky.

33 Then out of the great silence came a mighty thunder. For a brief interval the phenomena we had seen as light repeated themselves in terms of sound. It was the blast from thousands of blockbusters going off

simultaneously at one spot. The thunder reverberated all through the desert, bounced back and forth from the Sierra Oscuro, echo upon echo. The ground trembled under our feet as in an earthquake. A wave of hot wind was felt by many of us just before the blast and warned us of its coming.

34 The big boom came about one hundred seconds after the great flash—the first cry of a newborn world. It brought the silent, motionless silhouettes to life, gave them a voice. A loud cry filled the air. The little groups that had hitherto stood rooted to the earth like desert plants broke into a dance—the rhythm of primitive man dancing at one of his fire festivals at the coming of spring. They clapped their hands as they leaped from the ground—earthbound man symbolizing the birth of a new force that for the first time gives man means to free himself from the gravitational pull of the earth that holds him down.

35 The dance of the primitive man lasted but a few seconds, during which an evolutionary period of about 10,000 years had been telescoped. Primitive man was metamorphosed into modern man—shaking hands, slapping his fellow on the back, all laughing like happy children.

36 The sun was just rising above the horizon as our caravan started on its way back to Albuquerque and Los Alamos. We looked at it through our dark lenses to compare it with what we had seen.

37 "The sun can't hold a candle to it!" one of us remarked.

STUDY GUIDE

Organization and Rhetorical Effectiveness

This is a news report. The essential facts and their significance are stated briefly and dramatically in paragraph 1–5 and then an expanded chronological report on the final preparations and on the explosion itself is given in paragraph 6 to the end.

1. Show how the theater imagery sustained throughout paragraph 2 and 3 contributes to the dramatic effect.
2. How has the writer achieved the dramatic quality in paragraph 4 and 5?
3. Try to determine how suspense is built up to a climax in the second part of the report (paragraph 6 to the end).
4. Discuss the effectiveness of the similes and metaphors introduced into paragraph 28 to 32 to enable the reader to see the atomic explosion as the reporter saw them.
5. What type of sentence predominates in this selection? Does it contribute to the dramatic and emotional effect desired?
6. Using some of the technique of the author, try to write a report on some exciting event that you have witnessed.

A CREOLE COURTYARD

Lafcadio Hearn

An atmosphere of tranquility and quiet happiness seemed to envelop the old house, which had formerly belonged to a rich planter. Like many of the Creole houses, the façade presented a commonplace and unattractive aspect. The great green doors of the arched entrance were closed; and the green shutters of the balconied windows were half shut, like sleepy eyes lazily gazing upon the busy street below or the cottony patches of light clouds which floated slowly, slowly across the deep blue of the sky above. But beyond the gates lay a little Paradise. The great court, deep and broad, was framed in tropical green; vines embraced the white pillars of the piazza, and creeping plants climbed up the tinted walls to peer into the upper windows with their flower-eyes of flaming scarlet. Banana-trees nodded sleepily their plumes of emerald green at the farther end of the garden; vines smothered the windows of the dining room, and formed a bower of cool green about the hospitable door; an aged fig-tree, whose gnarled arms trembled under the weight of honeyed fruit, shadowed the square of bright lawn which formed a natural carpet in the midst; and at intervals were stationed along the walks in large porcelain vases—like barbaric sentinels in sentry-boxes—gorgeous broad-leaved things, with leaves fantastic and barbed and flowers brilliant as humming-birds. A fountain murmured faintly near the entrance of the western piazza; and there came from the shadows of the fig-tree the sweet and plaintive cooing of amorous doves. Without, cotton-floats might rumble, and street-cars vulgarly jingle their bells; but these were mere echoes of the harsh outer world which disturbed not the delicious quiet within—where sat, in old-fashioned chairs, good old-fashioned people who spoke the tongue of other times, and observed many quaint and knightly courtesies forgotten in this material era. Without, roared the Iron Age, the angry waves of American traffic; within, one heard only the murmur of the languid fountain, the sound of deeply musical voices conversing in the languages of Paris and Madrid, the playful chatter of dark-haired children lisping in sweet and many-voweled Creole, and through it all, the soft, caressing coo of doves. Without, it was the year 1879; within, it was the epoch of the Spanish Domination. A guitar lay upon the rustic bench near the fountain, where it had evidently been forgotten, and a silk fan beside it; a European periodical, with graceful etchings, hung upon the back of a

From *Creole Sketches* (Boston: Houghton Mifflin Company, 1924), pp. 78–81.

rocking-chair at the door, through which one caught glimpses of a snowy table bearing bottles of good Bordeaux, and inhaled the odor of rich West India tobacco. And yet some people wonder that some other people never care to cross Canal Street.

STUDY GUIDE

The purpose of many descriptive paragraphs, especially in fiction, is to create a dominant impression or atmosphere. Frequently this dominant impression is stated at the beginning of the paragraph and is then built up by concrete detail and imagery throughout the rest of the paragraph.

1. In this paragraph the dominant impression is the tranquility and quiet which pervade the old Creole courtyard. List all the phrases which contribute to this impression of sleepy calm.

2. In this description every one of the senses is appealed to.

A. List the phrases making the most vivid appeal to the sense of sight. In what sentences does the appeal to the sense of sight predominate?

B. What phrases appeal to the senses of smell and taste?

C. The appeal in sentences 7–9 is to the sense of hearing. List the phrases that make a strong appeal to the sense of hearing, and show how these sounds contribute to the tranquil atmosphere. Show how this atmosphere is intensified by the introduction of contrasting sounds in sentences 8 and 9.

D. Select several verbs whose kinetic connotations add to the atmosphere of unhurried, tranquil ease.

E. What two concrete objects have been used in the description to suggest an Old World atmosphere?

3. A. Why is the simile used in sentence 3 to describe the half-closed shutters appropriate to the dominant impression of tranquility?

B. Does the comparison describing the ornamental plants in their vases help us to see them and their position vividly? Is the connotation of "barbaric sentinels" as appropriate to the dominant impression of tranquility as is the comparison used in sentence 3?

Suggestions for Writing

To write successful description, you must be specific and concrete in your use of adjectives, nouns, and verbs; you must economize in your expression by using words which connote rather than merely state colors and precise actions; and you must see to it that all your diction and imagery contribute to the dominant impression you are trying to create.

1. Suppose you are preparing to describe the impression a garden makes on you on a stifling summer day.

A. List the specific trees, flowers, plants, and garden furniture that you would include in such a description.

B. Jot down the specific, connotative words or modifiers that you would use to make the reader see, feel, hear, and smell the objects of the scene as they have impressed you. Your impressions might include wilted hydrangeas, one listless robin drooping in the shade, the crackle of dry grass underfoot, and so on.

C. Do the same for the identical garden as it would impress you just after a heavy snow storm.

2. Write two paragraphs in which you state the dominant impression which these two scenes make on you in the opening sentences and in which you build up these impressions as vividly as you can by specific, concrete diction and imagery.

3. Sometimes it is not the scene or object which creates the dominant unifying impression in a description but the mood or interest of the writer. For instance, a person in a gay mood and another in a sad mood are apt to react quite differently to the same scene and put their divergent reactions into their description. So too, people with different interests will look at the same object or scene quite differently.

Draw up separate lists of details which would strike a hunter and a painter in the same woodland scene, and then write two paragraphs on the scene from the viewpoint of a hunter and of a painter.

THE CITY OF CHANDRAPORE

E. M. Forster

1 Except for the Marabar Caves—and they are twenty miles off—the city of Chandrapore presents nothing extraordinary. Edged rather than washed by the river Ganges, it trails for a couple of miles along the bank, scarcely distinguishable from the rubbish it deposits so freely. There are no bathing-steps on the river front, as the Ganges happens not to be holy here; indeed there is no river front, and bazaars shut out the wide and shifting panorama of the stream. The streets are mean, the temples ineffective, and though a few fine houses exist they are hidden away in gardens or down alleys whose filth deters all but the invited guest. Chandrapore was never large or beautiful, but two hundred years ago it lay on the road between Upper India, then imperial, and the sea, and the fine houses date from that period. The zest for decoration stopped in the eighteenth century, nor was it ever democratic. There is no paint and scarcely any carving in the bazaars. The very wood seems made of mud, the inhabitants of mud moving. So abased, so monotonous is everything that meets the eye, that when the Ganges comes down it might be expected to wash the excrescence back into the soil. Houses do fall, people are drowned and left rotting, but the general outline of the town persists, swelling here, shrinking there, like some low but indestructible form of life.

2 Inland, the prospect alters. There is an oval Maidan, and a long sallow hospital. Houses belonging to Eurasians stand on the high ground by the railway station. Beyond the railway—which runs parallel to the river—the land sinks, then rises again rather steeply. On the second rise is laid out the little civil station, and viewed hence Chandrapore appears to be a totally different place. It is a city of gardens. It is no city, but a forest sparsely scattered with huts. It is a tropical pleasance washed by a noble river. The toddy palms and neem trees and mangoes and pepul that were hidden behind the bazaars now become visible and in their turn hide the bazaars. They rise from the gardens where ancient tanks nourish them, they burst out of stifling purlieus and unconsidered temples. Seeking light and air, and endowed with more strength than man or his works, they soar above the lower deposit to greet one another with branches and beckoning leaves, and to build a city for the birds. Especially after the rains do they screen what passes below, but at all times, even when scorched or leafless, they glorify the city to the English people who inhabit the rise, so that new-comers cannot believe it to be as meagre as it is described, and have to be driven down to acquire disillusionment. As for the civil station itself, it provokes no emotion. It charms not, neither does it repel. It is sensibly planned, with a red-brick club on its brow, and farther back a grocer's and a cemetery, and the bungalows are disposed along roads that intersect at right angles. It has nothing hideous in it, and only the view is beautiful; it shares nothing with the city except the overarching sky.

STUDY GUIDE

Thought Structure

The description of the Creole courtyard begins with a statement of the dominant impression which is built up concretely in the rest of the paragraph. In these two descriptive paragraphs of the city of Chandrapore this method is reversed. Cumulative concrete details first create the dominant impression of the riverside and inland city, and then the impression is explicity stated toward the middle or end of the paragraphs.

1. What is the dominant impression of the separate parts of the city created by the author?
2. What sentences in each paragraph most clearly express this impression?

Diction and Imagery

No matter what the principle of organization in a descriptive paragraph is, if a dominant impression is to be created, the writer must see to it that his diction and imagery really build that impression.

1. An inexpert writer is apt to rely too much on descriptive adjectives which *state* the impression rather than on carefully selected nouns, adverbs,

and verbs which suggest it. One or two well-chosen nouns, adverbs, or verbs will frequently produce a fuller and more vivid impression than dozens of descriptive adjectives. For example, the verb *trails* in the phrase "it trails for a couple of miles along the bank" gives us a much more vivid impression of the city sprawling along the river than does the following phrase clotted with adjectives—"Chandrapore, a broad, irregular expanse of two miles or more along the river."

Explain why the following phrases employed by the author are better than the substituted phrases in parentheses, paying particular attention to the connotative value of the italicized words in each phrase: (1) "scarcely distinquishable from the *rubbish* it deposits so freely" (a dirty city); (2) "wide and *shifting panorama* of the stream" (wide and varied view of the stream); (3) "alleys whose *filth deters* all but the invited guest" (extremely dirty alleys); (4) "the *zest* for decoration" (the interest in decoration); (5) "The land *sinks* then *rises* again rather *steeply*" (there is a valley and then a steep hill); (6) "A *forest sparsely scattered* with *huts*" (innumerable trees and a few, shabby, dirty houses); (7) "The *toddy palms* and *neem trees* and *mangoes* and *pepul*" (the various tropical trees); (8) "They *rise* from the gardens . . . and *burst* out of the *stifling purlieus*" (they can be seen above the gardens and above the warm parks); (9) "they *soar* above the lower *deposit* to *greet* one another with branches and *beckoning* leaves" (they rise above the lower places to mingle their branches and leaves); (10) "They *screen* what passes below" (they cover what passes below); (11) "except the *overarching* sky" (except the expanse of sky).

2. Sometimes it is not so much the vivid sense impression but rather the atmosphere or emotional effect of a scene that a writer wishes to communicate in a description. In such case a comparison (simile or metaphor) is likely to serve him best. Comparisons, of course, can help to make a description vivid in sense appeal, but, when used for the purpose discussed here, they contribute not so much to the sense impression as to the emotional atmosphere.

A. In paragraph 1, Forster is trying to convey the depressing, sordid impression of the lower section of Chandrapore. All the concrete details contribute to that impression, but the sordid atmosphere is probably best conveyed in the following figurative phrases: "The very wood *seems made of mud,* the inhabitants of mud moving"; "wash the *excrescence* back into the soil"; and "the general outline of the town . . . swelling here, shrinking there, *like some low but indestructible form of life*." Why are these phrases an effective expression of the sordid impression of the dirty city?

B. Point out and discuss the comparisons in paragraph 2, sentences 7–9, to convey the general emotional impression of the upper city of Chandrapore.

C. Forster says the river seems to edge the city when seen from below and to *wash* it when seen from above. How do these verbs fit the general impression created of the two parts of the city?

Suggestion for Writing

Any city will impress you quite differently when approached from two different directions. It will give you one impression when viewed from the slums and coal yards through which a train passes, and quite another when viewed from a fine boulevard in one of the better residential districts.

Write a two-paragraph description of your home city as viewed from two such different points of view. Be sure to settle on the dominant impression in each case, and try to select your diction and imagery as carefully as Forster has to communicate your impressions.

MANDERLEY

Daphne du Maurier

1 Last night I dreamt I went to Manderley again. It seemed to me I stood by the iron gate leading to the drive, and for a while I could not enter for the way was barred to me. There was a padlock and a chain upon the gate. I called in my dream to the lodgekeeper, and had no answer, and peering closer through the rusted spokes of the gate I saw that the lodge was uninhabited.

2 No smoke came from the chimney, and the little lattice windows gaped forlorn. Then, like all dreamers, I was possessed of a sudden with supernatural powers and passed like a spirit through the barrier before me. The drive wound away in front of me, twisting and turning as it had always done, but as I advanced I was aware that a change had came upon it; it was narrow and unkept, not the drive that we had known. At first I was puzzled and did not understand, and it was only when I bent my head to avoid the low swinging branch of a tree that I realized what had happened. Nature had come into her own again and, little by little, in her stealthy, insidious way had enroached upon the drive with long, tenacious fingers. The woods, always a menace even in the past, had triumphed in the end. They crowded, dark and uncontrolled, to the borders of the drive. The beeches with white, naked limbs leant close to one another, their branches intermingled in a strange embrace, making a vault above my head like the archway of a church. And there were other trees as well, trees that I did not recognize, squat oaks and tortured elms that straggled cheek by jowl with the beeches, and had thrust themselves out of the quiet earth, along with monster shrubs and plants, none of which I remembered.

3 The drive was a ribbon now, a thread of its former self, with gravel surface gone, and choked with grass and moss. The trees had thrown out

From *Rebecca* (New York: Doubleday & Company, Inc., 1938), pp. 1–4.

low branches, making an impediment to progress; the gnarled roots looked like skeleton claws. Scattered here and again amongst this jungle growth I would recognize shrubs that had been land-marks in our time, things of culture and of grace, hydrangeas whose blue heads had been famous. No hand had checked their progress, and they had gone native now, rearing to monster height without a bloom, black and ugly as the nameless parasites that grew beside them.

4 On and on, now east now west, wound the poor thread that once had been our drive. Sometimes I thought it lost, but it appeared again, beneath a fallen tree perhaps, or struggling on the other side of a muddied ditch created by the winter rains. I had not thought the way so long. Surely the miles had multiplied, even as the trees had done, and this path led out to a labyrinth, some choked wilderness, and not to the house at all. I came upon it suddenly; the approach masked by the unnatural growth of a vast shrub that spread in all directions, and I stood, my heart thumping in my breast, the strange prick of tears behind my eyes.

5 There was Manderley, our Manderley, secretive and silent as it had always been, the grey stone shining in the moonlight of my dream, the mullioned windows reflecting the green lawns and the terrace. Time could not wreck the perfect symmetry of those walls, not the site itself, a jewel in the hollow of a hand.

6 The terrace sloped to the lawns, and the lawns stretched to the sea, and turning I could see the sheet of silver, placid under the moon, like a lake undisturbed by wind or storm. No waves would come to ruffle this dream water, and no bulk of cloud, wind-driven from the west, obscure the clarity of this pale sky. I turned again to the house, and thought it stood inviolate, untouched, and though we ourselves had left but yesterday, I saw that the garden had obeyed the jungle law, even as the wood had done. The rhododendrons stood fifty feet high, twisted and entwined with bracken, and they had entered into alien marriage with a host of nameless shrubs, poor, bastard things that clung about their roots as though conscious of their spurious origin. A lilac had mated with a copper beech, and to bind them yet more closely to one another the malevolent ivy, always an enemy to grace, had thrown her tendrils about the pair and made them prisoners. Ivy held prior place in this lost garden; the long strands crept across the lawns, and soon would encroach upon the house itself. There was another plant too, some half-breed from the woods, whose seed had been scattered long ago beneath the trees and then forgotten, and now, marching in unison with the ivy, thrust its ugly form like a giant rhubarb towards the soft grass where the daffodils had blown.

7 Nettles were everywhere, the van-guard of the army. They choked the terrace, they sprawled about the paths, they leant, vulgar and lank, against the very windows of the house. They made indifferent sentinels for in

many places their ranks had been broken by the rhubarb plant, and they lay with crumpled heads and listless stems, making a pathway for the rabbits. I left the drive and went on to the terrace, for the nettles were no barrier to me, a dreamer; I walked enchanted, and nothing held me back.

8 Moonlight can play odd tricks upon the fancy, even upon a dreamer's fancy. As I stood there, hushed and still, I could swear that the house was not an empty shell but lived and breathed as it had lived before.

9 Light came from the windows, the curtains blew softly in the night air, and there, in the library, the door would stand half open as we had left it, with my handkerchief on the table beside the bowl of autumn roses.

10 The room would bear witness to our presence. The little heap of library books marked ready to return, and the discarded copy of The Times. Ash-trays, with the stub of a cigarette; cushions, with the imprint of our heads upon them, lolling in the chairs; the charred embers of our log fire still smouldering against the morning. And Jasper, dear Jasper, with his soulful eyes and great, sagging jowl, would be stretched upon the floor, his tail a-thump when he heard his master's footsteps.

11 A cloud, hitherto unseen, came upon the moon, and hovered an instant like a dark hand before a face. The illusion went with it, and the lights in the windows were extinguished. I looked upon a desolate shell, soulless at last, unhaunted, with no whisper of the past about its staring walls.

12 The house was a sepulchre, our fear and suffering lay buried in the ruins. There would be no resurrection. When I thought of Manderley in my waking hours I would not be bitter. I should think of it as it might have been, could I have lived there without fear. I should remember the rose-garden in the summer, and the birds that sang at dawn. Tea under the chestnut tree, and the murmur of the sea coming up to us from the lawns below.

13 I would think of the blown lilacs, and the Happy Valley. These things were permanent, they could not be dissolved. They were memories that cannot hurt. All this I resolved in my dream, while the clouds lay across the face of the moon, for like most sleepers I knew that I dreamed. In reality I lay many hundred miles away in an alien land, and would wake, before many seconds had passed, in the bare little hotel bedroom, comforting in its very lack of atmosphere. I would sigh a moment, stretch myself and turn, and opening my eyes, be bewildered at that glittering sun, that hard, clean sky, so different from the soft moonlight of my dream. The day would lie before us both, long no doubt, and uneventful but fraught with a certain stillness, a dear tranquility we had not know before. We would not talk of Manderley, I would not tell my dream. For Manderley was ours no longer. Manderley was no more.

STUDY GUIDE

Description in Fiction

The descriptive essay as a separate literary form is not very popular with the modern reader. What description he does encounter is apt to be imbedded in his fictional reading—in short stories and novels. Such description may be used separately or combined with narrative either to provide the atmosphere and setting for the story or to bring the characters to life. This selection is the first chapter of the novel *Rebecca;* partly narrative and partly descriptive, it builds up a concrete picture of the neglected estate and creates an atmosphere of mystery about Manderley which plants the desire in the mind of the reader to get at the facts of the story which explain the neglect and solve the mystery.

Point of View

This selection is a good example of the shifting point of view. It passes over the scene like the eye of a movie camera.

1. Point out the successive shifts in point of view, and show how details have been carefully chosen to make us see vividly the scenes as they appear from these different points of view.
2. What has the author gained by assuming the general point of view of a dreamer throughout the description?

Dominant Impression and Selective Detail

It was pointed out above that the dominant impression created by this selection is one of neglect and mystery.

1. Select the verbs (both predicate verbs and verbals) that you think are particularly well chosen to create this atmosphere of wild growth and neglect.
2. Analyze the similes and metaphors that contribute to the atmosphere either of neglect or of mystery in paragraph 3, sentences 1 and 2; paragraph 4, sentence 1; paragraph 11, sentence 1; and paragraph 12, sentence 1.
3. Contrast has been used in several places in the selection to reinforce the atmosphere of neglect. Well-chosen concrete details do most to evoke pictures in strong contrast to the atmosphere of neglect and abandonment. For example, "the half-open door" and "the handkerchief on the table" beside the bowl of autumn roses set our imaginations working to create an image of an inhabited and tended Manderley that contrasts sharply with the image of present desolation and neglect. Point out the concrete details that you consider most effective in creating such contrasting pictures in paragraph 3, sentence 3; paragraph 6, sentence 7; paragraph 9; paragraph 10, sentences 2–4; paragraph 12, sentences 5 and 6; and paragraph 13, sentence 1.
4. Analyze the propriety of the sustained image in paragraphs 6 and 7 for emphasizing the atmosphere of neglect and wild growth.
5. What is the frame image employed in paragraph 5, sentence 2, which helps us visualize the actual position of Manderley in its surroundings?
6. One carefully selected word will often enable the imagination to paint a complete and exactly detailed picture. What word in paragraph 5 enables us to visualize the actual size of architecture in which Manderley is built?
7. Make a list of all the words and phrases that you think help build up a sinister and mysterious atmosphere about Manderley.

GURTH AND WAMBA

Sir Walter Scott

1 The human figures which completed this landscape were in number two, partaking, in their dress and appearance, of that wild and rustic character, which belong to the woodlands of the West-Riding of Yorkshire at that early period. The eldest of these men had a stern, savage, and wild aspect. His garment was of the simplest form imaginable, being of a close jacket with sleeves, composed of the tanned skin of some animal, on which the hair had been originally left, but which had been worn off in so many places, that it would have been difficult to distinguish, from the patches that remained, to what creature the fur had belonged. This primeval vestment reached from the throat to the knees, and served at once all the usual purposes of body-clothing; there was no wider opening at the collar than was necessary to admit the passage of the head, from which it may be inferred that it was put on by slipping it over the head and shoulders, in the manner of a modern shirt, or ancient hauberk. Sandals, bound with thongs made of boars' hide, protected the feet, and a roll of thin leather was twined artificially round the legs, and, ascending above the calf, left the knees bare, like those of a Scottish Highlander. To make the jacket sit yet more close to the body, it was gathered at the middle by a broad leathern belt, secured by a brass buckle; to one side of which was attached a sort of scrip, and to the other a ram's horn, accoutred with a mouthpiece, for the purpose of blowing. In the same belt was stuck one of those long, broad, sharp-pointed, and two-edged knives, with a buck's horn handle, which was fabricated in the neighbourhood, and bore even at this early period the name of a Sheffield whittle. The man had no covering upon his head, which was only defended by his own thick hair, matted and twisted together, and scorched by the influence of the sun into a rusty dark-red colour, forming a contrast with the over-grown beard upon his cheeks, which was rather of a yellow or amber hue. One part of his dress only remains, but it is too remarkable to be suppressed; it was a brass ring, resembling a dog's collar, but without any opening, and soldered fast around his neck, so loose as to form no impediment to his breathing, yet so tight as to be incapable of being removed, excepting by the use of the file. On this singular gorget was engraved, in Saxon characters, an inscription of the following purport:—"Gurth, the son of Beowulph, is the born thrall of Cedric of Rotherwood."

2 Beside the swineherd, for such was Gurth's occupation, was seated,

Reprinted from Sir Walter Scott, *Ivanhoe* (1820).

upon one of the fallen Druidical monuments, a person about ten years younger in appearance, and whose dress, though resembling his companion's in form, was of better materials, and of a more fantastic appearance. His jacket had been stained of a bright purple hue, upon which there had been some attempt to paint grotesque ornaments in different colours. To the jacket he added a shortcloak, which scarcely reached halfway down his thigh; it was of crimson cloth, though a good deal soiled, lined with bright yellow; and he could transfer it from one shoulder to the other, or at his pleasure draw it all around him, its width, contrasted with its want of longitude, formed a fantastic piece of drapery. He had thin silver bracelets upon his arms, and on his neck a collar of the same metal, bearing the inscription, "Wamba, the son of Witless, is the thrall of Cedric of Rotherwood." This personage had the same sort of sandals with his companion, but instead of the roll of leather thong, his legs were cased in a sort of gaiters, of which one was red and the other yellow. He was provided also with a cap, having around it more than one bell, about the size of those attached to hawks, which jingled as he turned his head to one side or other; and as he seldom remained a minute in the same posture, the sound might be considered as incessant. Around the edge of his cap was a stiff bandeau of leather, cut at the top into open work, resembling a coronet, while a prolonged bag arose from within it, and fell down on one shoulder like an old-fashioned night-cap, or a jelly-bag, or the headgear of a modern hussar. It was to this part of the cap that the bells were attached; which circumstance, as well as the shape of his head-dress, and his own half-crazed, half-cunning expression of countenance, sufficiently pointed him out as belonging to the race of domestic clowns or jesters, maintained in the houses of the wealthy, to help away the tedium of those lingering hours which they were obliged to spend within doors. He bore, like his companion, a scrip attached to his belt, but had neither horn nor knife, being probably considered as belonging to a class whom it is esteemed dangerous to intrust with edge-tools. In place of these he was equipped with a sword of lath, resembling that with which Harlequin operates his wonders upon the modern stage.

STUDY GUIDE

Order in Description

In enumerating the details which fill out the description of a place or person it is important to observe some definite order. In describing a scene, for instance, one might begin with the details of the terrain in the foreground and work up to the sky, or start with the sky and work down to some point of focus in the foreground. One may work in an orderly fashion from right to left or vice versa. It makes little difference what order is followed, but it is important that the details fall into some easily discernible pattern. The same is true for the description of the outward appearance of persons. One may begin, for instance, with the feet and work up to the head and face or vice versa; or one may begin with the most striking detail in the person's features or dress and then fill in the other details as they are related to this one, or begin with other details and end with the most striking detail.

Which of these principles of order does Scott follow in describing the appearance of Gurth and Wamba in these paragraphs?

Descriptions of External Appearance

Some desecriptions are concerned not so much with giving us the impression of the inner feeling and characters of the people described but rather of their external appearance. Here completeness and exactness of detail are what is needed.

Has Scott provided sufficient detail of color, size, shape, texture in these two descriptions to enable you to paint these characters accurately? That is the test of the success of his type of description.

Suggestion for Writing

Choose some striking person you have seen—perhaps a newsboy, beggar, soldier, farmer, or bus driver—and describe him as accurately as Scott describes Wamba and Gurth and in a similar orderly fashion.

SIRE DE MALÉTROIT

Robert Louis Stevenson

On a high chair beside the chimney, and directly facing Denis as he entered, sat a little old gentleman in a fur tippet. He sat with his legs crossed and his hands folded, and a cup of spice wine stood by his elbow on a bracket on the wall. His countenance had a strong masculine cast; not properly human, but such as we see in the bull, the goat, or the domestic boar; something equivocal and wheedling, something greedy, brutal, and dangerous. The upper lip was inordinately full, as though swollen by a blow or a toothache; and the smile, the peaked eyebrows, and the small, strong eyes were quaintly and almost comically evil in expression. Beautiful white hair hung straight all round his head, like a saint's, and fell in a single curl upon the tippet. His beard and mustache were the pink of venerable sweetness. Age, probably in consequence of inordinate precautions, had left no mark upon his hands; and the Malétroit hand was famous. It would be difficult to imagine anything at once so fleshy and so delicate in design; the tapered, sensual fingers were like those of one of

Reprinted from Robert Louis Stevenson, "The Sire de Malétroit's Door" in *The New Arabian Nights* (1882).

Leonardo's women; the fork of the thumb made a dimpled protuberance when closed; the nails were perfectly shaped, and of a dead, surprising whiteness. It rendered his aspect tenfold more redoubtable, that a man with hands like these should keep them devoutly folded like a virgin martyr—that a man with so intent and startling an expression of face should sit patiently on his seat and contemplate people with an unwinking stare, like a god, or a god's statue. His quiescence seemed ironical and treacherous, it fitted so poorly with his looks. Such was Alain, Sire de Malétroit.

STUDY GUIDE

Descriptive Detail and Inner Character

A good writer is rarely content with describing merely the outward appearance of his characters. He is rather interested in what their outward countenance, dress, and occupation reveal of their inner character and feelings. He is, therefore, careful to choose the details of outward appearance that will best reveal or suggest these inner characteristics.

1. What is the dominant impression of Sire de Malétroit's character that we get from Stevenson's description of him?

2. Show how the details in the description of his hands and countenance help create this impression.

3. Stevenson is not interested here in giving a detailed catalogue of Sire de Malétroit's whole appearance (he concentrates on his hands and face), but he does give us sufficient details to enable us to picture him in his proper age and size. Point out these details in the description.

4. Show how the equivocal or ironical appearance of Sire de Malétroit is emphasized by the comparisons used to describe him. For example, it is ironical that a person who has a brutal and dangerous looking countenance should have it framed with beautiful white hair like a saint's.

5. How does the detail of the spice wine on a bracket at Sire de Malétroit's elbow contribute to the dominant, ironic impression of him stated in sentence 10?

A NEW ENGLAND VILLAGE

William Dean Howells

1 The village stood on a wide plain, and around it rose the mountains. They were green to their tops in summer, and in winter white through their serried pines and drifting mists, but at every season serious and

Reprinted from William Dean Howells, *A Modern Instance* (1882).

beautiful, furrowed with hollow shadows, and taking the light on masses and stretches of iron-gray crag. The river swam through the plain in long curves, and slipped away at last through an unseen pass to the southward, tracing a score of miles in its course over a space that measured but three or four. The plain was very fertile, and its features, if few and of purely utilitarian beauty, had a rich luxuriance, and there was a tropical riot of vegetation when the sun of July beat on those northern fields. They waved with corn and oats to the feet of the mountains, and the potatoes covered a vast acreage with the lines of their intense, coarse green; the meadows were deep with English grass to the banks of the river, that, doubling and returning upon itself, still marked its way with a dense fringe of alders and white birches.

2 But winter was full half the year. The snow began at Thanksgiving, and fell snow upon snow till Fast Day, thawing between the storms, and packing harder and harder against the break-up in the spring, when it covered the ground in solid levels three feet high, and lay heaped in drifts, that defied the sun far into May. When it did not snow, the weather was keenly clear and commonly very still. Then the landscape at noon had a stereoscopic glister under the high sun that burned in a heaven without a cloud, and at setting stained the sky and the white waste with freezing pink and violet. On such days the farmers and lumbermen came in to the village stores, and made a stiff and feeble stir about their doorways, and the school children gave the street a little life and color, as they went to and from the Academy in their red and blue woollens. Four times a day the mill, the shrill wheeze of whose saws had become part of the habitual silence, blew its whistle for the hands to begin and leave off work, in blasts that seemed to shatter themselves against the thin air. But otherwise an arctic quiet prevailed.

3 Behind the black boles of the elms that swept the vista of the street with the fine gray tracery of their boughs, stood the houses, deep-sunken in the accumulating drifts, through which each householder kept a path cut from his doorway to the road, white and clean as if hewn out of marble. Some cross streets straggled away east and west with the poorer dwellings; but this, that followed the northward and southward reach of the plain, was the main thoroughfare, and had its own impressiveness, with those square white houses which they build so large in Northern New England. They were all kept in scrupulous repair, though here and there the frost and thaw of many winters had heaved a fence out of plumb, and threatened the poise of the monumental urns of painted pine on the gateposts. They had dark-green blinds, of a color harmonious with that of the funereal evergreens in their dooryards; and they themselves had taken the tone of the snowy landscape, as if by the operation of some such law as blanches the fur-bearing animals of the North. They seemed proper to its

desolation, while some houses of more modern taste, painted to a warmer tone, looked, with their mansard roofs and jig-sawed piazzas and balconies, intrusive and alien.

STUDY GUIDE

1. In a study of modern American prose style, the critic Walker Gibson discusses the difference between the type of description found in the traditional realistic novel such as *A Modern Instance* by Howells and the more expressionistic type found in a novel by Hemingway (and exemplified in the next selection). One of the differences is the point of view. Howells is observing the New England village from an omniscient point of view in both time and space. He sees the village from a height as if, Gibson says, he were floating above it in a balloon.[1] He sees the mountains on all sides, all the village, the whole plain, and the river as it curves through the whole plain. Read through the entire passage and select other details showing that the author is viewing the scene from a height.

2. The author, however, is not only seeing it from a height. He is omniscient; he knows how the scene looks in both summer and winter. The mountains are "green to the tops in summer, and in winter white through their serried pines and drifting mists." He knows also how the river slips away at last through an unseen pass. Select other details in the description that show that the author is describing the scene from the omniscient point of view in both space and time.

3. This passage might be described as *objective*. Howells keeps himself out of the picture and focuses attention on the physical details of the scene itself largely by providing such concrete, specific details that one could paint the scene accurately in all its shapes and colors. For example, the reader learns that the mountains are "*furrowed* with hollow shadows," and take the light "on *masses* and *stretches of iron-gray crag*." The fields wave "with *corn* and *oats* to the feet of the mountains" and the potatoes cover "a vaste acreage with the *lines of their intense, coarse green*." Go through the entire passage and pick out other concrete details that enable the reader to sense exactly the detailed appearance of the scene.

4. Part of the exactness of the description is achieved by the judicious choice of verbs, such as *furrowed* to describe the exact contour of the mountains and *swam* to describe the motion of the river across the plain. Find other examples of such connotative verbs in the passage.

5. There are evaluative adjectives and adjectival phrases in the passage that suggest the author's judgments on the scene. The mountains are "serious and beautiful." The features of the plain are "of purely utilitarian beauty." Find other examples of such evaluative modifiers in the passage. Such modifiers place the writer outside the scene, looking at it and making judgments about it, and they contrast with the Hemingway passage, where the writer is very much inside the scene, expressing chiefly his own personal feeling about it.

6. The sentence structure of this passage is characterized by fairly long,

[1] Walker Gibson, *Tough, Sweet, and Stuffy* (Bloomington, Ind.: Indiana University Press, 1966).

complex sentences. Make an estimate of the percentage of complex sentences in the selection and compare it to the Hemingway passage in this respect.

7. Find descriptive passages from other nineteenth-century novelists and make a similar study of their style.

AN ITALIAN VILLAGE IN SUMMER

Ernest Hemingway

1 In the late summer of that year we lived in a house in a village that looked across the river and the plain to the mountains. In the bed of the river there were pebbles and boulders, dry and white in the sun, and the water was clear and swiftly moving and blue in the channels. Troops went by the house and down the road and the dust they raised powdered the leaves of the trees. The trunks of the trees too were dusty and the leaves fell early that year and we saw the troops marching along the road and the dust rising and leaves, stirred by the breeze, falling and the soldiers marching and afterward the road bare and white except for the leaves.

2 The plain was rich with crops; there were many orchards of fruit trees and beyond the plain the mountains were brown and bare. There was fighting in the mountains and at night we could see the flashing from the artillery. In the dark it was like summer lightning, but the nights were cool and there was not the feeling of a storm coming.

3 Sometimes in the dark we heard the troops marching under the window and guns going past pulled by motor-tractors. There was much traffic at night and many mules on the roads with boxes of ammunition on each side of their pack-saddles and gray motor trucks that carried men, and other trucks with loads covered with canvas that moved slower in the traffic. There were big guns too that passed in the day drawn by tractors, the long barrels of the guns covered with green branches and green leafy branches and vines laid over the tractors. To the north we could look across a valley and see a forest of chestnut trees and behind it another mountain on this side of the river. There was fighting for that mountain too, but it was not successful, and in the fall when the rains came the leaves all fell from the chestnut trees and the branches were bare and the trunks black with rain. The vineyards were thin and bare-branched too and all the country wet and brown and dead with the autumn. There were

mists over the river and clouds on the mountain and the trucks splashed mud on the road and the troops were muddy and wet in their capes; their rifles were wet and under their capes the two leather cartridge-boxes on the front of the belts, gray leather boxes heavy with the packs of clips of thin, long 6.5 mm. cartridges, bulged forward under the capes so that the men passing on the road, marched as though they were six months gone with child.

4 There were small gray motor cars that passed going very fast; usually there was an officer on the seat with the driver and more officers in the back seat. They splashed more mud than the camions even and if one of the officers in the back was very small and sitting between two generals, he himself so small that you could not see his face but only the top of his cap and his narrow back, and if the car went especially fast it was probably the King. He lived in Udine and came out in this way nearly every day to see how things were going, and things went very badly.

5 At the start of the winter came the permanent rain and with the rain came the cholera. But it was checked and in the end only seven thousand died of it in the army.

STUDY GUIDE

1. Hemingway's type of subjective description is somewhat comparable to a landscape of expressionistic painting (see, for example, "Starry Night" or "Wheat Field with Cypresses" by the Dutch painter Vincent van Gogh). The expressionistic artist is not interested in giving an exact description of a scene but rather in communicating his own reaction to the scene and his feeling about it. For this reason, he selects details, exaggerates others, rearranges them, even distorts them, in order to communicate what the scene means to him or how he feels about it. His subject is more himself than the scene he is describing. Walker Gibson has pointed out that Hemingway partly achieves this subjective, expressionistic manner by the emphasis on the first person pronouns that persist throughout the passage.[1] The whole scene is presented only as it affected the narrator, Frederic Henry. Check the frequency of the first person pronoun in the passage.

2. Another sign of Hemingway's expressionistic manner is the selectivity of detail to communicate the impression of late autumn dryness and death. Indicate the various ways in which that impression is built up in the first paragraph. Note other impressions built up in the other paragraphs and indicate the choice of words by which they are created.

3. Since Hemingway is not trying to communicate an exact impression of the village but rather his narrator's reaction to it, he does not use multiple concrete detail. He speaks of a house but gives no details about what kind of house it is; he mentions trunks of trees but is not concerned about the kind of

[1] Walker Gibson, *Tough, Sweet, and Stuffy* (Bloomington, Ind.: Indiana University Press, 1966), pp. 30–42.

tree they are. He speaks of a village, the river, the plain, the mountains, and gives no qualifying details that suggest their shape, color, or size. Hemingway only provides such details when they contribute to the impression of dryness and bareness that he is building, for example, "the road *bare* and *white*" and the "dusty" trunks of trees. Study the whole passage and contrast it with that of Howells in this matter of concrete detail. Hemingway is not providing details that would enable readers to paint the scene, but only those details that impressed his narrator in the circumstances of a moment in the war.

4. The two passages are also greatly different in sentence structure. In length the sentences in the two excerpts are not very different. But Hemingway's are almost all short simple declarative sentences or compound sentences whose short clauses are strung together by *and*'s. Check on the predominance of this type of sentence in this passage and contrast it in its effect with the quotation from Howell where the complex sentence prevails.

5. The narrator here does not assume the omniscient point of view. He confines himself to what he can see and hear from the house he is occupying. These details of the moment are what affect him, and they are the only ones he communicates to the reader. Show that this more restricted viewpoint is maintained throughout the passage.

A SUMMER MORNING IN JEFFERSON

William Faulkner

1 It was a summer of wistaria. The twilight was full of it and of the smell of his father's cigar as they sat on the front gallery after supper until it would be time for Quentin to start, while in the deep shaggy lawn below the veranda the fireflies blew and drifted in soft random—the odor, the scent, which five months later Mr Compson's letter would carry up from Mississippi and over the long iron New England snow and into Quentin's sitting-room at Harvard. It was a day of listening too—the listening, the hearing in 1909 mostly about that which he already knew, since he had been born in and still breathed the same air in which the church bells had rung on that Sunday morning in 1833 and, on Sundays, heard even one of the original three bells in the same steeple where descendants of the same pigeons strutted and crooned or wheeled in short courses resembling soft fluid paint-smears on the soft summer sky. That Sunday morning in June with the bells ringing peaceful and peremptory and a little cacophonous—the denominations in concord though not in tune—and the ladies and chil-

dren, and house negroes to carry the parasols and flywhisks, and even a few men (the ladies moving in hoops among the miniature broadcloth of little boys and the pantalettes of little girls, in the skirts of the time when ladies did not walk but floated) when the other men sitting with their feet on the railing of the Holston House gallery looked up, and there the stranger was. He was already halfway across the Square when they saw him, on a big hard-ridden roan horse, man and beast looking as though they had been created out of thin air and set down in the bright summer sabbath sunshine in the middle of a tired foxtrot—face and horse that none of them had ever seen before, name that none of them had ever heard, and origin and purpose which some of them were never to learn. So that in the next four weeks (Jefferson was a village then: the Holston House, the courthouse, six stores, a blacksmith and livery stable, a saloon frequented by drovers and peddlers, three churches and perhaps thirty residences) the stranger's name went back and forth among the places of business and of idleness and among the residences in steady strophe and antistrophe: *Sutpen. Sutpen Sutpen. Sutpen.*

2 That was all that the town was to know about him for almost a month. He had apparently come into town from the south—a man of about twenty-five as the town learned later, because at the time his age could not have been guessed because he looked like a man who had been sick. Not like a man who had been peacefully ill in bed and had recovered to move with a sort of diffident and tentative amazement in a world which he had believed himself on the point of surrendering, but like a man who had been through some solitary furnace experience which was more than just fever like an explorer say, who not only had to face the normal hardship of the pursuit which he chose but was overtaken by the added and unforeseen handicap of the fever also and fought through it at enormous cost not so much physical as mental, alone and unaided and not through blind instinctive will to endure and survive but to gain and keep to enjoy it the material prize for which he accepted the original gambit. A man with a big frame but gaunt now almost to emaciation, with a short reddish beard which resembled a disguise and above which his pale eyes had a quality at once visionary and alert, ruthless and reposed in a face whose flesh had the appearance of pottery, of having been colored by that oven's fever either of soul or environment, deeper than sun alone beneath a dead impervious surface as of glazed clay. That was what they saw, though it was years before the town learned that that was all which he possessed at the time—the strong spent horse and the clothes on his back and a small saddlebag scarcely large enough to contain the spare linen and the razors, and the two pistols of which Miss Coldfield told Quentin, with the butts worn smooth as pickhandles and which he used with the precision of knitting needles; later Quentin's grandfather saw him ride at a canter around a sapling at

twenty feet and put both bullets into a playing card fastened to the tree. He had a room in the Holston House but he carried the key with him and each morning he fed and saddled the horse and rode away before daylight, where to the town likewise failed to learn, probably due to the fact that he gave the pistol demonstration on the third day after his arrival. So they had to depend on inquiry to find out what they could about him, which would of necessity be at night, at the supper table in the Holston House dining-room or in the lounge which he would have to cross to gain his room and the door again, which he would do as soon as he finished eating. The bar opened into the lounge too, and that would or should have been the place to accost him and even inquire, except for the fact that he did not use the bar. He did not drink at all, he told them. He did not say that he used to drink and had quit, nor that he had never used alcohol. He just said that he would not care for a drink; it was years later before even Quentin's grandfather (he was a young man too then; it would be years yet before he would become General Compson) learned that the reason Sutpen did not drink was that the did not have the money with which to pay his share or return the courtesy; it was General Compson who first realized that at this time Sutpen lacked not only the money to spend for drink and conviviality, but the time and inclination as well: that he was at this time completely the slave of his secret and furious impatience, his conviction gained from whatever that recent experience had been—that fever mental or physical—of a need for haste, of time fleeing beneath him, which was to drive him for the next five years—as General Compson computed it, roughly until about ninc months before his son was born.

3 So they would catch him, run him to earth, in the lounge between the supper table and his locked door to give him the opportunity to tell them who he was and where he came from what he was up to, whereupon he would move gradually and steadily until his back came in contact with something—a post or a wall—and then stand there and tell them nothing whatever as pleasantly and courteously as a hotel clerk. It was the Chickasaw Indian agent with or through whom he dealt and so it was not until he waked the County Recorder that Saturday night with the deed, patent, to the land and the gold Spanish coin, that the town learned that he now owned a hundred square miles of some of the best virgin bottom land in the country, though even that knowledge came too late because Sutpen himself was gone, where to again they did not know. But he owned land among them now and some of them began to suspect what General Compson apparently knew: that the Spanish coin with which he had paid to have his patent recorded was the last one of any kind which he possessed. So they were certain now that he had departed to get more; there were several who even anticipated in believing (and even in saying aloud, now that he was not present) what Sutpen's future and then unborn sister-in-

law was to tell Quentin almost eighty years later: that he had found some unique and practical way of hiding loot and that he had returned to the cache to replenish his pockets, even if he had not actually ridden with the two pistols back to the River and the steamboats full of gamblers and cotton- and slavedealers to replenish the cache. At least some of them were telling one another that when two months later he returned, again without warning and accompanied this time by the covered wagon with a negro driving it and on the seat with the negro a small, alertly resigned man with a grim, harried Latin face, in a frock coat and a flowered waistcoat and a hat which would have created no furore on a Paris boulevard, all of which he was to wear constantly for the next two years—the somberly theatric clothing and the expression of fatalistic and amazed determination—while his white client and the negro crew which he was to advise though not direct went stark naked save for a coating of dried mud. This was the French architect. Years later the town learned that he had come all the way from Martinique on Sutpen's bare promise and lived for two years on venison cooked over a campfire, in an unfloored tent made of the wagon hood, before he so much as saw any color or shape of pay. And until he passed through town on his way back to New Orleans two years later, he was not even to see Jefferson again; he would not come, or Sutpen would not bring him, to town even on the few occasions when Sutpen would be seen there, and he did not have much chance to look at Jefferson on that first day because the wagon did not stop. Apparently it was only by sheer geographical hap that Sutpen passed through town at all, pausing only long enough for someone (not General Compson) to look beneath the wagon hood and into a black tunnel filled with still eyeballs and smelling like a wolfden.

STUDY GUIDE

1. Everyone is familiar with the way in which a present sensation (an odor, a taste, a sound, a vivid color) can bring back a former experience of that sensation in all its detail. Faulkner makes good use of that associationistic device to kaleidoscope time and to bring the arrival of Sutpen in Jefferson vividly before the imagination of Quentin Compson in his room at Harvard College. What is the odor that starts memory working and, by association, summons up the whole experience of Sutpen's arrival with all its immediate circumstances and the many events that were to follow?

2. One of the most characteristic devices in Faulkner's writing is the way he kaleidoscopes time, frequently bringing the past into immediate proximity in the reader's consciousness with the present and sometimes pointing ahead to the future as well. Establish the present moment in time of the narrator in this passage, and then show how various dates in the past are brought into simultaneous consciousness in the imagination of the narrator and of the reader.

3. What sense experience besides smell is important in the associationistic

memory experience in this passage? How does it help to evoke some important details of the life in this Southern village?

4. Select a few well-chosen concrete details that are helpful in evoking characteristic features of this Southern village or of the people who live there.

5. Part of the mood of this piece is created by the sentence structure. The sentences are long and loosely structured—what the critics would call loose Senecan periods—and one phrase is tacked onto another in a way that is neither precise nor logical but just as they might be suggested to the mind. Why is that kind of sentence structure appropriate to the purpose of Faulkner here?

ALONG HIGHWAY 66

John Steinbeck

1 Along 66 the hamburger stands—Al & Susy's Place—Carl's Lunch—Joe & Minnie—Will's Eats. Board-and-bat shacks. Two gasoline pumps in front, a screen door, a long bar, stools, and a foot rail. Near the door three slot machines, showing through glass the wealth in nickels three bars will bring. And beside them, the nickel phonograph with records piled up like pies, ready to swing out to the turntable and play dance music, "Ti-pi-ti-pi-tin," "Thanks for the Memory," Bing Crosby, Benny Goodman. At one end of the counter a covered case; candy cough crops, caffeine sulphate called Sleepless, No-Doze; candy, cigarettes, razor blades, aspirin, Bromo-Seltzer, Alka-Seltzer. The walls decorated with posters, bathing girls, blondes with big breasts and slender hips and waxen faces, in white bathing suits, and holding a bottle of Coca-Cola and smiling—see what you get with a Coca-Cola. Long bar, and salts, peppers, mustard pots, and paper napkins. Beer taps behind the counter, and in back the coffee urns, shiny and steaming, with glass gauges showing the coffee level. And pies in wire cages and oranges in pyramids of four. And little piles of Post Toasties, corn flakes, stacked up in designs.

2 The signs on cards, picked out with shining mica: Pies Like Mother Used to Make. Credit Makes Enemies, Let's Be Friends. Ladies May Smoke But Be Careful Where You Lay Your Butts. Eat Here and Keep Your Wife for a Pet. IITYWYBAD?

3 Down at one end the cooking plates, pots of stew, potatoes, pot roast, roast beef, gray roast pork waiting to be sliced.

4 Minnie or Susy or Mae, middle-aging behind the counter, hair curled and rouge and powder on a sweating face. Taking orders in a soft low voice, calling them to the cook with a screech like a peacock. Mopping the counter with circular strokes, polishing the big shining coffee urns. The cook is Joe or Carl or Al, hot in a white coat and apron, beady sweat on white forehead, below the white cook's cap; moody, rarely speaking, looking up for a moment at each new entry. Wiping the griddle, slapping down the hamburger. He repeats Mae's orders gently, scrapes the griddle, wipes it down with burlap. Moody and silent.

5 Mae is the contact, smiling, irritated, near to outbreak; smiling while her eyes look on past—unless for truck drivers. There's the backbone of the joint. Where the trucks stop, that's where the customers come. Can't fool truck drivers, they know. They bring the custom. They know. Give 'em a stale cup a coffee an' they're off the joint. Treat 'em right an' they come back. Mae really smiles with all her might at truck drivers. She bridles a little, fixes her back hair so that her breasts will lift with her raised arms, passes the time of day and indicates great things, great times, great jokes. Al never speaks. He is no contact. Sometimes he smiles a little at a joke, but he never laughs. Sometimes he looks up at the vivaciousness in Mae's voice, and then he scrapes the griddle with a spatula, scrapes the grease into an iron trough around the plate. He presses down a hissing hamburger with his spatula. He lays the split buns on the plate to toast and heat. He gathers up stray onions from the plate and heaps them on the meat and presses them in with the spatula. He puts half the bun on top of the meat, paints the other half with melted butter, with thin pickle relish. Holding the bun on the meat, he slips the spatula under the thin pad of meat, flips it over, lays the buttered half on top, and drops the hamburger on a small plate. Quarter of a dill pickle, two black olives beside the sandwich. Al skims the plate down the counter like a quoit. And he scrapes his griddle with the spatula and looks moodily at the stew kettle.

6 Cars whisking by on 66. License plates. Mass., Tenn., R.I., N.Y., Vt., Ohio. Going west. Fine cars, cruising at sixty-five.

7 There goes one of them Cords. Looks like a coffin on wheels.

8 But, Jesus, how they travel!

9 See that La Salle? Me for that. I ain't a hog. I go for a La Salle.

10 'F ya goin' big, what's a matter with a Cad'? Jus' a little bigger, little faster.

11 I'd take a Zephyr myself. You ain't ridin' no fortune, but you got class an' speed. Give me a Zephyr.

12 Well, sir, you may get a laugh outa this—I'll take a Buick-Puick. That's good enough.

13 But, hell, that costs in the Zephyr class an' it ain't got the sap.

14 I don' care. I don' want nothing to do with nothing of Henry Ford's. I don' like 'im. Never did. Got a brother worked in the plant. Oughta hear him tell.

15 Well, a Zephyr got sap.

16 The big cars on the highway. Languid, heat-raddled ladies, small nucleuses about whom revolve a thousand accouterments: creams, ointments to grease themselves, coloring matter in phials—black, pink, red, white, green, silver—to change the color of hair, eyes, lips, nails, brows, lashes, lids. Oils, seeds, and pills to make the bowels move. A bag of bottles, syringes, pills, powders, fluids, jellies to make their sexual intercourse safe, odorless, and unproductive. And this apart from clothes. What a hell of a nuisance!

17 Lines of weariness around the eyes, lines of discontent down from the mouth, breasts lying heavily in little hammocks, stomach and thighs straining against cases of rubber. And the mouths panting, the eyes sullen, disliking sun and wind and earth, resenting food and weariness, hating time that rarely makes them beautiful and always makes them old.

18 Beside them, little pot-bellied men in light suits and panama hats; clean, pink men with puzzled, worried eyes, with restless eyes. Worried because formulas do not work out; hungry for security and yet sensing its disappearance from the earth. In their lapels the insignia of lodges and service clubs, places where they can go and, by a weight of numbers of little worried men, reassure themselves that business is noble and not the curious ritualized thievery they know it is; that business men are intelligent in spite of the records of their stupidity; that they are kind and charitable in spite of the principles of sound business; that their lives are rich instead of the thin tiresome routines they know; and that a time is coming when they will not be afraid any more.

19 And these two, going to California; going to sit in the lobby of the Beverly-Wilshire Hotel and watch people they envy go by, to look at mountains—mountains, mind you, and great trees—he with his worried eyes and she thinking how the sun will dry her skin. Going to look at the Pacific Ocean, and I'll bet a hundred thousand dollars to nothing at all, he will say, "It isn't as big as I thought it would be." And she will envy plump young bodies on the beach. Going to California really to go home again. To say, "So-and-So was at the table next to us at the Trocadero. She's really a mess, but she does wear nice clothes." And he, "I talked to good sound business men out there. They don't see a chance till we get rid of that fellow in the White House." And, "I got it from a man in the know—she has syphilis, you know. She was in that Warner picture. Man said she'd slept her way into pictures. Well, she got what she was looking for." But the worried eyes are never calm, and the pouting mouth is never glad. The big car cruising along at sixty.

20 I want a cold drink.
21 Well, there's something up ahead. Want to stop?
22 Do you think it would be clean?
23 Clean as you're going to find in this God-forsaken country.
24 Well, maybe the bottled soda will be all right.
25 The great car squeals and pulls to a stop. The fat worried man helps his wife out.
26 Mae looks at and past them as they enter. Al looks up from his griddle, and down again. Mae knows. They'll drink a five-cent soda and crab that it ain't cold enough. The woman will use six paper napkins and drop them on the floor. The man will choke and try to put the blame on Mae. The woman will sniff as though she smelled rotting meat and they will go out again and tell forever afterward that the people in the West are sullen. And Mae, when she is alone with Al, has a name for them. She calls them shitheels.
27 Truck drivers. That's the stuff.
28 Here's a big transport comin'. Hope they stop; take away the taste of them shitheels. When I worked in that hotel in Albuquerque, Al, the way they steal—ever' darn thing. An' the bigger the car they got, the more they steal—towels, silver, soap dishes. I can't figger it.
29 And Al, morosely, Where ya think they get them big cars and stuff? Born with 'em? You won't never have nothin'.
30 The transport truck, a driver and relief. How 'bout stoppin' for a cup a Java? I know this dump.
31 How's the schedule?
32 Oh, we're ahead!
33 Pull up, then. They's a ol' war horse in here that's a kick. Good Java, too.
34 The truck pulls up. Two men in khaki riding trousers, boots, short jackets, and shiny-visored military caps. Screen door—slam.
35 H'ya, Mae?
36 Well, if it ain't Big Bill the Rat! When'd you get back on this run?
37 Week ago.
38 The other man puts a nickel in the phonograph, watches the disk slip free and the turntable rise up under it. Bing Crosby's voice—golden. "Thanks for the memory, of sunburn at the shore—You might have been a headache, but you never were a bore—" And the truck driver sings for Mae's ears, you might have been a haddock but you never was a whore—
39 Mae laughs. Who's ya frien', Bill? New on this run, ain't he?
40 The other puts a nickel in the slot machine, wins four slugs, and puts them back. Walks to the counter.
41 Well, what's it gonna be?
42 Oh, cup a Java. Kinda pie ya got?

43 Banana cream, pineapple cream, chocolate cream—an' apple.
44 Make it apple. Wait—Kind is that big thick one?
45 Mae lifts it out and sniffs it. Banana cream.
46 Cut off a hunk; make it a big hunk.
47 Man at the slot machine says, Two all around.
48 Two it is. Seen any new etchin's lately, Bill?
49 Well, here's one.
50 Now, you be careful front of a lady.
51 Oh, this ain't bad. Little kid comes in late ta school. Teacher says, "Why ya late?" Kid says, "Had a take a heifer down—get 'er bred." Teacher says, "Couldn't your ol' man do it?' Kid says, "Sure he could, but not as good as the bull."
52 Mae squeaks with laughter, harsh screeching laughter. Al, slicing onions carefully on a board, looks up and smiles, and then looks down again. Truck drivers, that's the stuff. Gonna leave a quarter each for Mae. Fifteen cents for pie an' coffee an' a dime for Mae. An' they ain't tryin' to make her, neither.
53 Sitting together on the stools, spoons sticking up out of the coffee mugs. Passing the time of day. And Al, rubbing down his griddle, listening but making no comment. Bing Crosby's voice stops. The turntable drops down and the record swings into its place in the pile. The purple light goes off. The nickel, which has caused all this mechanism to work, has caused Crosby to sing and an orchestra to play—this nickel drops from between the contact points into the box where the profits go. This nickel, unlike most money, has actually done a job of work, has been physically responsible for a reaction.
54 Steam spurts from the valve of the coffee urn. The compressor of the ice machine chugs softly for a time and then stops. The electric fan in the corner waves its head slowly back and forth, sweeping the room with a warm breeze. On the highway, on 66, the cars whiz by.
55 They was a Massachusetts car stopped a while ago, said Mae.
56 Big Bill grasped his cup around the top so that the spoon stuck up between his first and second fingers. He drew in a snort of air with the coffee, to cool it. "You ought to be out on 66. Cars from all over the country. All headin' west. Never seen so many before. Sure some honeys on the road."
57 "We seen a wreck this mornin'," his companion said. "Big car. Big Cad', a special job and a honey, low, cream-color, special job. Hit a truck. Folded the radiator right back into the driver. Must a been doin' ninety. Steerin' wheel went right on through the guy an' lef' him a-wigglin' like a frog on a hook. Peach of a car. A honey. You can have her for peanuts now. Drivin' alone, the guy was."
58 Al looked up from his work. "Hurt the truck?"
59 "Oh, Jesus Christ! Wasn't a truck. One of them cut-down cars full a

stoves an' pans an' mattresses an' kids an' chickens. Goin' west, you know. This guy come by us doin' ninety—r'ared up on two wheels just to pass us, an' a car's comin' so he cuts in an' whangs this here truck. Drove like he's blin' drunk. Jesus, the air was full a bed clothes an' chickens an' kids. Killed one kid. Never seen such a mess. We pulled up. Ol' man that's drivin' the truck, he jus' stan's there lookin' at that dead kid. Can't get a word out of 'im. Jus rum-dumb. God Almighty, the road is full a them families goin' west. Never seen so many. Gets worse all a time. Wonder where the hell they all come from?"

60 "Wonder where they all go to," said Mae. "Come here for gas sometimes, but they don't hardly never buy nothin' else. People says they steal. We ain't got nothin' layin' around. They never stole nothin' from us."

61 Big Bill, munching his pie, looked up the road through the screened window. "Better tie your stuff down. I think you got some of 'em comin' now."

62 A 1926 Nash sedan pulled wearily off the highway. The back seat was piled nearly to the ceiling with sacks, with pots and pans, and on the very top, right up against the ceiling, two boys rode. On the top of the car, a mattress and a folded tent; tent poles tied along the running board. The car pulled up to the gas pumps. A dark-haired, hatchet-faced man got slowly out. And the two boys slid down from the load and hit the ground.

63 Mae walked around the counter and stood in the door. The man was dressed in gray wool trousers and a blue shirt, dark blue with sweat on the back and under the arms. The boys in overalls and nothing else, ragged patched overalls. Their hair was light, and it stood up evenly all over their heads, for it had been roached. Their faces were streaked with dust. They went directly to the mud puddle under the hose and dug their toes into the mud.

64 The man asked, "Can we git some water, ma'am?"

65 A look of annoyance crossed Mae's face. "Sure, go ahead." She said softly over her shoulder, "I'll keep my eye on the hose." She watched while the man slowly unscrewed the radiator cap and ran the hose in.

66 A woman in the car, a flaxen-haired woman, said, "See if you can't git it here."

67 The man turned off the hose and screwed on the cap again. The little boys took the hose from him and they upended it and drank thirstily. The man took off his dark, stained hat and stood with a curious humility in front of the screen. "Could you see your way to sell us a loaf of bread, ma'-am?"

68 Mae said, "This ain't a grocery store. We got bread to make san'-widges."

69 "I know, ma'am." His humility was insistent. "We need bread and there ain't nothin' for quite a piece, they say."

70 "'F we sell bread we gonna run out." Mae's tone was faltering.

71 "We're hungry," the man said.

72 "Whyn't you buy a san'widge? We got nice san'widges, hamburgs."

73 "We'd sure admire to do that, ma'am. But we can't. We got to make a dime do all of us." And he said embarrassedly, "We ain't got but a little."

74 Mae said, "You can't get no loaf a bread for a dime. We only got fifteen-cent loafs."

75 From behind her Al growled, "God Almighty, Mae, give 'em bread."

76 "We'll run out 'fore the bread truck comes."

77 "Run out, then, goddamn it," said Al. And he looked sullenly down at the potato salad he was mixing.

78 Mae shrugged her plump shoulders and looked to the truck drivers to show them what she was up against.

79 She held the screen door open and the man came in, bringing a smell of sweat with him. The boys edged in behind him and they went immediately to the candy case and stared in—not with craving or with hope or even with desire, but just with a kind of wonder that such things could be. They were alike in size and their faces were alike. One scratched his dusty ankle with the toe nails of his other foot. The other whispered some soft message and then they straightened their arms so that their clenched fists in the overall pockets showed through the thin blue cloth.

80 Mae opened a drawer and took out a long waxpaper-wrapped loaf. "This here is a fifteen-cent loaf."

81 The man put his hat back on his head. He answered with inflexible humility, "Won't you—can't you see your way to cut off ten cents' worth?"

82 Al said snarlingly, "Goddamn it, Mae. Give 'em the loaf."

83 The man turned toward Al. "No, we want ta buy ten cents' worth of it. We got it figgered awful close, mister, to get to California."

84 Mae said resignedly, "You can have this for ten cents."

85 "That'd be robbin' you, ma'am."

86 "Go ahead—Al says to take it." She pushed the waxpapered loaf across the counter. The man took a deep leather pouch from his rear pocket, untied the strings, and spread it open. It was heavy with silver and with greasy bills.

87 "May soun' funny to be so tight," he apologized. "We got a thousan' miles to go, an' we don't know if we'll make it." He dug in the pouch with a forefinger, located a dime, and pinched in for it. When he put it down on the counter he had a penny with it. He was about to drop the penny back into the pouch when his eye fell on the boys frozen before the candy counter. He moved slowly down to them. He pointed in the case at big long sticks of striped peppermint. "Is them penny candy, ma'am?"

88 Mae moved down and looked in. "Which ones?"

89 "There, them stripy ones."

90 The little boys raised their eyes to her face and they stopped breath-

ing; their mouths were partly opened, their half-naked bodies were rigid.

91 "Oh—them. Well, no—them's two for a penny."

92 "Well, gimme two then, ma'am." He placed the copper cent carefully on the counter. The boys expelled their held breath softly. Mae held the big sticks out.

93 "Take 'em," said the man.

94 They reached timidly, each took a stick, and they held them down at their sides and did not look at them. But they looked at each other, and their mouth corners smiled rigidly with embarrassment.

95 "Thank you, ma'am." The man picked up the bread and went out the door, and the little boys marched stiffly behind him, the red-striped sticks held tightly against their legs. They leaped like chipmunks over the front seat and onto the top of the load, and they burrowed back out of sight like chipmunks.

96 The man got in and started his car, and with a roaring motor and a cloud of blue oily smoke the ancient Nash climbed up on the highway and went on its way to the west.

97 From inside the restaurant the truck drivers and Mae and Al stared after them.

98 Big Bill wheeled back. "Them wasn't two-for-a-cent candy," he said.

99 "What's that to you?" Mae said fiercely.

100 "Them was a nickel apiece candy," said Bill.

101 "We got to get goin'," said the other man. "We're droppin' time." They reached in their pockets. Bill put a coin on the counter and the other man looked at it and reached again and put down a coin. They swung around and walked to the door.

102 "So long," said Bill.

103 Mae called, "Hey! Wait a minute. You got change."

104 "You go to hell," said Bill, and the screen door slammed.

105 Mae watched them get into the great truck, watched it lumber off in low gear, and heard the shift up the whining gears to cruising ratio. "Al—" she said softly.

106 He looked up from the hamburger he was patting thin and stacking between waxed papers. "What ya want?"

107 "Look there." She pointed at the coins beside the cups—two half-dollars. Al walked near and looked, and then he went back to his work.

108 "Truck drivers," Mae said reverently, "an' after them shitheels."

109 Flies struck the screen with little bumps and droned away. The compressor chugged for a time and then stopped. On 66 the traffic whizzed by, trucks and fine streamlined cars and jalopies; and they went by with a vicious whiz. Mae took down the plates and scraped the pie crusts into a bucket. She found her damp cloth and wiped the counter with circular sweeps. And her eyes were on the highway, where life whizzed by.

110 Al wiped his hands on his apron. He looked at a paper pinned to the wall over the griddle. Three lines of marks in columns on the paper. Al counted the longest line. He walked along the counter to the cash register, rang "No Sale," and took out a handful of nickels.

111 "What ya doin'?" Mae asked.

112 "Number three's ready to pay off," said Al. He went to the third slot machine and played his nickels in, and on the fifth spin of the wheels the three bars came up and the jack pot dumped out into the cup. Al gathered up the big handful of coins and went back of the counter. He dropped them in the drawer and slammed the cash register. Then he went back to his place and crossed out the line of dots. "Number three gets more play'n the others," he said. "Maybe I ought to shift 'em around." He lifted a lid and stirred the slowly simmering stew.

113 "I wonder what they'll do in California?" said Mae.

114 "Who?"

115 "Them folks that was just in."

116 "Christ knows," said Al.

117 "S'pose they'll get work?"

118 "How the hell would I know?" said Al.

119 She stared eastward along the highway. "Here comes a transport, double. Wonder if they stop? Hope they do." And as the huge truck came heavily down from the highway and parked, Mae seized her cloth and wiped the whole length of the counter. And she took a few swipes at the gleaming coffee urn too, and turned up the bottle-gas under the urn. Al brought out a handful of little turnips and started to peel them. Mae's face was gay when the door opened and the two uniformed truck drivers entered.

120 "Hi, sister!"

121 "I won't be a sister to no man," said Mae. They laughed and Mae laughed. "What'll it be, boys?"

122 "Oh, a cup a Java. What kinda pie ya got?"

123 "Pineapple cream an' banana cream an' chocolate cream an' apple."

124 "Give me apple. No, wait—what's that big thick one?"

125 Mae picked up the pie and smelled it. "Pineapple cream," she said.

126 "Well, chop out a hunk a that."

127 The cars whizzed viciously by on 66.

STUDY GUIDE

1. Two comparisons seem to be relevant to the type of descriptive passage exemplified in this selection from Steinbeck's *The Grapes of Wrath:* impressionistic painting and the cinema. In impressionistic painting bright strokes of color are applied to the canvas next to one another, and the eye of

the viewer blends these strokes into other shades of color at a little distance. In impressionistic description vivid images are thrust at the reader side by side, and he must himself derive from them what predication about the scene or person the writer is making. In such description the statement is generally not made explicit by the writer himself.

Today most people are familiar with this technique from adevrtising. An advertisement may show an attractive study where there is a whole series of period lamps ending with a modern bridge lamp; near this modern lamp are a bottle of a brand-name whiskey and a highball glass. In such an advertisement we do not need the text to tell us that this brand of whiskey has been the pleasant evening companion of men-in-the-know for generations. The mere juxtaposition of the images has made that predication for us. Images similarly juxtaposed in description can also make statements that are never verbally expressed. Steinbeck is making a number of predications about American society in this chapter, but they never become explicit. What is Steinbeck saying, for instance, by the detailed enumeration of the contents of the hamburger stands? It is not one stand he is describing, but all such stands—Al & Susy's Place—Carl's Lunch—Joe & Minne—Will's Eats. What is Steinbeck saying about these places?

2. Go through the entire passage and try to make explicit some of the things the author is saying about America and about some American people just by the impressionistic juxtaposing of concrete details in their description, and by presenting concrete action scenes of the waitress and cook, the truck drivers, the jalopie drivers, and the owners of Cadillacs. Without saying so, the author has strongly communicated to us where his sympathies lie. Where do they lie? How has he told us this impressionistically in the passage itself?

3. Why is it appropriate for the long descriptive passages here to be written entirely in phrases rather than in complete sentences?

4. Some actions and details are repeated frequently in the passage and become almost symbolic. What, for instance, are some of the things suggested by Mae's constant wiping of the counter and by the cars that whizz by on 66? How are the classes in American society symbolized in the cars that pull up to Al and Mae's place?

5. The cinematic techniques of the montage and the close-up also seem to have contributed to the structure of this passage. What have paragraphs 1–4 in common with a cinematic montage? What parts of the chapter take on the characteristics of a cinematic close-up, where the camera moves in on a scene and focuses on the action of the main character?

6. What are some of the intimate human (good and bad) characteristics that are revealed in Mae and Al in these close-ups?

7. What has Steinbeck said (without an explicit statement) by ending this passage with another set of truck drivers dropping into Al and Mae's place for a cup of java?

SECTION **11**

Understanding the Short Story

COMMUNICATION THROUGH THE PATTERN OF FICTION

Clayton Hamilton

1 Before we set out upon a study of the materials and methods of fiction, we must be certain that we appreciate the purpose of the art and understand its relation to the other arts and sciences. The purpose of fiction is to embody certain truths of human life in a series of imagined facts. The importance of this purpose is scarcely ever appreciated by the casual careless reader of the novels of the season. Although it is commonly believed that such a reader overestimates the weight of works of fiction, the opposite is true—he underestimates it. Every novelist of genuine importance seeks not merely to divert but also to instruct—to instruct, not abstractly, like the essayist, but concretely, by presenting to the reader characters and actions which are true. For the best fiction, although it deals with the lives of imaginary people, is no less true than the best history and biography, which record actual facts of human life; and it is more true than such careless reports of actual occurrences as are published in the daily newspapers. The truth of worthy fiction is evidenced by the honor in which it has been held in all ages among all races. "You can't fool all the people all the time"; and if the drama and the epic and the novel were not true, the human race

would have rejected them many centuries ago. Fiction has survived, and flourishes today, because it is a means of telling truth.

2 It is only in the vocabulary of very careless thinkers that the words truth and fiction are regarded as antithetic. A genuine antithesis subsists between the words fact and fiction; but fact and truth are not synonymous. The novelist forsakes the realm of fact in order that he may better tell the truth, and lures the reader away from actualities in order to present him with realities. It is of prime importance, in our present study, therefore, that we should understand at the very outset the relation between fact and truth, the distinction between the actual and the real.

3 A fact is a specific manifestation of a general law; this general law is the truth because of which that fact has come to be. It is a fact that when an apple-tree is shaken by the wind, such apples as may be loosened from their twigs fall to the ground; it is a truth that bodies in space attract each other with a force that varies inversely as the square of the distance between them. Fact is concrete, and is a matter of physical experience; truth is abstract and is a matter of mental experience. Actuality is the realm of fact; reality the realm of truth. The universe as we apprehend it with our senses is actual; the laws of the universe as we comprehend them with our understanding are real.

4 All human science is an endeavor to discover the truths which underlie the facts that we perceive; all human philosophy is an endeavor to understand and to appraise those truths when once they are discovered; and all human art is an endeavor to utter them clearly and effectively when once they are appraised and understood. The history of man is the history of a constant and continuous seeking for the truth. Amazed before a universe of facts, he has striven earnestly to discover the truth which underlies them—striven heroically to understand the large reality of which the actual is but a sensuously perceptible embodiment. In the earliest centuries of recorded thought the search was unmethodical; but in modern centuries certain regular methods have been devised to guide the search. The modern scientist begins his work by collecting a large number of apparently related facts and arranging them in an orderly manner. He then proceeds to induce from the observation of these facts an apprehension of the general law that explains their relation. This hypothesis is then tested in the light of further facts, until it seems so incontestable that the minds of men accept it as the truth. The scientist then formulates it in an abstract theoretic statement, and thus concludes his work.

5 But it is at just this point that the philosopher begins. Accepting many truths from many scientists, the philosopher compares, reconciles, and correlates them, and thus builds out of them an orderly view of the whole. But this total view remains abstract in the mind of the philosopher. It is now the artist's turn. Accepting the correlated truths which the scien-

tist and the philosopher have given him, he endows them with an imaginative embodiment perceptible to the senses. He translates them back into concrete terms; he clothes them in invented facts; he makes them imaginatively perceptible to a mind native and indued to actuality; and thus he gives expression to the truth.

6 This triple process of the scientific discovery, the philosophic understanding, and the artistic expression of truth has been explained at length, because every great writer of fiction must pass through the entire mental process. The fiction-writer differs from other seekers for the truth, not in the method of this thought, but merely in its subject matter. His theme is human life. It is some truth of human life that he endeavors to discover, to understand, and to announce; and in order to complete his work, he must apply to human life an attention of thought which is successively scientific, philosophic, and artistic. He must first observe carefully certain facts of actual life, study them in the light of extended experience, and induce from them the general laws which he deems to be the truths which underlie them. In doing this, he is a scientist. Next, if he be a great thinker, he will correlate these truths and build out of them an ordered view of the whole of human life. In doing this, he is a philosopher. Lastly, he must create imaginatively such scenes and characters as will illustrate the truths he has discovered and considered, and will convey them clearly and effectively to the minds of his readers. In doing this, he is an artist. . . .

7 Not only do the great characters of fiction convince us of reality; in the mere events themselves of worthy fiction we feel a fitness that makes us know them real. Sentimental Tommy really did lose that literary competition because he wasted a full hour searching vainly for the one right word; Hetty Sorrel really killed her child; and Mr. Henry must have won that midnight duel with the Master of Ballantrae, though the latter was the better swordsman. These incidents conform to the truths we recognize. And not only in fiction that clings close to actuality do we feel a sense of truth. We feel it just as keenly in fairy tales like those of Hans Christian Andersen, or in the worthiest wonder-legends of an earlier age. We are told of The Steadfast Tin Soldier that, after he was melted in the fire, the maid who took away the ashes next morning found him in the shape of a small tin heart; and remembering the spangly little ballet-dancer who fluttered to him like a sylph and was burned up in the fire with him, we feel a fitness in this little fancy which opens vistas upon human truth. Mr. Kipling's fable of "How the Elephant Got His Trunk" is just as true as his reports of Mrs. Hauksbee. His theory may not conform with the actual facts of zoological science, but at any rate, it represents a truth which is perhaps more important for those who have become again like little children.

8 Just as we feel by instinct the reality of fiction at its best, so also with a kindred instinct equally keen we feel the falsity of fiction when the

author lapses from the truth. Unless his characters act and think at all points consistently with the laws of their imagined existence, and unless these laws are in harmony with the laws of actual life, no amount of sophistication on the part of the author can make us finally believe his story; and unless we believe his story, his purpose in writing it will have failed. The novelist, who has so many means of telling truth, has also many means of telling lies. He may be untruthful in his very theme, if he is lacking in sanity of outlook upon the things that are. He may be untruthful in his characterization, if he interferes with his people after they are once created and attempts to coerce them to his purposes instead of allowing them to work out their own destinies. He may be untruthful in his plotting, if he devises situations arbitrarily for the sake of mere immediate effect. He may be untruthful in his dialogue, if he puts into the mouths of his people sentences that their nature does not demand that they shall speak. He may be untruthful in his comments of his characters, if the characters belie the comments in their actions and their words.

9 Even in the best fiction we come upon passages of falsity. There is little likelihood, however, of our being led astray by these; we revolt instinctively against them with a feeling that may best be expressed in that famous sentence of Ibsen's Assessor Brack, "People don't do such things." When Shakespeare tells us, toward the end of *As You Like It*, that the wicked Oliver suddenly changed his nature and won the love of Celia, we know that he is lying. The scene is not true to the great laws of human life. When George Eliot, at a loss for a conclusion to *The Mill on the Floss*, tells us that Tom and Maggie Tulliver were drowned together in a flood, we disbelieve her; just as we disbelieve Mr. J. M. Barrie when he invents that absurd accident of Tommy's death. These three instances of falsity have been selected from authors who know the truth and almost always tell it; and all three have a certain palliation. They come at or near the very end of lengthy stories. In actual life, of course, there are no very ends; life exhibits a continuous sequence of causation stretching on; and since a story has to have an end, its conclusion must in any case belie a law of nature. Probably the truth is that Tommy didn't die at all; he is living still; and always will be living. And since Mr. Barrie couldn't write forever, he may be pardoned a makeshift ending that he himself apparently did not believe in.

10 Arbitrary plotting, as a rule, is of no avail in fiction; almost always, we know when a story is true and when it is not. We seldom believe in the long-lost will that is discovered at last on the back of a decaying picture-canvas; or in the chance meeting and mutual discovery of long-separated relatives; or in such accidental circumstances as the one, for instance, because of which Romeo fails to receive the message from Friar Lawrence. The incidents of fiction at its best are not only probable but inevitable; they hap-

pen because in the nature of things they have to happen, and not because the author wants them to. Similarly, the truest characters of fiction are so real that even their creator has no power to make them do what they will not. It has been told of Thackeray that he grew so to love Colonel Newcome that he wished ardently that the good man might live happily until the end. Yet, knowing the circumstances in which the Colonel was enmeshed, and knowing also the nature of the people who formed the little circle around about him, Thackeray realized that his last days would of necessity be miserable; and realizing this, the author told the bitter truth, though it cost him many tears.

11 We are now touching on a principle which is seldom appreciated by beginners in the art of fiction. Every college professor of literary composition who has accused a student of falsity in some passage of a story that the student has sumbitted has been met with the triumphant but unreasonable answer, "Oh, no, it's true! It happened to a friend of mine!" And it has then become necessary for the professor to explain as best he could that an actual occurrence is not necessarily true for the purpose of fiction. The imagined facts of a genuinely worthy story are exhibited merely because they are representative of some general law of life held securely in the writer's consciousness. A transcription, therefore, of actual facts fails of the purposes of fiction unless the facts in themselves are evidently representative of such a law. And many things may happen to a friend of ours without evidencing to a considerate mind any logical reason why they had to happen.

12 It is necessary that the student should appreciate the importance of this principle at the very outset of his apprenticeship to the art. For it is only by adhering rigorously to the truth that fiction can survive. In every period of literature, many clever authors have appeared who have diverted their contemporaries with ingenious invention, billiant incident, unexpected novelty of character, or alluring eloquence of style, but who have been discarded and forgotten by succeeding generations merely because they fail to tell the truth. Probably in the whole range of English fiction there is no more skilful weaver of enthralling plots, no more clever master of invention or manipulator of suspense, than Wilkie Collins; but Collins is already discarded and well-nigh forgotten, because the reading world has found that he exhibited no truths of genuine importance, but rather sacrificed the eternal realities of life for mere momentary plausibilities.

13 But it is not any easy thing to tell the truth of human life, and nothing but the truth. The best of fiction-writers fall to falsehood now and then; and it is only by honest labor and sincere strife for the ideal that they contrive in the main to fulfill the purpose of their art. But the writer of fiction must be not only honest and sincere; he must be wise as well. Wisdom is the faculty of seeing through and all around an object of contempla-

tion, and understanding totally and at once its relations to all other objects. This faculty is not inherited; it has to be developed; and it is developed by experience only. Experience ordinarily requires time; and though most of the great short-story writers have been young, we are not surprised to notice that most of the great novelists have been men mature in years. They have ripened slowly to a realization of those truths which later they have labored to impart. Richardson, the father of the modern English novel, was fifty-one years old when *Pamela* was published; Scott was forty-three when *Waverly* appeared; Hawthorne was forty-six when he wrote *The Scarlet Letter*; Thackeray and George Eliot were well on their way to the forties when they completed *Vanity Fair* and *Adam Bede;* and these are the first novels of each writer.

14 Experience is of two sorts, extensive and intensive. A mere glance at the range of Mr. Kipling's subjects would show us the breadth of his extensive experience; evidently he has lived in many lands and looked with sympathy upon the lives of many sorts of people. But in certain stories, like his "They" for instance, we are arrested rather by the depth of his intensive experience. "They" reveals to us an author who not necessarily has roamed about the world, but who necessarily has felt all phases of the mother-longing in a woman. The things that Mr. Kipling knows in "They" could never have been learned except through sympathy.

15 Undoubtedly, very few people are always at home for every real experience that knocks upon their doors; very few people, to say the thing more simply, have an experiencing nature. But great fiction may be written only by men of an experiencing nature; and here is a basis for confession that, after all, fiction-writers are born, not made. The experiencing nature is difficult to define; but two of its most evident qualities, at any rate, are a lively curiosity and a ready sympathy. A combination of these two qualities gives a man that intensity of interest in human life which is a condition precedent to his ever growing to understand it. Curiosity for instance, is the most obvious asset in Mr. Kipling's equipment. We did not need his playful confession in the *Just So Stories*—

> I keep six honest serving men
> (They taught me all I knew):—
> Their names are What and Why and When
> And How and Where and Who—

to convince us that from his early youth he has been an indefatigable asker of questions. It was only through a healthy curiosity that he could have acquired the enormous stores of specific knowledge concerning almost every walk of life that he has displayed in his successive volumes. On the other hand, it was obviously through his vast endowment of sympathy that Dickens was able to learn so thoroughly all phases of the life of the lowly in London.

16 Experience gravitates to the man who is both curious and sympathetic. The kingdom of adventure is within us. We create adventure all around us when we walk the world inwardly aglow with love of life. Things of interest happened to Robert Louis Stevenson every day of his existence, because he had developed the faculty of being interested in things. In one of his most glowing essays, "The Lantern-Bearers," he declared that never an hour of his life had gone dully yet; if it had been spent waiting at a railway junction, he had had some scattering thoughts, he had counted some grains of memory, compared to which the whole of many romances seemed but dross. The author should cultivate the faculty of caring for all things that come to pass; he should train himself rigorously never to be bored; he should look upon all life that swims into his ken with curious and sympathetic eyes, remembering always that sympathy is a deeper faculty than curiosity; and because of the profound joy of his interest in life, he should endeavor humbly to earn that heritage of interest by developing a thorough understanding of its source. In this way, perhaps, he may grow aware of certain truths of life which are materials for fiction. If so, he will have accomplished the better half of his work; he will have found something to say.

STUDY GUIDE

Word Study

1. Is there any dictionary justification for the distinctions made between *fact* and *fiction, fact* and *truth,* and *actuality* and *reality* in paragraph 2?

2. With the help of your dictionary distinguish between *apprehend* and *comprehend* (paragraph 3).

3. What is the exact meaning of plausibility (paragraph 12)?

Thought Structure

1. State the main idea developed in this essay in one succinct sentence. What sentence or sentences in the essay come closest to expressing this idea?

2. Make a careful sentence outline of the entire essay which indicates major thought divisions and the line of thought development.

3. A. Study the use of contrast in the development of paragraph 3.

B. What is the method of development employed in paragraphs 7 and 9?

Content

1. What is it, according to the author's statements in paragraph 1, that gives fiction its real importance?

2. A. What does the author mean by saying in paragraph 2 that "the

novelist forsakes the realm of fact in order that he may better tell the truth"?

B. Why is the best fiction as true as the best history and biography, and more true than the actual occurrences published in the daily newspapers?

3. A. What do the scientist and philosopher, as they are discussed in paragraph 4–6, have in common?

B. What does the artist have in common with the scientist and philosopher? How does his purpose differ from theirs?

4. A. How does what Hamilton says about the business of the philosopher in paragraph 5, sentences 1–3, compare with Newman's statements about the liberally educated mind in "The Real Function of a University"?

B. What sentences in Newman's essay come closet to expressing the same thing that Hamilton has said about the philosopher?

C. How does wisdom as defined in paragraph 13 of Hamilton's essay compare with Newman's philosophic mind?

5. How do Hamilton's ideas about the *experiencing nature* (paragraph 15) compare with Eastman's ideas about the poetic character?

6. What is the difference between *curiosity* and *sympathy* discussed in paragraph 15? Why does sympathy imply a deeper and less selfish interest than mere curiosity? Does the etymology of sympathy suggest something of the reason for this?

ON THE SHORT STORY

Frank O'Connor

1 Definitions are a nuisance, but they prevent misunderstandings. When E. M. Forster wrote a book on the novel, he accepted a French definition of it as "a prose fiction of a certain length" which was incontrovertible, like saying it was written on paper, but not very helpful, as it implied that practically everything "of a certain length" was a novel and consequently that there was nothing useful to be said about it. Anthologies of short stories also suggest that everything "of a certain length" is a short story—squibs by Dorothy Parker or Saki, articles, essays, and plain shockers, and that nothing useful can be said about that, either. I don't share either view. I admit I am not at all clear what I mean by a short story, or else I should have much less trouble in writing it, but I am passionately clear about what I do *not* mean, and for me, anthologies are full of negative definitions.

2 A yarn, for instance, is not a short story, as—begging Mr. Forster's pardon—a medieval saga or romance is not a novel. Every literary form is, to

a certain extent, a convention; it is what people generally mean when they use the word that defines it, exactly as when a man says, "I'll meet you with the car," you expect to be met with an automobile, not a perambulator. A novel is *Tom Jones, Sense and Sensibility, Vanity Fair, War and Peace,* and *The Charterhouse of Parma,* and *not*—Mr. Forster's pardon again—*The Pilgrim's Progress, Marius the Epicurean,* or *Zuleika Dobson.* (When Mr. Forster launches into a discussion of *Zuleika Dobson,* I feel exactly as I should if the man who was to meet me with the car appeared with the perambulator.) By convention, the novel and the short story have both come to mean stories of real people in real situations, rather than what I call "The Cat's Whisker," the sort of yarn, so popular with magazine editors, which ends, usually in italics "*The face was the face of Minkie, the cat, but the whiskers were the whiskers of Colonel Claude Combpyne.*" If we must have a word for the thing, let us call it a "tale," and not mix it up with Chekhov's "Lady with the Toy Dog," with which it has nothing whatever in common but the fact that it is "a prose fiction of a certain length."

3 For me, what makes the short story what it is, is its attitude to Time. In any novel the principal character is Time—*Ulysses, The Informer,* and *Mrs. Dalloway* notwithstanding. Even in inferior novels and in books which are not strictly creative literature, the chronological ordering of events establishes a rhythm, which is the rhythm of life itself, and I have known novelists who sometimes wrote hundreds of pages until the novel proper began. But what to the novelist is the most precious element in his work is a nightmare to the short-story writer. He is all the while trying to get round the neccssity for describing events in sequence; the rhythm is too slow, and when novelists like Henry James and Hardy turn storytellers and use the rhythms of the novel, he finds the result disastrous. Hardy will cheerfully waste three pages getting his hero up the hill before he even begins to reveal what his story is about. Time the collaborator has become Time the gasbag.

4 Every great short story represents a struggle with Time—the novelist's Time—a refusal to allow it to establish its majestic rhythms ("Chapter I, A Walk on the Heath"). It attempts to reach some point of vantage, some glowing center of action from which past and future will be equally visible. The crisis of a short story *is* the short story, and not, as in the novel, the logical, inescapable result of everything preceding it, the mere flowering of events. I should almost say that in the story what precedes the crisis becomes a consequence of the crisis.

5 It is one of the weaknesses of the story writer that, because of his awareness of the importance of the crisis, he tends to inflate it, to give it artificial, symbolic significance. In teaching the short story, I have had to warn students that anyone using symbolism would be instantly expelled from the class. Joyce, who was fascinated by the problem, did use symbol-

ism, but being Joyce, used it in such a remote form that he manages to conceal it from most readers. In "Ivy-Day in the Committee Room," a satirical comment on Ireland after Parnell, we meet a few political figures consumed with rancor for the want of a drink. Then some bottles of stout appear, and the tone of their sentiment at once becomes nobler, till, in a mock-heroic parody of a Hero's funeral, a sentimental poem takes the place of a Dead March and three bottles of stout, placed before the fire to open, that of the three volleys fired over the Hero's grave.

6 The device of the muted symbol is superbly used in "The Dead." The events of the story have already long taken place, and were never very significant. A tubercular young man who sang a song called "The Lass of Aughrin" fell in love with a West of Ireland girl called Gretta. One night, she found him outside her window, wet and shivering, and soon after, he died. The story proper opens years later with the arrival of Gretta and her husband at a musical party given by two old music teachers in Dublin. As Gabriel Conroy, the husband, enters, he scrapes snow from his galoshes and cracks a joke with the maid about getting married. She retorts bitterly that "the men that does be there nowadays are nothing but old palaver and all they can get out of you." These two things—the snow and the maid's retort—form the theme of the story, and they are repeated in varied and more menacing forms until the climax.

7 "The men that does be there nowadays" cannot be great lovers; it is only the dead who can be perfect. The young Gaelic League girl with whom Gabriel chats about the West of Ireland—the subject, like the dead themselves, rising—may be charming, but she cannot have the courtesy and grace of the old music teachers who are passing into the shadow; Caruso —a subtle touch, this—may, for all we know, be a good singer, but he cannot be as great as Parkinson, the obscure English tenor, whom one of the old ladies once heard. And in the tremendous cadenza we realize that Gabriel, good husband though he may be, can never mean to his wife what the dead boy who once stood shivering beneath her window means— till he too has been buried under the snow which is Death's symbol.

8 This, of course, is only a way of saying that the short story is lyrical, not epic; that it springs from the heart of a situation rather than mounts up to and explains it. There is yet another way of expressing the same thing in relation to the novel. The novel, it is generally agreed, is the typical art of the middle classes which reached its highest development in the century of the middle classes, the nineteenth. The nineteenth-century novel in Europe had a peculiar geographical distribution. It is at its greatest in England, France, and Russia.

9 The distribution of the short story is quite different. Here, the Russians have the field to themselves; the French with Maupassant are barely in sight; while the English are still hovering round the starting post, eagerly

searching for the whiskers of Colonel Claude Combpyne. It is true that the great period of the short story didn't come until the decline of the novel, about 1880, but long before that Turgenev had done things with the short story which have never been bettered. This hints at a basic difference in approach between novel and story.

10 It is even more peculiar in our own times. Now, it is America which takes the place of Imperial Russia and produces both novels and short stories of the first rank. But Ireland, which has never produced a novel, has produced short stories of remarkable quality, and, in spite of Coppard and Pritchett, far superior to English short stories which still mainly investigate whiskers in italics. This suggests that the difference has something to do with the attitude that the two art forms impose on their writers. I have small doubt that the difference is in the attitude to society.

11 The thing which makes the Irish novel impossible is that the subject of a novel is almost invariably the relation of the individual to society, and Ireland does not have a society which can absorb the individual; as an American critic has put it, every good Irish novel ends on a ship to England or America. But the emotion of Gabriel Conroy in "The Dead" is not conditioned by society, and the loneliness of the people in Winesburg, Ohio, is not likely to be changed by any change in their social condition. Their troubles "are from eternity and shall not fail."

12 In fact, the short story, compared with the novel, is a lonely, personal art; the lyric cry in face of human destiny, it does not deal as the novel must do with types or with problems of moment, but with what Synge calls "the profound and common interests of life"; the little servant girl so weary of her nursing that she smothers the baby; the cabman so obsessed by his son's death that when one of his busy customers will not listen to his grief, he tells it to his old cab horse. It is not for nothing that some of the great storytellers like Gorki have been tramps. The story writer is not a soldier in the field, but a guerrilla fighter, fighting the obscure duels of a great campaign. He stands always somewhere on the outskirts of society, less interested in its famous and typical figures than in the lonely and gnarled and obscure individuals of Winesburg, Ohio, and Dublin, Ireland.

STUDY GUIDE

1. In spite of O'Connor's statement about the difficulty in defining the short story, he does try to arrive at a definition of it. What does he claim differentiates it from the tale and the novel?

2. What are some of the things that the novelist has room for that the short-story writer cannot afford?

3. What does O'Connor mean by saying that the short story is lyric rather than epic?

4. What do the short story and the lyric poem have in common? Where does O'Connor discuss this common element in this essay?

THE GENTLEMAN FROM SAN FRANCISCO

Ivan Bunin / TRANSLATED BY A. YARMOLINSKY

"Alas, alas that great city Babylon, that mighty city."
—REVELATION OF ST. JOHN

The Gentleman from San Francisco—neither at Naples or on Capri could any one recall his name—with his wife and daughter, was on his way to Europe, where he intended to stay for two whole years, solely for the pleasure of it.

He was firmly convinced that he had a full right to a rest, enjoyment, a long comfortable trip, and what not. This conviction had a two-fold reason: first, he was rich, and second, despite his fifty-eight years, he was just about to enter the stream of life's pleasures. Until now he had not really lived, but simply existed, to be sure—fairly well, yet putting off his fondest hopes for the future. He toiled unweariedly—the Chinese, whom he imported by thousands for his works knew full well what it meant, and finally he saw that he had made much, and that he had nearly come up to the level of those whom he had once taken as a model, and he decided to catch his breath. The class of people to which he belonged was in the habit of beginning its enjoyment of life with a trip to Europe, India, Egypt. He made up his mind to do the same. Of course, it was first of all himself that he desired to reward for the years of toil; but he was also glad for his wife and daughter's sake. His wife was never distinguished by any extraordinary impressionability, but then, all elderly American women are ardent travelers. As for his daughter, a girl of marriageable age, and somewhat sickly —travel was the very thing she needed. Not to speak of the benefit to her health, do not happy meetings occur during travels? Abroad, one may

Reprinted from Ivan Bunin, *The Gentleman from San Francisco and Other Stories* (1923).

chance to sit at the same table with a prince, or examine frescoes side by side with a multimillionaire.

The itinerary the Gentleman from San Francisco planned out was an extensive one. In December and January he expected to relish the sun of southern Italy, monuments of antiquity, the tarantella, serenades of wandering minstrels, and that which at his age is felt most keenly—the love, not entirely disinterested though, of young Neapolitan girls. The Carnival days he planned to spend at Nice and Monte Carlo, which at that time of the year is the meeting-place of the choicest society, the society upon which depend all the blessings of civilization: the cut of dress suits, the stability of thrones, the declaration of wars, the prosperity of hotels. Some of these people passionately give themselves over to automobile and boat races; others to roulette; others, again, busy themselves with what is called flirtation; and others shoot pigeons, which soar so beautifully from the dovecote, hover a while over the emerald lawn, on the background of the forget-me-not colored sea, and then suddenly hit the ground, like little white lumps. Early March he wanted to devote to Florence, and at Easter, to hear the Miserere in Paris. His plans also included Venice, Paris, bull-baiting at Seville, bathing on the British Islands, also Athens, Constantinople, Palestine, Egypt, and even Japan, of course, on the way back. . . . And at first things went very well indeed.

It was the end of November, and all the way to Gibraltar the ship sailed across seas which were either clad by icy darkness or swept by storms carrying wet snow. But there were no accidents, and the vessel did not even roll. The passengers—all people of consequence—were numerous, and the steamer, the famous *Atlantis*, resembled the most expensive European hotel with all improvements; a night refreshment-bar, Oriental baths, even a newspaper of its own. The manner of living was a most aristocratic one; passengers rose early, awakened by the shrill voice of a bugle, filling the corridors at the gloomy hour when the day broke slowly and sulkily over the grayish-green water desert, which rolled heavily in the fog. After putting on their flannel pajamas, they took coffee, chocolate, cocoa; they seated themselves in marble baths, went through their exercises, whetting their appetites and increasing their sense of well-being, dressed for the day, and had their breakfast. Till eleven o'clock they were supposed to stroll on the deck, breathing in the chill freshness of the ocean, or they played table-tennis, or other games which arouse the appetite. At eleven o'clock a collation was served consisting of sandwiches and bouillon, after which people read their newspapers, quietly waiting for luncheon, which was more nourishing and varied than the breakfast. The next two hours were given to rest; all the decks were crowded then with steamer chairs, on which the passengers, wrapped in plaids, lay stretched, dozing lazily, or watching the cloudy sky and the foamy-fringed water hillocks flashing beyond the sides of the vessel. At five o'clock, refreshed and gay, they drank strong, fragrant tea; at seven the sound of the bugle announced a dinner of nine courses. . . . Then the Gentleman from San Francisco, rubbing his hands in an onrush of vital energy, hastened to his luxurious state-room to dress.

In the evening, all the decks of the *Atlantis* yawned in the darkness, shone with their innumerable fiery eyes, and a multitude of servants worked with increased feverishness in the kitchens, dish-washing compartments, and wine-cellars. The ocean, which heaved about the sides of the ship, was dreadful, but no one thought of it. All had faith in the controlling power of the captain, a red-headed giant, heavy and very sleepy, who, clad in a uniform with broad golden stripes, looked like a huge idol, and but rarely emerged, for the benefit of the public, from his mysterious retreat. On the fore-castle, the siren gloomily roared or screeched in a fit of mad rage; but few of the diners heard the siren: its hellish voice was covered by the sounds of an excellent string orchestra, which played ceaselessly and exquisitely in a vast hall, decorated with marble and spread with velvety carpets. The hall was flooded with torrents of light, radiated by crystal lustres and gilt chandeliers; it was filled with a throng of bejeweled ladies in low-necked dresses, of men in dinner-coats, graceful waiters, and deferential maitres-d'hotel. One of these—who accepted wine orders exclusively—wore a chain on his neck like some lord-mayor. The evening dress, and the ideal linen made the Gentleman from San Francisco look very young. Dry-skinned, of average height, strongly, though irregularly built, glossy, with thorough washing and cleaning, and moderately animated, he sat in the golden splendor of this palace. Near him stood a bottle of amber-colored Johannisberg, and goblets of most delicate glass and of varied sizes, surmounted by a frizzled bunch of fresh hyacinths. There was something Mongolian in his yellowish face with its trimmed silvery moustache; his large teeth glimmered with gold fillings, and his strong, bald head had a dull glow, like old ivory. His wife, a big, broad and placid woman, was dressed richly, but in keeping with her age. Complicated, but light, transparent, and innocently immodest was the dress of his daughter, tall and slender, with magnificent hair gracefully combed; her breath was sweet with violet-scented tablets; and she had a number of tiny and most delicate pink dimples near her lips and between her slightly-powdered shoulder blades.

The dinner lasted two whole hours, and was followed by dances in the dancing hall, while the men—the Gentleman from San Francisco among them—made their way to the refreshment bar, where Negroes in red jackets and with eye-balls like shelled hard-boiled eggs, waited on them. There, with their feet on tables, smoking Havana cigars, and drinking themselves purple in the face, they settled the destinies of nations on the basis of the latest political and stock-exchange news. Outside, the ocean tossed up black mountains with a thud; and the snow-storm hissed furiously in the rigging grown heavy with slush; the ship trembled in every limb, struggling with the storm and ploughing with difficulty the shifting and seething mountainous masses that threw far and high their foaming tails; the siren groaned in agony, choked by storm and fog; the watchmen in their towers froze and almost went out of their minds under the superhuman stress of attention. Like the gloomy and sultry mass of the inferno, like its last, ninth circle, was the submersed womb of the steamer, where monstrous furnaces yawned with red-hot open jaws, and emitted deep, hooting sounds, and where the stokers, stripped to the waist, and purple with reflected flames bathed in their own dirty, acid sweat. And here, in the refreshment-bar, carefree men, with their feet, encased in dancing shoes, on the table, sipped cognac and liqueurs, swam in waves of spiced smoke, and exchanged subtle remarks; while in the dancing-hall everything sparkled and radiated light, warmth and joy. The couples now turned around in a waltz, now swayed in the tango; and the music, sweetly shameless and sad, persisted in its ceaseless entreaties . . . There were many persons of note in this magnificent crowd; an ambassador, a dry modest old man; a great millionaire, shaved, tall, of an indefinite age, who, in his old-fashioned dress-coat, looked like a prelate; also a famous Spanish writer, and an international belle, already slightly faded and of dubious morals. There was also among them a loving pair, exquisite and refined, whom everybody watched with curiosity and who did not conceal their bliss; he danced only with her, sang—with great skill—only to her accompaniment, and they were so charming, so graceful. The captain alone knew that they had been hired by the company at a good salary to play at love, and that they had been sailing now on one, now on another steamer for quite a long time.

In Gibraltar everybody was gladdened by the sun, and by the weather which was like early Spring. A new passenger appeared aboard the *Atlantis* and aroused everybody's interest. It was the crown-prince of an Asiatic state, who traveled incognito, a small man, very nimble, though looking as if made of wood, broad-faced, narrow-eyed in gold-rimmed glasses somewhat disagreeable because his long moustache, which was sparse like that of a corpse, but otherwise—charming, plain, modest. In the Mediterranean the breath of winter was again felt. The seas were heavy and motley like a peacock's tail and the waves stirred up by the gay gusts of the tramontane, tossed their white crests under a sparkling and perfectly clear sky. Next morning, the sky grew paler and the skyline misty. Land was near. Then Ischia and Capri came in sight, and one could descry, through an opera-glass, Naples, looking like pieces of sugar strewn at the foot of an indistinct dove-colored mass, and above them, a snow-covered chain of distant mountains. The decks were crowded; many ladies and gentlemen put on light-fur-coats; Chinese servants, bandy-legged youths—with pitch black braids down to the heels and with girlish, thick eyelashes—always quiet and speaking in a whisper, were carrying to the foot of the staircases, plaid wraps, canes, and crocodile-leather valises and handbags. The daughter of the Gentleman from San Francisco stood near the prince, who, by a happy chance, had been introduced to her the evening before, and feigned to be looking steadily at something far-off, which he was pointing out to her, while he was, at the same time, explaining something, saying something rapidly and quietly. He was so small that he looked like a boy among other men, and he was not handsome at all. And then there was something strange about him; his glasses, derby and coat were most commonplace; but there was something horse-like in the hair of his sparse moustache; and the thin, tanned skin of his flat face looked as though it were somewhat stretched and varnished. But the girl listened to him; and so great was her excitement that she could hardly grasp the meaning of his words; her heart palpitated with incomprehensible rapture and with pride that he was standing and speaking with her and nobody else. Everything about him was different: his dry hands, his clean skin, under which flowed ancient kingly blood, even his light shoes and his European dress, plain, but singularly tidy—everything had an inexplicable fascination and engendered thoughts of love. And the Gentleman from San Francisco, himself, in a silk-hat, gray leggings, patent leather shoes, kept eyeing the famous beauty who was standing near him, a tall, stately blonde, with eyes painted according to the latest Parisian fashion, and a tiny, bent peeled-off pet-dog, to whom she addressed herself. And the daughter, in a kind of vague perplexity, tried not to notice him.

Like all wealthy Americans he was very liberal when traveling; and he believed in the complete sincerity and goodwill of those who so painstakingly fed him, served him day and night, anticipating his slightest desire, protected him from dirt and disturbance, hauled things for him, hailed carriers, and delivered his luggage to hotels. So it was everywhere, and it had to be so at Naples. Meanwhile, Naples grew and came nearer. The musicians, with their shining brass instruments, had already formed a group on the deck, and all of a sudden deafened everybody with the triumphant sounds of a ragtime march. The giant captain, in his full uniform appeared on the bridge and, like a gracious Pagan idol, waved his hands to the passengers—and it seemed to the Gentleman from San Francisco, as it did to all the rest—that for him alone thundered the march, so greatly loved by proud America, and that him alone did the captain congratulate on the safe arrival. And when the *Atlantis* had finally entered the port and all its many-decked mass leaned against the quay, and the gang-plank began to rattle heavily—what a crowd of porters, with their assistants, in caps with golden galloons, what a crowd of various boys and husky ragamuffins with pads of colored postal cards attacked the Gentleman from San Francisco, offering their services. With kindly contempt he grinned at these beggars; and, walking towards the automobile of the hotel where the prince might stop, muttered between his teeth, now in English, now in Italian—"Go away. Via. . . ."

Immediately, life at Naples began to follow a set routine. Early in the morning breakfast was served in the gloomy dining-room, swept by a wet draught from the open windows looking upon a stony garden; while outside the sky was cloudy and cheerless; and a crowd of guides swarmed at the door of the vestibule. Then came the first smiles of the warm roseate sun, and from the high suspended balcony, a broad vista unfolded itself: Vesuvius, wrapped to its base in radiant morning vapors; the pearly ripple, touched to silver, of the bay, the delicate outline of Capri in the skyline; tiny asses dragging two-wheeled buggies along the soft, sticky embankment; and detachments of little soldiers marching somewhere to the tune of cheerful and defiant music.

Next on the day's program was a slow automobile ride along crowded, narrow, and damp corridors of streets, between high, many-windowed buildings. It was followed by visits to museums, lifelessly clean and lighted evenly and pleasantly, but as though with the dull light cast by snow; then to churches, cold, smelling of wax, always alike; a majestic entrance, closed by a ponderous, leather curtain, and inside—a vast void silence, quiet flames of seven-branched candlesticks, sending forth a red glow from where they stood at the farther end, on the bedecked altar—a lonely, old woman lost among the dark wooden benches, slippery gravestones under the feet, and somebody's "Descent from the Cross," infallibly famous. At one o'clock—luncheon, on the mountain of San-Martius, where at noon the choicest people gathered, and where the daughter of the Gentleman from San Francisco once almost fainted with joy, because it seemed to her that she saw the Prince in the hall; although she had learned from the newspapers that he had temporarily left for Rome. At five o'clock it was customary to take tea at the hotel, in a smart salon, where it was far too warm because of the carpets and the blazing fireplaces and then came dinner-time—and again did the mighty, commanding voice of the gong resound throughout the building; again did silk rustle and the mirrors reflect files of ladies in low-necked dresses ascending the staircases: and again the splendid palatial dining hall opened with broad hospitality; and again the musicians' jackets formed red patches on the estrade; and the black figures of the waiters swarmed around the maitre-d'hotel, who, with extraordinary skill, poured a thick pink soup into plates. . . . As everywhere, the dinner was the crown of the day. People dressed for it as for a wedding; and so abundant was it in food, wines, mineral waters, sweets and fruits that about eleven o'clock in the evening chambermaids would carry to all the rooms hot-water bags.

That year, however, December did not happen to be a very propitious one. The doormen were abashed when people spoke to them about the weather, and shrugged their shoulders guiltily, mumbling that they could not recollect such a year, although, to tell the truth, it was not the first year they mumbled those words, usually adding that "things are terrible everywhere"; that unprecedented showers and storms had broken out on the Riviera, that it was snowing in Athens, that Aetna, too, was all blocked up with snow, and glowed brightly at night, and that tourists were fleeing from Palermo to save themselves from the cold spell. . . .

That winter, the morning sun daily deceived Naples; toward noon the sky would invariably grow gray; and a light rain would begin to fall, growing thicker and duller. Then the palms at the hotel-porch glistened disagreeably like wet tin; the town appeared exceptionally dirty and congested; the museums too monotonous; the cigars of the drivers in their rubber raincoats, which flattened in the wind like wings, intolerably stinking; and the energetic flapping of their whips over their thin-necked nags —obviously false. The shoes of the signors, who cleaned the street-car tracks, were in a frightful state; the women who splashed in the mud, with black hair unprotected from the rain, were ugly and short legged; and the humidity mingled with the foul smell of rotting fish, that camc from the foaming sea, was simply disheartening. And so, early-morning quarrels began to break out between the Gentlemen from San Francisco and his wife; and their daughter now grew pale and suffered from headaches, and now became animated, enthusiastic over everything, and at such times was lovely and beautiful. Beautiful were the tender, complex feelings which her meeting with the ungainly man aroused in her—the man in whose veins flowed unusual blood, for, after all, it does not matter what in particular stirs up a maiden's soul: money, or fame, or nobility of birth. . . . Everybody assured the tourists that it was quite different at Sorrento and on Capri, that lemon-trees were blossoming there, that it was warmer and sunnier there, the morals purer, and the wine less adulterated. And the family from San Francisco decided to set out with all their luggage for Capri. They planned to settle down at Sorrento, but first to visit the island, tread the stones where stood Tiberius's palaces, examine the fabulous wonders of the Blue Grotto, and listen to the bagpipers of Abruzzi, who roam about the island during the whole month preceding Christmas and sing the praises of the Madonna.

On the day of departure—a very memorable day for the family from San Francisco—the sun did not appear even in the morning. A heavy winter fog covered Vesuvius down to its very base and hung like a gray curtain over the leaden surge of the sea, hiding it completely at a distance of half a mile. Capri was completely out of sight, as though it had never existed on this earth. And the little steamboat which was making for the island tossed and pitched so fiercely that the family lay prostrated on the sofas in the miserable cabin of the little steamer, with their feet wrapped in plaids and their eyes shut because of their nausea. The older lady suffered, as she thought, most; several times she was overcome with sea-sickness; and it seemed to her then she was dying; but the chambermaid, who repeatedly brought her the basin, and who for many years, in heat and in cold, had been tossing on these waves, ever on the alert, ever kindly to all—the chambermaid only laughed. The lady's daughter was frightfully pale and kept a slice of lemon between her teeth. Not even the hope of an unexpected meeting with the prince at Sorrento, where he planned to arrive on Christmas, served to cheer her. The Gentleman from San Francisco, who was lying on his back, dressed in a large overcoat and a big cap, did not loosen his jaws throughout the voyage. His face grew dark, his mustache white, and his head ached heavily; for the last few days, because of the bad weather, he had drunk far too much in the evenings.

And the rain kept on beating against the rattling window panes, and water dripped down from them on the sofas; the howling wind attacked the masts; and sometimes, aided by a heavy sea, it laid the little steamer on its side; and then something below rolled about with a rattle.

While the steamer was anchored at Castellamare and Sorrento, the situation was more cheerful; but even here the ship rolled terribly, and the coast, with all its precipices, gardens and pines, with its pink and white hotels and hazy mountains clad in curling verdure, flew up and down as if it were on swings. The rowboats hit against the sides of the steamer; the sailors, and the deck passengers shouted at the top of their voices; and somewhere a baby screamed as if it were being crushed to pieces. A wet wind blew through the door; and from a wavering barge, flying the flag of the Hotel Royal, an urchin kept on unwearyingly shouting "Kgoyal-al. Hotel Kgoyal-al. . . ." inviting tourists. And the Gentleman from San Francisco felt like the old man that he was—and it was with weariness and animosity that he thought of all these "Royals," "Splendids," "Excelsiors," and of all those greedy bugs, reeking with garlic, who are called Italians. Once, during a stop, having opened his eyes and half-risen from the sofa, he noticed in the shadow of the rock beach a heap of stone huts, miserable, mildewed through and through, huddled close by the water, near boats, rags, tin-boxes, and brown fishing nets—and as he remembered that this was the very Italy he had come to enjoy, he felt a great despair. . . . Finally, in twilight, the black mass of the island began to grow nearer, as though burrowed through at the base by red fires; the wind grew softer, warmer, more fragrant; from the dock-lanterns huge golden serpents flowed down the tame waves which undulated like black oil. . . . Then, suddenly, the anchor rumbled and fell with a splash into the water; the fierce yells of the boatman filled the air—and at once everyone's heart grew easy. The electric lights in the cabin grew more brilliant; and there came a desire to eat, drink, smoke, move. . . . Ten minutes later the family from San Francisco found themselves in a large ferryboat; fifteen minutes later they trod the stones of the quay, and then seated themselves in a small lighted car, which, with a buzz, started to ascend the slope; while vineyard stakes, half-ruined stone fences, and wet, crooked lemon-trees, in spots shielded by straw sheds, with their glimmering orange-colored fruit and thick glossy foliage, were sliding down past the open car windows. After rain, the earth smells sweetly in Italy; and each of her islands has a fragrance of its own.

The Island of Capri was dark and damp on that evening. But for a while it grew animated and lit up, in spots, as always in the hour of the steamer's arrival. On the top of the hill, at the station of the funiculaire, there stood already the crowd of those whose duty it was to receive properly the Gentleman from San Francisco. The rest of the tourists hardly deserved any attention. There were a few Russians, who had settled on Capri, untidy, absent-minded people, absorbed in their bookish thoughts, spectacled, bearded, with the collars of their cloth overcoats raised. There was also a company of long-legged, long-necked, round-headed German youths in Tyrolean costume, and with linen bags on their backs, who need no one's services, are everywhere at home, and are by no means liberal in their expenses. The Gentleman from San Francisco, who kept quietly aloof from both the Russians and the Germans, was noticed at once. He and his ladies were hurriedly helped from the car, a man ran before them to show them the way; and they were again surrounded by boys and those thickset Caprean peasant women, who carry on their heads the trunks and valises of wealthy travelers. Their tiny, wooden, foot-stools rapped against the pavement of the small square, which looked almost like an opera square, and over which an electric lantern swung in the damp wind; the gang of urchins whistled like birds and turned somersaults; and as the Gentleman from San Francisco passed among them, it all looked like a stage scene; he went first under some kind of mediaeval archway, beneath houses huddled close together, and then along a steep echoing lane which led to the hotel entrance, flooded with light. At the left, a palm tree raised its tuft above the flat roofs; and higher up, blue stars burned in the black sky. And again things looked as though it was in honor of the guests from San Francisco that the stony damp little town had awakened on its rocky island in the Mediterranean, that it was they who had made the owner of the hotel so happy and beaming, and that the Chinese gong, which had sounded the call to dinner through all the floors as soon as they entered the lobby, had been waiting only for them.

The owner, an elegant young man, who met the guests with a polite and exquisite bow, for a moment startled the Gentleman from San Francisco. Having caught sight of him, the Gentleman from San Francisco suddenly recollected that on the previous night, among other confused images which disturbed his sleep, he had seen this very man. His vision resembled the hotel keeper to a dot, had the same head, the same hair, shining and scrupulously combed, and wore the same frock-coat with rounded skirts. Amazed, he almost stopped for a while. But as there was not a mustard-seed of what is called mysticism in his heart, his surprise subsided at once; in passing the corridor of the hotel he jestingly told his wife and daughter about this strange coincidence of dream and reality. His daughter alone glanced at him with alarm, longing suddenly compressed her heart, and such a strong feeling of solitude on this strange, dark island seized her that she almost began to cry. But, as usual, she said nothing about her feeling to her father.

A person of high dignity, Rex XVII, who had spent three entire weeks on Capri, had just left the island; and the guests from San Francisco were given the apartments he had occupied. At their disposal was put the most handsome and skillful chambermaid, a Belgian, with a figure rendered slim and firm by her corset, and with a starched cap, shaped like a small, indented crown; and they had the privilege of being served by the most well-appearing and portly footman, a black, fiery-eyed Sicilian, and by the quickest waiter, the small, stout Luigi, who was a fiend at cracking jokes and had changed many places in his life. Then the maitre-d'Hotel, a Frenchman, gently rapped at the door of the American gentleman's room. He came to ask whether the gentleman and the ladies would dine, and in case they would, which he did not doubt, to report that there was to be had that day lobsters, roast beef, asparagus, pheasants, etc., etc.

The floor was still rocking under the Gentleman from San Francisco —so sea-sick had the wretched Italian steamer made him—yet he slowly, though awkwardly, shut the window which had banged when the maitre-d'hotel entered, and which let in the smell of the distant kitchen and wet flowers in the garden, and answered with slow distinctiveness, that they would dine, that their table must be placed farther away from the door, in the depth of the hall, that they would have local wine and champagne, moderately dry and but slightly cooled. The maitre-d'hotel approved the words of the guest in various intonations, which all meant, however, only one thing; there is and can be no doubt that the desires of the Gentleman from San Francisco are right, and that everything would be carried out, in exact conformity with his words. At last he inclined his head and asked delicately:

"Is that all, sir?"

And having received in reply a slow "Yes," he added that today they were going to have the tarantella danced in the vestibule by Carmella and Giuseppe, known to all Italy and to "the entire world of tourists."

"I saw her on post-card pictures," said the Gentleman from San Francisco in a tone of voice which expressed nothing. "And this Giuseppe, is he her husband?"

"Her cousin, sir," answered the maitre-d'hotel.

The Gentleman from San Francisco tarried a little, evidently musing on something, but said nothing, then dismissed him with a nod of his head.

Then he started making preparations, as though for a wedding: he turned on all the electric lamps, and filled the mirrors with reflections of light and the sheen of furniture, and opened trunks; he began to shave and to wash himself, and the sound of his bell was heard every minute in the corridor, crossing with other impatient calls which came from the rooms of his wife and daughter. Luigi, in his red apron, with the ease characteristic of stout people, made funny faces at the chambermaids, who were dashing by with tile buckets in their hands, making them laugh until the tears came. He rolled head over heels to the door, and, tapping with his knuckles, asked with feigned timidity and with an obsequiousness which he knew how to render idiotic:

"Ha sonata, Signore?" (Did you ring, sir?)

And from behind the door a slow, grating, insultingly polite voice, answered:

"Yes, come in."

What did the Gentleman from San Francisco think and feel on that evening forever memorable to him? It must be said frankly: absolutely nothing exceptional. The trouble is that everything on this earth appears too simple. Even had he felt anything deep in his heart, a premonition that something was going to happen, he would have imagined that it was not going to happen so soon, at least not at once. Besides, as is usually the case just after sea-sickness is over, he was very hungry, and he anticipated with real delight the first spoonful of soup, and the first gulp of wine; therefore, he was performing the habitual process of dressing, in a state of excitement which left no time for reflection.

Having shaved and washed himself, and dexterously put in place a few false teeth, he then, standing before the mirror, moistened and vigorously plastered what was left of his thick pearly-colored hair, close to his tawny-yellow skull. Then he put on, with some effort, a tight-fitting undershirt of cream-colored silk, fitted tight to his strong, aged body with its waist swelling out because of an abundant diet; and he pulled black silk socks and patent-leather dancing shoes on his dry feet with their fallen arches. Squatting down, he set right his black trousers, drawn high by means of silk suspenders, adjusted his snow-white shirt with its bulging front, put the buttons into the shining cuffs, and began the painful process of hunting up the front button under the hard collar. The floor was still swaying under him; the tips of his fingers hurt terribly; the button at times painfully pinched the flabby skin in the depression under his Adam's apple; but he persevered; and finally, with his eyes shining from the effort, his face blue because of the narrow collar which squeezed his neck, he triumphed over the difficulties—and all exhausted, he sat down before the pier-glass, his reflected image repeating itself in all the mirrors.

"It's terrible," he muttered, lowering his strong, bald head and making no effort to understand what was terrible; then, with a careful and habitual gesture, he examined his short fingers with gouty callosities in the joints, and their large, convex, almond-colored nails, and repeated with conviction, "It's terrible."

But here the stentorian voice of the second gong sounded throughout the house, as in a heathen temple. And having risen hurriedly, the Gentleman from San Francisco drew his tie more taut and firm around his collar, and pulled together his abdomen by means of a tight waistcoat, put on a dinner-coat, set to rights the cuffs, and for the last time he examined himself in the mirror. . . . This Carmella, tawny as a mulatto, with fiery eyes, in a dazzling dress in which orange-color predominated, must be an extraordinary dancer—it occured to him. And cheerfully leaving his room he walked on the carpet, to his wife's chamber, and asked in a loud tone of voice if they would be long.

"In five minutes, papa," answered cheerfully and gaily a girlish voice. "I am combing my hair."

"Very well," said the Gentleman from San Francisco.

And thinking of her wonderful hair, streaming on her shoulders, he slowly walked down along corridors and staircases, spread with red velvet carpets—looking for the library. The servants he met hugged the walls, and he walked by as if not noticing them. An old lady, late for dinner, already bowed with years, with milk-white hair, yet bare-necked, in a light-gray silk dress, hurried at top speed, but she walked in a mincing, funny, hen-like manner and he easily overtook her. At the glass door of the dining hall where the guests had already gathered and started eating, he stopped before the table crowded with boxes of matches and Egyptian cigarettes, took a great Manila cigar, and threw three liras on the table. On the winter veranda he glanced into the open window; a stream of soft air came to him from the darkness; the top of the old palm loomed up before him afar-off, with its boughs spread among the stars and looking gigantic; and the distant even noise of the sea reached his ear. In the library-room, snug, quiet, a German in round silver-bowed glasses and with crazy, wondering eyes, stood turning the rustling pages of a newspaper. Having coldly eyed him, the Gentleman from San Francisco seated himself in a deep leather arm-chair near a lamp under a green hood, put on his pince-nez, and, twitching his head because of the collar which choked him, hid himself from view behind a newspaper. He glanced at a few headlines, read a few lines about the interminable Balkan War, and turned over the page with an habitual gesture. Suddenly, the lines blazed up with a glassy sheen; the veins of his neck swelled; his eyes bulged out; the pince-nez fell from his nose. . . . He dashed forward, wanted to swallow air—and made a wild, rattling noise; his lower jaw dropped, dropped on his shoulder and began to shake, the shirt-front bulged out—and the whole body, writhing, the heels catching in the carpet, slowly fell to the floor in a desperate struggle with an invisible foe. . . .

Had not the German been in the library, this frightful accident would have been quickly and adroitly hushed up. The body of the Gentleman from San Francisco would have been rushed away to some far corner—and none of the guests would have known of the occurrence. But the German dashed out of the library with outcries and spread the alarm all over the house. And many rose from their meal, upsetting chairs; others growing pale, ran along the corridors to the library; and the question, asked in many languages, was heard: "What is it? What has happened?" And no one was able to answer it clearly; no one understood anything; for until this very day men still wonder most at death and most absolutcly rcfuse to believe in it. The owner rushed from one guest to another, trying to keep back those who were running and soothe them with hasty assurances, that this was nothing, a mere trifle, a little fainting-spell by which a Gentleman from San Francisco had been overcome. But no one listened to him; many saw how the footmen and waiters tore from the gentleman his tie, collar, waistcoat, the rumpled evening coat, and even—for no visible reason—the dancing shoes from his black silk-covered feet. And he kept on writhing. He obstinately struggled with death; he did not want to yield to the foe that attacked him so unexpectedly and grossly. He shook his head, emitted rattling sounds like one throttled, and turned up his eyeballs like one drunk with wine. When he was hastily brought into Number Forty-three—the smallest, worst, dampest, and coldest room at the end of the lower corridor—and stretched on the bed, his daughter came running, her hair falling over her shoulders, the skirts of her dressing-gown thrown open, with bare breasts raised by the corset. Then came his wife, big, heavy, almost completely dressed for dinner, her mouth round with terror.

In a quarter of an hour all was again in good trim at the hotel. But the evening was irreparably spoiled. Some tourists returned to the dining-hall and finished their dinner; but they kept silent, and it was obvious that they took the accident as a personal insult; while the owner went from one guest to another, shrugging his shoulders in impotent and appropriate irritation, feeling like one innocently victimized, assuring everyone that he understood perfectly well "how disagreeable this is," and giving his word that he would take all "the measures that are within his power" to do away with the trouble. Yet it was found necessary to cancel the tarantella. The unnecessary electric lamps were put out; most of the guests left for the beer-hall; and it grew so quiet in the hotel that one could distinctly hear the tick-tock of the clock in the lobby, where a lonely parrot babbled something in its expressionless manner, stirring in its cage, and trying to fall asleep with its paw clutching the upper perch in a most absurd manner. The Gentleman from San Francisco lay stretched in a cheap iron bed, under coarse woolen blankets, dimly lighted by a single gas-burner fastened in the ceiling. An ice-bag slid down on his wet, cold forehead. His blue, already lifeless face grew gradually cold; the hoarse, rattling noise which came from his mouth, lighted by the glimmer of the golden fillings, gradually weakened. It was not the Gentleman from San Francisco that was emitting those weird sounds; he was no more, someone else did it. His wife and daughter, the doctor, the servants were standing and watching him apathetically. Suddenly, that which they expected and feared happened. The rattling sound ceased. And slowly, slowly, in everybody's sight a pallor stole over the face of the dead man; and his features began to grow thinner and more luminous, beautiful with the beauty that he had long shunned and that became him well. . . .

The proprietor entered. "Gia e morto," whispered the doctor to him. The proprietor shrugged his shoulders indifferently. The older lady, with tears slowly running down her cheeks, approached him and said timidly that now the deceased must be taken to his room.

"O no, madam," answered the proprietor politely, but without any amiability and not in English, but in French. He was no longer interested in the trifle which the guests from San Francisco could now leave at his cash-office. "This is absolutely impossible," he said, and added in the form of an explanation that he valued this apartment highly, and if he honored her desire, this would become known over Capri and the tourists would begin to avoid it.

The girl, who had looked at him strangely, sat down, and with her handkerchief to her mouth, began to cry. Her mother's tears dried up at once, and her face flared up. She raised her tone, began to demand, using her own language and still unable to realize that the respect for her was absolutely gone. The proprietor, with polite dignity, cut her short: "If madam does not like the ways of this hotel, he dare not detain her." And he firmly announced that the corpse must leave the hotel that very day, at dawn, that the police had been informed, that an agent would call immediately and attend to all the necessary formalities. . . . "Is it possible to get on Capri at least a plain coffin?" madam asks. . . . Unfortunately not; by no means, and as for making one, there will be no time. It will be necessary to arrange things some other way. . . . For instance, he gets English soda-water in big, oblong boxes. . . . The partitions could be taken out from such a box. . . .

By night, the whole hotel was asleep. A waiter opened the window in Number 43—it faced a corner of the garden where a consumptive banana-tree grew in the shadow of a high stone wall set with broken glass on the top—turned out the electric light, locked the door, and went away. The deceased remained alone in the darkness. Blue stars looked down at him from the black sky; the cricket in the wall started his melancholy, care-free song. In the dimly lighted corridor two chambermaids were sitting on the windowsill, mending something. Then Luigi came in, in slippered feet, with a heap of clothes on his arm.

"Pronto?" he asked in a stage whisper, as if greatly concerned, directing his eyes toward the terrible door, at the end of the corridor. And waving his free hand in that direction, "Partenza," he cried out in a whisper, as if seeing off a train—and the chambermaids, choking with noiseless laughter, put their heads on each other's shoulders.

Then, stepping softly, he ran to the door, slightly rapped at it, and inclining his ear, asked most obsequiously in a subdued tone of voice:

"Ha sonata, Signore?"

And, squeezing his throat and thrusting his lower jaw forward, he answered himself in a drawling, grating, sad voice, as if from behind the door:

"Yes, come in. . . ."

At dawn, when the window panes in Number Forty-three grew white, and a damp wind rustled in the leaves of the banana-tree, when the pale-blue morning sky rose and stretched over Capri, and the sun, rising from behind the distant mountains of Italy, touched into gold the pure, clearly outlined summit of Monte Solare, when the masons, who mended the paths for the tourists on the island, went out to their work—an oblong box was brought to room number forty-three. Soon it grew very heavy and painfully pressed against the knees of the assistant doorman who was conveying it in a one-horse carriage along the white highroad which winded on the slopes, among stone fences and vineyards, all the way down to the seacoast. The driver, a sickly man, with red eyes, in an old short-sleeved coat and in worn-out shoes, had a drunken headache; all night long he had played dice at the eatinghouse—and he kept on flogging his vigorous little horse. According to Sicilian custom, the animal was heavily burdened with decorations: all sorts of bells tinkled on the bridle, which was ornamented with colored woolen fringes; there were bells also on the edge of the high saddle; and a bird's feather, two feet long, stuck in the trimmed crest of the horse, nodded up and down. The driver kept silence: he was depressed by his wrongheadedness and vices, by the fact that last night he had lost in gambling all the copper coins with which his pockets had been full—neither more nor less than four liras and forty centesimi. But on such a morning, when the air is so fresh, and the sea stretches nearby, and the sky is serene with a morning serenity—a headache passes rapidly and one becomes care-free again. Besides, the driver was also somewhat cheered by the unexpected earnings which the Gentleman from San Francisco, who bumped his dead head against the walls of the box behind his back, had brought him. The little steamer, shaped like a great bug, which lay far down, on the tender and brilliant blue filling to the brim the Neapolitan bay, was blowing the signal of departure—and the sounds swiftly resounded all over Capri. Every bend of the island, every ridge and stone was seen as distinctly as if there were no air between heaven and earth. Near the quay the driver was overtaken by the head doorman who conducted in an auto the wife and daughter of the Gentleman from San Francisco. Their faces were pale and their eyes sunken with tears and a sleepless night. And in ten minutes the little steamer was again stirring up the water and picking its way toward Sorrento and Castellamare, carrying the American family away from Capri forever. . . . Meanwhile, peace and rest were restored on the island.

Two thousand years ago there had lived on that island a man who became utterly entangled in his own brutal and filthy actions. For some unknown reason he usurped the rule over millions of men and found himself bewildered by the absurdity of his power; while the fear that someone might kill him unawares, made him commit deeds inhuman beyond all measure. And mankind has forever retained his memory; and those who, taken together, now rule the world, as incomprehensively and, essentially, as cruelly as he did—come from all the corners of the earth to look at the remnants of the stone house he inhabited, which stands on one of the steepest cliffs of the island. On that wonderful morning the tourists, who had come to Capri for precisely that purpose, were still asleep in the various hotels, but tiny long-eared asses under red saddles were already being led to the hotel entrances. Americans and Germans, men and women, old and young, after having arisen and breakfasted heartily, were to scramble on them; and the old beggarwomen of Capri, with sticks in their sinewy hands, were again to run after them along stony, mountainous paths, all the way up to the summit of Monte Tiberia. The dead old man from San Francisco, who had planned to keep the tourists company but who had, instead, only scared them by reminding them of death, was already shipped to Naples; and soothed by this, the travelers slept soundly, and silence reigned over the island. The stores in the little town were still closed, with the exception of the fish and green market on the tiny square. Among the plain people who filled it, going about their business, stood idly, as usual, Lorenzo, a tall old boatman, a carefree reveller and once a handsome man, famous all over Italy, who had many times served as a model for painters. He had brought and already sold—for a song—two big sea-crawfish, which he had caught at night and which were rustling in the apron of Don Cataldo, the cook of the hotel where the family from San Francisco had been lodged—and now Lorenzo could stand calmly until nightfall, wearing princely airs, showing off his rags, his clay pipe with its long reed mouth-piece, and his red woolen cap, tilted on one ear. Meanwhile, among the precipices of Monte Solare, down the ancient Phoenician road, cut in the rocks in the form of a gigantic staircase, two Abruzzi mountaineers were coming from Anacapri. One carried under his leather mantle a bagpipe, a large goat's skin with two pipes; the other, something in the nature of a wooden flute. They walked; and the entire country, joyous, beautiful, sunny, stretched below them; the rocky shoulders of the island, which lay at their feet, the fabulous blue in which it swam, the shining morning vapors over the sea westward, beneath the dazzling sun, and the wavering masses of Italy's mountains, both near and distant, whose beauty human word is powerless to render. . . . Midway they slowed up. Overshadowing the road stood, in a grotto of the rock wall of Monte Solare, the Holy Virgin, all radiant, bathed in the warmth and the splendor of the sun. The rust of her snow-white plaster-of-Paris vestures and queenly crown was touched into gold; and there were meekness and mercy in her eyes raised toward the heavens, toward the eternal and beatific abode of her thrice-blessed Son. They bared their heads, applied the pipes to their lips, and praises flowed on, candid and humbly-joyous, praises to the sun and the morning, to Her, the Immaculate Intercessor for all who suffer in this evil and beautiful world, and to Him who had been born of her womb in the cavern of Bethlehem, in a hut of lowly shepherds in distant Judea.

As for the body of the dead Gentleman from San Francisco, it was on its way home, to the shores of the New World, where a grave awaited it. Having undergone many humiliations and suffered much human neglect, having wandered about a week from one port warehouse to another, it finally got on that same famous ship which had brought the family, such a short while ago and with such a pomp, to the Old World. But now he was concealed from the living: in a tar-coated coffin he was lowered deep into the black hold of the steamer. And again did the ship set out on its far sea journey. At night it sailed by the island of Capri; and, for those who watched it from the island, its lights slowly disappearing in the dark sea, it seemed infinitely sad. But there, on the vast steamer, in its lighted halls shining with brilliance and marble, a noisy dancing party was going on, as usual.

On the second and the third night there was again a ball—this time in mid-ocean, during the furious storm sweeping over the ocean, which roared like a funeral mass and rolled up mountainous seas fringed with mourning silvery foam. The Devil, who from the rocks of Gibraltar, the stony gateway of two worlds, watched the ship vanish into night and storm, could hardly distinguish from behind the snow the innumerable fiery eyes of the ship. The Devil was as huge as a cliff, but the ship was even bigger, a many-storied, many-stacked giant, created by the arrogance of the New Man with the old heart. The blizzard battered the ship's rigging and its broad-necked stacks, whitened with snow; but it remained firm, majestic—and terrible. On its uppermost deck, amidst a snowy whirlwind there loomed up in loneliness the cozy, dimly lighted cabin, where, only half awake, the vessel's ponderous pilot reigned over its entire mass, bearing the semblance of a pagan idol. He heard the wailing moans and the furious screeching of the siren, choked by the storm; but the nearness of that which was behind the wall and which in the last account was incomprehensible to him, removed his fears. He was reassured by the thought of the large, armored cabin, which now and then was filled with mysterious rumbling sounds and with the dry creaking of blue fires, flaring up and exploding around a man with a metallic headpiece, who was eagerly catching the indistinct voices of the vessels that hailed him, hundreds of miles away. At the very bottom, in the underwater womb of the *Atlantis,* the huge masses of tanks and various other machines, their steel parts shining dully, wheezed with steam and oozed hot water and oil; here was the gigantic kitchen, heated by hellish furnaces, where the motion of the vessel was being generated; here seethed those forces terrible in their concentration which were transmitted to the keel of the vessel, by electricity, and looked like a gigantic cannon barrel, where slowly, with a punctuality and certainty that crushes the human soul, a colossal shaft was revolving in its oily nest, like a living monster stretching in its lair. As for the middle part of the *Atlantis,* its warm, luxurious cabins, dining-rooms, and halls, they radiated light and joy, were astir with a chattering smartly-dressed crowd, were filled with the fragrance of fresh flowers, and resounded with a string orchestra. And again did the slender supple pair of hired lovers painfully turn, twist, and at times clash convulsively amid the splendor of lights, silks, diamonds, and bare feminine shoulders: she—a sinfully modest pretty girl, with lowered eyelashes and an innocent hairdressing, he—a tall, young man, with black hair, looking as if it were pasted, pale with powder, in most exquisite patent-leather shoes, in a narrow-long-skirted dresscoat—a beautiful man resembling a leech. And no one knew that this couple had long since been weary of torturing themselves with a feigned beatific torture under the sounds of shamefully-melancholy music; nor did any one know what lay deep, deep, beneath them, in the very bottom of the hold, in the neighborhood of the gloomy and sultry maw of the ship, that heavily struggled with the ocean, the darkness, and the storm. . . .

STUDY GUIDE

Analysis

The theme, the basic idea of this story, is twentieth-century civilization has been dehumanized by materialism. The spiritual element that invested society with humane values and bound its members into corporate unity has been destroyed. The Christian affirmation that each man is his brother's keeper is cruelly mocked by the system of human relationship described in the story.

The *Atlantis,* the ship on which the Gentleman sails to Italy, is both a triumph of a materialistic civilization and a symbol of its cold heartlessness. It is a thing of power, but steel compartments shut off human beings from one another. In the radiant dining hall the Gentleman and the other members of the class "upon which depend all the blessings of civilization" sip rich wines; in the hold "the stokers, stripped to the waist, and purple with reflected flames, are bathed in their own dirty, acid sweat"; the lookouts "in their towers froze and almost went out of their minds."

The diseased condition of society is evidenced also in its artificiality. A young couple hired by the shipowners wearily play their role as lovers. The daughter of the Gentleman ("her breath was sweet with violet-scented tablets") thrills to the proximity of a wretched little man who possesses a title. She pretends not to notice her father who stands nearby, ogling a painted Parisian who addresses herself to a "peeled-off dog." Mechanically and joylessly the Gentleman and his family follow out their itinerary. The hotel servants, who hug the wall when the Gentleman meets them in the corridors, are always obsequiously courteous; but their regard is completely feigned. In a brief moment of perception even the Gentleman from San Francisco glimpses the bleakness of the unnatural system of human relationships that passes for society. "It's terrible," he muttered, and repeated with conviction, "It's terrible."

How terrible the system is becomes evident only after the Gentleman, preparing for the great materialistic ritual of dinner, succumbs to a heart attack. Hastily removed to the smallest, meanest room of the hotel, he passes away while "his wife and daughter, the doctors, the servants were standing and watching him apathetically." The hotel owner firmly refuses to permit the body to be returned to the room that had been engaged by the Gentleman. The proprietor states that there will be no time to make a coffin; he "gets English soda-water in big oblong boxes. . . . The partitions could be taken out from such a box. . . ."

In grim irony, the body of the Gentleman is taken away in an empty soda box. Past the stone house of Tiberius Caesar is carted the remains of one of those who "ruled the world as incomprehensibly and, essentially, as cruelly" as did Tiberius. But the world they rule is not of necessity a cruel and ugly place. Indeed, Bunin is eager to point out that it is ineffably beautiful:

> . . . the entire country, joyous, beautiful, sunny, stretched below them; the rocky shoulders of the island, which lay at their feet, the fabulous blue in which it swam, the shining morning vapors over the sea westward, beneath the dazzling sun, and wavering masses of Italy's mountains, both near and distant, whose beauty human word is powerless to render. . . .

Nor is human life intended to be ugly and cruel. Two simple peasants walk along a Capri road.

> Overshadowing the road stood, in a grotto of the rock wall of the Monte Solare, the Holy Virgin, all radiant, bathed in the warmth and splendor of the sun. The rust of her snow-white plaster-of-Paris vestures and queenly crown was touched into gold, and there were meekness and mercy in her eyes raised toward the heavens, toward the eternal and beatific abode of her thrice-blessed Son. They bared their heads, applied the pipes to their lips, and praises flowed on, candid and humbly—joyous praises to the sun and the morning, to her, the Immaculate Intercessor for all who suffer in this evil and beautiful world, and to Him who had been born of her womb in the cavern of Bethlehem, in a hut of lowly shepherds in distant Judea.

But in shaping their world the Gentleman and his class ignored the Judean Message. Their world is built upon physical values alone; in it they degraded their brothers and they themselves became joyless automatons. The Gentleman's body after being shunted from one port warehouse to another, finally is lowered deep into the hold of the *Atlantis* for return to the New World. In the engine room nearby, the great steel mechanism transmits its terrible forces to the colossal haft that revolves "with a punctuality and certainty that crushes the human soul." Here, in the engine room, we see an epitome of the society that was created by the Gentleman and his class at the beginning of the century. It is powerful and efficient but it "crushes the human soul."

Interpretation

A short story, says Cleanth Brooks, is a "tissue of significances." The writer has arranged a series of imagined incidents so that when we put them together they bring us, not only a human experience, but also they provide us with some understanding of human life. If we get only a portion of the author's revelation, we shall have only a portion of the experience he attempted to bring us. To guard against this we must read very attentively, remembering that the writer in his characterization, plot, and setting is constantly sending out a stream of signals as to what he means. Bunin, for example, does not give his leading character a name—"neither at Naples nor on Capri could anyone recall his name"—because names are personal, humane; and Bunin is stressing the impersonal, inhuman cast of materialistic society. Moreover, what is founded on materialism does not endure. Chaucer, writing five hundred years before Bunin, supplies the name of almost every one of the Canterbury pilgrims except the materialistic merchant; that name he cannot recall. San Francisco is given as the origin of the Gentleman because California represented, at the turn of the century, the raw, energetic materialism of the New World. Boston had long ago developed a considerable culture; Cleveland had mellowed; but San Francisco in 1912 was a citadel of crude Philistinism.

We must be careful to consider all the signals, or the communication becomes distorted. If we fix upon the freezing lookouts, the sweating stokers, and the cringing servants we may be misled into the impression that Bunin is simply castigating the wealthy for their maltreatment of the poor. Such an interpretation would leave dozens of incidents unexplained. Bunin expressly points out that the Gentleman himself is caught in the soulless machinery miscalled society. "It's terrible," he mutters darkly in one moment of half-realization. He derives no joy from the town; the trip to Capri is a nightmare; and he is in despair when he looks at the miserable stone huts that dot the Italy he has come to see. But, more than anything else, the structure of the story rules out the class-struggle theme. The first third of the story treats of the ship crossing; the second third, of the Italian tour; the last third, of the treatment accorded the Gentleman's corpse. If Bunin had been preoccupied with the class struggle, he would have ended his story with the death rattles in the Gentleman's throat. But to do this would be to leave his assertion incomplete. He patiently traces the undignified transit of the Gentleman's remains from the mean hotel room to its place in the dark hold of the ship. The cold inhuman system is all the more sharply demonstrated because its victim is a man who helped to shape it. In brief, Bunin uses the last third of the story to press upon us the fact that this materialistic society robs rich and poor alike of the dignity that belongs to creatures made in the image and likeness of God.

He loses no opportunity to stress this point. He selects winter as the season for his story because that season best reinforces the bleakness and coldness of a way of life based only on physical values. The headlines at which the Gentleman is looking when he is struck down tell of a war, another symptom of a diseased society.

The diction and imagery of the story supply further opportunities for the writer to concentrate on his message. Note, for example, the sentence describing the Gentleman's head. "There was something Mongolian in his yellowish face with its trimmed silvery moustache; his large teeth glimmered with gold fillings, and his strong bald head had a dull glow like old ivory." In a single sentence we meet with gold, silver, and ivory—all symbols of wealth, and all of them, like the Gentleman, hard. The adjective "Mongolian" brings to mind the Asiatic invaders who, centuries before, threatened Western civilization. The reference to "Large teeth" reinforces the predatory notion suggested by the adjective "Mongolian." The "yellowish" cast of the face both suggests disease and, because gold is yellow, hints at the nature of the disease. As another instance of the use of diction and imagery to further theme, note the terms in which the ship is described while the Devil is watching it pass Gibraltar. "The Devil was as huge as a cliff, but the ship was bigger, a many-storied, many-stacked giant, created by the arrogance of the New Man with the old heart." In comparing the ship to the Devil, Bunin is suggesting that this symbol of materialistic triumph is a thing of evil, that it is, indeed, a greater evil than men have known in the past. It is a "many-storied, many-stacked giant" with "fiery eyes"; in brief, it is, like a society with powerful body and shrivelled soul, a monstrosity.

Comparisons of Characters and Themes

An interesting comparison might be made between the character of the Gentleman from San Francisco and another gentleman described in the poem "Portrait" by Kenneth Fearing. In addition, students might read the drama *The Hairy Ape* by Eugene O'Neill and compare its view of social conditions with the treatment of this theme in "The Gentleman from San Francisco."

Note especially that Bunin and O'Neill both use the stratification of society on an ocean liner in developing this theme.

Norms for Evaluating Short Stories

In evaluating this, or any, short story the following norms, or measures, may be used. An excellent short story may be recognized by these norms:

1. *It involves a worthwhile idea.* In addition to the pleasure of the story the reader gains some new insight into or understanding of human life or human nature. This is not to say that the primary purpose of a piece of fiction is to teach a lesson. It is to say that any full-scaled human experience must engage the reader at the intellectual level.

2. *It is carefully integrated.* The story is made up of elements such as theme, plot, character, and setting, but all of these are tightly interrelated in their service of the basic idea.

3. *It reflects an awareness of the irony of life.* A competent writer does not paint his world in blacks and whites; he is willing to state the strongest case possible for the opposition. He never sets up straw men only to knock them over; the resolutions to his conflicts do not come readily or easily.

4. *It earns its emotional response by its own terms.* The characters provoke reactions in the reader directly by what they are and what they do. There is no necessity for the writer to provide stage directions telling the reader what he ought to feel (editorializing) or to prod him to feel more deeply than the situation warrants (sentimentalizing).

5. *It treats human beings as creatures possessed of intelligence and free will who determine their own fate for good or bad.* Such characters may fall, but they fall from a height. They do not fall off the floor, as must automatons jerked about by chance and instinct on a stage in which there are no moral dimensions.

MARY MULCAHY

Christopher La Farge

Lying quite still on her bed, so that the pain in her back was only a warning and not an actuality, Mary Mulcahy considered her problems. These were the matters of her back, of the broken novena, of Kathleen's hundred dollars, and most difficult to face, of this room. Whatever else she thought about, she was aware always of the room. Even while she lay thus, with her eyes closed, she could see its comforting detail, be aware of the fine light that swept in at the east window, of the huge ailanthus that grew in the next back yard. You might look and look in all that district of Manhattan and not find another room like this one, so convenient, so cheap, so clean and pretty, its own running water in the bright washbasin; a quiet room, in a jutting ell to an old house that looked out down the long reach of the back yards to trees and to privet bushes; a room into which the morning sun poured like a blessing from the dear Virgin.

Oh, but cheap as it was, it was the wasteful extravagance, surely! All the long summer, four solid months, she could, by living in one of the servants' rooms at the Park Avenue apartment where she worked, save the rent she was now paying. And so, without touching the savings that now mounted so slowly again toward security, she could set aside the money for Kathleen's wedding present. Hadn't she given a hundred dollars to the other nieces when they were married? To Rosie and to Agnes? But that was before the bad days, before the savings of a lifetime melted suddenly away. If you had asked her in 1929, she would have said she could stop work in another five years, living secure and content in such a room as this —if another such existed. Sixty years would have been the good age for stopping.

But there could be no stopping now. There was the present for Kathleen, and the savings that were so small, and always a little bit here and a little bit there for the blessed Church. You could not say no to a good man like Father Elliott, or to the sweet Sisters who knocked at your door, their lives in their faces, their smiles the reflection of the light of the Blessed Mother herself. She was lucky indeed to have so good a job; for taking care of the apartment in summer was within her powers and the half-days in winter were not that hard to do that she could not do them a while yet—if her back grew no worse. Last night it was so bad after she came home from the apartment that she had to lie down, as she had today; and, for all that her soul troubled her, she had stayed in her bed and so the novena was broken, and it in its eighth day. Surely Father Elliott would understand and be kind; there would be never a reproach to her; but within herself there was the knowledge that what she had set out to do for the glory of God and for the salvation of her own soul was left but partly done. It was like a warning, a portent. What if Mr. Gore, or indeed him and his wife too, should come to New York while she was like this now? How would she stand to fix their tea and to give them breakfast? Mrs. Gore was a beautiful, sweet woman and Mr. Gore the fine, big, strong man. It was a pleasure to make him comfortable and have things nice for him. They would be kind; they would understand; but wouldn't they say to themselves, "Mary Mulcahy is too old now"? Wouldn't they begin casting about for a young one who would not be ill to fail them?

I keep it clean and lovely, she thought, the lovely apartment; but if I am not there for them when they come, what good is the cleanness of it? It's well that I never married, indeed; for a fine wife I'd have been to the old husband in these the last years of his age.

So she lay on the bed, conscious of the warmth of the room, of its high ceiling, of the light beyond the window, the soft, glowing eastern light of the evening; and she felt the problems grow heavy in her breast. The smallness of the savings weighed and weighed on her; the present for Kathleen was a deadly weight; her back warned her, distantly but clearly, of the weight of her years. And behind it all, behind even the distress of the broken novena, lay the knowledge that if she gave up the room, lived in at the apartment, it would be all solved, all simple, and that once she let this room go, it would not be twenty-four hours before another would have it, and then, as sure as God was in His heaven, it would be gone forever. Weren't there people waiting for it now? Hadn't she waited for three years herself to get it? Hadn't she waited till Ellen Smith had died? Ellen had wanted never to move from it, and only death in the end had moved her. You live in house after house, room after room—life was a series of rooms in a long series of houses. Surely when a room at last said home to you, you had the good right to cling to it?

It was past six o'clock when she heard the knocking at her door. Something told her that the knocking had been going on for some time and that only now had she become fully conscious of it, and it frightened her.

"Come in," she called out. The door rattled.

"It's locked," said the mild voice of Mrs. Gustafson, her landlady.

It was necessary to rise, then, thought Mary Mulcahy. Slowly she began the process, easing herself up till she sat on the edge of her bed, pushing herself upright from there, one hand on her hip, the other hand clinging to the head of her bed. Her back ached painfully. Her left hand still pressed to her hip; she limped to the door, unlatched it and opened it.

"It's a telegram," said Mrs. Gustafson. "I'm sorry to get you up."

"A telegram!" cried Mary. "Oh!" she took the yellow envelope from Mrs. Gustafson. "Oh God!" She said.

"I hope it ain't some bad news," Mrs. Gustafson said patting her silver hair in the dusk of the hallway. "It's maybe nothing at all. Sometimes—"

"Aah," Mary said, "them things! You never know." She opened the envelope and read the message on the yellow slip aloud and slowly: " 'ARRIVED UNEXPECTEDLY AND SHALL SPEND THE NIGHT PLEASE BRING KEYS TO SILVER CLOSET.' It's himself. It's Mr. Gore."

"And you just home to rest!" said Mrs. Gustafson. "It's a shame!"

"No, no," Mary said. "He's a fine man. Sometimes he don't have a chance to send word before he has to come. I must go right around." She turned away.

"Can I help you?"

"Oh, no, I thank you," Mary said.

"You look sick, Miss Mulcahy."

"I'm all right," Mary said. "I'm all right. It's only I have the ache in my back. It's the weather, is all it is. It'll pass. It'll pass. It is nothing at all. I thank you for bringing up the telegram, Mrs. Gustafson."

"That's all right," Mrs. Gustafson said. "Let me know if I can help you. It's a shame when you were home already and lying down." She shut the door softly.

"Home already," Mary repeated as she put on her old black hat. Then she slipped her feet into a rather battered pair of white sneakers and left the room.

It was only six blocks to the apartment, so Mary walked it, as always. The beginning of the journey was worse than the end. She stopped at John O'Meara's and bought oranges and lemons and a pint of cream and a loaf of the Italian bread that Mr. Gore liked so well. Mr. Gore was waiting for her at the apartment when she let herself in at the kitchen entrance.

"Well, Mary," he said, "How are you?"

"Fine, fine," said Mary. "And how is yourself and the family?"

"All blooming," he said. "Sorry to rout you out like this. I'd no time to telegraph, even, till I arrived."

"Aah," she said, 'that's all right. That's all right. Will you have some tea now?"

"It's rather late," he said, looking at his watch.

"It'll do you good," she said.

"Well—it would. If it's not too much bother?"

"Not a bit of bother in the world," said Mary. "I'll have it for you in a minyute."

She bustled back to the kitchen, took off her hat and put on an apron, and made tea and toast. It was swiftly and competently done. She took the tray in to him, shuffling in her sneakers, the shuffling walk she had found was easier these days.

"And how is your niece, Kathleen?" he asked her.

"Fine, fine," said Mary. "She's to be wed in October."

"Indeed?" he said. "So soon? I could have wished she'd stayed on. Mrs. Gore liked her so much. A first-rate girl."

"Aah," said Mary, "the young ones today! They don't know when they're well off. All they think of is the men and the marrying."

"Natural enough," said Mr. Gore.

"To be sure," Mary said. "Natural enough. But there's many a one lives to regret it. She had a lovely place here, with lovely people; and she should have stayed in it. Then you know where you are. Aah, them young girls! They're all alike. What time will you be wanting breakfast, sir?"

"Call me at seven-thirty," he said, "Breakfast at eight. I'm off for home again tomorrow. I'll try to give you warning next time I come up. Leave the key of the silver closet on my dresser, will you? I'll give it back in the morning."

"I will," she said. "I will. Is there anything else now?"

"No," he said. "Good night, Mary. You toddle along home. I'll be out of here in half an hour."

"Good night, sir," she said.

She went to his bedroom then and turned down the bed for him, unpacked his bag, and laid out his toilet things and his pajamas. She drew him a warm bath and checked to be sure there were plenty of clean towels. She was pleased now that she'd put the fine, embroidered sheets on his bed, but it was lucky Mrs. Gore wasn't here too, for there'd only been the one pair home from the wash and on her bed were the plain ones. Then Mary went to the kitchen, made herself some tea, and sat down to wait for him to go. It was a long wait. She sat in a wooden chair instead of the upholstered wicker one, because it was easier to get up from, with her back and all, if he should ring for her.

When he had gone out at last she went to his room and hung up his suit, treed his shoes, and laid his underclothes neatly, ready for the morning. Then she cleaned the bathroom and straightened it up and rinsed out the tub, though that was painful, so painful it was frightening. But she was too busy to be really frightened. Then she collected the tea things and washed them and put ice in the ice carafe in the living room. She set out a tray with glasses and whisky and the carafe in the living room. She emptied his ashtray and plumped the cushions. When everything was done, when the apartment was as neat as a pin, proper and comfortable for his return, she looked around her and felt a sort of panic. Her occupations were over. There was nothing to divert her mind from her troubles now.

I'll stay here, she thought. I'll never get home and back. There's Cook's bed I can lie upon. That's the best.

Here she could lie down, lie down indeed. When she got up again, for all the pain, she would be here, where she had to be. There would be no stairs up, no stairs down, no six blocks to walk. She got a blanket from a bureau drawer and unrolled the mattress on the bed in the little, dark, viewless bedroom. Then she took off her sneakers, lay down on the bed, and pulled the one blanket over her. Lying there, she said her prayers twice through and begged the good God and His lovely Son and the Merciful Mother of Christ to forgive her that she hadn't the strength left in her to kneel to Their worship. When she lay still, her back was only a portent of pain.

In the morning, before Mr. Gore had left, Mary Mulcahy came to her decision. She told him merely that she was going to give up her room and sleep at the apartment. "Till you and Madam come back in October," she said.

"That's good," he said. "I should think that much more convenient and economical."

"It is, it is," she said. That was all. There was no use bothering him with your own little problems and him probably bowed down with his great ones. And how could you tell a man in his lovely ten-room apartment what a room in a rooming house might mean to you?

When she had everything clean and in order, she put on her hat and left the apartment. On her way home she went by way of St. Anthony's, entered the church, and, going to the Lady Chapel, she knelt there and said many prayers and many of them over. She prayed the Virgin for strength to continue and for forgiveness for her sins. If she had seen Father Elliott, she would have told him about her back and the novena; but there was no one around but the old sacristan, dusting and dusting. All he did, she thought, was move the blessed dust from one place to another. Then she left and walked home.

When she had packed her two old, battered suitcases, she found Mrs. Gustafson in her kitchen.

"I've got to go," she said. "I've got to give up the room. I must live in till October."

"Oh!" cried Mrs. Gustafson. "Why, Miss Mulcahy, I thought you would be here for always now."

"It's a lovely room," Mary said. "A lovely, lovely room. But it's my niece is to be married and so on and so on. And my people come often to the apartment and all."

"Well," said Mrs. Gustafson. "If you must, you must. I hate to have you going, Miss Mulcahy. Till October, you say?"

"Till October," Mary said. "That's the truth. I'll want a room then, if you've a vacancy, Mrs. Gustafson. Here's what I owe you." She held out a small wad of crumpled bills.

Mrs. Gustafson took it and counted it. "That's right," she said, and smiled. "We'll be waiting for you. Good-by. Good luck."

"Good-by," Mary said.

She said the same thing in a whisper to her room as she left it. The leavetaking was not prolonged. That would have been sinful, and useless. She picked up the two bags and looked at the room around her and said, in a whisper, "Good-by." That was all. Then she began the painful descent of the stairs. The pain reassured her now. It was so right to go. She opened the front door and stepped out onto the high stoop. She was just going to close the door behind her when Mrs. Gustafson appeared.

"See," said Mrs. Gustafson awkwardly. "We are not young now. Life ain't all money, money. Isn't it? When you come back to me, when you come back in October, the little room will be for you. So."

"Aah," Mary said. "My room! God will remember you, Mrs. Gustafson. It's a lovely thing, it is. A lovely thing. You put the heart back into me."

"It is nothing," said Mrs. Gustafson. "Till October, when you come home. We will expect you, Miss Mulcahy. So long." She closed the door then, rather abruptly.

Mary picked up the suitcases again and descended the stoop. There were tears in her eyes and she had to stop when she reached the sidewalk, put down the cases, and wipe her eyes. "The kind woman," she said aloud. "The lovely, kind woman."

John O'Meara's delivery boy, Julian, pushing his cart, stopped beside her.

"You off to the apartment, Miss Mulcahy?" he said.

"I am," she said. "I am. Good morning, Julian."

"I'll put your bags in and take them up," he said.

"Aah," she said, "it's out of your way, then."

"No," he said. "Never a bit." He took the two suitcases and put them in his cart and together they began walking toward Park Avenue, he in his thick shoes, lightly, as a young man; she in her white sneakers, shuffling.

"The Lord is my shepherd," said Mary Mulcahy.

STUDY GUIDE

1. What is the problem confronting Mary Mulcahy?

2. Why does she wish to retain her room at Mrs. Gustafson's through the summer?

3. How does Kathleen's wedding present bear on the problem?

4. How does Mary Mulcahy's aching back bear on the problem?

5. What kind of man is Mr. Gore? What is Mary's estimate of him as stated? How is her estimate implied in her actions, particularly in her decision about the room?

6. How is the little conversation between Mary and Mr. Gore functional in the story? What does it tell the reader about Mr. Gore? About Mary's attitude toward her job? About what factor in Mary's problem does it remind the reader? What does it suggest about the relationship between Kathleen and the Gores?

7. Why doesn't Mary tell Mr. Gore about the room problem that is vexing her? About the distress her back is causing her?

8. Why doesn't La Farge end his story with Mary's decision? What two additional human relationships does he wish his readers to see? What is the nature of these relationships? What is the nature of the relationship between Mary Mulcahy and the Gores? What characterizes all three relationships that you see in the story?

9. Compare the human relationships you meet in this story with those you met in "The Gentleman from San Francisco."

10. What is the source of the toxin with which the Gentleman poisons the human relationships around him?

11. Is there such a thing as "good infection"? Is Mary Mulcahy a carrier of good infection?

12. What is the source of Mary's good infection? Is the expression that closes the story, "The Lord is my shepherd," merely a pious ejaculation, or is it the key to Mary Mulcahy and the good infection she spreads?

13. Write a paper in which you make a comparison between the character of Achilles in the *Iliad* and that of the Gentleman from San Francisco, Mr. Gore, and Mary Mulcahy.

THE SCULPTOR'S FUNERAL

Willa Cather

A group of the townspeople stood on the station siding of a little Kansas town, awaiting the coming of the night train, which was already twenty minutes overdue. The snow had fallen thick over everything; in the pale starlight the line of bluffs across the wide, white meadows south of the town made soft-smoke-coloured curves against the clear sky. The men on the siding stood first on one foot and then on the other, their hands thrust deep into their trousers pockets, their overcoats open, their shoulders screwed up with the cold; and they glanced from time to time toward the southeast, where the railroad track wound along the river shore. They conversed in low tones and moved about restlessly, seeming uncertain as to what was expected of them. There was but one of the company who looked as if he knew exactly why he was there, and he kept conspicuously apart; walking to the far end of the platform, returning to the station door, then pacing up the track again, his chin sunk in the high collar of his overcoat, his burly shoulders drooping forward, his gait heavy and dogged. Presently he was approached by a tall, spare, grizzled man clad in a faded Grand Army suit, who shuffled out from the group and advanced with a certain deference, craning his neck forward until his back made the angle of a jack-knife three-quarters open.

"I reckon she's a-goin' to be pretty late agin tonight, Jim," he remarked in a squeaky falsetto. "S'pose it's the snow?"

"I don't know, responded the other man with a shade of annoyance, speaking from out an astonishing cataract of red beard that grew fiercely and thickly in all directions.

The spare man shifted the quill toothpick he was chewing to the other side of his mouth. "It ain't likely that anybody from the East will come with the corpse, I s'pose," he went on reflectively.

Reprinted from *Youth and the Bright Medusa*, by Willa Cather, courtesy of Alfred A. Knopf, Inc.

"I don't know," responded the other, more curtly than before.

"It's too bad he didn't belong to some lodge or other. I like an order funeral myself. They seem more appropriate for people of some repytation," the spare man continued, with an ingratiating concession in his shrill voice, as he carefully placed his toothpick in his vest pocket. He always carried the flag at the G.A.R. funerals in the town.

The heavy man turned on his heel, without replying, and walked up the siding. The spare man rejoined the uneasy group. "Jim's ez full ez a tick, es ushel," he commented commiseratingly.

Just then a distant whistle sounded, and there was a shuffling of feet on the platform. A number of lanky boys, of all ages, appeared as suddenly and slimily as eels wakened by the crack of thunder; some came from the waiting-room, where they had been warming themselves by the red stove, or half asleep on the slat benches; others uncoiled themselves from baggage trucks or slid out of express wagons. Two clambered down from the driver's seat of a hearse that stood backed up against the siding. They straightened their stooping shoulders and lifted their heads, and a flash of momentary animation kindled their dull eyes at that cold, vibrant scream, the world-wide call for men. It stirred them like the note of a trumpet; just as it had often stirred the man who was coming home tonight, in his boyhood.

The night express shot, red as a rocket, from out the eastward marsh lands and wound along the river shore under the long lines of shivering poplars that sentinelled the meadows, the escaping steam hanging in grey masses against the pale sky and blotting out the Milky Way. In a moment the red glare from the headlight streamed up the snow-covered track before the siding and glittered on the wet, black rails. The burly man with the dishevelled red beard walked swiftly up the platform toward the approaching train, uncovering his head as he went. The group of men behind him hesitated, glanced questioningly at one another, and awkwardly followed his example. The train stopped, and the crowd shuffled up to the express car just as the door was thrown open, the man in the G.A.R. suit thrusting his head forward with curiosity. The express messenger appeared in the doorway, accompanied by a young man in a long ulster and travelling cap.

"Are Mr. Merrick's friends here?" inquired the young man.

The group on the platform swayed uneasily. Philip Phelps, the banker, responded with dignity: "We have come to take charge of the body. Mr. Merrick's father is very feeble and can't be about."

"Send the agent out here," growled the express messenger, "and tell the operator to lend a hand."

The coffin was got out of its rough-box and down on the snowy platform. The townspeople drew back enough to make room for it and then formed a close semicircle about it, looking curiously at the palm leaf which lay across the black cover. No one said anything. The baggage man stood by his truck, waiting to get at the trunks. The engine panted heavily, and the fireman dodged in and out among the wheels with his yellow torch and long oil-can, snapping the spindle boxes. The young Bostonian, one of the dead sculptor's pupils who had come with the body, looked about him helplessly. He turned to the banker, the only one of that black, uneasy, stoop-shouldered group who seemed enough of an individual to be addressed.

"None of Mr. Merrick's brothers are here?" he asked uncertainly.

The man with the red beard for the first time stepped up and joined the others. "No, they have not come yet; the family is scattered. The body will be taken directly to the house." He stooped and took hold of one of the handles of the coffin.

"Take the long hill road up, Thompson, it will be easier on the horses," called the liveryman as the undertaker snapped the door of the hearse and prepared to mount to the driver's seat.

Laird, the red-bearded lawyer, turned again to the stranger: "We didn't know whether there would be any one with him or not," he explained. "It's a long walk, so you'd better go up in the hack." He pointed to a single battered conveyance, but the young man replied stiffly: "Thank you, but I think I will go up with the hearse. If you don't object," turning to the undertaker, "I'll ride with you."

They clambered up over the wheels and drove off in the starlight up the long, white hill toward the town. The lamps in the still village were shining from under the low, snow-burdened roofs; and beyond, on every side, the plains reached out into emptiness, peaceful and wide as the soft sky itself, and wrapped in a tangible, white silence.

When the hearse backed up to a wooden sidewalk before a naked, weather-beaten frame house, the same composite, ill-defined group that had stood upon the station siding was huddled about the gate. The front yard was an icy swamp, and a couple of warped planks, extending from the sidewalk to the door, made a sort of rickety foot-bridge. The gate hung on one hinge, and was opened wide with difficulty. Steavens, the young stranger, noticed that something black was tied to the knob of the front door.

The grating sound made by the casket, as it was drawn from the hearse, was answered by a scream from the house; the front door was wrenched open, and a tall, corpulent woman rushed out bareheaded into the snow and flung herself upon the coffin, shrieking: "My boy, my boy! And this is how you've come home to me!"

As Steavens turned away and closed his eyes with a shudder of unutterable repulsion, another woman, also tall, but flat and angular, dressed entirely in black, darted out of the house and caught Mrs. Merrick by the shoulders, crying sharply: "Come, come, mother; you mustn't go on like this!" Her tone changed to one of obsequious solemnity as she turned to the banker: "The parlour is ready, Mr. Phelps."

The bearers carried the coffin along the narrow boards, while the undertaker ran ahead with the coffin-rests. They bore it into a large, unheated room that smelled of dampness and disuse and furniture polish, and set it down under a hanging lamp ornamented with jingling glass prisms and before a "Rogers group" of John Alden and Priscilla, wreathed with smilax. Henry Steavens stared about him with the sickening conviction that there had been a mistake, and that he had somehow arrived at the wrong destination. He looked at the clover-green Brussels, the fat plush upholstery, among the hand-painted china placques and panels and vases, for some mark of identification,—for something that might once conceivably have belonged to Harvey Merrick. It was not until he recognized his friend in the crayon portrait of a little boy in kilts and curls, hanging above the piano, that he felt willing to let any of these people approach the coffin.

"Take the lid off, Mr. Thompson; let me see my boy's face," wailed the elder woman between her sobs. This time Steavens looked fearfully, almost beseechingly into her face, red and swollen under its masses of strong, black, shiny hair. He flushed, dropped his eyes, and then, almost incredulously, looked again. There was a kind of power about her face—a kind of brutal handsomeness even; but it was scarred and furrowed by violence, and so coloured and coarsened by fiercer passions that grief seemed never to have laid a gentle finger there. The long nose was distended and knobbed at the end, and there were deep lines on either side of it; her heavy, black brows almost met across her forehead, her teeth were large and square, and set far apart—teeth that could tear. She filled the room; the men were obliterated, seemed tossed about like twigs in an angry water, and even Steavens felt himself being drawn into the whirlpool.

The daughter—the tall, raw-boned woman in crepe, with a mourning comb in her hair which curiously lengthened her long face—sat stiffly upon the sofa, her hands, conspicuous for their large knuckles, folded in her lap, her mouth and eyes drawn down, solemnly awaiting the opening of the coffin. Near the door stood a mulatto woman, evidently a servant in the house, with a timid bearing and an emaciated face pitifully sad and gentle. She was weeping silently, the corner of her calico apron lifted to her eyes, occasionally suppressing a long, quivering sob. Steavens walked over and stood beside her.

Feeble steps were heard on the stairs, and an old man, tall and frail, odorous of pipe smoke, with shaggy unkept grey hair and a dingy beard, tobacco stained about the mouth, entered uncertainly. He went slowly up to the coffin and stood rolling a blue cotton handkerchief between his hands, seeming so pained and embarrassed by his wife's orgy of grief that he had no consciousness of anything else.

"There, there, Annie, dear, don't take on so," he quavered timidly, putting out a shaking hand and awkwardly patting her elbow. She turned and sank upon his shoulder with such violence that he tottered a little. He did not even glance toward the coffin, but continued to look at her with a dull, frightened, appealing expression, as a spaniel looks at the whip. His sunken cheeks slowly reddened and burned with miserable shame. When his wife rushed from the room, her daughter strode after her with set lips. The servant stole up to the coffin, bent over it for a moment, and then slipped away to the kitchen, leaving Steavens, the lawyer, and the father to themselves. The old man stood looking down at his dead son's face. The sculptor's splendid head seemed even more noble in its rigid stillness than in life. The dark hair had crept down upon the wide forehead; the face seemed strangely long, but in it there was not that repose we expect to find in the faces of the dead. The brows were so drawn that there were two deep lines above the beaked nose, and the chin was thrust forward defiantly. It was as though the strain of life had been so sharp and bitter that death could not at once relax the tension and smooth the countenance ino perfect peace—as though he were still guarding something precious, which might even yet be wrested from him.

The old man's lips were working under his stained beard. He turned to the lawyer with timid deference: "Phelps and the rest are comin' back to set up with Harve, ain't they?" he asked. "Thank 'ee, Jim, thank 'ee." He brushed the hair back gently from his son's forehead. "He was a good boy, Jim; always a good boy. He was ez gentle ez a child and the kindest of 'em all—only we didn't none of us ever onderstand him." The tears trickled slowly down his beard and dropped upon the sculptor's coat.

"Martin, Martin! Oh, Martin! come here," his wife wailed from the top of the stairs. The old man started timorously: "Yes, Annie, I'm coming." He turned away, hesitated, stood for a moment in miserable indecision; then reached back and patted the dead man's hair softly, and stumbled from the room.

"Poor old man, I didn't think he had any tears left. Seems as if his eyes would have gone dry long ago. At his age nothing cuts very deep," remarked the lawyer.

Something in his tone made Steavens glance up. While the mother had been in the room, the young man had scarcely seen any one else; but now, from the moment he first glanced into Jim Laird's florid face and bloodshot eyes, he knew that he had found what he had been heartsick at not finding before—the feeling, the understanding, that must exist in some one, even here.

The man was red as his beard, with features swollen and blurred by dissipation, and a hot, blazing blue eye. His face was strained—that of a man who is controlling himself with difficulty—and he kept plucking at his beard with a sort of fierce resentment. Steavens, sitting by the window, watched him turn down the glaring lamp, still its jangling pendants with an angry gesture, and then stand with his hands locked behind him, staring down into the master's face. He could not help wondering what link there had been between the porcelain vessel and so sooty a lump of potter's clay.

From the kitchen an uproar was sounding; when the dining-room door opened, the import of it was clear. The mother was abusing the maid for having forgotten to make the dressing for the chicken salad which had been prepared for the watchers. Steavens had never heard anything in the least like it; it was injured, emotional, dramatic abuse, unique and masterly in its excruciating cruelty, as violent and unrestrained as had been her grief of twenty minutes before. With a shudder of disgust the lawyer went into the dining-room and closed the door into the kitchen.

"Poor Roxy's getting it now," he remarked when he came back. "The Merricks took her out of the poor-house years ago; and if her loyalty would let her, I guess the poor old thing could tell tales that would curdle your blood. She's the mulatto woman who was standing in here a while ago, with her apron to her eyes. The old woman is a fury; there never was anybody like her. She made Harvey's life a hell for him when he lived at home; he was so sick ashamed of it. I never could see how he kept himself sweet."

"He was wonderful," said Steavens slowly, "wonderful; but until tonight I have never known how wonderful."

"That is the eternal wonder of it, anyway; that it can come even from such a dung heap as this," the lawyer cried, with a sweeping gesture which seemed to indicate much more than the four walls within which they stood.

"I think I'll see whether I can get a little air. The room is so close I am beginning to feel rather faint," murmured Steavens, struggling with one of the windows. The sash was stuck, however, and would not yield, so he sat down dejectedly and began pulling at his collar. The lawyer came over, loosened the sash with one blow of his red fist and sent the window up a few inches. Steavens thanked him, but the nausea which had been gradually climbing into his throat for the last half hour left him with but one desire—a desperate feeling that he must get away from this place with what was left of Harvey Merrick. Oh, he comprehended well enough now the quiet bitterness of the smile that he had seen so often on his master's lips!

Once when Merrick returned from a visit home, he brought with him a singularly feeling and suggestive bas-relief of a thin, faded old woman, sitting and sewing something pinned to her knee; while a full-lipped, full-blooded little urchin, his trousers held up by a single gallows, stood beside her, impatiently twitching her gown to call her attention to a butterfly he had caught. Steavens, impressed by the tender and delicate modelling of the thin, tired face, had asked him if it were his mother. He remembered the dull flush that had burned up in the sculptor's face.

The lawyer was sitting in a rocking-chair beside the coffin, his head thrown back and his eyes closed. Steavens looked at him earnestly, puzzled at the line of the chin, and wondering why a man should conceal a feature of such distinction under that disfiguring shock of beard. Suddenly, as though he felt the young sculptor's keen glance, Jim Laird opened his eyes.

"Was he always a good deal of an oyster?" he asked abruptly. "He was terribly shy as a boy."

"Yes, he was an oyster, since you put it so," rejoined Steavens. "Although he could be very fond of people, he always gave one the impression of being detached. He disliked violent emotion; he was reflective, and rather distrustful of himself—except, of course, as regarded his work. He was sure enough there. He distrusted men pretty thoroughly and women even more, yet somehow without believing ill of them. He was determined, indeed, to believe the best; but he seemed afraid to investigate."

"A burnt dog dreads the fire," said the lawyer grimly, and closed his eyes.

Steavens went on and on, reconstructing that whole miserable boyhood. All this raw, biting ugliness had been the portion of the man whose mind was to become an exhaustless gallery of beautiful impressions—so sensitive that the mere shadow of a poplar leaf flickering against a sunny wall would be etched and held there for ever. Surely, if ever a man had the magic word in his finger tips, it was Merrick. Whatever he touched, he revealed its holiest secret; liberated it from enchantment and restored it to its pristine loveliness. Upon whatever he had come in contact with, he had left a beautiful record of the experience—a sort of ethereal signature; a scent, a sound, a colour that was his own.

Steavens understood now the real tragedy of his master's life; neither love nor wine, as many had conjectured; but a blow which had fallen earlier and cut deeper than anything else could have done—a shame not his, and yet so unescapably his, to hide in his heart from his very boyhood.

And without—the frontier warfare; the yearning of a boy, cast ashore upon a desert of newness and ugliness and sordidness, for all that is chastened and old, and noble with traditions.

At eleven o'clock the tall, flat woman in black announced that the watchers were arriving, and asked them to "step into the dining-room." As Steavens rose, the lawyer said dryly: "You go on—it'll be a good experience for you. I'm not equal to that crowd tonight; I've had twenty years of them."

As Steavens closed the door after him he glanced back at the lawyer, sitting by the coffin in the dim light, with his chin resting on his hand.

The same misty group that had stood before the door of the express car shuffled into the dining-room. In the light of the kerosene lamp they separated and became individuals. The minister, a pale, feeble-looking man with white hair and blond chin-whiskers, took his seat beside a small side table and placed his Bible upon it. The Grand Army man sat down behind the stove and tilted his chair back comfortably against the wall, fishing his quill toothpick from his waistcoat pocket. The two bankers, Phelps and Elder, sat off in a corner behind the dinner-table, where they could finish their discussion of the new usury law and its effect on chattel security loans. The real estate agent, an old man with a smiling, hypocritical face, soon joined them. The coal and lumber dealer and the cattle shipper sat on opposite sides of the hard coal-burner, their feet on the nickel-work. Steavens took a book from his pocket and began to read. The talk around him ranged through various topics of local interest while the house was quieting down. When it was clear that the members of the family were in bed, the Grand Army man hitched his shoulders and, untangling his long legs, caught his heels on the rounds of his chair.

"S'pose there'll be a will, Phelps?" he queried in his weak falsetto.

The banker laughed disagreeably, and began trimming his nails with a pearl-handled pocket-knife.

"There'll scarcely be any need for one, will there?" he queried in his turn.

The restless Grand Army man shifted his position again, getting his knees still nearer his chin. "Why, the ole man says Harve's done right well lately," he chirped.

The other banker spoke up. "I reckon he means by that Harve ain't asked him to mortgage any more farms lately, so as he could go on with his education."

"Seems like my mind don't reach back to a time when Harve wasn't bein' edycated," tittered the Grand Army man.

There was a general chuckle. The minister took out his handkerchief and blew his nose sonorously. Banker Phelps closed his knife with a snap. "It's too bad the old man's sons didn't turn out better," he remarked with reflective authority. "They never hung together. He spent money enough on Harve to stock a dozen cattle-farms, and he might as well have poured it into Sand Creek. If Harve had stayed at home and helped nurse what little they had, and gone into stock on the old man's bottom farm, they might all have been well fixed. But the old man had to trust everything to tenants and was cheated right and left."

"Harve never could have handled stock none," interposed the cattleman. "He hadn't it in him to be sharp. Do you remember when he bought Sander's mules for eight-year olds, when everybody in town knew that Sander's father-in-law give 'em to his wife for a wedding present eighteen years before, an' they was full-grown mules then?"

The company laughed discreetly, and the Grand Army man rubbed his knees with a spasm of childish delight.

"Harve never was much account for anything practical, and he shore was never fond of work," began the coal and lumber dealer. "I mind the last time he was home; the day he left, when the old man was out to the barn helpin' his hand hitch up to take Harve to the train, and Cal Moots was patchin' up the fence; Harve, he come out on the step and sings out, in his ladylike voice: 'Cal Moots, Cal Moots! please come cord my trunk.' "

"That's Harve for you," approved the Grand Army man. "I kin hear him howlin' yet, when he was a big feller in long pants and his mother used to whale him with a rawhide in the barn for lettin' the cows git foundered in the cornfield when he was drivin' 'em home from pasture. He killed a cow of mine that-a-way onct—a pure Jersey and the best milker I had, an' the ole man had to put up for her. Harve, he was watching the sun set acrost the marshes when the anamile got away."

"Where the old man made his mistake was in sending the boy East to school," said Phelps, stroking his goatee and speaking in a deliberate, judicial tone. "There was where he got his head full of nonsense. What Harve needed, of all people, was a course in some first-class Kansas City business college."

The letters were swimming before Steavens's eyes. Was it possible that these men did not understand, that the palm on the coffin meant nothing to them? The very name of their town would have remained for ever buried in the postal guide had it not been now and again mentioned in the world in connection with Harvey Merrick's. He remembered what his master had said to him on the day of his death, after the congestion of both lungs had shut off any probability of recovery, and the sculptor had asked his pupil to send his body home. "It's not a pleasant place to be lying while the world is moving and doing and bettering," he had said with a feeble smile, "but it rather seems as though we ought to go back to the place we came from, in the end. The townspeople will come in for a look at me; and after they have had their say, I shan't have much to fear from the judgment of God!"

The cattleman took up the comment. "Forty's young for a Merrick to cash in; they usually hang on pretty well. Probably he helped it along with whisky."

"His mother's people were not long lived, and Harvey never had a robust constitution," siad the minister mildly. He would have liked to say more. He had been the boy's Sunday-school teacher, and had been fond of him; but he felt that he was not in a position to speak. His own sons had turned out badly, and it was not a year since one of them had made his last trip home in the express car, shot in a gambling-house in the Black Hills.

"Nevertheless, there is no disputin' that Harve frequently looked upon the wine when it was red, also variegated, and it shore made an oncommon fool of him," moralized the cattleman.

Just then the door leading into the parlour rattled loudly and every one started involuntarily, looking relieved when only Jim Laird came out. The Grand Army man ducked his head when he saw the spark in his blue, blood-shot eye. They were all afraid of Jim; he was a drunkard, but he could twist the law to suit his client's needs as no other man in all western Kansas could do, and there were many who tried. The lawyer closed the door behind him, leaned back against it and folded his arms, cocking his head a little to one side. When he assumed this attitude in the court-room, ears were always pricked up, as it usually foretold a flood of withering sarcasm.

"I've been with you gentlemen before," he began in a dry, even tone, "when you've sat by the coffins of boys born and raised in this town; and, if I remember rightly, you were never any too well satisfied when you checked them up. What's the matter, anyhow? Why is it that reputable young men are as scarce as millionaires in Sand City? It might almost seem to a stranger that there was some way something the matter with your progressive town. Why did Ruben Sayer, the brightest young lawyer you ever turned out, after he had come home from the university as straight as a die, take to drinking and forge a check and shoot himself? Why did Bill Merrit's son die of the shakes in the saloon in Omaha? Why was Mr. Thomas's son, here, shot in a gambling-house? Why did young Adams burn his mill to beat the insurance companies and go to the pen?"

The lawyer paused and unfolded his arms, laying one clenched fist quietly on the table. "I'll tell you why. Because you drummed nothing but money and knavery into their ears from the time they wore knickerbockers; because you carped away at them as you've been carping here tonight, holding our friends Phelps and Elder up to them for their models, as our grandfathers held up George Washington and John Adams. But the boys were young, and raw at the business you put them to, and how could they match coppers with such artists as Phelps and Elder? You wanted them to be successful rascals; they were only unsuccessful ones—that' all the difference. There was only one boy ever raised in this borderland between ruffianism and civilization who didn't come to grief, and you hated Harvey Merrick more for winning out than you hated all the other boys who got under the wheels. Lord, Lord, how you did hate him! Phelps, here, is fond of saying that he could buy and sell us all out any time he's a mind to; but he knew Harve wouldn't have given a tinker's damn for his bank and all his cattlefarms put together; and a lack of appreciation, that way, goes hard with Phelps.

"Old Nimrod thinks Harve drank too much; and this from such as Nimrod and me!

"Brother Elder says Harve was too free with the old man's money—fell short in filial consideration, maybe. Well, we can all remember the very tone in which brother Elder swore his own father was a liar, in the county court; and we all know that the old man came out of that partnership with his son as bare as a sheared lamb. But maybe I'm getting personal, and I'd better be driving ahead at what I want to say."

The lawyer paused a moment, squared his heavy shoulders, and went on: "Harvey Merrick and I went to school together, back East. We were dead in earnest, and we wanted you all to be proud of us some day. We meant to be great men. Even I, and I haven't lost my sense of humour, gentlemen, I meant to be a great man. I came back here to practise, and I found you didn't in the least want me to be a great man. You wanted me to be a shrewd lawyer—oh, yes! Our veteran here wanted me to get him an increase of pension, because he had dyspepsia; Phelps wanted a new county survey that would put the widow Wilson's little bottom farm inside his south line; Elder wanted to lend money at 5 per cent. a month, and get it collected; and Stark here wanted to wheedle old women up in Vermont into investing their annuities in real-estate mortgages that are not worth the paper they are written on. Oh, you needed me hard enough, and you'll go on needing me!

"Well, I came back here and became the damned shyster you wanted me to be. You pretend to have some sort of respect for me; and yet you'll stand up and throw mud at Harvey Merrick, whose soul you couldn't dirty and whose hands you couldn't tie. Oh, you're a discriminating lot of Christians! There have been times when the sight of Harvey's name in some Eastern paper has made me hang my head like a whipped dog; and, again, times when I liked to think of him off there in the world, away from all this hog-wallow, climbing the big, clean upgrade he'd set for himself.

"And we? Now that we've fought and lied and sweated and stolen, and hated as only the disappointed strugglers in a bitter, dead little Western town know how to do, what have we got to show for it? Harvey Merrick wouldn't have given one sunset over your marshes for all you've got put together, and you know it. It's not for me to say why, in the inscrutable wisdom of God, a genius should ever have been called from this place of hatred and bitter waters; but I want this Boston man to know that the drivel he's been hearing here tonight is the only tribute any truly great man could have from such a lot of sick, side-tracked, burnt-dog, land-poor sharks as the here-present financiers of Sand City—upon which town may God have mercy!"

The lawyer thrust out his hand to Steavens as he passed him, caught up his overcoat in the hall, and had left the house before the Grand Army man had had time to lift his ducked head and crane his long neck about at his fellows.

Next day Jim Laird was drunk and unable to attend the funeral services. Steavens called twice at his office, but was compelled to start East without seeing him. He had a presentiment that he would hear from him again, and left his address on the lawyer's table; but if Laird found it he never acknowledged it. The thing in him that Harvey Merrick had loved must have gone under ground with Harvey Merrick's coffin; for it never spoke again, and Jim got the cold he died of driving across the Colorado mountains to defend one of Phelps's sons who had got into trouble out there by cutting government timber.

STUDY GUIDE

1. Although this story is cntitled "The Sculptor's Funeral," it is as much centered on Jim Laird, the lawyer, as on Harvey Merrick. Laird is set apart from the rest of the townspeople at the very beginning. Show how Willa Cather creates this opposition in the opening of the story at the railroad station and intensifies it until the story reaches a climax when Laird faces the townspeople at the wake and gives his scathing evaluation of each of them. Since this was his judgment of his fellow townsmen, why did Laird stay there and why did he catch the cold from which he died "driving across the Colorado mountains to defend one of Phelp's sons who had got into trouble out there by cutting government timber"?

2. Although it is true that much of the dramatic tension centers around Jim Laird, the story is still about the sculptor's funeral because it is the funeral of the sculptor Harvey Merrick and his character, interests, talent, profession, achievements, and death that act as a kind of catalytic agent bringing into focus the characters and values of everyone else. Through the experience of his student at the wake the reader learns of the tension that existed in Harvey's own family—the destructive contrast between his domineering mother and vacillating father. Point out details of the description and action of the father and mother that masterfully reveal their character traits. How did each of them react to the career of Harvey? To his death? How do these reactions reveal their own characters?

3. Harvey's father remarks that "we didn't none of us ever onderstand

him." Is there any evidence in the story that the father came closer to understanding Harvey Merrick than anyone else in the family?

4. Do you see a parallel between the father and Jim Laird on the one hand and the mother, daughter, and the other townsfolk on the other in their relationship and attitudes toward Harvey?

5. Show some of the ways in which Miss Cather highlights the artistic sensitivities of Harvey from his earliest days and contrasted them with the gross insensitivities of most of his fellow townsfolk.

6. In this connection, what is the significance of the "bas-relief of a thin, faded old woman, sitting and sewing something pinned to her knee; while a full-lipped, full-blooded urchin, his trousers held up by a single gallows, stood beside her, impatiently twitching her gown to call her attention to a butterfly he had caught"?

7. Harvey had told his pupil before he died that when he had died "the townspeople will come in for a look at me; and after they have had their say, I shan't have much to fear from the judgment of God!" Relate this to what his townspeople actually did say about him at his wake. Was Harvey's evaluation of them accurate? How does it relate to Jim Laird's evaluation of them?

8. This story is noteworthy for its many expressive images. For example, why are the boy's waiting to meet the casket of Harvey at the railroad station appropriately compared to eels? Comment on the propriety of the images in the following passages: "She filled the room; the men obliterated, seemed tossed about *like twigs in an angry water*, and even Steavens felt himself *being drawn into the whirlpool*"; "he . . . continued to look at her with a dull, frightened, appealing expression, as a spaniel looks at the whip"; "he could not help wondering what link there had been between *the porcelain vessel* and *so sooty a lump of potter's clay*"; "*A burnt dog dreads the fire.*"

THE GREAT MOUNTAINS

John Steinbeck

In the humming heat of a midsummer afternoon the little boy Jody listlessly looked about the ranch for something to do. He had been to the barn, had thrown rocks at the swallows' nests under the eaves until every one of the little mud houses broke open and dropped its lining of straw and dirty feathers. Then at the ranch house he baited a rat trap with stale cheese and set it where Doubletree Mutt, that good big dog, would get his nose snapped. Jody was not moved by an impulse of cruelty; he was bored with the long hot afternoon. Doubletree Mutt put his stupid nose in the trap and got it smacked, and shrieked with agony and limped away with blood on his nostrils. No matter where he was hurt, Mutt limped. It was just a way he had. Once when he was young, Mutt got caught in a coyote trap, and always after that he limped, even when he was scolded.

When Mutt yelped, Jody's mother called from inside the house, "Jody! Stop torturing that dog and find something to do."

Jody felt mean then, so he threw a rock at Mutt. Then he took his slingshot from the porch and walked up toward the brush line to try to kill a bird. It was a good slingshot, with store-bought rubbers, but while Jody had often shot at birds, he had never hit one. He walked up through the vegetable patch, kicking his bare toes into the dust. And on the way he found the perfect slingshot stone, round and slightly flattened and heavy enough to carry through the air. He fitted it into the leather pouch of his weapon and proceeded to the brush line. His eyes narrowed, his mouth worked strenuously; for the first time that afternoon he was intent. In the shade of the sagebrush the little birds were working, scratching in the leaves, flying restlessly a few feet and scratching again. Jody pulled back the rubbers of the sling and advanced cautiously. One little thrush paused and looked at him and crouched, ready to fly. Jody sidled nearer, moving one foot slowly after the other. When he was twenty feet away, he carefully raised the sling and aimed. The stone whizzed; the thrush started up and flew right into it. And down the little bird went with a broken head. Jody ran to it and picked it up.

"Well, I got you," he said.

The bird looked much smaller dead than it had alive. Jody felt a little mean pain in his stomach, so he took out his pocketknife and cut off the bird's head. Then he disemboweled it, and took off its wings; and finally he threw all the pieces into the brush. He didn't care about the bird, or its life, but he knew what older people would say if they had seen him kill it; he was ashamed because of their potential opinion. He decided to forget the whole thing as quickly as he could, and never to mention it.

The hills were dry at this season, and the wild grass was golden, but where the spring-pipe filled the round tub and the tub spilled over, there lay a stretch of fine green grass, deep and sweet and moist. Jody drank from the mossy tub and washed the bird's blood from his hands in cold water. Then he lay on his back in the grass and looked up at the dumpling summer clouds. By closing one eye and destroying perspective he brought them down within reach so that he could put up his fingers and stroke them. He helped the gentle wind push them down the sky; it seemed to him that they went faster for his help. One fat white cloud he helped clear to the mountain rims and pressed it firmly over, out of sight. Jody wondered what it was seeing, then. He sat up the better to look at the great mountains where they went piling back, growing darker and more savage until they finished with one jagged ridge, high up against the west.

Curious secret mountains; he thought of the little he knew about them.

"What's on the other side?" he asked his father once.

"More mountains, I guess. Why?"

"And on the other side of them?"

"More mountains. Why?"

"More mountains on and on?"

"Well, no. At last you come to the ocean."

"But what's in the mountains?"

"Just cliffs and brush and rocks and dryness."

"Were you ever there?"

"No."

"Has anybody ever been there?"

"A few people, I guess. It's dangerous, with cliffs and things. Why, I've read there's more unexplored country in the mountains of Monterey County than any place in the United States." His father seemed proud that this should be so.

"And at last the ocean?"

"At last the ocean."

"But," the boy insisted, "but in between? No one knows?"

"Oh, a few people do, I guess. But there's nothing there to get. And not much water. Just rocks and cliffs and greasewood. Why?"

"It would be good to go."

"What for? There's nothing there."

Jody knew something was there, something very wonderful because it wasn't known, something secret and mysterious. He could feel within himself that this was so. He said to his mother, "Do you know what's in the big mountains?"

She looked at him and then back at the ferocious range, and she said, "Only the bear, I guess."

"What bear?"

"Why the one that went over the mountain to see what he could see."

Jody questioned Billy Buck, the ranch-hand, about the possibility of ancient cities lost in the mountains, but Billy agreed with Jody's father.

"It ain't likely," Billy said. "There'd be nothing to eat unless a kind of people that can eat rocks live there."

That was all the information Jody ever got, and it made the mountains dear to him, and terrible. He thought often of the miles of ridge after ridge until at last there was the sea. When the peaks were pink in the morning they invited him among them: and when the sun had gone over the edge in the evening and the mountains were a purple-like despair, then Jody was afraid of them; then they were so impersonal and aloof that their very imperturbability was a threat.

Now he turned his head toward the mountains of the east, the

Gabilans, and they were jolly mountains, with hill ranches in their creases, and with pine trees growing on the crests. People lived there, and battles had been fought against the Mexicans on the slopes. He looked back for an instant at the Great Ones and shivered a little at the contrast. The foothill cup of the home ranch below him was sunny and safe. The house gleamed with white light and the barn was brown and warm. The red cows on the farther hill ate their way slowly toward the north. Even the dark cypress tree by the bunkhouse was usual and safe. The chickens scratched about in the dust of the farmyard with quick waltzing steps.

Then a moving figure caught Jody's eye. A man walked slowly over the brow of the hill, on the road from Salinas, and he was headed toward the house. Jody stood up and moved down toward the house too, for if someone was coming, he wanted to be there to see. By the time the boy had got to the house the walking man was only halfway down the road, a lean man, very straight in the shoulders. Jody could tell he was old only because his heels struck the ground with hard jerks. As he approached nearer, Jody saw that he was dressed in blue jeans and in a coat of the same material. He wore clodhopper shoes and an old flat-brimmed Stetson hat. Over his shoulder he carried a gunny sack, lumpy and full. In a few moments he had trudged close enough so that his face could be seen. And his face was as dark as dried beef. A mustache, blue-white against the dark skin, hovered over his mouth, and his hair was white too, where it showed at his neck. The skin of his face had shrunk back against the skull until it defined bone, not flesh, and made the nose and chin seem sharp and fragile. The eyes were large and deep and dark, with eyelids stretched tightly over them. Irises and pupils were one, and very black, but the eyeballs were brown. There were no wrinkles in the face at all. This old man wore a blue denim coat buttoned to the throat with brass buttons, as all men do who wear no shirts. Out of the sleeves came strong bony wrists and hands gnarled and knotted and hard as peach branches. The nails were flat and blunt and shiny.

The old man drew close to the gate and swung down his sack when he confronted Jody. His lips fluttered a little and a soft impersonal voice came from between them. "Do you live here?"

Jody was embarrassed. He turned and looked at the house, and he turned back and looked toward the barn where his father and Billy Buck were. "Yes," he said, when no help came from either direction.

"I have come back," the old man said. "I am Gitano, and I have come back."

Jody could not take all this responsibility. He turned abruptly, and ran into the house for help, and the screen door banged after him. His mother was in the kitchen poking out the clogged holes of a colander with a hairpin, and biting her lower lip with concentration.

"It's an old man," Jody cried excitedly. "It's an old *paisano* man, and he says he's come back."

His mother put down the colander and stuck the hairpin behind the sink board. "What's the matter now?" she asked patiently.

"It's an old man outside. Come on out."

"Well, what does he want?" She untied the strings of her apron and smoothed her hair with her fingers.

"I don't know. He came walking."

His mother smoothed down her dress and went out, and Jody followed her. Gitano had not moved.

"Yes?" Mrs. Tiflin asked.

Gitano took off his old black hat and held it with both hands in front of him. He repeated, "I am Gitano, and I have come back."

"Come back? Back where?"

Gitano's whole straight body leaned forward a little. His right hand described the circle of the hills, the sloping fields and the mountains, and ended at his hat again. "Back to the rancho. I was born here, and my father too."

"Here?" she demanded. "This isn't an old place."

"No, there," he said, pointing to the western ridge. "On the other side there, in a house that is gone."

At last she understood. "The old 'dobe that's washed almost away, you mean?"

"Yes, *señora.* When the rancho broke up they put no more lime on the 'dobe, and the rains washed it down."

Jody's mother was silent for a little, and curious homesick thoughts ran through her mind, but quickly she cleared them out. "And what do you want here now, Gitano?"

"I will stay here," he said quietly, "until I die."

"But we don't need an extra man here."

"I can not work hard any more, *señora.* I can milk a cow, feed chickens, cut a little wood; no more. I will stay here." He indicated the sack on the ground beside him. "Here are my things."

She turned to Jody. "Run down to the barn and call your father."

Jody dashed away, and he returned with Carl Tiflin and Billy Buck behind him. The old man was standing as he had been, but he was resting now. His whole body had sagged into a timeless repose.

"What is it?" Carl Tiflin asked. "What's Jody so excited about?"

Mrs. Tiflin motioned to the old man. "He wants to stay here. He wants to do a little work and stay here."

"Well, we can't have him. We don't need any more men. He's too old. Billy does everything we need."

They had been talking over him as though he did not exist, and now, suddenly, they both hesitated and looked at Gitano and were embarrassed.

He cleared his throat. "I am too old to work. I come back where I was born."

"You weren't born here," Carl said sharply.

"No. In the 'dobe house over the hill. It was all one rancho before you came."

"In the mud house that's all melted down?"

"Yes. I and my father. I will stay here now on the rancho."

"I tell you you won't stay," Carl said angrily. "I don't need an old man. This isn't a big ranch. I can't afford food and doctor bills for an old man. You must have relatives and friends. Go to them. It is like begging to come to strangers."

"I was born here," Gitano said patiently and inflexibly.

Carl Tiflin didn't like to be cruel, but he felt he must. "You can eat here tonight," he said. "You can sleep in the little room of the old bunkhouse. We'll give you your breakfast in the morning, and then you'll have to go along. Go to your friends. Don't come to die with strangers."

Gitano put on his black hat and stooped for the sack. "Here are my things," he said.

Carl turned away. "Come on, Billy, we'll finish down at the barn. Jody, show him the little room in the bunkhouse."

He and Billy turned back toward the barn. Mrs. Tiflin went into the house, saying over her shoulder, "I'll send some blankets down."

Gitano looked questioningly at Jody. "I'll show you where it is," Jody said.

There was a cot with a shuck mattress, an apple box holding a tin lantern, and a backless rocking-chair in the little room of the bunkhouse. Gitano laid his sack carefully on the floor and sat down on the bed. Jody stood shyly in the room, hesitating to go. At last he said,

"Did you come out of the big mountains?"

Gitano shook his head slowly. "No, I worked down the Salinas Valley."

The afternoon thought would not let Jody go. "Did you ever go into the big mountains back there?"

The old dark eyes grew fixed, and their light turned inward on the years that were living in Gitano's head. "Once—when I was a little boy. I went with my father."

"Way back, clear into the mountains?"

"Yes."

"What was there?" Jody cried. "Did you see any people or any houses?"

"No."

"Well, what was there?"

Gitano's eyes remained inward. A little wrinkled strain came between his brows.

"What did you see in there?" Jody repeated.

"I don't know," Gitano said. "I don't remember."

"Was it terrible and dry?"

"I don't remember.

In his excitement, Jody had lost his shyness. "Don't you remember anything about it?"

Gitano's mouth opened for a word, and remained open while his brain sought the word. "I think it was quiet—I think it was nice."

Gitano's eyes seemed to have found something back in the years, for they grew soft and a little smile seemed to come and go in them.

"Didn't you ever go back in the mountains again?" Jody insisted.

"No."

"Didn't you ever want to?"

But now Gitano's face became impatient. "No," he said in a tone that told Jody he didn't want to talk about it any more. The boy was held by a curious fascination. He didn't want to go away from Gitano. His shyness returned.

"Would you like to come down to the barn and see the stock?" he asked.

Gitano stood up and put on his hat and prepared to follow.

It was almost evening now. They stood near the watering trough while the horses sauntered in from the hillsides for an evening drink. Gitano rested his big twisted hands on the top rail of the fence. Five horses came down and drank, and then stood about, nibbling at the dirt or rubbing their sides against the polished wood of the fence. Long after they had finished drinking an old horse appeared over the brow of the hill and came painfully down. It had long yellow teeth; its hoofs were flat and sharp as spades, and its ribs and hip-bones jutted out under its skin. It hobbled up to the trough and drank water with a loud sucking noise.

"That's old Easter," Jody explained. "That's the first horse my father ever had. He's thirty years old." He looked up into Gitano's old eyes for some response.

"No good any more," Gitano said.

Jody's father and Billy Buck came out of the barn and walked over.

"Too old to work," Gitano repeated. "Just eats and pretty soon dies."

Carl Tiflin caught the last words. He hated his brutality toward old Gitano, and so he became brutal again.

"It's a shame not to shoot Easter," he said. "It'd save him a lot of pains and rheumatism." He looked secretly at Gitano, to see whether he noticed the parallel, but the big bony hands did not move, nor did the dark eyes turn from the horse. "Old things ought to be put out of their misery," Jody's father went on. "One shot, a big noise, one big pain in the head maybe, and that's all. That's better than stiffness and sore teeth."

Billy Buck broke in. "They got a right to rest after they worked all of their life. Maybe they like to just walk around."

Carl had been looking steadily at the skinny horse. "You can't imagine now what Easter used to look like," he said softly. "High neck, deep chest, fine barrel. He could jump a five-bar gate in stride. I won a flat race on him when I was fifteen years old. I could of got two hundred dollars for him any time. You wouldn't think how pretty he was." He checked himself, for he hated softness. "But he ought to be shot now," he said.

"He's got a right to rest," Billy Buck insisted.

Jody's father had a humorous thought. He turned to Gitano. "If ham and eggs grew on a side-hill I'd turn you out to pasture too," he said. "But I can't afford to pasture you in my kitchen."

He laughed to Billy Buck about it as they went on toward the house. "Be a good thing for all of us if ham and eggs grew on the side-hills."

Jody knew how his father was probing for a place to hurt in Gitano. He had been probed often. His father knew every place in the boy where a word would fester.

"He's only talking," Jody said. "He didn't mean it about shooting Easter. He likes Easter. That was the first horse he ever owned."

The sun sank behind the high mountains as they stood there, and the ranch was hushed. Gitano seemed to be more at home in the evening. He made a curious sharp sound with his lips and stretched one of his hands over the fence. Old Easter moved stiffly to him, and Gitano rubbed the lean neck under the mane.

"You like him?" Jody asked softly.

"Yes—but he's no damn good."

The triangle sounded at the ranch house. "That's supper," Jody cried. "Come on up to supper."

As they walked up toward the house Jody noticed again that Gitano's body was as straight as that of a young man. Only by a jerkiness in his movements and by the scuffling of his heels could it be seen that he was old.

The turkeys were flying heavily into the lower branches of the cypress tree by the bunkhouse. A fat sleek ranch cat walked across the road carrying a rat so large that its tail dragged on the ground. The quail on the side-hills were still sounding the clear water call.

Jody and Gitano came to the back steps and Mrs. Tiflin looked out through the screen door at them.

"Come running, Jody. Come in to supper, Gitano."

Carl and Billy Buck had started to eat at the long oilcloth-covered table. Jody slipped into his chair without moving it, but Gitano stood holding his hat until Carl looked up and said, "Sit down, sit down. You might as well get your belly full before you go on." Carl was afraid he might relent and let the old man stay, and so he continued to remind himself that this couldn't be.

Gitano laid his hat on the floor and diffidently sat down. He wouldn't reach for food. Carl had to pass it to him. "Here, fill yourself up." Gitano ate very slowly, cutting tiny pieces of meat and arranging little pats of mashed potato on his plate.

The situation would not stop worrying Carl Tiflin. "Haven't you got any relatives in this part of the country?" he asked.

Gitano answered with some pride, "My brother-in-law is in Monterey. I have cousins there, too."

"Well, you can go and live there, then."

"I was born here," Gitano said in gentle rebuke.

Jody's mother came in from the kitchen, carrying a large bowl of tapioca pudding.

Carl chuckled to her, "Did I tell you what I said to him? I said if ham and eggs grew on the side-hills I'd put him out to pasture, like old Easter."

Gitano stared unmoved at his plate.

"It's too bad he can't stay," said Mrs. Tiflin.

"Now don't you start anything," Carl said crossly.

When they had finished eating, Carl and Billy Buck and Jody went into the living-room to sit for a while, but Gitano, without a word of farewell or thanks, walked through the kitchen and out the back door. Jody sat and secretly watched his father. He knew how mean his father felt.

"This country's full of these old *paisanos*," Carl said to Billy Buck.

"They're damn good men," Billy defended them. "They can work older than white men. I saw one of them a hundred and five years old, and he could still ride a horse. You don't see any white men as old as Gitano walking twenty or thirty miles."

"Oh, they're tough, all right," Carl agreed. "Say, are you standing up for him too? Listen, Billy," he explained, "I'm having a hard enough time keeping this ranch out of the Bank of Italy without taking on anybody else to feed. You know that Billy."

"Sure, I know," said Billy. "If you was rich, it'd be different."

"That's right, and it isn't like he didn't have relatives to go to. A brother-in-law and cousins right in Monterey. Why should I worry about him?"

Jody sat quietly listening, and he seemed to hear Gitano's gentle voice and its unanswerable, "But I was born here." Gitano was mysterious like the mountains. There were ranges back as far as you could see, but behind the last range piled up against the sky there was a great unknown country. And Gitano was an old man, until you got to the dull dark eyes. And in behind them was some unknown thing. He didn't even say enough to let you guess what was inside, under the eyes. Jody felt himself irresistibly drawn toward the bunkhouse. He slipped from his chair while his father was talking and he went out the door without making a sound.

The night was very dark and far-off noises carried in clearly. The hamebells of a wood team sounded from way over the hill on the county road. Jody picked his way across the dark yard. He could see a light through the window of the little room of the bunkhouse. Because the night was secret he walked quietly up to the window and peered in. Gitano sat in the rocking-chair and his back was toward the window. His right arm moved slowly back and forth in front of him. Jody pushed the door open and walked in. Gitano jerked upright and, seizing a piece of deerskin, he tried to throw it over the thing in his lap, but the skin slipped away. Jody stood overwhelmed by the thing in Gitano's hand, a lean and lovely rapier with a golden basket hilt. The blade was like a thin ray of dark light. The hilt was pierced and intricately carved.

"What is it?" Jody demanded.

Gitano only looked at him with resentful eyes, and he picked up the fallen deerskin and firmly wrapped the beautiful blade in it.

Jody put out his hand. "Can't I see it?"

Gitano's eyes smoldered angrily and he shook his head.

"Where'd you get it? Where'd it come from?"

Now Gitano regarded him profoundly, as though he pondered. "I got it from my father."

"Well, where'd he get it?"

Gitano looked down at the long deerskin parcel in his hand. "I don't know."

"Didn't he ever tell you?"

"No."

"What do you do with it?"

Gitano looked slightly surprised. "Nothing. I just keep it."

"Can't I see it again?"

The old man slowly unwrapped the shining blade and let the lamplight slip along it for a moment. Then he wrapped it up again. "You go now. I want to go to bed." He blew out the lamp almost before Jody had closed the door.

As he went back toward the house, Jody knew one thing more sharply than he had ever known anything. He must never tell anyone about the rapier. It would be a dreadful thing to tell anyone about it, for it would destroy some fragile structure of truth. It was a truth that might be shattered by division.

On the way across the dark yard Jody passed Billy Buck.

"They're wondering where you are," Billy said.

Jody slipped into the living-room, and his father turned to him. "Where have you been?"

"I just went out to see if I caught any rats in my new trap."

"It's time you went to bed," his father said.

Jody was first at the breakfast table in the morning. Then his father came in, and last, Billy Buck. Mrs. Tiflin looked in from the kitchen.

"Where's the old man, Billy?" she asked.

"I guess he's out walking," Billy said. "I looked in his room and he wasn't there."

"Maybe he started early to Monterey," said Carl. "It's a long walk."

"No," Billy explained. "His sack is in the little room."

After breakfast Jody walked down to the bunkhouse. Flies were flashing about in the sunshine. The ranch seemed especially quiet this morning. When he was sure no one was watching him, Jody went into the little room, and looked into Gitano's sack. An extra pair of long cotton underwear was there, an extra pair of jeans and three pairs of worn socks. Nothing else was in the sack. A sharp loneliness fell on Jody. He walked slowly back toward the house. His father stood on the porch talking to Mrs. Tiflin.

"I guess old Easter's dead at last," he said. "I didn't see him come down to water with the other horses."

In the middle of the morning Jess Taylor from the ridge ranch rode down.

"You didn't sell that old gray crowbait of yours, did you, Carl?"

"No, of course not. Why?"

"Well," Jess said. "I was out this morning early, and I saw a funny thing. I saw an old man on an old horse, no saddle, only a piece of rope for a bridle. He wasn't on the road at all. He was cutting right up straight through the brush. I think he had a gun. At least I saw something shine in his hand."

"That's old Gitano," Carl Tiflin said. "I'll see if any of my guns are missing." He stepped into the house for a second. "Nope, all here. Which way was he heading, Jess?"

"Well, that's the funny thing. He was heading straight back into the mountains."

Carl laughed. "They never get too old to steal," he said. "I guess he just stole old Easter."

"Want to go after him, Carl?"

"Hell no, just save me burying that horse. I wonder where he got the gun. I wonder what he wants back there."

Jody walked up through the vegetable patch, toward the brush line.

He looked searchingly at the towering mountains—ridge after ridge after ridge until at last there was the ocean. For a moment he thought he could see a black speck crawling up the farthest ridge. Jody thought of the rapier and of Gitano. And he thought of the great mountains. A longing caressed him, and it was so sharp that he wanted to cry to get it out of his breast. He lay down in the green grass near the round tub at the brush line. He covered his eyes with his crossed arms and lay there a long time, and he was full of a nameless sorrow.

STUDY GUIDE

1. What have the great mountains to do with the central character trait of Jody in this story? What do they symbolize that both Jody and Gitano have in common?

2. Point out specific details in the opening paragraphs that make Jody a very convincing boy for the reader.

3. Discuss the contrasted character traits in Billy Buck, Carl Tiflin, and Mrs. Tiflin that are revealed by their individual reactions to Gitano.

4. Show how the contrasted attitudes of Billy and Carl toward the old horse Easter reveal fundamental character differences in the two men. How do these attitudes toward the horse operate somewhat symbolically in the story?

5. What does Gitano's rapier symbolize? What trait does it show that he shares with Jody?

6. Read "The Death of the Hired Man" by Robert Frost, a poem that has a theme similar to that of "The Great Mountains." Compare and contrast Steinbeck's handling of this theme in his prose narrative with Frost's poetic treatment of it. Note especially the greater use of symbolism in the poem.

TAKE PITY

Bernard Malamud

Davidov, the census-taker, opened the door without knocking, limped into the room and sat wearily down. Out came his notebook and he was on the job. Rosen, the ex-coffee salesman, wasted, eyes despairing, sat motionless, cross-legged, on his cot. The square, clean but cold room lit by a dim globe was sparsely furnished: the cot, a folding chair, small table, old unpainted chests—no closets but who needed them?—and a small sink with a rough piece of green, institutional soap on its holder—you could smell it across the room. The worn black shade over the single narrow window was drawn to the ledge, surprising Davidov.

"What's the matter you don't pull the shade up?" he remarked.

Rosen ultimately sighed. "Let it stay."

"Why? Outside is light."

"Who needs light?"

"What then you need?"

"Light I don't need," replied Rosen.

Davidov, sour-faced, flipped through the closely scrawled pages of his notebook until he found a clean one. He attempted to scratch in a word with his fountain pen but it had run dry, so he fished a pencil stub out of his vest pocket and sharpened it with a cracked razor blade. Rosen paid no attention to the feathery shavings falling to the floor. He looked restless, seemed to be listening to or for something, although Davidov was convinced there was absolutely nothing to listen to. It was only when the census-taker somewhat irritably and with increasing loudness repeated a question, that Rosen stirred and identified himself. He was about to furnish an address but caught himself and shrugged.

Davidov did not comment on the salesman's gesture. "So begin," he nodded.

"Who knows where to begin?" Rosen stared at the drawn shade. "Do they know here where to begin?"

"Philosophy we are not interested," said Davidov. "Start in how you met her."

"Who?" pretended Rosen.

"Her," he snapped.

"So if I got to begin, how you know about her already?" Rosen asked triumphantly.

Davidov spoke wearily, "You mentioned before."

Rosen remembered. They had questioned him upon his arrival and he now recalled blurting out her name. It was perhaps something in the air. It did not permit you to retain what you remembered. That was part of the cure, if you wanted a cure.

"Where I met her—?" Rosen murmured. "I met her where she always was—in the back room there in that hole in the wall that it was a waste of time for me I went there. Maybe I sold them a half a bag of coffee a month. This is not business."

"In business we are not interested."

"What then you are interested?" Rosen mimicked Davidov's tone.

Davidov clammed up coldly.

Rosen knew they had him where it hurt, so he went on: "The husband was maybe forty, Axel Kalish, a Polish refugee. He worked like a blind horse when he got to America, and saved maybe two—three thousand dollars that he bought with the money this pisher grocery in a dead neighborhood where he didn't have a chance. He called my company up for credit and they sent me I should see. I recommended okay because I felt sorry. He had a wife, Eva, you know already about her, and two darling girls, one five and one three, little dolls, Fega and Surale, that I didn't want them to suffer. So right away I told him without tricks, 'Kiddo, this is a mistake. This place is a grave. Here they will bury you if you don't get out quick!' "

Rosen sighed deeply.

"So?" Davidov had thus far written nothing, irking the ex-salesman.

"So?—Nothing. He didn't get out. After a couple months he tried to sell but nobody bought, so he stayed and starved. They never made expenses. Every day they got poorer you couldn't look in their faces. 'Don't be a damn fool,' I told him, 'go in bankruptcy.' But he couldn't stand it to lose all his capital, and he was also afraid it would be hard to find a job. 'My God,' I said, 'do anything. Be a painter, a janitor, a junk man, but get out of here before everybody is a skeleton.'

"This he finally agreed with me, but before he could go in auction he dropped dead."

Davidov made a note. "How did he die?"

"On this I am not an expert," Rosen replied. "You know better than me."

"How did he die?" Davidov spoke impatiently. "Say in one word."

"From what he died?—he died, that's all."

"Answer, please, this question."

"Broke in him something. That's how."

"Broke what?"

"Broke what breaks. He was talking to me how bitter was his life, and he touched me on my sleeve to say something else, but the next minute his face got small and he fell down dead, the wife screaming, the little girls crying that it made in my heart pain. I am myself a sick man and when I saw him laying on the floor, I said to myself, 'Rosen, say good-bye, this guy is finished.' So I said it."

Rosen got up from the cot and strayed despondently around the room, avoiding the window. Davidov was occupying the only chair, so the ex-salesman was finally forced to sit on the edge of the bed again. This irritated him. He badly wanted a cigarette but disliked asking for one.

Davidov permitted him a short interval of silence, then leafed impatiently through his notebook. Rosen, to needle the census-taker, said nothing.

"So what happened?" Davidov finally demanded.

Rosen spoke with ashes in his mouth. "After the funeral—" he paused, tried to wet his lips, then went on, "He belong to a society that they buried him, and he also left a thousand dollars insurance, but after the funeral I said to her, 'Eva, listen to me. Take the money and your children and run away from here. Let the creditors take the store. What will they get?—Nothing.'

"But she answered me, 'Where will I go, where, with my two orphans that their father left them to starve?'

" 'Go anywhere,' I said. 'Go to your relatives.'

"She laughed like laughs somebody who hasn't got no joy. 'My relatives Hitler took away from me.'

" 'What about Axel—surely an uncle somewheres?'

" 'Nobody,' she said. 'I will stay here like my Axel wanted. With the insurance I will buy new stock and fix up the store. Every week I will decorate the window, and in this way gradually will come in new customers—'

" 'Eva, my darling girl—'

" 'A millionaire I don't expect to be. All I want is I should make a little living and take care on my girls. We will live in the back here like before, and in this way I can work and watch them, too.'

" 'Eva,' I said, 'you are a nice-looking young woman, only thirty-eight years. Don't throw away your life here. Don't flush in the toilet—you should excuse me—the thousand poor dollars from your dead husband. Believe me, I know a graveyard when I smell it. Go better some place and find a job. You're young yet. Sometime you will meet somebody and get married.'

" 'No, Rosen, not me,' she said. 'With marriage I am finished. Nobody wants a poor widow with two children.'

" 'This I don't believe it.'

" 'I know,' she said.

"Never in my life I saw so bitter a woman's face.

" 'No,' I said. 'No.'

" 'Yes, Rosen, yes. In my whole life I never had anything. In my whole life I always suffered. I don't expect better. This is my life.'

"I said no and she said yes. What could I do? I am a man with only one kidney, and worse than that, that I won't mention it. When I talked she didn't listen, so I stopped to talk. Who can argue with a widow?"

The ex-salesman glanced up at Davidov but the census-taker did not reply. "What happened then?" he asked.

"What happened?" mocked Rosen. "Happened what happens."

Davidov's face grew red.

"What happened, happened," Rosen said hastily. "She ordered from the wholesalers all kinds goods that she paid for them cash. All week she opened boxes and packed on the shelves cans, jars, packages. Also she cleaned, and she washed, and she mopped with oil the floor. With tissue paper she made new decorations in the window, everything should look nice—but who came in? Nobody except a few poor customers from the tenement around the corner. And when they came? When was closed the supermarkets and they needed some little item that they forgot to buy, like a quart milk, fifteen cents' cheese, a small can sardines for lunch. In a few months was again dusty the cans on the shelves, and her thousand was gone. Credit she couldn't get except from me, and from me she got because I paid out of my pocket the company. This she didn't know. She worked, she dressed clean, she waited that the store should get better. Little by little the shelves got empty, but where was the profit? They ate it up. When I looked on the little girls I knew what she didn't tell me. Their faces were white, they were thin, they were hungry. She kept the little food that was left, on the shelves. One night I brought in a nice piece of sirloin, but I could see from her eyes that she didn't like that I did it. So what else could I do? I have a heart and I am human."

Here the ex-salesman wept.

Davidov pretended not to see though once he peeked.

Rosen blew his nose, then went on more calmly, "When the children were sleeping we sat in the dark there, in the back, and not once in four hours opened the door should come in a customer. 'Eva, for Godsakes, *run away*,' I said.

" 'I have no place to go,' she said.

" 'I will give you where you can go, and please don't say to me no. I am a bachelor, this you know. I got whatever I need and more besides. Let me help you and the children. Money don't interest me. Interests me good health, but I can't buy it. I'll tell you what I will do. Let this place go to the creditors and move into a two-family house that I own, which the top floor is now empty. Rent will cost you nothing. In the meantime you can go and find a job. I will also pay the downstairs lady to take care of the girls—God bless them—until you will come home. With your wages you will buy the food, if you need clothes, and also save a little. This you can use when you get married someday. What do you say?

"She didn't answer me. She only looked on me in such a way, with such burning eyes, like I was small and ugly. For the first time I thought to myself, 'Rosen, this woman don't like you.'

" 'Thank you very kindly, my friend Mr. Rosen,' she answered me, 'but charity we are not needing. I got yet a paying business, and it will get better when times are better. Now is bad times. When comes again good times will get better the business."

" 'Who charity?' I cried to her. 'What charity? Speaks to you your husband's a friend.'

" 'Mr. Rosen, my husband didn't have no friends.'

" 'Can't you see that I want to help the children?'

" 'The children have their mother.'

" 'Eva, what's the matter with you?' I said. 'Why do you make sound bad something that I mean it should be good?'

"This she didn't answer. I felt sick in my stomach, and was coming also a headache so I left.

"All night I didn't sleep, and then all of a sudden I figured out a reason why she was worried. She was worried I would ask for some kind payment except cash. She got the wrong man. Anyway, this made me think of something that I didn't think about before. I thought now to ask her to marry me. What did she have to lose? I could take care of myself without any trouble to them. Fega and Surale would have a father he could give them for the movies, or sometime to buy a little doll to play with, and when I died, would go to them my investments and insurance policies.

"The next day I spoke to her.

" 'For myself, Eva, I don't want a thing. Absolutely not a thing. For you and your girls—everything. I am not a strong man, Eva. In fact, I am sick. I tell you this you should understand I don't expect to live long. But even for a few years would be nice to have a little family.'

"She was with her back to me and didn't speak.

"When she turned around again her face was white but the mouth was like iron.

" 'No, Mr. Rosen.'

" 'Why not, tell me?'

" 'I had enough with sick men.' She began to cry. 'Please, Mr. Rosen. Go home.'

"I didn't have strength I should argue with her, so I went home. I went home but hurt me my mind. All day long and all night I felt bad. My back pained me where was missing my kidney. Also too much smoking. I tried to understand this woman but I couldn't. Why should somebody that her two children were starving always say no to a man that he wanted to help her? What did I do to her bad? Am I maybe a murderer she should hate me so much? All that I felt in my heart was pity for her and the children, but I couldn't convince her. Then I went back and begged her she should let me help them, and once more she told me no.

" 'Eva,' I said, 'I don't blame you that you don't want a sick man. So come with me to a marriage broker and we will find you a strong, healthy husband that he will support you and your girls. I will give the dowry.'

"She screamed, 'On this I don't need your help, Rosen!'

"I didn't say no more. What more could I say? All day long, from early in the morning till late in the night she worked like an animal. All day she mopped, she washed with soap and a brush the shelves, the few cans she polished, but the store was still rotten. The little girls I was afraid to look at. I could see in their faces their bones. They were tired, they were weak. Little Surale held with her hand all the time the dress of Fega. Once when I saw them in the street I gave them some cakes, but when I tried the next day to give them something else, the mother shouldn't know, Fega answered me, 'We can't take, Momma says today is a fast day.'

"I went inside. I made my voice soft. 'Eva, on my bended knee, I am a man with nothing in this world. Allow me that I should have a little pleasure before I die. Allow me that I should help you to stock up once more the store.'

"So what did she do? She cried, it was terrible to see. And after she cried, what did she say? She told me to go away and I shouldn't come back. I felt like to pick up a chair and break her head.

"In my house I was too weak to eat. For two days I took in my mouth nothing except maybe a spoon of chicken noodle soup, or maybe a glass tea without sugar. This wasn't good for me. My health felt bad.

"Then I made up a scheme that I was a friend of Axel's who lived in Jersey. I said I owed Axel seven hundred dollars that he lent me this money fifteen years ago, before he got married. I said I did not have the whole money now, but I would send her every week twenty dollars till it was paid up the debt. I put inside the letter two tens and gave it to a friend of mine, also a salesman, he should mail it in Newark so she would not be suspicious who wrote the letters."

To Rosen's surprise Davidov had stopped writing. The book was full, so he tossed it onto the table, yawned, but listened amiably. His curiosity had died.

Rosen got up and fingered the notebook. He tried to read the small distorted handwriting but could not make out a single word.

"It's not English and it's not Yiddish," he said. "Could it be in Hebrew?"

"No," answered Davidov. "It's an old-fashioned language that they don't use it nowadays."

"Oh?" Rosen returned to the cot. He saw no purpose to going on now that it was not required, but he felt he had to.

"Came back all the letters," he said dully. "The first she opened it, then pasted back again the envelope, but the rest she didn't even open."

" 'Here,' I said to myself, 'is a very strange thing—a person that you can never give her anything.—*But I will give.*'

"I went then to my lawyer and we made out a will that everything I had—all my investments, my two houses that I owned, also furniture, my car, the checking account—every cent would go to her, and when she died, the rest, would be left for the two girls. The same with my insurance. They would be my beneficiaries. Then I signed and went home. In the kitchen I turned on the gas and put my head in the stove.

"Let her say now no."

Davidov, scratching his stubbled cheek, nodded. This was the part he already knew. He got up and before Rosen could cry no, idly raised the window shade.

It was twilight in space but a woman stood before the window.

Rosen with a bound was off his cot to see.

It was Eva, staring at him with haunted, beseeching eyes. She raised her arms to him.

Infuriated, the ex-salesman shook his fist.

"Whore, bastard, bitch," he shouted at her. "Go 'way from here. Go home to your children."

Davidov made no move to hinder him as Rosen rammed down the window shade.

STUDY GUIDE

1. The chief interest in this story lies in the character of Rosen. What is his dominant character trait? How does this come through in his action in the story? What connection has the title of the story with this trait?

2. Why does Eva so persistently refuse all the help offered by Rosen?

3. What is the significance of the drawn shade in Rosen's room? Show how references to this punctuate the whole narrative.

4. The author is not very explicit about the setting of the story. What meager details reveal that it takes place in a room in an institution for the mentally disturbed?

5. Why does Davidov's curiosity about Rosen's situation die down? Is it lack of interest, lack of sympathy, or what?

6. What is the significance of the unexpected response by Rosen to Eva's sudden appearance at the window at the end of the story?

7. Part of the atmosphere of this story is created by the convincing Jewish dialect in which it is written. Point out some of the features of syntax that characterize the speech of both Rosen and Eva.

A ROSE FOR EMILY

William Faulkner

I

When Miss Emily Grierson died, our whole town went to her funeral: the men through a sort of respectful affection for a fallen monument, the women mostly out of curiosity to see the inside of her house, which no one save an old manservant—a combined gardener and cook—had seen in at least ten years.

It was a big, squarish frame house that had once been white, decorated with cupolas and spires and scrolled balconies in the heavily lightsome style of the seventies, set on what had once been our most select street. But garages and cotton gins had encroached and obliterated even the august names of that neighborhood; only Miss Emily's house was left, lifting its stubborn and coquettish decay above the cotton wagons and the gasoline pumps—an eyesore among eyesores. And now Miss Emily had gone to join the representatives of those august names where they lay in the cedar-bemused cemetery among the ranked and anonymous graves of Union and Confederate soldiers who fell at the battle of Jefferson.

Alive, Miss Emily had been a tradition, a duty, and a care; a sort of hereditary obligation upon the town, dating from that day in 1894 when Colonel Sartoris, the mayor—he who fathered the edict that no Negro woman should appear on the streets without an apron—remitted her taxes, the dispensation dating from the death of her father on into perpetuity. Not that Miss Emily would have accepted charity. Colonel Sartoris invented an involved tale to the effect that Miss Emily's father had loaned money to the town, which the town, as a matter of business, preferred this way of repaying. Only a man of Colonel Sartoris' generation and thought could have invented it, and only a woman could have believed it.

When the next generation, with its more modern ideas, became mayors and aldermen, this arrangement created some little dissatisfaction. On the first of the year they mailed her a tax notice. February came, and there was no reply. They wrote her a formal letter, asking her to call at the sheriff's office at her convenience. A week later the mayor wrote her himself, offering to call or to send his car for her, and received in reply a note on paper of an archaic shape, in a thin, flowing calligraphy in faded ink, to the effect that she no longer went out at all. The tax notice was also enclosed, without comment.

They called a special meeting of the Board of Aldermen. A deputation waited upon her, knocked at the door through which no visitor had passed since she ceased giving china-painting lessons eight or ten years earlier. They were admitted by the old Negro into a dim hall from which a stairway mounted into still more shadow. It smelled of dust and disuse—a close, dank smell. The Negro led them into the parlor. It was furnished in heavy, leather-covered furniture. When the Negro opened the blinds of one window, they could see that the leather was cracked; and when they sat down, a faint dust rose sluggishly about their thighs, spinning with slow motes in the single sun-ray. On a tarnished gilt easel before the fireplace stood a crayon portrait of Miss Emily's father.

They rose when she entered—a small, fat woman in black, with a thin gold chain descending to her waist and vanishing into her belt, leaning on an ebony cane with a tarnished gold head. Her skeleton was small and spare; perhaps that was why what would have been merely plumpness in another was obesity in her. She looked bloated, like a body long submerged in motionless water, and of that pallid hue. Her eyes, lost in the fatty ridges of her face, looked like two small pieces of coal pressed into a lump of dough as they moved from one face to another while the visitors stated their errand.

She did not ask them to sit. She just stood in the door and listened quietly until the spokesman came to a stumbling halt. Then they could hear the invisible watch ticking at the end of the gold chain.

Her voice was dry and cold. "I have no taxes in Jefferson. Colonel Sartoris explained it to me. Perhaps one of you can gain access to the city records and satisfy yourselves."

"But we have. We are the city authorities, Miss Emily. Didn't you get a notice from the sheriff, signed by him?"

"I received a paper, yes," Miss Emily said. "Perhaps he considers himself the sheriff . . . I have no taxes in Jefferson."

"But there is nothing on the books to show that, you see. We must go by the—"

"See Colonel Sartoris. I have no taxes in Jefferson."

"But, Miss Emily—"

"See Colonel Sartoris." (Colonel Sartoris had been dead almost ten years.) "I have no taxes in Jefferson. Tobe!" The Negro appeared. "Show these gentlemen out."

II

So she vanquished them, horse and foot, just as she had vanquished their fathers thirty years before about the smell. That was two years after her father's death and a short time after her sweetheart—the one we believed would marry her—had deserted her. After her father's death she went out very little; after her sweetheart went away, people hardly saw her at all. A few of the ladies had the temerity to call, but were not received, and the only sign of life about the place was the Negro man—a young man then—going in and out with a market basket.

"Just as if a man—any man—could keep a kitchen properly," the ladies said; so they were not surprised when the smell developed. It was another link between the gross, teeming world and the high and mighty Griersons.

A neighbor, a woman, complained to the mayor, Judge Stevens, eighty years old.

"But what will you have me do about it, madam?" he said.

"Why, send her word to stop it," the woman said. "Isn't there a law?"

"I'm sure that won't be necessary," Judge Stevens said. "It's probably just a snake or a rat that nigger of hers killed in the yard. I'll speak to him about it."

The next day he received two more complaints, one from a man who came in diffident deprecation. "We really must do something about it, Judge. I'd be the last one in the world to bother Miss Emily, but we've got to do something." That night the Board of Aldermen met—three graybeards and one younger man, a member of the rising generation.

"It's simple enough," he said. "Send her word to have her place cleaned up. Give her a certain time to do it in, and if she don't . . ."

"Dammit, sir," Judge Stevens said, "will you accuse a lady to her face of smelling bad?"

So the next night, after midnight, four men crossed Miss Emily's lawn and slunk about the house like burglars, sniffing along the base of the brickwork and at the cellar openings while one of them performed a regular sowing motion with his hand out of a sack slung from his shoulder. They broke open the cellar door and sprinkled lime there, and in all the outbuildings. As they recrossed the lawn, a window that had been dark was lighted and Miss Emily sat in it, the light behind her, and her upright torso motionless as that of an idol. They crept quietly across the lawn and into the shadow of the locusts that lined the street. After a week or two the smell went away.

That was when people had begun to feel really sorry for her. People in our town, remembering how old lady Wyatt, her great-aunt, had gone completely crazy at last, believed that the Griersons held themselves a little too high for what they really were. None of the young men were quite good enough to Miss Emily and such. We had long thought of them as a tableau; Miss Emily a slender figure in white in the background, her father a spraddled silhouette in the foreground, his back to her and clutching a horsewhip, the two of them framed by the back-flung front door. So when she got to be thirty and was still single, we were not pleased exactly, but vindicated; even with insanity in the family she wouldn't have turned down all of her chances if they had really materialized.

When her father died, it got about that the house was all that was left to her; and in a way, people were glad. At last they could pity Miss Emily. Being left alone, and a pauper, she had become humanized. Now she too would know the old thrill and the old despair of a penny more or less.

The day after his death all the ladies prepared to call at the house and offer condolence and aid, as is our custom. Miss Emily met them at the door, dressed as usual and with no trace of grief on her face. She told them that her father was not dead. She did that for three days, with the ministers calling on her, and the doctors, trying to persuade her to let them dispose of the body. Just as they were about to resort to law and force, she broke down, and they buried her father quickly.

We did not say she was crazy then. We believed she had to do that. We remembered all the young men her father had driven away, and we knew that with nothing left, she would have to cling to that which had robbed her, as people will.

III

She was sick for a long time. When we saw her again, her hair was cut short, making her look like a girl, with a vague resemblance to those angels in colored church windows—sort of tragic and serene.

The town had just let the contracts for paving the sidewalks, and in the summer after her father's death they began the work. The construction company came with niggers and mules and machinery, and a foreman named Homer Barron, a Yankee—a big, dark, ready man, with a big voice and eyes lighter than his face. The little boys would follow in groups to hear him cuss the niggers, and the niggers singing in time to the rise and fall of picks. Pretty soon he knew everybody in town. Whenever you heard a lot of laughing anywhere about the square, Homer Barron would be in the center of the group. Presently we began to see him and Miss Emily on Sunday afternoons driving in the yellow-wheeled buggy and the matched team of bays from the livery stable.

At first we were glad that Miss Emily would have an interest, because the ladies all said, "Of course a Grierson would not think seriously of a Northerner, a day laborer." But there were still others, older people, who said that even grief could not cause a real lady to forget *noblesse oblige*—without calling it *noblesse oblige*. They just said, "Poor Emily. Her kinsfolk should come to her." She had some kin in Alabama; but years ago her father had fallen out with them over the estate of old lady Wyatt, the crazy woman, and there was no communication between the two families. They had not even been represented at the funeral.

And as soon as the old people said, "Poor Emily," the whispering began. "Do you suppose it's really so?" they said to one another. "Of course it is. What else could . . ." This behind their hands; rustling of craned silk and satin behind jalousies closed upon the sun of Sunday afternoon as the thin, swift clop-clop-clop of the matched team passed: "Poor Emily."

She carried her head high enough—even when we believed that she was fallen. It was as if she demanded more than ever the recognition of her dignity as the last Grierson; as if it had wanted that touch of earthiness to reaffirm her imperviousness. Like when she bought the rat poison, the arsenic. That was over a year after they had begun to say "Poor Emily," and while the two female cousins were visiting her.

"I want some poison," she said to the druggist. She was over thirty then, still a slight woman, though thinner than usual, with cold, haughty black eyes in a face the flesh of which was strained across the temples and about the eye-sockets as you imagine a lighthouse-keeper's face ought to look. "I want some poison," she said.

"Yes, Miss Emily. What kind? For rats and such? I'd recom—"

"I want the best you have. I don't care what kind."

The druggist named several. "They'll kill anything up to an elephant. But what you want is—"

"Arsenic," Miss Emily said. "Is that a good one?"

"Is . . . arsenic? Yes, ma'am. But what you want—"

"I want arsenic."

The druggist looked down at her. She looked back at him, erect, her face like a strained flag. "Why, of course," the druggist said. "If that's what you want. But the law requires you to tell what you are going to use it for."

Miss Emily just stared at him, her head tilted back in order to look him eye for eye, until he looked away and went and got the arsenic and wrapped it up. The Negro delivery boy brought her the package; the druggist didn't come back. When she opened the package at home there was written on the box, under the skull and bones: "For rats."

IV

So the next day we all said, "She will kill herself"; and we said it would be the best thing. When she had first begun to be seen with Homer Barron, we had said, "She will marry him." Then we said, "She will persuade him yet," because Homer himself had remarked—he liked men, and it was known that he drank with the younger men in the Elks' Club—that he was not a marrying man. Later we said, "Poor Emily" behind the jalousies as they passed on Sunday afternoon in the glittering buggy, Miss Emily with her head high and Homer Barron with his hat cocked and a cigar in his teeth, reins and whip in a yellow glove.

Then some of the ladies began to say that it was a disgrace to the town and a bad example to the young people. The men did not want to interfere, but at last the ladies forced the Baptist minister—Miss Emily's people were Episcopal—to call upon her. He would never divulge what happened during that interview, but he refused to go back again. The next Sunday they again drove about the streets, and the following day the minister's wife wrote to Miss Emily's relations in Alabama.

So she had blood-kin under her roof again and we sat back to watch developments. At first nothing happened. Then we were sure that they were to be married. We learned that Miss Emily had been to the jeweler's and ordered a man's toilet set in silver, with the letters H. B. on each piece. Two days later we learned that she had bought a complete outfit of men's clothing, including a nightshirt, and we said, "They are married." We were really glad. We were glad because the two female cousins were even more Grierson than Miss Emily had ever been.

So we were not surprised when Homer Barron—the streets had been finished some time since—was gone. We were a little disappointed that there was not a public blowing-off, but we believed that he had gone on to prepare for Miss Emily's coming, or to give her a chance to get rid of the cousins. (By that time it was a cabal, and we were all Miss Emily's allies to help circumvent the cousins.) Sure enough, after another week they departed. And, as we had expected all along, within three days Homer Barron was back in town. A neighbor saw the Negro man admit him at the kitchen door at dusk one evening.

And that was the last we saw of Homer Barron. And of Miss Emily for some time. The Negro man went in and out with the market basket, but the front door remained closed. Now and then we would see her at a window for a moment, as the men did that night when they sprinkled the lime, but for almost six months she did not appear on the streets. Then we knew that this was to be expected too; as if that quality of her father which had thwarted her woman's life so many times had been too virulent and too furious to die.

When we next saw Miss Emily, she had grown fat and her hair was turning gray. During the next few years it grew grayer and grayer until it attained an even pepper-and-salt iron-gray, when it ceased turning. Up to the day of her death at seventy-four it was still that vigorous iron-gray, like the hair of an active man.

From that time on her front door remained closed, save for a period of six or seven years, when she was about forty, during which she gave lessons in china-painting. She fitted up a studio in one of the downstairs rooms, where the daughters and granddaughters of Colonel Sartoris' contemporaries were sent to her with the same regularity and in the same spirit that they were sent to church on Sundays with a twenty-five cent piece for the collection plate. Meanwhile her taxes had been remitted.

Then the newer generation became the backbone and the spirit of the town, and the painting pupils grew up and fell away and did not send their children to her with boxes of color and tedious brushes and pictures cut from the ladies' magazines. The front door closed upon the last one and remained closed for good. When the town got free postal delivery, Miss Emily alone refused to let them fasten the metal numbers above her door and attach a mailbox to it. She would not listen to them.

Daily, monthly, yearly we watched the Negro grow grayer and more stooped, going in and out with the market basket. Each December we sent her a tax notice, which would be returned by the post office a week later, unclaimed. Now and then we would see her in one of the downstairs windows—she had evidently shut up the top floor of the house—like the carven torso of an idol in a niche, looking or not looking at us, we could never tell which. Thus she passed from generation to generation—dear, inescapable, impervious, tranquil, and perverse.

And so she died. Fell ill in the house filled with dust and shadows, with only a doddering Negro man to wait on her. We did not even know she was sick; we had long since given up trying to get any information from the Negro. He talked to no one, probably not even to her, for his voice had grown harsh and rusty, as if from disuse.

She died in one of the downstairs rooms, in a heavy walnut bed with a curtain, her gray head propped on a pillow yellow and moldy with age and lack of sunlight.

V

The Negro met the first of the ladies at the front door and let them in, with their hushed, sibilant voices and their quick, curious glances, and then he disappeared. He walked right through the house and out the back and was not seen again.

The two female cousins came at once. They held the funeral on the second day, with the town coming to look at Miss Emily beneath a mass of bought flowers, with the crayon face of her father musing profoundly above the bier and the ladies sibilant and macabre; and the very old men—some in their brushed Confederate uniforms—on the porch and the lawn, talking of Miss Emily as if she had been a contemporary of theirs, believing that they had danced with her and courted her perhaps, confusing time with its mathematical progression, as the old do, to whom all the past is not a diminishing road but, instead, a huge meadow which no winter ever quite touches, divided from them now by the narrow bottle-neck of the most recent decade of years.

Already we knew that there was one room in that region above stairs which no one had seen in forty years, and which would have to be forced. They waited until Miss Emily was decently in the ground before they opened it.

The violence of breaking down the door seemed to fill this room with pervading dust. A thin, acrid pall as of the tomb seemed to lie everywhere upon this room decked and furnished as for a bridal; upon the valence curtains of faded rose color, upon the rose-shaded lights, upon the dressing table, upon the delicate array of crystal and the man's toilet things backed with tarnished silver, silver so tarnished that the monogram was obscured. Among them lay a collar and tie, as if they had just been removed, which, lifted, left upon the surface a pale crescent in the dust. Upon a chair hung the suit, carefully folded; beneath it the two mute shoes and the discarded socks.

The man himself lay in the bed.

For a long while we just stood there, looking down at the profound and fleshless grin. The body had apparently once lain in the attitude of an embrace, but now the long sleep that outlasts love, that conquers even the grimace of love, had cuckolded him. What was left of him, rotted beneath what was left of the nightshirt, had become inextricable from the bed in which he lay; and upon him and upon the pillow beside him lay that even coating of the patient and biding dust.

Then we noticed that in the second pillow was the indentation of a head. One of us lifted something from it, and leaning forward, that faint and invisible dust dry and acrid in the nostrils, we saw a long strand of iron-gray hair.

STUDY GUIDE

1. This story is so structured that the reader is kept in suspense until the final paragraphs before he grasps the whole of Emily's situation. There are, however, many clues that build toward the final revelation. Study, for instance, the hints of something odd in the situation that the following details provide: the smell in the Grierson house, the closed house, Emily's life as a recluse, the references to insanity in the Grierson family, the purchase of arsenic, the mysterious disappearance of Homer Barron.

2. The story is a kind of macabre love story. Show how Faulkner gradually builds the strange love life of Emily to an utterly macabre ending. What is the meaning of the title "A Rose for Emily" in this connection? Discuss the significance of the faded rose-colored curtains and lamp shades in the last episode in this connection.

3. In spite of her macabre qualities, Emily is made a convincing, even a rather fascinating person. She won "the respectful affection" of the men of the town. What are some of the qualities that won her that respect?

4. Faulkner knew small-town life well, where everybody's business is everybody else's business and where gossiping is apt to be a full-time job—especially for the women. Show how Faulkner gives a realistic, sustained, and ironic—if not satiric—picture of this aspect of small-town life in the story.

5. What aspects of Emily's life stimulated gossip in Jefferson?

6. Faulkner also knew the realities, good and bad, of Southern culture in decay. He speaks of Emily's house as showing "stubborn and coquettish decay." This might be said of Emily herself and some of the other characters in the story. Point out examples of attempts, on the part of some of the characters, to save the surface graces and courtesies of the Old South.

7. Faulkner builds to a climax in his treatment of Emily's facial features. Study in detail the sense of tension and change that is revealed in the successive descriptions of Emily's face.

8. A similar effect is achieved through the successive treatment of her hair. Relate this to the love theme and the macabre detail of the "strand of iron-gray hair" in the final revelation of the story.

EVERYTHING THAT RISES MUST CONVERGE

Flannery O'Connor

Her doctor had told Julian's mother that she must lose twenty pounds on account of her blood pressure, so on Wednesday nights Julian had to take her downtown on the bus for a reducing class at the Y. The reducing class was designed for working girls over fifty, who weighed from 165 to 200 pounds. His mother was one of the slimmer ones, but she said ladies did not tell their age or weight. She would not ride the buses by herself at night since they had been integrated, and because the reducing class was one of her few pleasures, necessary for her health, and *free*, she said Julian could at least put himself out to take her, considering all she did for him. Julian did not like to consider all she did for him, but every Wednesday night he braced himself and took her.

She was almost ready to go, standing before the hall mirror, putting on her hat, while he, his hands behind him, appeared pinned to the door frame, waiting like Saint Sebastian for the arrows to begin piercing him. The hat was new and had cost her seven dollars and a half. She kept saying, "Maybe I shouldn't have paid that for it. No, I shouldn't have. I'll take it off and return it tomorrow. I shouldn't have bought it."

Julian raised his eyes to heaven. "Yes, you should have bought it," he said. "Put it on and let's go." It was a hideous hat. A purple velvet flap came down on one side of it and stood up on the other; the rest of it was green and looked like a cushion with the stuffing out. He decided it was less comical than jaunty and pathetic. Everything that gave her pleasure was small and depressed him.

She lifted the hat one more time and set it down slowly on top of her head. Two wings of gray hair protruded on either side of her florid face, but her eyes, sky-blue, were as innocent and untouched by experience as they must have been when she was ten. Were it not that she was a widow who had struggled fiercely to feed and clothe and put him through school and who was supporting him still, "until he got on his feet," she might have been a little girl that he had to take to town.

"It's all right, it's all right," he said. "Let's go." He opened the door himself and started down the walk to get her going. The sky was a dying violet and the houses stood out darkly against it, bulbous liver-colored monstrosities of a uniform ugliness though no two were alike. Since this had been a fashionable neighborhood forty years ago, his mother persisted in thinking they did well to have an apartment in it. Each house had a narrow collar of dirt around it in which sat, usually, a grubby child. Julian walked with his hands in his pockets, his head down and thrust forward and his eyes glazed with the determination to make himself completely numb during the time he would be sacrificed to her pleasure.

The door closed and he turned to find the dumpy figure, surmounted by the atrocious hat, coming toward him. "Well," she said, "you only live once and paying a little more for it, I at least won't meet myself coming and going."

"Some day I'll start making money," Julian said gloomily—he knew he never would—"and you can have one of those jokes whenever you take the fit." But first they would move. He visualized a place where the nearest neighbors would be three miles away on either side.

"I think you're doing fine," she said, drawing on her gloves. "You've only been out of school a year. Rome wasn't built in a day."

She was one of the few members of the Y reducing class who arrived in hat and gloves and who had a son who had been to college. "It takes time," she said, "and the world is in such a mess. This hat looked better on me than any of the others, though when she brought it out I said, 'Take that thing back. I wouldn't have it on my head,' and she said, 'Now wait till you see it on,' and when she put it on me, I said, 'We-ull,' and she said, 'If you ask me, that hat does something for you and you do something for the hat, and besides,' she said, 'with that hat, you won't meet yourself coming and going.' "

Julian thought he could have stood his lot better if she had been selfish, if she had been an old hag who drank and screamed at him. He walked along, saturated in depression, as if in the midst of his martyrdom he had lost his faith. Catching sight of his long, hopeless, irritated face, she stopped suddenly with a grief-stricken look, and pulled back on his arm. "Wait on me," she said. "I'm going back to the house and take this thing off and tomorrow I'm going to return it. I was out of my head. I can pay the gas bill with that seven-fifty."

He caught her arm in a vicious grip. "You are not going to take it back," he said. "I like it."

"Well, " she said, "I don't think I ought . . ."

"Shut up and enjoy it," he muttered, more depressed than ever.

"With the world in the mess it's in," she said, "it's a wonder we can enjoy anything. I tell you, the bottom rail is on the top."

Julian sighed.

"Of course," she said, "if you know who you are, you can go anywhere." She said this every time he took her to the reducing class. "Most of them in it are not our kind of people," she said, "but I can be gracious to anybody. I know who I am."

"They don't give a damn for your graciousness," Julian said savagely. "Knowing who you are is good for one generation only. You haven't the foggiest idea where you stand now or who you are."

She stopped and allowed her eyes to flash at him. "I most certainly do know who I am," she said, "and if you don't know who you are, I'm ashamed of you."

"Oh hell," Julian said.

"Your great-grandfather was a former governor of this state," she said. "Your grandfather was a prosperous landowner. Your grandmother was a Godhigh."

"Will you look around you," he said tensely, "and see where you are now?" and he swept his arm jerkily out to indicate the neighborhood, which the growing darkness at least made less dingy.

"You remain what you are," she said. "Your great-grandfather had a plantation and two hundred slaves."

"There are no more slaves," he said irritably.

"They were better off when they were," she said. He groaned to see that she was off on that topic. She rolled onto it every few days like a train on an open track. He knew every stop, every junction, every swamp along the way, and knew the exact point at which her conclusion would roll majestically into the station: "It's ridiculous. It's simply not realistic. They should rise, yes, but on their own side of the fence."

"Let's skip it," Julian said.

"The ones I feel sorry for," she said, "are the ones that are half white. They're tragic."

"Will you skip it?"

"Suppose we were half white. We would certainly have mixed feelings."

"I have mixed feelings now," he groaned.

"Well let's talk about something pleasant," she said. "I remember going to Grandpa's when I was a little girl. Then the house had double stairways that went up to what was really the second floor—all the cooking was done on the first. I used to like to stay down in the kitchen on account of the way the walls smelled. I would sit with my nose pressed against the plaster and take deep breaths. Actually the place belonged to the Godhighs but your grandfather Chestny paid the mortgage and saved it for them. They were in reduced circumstances," she said, "but reduced or not, they never forgot who they were."

"Doubtless that decayed mansion reminded them," Julian muttered.

He never spoke of it without contempt or thought of it without longing. He had seen it once when he was a child before it had been sold. The double stairways had rotted and been torn down. Negroes were living in it. But it remained in his mind as his mother had known it. It appeared in his dreams regularly. He would stand on the wide porch, listening to the rustle of oak leaves, then wander through the high-ceilinged hall into the parlor that opened onto it and gaze at the worn rugs and faded draperies. It occurred to him that it was he, not she, who could have appreciated it. He preferred its threadbare elegance to anything he could name and it was because of it that all the neighborhoods they had lived in had been a torment to him—whereas she had hardly known the difference. She called her insensitivity "being adjustable."

"And I remember the old darky who was my nurse, Caroline. There was no better person in the world. I've always had a great respect for my colored friends," she said. "I'd do anything in the world for them and they'd . . ."

"Will you for God's sake get off that subject?" Julian said. When he got on a bus by himself, he made it a point to sit down beside a Negro, in reparation as it were for his mother's sins.

"You're mighty touchy tonight," she said. "Do you feel all right?"

"Yes I feel all right," he said. "Now lay off."

She pursed her lips. "Well, you certainly are in a vile humor," she observed. "I just won't speak to you at all."

They had reached the bus stop. There was no bus in sight and Julian, his hands still jammed in his pockets and his head thrust forward, scowled down the empty street. The frustration of having to wait on the bus as well as ride on it began to creep up his neck like a hot hand. The presence of his mother was borne in upon him as she gave a pained sigh. He looked at her bleakly. She was holding herself very erect under the preposterous hat, wearing it like a banner of her imaginary dignity. There was in him an evil urge to break her spirit. He suddenly unloosened his tie and pulled it off and put it in his pocket.

She stiffened. "Why must you look like *that* when you take me to town?" she said. "Why must you deliberately embarrass me?"

"If you'll never learn where you are," he said, "you can at least learn where I am."

"You look like a—thug," she said.

"Then I must be one," he murmured.

"I'll just go home," she said. "I will not bother you. If you can't do a little thing like that for me . . ."

Rolling his eyes upward, he put his tie back on. "Restored to my class," he muttered. He thrust his face toward her and hissed, "True culture is in the mind, the *mind*," he said, and tapped his head, "the mind."

"It's in the heart," she said, "and in how you do things and how you do things is because of who you *are*."

"Nobody in the damn bus cares who you are."

"I care who I am," she said icily.

The lighted bus appeared on top of the next hill and as it approached, they moved out into the street to meet it. He put his hand under her elbow and hoisted her up on the creaking step. She entered with a little smile, as if she were going into a drawing room where everyone had been waiting for her. While he put in the tokens, she sat down on one of the broad front seats for three which faced the aisle. A thin woman with protruding teeth and long yellow hair was sitting on the end of it. His mother moved up beside her and left room for Julian beside herself. He sat down and looked at the floor across the aisle where a pair of thin feet in red and white canvas sandals were planted.

His mother immediately began a general conversation meant to attract anyone who felt like talking. "Can it get any hotter?" she said and removed from her purse a folding fan, black with a Japanese scene on it, which she began to flutter before her.

"I reckon it might could," the woman with the protruding teeth said, "but I know for a fact my apartment couldn't get no hotter."

"It must get the afternoon sun," his mother said. She sat forward and looked up and down the bus. It was half filled. Everybody was white. "I see we have the bus to ourselves," she said. Julian cringed.

"For a change," said the woman across the aisle, the owner of the red and white canvas sandals. "I come on one the other day and they were thick as fleas—up front and all through."

"The world is in a mess everywhere," his mother said. "I don't know how we've let it get in this fix."

"What gets my goat is all those boys from good families stealing automobile tires," the woman with the protruding teeth said. "I told my boy, I said you may not be rich but you been raised right and if I ever catch you in any such mess, they can send you on to the reformatory. Be exactly where you belong."

"Training tells," his mother said. "Is your boy in high school?"

"Ninth grade," the woman said.

"My son just finished college last year. He wants to write but he's selling typewriters until he gets started," his mother said.

The woman leaned forward and peered at Julian. He threw her such a malevolent look that she subsided against the seat. On the floor across the aisle there was an abandoned newspaper. He got up and got it and opened it out in front of him. His mother discreetly continued the conversation in a lower tone but the woman across the aisle said in a loud voice,

"Well that's nice. Selling typewriters is close to writing. He can go right from one to the other."

"I tell him," his mother said, "that Rome wasn't built in a day."

Behind the newspaper Julian was withdrawing into the inner compartment of his mind where he spent most of his time. This was a kind of mental bubble in which he established himself when he could not bear to be a part of what was going on around him. From it he could see out and judge but in it he was safe from any kind of penetration from without. It was the only place where he felt free of the general idiocy of his fellows. His mother had never entered it but from it he could see her with absolute clarity.

The old lady was clever enough and he thought that if she had started from any of the right premises, more might have been expected of her. She lived according to the laws of her own fantasy world, outside of which he had never seen her set foot. The law of it was to sacrifice herself for him after she had first created the necessity to do so by making a mess of things. If he had permitted her sacrifices, it was only because her lack of foresight had made them necessary. All of her life had been a struggle to act like a Chestny without the Chestny goods, and to give him everything she thought a Chestny ought to have; but since, said she, it was fun to struggle, why complain? And when you had won, as she had won, what fun to look back on the hard times! He could not forgive her that she had enjoyed the struggle and that she thought *she* had won.

What she meant when she said she had won was that she had brought him up successfully and had sent him to college and that he had turned out so well—good looking (her teeth had gone unfilled so that his could be straightened), intelligent (he realized he was too intelligent to be a success), and with a future ahead of him (there was of course no future ahead of him). She excused his gloominess on the grounds that he was still growing up and his radical ideas on his lack of practical experience. She said he didn't yet know a thing about "life," that he hadn't even entered the real world—when already he was as disenchanted with it as a man of fifty.

The further irony of all this was that in spite of her, he had turned out so well. In spite of going to only a third-rate college, he had, on his own initiative, come out with a first-rate education; in spite of growing up dominated by a small mind, he had ended up with a large one; in spite of all her foolish views, he was free of prejudice and unafraid to face facts. Most miraculous of all, instead of being blinded by love for her as she was for him, he had cut himself emotionally free of her and could see her with complete objectivity. He was not dominated by his mother.

The bus stopped with a sudden jerk and shook him from his meditation. A woman from the back lurched forward with little steps and barely escaped falling in his newspaper as she righted herself. She got off and a large Negro got on. Julian kept his paper lowered to watch. It gave him a certain satisfaction to see injustice in daily operation. It confirmed his view that with a few exceptions there was no one worth knowing within a radius of three hundred miles. The Negro was well dressed and carried a briefcase. He looked around and then sat down on the other end of the seat where the woman with the red and white canvas sandals was sitting. He immediately unfolded a newspaper and obscured himself behind it. Julian's mother's elbow at once prodded insistently into his ribs. "Now you see why I won't ride on these buses by myself," she whispered.

The woman with the red and white canvas sandals had risen at the same time the Negro sat down and had gone further back in the bus and taken the seat of the woman who had got off. His mother leaned forward and cast her an approving look.

Julian rose, crossed the aisle, and sat down in the place of the woman with the canvas sandals. From this position, he looked serenely across at his mother. Her face had turned an angry red. He stared at her, making his eyes the eyes of a stranger. He felt his tension suddenly lift as if he had openly declared war on her.

He would have liked to get in conversation with the Negro and to talk with him about art or politics or any subject that would be above the comprehension of those around them, but the man remained entrenched behind his paper. He was either ignoring the change of seating or had never noticed it. There was no way for Julian to convey his sympathy.

His mother kept her eyes fixed reproachfully on his face. The woman with the protruding teeth was looking at him avidly as if he were a type of monster new to her.

"Do you have a light?" he asked the Negro.

Without looking away from his paper, the man reached in his pocket and handed him a packet of matches.

"Thanks," Julian said. For a moment he held the matches foolishly. A NO SMOKING sign looked down upon him from over the door. This alone would not have deterred him; he had no cigarettes. He had quit smoking some months before because he could not afford it. "Sorry," he muttered and handed back the matches. The Negro lowered the paper and gave him an annoyed look. He took the matches and raised the paper again.

His mother continued to gaze at him but she did not take advantage of his momentary discomfort. Her eyes retained their battered look. Her face seemed to be unnaturally red, as if her blood pressure had risen. Julian allowed no glimmer of sympathy to show on his face. Having got the advantage, he wanted desperately to keep it and carry it through. He would have liked to teach her a lesson that would last her a while, but there seemed no way to continue the point. The Negro refused to come out from behind his paper.

Julian folded his arms and looked stolidly before him, facing her but as if he did not see her, as if he had ceased to recognize her existence. He visualized a scene in which, the bus having reached their stop, he would remain in his seat and when she said, "Aren't you going to get off?" he would look at her as at a stranger who had rashly addressed him. The corner they got off on was usually deserted, but it was well lighted and it would not hurt her to walk by herself the four blocks to the Y. He decided to wait until the time came and then decide whether or not he would let her get off by herself. He would have to be at the Y at ten to bring her back, but he could leave her wondering if he was going to show up. There was no reason for her to think she could always depend on him.

He retired again into the high-ceilinged room sparsely settled with large pieces of antique furniture. His soul expanded momentarily but then he became aware of his mother across from him and the vision shriveled. He studied her coldly. Her feet in little pumps dangled like a child's and did not quite reach the floor. She was training on him an exaggerated look of reproach. He felt completely detached from her. At that moment he could with pleasure have slapped her as he would have slapped a particularly obnoxious child in his charge.

He began to imagine various unlikely ways by which he could teach her a lesson. He might make friends with some distinguished Negro professor or lawyer and bring him home to spend the evening. He would be entirely justified but her blood pressure would rise to 300. He could not push her to the extent of making her have a stroke, and moreover, he had never been successful at making any Negro friends. He had tried to strike up an acquaintance on the bus with some of the better types, with ones that looked like professors or ministers or lawyers. One morning he had sat down next to a distinguished-looking dark brown man who had answered his questions with a sonorous solemnity but who had turned out to be an undertaker. Another day he had sat down beside a cigar-smoking Negro with a diamond ring on his finger, but after a few stilted pleasantries, the Negro had rung the buzzer and risen, slipping two lottery tickets into Julian's hand as he climbed over him to leave.

He imagined his mother lying desperately ill and his being able to secure only a Negro doctor for her. He toyed with that idea for a few minutes and then dropped it for a momentary vision of himself participating as a sympathizer in a sit-in demonstration. This was possible but he did not linger with it. Instead, he approached the ultimate horror. He brought home a beautiful suspiciously Negroid woman. Prepare yourself, he said. There is nothing you can do about it. This is the woman I've chosen. She's intelligent, dignified, even good, and she's suffered and she hasn't thought it *fun*. Now persecute us, go ahead and persecute us. Drive her out of here, but remember, you're driving me too. His eyes were narrowed and through the indignation he had generated, he saw his mother across the aisle, purple-faced, shrunken to the dwarf-like proportions of her moral nature, sitting like a mummy beneath the ridiculous banner of her hat.

He was tilted out of his fantasy again as the bus stopped. The door opened with a sucking hiss and out of the dark a large, gaily dressed, sullen-looking colored woman got on with a little boy. The child, who might have been four, had on a short plaid suit and a Tyrolean hat with a blue feather in it. Julian hoped that he would sit down beside him and that the woman would push in beside his mother. He could think of no better arrangement.

As she waited for her tokens, the woman was surveying the seating possibilities—he hoped with the idea of sitting where she was least wanted. There was something familiar-looking about her but Julian could not place what it was. She was a giant of a woman. Her face was set not only to meet opposition but to seek it out. The downward tilt of her large lower lip was like a warning sign: DON'T TAMPER WITH ME. Her bulging figure was encased in a green crepe dress and her feet overflowed in red shoes. She had on a hideous hat. A purple velvet flap came down on one side of it and stood up on the other; the rest of it was green and looked like a cushion with the stuffing out. She carried a mammoth red pocketbook that bulged throughout as if it were stuffed with rocks.

To Julian's disappointment, the little boy climbed up on the empty seat beside his mother. His mother lumped all children, black and white, into the common category, "cute," and she thought little Negroes were on the whole cuter than little white children. She smiled at the little boy as he climbed on the seat.

Meanwhile the woman was bearing down upon the empty seat beside Julian. To his annoyance, she squeezed herself into it. He saw his mother's face change as the woman settled herself next to him and he realized with satisfaction that this was more objectionable to her than it was to him. Her face seemed almost gray and there was a look of dull recognition in her eyes, as if suddenly she had sickened at some awful confrontation. Julian saw that it was because she and the woman had, in a sense, swapped sons. Though his mother would not realize the symbolic significance of this, she would feel it. His amusement showed plainly on his face.

The woman next to him muttered something unintelligible to herself. He was conscious of a kind of bristling next to him, a muted growling like that of an angry cat. He could not see anything but the red pocketbook upright on the bulging green thighs. He visualized the woman as she had stood waiting for her tokens—the ponderous figure, rising from the red shoes upward over the solid hips, the mammoth bosom, the haughty face, to the green and purple hat.

His eyes widened.

The vision of the two hats, identical, broke upon him with the radiance of a brilliant sunrise. His face was suddenly lit with joy. He could not believe that Fate had thrust upon his mother such a lesson. He gave a loud chuckle so that she would look at him and see that he saw. She turned her eyes on him slowly. The blue in them seemed to have turned a bruised purple. For a moment he had an uncomfortable sense of her innocence, but it lasted only a second before principle rescued him. Justice entitled him to laugh. His grin hardened until it said to her as plainly as if he were saying aloud: Your punishment exactly fits your pettiness. This should teach you a permanent lesson.

Her eyes shifted to the woman. She seemed unable to bear looking at him and to find the woman preferable. He became conscious again of the bristling presence at his side. The woman was rumbling like a volcano about to become active. His mother's mouth began to twitch slightly at one corner. With a sinking heart, he saw incipient signs of recovery on her face and realized that this was going to strike her suddenly as funny and was going to be no lesson at all. She kept her eyes on the woman and an amused smile came over her face as if the woman were a monkey that had stolen her hat. The little Negro was looking up at her with large fascinated eyes. He had been trying to attract her attention for some time.

"Carver!" the woman said suddenly. "Come heah!"

When he saw that the spotlight was on him at last, Carver drew his feet up and turned himself toward Julian's mother and giggled.

"Carver!" the woman said. "You heah me? Come heah!"

Carver slid down from the seat but remained squatting with his back against the base of it, his head turned slyly around toward Julian's mother, who was smiling at him. The woman reached a hand across the aisle and snatched him to her. He righted himself and hung backwards on her knees, grinning at Julian's mother. "Isn't he cute?" Julian's mother said to the woman with the protruding teeth.

"I reckon he is," the woman said without conviction.

The Negress yanked him upright but he eased out of her grip and shot across the aisle and scrambled, giggling wildly, onto the seat beside his love.

"I think he likes me," Julian's mother said, and smiled at the woman. It was the smile she used when she was being particularly gracious to an inferior. Julian saw everything lost. The lesson had rolled off her like rain on a roof.

The woman stood up and yanked the little boy off the seat as if she were snatching him from contagion. Julian could feel the rage in her at having no weapon like his mother's smile. She gave the child a sharp slap across his leg. He howled once and then thrust his head into her stomach and kicked his feet against her shins. "Be-have," she said vehemently.

The bus stopped and the Negro who had been reading the newspaper got off. The woman moved over and set the little boy down with a thump between herself and Julian. She held him firmly by the knee. In a moment he put his hands in front of his face and peeped at Julian's mother through his fingers.

"I see yoooooooo!" she said and put her hand in front of her face and peeped at him.

The woman slapped his hand down. "Quit yo' foolishness," she said, "before I knock the living Jesus out of you!"

Julian was thankful that the next stop was theirs. He reached up and pulled the cord. The woman reached up and pulled it at the same time. Oh my God, he thought. He had the terrible intuition that when they got off the bus together, his mother would open her purse and give the little boy a nickel. The gesture would be as natural to her as breathing. The bus stopped and the woman got up and lunged to the front, dragging the child, who wished to stay on, after her. Julian and his mother got up and followed. As they neared the door, Julian tried to relieve her of her pocketbook.

"No," she murmured, "I want to give the little boy a nickel."

"No!" Julian hissed. "No!"

She smiled down at the child and opened her bag. The bus door opened and the woman picked him up by the arm and descended with him, hanging at her hip. Once in the street she set him down and shook him.

Julian's mother had to close her purse while she got down the bus step but as soon as her feet were on the ground, she opened it again and began to rummage inside. "I can't find but a penny," she whispered, "but it looks like a new one."

"Don't do it!" Julian said fiercely between his teeth. There was a streetlight on the corner and she hurried to get under it so that she could better see into her pocketbook. The woman was heading off rapidly down the street with the child still hanging backward on her hand.

"Oh little boy!" Julian's mother called and took a few quick steps and caught up with them just beyond the lamppost. "Here's a bright new penny for you," and she held out the coin, which shone bronze in the dim light.

The huge woman turned and for a moment stood, her shoulders lifted and her face frozen with frustrated rage, and stared at Julian's mother. Then all at once she seemed to explode like a piece of machinery that had been given one ounce of pressure too much. Julian saw the black fist swing out with the red pocketbook. He shut his eyes and cringed as he heard the woman shout, "He don't take nobody's pennies!" When he opened his eyes, the woman was disappearing down the street with the little boy staring wide-eyed over her shoulder. Julian's mother was sitting on the sidewalk.

"I told you not to do that," Julian said angrily. "I told you not to do that!"

He stood over her for a minute, gritting his teeth. Her legs were stretched out in front of her and her hat was on her lap. He squatted down and looked her in the face. It was totally expressionless. "You got exactly what you deserved," he said. "Now get up."

He picked up her pocketbook and put what had fallen out back in it. He picked the hat up off her lap. The penny caught his eye on the sidewalk and he picked that up and let it drop before her eyes into the purse. Then he stood up and leaned over and held his hands out to pull her up. She remained immobile. He sighed. Rising above them on either side were black apartment buildings, marked with irregular rectangles of light. At the end of the block a man came out of a door and walked off in the opposite direction. "All right," he said, "suppose somebody happens by and wants to know why you're sitting on the sidewalk?"

She took the hand and, breathing hard, pulled heavily up on it and then stood for a moment, swaying slightly as if the spots of light in the darkness were circling around her. Her eyes, shadowed and confused, finally settled on his face. He did not try to conceal his irritation. "I hope this teaches you a lesson," he said. She leaned forward and her eyes raked his face. She seemed trying to determine his identity. Then, as if she found nothing familiar about him, she started off with a headlong movement in the wrong direction.

"Aren't you going on to the Y?" he asked.

"Home," she muttered.

"Well, are we walking?"

For answer she kept going. Julian followed along, his hands behind him. He saw no reason to let the lesson she had had go without backing it up with an explanation of its meaning. She might as well be made to understand what had happened to her. "Don't think that was just an uppity Negro woman," he said. "That was the whole colored race which will no longer take your condescending pennies. That was your black double. She can wear the same hat as you, and to be sure," he added gratuitously (because he thought it was funny), "it looked better on her than it did on you. What all this means," he said, "is that the old world is gone. The old manners are obsolete and your graciousness is not worth a damn." He thought bitterly of the house that had been lost for him. "You aren't who you think you are," he said.

She continued to plow ahead, paying no attention to him. Her hair had come undone on one side. She dropped her pocketbook and took no notice. He stooped and picked it up and handed it to her but she did not take it.

"You needn't act as if the world had come to an end," he said, "because it hasn't. From now on you've got to live in a new world and face a few realities for a change. Buck up," he said, "it won't kill you."

She was breathing fast.

"Let's wait on the bus," he said.

"Home," she said thickly.

"I hate to see you behave like this," he said. "Just like a child. I should be able to expect more of you." He decided to stop where he was and make her stop and wait for a bus. "I'm not going any farther," he said, stopping. "We're going on the bus."

She continued to go on as if she had not heard him. He took a few steps and caught her arm and stopped her. He looked into her face and caught his breath. He was looking into a face he had never seen before. "Tell Grandpa to come get me," she said.

He stared, stricken.

"Tell Caroline to come get me," she said.

Stunned, he let her go and she lurched forward again, walking as if one leg were shorter than the other. A tide of darkness seemed to be sweeping her from him. "Mother!" he cried. "Darling, sweetheart, wait!" Crumpling, she fell to the pavement. He dashed forward and fell at her side, crying, "Mamma, Mamma!" He turned her over. Her face was fiercely distorted. One eye, large and staring, moved slightly to the left as if it had become unmoored. The other remained fixed on him, raked his face again, found nothing and closed.

"Wait here, wait here!" he cried and jumped up and began to run for help toward a cluster of lights he saw in the distance ahead of him. "Help, help!" he shouted, but his voice was thin, scarcely a thread of sound. The lights drifted farther away the faster he ran and his feet moved numbly as if they carried him nowhere. The tide of darkness seemed to sweep him back to her, postponing from moment to moment his entry into the world of guilt and sorrow.

STUDY GUIDE

1. This story by Flannery O'Connor is built around the complexities of human relations. One of these complexities is revealed in the relationship between Julian and his mother. The mother is seen chiefly through Julian's unsympathetic eyes. What are some of the things about his mother of which he has become critical? What do the mother's hat and gloves and Julian's

removing his necktie reveal about the nature of the conflict between Julian and his mother?

2. How are some of the typical aspects of race prejudice and class consciousness revealed in the conversation and action of Julian's mother? In those of other characters on the bus?

3. Is Julian really as free from race prejudice and class consciousness as he says he is? What evidence do you have to the contrary? Does he really have deep respect for Negroes, or is he using them for his own purposes? Give evidence for your answer from his actions in the story. Why had he never succeeded in making any Negro friends?

4. Is Julian as contemptuous of the old aristocratic traditions as he says he is, or is he secretly treasuring them? What evidence is there in the story for this?

5. What is the significance and dramatic effect of Julian's mother and the Negro woman wearing identical hats? Does this, in one respect, put the two women on the same level? Have they, in the words of the title of the story, accidentally converged?

6. Early in the story, Julian is compared to St. Sebastian waiting to be pierced by arrows, and later he speaks of himself as a martyr. To what does he think he is being sacrificed?

7. Julian's mother thinks she is superior to the Negroes and Julian thinks he is superior to his mother. Why does he think so? Does he still think so at the end of the story? What is the sense of guilt that is overtaking him as the story ends?

8. Why does the Negro woman react so violently to the offer of the penny? Why does her violence so shatter the mind of Julian's mother and lead to her death? Discuss some of the facets of race relationships revealed in Julian's mother's attitude toward, and treatment of, the Negro boy and the boy's attitude toward her, in the attitude of the mother toward the Negro woman and other Negroes on the bus; and in the attitude of the Negro woman toward Julian's mother.

9. Do you think that Julian's mother understood why the Negro woman was so offended at her offering the boy a penny? What is the significance of Julian's mother talking about going "home" and asking for her grandfather to come get her? What is "home" to her?

10. What does the following remark of the author reveal about the subconscious attitude of Julian toward his aristocratic background at the very moment when he is telling his mother that "the old manners are obsolete and your graciousness is not worth a damn"? The author's remark: "He thought bitterly of the house that had been lost for him."

11. The title of the story, "Everything that Rises Must Converge," is based on an idea that Teilhard de Chardin expressed in the following passage:

> To be fully ourselves it is in the opposite direction, *in the direction of convergence with all the rest,* that we must advance—towards the "other!" the goal of ourselves, the acme of our originality is not our individuality but our person; and according to the evolutionary structure of the world, we can only find our person by uniting together. There is no mind without synthesis. The same law holds good from top to bottom. The true ego grows in inverse proportion to "egoism."

Show how this idea is applicable to Julian's mother and to Julian's own attitudes, action, and change. The Negroes in the story had risen to some extent

—the buses had been integrated—but did Negroes and white people converge in the Teilhardian sense of personal encounter?

12. Show how Flannery O'Connor used her shock technique as an actual grace shaking Julian into a consciousness of his excessive egoism, into "the world of guilt and sorrow."

A & P

John Updike

In walks these three girls in nothing but bathing suits. I'm in the third checkout slot, with my back to the door, so I don't see them until they're over by the bread. The one that caught my eye first was the one in the plaid green two-piece. She was a chunky kid, with a good tan and a sweet broad backside with those two crescents of white just under it, where the sun never seems to hit, at the top of the backs of her legs. I stood there with my hand on a box of HiHo crackers trying to remember if I rang it up or not. I ring it up again and the customer starts giving me hell. She's one of these cash-register-watchers, a witch about fifty with rouge on her cheekbones and no eyebrows, and I know it made her day to trip me up. She'd been watching cash registers for fifty years and probably never seen a mistake before.

By the time I got her feathers smoothed and her goodies into a bag—she gives me a little snort in passing, if she'd been born at the right time they would have burned her over in Salem—by the time I get her on her way the girls had circled around the bread and were coming back, without a pushcart, back my way along the counters, in the aisle between the checkouts and the Special bins. They didn't even have shoes on. There was this chunky one, with the two-piece—it was bright green and the seams on the bra were still sharp and her belly was still pretty pale so I guessed she just got it (the suit)—there was this one, with one of those chubby berry-faces, the lips all bunched together under her nose, this one, and a tall one, with black hair that hadn't quite frizzed right, and one of these sunburns right across under the eyes, and a chin that was too long—you know, the kind of girl other girls think is very "striking" and "attractive" but never quite makes it, as they very well know, which is why they like her so much—and then the third one, that wasn't quite so tall. She was the queen. She kind of led them, the other two peeking around and making their shoulders round. She didn't look around, not this queen, she just walked straight on slowly, on these long white prima-donna legs. She came down a little hard on her heels, as if she didn't walk in her bare feet that much, putting down her heels and then letting the weight move along to her toes as if she was testing the floor with every step, putting a little deliberate extra action into it. You never know for sure how girls' minds work (do you really think it's a mind in there or just a little buzz like a bee in a glass jar?) but you got the idea she had talked the other two into coming in here with her, and now she was showing them how to do it, walk slow and hold yourself straight.

She had on a kind of dirty-pink—beige maybe, I don't know—bathing suit with a little nubble all over it and, what got me, the straps were down. They were off her shoulders looped loose around the cool tops of her arms, and I guess as a result the suit had slipped a little on her, so all around the top of the cloth there was this shining rim. If it hadn't been there you wouldn't have known there could have been anything whiter than those shoulders. With the straps pushed off, there was nothing between the top of the suit and the top of her head except just *her*, this clean bare plane of the top of her chest down from the shoulder bones like a dented sheet of metal hanging in the light. I mean, it was more than pretty.

She had sort of oaky hair that the sun and salt had bleached, done up in a bun that was unravelling, and a kind of prim face. Walking into the A & P with your straps down, I suppose it's the only kind of face you *can* have. She held her head so high her neck, coming up out of those white shoulders, looked kind of stretched, but I didn't mind. The longer her neck was, the more of her there was.

She must have felt in the corner of her eye me and over my shoulder Stokesie in the second slot watching, but she didn't tip. Not this queen. She kept her eyes moving across the racks, and stopped, and turned so slow it made my stomach rub the inside of my apron, and buzzed to the other two, who kind of huddled against her for relief, and then they all three of them went up the cat-and-dog-food-breakfast-cereal-macaroni-rice-raisins-seasonings-spreads-spaghetti-soft-drinks-crackers and-cookies aisle. From the third slot I look straight up this aisle to the meat counter, and I watched them all the way. The fat one with the tan sort of fumbled with the cookies, but on second thought she put the package back. The sheep pushing their carts down the aisle—the girls were walking against the usual traffic (not that we have one-way signs or anything)—were pretty hilarious. You could see them, when Queenie's white shoulders dawned on them, kind of jerk, or hop, or hiccup, but their eyes snapped back to their own baskets and on they pushed. I bet you could set off dynamite in an A & P and the people would by and large keep reaching and checking oatmeal off their lists and muttering "Let me see, there was a third thing, began with A, asparagus, no, ah, yes, applesauce!" or whatever it is they do mutter. But there was no doubt, this jiggled them. A few houseslaves in pin curlers even looked around after pushing their carts past to make sure what they had seen was correct.

You know, it's one thing to have a girl in a bathing suit down on the beach, where what with the glare nobody can look at each other much anyway, and another thing in the cool of the A & P, under the fluorescent lights, against all those stacked packages, with her feet paddling along naked over our checkerboard green-and-cream rubber-tile floor.

"Oh, Daddy," Stokesie said beside me. "I feel so faint."

"Darling," I said. "Hold me tight." Stokesie's married, with two babies chalked up on his fuselage already, but as far as I can tell that's the only difference. He's twenty-two, and I was nineteen this April.

"Is it done?" he asks, the responsible married man finding his voice. I forgot to say he thinks he's going to be manager some sunny day, maybe in 1990 when it's called the Great Alexandrov and Petrooshki Tea Company or something.

What he meant was, our town is five miles from a beach, with a big summer colony out on the Point, but we're right in the middle of town, and the women generally put on a shirt or shorts or something before they get out of the car into the street. And anyway these are usually women with six children and varicose veins mapping their legs and nobody, including them, could care less. As I say, we're right in the middle of town, and if you stand at our front doors you can see two banks and the Congregational Church and the newspaper store and three real-estate offices and about twenty-seven old freeloaders tearing up the main street because the sewer broke again. It's not as if we're on the Cape; we're north of Boston and there's people in this town haven't seen the ocean for twenty years.

The girls had reached the meat counter and were asking McMahon something. He pointed, they pointed, and they shuffled out of sight behind a pyramid of Diet Delight peaches. All that was left for us to see was old McMahon patting his mouth and looking after them sizing up their joints. Poor kids, I began to feel sorry for them, they couldn't help it.

Now here comes the sad part of the story, at least my family says it's sad, but I don't think it's so sad myself. The store's pretty empty, it being Thursday afternoon, so there was nothing much to do except lean on the register and wait for the girls to show up again. The whole store was like a pinball machine and I didn't know which tunnel they'd come out of. After a while they came around out of the far aisle, around the light bulbs, records at discount of the Caribbean Six or Tony Martin Sings or some such gunk you wonder they waste the wax on, sixpacks of candy bars, and plastic toys done up in cellophane that fall apart when a kid looks at them anyway. Around they come, Queenie still leading the way, and holding a little gray jar in her hand. Slots Three through Seven are unmanned and I could see her wondering between Stokes and me, but Stokesie with his usual luck draws an old party in baggy gray pants who stumbles up with four giant cans of pineapple juice (what do these bums *do* with all that pineapple juice? I've often asked myself) so the girls come to me. Queenie puts down the jar and I take it into my fingers icy cold. Kingfish Fancy Herring Snacks in Pure Sour Cream: 49¢. Now her hands are empty, not a ring or a bracelet, bare as God made them, and I wonder where the money's coming from. Still with that prim look she lifts a folded dollar bill out of the hollow at the center of her nubbled pink top. The jar went heavy in my hand. Really, I thought that was so cute.

Then everybody's luck begins to run out. Lengel comes in from haggling with a truck full of cabbages on the lot and is about to scuttle into that door marked MANAGER behind which he hides all day, when the girls touch his eye. Lengel's pretty dreary, teaches Sunday school and the rest, but he doesn't miss that much. He comes over and says, "Girls, this isn't the beach."

Queenie blushes, though maybe it's just a brush of sunburn I was noticing for the first time, now that she was so close. "My mother asked me to pick up a jar of herring snacks." Her voice kind of startled me, the way voices do when you see the people first, coming out so flat and dumb yet kind of toney, too, the way it ticked over "pick up" and "snacks." All of a sudden I slid right down her voice into her living room. Her father and the other men were standing around in ice-cream coats and bow ties and the women were in sandals picking up herring snacks on toothpicks off a big glass plate and they were all holding drinks the color of water with olives and sprigs of mint in them. When my parents have somebody over they get lemonade and if it's a real racy affair Schlitz in tall glasses with "They'll Do It Every Time" cartoons stencilled on.

"That's all right," Lengel said. "But this isn't the beach." His repeating this struck me as funny, as if it had just occurred to him, and he had been thinking all these years the A & P was a great big dune and he was the head lifeguard. He didn't like my smiling—as I say, he doesn't miss much—but he concentrates on giving the girls that sad Sunday-school-superintendent stare.

Queenie's blush is no sunburn now, and the plump one in plaid, that I liked better from the back—a really sweet backside—pipes up, "We weren't doing any shopping. We just came in for the one thing."

"That makes no difference," Lengel tells her, and I could see from the way his eyes went that he hadn't noticed she was wearing a two-piece before. "We want you decently dressed when you come in here."

"We *are* decent," Queenie says suddenly, her lower lip pushing, getting sore now that she remembers her place, a place from which the crowd that runs the A & P must look pretty crummy. Fancy Herring Snacks flashed in her very blue eyes.

"Girls, I don't want to argue with you. After this come in here with your shoulders covered. It's our policy." He turns his back. That's policy for you. Policy is what the kingpins want. What the others want is juvenile delinquency.

All this while, the customers had been showing up with their carts but, you know sheep, seeing a scene, they had all bunched up on Stokesie, who shook open a paper bag as gently as peeling a peach, not wanting to miss a word. I could feel in the silence everybody getting nervous, most of all Lengel, who asks me, "Sammy, have you rung up their purchase?"

I thought and said "No" but it wasn't about that I was thinking. I go through the punches, 4, 9, GROC, TOT—it's more complicated than you think, and after you do it often enough, it begins to make a little song, that you hear words to, in my case "Hello (*bing*) there, you (*gung*) hap-py *pee*-pul (*splat*)!" the *splat* being the drawer flying out. I uncrease the bill, tenderly as you may imagine, it just having come from between the two smoothest scoops of vanilla I had ever know were there, and pass a half and a penny into her narrow pink palm, and nestle the herrings in a bag and twist its neck and hand it over, all the time thinking.

The girls, and who'd blame them, are in a hurry to get out, so I say "I quit" to Lengel quick enough for them to hear, hoping they'll stop and watch me, their unsuspected hero. They keep right on going, into the electric eye; the door flies open and they flicker across the lot to their car, Queeny and Plaid and Big Tall Goony-Goony (not that as raw material she was so bad), leaving me with Lengel and a kink in his eyebrow.

"Did you say something, Sammy?"

"I said I quit."

"I thought you did."

"You didn't have to embarrass them."

"It was they who were embarrassing us."

I started to say something that came out "Fiddle-de-doo." It's a saying of my grandmother's, and I know she would have been pleased.

"I don't think you know what you're saying," Lengel said.

"I know you don't," I said. "But I do." I pull the bow at the back of my apron and start shrugging it off my shoulders. A couple customers that had been heading for my slot begin to knock against each other, like scared pigs in a chute.

Lengel sighs and begins to look very patient and old and gray. He's been a friend of my parents for years. "Sammy, you don't want to do this to your Mom and Dad," he tells me. It's true, I don't. But it seems to me that once you begin a gesture it's fatal not to go through with it. I fold the apron, "Sammy" stitched in red on the pocket, and put it on the counter, and drop the bow tie on it. "You'll feel this for the rest of your life," Lengel says, and I know that's true, too, but remembering how he made that pretty girl blush makes me so scrunchy inside I punch the No Sale tab and the machine whirs "pee-pul" and the drawer splats out. One advantage of this scene taking place in summer, I can follow this up with a clean exit, there's no fumbling around getting your coat and ear muffs, I just saunter into the electric eye in my white shirt that my mother ironed the night before, and the door heaves itself open, and outside the sunshine is skating around on the asphalt.

I look around for my girls, but they're gone, of course. There wasn't anybody but some young married screaming with her children about some candy they didn't get by the door of a powder-blue Falcon station wagon. Looking back in the big windows, over the bags of peat moss and aluminum furniture stacked on the pavement, I could see Lengel in my place in the slot, checking the sheep through. His face was dark gray and his back stiff, as if he'd just had an injection of iron, and my stomach kind of fell as I felt how hard the world was going to be to me hereafter.

STUDY GUIDE

1. Part of the humor of this story by John Updike resides in the point of view from which it is narrated—that of Sammy, a teen-age checker in an A & P store. Show how the language of the story throughout keeps the reader aware of this fact.

2. The incongruity of the situation (a trio of girls in two-piece bathing suits in a midtown A & P store, weaving in and out of the counters of packaged food) is emphasized by the reaction of various groups and individuals in the store. Discuss the effect of this incongruity on the narrator, on Stokesie, on the "sheep," on the "house slaves in pin curlers," and on the manager, Lengel.

3. There is in the reaction of the narrator to the leader of the three girls a hint of class—of the commoner falling for the charming princess. Point out these hints in the description of the girl herself and what runs through Sammy's mind when he learns the nature of her purchase.

4. Is there something of adolescent gallantry in the action of the narrator at the end of the story?

5. Why is Sammy's gallantry somewhat ironic? Are the girls really aware of either an offense that needs his gallant defense, or even of the fact that he has defended them?

APPENDIX

Some Notes on Rhetoric

The term *rhetoric* today generally means the art of writing logically and emotionally *effective* prose, as distinct from merely *correct*, grammatical sentences. A knowledge of rhetoric makes a person sensitive not merely to the correctness of his diction and syntax but also to the effect on readers of his over-all thought structure, of the shape and form of his sentences, and of the connotation of individual words, images, and rhythms.

In the past, rhetoric was more narrowly associated with the realm of oratory. For such great rhetoricians as Aristotle, Cicero, and Quintilian, rhetoric was the art of logical and emotionally effective persuasion. It dealt with matters about which there was room for different opinions, and it was the purpose of the orator to marshal his material in a manner that would induce his listeners to accept his opinion. There was always a considerable appeal to the emotions in the process. The art that developed this skill in composing persuasive oratorical prose formed one of the three important disciplines in ancient, medieval, and renaissance education; in fact, the art of rhetoric continued to be an important part of educational practice down to the middle of the nineteenth century. It was one of the elements of the *trivium*, a division of the curriculum in medieval schools. In the trivium, grammar was not what it later became—a study of the logic of language, its parts of speech and syntax—but a broad training in the sensitive reading of a text, which today would be called practical criticism; dialectic was a training in the art of correct thinking; and rhetoric was a training in the art of effective or moving expression.

Rhetoric itself was divided into several parts: *inventio* was concerned with the discovery of the material for the oration; *dispositio*, with the effective organization or arrangement of the material; *eloquentia*, with matters of style, such as diction, imagery, rhythm; *memoria*, with the memorization of the finished oration; and *traditio*, with its actual delivery.

It is apparent that these parts of rhetoric, especially the first three parts, are the chief concerns of any writer at any time: he must have something to say and know how to say it. *Inventio* taught him how to discover the "what"; *dispositio* and *eloquentia*, the "how." The suggestions made by the old rhetoricians about both the "what" and the "how" are still helpful to writers today.

Different occasions demanded different types of oratory. The two chief forms that developed were the forensic, or argumentative, and the epideictic, or occasional. The former tried to prove a point or persuade an audience to accept a definite opinion about something; the latter presented, in a combined narrative-expository manner, the bases for the praise or acclaim that was being solicited for the person or occasion honored by the epideictic or laudatory oration. Out of the forensic oration developed argumentative prose and from the epideictic oration, straight expository prose.

But whatever the nature of the occasion, the oration itself was always built into an organic whole; so much so that it became the exemplar of organic unity in prose compositions in general. To achieve organic unity in any piece of writing, Aristotle says in his *Poetics*, one must see that it has a beginning, a middle, and an end. And these parts are not interchangeable; one part must develop from the other.

The typical classical oration eventually came to be structured in a set pattern. It always began with a *poemium*, or introduction, which was to render the audience benevolent and introduce the main topic, and it ended with an *exordium*, which summarized the main body of the oration and brought it to a conclusion. The body of the oration itself was made up of a *narratio*, or preliminary exposition of the main idea; of the *propositio*, or very succinct statement of the main point; of the *confutatio*, or proof, which marshaled the chief arguments for the position presented in the oration; and then the *reprehensio*, or answer to the objections that might be brought against the position defended in the oration. Sometimes a *digressio* was introduced after the main proof or *confutatio*, and this part often added the evidence of a case parallel to that developed in the main proof. This typical structure is well exemplified in Swift's "A Modest Proposal." It is impossible to exaggerate the importance of this oratorical structure in developing a sense of logical organization in prose composition. It is readily apparent that here are the chief elements of all organized expression—a beginning, a middle, and an end.

In the development of the body of the oration most of the important rhetorical methods of developing an idea were already exemplified. There are actually not many things that you can do with an idea. You can *define* it; you can *analyze* it into its component parts; you can illuminate it by an *analogy*; you can *contrast* it with its opposite or *compare* it to something resembling it; you can give a *concrete example* of it or a whole *series of concrete examples* and thus build up some of the cogency of a logical induction; or you can explain it by elaborating on either its *causes* or its *effects*. These continue to be the main methods of developing an idea.

Forms of Discourse

The form of discourse is chiefly determined by the purpose of the writer. If the writer wishes to tell his readers about a series of events that have taken place, he writes a *narrative*; if he wishes to share with them a sight he has seen—a person, place, or situation—he writes a *description*; if he wants to convince them of some definite assertion, he builds an *argumentation*; and, finally, if he desires to explain an idea or a process, he composes a piece of *exposition*.

NARRATIVE

The purposes of various forms of discourse also partly determine the order in which the material is arranged. In a narrative the detailed events are frequently arranged chronologically, that is, in the order in which they occurred. But sometimes, especially in fictional narrative, the story begins in the midst of the action and then supplies the preceding events in dramatic flashbacks. This latter is the order followed in the epic and in many novels.

DESCRIPTION

The general purpose of description is to enable the reader to experience vicariously what the writer has himself seen, heard, smelled, touched, or tasted, or what he wants the reader to sense in the specific context of his work. That context, however, can vary greatly. The author may be writing a descriptive essay in which he mainly wants the reader to see as accurately as possible whatever he is describing—a scene, an object, a situation, a person, or all of these together. For such a purpose he can order the details of his description in a variety of ways. In a landscape, for instance, he can move from top to bottom or from the bottom to the top, from right to left or left to right, or from the foreground to the background or vice versa. Or he can select only the most important details of the scene and ignore the less important ones. In describing a person a similar variety of order is available to the writer. But he may not want to supply a complete catalog of all the details of the character's appearance; he may prefer to focus on a single detail of dress or action that reveals the dominant character trait of the person being described.

Exclusively descriptive essays are seldom written today; but descriptive passages often occur in such semi-expository essays as those on Stonehenge, the Bessemer process, and the first explosion of the atomic bomb in this collection. Description, however, is indispensable to the fiction writer; he needs it to create the setting and characters of his narrative. But he uses it in widely divergent ways and for very different purposes. Many nineteenth-century novelists, for instance, used it to build up realistic and objective impressions of the setting for their story. They provided many concrete details, complete and exact enough to enable a reader to paint the scene or person described accurately. They also often assumed an omniscient point of view. For instance, the speaker in the description of a New England village, from Howells' *A Modern Instance*, knows what the village looks like in winter as well as in summer, and he sees it not only from the ground but also from a bird's-eye view. In such descriptions the writer may describe what he sees from a fixed point or adopt a shifting or roving point of view in which his eye wanders over the scene like the eye of a motion-picture camera on a moving camera truck. The selection from Hemingway's *A Farewell to Arms* exemplifies the fixed point of view (the author describes only what Frederic Henry can see from the door of his house), while the selection from Du Maurier's *Rebecca* exemplifies both the roving and the omniscient point of view (the speaker moves all the way up the driveway to Manderley and sees the driveway and the mansion both as they were before the fire and as they are now). Some writers, such as Steinbeck in sections of *The Grapes of Wrath*, perfected an impressionistic type of description in which vivid sense impressions, juxtaposed in predicateless phrases, frequently suggest much more about setting, character, and theme than would be expressed in any kind of explicit predication. And in much modern fiction, again well exemplified in the selection from Hemingway's *A Farewell to Arms*, the purpose of the descriptive passages is not to recreate a realistic picture of the scene but rather to communicate the impression and emotional impact it made on the speaker. This is a subjective and expressionistic type of description, and again the selection from Hemingway's *A Farewell to Arms* is a good example. It is analagous to the paintings of such an Expressionistic artist as Vincent van Gogh where the colors, lines, and masses of the composition are chosen to express the artist's emotional reaction to the scene rather than to communicate an objective impression of it.

ARGUMENTATION

Except in formal debates, there are not many occasions when formal argumentation is demanded of writers today. But the methods of logical proof are frequently helpful and are closely related to certain methods of rhetorical development. The two chief methods of logical proof are *induction* and *deduction*, which were discussed in some detail in Section 2 of this text (pages 63–64), and there is no need to repeat the discussion. An induction, which gains its cogency by working from a sufficient number of identical single incidents to the general conclusion that under like circumstances the same thing will always occur, is analogous to the rhetorical method of developing an idea by *multiple example*. And an idea developed by multiple examples, therefore, has some of the cogency of a logical induction. A deduction, of course, proceeds in the opposite direction from a general premise to a particular conclusion, and it is, in its most exact form, expressed in the syllogism. Although a writer seldom has the occasion for using the deductive method in its full syllogistic form, he frequently employs the logical order of proof or argumentation from a generic principle to a particular application of it. In fact, the rhetorical development of an idea by arguing to the *causes of a known effect* or to the *effects of a known cause* has something of the method of a logical deduction about it.

EXPOSITION

But for most people the form of discourse for which there is the greatest and most frequent need is *exposition*. The purpose of exposition is to explain an idea or process. And it is this purpose that dictates all the methods of development in expository prose. These methods are really merely ways of answering various questions. A writer may ask about a subject that he is trying to explain: What is it? *Definition*. What are its various parts? *Analysis*. What is a good example of it? *Illustration* and *concrete example*. What is it like? *Comparison*. How is it different from other things? *Contrast*. What are some of its logical relationships: What is it for? *Purpose*. Why does it act the way it does? What are its causes? *Effect to cause*. What are its effects? *Cause to effect*. Actually, if a writer gets into the habit of asking himself these questions about any subject he is trying to explain, he will be surprised at how much he already knows—and he will also quickly discover the areas in which his knowledge is inadequate and in which he will have to do further work before he can write intelligently. It is these types of questions with which rhetorical *inventio* (discovery) was always concerned; questions that helped the writer discover the material for his composition. Some or all of these questions may have to be answered in the process of developing a good piece of expository prose. As the essays in this collection show, it is generally by a combination of these methods of development that a good expository essay is built. Methods of development are really concerned with the second part of rhetoric—*dispositio*, or the principles guiding the arrangement of material once it is discovered.

DEFINITION Since the purpose of exposition is to explain or clarify something, it almost always involves a *definition* of what is being explained. The term *definition* itself means to put limits about something and therefore to set it off from something else. That is what every good definition does: It enables us to delimit the meaning of a word, of an idea, or an object, that is, to specify positively what the object defined is and what distinguishes it from other objects that are like it.

A *logical definition* provides this information in a very succinct and formal way. It tells, first, the general class or *genus* to which the object defined belongs and, second, the ways in which it differs from other objects in the same class (the species or specific difference). For instance, this is a logical definition of man: *man is a rational animal.* This definition provides the information that man belongs to the general class (*genus*) of animals. This already delimits him and sets him off from pure spiritual beings above him and from plants and the nonliving realm below him. But the added qualification *rational*—what the philosophers call the *specific difference*—further delimits man and tells how he differs from all other animals, namely by possessing reason.

Logical definitions define the objects or ideas lying behind words. *Dictionary definitions* are more concerned with delimiting the various possible meanings of the words themselves. A dictionary gives not just one meaning of a word but all the various meanings that it can have today in different contexts (the word *bay*, for instance, means one thing when it refers to a body of water but quite another when it refers to a part of a building or to a horse of a particular color). A dictionary also lists the various meanings that a word has had in the past, and in addition, it usually provides examples of the various usages in complete sentences. Another type of dictionary definition is the *etymological*, the root meaning of the word in the language from which it was derived. This is sometimes related to the present meaning of the word and sometimes not, depending on what has happened to it since its entrance into English. As Stuart Robertson and Frederic Cassidy have pointed out in their essay "Changing Meanings and Values in Words," etymology is sometimes a dangerous guide to current meanings. However, it is always interesting to know where a word came from, and sometimes etymology helps readers to grasp and retain the exact denotation of a word whose meaning has not changed from its root meaning. For instance, the etymology of *definition* (*de* + *finire*, to put limits about) still deepens our understanding of what a definition does. On the other hand, when the meaning of a word has changed, the etymology may help fill out the exact life-story of the word. It is interesting to note, for instance, that the etymological and original meaning of "politician" (from the Greek *politēs*, citizen) was a man devoted to the welfare of the city and its citizens, and it leads to speculations on how the word came to have its present connotation of a man who manipulates citizens for his own welfare.

But as helpful and sometimes necessary as these logical and dictionary definitions are to the expository writer, they are generally not sufficient to accomplish his purpose of defining and explaining a subject fully. To achieve his purpose he must almost always resort to an *extended definition.* In other words, he must extend his definition by employing some of the other methods of rhetorical development.

It has been said that one good *concrete example* or one *good picture* is often better than ten definitions to clarify a topic. For instance, if I were trying to define a Byzantine church, I would begin by saying that it is a type of church edifice (*genus*) made up of a series of domes resting upon square supports (*specific difference*), but I could expect to be understood better if I cited Hagia Sophia in Istanbul or Saint Mark's in Venice as concrete examples of the Byzantine style. I would be even better understood if I provided pictures of these two buildings.

Every definition involves a clarification about what the object being defined is. Since this precise quality may be very new and unfamiliar to a reader, an author may help him to understand the definition if the author extends it through a *comparison* to something with which the reader is familiar. For instance, the reader may know nothing at all about the structural principles of a Byzantine church, but he does know what round arches are and what a dome is. If I tell him that a Byzantine building is constructed by arranging four Roman arches in a square and then resting the dome, like an inverted half eggshell or cup, on the tops of the arches, he will have a fairly clear visual impression of the skeletal structure of a Byzantine church. Comparison is almost a necessity for extending the positive side of a definition of unfamiliar things.

But a definition also involves a specific difference—the way in which the thing defined differs from objects or ideas excluded from the definition. To extend this part of the definition, *contrast* is often very useful. In my definition of a Byzantine church the specific detail that differentiates this style from other types of church architecture is the structural principle of domes resting directly on the tops of round arches. This specific difference could be extended by contrasting Byzantine churches with the basilica church, which has no dome, or with the domed Renaissance church, in which the dome rests not directly on the tops of arches but on a circular drum which in turn rests on the tops of the four arches. Here again, this extension of the definition by *contrast* would be much enhanced by extending it still further by citing *concrete examples* of these two forms of domed structures—Hagia Sophia, a domed structure without a drum, and Saint Peter's, a domed structure with one.

Frequently what is being defined is an abstract idea such as patriotism. However clear and exact a writer may make his logical definition of such an abstract idea, it will be very much clarified and intensified by an *illustration*, or concrete anecdote, in which he shows patriots in action. Patriotism in simplest terms is love (*genus*) for one's country (*specific difference*), which differentiates it from love for family. But what patriotism is would be made much more meaningful by an illustration of it from the life of a great patriot, such as George Washington, Abraham Lincoln, or Winston Churchill.

A definition may also be extended by a process of *analysis*, that is, by dividing the object into its physical or logical components. I might, for instance, extend the definition of a basilica-type church by enumerating its physical parts. It is made up of the entrance way, or *atrium*, on the west end; the long rectangular body of the church, or nave of three or five aisles; two side wings, or transepts; and, finally, at the east end, a semicircular apse. If I wish to clarify the ground plan further, I might add a *comparison* and say that the parts taken together form a Roman cross. Or, if I am trying to define patriotism, I might extend the logical definition, *love for one's country*, by enumerating the elements that may enter into that love. I might say, for instance, that it is partly a matter of pride in one's native country or nationality, partly a love for the place of one's origin, partly an emotional association with home and family, partly a sense of one's identity with a group separate from all outside groups or foreign nationalities, and a willingness to sacrifice oneself in defense of or for the preservation of all these things one loves. Such details help to extend the naked idea of patriotism as stated in the logical definition.

Another way of extending a definition is to go into the logical matters of *cause* and *effect*. If I were trying to give a complete explanation of a basilica church, for instance, I might want to explain why that particular form of building was adopted by early Christians as a place of worship. In other words, I would be providing the *cause* of a particular effect. In doing so, I would explain the need early Christians had for a building accommodating large crowds of worshipers and then show how the basilica filled that need.

It is evident, then, that to develop an extended definition, one combines the various rhetorical methods of development. Many examples of the various ways of combining these methods to extend a definition can be found in the expository essays of this collection. Particularly good examples occur in De Quincey's "The Literature of Knowledge and the Literature of Power," F. L. Lucas' "What Is Style?," T. H. Huxley's "Inductive and Deductive Reasoning," L. M. Myers' "What Is Language?," Roger Troisfontaines' "What Is Existentialism?," and John Henry Newman's "Communication through Literature."

ANALYSIS In addition to logical definition and the various methods of writing an extended definition, there are other ways of developing expository prose. Chief among them is *analysis.* A definition of any kind attempts to present what it defines as a whole and to determine what sets it off from all other things. Analysis, on the other hand, breaks down the whole into its component parts. It does not create these parts but discovers those already in the thing being analyzed. Analysis is certainly one of the most helpful steps by which to arrive at an understanding of any problem, and it is almost always necessary for the successful development of a piece of expository prose.

Analysis is usually divided into two main types: *partition* and *classification.* Partition is the division of an object that is ordinarily thought of as one whole into its component parts. A basilica church, to continue the same illustration, is ordinarily thought of as one entity. The division of it into *atrium* or entrance way, nave or body, transepts or side wings, and apse is a partition of it. People ordinarily think of the United States government as one entity, but it can be analyzed by partition into the legislative, judicial and executive branches. This kind of analysis helps a writer to order what he wants to say about his subject. An entire expository essay could be written about the basilica by discussing each part consecutively and by describing its shape and function, and another about the United States government by discussing in order the function of each of its branches.

Analysis by classification proceeds by grouping into wholes elements that ordinarily exist separately. A book is a single whole and can be analyzed by partition into its introduction, table of contents, chapters, conclusion, and index. Moreover, a whole group of books can be analyzed by classification in various ways: by subject matter (all books on history, literature art), by size (quarto and folio volumes), by date of publication, by language, and so on. Analysis by classification is a means of organizing or controlling material. In discussing buildings, for instance, I might group them by style—romanesque, Gothic, high Renaissance, Baroque; by structural principles—the post and lintel, the arch, the cantilever, or reinforced concrete structure; by function—dwellings, schools, factories, churches, office buildings. Any of these classifications might provide an orderly framework in which to discuss the topic of buildings. But I must be consistent and not mix my classifications. For example, I should not classify —in one and the same line of discussion—buildings according to various principles, for example, large buildings, reinforced concrete buildings, and office buildings. Such a mixture of classification would confuse rather than clarify my discussion of the topic.

OTHER METHODS OF DEVELOPMENT The other most important methods of developing an idea were mentioned in the discussion of methods for extending a definition: *illustration, multiple concrete examples, comparison and contrast,* and *cause-and-effect relationships.* These methods, of course, need not be employed merely as means of extending definitions. A whole essay, or large parts of it, or just individual paragraphs may be developed by any one of these methods, and generally good expository prose is made up of a combination of them. Most of the expository essays in this book, as a matter of fact, employ a combination of several of these methods of development.

Narrative and *description* also occasionally serve a purpose in expository prose, especially in developing a sustained illustration or concrete example and in explaining a process.

The Elements of Style

In the traditional rhetorics, style, or eloquentia, dealt with the effectiveness of *sentence structure, diction, imagery,* and *rhythm.* The effectiveness of any of these matters must be judged by the purpose of the writer. Because the traditional rhetoric generally dealt with an oratorical purpose, it countenanced much more of an emotional appeal than is favored today in expository prose. Today, in most instances, a writer's purpose is primarily to explain or clarify a topic or idea. Hence the norm of successful sentence structure, diction, imagery, or rhythm in such prose is simply this: Does the sentence structure, the word, the image, or the rhythm help clarify, emphasize, or intensify the idea the writer is trying to communicate? But in order to guarantee that these elements of discourse do contribute to the effectiveness of his communication, the writer must know their potentialities.

SENTENCE STRUCTURE

A writer must know that sentences communicate meanings to readers not only by *what* they say but also by *how* they say it. He must recognize, for example, the different nuances of meaning and tone that exist among the *declarative, interrogative, imperative* and *exclamatory* forms of the sentence. The sentences of expository prose will ordinarily be largely declarative because it deals with straightforward statement of fact. But there is also room for all the other types of sentence in exposition. Well-placed interrogatives at the beginning of an essay or at the the opening of a new thought division can alert the reader to the question the writer is attempting to answer in the whole essay. Exclamations and imperatives carry special connotations and suggest special relationships between writer and reader, and hence must be used with caution. Imperatives that are employed too early may be resented by the reader. They come best toward the end of an essay, after the author has revealed his knowledge of the subject and has established his right to speak authoritatively about it. Exclamations may serve a purpose in an introduction or at important thought junctures of the essay, but they, too, will be accepted more readily after the author's exposition has brought the reader to a sufficient understanding of and enthusiasm for or criticism of his subject to warrant an emotional exclamation.

Simple, compound, and *complex* sentences also mirror the thought they express. Often a mere listing or summary of details is emphasized by a series of simple declarative sentences in parallel structure. But not all simple sentences are short. Often a sense of urgency, intensity, or climax can be achieved by a simple sentence with an accumulative, compound predicate. As a matter of fact, the use of compound predicates can also result in an economy of expression and reduce wordiness. Where an author is concerned with expressing exact thought relationships, such as conditions, causes, time elements, as he frequently is in expository prose, the complex sentence is an absolute necessity. And often, because exposition frequently involves careful comparisons and contrasts, these balanced thought relationships are best expressed in parallel sentence structure. *Parallelism,* as a matter of fact, between the structure of successive sentences or between successive clauses and phrases of the same sentence is one of the most characteristic features of expository prose.

Another classification of sentences is the *curt, loose,* and *periodic.* A prevalence of one or the other can create a very specific tone in a piece of writing and actually help communicate meaning. The periodic *sentence,* in which the full meaning is suspended until the end, is achieved easily enough in English by simply beginning a complex sentence with the subordinate clause or clauses. This puts the main clause, expressing the main idea, at the end of the sentence. The periodic sentence creates a rolling, rotund rhythm, and sense of climax that is, perhaps, more appropriate for oral than for written discourse. But it can serve a useful purpose in expository prose to create an emotional emphasis, a sense of climax, or an impressive summary statement. It particularly characterized the style of many writers in the late eighteenth and early nineteenth centuries. Examples of it will be found in the selections from Burke, Macaulay, and Newman.

The *loose period* is less logically organized. It generally begins with a clause stating the main idea, and then from that, like the segments of a telescope, stretch any number of relative clauses, and participial modifiers. The loose period expresses successive thoughts in the loose-jointed, impressionistic manner in which they occur in the mind; it does not rearrange them in the logical and climactic order of the periodic sentence. Baroque writers like Sir Thomas Browne in the seventeenth century and Faulkner in the twentieth century exemplify the style.

The *curt style* is made up of short staccato sentences, generally just simple declarative sentences, or compound sentences the clauses of which are strung together with "ands" or without any connectives at all. It is almost always the style in which a writer expresses his ethical observations on life. The brevity, pithiness, and proverbial quality of the curt style make it particularly suitable for this purpose. Its staccato movement jolts the reader into thinking about what its terse statements have to say. It is exemplified in the selections from Bacon's early *Essays,* in the essay by Emerson, and in the quotation from Marshall McLuhan's and Quentin Fiore's *The Medium is the Massage.* It is also employed for a very different purpose in the fictional writing of Hemingway and many other modern writers influenced by him.

DICTION

Diction merely means the choice of the right word for one's purpose. Words have both *denotations* and *connotations,* and for a word to be effective a writer must be concerned about both. The denotation is the exact dictionary meaning of the word and is relatively definite and fixed, while the connotation is that whole series of associations or meanings that the mention of any word is apt to bring to the mind of the reader. When you drop a pebble into water, it creates a fixed dot where it sinks, but immediately a series of rings starts moving out from that point and these rings will eventually stretch out to the extreme edge of the whole body of water. Denotation is like that central spot, exact and fixed; connotations are like the centrifugal rings. Some of them are very close to the central spot or denotation, but for each of us they increasingly move farther and farther away from that central point. Thus the word *tulip* denotes a brightly colored flower with a chalice-shaped blossom growing from a bulb on a single stem. But because of its history, the mere mention of tulip will almost certainly connote to everyone Holland and windmills. For some the rings may move farther out to connote wooden shoes and Dutch Cleanser. Certain connotations a writer can be sure that almost any reader will have; others, more personal to himself, he cannot expect his readers to grasp unless he provides a context that will suggest them.

Words are also *generic* or *specific, abstract* or *concrete. Building* is generic; *house* is specific. *Building* is also abstract. It is an idea in the mind —elastic enough to embrace houses, barns, churches, factories. We do not sense (see, hear, touch, taste, smell) abstractions. We sense only the concrete object. We have never seen a house—only palaces, bungalows, cottages, duplex flats, brownstone mansions, and ranch houses. Since it is only *concrete* objects—robins, not birds, cottages, not houses—that we actually sense, and since it is the concrete sense experience that is richest in connotations and emotional associations, a writer must use the concrete and connotative word, if he wishes to make an emotional appeal in his writing. It goes without saying that the writer of description, whose chief purpose is to enable his reader to recreate a sense experience of an object, scene, or person, must use concrete language if he is to be successful. But the writer of expository prose finds the concrete helpful too; it is the concrete example or the concrete comparison that is frequently the most effective way of clarifying an unfamiliar idea. It brings the unfamiliar within range of our everyday experience. Because the concrete often connotes so much more than it actually expresses, it is also another means of achieving economy in expression. This does not mean, however, that abstract diction is lacking in effect. When one is discussing abstract ideas, the abstract word, of course, is frequently the only *exact* word. Any word is effective if it clearly expresses the idea.

English is rich in synonyms because it has assimilated vocabulary from so many sources. The two main sources, of course, are Anglo-Saxon and Latin, much of the latter arriving through French. Words of Anglo-Saxon origin tend to be *shorter,* even *monosyllabic;* those from Latin, *longer* and *polysyllabic.* It is the difference between *think* and *cogitate, house* and *habitation, root* and *derivation.* Writing that favors the shorter Anglo-Saxon vocabulary creates an impression of greater simplicity and naturalness than one that leans toward the more polysyllabic Latinate vocabulary. But here again, there are no absolutes. Because all the words of our language have taken on very individual nuances of meaning, the only thing that can determine which is the right word in a given sentence is the precise idea and tone that the writer is attempting to communicate at that moment.

IMAGERY

Imagery in the widest sense is any word or phrase that makes a vivid appeal to any one of the senses. Hence a concrete term is by its nature an image in this broad sense. "Little houses could be seen all along the roadside" is an abstract statement of fact without imagery. "Little thatched cottages nestled behind hawthorne hedges along the country lane" describes the same setting, but the phrases "thatched cottages," "hawthorne hedges," and "country lane" in their concreteness enable the reader to experience the scene in detail. Here is another example. "The fish moved out of sight" is an exact statement of fact, but "the trout swished under the rocks" enables the reader to see and perhaps even hear the quick movement of a specific kind of fish. This kind of imagery is absolutely necessary for effective description, but it is also frequently helpful for enlivening exposition.

Ordinarily, however, imagery is regarded as synonymous with *figurative language*—what the old rhetoricians called *tropes.* The word came from the Greek verb τρεπειν, meaning *to turn* or *twist.* A trope was a turn or twist given to expression; and there were two types—a turn of thought and a turn of language: *schemata rerum* (patterns of thought) and *schemata verborum* (patterns of words). The "turns" of words were sound patterns, such as *alliteration*—identical consonants repeated at the beginning of words in close proximity to one another. The "turns" of thought were what today is called figurative language, in which the turn or twist is in the thought expressed by the words rather than in the mere sound of the words. The chief figures of thought, of course, are *simile, metaphor, synecdoche,* and *metonymy.*

A *simile* is an expressed comparison, but not every comparison is a simile. To say that John is like his brother James is not a simile but a simple comparison. In a simile the two things compared must be essentially different. Actually, a simile is defined as an expressed likeness between two things which are essentially different but which have some points in common. These common points consist either in qualities that the two things share or in actions that they both perform. Thus I might say of an attractive girl: "Clara entered like a spring breeze." The girl, Clara, is essentially different from a spring breeze, but they have things in common. Every simile can be diagramed in the following fashion: the two things being compared are expressed by nouns; the qualities or actions which they share and which are the basis of the likeness are expressed by adjectives and verbs. The example above could be diagramed in this way:

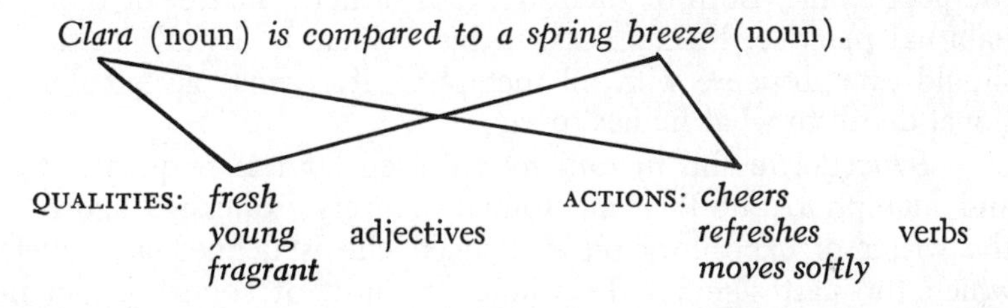

A *metaphor* differs from a simile in this: It does not state a likeness between two objects which are essentially different from one another; it rather *identifies* the two objects. A metaphor gives the nature of one to the other and hence enables it to show the qualities and perform the actions of the other. Thus I might say: "John was a veritable lion. He roared into the room and clawed to tatters the reputation of everyone in it." Here I do not say that John was *like* a lion; I say that he *was* a lion. I identify him and the lion, and hence I can represent him as *roaring* and *clawing*—actions appropriate to the lion. Metaphors can also be diagramed like similes. This one would appear in a diagram thus:

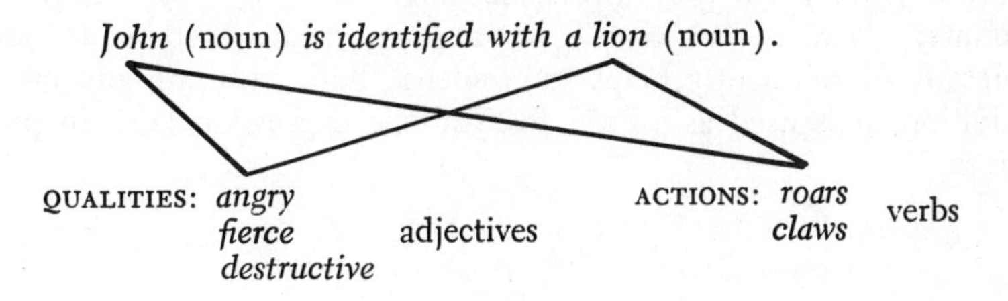

Since metaphors *identify* objects which are essentially different from one another, their immediate effect is to obscure identities; at the same time, they can be very expressive because one object has taken on the nature of the other and hence can perform as it does. John *roars* and *claws* —action that he cannot perform in the same way in his own nature. A metaphor is apt to be more emotionally intense than a straight simile. For that reason it has always been recognized as the chief tool of the poet. The simile, on the other hand, because it keeps the two things being compared separate from one another is apt to be a more useful tool for the writer of expository prose, who is trying primarily to clarify rather than intensify an idea. He borrows the familiar to make the unfamiliar less so. Thus, when William L. Laurence is trying to explain the process of atomic fission in his essay "The Truth about the Bomb" he says that the process is *like* lighting a match, and then goes on to show in how many ways the two processes are alike. Here Laurence is working with simile and not metaphor. It would probably be less helpful to express that idea in a metaphor because atomic fission is *not* lighting a match, and to say that it is would confuse rather than clarify what the process really is. This does not mean, however, that the writer of exposition never uses metaphor, nor the poet simile. Both of them do; it is rather a matter of their usual and habitual practice. F. L. Lucas, in his "What Is Style?" insists, no writer should ever dispense with all metaphor; it is what gives color and emotional depth to what he has to say.

Synecdoche and *metonymy* are used far less frequently than simile and metaphor, but they are sometimes very expressive figures, even for the writer of expository prose. Synecdoche is defined as a metaphor in which the part signifies the whole. It must, of course, be an important part of the whole and must be closely associated with the subject under discussion. Thus *motor* is important enough to stand for automobile; *tire* would hardly do. *Hands* would serve for laborers; *heads* would not. This figure of speech is frequently used by poets and satirists to depersonalize an action. Thus, to emphasize the impersonal *use* of human beings as tools in the factory system in the nineteenth century, a writer might say: "More than three thousand hands were needed in order to keep the looms running."

Metonymy is a figure of speech which transfers the name of one object to another object closely associated with it. Thus people speak of "the crown" when they mean the king; "the flag" when they mean the country; "sweat and tears" when they mean hard labor and grief. Metonymy frequently helps to condense both meaning and emotion. In addition, it is used as an aid to symbolic expression both in poetry and prose.

RHYTHM

Rhythm in general is the regular repetition of anything. It is ordinarily associated with poetic expression, but prose has its rhythm, too. The repeat of prose rhythm is less predictable than that of poetry; but it is there nonetheless, and contributes both meaning and emotional tone to expression.

Sentences have rhythm. There is a swelling rotundity to the full-mouthed *periodic sentence* that gives a solemnity and sense of climax to whatever it expresses. It contributes a formality to expression which is probably not very congenial to modern tastes; it smacks of the oratorical and flourishes in ages and places where oratory is in vogue. The shorter, less formally structured sentence is more agreeable to modern taste; it lacks the formality of the periodic sentence but seems more natural to us because it reflects some of the movement of our everyday conversation.

In exposition the frequent need of relating, comparing, and contrasting ideas often results in a rhythmic pattern created by the repetition of clauses and phrases built in parallel structure—framing parallel ideas, comparisons, and contrasts. This makes for a definite *balanced movement* in the sentences where the parallel pattern occurs. Note, for example, the rhythm in prose as well as in poetry. *Alliteration* can often call attention from Orwell's "Politics and the English Language":

> Thus political language has to consist largely of euphemism, question-begging and sheer cloudy vagueness. Defenceless villages are bombarded from the air, the inhabitants driven out into the countryside, the cattle machine-gunned, the huts set on fire with incendiary bullets: this is called *pacification*. Millions of peasants are robbed of their farms and sent trudging along the roads with no more than they can carry: this is called *transfer of population* or *rectification of frontiers*. People are imprisoned for years without trial, or shot in the back of the neck or sent to die of scurvy in Arctic lumber camps: this is called *elimination of unreliable elements*. Such phraseology is needed if one wants to name things without calling up mental pictures of them.

Or note how the comparison in this passage from the same essay is strengthened by the balanced structure of the sentences which express it:

> A man may take to drink because he feels himself to be a failure, and then fail all the more completely because he drinks. It is rather the same thing that is happening in the English language. It becomes ugly and inaccurate because our thoughts are foolish, but the slovenliness of our language makes it easier for us to have foolish thoughts.

To neglect this kind of rhythmic structure in writing expository prose is to weaken one's thought as well as one's expression.

Very often an expressive rhythm can be created in a passage of expository prose by the repetition of just one word. One of the most famous examples of this kind of rhetorical emphasis is the thirteenth chapter of St. Paul's First Epistle to the Corinthians, where the repetition of the word *charity* binds together the whole chapter into a beautifully textured untiy. Note a similar effect created by the repetition of *exactly* and *right* in the following passage from H. L. Mencken's "American Culture" (the italics are mine).

> . . . [the American bogus aristocrat] is made even more tremulous, for what he faces within the gates is a scheme of things made up almost wholly of harsh and often unintelligible taboos, and the penalty for violating even the least of them is swift and disastrous. He must exhibit *exactly* the *right* social habits, appetites and prejudices, public and private. He must harbor *exactly* the *right* enthusiasms and indignations. He must have a hearty taste for *exactly* the *right* sports and games. His attitude toward the fine arts must be propertly tolerant and yet not a shade too eager. He must read *exactly* the *right* books, pamphlets and journals. He must put up at the *right* hotels when he travels. His wife must patronize the *right* milliners. He himself must stick to the *right* haberdashery. He must live in the *right* neighborhood. He must even embrace the *right* doctrine of religion. It would ruin him, for all society column purposes, to move to Union Hill, N.J., or to drink coffee from his saucer, or to marry a chambermaid with a golden tooth, or to join the Seventh Day Adventists.

Even the repetition of individual letters can create a reinforcing rhythm in prose as well as in poetry. *Alliteration* can often call attention to words expressing ideas that the writer wants us to consider together. For instance, in this phrase of Mencken: "*b*ogus [English] counts coming over to work their magic upon the daughters of *b*reakfast-food and *b*athtub kings," the *b*'s pull *bogus, breakfast-food,* and *bathtub* together and make us think of bogus counts and commercial heiresses together.

There are actually families of consonants and each family has its own connotations. A prevalence of one or other family in a given passage can create a definite emotional tone. If that tone is appropriate to what is being expressed in the passage, it can add to its effectiveness. The chief families of consonants are the following:

1. The plosives—*b, d, g, k, p, t*—pronounced by releasing the breath from compressed lips with an explosion
2. The fricatives—*c, f, h, g*—pronounced with less stricture of the lips but with some constriction
3. The sibilants—*ch, s*—pronounced with a hissing sound
4. The liquids—*l, r*—pronounced smoothly off the tongue
5. The nasals—*m, n, ng*—pronounced with a humming sound through the nose.

Note, for instance, the effect of the alliterated fricatives and plosives in the following lines from Gerard Manley Hopkins' "The Leaden Echo and the Golden Echo":

> "O why are we so *h*aggard at the *h*eart,
> so *c*are-coiled, *c*are *k*illed, so *f*agged
> so *f*ashed, so *c*ogged, so *c*umbered."

These refinements of sound, it is true, are more usual in poetry than in prose, but they are also occasionally used in prose for emphasis or to create an emotional tone. Note, for instance, how the plosive *b*'s in the following sentence helps to express Mencken's contempt for pseudo-aristocracy: "But this *b*ugaboo aristocracy is actually *b*ogus, and the evidence of *b*ogusness lies in its insecurity."

Similarly, there are families of *vowel sounds*, ranging from high to low pitch. *Pitch* is determined according to where the sound originates in the vocal cavity. High-pitched vowels originate in the fore part of the mouth. As the sound lowers in pitch, it originates farther back in the mouth, until, finally, extremely low-pitched vowels originate far back in the throat. The following words are arranged to illustrate a movement from very high-pitched vowels through vowels of middle pitch to very low-pitched ones:

1. rite, mete, date, hit, due
2. hat, set
3. dot, tar, foot, boil, hut
4. nor, food, brow, urn
5. tall, note.[1]

A passage of either poetry or prose composed of words of predominantly high, middle, or low pitch can create a rhythmic accompaniment to what is being said that can induce a mood in the reader very much as mood music does in a cinema. Accomplished prose writers are as sensitive to this element of their expression as poets.

The writer of prose, as well as the poet, must be conscious of what his writing sounds like as well as of what it says; he must, in other words, strive for euphony in his expression. Somerset Maugham wrote in this connection:

> Many writers without distress will put two rhyming words together, join a monstrous long adjective to a monstrous long noun, or between the end of one word and the beginning of another have a conjunction of

[1] Reprinted from James H. Smith, *Reading of Poetry* (Boston: Houghton Mifflin Company, 1939).

> consonants that almost breaks your jaw. These are trivial and obvious instances. I mention them only to prove that if careful writers can do such things, it is only because they have no ear. Words have weight, sound, and appearance; it is only by considering these that you can write a sentence that is good to look at and good to listen to.

It goes without saying that all these elements of style—sentence structure, diction, imagery, and rhythm—just briefly touched on here, are exemplified in many of the selections in this book. It is part of the responsibility of a sensitive reader to become aware of how the writer has used all these resources of his language to make his expression more effective. If the reader becomes aware of the sources of some of the effectiveness in the writing of others, he may begin at last to exploit some of these resources in his own writing.

Index of Authors and Titles*

* Titles are italicized